THE
SUPPLY
MANAGEMENT
HANDBOOK

SEVENTH EDITION

JOSEPH L. CAVINATO, PH.D., C.P.M.

ANNA E. FLYNN, PH.D., C.P.M.

RALPH G. KAUFFMAN, PH.D., C.P.M.

McGraw-Hill
New York   Chicago   San Francisco   Lisbon   London   Madrid
Mexico City   Milan   New Delhi   San Juan   Seoul
Singapore   Sydney   Toronto

The **McGraw·Hill** Companies

3 4 5 6 7 8 9 0   DOC/DOC   0

ISBN 0-07-144513-7

This publication is designed to provide accurate and authoritative information in regard to the subject matter covered. It is sold with the understanding that the publisher is not engaged in rendering legal, accounting, or other professional service. If legal advice or other expert assistance is required, the services of a competent professional person should be sought.
>   —*From a declaration of principles jointly adopted by a Committee*
>   *of the American Bar Association and a Committee of Publishers.*

McGraw-Hill books are available at special quantity discounts to use as premiums and sales promotions, or for use in corporate training programs. For more information, please write to the Director of Special Sales, Professional Publishing, McGraw-Hill, Two Penn Plaza, New York, NY 10121-2298. Or contact your local bookstore.

This book is printed on recycled, acid-free paper containing a minimum of 50% recycled, de-inked fiber.

C O N T E N T S

PREFACE

LOOKING FORWARD INTO THE FIELD

Welcome to the 2006 edition of the Institute for Supply Management™ (ISM)/ McGraw-Hill's *Supply Management Handbook*. This edition brings a new title to its long history stretching back to the 1920s. Many editions have been lost in history, but since 1958 nine separate ones in this string have been published with the general title of *Aljian's Purchasing Handbook*, or just plain *Purchasing Handbook*. But the 2000 edition and this one have taken a different tack from the previous ones.

This handbook's history was deeply rooted in capturing the best and most appropriate practice at the time. For decades the industry leaders were invited to contribute the best way to perform the many various tasks in the complex world of buying, or purchasing as it evolved into in later years. The 2000 edition and this one turn from the best of the current to instead looking from today forward. Thought leaders have been invited to contribute what they are seeing today and cast their observations and syntheses forward to the five-year span of the last half of this decade. Thus, the book projects the field into what it is becoming, and how one can fit within this dynamic.

The rationale for this directional shift with the book comes from many angles. For one, the ISM's annual meeting content and participants have sought forward-looking topics in recent times. Also, the popular articles in *Inside Supply Management*® are ones that point toward improving supply management by doing the best today with an eye toward meeting the demands of tomorrow. In addition, we've noted a dramatic move toward changes in purchasing department and professionals' titles toward ones containing the word *supply*. And, the ISM's A.T. Kearney Center for Strategic Supply Leadership is growing in activity with research and program content oriented toward supply leaders' issues and opportunities three to five years into the future.

The ISM/McGraw-Hill Supply Management Handbook takes a leadership thrust in presenting the best of today and how to meet the demands of tomorrow at the same time. The book is divided into seven sections. Part 1, *Supply: The Expanding Edges of Purchasing*, presents four chapters focusing upon the recent and evolving changes in the field and how organizations are setting their sights for new environments and demands. Part 2, *Going to Market with Today's Crucial Imperatives*, covers how organizations are and can shape and implement supply strategies. Part 3, *The Four Core Supports of Every Supply Chain*, includes chapters focusing upon the four pillars of supply chains today. These are the subarchitectures of physical, financial, informational, and relationally focused supply chain constructs. Part 4, *Emerging Issues and Opportunities in Supply*, presents the building blocks of supply-focused supply departments and organizations. Part 5, *Components and Capabilities*, delves into the state of the art and practice in the core areas of the profession. Part 6, *Item and Industry Practice*, provides updates and insights into special areas of the field. And finally, Part 7, *Supply Management Information Resources: Institute for Supply Management*™, describes the resources available to the supply management executive through the institute.

Joseph L. Cavinato, Ph.D., C.P.M.
Anna E. Flynn, Ph.D., C.P.M.
Ralph G. Kauffman, Ph.D., C.P.M.

C O N T R I B U T O R S

Dennis R. Arter, PE
Certified Quality Auditor
Columbia Audit Resources
Kennewick, Washington (Chap. 27)

Johnathon Baker
Director, Supply Chain Management
Corporate Operations and
Supply Chain Strategy
Delta Air Line
Atlanta, Georgia (Chap. 40)

Patsy Ball-Brown
Brown & Associates Quality
Consulting, Inc.
Pine Bluff, Arkansas (Chap. 27)

Jack Barry
Managing Director
Pegasus Global, Inc.
Fairfield, Connecticut (Chaps. 8 and 13)

Laura Birou, Ph.D.
Senior Consultant
ADR International
Tampa, Florida (Chap. 15)

John D. Blascovich
Vice President
A.T. Kearney, Inc.
New York (Chap. 2)

Lee Buddress, Ph.D., C.P.M.
Associate Professor and Director
Supply and Logistics Management Program
Portland State University
Portland, Oregon (Chaps. 22 and 35)

Craig R. Carter, Ph.D.
Assistant Professor of Supply Chain Management
College of Business Administration
University of Nevada
Reno, Nevada (Chap. 20)

Joseph R. Carter, DBA, C.P.M.
Avnet Professor and Chair of Supply Chain
Management Department, W. P. Carey School
of Business, Arizona State University
Tempe, Arizona (Chap. 5)

Phillip L. Carter, DBA
Professor of Supply Chain Management and
Harold E. Fearon Chair of Purchasing
W. P. Carey School of Business
Arizona State University, and Executive Director
CAPS: Center for Strategic Supply Research
Tempe, Arizona (Chaps. 11 and 21)

Joseph L. Cavinato, Ph.D., C.P.M.
Institute for Supply Management™
ISM Professor of Supply Management at
Thunderbird, The Garvin School of International
Management and Director, A.T. Kearney Center
for Strategic Supply Leadership at the Institute
for Supply Management™
Tempe, Arizona (Chaps. 1 and 12)

Lawrence J. Clark, C.P.M.
Sodus Central Schools
Sodus, New York (Chap. 28)

Dan Creinin
Product Manager
Böwe Bell & Howell
Wheeling, Illinois (Chap. 27)

Thomas A. Crimi, C.P.M.
Chevron International Exploration and
Production Inc.
CIEP Learning and Development Coordinator
Houston, Texas (Chap. 41)

S. R. (Randy) Dean
Supply Manager
BHP Billiton/New Mexico Coal
Farmington, New Mexico (Chap. 41)

Aaron D. Dent
Former Vice President
Supply Chain Management
Delta Air Lines
Atlanta, Georgia (Chap. 40)

Roberta J. Duffy
Editor
Inside Supply Management®
Institute for Supply Management™
Tempe, Arizona (Chap. 4)

Robert J. Easton
Partner and Global Supply Chain Management
Lead for Financial Services
Accenture, Kronberg, Germany (Chap. 3)

Lisa M. Ellram, Ph.D., C.P.M., CMA
Richard and Lorie Allen Professor of Business
Professor of Supply Chain Management
College of Business, Colorado State University
Fort Collins, Colorado (Chap. 23)

M. Theodore Farris, II, Ph.D., CTL
Associate Professor of Logistics and Executive
Director, TLEF Center for Logistics Education
and Research, University of North Texas
Denton, Texas (Chap. 30)

Donavon Favre
Adjunct Professor
North Carolina State University
Cary, North Carolina (Chap. 3)

Stanley E. Fawcett, Ph.D.
Professor, Global Supply Chain Management
Marriott School of Management
Brigham Young University
Provo, Utah (Chap. 17)

Anna E. Flynn, Ph.D., C.P.M.
Associate Professor
Institute for Supply Management™
Tempe, Arizona (Chap. 7)

Ernest G. Gabbard, JD, C.P.M., CPCM
Director, Strategic Sourcing
Allegheny Technologies
Pittsburgh, Pennsylvania (Chap. 26)

Henry F. Garcia, C.P.M.
Consultant and Trainer
Asentrene
San Antonio, Texas (Chap. 42)

Linda Howe Garriz
Manager, Quality Assurance
Alcon Manufacturing, Ltd.
Irvine, California (Chap. 27)

Jules A. Goffre
Vice President
A.T. Kearney, Inc.
Munich, Germany (Chap. 6)

Richard A. Gould
Chief Solution Provider
R G Management Solutions
Surprise, Arizona (Chap. 27)

Mary Lu Harding, C.P.M., CPIM, CIRM
Consultant
Harding & Associates
Lincoln, Vermont (Chap. 33)

Michael Harding, C.P.M., CPIM
Consultant
Harding & Associates
Lincoln, Vermont (Chap. 33)

Ralph G. Kauffman, Ph.D., C.P.M.
Associate Professor and Coordinator
Supply Chain Management Program
University of Houston–Downtown
Houston, Texas (Chap. 25)

Dana Kendall
Former Program Manager
A.T. Kearney Center for Strategic Supply
Leadership at the Institute for Supply
Management™
Tempe, Arizona (Chap. 4)

H. Ervin Lewis, C.P.M.
President
Lewis and Associates
Florence, South Carolina (Chap. 34)

Brian G. Long, Ph.D., C.P.M.
President
Marketing and Management Institute, Inc.
Kalamazoo, Michigan (Chap. 24)

Edward M. Lundeen, C.P.M., CPIM
Director, Contracts
Eclipse Aviation
Albuquerque, New Mexico (Chap. 10)

Gregory M. Magnan, Ph.D.
Associate Professor of Operations
Management
Albers School of Business and Economics
Seattle University
Seattle, Washington (Chap. 17)

Leslie S. Marell
Attorney at Law
Law Offices of Leslie S. Marell
Hermosa Beach, California (Chap. 36)

William J. Markham
Principal
A.T. Kearney, Inc.
Chicago, Illinois (Chap. 2)

Casey P. McDowell
Chief Procurement Officer
The Auto Club Group
Dearborn, Michigan (Chap. 11)

William S. McKinney III
President, McKinney and Associates, LLC
Director, Source One Management, LLC
Philadelphia, Pennsylvania (Chap. 16)

Robert M. Monczka, Ph.D., C.P.M.
Research Professor of Supply Chain Management
W.P. Carey School of Business, Arizona State
University, and Director, Strategic Sourcing
& Supply Chain Strategy
CAPS: Center for Strategic Supply Research
Tempe, Arizona (Chap. 11)

R. David Nelson, C.P.M., A.P.P.,
Vice President
Global Supply Management
Delphi Corporation
Troy, Michigan (Chap. 18)

Kenneth J. Petersen, Ph.D.
Associate Professor of Management
College of Business
Colorado State University
Fort Collins, Colorado (Chaps. 11 and 21)

Gil Pilz
Director of Security and Directory Services
E2open, Inc.
Redwood City, California (Chap. 14)

Helen M. Pohlig, J.D.
Patagonia, Arizona (Chap. 31)

Alan Raedels, Ph.D., C.P.M.
Professor Emeritus of Supply and
Logistics Management
Portland State University
Beaverton, Oregon (Chap. 29)

Craig Reed
Director, Supply Chain Management
Fuel & Airport Services
Delta Air Lines
Atlanta, Georgia (Chap. 40)

Mark Schenecker
Director, Standards Architecture
SAP
Palo Alto, California (Chap. 14)

Thomas I. Schoenfeldt
President
Schoenfeldt Services, Inc.
Livonia, Michigan (Chap. 27)

Thomas H. Slaight
Vice President
A.T. Kearney, Inc.
New York, New York (Chaps. 2 and 6)

Michael E. Smith, Ph.D., CQA
Associate Professor of Management &
International Business
MBA Program Director
Western Carolina University
Cullowhee, North Carolina (Chaps. 22 and 35)

Gary L. Stading, Ph.D.
Assistant Professor
University of Houston–Downtown
Houston, Texas (Chap. 32)

Jonathan R. Stegner
General Director, Global Supply Management
Delphi Corporation
Troy, Michigan (Chap. 18)

Anthony Tarantino, Ph.D. C.P.I.M.
Senior Manager
BearingPoint
Mountain View, California (Chap. 14)

Traci Van Arsdale
TVA Associates
Baltimore, Maryland (Chap. 27)

Bruce J. Wright*
President
B. Wright & Associates and Total Systems, Inc.
Sandy, Utah (Chaps. 37 and 39)

Lori Yelvington, CPCU
Assistant Vice President
Procurement Governance
Allstate Insurance Company
Northbrook, Illinois (Chap. 38)

Richard R. Young, Ph.D., C.P.M.
Associate Professor of Supply Chain
Management
The Pennsylvania State University
Capital College
Lancaster, Pennsylvania (Chap. 9)

George A. Zsidisin, Ph.D., C.P.M.
Assistant Professor
The Eli Broad College of Business
Michigan State University
East Lansing, Michigan (Chap. 19)

*Deceased

ABOUT THE
EDITORS-IN-CHIEF

JOSEPH L. CAVINATO, PH.D., C.P.M., is the ISM Professor of Supply Management at Thunderbird, The Garvin Graduate School of International Management, and Director of the A.T. Kearney Center for Strategic Supply Leadership at the Institute for Supply Management™. Cavinato was a professor of business logistics at The Pennsylvania State University from 1978 until 1999 with teaching, executive management, and research activities in the areas of business futures, strategic development, supply/value and business model analyses, and international business.

He is a member of ISM, the World Future Society, the International Center for Organizational Effectiveness, and the Council of Supply Chain Management Professionals and is listed in *Who's Who in Industry and Finance*, *Who's Who in American Education*, *Who's Who in the World*, and *International Biographies*.

Cavinato received a doctorate in business from The Pennsylvania State University and a bachelor's and MBA from The American University. He received the A.T. Kearney Doctoral Dissertation Award for a study of multifirm supply chain system total cost measurement systems, the first research believed to be conducted on supply chains.

He has been engaged in consulting and management development program activities with major corporations and not-for-profit organizations on six continents. The A.T. Kearney Center for Strategic Supply Leadership at the Institute for Supply Management™ is a research-based organization devoted to identifying and uplifting leadership capabilities in supply management.

In addition, Cavinato is the author of *Supply Chain/Transportation Dictionary*, *Finance for Transportation Distribution Managers*, and *Purchasing and Materials Management: Integrative Strategies*. He is coauthor of the texts *Logistics in the Service Industries*, *Transportation*, and *Traffic Management* and coeditor of *The Purchasing Handbook*, 6th edition. He has written over 180 cases in strategy, interorganization linkages, purchasing, and value chain management.

ANNA E. FLYNN, PH.D., C.P.M., is vice president and associate professor at the Institute for Supply Management™ (ISM). Prior to joining ISM, Dr. Flynn was senior lecturer and director of the undergraduate program in Supply Chain Management (SCM) at Arizona State University. Dr. Flynn is coauthor of the 13th edition of *Purchasing and Supply Management* (2006) with Leenders, Johnson, and Fearon; coauthor of volume 4 of the *ISM Supply Management Knowledge Series: The Supply Management Leadership Process;* and coauthor of *Value-Driven Purchasing: Managing the Key Steps in the Acquisition Process.* She earned a bachelor's degree in international studies from the University of Notre Dame and an MBA and a Ph.D. in learning and instructional technology from Arizona State University.

RALPH G. KAUFFMAN, PH.D., C.P.M., is associate professor of management and coordinator of the Supply Chain Management Program at the University of Houston–Downtown. Prior to entering academia, he gained more than 27 years of purchasing and supply management experience with Oryx Energy Co. as manager of procurement and materials management, and, prior to that, with Sun Company.

Currently, Kauffman is chair of the ISM Non-Manufacturing Business Survey Committee. He conducts monthly surveys of more than 350 committee members and prepares the monthly Non-Manufacturing ISM *Report On Business®*. From 1994 to 1996, he served as chair of the ISM Manufacturing Business Survey Committee. He is also coeditor of the sixth edition of *The Purchasing Handbook.*

He has published articles in management journals including the *Academy of Management Journal,* the *Journal of Supply Chain Management,* and the *Journal of Business and Industrial Marketing.* He has presented papers at national and international academic and professional conferences, including the ISM Annual International Supply Management Conference. He is also a frequent guest speaker at professional conferences and seminars. In 2002 he received the J. Shipman Gold Medal, ISM's most distinguished award.

Kauffman received a bachelor's degree in engineering from Lehigh University and an MBA degree in transportation management from Northwestern University. He received his doctorate in management science from the University of Texas at Dallas. He is a member of NAPM–Houston, Inc., the American Marketing Association, the Institute for Operations Research and Management Sciences, and the Southeast Texas Association of Public Purchasing.

PART 1

SUPPLY: THE EXPANDING EDGES OF PURCHASING

This book has a history that dates to the early 1920s as a buying handbook. Its purpose was to provide an A to Z encyclopedia of how to understand and do the standard activities of the field. It was what some writers refer to as a conformist's reference. It described each and every step to the buying process. But in today's organizations, few things remain the same from year to year. What worked in the past often has to be altered for the next time. And, what needs to be done next is often in uncharted waters.

The field is now in a continuous period of expansion. While many of the traditional things remain as part of the basic core, each year new practices come to light in new areas with successes that translate into positive organizational performance.

This section of the book takes a forward look at where eight thought leaders see the field today and where further opportunities lie for the profession over the next five years.

The four chapters that follow start with insights into the Institute for Supply Management's scan of the profession in its expansion from buying to purchasing to supply. The next two chapters contain insights from leading consulting firms in the field as to their observations of the strategic directions and opportunities for supply. The last chapter provides a synthesis of what the nature of the leading roles and jobs are as they are evolving today. This chapter is based on several forums conducted by the A.T. Kearney Center for Strategic Supply Leadership at ISM which focused on defining the nature of the field's leadership three to five years hence.

SUPPLY MANAGEMENT: ISM'S LEADERSHIP VIEW

Joseph L. Cavinato, Ph.D., C.P.M.
ISM Professor of Supply Management
Thunderbird, The Garvin School of International Management
and
Director
A.T. Kearney Center for Strategic Supply Leadership
Institute for Supply Management™

The significant changes in purchasing traditionally came from within the field, but today they originate from outside the company or organization, from other fields, as well as from within the field of purchasing itself. It is no longer a field defined unto itself, but is a human and system organism that remains exists or thrives by fulfilling the needs of others. This context defines today's supply management. If one concept characterizes supply management today and into the future, it is integration: both integrating and integrative. Supply management is linked hand in hand with suppliers, other departments, and customers and has a leadership role in taking the initiative to find value for customers and business performance. This chapter explores the underlying roots of "new" purchasing, or supply management, as it is increasingly named, and presents many of its characteristics as observed in ongoing research at the Institute for Supply Management (ISM) into the current state and directions of the field.[1]

This chapter is divided into two major parts: (1) how the field got to the midpoint of the first decade of the twenty-first century and (2) where the field is going. Within this background is an analysis of major trends that shaped the field in the past two decades and continue to do so, a research debrief of senior managements' attitudes toward their purchasing and supply, and why the ISM reoriented itself toward a forward role in the field and profession. As to where the field is going, we look at the nature of supply chains and networks, both where they are today and where they seem to be evolving; examine the megatrends and

---

1 Much of this research is conducted by the A.T. Kearney Center for Strategic Supply Leadership at ISM. This organization is dedicated to discover, interpret, and disseminate the "next" practices of the field. The CSSL researchers have conducted interviews in over 705 firms and organizations worldwide since 1990 involving over 4,900 interviews.

implications affecting the field; and look at the supply manager of 2005 to 2010 based upon evidence that already exists.

HOW WE GOT TO WHERE WE ARE TODAY

As several other chapters in this book mention, purchasing was long a function that kept to itself. Others in a company were forced to conform to it, and purchasing was under the control of manufacturing or accounting. It was an activity- and task-focused field where new people were told, "When you learn how we do it around here, then we'll give you some responsibilities." That worked in a long period of stability, where competitive forces were slow to shift and the landscape rarely changed. The challenge of the complexity of purchasing was to learn it, stabilize it, and keep it on course. Most of all, the expectations of senior managements and other departments didn't change much either.

By the 1970s commodity shortages brought new ways to acquire goods. Figure 1–1 presents some major developments in the expansion of purchasing on a timeline related to a change scale. Some companies learned that by changing the way they approached the supply market they didn't need to use volume in order to get the best buying power in the market. Many learned a new principle that by consolidating, using fewer suppliers, and standardizing specifications to industry norms they could reap price benefits.

F I G U R E   1–1

The Changing Ways of How Organizations Acquire Things

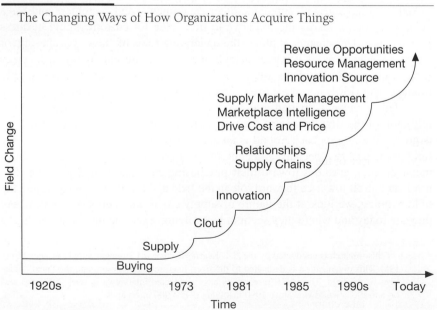

FIGURE 1–2

Eras of Purchasing Development

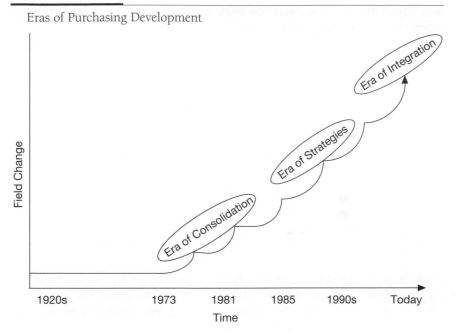

In the faster-paced industries, the shortening of product life cycles posed a problem for product development cycles as well. No longer could companies do everything from concepting to design to market testing and launch alone. When life cycles became shorter than development cycles, companies had to look to suppliers and other outsiders for input to their creation of value. Purchasing in some companies became very active in these new relationships and roles. Some companies found that by approaching suppliers with relationships different than arm's-length ones that other forms of added value could result. Too, by expanding the scope of purchasing from starting at requisitions and ending with closeout toward logistics, supplier activities, and even customer (internal and external) matters, that purchasing could bring additional value to the competitiveness of products and services and the performance of the firm. At this point, as Figure 1–2 shows, buying was still a mainstay of the field. These other practices were being done in addition to it.

Around 1990 even more sophisticated forms of purchasing practice were being implemented. Cost-driven pricing became popular as did a look into the longer-term supply market situation (which supplier will not be here in three to five years? etc.), and purchasing took the initiative of influencing suppliers' investments, innovation, supply chain practices, and more. Later in the 1990s some purchasing departments started to become involved in being the group to seek out innovation opportunities with suppliers, be evaluated upon new product and service revenue, and take charge of outsourcing. Figure 1–2 presents all these practices in a macro way starting with an era of consolidation, then strategies, and now integration. The field was and is expanding in the form of more and more nontraditional practices and broadening its scope in both directions of the supply chain.

Senior Management Pulse of Purchasing and Supply

The Center for Strategic Supply Leadership's ongoing interviews with CEOs and other senior managers reveal their following perceptions of the field by mid-2005.[2] Many of them overlap.

60 percent look to purchasing to minimize purchase price and maintain purchase price variances (PPV)

35 percent want their purchasing and supply groups to expand into the supplier side of their supply chains as well as into their own companies and organizations to seek supply chain cost takeout and speed up cycle times. This group often mentions the cash-to-cash cycle and attendant working capital gains.

20 percent mention that their purchasing and supply groups should be active in seeking top-line revenue product and service innovation opportunities. Both this group and the previous one want purchasing to take these initiatives without being ordered to do so.

This data indicates that 60 percent look to purchasing to play the traditional role of performing administrative buying services and continually meet or beat PPV. On the other hand 55 percent of them want purchasing and supply to take on expansive roles for value-adds to their companies and organizations. Many revealed in the interviews, however, that they did not know what purchasing could or should do in this regard. But the message is clear that they want a supply management group that identifies opportunities for the organization as a whole and takes an extraverted role in bringing benefits to it.

ISM's Leadership Approach to the Field

In 2000 the National Association of Purchasing Management (NAPM) was starting to identify some of these same needs from within and outside the field. Long an organization that was built from the ground up to serve the needs that members identified, it renamed itself (now Institute for Supply Management™) and took on a new governance role as a leadership organization for the profession. So

2 Between 2000 and 2004 a total of 67 CEOs of firms between the size of $2 billion in annual revenues and $140 billion were interviewed. The figures presented herein represent those interviewed in 2004.

many changes were on the horizon that what was needed was a role of detecting, interpreting, and providing educational content to assist professionals in the field to develop further. The view was to provide visions and means for professionals in the field to attain greater contributions for their companies and organizations.

The common themes revealed to the NAPM/ISM researchers called for new and evolving roles of purchasing as defined in the following supply management definition: *the identification, acquisition, access, positioning, and management of resources the organization needs or potentially needs in the attainment of its strategic objectives.* Taken apart, this definition of supply shows some greatly enhanced and value-contributing roles for the organization.

> *Identification* refers to identifying opportunities in the marketplace, whether they are new materials, new technologies, unknown suppliers, or even different paradigms for creating the organization's products and services.

> *Acquisition* is the act of obtaining, which is much broader than buying. It includes identifying and creating strategies for seeking and using sources. It means developing the appropriate relationships, acquisition methods, and chain processes that range from traditional buying to that of enabling others in the organization to develop and manage the process efficiently and effectively. It further extends to the creation and leadership role of very broad organization-to-organization interactions (inside and outside the organization).

> *Access* means gaining use or potential use of something of value. This is often a search-and-interpretation role for potential suppliers, potential supply methods and services, and technologies that could be competitively used by the organization rather than have them go to competitors. It also means accessing resources and assets available in the market that the organization does not have and does not want to invest in but does want to use.

> *Positioning* the organization for marketplace competitive advantage is a key strategic activity today. Like that of marketing and sales personnel who attempt to position the organization competitively in the demand marketplace, a mirror role is also needed on the supply side using macro- and microlevel marketplace intelligence tools to position the organization for long-run supply assurance, price/cost advantage, and innovation access. This is a greatly enhanced role from that of narrow supply base assessment, buying, and supplier management. Instead, this includes the leadership and management of suppliers and extends to that of positioning the organization favorably in the market.

> *Supply* involves many processes. It is a cost takeout and product and service enhancement role. It involves a scan of all organizations and processes in the chain from original creation of products and services through to the

organization obtaining and/or using the products and services and all the way out to the customer eventually acquiring and consuming them. This involves analyzing steps and flows, handlings, movements, transactions, costs, and information. Some organizations attain 20 to 30 percent cost takeout of the business by placing attention to this area. Up until a few years ago most organizations had no one overseeing these activities and costs. It requires viewing costs in a total sense whether it be those of the suppliers, the organization, and/or of customers. SAirGroup, for one, is accomplishing significant cost takeout by developing talent, expertise, processes, oversight, and leadership in this area.

The attainment of strategic objectives calls for a highly proactive role within the organization. Supply management is the one department that has vast networks of eyes, ears, and antennas on the supply market. Much of the advantage of this information and intelligence, however, tends not to go farther into the organization where it can be of additional competitive benefit. Most of these objectives must be championed. In an extraverted role, supply management has to develop and hone its influence and reach throughout the organization for greater contribution and impact.

These new demands mean that titles and names such as *buyer, buying, purchasing,* and *procurement* are being challenged within the expanded scope for supply roles of today and tomorrow. A small number of organizations are exploring new titles and names. *Acquisition, access,* and *supply* appear to be evolving into greater use. There is little consensus, but questions are being raised as to what to call the field as it is evolving today. The ISM's research has determined that the term *supply* captures the breadth and depth of these new expanded purchasing field roles. This is in line with an increasing number of CEOs who refer to the "supply side" of their organization both from an organizational span standpoint as well as a breadth of managerial oversight and control standpoint.

What This All Means

Three key points are obvious from these trends and changes. One is that supply chains are different today than they were seen and applied in the past. Two is that impacts upon the field continue to take place from outside the field to which it must adapt to and position for added value. Three, the successful buyer of yesterday has shifted into a supply manager in this decade with many new and highly contributive roles.

NATURE OF SUPPLY CHAINS TODAY

Supply chains are the investments, processes, and flows of goods designed to meet the needs of a set of ultimate customers or consumers. They traditionally were viewed as a connection of physical parts in a flow that consisted of transportation, warehousing, and inventories. Customer service and order management later became seen as key components of them. These were the outbound flows from the company to the customer. In the 1980s materials management and purchasing were added to this concept. In the 1990s senior and nonfield managers began to see supply chains as how the company gets its products or services to the market, and in this way they perceived it to be an embodiment of the company's operational business model.

Although *supply chain* and *supply chain management* became popular business buzzwords, differing opinions of what a supply chain is may actually hinder an organization's ability to manage it. Understanding the characteristics of supply chains and supply chain management enables an organization to customize its initiatives to fit its business. Characteristics of supply chains and supply chain management are described in the following statements.

- Supply chains are multitiered—they span beyond an organization's immediate suppliers and customers.
- Supply chains are customer driven.
- Supply chains exist externally and internally, requiring cross-functional effort.
- Supply chain management is an ongoing journey—not a destination.
- Supply chain management activities include good purchasing activities, but good purchasing activities are not necessarily true supply chain management activities (such as logistics or distribution).

An important feature of supply chains is the involvement of multiple tiers of suppliers and customers—both internal and external.

A supply chain only makes sense within the framework of the company's business model. The business model makes sense within the perspective of how the company competes in its marketplaces. Thus, some supply chains are built to emphasize manufacturing efficiencies (e.g., chemicals), while others are balancing suppliers and customers (common in branded food companies), while others are focused upon serving a strong and final retail network. Still others emphasize innovation and time-to-market. Supply chains in the financial service industries are created for performance related to information availability, network linkages, and transaction efficiencies. Thus, a supply chain makes sense only within the context within which the company is competing.

To achieve an optimized supply chain, the supply chain must be documented—or mapped. Mapping helps to generate an awareness of the other members and how directly they're impacted by an organization's decisions. Most supply chains, when mapped, look quite complex with many elements. The resulting supply chain is not a concise, linear graphic. In fact, this is why some organizations refer to their supply chains as supply networks with all elements pointing in the direction of the end customer.

FIGURE 1-3

Hypothetical Hotel Supply Chain

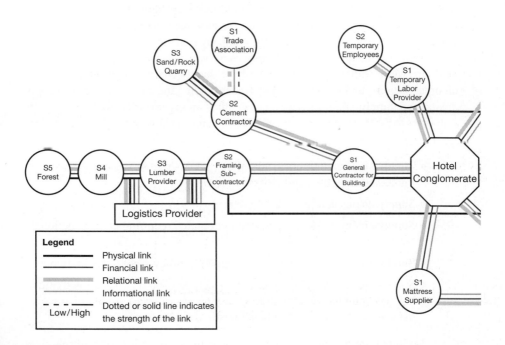

Figure 1-3 outlines a few of the many supply chain relationships that exist within and outside of an organization. It maps a hypothetical chain in the hotel industry. While many elements are captured in this one graphic, other organizations may find it more valuable to map their own generic templates to apply to individual supply chains, or they may map several supply chains within their organization. Supply chains can be mapped by commodity (such as the supply chain associated with temporary labor), by the product or service that is provided by an organization (such as the supply chain associated with providing hotel service to the leisure traveler), or by relationship (such as the supply chains associated with physical, financial, relational, and/or informational flows). In the sample, many of these components are combined on one diagram.

Supply chain maps may also demonstrate a lengthy chain of suppliers (fourth- and fifth-tier suppliers) that eventually reach the customer. In the figure, the example of lumber to build a new facility is used as are such things as the trade association, local unions, and chamber of commerce. Any and all resources that add to or impact the creation of eventual customer satisfaction, and company performance are legitimate components of the supply chain.

FIGURE 1–3

(Continued)

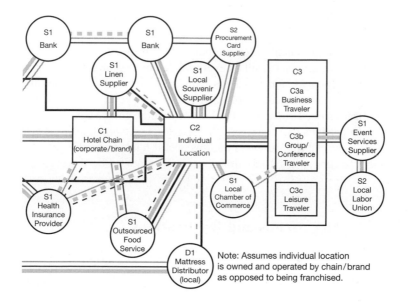

Note: Assumes individual location is owned and operated by chain/brand as opposed to being franchised.

The physical mapping of the extended hotel supply chain shown in Figure 1–3 is just one part of the overall supply chain architecture. Aside from the physical structure, there are four additional subarchitectures underlying every supply chain (whether or not the managers of it perceive and manage them). These five subarchitectures are as follows:

- *Physical.* The actual movements and flows within and between firms, transportation, service mobilization, delivery movement, storage, and inventories.

- *Financial.* The flows of cash between organizations, the incurrence of expenses, and the use of investments for the entire chain (or network), settlements, and accounts receivable and accounts payable processes and systems.

- *Informational.* The processes and electronic systems, data movement triggers, access to key information, capture and use of data, enabling processes, and market intelligence.

- *Relational.* The appropriate linkage between a supplier, the organization, and the organization's customers for maximum benefit, including
  internal supply matter relationships throughout the organization.

- *Innovational.* Who and how product and service innovations are developed
  and come to market for those companies and parties within the supply
  chain. This is increasingly pertinent today where supply management is
  involved in orchestrating supplier's activities for the company's new
  offerings in the market.

By seeing the supply chain in an extended way from original sources to
final customers and consumers as well as eventual disposition and viewing it in
the above five ways, supply chain managers gain the benefit of seeing the total
efficiency and performance outcomes of each party and overall chain. That is
why in some industries one firm at a particular point in the chain seems to dominate many of the decisions and actions of the entire set of companies today. In
retailing, it tends to be the final stores; in aerospace, it tends to be the airframe
and aircraft manufacturers; in information systems it tends to be the software
providers.

Megatrends and Implications

Several driving forces are at play in the mid-2000s that will significantly impact
supply managers in terms of their roles and opportunities. Each of these driving
forces is of such significance that together they are bringing permanent change to
the field.

1. *Globalization.* Companies are seeking the lowest-cost production or
   service points in the world, all made possible with easier transportation
   and transactions as well as greatly improved telecommunications and
   information linkages. Too, the globalization shift is taking place to tap
   markets. The wealthy Group of Eight (G-8) countries represent markets
   of slow consumer spending growth for the next several decades, so
   companies seeking to grow and remain financially competitive must
   seek out other markets in the world. China, India, the former Soviet
   Union, Latin America, and many emerging countries of Africa represent
   these new areas of focus. Supply managers are generally the ones in a
   company at the service point when opening up a new country for their
   companies. This changes the nature of how the group performs its work
   in terms of geographic and time zone spread, use of management time
   with extended suppliers, and longer and more complex supply chains.
   This trend will not reverse, and the supply managers who become effective and comfortable with this new environment will be in demand.

   In Europe the opening of 10 additional countries to the European
   Union poses new supply opportunities at lower costs. Too, these add a
   complexity in supply chain linkages, but this trend will continue with

even more countries being added in the near future. There is also consideration being proposed for a new trading bloc of China, Japan, and India.

2. *Technologies.* The unit cost of information will continue to drop and become nearly infinitely available. In this environment information will increasingly be used to impact efficient inventory, production, design, flow, distribution, and sales activities. One facet of this area that is changing is the purchasing of technologies. Companies are less prone to purchasing complex information technology (IT) systems up front anymore, and instead are increasingly seeking pay-as-you-go arrangements for enterprise resource planning and linkage systems. This brings increased flexibility for the buying and using company. Given that supply chains are vastly information rich and dense, today's supply manager must stay at the forefront of developments, applications, and potentials in this area.

3. *Regulatory policies and issues.* These will continue to dominate overall corporate and organization performance, and supply will be involved in many ways. In the United States, the Sarbanes–Oxley Act requires companies to develop and maintain an integrity to their core financial processes as well as identify and reveal to investors areas of risk that could materially impact the company's performance. Supply chains and supply are central to both of these requirements in terms of systems that are transparent and robust and identifying areas of vulnerability with suppliers and customers.

   Social responsibility is another area of rising interest, and supply managers are involved as their suppliers might affect their companies. This started with the use of child labor in third- and fourth-tier suppliers in overseas countries, but it points to supply chain transparency, corporate image, and attitudes of acceptable practices.

4. *Management shifts.* The management of all functions is increasingly demanding in terms of speed of competitive pressures, increased need for innovation, and constant reconfiguring of the business structures and processes. Except for start-ups nearly every company is seeking ways to reduce head count. Supply managers are having to deal with suppliers at farther distances and to use more complex supply chains, and all at faster rates of change. Where yesterday's purchasing manager overlooked a stable set of buying tasks where the items bought and available suppliers rarely changed, today there is greater complexity.

Supply Manager of This Decade

Center for Strategic Supply Leadership (CSSL) research reveals six key tenants of the supply manager's duties and challenges during the remainder of this decade.

It's no longer about overseeing a buying function. It is more complex and contributive than that.

1. *Supply is at the forefront of the company.* Where buying played a passive
   role at the end of a string of decisions in the past, today's supply is
   under the magnifying glass of senior managements for performance
   affecting corporate finances and competitiveness. More is expected of
   supply, whether it is to reduce complexity, speed product to market,
   find new sources of innovation, or protect the company from unknown
   risks. *Bottom line:* What makes sense in supply chains is defined by
   how the company is competing in its marketplaces, and by their very
   nature supply chain managers are now visible leaders and managers of
   part of the company's competitiveness or not-for-profit organization's
   missions.

2. *Top-line revenue is now a performance expectation of supply.*
   Corporate growth is a necessity today, and competitive pressures
   dictate that companies seek innovation speedily and effectively.
   Increasingly this is coming from suppliers rather than being done
   exclusively in-house. This puts supply in the position of accessing
   innovation by knowing where it might be possible to tap and bringing
   it into the organization. Top-line revenue is part of supply's performance metrics in addition to reducing costs for profit enhancement and
   assets for the balance sheet health. *Bottom line:* By its very nature this
   aspect of supply requires exploring for innovation sources as well as
   maintaining strong relationships with those that are in use.

3. *Slim and extend the supply chains.* Several things are apparent in this
   challenge. For one, there is a constant need to reduce complexity and
   unneeded costs, processes, and assets. There is also a need to extend
   supply chains globally, across tiers and time zones, and into and
   through the company out to the customer side. *Bottom line:* Supply
   chain efficiency means taking costs and assets out of the entire flow
   for reduced product/service and business cost structure benefits, and
   the greater use of outsiders to tap resources and performance enhancements. This will require skills of influence and reach in order to garner
   needed activities from others as well as knowing where to find and
   utilize them.

4. *Managing risk.* Risk was usually a problem of a supplier plant fire or a
   truck strike. The risks were known and usually short lived. Today, supply chains are longer; we know less about overseas suppliers than the
   domestic ones, and inbound transport flows are subject to many disruptions or uncertainties. *Bottom line:* Planning must be made farther
   into the supply chain, oversight must be maintained, and contingency
   actions identified and made ready.

5. *Supply managers are CFOs of the supply chains.* Companies are finan-cial entities in terms of performance and measurement. By viewing supply chains and supply activities as financial ones the supply man-ager enhances his or her credibility and results. More opportunities for improvement become obvious than when just viewing a chain as a physical flow entity. Too, discussions with senior and other C-level managements on a financial plane greatly lift the perception of supply as a partner in business performance. *Bottom line:* Finance and accounting knowledge and use of these languages are essential to being regarded as an effective supply professional.

6. *Take the initiative with opportunities and problems.* Purchasing used to be a passive function, waiting for others to give it requisitions or by working off of annual plans. No longer. Everyone in the company is expected to scan for opportunities and problems that cut into organiza-tional performance. Supply is no exception. There are no boundaries to supply. *Bottom line:* Professional supply management and leader-ship means taking the initiative in ways that bring new revenues to the business, remove unnecessary steps, assets, and costs, and reduce risks. In increasingly integrated businesses it is supply that sees across the departments and boundaries, and this is what gives it the ability and license to take these initiatives.

SUMMARY

Purchasing has shifted from having a passive, vertical function of performing administrative buying services to having a highly integrative, initiative-seizing set of leadership roles. The field will continue to evolve in many ways. The ISM supports professionals in this new setting. The remaining chapters of this book discuss topics, concepts, tools, and methodologies for the challenges and oppor-tunities of supply management for the remainder of this decade.

STRATEGIC DIRECTIONS FOR SUPPLY MANAGEMENT

John D. Blascovich
Vice President
A.T. Kearney, Inc.

William J. Markham
Principal
A.T. Kearney, Inc.

Thomas H. Slaight
Vice President
A.T. Kearney, Inc.

Powerful market forces continue to elevate expectations for supply management. Ever-increasing customer demands, quantum advances in technology, changes to industry structure, heightened economic challenges, the global economy, and enhanced risks to business continuity are collectively bringing waves of change that will severely test traditional approaches to supply management.

These future forces present a mandate for change in how a company manages the roles, relationships, processes, and performance expectations of its supply base. Successful supply management organizations will adopt a new strategic approach, while others risk slipping into irrelevancy. A proactive philosophy and willingness to change will allow companies to take advantage of increased opportunities and expectations to create and capture value from supply relationships. At the same time, supply management will become a catalyst for greater integration within and across value chains.

Supply management leadership will need to create new strategies while extracting maximum value through the execution of today's proven strategies. In this new era, the winners will be those that both anticipate and adapt to radical changes and make breakthroughs at opportune moments while also effectively bringing about continuous improvements.

THE IMPACT OF FUTURE FORCES

A number of forces will shape future strategies for supply management. Individually, each may appear manageable; viewed collectively, they sound an urgent call for supply management leaders to rethink their core strategies and take bold action.

Ever-Increasing Customer Demands

Increasingly, customers seem to want it all: superior value for price, innovative and highly customized products and services, and flawless life-cycle service. And, in many industries, it has become a buyer's market in which customers can exploit their full buying power from suppliers that are faced with significant over-capacity and hungry competitors around the world. These companies, in turn, then pressure their own suppliers for "more, faster, cheaper."

These customer demands will place radically different demands on a company's own operations, and in turn, on its supply base. Vastly increasing volumes of individual orders in decreasing order quantities will greatly affect manufacturing strategies and distribution patterns and dramatically change the role of suppliers. Suppliers will need to be more responsive than ever, striving to satisfy demand under rapidly changing market conditions. They will have to become more agile, adapting swiftly to optimize cost and service levels while minimizing waste.

Similarly, customers of service industries (e.g., financial institutions, health care, and telecommunications) will demand increasingly sophisticated and tailored service offerings. In turn, these industries will raise the bar for their suppliers of equipment, business services, consumables, and a range of other goods and services, boosting expectations for speed of response, reliability of service, and quality of customer interaction.

Finally, across all industries, suppliers will need to increase the pace and level of innovation to help their customers anticipate end-customer needs and to satisfy future requirements. In the latest edition in its global *Assessment of Excellence in Procurement* research series,[1] A. T. Kearney reports that leading companies are relying on suppliers for new product ideas. For example, at the Global Baby Care business unit of consumer products giant Procter & Gamble, 50 percent of innovation in the next few years is expected to come from suppliers.

Finding and developing suppliers with these types of capabilities will be a key goal of supply management organizations going forward.

Suppliers will also have to develop a better understanding of what drives customer demands—considering, for instance, whether a key customer is simply squeezing the margins or actually shifting strategies. Also of paramount importance is the balance between service and costs: not all demands are equally important to the customer, who can sometimes be appeased by a lower-cost alternative.

---

1 *Creating Value Through Strategic Supply Management, The 2004 Assessment of Excellence in Procurement*, A.T. Kearney, Inc.

Beyond knowing *what* the customer buys and trying to meet demand, the smart supplier will look to see *why* the customer purchases certain goods.

The Breakneck Pace of Technology Change

Technological change will continue to bring about radical shifts in certain industries and is likely to impact multiple facets of every value chain. Innovations in materials science, communications, and computing will shatter our current assumptions about product design, manufacturing technologies, and operational processes.

Photo imaging offers a good case in point. Over the past decade, the development and rapid adoption of digital photography has had an impact on the types of products being made, as well as on the participants in the value chain. The purchasing pattern has shifted: where the photo-processing market was long dominated by labs that purchased chemicals and light-sensitive paper, there is now a sizable market of home users who purchase glossy paper and printer ink from computer, office supply and other big-box stores, circumventing the traditional process. Kodak's ongoing shift away from traditional photo-processing goods in favor of digital products is but one example of the changes in this industry.

The radio frequency identification (RFID) tag that retailers like Wal-Mart and Target and the U.S. Department of Defense require suppliers to use in order to identify pallets and boxes is but the tip of the iceberg where microchip technology and microelectromechanical systems (MEMS) are concerned. In coming years, chips will go beyond merely noting an object's identity and allow objects to act autonomously or in concert with other "thinking" objects.

For example, machinery will have powerful built-in self-diagnostics systems capable of monitoring for and predicting failures and able to trigger proactive maintenance. This will significantly change what types of equipment a business will buy, how life-cycle costs are calculated, what additional products or services are purchased, and, most importantly, who the suppliers will be.

New Manufacturing Capabilities and Product Design

Future manufacturing capabilities and product design will change how and what companies purchase. New technologies will come to change supplier economics and impact their own manufacturing plants along with the related supply lines supporting them.

Already, automobile tire manufacturers are envisioning a switch toward units of one, as the day is not too far off when retail stores will be able to mix the appropriate compounds, build a tire carcass, and then vulcanize and finish a tire while the customer waits—all without incurring a cost penalty. Even more compelling is digital fabrication, which is currently used for model development and prototyping in many manufacturing settings. Author Neil Gershenfeld predicts that advances in IT and manufacturing technologies will allow individuals to design and produce custom products in their own homes using personal fabricators.[2] Already "fab labs" exist that allow individuals to design and create affordable "units of one" for applications as varied as the monitoring of food safety, creating custom musical instruments, and tracking the efficiency of agricultural equipment.

Changes in Industry Structure

Many industries are undergoing fundamental changes that alter traditional economics, drive consolidation, and redefine value chain relationships. Supply management organizations must understand how these changes affect their supply markets and plan accordingly. However, to fully plan for future supply needs, leading companies will also need to examine how changes in their own industries, and those of their customers, are affecting competitive dynamics and future expectations for supply.

For example, excess capacity continues to plague many industries in both the industrial and service sectors. Three main factors are driving this overcapacity: timing within the economic cycle, long-term industry trends, and the emergence of new capacity in emerging markets. As a result, companies within many supply markets are addressing overcapacity in an attempt to restore shareholder value. For instance, a move to rationalize production units across a network can free up whole units of productive capacity, such as an assembly line, a paper machine, or an entire plant. Unused assets can then be sold or written off.

Awareness of the ways in which new manufacturing technologies can change underlying industry economics, and the taking of appropriate actions in response, also brings benefits. For instance, by commercializing steel minimill technology, Nucor added to industry overcapacity while accelerating asset obsolescence for competitors that were relying on integrated mills.

Overcapacity also fuels aggressive consolidation. Ongoing consolidation will have broad effects on supplier relations, and success will hinge on the ability to forge strategic relationships.

Of course, not all industries are changing at the same rate. Where the pace is slower, supply markets can be leveraged to improve the current business. In fast-changing industries, supply executives must take on an active leadership role in a company's evolution.

The trend of companies focusing solely on what is key to delivering value to customers—the heart of their business—and outsourcing non-mission-critical functions is also driving industry restructuring. This phenomenon is leading to the emergence of value networks, groupings of companies that use complementary capabilities to deliver value to customers.

---

2 *FAB*, Neil Gershenfeld, Basic Books, 2005.

Within these value networks, each company must perform at a best-in-class level, be it in manufacturing, fulfillment, design, or service. Control must give way to cooperation within the network, where management happens collaboratively. The need to develop and maintain customer relationships and assemble and orchestrate appropriate teams has led to the emergence of a new role, the value network integrator. Taking on this role requires a company to have powerful ideas, to be quick to market so as to link up to and lock up with top-notch players, and to orchestrate operations across this extended enterprise.

The World Economy and Geopolitical Shifts

World economic and geopolitical changes pose yet another challenge. Increasingly, companies have to understand and attempt to anticipate the future direction and pace of globalization, the impact of social forces, changes in business regulation, and the potential impact of global security threats.

Globalization is occurring at a start-and-stop pace, speeding up when, for instance, new countries join the World Trade Organization and receive an influx of capital from foreign investment, and then slowing due to factors like variance in gross domestic product (GDP) growth and the implementation of new tariffs.

Companies have long grappled with the operational complexities brought about by globalization. They seek the right product mix, supply sources, and network of facilities with which to enter and serve geographically dispersed, economically diverse, and culturally different markets. At the same time, they are required to continue to balance logistical considerations, fluctuating currencies, tax differences, and regulatory inconsistencies.

Globalization raises new issues that affect how companies operate. In emerging-market countries, for example, limited income and distribution constraints are leading companies to adopt nontraditional solutions. Consider that in India, a Unilever PLC subsidiary manufactures and distributes single-serve packs of personal care products priced at the equivalent of a few American pennies. In this same country, Arvind Mills sells ready-to-sew kits of blue jeans components through a network of thousands of local tailors. Low costs and widespread distribution have made Arvind the market leader.

Recently, globalization has amplified as many companies pursue offshoring, seeking lower costs, higher productivity, more flexibility, improved service, and access to additional technical skills. With it come increased challenges of working with suppliers in distant markets with unfamiliar cultures for activities such as engineering and technical services, information technology (IT) management, customer contact centers, and finance and accounting.

Financial and legal issues also pose challenges. Unusual, sometimes opaque accounting standards can cast doubt on the viability of customers and suppliers in foreign lands. In other cases, companies operating globally may face newly stringent control and reporting requirements, such as those that have been brought about in the United States by the Sarbanes-Oxley Act of 2002. Intellectual property protection varies widely, especially between developed and developing countries, which can undermine investments in brand and technology. Also, no rules exist yet to govern the "virtual companies" being formed by new cross-border alliances and relationships.

In coming years, a number of "hot spots" will have a strong effect on global trade. Some of these are political, such as the situation between Israel and the Palestinians, Iraq's movement toward democracy, and ongoing tensions between India and Pakistan. Others involve scarcity of resources, such as oil and fresh water. Key transit chokepoints, such as the Panama and Suez canals and pipelines in Russia and the Turkish straights, may also play a role. China's explosive growth rate places increased demands for basic materials, absorbing unused capacity in some markets, and taxing tight capacity in others in the short term and potentially driving step-change capacity increases longer term. Finally, demographics issues, such as the aging populations of North America and Europe and the growing number of opportunity-starved young people in the so-called arc of instability that spans the Middle East, North Africa, and South Asia, will also reshape supply and demand markets.

To prepare themselves, companies should consider the impacts of working in potentially very different global business environments in the next several years. For example, three such scenarios for the decade ahead are

1. *Circle the wagons.* Under this scenario, the United States turns inward and isolationist, while European nations draw closer together to form a counterweighing coalition to the United States. China flexes its muscles, potentially leading to tensions with India and/or the United States. Terrorism remains a prevalent problem.

2. *Patchwork world.* In this model, the United States participates in world affairs, while alternately cooperating and quarreling with Europe. Rivalries between the world's powers cause tension, but remain under control. Terrorism and local conflicts flare up.

3. *Open society.* In this state, the United States is active on the world stage and works closely with Europe to collaborate on issues and emphasize multilateral solutions to problems. Working relations are maintained among the world's power rivals (United States, India, and China). Multilateral coalitions counter terrorism and localized conflicts.

Each one of these scenarios would affect supply markets in different ways and require varying levels of contingency planning and careful management of risks. Companies increasingly depend on a complicated network of global suppliers and partners, which boosts the risk of system failure if a key member of the network shuts down, even temporarily. Businesses face the challenge of balancing the benefits and risks inherent in this way of working. In looking at the global picture, companies have a growing need to reevaluate how their products sold will differ by region, where supply sources must be located, and what local requirements must be met.

Risks to Business Continuity

However optimistically or pessimistically one may view the future business environment, working in a global economy presents clear risks to business continuity—risks that require companies to develop actionable risk management strategies. Expansion into foreign markets, global sourcing, and a reduced supplier base bring enormous benefits to the companies utilizing these strategies, but they also create additional points of exposure to harm and increase the potential impact from a disaster.

Just-in-time and lean approaches to supply and manufacturing leave companies highly vulnerable to disruptions that can shut down factories. This became clear in 2002, when the port shutdown on the U.S. West Coast forced Toyota and General Motors' joint manufacturing plant in Fremont, California, to shut down just four days into the work stoppage for lack of parts, which were sitting offshore aboard inbound cargo ships.

Although suppliers in developing economies are often the lowest-cost producers, global sourcing involves lengthened lead times, increased uncertainty, and heightened security concerns. Goods coming from these countries can pass through nearly a dozen middlemen, greatly increasing the risk of disruption along any one of these points.

While the outsourcing of noncore activities is delivering benefits in both cost and service levels, it also compounds risk. With critical operations, from order management and manufacturing through to distribution being managed outside the company, the number of interfaces—and potential points of risk—increases.

Finally, supplier and supply location consolidation carries both benefits and risks. While strategic supply partnerships and consolidated manufacturing locations bring about economies of scale, they also increase the potential impact of a disruption, with few or no readily available backups or substitutes. Similar issues exist in service industries as well. For example, financial institutions with sole operating locations in lower Manhattan were unable to function following the September 11th attack as communications lines were cut and data centers abandoned. Other financial institutions had worked with suppliers to set up backup operations outside Manhattan and were functioning again in a matter of hours.

There is no easy answer to navigating through these hazards, so companies must keep these in mind as they make strategy decisions. Balancing benefits and risks has always been a key business challenge, but this is true now more than ever.

Capturing the New Opportunities

To respond to the changing environment, supply management executives and their organizations will need to extend beyond their current capabilities to define and execute a new, compelling strategic supply management vision. Living up to this new vision will require the following:

1. Build a foundation for achievement.

2. Focus on delivering value.

3. Exploit changes in the business environment to define breakthrough strategic supply management strategies.

Each individual company's preparedness to perform these tasks varies, but failure to do so will significantly detract from their chances of future success.

Build a Foundation for Achievement

Adapting proven leadership practices is key to fully exploiting the advantages achievable through supply management. A.T. Kearney developed the House of Purchasing and Supply framework (Figure 2–1) to illustrate the components that collectively build the foundation for achievement.

The quest for excellence begins with direction setting through a supply management strategy that fully integrates with the corporate strategy, and capitalizes on supply market opportunities to drive value creation through innovation, cost leadership, and marketing and revenue realization. Supporting this strategy is organiza-

FIGURE   2–1

A.T. Kearney's House of Purchasing and Supply®

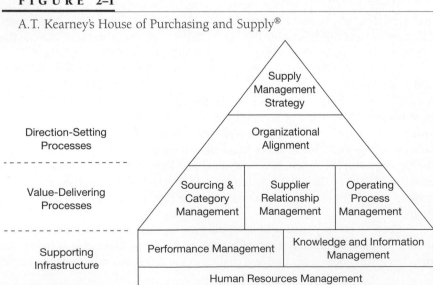

tional alignment, which enables supply management strategies, policies, skills, and knowledge to become embedded in a company's key business processes.

Value-delivering processes allow companies to execute their strategies in an effective manner. Advanced sourcing techniques leverage the full value potential across the entire expenditure base, thus helping the company to better exploit its own core competencies. Supplier relationship management manages the tension between the value-creation potential and inherent risks of each relationship. Operating process management entails the aggressive and innovative use of management policies and e-supply management tools to automate and streamline the full range of requisition-to-payment processes.

The supporting infrastructure positions a company for ongoing successes. Performance management links supply management metrics with corporate results and strategic objectives by making supply's contribution to results transparent. Knowledge and information management continuously captures and shares best practices, databases, and analytical tools across processes, geographies, business units, and external relationships. Human resource management creates "ambassadors" of supply management excellence through training, incentives, and aggressive rotation of high-potential professionals throughout the organization.

Focus on Delivering Value
A solid foundation helps supply management leaders address their single-most important priority: a relentless focus on value delivery. The scope of this delivery refers not to single tasks (e.g., placing an order) but to the broader strategic processes that dictate how tasks are carried out (e.g., strategic sourcing, supplier development). Several components are crucial to achieving this, beginning with the quest to attain "perfect information."

Knowledge is a highly strategic asset, and companies need to continue to nurture and reward quality data and invest in the tools required for effective decision support. For example, one telecommunications company has undergone a significant mindset change to stay abreast of the technology curve that is so crucial to its industry. To keep informed about new developments, the company has developed relationships with venture capitalists and next-generation technology firms, while adding resources dedicated to identifying, testing, and integrating new technology. The upshot? Additional capacity and capability are being added to the company's network ahead of its competitors.

As well, growth and innovation opportunities need to be relentlessly pursued and captured. Companies need to look outside themselves to uncover sources of innovation, and to consider how suppliers can be further leveraged for collaborative innovation—and potentially even for help generating revenues.

Supply management leaders will need to take cost reduction to the next level. New sources of value can be captured by working across functions such as engineering, research and development, and marketing. Because cost reduction opportunities are greatest in the conceptual design and detailed design life-cycle stages, next-level cost reduction will require early life-cycle involvement by all pertinent parties. A step-change approach to cost reduction has proven successful for many companies in the automotive industry. A deep understanding of cost drivers—both within the company and within the supplier's value chain—helps to set the targets for cost reduction. Some manufacturing companies have found that design and specification changes can lead to an additional 25 percent improvement in cost reduction above and beyond the levels attainable through supplier process and price improvement efforts. Furthermore, joint efforts between supply management and engineering can bring an additional cost savings of some 10 percent, doubling the increase typically attained when the two functions undertake independent efforts.

Companies can also find value by collaborating in innovative ways with other companies and with their suppliers. General Mills is a notable leader in this area. In one example, it worked together with both its supplier of corrugated cardboard and a U.S.-based beverage manufacturer to pool demand on a common cardboard box size that both companies use. The supplier was thus able to establish a dedicated corrugated line solely for the two companies, with all three benefiting from the resulting economies of scale. In another situation General Mills, which uses egg whites for many products, teamed up with a noodle manufacturer, which only uses the yolks, to coordinate purchases from a single supplier. In collaborating on product specifications, they were able to lower the supplier's costs, with all three participants sharing the savings. General Mills also leveraged its grain-purchasing experience to lower the egg supplier's cost for its most costly raw material, chicken feed, fueling further savings for all involved parties.

Additional opportunities for cost reduction can come through the outsourcing of specific supply management elements, both in terms of supply activities and specific types of purchases. Already, companies report that external providers are handling transaction processing, day-to-day supplier management, and even the strategic direction for purchasing certain categories. Indirect purchases, services, and maintenance and repair operations are among the broad spend categories being handled by these supply management experts, often through consortia and other tools that leverage large spend pools.

Finally, companies can gain value by pursuing step-change cost reduction from supplier development and integration. For example, retailer Sears and tire manufacturer Michelin teamed on a collaborative supply chain effort in which they implemented Collaborative Planning, Forecasting and Replenishment (CPFR). Through CPFR, they jointly benefited from a 4.3 percent increase in store in-stock levels, higher order fill rates (10.7 percent improvement), improved margins through proactive exceptions management, and improved productivity along the supply chain.

Exploit Changes in the Business Environment to Define Breakthrough Strategic Supply Management Strategies

As the business environment evolves, companies must be both willing and able to exploit the changed environment to survive and prosper. For instance, the rapid pace and multitude of technology changes requires that companies seek out and capitalize on technology innovation with their suppliers. Supply managers and suppliers alike can begin by developing a clear strategy for employing e-supply management technology across all the core business processes that are impacted by supply management (design collaboration, sourcing, category management, electronic transaction processing, and supply chain collaboration). Additionally, there is an ongoing need to anticipate the implications of radically new technologies on businesses, products, processes, and geographies.

To meet ever-increasing customer demands, companies will need to proactively align supply capabilities by transferring some of these demands to suppliers—essentially requiring suppliers to contribute to and support a more efficient value chain. An example of this is the partnership between BMW and Magna Steyr. Several years ago, BMW awarded Magna Steyr a contract to engineer its X3 sports activity vehicle while retaining responsibility for design, engine construction, supply management, and customer service in-house. BMW then drew its new partner even closer when, in a move unprecedented in its history, it announced that Magna Steyr would also assemble the X3, thus engaging its partner at multiple points on the value chain.

Finally, in order to face economic and geopolitical shifts, companies will have to consistently monitor how supply strategies address world economy pressures and create contingency plans for high-risk markets. For example, one consumer products company turned to a supply chain reexamination to fuel growth. Finding the local cost of a crucial ingredient so high that it posed a barrier to its European market-entry strategy, the company extensively examined raw material prices and supplier processing costs. It then worked with suppliers to obtain raw materials and helped processors improve their own manufacturing process to reduce costs. Doing so allowed the company to make a successful entrance into this new market.

Supply management executives will need to identify the next levels of value capture and value creation throughout the value chain, including all existing and potential value chain components. Examples where this applies include the successful transition of supply bases to emerging markets with lower labor rates (e.g., fabrication and machining components), pursuit of more integrated solutions to structural cost problems (e.g., airline maintenance and repair operations), collaborative sourcing with first-, second- and even third-tier suppliers, and more effective leverage of capabilities from all partners in the value chain (e.g., automotive design, manufacturing, and assembly).

Market intelligence will be another key component. For example, a leading global technology firm surpassed its competitors when it created an advantage three levels back in its supply chain by locking in the supplier of a critical component. Best practices in obtaining market intelligence today require the leveraging of dramatic improvements in information availability, broadening the understanding of the supplier market to a global level and deepening the understanding of core suppliers.

Another priority in setting strategies is a reexamination of the company's core competencies in light of the marketplace forces cited earlier in this chapter. This may require outsourcing noncore processes and shifting activities to an industry leader with both the scale and expertise to reduce cost. The recent wave of companies engaging in outsourcing and offshoring functions like information technology, manufacturing, and logistics clearly illustrates this trend.

The supply management team has a major role to play throughout the strategic outsourcing process: supporting strategy and planning, contributing to analysis of options and decision making, structuring the relationship and contractual arrangements, transitioning and implementing, and handling ongoing management, and measurement. In fact, the supply management organization's involvement was cited as a key factor in determining the success or failure of outsourcing activity, as A.T. Kearney, CAPS, and Arizona State University found in a 2004 study of strategic outsourcing involving 165 companies around the world.[3]

For many companies that participated in the research study, the supply management function had already assumed a strong role in outsourcing activities like procurement and supply management, manufacturing, and distribution and fulfillment, as well as such corporate support functions as information technology, human resources, and finance and accounting. Supply management organizations with a track record of success in strategic outsourcing can use this as a springboard to boost involvement in other outsourcing growth areas such as engineering, product and service development, and customer call centers.

Opportunities remain for supply management to extend its reach deeper into the outsourcing process. While supply currently has a high degree of involvement on the front end of the strategic outsourcing process (strategy and planning, analysis and decision making, and structuring the relationship and contract) at a majority of companies, there is room for supply management to expand its role in transitioning and implementing as well as ongoing management and measurement.

THE EVOLVING ROLE
OF THE SUPPLY MANAGEMENT FUNCTION

The supply management organization currently faces a turning point, similar to the situation that faced information technology departments several decades ago. While most companies may ultimately choose to outsource some portion of their procurement activities, supply management leadership should have a strong say in these and many other outsourcing decisions. As supply management becomes more strategic, the individuals leading this charge will themselves have to be among the most capable people in the organization.

3 Monczka, Ph.D., R. M., J. R. Carter, DBA, C.P.M., W. J. Markham, J. D. Blascovich, and T. H. Slaight (2005). *Outsourcing Strategically for Sustainable Competitive Advantage*, Tempe, AZ: CAPS and A.T. Kearney, Inc.

Lessons Learned from the IT Experience

In the 1970s and early 1980s, the broad availability of computing power seemed to hold great promise even as it created enormous competitive risks. At the time, IT was viewed as a significant competitive weapon, but time has proven that this was not the case for all companies.

The popular view of IT diverged rapidly, with three different paths or models evolving for this function circa 1985:

1. Develop into a strategic weapon.

2. Become an internal utility.

3. Transition to an outsourced service.

A combination of factors led each different companies to pursue one of these paths, but the IT executives generally had a strong influence on their enterprises' decision-making processes based on their ability to demonstrate value and how well they were able to articulate a strategic role for the future. Similarly, today's supply management heads will play a major role in determining their departments' fate, though best-in-class companies will tend to lean toward a blended model.

For information technology, the trigger point for this function's fate was the personal computer, as small-scale computing came to strip away much of the traditional mystique from data processing. For supply management, the trigger is still somewhat elusive. The increasing availability and power of Internet tools, increased volume and quantity of information about supply needs and options, and increasingly transparent market economics all may well be this trigger. Alternately, the trigger could come about as a result of companies reaching a "tipping point" in their value chain structure. As a greater percentage of the value chain is out-sourced, companies will be forced to rethink how they will manage their portfolio of external supplier relationships going forward.

Consider that until recently, the supply market was a realm that could only be accessed by diligent practitioners working in offices stacked floor to ceiling with supplier catalogs. Now, the supply marketplace has an electronic billboard online that faces the world: an interface available to *everyone*, not just the purchasing agent. Companies now want virtually all the goods and services they rely on to be sourced effectively, managed well, and purchased efficiently.

Far from what we may expect in these still-early, pioneering days of the Internet-purchasing interface, the supply models of the future are likely to parallel the evolution of the information technology function. For supply management, a model similar to information technology will likely apply over the coming years. Leaders will transform supply management into a strategic weapon by providing customer-facing innovation and revenue and create strategic cost advantage under the leadership of a key executive. In other areas, a utility or shared services approach that manages for optimal efficiency and cost will be employed. Finally, it is likely that large portions of companies' buys will transition to an outsourced service that can capitalize on its own expertise and advantages of scale.

The Future-State Supply Management Organization and the Supply Management Executive's Role

There are almost as many questions as answers concerning the design of tomorrow's supply management organization, from the top on down. One challenge companies will face involves the balance between center-led and centralized leadership structures for supply—part of this equation will be solved according to how standardized a given business functions from market to market. Lower on the reporting structure, many capabilities and skills will be embedded into processes across the organization, displacing clerical activities within supply management as users are given access to online purchasing catalogs, especially for purchases of indirect category items.

Single-point-of-contact relationships between buyers and suppliers will virtually disappear. Indeed, the prevalence of outsourcing and alliance arrangements will require an emphasis on managing external resources as new, nontraditional relationships are developed and nurtured. And, as supply management takes on increased roles in supporting areas like finance, information technology, and marketing, there will be even greater use of cross-functional, cross-company teams.

To make a global supply strategy work, leaders will need a deep understanding of other markets, preferably gained by first-hand exposure to other cultures. Supply leaders will be best served by working in different positions around the world throughout their careers to develop into truly global thinkers.

Even in today's interconnected Internet world, ensuring that the organization can manage a global supply network will require a blend of information systems to enable communications and provide visibility and local (offshore) offices to troubleshoot, manage relationships, and explore new opportunities.

"Smaller, smarter" will be the order of the day, with an increased emphasis on training and knowledge transfer across the organization. A firm grasp of technology is already a must for supply management. Additionally, leaders need to think like strategists and be prepared to lead change management efforts as their companies move to more advanced techniques.

With so many demands being put on supply, there is some question as to whether there will be enough talent to go around, as the broad skill set and deep knowledge required may make for a limited talent pool. In the short term, this may well extend the careers of experienced supply management stars who might otherwise be contemplating retirement.

ASSESSING READINESS FOR TOMORROW

Table 2–1 is a self-assessment that offers a quick indicator of how prepared a company is for the changes ahead. It examines whether the company has developed

TABLE 2–1

Are You Ready for Tomorrow?

Do You Have an "Evergreen" Process to … ?	Yes	No
Investigate the potential for value creation from supply markets?		
Define targets for supply management in corporate value creation?		
Link supply strategy to business strategy and pace of change for industries you buy from, sell to, and compete in?		
Align supply capabilities to support customers that want it all and want it now?		
Seek out and capitalize on innovation from traditional and nontraditional supply markets?		
Anticipate the supply implications of new technologies on businesses, products, and processes?		
Adapt supply strategies to reflect industry restructuring?		
Manage supply market risks to business continuity?		
Address globalization challenges via supply strategies?		
Tailor category sourcing strategies to reflect value potential and market dynamics?		
Manage supplier relationships to maximize value potential?		
Develop and refresh strategic skills within the supply market team?		
Integrate supply management with other core business processes?		
Pursue outsourcing of low-value supply management activities?		
Evaluate performance against strategic goals and define next actions?		
Total		

Number of Yes Replies	Readiness for the Future
12 or more	On track. Well on the way toward a robust, renewable supply management strategy. Should be able to anticipate and keep ahead of new challenges.
6 to 11	Questionable. Key elements not yet in place. In danger of being blindsided by forces of change.
0 to 5	At risk. Supply management strategy is obsolete. Company is not ready for changes ahead. Immediate action required.

and deployed "evergreen" processes to continuously keep the supply management strategy aligned with the business strategy, address the challenges posed by future forces via the supply management strategy, and support the supply strategy via sound execution capabilities.

Assessing your company against these criteria is an important early step in determining whether your supply management organization will develop into a strategic weapon, become an internal utility, or be transitioned to an outsourced service.

CONCLUSION

In summary, supply management will continue to face dramatic changes, but many of the fundamental drivers of value will remain the same: leveraging the supply base to achieve cost leadership, fuel innovation, and support revenue growth. Leaders in supply management will be those that know how to turn changes and threats into opportunities and capitalize on them for competitive advantage. The real challenge for supply management executives will ultimately lie in finding and maintaining an effective balance between a relentless execution of proven approaches and the necessary "creative destruction" of today's practices to deal in tomorrow's world.

INNOVATION AND OPPORTUNITY: WHAT'S AHEAD IN SUPPLY MANAGEMENT

DONAVON FAVRE
Adjunct Professor
North Carolina State University

ROBERT J. EASTON
Partner, Accenture Procurement Solutions, Accenture

INTRODUCTION

Research has shown that companies with well-managed, innovative, relationship-focused supply management practices outperform other companies in financial terms (total shareholder return, return on equity, return on assets, cash flow, return on investment) and in productivity terms (sales per employee, income per employee, real growth in sales).

The reason is simple: in most manufacturers, purchased materials and services account for at least 50 percent of the cost of goods sold. So it stands to reason that supply-management-savvy businesses generally are more successful. Consider a company whose purchased materials comprise 55 percent of its cost of goods sold: a mere 1 percent reduction in that figure will produce the same margin lift as a 12 to 18 percent rise in sales growth.

Like never before, the potential to meet and exceed that 1 percent reduction is available to companies of all types and sizes. The reasons are multifold: new and better technology, more companies and countries from which to source products, and increasingly sophisticated approaches to managing the supply management function (e.g., outsourcing and shared services). Supply management performance opportunities also are abundant because more and more enterprises—service and governmental entities, for example—are working to do it better.

The net effect—and the focus of this chapter—is an exciting and productive future for supply management. Just around the corner, look for manufacturers, service providers, and governments to leverage new technologies, contact and collaborate with a wider swath of suppliers, and successfully apply a host of new operating models for supply management and sourcing.

NEW TECHNOLOGIES:
TOMORROW'S SUPPLY MANAGEMENT TOOLS

Procurement technologies have advanced considerably. So much so, in fact, that virtually any company now has the potential to benefit from more-modern procurement or sourcing tools. However, if procurement technology has gained so much ground in the last few years, what should companies expect in the *next* few? This section looks at four of the most promising trends.

Maturing and Scaling of Procurement Technology

Early on, procurement technologies concentrated largely on the acquisition of indirect materials using electronic catalogs and work-flow tools from established names such as SAP and Ariba. More recently, solution providers expanded their range to address direct materials—a move that has helped many companies improve their operational performance. But down the road, challenges pertaining to *services procurement* will produce the greatest changes in procurement technology.

Services procurement is particularly valuable because of the growing complexity of service-related category management and the rising importance of service providers to the enterprise in general. Additionally, more companies are outsourcing service activities that used to be done in-house. All in all, more than 33 percent of a typical organization's current spending now is on services, such as contractors, temporary labor, travel, training, and marketing. Supply management departments typically manage less than 10 percent of this spending, and compliance with preferred providers is often low. The net effect is a wide-open field for services-savvy procurement applications that can help companies curtail rogue spending, work efficiently with a wider range of suppliers, simplify the sourcing process, and actively manage total costs.

A good example is contract labor—an area where coordinated procurement is arduous and compliance with preferred agreements is particularly poor. Much of the problem is due to the complexities of identifying and hiring appropriate temporary labor, and the subjective nature of hiring decisions. These challenges have made it difficult for supply managers to embed procurement and negotiating rules when electronically acquiring temporary labor services. However, new service-focused capabilities in e-procurement software will soon help companies overcome such obstacles.

Like e-procurement, e-*sourcing* technologies are becoming more powerful and (consequently) more popular. Originally designed to support the reverse auction (e-auction) process, e-sourcing capabilities are starting to find their way into core applications, including enterprise resource planning (ERP) offerings from suppliers such as SAP. As this continues, work flow and knowledge-management functionality will become more sophisticated, thus enhancing the sourcing process.

In addition, increasingly robust analytical tools will help companies proactively assess sourcing opportunities, identify alternatives, and evaluate proposals from prospective suppliers. Making the latter possible will be increasingly sophisticated modeling tools that allow companies to better determine and manage total cost of ownership across a wide array of categories.

Specialized capabilities in e-sourcing also will advance. A good example is the back-and-forth interaction required to reach agreement about the specific wording in contract documentation. Applications are emerging that allow companies to negotiate contract language over the Web by evaluating and marking up documents online, thereby resolving contract issues in something closer to real time and leaving a clear audit trail. Another promising area exists in the decision support function—specifically optimization solutions that evaluate numerous variables on a large scale. When procuring transportation services, for example, supply managers will be more able to present complex, multivariant scenarios, including specific business constraints. Suppliers will be able to respond with multiple bid variants of their own, including different price-break points and discount percentages that vary by volumes, sites, and so forth. These powerful combinatorial decision-support systems allow companies to create and understand more possible combinations than can logically exist in a typical e-auction system, and to scrutinize all possible combinations to know which scenarios best fit their business needs.

As noted later in this section, e-sourcing tools will become more valuable as their integration with other technologies is enabled and as organizations regroup to take advantage of these capabilities. Contract management, for example, is an e-sourcing capability of burgeoning importance; yet its success requires tight integration across procurement and financial systems. When companies pull information from enterprise applications, a new potential arises for them to monitor performance, enforce compliance, and become more attuned to milestones, aberrations, and expiration dates

Lastly, look for niche suppliers and ERP companies to focus more on applications that use standard capabilities to solve nonstandard problems—avoiding the need to create expensive overcustomized software. One such solution—an application for sourcing and managing complex services on an ongoing basis—is being developed by a company called Elance. Rather than build a new application for every service-related commodity, Elance has developed a powerful, generalized framework that allows supply managers to address high levels of complexity for commodities such as marketing and temporary labor. The solution addresses the strategic sourcing requirement and the tactical buying need—where business users construct, approve, and procure complex services orders (which are almost always different every time). A simple example would be an agreement for print services, where negotiation off the rate card is a complicated endeavor addressed through strategic sourcing, but significant value is captured by accurately *following* the rate card for custom print service jobs. Today, these requirements are not adequately addressed by traditional e-procurement systems.

More Sophisticated Business Intelligence

In the near future, procurement systems will be a lot smarter about gathering, inter-preting, and communicating relevant procurement-related information. To date, procurement-reporting capabilities generally have been weak. This means that the potential for better procurement analytics is enormous—even in the short term, with supply managers able to capture savings that they previously were unaware of. For example, spend-aggregation opportunities across departments or business units are less likely to be lost, and off-contract purchases can be identified more easily and addressed more proactively. Further down the road, such capabilities will allow companies to perform more in-depth analyses in less time, thus maxi-mizing their ability to negotiate with suppliers, manage supplier performance, and free up supply managers to concentrate on more strategic activities.

The greatest value, however, will be improving the speed of decision mak-ing, with alerts, triggers, and reports customized by end users—along with the ability to "slice and dice" procurement information at will. With this capability, the supply management function becomes more proactive—identifying problems before they get serious and flagging cost-reduction opportunities before the com-pany reaches its annual round of "let's go find the money." In effect, continuous improvement becomes more of a reality. You could also say that better supply management intelligence democratizes a company's information management capa-bilities by putting more powerful tools in the hands of those with the business insight to use them productively.

Before these milestones can happen, however, most companies will require much more granular data and significantly improved classification schemes for content. Many should also plan to increase the granularity of item information captured in reporting and analysis solutions (e.g., complete supplier data and/or line-item data from their bills of materials). Others will need to develop a clear and deep understanding of their services spend. These efforts—combined with technology improvements—will translate into real money very quickly.

Integration of Technology Functions with Other Parts of the Business

A natural analogue exists between increasing supply management's business intelligence and tightening procurement technology's integration with other busi-ness systems. Both ERP and best-of-breed suppliers have made this a priority, linking procurement technology more fully to financial, logistics, and even prod-uct life cycle management (PLM) systems.

The PLM connection is particularly relevant to direct-material sourcing (where more and more companies are pursuing cost reductions and new capabil-ities) and to the increase in global sourcing being undertaken by companies across commodity categories. Consider that the connection between product development and supply management is innate: up to 80 percent of direct material costs are locked up in the design and prototyping phases. However, better linkages with e-sourcing systems have strong potential to extend near- and long-term benefits for product development and supply management. These advantages include improvements in part reuse, streamlined item acquisition and availability, expanded sources of supply, improved access to preferred suppliers, and greater economy at the design stage—all without compromising designer priorities such as quality, functionality, and manufacturability. In effect, better connectivity with PLM tools means new chances to design costs out of new products and leapfrog the competition.

Although immediate cost reductions are not the mission of supplier portals, better integration with procurement technologies is another important advancement. The key benefits here are better collaboration with suppliers and the potential to automate basic transactions, such as purchase orders, purchase order acknowledgments, advance shipping notices, and invoices.

Primarily focused on evaluating supplier performance, radio frequency identification systems (RFID) applications are another procurement-integration target. To date, supplier-performance evaluations generally have been shallow, manual, and largely subjective: "Did they hit their delivery window?" "Were orders complete?" etc. However, linkages between RFID and procurement applications have the potential to inform supply chain decision makers in real time about actual reject rates, improve item tracking to accelerate recalls and warranty-management processes, and even abet supplier-managed inventory processes (i.e., deployment or removal of an item immediately triggers an order for a replacement item).

Lastly, planning and forecasting are tremendously important parts of the entire procurement life cycle—particularly in direct materials. For this reason, integrating supply management capabilities with planning, forecasting, and MRP systems will be a major supplier priority. This connection will effectively "close the loop"—reducing overall costs by providing future materials requirements to suppliers who, in turn, will be able to respond quickly without maintaining excessive inventories or suboptimizing manufacturing capacity to deal with unanticipated crises.

Stronger Influence of Web Services on Supply Management

Today, supply management professionals access various procurement portals to acquire materials, check status, complete transactions, research potential suppliers, and manage e-sourcing events. In the near future, a greater percentage of those interactions will happen transparently *between systems*, with software that uses open standards to connect applications and data sources over the Internet on demand, instead of through custom interfaces developed on proprietary networks. For example, when an item is ready to ship, the supplier's system will have the ability to automatically generate and submit an advanced shipment notice (ASN)

Later, the same automatic process will help trigger the generation and forwarding of an invoice. Basically it's the promise of electronic data interchange (EDI), but without proprietary networks and proprietary software.

Right now, the focus for Web services development is on building infrastructure and developing standards. In the near future, however, emphasis will shift to actual application components, such as industry-specific content. Shortly thereafter, early-adopting companies will be able to

- Simplify the connection of disparate systems to reduce connection costs and enhance collaboration with suppliers.
- Readily access new applications, thus extending information transparency and granularity.
- Connect to myriad suppliers in a single, uniform manner through a "Web services interface."
- Share more (and more detailed) procurement-related information with select suppliers, thereby reducing costs and fostering more long-term relationships.

Improved transaction and content management, as well as planning and scheduling processes, also will be major beneficiaries of advanced Web services. Today, for example, the process of planning and scheduling often requires companies to log onto a supplier's system, download a forecast, and then read and react to it manually. In a Web services environment, forecasts and plans will be shared, updated, and enhanced in a more real-time fashion. Design, financial, manufacturing, and logistical information will (with the proper authorizations) be ubiquitous.

NEW VENUES:
GLOBAL SOURCING AND SUPPLY MANAGEMENT

Global sourcing—seeking to acquire materials from "low-cost countries"—is not a new concept. Many companies have been doing it for years to reduce overall costs and capture other strategic benefits. Recently, however, there have been large increases in (1) the number of companies pursuing a more global supply base, (2) the variety of countries being considered as sourcing candidates, and (3) the quantity and variety of items being pursued and acquired. This trend is virtually certain to continue and grow. In fact, a 2003 Accenture survey reported that 91 percent of all respondents plan to increase their sourcing from low-cost countries or regions. Like global operations, global sourcing will be a hallmark of twenty-first century business.

Among all the low-cost countries on the world's radar screen, none has received more attention than China. And there is no other country whose continued growth is more certain or more massive. This section focuses on the characteristics that have made China one of the world's premier sources of supply. However, its lessons and observations apply to companies looking to tap *any* of the world's emerging sources of supply, including central and eastern Europe, Mexico, India, or other countries along the Pacific Rim.

Why Companies Are Seeking Alternative Sources of Supply

As shown in Figure 3–1, price and competitive pressures continue to be the motivators that most companies cite for acquiring more items from low-cost countries. According to the 2003 Accenture survey, globalization of suppliers (that is, a supplier relocating to a low-cost region or country) also is an important driver. In the high-tech industry, for example, most suppliers already have moved their operations to low-cost countries, such as China.

The flip side of the equation is the increasing attractiveness of countries from which new sources of supply might emanate. The following five criteria are largely universal, although the examples refer to China specifically.

- *Abundance of low-wage labor.* China has 941 million citizens between the ages of 15 and 59 (64 percent of its total population). The country's average hourly wage for manufacturing is about 60 cents.

- *Worker education.* Almost 49 percent of China's population has attained a middle school or higher education.

FIGURE 3–1

Price and Competitive Pressures Are the Top Two Motivators for Companies Seeking to Obtain Items from Low-Cost Countries
SOURCE: Accenture Low Cost Country Sourcing Survey, 2003.

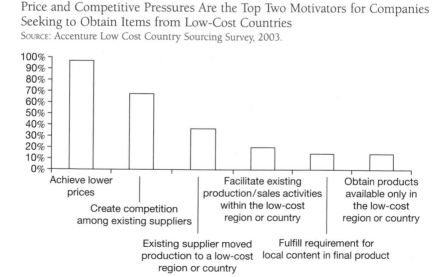

- *Size of domestic and export market.* According to the China National Statistics Bureau, the country's total domestic consumption reached $495 billion in 2003—an 8.8 percent increase from 2001. Total exports reached $326 billion—a 22.3 percent increase from 2001.

- *Market liberalization.* In conjunction with regulatory changes, such as its entry into the World Trade Organization (WTO), China has committed to reduce tariffs from the current average of 24.6 percent to 9.4 percent by 2005.

What Kinds of Products Will Be Best Suited to Global Sourcing?

"Traditional" labor-intensive products—items geared to leveraging a country's abundance of low-cost labor—used to represent the bulk of low-cost, country-sourced products (Figure 3–2). As shown, the momentum is toward higher-technology products and components. Note that natural resource exports are decreasing. This is because China's swift economic growth is placing greater internal-demand pressures on natural resources. In China, for example, consumer goods, clothing, and textiles were the largest export product categories. However, products with higher-technology content increasingly are being exported, as the Chinese manufacturing industry matures and as more and more global companies start sourcing directly from China. This is the direction that most low-cost countries will likely take: ramping up with labor-intensive manufacturing, and migrating slowly toward more skilled, higher-value products and services.

Global Sourcing Differences and Challenges

Dramatic differences in low-cost countries' culture, organization, relationships, and technology prowess pose significant challenges for global sourcing. Some of those challenges include:

- *Supplier relationships and identification.* Most companies have spent a great deal of time, energy, and money building a network of productive supplier contacts and relationships. In effect, they have created a system that works. Disrupting that system in favor of new sourcing opportunities (which many companies will have to do to remain competitive) is a formidable task. The process of supplier identification, for example, often is taken for granted in North America, since comprehensive information on suppliers generally exists, as does a standardized business language. Most companies also have experienced supply management and sourcing teams working in "familiar territory." However, in low-cost countries such as China, supplier information is far more fragmented and thus more difficult to obtain and compare. These complications are enhanced

FIGURE 3-2

Growth Rate and Strategic Importance for China's Exporting Business by Industry

SOURCE: WTO Statistics, 2002.

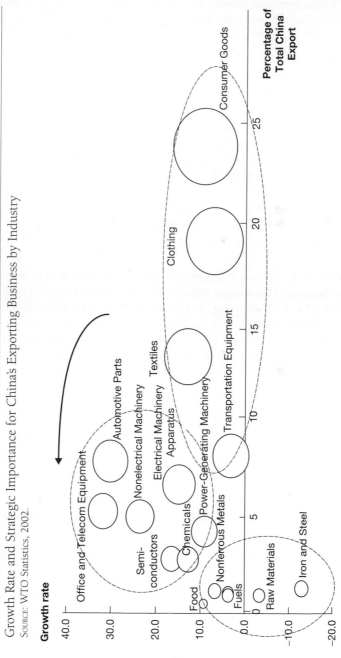

by language differences and the need for new or retrained professionals who have experience dealing with international supply managers and suppliers.

- *Technology and information systems.* Information technology (IT) systems and infrastructures are significantly less advanced and integrated in China, as they are across most low-cost countries and regions.

- *Supplier short-listing.* During the solicitation, screening, and short-listing process, stateside supply management teams also have come to expect a generally high level of sophistication from their prospective suppliers. There are numerous reasons why this will change when they work with Asian, central and eastern European, or even Mexican suppliers. In all these venues, for example, information is harder to acquire, consolidate, and present due to systems limitations and language barriers. Quality standards and legal oversight may be lax, which means that due diligence responsibilities rest more heavily with the supply manager.

- *Relationship-based negotiation.* Companies will need to incorporate an understanding of local business culture and relationships when negotiating for quality, service, and price. This is particularly true in China, but it also is common to many less-developed countries. Without the right *guanxi* (relationships), for example, priority-customer treatment in China is unlikely. The reality is that China's emphasis on relationships often trumps commercial realities. This is changing, but not quickly.

APPROACHES TO GLOBAL SOURCING

Multinational companies generally have used one of three business models to source products from China and other countries. As shown in Figure 3–3, the key difference is the degree of sourcing commitment:

1. *Trading agent.* Companies source products via trading agents, who help identify local suppliers, negotiate prices, and follow up on order fulfillment and logistics.

2. *Local joint ventures and wholly owned foreign enterprises.* Companies work with (and potentially invest in) in-country enterprises to develop an in-country presence.

3. *International supply management office.* Companies set up international supply management offices to identify, assess, and develop local suppliers.

Of the three alternatives, establishing an international supply management office tends to be the most widely practiced and successful approach. In addition to the basic benefits noted in Figure 3–3, international supply management offices will

FIGURE 3-3

Alternative Business Models for Sourcing Products from China

Typical Approach	Example	Benefits	Success Factors (Risks)
Trading agent	Textiles, clothing, and other consumer goods sourced via companies such as Li & Fung and Chinese import & export companies	▪ Smaller investments ▪ Simple operations ▪ Broad connectivity provided by local agents	▪ Ability to control quality and responsiveness ▪ Specialized products could be difficult to source due to the lack of technical knowledge and long-term commitment of the trading agents
Local joint venture/wholly owned foreign enterprise	ABB, Siemens, Philips	▪ Better understanding of suppliers ▪ Better control of quality ▪ Ability to form long-term relationships with suppliers	▪ Ability to coordinate sourcing programs across plants in different continents ▪ Ability to balance interests between different plants ▪ Ability to manage logistics and order fulfillment
International supply management office	3M China Ltd, Bosch, Carrefour, DuPont, GE, GM	▪ Specialized sourcing team ▪ Shared services for all business units ▪ Dedicated order and logistics management functions	▪ Sponsorship from all related business units ▪ Commitment to the success of the international procurement office ▪ Ability to manage in-house or outsourced logistics function

Low ← Degree of Sourcing Commitment → High

continue to offer most companies the best chance of reducing overall sourcing costs while limiting sourcing cycle times. The presence of an international supply management office also helps to ensure that all forms of supply information are communicated to corporate business units worldwide. Basically, they are the surest way to incorporate a new sourcing region or country into an established global supply chain. Typical capabilities of an international supply management office include:

- Local supplier identification, screening, and negotiation
- Purchase order management
- Sampling, design, and engineering support
- Logistics coordination and management
- Quality assurance and control

Some companies have successfully begun their sourcing journey by establishing a joint venture to ramp up local production and serve a local market. A year or so later, they launch an international supply management office that serves global as well as local markets, and increases overall sourcing value by accessing a broader range of sourced materials. This approach will continue to make sense in the future because it limits initial investments, identifies small problems before they become big ones, and resolves issues before regulatory approvals and licenses are obtained.

THE FUTURE IS NOW

Major global sourcing announcements by many of the world's leading companies are evidence of a trend that will fundamentally alter most companies' supply chain models and competitive cost positions. Nevertheless, there is no universal approach to managing sourcing operations in China or any other market. However, all global sourcing initiatives generally should begin with the same sort of business-case-driven approach. In other words, the first critical steps are to identify and quantify the need and then develop an overall low-cost-country sourcing strategy—determining which item categories are most suitable for alternative low-cost-country sourcing models and opportunities. Most companies then will need to perform a "strategic sourcing" exercise, during which they

1. Map current and optimal sourcing processes
2. Analyze total spend for each category
3. Develop a list of selection factors for assessing the value of current and prospective suppliers
4. Quantify the value and economy provided by the company's current stable of suppliers
5. Identify potential new suppliers and assess their ability to meet the company's needs with greater efficiency and lower prices

6. Develop a global (standardized) negotiation strategy

7. Develop a global (standardized) request for quotation

8. Develop and send requests for proposal to current and prospective suppliers

9. Analyze bids returned by interested suppliers and develop a "short list" of candidates

10. Negotiate with short-listed suppliers and make final choices

Like most business initiatives, the success of most twenty-first century global sourcing efforts will depend on how well they mesh with a company's business strategy, the degree of management buy-in, and the overall business case. But regardless of economic or political conditions, continued development of global sourcing capabilities and venues is inevitable.

NEW APPROACHES:
THE RISE IN PROCUREMENT OUTSOURCING

By 2005, all of North America's major companies likely will outsource at least some of their IT functions. In procurement, the trend is equally clear: the amount companies spend to outsource their complete procurement operations is projected to grow by 500 percent by the end of 2006 (Figure 3–4). Growth projections are reasonably consistent across all major regions of the world (North America, Europe, and Asia-Pacific). Moreover, nearly 40 percent of respondents to a recent international survey expect their spending on outsourced procurement to rise within 12 months.

Procurement Outsourcing Defined

Procurement outsourcing involves the transfer of all or part of an organization's purchasing activities to a third party that—by leveraging advanced technology, centralized operations, and the ability to translate the purchases of multiple clients into more economical buys—can offer improved procurement performance. Organizations outsource their procurement operations for a number of reasons; for example, an organization might outsource to reduce overall costs or to increase its focus on core competencies. Regardless of motivation, procurement outsourcing generally is

- A multiyear agreement
- More correctly associated with the provision of third-party services than with a complete transfer of control
- Contractually linked to explicit benefit targets, such as cost reduction and service enhancement
- Geared to continuous, step-change improvements in performance

FIGURE   3–4

Worldwide Procurement Outsourcing: Current Deployment Levels and
Projected Growth through 2006
Source: IDC 2003, Aberdeen 2002, Accenture Estimates.

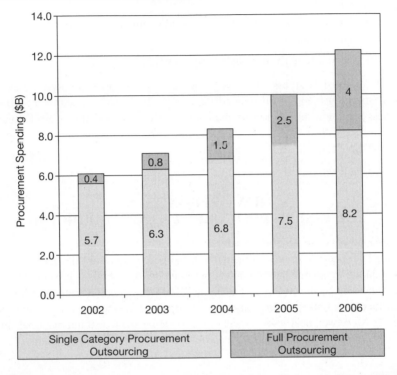

Outsourcing of the procurement function can occur on several levels (Figure
3–5). The most basic level involves a migration of infrastructure—primarily procurement technology and other tactical components of the procurement organization.
At the next level, an outsourcing services provider might also assume responsibility
for one or more transaction-type processes, such as requisitioning and procure-to-
pay. Higher still are value-added functions, including strategic sourcing (identifying,
selecting, and shaping supplier relationships and value propositions). Outsourcing
relationships that encompass these high-level activities may also involve the third
party's assumption of certain strategic responsibilities, such as the formulation of
business rules.

Why Procurement Outsourcing Will Increase

Historically, businesses have outsourced functions that are not part of their core
competencies—functions that could be performed more effectively by an organization for which the work *is* a core competency. For most organizations, pur-

FIGURE 3–5

A Pyramid of Increasingly Strategic Processes and Enablers and Assets
Demonstrates the Various Levels of Procurement Outsourcing

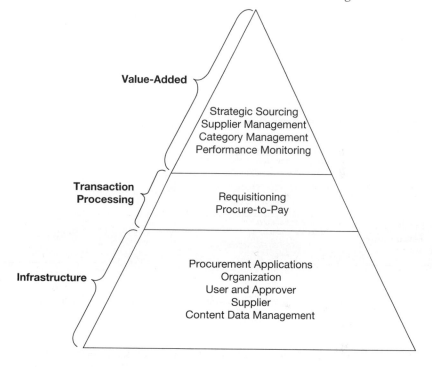

chasing indirect or noncritical materials—or managing basic processes such as procure-to-pay—are not core competencies.

However, more and more businesses are coming to realize that outsourcing also is an opportunity to increase efficiency. This acknowledgment, more than any other, is responsible for the dramatic usage increases projected over the next few years. As shown in Figure 3–6, cost reductions of 5 to 18 percent can result from an organization's ability to

- *Drive contract compliance.* Increasing on-contract buys from, for example, 60 to 95 percent can reduce an organization's costs by up to 3 percent.

- *Source effectively.* Since outsourcing providers procure materials and services for many clients, new opportunities arise to save money because of access to deeper category expertise and aggregated agreements.

- *Connect with a larger base of suppliers.* Outsourcing providers manage a broad pool of suppliers, which provides them with additional opportunities to capture lower prices and achieve a better fit with clients' procurement needs.

F I G U R E   3-6

Outsourcing Procurement Represents Significant, Ongoing Cost Savings through Scale Economics

Procurement Activity	Challenge	Opportunity, % Spend Reduction	Savings Implications per $1B in Spend
Sourcing	• Most entities do not follow a rigorous strategic sourcing approach • Most entities have not attracted top talent to procurement • Most entities do not have leading-edge tools (e-sourcing, e-auctions, etc.)	• 5 – 10	• $50M to $100M
Supplier Management	• Limited supplier qualification • Limited supplier integration • Opportunity to leverage aggregated buys for midsized and smaller entities • Lack of compliance with supply contracts	• 2 – 3	• $20M to $30M
Procurement Process	• Efficient sourcing-to-payment • Effective management of payment terms and settlement processes	• 2 – 3	• $20M to $30M
Procurement Technology	• Few entities have any form of procurement automation • Solution-selection and support skills are often lacking	• 1 – 2	• $10M to $20M

- *Operate more efficiently.* Third-party service providers distinguish themselves through exceptional levels of process rigor, discipline, and control.

- *Address complex services spend.* More than 33 percent of a typical organization's spend is on services, such as contractors, temporary labor, travel, and marketing. Purchasing departments typically manage less than 10 percent of this spend, and compliance with preferred providers is low. Outsourcing providers have solutions to manage a wide range of service categories.

- *Leverage technology more effectively.* Outsourcing providers have more access to and greater proficiency in the latest and best technologies. For example, they can use their experience with e-procurement and e-sourcing technologies to intensify supplier competition and deliver better prices.

Improved operational effectiveness is another characteristic that will spur adoption of outsourced procurement models. For example, outsourcing providers generally are better equipped to take advantage of early-payment discounts (potentially amortized across multiple buyers) and to optimize invoice matching and processing. Process controls and reporting efficiencies also may be enhanced by tighter procedures and better visibility of spend precommitments. Additionally, outsourcing providers can deliver a better cost model by using a blended workforce, which can include onshore, nearshore, and offshore resources.

Lastly, outsourced procurement will continue to gain popularity because it helps executives overcome the challenges they face when attempting to drive change through their organization. In recent years, most major organizations have worked to improve their procurement capabilities—usually by hiring new people or improving processes and technologies. However, organizations undertaking such change often are hampered by culture clashes and corporate inertia. In an outsourced procurement environment, change can be enacted more quickly, more efficiently, and with less resistance. Innovation is encouraged because the outsourcing provider continuously strives to reduce costs and increase service levels.

What Will Tomorrow's
Outsourced Procurement Environment Look Like?

In tomorrow's outsourced procurement environment, "service center" approaches will dominate—replacing today's distributed-procurement models that emphasize multiple individuals at multiple locations. In fact, centralization is the key component of procurement outsourcing: employees interact with a central buying function that, in turn, reaches out to a worldwide group of suppliers. Resources are shared across business units and even across organizations. This operating model requires rigor and discipline to achieve the needed level of collaboration among centralized sourcing specialists and end users.

As noted earlier, procurement outsourcing also is a compliance-intensive environment: more commodity categories and suppliers are tied to aggregated contracts, so there will be fewer tactical decisions for users to make. From the supplier's view, these changes usually will accelerate order, invoicing, and payment cycles.

Not surprisingly, the new environment will be more automation-intensive: the client organization's staff works largely in a self-service mode, transmitting orders electronically and using Web-based tools to access information about order status, supplier profiles, and contracted terms and conditions. Sourcing and quoting tools are equally prevalent: instead of phoning, faxing, or mailing requests for quotation (RFQs) to suppliers, client organizations will take advantage of electronic bidding and quoting. High levels of automation also will be necessary to ensure that up-to-the-minute information reaches online catalogs, inventory management systems, and accounts receivable and accounts payable functions.

Lastly, organizations can expect an intense focus on operating metrics, since outsourcing contracts and fee structures typically are tied to measurable results, such as cost savings or service improvements. As the outsourcing program is implemented, these metrics become the basis for quantifying the performance of individual business units against the broader set of organization-wide objectives. Business units that are not performing up to their targeted level are identified for focused performance-improvement programs.

NEW ADHERENTS: SUPPLY MANAGEMENT IN GOVERNMENT AND FINANCIAL SERVICES

Having engendered enormous benefits for manufacturers, strategic approaches to supply management are certain to be adopted by more and more nonmanufacturing entities. To date, organizations of this type have been less aggressive about supply management, probably because they view it as less critical and because they typically have fewer "direct materials." This will change. In the future, manufacturers and nonmanufacturers will work equally hard on supply management innovations that help them reduce spending, deliver enhanced services, and dramatically enhance their overall operating performance. To help understand how and why these efforts will become more widespread, this section looks at two nonmanufacturing examples—government agencies and the financial services industry.

Government

"Supply management excellence" used to be synonymous with cost efficiency. Now, however, most of the world's private-sector leaders (particularly manufacturers) emphasize supply management because they know that the term *strategic supply management* implies—and even helps create—advantages in operational effectiveness, customer satisfaction, and overall business performance. Many of the world's public-sector agencies have come to the same conclusion; and in the near future, many more will do the same.

Contrary to traditional bid/quote systems, which reconcile the lowest price against some basic minimum requirements, strategic supply management emphasizes understanding customer requirements and actively partnering with suppliers to obtain beneficial pricing and superior service and thereby reducing the total cost of ownership for goods and services. A top public trendsetter in this area is the New York City Department of Education (NYCDOE), which successfully used analytical methods to understand its spending habits and facilitate its sourcing of commodities: IT hardware, telecommunications, software, office supplies, office equipment, instructional supplies, food, fuel, and maintenance and custodial supplies. Once all these measures have been fully implemented, savings are expected to exceed $70 million per year. However, NYCDOE achieved further operational savings by improving Web-based ordering and consolidating its invoicing. And it also secured significant service-related improvements, including better warranties; asset-management, repair, and maintenance agreements; and service-delivery guarantees.

These accomplishments do not exaggerate strategic supply management's potential benefits to the public sector. Consider that the U.S. federal government collected approximately $2.1 trillion in tax revenue for the 2001 tax year.[1] During

---

1 Source: Internal Revenue Service, 2002.

that same period, Wal-Mart Stores, Inc., the world's largest company, generated $220 billion in revenue.[2] Moreover, procurement savings as a percentage of revenue could be even higher for governments since, to date, few agencies have been as rigorous about efficiency as private-sector companies such as Wal-Mart.

What Will Be
Looking ahead, innovative public-sector entities will be more likely than ever before to engage in the following supply management practices.

Leverage Purchasing Power. Forward-thinking public-sector organizations will use their size and scale to forge consolidated and collective agreements that help drive better deals.

Like the private sector, many public entities defer purchasing and contracting to a site, group, department, or functional area. In the absence of organization-wide contracts or agreements, each buying entity has sole purchasing authority. Not surprisingly, this has lead to suboptimized pricing, transactional-based supplier relationships, and an unhealthy proliferation of the supply base—a clear disadvantage when attempting to negotiate more cost-effective and service-oriented contracts and agreements.

Even public-sector entities that do possess a formal contracting or supply management organization often have found themselves hamstrung when it comes to leveraging purchasing power. This is because such groups often are required to execute competitive bid events solely to identify low-cost bidders—a process that leaves little room for strategically negotiated agreements focused on leveraging the total organization's size and scale. This bid/quote approach is markedly different from the strategic supply management approach (negotiating contracts based on market intelligence, cross-organization collaboration, and total cost of ownership) practiced by tomorrow's (and a few of today's) leaders.

Before its supply-management-rationalization initiative, each school district in the New York City Department of Education controlled its own computer purchases. This fragmentation (711 different IT suppliers) created many problems, including unmanaged acquisition practices, lack of access to key data points, severe maintenance and customer-service shortcomings, and a lack of market-comparable pricing and service. As part of the initiative, NYCDOE defined four standard laptop and desktop specifications to simplify requirements and aggregate demand for approximately 13,000 machines. It then placed this volume out for competitive bid, which resulted in savings of more than 30 percent across all platforms, along with stronger commitments for delivery, software imaging, asset tracking, installation, next-day maintenance, and warranty services. In effect, the approach transferred channel power from supplier to purchaser, thus giving NYCDOE the ability to better control product, price, and service requirements.

---

2 Source: Time, Inc., 2002 (Fortune.com).

Practice Cost Avoidance. The enormity and inherent complexity of public-sector organizations means that more-efficient purchasing principles have great potential to eliminate costly and unnecessary purchases.

Cost avoidance is not merely a blind reduction in spend (which tends to compromise an organization's ability to perform its job effectively). Instead, cost avoidance implies the targeted reduction of "waste spending" by identifying and eliminating noncritical costs. In the future, more and more public-sector entities will work harder to build a higher level of understanding about their purchasing practices, priorities, and beneficiaries. The NYCDOE performed such an assessment, focusing on supplier concentration, top-spending districts, and frequently ordered items. The analysis revealed opportunities to promote cost savings through targeted renegotiations, restructured price agreements, increased supplier management, and improved communication with end users.

Know the Market. Leading public-sector entities will make better supply management decisions by working first to understand market dynamics and conduct necessary due diligence.

By developing a deep knowledge of specific industries, supply management decision makers can discover new opportunities for cost savings and service improvements. Understanding market dynamics also is important for shifting the locus of power from sellers to buyers—knowing about the latest and greatest services is central to finding the best deals at the best prices.

Toward this end, NYCDOE software- and hardware-commodity teams began working with the internal IT organization to source and develop software. Soon after, the group discovered that operating system licenses often were being purchased individually, resulting in extra expense and multiple license agreements. Changes to this approach reduced NYCDOE costs per license by more than 80 percent. By analyzing existing contracts, the Department also determined that suppliers were allowed to charge up to 5 percent of the retail price for freight. After implementing single-user license agreements, freight charges were virtually eliminated.

Overcome Legislative Burdens. Today's public agencies often are limited by legislative constraints requiring that decisions be made solely on product price. In the future, commodity strategies will require a total-cost-of-ownership perspective.

Formal policies frequently keep today's government purchasers from applying the most current and innovative supply management techniques. As a result, public-sector agencies often are hesitant to conduct online auctions, close off traditional sources of supply, exploit the advantage of spot markets, and implement aggressive supplier-management programs.

Overcoming these obstacles requires a deep understanding of current legislative constraints and a thorough knowledge of market dynamics. For example, existing NYCDOE procurement rules preclude the awarding of bids based on best value—focusing instead on cost exclusively. However, by expanding the use of requests for proposal, NYCDOE was able to include additional services and evaluate proposals according to the total cost of ownership of the goods and services purchased. These changes to the norms of bidding were critical to the overall success of the initiative. And in each case, they reduced NYCDOE's total cost of ownership.

Build Confidence in Strategic Supply Management. Gaining the trust of internal end users is critical to structuring effective agreements with suppliers. To realize the benefits of new sourcing agreements, tomorrow's leading public-sector entities will provide incentives that encourage end users to adopt better purchasing behaviors.

Public-sector organizations generally spend according to fixed yearly funding allocations. As part of the approval process, reviews are made of the previous year's spending, which plays an important part in determining future allocations. As a result, organizations are implicitly encouraged to spend all budget allotments—regardless of need—in order to avoid budget cuts in ensuing fiscal years. This approach reduces the motivation of end users to work with a central contract just because it is lower cost.

To change this paradigm, enlightened public-sector administrators will develop policies and priorities that more actively incorporate end-user requirements. As part of its strategic supply management initiative, the New York City Department of Education leveraged end-user motivation to drive compliance. For example, easier ordering mechanisms, such as Web-based ordering and convenience cards, were implemented to encourage use of preferred suppliers. Additionally, new suppliers were associated with superior services, such as guaranteed next-day delivery and higher fill rates—thus contributing to higher end-user satisfaction, more concentrated spend, and greater annualized cost savings.

Improve Supplier Management. Strategic supply management advocates a buyer-centric model. The most successful public-sector organizations will actively monitor supplier performance to ensure adherence to agreed-upon terms and to identify additional savings opportunities.

The principal objective of strategic supply management is to develop agreements with suppliers that promote cost-efficiency, while meeting or exceeding the requirements of end users. However, supply management professionals must constantly monitor and manage supplier performance and adherence to agreed-upon terms if they expect to fully realize the promised benefits.

Changing the Way Government Purchases

Perhaps most important, supply management organizations in all sectors will put more effort and imagination into finding ways to reduce total cost of ownership. These initiatives will include the benefits previously mentioned (strategic sourcing, procedural changes, new purchasing efficiencies, etc.). But they also will need to include newer processes and technologies such as reverse auctions, e-procurement, and e-sourcing. Better training, professional development, professional recruiting, and other organization and people enhancements can create even more benefits. And longer-term initiatives, such as policy and legislative reform, agencywide education, and financial reform, also will be needed to change the overall perception and environment of public-sector purchasing.

Financial Services

In today's highly competitive markets, the survival of financial institutions often depends on their ability to source and distribute capital at attractive prices, with the right service package. At the same time, they face unrelenting challenges to lower their cost base and streamline operations. In such an environment—with margins shrinking and customers wary—senior executives must pay close attention to any initiative with the potential to lift their businesses above the pack and deliver shareholder value.

In the near future, many more financial services companies will look to strategic supply management to help them achieve these goals. The main reason is an opportunity to improve the total cost of ownership of indirect materials. But supply management leaders in virtually all industries know that other customer-service-, time-, and labor-enhancing benefits nearly always accompany an aggressive, imaginative procurement-optimization initiative. Following are some supply management initiatives that will make a significant difference in financial services firms' operating performance over the next several years.

Optimize Sourcing. Compared to companies in other industries, financial services entities tend to exhibit less maturity in their sourcing practices. As a result, sourcing will continue to be an area of focus for these organizations—helping them to cut procurement costs by as much as 15 percent on their addressable spend base. A good example is Société Générale Group, the sixth largest bank in the Euro Zone. To respond to falling banking income—and to create a hedge against further degradation of the business climate—Société Générale launched an aggressive cost-reduction program. A cornerstone of that program was a strategic sourcing initiative during which the bank used a formal methodology to identify the widest range and mix of suppliers, map current sourcing processes, rationalize the current supplier base, and negotiate or renegotiate contracts to reduce overall cost of ownership. Among the 16 categories addressed by the initiative were market data, travel, marketing and communication, and legal and human resources (HR) services. This particular effort has helped Société Générale reduce its total spend by an average of 5 percent.

Rebuild the Procure-to-Pay Model. There is more than one way to fix what is broken in supply management, but it always is appropriate to take a holistic view of all components: people, technology, and processes. And one of the systemic problems that this view typically reveals is a flawed procure-to-pay model.

Traditional procure-to-pay approaches divide procurement into a series of steps, each of which is handled by a different unit or department. From requisition through payment, the result is too many hands and too many handoffs, all of which add unnecessary expense, delay, and errors. Financial services companies often are dogged by this problem because, on balance, they have less supply management expertise than companies that routinely make large direct-materials purchases. For both entities, however, the solution is the same: a procure-to-pay model that spans all capabilities, IT infrastructure, applications, and processes.

Increase Use of Electronic Tools. Financial services companies will increasingly take advantage of electronic tools such as e-sourcing, e-auctions, and spend-management applications—thus achieving cost savings by adding discipline to their sourcing approaches, shortening process cycle times, and better understanding their spend patterns. Société Générale created an electronic procurement portal to provide structured, companywide access to purchasing information, such as contracts, terms and conditions, best practices, and policies.

Apply Best Practices to Overlooked Spend Categories. A number of spend categories tend to be unique to financial services. And there are several others that, for a variety of reasons, have historically been underattended by the industry. As more and more financial services firms design and implement sophisticated supply management solutions, they will work harder to accommodate the unique requirements of categories such as

- Brokerage, clearance, and exchange fees
- Market data expenses
- Legal fees
- Marketing and advertising expenses
- Property and casualty claims replacement

Maximize Compliance. Compliance is critical to sustaining the savings gained from the strategic sourcing process. Recognizing this, more and more financial services companies will focus specifically on the activities that drive compliance, including benefit tracking, data mining, integrating processes end-to-end, facilitating user compliance, and communicating issues upstream to suppliers. Société Générale, for example, developed a "compliance dashboard" to track buyer non-compliance to existing procurement contracts at all levels of the organization. On a monthly basis, each business unit manager now receives compliance indicators, such as percentage of (economically unjustifiable) short flights and monthly spend per employee profile (manager, assistant, etc.).

Develop Shared Services Programs. Supply management is fast becoming one of the top areas of focus for financial services companies when it comes to achieving cost savings and operational efficiency. As this focus continues to expand, more and more financial services companies will develop shared services units to manage the function.

Outsource All or Part of the Supply Management Function. Achieving supply management excellence can be a complex undertaking. Recognizing this, more and more financial services companies will follow the lead of Deutsche Bank and outsource their procurement operations. Deutsche Bank recently outsourced all its global procurement and accounts payable processing functions. The third party has assumed total management of the organization's indirect spend and tactical sourcing.

CONCLUSION: DEFINING AND LEVERAGING SUPPLY MANAGEMENT LEADERSHIP

Recognizing and leveraging opportunities is key to developing a supply management function that is both cost efficient and business-results oriented. But what characteristics typify those companies that consistently do this best? Generally speaking, supply management leaders excel in most or all of the following six areas: (1) leadership, strategy, and governance, (2) organizational structure, (3) cross-enterprise integration, (4) resource management and development, (5) stakeholder relationship management, and (6) application of supply management metrics. This chapter concludes with a brief examination of each these traits.

1. *Leadership, strategy, and governance.* The initial (and overriding) task of a visionary, supply-management-focused procurement leader is to establish a global supply management strategy. Generally speaking, that strategy will frame the company's practices, policies, priorities, and approaches to the organization's direction, execution, and enablement:

   - *Direction.* How do we want to acquire materials and services?
   - *Execution.* What do we need to do to raise our level of performance?
   - *Enablement.* How will we make it happen?

2. *Organizational structure.* The organizational structure most commonly used by supply management leaders is grouping by like commodities. This approach allows companies to consolidate enterprisewide volume and to concentrate (narrow) the supply base—two important ways to leverage volume and save money. Grouping by like commodities also helps supply managers to develop deep industry, commodity, and supplier expertise and to speak with one, consistent (enterprise-level) voice to suppliers.

3. *Cross-enterprise integration.* To ensure that an efficient, enterprise view of procurement takes precedence, supply management leaders

frequently rely on cross-functional sourcing teams. These teams include representatives from the supply management organization, manufacturing, engineering, and product development; although finance, sales, distribution, and IT people may be involved from time to time. Working together, they determine strategic sourcing priorities, devise total cost of ownership (TCO) models, develop category strategies, and design supplier-selection decision matrices that identify and weigh supplier-selection factors. They also may take responsibility for issuing and evaluating requests for information and requests for proposal.

4. *Resource management and development.* Supply management leaders recognize that acquiring, developing, and retaining talent is critical. They also follow through—with comprehensive, customized descriptions of the skills needed to build and remain supply management leaders. For example, their job and skill set profile for negotiation may be "prepares, coordinates, and conducts negotiations with suppliers. . . . Also negotiates agreements to achieve results that support sourcing strategies and enterprise business objectives."

5. *Stakeholder relationship management.* In virtually all companies, a supply management organization's primary stakeholders are internal customers, department employees, and suppliers. However, supply management leaders generally do a better-than-average job of weaving each group's point of view into their gap analyses, opportunity assessments, and supply strategies. Not surprisingly, they also communicate more effectively and frequently with their stakeholders. In fact, to ensure the delivery of (and adherence to) key messages, many have developed formal communication matrices consisting of stakeholders, target audiences, key messages, timing, communication channels, desired outcomes, and responsibilities.

6. *Metrics.* Supply management leaders insist that all decision makers apply the same assessment formulas. Toward this end, many deploy a Balanced Scorecard to ensure that everyone reads from the same book, speaks the same language, and interprets information in largely the same way. Examples of balanced metrics might include supply management employees as a percentage of company employees, sales per supply management employee, total supply dollars per supply management employee, active suppliers per supply management employee, and annual training hours received per supply management employee.

CHAPTER 4

THE THREE- TO FIVE-YEAR OUTLOOK: ANTICIPATING THE FUTURE IS NO LONGER ONLY SENIOR MANAGEMENT'S CONCERN

Dana Kendall
Former Program Manager
A.T. Kearney Center for Strategic Supply Leadership
Institute for Supply Management™

Roberta J. Duffy
Editor
Inside Supply Management®
Institute for Supply Management™

In a recent quote, "Dilbert" creator Scott Adams accurately depicted two main methodologies to perfectly predict the future: (1) reading tarot cards or tea leaves, otherwise known as the "nutty methods" or (2) using sophisticated computer models to crunch statistics and well-researched facts, which he refers to as a complete waste of time! Predicting the future is tumultuous territory, especially in today's accelerated business environment. But no matter how daunting, senior executives commit significant time and resources to it. What's more, if you're not devoting energy to considering what's next, you'll be left behind while the successful pass you by. Identifying today's necessary actions to meet future challenges and opportunities is no longer a task solely for entrepreneurs and visionaries, but an expectation at all levels.

This chapter focuses on three areas: (1) chief executive officers' (CEOs) expectations for the next three to five years and the implications of these expectations for supply management, (2) the three- to five-year expectations of chief purchasing officers (CPOs) for supply management, and (3) the competencies and proficiencies needed to meet these expectations. Of particular interest is the contribution supply can make in the near term, and the influence supply can have on CEOs' perspectives and, consequently, on organizational strategy.

When considering the future, one thing that is fairly predictable is that leaders' visions will trickle down the corporate hierarchy and become tomorrow's reality.

This chapter begins with an overview of why it is important to consider the future, continues with a discussion of leaders' visions for the future, and concludes with the competencies and proficiencies needed to prepare for and excel in the future.

THE FUTURE IS NOW

Why does the future matter, and why is it important right now? The answer is simple. Successful leaders anticipate, appreciate, and address future opportunities and challenges, and they begin adapting now to create competitive advantage before the future is reality. Those who do not do so are left supporting those who do. Future potential is where leaders make their mark. It is no longer enough to merely focus on and solve today's problems.

Why should supply management professionals prioritize and analyze an obscure future, given the volume of critical challenges faced today? There are no guarantees about the future. Even at the CEO level, there is disagreement on what the future holds. However, leaders agree that competitive advantage can be gained from understanding the future faster than the competition does. This is a challenging task at best, especially given the complexity added by new and dynamic commerce models, the speed of information flows, and the rate of technological innovation.

Natural organizational culture can also be a hindrance. There is an inherent behavioral challenge in trying to dedicate today's resources in anticipation of an opportunity or challenge that has not yet surfaced and will not for upward of five years. However, the reality is that it takes three to five years to get major initiatives off the ground; therefore, the key is anticipating and budgeting for them now.

Prioritization is also a factor. There are many strategic initiatives that are driven by and impact supply management, and many professionals are uncertain about which direction to steer—it is like trying to navigate an airplane with a compass instead of a global positioning system. In large companies, this adds incalculable complexity, especially given the propensity for strategic initiatives to contradict one another, leaving the decision makers at a crossroads.

Finally, the ambiguity and uncertainty of trying to contemplate the future deters many people from spending time considering "what could be?" Assessing whether predicted threats and opportunities are materializing or morphing is both time consuming and difficult.

Nonetheless, considering the future is an imperative for all leaders. It all comes down to this: someone in the company must address future-oriented issues. Given supply management's edge-to-edge reach, from the organization's customer's customers to our supplier's suppliers, who better to lead the organization through complex times? Even in organizations where the chief financial officer holds the reigns, the broadening umbrella of supply management dictates that there is opportunity to surpass the status quo at all levels.

As Cece Webster, vice president of procurement at Coca-Cola, stated, "I want to get a mirror out there and see what's around the corner. I've got other people in the organization who can identify current best practices. I need to know what's going to be out there a couple years from now."

What does the future hold? As we have derived, there is no single clear-cut answer. However, one thing we can be sure of is that CEOs' expectations for the future will drive business priorities and become strategy. These priorities will fan out to all business functions and influence key business processes including those led by the chief purchasing officers (or equivalent) and continue downward into the organization. Therefore, much can be learned from CEOs' expectations for the next five years, and this is the logical place to begin.

CHIEF EXECUTIVE OFFICERS' EXPECTATIONS

The Conference Board's annual publication, the *CEO Challenge*, is dedicated to answering the question of what CEOs think are current forces in the marketplace and the trends they expect to face in five years. Interestingly, the 2003 report clearly indicated that supply management will play an ever-increasing role on CEOs' radars. The top five areas were

- Today's cost/price crunch will become a way of life.
- Strategic focus will be on brand.
- Technology will hit a wall.
- Global commerce will be the single driving force that dominates all aspects of competition.
- Industry consolidation will be inevitable and widespread.[1]

Implications for Supply Management

Each of these five projections has implications for supply strategy and execution. Supply management leaders must determine the extent of the impact of these projections on their company and industry and devise effective strategies to increase the organization's competitive advantage.

---

1 E. V. Rudis (2003). "The CEO Challenge 2003: Top Marketplace and Management Issue," *The Conference Board*, www.conference-board.org.

Cost and Price Focus

In the last decade the emphasis was on reducing the costs of processes, labor, and purchased goods and services. Today, many supply leaders agree that they have largely taken out avoidable costs in people, purchasing, and processes. The emphasis must now shift toward institutionalizing the behavior while incrementally improving contributing factors at every opportunity. The implications are that cost-cutting will become normative; costs and pricing will become transparent to customers.

The implications of the cost and price focus for supply management are that new means of negotiation must be developed—both when dealing with suppliers and within companies to respond to the organization's customers. The focus becomes the development and maintenance of lean supply chains rather than special cost-reduction projects to reach a specified savings target. Furthermore, continuous investment is required to make supply chains more efficient and effective versus isolated deals. Transparency in supply chains increases because of more sharing of and access to data and information making it progressively easier to identify opportunities and cooperate to remove unnecessary costs. Leaders are more concerned with crafting productive interactions among supply chain partners to improve cost structures than in achieving isolated price reductions.

Brand Focus

Five years from now, branding will be challenging and even riskier due to speed, lack of barriers to new market entrants, institutionalized cost management, transparency, and downward pricing pressure from rising Asian competitors.[2]

For supply management, the focus on brand means that supply managers must move beyond the current question of "How can we directly contribute to the bottom line?" to those of "How can we contribute to and build our company's brand?" "How can supply deliver brand-building value to our customers?" and "How will our sourcing decisions build our brand?" Intel is a perfect example of a company that has used supply innovation to contribute to customers' brands. Computers with Intel chips use the Intel Inside logo in both advertising and on the product. Like it or not, supply management professionals must get in touch with their marketing roots.

Technology Stagnation

Predicting the next Internet-magnitude trend would be foolish. Skeptics predict that IT innovation will run out of steam after reaching the limits of possibility directed by the laws of physics. If this happens, there will be discontinuity and adaptation pains as the world adjusts. Of course, there is always the possibility that new breakthroughs will mitigate this risk. The likely time lag will probably leave some sort of a gap.

---

2 Ibid.

As efficiencies are achieved through business-to-business e-commerce, supply leaders look for the next win. AMR Research reports expected growth in the sale and use of supply chain management software as manufacturing companies increase their supply chain IT investments. Beyond the expected consolidation, which will most likely result within the maturing ERP supply base, the next technology shift the supply management profession is most likely to observe is a surge in partner data-sharing solutions.[3]

Global Commerce Dominates Competition

Perfect competition is discussed in economics, but only because the real world is so dynamic that it is too difficult to conceptualize. By 2008, perfect competition may be a reality, given driven-down pricing and access to information at the touch of a keyboard. Among all the fast-rising Asian markets commanding attention, none will influence cost and price beyond China due to its labor sophistication and manufacturing capabilities minus the cost burden of legacy technologies and infrastructures of developed nations. Beyond China and India, Europe, Russia, east and central Asia, and Latin America are expected to be the hot spots five years from now. [4]

The implication of global competition is greater development and sophistication of global supply chains. Clearly, supply chains that can easily adapt to new markets will prevail. But the real magic here will be the emphasis on global geographies that reshape every aspect of the way our organizations operate, even those companies that are already multinationals. In periods of unrest, oftentimes we revert to time-tested fundamentals, but will they be applicable in the globally reshaped landscape? Typically, U.S. majority-owned organizations have had the luxury of functioning with processes and protocols based largely on a U.S.-oriented foundation, with local cultural influences overlaid upon them. "Developed environments function significantly differently than undeveloped, even in controlled markets like China's."[5] As organizations shift more of their resources to overseas locations, U.S. employees must learn to adapt to new processes and protocols, creating new challenges for organizational culture.

The bottom line is that the question that will have to be answered by supply leaders goes far beyond "How do we optimally source globally?" to "How do we organize virtually across the world, while balancing the fine line between the importance of consistent organizational culture worldwide (proven to be a contributor to competitive advantage) and the importance of integrating local cultures, all-the-while enabling U.S. employees to cope with the change in management issues that will accompany the redefinition of company protocols?"

---

3 AMR Research (2004). *Annual Market Analytic Market Sizing Report*. Series 2004.
4 Conference Board. *CEO Challenge 2003*. November 2003, www.conference-board.org.
5 Ibid.

Mass Industry Consolidation

Mass industry consolidation will result from growth through acquisitions instead of growth from the ground up. According to the Conference Board survey of CEOs, size buys power to invest in the assets needed for growth and differentiation, resulting in pricing power or at least the slowdown of its loss.[6]

The implication for supply is twofold. First, industry expertise will be replaced by expertise in analyzing new chains of commodities. Second, company-specific benchmarking will not be as relevant as it is today. Supply management professionals will have to learn to excel at extracting benchmarking nuggets and developing the critical thinking skills that will enable them to apply the lessons learned from those nuggets to their individual, complex supply chains.

CHIEF PURCHASING OFFICERS' EXPECTATIONS

The evolution of the supply management profession is akin to that of the IT boom and IT's emergence from technical support to a strategic seat at the boardroom table. In the last 10 years alone, supply management has evolved from purchasing to procurement to supply chain management to supply management. The evolution reflects the difference between a vocation and a profession. Supply management leaders lobby for their discipline to be viewed as a profession but realize they are still struggling with it being seen as a vocation. Because of this, in addition to the acceleration in the business environment, the scope of critical issues supply management executives will face in the next few years barely resembles what they would have in the past.

The era has passed when automating processes, leveraging spend, and negotiating lower prices defined supply management success. The tactical day-to-day victories, while still necessary for operational efficiency, have given way to strategic challenges that reflect the growing role of the function: understanding all the inputs required for the business, identifying new business opportunities, orchestrating mergers and acquisitions, and managing and mitigating risk—both internally and from business partners (suppliers). Supply management is now impacting the core competency of the organization like never before.

However, there is still a spectrum of sophistication levels across companies and their supply organizations. The level of supply sophistication largely depends on where you sit and the culture of the company for which you work. There are companies where supply management has never been looked upon as anything less than key to the firm. In others, supply management has only recently evolved to claim a seat among senior management. Historically, procurement activities have ultimately fallen under other functions, such as finance. While this might have made sense when purchasing's main function was to support operations, this

---

6 Ibid.

function now influences both sides of the business: supplying the firm and creating new business. Furthermore, many of the activities that traditionally fell to finance, such as outsourcing decisions, are competencies in which supply management now excels.

> I really think it is a mixed bag as far as understanding the importance and value of supply management. Some senior management still view the profession as purely a support function to execute tactical activities at the beck and call of the end user. Other senior management members call upon supply management to be an integral part of the strategic team for their organization. They see supply management as an asset that can be a competitive advantage at the executive level to enhance profitability and, yet at the same time, be attuned to the operational requirements and deliverables for the organization.

ANTHONY NIEVES, C.P.M., CFPM
Senior Vice President, Supply Management
Hilton Hotels Corporation

A Shared Vision

Over the next three to five years my vision is supply management will become, and be viewed as, an enabler to increasing market share for the enterprise. Our focus in the past has been one dimensional and narrow in focus, that being price reduction. However, the focus has been directed rather than open to innovation. The role of the organization will be to provide innovative solutions to customer-focused problems that are related to the supply chain. This could be in the way parts are designed, manufactured, shipped, stored or sold. The areas of influence primarily will be in product costing and supply chain design, but the involvement will be at a much higher level in the organization. This new role will force a change in how engineering, sales, manufacturing and other organizations interact and communicate with supply management. In some instances, supply management will be integrated into these organizations as a cohesive complementary component. Based on the current economic conditions and the ever-increasing need to grow, even in these desperate times, there is high potential for the above referenced changes. Many companies are already seeing the need and taking the opportunity to elevate their supply management operations to a position of a strategic member of the team.

ALEX BROWN
Vice President, Global Supply Management
Advanced Micro Devices, Inc. (AMD)

The supply management profession is rapidly evolving. The function is getting closer to the boardroom as we inch our way up the organization chart of Fortune 100 companies. With 50–80 percent of a company's revenue going to suppliers, the role of supply management has never been so critical … and it will continue to grow in importance as companies outsource more and more services and manufacturing. Suppliers are suddenly doing things that were done by employees. Supply management will have more say in what gets outsourced. Supply management will sit on the most senior strategic decision-making boards in successful companies. Supply management will influence product portfolios and product design to ensure maximum leverage and maximum supply-chain flexibility while achieving a minimum risk for their company. Optimizing the business around supply management will emerge as a best practice—after all, 50–80 percent of revenue dollars flow through supply management.

THERESA METTY, C.P.M.
Former Senior Vice President and Chief Procurement Officer
Motorola, Inc.

Supply management will have a seat at the head table with other business-critical functions like R&D, product development, engineering, marketing and finance. A proactive supply management organization, with proper leadership, has the unique opportunity to influence the company's cost structure. Integration of the supply base with R&D, product development and engineering will create advantages in reduced costs, improved quality and output, and shorter cycle times. Supply management must develop sourcing and supply management approaches that will vary for their different spend categories. The world is today's marketplace and good supply management organizations will be looking globally to source new and lower-cost suppliers. Finding new suppliers also fits well with many companies' plans to globalize their product manufacturing.

JACK FUTCHER
Senior Vice President and Deputy Project Director
Bechtel Corporation

In February of 2004, 30 CPOs, senior vice presidents (SVP), and vice presidents (VP) from a cross section of industries convened to discuss their three- to five-year vision of supply and delve into the implications of this vision. Each leader had his or her vantage point, creating a tapestry of perspectives, none of which is mutually exclusive. The common theme that emerged was that the critical issues supply faces in three to five years look completely different than those of just the past three years. This section explores the common threads that will become tomorrow's reality.

Supply Management Is a Core Organizational Capability

Increasing complexity will drive supply management competencies to become core capabilities of the organization. The scope of supply management will be amplified as organizations hone "traditional" supply management skills. Even those areas that the supply management team may already excel at, for example, negotiations and cost and project management, will demand greater refinement and proficiency to bring even more value to the company. Negotiations will involve a larger scale, cost management will have deeper impacts, and projects will be chartered around more intricate objectives. As these competencies transform into core capabilities, organizations will become more and more nimble to address the acceleration in business complexity.

Business complexity can be thought of as a three-dimensional cube, with the three axes representing complexity, global opportunities, and whatever dynamics are evolving in any given industry. In the future, this cube just gets bigger, creating additional layers and permutations within, all directly impacting supply management. Competencies, such as value engineering, cost analysis, spend management, process integration, and information technology aptitude, will all be involved and applied to a more complex world to the point where they become capabilities and the sum of the whole creates added competitive advantages. "We're going to be playing in a bigger bucket," said one supply executive.

The critical strategic questions that supply management professionals must ask are

- What business are we in?

- What are the ways to go to market?

- What are the business models we could use?

- What are the supply chains that then make sense given those business models?

- How can I synthesize existing best practices with regard to those supply chains to enable and optimize them for today and tomorrow?

- More importantly, what "next" best practices should our organization create for competitive advantage?

RISK MANAGEMENT LEADER

Supply management will lead analysis and management of risk for the company at all levels. Risk management has always been important, but not always a priority at all levels. With the advent of the Sarbanes-Oxley legislation, the processes and facets are even more prescribed. This scrutiny aligns directly with supply management's scope and activities—it is yet another opportunity for supply management to step to the forefront of business strategy.

The key, however, will be to think of all things in terms of risk. Rather than an isolated competency, risk analysis and risk management processes will be established throughout all functions, acting as a filter through which all business decisions will pass. This raises the process's level of sophistication and gives risk its required attention. For example, total costs, supply decisions, and asset management can be measured in terms of risk.

There is a shift in the focus on risk from mitigation to optimization. In the past, supply management has focused on mitigating risk for the company through its exposure to supply-side threats. However, many companies are realizing that there is enormous opportunity in understanding risk and determining acceptable levels to maximize return on investment (ROI). Companies will excel if they formally establish acceptable levels of risk, communicate these levels throughout the enterprise, and educate employees about how to weigh acceptable risk levels when making decisions. The real challenge is communicating with employees and educating them about acceptable levels of risks and the use of these levels to effectively measure risks and make good decisions.

Another relevant and important angle on the topic of risk is the need for supply managers to uncover and identify potential future risk. Historically, supply risks were managed by carrying inventory and using multiple suppliers. Unnecessary carrying costs and redundant suppliers were eliminated through the successful implementation of just-in-time (JIT) manufacturing and the application of lean thinking. However, numerous new crevices for risk to hide and evolve have resulted. "Risks lurk along the entire length of the supply chains and are as diverse as political instability, exchange rates, carriage capacity, shelf life and customer demand."[7] Given today's instability because of terrorist activity and political strife (which is expected to continue) combined with increased globalization as we move toward 2008, supply managers will not only increase their ability to analyze risk, but will have to become experts at identifying where risks exists.

As one Miami executive indicated,

> Risk will be anything that affects the continuity and integrity of supply. We must deal with the known issues, but also with the issues that we don't even know about yet. That's what makes it difficult to define. We must challenge everyone to analyze even those areas currently believed to be full of integrity. Risks will arise out of areas that are overlooked because they're assumed to be risk-free.

Global sourcing issues fall within the realm of risk management for supply. The world market lures with opportunity, but every venture carries with it critical junctures for risk assessment. Should you expand into new global arenas for market and/or supply advantages? Where should your resources be? What are the legal issues? Are you too dependent on certain areas? What are the drivers behind the risks? Does this venture align with your corporate citizenship values? These are all questions that supply leaders must answer.

Functional Outsourcing

Every function within the company will be looked at from a make-versus-buy perspective. Surveying the marketplace for the best source of supply, monitoring the product or service coming in through the supply line, and ensuring that the customer's objectives are continually met are typical supply-side activities. In its more sophisticated form, it is outsourcing.

Outsourcing, a common theme in today's organizations, will be applied further to include outsourcing of complex subsystems, such as design engineering or

---

7 D. Stauffer (2003). "Supply Chain Risk: Deal with It," *Harvard Business Review,* April 28.

new product development. Functional services will come under the microscope to see if they can benefit from third-party expertise. In each case, supply management is taking the calculated path of letting industry experts (the outsourcers) process the details and return significant benefit. "Letting go to get more" will become an organization mantra.

As one executive put it, "We need to keep the company from doing dumb outsourcing and help the company do smart outsourcing; we need to be able to manage the outsourcing operations after we've made the decision." Smart versus dumb is making certain that the outsourced relationship provides true ultimate value and that it is not just based on a quick glance at a balance sheet.

Translucent Borders

Borders between the extended enterprise, the firm, and its suppliers will become increasingly translucent. Throughout the process, the goal is to operate like a synergistic network. Therefore, organizations must develop and adopt shared supply chain measurements that cover total costs, improvements, and benefit generation. Attainment of these metrics breeds sustainable competitive advantage for the entire network. As one executive put it, "It's okay to share best practices and ideas with others in the industry; you don't need to keep it a secret, you just need to stay ahead."

Such an integrated environment changes the dynamic of supply network relationships. It may mean taking unprecedented steps with a supplier to help them improve. One firm recognized that its supplier, while relatively strong, was weaker on the West Coast. The firm exercised its influence and advised the supplier to purchase another operation in that region so that it could enhance its expertise and capabilities, strengthening the chain and ultimately benefiting the customer in the process.

The more integrated the supply chain or network becomes, the more difficult it will be to know where customers end and suppliers begin, particularly in instances of colocation or shared resources. The network becomes one cohesive unit striving for common goals. In a perfect world, these supply chain maximizing efforts go smoothly, but the reality is that as the lines between functions become blurred, some may feel threatened by the loss of control. Therefore, the challenge is in bridging those disconnects and continually reiterating the positive results and purposes.

Top-Line Focus

The focus will shift from the bottom line to the top line. Generating revenue will no longer be a goal left to sales and marketing. Supply management will play an increasingly larger role in top-line growth. As a corporate executive concerned with the overall success of the business, revenue generation is a legitimate priority for supply leaders.

Supply management's contribution in this area may come in the form of recognizing new revenue streams through supply base investigation. What capabilities exist in the supply base that your company can capitalize upon? It may be a supplier's product or engineering process that you can add value to for a niche market. Or the scope of service processes can expand to include for-profit streams. Consider the hotel chain that already has massive laundry facilities in place to meet its own needs. It now also charges for this service to outside parties (including competitors) to reap revenues on the investment.

The emerging trend for procurement services to be made available on a commercial basis to other firms will continue to expand. Think of it as a high-quality product developed for in-house use but now appreciated for its market value. This type of revenue stream might not have been on the radar screen in years past.

What both of these scenarios have in common is supply management's closer proximity to the customer. In the past, supply management has used customer needs and wants to help shape supply strategy. Now, the dissection of customer desires creates entirely new products or services. It is not so much figuring out the best road to take to reach the customer as it is putting whole new roads on the map—roads that go to new customers and stop at the bank along the way. Being successful at revenue-generating activities will require supply management to have the utmost knowledge about the products and services the firm currently offers.

Some leading-edge firms already inherently understand the value of being in tune with market pulses. One consumer electronics company was asked to describe its organizational chart. Not only were the traditional labels of functional silos missing and replaced with process-oriented components ("manufacturing" becomes "conversion" and "service" becomes "configuring"), but it was evident that ideas and innovation could come from any area. Also, when asked about the most important component of the enterprise, it was unanimous: any portion that culled information from customers and funneled the ideas back to the innovation stage and resulted in new products.

The bottom line about the top line is that supply management professionals at all levels will learn to think like "business" executives and not just "supply" executives.

High-Potential Candidates Work in Supply Management

Supply management will become the go-to area and *the* function for high-potential candidates in the company—the real up-and-comers, the ones who make things happen and have credibility and respect. Supply management has been transformed a great deal over the last few decades, but there is still more to come.

Part of the transformation process is speaking the language of the CEO, or translating supply management impacts in terms of earnings. You can do this if you claim market capitalization. Additionally, the ratios you develop need to be understood and standardized so that valid comparisons can be made term over term. Reporting of these ratios and gains must be accurate and prominent—imagine the day when each firm's annual report contains a section on "Supply Management's Contributions."

Beyond numbers, CEOs need supply management's competencies as a leading profession and proactive resource. CEOs do not want to wait until they have to ask purchasing what is going on. They need businesspeople in supply management who will think of things on their own. CEOs want leaders they can trust and who can bridge the gap between supply chain components.

Credibility must also run laterally and down through the organization. Supply managers need the respect of other business unit leaders and employees throughout the organization. As with the case of the CEOs, reverence must be earned. By making steady progress from a mere negotiator to a consultative authority, supply will be able to extend its capabilities within a company and deliver sustainable competitive advantage. It will then be recognized as the discipline and business partner that

- Owns strategy and execution
- Thinks beyond a gatekeeper mentality
- Is proactive
- Understands financial capabilities and viabilities
- Is a key player in company decisions

The ability to attract and retain quality talent is another ancillary (but necessary) requirement of raising the perception of supply management on an enterprise-wide basis. While not historically viewed as the fast track to C-level positions, supply management will attract rising business stars with its new influential, leadership role. Once attracted, however, it is vital that the training tools are in place to groom high-potential candidates as supply management leaders.

REQUIREMENTS FOR TRANSFORMATION

What will be required? How do we get there? How will supply management need to transform?

> How supply management is organized and the authority given to it is key in achieving its potential. Supply management must have top talent and people with the new skill sets in order to achieve the vision.

CHRISTINE S. BREVES, C.P.M.
Chief Procurement Officer
Alcoa Inc.

Looking toward the future, it is clear that supply management needs to become integral to activities that were long thought of as outside the realm of this profession. These opportunities set the stage for supply management to become the core business asset. The obvious next question is, "How?" According to the leaders at the Miami Executive Summit it requires reach, measurement, innovation, value extraction, global business, and diversity.

Reach

We need to develop better and better communication tools to articulate the business case for supply management, up, down and sideways, for every corner of the business.

Measurement

You're going to be measured by how well you do compared to competitors. Period. Even if you've been successful in getting the level of procurement raised and been able to demonstrate some positive supply management benchmarks, it's challenging because you're not going to be measured against those benchmarks.

Innovation

Supply management must get involved in innovation and involve their suppliers in innovation. This also means getting suppliers to be innovative.

Extracting Value

Seven or eight times out of 10, our suppliers know more about what they're providing than we do. We need to ensure we're getting the fullest value from this. . . . That's what keeps me up at night.

Supply management does a good job of rationalizing the supply base, getting exactly what it needs out of suppliers and all the while squeezing their margins. We now need to consider "What if we wake up one morning and discover the supplier is out of business because we squeezed too hard?"

We want to be flexible and nimble in responding to customer demands. We need to create an environment and supply chain where we can be in—and out—of markets quickly. We need to be nimble.

Global Business

We're going to have to have tremendous social awareness. The future will no longer be about the implications of sourcing in the country of origin. The question we need to ask will be: "What will be the implications of *not* sourcing in the country of origin?"

Diversity

We need to grow with our customers, but as they serve more diverse populations, we're impacted by their need for more diversity and inclusion in their supply base.

Overall, supply managers will reach beyond traditional skills and develop the ability to integrate processes and manage knowledge, people, and relationships. The following is just a smattering of the expectations for the roles of supply managers in the next three to five years. Each individual area on its own may not seem like new news; rather it will be through the combination and integration of all these roles that tomorrow's supply management leader will emerge.

- Facilitate information flows through the extended enterprise.
- Align collaborative relationships, including demand management initiatives.
- Help suppliers eliminate waste through supplier development engineering.
- Educate others in your firm and your suppliers.
- Scan business (physical and financial aspects) and systems for cost removal opportunities.
- Cull innovative solutions from the supply base.
- Seek out other sources of competitive advantage. Source revenue and business growth opportunities.
- Open dialogues with business partners. Link suppliers' innovation to your design organization.
- Develop an intuitive pulse of the extended enterprise and the world.
- Create and cultivate relationships that extend beyond price and cost.
- Apply supply advantages across the business.
- Contribute to merger-and-acquisition decisions at lower levels.
- Create partnerships within the supply chain for collective buying power.
- Leverage key competencies of the firm with both customers and suppliers (i.e., financial).
- Delegate routine purchasing where supply management cannot add value.
- Send key team members to other groups for work.[8]

Given the magnitude of these requirements, change in management initiatives will be abundant—changing process, strategies, and, of course, people. Another environmental element will be the constant balancing act among short-, medium-, and long-term strategies and initiatives with regard to personnel, time, money, and focus.

"For years, we were a function that managed a function, but now we need to think more like an entrepreneur and take ownership of areas that aren't necessarily part of our function. We need to understand how to reach in and influence those," stated one executive at the February 2004 CSSL Miami Executive Summit.

---

8 J. Cavinato (2004). *Supply Manager of 2015*. CSSL Leadership Report.

How will the new supply management organization look and what type of talent will be needed? The following are some characteristics:

- High visibility. A company executive at the top of the pyramid will need to sponsor the changes and new roles.

- Expertise in managing projects to generate results (rather than in one core competency), knowing where to find expertise, and how to facilitate groups of experts to reach the end goal.

- Ability to educate and influence upward. During times of transformation, immediate supervisors can block progress; the successful professionals will be those who can educate upward, downward, and to the sides about business acumen. Fortunately with time, the pyramid will flatten further, eliminating hierarchical roadblocks.

- Enablers, not managers. The new breed of supply managers will describe themselves as the "glue and lubricant" of the firm but will not necessarily have people reporting to them. These people will have tremendous personal relationships throughout the company and know that it will take influence and research to exercise those contacts.

- Influence without authority will be critical. A supply manager will be required to motivate others to take action even when he or she has no direct authority over them.

- Extroverts, move over! To influence and advise the CEO, a supply manager must be able to do so without pride and without causing embarrassment.

- Well-rounded. A wealth of understanding, not necessarily expertise, about how a range of business functions operate and intersect will be critical to maneuver both the physical and political network.

You may recognize these people in your firm. If you were to map out how informal communications flow when problems need to be resolved, you would be able to see the junctures or people that serve as human portals. "These are the ones who, if they left the organization, would leave behind gaping holes," confirms one supply executive.

Personal Development

What should your personal development plan look like? General skill, ability, and experience as a buyer or commodity manager are no longer sufficient; specific competencies will be sought by leaders. There is no single mold—organizations will require a mélange of professionals with complementary profiles. The 30 senior leaders at the CSSL Miami Executive Summit set the framework for grouping the desired competencies into four groups: entrepreneurs, strategic thinkers, results-drivers, and recruiters. Each will add distinct value. The competencies that will be required for each are listed here.

Entrepreneurs

The entrepreneurial executive will need to demonstrate and be proficient in terms of

- Broad thinking. If you have excelled at a particular sourcing activity, stretch your thinking to determine how to leverage that value elsewhere.

- Long-term focus on network profitability and cost management.

- Ability to align strategies across departments and network firms.

- Financial knowledge. Comfortable conversing with the CFO on a peer level.

- Business acumen. Deep and accurate understanding of every part of the business environment. Regardless of industry, you must learn the drivers and inner workings.

- Multilingual skills, in order to speak the language of various functions, including finance, manufacturing, and marketing. Define and track benefits in terms used by those working in these areas.

"As our role increases and we get more access, we become more of a sponsor and strategy communicator to the outside world."

Strategic Thinkers

The high-level company representative will need to demonstrate and be proficient in terms of

- Communication skills and the ability to convey where the business is going. You'll need to do this across industries, speaking in terms others will appreciate.

- Appropriate "hunter and farmer" skills. You'll need to ascertain when it is best to seek out new relationships and when it is best to cultivate existing ones.

"People talk about the value of procurement in terms of savings. But there are so many other values (less tangible) that supply brings."

Results-Drivers

The executive that "gets it done" in terms of supply, bringing value to the company and the supply process, will need to demonstrate and be proficient in terms of

- Having the ability to define, predict, measure, and track quantitative benefits of supply management. Measuring your success against your prediction builds credibility.

- Marketing and selling supply management's capabilities to increase overall value to the organization.

- Managing expectations. The golden rule is to underpromise and over-deliver.

- Continuous-improvement focus.

- Cost management ownership, including understanding industry costs and knowing what's best-in-class.

- Lean expertise. Be able to analyze opportunities for effectiveness and efficiency.

- Negotiation skills. Film mock negotiation scenarios and role play with colleagues to continually improve.

- Understanding nuances, particularly as they relate to outsourcing. In general, outsourcing will increase, but each relationship will be slightly different, and you need to know how to manage each appropriately.

- Operations experience, beyond manufacturing, to include engineering and product development and project management.

- Internal integration skills.

- International management skills, with a global mindset and sensitivity.

- Market intelligence skills. Constantly scan the environment and use a global vision; picking up trends, signals, and early warnings.

"Get the right people into your organization—locate, attract, hire, retain and then train to make them better. Train for performance."

Recruiters
In order to draw the best people into the organization and have them thrive, supply executives as recruiters will need to demonstrate and be proficient in terms of

- Organizational skills.

- Performance measurements to reward and recognize key people.

- Ability to hone in on the right skills needed for any given position.

- Advocacy skills, to promote the area for which they are recruiting.

- Conviction to rotate people out of their area so they can come back with cross-functional experience.

- People development skills to bring out the best in others.

"We can't influence the direction of our firm without being able to influence and lead. That's key."

Leadership

The supply management executive whom others will follow will need to demonstrate and be proficient in terms of

- Change management skills, to get people out of their comfort zone to where they say change is good and to go beyond where they just cope.

- Understanding and effecting culture change. Get beyond pushback and old ways.

- Humility. Pass credit and take blame. Seek problem resolution, not finger-pointing.

- Trust and communication skills.

- Salesmanship, to gain support for initiatives.

- Influence. No one exists on an island, and one can't operate effectively without allies.

- Relationships and networking skills.

- Implementation skills.

- Ability to deal with "unreasonable" expanding expectations.

- Cross-functional consensus-building skills.

- High-level communication skills, to bring convergent groups together.

- Process management and vision. It's important to define and articulate the vision and move incrementally, but constantly, toward it.

As a backdrop to all the competencies listed, one other important attribute is the ability to recognize new skills that emerge as critical in the coming years. In other words, we need to consider what has not yet been identified and continuously update this list.

CRITICAL SUCCESS FACTORS

The following factors will be required for this vision to become a reality:

1. Visionary or open-minded CEO or CFO.

2. Corporate governance designed to open doors and enforce rules.

3. Strong supply management leadership with a willingness to take great leaps.

4. Systems to enable analytical assessment of enterprise data.

5. Trained and engaged supply management professionals with the ability to deliver on the promise.

This will require individuals to have a changed view of supply management to attract the best thinkers and executors. The incumbents are required to focus on the future while executing against the current reality of supply management. We will have to continue a focus on education of both individuals and organizations. Organizations will have to continue to upgrade their e-procurement capabilities and acceptance of system solutions. Investments will have to be made in supply management to improve capabilities and enhance innovation just as investments are made in the factory for increased capacity and to product innovation. As referenced above, upper/executive management is a key enabler to the vision.

ALEX BROWN
Vice President, Global Supply Management
Advanced Micro Devices, Inc. (AMD)

THE NEXT STEP

Where do we go from here? The opportunities and challenges for supply management in the next three to five years are incalculable. As CEOs and their CPOs grapple with the space where addressing today's challenges and opportunities intersects with ramping up to meet tomorrow's, we are all called to identify those areas within our circles of influence. Successful leaders will not be left stammering and fading into the shadows when they get that two minutes alone in the elevator with their CPO who asks "What is your vision for the next three to five years?" It is no longer only senior management's concern.

> [In the next three to five years, supply management will focus more on] creating value for our customers; eliminating waste in both our own and our suppliers' processes; better defining the connections between our processes, our internal customers, and our suppliers; and in general working more collaboratively with our suppliers. Supply management will contribute to top-line growth, as well as cost reduction, and other areas such as working capital management and asset management. Ensuring that supply management personnel have the new skill-sets required will be essential. The new skills include being well-rounded in other disciplines, as well as current supply management competencies.

CHRISTINE S. BREVES, C.P.M.
Chief Procurement Officer
Alcoa Inc.

PART 2

GOING TO MARKET WITH TODAY'S CRUCIAL IMPERATIVES

What does the unfolding and expanding future of purchasing and supply look like? For one, in recent times there has been a noticeable drop in the use of the terms *buying*, *purchasing*, and *procurement*. More and more the titles of groups and persons have the word supply in them. This represents a shift from buying or purchasing for the organization to identifying, acquiring, leading, and managing supply. This broader scope of work means there are more and different things in the profession's realm.

The chapters in this section provide insights into these new imperatives. Supply strategies set the stage for the longer term, and this is much farther in span than just the next upcoming contract term and renegotiation. Strategic sourcing is more aligned with the needs of the organization and the evolving supply markets. Today, supply strategies and sourcing requires a new area of knowledge management throughout the organization and also greater insights into the supply market. Sourcing is more than just picking one out of many similar suppliers in that it seeks deeper insights into which supplier is best for today and the long term. Because nearly every organization has global competitors and global customers, these organizations are also in a global supply marketplace. The chapter devoted to this subject explores the nature of these global supply networks.

Outsourcing became popular with corporate overhead items in the 1980s and more and more of the line activities, products, and services of the organization in the 1990s. The trend continues, and the chapter covering this topic presents challenges, opportunities, and methods of pursuing and managing these relationships.

Lastly, the viable organization today must constantly look at its competitors and peers for benchmarking the best of the best. The final chapter in this section presents Project 10X, a major initiative in this area.

DEVELOPING AND IMPLEMENTING SUPPLY STRATEGIES

Joseph R. Carter DBA, C.P.M.
Avnet Professor and Chair, Supply Chain Management Department
W. P. Carey School of Business
Arizona State University

INTRODUCTION

Supply strategy development is a business process. This may seem like an obvious statement, but it is important to consider what this means before proceeding with the study of this topic. Any particular business process is an integrated set of business activities. One process operates within the context of other processes to meet the organization's ultimate goals of competitive advantage and satisfactory return on investments.

To understand this comprehensive and systematic process, each component is briefly reviewed in this chapter. It is necessary to note that many different strategy-development models have been created to fit individual companys' needs; however, they generally have the same basic components. An important point worth repeating is that this model may differ slightly from others. However, the major components are similar. The critical factor is that the general process should be followed in a comprehensive and systematic manner. During the following overview of the supply strategy development and implementation process, reference is made to specific products. However, this entire process applies to many goods or services.

SEGMENTATION

As more and more firms are discovering, positioning the supply management process into a segmenting of different supply strategies, supply tactics, and supply management approaches is the only way to effectively link supply strategies with overall firm goals, product marketing strategies, and competitive efforts. This differentiation process is often referred to as "supply segmentation."

The supply segmentation technique provides a mechanism for discriminating between the various items and services that are purchased by a firm with the goal of developing specific strategies to meet the needs of the organization with respect to separate and logical categories of items. Supply segmentation is an excellent marketing tool for convincing senior management of the critical role that supply management can and does play in the support of corporate-level strategies and firm profitability.

This chapter will begin with a discussion of "category analysis" including Risk, Value, and Spend Analysis as applied to the purchase of goods and services and its limitations. A discussion of the supply segmentation approach to supply strategy development will follow including development of a spend analysis and categorization of purchases. The chapter will end with a discussion of supply management goals and the supplier relationship strategy development process.

RISK AND VALUE

During the first stage of this process, the question is asked, "What kind of good or service is being sourced?" This question is *not* answered in terms of specifications or attributes such as janitorial services, paper, solvents, or resins. This question is answered in the business terms of value, risk, internal usage, and external markets.

First, the internal use of the good or service must be considered. Think in terms of two concepts—risk and value (as presented in Figure 5–1).

Risk is the extent to which the company will suffer negative outcomes if the good or service has poor quality or is priced too high or if the available supply of

FIGURE 5–1

Supply Risk and Value: Restaurant Chain

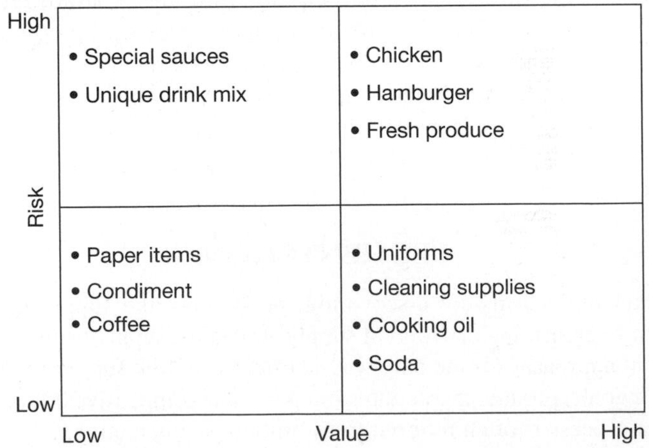

the good or service becomes depleted. For instance, a heart pacemaker manufacturer uses highly sensitive electronic connectors that cost only a few dollars each. However, the supplier unexpectedly went out of business, so even though the switch was relatively low cost, the company had to stop production until it could find another supplier. The heart pacemaker was put at high risk because of the switch in suppliers.

The other continuum represents cost/value. Cost/value is generally equated to dollars, but it could be the extent to which a component adds intrinsic value to the total finished good. For instance, the fabric durability on a first-class airplane seat is extremely valuable for overall appearance. However, the cost of the fabric is relatively low compared to the overall aircraft; but this is what the customer sees. High dollar value is represented by the screen of a plasma high-definition TV because this is a major cost element of the finished television.

The risk and value can be placed from high to low on these two continuums. The product or service will then be placed in the appropriate category or quadrant. The importance of these quadrants becomes more apparent when we begin to discuss the balancing of the sourcing portfolio.

Figure 5–1 presents the various products that would be appropriate for a quick service restaurant chain featuring such items as hamburgers, fries, milk shakes, and chicken sandwiches. The company advertises its unique sandwich sauces and differentiates itself on the quality of its products; in particular, its hamburger is low fat, and its chicken breast sandwiches are much thicker than its competitors. But how does a company populate the matrix?

THE SPEND ANALYSIS

To begin constructing a supply segmentation portfolio the firm must develop a "spend" analysis of all the goods and services that are purchased by the firm. Total purchases must be aggregated across divisions and/or strategic business units (SBUs) for both individual items and services and by individual suppliers. The spend analysis can be a laborious and tedious undertaking, but it is critical nonetheless. There are outside suppliers, such as Dun & Bradstreet, that will assist a firm in developing the spend analysis.

The concluding step is to graph each of these stockkeeping units (SKUs) and service categories on a chart in which the horizontal (X) axis represents the relative cost/value of the item or service and the vertical (Y) axis represents supply market complexity as pictured in Figure 5–2. In many cases, individual items and/or services can be grouped into commodity categories and then plotted, where such a grouping is relevant.

As mentioned, the cost/value axis represents the importance of the item, service, or commodity in terms of its annual dollar spend within the firm. Cost/value is usually measured as the total annual dollar amount purchased for each item or service. For example, a million items at $20 each totals to a $20 million annual

FIGURE 5–2

Spend Analysis Matrix

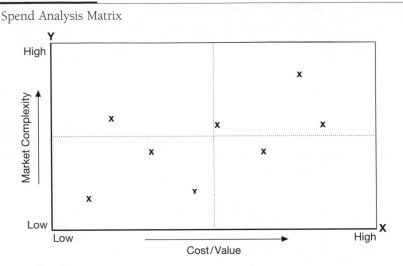

spend and is plotted as such. The total annual purchase amount can be adjusted higher or lower if there are any factors of cost that are not captured by the spend analysis, for example, import duties and some transportation and warehouse costs.

Each firm must define the market complexity axis according to its own situation and needs. For most it will be a mixture of technological factors, supply availability, technical requirements, and environmental issues.

The initial spend analysis can be the subject of heated debate as individual managers from various business units may have different views as to the relative importance and exposure of some items, commodities, or services. For example, one business unit could view application-specific integrated circuits (ASICs) as a commodity purchase while another business unit could view ASICs as a critical technology. In such cases, it may be wise to split the item's purchases into two distinct commodity groups.

MARKET COMPLEXITY

The nature of the market from which a product is being purchased should be thoroughly analyzed to determine the market structure and trends. During a market analysis, one should determine

- Major competitors
- Number of suppliers in relationship to the number of buyers
- Potential substitute products for the one being sourced
- Potential new competitors in the market

FIGURE 5-3

Market Complexity

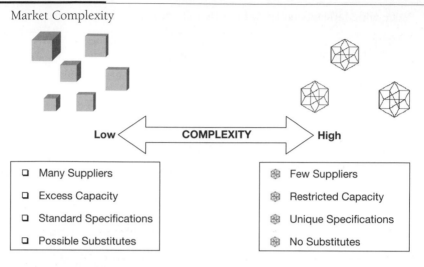

| Low < **COMPLEXITY** > High |

❏ Many Suppliers		▦ Few Suppliers
❏ Excess Capacity		▦ Restricted Capacity
❏ Standard Specifications		▦ Unique Specifications
❏ Possible Substitutes		▦ No Substitutes

- Pricing trends
- Technology trends
- Cost drivers
- Long-term and short-term capacity issues

After the market analysis, it will be possible to determine the appropriate supply strategy, the supplier strategy, and how to best structure a fact-based brief for the negotiation, and ultimately the best approach for managing the supplier. For instance, there are two or three companies in the entire world that produce advanced radar control systems for commercial airlines. The market for this type of a system is much different than that of television monitors where there are many suppliers and a worldwide surplus.

As seen in Figure 5–3, a simple market has many suppliers, and sufficient capacity exists. Therefore, the product specifications are relatively easy to identify, and substitute products are available. On the other end of the continuum, a complex market has only a few suppliers, capacity is restricted, product specifications are unique, and no substitutes are available.

It is much more difficult to source from complex markets; as a result, the negotiation plan and supplier management approach will be different than in a simple or low-complexity market.

COST/VALUE

The relationship between market complexity and value can also be demonstrated with a diagram. Figure 5–4 depicts the products for a hypothetical chip

FIGURE 5–4

Value and Market Complexity for a Hypothetical Chip Manufacturer

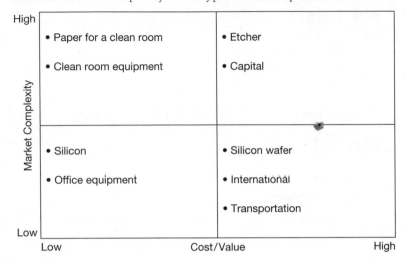

manufacturer. These product placements may vary from one company to another depending on its perception of the market but the placement should drive much of the remaining sourcing strategy.

For instance, a product placed in the upper right-hand quadrant would probably need a long-term supplier alliance strategy because of a large investment in the product and the limited number of suppliers. A product in the lower left-hand quadrant might be best managed with a supplier or a spot buy because there are many suppliers and the investment is relatively small. In addition, the best way to negotiate with suppliers for products in the upper right-hand quadrant would be to use a collaborative approach, whereas a power-based arm's-length approach might be best for items in the left-hand quadrant.

To ensure the best approaches are used throughout the strategic sourcing process, the category analysis and market analysis should be done before proceeding to the next steps of the strategic sourcing model.

SUPPLY SEGMENTATION ANALYSIS

With the initial spend analysis complete, the next step is to segment the purchases by dividing the chart into four or more categories as depicted in Figure 5–5. Each category has been assigned a name that describes the supply imperative of the items and services classified within it.

The items and services represented in quadrant I, low market complexity and low cost/value, are referred to as *tactical*. These are the routine items, commodities, or services that do not enter into the direct value-added price of the fin-

FIGURE 5-5

Supply Segmentation Matrix

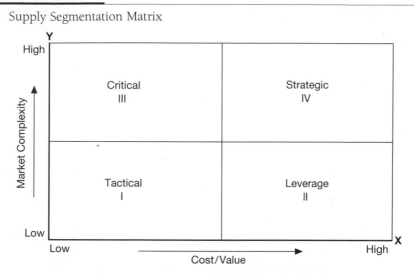

ished products of the firm. Their cost/value is low, and the potential harm through disruption to the firm due to supply availability issues is low. These are commonly standardized items in plentiful supply from a wide number of suppliers. Many maintenance, repair, and operating (MRO) items and services, office supplies, and administrative items are examples of tactical items and services.

The items and services categorized in quadrant II, low market complexity and high relative cost/value, are referred to as *leverage*. These items and services are true generic, basic purchases that represent high dollar expenditures but a low risk to the firm. Corrugated packaging, basic production goods, fasteners, and some coatings are examples of items that would fall into this quadrant of items and services. Because there can be little difference between competing brands of these items and services, suppliers often attempt to differentiate themselves to the purchaser through service-related attributes.

The items and services categorized in quadrant III, high market complexity and low cost/value, are referred to as *critical*. These are low relative cost/value items and services that provide a potential market difficulty and resulting high market complexity to the firm. Examples may be spare parts that are available from only very few suppliers with long lead times or backlogs, critical services such as specialty heat treatment, and specialty chemicals. The market complexity to the firm is high, yet the final customer either does not care for the special purchase nature of the item or service or is not aware of it.

The items and services categorized in quadrant IV, high market complexity and high cost/value, are referred to as *strategic*. Strategic items and services provide a firm's products with competitive or distinctive advantage in the marketplace. Such items provide the firm with both a high market complexity and high relative cost/value environment. Examples of these items may be any unique custom-designed item, a component that permits a lower total cost, higher reliability, a more environmentally friendly operation for the final customer, or a unique advertising campaign tied to the final product. The value of these items and services is measured in terms of customer satisfaction and the value-add for them, and not in terms of the purchase price.

By segmenting purchased items and services in this way, it becomes easier to delineate the required strategies and tactics to apply in various supply markets and environments. Each of these quadrants has a uniquely different competitive and operating impact upon the firm. In contrast to ABC analysis, which focuses upon dollar volume and high-unit-cost items, the supply segmentation approach captures the interaction between supply market complexity and the cost/value impact to the firm. Using the supply segmentation approach, supply management can see clearly how various items and services actually impact the competitiveness and profitability of the firm.

SUPPLY MANAGEMENT TARGETS

The items and services segmented into the four quadrants have considerably different supply market characteristics. Not surprisingly the supply management goals associated with these items and services will be quite different as shown in Figure 5–6.

The greatest number of parts and services will end up being classified as tactical. These items, being of low cost/value and having low market complexity, are those on which resources expended should be minimized. The supply management target is to dramatically increase the efficiency of the purchasing process, thereby significantly reducing transaction costs.

Individual item or service purchase price is of little importance in this category. A large improvement in the purchase cost of the tactical items will result in a relatively small saving in total spend, whereas a small improvement in the total purchase cost of items that have high cost/value will result in a larger proportional savings.

Critical items and services, while being of low value, are nonetheless very important to the effective operation of the firm. Here the major goal will be to reduce the risk or exposure to the firm of any supply disruptions, even at a premium price. In general, the business is relatively insensitive to the price of these items. Nevertheless, these items should be kept under frequent review to ensure that they do not become a major cost item and thus move into quadrant IV. Also, every effort should be made to find ways of moving these items and services down into quadrant I, that is, reclassifying them as tactical. Supply managers should constantly assess the supply market, watching out for changes in the supply base and the global economy.

Leverage items and services are of high cost/value but have no major complications that would increase the resulting level of complexity. Frequently,

F I G U R E 5–6

Supply Segmentation Purchasing Goals

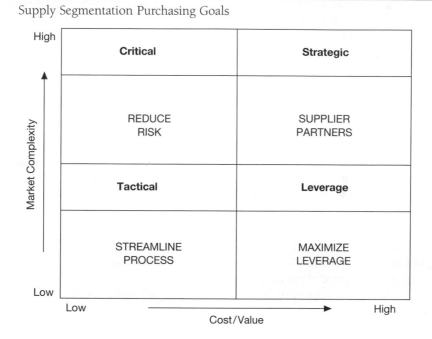

there will be an acceptable number of competitive suppliers. It is in this area that supply managers can seek out opportunities to reduce total landed cost and improve the profit contribution of these items and services. With a secure supply market, supply managers can afford to leverage their buy with a single source, that is, to reasonably increase the level of risk in order to gain volume efficiencies.

The situation in quadrant IV is very different. Strategic items and services are of high cost/value and every effort must be made to prevent any potential negative financial impact upon the firm. But the use of volume leveraging as a weapon may not be wise. These items and services also exhibit a high level of supply market complexity for the firm, which suggests that volume leveraging in a single source of supply might not be logical. These items and services lend themselves to a longer-term planning horizon and "partnering" mentality. These items and services should be managed for their value-adding impact on the firm's products and market share.

PRICE VERSUS COST IN THE SEGMENTATION ARENA

Price is only a small part of the total acquisition cost of an item or service. This fact vividly applies to the supply segmentation approach to supply strategy development. The following paragraphs will address this concept in more detail.

Leverage items and services are frequently benchmarked on the basis of price, but today price should include several other aspects of costs. For example, freight costs, payment terms, delivery expenses, warehouse charges, and inventory carrying costs are frequently used as a direct addition to the supplier's quoted price. Freight costs are being factored into the purchase cost, and many suppliers are asked to quote a "landed cost," which adds most movement and inbound storage costs to the purchase price. Payment terms, including the currency of payment, can significantly impact cash flow, cost of capital, and product cost integrity. Inventory costs, arising from lot sizing and timing of purchase decisions, are increasingly being added into the overall cost equation for these types of items and services.

Tactical items and services are significantly impacted by the transactional nature of the buying process. In addition to the supplier's quoted price, the cost of managing the acquisition process is of concern. For example, in many firms the cost of managing and generating a purchase order can exceed $200 per transaction. Given the low dollar volumes purchased in this category, the acquisition cost can exceed the supplier's quoted price per order. It is imperative that the acquisition cost of tactical items and services be measured accurately and be compared to the purchase price of the commodity.

The segmentation costs of critical items and services comprise the cost of plant or equipment downtime and utilization costs when the critical items or services are unavailable. Should a custom-designed item or service be purchased in this category? In some cases, the benefit of using a custom-designed item or service diminishes in comparison to the risk or exposure of not having that critical item or service available when needed.

The costs of strategic items and services are often measured as part of customer value-adds or in terms of their impact on ultimate customer service and satisfaction. These items and services often provide the key decision point that determines why the customer purchases from your firm instead of a competitor. Key metrics applied to these items and services are maintainability and reliability costs or even avoidance costs.

THE SUPPLY STRATEGY DEVELOPMENT PROCESS

The supply segmentation approach highlights the need for different supply strategies for each quadrant of the matrix. Figures 5–7 and 5–8 present examples of certain strategic approaches to managing the cost of items and services purchased based on the technical complexity and cost/value of the item purchased (Figure 5–7) and the level of market complexity and cost/value of the items and services purchased (Figure 5–8).

The supply strategies applied to tactical items and services should involve streamlining the acquisition process. For example, this can be measured in terms of the purchasers' time expended in the entire order process cycle. These are low-

FIGURE 5–7

Material Cost Reduction Strategies Based on the Level of Technical Complexity and Value

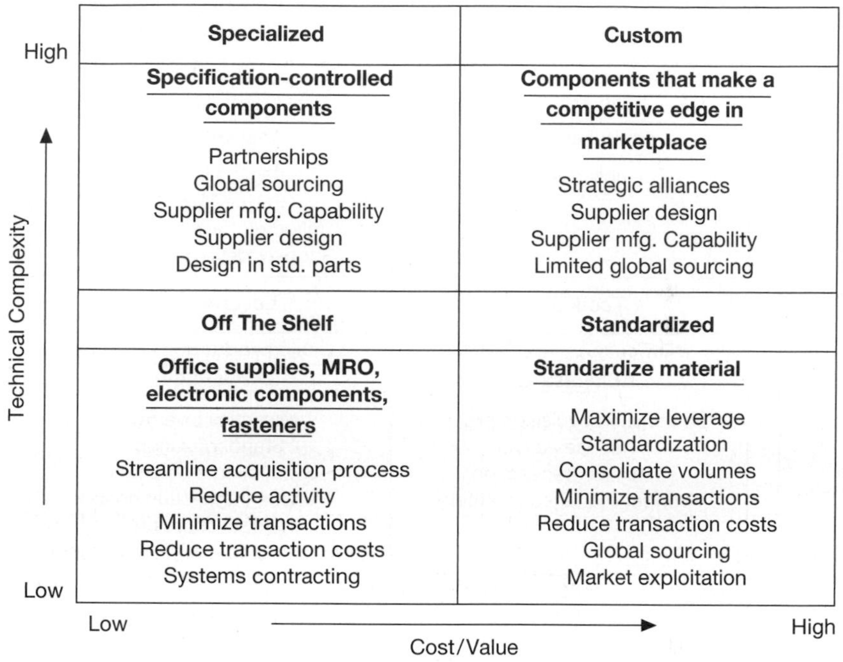
Specialized
Custom
High
Specification-controlled components
Partnerships
Global sourcing
Supplier mfg. Capability
Supplier design
Design in std. parts
Components that make a competitive edge in marketplace
Strategic alliances
Supplier design
Supplier mfg. Capability
Limited global sourcing
Technical Complexity
Off The Shelf
Standardized
Office supplies, MRO, electronic components, fasteners
Streamline acquisition process
Reduce activity
Minimize transactions
Reduce transaction costs
Systems contracting
Standardize material
Maximize leverage
Standardization
Consolidate volumes
Minimize transactions
Reduce transaction costs
Global sourcing
Market exploitation
Low
Low
Cost/Value
High

value activities that contribute very little to the strategic directions of the firm. The acquisition process should be minimized, eliminated, or outsourced. Many integrated supplier relationships, such as electronic data interchange, supplier bar coding, electronic funds transfer, and supplier-managed inventory systems are available. A key supply management goal is to reduce the time spent by personnel in the firm on the acquisition, delivery, stockkeeping, and payment of these items and services.

The supply strategies applied to leverage items and services are mainly traditional. The appropriate supply strategies within the leverage quadrant should focus upon short-term contracts to enable the buyer to constantly seek out and change to lower-cost sources. Supply managers should pursue a proactive supply strategy to find new suppliers and/or substitute products globally. Supply managers should be driven by the need to make a significant contribution to corporate profit by reducing costs in this high-volume quadrant.

Overall, the supply management emphasis placed on leverage items and services will be to increase the profit margin, that is, to use competitive supply management practices to increase corporate profitability. As a result, the firm should expect to see decreases in unit costs, increased market security, and detailed supplier

FIGURE 5-8

Material Cost Reduction Strategies Based on the Level of Complexity and Value

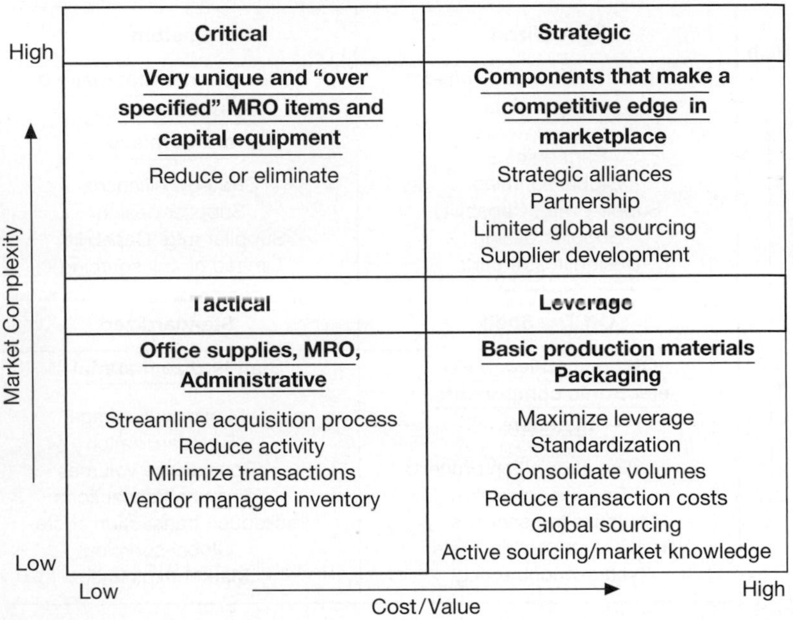

	Critical	Strategic
High	**Very unique and "over specified" MRO items and capital equipment** Reduce or eliminate	**Components that make a competitive edge in marketplace** Strategic alliances Partnership Limited global sourcing Supplier development
	Tactical	Leverage
	Office supplies, MRO, Administrative Streamline acquisition process Reduce activity Minimize transactions Vendor managed inventory	**Basic production materials Packaging** Maximize leverage Standardization Consolidate volumes Reduce transaction costs Global sourcing
Low		Active sourcing/market knowledge

Market Complexity (vertical axis, Low to High)

Low ———————————————————→ High
Cost/Value

knowledge. Supply management should expect to see an increase in supply market knowledge and the number of orders, a better timing and sensitivity of order placement, and possible supplier change. The supply base will range from local to national to global sources of supply.

Critical items and services should be analyzed for elimination. Early supplier design involvement where needed, early supply management design involvement, and close communication with engineering and users during the design phase for the product or service can help reduce the custom-designed nature of these items and services before they are "locked in." For existing items and services, value analysis and value engineering techniques can be effectively used to eliminate or, at least, reduce the need for these items and services. The supply strategy is to make changes that will shift these items and services to either the tactical (lower their market complexity) or leverage (lower their market complexity and increase their value) quadrants, or turn them into strategic items or services (increase their value) that have market impact or lend competitive advantage (see Figure 5-9).

Items and services in the strategic quadrant require the highest level of supply management competence. In some instances, long-term contracts may be very suitable, but in other circumstances medium-term contract lengths are pre-

FIGURE 5-9

Supply Segmentation Movement Goals for Critical Items and Services

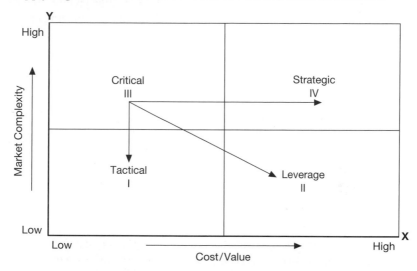

ferred. Supply management teams need to obtain detailed information on individual suppliers and work to develop them for mutual advantage. It is in this quadrant where the "supplier strategic alliance" concept can most effectively be implemented. The total cost of ownership (TCO) of each item or service must be closely monitored and controlled using competitive benchmarking techniques and price and cost auditing. All the items and services categorized in this quadrant need to be kept under continuous review to ensure that suppliers continue to supply at high levels of customer service and that costs are kept within targeted limits (target costs).

The supply management emphasis applied to items and services found in the strategic quadrant is to maximize competitive advantage. This is broader than just price advantage and includes rapid innovations, earlier time-to-market, and superior product quality, to name a few. The value-added nature of strategic items and services should be enhanced in any way possible.

OTHER QUADRANT STRATEGIES

The supply segmentation approach assists in the development of realistic functional-level (namely, supply management) strategies. Once again, Figures 5–7 and 5–8 provide examples of a few specific supply strategies. A further discussion of the supply management strategy development process follows.

Many of the specific supply management strategies for tactical-quadrant items and services call for increased involvement of suppliers both on-site and off-site.

While these items and services account for a small percentage of purchasing dollar expenditures, they frequently account for the vast majority of purchasing transactions and the resulting administrative costs of managing the acquisition process. The issue that drives all supply management strategies in this quadrant is minimizing the number of transactions and thereby lowering the resulting administrative cost of acquisition. With acquisition cost per transaction approaching $200 for the typical order, acquisition cost can be 50 percent or more of the total order cost. The main supply management strategy is to minimize the number of separate transactions through the consolidation of large numbers of orders with fewer suppliers by using blanket orders and other supply base rationalization and order-reduction strategies. The use of procurement cards (P-cards) is a frequently implemented and rewarding strategy. With P-cards, users can order directly from suppliers by telephone to a certain dollar authorization level specific to each firm. This dramatically reduces transaction levels since orders are summarized on the card's monthly statement and a single monthly payment is made to a financial institution instead of directly to numerous suppliers. For more commonly and frequently ordered items and services, the use of integrated suppliers and outsourcing strategies may be appropriate. The use of electronic data interchange (EDI) linkages with suppliers, although not common with items and services within this quadrant, is certainly an option to consider for higher-volume purchases. Supplier-managed inventories and consignment inventories are two other supply strategies applied to items and services categorized within this quadrant.

In summary, some example strategies for tactical-quadrant items are

- Use of the procurement card
- Supplier-managed inventories
- Systems contracting
- Electronic data interchange (EDI)
- Lean inventories

Supply strategies for leverage-quadrant items and services stress the minimization of the total landed costs of purchased items or services. This entails volume leveraging where appropriate with additional spot buys to meet unplanned capacity need variations. Supplier partnering strategies are of less importance with these suppliers, since traditional purchasing techniques seem effective. The items and services in this quadrant should be viewed as being generic in nature. This reflects the nature of the supply market environment and the characteristics of the items and services. For example, the supply market for these items and services is characterized by low barriers to entry resulting in several sources of supply for each item or service. The buying firm has low switching costs to move volumes across suppliers resulting in a low loyalty to any one source of supply. The total landed cost is the major supplier selection determinant. Supply strategies should all involve some sort of volume leveraging, such as concentrating purchases across diverse business units and adding potential volume to the supplier equation by suggesting longer-term contracts.

The leverage quadrant is where much of the purchase dollars are expended. Therefore, cost reductions, cash flow management through dollar cost averaging, and volume timing supply strategies are of critical importance. Just-in-time supply management strategies were developed for items located in this quadrant. Also, supplier quality assurance strategies are in frequent use.

In summary, some example strategies for leverage-quadrant items are

- Leverage the company buy in order to increase volume discounts.

- Use short-term contracts in order to remain flexible as prices or costs change.

- Join with horizontal consortiums.

- Actively analyze the supply base to find viable new suppliers.

- Assure continuity of supply.

The supply strategies pertaining to critical-quadrant items and services pertain to decreasing product and service variety. In a retail environment this means reducing the number and variety of stockkeeping units. In a manufacturing environment the supply strategies involve developing item and service standardization, using value analysis or value engineering techniques, and using cross-functional teams to improve and develop efficient processes to manage assets over their useful life. Custom-designed tools, capital equipment, and support items and services form the majority of items and services in this quadrant. While these items and services represent a small portion of the total annual spend by supply management, they represent those that require frequent interaction between supply management personnel and other user functions. Even though the cost savings potential is limited, the potential for bad publicity for supply management should something go wrong is great. These items, therefore, command more purchasing time and attention then they are "worth." What can supply managers do?

In order to add value to items and services found in the critical quadrant, supply management involvement in the order cycle must begin as early as possible, preferably even in the design stage. The supply management strategies must reflect this need through implementing early supplier design involvement and supplier research and development. Supply management can proactively support the user by reducing the number of sources through exclusivity of design and simultaneous engineering concepts. Nonitem costs, such as inventory carrying, training, transport, and maintenance costs, become a critical issue in the supplier selection and evaluation process. The cost of acquisition, in contrast to quadrant I items and services, is a very small proportion of the total item cost. Technical expertise and teaming skills are critical for supply management personnel involved with these items and services.

In summary, some example strategies for critical-quadrant items and services are

- Use long-term contracts to guarantee the supply.

- Maintain higher inventory levels.

- Find possible substitutes.
- Identify or develop new possible sources.

Developing supply strategies for strategic-quadrant items and services involves gaining competitive advantage through new technology access and development and fostering a high level of unique services from suppliers. This quadrant is full of critical items and services that the firm needs to maintain operations and market share. These are commonly unique items, services, and technologies without easy substitution. Many of these items are sole sourced. The costs of materials, acquisition, inventory, and transport are frequently of secondary consideration. Supply strategies must be to deepen the buyer-supplier relationship through sole sourcing, alliance partnering, and joint ventures, especially with foreign suppliers.

Total landed cost is not the driver of relationship development for items and services in this quadrant. Much of the negotiations revolve around cost-sharing discussions between the buyer and supplier to determine which firm is better situated to perform which activity within the supply chain. The managerial focus of supply management is placed upon customer service innovation and product and service enhancement.

In summary, some example strategies for strategic-quadrant items and services are

- Create a long-term contract with gains sharing.
- Establish a strategic partnership with the supplier.
- Develop alternative suppliers.
- Search aggressively for substitute products.

SUPPLIER RELATIONSHIP STRATEGY

A good way to think about supplier relationship strategy is presented in Figure 5–10. On one end of the continuum is the transaction focus, and on the other end is the collaboration focus. Strategies with a transaction focus generally have a short-term, arm's-length arrangement, whereas strategies with a collaboration focus generally have a long-term, highly interactive focus. Another way to think of the transaction focus is by referring to it as "cash-and-carry" in that the goal is to simply complete the transaction. However, the collaboration approach is much more involved.

CHOOSING AN APPROACH

Figure 5–11 depicts when the appropriate approach should have a transaction focus compared to a collaboration focus. Low-value, low-risk products sourced from a low-complexity market should have a transaction focus. Meanwhile, high-

FIGURE 5–10

Supplier Relationship Strategy

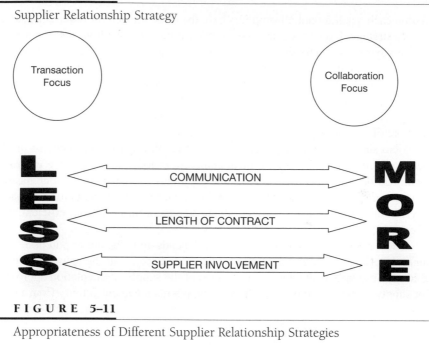

FIGURE 5–11

Appropriateness of Different Supplier Relationship Strategies

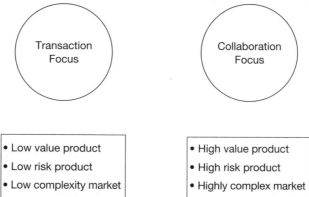

value, high-risk products sourced from a high- complexity market should have a collaboration focus.

This step closely relates to the earlier steps in the strategy development process—the appropriate supplier relationship strategy depends on the product, market, and supply strategy goals. Because one step in the strategy development process leads to the next step, it is vital that they be completed in a systematic manner. Neither a fact-based negotiation plan nor the supply management approach can be devised until the earlier process steps have been completed.

SUMMARY

Within each quadrant not all suppliers have the same impact nor require the same supply strategy. Experience has shown that within each quadrant there is a limited number of suppliers that accounts for the majority of supply management's resource expenditure activity. Key account suppliers must be actively managed. One individual or team—for example, a commodity team—should have the responsibility across strategic business units for the key supplier(s) of that commodity group. This will mean the use of all supply management strategies across the plethora of commodity groups sourced globally.

No single strategic approach is appropriate throughout the range of products and services used by the typical company in today's competitive environment. Unlike the historical purchasing paradigm that treated the purchasing process for most goods and services the same, the supply segmentation approach toward supply strategy development delineates them into differing efficient and effective strategies.

The extent of usage of this technique depends upon the dollar purchase volume, the criticality of the items and services purchased, and the resources available within supply management. The usage of the supply segmentation approach for supply strategy development can shift supply management activity from a tactical orientation into a strategic role within the firm, contributing significantly to profit, value-added, and market penetration.

The advantage of using the supply segmentation approach is that supply strategies can be aligned with corporate strategy, thereby exploiting supply management expertise for company advantage.

BIBLIOGRAPHY

Elliott-Shircore, T. I., and P. T. Steele (1985). "Procurement Positioning Overview," *Purchasing and Supply Management, Official Journal of the Institute of Purchasing and Supply* (December) pp. 23–26.

Porter, Michael E. (1996). "What Is Strategy?" *Harvard Business Review* (November–December), pp. 61–78.

Steele, Paul, and Brian Court (1996). *Profitable Purchasing Strategies: A Manager's Guide for Improving Organizational Competitiveness Through the Skills of Purchasing,* London: McGraw-Hill Book Company.

Vollmann, T. E., W. L. Berry, and D. C. Whybark (1997). *Manufacturing Planning and Control Systems,* 4th ed., New York: Irwin/McGraw-Hill.

CHAPTER 6

STRATEGIC SOURCING: WHERE DID IT COME FROM? WHAT HAS IT ACCOMPLISHED? WHERE IS IT GOING?

THOMAS H. SLAIGHT
Vice President
A.T. Kearney, Inc.

JULES A. GOFFRE
Vice President
A.T. Kearney, Inc.

Strategic sourcing began in the decade of the 1990s as a euphemism. Descriptions have shifted from tactical to more strategic over the last decade. The purchasing function became more "supply management." The buying activity became "sourcing." Sourcing used to be considered as identifying and qualifying potential suppliers of a company's purchased materials and services. By adding "strategic" to its description, its meaning was extended to a systematic, repeatable process to identify, qualify, specify, negotiate, and select suppliers for categories of similar spend.

For supply managers, strategic sourcing has become an organized, systematic, collaborative way to identify competitive suppliers for longer-term agreements to buy materials and services that firms need for direct and indirect purposes. Simply put, strategic sourcing is organized corporate buying. A little more than a decade ago, purchasing managers were struggling to make their impact felt within their own companies. Except for key materials, senior executives didn't view suppliers as strategic. Market price was what it was, and competitive advantage had to be gained through a collaborative, process-improvement approach with key suppliers. Key users within the organization, people in manufacturing, engineering, marketing, and information technology, often treated purchasers as tactical negotiators and keepers of contract terms and conditions. Too often, purchasing managers sank into a procedural, bureaucratic role of tracking requisitions and approvals, becoming a nonvalue barrier between the people who needed something and the suppliers who provided it.

But times changed; leading-edge firms are now recognizing supply managers and strategic sourcing as a value-added process that provides competitive advantage. In order for the process to work it must be organized, systematic, and collaborative. These may be elements of effective and successful strategic sourcing, but what do they mean?

Organized means that sourcing is part of an ongoing enterprise process. It covers all spend categories for materials and services. Sourcing strategies are reviewed and updated periodically by supply managers and by the executives for whom the spend is purchased. Suppliers are invited to be part of the process to varying degrees, depending on the class of category or market dynamics. Senior corporate executives are briefed on key spend categories and may enter the process when the financial or operating impact of an option is significant.

Systematic means that the firm has an agreed-upon process for pursuing strategic sourcing, and it's applied to all spend category teams in all business units. The systematic process is a key component of the organization's supply management training—in great detail for supply management professionals, in summary for collaborating using departments. Strategic sourcing results are tracked in terms of non-cost-performance metrics as well as cost savings. Knowledge from applying the process to spend categories is captured, ensuring continuous improvement for future sourcing teams. Systematic also means that the process is regularly reviewed to incorporate new sourcing tools and approaches, new supplier market opportunities, and developments in benchmarking and best practices.

Collaborative means that supply managers collaborate internally, with department managers who use the materials and services purchases and with senior executives on key spend categories, and externally, with key suppliers, incumbent or potential, on major new supply opportunities. Collaboration demonstrates the value of supply management. The effective supply manager will not only "get a seat at the table," but will be viewed as a "value advisor" on strategic supply issues.

WHERE HAVE WE COME FROM?

The elements of being organized, strategic, and collaborative are key to strategic sourcing now, but how did this proven way of providing better supply management for business evolve? It came from purchasing—as viewed by 1970s era managers and executives. Perhaps you're familiar with those antiquated perceptions: Purchasing people were brought in to finalize terms and conditions with the supplier someone had already selected—someone who knew far better what supplier would be best. Production planning had the important job of deciding when and how much product should ship to the factories; purchasing ensured on-time delivery. Engineers decided, manufacturers scheduled, quality checked, finance paid, and purchasing negotiated the terms and conditions.

In the 1980s, there were signs of change. For example, in the automotive industry, leading thinkers at a few companies started to investigate alternative sources of supply, outside the domestic, local suppliers qualified by the engineers.

The alternative was called "global sourcing." By challenging the selection process, by taking suppliers and engineers out of their comfort zone, supply managers provided improved pricing, prompt delivery, and higher quality, making that car company more competitive than it had been.

This was all happening during the decade of "reengineering," when organizations were downsizing without the connected requirement of removing work from internal processes. The great "hollowing out" of business organizations had begun. When business consultants realized that addressing the 50 to 80 percent of a firm's cost structure that came in from the outside might be less painful and more rewarding than identifying people to be downsized, the response from firms was alarming: "We don't know what we are spending beyond major suppliers. Aren't we already getting the best prices set by the market?" Department managers were defensive: "We can't afford to challenge those suppliers; we depend on them to keep our factories going, our computers running, our sales flowing, our warehouses full." Purchasing managers were frightened: "I've spent years trying to get a seat at the table and now you are going to ruin it. If you get better pricing than me, they'll fire me!"

The 1990s brought a three-pronged approach that began to make some headway with organizations that wanted to improve their competitiveness through better corporate buying. A business consultant could come in and address the above-mentioned concerns:

1. *Executive involvement.* Mr/s. Executive: You're spending more than you think. Key suppliers are not as large a proportion of that spend as you think. We can address some of the unimportant spend categories with your people to save you significant dollars.

2. *Department manager involvement.* Mr/s. Administration, Information Technology, Marketing, Logistics: We can combine with your people to identify supplier requirements and apply a "proven" process, saving money and negating the need for downsizing.

3. *Purchasing acquiescence.* Mr/s. Purchasing Director: We will work with you to apply a "proven" process that will build your credibility with department heads and senior executives, thereby increasing the amount of spend that you influence and bringing you credit for achieving enormous savings.

What would this "proven" process be called? "Global sourcing" incorrectly implied the necessity of foreign suppliers; "aggressive sourcing" sounded too literal. Finally, "strategic sourcing" was chosen because any approach that produced that extent of results had to be strategic, or *should be.*

The proven process was the seven-step process described later in this chapter. One key lever behind the process was the use of multidisciplined teams to apply it (teams that included other departments in addition to supply management. Most of the time, the teams were led by non-supply-management people.). Another key lever, and most important, was a corporatewide program of "waves" of sourcing categories sponsored by a committed senior executive. The wave structure enabled the communication of significant improvement and the recruiting of a cadre of successful sourcing "ambassadors" to the rest of the (still nonbelieving) company.

WHAT HAS WORKED?

For the next 10 years, this formula worked. It worked in manufacturing companies and consumer products companies. It worked in retailers, telephone companies, and pharmaceutical companies. It even worked in banks and other financial institutions. There has been no reason for it not to work in all companies; unfortunately, it has only been applied successfully in around 30 percent of North American companies, 20 percent of European companies, and less than 10 percent of companies in the Asia-Pacific geography.

Why hasn't it worked in a higher proportion of firms? There are three types of factors, with many individual reasons. The three factors are connected to philosophy, organization, and technology. Let's discuss these briefly before looking into our crystal balls to see what lies in the future.

Philosophical Tension

There has always been a philosophical tension between the ideas around competition and collaboration with suppliers. Proponents of competition make the case that a competitive supply market uses economic laws to ensure the lowest possible price at a set quality and service level demanded from buying communities. Suppliers will adjust their plans and performance to meet market requirements, or they will exit the market. Proponents of collaboration make the case that a strong supply or value chain requires the identification of best-of-breed innovation from a supply base that partners with its customers to provide best value to its end customers. Proponents of collaboration seem to be as much fearful of the misuse of competition as they are of the benefits of collaboration. Toyota is often used an example of a company that has managed to be competitive and collaborative at the same time. AT&T, prior to divestiture, might be an example of a planned, collaborative value chain that was slow to introduce innovation, keeping higher consumer prices while maintaining inefficiencies in its supply base. A balanced approach between competition and collaboration is the ideal, but companies continue to avoid the benefits of one for fear of misusing the other.

Organizational Misalignment

Organizational misalignment has also been a continuing deterrent to more widespread use of strategic sourcing. Senior executives lose interest after the first several waves of sourcing have taken place. A senior executive will think, "I thought I fixed that—aren't we still using an organized, systematic, collaborative approach for supply cost competitiveness?" In addition, a corporate executive may be challenged by a divisional executive who resists complying with a corporate purchasing program. In fact, when there is an opportunity to leverage corporate spend and processes to improve a division's competitiveness, there is no reason not to participate, particularly when it applies to noncore spending. Unfortunately, department managers gradually return to the less-cooperative practices of the past. Those who did not participate in the original waves of sourcing have not experienced the value from the program. They are less willing to collaborate with supply management to identify alternative suppliers or create improved supply chain and commercial opportunities. Supply managers also may lapse into presourcing behavior—taking shortcuts in the seven-step process, avoiding the rigor in conducting the analysis, and giving alternative suppliers the impression that they're only being used to hammer on the incumbents. Supply management executives have to continue to raise their level of performance, demonstrating that they have much more to offer than traditionally thought.

Tools and Technology

Finally, tools and technology are often blamed for incomplete application of the process. "If we only knew what we spent by category, by supplier, by business unit, we could. . . . We don't have the time to determine all the potential suppliers, all the required specifications, all the various proposals. . . . " In fact the tools and technology have overcome most of the objections that were originally made against the software as it was introduced. The Internet *is* fast enough, secure enough, and widespread enough. Suppliers *will* participate, users *will* report, and finance *will* fund investments. Tools and technology continue to support and accelerate the process. The tools get better and better each year—it is the unwillingness of executives, department managers, and supply management executives to deal with change that is the barrier to their use, not the technology itself.

WHERE DO WE GO FROM HERE?—SUSTAINABILITY

Although companies made great inroads in institutionalizing sourcing in their organizations in the eighties and nineties, they still are struggling to make the process sustainable, repeatable, and less subject to human factors. The concept of the sourcing factory as shown in Figure 6–1 was born out of the desire to industrialize the sourcing process, to the extent possible and meaningful.

Imagine the following factory, where the category manager is the foreman, responsible for the machine shop. For simplicity, the machine shop is constituted of several machining centers: spend analysis, e-RFx, and e-auction.

FIGURE 6-1

Sourcing Factory

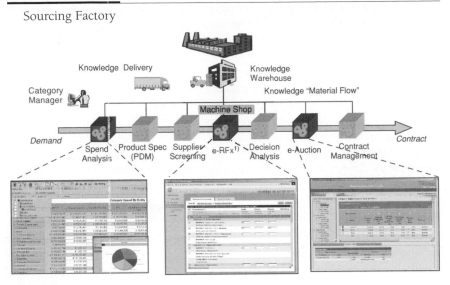

At the push of a button, these machines deliver the desired output. The Spend Analysis machine, for example, delivers the aggregate spend of all company locations, with the appropriate specifications, prices, past spend, future spend, and suppliers. The output of the spend analysis machine then goes as input into the e-RFx machine, which sends out the specifications to the targeted suppliers, and so on. The setup of these machines highly depends on the categories and category strategies that are pushed through. The configuration is made with the help of intellectual capital (IC). Fast configuration can be done with the help of existing categorizations, supplier long and short lists, e-RFx templates, eAuction builds, evaluation models, and sample modular contracts. The machines are each highly dependable, and inputs can be easily baselined and outputs can be easily benchmarked. The process is predictable, and the outcome is of the highest quality.

Is this a vision or reality? Well, for the most part still a vision. Yet many companies are making progress in making this vision a reality. This development is driven by five major factors:

1. *Core competence.* Supply management effectiveness has steadily increased throughout the years. By automating and making more efficient certain repeatable processes, supply management can devote more time to strategic thinking, cross-functional coordination, and work to create value beyond cost cutting.

2. *Compliance.* In view of the bankruptcies of recent years, process stringency is required above and beyond the existing codes of con-

ducts and ethics. Clear rules, guidelines, transparent decision-making criteria, and an audit trail of bids make it necessary to automate the sourcing process.

3. *Velocity.* Several sourcing categories require sourcing in relatively short intervals, due to the nature of the commodity: electronic components, certain raw materials, and spot freight. This means that companies must be able on demand to quickly source these items at a favorable point in time or based on a sudden surge of required capacity. Speed can be a strategy in itself to lock in the prices at a certain point in time. Take a high-tech company with 20 locations in three different business units. For certain direct materials, the sourcing process is run on a monthly or even weekly basis. Process automation is absolutely crucial. Companies that are not able to quickly aggregate spend and tender out the volumes are at a clear disadvantage.

4. *Local spend.* Several sourcing categories are local spend categories and cannot be sourced centrally: civil works, installation services, and value-added reselling, just to name a few. Similarly to a fast-food restaurant, purchasing needs to franchise the sourcing process to ensure that the output is of consistent quality, even in remote locations. Leading companies ensure that best practices are documented, audited, and rolled out, and that local organizations use the tools and structures prescribed centrally.

5. *Governance structures.* An important element of sustainability is the organization and the governance of sourcing. Strategic sourcing is a process requiring clear multifunctional and sometimes multidivisional involvement. Governance structures need to reflect this. Besides the cross-functional teams, there is a need for cross-functional demand committees to ensure buy-in of key stakeholders and rapid decision making. Without the proper decision and escalation structures, it is very difficult to implement an effective sourcing process. Additional complications come about when on top of the cross-functional involvement, the supply management function must source across business units or divisions. The right trade-offs need to be made in order to make the process manageable and the sourcing factory implementation a success.

The setup of a sourcing factory has two implementation planks: information technology and professional development.

1. *Information technology.* There are a number of applications or systems that need to be put in place in order to build the sourcing factory. The following table lists the applications and limitations today to fully automate the sourcing process for each process step.

Sourcing Step	Enabling Applications	Today's Typical Limitations
Conduct internal assessment	ERP transaction systems	Multiple local system instances Focus on existing suppliers
	PDM systems	Contain technical specifications but limited commercial information
	Data warehouses or spend management systems	Can establish links across disparate systems, but are only as good as the input data itself Need for content management, i.e., cleaning, categorization, validation, and data aggregation
	Excel and shared files and e-rooms	Highly manual and dependent on individual contributors
	Collaborative sourcing platforms	Requires configuration by category
Conduct external assessment	Supplier and purchasing portals	Need to attract suppliers on own platform
	External databases and service providers	Requires integration, collaboration, and continuous updating for new capabilities
Collect supplier information	Supplier and purchasing portals	Need to attract suppliers on own collaboration tool
	RFx tools	Need to customize and catalog templates to each spend category
Develop sourcing strategy	Some point solutions based on game theory, constraint optimization, etc.	Must capture successful, preceding approaches into a sourcing history feature
Solicit and evaluate bids	RFx tools	Need to customize templates to each spend category
Negotiate and select suppliers	Auction tools	Need to customize auction builds to each spend category, mostly point solutions in place
Implement recommendations	Contract management	Need for different contract clauses and T&Cs by country and unit Need a contract calendar feature linked to sourcing plan
	ERP transaction systems	Need flexible implementation features for local systems with local master records
	Catalog buying systems	Multiple back-end linkages to ERP systems

Note: ERM = enterprise resource management; ERP = enterprise resource planning; PDM = product data management; RFx = request for quotation, information or proposal; T&C = terms and conditions.

Although there are some important limitations, some software providers are working on integrated supplier relationship management (SRM) solutions to cover part of these shortcomings. A seamless full integration will not be in sight for the next five years, due to the disparity of systems and sources of information. Until this is achieved many companies are looking for nonintegrated best-of-breed point solutions to best cover the functionalities needed. What can be said is that all solutions require a good degree of customization to cater for category-specific needs. Alternatively, companies are having recourse to category-specific end-to-end solutions like in the area of print or travel.

2. *Professional development.* Regardless of the level of automation, the sourcing process depends vastly on the people executing it. Internal and external skills training and certification ensures consistency of the process. Strategic sourcing done right is a process requiring subject matter expertise, creativity, analytical skills, negotiation, project management skills, and much more! Leading companies have set up "sourcing universities" to cater to the professional development needs of their employees. The right combination of internal and external training, Web casts, and hard and soft skills is essential to have a program that caters to all development needs. Certifications in certain learning fields allow supply management leadership to better match job descriptions to capabilities, develop personal development programs, and provide a more objective base for career progressions. Whereas purchasing in the last decades was rather undifferentiated, that is, the buyer did everything from sourcing to operational buying, we have proceeded to a more skills-based functional development. A modern supply management department includes specialists like e-procurement professionals, data and spend management specialists, controlling and benefits tracking managers, consultants, advanced purchasing engineers (to optimize specifications in interaction with R&D and marketing), category managers, key account managers (for suppliers), and global sourcing managers. In addition, the cross-functional requirements have increased, so broader training in subject matter that goes beyond sourcing is necessary. Any sourcing factory implementation will require substantial re-qualification and change management.

MAKING IT WORK: THE SEVEN-STEP SOURCING PROCESS

At the heart of strategic sourcing is a seven-step process (see Figure 6–2). It can be applied to each of an organization's spend categories. However, even before beginning with the first step with a particular category, *the methodology begins with a diagnostic of a company's spend.* The diagnostic divides the total corporate spend into categories that roughly relate to the supplier markets that provide the company's needs. It typically further divides spend categories by the business units or locations, and it identifies each supplier. The diagnostic seeks only an 80 percent precision, not Six Sigma standards. You will see that in step 3, beyond the initial diagnostic, when sourcing teams need to refine spend data for each category, the supplier may be a more accurate source (even if supply managers are embarrassed to use it).

The diagnostic provides a spend map by category. Spend categories are then classified by the competitiveness for the supplier marketplace compared to their internal impact. This results in a spend category positioning matrix (the familiar four-quadrant grid), which directs supply managers to a potential sourcing strategy for the category. The matrix plots categories as *critical* (low supply market competitiveness, high business impact), *leveraged* (high supply market competitiveness, high business impact), *bottleneck* (low supply market competitiveness, low business impact), and *noncritical* (high supply market competitiveness, low business impact).

Once the diagnostic is complete, companies must decide which categories to address immediately and which to delay until internal and external conditions are better. For those categories it chooses to address, the seven-step process begins.

STEP 1: CONDUCT INTERNAL ASSESSMENT

The first three steps are conducted concurrently by the sourcing team. In step 1, the team ensures it understands everything about the spend category itself. For example, if the category is corrugated packaging at a consumer products company, the team will make sure that it understands the definition of the category, confirms usage information, and knows why the types and grades of corrugated packaging were specified. Company consumers at all operating units and physical locations would be identified; other people with an interest in corrugated packaging would be identified—logistics people who need to know strength and other shipping specification, and marketing staff who need to understand visual and quality or environmental characteristics (if applicable). Existing supplier relationships should be cataloged and understood, as well as the existing purchasing processes that users and suppliers are familiar with, *because there will likely be changes to them.*

STEP 2: CONDUCT SUPPLIER MARKET ASSESSMENT

At the same time, step 2 begins. Additional suppliers, other than incumbents, are identified. Key supplier marketplace dynamics are identified, and supplier and user should-cost information is determined. Major supplier cost components are evaluated, and the supplier marketplace is analyzed for risks and opportunities. In the corrugated category example, it will be particularly important to set up a map of potential serving locations (versus need locations) due to the impact of transportation costs on the category.

The Seven-Step Sourcing Process

1. Conduct Internal Assessment
- Confirm category definition
- Validate baseline information
- Identify company consumers
- Identify key constituencies
- Identify existing supplier relationships
- Understand current purchasing processes

2. Conduct Market Assessment
- Analyze market dynamics/trends
- Identify supplier universe

3. Collect Supplier Information
- Develop supplier survey
- Develop evaluation criteria
- Verify spend data

4. Develop Sourcing Strategy
- Develop specifications
- Identify sourcing levers
- Develop end-state scenarios
- Determine potential mega-supplier approaches

5. Solicit/Evaluate Bids
- Develop RFP evaluation criteria
- Develop supplier messages
- Develop RFP
- Short list suppliers

6. Negotiate/Select suppliers
- Negotiate with suppliers
- Select suppliers

7. Implement Recommendations
- Develop category implementation plans
- Develop communication plan
- Develop measurement
- Capture intellectual capital

Ensure Compliance

Capture Learning

Measure and Report

SOURCE: A.T. Kearney

STEP 3: COLLECT SUPPLIER INFORMATION

In step 3, the sourcing team develops a supplier survey for both incumbent and potential alternative suppliers. The survey helps evaluate each supplier's capabilities to serve, as well as its costs to serve. At this time, the team will also verify spend information with the data that incumbent suppliers may have from their sales systems.

STEP 4: DEVELOP SOURCING STRATEGY

The combination of the first three steps—conduct the internal assessment, conduct the market assessment, and update supplier information—provide important input to developing a sourcing strategy in step 4 of the process.

The sourcing strategy for the category will depend on the answers to the following questions:

1. How competitive is the supplier marketplace?

2. How aligned are your organization's users on the need versus opportunity to test incumbent relationships?

3. What alternatives to a competitive assessment exist for your organization in this or connected categories?

How Competitive Is the Supplier Marketplace?

Armed with the information from step 2 (incumbents, alternatives, and a "five forces" competitive positioning model (derived from *Competitive Strategy: Techniques for Analyzing Industries and Competitors*, 1980, Michael E. Porter, Free Press), you are ready to build the competitive tension in the supplier marketplace. This will demonstrate the "size of the prize" to be won to motivate alternative suppliers and to communicate the seriousness of a potential sourcing exercise to your incumbents.

How Aligned Are Your Organization's Users to the Need Versus Opportunity to Test Incumbent Relationships?

The sourcing team has two sets of constituencies: (1) the people who use the things that are bought and (2) the executives that manage overall costs. The people who use the spend category accept cost reductions as long as they start in another department, don't change incumbent suppliers, and don't create any complaints from the supply base that might affect any part of the relationship—delivery reliability, service, or payments. For users, all change is bad.

For executives, cost and service competitiveness is a key objective, but they too are users of various corporate services, so they often have a split personality between executive pursuit of cost improvement and being users who resist change.

("Get better costs for my key components, but don't change my travel agent" is a typical manifestation of this split personality.)

In order to mobilize users and executives to support the category sourcing strategy, it is necessary to communicate benefits (particularly to the executive) and overcome potential risks (particularly to the users).

What Alternatives to a Competitive Assessment Exist for Your Organization in This or Connected Categories?

If the supply base is competitive, you will be able to harness those forces for better pricing or terms due to increased volume of streamlined product specification. Once the result of the competitive sourcing effort is determined, you will then set up a collaborative program that will continue until the next logical, appropriate competitive sourcing event takes place.

If you don't use a competitive approach to sourcing, what are your alternatives? The alternatives consist of collaborating with suppliers (1) to reduce complexity to build increased productivity into their process, (2) to create joint process improvements that reduce the cost of doing business, and (3) to set up relationship restructuring where firms invest in supplier operations to guarantee access to supply, new technology, or process improvements. These alternatives are typically pursued where the buying company has little leverage over its supply base; consequently, buying companies are relying on good-faith sharing of benefits from their suppliers.

Your sourcing strategy will be an accumulation of the levers depicted in the "sourcing gemstone" in Figure 6–3. A high-buying, cost-based power approach toward the competitive marketplace will enable global alternatives, best-price comparison, volume concentration advantages, and perhaps, product specification improvements. Collaboration will begin to be addressed by competitive proposals and will continue after supplier selection.

STEP 5: SOLICIT AND EVALUATE BIDS

For most of the spend categories, a competitive approach is used. This requires step 5, preparing a request for proposal (RFP) and preparing and soliciting bids. This will define the basis for competition to the prequalified suppliers. It includes product or service specifications, delivery and service requirements, evaluation criteria, pricing structure, and financial terms and conditions. Also in this step, a communication plan will be executed that will attract maximum supplier interest, ensure that every supplier will be competing on a level playing field, and enable the buying organization to come to an optimum selection decision. The RFP is then sent out to all suppliers, and they are given enough time to respond completely, with follow-up messages sent to encourage supplier response and to field questions.

FIGURE   6–3

Strategic Sourcing Approaches

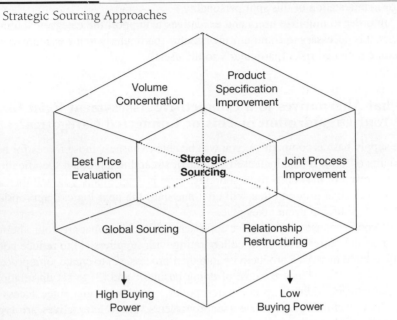

STEP 6: NEGOTIATE WITH AND SELECT SUPPLIERS

In step 6, the sourcing team applies its evaluation criteria to the supplier responses. If more information beyond the RFP response is needed, it's requested. The negotiation process is conducted first with a larger set of suppliers and then narrowed to a few finalists, if it is done manually. If the sourcing team uses an electronic negotiation tool, more suppliers may be kept in the process longer, giving alternative or diversity suppliers a greater chance at winning the business. Award scenarios are conducted to compare a series of outcomes in terms of total value or implementation cost differences. Using departments are brought into the final selections process. Senior executives are briefed on the selection outcome; their approval is obtained, and they understand the rationale so that they are prepared to receive calls from any disappointed suppliers.

STEP 7: IMPLEMENT RECOMMENDATIONS

Finally, the winning supplier(s) are notified and invited to participate in step 7, implementing recommendations. Implementation plans vary depending on the degree of supplier switches. For incumbents, there will be a communication plan that will include any changes in specifications, improvements in delivery, or service requirements or pricing. These are communicated to the users as well. The company may have received significant improvements from the process; it's important that these are recognized by the company and by the supplier.

For new suppliers, a communication plan has to be developed that manages the transition from old to new supplier at every point in the company's process that is touched by the spend category. Receiving docks, using department, finance, and customer service are often impacted by a change, and their risk antennae will be up during this period. It is particularly important to measure the new supplier closely in the first several weeks of performance. Being able to demonstrate to your organization that the new supplier's performance is equal to or better than that of the former incumbent will be particularly important during that sensitive time.

It is also important to capture intellectual capital that your sourcing team has developed during the seven-step process, for the next time the category is sourced and to refresh corporate memories should questions arise.

There are three important *feedback loops* in the seven-step process:

1. *Measure and report* is a way to measure the benefits from the sourcing exercise through the life of the new arrangement and report results to using departments and executive groups, addressing all-too-frequent comments like, "They say they saved a lot in that category, but I've never seen it."

2. *Capture learning* begins with the internal and external assessments in steps 1 and 3 and continues to capture learning throughout the process. Supplier market dynamics change, supplier contacts change, new entrants appear in supplier marketplaces, and people change in using departments—all need to be captured. Some of the spend analysis and e-sourcing tools available today have such electronic means.

3. *Ensure compliance* is aimed at the supplier, the using department, and supply management. The supplier must be measured against performance metrics that were agreed upon in the sourcing process. The using department must not solicit new suppliers or alter the performance terms that were agreed on. Supply management must maintain contact with the supplier to build on the relationship during the ongoing relationship.

Used accurately and thoroughly, this seven-step proven process for strategic sourcing can give enterprises the competitive advantage that ultimately elates corporate executives, users, and supply management professionals alike.

THE PROCUREMENT INTENSITY CONTINUUM: HOW AGGRESSIVE ARE WE AND SHOULD WE BE AT SOURCING?

As firms approach strategic sourcing methodologies and initiatives to better create supply management value, the extent to which they embrace the process will be influenced by factors both internal and external to the organization.

INTERNAL INFLUENCES

The internal influences are characterized by the attitudes and mindsets detailed in step 4 of the seven-step process (see pags 110–111). Sourcing teams are charged with satisfying both internal users who might be fearful of change and executives who expect cost savings and added value. Well-established routines, "selling" supply management, demonstrating return on investment, and aligning with corporate objectives along the way all influence a supply manager's choices about how aggressive to be in strategic sourcing.

EXTERNAL INFLUENCES

In addition, external forces will also have impacts as well. Competitiveness of supplier marketplaces follows the economic classifications seen in Figure 6–4 in the supply competitive continuum. Too often, sourcing teams automatically shy away from supplier markets on the left side of the supply competitiveness continuum. All supplier markets have opportunities for those who are willing to look for them.

In what a pharmaceutical company thought was a pure *monopoly* situation, its sourcing team worked with a supplier of patented active ingredients to provide additional marketing funds to grow volume in exchange for patent expiration concessions. The sourcing strategy included demonstrating to supplier senior management the economic value added for their company of added market share from its product.

For a regional telephone company that had standardized its network on a *single source,* the sourcing team developed a megasupplier strategy that linked the single-source categories with other competitive categories to demonstrate the company's willingness and capability to execute a multicategory sourcing strategy. The supplier did not believe that the telephone company could execute the strategy, so a few of the incumbent's competitive categories were put out to bid, reducing the incumbent's share.

FIGURE 6–4

Supply Competitiveness Continuum

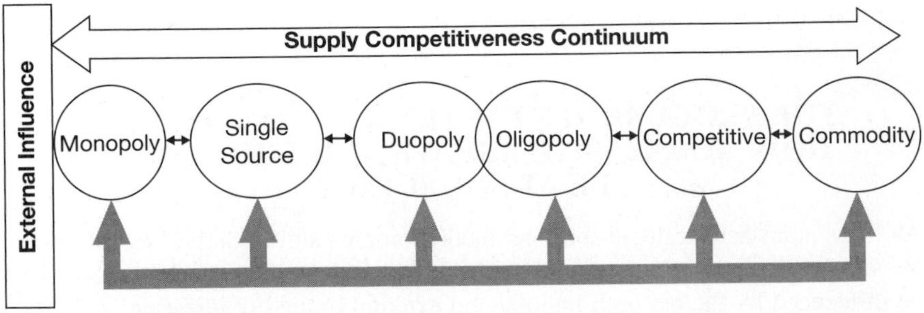

Source: A.T. Kearney

For an industrial products assembler and distributor who was supplied by an *oligopoly,* the sourcing team created a blind price competition where suppliers competed by price rank rather than price level. The key to executing this strategy was aligning the company's sourcing, manufacturing, marketing, and executive teams to demonstrate to the oligopoly that its members could neither dictate the terms of the competition nor go around the process to other customer contacts.

In a *competitive* situation, the key is to retain credibility with all members of the competitive cohort. Fairness to the group of suppliers is more important than fairness to one or another. Maintaining balance in the supplier group is more valuable than supporting one or the other. Letting too many suppliers merge or go out of business is counter to maintaining the competitive tension in these categories, so the sourcing team has to be willing to give business to nonincumbents to demonstrate its willingness to maintain the competitive group of suppliers.

In a *commodity* supplier market situation, the sourcing team must make sure that it has accurate visibility on the commodity supplier market pricing and must determine supply chain opportunities to gain advantage through the commodity's pricing structure. Too often, we see company's who understand the category's commodity nature but who misread the commodity's actual pricing by not understanding the real price or by being unaware of supply chain features that are giving its own competitors' advantage.

PUTTING IT ALL TOGETHER

From the combination of the external and internal situations, companies develop an accepted behavior with their suppliers over time—explicitly or tacitly. There is a procurement intensity continuum at each company and for each spend category that must be addressed and may have to be shifted to produce results. If you could picture the range of behaviors that are possible in terms of sourcing and investigating potential supply sources, it might include the following.

At the far left end is "scorched earth" sourcing: This would be characterized by aggressive investigation and assessment of the supply market, an eager openness to seeking out new suppliers, a tendency toward short-term gains, a constant focus on what else is available in the market, and a fervent attitude of "Can we be getting better value from a different supplier(s)?"

At the far right end is "smooth water" sourcing: This environment is characterized by the status quo. There is little or no encouragement or acknowledgment of new supply base opportunities, or opportunities are scarce due to market conditions. People are generally pleased just to adhere to known suppliers, where the process and interpersonal relationships are familiar. The threatening idea of change causes resistance to new ideas and often wins out over any cost, quality, or value improvements that might be possible with new suppliers.

Somewhere in between lies a firm's "zone of acceptability." This might be different for any given firm, though there may be some tendencies overall for industries. It indicates the market's and a firm's tolerance and general attitude toward new sourcing opportunities and is influenced by what the external market situation will tolerate, the firm's strategies and goals around supplier relationships, short- and long-term priorities and requirements, and general aptitude for change.

Detailing this range of procurement intensities may seem fairly academic in nature, but it does exist. Suppliers also recognize these behavior patterns and respond to them in a variety of ways. Often when a buying firm begins a sourcing improvement program, it is making a conscious intentional shift toward the left end, away from smooth waters, and moving closer to scorched earth.

Typically, the zone of acceptability is too far to the right toward smooth water sourcing. The influence of users who find reasons not to encourage new suppliers to create competitive tension to reduce costs has usually overcome executives' desire for lower costs and purchasing's willingness to set up a sourcing exercise.

Occasionally, we hear evidence that executives in a particular industry or spend category have moved the zone of acceptability too far to the left toward scorched earth sourcing. There has been much discussion in the automotive industry that original equipment manufacturers (OEMs), beginning with the tactics of Ignacio Lopez (first at General Motors, and then at Volkswagen), have used strong-arm tactics too heavily on tier-one automotive suppliers, so much so that these suppliers are in danger of going out of business. On the other hand, OEMs have shown no signs of regular, systematic sourcing approaches for their indirect spend.

Recognizing the internal and external forces that will impact the strategic sourcing initiative will help supply managers approach and implement the process with greater success.

THE NEXT FRONTIER—VALUE-BASED SOURCING: WHAT DOES THIS ENTAIL?

One could say: strategic sourcing is focused on getting the best deal for a given spend item (a good or service). The best deal can be the lowest price in the case of a commodity item, but can also be getting the greatest value out of a more broadly defined supplier relationship. It is the latter which is at the heart of value-based sourcing.

Example: When Hella, an automotive supplier, developed the new ring-shaped headlights with BMW for its new 5 series car, it brought much more than a new headlight to the market. It enabled BMW to strengthen its brand equity and identity. Until then it was very difficult to distinguish a car at night, driving on the

Source: BMW and Hella Internet sites

motorway. With this innovation, car drivers can easily recognize a BMW coming from behind, thus increasing the brand awareness.

This example underscores the need to look at value beyond the immediate scope of purchase to other capabilities and other sources of value. This constitutes the next challenge for the supply management community as procurement professionals have been traditionally focusing on their responsibility area: the sourcing of goods and services. Value-based sourcing implies figuring out what are the other assets, capabilities or benefits a supplier can bring to the table than just the product or service itself. Figure 6–5 shows that value-based sourcing defines clearly new boundaries for supply management.

When going down this road, the supply management professional must be involved in addressing more strategic questions:

- Is my supplier better capable to take over certain activities, which are currently in my company's responsibility, like product and service development, inventory management, or after-sales servicing?

- Can my supplier help de-risk my goods supply in terms of bottlenecks, supply chain disruptions, exchange rate risks?

- Can my supplier provide me with a competitive advantage by providing me with a unique feature set which helps me differentiate with respect to the competition?

- Can a potential supplier help me expand my offerings portfolio to address new customer segments or needs?

F I G U R E   6–5

Evolution of the Strategic Sourcing Confines

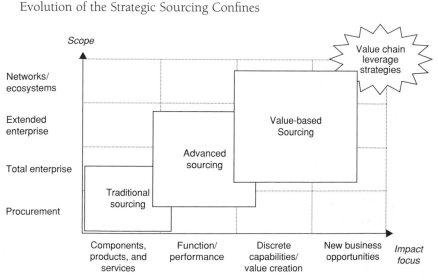

Source: A.T. Kearney

• Can an existing or new supplier help me get my goods or services quicker to the market?

The positive aspect of addressing these more strategic questions is that the role of the supply management professionals will be further strengthened in the company's organization. The drawback is that few are prepared to assume this expanded role.

Although some leading companies have embarked on this route, many are struggling with the transition from a more traditional strategic sourcing to the value-based approach. Some of these challenges are highlighted in Figure 6–6.

THE FUTURE TODAY?

Some leaders in some industries are adopting quite quickly the value-based sourcing approach. At a leading computer hardware manufacturer, the supply management function is now focusing its attention on the strategic part of the external value chain. This encompasses the design, manufacturing, sourcing, quality management, and logistics of key components and systems like the CPU, power management, or storage devices. The responsibility spans much more than traditional sourcing in order to address all sources of value like: time-to-market performance with new feature sets, management of configuration complexity, or new product introduction to new niche segments. One can say the role of the supply management function has evolved to that of a value chain integrator. Other spend items, e.g., for the assembly plant, are now being managed by the plant itself and the supply management function is only involved in recruiting the procurement professionals, training them and providing them with the state-of-the-art tools and processes. This company has clearly pushed the envelope of strategic sourcing to the next level.

FIGURE 6–6

Transition from Traditional Sourcing to Value-Based Sourcing

Traditional Sourcing	Value-Based Sourcing
■ Focus on prices	■ Focus on value
■ Total Cost of Ownership	■ Total Contribution of Ownership
■ Process-driven sourcing approach	■ Strategic intent-driven sourcing approach
■ Seek comparability	■ Seek differentiation
■ Involvement in spec definition phase	■ Involvement in strategic decisions
■ CPO reports to Executive Committee	■ CPO is Executive Committee member
■ Procurement skills	■ Business skills
■ Procurement is "independant" and acts as a counter party	■ Procurement is aligned and intrinsically linked with business stakeholders

Caveat: there still is the need for traditional sourcing!

SOURCE: A.T. Kearney

Although not all companies are this far, we expect other leading companies to rapidly follow suit and become more strategic in their sourcing, without of course neglecting less strategic spend areas.

For most companies though, strategic sourcing will continue as the organized, systematic, collaborative process for establishing and maintaining spend category relationships with suppliers. It will struggle with getting the attention that it deserves with executives and using departments and will constantly seek balance between competition and collaboration. Those who thought it was another management fad are mistaken. It has endured for at least a decade, and it will continue to be an important component of supply management well into the future.

CHAPTER 7

KNOWLEDGE-BASED SUPPLY MANAGEMENT

ANNA E. FLYNN, PH.D., C.P.M.
Associate Professor
Institute for Supply Management™

Knowledge-based supply management is a process that is driven by knowledge about customers, organization strategy, the economy, the supply base, and other factors that influence the ability of supply and suppliers to contribute to the long-term success of an organization. Supply is uniquely positioned to synthesize information and input from three distinct sources: (1) internal business partners, (2) the supply base, and (3) the customer base. It is the individual and collective efforts of supply professionals to synthesize and act on the information derived from these three sources that sets apart the strategic supply organization from the tactical. How members of the supply group attain, organize, manage, and use knowledge to develop and implement supply strategies throughout the process is a vital aspect of organizational success.

This chapter addresses three components of a successful supply management process: sourcing, evaluating and selecting suppliers, and measuring supplier performance. First, it addresses three sourcing models that can be used to categorize and define organizational needs. Next, it focuses on the sourcing process, including the strategic questions that the sourcing team should consider when assembling a short list of sources and the typical factors that are then analyzed to make the final selection. Finally, it presents several approaches to measuring supplier performance and using those metrics to drive continuous improvement.

CONTEMPORARY SOURCING MODELS

Sourcing is the process of identifying potential sources that could provide needed products or services. One challenge of the sourcing process is ensuring that organizational, and ultimately customer, needs are met effectively in the short and long term. To determine the capability of potential sources, supply strategies must be aligned with organizational strategies which must be aligned with customer needs. Strategic supply management is the development of this seamless linkage between customers and tiers of suppliers. The ability or inability of supply to make and sustain this link is a key determinant of the overall value-adding capability of supply. Three approaches to sourcing are discussed: spend-driven, risk-driven, and strategy-driven.

Spend-Driven Sourcing Model

In companies that adopt a spend-driven approach to sourcing, the sourcing team starts with data derived from spend analysis. This data includes . what is bought, from whom, in what quantities, and under what terms and conditions. Resources, including managerial time and attention, are allocated to those purchases that consume the greatest spend annually. This approach has led to greater involvement of supply and a wider application of a structured sourcing process to what are often referred to as nontraditional purchases such as benefits, energy, travel, and other service categories. Figure 7–1 depicts the typical sourcing process starting with spend analysis.

Spend Categories
Spend analysis results in a better understanding of organizational spend by category. These categories may be designated A, B, and C using a Pareto analysis or as commodity categories based on the type of purchase. Policies and procedures are then established to manage each category. Typically, more managerial time, effort, and funds are allocated to higher spend categories. For example, in a packaged foods company that makes breads, cakes, and cookies, the raw materials such as flour, sugar, and butter are A items and typically receive more planning and managerial attention than B or C items. Subcategories can also be classified within the three broad classifications depending on how finely management wishes to stratify purchases.

Additionally, spend categories can be defined according to the type of purchase, including raw materials (metals, agricultural products), purchased parts (components and semifinished goods), packaging (paper, plastic, glass, corrugated), MRO (maintenance, repair, and operating supplies like paint, spare parts, lubricants), services (travel, janitorial, security, consulting, benefits), capital equipment

FIGURE 7–1

Spend-Driven Sourcing Model

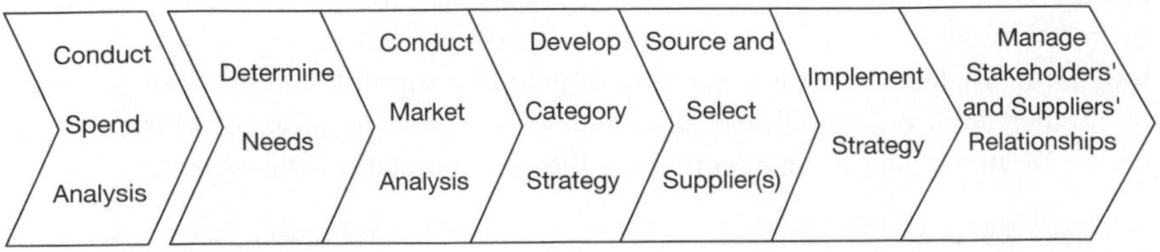

(machinery, office equipment, vehicles), and resale (finished goods, like private-label audio systems). The sourcing team should be knowledgeable about the assigned category, including the supply base, emerging technology, logistics, market conditions, cost structure, price trends, and industry practices. Knowledge from the spend analysis is used to develop a strategy to meet the short- and long-term needs of the organization, and satisfy final customers.

Operationally, the goal is to ensure that "the right good or service is delivered to the right place at the right time and at the right service level, in the right quantity, at the right price from the right source" in the short and long term. How this goal is achieved is influenced by spend category. Supply assurance, quality, and delivery may be as important for B or C requirements as A, but these would be managed differently. Cycle time, documentation, and personnel may be reduced by using tools such as e-procurement and supplier-managed inventory. Effectively implemented, spend analysis may free up time to focus on the strategic aspects of the process.

Risk-Driven Sourcing Model

In companies that adopt a risk-assessment approach to sourcing, the sourcing team starts with data from the organization's risk profile. The risk profile is derived from the identification of significant risks faced by the organization along with quantitative and qualitative analyses of the exposure levels. Ideally, supply base risk assessment is one area of exposure that is aggregated to generate the organization's risk profile. At a minimum, supply management leadership should conduct supply base risk assessment and align risk-mitigation strategies on the supply side to the overall risk profile. Understanding the organization's mission and culture assists in aligning risk taking and risk mitigation with organizational risk aversion. One aspect of supply's role as a strategic contributor is to assess the enterprisewide impact of a supply initiative. Resources, including managerial time and attention, are allocated to those purchases that are deemed riskiest to acquire in the marketplace and of greatest expected return to the organization as a whole.

This approach focuses internal resources (supply professionals and internal business partners) and key suppliers on identifying and dealing with root causes of risk. Each sourcing decision should be considered in the context of the organization's risk profile. Risk is perceived to be higher with new purchases or suppliers and with increased dollar amounts and higher levels of customization. Risk-mitigation strategies include efforts to mitigate, limit, transfer, ensure against, or explicitly take the risk. Risk can be transferred by working in a cross-functional team, for example, with engineering and finance, or by seeking additional information, including placing a trial order or hedging in the commodities market. Requiring bid bonds, performance bonds, or payment bonds ensures against risk. By not doing business with suppliers in certain countries, the team avoids risk. Dual or multiple sourcing rather than single sourcing mitigates risk. Negotiating payment terms that allow progress payments when certain milestones are met, and that withhold a percentage of the payment until completion and acceptance of the service, limits risks. When a supply manager takes an action such as selecting a supplier or switching suppliers or agreeing to certain terms and conditions, he or she should take these actions with the explicit understanding of both the risk at which the decision puts the organization, the return expected, and the balance between the two. The assessment of the trade-off between risk and reward in isolation and in the aggregate should guide the sourcing manager or team's decisions.

An organization's risk profile is influenced by both internal and external factors. Internal factors include changes in organization structure or leadership, new strategies, new or improved products, technology, distribution channels, or processes. It is also significant if individuals in other functional areas fail to take into account the strategic value of the organization's suppliers, supply base, and supply chains or networks. External risk factors include changes in the economy, competitive factors, legislative and regulatory changes, and new technology.

An organization's risk profile is reflected in its initiatives. Early adopters have assessed internal and external risks and decided that, given the level of organizational risk aversion, to adopt an innovation earlier than others. An organization with a highly risk averse management and culture may conclude from a similar assessment that a wait-and-see approach is best. For example, the adoption of e-auctions varies considerably even within an industry because the conclusions drawn from risk assessments are different.

Risk assessment is the foundation of solid strategy development. Portfolio analysis focuses attention on the value-generating capability of a purchase in light of the risks of acquiring the purchase in the marketplace. One benefit of this approach over Pareto analysis is that it captures risky smaller-dollar purchases. Figure 7–2 is adapted from the classic matrix first developed by Peter Kraljic.[1] Purchased items are placed in the appropriate quadrant and strategies are developed by quadrant and by specific commodity within a quadrant.

Noncritical and Leverage Purchases

Noncritical and leverage purchases are standard goods and services that are low to medium risk to acquire. There are multiple suppliers, quality is comparable, substitutes are available, and market forces keep prices competitive. Therefore, easy and low-cost acquisition and delivery systems may be the most important decision criteria in the sourcing process. Higher volume (leverage quadrant) gives the buying organization power in the marketplace, so supply strategies focus on

---

1 Peter Kraljic (1983). "Purchasing Must Become Supply Management," *Harvard Business Review*, September 1. pp 109–117.

F I G U R E   7–2

Characteristics of the Four Quadrants

High		
Risk of Acquisition	*Bottleneck* • Unique specification • Supplier's technology is important • Production-based scarcity: low demand and/or few sources of supply • Substitution is difficult • Switching suppliers is difficult • Usage fluctuates and is unpredictable	*Strategic* • Continuous availability is essential • Custom design or unique specifications • Supplier technology is important • Few suppliers with technical capability or capacity • Switching suppliers is difficult • Substitution is difficult
	Noncritical • Standard specification or "commodity" type items • Substitutes readily available • Competitive supply market: many sources	*Leverage* • Standard specification or "commodity" type items • Volume-price breaks: price/unit is key • Substitution is possible • Competitive supply market: several sources
Low		
	Low	**Value** High

leveraging volume and scale and reducing the supply base. The supply manager generates price savings that free up cash for other uses such as reallocating to support or generate top-line or revenue growth or returning it to the bottom line.

Bottleneck and Strategic Purchases

Bottleneck and strategic purchases are medium to high risk to acquire because of a unique or customized specification or the need for access to a patented, copyrighted, or trademarked item. Risk can be lowered by reducing or eliminating uniqueness without negatively affecting the final customers. Typically, a cross-functional and often cross-organizational team is required because of the high risk of alienating end customers.

Strategic purchases represent the greatest risk and reward opportunity for an organization and its supply network because of the potential impact on the organization's mission. The trend is toward joint ownership of goals, strategies, and metrics. Supply's process expertise, supply base knowledge, negotiation and contract management skills, and the ability to build and manage long-term relationships complements the internal business partner's technical knowledge.

Strategy-Driven Sourcing Model

In companies that adopt a strategy-driven approach, the team starts with the organization's strategic plan. Since supply management brings in-depth knowledge and understanding of the external marketplace, as well as of the organization's suppliers and competitors, it is critical that supply provide inputs to the corporate strategic plan just as its counterparts in marketing or operations. Resources, including managerial time and attention, are allocated to purchases that have the greatest potential impact on strategic success. Efforts are undertaken to maximize the opportunities and minimize and manage the risks of achieving strategic success. Supply strategy, like organizational strategy, is driven from customer analysis (see Figure 7–3).

The sourcing team should first determine whether the requirement is strategic or operational. Operational purchases affect the ability of the organization to continue day-to-day operations with little or no impact on final customers. For example, office supplies may represent a high-dollar spend category and be important for daily operations but have little or no impact on final customers. A good strategy is to establish an operational partnership with a single source with electronic catalog management capabilities for a long-term contract. A category or commodity team would manage the partnership, but senior management would probably be uninvolved.

A strategic purchase affects the ability of the organization to serve its external customers or significantly affects the bottom line or financial health of the organization. Major dollar requirements are often strategic because of their bottom-line impact. A relatively low dollar value purchase, for example, a unique raw material that, in small quantities, enhances the performance of a much larger batch of raw material or of a piece of machinery, may also have strategic significance. Competitive advantage may be gained in tight supply situations. Strategic partnerships and alliances should be structured and managed differently than operational ones.

The interdependency between and among major strategy areas in an organization, including enterprisewide, operational, financial, marketing, and supply strategies, supports a process rather than a functional orientation. This interrelatedness requires strong internal business partnerships between and among strategy and process owners.

The chosen sourcing model influences the organization of the supply department and the knowledge and skill sets required of personnel. For example, a spend analysis approach requires expertise in each spend category; a risk-management

FIGURE 7–3

Information Flow

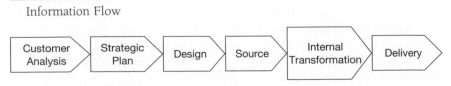

approach requires analytical skills and knowledge to assess risk and develop and implement risk-mitigation strategies; and a strategy alignment approach requires strategic thinkers who can develop and align supply strategies with organizational strategies and develop an efficient and effective process that allows focus on strategic purchases. Clearly, these three approaches can be incorporated into one. However, the primary approach will drive the organization of the supply department as well as the behavior and decisions. Once established, the supply department must determine how it will source potential suppliers and on what basis supplier selection decisions will be made.

EVALUATING SUPPLIERS TODAY AND FOR TOMORROW [2]

Sourcing is when alternatives are generated and the decision is made to include or exclude suppliers from the pool of candidates. Research on decision making suggests that a failure to generate a wide range of alternatives often results in a suboptimal decision. Therefore, sourcing is a critical juncture in the acquisition process because of the effect on the final outcome.

   An accurate description of the need, service, or good is essential to an effective and efficient sourcing process. The sourcing team or the buyer and internal user share responsibility for developing the appropriate specifications, performance terms and acceptance criteria in light of organizational and supply strategy. Developing these descriptions focuses the sourcing team, whose members may have conflicting goals and objectives, to reach consensus on the requirement. While the process is heavily front-end loaded, it provides opportunities to avoid building in unnecessary costs, creates a united voice when communicating with suppliers, and more accurately communicates the specification. Sourcing can be viewed as a two-stage process: (1) identify a broad range of suppliers that might be worthy of consideration, and (2) narrow the list to a reasonable number for more in-depth analysis and selection.

First-Cut Strategic Considerations

Working from the category strategy, the sourcing team establishes initial criteria for identifying potential sources. Strategic or high-level considerations are related to the nature of the purchase, its relative importance to the organization as a whole, and the urgency associated with the requirement. Based on the organization's approach to sourcing, purchases will have been classified as high, medium, or low dollar spend; high, medium, or low risk; or strategic or operational. Some organizations may combine these assessments for more detailed classifications such as medium dollar, high risk, and high strategic importance. For example, if

2 Michiel R. Leenders, P. Fraser Johnson, Anna E. Flynn, and Harold E. Fearon (2006). "Supplier Selection," Chapter 10 in *Purchasing and Supply Management,* 13th ed., McGraw-Hill/Irwin, New York.

the purchase is of high strategic importance, then a single source and the development of a long-term strategic relationship may be desirable. If the purchase is high dollar, medium risk, and operationally important, then a long-term volume contract with a single source may be desirable.

Typically, the strategic issues the buying team should consider include the following:

1. *Existing or new supplier.* Is the existing supplier performing adequately, or should the sourcing team consider other sources?

2. *Number of suppliers.* Can the risks be minimized and the opportunities maximized best through a single source or multiple sources? Supply base rationalization means determining the optimal number of suppliers for any given requirement. In some cases this may mean adding, not eliminating, suppliers.

3. *Size of supplier.* Will the short- and long-term needs of the organization, and ultimately those of the final customer, be met best by a small, medium, or large supplier?

4. *Location and proximity.* Will a local, national, or global supplier best serve the needs of the buying organization? Does proximity matter? If so, how close does the supplier or one of its facilities need to be in relation to the buying organization or one of its facilities?

5. *Type of relationship.* What type of buyer-supplier relationship should be developed? Is an alliance or partnership warranted? Is the purchase of strategic or operational importance?

6. *Contract length.* Is the contract (relationship) designed to be short, medium, or long term?

7. *Type of supplier.* Can the need be met best by a manufacturer, wholesaler, reseller, contract manufacturer, or other outsourced third party?

8. *Social, political, and environmental considerations.* Are there any social, political, or environmental concerns that might heavily influence the list of potential sources?

9. *Financial stability.* At a high level, are the potential sources financially viable?

Existing versus New Suppliers

By assessing changing market conditions such as price, availability, and entries and exits from the supply base, the team can analyze the competitive environment and determine whether a change is needed. Cost analysis will indicate whether the cost of switching suppliers will be offset by projected improvements from a new one.

New sources may be preferred if quality, service, delivery, price, cost, or other standards have not been met; uniformity and continuity of supply is of little importance; products or services are of low complexity; and access is needed to technology, patents, copyrights, and trademarks not owned by existing suppliers. Low urgency for the requirement; adequate lead time to evaluate, select, and transition to a new supplier; and no prior commitments or long-term contracts makes it easier to transition to a new supplier. Major organizational changes in either the existing supplier or the buying organization, such as changes in strategic direction or key personnel or mergers and acquisitions, may cause a disruption or change in requirements. Anticipated or actual changes may affect the risk assessment and lead to a decision to split business among several suppliers. If a suitable source does not exist, the team may need to develop or create a source to meet a current or future requirement. Political, economic, or environmental reasons may also drive change.

Number of Suppliers

The sourcing team decides if cooperation or competition will be most effective. There are several types of competition. Full and open competition (many buyers and sellers) promotes product or service improvements and price containment. Limited competition (few sellers) promotes fixed or firm pricing and may discourage improvements. Limited competition occurs nationally if demand is great and locally if the few sellers copy behaviors and pricing. Technical competition exists when many suppliers provide the technology. Patents, copyrights, and trademarks limit competition. A sole source is the only source available, and no competition exists. The interaction of the external environment and the buyer's needs determines the degree of competition. It is a continuing challenge to balance the desire for competition with the benefits of cooperation.

Multiple sourcing maintains competition and hedges the risk of relying on one supplier for a requirement. It may be preferred if the assessed risk of a single source is too high given the strategic goals of the organization. It also allows new suppliers to be tested at fairly low risk, assures supply, may lead to better pricing and service, provides flexibility and access to unused capacity, or meets government regulations.

Single sourcing (one supplier is chosen; many are available) fosters cooperation and enables the development of closer relationships with a few key suppliers. Typically, a partnership or strategic alliance is developed. It may be preferred if it is believed that a close relationship with one source will generate mutual benefits such as superior quality, cost reductions, avoidances, or savings through continuous improvement initiatives, price or freight discounts, easier planning and scheduling, coordinated forecasting, just-in-time (JIT) systems, or supplier-managed inventory. It may be required if the order is too small to split or a long-term contract already exists.

Size of Supplier

The size relationship between the buying and selling organizations may affect the supplier's ability to meet the buyer's short- and long-term needs. If the supplier is too small relative to the buying organization's demand, it may become overly dependent on the customer for its survival, putting both organizations at unnecessarily high risk. If the supplier is too large relative to the customer, the customer's business may be of less value to the supplier and may receive less attention or the attention of lower-level or less-qualified staff than would a key customer. The trend toward national and global contracts has often made it more difficult for smaller suppliers to compete.

Location and Proximity

The team must also consider the location, domestic or international, and proximity of the source. The globalization of business has increased the need for suppliers to have the capability to provide products and services across a wide geographical area. Buying from national or international sources rather than local ones increases competition and may provide better quality, lower prices, and a wider range of goods and services. Domestic sources may be preferred since the same laws, transportation links, and communications apply for the purchaser and supplier. If sourcing internationally, the team must consider exchange rates, payment processes, duties, transportation costs, timing, laws, and social responsibility issues. JIT systems require close proximity.

Type of Supplier Relationship

The sourcing team should also consider the type of buyer-supplier relationship it intends to foster. A primary consideration is the degree to which the purchase is operationally or strategically important. Typically, a purchase is strategic if it has the potential to affect the organization's ability to achieve its mission, and operational if it has the potential to affect the day-to-day operations without adversely affecting the final customers. Often, this distinction is blurred. For example, in many organizations supply has established a single-source relationship with an office supply provider and labeled the relationship a strategic alliance even though office supplies, although a large spend category and important to daily operations, have little or no strategic significance.

The main types of buyer-supplier relationships are strategic and operational partnerships and alliances, and preferred, approved, prequalified, or certified suppliers. Strategic and operational partnerships and alliances are typically marked by long-term arrangements and volume commitments. They are based on mutual trust and support, information sharing, and joint continuous-improvement initiatives. The differences are that strategic relationships also involve joint product or service development, close coordination throughout the supply chain, and joint long-term planning. Strategic relationships allow both parties to leverage their strength and pool their resources to create competitive advantage. One of the hallmarks of strategic alliances is that senior management recognizes them as critical to organizational success. If the relationship is truly strategic, then communication should occur at multiple levels, including the CEOs and other senior executives as well as operational personnel. If the strategic relationship depends on a supply manager and a sales representative, there is a high degree of risk because the relationship has not been institutionalized. Even if these individuals work well together, both organizations are at risk if either party leaves. In many organizations, stronger internal business partnerships and greater understanding of the contribution of strategic supplier partners to organizational success is needed.

One of the advantages of strategic alliances is early supply and supplier involvement in new product or service development and design. Working closely with a supplier from product or service concept to actual production or delivery allows designers to tap additional resources to ensure design for procurability and manufacturability as well as meeting quality, cost, and time targets. The cross-organizational team focuses on developing defect-free products, flawless launches, and speedier time-to-market while achieving significant cost reductions and improvements in customer service. By creating a seamless relationship with key suppliers, the team or supply manager in effect turns the supplier into an extension of the buying organization.

Preferred, approved, prequalified, and certified supplier classifications streamline the purchasing process for operational purchases. Certification typically refers to a supplier, whose quality control system is integrated with the purchaser's system, reducing the total costs of quality assurance by eliminating duplication. Preferred, approved, and prequalified suppliers have typically undergone a thorough evaluation and performed satisfactorily. An in-depth analysis of the supplier's financial strength, facilities, location, size, technology, labor status, management, costs, terms, references, and other factors is performed. These suppliers can then be awarded business without additional analysis and often by internal users via an e-procurement system.

Contract Length
The team must consider what contract length is appropriate. This decision is linked closely with the other strategic considerations, especially the goals of the buyer-supplier relationship.

Type of Supplier
The sourcing team may also need to consider the type of supplier, manufacturer, or reseller that will best meet short- and long term organizational needs. Buying from a manufacturer may be desirable if the volume is high, the distributor provides little or no value-added services, and design or technical support is needed from the manufacturer. Manufacturers often have little interest in selling direct and require the use of a distributor or price to encourage it. Resellers, including distributors, wholesalers, and retailers, may be preferred if the buyer has limited warehouse facilities, needs only a small quantity, or needs to purchase small amounts of a wide range of products by many different suppliers. The decision is often based largely on the need for services, such as vendor- or supplier-managed inventory. Total cost may be less when using distributors or wholesalers because marketing costs are spread over a variety of items and transportation costs may be less for distributors since they can buy in car or truckload lots.

Social, Political, and Environmental Considerations

There are social, political, and environmental issues to evaluate when sourcing. Government legislation, social responsibility, and the desire to develop alternate sources may lead to the development of supplier diversity programs. Diversity may be narrowly defined to mean minority-owned businesses or expanded to include women-owned, small, economically disadvantaged, or historically under-utilized businesses.

Environmental considerations may be mandated by law or determined by organizational strategy. Federal regulations for the use, transportation, and disposal of hazardous materials, workplace right-to-know laws, and emergency prepared-ness requirements significantly impact the acquisition process. The main questions are (1) How can supply decrease environmental concerns? and (2) Which suppliers and supply chains lessen the potential liability from environmental issues?

Financial Stability

The overall financial stability of potential sources may be assessed at a high level to ensure that the supplier is not a high risk. The prescreening may include the supplier's credit rating by a third-party financial organization such as D&B or assess-ment by an automated financial risk-assessment model. Tools such as profitability, liquidity, asset management, financial leverage, market valuation, cash flow, and bankruptcy indicator ratios as well as qualitative factors and industry comparisons may be included. The supplier is scored as a low, medium, or high risk.

Ability to Perform

The decisions based on these strategic issues formulate the foundation of the buy-ing strategy for a particular category. Once made, the sourcing team can narrow the field and then conduct a more in-depth analysis of the short-listed sources to make a final selection.

Ultimately, the sourcing team's goal is to select suppliers that meet current and forecasted operational and strategic needs to enable the organization to satisfy its customers. To do this, the team must determine the ability of potential sources to per-form. Numerous factors may be assessed, including financial position, quality con-trol and quality assurance systems, information technology systems, organization, and management. In addition, operational capabilities may be relevant, including capacity, capability, cycle time to process orders, delivery and distribution sys-tems, degree of electronic business enablement, and product and service expertise. Suppliers are typically evaluated based on internal data from past performance, objective data from third parties, and supplier-provided data in bids, proposals, and site visits. The team must determine the relative importance of each factor and establish a process for consistently assessing each potential supplier against the same criteria, with the same weightings and using the same rating system. Consistency is a key driver in developing a fair and objective repeatable process.

Quality Assurance and Quality Control Systems

Materials and services must arrive at the preestablished quality standard consistently. There needs to be a commitment, if not an actual plan, for continuous quality improvement. For goods, the manufacturing process, quality control systems, procedures, and statistical process control (SPC) programs should be assessed as well as acceptance and rejection history, traceability, and calibration dates on gauges and test devices. For services, provider qualifications, experience, and track record, and other aspects of the particular service that directly impact service quality should be assessed.

Operational Capability and Capacity

The supplier's operational capability must fit with the requirements of the buying organization and its customers. The specific areas for assessment are driven by the context of the purchase and the supply strategy employed. Typically, the review includes the customer category, the supplier's operational and process cycle time, technical and operational expertise and experience, and capacity. The supply manager should determine how long, on average, it takes the supplier to process orders, if deadlines are usually met, and how much, if any, follow-up or expediting will likely be required. All these factors influence total cost of ownership.

The supply manager should determine the company's production or service delivery capacity. Is it underutilized, overutilized, operating efficiently, or backlogged? The ability to analyze the supplier's capacity is dependent on the accuracy of the sourcing team's forecasts, which depends in part on how far in advance the decision must be made. The decision of how much to buy is complicated by several factors, including timing, scheduling, volume-price breaks, carrying cost of inventories, desired service levels, and possibility of shortages. Underestimating requirements may result in higher costs to meet unanticipated needs, and overestimating may result in higher levels of inventory and carrying costs or overuse of services.

Forecasts are essential and usually unreliable. Forecasts are derived from knowledge of the customer's needs and wants worked through the entire organization (including sales, purchasing, and logistics) and supply network. Who makes the forecast and how it is derived and monitored has a tremendous impact on the entire supply network. It is critical for the sourcing team to monitor the forecast against actual requirements and devise a procurement plan that takes into consideration the probability of all possible outcomes. Timely information flows between the sourcing team and tiers of suppliers may be more important and more realistic than improvements in forecast accuracy. Information may relate to the timing of delivery needs, production and service process flow, supply chain issues, supplier's lead time, and final customer changes.

Logistics and Distribution System

The team may also need to analyze the potential source's ability to deliver according to the projected schedule, the flexibility of its systems and people when schedules change, and its ability to provide inventory management or continuous replenishment. Information management systems and e-business capabilities and experience may play an important role in the suppliers' capabilities.

Service Capability

Service may refer to many aspects of a supplier's capabilities, including responsiveness, flexibility, and adaptability. Clearly defining the desired service level is often more difficult than establishing the quality level of a product or component. Highly intangible services are the most difficult to assess. Typically, the evaluator will rely on surrogate indicators to assign a rating for a potential supplier's service. For example, educational levels, years of experience, and a client list may be used to indicate that the supplier's service level will be acceptable.

Financial Status

Supplier financial assessments can be done from a number of angles, starting with the supplier's financial and cost data. Information may be obtained from independent third parties such as industry analysts and financial organizations. A sole source or a privately held company may not be willing to provide financial information. The assessment leads to a rating or score that indicates the financial risk of one potential source relative to other sources, or each potential source may be categorized as a low, medium, or high financial risk. These results are then weighted according to the team's plan and incorporated in the final selection decision.

A number of analytical tools are available, including a review of a supplier's income statement (earnings for a period of time, usually one year) and the balance sheet which shows the supplier's financial position (assets and liabilities) at a given point in time. Ratio analysis can be conducted using this information. Ratios can be grouped into four major areas: (1) financial efficiency, (2) profitability, (3) liquidity, and (4) leverage and solvency. Financial efficiency is measured by asset turnover, inventory turnover, and average accounts receivable turnover. Liquidity is measured by working capital, cash flow, current or quick ratio, and operating expense ratio. Profitability is measured by net income, earnings per share, gross profit and operating profit margin, return on assets, and return on equity. Leverage or solvency is measured by debt-to-equity ratio, times interest earned ratio, cash flow coverage, and debt to assets.

Other potentially relevant data includes off-balance-sheet items; special charges and extraordinary items; earnings projections; accounting policies, cost reduction, avoidance, savings initiatives; revenue-generating initiatives; mergers, acquisitions and divestitures; intangibles; cost structure; CFO discussions; and parent, subsidiary, and affiliate structure. The company's annual report also includes information on the company's outlook, new products and new developments, outstanding stock, acquisitions, and debt. A 10-K report provides more detailed financial information about a publicly held company than an annual report.

Data from external sources includes trend analysis; comparison with peers and the industry (Hoover's, Factiva, Nasdaq); reports from analysts, banks, and rating agencies (S&P, Moody's, Fitch); auditor's opinion and issues; litigation; and stock price relative to peers. Credit ratings provide a picture of the supplier's financial history and clues to its future viability. Excessively large debt or accounts payable and poor cash flow would suggest an inability to secure loans and, perhaps, an inability to generate the resources to meet the supply manager's needs.

Organization and Management

The team may also review the strengths and weaknesses of the supplier's structure; the stability and qualifications of senior management; and corporate controls, strategies, and policies and procedures. Technical competence and innovative ability is indicated by the educational background, work experience, and stability of its workforce, a well-supported training program and state-of-the-art equipment and technology. Business publications and references provide information on the supplier's general reputation and industry standing. The willingness to commit services and support and to invest in developing the buyer-supplier relationship indicates customer commitment. Supplier violations of employment or environmental laws may taint the reputation and image of the buying organization. If the supplier is acquiring a high dollar volume of inputs, the team should review the supplier's procurement system and organization.

Labor Status

The supply manager should be concerned with three areas of a supplier's labor: employee skills, unionization, and contract expiration date. The team should assess the stability, skills, training, experience, and competence of the workforce. Commitment to employee training and development may indicate willingness and ability to head off potential problems. If the workforce is unionized, the status of union contracts, history and threat of strikes, backup plans in case of delays or disruptions during strikes, and the general tenor of the labor-management relationship should be reviewed.

Legal and Regulatory Environment

To ensure lowest total cost of ownership, the sourcing team may also need to consider compliance with laws and regulations such as the Occupational Health and Safety Act (OSHA) and the Consumer Product Safety Act. The environmental impact of items a company buys and how the waste products from these items, after their usage, will be disposed of may also be a concern. Environmental supply chain strategies range from avoiding violations to including environmental issues from the design stage forward.

Visits to Supplier's Facilities

A site inspection gives a first-hand look at the supplier's facilities, level of technology, education and training of staff, employees' attitudes toward their work, and overall effectiveness. The investment against future problems may be greater than the costs of time and travel. An unaudited supplier with poor facilities, old technology, insufficient capacity, or a poorly qualified staff may result in downtime or lost production and limited assets for future growth. Discussions should focus on operational and strategic needs, value improvements, and issues specific to the situation.

ANALYZING SUPPLIER PERFORMANCE

A structured and formal supplier performance measurement program adds greater discipline, consistency, and focus to the supply management process. Collection and analysis of performance data allows for more intelligent sourcing decisions and more useful feedback to support continuous-improvement initiatives, such as better pricing, quality, supply assurance, cost reductions, and revenue growth through improved customer service. The primary goal is to create competitive advantage through the contribution of suppliers. Without a disciplined and structured assessment process, it is difficult to know if suppliers have made a meaningful contribution. A successful supplier performance measurement system helps ensure that (1) the organization delivers customers' wants and (2) organizational expectations are clearly and consistently communicated to the supplier.

Characteristics of a Successful Program

Measurement takes time and resources. Cooperation and collaboration with internal business partners and key suppliers ensures that these stakeholders provide information, participate in the analysis, and use the results in their execution and planning. The program needs to be integrated into other corporate initiatives and programs to get companywide cooperation, buy-in, and input. Management support at the global, regional, and site levels ensures resource allocation. Top managers must persuade employees, customers, and suppliers that the return from measuring performance across the supply chain is worth substantial effort. This may be difficult if the system does not show immediate, measurable impact on getting products or services to customers or if time and energy is devoted to daily challenges and emergencies. The ability to effectively manage change, internally and externally, supports the process. An efficient and effective system allows for conducting more supplier performance reviews with less effort.

Suppliers must perceive the process as fair and objective. This requires regular, specific, and timely feedback on performance so that improvements can be made and the business relationship can be enhanced. The sourcing team must make decisions and take actions based on scorecard data, or the integrity of the program will be quickly compromised. Supply personnel must understand the process, learn to evaluate by numbers, and seek improvements across functional boundaries. Without internal training and commitment, employees may become sloppy about data entry and accuracy. Externally, suppliers may lose motivation.

Valid and reliable data, not opinions and perceptions, must be used on score-cards with a link between data and decisions to avoid the costs of capturing use-less information. Inaccurate data damages the credibility and effectiveness of the program. Information technology (IT) capabilities must be used to their fullest extent to gather data and assist in analysis. Automation of real-time metrics, such as on-time delivery measures, and careful selection of more time-consuming data collection activities helps to reduce the time spent measuring results. Challenges include lack of IT support or solutions and poor data integrity.

Key Performance Indicators

Key performance indicators (KPI) are the designated metrics used to distinguish between and among suppliers used consistently across the organization and supply base. Determining what to report, the frequency of reporting, and how to report requires careful analysis. KPIs should align with organizational strategy, be clearly defined and prioritized, and encourage desired behaviors. Complex KPIs are difficult to measure and explain and complicate developing corrective action plans. Suppliers need time to review data and resolve disputes before the scorecard is finalized.

KPIs may be related to cost, quality, delivery, technology, supply assurance, and so on, and may include on-time delivery; number of rejects; the increase in sales after a marketing campaign; and cycle time for new product, service, and tech-nology development. Performance standards typically reflect the costs incurred, supplier by supplier, in satisfying requirements. Softer metrics, such as commit-ment to the relationship, responsiveness, and flexibility, are often harder to meas-ure, but equally important. A summary statement may include the supplier's cost performance relative to the should cost or ideal cost, quality and timeliness per-formance and a compilation of satisfaction surveys, real-time metrics, variances, and other contract-related terms.

Price and Cost Metrics

Price is one of the most common metrics in a supplier performance assessment. There are a number of different ways to measure price performance, including old price versus new price, lowest acceptable initial bid versus final price, actual ver-sus budget, and supplier quote versus final quote. The reasonableness of prices paid can be assessed by comparing actual price to an index of market prices to compare prices paid to the overall market.

Overemphasis on price metrics may undermine efforts to focus on cost struc-tures and total cost of ownership. More effective means of conducting cost analy-sis, capturing the results of strategic cost management initiatives, and getting internal validation from finance and internal business partners are being developed. Cost analysis provides a more detailed analysis of the cost elements in the price and may result in a better evaluation and comparison of price quotes. Better yet, cost analysis and tracking of cost savings, cost reductions, and cost avoidance may help to refocus the attention of internal business partners, suppliers, and supply managers on needed initiatives. Comparing actual costs to should cost and ideal cost provides opportunities to benchmark a supplier's cost performance against several baselines, discuss the supplier's performance up front, and measure it in-process and after the fact. This approach may contribute to longer-lasting relationships, greater cost transparency and knowledge of cost drivers.

Delivery

The costs of improper delivery must be calculated. A weighted cost factor can be assigned to the different delivery possibilities on the early and late side of on-time. Costs could be the expense of extra inventory, space and handling, idle operations time, and the replanning caused by delinquent shipments, and travel, telephone, and living expenses created by having to expedite the delivery.

Quality

Quality can be defined in many ways. In absolute terms, quality is a function of excellence, intrinsic value, or grades as determined over time by society generally or by designated bodies in specialized fields. The simplest definition is that the item or service meets specifications. However, the ultimate test is whether or not the good or service performed in actual use to the requirements regardless of conformance to specification. If not, the original specification may be at fault, not the supplier. Specification development, communication, and early supplier involvement are critical.

Determining whether a product meets specifications is accomplished through acceptance testing, such as the percent of defective items from a given supplier multiplied by a disposition factor. The number of defects can be determined by sampling, and the disposition factor is based on the cost of disposing of defective material by scrapping the material and reordering, returning the material and reordering, reworking the material, or even using it as is. The cost of dealing with defective material varies with the disposition method chosen. If the defective item is used, the cost may include writing a quality data report and holding a conference with possibly the quality control engineer, the project engineer, the incoming materials inspector, and the supplier. Scrapping and reordering costs may include writing a quality report, sending a letter to the supplier, disposing of the defective materials, issuance of a second purchase order, and a second incoming inspection. Returning and reordering may involve the cost of writing a quality report and a letter to the supplier, a shipping notice, packaging of the material, issuance of a replacement order, and a second incoming inspection.

Service

Service factors might include cooperation and assistance in problem resolution; the promptness with which rejected material, requests for quotations, and acknowledgments are handled; quality of technical and training assistance; responsiveness; and voluntary suggestions for value improvement. Service evaluation is often based on a judgment which the supplier may consider subjective and unfair. Service aspects should be clearly defined in the initial request for quote (RFQ) or request for proposal (RFP) reinforced in the contract terms and conditions, and captured in the most objective way possible in the scorecard.

Supplier Performance Rating Methods

The three principal formal techniques for rating suppliers are the categorical method, the weighted-point method, and the cost-ratio method.

Categorical Method

The categorical method is a qualitative approach to supplier evaluation. The supplier keeps a record of all suppliers and their products and services. The purchaser establishes a list of factors and then grades each supplier, usually on a scale of plus, minus, and neutral. Departments or personnel involved with the supplier also grade the supplier. The evaluators review the ratings in periodic evaluation meetings. Each supplier is then assigned an overall group rating, suppliers are notified of their rating, and improvement plans are developed.

Weighted-Point Method

The weighted-point method is a quantitative approach to supplier evaluation. Each performance factor is assigned a weight that reflects the team's consensus about the relative importance of the specific performance factor. For example, quality might rate 50 percent, delivery 25 percent, price 15 percent, and service 10 percent. Before assessing suppliers, the team must develop a formula or procedure for measuring actual supplier performance. Each overall rating is determined by multiplying each factor weight by the corresponding performance rating, and adding the results. This minimizes subjective evaluation and can include categories to cover qualitative factors.

Cost-Ratio Method

The cost-ratio method relates all identifiable purchasing and handling costs to the value of each shipment received from a supplier. The lower the ratio of costs to shipments, the higher the rating for the supplier; and conversely, the higher the ratio of costs to shipments, the lower the rating.

The steps normally taken in the cost-ratio method are as follows: (1) Determine the costs for quality, delivery, and service for each supplier. (2) Convert these costs to a cost ratio expressing the cost as a percentage of total order cost for each category. (3) Compute each supplier's overall cost ratio. (4) Adjust each supplier's price by the following formula: Adjusted price = Price $\times$ (1 + Overall cost ratio). (5) Use the adjusted price as a basis for evaluating supplier performance.

Applying Metrics to Modify and Shape Performance

It is important to build in a continuous-improvement effort to ensure that the performance metrics and the system itself remains relevant and contributes to capturing the full contribution of the supply base. Supplier performance information can be used more aggressively to increase supply chain efficiency and effectiveness, adjust supplier incentives, and develop more systematic and seamless processes. If performance measurement system data does not drive continuous improvement, then there is little point in investing resources in the process.

The measurement process itself can be improved by integrating scorecard data into the data warehouse for easier and faster accessibility and use in different formats. Metrics and weightings may be adjusted to ensure the scorecard accurately reflects expectations and priorities. For example, if an organization's main focus is on supply assurance, then the most heavily weighted metrics may be on-time delivery and lead time with continuous-improvement efforts focused on lead-time reduction. If, however, business conditions change and the main focus shifts to more competitive pricing, decreased inventory liabilities, and increasing inventory turns, then the most heavily weighted performance metrics might become price competitiveness, cost reductions, better supplier terms and conditions, and replenishment programs. The supplier scorecard system must be flexible and reviewed periodically to adjust the metrics as business conditions change.

MARKET INTELLIGENCE

A strategically oriented supply organization must possess the capability to acquire, verify, analyze, and transform data and information into actionable knowledge. What will the market look like in the next three to five years? Will the organization have the supply base it needs to achieve its longer-term goals and objectives? Which suppliers will grow? Which ones will go out of existence? The purpose of market intelligence is better supply decisions that contribute to competitive advantage through revenue enhancement or cost or asset management.

Sales and marketing professionals forecast demand, and supply professionals forecast supply requirements. A critical piece of market intelligence is the acquisition of knowledge about future prospects for key materials and suppliers. How far into the future the supply organization forecasts depends on the type and nature of the purchase and the market. The team must develop a clear picture of the organization's intelligence requirements and develop strategies to protect and improve the company's position. There are three key intelligence areas: (1) the identification of supply opportunities, (2) the prediction of future trends that affect supply, and (3) the identification of lower total cost alternatives that deliver the functionality required by customers.

Market intelligence is especially important for new product or service development, especially when risk is high. These situations reinforce the need for early supply and supplier involvement in new product and service development processes where risks may be related to uncertainty about quality, lead times, start-up and ramp-up time, cost structure fluctuations, and technology changes. The intelligence team must be capable of recognizing risks, assessing the probability of occurrence, and developing risk-mitigation strategies. For products or services in the maturity phase of their life cycle, there may be less of a need for extensive market analysis.

Unstable markets are typically the focus of market analysis. Instability may be caused by high levels of entries and exits from the marketplace, rapid changes in technology, uncertain supply lines, and civil and political unrest. The changing forces of supply and demand can lead to fluctuations in availability, price, quality, and so on. Analysts gather and interpret supply and demand data, economic forecasts, capacity utilization, cost factors, degree of competition, and the possibility of new sources as inputs into their strategy development.

Industry analysis is another aspect of market intelligence. The team may decide to profile the growth potential of the industry based on technological change, commercial competition, and the ease of entry into domestic and international markets.

The Intelligence-Gathering Process

A sustainable intelligence process is required to successfully and continuously turn information and data into usable and actionable knowledge. Alignment of supply strategy with organizational strategy is the first step in developing a market intelligence capability. While there are multiple purposes for data gathering, first and foremost supply market intelligence must support and contribute to the long-term strategy, goals, and objectives of the organization.

The greatest opportunity to add value is when products or services are designed and developed. Supply organizations that have the capability of actively participating at this stage are most likely to contribute the greatest to the organization's competitive advantage. Knowledge of the existing supply base and potential suppliers that may be attractive supply chain members can speed up the time-to-market by reducing the design and development cycle, can lead to the greatest value to the final customer at the lowest cost structure, and can result in long-term alliances with key suppliers whose management is committed to a long-term relationship.

CONCLUSION

To optimize the contribution of supply and suppliers to the organization, supply professionals must acquire and maintain the knowledge and skills to align supply strategies vertically with organizational strategies and horizontally with strategies of other key business processes and functions. By linking sourcing to final customer satisfaction and working to align suppliers at multiple tiers in the supply network with customers, supply can enhance its role as a strategic player in the organization. Therefore, sourcing, evaluating, and selecting suppliers, and measuring supplier performance are critical components of a successful supply management process.

SUPPLY CHAIN SELF-MEASUREMENT

Jack Barry
Managing Director
Pegasus Global, Inc.

SUPPLY CHAINS: MEASUREMENTS AND EVALUATION

Introduction

Procurement and supply management professionals operate in a highly competitive and visible environment. The past decades have put an increased demand on the contributions from supply management.[1] Many enterprises now see the contribution from supply management as the most critical factor in continued prosperity and growth. While supply management's contribution is best optimized as a trade-off between value and risk, the recent emphasis has been on the value side of the trade-off. This is changing.

For the last 50 years global economies have benefited from the stability afforded by the longest period of uninterrupted economic advance. The compromise of communism, the market-driven economies in China and Russia, the breakup of colonialism in Africa, and the growth of economic communities in Europe, Southeast Asia, Africa, and the Americas have all encouraged an open society. Innovation and technology now flow as freely in Dubai as they do in Detroit.

Globalization has resulted in a lowering of overall costs, but that has occurred in a stable world environment. The world is no longer stable. Because the scope of supply management sources and markets is global, so is the risk. There must be an impact on supplier relationships associated with the higher risk level of a global supply chain.[2] The world is at risk, and supply management is not exempt. Globalization requires supply professionals to manage risk better.

---

1 According to the Institute for Supply Management, supply management is defined to include, at a minimum, the functions of procurement and purchasing, physical distribution, transportation, logistics, materials management, quality, inventory management, production control, packaging, product and service development, receiving, warehousing, and customer service.

2 Supply chains are defined as both internal enterprise-wide supply activities and the external supply activities of suppliers. This definition recognizes that effective supplier measurement and evaluation must include both aspects of internal and external supply activities.

The most critical risk aspect of supply management is avoiding disruptions to the continuity of supply. Supply management starts with the visibility and accuracy of measurement and evaluation, which is a systematic approach to reduce risk by

- Initially qualifying sources of supply
- Establishing both quantitative and qualitative measures and standards to rank and compare against other known or potential sources of supply and existing or future expectations
- Specifying to the criticality and priority of performance criteria and operational requirement
- Identifying and evaluating the value and risk
- Correlating those values and risks to performance expectations, perform-ance improvements, and innovation
- Formalizing expectations as a measurable aspect of key supply manage-ment

Supply professionals no longer have the luxury of not knowing what best practices are and how their operations (and supply chains) compare to those practices. Supply professionals must have a realistic and accurate assessment of how their supply chains' functional, strategic, operational, and financial performance ranks against world-class best standards. The intent is to create a baseline of assessment and evaluation requirements that would allow the supply professional to make realistic selections based on comparisons against world-class best standards. This requires a differentiated approach to supply management.

The differentiated approach distinguishes the firm's goods and services according to the different levels of value and risk they represent.[3] This is depicted graphically in Figure 8–1. Differentiation is a departure from the traditional way of looking only at the highest-cost or highest-volume items and often ignoring the rest.

This approach to supply measurements identifies just how important each product or service is to the firm and points to effective supply measurement management for each. It recognizes that product and service groups often need different strategies, tactics, measurement, and incentives.

Scope of the Measurement and Evaluation Process

Although supply measurement and evaluation is a collaborative process involving many interdisciplinary entities (both internal and external), the supply pro-

---

3 P. Kraljic (1983). "Purchasing Must Become Supply Management," *Harvard Business Review*, September–October. pp. 109–117.

FIGURE 8–1

Degrees of Value and Risk

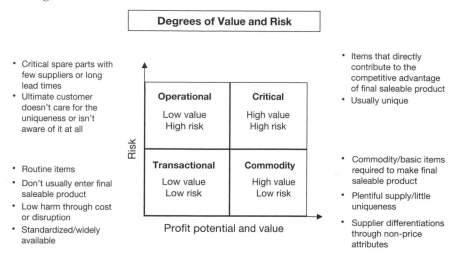

fessional must be the prime creator and owner of this aspect of measurement and evaluation management. This creates unique challenges for the procurement and supply professional. No longer is supply measurement and evaluation management limited to a buyer-and-seller environment—it must involve multilevels and multirequirements from all the stakeholders of supply management—both internal and external to the enterprise. Supply professionals must orchestrate and consolidate these requirements and expectations from a wide range of stakeholders.

As Figure 8–2 indicates, the traditional single point of contact between buyer and sales representative has been replaced by multiple contact points across the enterprises. The buyer's job has been redirected from the gatekeeper controlling supply measurement to the facilitator managing multiple relationships. Additionally, supply chains are often just one level of linkage in a supply chain continuum. Few supply chains are so vertically integrated that they can provide all materials and services without using second-tier supply chains. It is necessary to not only assess the performance of the supplier (and its supply chains) but also to measure how well the supply manages its supply chains—that is, its supply chain supply management performance.

- How effectively are you able to measure how well your supply chain supply management organization sources materials and services needed to fulfill requirements?

- Do you have visibility to your supply chain's supply chains, and can you measure their performance?

FIGURE 8–2

Enterprise Contact Points

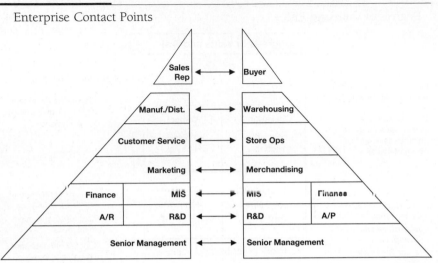

Many supply professionals now answer these key (and many more) questions with a formal self-measurement and evaluation program.

Supply Profiles

Supply measurement should set standards for qualitative and quantitative criteria to evaluate the "form, fit, and functionality" of the materials provided and services performed by the supply chains. The supply professional must understand the following:

- The concept of supply measurement and how measurements are applied in the supply management and procurement processes.
- The key elements and implications of qualitative and quantitative measurements.
- How effective supply measurement will facilitate improved contribution, profits, and innovation.
- When to apply incentive-based performance measurements and the valuation of the contribution and resources.
- The impact of supply measurements to set standards for development and long-term relationships.

The emphasis of supply measurement is the development of a supplier assessment and evaluation profile that quantitatively and qualitatively measures capabilities and performance—both an initial baseline and continuously updated analysis. It recognizes the need to have well-defined and realistic measurement criteria.

The first step is the development of a profile that includes the underlying infrastructure, resources, skill bases, systems, and business processes that identify how business is conducted—both internally and with key supply chains. Key questions to ask when developing a profile are

1. What is the organizational structure and levels of the key divisions, plants, departments, or operating units with whom you will interact, for example, order entry, sales, research and development (R&D), accounts receivable and payable, engineering, and supply management. It is critical to establish where functional activities and processes reside organizationally. Additionally, if the supplier is part of a larger conglomerate or organization, what is the reporting structure and interdependence?

2. What are the informational systems (software and hardware) and operating protocols, and how do they benchmark against other internal infrastructure?

3. Where are the locations (domestic and international) of physical assets, plants, and equipment—which plants or units produce what and where? What are the R&D capabilities?

4. What is the supply chain's relationship with its supply chains? Are there "tier" relationships where one set of supply chains manages a subset of other supply chains; does the supplier outsource functions, and if so, what and to whom? Does the supplier utilize third-party logistics (3PL) providers, and if so, whom and for what?

5. What is the financial health of the supplier? This should far exceed a simple Dun & Bradstreet report. What is the debt structure? What are the major organizational or enterprise owners of the supply chain? What other companies does the supplier own? What are the banking relationships and governances that would impact your relationship? Is the supplier properly insured and protected against risks? What provisions are established to protect any assets, work-in-progress, or intellectual property in the case of failure of the supply?

6. Who is on the management team, including board members? Are there conflicts of interest with your competitors? Are key management executives experienced and stable in their positions?

The profile will show how the supply chain manages the following:

- *Order management.* The ability to accurately accept orders and communicate status.

- *Inventory.* The substitution of information to reduce the buffers of excess inventory.

- *Finances.* The reconciliation process that conserves working capital and reduces excess administrative costs.

- *Social responsibility.* The commitment to operate in an ethical and socially responsible manner.

- *Logistics.* The infrastructure and procedures that optimize the physical supply chains.

- *Quality.* As an integral part of an overall effort to improve quality.

- *Commitment.* As a statement of managerial vision and responsibilities.

- *Supply commitment.* The expectation of future problem solving and improvement cooperation.

- *Customer service.* The formal process to ensure accurate order fulfillment.

- *Cost competitiveness.* The mutual effort to eliminate waste and reinforce cost reductions

- *Cash flow and the financial supply chain.* The direct impact of processing costs and the ability to receive substantial discounts.

- *Engineering, R&D, and technology.* The critical link to make innovation transfer a measure of success.

- *Management and personnel development.* As a framework for continuous improvement by investment in human capital.

- *Compliance.* Particularly with health, safety, and environmental standards, and the assurances that supply chain programs protect against unnecessary risk.

- *Project management.* The quality check that outsourced and contractor-managed projects are effectively controlled and that key interests are protected.

Supplier Visits

A supplier visit, audit, or evaluation is a technique employed by a supply professional to determine if business should be placed with a new or previous supplier. A supplier visit gives the supply professional a first-hand look at the organization's facilities, and should answer the majority of questions about the level of technology at the facility, the education and training of the staff, the employees' attitudes toward their work, and the overall effectiveness of the supplier. If the organization does not make a sincere effort to show its best side during this visit and cooperate fully, it can be assumed that the organization probably will not do so for the supply manager in the future.

Costs versus Benefits of Visits

Although such visits may be costly in terms of time, airfare, food, and lodging, such expenditures are sound investments against future problems. An unaudited supplier with poor facilities, old technology, insufficient capacity, or an under-qualified staff may experience increased downtime and or lost production. Such an organization is also likely to have limited assets for future growth. Such factors will affect the supply continuity to the supply manager's organization.

Site Inspection Team

A carefully selected cross-functional audit team consisting of individuals from supply management, quality assurance, operations, and engineering will provide the expertise necessary to recognize problems at the supplier's plant and make suggestions for corrective actions.

Factors Appraised at Site Visits

Approved suppliers should be visited at intervals commensurate with their performance. A superior supplier will not be visited as often as one that frequently ships late and experiences quality problems. Critical suppliers should be visited at least semiannually.

CREATING THE SUPPLIER DATA BASELINE PROFILE

Creating the initial and expanded supplier data baseline profile is a continuing task. It is not a one-time effort but an active and changing profile that reflects the active and changing status of key suppliers. It is best created in a digital format that would allow you to manage and customize the data baseline. Its utilization has many aspects:

- Self-assessment of internal capabilities and attributes

- Comparative analysis of multiple suppliers to rank and prioritize

- Benchmarking effort to identify world-class programs

- Competitive analysis of the suppliers near and potential competitors

- An identification of potential market opportunities where the supplier's capabilities and attributes fill a gap, provide superior offerings, or provide a competitive advantage

The development of the data baseline is from two primary sources, existing research and original research. Existing research includes published research reports, such as AMR Research, Gardner, and others that track companies; financial and brokerage reports, such as Dun & Bradstreet, Morgan Stanley, Hoover's, and ValueLine, which report on individual companies; Internet search engines, like Google, that provide a wealth of information on specific companies; published reports from the supplier, notably the last three to five years of annual reports and 10-Ks to identify problems and trends; benchmarking studies, such as those generated by CAPS: Center for Strategic Supply Research (sponsored by the Institute for Supply Management and Arizona State University), that give, by industry group, ranges of profile data baselines.

Original research includes supplier visits; extensive preparation and coordination of the supply manager's team and its detailed functional focus; references from at least 10 existing and past suppliers and 10 customers (5 of each chosen by the supply manager) to forecast the future relationship with the supplier; and formal supplier questionnaires or self-assessment profiles. This process provides the basis of both a quantification and qualification of the supplier's capabilities and attributes.

KEY SUPPLIER PERFORMANCE MATRICES

The following supplier performance matrices address the key aspects of a supplier self-measurement and evaluation program. The key aspects are on-time delivery, cost effectiveness, inventory accuracy, supply chain alignment with stakeholders' requirements, and cycle time reductions. This is an enterprise concept; that is, it includes both internal supply activities and external key supplier activities.

Deliver Requested Materials or Services on Time

The primary performance measure is delivery. No other measure has the significance of this basic fulfillment metric: Did the enterprise deliver the required materials or services on time? Subsequent responsibilities such as cost, quality, control, and standards, while valid measurements, are meaningless if delivery is not accomplished. It is the basis of trust and confidence not only between the supplier and supply manager but also critically between the supply manager and the supply manager's internal customers.

One innovative company developed a monthly graphic display of how well the individual supplier's on-time delivery goals were accomplished (see Figure 8–3). Early and late deliveries were considered unacceptable. Poor performance was if the supplier delivered less than 5 percent on time one day early or late. Penalties were imposed if the supplier's delivered between 5 and 10 percent on time two days early or late. Unacceptable performance resulted in part of the enterprise volume being moved to competitive sources, while probation suspended all volume to the enterprise for a specific period. Continued unacceptable performance resulted in termination of the relationship.

Delivery Performance Measurements

Delivery performance includes other measures besides timeliness. A key first step in measuring these other attributes of delivery performance is to identify and prioritize (scale of 1 = low and 10 = high) all the critical measurement criteria that define delivery performance. In a multiorganizational measure, different organizational entities may place a different weighted priority for each measurement

On-Time Delivery Graphic

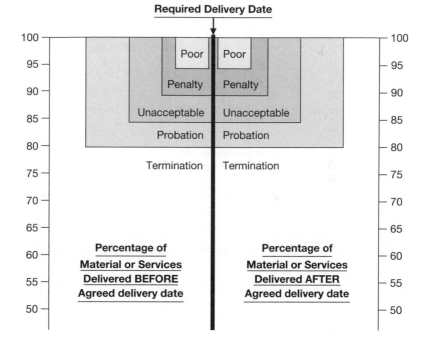

criteria (see Figure 8–4). Again, a segmentation approach to measuring supply chains may also place a different weighted priority for each measurement criteria. This weight-averaging technique is also very useful in initial supply selection and comparisons against other potential supply chains.

The next step is to rank how well the individual supply performs against those delivery performance measurement criteria; first individually and then against competitive and alternative supply chains.

Cost-Effective Materials and Services

The supply organization, including external suppliers, must be an active participant in cost-reduction efforts. There is a danger of losing credibility when savings' reports from supply organization identify high cost savings while the finance department issues negative purchase price variance reports and increasing standard costs-per-material cost accounting statements. Supply chain savings should be measured on a "market basket" approach to identify the total impact of competitive pricing. The basket consists of the top 20 to 25 purchased commodities

FIGURE 8–4

Weighted Averaging Technique

Performance Measure / Supplier	Order Turnaround	Order Fill Rate	Shipping Frequency	Split Ship OK?	Order Status	Delivery Reliability	Ease of Ordering	Invoice Accuracy	Weighted Average
Organization A	6	7	5	9	8	10	8	4	
Organization B	4	6	7	5	9	8	10	8	
Organization C	8	4	6	7	5	9	8	10	
Organization D	0	7	6	9	8	10	8	4	
Organization E	5	9	8	10	8	4	7	6	
Organization F	6	7	5	9	8	10	8	4	
Total Weighted Average									

(materials or services), which collectively account for in excess of 80 to 90 percent of the total annual spend for purchased materials and/or services supply. There are three separate types of materials or services to be tracked individually by supply: A items are the significant total dollar expenditures (unit price times volume); B items are those high single-unit cost items; and C items are neither necessarily high-volume nor high-unit costs but items critical to overall profits and efficiencies. For each commodity and collectively for the entire basket, statistical process control charts are developed and tracked against the targeted range (see Figure 8–5). The targeted range is developed quarterly by the head of supply and approved by the heads of finance and manufacturing. The target range represents historical projections and engineered or benchmarked goals that consider the estimated total usage. Quarterly reported improvements below the target areas are considered hard savings.

This market basket technique is also effective when measuring expected versus actual price adjustments of contracts. The tracking and reporting of this cost savings measurement becomes a credible indicator of overall supplier performance to predict and reduce costs. Contractual penalties and incentives should be based on these performance indexes.

Inventory Accuracy

The challenge with inventory is to measure both the absolute change and the relative improvement against an ever-tightening target. The emphasis is on finding

FIGURE 8–5

The Market Basket Approach

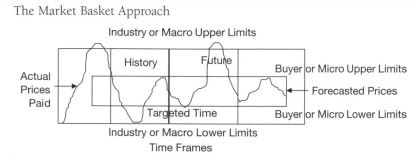

FIGURE 8–6

Measuring Inventory Accuracy

			Absolute		Relative						
Measuring Inventory Accuracy											
Class	**Date Counted**	**Item Counted**	*Items with Errors*		*Percentage Level of Inaccuracy*						
			Number	**Percent**	**0-2%**	**3-5%**	**>5%**	**>10%**	**>20%**	**>30%**	**>50%**
"A"	12/13	30	3	10.0%	-	3	1	-	-	-	-
"B"	12/13	300	25	8.3%	18	3	3	1	1	-	-
"C"	12/13	400	30	7.5%	24	2	2	2	1	1	-
			Drive to zero		*Drive to zero*						

the systemic causes—not just to correct mismatches. Inventory accuracy is the baseline for success in any enterprise resource management (ERP) or materials requirements planning system (MRP) system. Millions are spent for sophisticated software that will not work effectively unless inventory accuracy is over 95 percent. No system—manual or electronic—can operate without inventory accuracy. Beware; if the record indicates 100 items are on hand and there are actually 98 items on hand, inventory accuracy is zero—not 98 percent. Quarterly or yearly wall-to-wall inventory counts only reconcile the financial records. Cycle counting is an effective method of measuring inventory accuracy. The weekly effort should include all A items, 25 percent of all B items, and 5 percent of all C items (note the B and C items change with each count and are randomly selected). Use special teams of supply personnel to conduct a cycle count of selected items. The count should be conducted during a regular working period. On Figure 8–6, the absolute scale measures the 0 or 100 percent values, while the relative scale measures the number of inaccurate cycle count items within predetermined ranges of inaccuracy. Both scales graphically show that the goal of cycle counting is to improve inventory accuracy, absolute and relative, to zero percent inaccurate.

Measure Supply Chain Performance against Changing Stakeholder Requirements

The process of supply measurement and evaluation has two basic tenets. One, it should measure both quantitative and qualitative performance. Two, it should be an ongoing measurement identifying trends and changing requirements—not just a one-time effort. Supply management and the internal users are both customers of the supply chains. It is supply management's responsibility, however, to formalize the measurement process to identify those significant and changing requirements. This is best accomplished with a weekly survey of users conducted by both the supply personnel and the internal user at all levels of the organization. The survey should consist of three parts. Part One should be 10 to 15 standard questions to evaluate how supply is meeting the desired performance based on actual performance (see Figure 8–7). Part Two should be 5 to 10 questions that reflect the unique and current concerns of the specific supply management activity or the internal user. These questions differ weekly and are different for each supply; for example, the supply manager's team interviewer should ask the supplier about any new changes to the order-entry system that may impact confirmation orders and scheduling. Part Three is an open-ended question from supply that allows the supply management and internal users to answer the question, "How is supply doing?"

F I G U R E   8–7

Customer Responsiveness

Satisfiers	Total # Respondents	Current Performance	Average Rating	
			Desired Performance	Performance Gap
Forecasting	21	1.1	3.9	2.8
Timeliness	37	1.1	3.8	2.7
Delivery	62	1.8	3.9	2.1
Service to Clients	76	1.9	3.9	2.0
Processes & Procedures	34	1.5	3.5	2.0
Skill Development/Training	18	1.8	3.8	2.0
ID New Sources/Products	17	1.2	3.2	2.0
Support	39	1.8	3.2	1.9
Supply Continuity	18	2.2	3.9	1.7
Cost Reduction	63	2.1	3.6	1.5
Quality	36	2.6	3.9	1.3

Cycle Time Reductions in Processes and Resources

The basic lessons of just-in-time (JIT) and quality control initiatives are that reductions in process cycle time expose problems, improve resource management, and reduce overall costs. Since over 50 percent of the operational process is performed by supply chains (either as provided materials or services performed), the supplier must be a critical part of the effort to reduce cycle time. In many cases, the longest cycle time is the acquisition administrative process and the lead times for delivery. It is blatantly unfair to burden the supply management organization solely with these responsibilities, since most of the factors are beyond its control. However, few internal management functions have the power to reduce cycle times as does the supply organization.

Supply chains should initiate measurable programs in process time reductions, material delivery times, and acquisition cycle time frames. Reducing process cycle time is the supremely critical success factor. It is the most important task—reduce cycle time, and costs will decrease and productivity and quality will increase (see Figure 8–8). If you can only accomplish one effort, forget technology; just reduce process cycle time. Reduced process cycles and lead times will generate benefits in several areas:

- Lower inventories of work-in-progress and finished goods

- Improved responsiveness to customer needs achieved with production flexibility

FIGURE 8–8

Changing Time Patterns

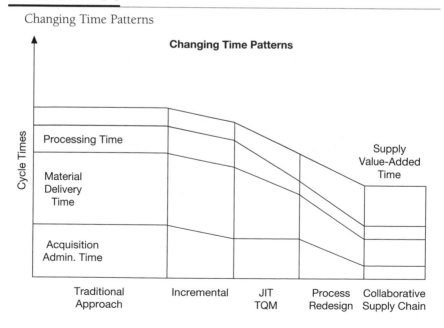

- Improved quality due to a shorter defect pipeline
- Greater operating efficiencies

Innovative techniques for managing time have evolved as a powerful source of competitive advantage. Supply chains focused on reducing time-consuming functions in every aspect of their business often outperform their competitors.

CREATING A BALANCED SCORECARD WITH KEY PERFORMANCE INDICATORS

Supplier performance measures provide supply professionals with important signals about the objectives of the buying organization and are important in driving supply behavior. Inclusion of a specific measure will imply to the supply organization that its performance in this area makes an important contribution to the overall objectives of the relationship, and it will focus on achieving high performance in this area. Conversely, exclusion of a particular measure will lead the supplier to believe that the area is not critical and will lead to a lower degree of focus.

Because of the impact of supplier performance measures on supply chains' actions, measurements should be developed in the context of the broader objectives of the relationship as a whole. When developing the performance measurement scorecard, the relationship holder should review the strategy and objectives of the relationship and understand how the supplier will make a contribution to these objectives. By ensuring that the supply chain performance measures tie directly into the businesses' operating objectives, the relationship holder can ensure that it is motivating the right behavior.

Supplier performance measures are as follows:

- Provide all parties with an indication of contract performance and progress.
- Communicate to supply the aspects of its performance that are important to the buying organization.
- Establish benchmarks for performance that both parties understand and that can be measured.
- Provide early indication of potential contract management issues and root causes.
- Provide a means of comparing supply chains on a factual basis.

It is also important to note that performance reporting does not only include historic performance; it also drives behavior. Establishing the right supplier performance measurement system can be a major contributor to success. If the system measures the wrong aspects of performance, or fails to recognize some important aspects, this will represent a major handicap in successful execution throughout the life of the relationship. An effective performance measurement system must include

- The principles and processes behind establishing a supplier performance measurement system.
- How business performance is reviewed on a periodic basis with supply chains.
- The overall reporting requirements for a supplier during the execution of the contract.
- Review and action planning based on supply reporting.
- Specific aspects of reporting such as valuations and milestone payments, and penalties and incentives.

A widely used mechanism for supplier performance measurement is a balanced scorecard.[4] The scorecard brings together a set of measures identified by the buying organization against which the supplier will be assessed. In a balanced scorecard, groups of measures that contribute to particular objectives are brought together. Typical key performance indicators (KPIs) for measurement would include health, safety, and the environment (HSE), quality, technology, innovation, responsiveness, value improvement, innovation, and cost competitiveness. Often, those KPI elements are graphically depicted as a "spider" diagram (see Figure 8–9). This display allows the evaluator to graphically compare prior and future performance and to evaluate various supply chains against the same measurement criteria.

CONCLUSION

The identification and quantification of supply chains' self-evaluation and measurement programs provides benefits such as

1. Reducing the risks of nonperformance by prescreening and ranking supply chains against a standard set of benchmarks.
2. Promoting new sources of supply, and reducing cost, administration, and cycle time, while increasing competition, diversity, and innovation.
3. Setting comparative standards and minimum-requirement expectations for providers of materials and services.

Additionally, the same data baselines are also applicable as self-assessment tools of internal capabilities and attributes, comparative analyses of multiple supply

---

4 R. S. Kaplan and D. P. Norton (1996). *The Balanced Scorecard: Translating Strategy into Action.* Boston: Harvard Business School Press.

FIGURE 8–9

Sample Spider Diagram

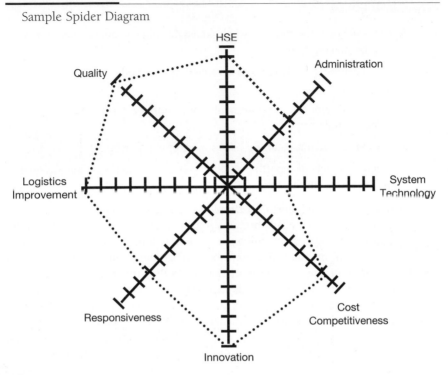

chains, benchmarking tools to identify world-class programs, competitive analyses of related companies and industry segments, and qualification for approved supply chains to use in sourcing programs with other customers.

Enterprises need a supplier measurement program, for example, to depict comparisons of various components of the key performance indicators of measurement between internal supply activities and external supplier activities (see Figure 8–10).

Industry Case Example— Supplier Self-Measurement Programs

Many firms are pursuing new global and domestic sources of supply and reassessing existing supplier relationships, including challenging sole-source providers. Firms are also actively seeking new supply chains to achieve volume advantages

FIGURE 8-10

Internal and External Performance Indicators

Elements of Key Performance Indicators (KPIs) in Ranked Importance as Perceived by the Users	Ranking of Importance	Performance							
		Low ◄——————————► High							
		0	1	2	3	4	5	6	7
Order Accuracy	9.0								
Order Completeness	9.0								
Delivery Reliability	8.0								
	8.0								
	7.5								
	7.5								

FIGURE 8–11

Supply Chain Self-Measurement

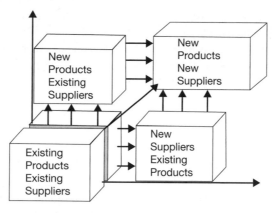

in price reductions and, more importantly, to gain access to new and emerging technological innovations from world-class supply chains. Firms are also seeking an aggressive approach to identify and qualify new sources of supply, including the use of online auctions and e-markets, collaboration with a buying consortium, and the use of third-party outsourcing providers. Many have performed the first step by developing a set of requirements, standards, blueprints, bills of materials, drawings, and specifications that allow new supply chains to effectively understand and quote on requirements.

The challenge is evaluating and measuring new potential sources of supply, especially unknown supply chains and/or global supply chains with whom the firm and its marketplace have no effective experience. How will the credibility, capabilities, and reputation of an unknown supply that responds to specifications via an auction or e-marketplace be validated?

Most firms rely on supply chains to provide the required materials and services. The interrelationship is based on a conviction that supply chains are in full compliance with all applicable regulations that govern the industry. The risk is too high to fully rely on that conviction. Firms must establish an effective compliance monitoring system that initially establishes compliance and then provides for periodic audits, continuous monitoring, reassessments, and reporting mechanisms to ensure that compliance remains valid.

Global firms have unique social and regulatory requirements that underlie the public's trust. Supply chains are held to a higher standard of integrity and compliance with local, state, and federal regulations. It is the stewardship of this responsibility that mandates that supply chains are also held to those higher standards of compliance.

An important aspect of supply management programs is a framework for mutual business process improvement and seamless, accurate, and timely integration of compliance efforts between the internal and external aspects of the enterprise. The task of compliance monitoring can be daunting because most firms have literally thousands of current and future supply chains that may be subject to a wide variety of rules, regulations, and compliance requirements. The criticality of the market demands that any changes to supply chain compliance be immediately known and the risk analyzed.

Firms require real-time access to individual and collective supply chain compliance status plus the ability to monitor and rank supply chains based on their performance levels. The examples in Appendix A identify the key areas that many firms have outlined to ensure supply chain compliance. These areas are part of a supplier self-evaluation program and are managed electronically.

Supply Chain Order Management

The primary point of contact between the supply organization and the supplier's supply chain's fulfillment is the supply chain order management activity. It establishes priorities and lead times and confirms or modifies requirements. It is the entry point for all downstream supply activities and the point where most errors occur. Poor order management processes and resources can effectively dilute the supply chain measurements. It is critical that an assessment of supply chain order management capabilities be a prime element in any supply measurement program. Key questions are

- Is the supply chain order management system part of a large enterprisewide system?
- Does the supply relationship allow your organization to make payment using a procurement card?
- Does the supply relationship have the capability to allow your organization to order electronically?
- Does the supply relationship have the ability to
  - Immediately link its order management process to other internal financial and operational processes?

- Link its internal ordering, delivery, and payment processes to your organization's customers and/or the complete supply chains?
- Gain increased inventory visibility internally and the ability to link that visibility to your organization while gaining access to the supplier's levels of inventory or ordering status?
- Receive any medium of order and translate it into a standard digital format?
- Eliminate a three-way match by providing electronic versions of the documents indemnified by a financial third party (e.g., bank)?
- Provide a propriety ordering process including customized catalogs, pricing, product availability, approvals, and performance data?
- Provide electronic shipping status including the actual and detailed in-box contents of the shipment?
- View inventory levels in all areas including the supplier's supply chains and your customers?
- Track shipments through the delivery process, and settle claims and returns online?

- Does the supply relationship allow all payment options, including electronic funds transfer (EFT), automated clearinghouse (ACH) services, and purchase cards?

- How does the supply relationship communicate buyer order fulfillment cycle times and changes?

- How does the process differ for routine off-the-shelf items versus made-to-order noninventoried items?

- What percentage of the payments made for materials bought and payments received are paid electronically?

- How does the supply chain report problems to your organization?

- How does the supply relationship track and measure product availability, order-entry errors, invoicing errors, pricing errors, warehouse (packing errors), shipping damage, incomplete paperwork, and product returns on a regular, ongoing basis?

- Does the supplier provide customer-service call center operations, customer needs forecasting, and customer database management?

APPENDIX B

Industry Case Example— Self-Measurement and Evaluation Program

Many firms are aggressively pursuing quality initiatives to provide increased value of products and services to their customers. The business strategy is to develop a strong partnership relationship with key supply chains. Most of these supply chains have been active for many years. In many cases, the relationship is personal and informal—without structured measurements, rankings, or profiles.

Firms are attempting to provide increased value and reduced risk of their high-scale materials and services at lower cost. It is hoped that many of the original supply chains will be able to participate with the firms in this expansion. It is also accepted that many new and unknown supply chains, worldwide, must be included in the firms' supply relationships.

Many firms have decided to implement a supplier self-evaluation program. Some firms have developed over 1,000 performance attributes (questions) that allow a supplier to self-evaluate its performance in both strategic directions and functional operations. These performance attributes are segmented in the categories in Figure 8–12.

FIGURE 8–12

Performance Attributes

Strategic Objectives Self-Assessment	Business Process Self-Assessment
Risk Strategies	Quality Management
Relational Strategies	Financial Management
Informational Strategies	Social Responsibility Management
Operational Strategies	Application and Enterprise Systems Management
Financial Strategies	Measurement Management
Enterprise Strategies	Training Management
Alliance and Partnership Strategies	Organizational Management
Competencies Strategies	Compliance: Health Safety and Environment
Leadership Strategies	
Enterprise Supplier Self-Assessment	**Logistics Operation Self-Assessment**
Procurement Management	Inventory Management
Sourcing Management	Asset Management
Cost Management	Distribution Management
Enterprise Supply Management	Transportation Management
Service Procurement Management	Warehouse Management
Contract Administration	Transportation Management
Contractor, Outsourcer, Third Party Management	Warehouse Management
Order Management	

The self-assessment and measurement quantitatively and qualitatively measures capabilities and performance as an initial baseline and as a continuously updated analysis. Each performance attribute is a detailed description of a process or activity that allows the buyer to measure how effectively the supply chain program or effort contributes to the improvement of each of the major categories of self-evaluation.

Each functional grouping of activities, processes, and initiatives consists of a series of evaluative questions or attributes. To assist the supplier in selecting the most appropriate rating reflecting the supply chain level of capabilities or performance for each attribute, each attribute has eight situational qualitative statements (similar in concept to the Malcolm Baldrige National Quality Award's self-evaluative conditional statements) that describe the conditions that are representative of each rating. Using these conditional statements as a guide, the supplier is asked to select the descriptive situational qualitative statement that best matches the supply chain capabilities or performance.

Many firms have developed a Web-based version for the supplier to submit responses electronically. This Web-based format allows those firms to easily compare, benchmark, and profile multiple supply chains. It offers to each supply the opportunity to benchmark its responses against those submitted by other supply chains.

Many firms have also gained considerable value from a supplier measurement program as a guideline to internal improvements within those firms from

- Benchmarking the supply performance against measures of internal performance.
- Recognizing competitive advantages and disadvantages from the supply chains' operational performance.

Firms that use the profiles and measurements of key supply alliances internally are able to develop specific operational toolkits for improved management and administration. Examples of these profiles and measurements are

RFx prequalification and evaluations standards. (RFx includes all the applicable responses from bidders or suppliers to RFP, RFI, RFQ, and other requests for information in a bidding or contractual process.) These subsets of the supplier self-evaluation documentation can be used to provide standard supplier prequalification criteria. Use of an electronic format for responses allows easy comparisons and evaluations of the functionality and qualifications of prospective bidders (supply chains) with particular emphasis on the functional and operational requirements that are specific to the RFx. Use of a standardized set of performance attributes (self-evaluative questions) eases the administrative burden of RFx and contract management and creates an historical baseline for use in future RFx events.

Ad hoc criteria. These subsets can be used as specific ad hoc toolkits for benchmarking efforts to address particular issues or requirements, for

F I G U R E   8–13

Sample Self-Evaluation Item

No.	Does your Enterprise Supplier maintain and provide	
13.58[1]	up-to-date and accurate information on expected	Weight
	shipments and delivery dates for outstanding orders?	Level $= 6^2$

Don't Know	1	2	3	4	5	6	7
☐	☐	☐	☐	☐	☐	☐	☐

Percentage of responses from supply enterprises that fall in this level	Select	Conditional Statement that most accurately describes the Enterprise Supply Chains situations—performance, capabilities, or processes.
Btwn 0% and 5%	○	Do not know or do not use.
Btwn 6% and 15%	○	Management sees little value, thus little or no program or initiative is present. There are no effort or poor results in the area. Trend data are either not reported. Little or no deployment of an approach is evident. No evidence of an improvement orientation; improvements is achieved through reaction to problems. No organizational alignment is evident; individual areas or work units operate independently.

---

[1] The number is a reference to the placement of the questions within the larger base of over 600 questions.

[2] The "Weight Level" code refers to the weighting of each attribute within an over-all priority sequence for each functional grouping of activities, processes, and initiatives. Thus a "weight level of 10" is weighted at 1.0; while a weight level of 8 is weighted at .80 scale. The intent is to give greater value to those attributes that are considered more important.

F I G U R E   8–13

(Continued)

Btwn 16% and 25%	O	Some activity, initiative, or compliance exists but decisions and efforts are ad hoc and based on individual manager's commitment. There are no standards or measures of performance nor is there a consistency of applications. No reporting is present.
Btwn 26% and 35	O	There is general acceptance of the value and contribution by effective performance in this area. There is progress in establishing a consistent definition of superior performance. There are no standards for compliance or reporting.
Btwn 36% and 55%	O	Most areas of the enterprise have established a consistent approach to performance and measurements in this area. There is, however, no requirement for compliance nor any over-all measurement and reporting.
Btwn 56% and 75%	O	Consistent policies and procedures exist and are applied. Non-compliance is infrequent and a subject of managerial concern. Performance standards are clearly defined and well supported. While no over-all measurement and reporting definitions exist, local managers have established independent compliance and reporting.
Btwn 76% and 85%	O	Managers have instituted effective problem solving processes to achieve higher performance in this area. All activities, initiatives, measurements, and compliance are consistent and standardized. Both local and consolidated levels of responsible groups and/or individuals have been established and tasked to monitor and achieve improvements in this area.
Btwn 86% and 100%	O	There is a strong executive commitment to success in this area. Measurements, reporting, performance criteria are all linked to effectiveness in this area. It is one of the highest managerial priorities and is effectively supported with visibility, assets, and key personnel.

> example, digital enablement, quality commitment, cost reduction efforts, information technology assessment, or regulatory compliance.
>
> *Supply management functional self-assessments.* These subsets can be used to self-evaluate and rank the performance of the buyer's supply management organization.
>
> *Functional profile analyses.* These subsets can be used to profile functional responsibilities and capabilities, for example, logistics, financial, and order management.

Figure 8–13 shows one example of the format of the 1,000 questions that have been used by leading firms to self-evaluate supply chains. One example of the procurement module of the supplier self-evaluation is in Appendix A, and additional examples of other functional modules may be viewed as a PDF or electronic file by visiting the Pegasus Global Web site for at www.pegasusglobal.com.

GLOBAL SUPPLY CHAIN NETWORKS

RICHARD R. YOUNG, PH.D., C.P.M.
Associate Professor of Supply Chain Management
The Pennsylvania State University
Capital College

INTRODUCTION

Earlier U.S. economic history saw manufacturers develop an increasing dependency on certain foreign basic raw materials because they were not being found at home. Some examples include cocoa, coffee beans, bauxite for manufacturing aluminum, platinum, palladium, chromium, titanium, nitrates, and natural latex. As technology found replacements for some materials, new demands for even more exotic materials emerged. Political and economic factors added complexity to supply lines that were already fragile due to the vagaries of transit time as well as shear volume.

With the industrial rebuilding of Europe and much of Asia during the second half of the last century and continuing to the present day, other nations began producing higher value-added materials as well as consumer products. The nature of U.S. imports underwent a major shift as these goods began to take a dominant share of the overall value imported. At the same time improved transportation provided the necessary capacity and speed with the advent of ever larger containerships and jumbo jet aircraft. The nature of a firm's supply chains has become significantly more complex as the potential number of suppliers has skyrocketed along with the number of items.

For the United States, international trade has risen dramatically, and since the 1960s has averaged nearly 8 percent or double the growth in gross domestic product (GDP) for the same period.[1] Part of this phenomenon could be explained as the labor cost chase as buyers went from nation to nation in pursuit of low hourly wages for high-labor-content items. In Asia, the United States initially looked to Japan, but the emphasis eventually shifted to South Korea, Taiwan, and

---

1 The Economist (1994). *Guide to Global Economic Indicators*, London, England: The Economist
    Books, pp. 125–128.

Singapore. Later it became Thailand, Malaysia, and Indonesia, but also Eastern Europe in the early 1990s as well as Brazil.

However, there have also been three additional variables in the equation: the technology chases, a customer service element, and access to the huge potential markets of India and especially China. These needs, when coupled with several key enablers, suggest that the trend toward even more global sourcing will not ebb anytime soon. These enablers include a steady downward trend in import tariffs including a continuing agglomeration of nations into trading blocs, rapidly advancing information technology, and improved communications, as well as further expanded sealift and airlift capacities.

For firms of all types, these economic developments raise three key issues:

1. The need for global sourcing and supply

2. How to go about sourcing and building global linkages

3. How to assert continuous leadership and management of extended global supply networks

THE NEED FOR GLOBAL SOURCING AND SUPPLY

Global sourcing places great demands on supply managers from within the organization because there is the expectation that they will have an understanding of the marketplace: which suppliers possess what technologies, capabilities, and capacities no matter where they may be located. But on a strategic level the firm may elect to source globally because it wants access to sell into particular markets. Blending such strategic decisions into supply management can present a conundrum that needs to place short-term cost interests into a secondary role.

Technologies

All nations possess certain factor endowments. Some are due to geography such as deposits of raw materials or other forms of natural resources that could include growing seasons, rainfall and soil fertility for agriculture, or access to key infrastructure such as seaports. Other factor endowments can be acquired, including an educated workforce. While some technologies may represent advantageous positions in natural resources, most are now based on intellectual capital that results in a geographic clustering of technologies. Witness Silicon Valley as a center for microelectronics or north central Pennsylvania for powdered metallurgy. Internationally, Scandinavia has become a technology cluster for cellular telephony, not only due to the presence of Ericsson and Nokia, but smaller firms that may be included among their first- and second-tier suppliers. Such advantage is highly transitory as witnessed by the former pole position held by the German firms BASF, Bayer, and Hoechst in dyes and pigments; and the Swiss firms Ciba, Roche, and Sandoz in pharmaceuticals. In one form or another they're all still important, but each firm's franchise has been diluted as the industries have become more dispersed.[2,3]

Therefore, assessing technology becomes a problem of strategic positioning and cannot be measured by such traditional means as discounted cash flow analysis or simple payback calculations let alone the favored longstanding purchasing measure, purchase price variance (PPV), or even total cost. Instead, supply managers must consider sourcing decisions for technology based on where it may potentially position the firm 5 and 10 years hence rather than today.[4]

Assessing the technology, capabilities, and capacities of potential suppliers is a complex undertaking that requires a sophisticated understanding of what is needed today plus good insights for what will be required tomorrow. Global sourcing plays a role in providing a significantly wider array of opportunities from which the supply manager may draw; however, those opportunities must be weighed by using factors drawn from myriad sources.[5]

Market Access
Global sourcing may be a prerequisite for being given access to sell in a particular market. The major aircraft makers have done this for some time by sourcing certain components with the objective of increasing a specific nation's local content in order that aircraft will become more attractive to a particular national airline. A twist to this strategy has been the construction of polymer plants in China where initial product is supplied to the U.S. market; however, the long-term strategy is to serve the now rapidly growing Chinese demand for molding resins.

These decisions are not just complex; they also require a divergence from prevailing supply management thinking, not only because it is about the future rather than the present, but because it also cuts across contemporary supply management measurement criteria. To succeed in global markets, firms will need to be able to successfully access global suppliers and to assure that such selected suppliers will serve both the present and future needs of the firm.

ESTABLISHING GLOBAL SOURCES AND SUPPLY CHAIN LINKAGES

The identification and qualification of potential suppliers in a global context represents a key part of the sourcing process. Closely related is the forging of physical

2 Ernst Bäumler (1968). *A Century of Chemistry*, Düsseldorf: Econ Verlag, pp. 209–246.

3 Kurt Lanz (1980). *Around the World with Chemistry*, New York: McGraw-Hill, pp. 37–50.

4 Kant Rao, Alan J. Stenger, and Richard R. Young (1988). "Corporate Framework for Developing and Analyzing Logistics Strategies," *Proceedings of the Annual Meeting of the Council of Logistics Management*, Council of Logistics Management, Oak Brook, IL, pp. 243–262.

5 Richard R. Young (2000). "Knowledge of Supply Markets." In Joseph L. Cavinato and Ralph G. Kauffman, *The Purchasing Handbook*, 6th ed., New York: McGraw-Hill, pp. 99–126.

and information linkages that provide continuity through efficient and effective access to materials and products. Without carefully constructing this network, nothing that subsequently occurs can compensate for poor decision making at this stage. It is this part of the process that requires a close working relationship between supply managers and their logistics counterparts. Both need to view the process holistically with an appreciation for present requirements as well as an understanding of the future needs of their firms. The amount of complexity is severalfold that of domestic sourcing situations as suggested in Table 9–1.

Sourcing

All the information that a supply manager must know about potential domestic suppliers is also true of global ones, but this becomes only the baseline. All elements include macroeconomic, industry-specific, and supplier-specific information, plus from the logistics side, network-specific information. While relatively simple to obtain for domestic suppliers, this information is far more difficult with respect to those lying offshore. While the information provided here applies specifically to foreign sources, the reader is also referred to the "Knowledge of Supply Markets" section appearing in *The Purchasing Handbook,* 6th ed., to use as a baseline.[6]

Supply managers are again referred to Table 9–1 and cautioned that the level of complexity that they may design into their global supplier network will add both variation and added cost for which they will need to account. As a template, Figure 9–1 provides a catalog of factors that is useful in identifying those areas where supply managers may not have control. This part of the discussion, however, focuses on the prerequisites for establishing sources, or what Figure 9–1 attributes to *source complexity.*

Macroeconomic

The economic, social, and legal environments of other nations generally do not mirror those of the United States. While there is a great temptation to want to pursue low prices quoted by a foreign supplier whose product has already passed quality trials, there remains a lengthy list of matters that need to be assessed. Note that these are only the basic or key criteria. Others may also play a role, but they may likely be either industry- or supplier-specific:

1. Economic stability

2. Political stability

3. Legal and fiscal structures

4. Technology and infrastructure

5. Cultural implications

---

6 Ibid.

TABLE 9–1

Comparison of Parties to Supply Transactions

Domestic	Variables	Key Flow
Supplier	Price Avg. lead time Lead time variance	Physical
Inbound carrier	Transport cost Avg.transit time Transit time variance	Physical

Global	Variables	Key Flow
Supplier	Price Avg. lead time Lead time variance	Physical
Freight forwarder	Transaction price Avg. processing time Processing time variance	Information
Foreign access carrier	Transport cost Avg. transit time Transit time variance	Financial
Government export agency	Processing fee Avg. processing time Processing time variance	Information
Port of loading	Port processing fee Loading or stevedoring fee	Physical
Line haul carriers	Transport cost Avg. transit time Transit time variance	Physical
Port of arrival	Port processing fee Unloading or stevedoring fee	Physical
Customs agencies	Import duty Merchandise processing fee Harbor maintenance tax	Financial
Customs house broker	Processing fee Avg. processing time Processing time variance	Information
Inland carrier	Transport cost Avg. transit time Transit time variance	Physical
Cooper (restow container after Customs inspection)	Operations charge Avg. operations time Operations time variance	Physical
Insurance carrier	Premium costs	Financial

FIGURE 9–1

Principal Components of Supply Chain Complexity

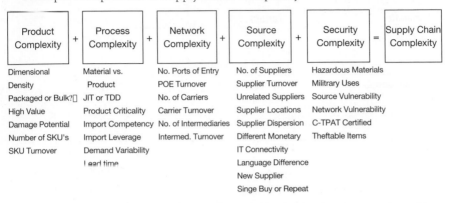

Product Complexity	+	Process Complexity	+	Network Complexity	+	Source Complexity	+	Security Complexity	=	Supply Chain Complexity

Product Complexity	Process Complexity	Network Complexity	Source Complexity	Security Complexity
Dimensional	Material vs.	No. Ports of Entry	No. of Suppliers	Hazardous Materials
Density	Product	POE Turnover	Supplier Turnover	Military Uses
Packaged or Bulk?	JIT or TDD	No. of Carriers	Unrelated Suppliers	Source Vulnerability
High Value	Product Criticality	Carrier Turnover	Supplier Locations	Network Vulnerability
Damage Potential	Import Competency	No. of Intermediaries	Supplier Dispersion	C-TPAT Certified
Number of SKU's	Import Leverage	Intermed. Turnover	Different Monetary	Theftable Items
SKU Turnover	Demand Variability		IT Connectivity	
	Lead time		Language Difference	
			New Supplier	
			Singe Buy or Repeat	

SOURCE: Richard R. Young, "Managing International Supply Chain Complexity," Proceedings of the 15th Annual North American Research and Teaching Symposium, Tempe, AZ, 2004, pp. 633–650.

The following add some level of specific detail to understanding each of these key criteria:

1. Economic stability is usually thought of as the inflation rate. Other nations may have differing levels of inflation due to individual decisions that their governments have made for fiscal and monetary policies. High inflation may make foreign suppliers vulnerable because their suppliers need to be paid in ever-cheapening currency units. A profitability squeeze is created when suppliers provide fixed selling prices and buy materials at essentially floating prices.

2. A somewhat related matter is the currency exchange rate. If the currency is one that is officially pegged to the U.S. dollar, exposure is substantially minimized. Similarly, nations using established trading currencies (e.g., pound sterling, euro, or Japanese yen) will typically pose minimal problems as well. Global supply markets; however, have opened up.

3. Supply continuity can be adversely affected by current events. Some nations as well as regions tend to be less stable than others. While the loss of a supplier can be a single catastrophic event, a series of less serious events disturbs many parts of fragile global supply chains. The requirements that U.S. Customs has now placed on global purchasers to have full knowledge of their suppliers raises new questions about supplier due diligence, especially when they may be located in unstable areas or of equal concern when purchased materials or products must traverse such areas en route. Supply managers considering engaging in a regular flow of imports no matter what the source should investigate the practicality of complying with and seeking certification under the

Customs-Trade Partnership Against Terrorism (C-TPAT) in order to reduce the adverse time impact and administrative burdens of cargo inspections on these supply chains.[7]

4. A positive development for supply managers engaging in global sourcing is the emergence and continuing development of trading blocs. NAFTA is perhaps the best known to those in the United States, but the European Union (EU) is a significant force in reducing the complexities of trading between member states. Others showing much promise are the Association of Southeast Asian countries (ASEA) and MERCOSUR in South America. Added to this is the number of bilateral trade agreements between the United States and a growing list of nations including Israel, Jordan, Singapore, and Chile. Where the United States does not have trade agreements, potential global purchasers should investigate whether specific countries and intended commodities are listed on the General System of Preferences for either duty reduction or elimination.[8] Conversely, the United States periodically updates the list of those nations with whom trade is prohibited.

5. Legal and fiscal issues address the problem of compliance and the payment of taxes and fees related to suppliers' exports. Exports are not dutiable per international agreement, specifically the General Agreement on Tariffs and Trade; however, many nations may require export licenses before goods can move. Efficiency may not be a high priority in many nations where government employment is often a key social program. Many nations may not yet have the information technology solutions necessary for the efficient movement of goods. Moreover, the assortment of fees may be onerous making compliance difficult, expensive, and a significant source of cycle time variance.

6. In the United States, technology and infrastructure work because a level of competition exists. Where competition is suppressed or where governments may be the sources of communication and transport infrastructure, this is not the case. For example, although rapidly improving in many parts of the world, many phone systems will not support high-speed computer modems. Some may yet have only analog service.

7. Transportation infrastructures differ widely even among developed nations. Highways, railways, airports, and harbors may be modern, but subtle differences become important factors. One example is the limitation on shipping high-cube ocean containers on many European railways. A combination of overhead electrification and low clearance in tunnels dimensionally precludes these transport options.

---

7 http://cbp.gov/xp/cgov/import/commercial_enforcement/ctpat/importers/.

8 http://www.ustr.gov/Trade_Development/Preference_Programs/GSP/Section_Index.html.

8. Cultural differences permeate everything and are often manifested by religion, language, and local customs. Regulations, hours of operation, holidays, and the value placed on time are but a few examples. Response times for answering inquiries as well as differences in time zones add complexity. So does language, and even though many nations have adopted English as their lingua franca, such should not be a universal assumption.

Industry-Specific. The principal concerns at the industry level are limited to ownership, financing, and size or capacity. All these can also be viewed as inter-related because the ownership issue impacts access to funds and whether there may be a policy of supporting export business.

1. Fundamental to the ownership issue is whether governments or other corporations own a significant share of the industry. When government is an owner, the question becomes one of long-term intent and potential changes as public policy may shift after a change in regime potentially disenfranchising the state-owned company. Changes from private to state ownership or control, or vice versa, have often proved to be traumatic events leaving such firms incapable of supplying basic goods or services. Investigating the ownership question need not be a daunting task. Among publicly traded companies with some state ownership this is disclosed in their annual reports or other publicly available records (e.g., French government equity stakes in Aventis, the major pharmaceutical company). When considering major supply arrangements in less democratic settings, the U.S. Central Intelligence Agency collects and readily makes economic intelligence available for commercial purposes.

2. Size and capacity issues are considerations relative to the business cycle. Whether state-owned or publicly traded, suppliers look to establish export business because recessionary times in the home market may force them to seek other outlets in order to keep capacity filled. The question then becomes what happens when the domestic market recovers? Some industries, such as chemicals and other process types, do not have processes that lend themselves to significantly lower levels of throughput and are fundamentally in a state of either operating or being shut down. If the decision is made to continue operations, output will need to be inventoried or exported, or perhaps some combination of the two. The ownership issue may also affect how capital investments will be made. No matter how successful the state-controlled firm, public money competes for other types of public needs thereby relegating capital expansion plans to a secondary role.

Supplier-Specific. Although all the questions that comprise due diligence actions for domestic suppliers apply to offshore firms, there is also a list of concerns that needs to be expanded upon if the addition of a particular firm is to be a successful and appropriate addition to the global supplier network. Most of these concerns could be categorized as communications-related and include lingua franca, IT sophistication, and security interests. These are over and above the issues of capacity, product range, pricing and profit, capital sources, benchmarking partners, technologies, processes employed, and management.[9]

1. The language of business or *lingua franca* is the basic facilitator of communications. It is paramount for establishing and maintaining relationships. When one trading partner does not have the equivalent language, the provision must be made for translations. Even with translation capabilities, the resolution of misunderstandings rapidly becomes an expensive undertaking as poor product quality or unsatisfactory delivery performance problems persist. Global purchasers may frequently overlook the costs incurred due to longer learning curves.

2. The ability to expeditiously exchange information on a computer-to-computer basis is now relatively inexpensive. Globally, even electronic data interchange (EDI) applications have been replaced by Web-based applications. Many firms have bypassed the EDI stage altogether and gone directly to the Internet.

3. Security issues are the latest, and in many instances the greatest, concerns now facing global purchasers. The extent to which purchasers must know their suppliers has changed from just knowing their manufacturing processes and the name of their respective freight forwarders. When a supplier's manufactured products are attractive to tampering because they will become part of the food chain or because the containers will not be secure en route, the extent to which a purchaser knows about its suppliers, the arrangements that those suppliers have with their suppliers, and their physical facilities becomes a new informational hurdle.

Constructing the Network

Global supply chain networks are fragile because there are a great many active variables. Many of these may be controllable to some extent; however, supply management and logistics functions may elect to make periodic changes that potentially prove disruptive. Table 9–2 provides some insight into the number of parties that a purchaser firm may need to employ when sourcing globally, although even it may substantially understate the problem. A single domestic source typically represents two relationships: the supplier and the transportation firm. A single global supplier could have 12 relationships. Increase this from one to five suppliers, and the domestic model ranges from 6 to 10 relationships, while the global scenario may range from 20 to nearly 50 depending on the freight terms stipulated.

---

9 Young, "Knowledge of Supply Markets."

TABLE 9-2
Network Complexity

Parties	Number of parties count within the network					
	Scenario 1	Scenario 2	Scenario 3	Scenario 4	Scenario 5	Scenario 6
Suppliers	1	1	5	5	5	100
Freight forwarders	0	1	1	5	5	20
Foreign inland carriers	0	1	5	5	5	20
Government export agencies	0	1	1	5	5	20
Ports of loading	0	1	1	5	5	20
Line haul carriers	0	1	1	5	5	5
Ports of arrival	0	1	1	1	5	5
Customs agencies	0	1	1	1	1	1
Customs house brokers	0	1	1	1	1	1
Inland or inbound carriers	1	1	1	1	5	5
Cooper	0	1	1	1	5	5
Insurance carriers	0	1	1	1	1	1
Total Parties to Transactions	2	12	20	36	48	203

Network Summary						
Importer's inland destinations	1	1	1	1	5	5
Active Unique Supply Chains	1	1	5	5	25	500

Scenario 1   Domestic only. Single supplier and a single inbound carrier selected.

Scenario 2   Single foreign supplier only. Importer controls logistics on an ex works basis.

Scenario 3   Five foreign suppliers all located in the same country with the importer responsible for all. logistics on an ex works basis.

Scenario 4   Five foreign suppliers, but each located in a different country. Importer controls logistics on an ex works basis.

Scenario 5   Same as Scenario 4, except importer is a geographically dispersed and a multi-plant operation. Assume that logistics has selected a single nationwide customshouse broker.

Scenario 6   Same conditions as Scenario 5 except with 100 suppliers dispersed across 20 countries. All suppliers ship to all of the importer's plant locations.

An even more compelling argument for giving the *fragile* label to global supply chains is the manner in which permutations can grow. In Table 9–2, Scenario 6 suggests that a firm with five operations has 100 foreign suppliers distributed across 20 countries and serving only five U.S. locations. Assuming that the logistics activities of the firm have rationalized the number of transportation providers, the customhouse broker, and the ports of entry, the result is only 500 supply chain permutations. It is not uncommon for U.S.-based multinational firms to have 1,000 suppliers distributed across 50 nations serving 20 domestic locations.

Managing such a level of complexity becomes a daunting task. However, at this point some further explanation of each of the parties to a global supply chain is required. For simplicity, the applicable Incoterms will be ex works meaning that the customer has full responsibility for all elements of the supply chain.[10] Figure 9–1 (shown earlier) highlights the participants by name, their respective impacts, and the type of principal flow that they control.

Supply chain management has evolved on the basis that there are three flows—physical, informational, and financial—which while distinct still must function with a high level of interdependence as shown in Figure 9–2. Clearly, physical flows require well-functioning information flows that contain forecasts, purchase order information, order acknowledgments, advance shipping notices, invoices, bills of lading, plus various documents required by government agencies. Any delays or failure to the information flow has an adverse impact on the physical flow including delays, wrong product, or other assets of the supply chain not being deployed when needed. Similarly, financial flows may be adversely affected by malfunctioning information flows or physical flows.

F I G U R E   9–2

Categories of Flows within Supply Chains

Physical Flow

Information Flow

Financial Flow

Relationships   • The objective is to have a physical flow with the least amount of variation in that its flow is unimpeded and goods arrive in the right quantity at the right time and place.

• Physical flows are enabled by the appropriate flows of information, but both flows are enabled by the appropriate flow of funds from buyer to supplier, whether in payment for goods or services.

10 International Chamber of Commerce (1990). *Incoterms*, Paris: ICC Publishing, pp. 16–23.

Participants

Each of the participants has a specific role, some legally defined, but in most cases the roles also represent competencies that global purchasers elect to not establish internally. The following discussion addresses those roles and the amount of cost and variation that each represents to the supply chain.

1. *Foreign freight forwarders.* For matters and filers of information, selection of this intermediary should be done based on access to information, ability to prepare documentation accurately, and in a timely fashion and for the connections that they have in their particular locale. Globally, this industry continues to consolidate as smaller firms frequently lack the financial ability to invest in information technology or because of the leverage that larger firms represent in the marketplace. The out-of-pocket costs are on a transaction-by-transaction basis; however, the true costs of using these firms need to include the customer service and potential inventory requirements necessary to cover instances when the performance falters. Ancillary services include selection and/or coordination of the local access carriers, booking line haul transportation, translation services, coordinating banking, and obtaining special permits and licenses.

2. *Foreign inland carrier.* Whether the predominant mode of international transport is air or ocean, access to that mode will ultimately be by road. One of the simplest transportation services, its failure often comes from its inability to obtain empty containers in a timely fashion or to similarly gain port access with cargo. Engaged on a transaction-by-transaction basis, like the forwarder a service failure can result in substantial costs frequently not foreseen at the outset of the business relationship.

3. *Government export agencies.* While not normally considered a discretionary cost, individual offices or units may be more user-friendly than others. Consequently, ports may be selected on the basis of government agency efficiency. Overall, these agencies represent administrative fees that are direct costs. Potential shipment delays due to variations in administrative processes may ultimately result in poor customer service and the need to carry larger inventories.

4. *Ports of loading.* Conventional wisdom has been to select that port closest to the exporter; however, other considerations include which shipping lines make port calls and at what frequency, connections to other modes of transportation, which forwarders are located there, and the efficiency of the government agencies for clearing cargo. Additionally, there are the issues of storage facilities, if required; throughput efficiency; and effectiveness in tracking cargoes. Although port charges are direct costs such as "terminal loading charges," the efficiency issue means customer service and inventory issues for the global purchaser.

5. *Line-haul carriers.* As either international airlines or ocean carriers, line-haul has substantial cost implications of both temporal and spatial dimensions. Aside from the obvious question of whether a carrier serves the origin and destination ports selected, there are also the issues of consistently available capacity, appropriate capability for the materials or products being transported (e.g., refrigerated service, heavy lift, or roll-on/roll-off services), and equipment reliability. Many importers by ocean may overlook the problem of vessel rotation—the route that is followed from port to port on its sailing schedule—and how it will add to average transit times with implications for inventory levels. Carriers charge by weight and cube, but their ability to impact total cost is substantially more far-reaching.

6. *Ports of arrival.* Although much of the same criteria that were discussed previously for ports of loading apply to ports of arrival, the geographic size of the United States offers more options. Efficiency and the ability to move goods from ports to final destinations is one of these. As an example, a global purchaser in northern New Jersey would regularly opt to use the Port of Philadelphia instead of the Port of New York–New Jersey because the latter was congested at the time and despite the longer and more expensive inland transportation, possession of imports could be had days sooner. In a similar example, the last U.S. port of call for many vessels coming from Europe has historically been Wilmington, North Carolina, meaning that some global purchasers in Charlotte would opt to unload freight at Savannah or Charleston to save time.

7. *Customs agencies.* Selecting a port where Customs provides a more efficient service is an important consideration. Larger importers with consistent levels of import activity have greater leverage for obtaining more consistent service from Customs. Eastman Kodak, for example, prefers to use the Port of Rochester, New York, because of the proximity. Another Customs issue is the harbor maintenance fee which is an ad valorem charge on imports arriving at U.S. seaports. Importing into Halifax or Montreal and then trucking or railing to inland U.S. destinations will preclude an importer from paying this tax.

8. *Customs house brokers.* Selection of these firms is based essentially on the same criteria as the selection of freight forwarders. Transaction-by-transaction fees are the basis for the obvious costs, but effective and efficient processing clearly precludes additional customer service and inventory investment costs. Ineffective brokers may create compliance problems whereby importers are repeatedly sent inquiries about specific imports, have shipments regularly subject to intensive examinations, must make postimportation amendments to documentation, and undergo lengthy audits by the Customs Service. Difficult to measure, these administrative overhead problems represent substantial costs.

9. *Inland carriers.* These are exactly the same issues facing the inland carriers at the beginning of the import process. Delays are the most costly element.

10. *Coopers.* Perhaps an outmoded term, but the barrel makers of old are those who are employed to restow and secure cargoes that have undergone intensive Customs inspection. They charge on a shipment-by-shipment basis, but their true costs to the global purchaser may be found in the time factor impact on service and inventory levels.

11. *Insurance carriers.* While unlikely to delay a shipment, the costs of providing insurance coverage for goods in international transit are still incurred. Moreover, it also has a small administrative overhead issue.

Duty Management

Duty management is included in the structuring section because the nonsourcing initiative requires some physical and/or administrative infrastructure. Duty management contains opportunities for duty reduction, avoidance, delaying payment, and refunds. Some considerations for reducing costs through these are as follows:

1. *Duty reduction.* The principal method other than changing sources of supply is through careful tariff classification of the goods. Alternatively a global purchaser may elect to use a foreign trade zone (FTZ) to transform the goods into a product with a lower duty rate. Manufacturing, assembly, packaging, assorting, and marking are the more common activities carried out in FTZs. The process for establishing use may be complex, but for larger importers moving substantial volumes, the payoffs are clearly advantageous.

2. *Duty avoidance.* Importing goods where it is known that they will be subsequently exported offers a couple of opportunities. Temporary import bonds (TIBs) allow for goods to be imported and used for such purposes as research and development. Under the law, the TIB requires that the goods be subsequently exported or alternatively destroyed under Customs supervision. After importation, goods may be placed in a bonded warehouse and then exported without incurring any duty payment. There is, however, a cost for storing goods in a bonded facility. Administrative overhead is always an issue.

3. *Delaying payment.* From a cash flow standpoint, delaying duty payment may be an appropriate strategy. Placing goods in a bonded warehouse and not withdrawing them until such time that they are needed is clearly one of them. An FTZ will offer the same opportunity along with the possibility to change their physical condition. Administrative overhead remains an issue for these initiatives as well.

4. *Duty refunds.* For nearly 200 years Congress has provided a mechanism for obtaining refunds of duty on imported goods that are subsequently

exported. Duty drawback provides such relief whether goods are exported in their exact imported state or whether they have been used in the manufacture of some other product. The record-keeping requirements are extensive requiring documentation of the import, the export, and the intervening manufacturing processing. Additionally, preparation of the drawback entry or application for refund requires additional administrative costs and, similar to the issues in the previous section concerning Customs brokers, the potential for specialized Customs audits increases as well.

The Hazards of Disconnects

When supply management and logistics are not organizationally connected or if their respective measurement criteria cause suboptimization at the firm level, the result is a dysfunctional supply chain. One example of this is the U.S. subsidiary of a global industrial equipment manufacturer that had a supply management department switch from a domestic supplier to one in Brazil. Although the 20 percent price savings was attractive, there was no supply-logistics coordination and no landed cost model employed. Unfortunately, the only transportation cost considered was ocean freight; neither U.S. inland freight nor terminal handling charges were considered. While Customs duty was calculated, the fees paid on a per-transaction basis to the broker were not. The four-week lead time from the foreign supplier (significantly longer than the domestic supplier's one week) resulted in the necessity of carrying more cycle stock inventory. With manufacturing previously accustomed to just-in-time deliveries, there was no available space for the added stocks. Sailing schedules from São Paulo to Baltimore caused a significant variance in lead times thereby necessitating that safety stocks increase from a matter of hours to days. Moreover, the added distance precluded any advantage that supplier flexibility could offer, and the physical properties of the item meant that airfreight was out of the question. While the supply management department was pleased with the price savings, the change shut down production several times, and when all other factors were considered, the supposed savings were actually cost increases. This manufacturing firm is now busily constructing a more reliable landed cost model.

Sophisticated Landed Cost Models

A basic landed cost model contains several principal variables: cycle stock inventory, administrative overhead inclusive of fees paid to intermediaries, in-transit inventory, duties, and taxes, and transportation costs. Additionally, variation in lead time adds a safety stock component. The most sophisticated importers develop landed cost models as decision support tools to assure that they (1) capture all relevant costs, and (2) are able to make informed tradeoffs when considering new global sourcing opportunities.

CONCEPT OF SUPPLY CHAIN COMPLEXITY

As shown earlier in Figure 9–2, the basic building blocks of global supply chain complexity are product complexity, process complexity, network complexity, source complexity, and security complexity. While each component is not equally weighted and the variables are not equally weighted within each component, all potentially contribute to cost and variation. Competing suppliers can be compared using the model as a checklist for identifying where problems may exist. Subsequently, these can be further investigated for the cost impacts of each factor.[11,12] Individual components are discussed in the following.

Product Complexity

Supply managers, even when they have been actively engaged in early procurement involvement or otherwise been able to affect material specifications, may have relatively little control over the physical nature of the product or material being imported. Each of these, however, represents a variable that impacts physical flow. Dimensional characteristics—height, width, and length—affect stowability in transit and the selection of those transport modes must be capable of handling the cargo. Density and whether a shipment is bulk or packaged freight are other determinants. High-value items and those that are easily damaged in transit tend to suggest higher cost modes and smaller packaging, and ultimately may even extend to some concern for security. Large firms engaged in assembly operations typically are dealing with a high number of stockkeeping units (SKUs) that inherently add a quantity problem to product complexity, but depending on the industry may also pose a coloading problem because certain items may be incompatible with others. For example, incompatibility for shipping and storage has been and remains a significant problem for the chemical industry.

Process Complexity

Process complexity represents the importance that the customer has placed on a particular product or material. Those using just-in-time (JIT) and time definite delivery (TDD) initiatives place a premium on the temporal performance of global supply chains. Large retailers are concerned about the costs of missing specific seasonal market opportunities when it comes to the delivery of specific products. However, when deliveries of raw materials and assembly components are late for manufacturers, the result can be disrupted operations, loss of revenue, and, depending on their labor contract, idled workers.

---

11 Kant Rao and Richard R. Young (1994). "Global Supply Chains: Factors Influencing Outsourcing of Logistics Functions," *International Journal of Physical Distribution and Logistics Management*, 24:6, pp. 11–19.

12 Richard R. Young (2004). "Managing International Supply Chain Complexity," *Proceedings of the 15th Annual North American Symposium on Purchasing and Supply Management*, Arizona State University, Tempe, AZ, pp. 633–650.

Network Complexity

Principally the domain of logistics management, network complexity reflects the structure of the relationships between the various intermediaries and transportation firms in the supply chain. It deals with the flows of physical goods, information, and finance. It can have so many nodal and linkage variables as to become unwieldy and extremely difficult to manage and is, therefore, one of the most unique components of complexity because of the discretion that firms have—more so than with any other complexity. From a nodal standpoint, all elements of network complexity are derived from the demand for transportation and related services created though supply management's creation of foreign sources.

Source Complexity

Source complexity is closely allied with network complexity also because of the amount of discretion that firms have over its creation. The number of suppliers and their locations are the primary drivers; however, these decisions lead to other complexity issues such as monetary units, language differences, and cultural differences. New suppliers imply the existence of an active learning curve. The lack of learning curves precludes the benefits of learning from experience, and the use of a given supply chain is a singular event. Similarly, related parties have advantages in common information systems, ease of transactions, and common language.

Security Complexity

Following the events of 9/11, security issues have increased. The principal concerns from a regulatory standpoint are the nature of the goods and their origins. Clearly, some materials and products have more "tamper appeal" than others such as when they are hazardous materials, high-value goods, or those goods that might hold some potential military applications. Some origins of goods hold more risk than others, but no place is totally safe from unwanted tampering. Whether goods can be tampered with at a supplier location or while in transit is an issue that concerns both governments and importing firms alike. One part of a solution is the Customs-Trade Program Against Terrorism mentioned earlier.

CONTINUOUS LEADERSHIP AND MANAGEMENT OF EXTENDED GLOBAL SUPPLY CHAINS

In the preceding discussion prospective global purchasers were cautioned to find ways to build global supply chains that would not only minimize out-of-pocket costs but would reduce the potential for increased or unnecessary administrative overhead. Moreover it was cautioned that the selection of suppliers, transportation providers, and other intermediaries needed to be carried out with a concern for cycle time throughout the system as well as for variations in cycle time because these impact overall inventory levels and safety stocks, respectively.

This section specifically addresses how firms may reduce, if never totally eliminate, additional sources of variation and complexity from their global supply chains. Some may be eliminated organizationally, while others will require a change in the paradigm for supplier relationships.

Using Foreign Affiliates

Some of the variation in global supply chains stems from the complexity of translations, not only of languages, but of information systems, time zones, telephone communication protocols, legal systems, monetary systems, and business cultures. One of the most effective methods for reducing the impact of these is through the skillful use of affiliated companies provided that these do in fact exist. Their use replaces a single transaction between a supplier and purchaser with a pair of transactions: an international one between the two affiliates, and a domestic one between foreign affiliate and the supplier. This reduces complexity in two ways: communications between affiliated companies is typically facilitated with common information systems, simplified currency exchange mechanisms that usually do not entail letters of credit, and a lingua franca. On this last point, firms will standardize on the home language with U.S. firms adopting English, although Hoechst AG, the former German chemical giant used German worldwide (even for business being conducted between its affiliates in Taiwan and Colombia, neither Chinese or Spanish was used).

Domestic transactions between the foreign affiliate and the supplier can be carried out in the local language, using local currency, and under local laws by people living in the same time zone. Where face-to-face meetings are required, the cost and frequency of their occurrence need not be a major undertaking.

Reducing Variation in Supply Chains

While there is ample variation in the supply chain, it may be due to many firms still clinging to policies that require (1) multiple sources for goods and services, (2) periodic contract renewal for suppliers, and (3) similar contract rebidding or renewal for providers of transportation services and intermediaries. Breaking this paradigm is a major undertaking, but has several dramatic effects. First, the trade literature is rife with articles about supply base rationalization. Return to Table 9–2 and replace the numbers in Scenario 6 with the example of 1,000 suppliers in 50 countries, serving 20 U.S. plant locations. Other variables can remain constant, but observe the number of relationships that the global purchaser must now be able to service. The quality literature of the mid-1980s addressed the variability problem vis-à-vis the supply base extensively.[13]

The other self-defeating practice is the periodic turnover in suppliers. The global network, as previously suggested, is extremely fragile. Suppliers should be

---

13 W. Edwards Deming (1982). *Out of the Crisis*, Cambridge, MA: MIT Center for Advanced Engineering Study, pp. 35–40.

changed when strategic, technical, or compelling economic necessity is apparent. That circumstance is only achieved when the total costs of the entire network are available for analysis—not a simple univariate task. Continuing with the example in Table 9–2, deleting one supplier will be a simple proposition, but inserting another should it be in a different country or region may entail as many as five changes—supplier per se, inland carrier, freight forwarder, government agency, and line-haul carrier.

By contrast, should logistics management chose to rebid and ultimately replace the customhouse broker in Scenario 6 of Table 9–2, they have actually not only replaced one participant with five different offices, but also impacted the functioning of as many as 500 supply chains even though many of those chains share a common node.

Other Sources of Variation

While not within the scope of supply management to control, the other components in Figure 9–1 add a level of global supply chain complexity that must be nevertheless addressed. Specifically, in industries with rapidly advancing technology or consumer goods companies where frequent new items continue to be spawned as product extensions, the additions represent new items to be potentially sourced as well as to be assessed for duty classification. New products may have new weights, packages, stowability issues, values, and handling characteristics. Moreover, many such firms will frequently retire some products thereby removing these stockkeeping units from their active files after a period of time.

Customers not only change, but existing customers change their business processes. Among those business-to-business transactions, purchasers are increasingly looking to economize on inventories with the result being a continuing increase in JIT and TDD types of initiatives.

Supply managers clearly need to be able to access an array of sources, not just domestically, but wherever they may be found worldwide. Achieving continuity requires that they assume leadership in maintaining these extended global supply chains for maximum competitive advantage. Leadership in this sense means understanding the dynamics of the supply chain network, all the variables that enable it to function or fail, all the different dimensions of cost, and the impacts of change to any of the supply chain's variables. Leadership means building bridges to other parts of the organization, specifically logistics management, to assure that decisions affecting the integrity of the supply chain are devised and executed in a holistic manner and that a suboptimal decision is not impetuously initiated that will prove detrimental to the global supply chain's fragile nature. Directly related to this organizational issue is the need to establish meaningful performance metrics that encourage all parts of the organization to act in ways that allow for developing competitive supply chains, but also for protecting their integrity. Finally, the supply manager's leadership role demands a cognizance of corporate strategy and how certain sourcing decisions may fit despite their appearing to be uneconomic on the surface.

Achieving Leadership

To avoid the possibility of suboptimizing the supply chain, supply management must take a leadership role in evaluating the true total cost of any offshoring initiatives. It must move beyond purchase price variance in its evaluation of any sourcing opportunity by including the costs associated with any of the potential intermediaries. Such costs, however, are not just denominated in dollars, but in the implications of the time involved. Time, at least in this context, is not only the average lead time, but the variance in that lead time that ultimately gets translated into increased inventory and additional administrative overhead.

Where the leadership issue needs to be addressed first is in the performance metrics because the true total costs span the activities of supply and logistics. Logistics, as a derived demand activity, is dependent upon those sourcing decisions made by supply management. It is for this reason that global sourcing initiatives, to become effective, must embrace the cost issues that face both supply and logistics activities. Any determination otherwise will result in higher costs, poor delivery performance to the firm's own customers, and unacceptable levels of administrative effort.

SUMMARY

The management of global supply chain networks is substantially different than that of their domestic counterparts in part because global supply networks require many more participants in order to function, but also because they may be established to access specific technologies, allow the firm to access particular markets, or for cost advantage.

The global supply chain is both fragile and complex. Its many variables offer ample opportunities for the loss of cost advantages because of additional administrative processes as well as added cycle times, especially as pertains to transportation, to spawn higher levels of inventory investment. As with all complex systems, management of global supply chains is best achieved though dividing them into discrete units that focus on product characteristics, process or character of demand, supplier characteristics, spatial and temporal variables in the transportation network, and those attributes that potentially raise security concerns.

Variation is often mentioned as the nemesis of quality. A global supply chain that is to consistently perform up to quality expectations will be one where variation has been consciously reduced. Some parts of the global supply chain inherently contain variation: those must be recognized. Other parts of the supply chain possess elements that have been historically managed in suboptimal ways that have often increased variation: those approaches must be revised. Supply chains are like living organisms; they are in a constant state of change. Leadership will be in recognizing those changes and where appropriate, countering or accommodating those changes.

CHAPTER 10

OUTSOURCING: CHALLENGES AND OPPORTUNITIES

Edward M. Lundeen, C.P.M., CPIM
Director, Contracts
Eclipse Aviation

INTRODUCTION

The topic of outsourcing has been much discussed in boardrooms across America, on the evening news, and in union-organizing campaigns especially when the outsourced activity is offshore. The boardroom perspective suggests outsourcing, especially when done offshore, is a means for companies to achieve cost reductions and cost avoidances in order to compete in the marketplace (see Table 10–1). The rhetoric views outsourcing as a drain to the domestic economy by shifting work to offshore companies in economically depressed countries and regions, all at the cost of the domestic workforce.

This chapter takes a practitioner approach to outsourcing. It discusses the process-related mechanics from inception of the process, to critical considerations in developing a comprehensive agreement and statement of work, to management of the relationship. The intent herein is to provide information about the outsourcing process and not to take a position regarding the rhetoric surrounding the outsourcing debate.

Overview

Outsourcing is an excellent method for organizations to use to discontinue activities that are not part of its core competency, thereby permitting a shift from a fixed-cost business model to a variable-cost model, potentially reducing unit cost of performance and minimizing capital acquisition and ownership costs (see Table 10–2).

As organizations recognize and differentiate their core and noncore competencies, their ability to influence and impact their supply networks increase as they opt to outsource noncore activities and functions. Negotiating and contracting for outsourced business activities is markedly different from routine services agreements, especially if, for example, intellectual property ownership, warranties, creative

T A B L E   10–1

ISM Outsourcing Survey Results

ISM recently conducted a survey of chief procurement and supply officers of medium and large organizations at the request of the Department of Commerce to determine the impact of outsourcing/offshoring jobs. The survey findings included the following:

- Thirty four percent of respondents moved production activities outside of the United States in the past year.

- Labor costs were the most often cited reason for outsourcing.

- In about half the cases, outsourced production activities services NAFTA countries.

- Half of the companies that outsourced production activities relocated them to either China or India.

- In about two-thirds of companies that outsourced activities, information technology was cited as playing an "important" or "very important" role in the decision to relocate; transportation costs played such roles in less than half the cases.

- Only 4 percent of companies moved production activities into the United States from suppliers abroad in the past year.

- Firms that outsourced many jobs in the past year expect to outsource fewer in the coming year; and vice versa.

- There is no clear relationship between firm employment size and the likelihood of outsourcing jobs.

Source: Inside Supply Management March 2004

design, works-for-hire, epidemic failure, data ownership, liability, and indemnity provisions are involved. Considerations regarding key performance indicators, metrics, service-level agreements, disaster recovery, and exit strategies become contract critical.

This chapter examines the processes, mechanics, and considerations specific to developing, negotiating, and managing outsourcing agreements. Further, the chapter will present concepts, methods, templates, tools, and approaches to use when developing and negotiating outsourcing agreements.

HOW DOES OUTSOURCE CONTRACTING VARY FROM TRADITIONAL SERVICES CONTRACTING?

Traditional services contracting is typically focused on an individual task or a range of tasks to be completed in a specific time frame. Annual agreements for traditional services have similarities to outsource contracting in that both require general terms and conditions and a statement of work; beyond that, there are significant differences. The key distinction is that many companies contract traditional service providers to supplement their workforce or to perform specialized services

TABLE   10–2

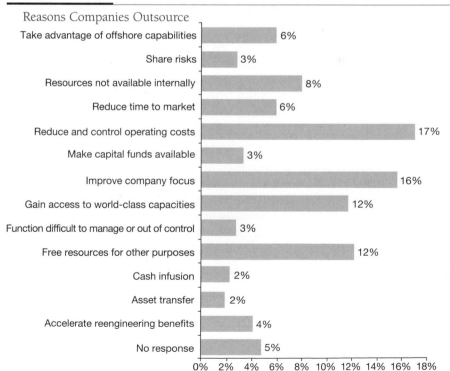

Reasons Companies Outsource

Take advantage of offshore capabilities	6%
Share risks	3%
Resources not available internally	8%
Reduce time to market	6%
Reduce and control operating costs	17%
Make capital funds available	3%
Improve company focus	16%
Gain access to world-class capacities	12%
Function difficult to manage or out of control	3%
Free resources for other purposes	12%
Cash infusion	2%
Asset transfer	2%
Accelerate reengineering benefits	4%
No response	5%

0%   2%   4%   6%   8%   10% 12% 14% 16% 18%

From The Outsourcing Institute's *8th Annual Outsourcing Index*, a Survey of 1,410 oursourcing buyers.

(e.g., temporary labor, construction, garbage collection, creative work, or contractors for short-term projects), whereas outsource contracting typically takes a group of tasks or functions, historically performed by the contracting company (see Table 10–3), and moves that group on an intended long-term basis to an outsource services provider (e.g., security, payroll, accounts payable, call centers, software development). This longer-term aspect associated with outsourcing requires more detailed planning for activity transition, work requirements scoping, performance measurement, developing baseline metrics, disaster recovery, and exit strategies than does casual or traditional services contracting. Further, frequently when companies outsource, there is a corresponding reduction in the existing workforce, thus adding barriers and degrees of difficulty if a company should choose to reverse the process at a later date ("insourcing"). These barriers, degrees of difficulty, and complexity are often due to poor planning (and lack of anticipation of evolving business needs) that ultimately results in the loss of knowledge base (e.g., process knowledge, corporate knowledge, disruption in data collection, insufficient systems and infrastructure, and the loss of the previously skilled in-house workforce).

Aspects that are critical to effective outsourcing include the following points for consideration and action. [Note that the use of the term *services* implies that the work to be performed is a service-based activity; that is, it may be an activity such as outsourcing a function historically performed by proprietary employees (accounting, call centers, security, etc.) or it may be much broader to include activities such as contract manufacturing of products.]

1. Developing a comprehensive statement of work (SOW) that accurately describes the expected outcomes that are essential and required. Frequently, this is in the form of describing services that require performance and processes that require completion, but not necessarily the methods necessary to accomplish the work activity.

2. Establishing baseline (referential) metrics for the services to be provided. It is exceedingly difficult to establish baseline metrics once the process is already under way to transition work to a new or different services provider. Also, if in-house employees are aware that work may be outsourced (or if an incumbent services provider perceives they may be losing a contract), it potentially introduces bias into the process to collect and validate baseline metrics. These baseline metrics are essential in order to gauge the performance of the future services provider.

3. Developing service-level agreements (SLAs) to define responsibilities and minimum acceptable standards and developing key performance indicators (KPIs) to effectively measure performance against requirements, standards, or baseline metrics is critical to successful performance management, process improvement, and cost reduction. There is an anonymous quote stating, "What gets measured, gets managed." The experience of those who outsource substantiates this quote. Those

functional elements that have KPIs and SLAs get closely managed; those that don't, tend to get lost in the shuffle.

4. Establishing an effective costing methodology (identifying, qualifying, quantifying, and classifying fixed and variable cost elements) to address current as well as future (expected and unexpected) requirements (those in the SOW as well as those that were not contemplated in advance) will serve to minimize conflict, unnecessary negotiations, and disputes relative to cost and expense. Those negotiating outsourcing agreements should make it an imperative that any costing methodology used in the final agreement be scalable to permit upside and downside volume fluctuations, significant changes in economics and market conditions, as well as other variables that may materially impact the cost/expense category of the agreement.

5. Separation of responsibilities (between the company contracting for outsourcing and the outsource contractor) must be defined to address issues such as when, where, and how data, information, and reports will be exchanged between the parties (not only at the start of the agreement but on a sustaining basis). Further, the SOW needs to be unequivocal in identifying responsibilities for specific tasks, processes, events, and activities. In this regard, going through the painstaking activity to process-map the activities to be outsourced, including the inputs and outputs to the processes and the interrelated activities, significantly assists to scope, identify, clarify, and describe the responsibilities and logical hand-offs.

6. The previously mentioned process mapping will assist in any planned business process reengineering and in determining (at a macro level) requirements for integration of systems, protocols, methods, and, possibly, data structure.

7. The inclusion of a predetermined process for dispute or conflict resolution is very important. The astute supply manager should include a process that involves management at least one to two levels removed from those who provide daily management and administration of the agreement so that disputes can be equitably resolved by parties who did not substantially create the dispute initially. Such a process will save time, money, and functional relationships while mitigating the unnecessary expense of arbitrators, mediators, and lawyers.

8. Prior to awarding this outsourcing agreement, the supply manager should already be thinking about the contractual prenuptial agreement and how to exit the agreement and transition the work in the event of a commercial divorce, force majeure event, bankruptcy, change in control, and so forth.

TABLE 10–3

What's Being Outsourced?

From The Outsourcing Institute's *8th Annual Outsourcing Index*, a Survey of 1,410 oursourcing buyers.

WHAT ARE SOME OF THE KEY POINTS FOR THE SOW, THE REQUEST FOR PROPOSAL (RFP), AND THE ULTIMATE BASE OUTSOURCING AGREEMENTS?

Outsourcing should not (necessarily) attempt to duplicate services *exactly* as they were performed by the company seeking the services. Presuming the supply manager selected the outsource contractor based on core competency (and, hopefully, not based solely on the economics of the contractor's proposal), theory holds the outsource contractor should possess methods, techniques, tools, processes, and resources to more effectively manage the outsourced functions and activities better than the company seeking the services. Accordingly, the RFP and accompanying SOW should be crafted so as to describe expected outcomes (i.e., requirements), not a step-by-step approach to describe, in detail ad nauseam, the process that is being outsourced.

The following should be considered when crafting the RFP and draft agreement (including the terms and conditions, SOW, exhibits, metrics, process maps, etc.). The mechanics of the agreement (considering who, what, where, when, and how) should contemplate the work outcomes (i.e., requirements of the work to be performed) including timing and milestones for the activities and outcomes; expected hand-off points for activities, reports, data, and product; timing associated with activities, outcomes, reports, reporting, and work activity; an outcome "acceptance process" (if appropriate); key measures specific to the services to be performed (i.e., metrics, KPIs, and SLAs); scheduled business reviews; and, risk-reward provisions (if any). Of course, in addition to the normal legalese, it will be necessary to address additional terms such as ownership of intellectual property; works for hire and work product considerations; a remedy process for unacceptable outcomes; dispute resolution methodology; indemnity; limitation of liability; and insurance (e.g., workers' compensation, general liability, product liability, property damage, and errors and omissions) just to name a few.

Next, what extenuating circumstances warrant special consideration and foresight?

- How will the company transition away from this outsource contractor in the event of a commercial divorce?

- Does the outsourcing agreement contain a termination for convenience provision? If so, how much time is permitted for the transition?

- Will the future ex-outsource contractor "bridge" services requirements until the replacement outsource contractor is in place?

- Will the future ex-outsource contractor provide training or support for the new outsource contractor?

- Will the company be able to recover any of its initial (sunk) setup, start-up, or training costs?

- What if the outsource contractor experiences a change in control and has a successor or there is an assignment of their business?

- What if the successor company is a competitor to the company that is outsourcing the services (remember, they are performing work that may not quickly or easily transition, and they may have access to confidential information about the company that is contracting for outsourced services)?

- What if the outsource contractor goes into a reorganization or bankruptcy chapter filing?

- Does the agreement require both parties approval for any changes in control or ownership?

- Does the agreement have a noncompete clause (unless your state prohibits them)?

- Can the company who is outsourcing prevent its outsource contractor from directly recruiting the company's key employees?

- If the outsource contractor agreed to hire employees from the company that is outsourcing (not unusual) to transition the business, does the contractor also have the right to rehire or transition the employees to a new outsource contractor (assuming the employees also agrees)?

- Does the outsource contractor have the ability to remove or reassign the key employees on the account without the knowledge or consent of both parties (other than for a violation of the law or material violations of the outsource contractor's company rules and regulations)?

- Does the company that is outsourcing have the right to review, interview, and approve of new key employees assigned to the account?

- Will the company that is outsourcing have the needed resources to take the activity back in-house if necessary?

- Does the company that is outsourcing have the right to audit the records of the outsource contractor for possible overcharges, underpayments, inaccurate work, or physical inventory (if appropriate)?

- Who owns the data, databases, knowledge base, work in progress, work product, work papers, and so forth, that the outsource contractor will generate during this agreement?

- Does the outsource contractor have the ability to employ the information or knowledge it gained from the company that is outsourcing in any fashion related or unrelated to the business?

- Does the definitive agreement contain a provision for the return and/or destruction of records (paper and digital format) in the event of termination of the agreement?

- Were nondisclosure agreements in place *prior* to the start of the engagement?

- Is there a continuous process in place to track the financial health of the outsource contractor (or any type of system that would provide an early warning of impending change in business condition)?

WHAT IS A SERVICE-LEVEL AGREEMENT AND HOW IS IT USED?

Service-level agreements (SLAs) are frequently developed to amplify and clarify an SOW by specifying in great detail which organization (company or outsource contractor) has the responsibility for specific activities, events, and tasks. The SLA format may simply be a text document with the heading "Company Responsibilities" with a bulleted listing of the responsibilities, followed by another heading "Outsource Contractor Responsibilities," followed by another bulleted listing; or it may be in matrix format with columns for elements such as event, timing and milestone, responsibility, and frequency; or it may be a mix of both bullets and a matrix. Further, SLAs may be used to define or describe minimal levels of work or work activities that must take place within a prescribed time or sequence. SLAs, while frequently used as a stand-alone, may also be tied to metrics.

One benefit of incorporating the SLA as an exhibit or a schedule to the agreement is that as the relationship evolves and matures, the SLA will invariably need to be modified and updated.

An example of a text format SLA follows.

Service-Level Agreement

Scope and Definition

Outsource contractor shall "own" continuation engineering for mature products, as agreed upon by the company and the outsource contractor. This will enable outsource contractor to design the product for a high-volume assembly environment and with component parts sourced to take advantage of outsource contractor purchasing leverage. This is expected to drive significant cost reductions in future products.

Company Responsibilities

- Develop, maintain, and provide customer requirement specification.
- Approve key technology and engineering changes initiated by outsource contractor.
- Provide all specifications, artwork, and packaging design to support the development, procurement, manufacture, test, and packaging of the products.
- Provide firmware support for outsource contractor-initiated and Company-approved engineering changes.

Outsource Contractor Responsibilities

- Release bill of material for new stockkeeping unit (SKU).
- Assume responsibility for initiating, executing, and implementing engineering change orders in support of ongoing product and product enhancements.
- Perform cross-functional cost reduction and product improvement activities.
- Provide technical assistance to Company in effecting resolutions to product quality problems.
- Provide a cost reduction plan to Company. The plan should include a feasibility report, design study, and analysis of specifications.
- Support product "end of life" activities to minimize scrap and obsolescence
- Review and approve component-level first article inspection.

T A B L E　10–4

Performance Indicator	Definition	Criteria or Limit
Sales Order acknowledgment	All sales orders are to be acknowledged to company within two (2) working days	100%
Order fulfillment	Shipment on committed date.	95%
Admin claim performance	Process all claims within five (5) working days of receipt of claim	98%
JIT delivery	Delivery within four (4) hours upon request.	100%
Cancellation of orders	Cancellation of orders within the order system within two (2) business days of receipt	100%

WHAT ARE KEY PERFORMANCE INDICTORS?

Key performance indicators (KPIs) and metrics are used to define, describe, and measure specific performance requirements that are to be met by the outsource contractor (as well as the company who outsourced the services). More specifically, they are measurements that monitor whether or not the outsource contractor is performing the right service, at the right time, in the right place, at the correct (agreed upon) cost, and at the right quality level.

Typically, the benchmark used for these measures is, at a minimum, consistent with the company's historical performance measures before it outsourced the activity. On occasion (rarely), industry standards may be available for a benchmark or reference point. KPIs may be as simple as those reflected in Table 10–4.

The benefits of using KPIs formatted like those reflected in Table 10–4 are that they are easy to track, measure, report, and understand.

KPIs should be established to effectively measure activities and outcomes without unduly burdening the outsource contractor with so much data collection that the contractor must increase billable costs merely to collect the data.

Suggested areas in which KPIs may be employed include:

- Process time
  - Turnaround time
  - Cycle time
  - Transformation time

- Price/cost reductions
  - Unit/purchase cost reductions
  - Scrap percentage
  - Rework percentage

- Quality
  - Warranty returns
  - Epidemic failures
  - Defects
    - Defective parts per million (DPPM) on incoming inspection
    - Material review board activity (MRB)
    - Annualized failure rate (AFR)
    - Line reject rates

- Delivery
  - On time, early, late
  - Shipping compliance or nonconformances

- Processing metrics
  - Units completed per period
  - Cost per unit processed

SHOULD RISK-REWARD PROVISIONS BE INCLUDED IN OUTSOURCING AGREEMENTS?

Some supply chain practitioners feel strongly regarding the topic of employing (or not employing) penalty-incentive or risk-reward provisions in outsourcing agreements. While many are not in favor of using such risk-reward provisions (specific to outsourced services agreement), the cases where some may be inclined to use such risk-reward provisions are when the baseline metrics are solid and verifiable and there is a strong financial incentive (or disincentive) for variations in the metrics due to performance or lack of performance.

As a comparative example let's assume a new proprietary employee is being hired. The new employee likely will be provided with a job description, the instructions needed in order to perform the work (including training), and an agreement upon the amount of pay expected if the employee performs the work. If the work is well defined and there are reasonable work standards (e.g., industrial engineering assessments, time and motion studies, or empirical data of similar work performed with expected or normative outcomes), why should an organization agree to pay a premium (reward or incentive) beyond that which was already agreed in order to compensate the employee? Isn't that what the salary or wage rate is for? If the new employee doesn't or can't perform, the option is to replace them. This does not say there isn't room for improvement or ingenuity in the process; there may be, but rewards and incentives that are not well conceived will turn out to be unnecessary profit centers for the outsource contractor. Frequently, the outsource contractors focus primarily (almost solely) on those metrics and elements that will provide them with additional incentives versus judiciously managing the entire suite of responsibilities.

Risk-reward provisions should (1) be used sparingly, (2) be very well thought out, (3) have a time limit on them, (4) have a dollar cap, and (5) be bilateral (i.e., if outsource contractor doesn't meet a predefined threshold of performance, they risk losing money for not effectively performing the services).

Risk-reward provisions work well when there are rock solid standards (supported by irrefutable baseline data) and the risk-reward (incentive or penalty) does not become applicable until a specific threshold has been reached (e.g., above 120 percent or below 80 percent of expected performance levels). An outsource contractor should not receive a reward for marginally exceeding a metric nor should they be penalized for marginally missing a metric.

Another consideration is when an outsource contractor is able to reduce purchase costs or increase utilization (i.e., reduce waste or scrap) of a product or service. Frequently, an approach is employed wherein the outsource contractor is permitted to share the cost reductions (maybe even as much as 100 percent of the savings for a specific period of time) and then the future savings (in full or in part) pass through to the company who is contracting for the outsource contractor.

The use of risk-reward provisions may increase costs and undoubtedly will increase the degree of complexity (not to mention the potential for disputes) to manage, administer, and audit the outsourcing agreement. Properly conceived and applied, risk-reward provisions can mutually benefit both the company and the outsource contractor.

IF THE OUTSOURCE SUPPLIER IS BASED OFFSHORE, WHAT ADDITIONAL CONCERNS OR ISSUES SHOULD BE CONSIDERED?

Many companies are intentionally selecting offshore suppliers due to low labor cost markets and tax considerations. In addition to all the same issues and considerations that apply to domestic outsource services providers, the following points should be considered:

- In which currency will the agreement be quoted, negotiated, and invoiced? Will currency exchange rate fluctuations affect the economics of the agreement? Will the agreement permit escalation and deescalation due to fluctuations that exceed a predetermined level?

- Will the offshore supplier be able to obtain the types and amounts of insurance that are required or necessary to perform the work and will it be with an insurance carrier with a Best's rating that is acceptable? Some types of insurance that are standard or routine in the United States are not available in some countries. Further, if bonds or bonding (i.e., performance or payment bonds) is a requirement, this may prove problematic for the supply manager as bonding practices in the United States may not be consistent with bonding practices (or availability) in some countries.

- A strong consideration should be made to have the agreement contain governing law and venue citing U.S. courts and venues, not only for any legal actions but for disputes as well. Unless the supply manager's company has legal resources in the country where the services are being performed, this can result in a significant expense and an unmanageable situation in the event of a dispute or legal action. Foreign courts do not always look favorably upon U.S. companies, especially in the event of a dispute with a local company. Alternative considerations are available for Swiss law and arbitration or mediation in Geneva, but again, this can become a very expensive proposition.

- If the offshore company also has a U.S. affiliate, there may be benefit and value in contracting with the U.S. entity versus the offshore corporation. The supply manager should consult with counsel to determine which legal entity would be most beneficial with which to contract.

- Will the agreement require that all outsourced services be provided in any specific language(s)? Will the agreement have minimal requirements as to language proficiency? Does the supply manager's company have personnel proficient in the language of the outsourced company?

- Time-zone differentials (between where the supply manager's company is located and where the outsourced company is located) can be a significant benefit as well as a substantial detriment depending on the type of work activity being performed.

THE UGLY SIDE OF OUTSOURCE CONTRACTING: DISASTER RECOVERY, BUSINESS DOWNTURN, AND EXIT STRATEGIES

When supply chain and contracting professionals speak with suppliers' sales representatives regarding new business opportunities, the tendency is to focus on the positive aspects of the future relationship. Forecasts are provided that are optimistic, typically rounded-up, and with positive trends. Generally, talk is in terms of expansion, new products or services, growth, and opportunity. Written agreements, all too often, focus on capturing the obligatory legalese and the positive aspects of the future or expected relationship. While this is a preferable situation to be in, experience has proven otherwise.

Given the general business climate since the dot-com bust (downturn in business, business failures, acquisitions, etc.), many suppliers have been discouraged with underperforming accounts and supply managers have been pressed to provide more realistic forecasts of their future requirements. More importantly if the supply manager is in a take-or-pay agreement or a requirements contract that had volume purchase requirements (monthly or quarterly) or guaranteed purchase commitments (in terms of dollars), even if the buying organization didn't consume the product or service, it was in a commercially vulnerable position and likely paid premiums (or possibly liquidated damages) for products or services that were not consumed.

Typically, it isn't until such a situation arises that there is recognition that the proverbial "an ounce of prevention is worth a pound of cure" analogy should have been contemplated with regard to the language in the agreement.

Given the foregoing, the following question should be asked when negotiating and drafting agreements: What can possibly go wrong in this agreement and what language should be negotiated and inserted in the agreement now to mitigate those undesirable, yet potential, future events? When anticipating all that could possibly go wrong with an agreement, put your most pessimistic hat on and try to imagine all the conceivable what-if type scenarios and then, test those scenarios against the language of the planned agreement to see if it provides the relief or protection that is necessary in order to mitigate unnecessary risk.

How Should Disaster Recovery Be Addressed in the Outsourcing Agreement?

Companies have become somewhat proficient at developing and testing disaster recovery plans, especially those related to data management (IT). Industries with unusual risk exposures (e.g., petrochemical plants, nuclear generation, and airlines) have developed and tested comprehensive plans to deal with disaster management, disaster containment, media management, key contacts, and so forth.

What if the outsource contractor were to experience a significant event (e.g., fire, flood, earthquake, tornado, hurricane, or strike) and invoked a force majeure clause? How will the supply manager recover, especially if the services being performed by the outsource contractor are mission critical to the business? If the supply manager has outsourced, for example, the accounts receivable function and the outsource contractor is unable to perform, what will happen to the company's revenue stream and the associated banking and accounting management functions? If the supply manager outsources the company's call center and the facility providing the services is severely damaged in a natural disaster, can the company afford to stop supporting its customers until the facility is repaired? What if the outsource contractor declares bankruptcy and is unable to continue providing the services?

In a traditional services agreement, the supply manager would rapidly switch to an alternate contractor or might take work back in-house, but in the case of an outsource contract, the scope and complexity is frequently so cumbersome that it is not practical on short notice (for the company contracting for outsourcing) to move the activity or to bring it back inside. The outsource contractor should provide a comprehensive disaster recovery and business continuity plan to be incorporated into the agreement. A sample plan might include some of the following points:

Disaster Recovery and Business Continuity Plan

Scope and Definition

Outsource contractor shall develop and implement a plan for the prevention and mitigation of business interruptions due to natural disasters or other causes that prevent normal business operations for more than xx consecutive hours [or some specified period of time that the supply manager determines that the company can afford to be without this service]. Outsource contractor shall make all reasonable efforts to prevent and recover from such events to ensure the continuity of business operations.

Outsource Contractor Responsibilities

- Make all reasonable efforts to ensure the continuity of operations through implementation of the disaster recovery and business continuity plan.

- Develop a more detailed and comprehensive plan to assure business continuity in the event of natural or other events that may cause services, supply chain, delivery, or performance interruptions. Plan must address those activities required to resume operations at an alternate location within xx days of a catastrophic event at 100 percent of normal operating levels. Examples of the activities to address are

  - Disaster response overview
  - Organization
  - List of key contacts, names, titles, phone numbers (work, cell, and home)
  - Risk identification and mitigation
  - Response strategies and timing
  - Prevention and mitigation efforts
  - Supply base continuity, especially for critical or single-sourced materials or services
  - Recovery of information systems and storage of critical information

A disaster recovery and business continuity plan will not prevent disasters from occurring, but it should provide the logic, thought process, business planning, and recovery considerations required, in advance of a business interruption, to mitigate extended loss of services, business, and revenue.

Business Downturn Provisions: What Are They and How Do They Work?

The provisions of an outsourcing agreement (forecast, volumes, costs, etc.) should be based on the expected or normal operating conditions. Further, the term of the agreement will typically be set to allow the outsource supplier to recover its initial investments and to enjoy some level of profitability. Frequently, the upfront costs of a start-up outsourcing agreement may be shared by the parties in the form of a nonrecurring expense or charge. If the contract is structured in an equitable fashion, it likely contains a price-cost matrix that has variability considerations given fluctuations in volume or product-services mix.

What if the outsourcing agreement has a fixed price table (without consideration for variations in volume) and contains minimum periodic (daily, weekly, monthly, quarterly) volumetric requirements? And, what if the business declines and the company that is outsourcing no longer has a demand consistent with the required minimums? How does the supply manager reconcile the differences? An attempt can be made to renegotiate at the time of the event, but the supply manager will not be in a position of power for the negotiation. In a situation like this, the negotiating power and leverage resides with the outsource supplier.

How should the agreement be postured to mitigate events such as this? One consideration is to include a business downturn provision in the agreement. Such a provision is invoked in the event of a predefined demonstrable change in business. For example, the provision may state that if company sales decline by some predetermined percentage in any given period of time (business quarter, rolling 13-week period, etc.) then the minimum periodic purchase requirement declines proportionately. Sometimes, the downturn provision serves as an opener to renegotiate the terms without predetermining the outcome or, if the change in business is significant enough, may initiate a contract termination action (this is not necessarily a bad thing).

There is significant flexibility in drafting downturn provisions, and the only limitation is the creativity of the individuals negotiating the agreement. Importantly, the critical juncture is recognizing on the front end of the negotiations (before an agreement is signed) that business downturn is a realistic consideration and anticipating which business and financial metrics are relevant in determining and invoking the downturn provision.

What Should Be Contemplated Regarding Exit Plans?

View an exit plan as a sort of prenuptial agreement. This requires the supply manager's organization to consider the what-if scenarios regarding a commercial divorce and should be treated as another form of business continuity plan. Be practical; nothing—including partnerships, business relationships, alliances, and contracts—is forever. The supply manager must consider alternatives well in advance of the need to employ them, especially with items related to outsourcing agreements. If a company must transition its business to another outsource contractor or move it back in-house, what are the implications?

An exit plan sets forth the terms and conditions under which the company and the outsource contractor will carry out the activities and responsibilities required in order to effect an orderly transition of business activities provided by the current outsource contractor to another outsource contractor (or back in-house). Upon either the expiration or termination of the agreement, for whatever reason, the company and the outsource contractor must agree to follow the terms and conditions set forth in the exit plan.

Exit plans should include provisions for the (future) ex-outsource contractor agreeing to:

1. Prepare, package, and ship all company-owned property either back to the company or to the new outsource contractor.

2. Provide training and support the new outsource contractor for a specified period of time.

3. Provide "bridging" services until the new outsource contractor has resumed daily production at current production levels.

4. Maintain the current level of services and named resources on the account until the completion of services.

When drafting an exit plan,

1. Develop a detailed listing of events or activities that must transpire.

2. Determine who is responsible to ensure the activity takes place and is completed.

3. Determine who is financially responsible for the activities on the listing.

4. Determine who will hold title to specifically identified goods and materials after the exit plan is effected.

The following questions should be resolved:

1. Who will own the data and information?
   a. Databases built during agreement.
   b. Databases generated during the agreement.
   c. Reports and reporting.
   d. Test scripts.
   e. Manufacturing instructions.
   f. Records of customers and customer account data.
   g. Purchasing records.
      (1) Approved vendor list (AVL)
         (a) Spend data by outsource contractor
         (b) Spend data by commodity
         (c) Lead-time data
      (2) Historical (recent and trend) price data
         (a) Spend data by outsource contractor
         (b) Spend data by commodity
         (c) Component-level costing data
         (d) Lead-time data
   h. Manufacturing process instructions (MPI).
   i. Manufacturing maintenance instructions (MMI).
   j. Company-unique production software, including source files, executable files, and test scripts.
   k. Manufacturing test engineering (MTE) database.
   l. Historical production and product design databases.
   m. Company proprietary engineering notebooks, technical reports, and engineering analysis.

    n. Production "gold masters" and standards used in production and failure analysis.

    o. Any other records and documentation developed jointly, independently, and/or obtained from the company that would be necessary for the continued manufacturing of the company's products and are within outsource contractors' legal rights to provide.

2. Which intellectual property should be returned or authorized for destruction?
   a. Prints, drawings, and diagrams
   b. Source code and object code
   c. Samples and prototypes

3. Who will own the capital assets?
   a. Manufacturing equipment
   b. Test equipment
   c. Tooling, jigs, dies, molds, etc.

4. How will the price/cost at which assets will be transferred or sold be determined?
   a. Appraised or fair market value
   b. Net book or depreciated value

5. What are the conditions for return of consigned or loaned materials, property, etc.?

6. What are the provisions for purchasing the capital assets and transfering them to another party for use?

7. How will inventories be dispositioned?
   a. Raw materials
   b. Components
   c. Residual items, finished goods, work in process, and materials not purchased by company

8. Who will have access to and/or copies of pertinent accounting and financial records?

9. How will this outsource contractor fulfill warranty obligations and the other survivor clauses (especially if the supply manager is transferring all the manufacturing equipment, etc.)?

10. Will the current outsource contractor or another supply manager train the new outsource contractor (engineering, production, manufacturing, testing, etc.)? If it will be the current outsource contractor, predetermine the cost components, charges, and fees for this activity.

11. What will be the cost of labor, packaging, palletizing, freight, permits, taxes, tariffs, duties, and so forth for moving the plant, equipment, and inventories from their current location to a new location?

12. What will be the cost of facilitization, unpacking, reinstallation, calibration, alignment, verification, and certification of the plant and equipment at the new location?

The following is recommended for the negotiation: Since the company and the outsource contractor equally benefit over the term of the agreement, upon expiration of the agreement or termination by mutual agreement, the company and the outsource contractor should share costs associated with the exit plan, unless one company unilaterally terminates early for its convenience. In such a case, consideration should be for the early terminating company (if termination is for convenience and not cause) to pay the majority, if not all, of the costs.

WHAT ARE SOME EFFECTIVE TECHNIQUES, METHODS, AND PRACTICES FOR MANAGING OUTSOURCING AGREEMENTS?

There is no magic in managing outsourcing agreements, just the basics. A supply manager would not hire employees and then not spend time assisting them through the learning curve and working to develop and support their future success. It is no different with an outsource contractor. Some key considerations are

- Have a single point of contact or management representative for each company.
- Have scheduled quarterly business reviews (QBRs) to assess progress, review and resolve open issues, discuss performance (by both the company and the outsource contractor), review SLA progress, review KPI performance, set goals, discuss the future business horizon, and so forth.
- On an annual basis, have an extended QBR and include executives from each company and have each organization discuss the "state of the company," plans, projections, product road maps, opportunities, and so forth.
- Coordinate regular site visits.
- Have an assigned executive sponsor from each company.
- Keep the metrics, KPIs, and SLAs current; as business changes, consider revising the KPIs, SLAs and metrics.
- *Bottom line:* communicate, communicate, communicate.

SUMMARY

Contracting for outsourcing requires additional contemplation, thoughtfulness, consideration, and planning which eclipse that normally associated with traditional services agreements (this is not a "three bids in a cloud of dust approach"). Specific to this point are the following:

- A comprehensive SOW is essential to ensure that requirements are well defined.

- SLAs specify in great detail the specific requirements of the SOW and define which party has the responsibility for specific tasks, functions, and requirements.

- KPIs and metrics are critical to effectively measure the outsource contractor's performance (and the company's in some cases) specific to contract requirements and outcomes.

- The costing portion of the agreement needs to be scalable given the likelihood of variations in volume and changes in requirements.

- Costing variables should be predetermined (as much as is practical), especially for potential out-of-scope work activities.

- The supply manager who hires an outsource contractor that is recognized for its "best practices" should let it assist in process reengineering. Don't tell the contractor how to do the work; tell it what outcomes the company requires.

- The agreement will need to be very specific on critical topics dealing with remedies; indemnity; limitation of liability; termination provisions; successors and assigns; noncompete provisions; hiring and rehiring of employees; audit; ownership of data; ownership of work product; ownership of tooling, molds, jigs, drawings, and prints; and nondisclosure among many others.

- A disaster recovery and business continuity plan is essential to any agreement where mission critical activities are outsourced.

- A business downturn plan and an exit plan should be part of an outsourcing agreement to address issues that will likely be encountered due to changes in business requirements and volume fluctuations or at the end of the agreement.

- Risk-reward provisions have limited value in many outsourcing agreements; however, there are business cases where they are appropriate.

- Management of outsourcing agreements is a function of effective, timely, and candid communications. Executive sponsorship and participation is essential to success.

- Planning, process mapping, and scenario analysis (what-if analysis) are important to understand the processes of the supply manager's company, successfully communicate the processes to potential suppliers, and to anticipate problem areas before they become problems.

CLOSING COMMENTS

The following section contains references that may prove helpful for supply managers who are attempting outsourcing for the first time or are interested in improving upon the outsourcing business model or processes currently in use within their organization. Four helpful organizations are

CAPS: Center for Strategic Supply Research hosts a robust search engine that has an excellent index of outsourcing reports, benchmark studies, academic works, and access to practitioners submittals. Further, CAPS has conducted studies on outsourcing critical success factors as well as on outsourcing benchmarks.

The Outsourcing Institute as an exceptional library of referential information and white papers on outsourcing topics. Many of these papers and reports are available for free, and there is an expanded research area available on a membership basis.

Caucus is a membership-based organization that offers white papers and reports as well as training and an interactive chat room where practitioners post requests for information and member subscribers share ideas and concepts, draft language, and provide general support to fellow members.

Institute for Supply Management™ has a database containing many articles focused on outsourcing that are available to the members of the institute.

References for these and others are listed in the section Web-Based Resources at the end of this chapter.

Glossary of Terms and Acronyms Used in This Chapter

AFR: annualized failure rate

AVL: approved vendor list

DPPM: defective parts per million

KPI: key performance indicators

MRB: material review board

QBR: quarterly business review

RFP: request for proposal

RFQ: request for quotation

SKU: stockkeeping unit

SLA: service-level agreement

SOW: statement of work or scope of work

Web-Based Resources

A.T. Kearney (www.atkearney.com/main.taf?p=5,6,1,12).

Arizona State University (wpcarey.asu.edu/pubs/pub_dept.cfm?dept=scm). Search on key word *outsource* or *outsourcing.*

CAPS: Center for Strategic Supply Research (www.capsresearch.org/publications/index.htm). Search on key word *outsource* or *outsourcing.*

Caucus (www.caucusnet.com).

Gartner (outsourcing book) (www4.gartner.com/pages/section.php.id.2215.s.8.jsp).

Institute for Supply Management™ (www.ism.ws/SiteSearch/index.cfm). Search on key word *outsource* or *outsourcing.*

Michigan State University (www.bus.msu.edu/search.html). Search the BROAD Web site and use the key word *outsource* or *outsourcing.*

Outsourcing Institute (www.outsourcing.com).

Outsourcing Journal (www.outsourcing-journal.com).

Outsourcing Benchmarking Association (www.obenchmarking.com).

CHAPTER 11

PROJECT 10X: THE VALUE PROPOSITION AND STRATEGIC IMPACT TO SOURCING AND SUPPLY EFFECTIVENESS

ROBERT M. MONCZKA, PH.D.
Research Professor of Supply Chain Management
W. P. Carey School of Business
Arizona State University
and
Director, Strategic Sourcing & Supply Chain Strategy
CAPS: Center for Strategic Supply Research

PHILLIP L. CARTER, DBA
Professor of Supply Chain Management
Harold E. Fearon Chair of Purchasing
W. P. Carey School of Business
Arizona State University
and
Executive Director
CAPS: Center for Strategic Supply Research

KENNETH J. PETERSEN, PH.D.
Associate Professor of Management
College of Business
Colorado State University

CASEY P. MCDOWELL
Chief Procurement Officer
The Auto Club Group

PROJECT 10X BACKGROUND

Project 10X is an ongoing strategic sourcing and supply chain research and benchmarking initiative combining leading-edge information and Web-based deployment systems to help organizations continuously transform to world-class performance. Information, collected from firms around the world, is leveraged to create content knowledge about current and emerging sourcing and supply chain strategies, practices, and performance for 30 critical strategy areas. The Project 10X Knowledge Management System (KMS.2) enables firms to apply leading-edge knowledge content, conduct internal and external benchmarking, and develop unique and confidential content and assessment questions. KMS.2 is available 24/7 on a worldwide basis. (At this writing, KMS.2 is available only to companies that are major donors to CAPS: Center for Strategic Supply Research.)

Project 10X was established in 2001 by CAPS: Center for Strategic Supply Research under the direction of Robert M. Monczka, Ph.D., to assist companies in their transformation process to leading-edge performance. This continuous-improvement initiative provides the knowledge and tools to organizations to enable them to (1) apply leading-edge strategies and practices established by the Project 10X team from sources worldwide, (2) assess existing internal strengths and weaknesses, share best practices, and conduct external benchmarking with other firms (open or anonymous), (3) apply deployment guidance enabling organizations to incorporate strategic sourcing and supply strategies and practices leading to potential performance improvements of 5 to10 times, and (4) utilize KMS.2, the Web-based knowledge management system to assist in overall or specific transformation processes. See Figure 11–1. (Note: The multiple-of-10 concept does not necessarily imply that an organization must transform to this level in a one-year period.)

Project 10X comprised three ongoing key processes.

1. *Continuous development of leading-edge information and knowledge creation.* Critical approaches utilized by Project 10X to develop the sourcing supply knowledge base include
   - Global vision sessions with leading company executives
   - Survey assessments and results
   - Focused field research
   - Benchmarking
   - Research forums

FIGURE 11–1

Project 10X Elements

| Knowledge Creation | + | KMS.2 | = | Accelerated Transformation and Breakthrough Opportunities |

The Knowledge Creation process leverages Information from firms and sources worldwide using a maturity model structure

Knowledge Management System facilitating data collection assessments, knowledge sharing, collaboration, and project management

- E-research regarding leading-edge practices
- CAPS: Center for Strategic Supply Research
- Other research

    Data and information are regularly updated leading to relevant and current knowledge reflecting latest sourcing and supply strategies and practices.

2. *Creation of value from data and knowledge applied to the sourcing and supply transformation.* The creation of specific strategies, processes, and insights across a broad spectrum of sourcing and supply functions and processes is focused on assisting firms in their transformation efforts. Implementation guidance and good strategy and practice company examples are provided throughout the knowledge content and deployed through KMS.2.

3. *Data and information collection, analysis, and deployment.* The Project 10X team has developed a Web-based knowledge management system (KMS.2) designed to help CAPS member companies access and use data and knowledge for the purpose of understanding and deploying leading-edge sourcing and supply strategies. KMS.2 functionality is detailed in Project 10X KMS.2 tutorials, Web casts, and roundtables conducted on a worldwide basis.

Figure 11–2 provides a detailed overview of Project 10X.

PROJECT 10X KNOWLEDGE CONTENT

Project 10X knowledge content is organized into three areas. Each of these areas contains current information enabling companies to achieve leading-edge performance. These areas are

- The Strategic Sourcing and Supply Chain Excellence (S^3E) Leadership and Management Model and its elements
- 10X assessment questions and ratings
- Ongoing research driving innovation and breakthrough strategies

The S^3E Leadership and Management Model

The Strategic Sourcing and Supply Excellence (S^3E) Leadership and Management Model provides a framework to help understand the strategies necessary to achieve leading-edge performance and the basis on which to organize data and information and new knowledge within KMS.2. Sustainable competitive advantage is the desired end result of transformation within any or all of the critical strategy areas (CSAs) included in the S^3E leadership model. Five key elements make up the

FIGURE   11–2

Project 10X Overview Detail

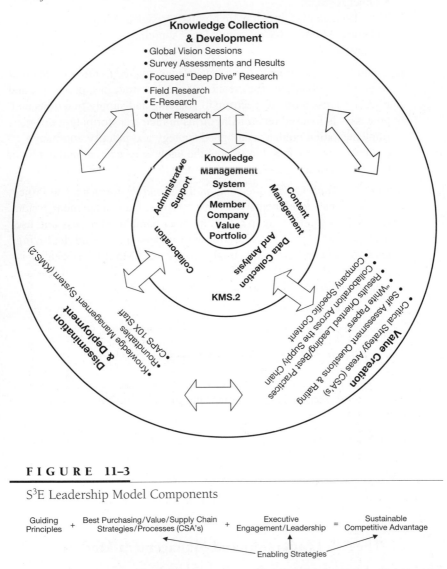

FIGURE   11–3

S³E Leadership Model Components

model, each consisting of multiple CSAs. The basic components of the leadership model are depicted in Figure 11–3.

Figure 11–4 presents specific CSAs for each of the components of the S³E leadership model. Organizations should consider each of the CSAs when developing their strategic plan. This has been found to be important, in varying degrees, to sourcing and supply chain effectiveness.

The Strategic Sourcing and Supply Excellence (S³E) Leadership Model

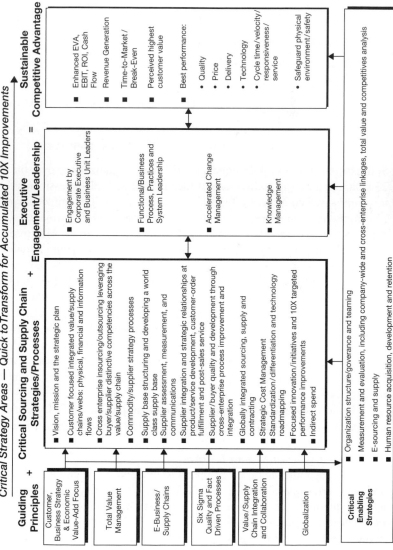

Critical Strategy Areas — Quick toTransform for Accumulated 10X Improvements

Guiding Principles + **Critical Sourcing and Supply Chain Strategies/Processes** + **Executive Engagement/Leadership** = **Sustainable Competitive Advantage**

Customer, Business Strategy & Economic Value-Add Focus

Total Value Management

E-Business/ Supply Chains

Six Sigma Quality and Fact Driven Processes

Value/Supply Chain Integration and Collaboration

Globalization

- Vision, mission and the strategic plan
- Customer focused integrated value/supply chains/webs: physical, financial and information flows
- Cross enterprise insourcing/outsourcing leveraging buyer/supplier distinctive competencies across the value/supply chain
- Commodity/supplier strategy processes
- Supply base structuring and developing a world class supply base
- Supplier assessment, measurement, and communications
- Supplier integration and strategic relationships at product/service development, customer-order fulfillment and post-sales service
- Supplier/buyer quality and development through cross-enterprise process improvement and integration
- Globally integrated sourcing, supply and contracting
- Strategic Cost Management
- Standardization/differentiation and technology roadmapping
- Focused innovation/initiatives and 10X targeted performance improvements
- Indirect spend

- Engagement by Corporate Executive and Business Unit Leaders
- Functional/Business Process, Practices and System Leadership
- Accelerated Change Management
- Knowledge Management

- Enhanced EVA, EBIT, ROI, Cash Flow
- Revenue Generation
- Time-to-Market / Break-Even
- Perceived highest customer value
- Best performance:
  - Quality
  - Price
  - Delivery
  - Technology
  - Cycle time/velocity/ responsiveness/ service
  - Safeguard physical environment/safety

Critical Enabling Strategies

- Organization structure/goverance and teaming
- Measurement and evaluation, including company-wide and cross-enterprise linkages, total value and competitives analysis
- E-sourcing and supply
- Human resource acquisition, development and retention

The knowledge content within each CSA is regularly updated and is structured in KMS.2 as follows:

- CSA definition
- Critical attributes, enablers, and best characteristics
- Key strategies, processes, and practices for the CSA, including implementation steps
- Resulting benefits, where identifiable
- Evolution (future innovation) of the CSA
- Supplemental information from 10X and CAPS studies, benchmarking findings, and research from other sources

In addition, company best practices are provided throughout each CSA.

Maturity Models and 10X Assessment

Self-assessments have been conducted by many organizations over the past 20 to 25 years. In the early 1990s General Electric utilized self-assessments throughout the company. The Malcolm Baldridge process and SCOR utilize assessments to determine the quality level of strategies, practices, and performance. Consulting firms and service providers such as PWC, IBM, A.T. Kearney, McKinsey and Co., and Booz Allen Hamilton utilize assessment questions and methodologies to determine the "current state" of a firm's sourcing and supply strategies and practices. The objective of the assessment process is to establish the baseline (current state) from which to develop recommendations and action plans to achieve the desired state.

These assessments are generally aligned to a "maturity model," which segments a firm's strategies and practices into a number of classifications (generally three or four). Figure 11–5 illustrates a maturity model at a macro level. Naturally, each of the strategy and practice areas is further detailed into lower-level maturity models requiring self-assessment, external review, and possibly internal and external benchmarking.

Project 10X and KMS.2 provides for the application of self-assessments and other approaches to determining the current and future states on a worldwide basis.

Assessment Questions and Ratings

This 10X capability allows a company to evaluate its strengths and weaknesses and the "current state" in each of the CSAs by conducting a self-assessment using a set of questions (typically around 15) based on leading-edge strategy and practice. These assessment questions are driven by the maturity model concept. The highest rating on the rating scales depicts the most innovative and leading-edge strategies. The lowest-rated areas indicate a beginning or early stage.

These assessments may then be compared to multiple internal assessments across chosen areas, business units, and so forth, in a benchmarking and best-practice sharing initiative or to external companies by specific CSAs. Objective performance

FIGURE 11–5

Stages of Sourcing and Supply Chain Strategy Evolution: Macromodel

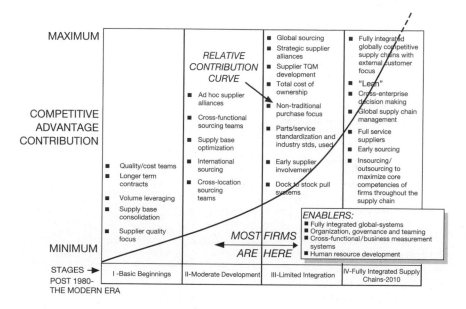

measures are also available, for example, price reduction, inventory, cash-to-cash cycle, and time-to-market. Internal change and improvement can also be tracked over time by applying assessments over periodic intervals.

ONGOING RESEARCH

Field, survey, and other research focused on innovation and breakthrough thinking at leading companies regarding the CSAs continue to be conducted. The results of this ongoing work provide early and robust insights into future developing areas that significantly impact sustainable competitive advantage provided by sourcing and supply. Key insights and leading and best practices from these research findings are incorporated into the knowledge content (see Figure 11–6) and provided through KMS.2.

Organizations and World-Class Sourcing and Supply Performance

Studies and personal observation suggest that sourcing and supply chain organizations often perceive themselves to be more advanced in their sourcing and supply strategies implementation and competitive positioning than is the actual case. When companies fully understand implemented and potential strategies and benchmark

FIGURE 11–6

The Knowledge Components

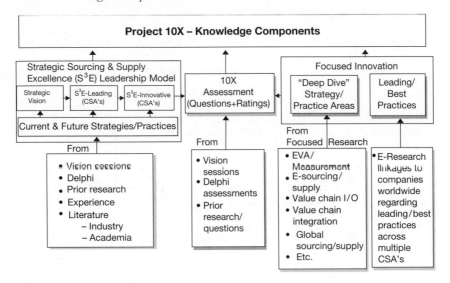

FIGURE 11–7

Degree of Innovation and Implementation

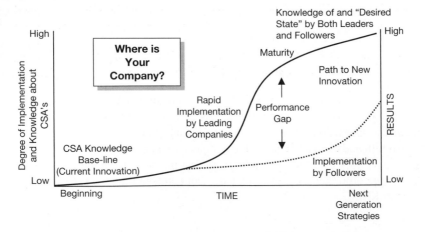

their implemented strategies, and process internally and with other companies viewed as industry leaders, they frequently realize that they are not as advanced as they initially believed.

Figure 11–7 illustrates differences between known and implemented strategies and suggests that knowing about specific strategies and practices is not the same as implementing these strategies and obtaining results. Project 10X through its knowledge content, assessment capabilities, and KMS.2 further provides a firm with both insight into leading-edge strategies and the ability to measure actual implementation.

THE PROJECT 10X VALUE PROPOSITION

Why and how should a company utilize the 10X S³E and the KMS.2? The over-arching goal of Project 10X is to enable significant strategic sourcing and supply transformations and performance improvement (up to 5 to 10 times) in an acceler-ated time frame. Through utilization of the 10X KMS.2, with its knowledge con-tent, assessment tools, and deployment capabilities, companies can drive their transformation processes by leveraging global, leading-edge ideas and infor-mation. In addition, internal and external benchmarking initiatives can be under-taken, collaborative efforts with customers and suppliers facilitated, transformation projects managed, and information confidential to individual companies created and utilized.

The key driver of any transformation initiative is to improve shareholders' and stakeholders' value. The economic value-add (EVA) model best illustrates the high-impact areas to which sourcing and supply must significantly contribute to maximize the organization's EVA (see Figure 11–8). Project 10X can assist com-panies in enhancing their sourcing and supply organization's contribution to EVA by not only providing insights about strategies and practices focused on reducing cost but also by additional insights relevant to enhancing value through revenue enhancement and asset utilization.

In addition, Project 10X's knowledge content and KMS.2 can be applied within a business case framework as illustrated in Figure 11–9. Both the 10X

FIGURE 11–8

Economic Value-Add Structure

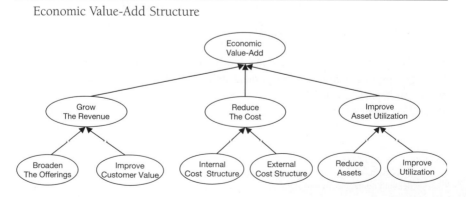

Project 10X Business Case Framework

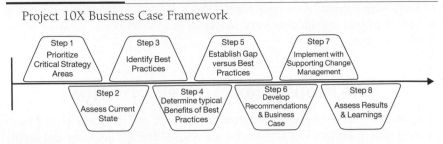

knowledge content and KMS.2 will provide useful information, data collection, and analysis capabilities for each step of the business case analysis (additional applications of 10X knowledge content and KMS.2 will be described in following sections).

Benefits of the 10X business case framework include the following:

- Provides a structured approach that accelerates development of a business case while offering company-specific flexibility

- Uses cross-industry best practices and improvement levers[1] to improve the credibility of the analysis and recommendations

- Serves as the foundation of a systematic transformation process

- Encourages a single-view opportunity assessment (versus multiple assessments) across the company

- Provides Web-based access and an integrated knowledge management system to improve worldwide use

- Provides evergreen updates to best practices by industry, academia, and consultants

KMS.2: A CRITICAL ENABLER

KMS.2 is a user-friendly, Web-based interactive knowledge management system. Content management, data collection, analysis, dissemination, collaboration, and project management capabilities exist. KMS.2 may be used by individuals, natural work groups, leadership and management, and value chains and networks to achieve world-class performance.

KMS.2 offers a variety of robust functionality enabling numerous practical applications of 10X knowledge content, assessments, and collaboration. However,

---

1 A lever is defined as a tool or action that can significantly improve business performance (e.g., demand management and supplier development).

FIGURE 11–10

Project 10X: KMS.2 Structure and Capability Profile

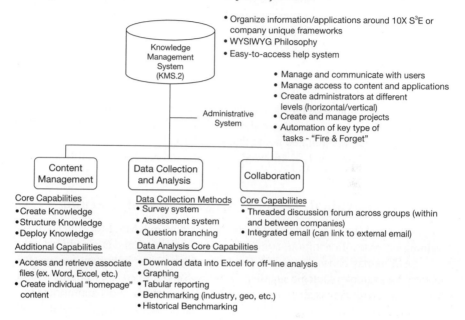

companies will find many unique ways to apply 10X knowledge content and KMS.2 beyond the applications to be described.

Figure 11–10 provides the KMS.2 structure and insight into its use.

PROJECT 10X AND KMS.2 APPLICATIONS

The following are selected primary 10X knowledge content and KMS.2 application areas that individually or collectively can be used by an organization to transform its strategic sourcing and supply processes.

1. Individual, team, or organization learning

2. Internal assessments and benchmarking

3. External benchmarking

4. Unique knowledge and/or assessment creation, including surveys

5. Data analysis

6. Consensus building

7. Forum creation for internal and external collaboration

8. Priority setting

   9. Strategy development and alignment

   10. Strategy deployment

   11. 10X white paper presentation and deployment of other research reports from CAPS

   12. Continuous evaluation for innovation or breakthrough improvement opportunities

We now provide a brief discussion and one or more example scenarios with details about potential uses for each application area. Actual or "armchair" company scenarios are used to demonstrate the practical use of the Project 10X–KMS.2 leadership model. It should be noted that these examples are not intended to capture all potential uses of 10X knowledge content and KMS.2 capabilities.

1. Individual, Team, or Organizational Learning

Organizations can use the knowledge content residing in KMS.2 for education and training purposes. In addition, company-unique information can also be added.

A firm may choose a specific critical strategy area as important for transformation, for example, strategic supplier alliances (SSAs). To ensure a common baseline of knowledge across all company stakeholders about the most appropriate way to deploy SSAs, all persons would be asked to access KMS.2 and review the SSA knowledge content, including the implementation steps. Each person would be asked to add any additional information regarding SSAs unique to the company for stakeholder review. SSA implementation consensus could then be developed through a series of forums, e-mails, and telephone conferences or videoconferences facilitated by KMS.2.

Firms can also use KMS.2 knowledge content deployment features to conduct educational and training sessions across the firm for any or all CSAs. These sessions can be facilitated by sourcing and supply leaders.

2. Conduct Internal Assessments

KMS.2 provides an internal assessment capability, whereby companies can assess their current state by responding to specific questions for each CSA. They can also establish their desired state based on the assessment questions and CSA content knowledge. Assessment questions and KMS.2 can also be used by organizations to establish gaps between their current and potential future state (maturity model), across business units or other defined areas within a company (internal assessment and benchmarking), or between different companies and geographies (external benchmarking), which is discussed in more detail in the following section.

Member companies can also create additional assessment questions and/or modify existing questions creating a customized approach to meet company-specific situations. Organizations overall, including those with multiple locations and functions, can individually or collectively conduct internal assessments providing a spectrum of results and ultimately a baseline for future actions or validation of previously implemented strategies and initiatives. The process includes five steps:

1. Target several critical strategy areas from the 10X S^3E leadership model for assessment.

2. Select appropriate individuals in each business unit to complete the assessments by a specified date (each assessment can be done by a team or an individual).

3. Identify key strengths and weaknesses within each relevant CSA and establish the current state.

4. Develop and execute action plans to close gaps with a desired state.

5. Measure and track progress.

Assessment Question Structure

Each person or team answers approximately 15 assessment questions for each chosen CSA. For each question, a rating from 1 to 12 is given using the scale shown, which depicts four maturity model stages.

1 2 3	4 5 6	7 8 9	10 11 12
Basic	Moderately advanced	Very advanced	Future leading-edge and innovative

Scenario 1: Conduct Internal Assessments Against Existing Performance. A leadership team within a distribution company decided to assess the company's current state for structuring and maintaining a world-class supply base. A representative for each of 11 global site locations was identified by the team leader, and an assessment was initiated using the KMS.2. The following is a sample assessment question rated by each respondent (question 7 out of 16):

> Are the detailed determination, evaluation and ratings of current suppliers formalized and utilized to increase supply base contribution to EVA (economic value-add) and drive toward a world-class supply base?

The possible responses were

> *Rating of 1, 2, or 3 (basic).* Detailed supplier selection processes do not exist. Internal systems and structures are not in place that link supplier performance to organizational goals and objectives. The ability to gather aggregated company supplier data is limited.

> *Rating of 4, 5, or 6 (moderately advanced).* Your organization recognizes the need to aggregate data globally to compare commodity or purchase family total cost of ownership (TCO). Quality processes are developed and beginning to be deployed to evaluate and rate specific supplier performance against established goals and objectives. Supplier prioritization

activities occur based on EVA, and supplier globalization and reduction efforts are becoming ongoing business practice.

Rating of 7, 8, or 9 (very advanced). Your organization has a highly advanced supplier selection process and associated performance metrics. These processes are used to ensure quality. Global suppliers are aligned with company goals and objectives. The supply chain processes enable cross-enterprise collaboration and multitiered supply chain information transfers to improve cash flow, financial performance, quality, cycle times, and product and service development. Poorly performing suppliers that cannot meet continuing challenges are eliminated.

Rating of 10, 11, or 12 (future leading edge and innovative). Your organization has a strategic and detailed supplier selection and measurement process. Cross-functional and cross-organizational teams develop goals and objectives. These processes are e-enabled to collaborate with real-time data internally and externally. You have achieved virtual integration with the supply base.

The distribution company completed this assessment, and the KMS.2 calculated an average rating of 4.37. Additionally, KMS.2 reported that the 90th percentile for all company responses in this critical strategy area was 7.14. Recognizing the opportunity to improve, despite a few individual questions on which the company scored high, a formalized action plan was developed based on the gaps against the identified desired state. This company reduced its supply base by 30 percent while adding strategic suppliers in more competitive regions and created a more disciplined and aligned set of category and commodity strategies with which to execute future strategies. Six months following the improvement initiative, the same respondents completed the same assessment and rated their performance at 8.59. A clear improvement with measurable results provided a platform for repeating this process for other critical strategy areas.

Scenario 2: Establish Baseline Performance from Self-Assessments. A similar approach as in Scenario 1 was performed by another company that determined its average rating to be 7.44. It also determined that there were opportunities to improve in specific areas related to the specific questions in the self-assessment. However, based on other critical strategy areas that the company perceived to require more dedicated effort, they decided to place this on the "back burner" until a later date with only minor actions taken by this group.

Scenario 3: Develop Strategies and Business Plans Utilizing CSAs as a Foundation. A supply chain organization within a consumer or commercial technology-based company wanted to develop one-, three-, and five-year business plans for transforming its purchasing and supply organization from a tactically driven operation to a strategically focused organization. This firm had a few documented sourcing and supply strategies in place such as cost savings, supplier assessment and measurement, and commodity category and supplier strategy process, but wanted to compare its overall functional strategy with the critical strategy areas provided by Project 10X. The company utilized KMS.2 by specifically focusing on the CSAs knowledge content to establish a baseline of leading and innovative strategies and practices versus its current state. The leadership group divided the reviews throughout the organization based on subject matter expertise. Each team had five strategy areas for which it was asked to complete a comparison of the existing strategies with those outlined in the S3E leadership model. In many areas this company did not have any strategy outlined, and therefore the Project 10X strategy defaulted as the strategy to use until further review. Each team outlined the gaps with the existing strategies to those provided within the CSAs. From this the teams were able to identify where the company was strongest and where more focus and attention needed to be placed. The teams completed the one-, three-, and five-year business plans based on the outcomes of this initiative and greatly improved the company's focus in setting and meeting savings targets (8 percent in the first year), achieved a stronger alignment to enterprise objectives creating a stronger perception of the organization among company and functional leadership, and provided greater clarity to the supply management staff resulting in greater productivity.

3. Conduct External Benchmarking

External benchmarking is similar to internal benchmarking (across internal business units). However, with external benchmarking a company can compare its ratings for and within a particular CSA with anonymous external company responses. It can be useful to benchmark external companies to better gauge the current state and potential importance or value associated with undertaking a transformation in a particular area. A company might conclude that what it thought was a good process through internal assessments is far behind other organizations. Alternatively, a company might determine what it thought was a poor process is considerably higher rated when compared externally. A company might conclude that it is doing much better on average than most other companies and decide not to take immediate action or may chose to address an area much sooner to close a specific gap and benefit from potential results.

External (and internal) benchmarking results show the assessment question, company rating, number of responses, average rating of all respondents, and the 90th percentile across respondent ratings. A company benchmarking against external companies has the ability to select potential partners and send a confidential, anonymous request through the KMS.2 communication platform or simply select a profile based on the five segments that follow to compare responses from other companies. This can also be conducted in an "open" format where the parties agree to an external benchmark with all known users. Just like the internal assessment format, a company is able to structure and compare responses by

1. Geography
2. Industry

3. Product or service type

4. Business type

5. Purchase type

Scenario 1: Conduct Anonymous External Benchmarking The same company that completed an internal assessment earlier and judgmentally determined that it was fairly strong based on that assessment decided to compare its ratings against external organizations. The company discovered that despite a favorable rating based on the internal assessment (7.14 at the 90th percentile), the external companies it benchmarked against had 9.14 at the 90th percentile. In an effort to achieve a leadership position this organization initiated greater focus and aggressive actions to improve its position. Actions included supply base reduction by another 20 percent by consolidating supply opportunities combined with an enhanced supplier and functional performance measurement system. Eight months later, after completion of the series of improvement initiatives, another external assessment was conducted, and the company's rating increased to 8.93 placing it near the 90th percentile. Additional actions continued to be taken with anticipation that another external assessment would be completed at a later date to gauge the company's improvement toward a leadership position within this critical strategy area.

Scenario 2: Conduct Open-Forum Benchmarking Supply leaders from six different companies decided at a CAPS Research executive roundtable meeting that they were collectively interested in conducting an external benchmarking assessment in the area of insourcing and outsourcing strategies. They coordinated an effort to have one key function within each of their companies complete the 10X insourcing and outsourcing assessment and allowed the ratings to be made available to each company with identification. The results showed that four of the six companies had strengths (ratings ranging from 9 to 12) in at least one of every question area, and the two remaining companies had ratings from 7 to 9. Based on these findings, a conference call was conducted with each company sharing insights into its processes. Two separate one-on-one benchmarking sessions were also conducted among four of the companies allowing for specific content areas to be delved into more deeply. Each company derived value from the external benchmarking, and each has shown significant improvements from the initial assessments.

4. Create Unique and Confidential Knowledge and Assessments

Knowledge content in KMS.2 consists of knowledge specific to each of the critical strategy areas. The knowledge is organized into definitions, critical attributes, a process model, results, and evolution and breakthroughs for each CSA. The CSAs can be imported to a company's private work space (confidential to the organization) and modified to better align to a specific environment as necessary. In addition, the self-assessments can also be modified or additional questions added that might be particularly meaningful to a specific organization or company situation (again, without visibility by other companies). An added feature of KMS.2 is the ability to develop and conduct specific surveys of topical interest to the organization.

Scenario 1: Customize Assessment Questions for a Company's Specific Needs The leadership team at an energy services company decided to use the 10X knowledge management system as a focal point of the supply management organization's strategic plan. The company added a link to 10X on its supply management intranet site for easy access and to encourage regular use of the knowledge management system and the knowledge content. To avoid creating a separate company-specific knowledge base, the 10X KMS.2 provides for unique company content and CSAs to be added to the company site. The company site administrator can add any content to the system that the leadership team wants accessible to internal users. For example, in the global sourcing and the supplier development CSAs, the company added four additional questions to each of these strategy area assessments that pertained specifically to its installed supplier relationship management (SRM) software. This helped the company to determine how respective users were utilizing the various functions of this new software in addition to the assessment questions that already existed. The company determined that its SRM strategy was being accepted by the organization. It also found that certain aspects of the software were not being utilized to the full extent possible. Actions were then put in place to ensure full utilization of all functionality.

Scenario 2: Customize CSAs to Meet a Company's Needs A company can modify specific components of particular knowledge content for a CSA within its own Web or work space and allow access only to company employees. One example was a food manufacturer who generally liked the indirect procurement CSA content, but wanted to add specific company information and knowledge to a few sections of this strategy area to reflect company policy and practice. The manufacturer was able to customize the sourcing process to include some direct goods and services that would not normally be defined as an indirect procurement function. This was easily accommodated by creating a direct link to the 10X KMS.2 and adding this company-unique knowledge, importing the appropriate 10X CSA, and making modifications. Only this company had access to the modifications. The result was that this company now had a documented strategy that was reflective of its business structure and provided greater clarity for the supply management organization.

Scenario 3: Develop a Survey to Assist in Capturing Leading and Best-Practice Knowledge A medical services provider was looking for specific insights about an e-procurement solution to implement across 44 locations. Its initial due diligence included working with several application solution providers, which proved valuable for gathering information but was inadequate for defining the services it should initially pursue. The medical services provider decided to create a survey using 10X KMS.2 functionality and deployed the survey to 10 member companies who had agreed to participate. After the completed surveys were received and the results analyzed, it was clear that the majority of companies surveyed chose to initially implement a basic catalog approach before migrating to more extensive solutions such as reverse auction and supply planning. This aligned well with this medical services provider's needs and provided for a full implementation of catalog ordering in less than six months.

5. Conduct Data Analysis

An important aspect of determining priorities, developing strategies, and seeking leadership approval and buy-in is the ability to capture data, conduct analyses, and display the results in a meaningful manner. KMS.2 has various functionalities that allow companies to create a variety of reports or export data to other programs for more complex statistical analysis. Results can be displayed graphically as spider charts, lists, circle diagrams, bar charts, and so forth.

6. Consensus Building

Building consensus among key persons is critical when change is undertaken. This is especially so when resistance to the change is expected. One way to gain acceptance of change is through a collaborative forum of internal and/or external participants who are made part of the approval process or who are impacted by the change. The following scenarios illustrate this point.

Scenario 1: Develop a Survey to Assist in Capturing Broad Organizational Input
A newly appointed vice president of supply management wanted to quickly build consensus among her leadership team about the future direction of the supply organization. As a member company of CAPS she had access to the Project 10X KMS.2. She asked each of her direct reports to review all critical strategy areas and list the top 10 for their company. This was accomplished by creating a survey using KMS.2 functionality and sending the survey to predefined groups or teams. Each group provided its input via this online tool.

From the survey results, she was able to quickly understand the leadership team's perspectives about the most critical strategy areas. From this starting point, she conducted several strategy development sessions with the team to gain agreement about which strategy areas to focus on in the short and long term. The 10X knowledge management system provided a focal point for the team to move quickly forward.

Scenario 2: Using KMS.2 as an Educational Platform to Develop a Team Solution
A vice president of supply management wanted to quickly implement a strategic supplier alliance program for a key commodity. It had been determined that the supply organization lacked experience in developing partner relationships that could lead to mutual gains for the buying and supplying organizations. To remedy the situation, key people from various cross-functional business units were given access to 10X KMS.2 and instructed to review the knowledge and processes related to supplier alliances.

Commodity team members, with representatives from all business units, then collaborated to identify those aspects of the buyer-supplier relationship that were missing and develop a relationship-building process appropriate to the company's culture, past relationships, and future goals.

7. Develop a Forum (Collaborate Internally and Externally)

KMS.2 has the capability to post a question(s) and allow "threaded" responses to be accumulated over a defined period of time. This discussion can be conducted internally within a sourcing and supply chain function, among cross-functional organizations, or between a company and its external customers and suppliers. The system also accommodates the capability to send new responses directly to an individual's e-mail address. This ensures that the opportunity to comment is not ignored even if the person is not actively reviewing the forum functionality of KMS.2.

Scenario 1: Utilization of the Forum Function to Allow for Open Dialogue for Developing and Evaluating a New Strategy A supply chain organization considered an e-sourcing and supply strategy that was centered around reverse auctions. However, leaders were concerned that suppliers would view this negatively and would believe that price was the only determinant in sourcing decisions. Since the supply base was far too large for a face-to-face conference, the company decided to pose a series of questions related to anticipated concerns the suppliers would have about reverse auctions. They decided to utilize KMS.2 forum capability. The forum window was open for one week allowing for an active exchange of ideas, a format to debate specific points, and all concerns to be addressed. This forum proved to be worthwhile, as many of the suppliers were much more comfortable with the approach based on the types of commodities intended for this auction process. In addition, the suppliers appreciated being asked for their comments and the opportunity to convey their concerns.

8. Establish Priorities

Companies have identified determining sourcing and supply priorities as one of their primary issues. The 10X assessment (both internal and external) process often helps determine priorities by identifying CSA weaknesses and strengths. The CSAs can then be prioritized based on the various factors that companies evaluate when making "transformation investments."

One of the first priority-setting tasks of any leadership team is to select three or four critical strategy areas on which to focus. The thought process that the team must engage in to select the most promising CSAs from the full set of 10X strategy opportunities is shown in Figure 11–11. This figure illustrates selected factors that influence priority setting and the resulting 10X CSA focus for transformation. The following steps directionally lead to the appropriate quadrant.

Priority-Setting Steps

Step 1. Identify those CSAs that are significant problem areas or offer obvious opportunity.

Step 2. Conduct a second screening whereby both the *business and strategic impact* and *complexities of implementation* are fully determined by the sourcing and supply leadership team and other key personnel.
Suggested factors for analysis for each of these include the following:
- Business and strategic impact
    1. Is this a core competency of sourcing and supply to contribute to the competitive advantage of the firm?
    2. What is the financial impact on the firm of performing the CSA well or poorly—on revenue, assets, cost?
    3. Does the customer demand excellence in the CSA for the firm to be a key supplier?

FIGURE 11–11

Project 10X: CSA Priority-Setting Process

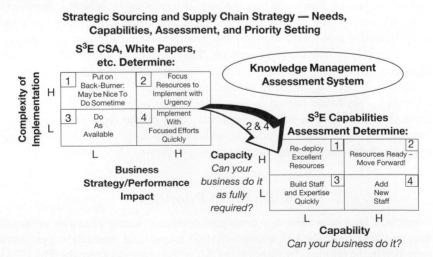

4. Does the firm have to do well to have a strong supply base in critical commodity areas?
5. How well does the firm have to perform in a CSA to create the correct internal and external perceptions?
- Complexity of implementation
    1. Availability of required data and knowledge
    2. Narrow or broad cross-functional changes
    3. Number and complexity of process steps
    4. Available human resources with knowledge and skill capability
    5. Available financial resources and/or what ability to obtain
    6. Culture and attitude toward change
    7. Company's organizational structure

Step 3. Assign a low or high rating to each CSA in terms of the impact on business strategy and performance—from 1 low to 10 high.

Step 4. Assign a low or high rating to the complexity of implementation—from 1 low to 10 high.

Step 5. Based on steps 1 and 2, establish the quadrant for each CSA.

Step 6. CSAs that fall into quadrant 1 (Implement Quickly) or quadrant 2 (Focus Resources to Implement with Urgency) would then be subjected to an assessment of capabilities.

Step 7. Assign a low or high rating to capability. High capability means the organization has the resources and infrastructure to implement the CSA.

Step 8. Assign a high or low rating to capacity. High capacity means business can implement the CSA as required.

Step 9. Determine which quadrant the CSA is in and take appropriate action.

Scenario 1: Establishing Priorities through Assessments and Collaboration
The newly hired senior supply chain executive of an electronics company wanted to identify those strategic initiatives requiring top priority. After about a month on the job, she determined that of the total critical strategy areas identified in Project 10X (the company was an existing CAPS member) the company should focus on 10 areas. However, with limited staff and budget constraints, it became clear that only three to four CSAs could immediately be addressed. She assigned subteams to conduct self-assessments for each of the 10 strategy areas. Once the assessment ratings were determined and the lower-rated strategy areas revealed, she reviewed these strategies against the company's objectives, budget, resources, capacity, and systems available. (This is similar to the approach displayed in Figure 11–11.) Combining all factors and interactive and collaborative input (via the forum function within KMS.2) from supply chain–activated personnel and from other functions in the firm, the top four strategy areas were determined. This same approach was used six months later as the next four strategies were being determined. The result

was a prioritized set of action plans that were aligned with business needs, organizational recommendations, and the executive's leadership judgment.

9. Develop and Align Strategy

Once the leadership team has set priorities for the next planning period, the 10X knowledge content can be used to develop the approach to implement leading-edge practices. For example, suppose the team selected strategic supplier alliances as one of the company's critical strategy areas. The process for developing a transformation strategy might include the following:

1. Review the integrated PowerPoint presentation on strategic supplier alliances.

2. Conduct an in-depth study of the content about strategic supplier alliances, including
   a. Definition
   b. Critical attributes
   c. Process model
   d. Results
   e. Evolution and breakthroughs, including company best practices

3. Determine where the company is currently positioned (current state and desired state) in the CSA by having a number of individuals complete the self-assessment for this area.

4. Apply the prescribed appropriate implementation steps to achieve the defined future state. The process for implementing strategic supplier alliances includes six steps.
   Step 1. Establish business needs and requirements.
   Step 2. Define sourcing strategies for purchase families.
   Step 3. Define alliances and supplier alliance criteria.
   Step 4. Identify, assess, and select allied partners.
   Step 5. Structure and develop alliance relationships.
   Step 6. Implement, manage, and assess alliance relationship.

Each of the CSAs included in 10X provides a comprehensive structure for each of the strategies. A company may decide that the CSA can be incorporated (aligned) as it is presented or that there are some unique company characteristics that require modification to the CSA. The 10X CSAs provide companies a foundation on which unique considerations and processes may be built.

Scenario 1: Customization of CSAs to Meet S pecific Requirements and Needs
In the scenario presented, four strategies were to be implemented. However, one of the strategy areas required additional detail and customization to capture unique aspects of the company's business. KMS.2 allows modifications without any tech-

nical support or unique programming requirements. Although this strategy required modification to meet company needs, significant time was saved by having a baseline strategy.

10. Deploy Strategy

In developing company sourcing and supply strategies, 10X CSAs provide guidance in strategy development and deployment. However, since every organization and company has numerous factors to manage, strategy modifications are not unusal.

In addition, KMS.2 provides project management capability for organizations to track and enhance deployment of the strategic plan. Functionality such as forums, e-mails, tracking to schedule, and strategy and practice enhancement significantly assist in deployment. Other functions are also able to review strategies and their deployment and provide enhancement suggestions.

11. Review White Papers, Vision Session Findings, and Other Leading-Edge Research Provided by Project 10X, CAPS Studies, and Others

In addition to current critical strategy areas, Project 10X and CAPS continually conduct research focused on progressive and emerging strategies, best practices, and other meaningful topics that firms find timely and useful. It is recommended that these other research outputs be reviewed on a periodic basis to allow a firm to take advantage of leading and innovative information. Many companies are finding a host of benefits from these white papers, deep-dive studies, and leading-edge practices. Companies recognize that a strategy gains additional credibility within their organizations if they provide evidence that the strategy has provided positive results at other companies. Importantly, Project 10X is dynamic and provides information that is continually updated, global, and leading-edge to assist ongoing transformations at companies worldwide.

12. Evaluate Process for Innovation and Continuous-Improvement Opportunities

CSAs focus on innovation and processes companies should use to achieve 5 to 10 times improvement. In addition, Project 10X, by combining knowledge content and KMS.2 functionality, provides a continuous and dynamic means for companies to gain access to leading-edge strategies and practices enabling sourcing and supply transformations. Leading supply chain management companies are increasingly considering Project 10X as one of their primary approaches to obtain leading and innovative strategies and processes for driving their sourcing and supply organization's transformation to world-class leadership.

CONCLUDING COMMENTS

Project 10X, combining leading-edge knowledge content and KMS.2, provides one means for companies to achieve leading-edge performance in sourcing and supply. Project 10X can be applied to each of the following "keys to success" of a sourcing and supply transformation initiative. Developed over time, these keys are based on successful company experience.

Keys to Success (Experience Based)

- Absolute (or relative) identification of leading-edge, best, and good strategies and practices (the model)
- Conducting valid assessments—current and future
- Establishing correct action plans, including resources—leadership team driven
- Priority setting
- Total vertical and horizontal communication and achieving buy-in
- Project management
- Measurement and rewards
- Learning
- Focus, focus, focus on the priorities established

Project 10X
The Project 10X Web site is at www.caps10x.org, for sponsor companies or you can go to www.capsresearch.org for information about CAPS.

CAPS: Center for Strategic Supply Research
CAPS: Center for Strategic Supply Research asks each sponsoring corporation to provide $12,500 annually to support the research program. Sponsors receive invitations to the annual executive roundtables, best-practices workshops, and critical issues/partnership conferences. Sponsors have access to Project 10X and are provided with published focus studies, benchmarking reports, and best-practices studies.

THE FOUR CORE SUPPORTS
OF EVERY SUPPLY CHAIN

Whether an organization recognizes it or not, it has a supply chain. For many years the concept of a supply chain was illustrated using a physical chart showing the organization in the middle with suppliers on one side and customers on the other. Today, the design of a supply chain, or supply chains, includes the physical flows and also financial ones. These include the settlement processes, flows of cash, investments in assets, and presence of debt. Too, supply chains have a subcomponent of an informational flow and network. These include order processes to suppliers and from customers but also the triggering of inventory and service movements within the organization. Relationships are the natures of interactions with outsiders as well as with those throughout the entire organization.

The chapters in this part provide the four building blocks of all supply chains. Once the chain is defined strategically, from Part 2, then the specific physical, financial, informational, and relational component chains can be defined.

CHAPTER 12

PHYSICAL SUPPLY CHAIN DESIGN AND LINKAGES

Joseph L. Cavinato, Ph.D., C.P.M.
Professor of Supply Management
Thunderbird, The Garvin School of International Management
and
Director
A.T. Kearney Center for Strategic Supply Leadership
Institute for Supply Management™

Supply is about acquiring and accessing goods and services. Its final boundary traditionally ended when the order was placed; leaving the transportation and delivery to the supplier. In recent decades the beginning and end of supply has expanded from buying to orchestrating and obtaining value throughout newly identified chains and networks. This chapter presents concepts, tools, and trends involving the physical attributes of supply chains.

The physical parts of supply chains involve the actual movement and flows of goods and services into, through, and out of the firm. Early transportation deregulation in the United States and more recently in other countries has brought the traffic and transportation function into purchasing. Physical supply chains were then considered a key organizational service to be purchased, and it was logical to combine their purchase with that of the sourcing, negotiating, and transacting of other goods and services. In recent years, the field has expanded to where supply professionals are overseeing the entire flow for seeking landed cost, time cycle, agility, and other value efficiencies.

This chapter presents the core physical supply chain components, which are manufacturing, transportation, warehousing, inventories, and logistics information systems that directly deal with product and service flows. Too, the use of third-party logistics providers is discussed in the transportation and warehousing sections. It also presents how they are often crafted together into a system by companies. The chapter finishes with supply chain agility, a new attribute that is increasingly needed in today's quickening globalization and dynamism.

PHYSICAL SUPPLY CHAIN COMPONENTS

This section presents each of the components in terms of (1) the key points of efficiency and value and (2) the megatrends associated with them.

Manufacturing

The production of goods is increasingly viewed as a key activity within the supply chain. This is a departure from 100 years of viewing manufacturing as being central to a company. Many firms today view their manufacturing as being one of the possible product supply sources for providing customers with its salable goods. Outside manufacturers are the alternative ones.

Two key points of efficiency for manufacturing that are important today are the quest for low-cost labor and the quest for consistently high quality of product. The low-cost labor quest started in the 1950s when American manufacturing (the only industrial sector in the world not destroyed in World War II) sought to minimize the effects of unionization and higher wages. This started a shift toward low-cost labor in the following areas as listed by decade:

1950s. U.S. South

1960s. Japan

1970s. Korea, Taiwan, Hong Kong, and Singapore

1980s. Mexican maquiladoras, Malaysia, Thailand, Philippines

1990s. Vietnam, China, India

2000–2005. China, India, Bangladesh

Each decade brought a shift toward other geographies, and purchasing managers in this period were continually finding and developing manufacturing sources in an ever-widening and more complex global setting. The low-cost labor quest caused unique growth in the countries involved. The initial objective was to reduce labor costs, but this progressed into the need to develop manufacturing depth with quality enhancement, and then finally to today's emphasis on technology and innovation.

Quality consistency is a key need today. With decades of quality initiatives [e.g., quality circles, statistical process control (SPC), reengineering, Six Sigma, and the International Organization for Standardization (ISO)], the demand today is for a known and consistent quality. Even in today's low-cost countries there is an emerging trend toward automation, not so much for the further lowering of labor cost, but for the need for consistent quality output for global product success.

Manufacturing Megatrends

Several key trends are afoot in this decade related to manufacturing that affect supply managers. One is that manufacturing is decreasingly viewed as something special or core that a firm must do itself. Many forces have caused this senior management perception including the drive to reduce assets and head count as well as the need to increase flexibility in seeking new capabilities and technologies. This has caused a rise in outsourcing, offshoring, and other uses of outsiders. Supply managers have moved from buying raw materials to feed their plants to seeking, leading, and managing outside manufacturing even at great distances.

A second megatrend, one that is inside manufacturing, is toward simplification and increased efficiency of operations. This is found in many forms. Development and launch cycles will be more and more compressed. Flatter bills of material will be sought so as to reduce manufacturing complexity within the organization, especially with the higher-labor-cost original equipment manufacturers (OEMs) at the end of production supply chains such as automobile assembly, machinery, and even electronics. Noncritical items will be increasingly outsourced. Examples in manufacturing are maintenance as well as purchasing and inventory management of maintenance, repair, and operating (MRO) supplies. Still another is the reduction in switchover in production from one product line to another. One paper company used to take eight hours to switch from running one form of pulp-to-paper line to another; today it takes less than an hour. The efficient production run of one lot size of one unit (as opposed to large production runs) is a sought-after goal in many industries such as computer assembly and other electronics. These all require increased flexibility. They also expose the factory to the customer. In fewer industries is the produce-to-stock mode of planning used. Today it is increasingly the produce-to-order mode, and manufacturing flexibility is the key to this end.

These trends are leading to new thinking about widespread manufacturing. A growing number of global firms are seeking ways to make management over many time zones and deepening sets of supplier tiers more efficient. Addressing this complexity is central to the management efficiency of seeking the benefits of global manufacturing and presence. Another new thinking is now balancing the initial push to low-cost manufacturing in terms of identifying a global total cost of doing business. A few companies have noted that the advantage of a lower cost of labor was in their case eaten up with the increased cost of capital and inventory afloat in the world. Some companies have actually brought back some manufacturing to Europe and the Americas as it is more cost efficient when factoring in shipping times and customer response needs. This is leading some companies to create or outsource manufacturing in the three daylight time zones of the world: (1) Asia, (2) Europe, Africa, Middle East, (3) and the Americas. This gives rise to an opportunity for supply professionals to identify and educate the rest of their organizations about a total cost of business from a sourcing, manufacturing, and landed product and service standpoint.

Transportation

After manufacturing, transportation is often the second-largest supply chain cost in a company. In some industries it is a key cost driver that impacts sourcing and the ability of a company to compete in certain customer markets. The complexity of transportation is in its many choices and varieties. These range from various forms of ocean transport to air and sea trade-offs, and many land options. Too, transportation is very sensitive to labor costs (the highest cost component in most transportation modes) and energy (often the second highest cost).

Transportation Megatrends

Transportation comprises many individual subindustries and presents a mosaic of choice for supply professionals. Each and all share some common trends for the remainder of this decade.

Security is an overriding concern today. There are over 10,000 ships in the world. The United States has 5,000 coastal facilities and 361 ports. Post-9/11 actions have identified and tightened oversight of product flows not only in the United States but in other parts of the world as well. The current time represents one in which new administrative regulations and systems are being rolled out and shippers and receivers are required to learn what they are and to adopt them. The United States, for example, requires prenotification of shipments being loaded onto ships and planes bound for the United States. Too, inspection of ships 96 hours prior to arrival at port all slow down the supply chain speed. These effects tend to be in the forms of increased compliance requirements, lengthening of transit times, and increased documentation. In the food industry there are trends emerging in the food supply chain toward documenting and attesting to the integrity of the goods from field to table.

Congestion is another megatrend as a result of inadequate planning and investment in many of the transportation infrastructures in the world. One example is European railroads and highways. The opening of EU borders in 1992 brought greatly increased traffic flows without increases in rail and highway rights-of-way. One estimate has the prime origin-destination highway routes as being 60 percent congested by 2010, up from 35 percent in 2002. In this United States the 95 prime interstate highway origin-destination routes are now 5 percent congested, which is expected to rise to 30 percent by 2010. Congestion deteriorates delivery reliability and raises the cost per mile or kilometer of anything that is being moved (as well as the return of the vehicle from deliveries). Too, dock congestion is plaguing U.S. West Coast, Chinese, and many European ports. This congestion is linked with inadequate rail and highway capacity to deliver inland. As supply chains lengthen and involve many more suppliers in different regions, transportation capacity and transit times will increasingly have to be factored in and not taken for granted.

Transportation costs are a continuing supply chain element and require constant attention. The two prime drivers here are labor and energy. Transportation costs tend to be specific to a country or to a home flag carrier's labor costs. Sourcing goods in a low-cost labor market will still require ocean carriage and land transportation, which are influenced by the costs of various transport labor markets. In the United States there is a shortage of qualified and licensed truck drivers and rail workers. Europe enjoys a greater percentage of owner-operators who tend to be lower in cost, but the congestion and capital cost of their vehicles outweigh that labor advantage. Energy costs are dominated by the price of a barrel of oil, and many estimates state that the days of $10 per barrel are over and that $40 to $50 will be the norm from here on out. In the EU a new environmental tax started in 2004 and charged to truckers has caused an upward of 45 percent increase in vehicle cost per kilometer (depending upon the country). This increases the cost per mile and causes carriers to wait hours or days to fully load their vehicles, trains, or planes; and all this impacts tightly orchestrated just-in-time (JIT) inventory flow systems.

Ocean shipping is experiencing mid-decade dynamics that supply professionals need to factor in when making any long-term plans. Trans-Pacific traffic imbalances have ships at full capacity eastbound and often only at 30 percent of full capacity westbound, but they may appear full westbound because the containers must be returned to shipment origin points in Asia. Larger and larger container ships are being built. While 2,000-TEU (20 ft × 20 ft × 8 ft size) ships were the norm in the 1980s, today 8,000-TEU ships are entering into the trade and some 10,000-TEU ships are being built. Where flows from Asia to the U.S. West Coast and then by minibridge flow to the East Coast were common, congestion at ports is leading to all-water physical supply chains. *Bottom line:* What was yesterday's optimal flow must, today, be recalibrated.

For the rest of the decade there are two overriding factors for supply chain professionals to consider. One is that in spite of the current high traffic volumes enjoyed by ocean, truck, and rail carriers in the United States at mid-decade, most carriers in the world continue to fail to earn a return to their cost of capital. This causes continual flux in investments, ownership, and services. The second point is that with transportation, it is all about volume buying power. Synergies among business units and even with other companies, as well as with third-party logistics providers, are the ways to garner this buying power strength for price efficiencies and service offerings.

Warehousing

Warehouses serve many value-added roles as locations where inventory rests for different purposes. One is for stock-spotting purposes in order to position inventory at or near a point of need. This is a common use with supplier-managed inventory situations. The original prime motive for most warehouses was, and still is, for distribution economy purposes utilizing differences in transportation pricing for cost motives. This second use is often referred to as a distribution center. Rather than ship small-lot (expensive transportation costs per unit) customer deliveries long distances, a distribution center is built near major markets where the goods are shipped in large-lot (low transportation cost per unit) shipments. Customer deliveries are then made in final short-distance deliveries. The total cost of the distribution center system option is lower than that of the combined cost of many direct small shipments. A third form of warehousing is for inbound consolidation, or a reverse of the distribution center flow. Rather than have many small and longer-distance inbound moves, the inbound consolidation center collects these shipments central to many inbound sources and consolidates them for long haul to their common destination.

Warehousing Megatrends

As with all supply chain logistics components, warehouses are also undergoing many dynamics that require supply chain professionals to keep a vigilant oversight related to them.

One megatrend applies to warehouses that are owned and operated by manufacturing companies: senior managers increasingly seek to eliminate them from the company. Warehouses are high-asset investments that are also often labor intensive. The trend is to use outside warehouse companies (third-party logistics entities) who provide this service as their core activity so that the client company is able to release many fixed costs and decrease head count. Moving to a third-party company also shifts many of what would otherwise be fixed costs into a cost or fee per use or per unit of product.

Another megatrend is the greater use of warehouses for postmanufacturing and other forms of product transformation, assortment, and value-add. This relieves factories of production complexity, and it greatly increases the ability to offer and satisfy specific customer demands. Product postponement is a major example of this trend. Many electronics products are partially produced in common form and distributed to regional distribution centers. When specific country orders are placed, the distribution center completes the products with country-specific electrical plugs and power packs as well as language-specific manuals and labeling. This product postponement greatly reduces the amount of total inventory in the supply line and increases customer service response.

For the remainder of this decade, warehousing will continue to be seen as an outside value option. Generally, major retail brands will continue to invest in local and regional distribution centers for final supply chain deliveries to stores. Other than these entities, the trend is toward increasing use of third-party logistics and warehousing providers. The supply chain professional's challenge will be to be aware of the logistics dynamics and markets and be ready to change flow and warehouse role options when and where appropriate.

Inventories

Inventories are physical goods in various forms, from raw materials to components to finished goods. They also exist as final goods purchased and ready for resale in their current form. For many decades they were not measured other than in terms of ensuring there were sufficient amounts so as to reduce stock-outs. Today, inventories are seen as substitutes for cash and as a result are under close scrutiny and measurement in the quest to manage them as tightly as possible.

Inventory Megatrends

Inventory velocity and visibility represent a key megatrend in most industries in the world today. Inventory has little value when sitting other than to be available for use or demand. Most business applications seek to have it continually moving from raw form to final sale. Speeding up the cash-to-cash cycle is the motivation for this trend. The faster that inventory turns over, the less chance there is for it to become obsolete in the market. Too, when inventory moves faster and is visible throughout the chain, the chance for lost sales and inventory write-offs due to spurs in demand or slackening of markets is minimized.

The need to manage inventory more tightly and have it move faster has given rise to investments and practices that lead to inventory visibility throughout the entire supply chain. Visibility of inventories in supplier firms as well as at customer locations is becoming a major trend for new information investments and firm-to-firm linkages.

For the rest of this decade inventory management initiatives appear to be directed toward combining inventories with working-capital measurement systems. An example of this is seen with the lessening of measurement of inventory turnover toward that of capturing days of sales outstanding (DSO) and measuring inventories in terms of when they were paid for versus when their sales will be received in customer payments. This more closely aligns inventory flows with the financial flows of the organization.

Logistics Information Systems

Most original information systems were built as vertical functional data collecting and summarizing reporting devices. They were vertical in that there was one for sales, another for accounts receivables and collections, still another for distribution inventories, and so on with manufacturing scheduling, materials management inventories, and purchasing. During the 1990s third-party firms, such as SAP and Manugistics, rose to provide horizontal function-linking information systems. Currently, the overall goal is still to provide company-to-company linkages whereby everything from order entry through to purchase order placement is combined, but this may be many years off. In the meantime, functions are slowly being integrated toward this goal.

Logistics Information Systems Megatrends

There is much promise and associated investment taking place in the area of logistics information systems such that many trends are relevant for tomorrow's supply professional. One megatrend is the use of the Web for company order management systems. Selling companies find that any action that makes customer orders easier and more value-added with deeper and richer information availability helps with their competitiveness. In addition to acting as portals for customer ordering, they often provide tracking, billing, and product and service information. Another trend that is emerging is multidepartmental information integration with such initiatives as collaborative planning forecasting and replenishment (CPFR). This originally started between major retailers and key suppliers as a means to share forecasts and have near-instant volume demand changes reflected in similar production and distribution flows. Similar types of linkages are being built in other industries with promising results. This will no doubt continue throughout this decade.

Radio frequency identification systems (RFID) are being implemented at great speed at mid-decade. Spurred by Wal-Mart, the U.S. Department of Defense, Micro supermarket in Germany, and the Chinese government, the use of electronic tags that can read and transmit information about the inventory item promises to greatly reduce inventory loss and increase its visibility and access. As of this writing, RFID tags still cost about $0.80, but as convergence of the technology takes place and economies of scale come about, the technology is expected to become widespread when the price drops to $0.05 and less. The key benefit of RFID is inventory site and disposition capture for transmission to places and organizations that can manage it efficiently.

For the rest of this decade one key attribute can be noted. That is, companies are less willing to invest upfront in large software and other technology solutions. The recent history of Y2K and other past huge investments has thinned capital budgets in this area. This has led to a trend of acquiring new systems from providers on a pay-as-you-use basis per transaction. This places much of the functional usability risk onto the information system supplier, but it releases budgets in the purchasing company for other uses.

SUPPLY CHAINS ARE NOT ALL THE SAME— BE CAREFUL WHAT YOU BENCHMARK FOR

Supply chains have traditionally been built from the bottom up. Since the 1960s, the quest was to look at how others performed their transportation, warehousing, inventory, and other functions and to copy and apply those practices that seemed to be best. While this is always a valid pursuit, evidence is now beginning to emerge that suggests that this can lead a company into doing something right, but that it might not be the right thing to do.

One benefit of the dot-com bubble era was that it changed senior managements' views of their companies in terms of business models. This has led to a topdown view of companies today in ways that point to the right supply chains to invest in and apply in the marketplace.

The process begins with *identifying the concept of the business.* Is the company or organization in business to be a low-cost provider, a high-innovation producer, an integrator in the industry, or some other concept? Southwest Airlines, for example, was built as a low-cost provider, and all its investments and activities are directed toward that end. The concept of the business then *defines the strategy* or strategies that the company or organization can pursue in its marketplace. The strategies create a focus upon what is core, what is not core, what is important to invest into, what to have others perform, and so forth, as well as to create an organization-wide alignment of resources, people, and systems. This strategy then is used to define the *business model(s)* to apply in the marketplace. The business model(s) then define the *supply chain(s)*. Thus supply chains only make sense within the context of the company's business model, strategies, and concept. Thus, what is observed in one company or organization might not easily fit and apply in another.

Common forms of supply chains with their major emphases are as follows:

Nanosupply chains. Flow materials to the production line as efficiently as possible.

Microsupply chains. Balance costs and flows starting with purchasing through to shipment of finished goods to customers.

Extended supply chains. Coordinate suppliers, organization processes, and customer demands and needs.

Project logistics supply chains. Complete a project at a certain point in time (found in construction and military settings; oil and gas projects are examples).

Synergistic chains. Combine the various supply and other activities of all organizations within a decentralized and/or multinational company to attain optimum buying power and financial coordination.

Innovation chains. Access new technologies and product opportunities through networks of outsiders.

These are just some of the many generic forms of supply chains or networks that seem to be evolving in visible form in this decade. Each one demands different emphases from the supply department and supply professionals. These range from straight buying and seeing to delivering through to searching for and creating high-value-added relationships.

AGILE SUPPLY CHAINS AND NETWORKS: MANTRA FOR THE DECADE AND BEYOND

The speed of product innovation, increasing competition among firms, and economically rapidly rising regions and countries, among other things, all point to a need for supply chains to become increasingly more flexible in design and daily execution. In the past, a supplier that could ramp up volume when needed or could reduce it without negatively impacting the buying firm was the concern. Today, a supply chain that can handle such things as troublesome risk events in the world, transport bottlenecks, and quickly shifting customer demands requires constant vigilance and the ability to shift to new tactics and even strategies.

Supply professionals are at the center of this heightening business need. As builders of the flow systems, they are the architects of the supply chains and networks. Thus they have the responsibility and expected authority to oversee and make changes and shifts when and where needed. This is a far cry from years ago when the field consisted of buyers who were hired to learn the job of buying.

CHAPTER 13

THE FINANCIAL
SUPPLY CHAIN

Jack Barry
Managing Director
Pegasus Global, Inc.

Until recently, there was little management pressure to commit the investments necessary to improve financial supply chain processes. The financial supply chain is the flow of cash, investments, and monetary commitments from one firm to another along revenue-producing networks and chains. It also includes the investments, costs, and economics of business models applied in the creation and delivery of value to customers and consumers.

It is a new management process and emphasis that integrates existing non-coordinated functions within the order-to-cash cycle. It links the ordering processes with the invoicing and delivery processes. The goal is to substantially reduce the delays in financial settlement caused by invoices that are difficult to reconcile—estimates are that over 20 percent of all invoices have data errors that will delay payments.

THE CFO PARADOX

Chief financial officers (CFOs) today face unprecedented challenges and opportunities. The CFO's job is much larger today than it once was. CEOs now demand that CFOs discuss strategic issues, not just financial issues, when they sit at the table. The enterprise does business in more countries, with more customers and banks, and through more channels of distribution. The CFOs must support these new demands with only modest increases in resources. The result is that CFOs must do more with less.

CFOs need solutions to significantly advance the workings of their company's financial supply chain (FSC). FSC solutions enable CFOs to accurately manage their receivables, forecast their company's financial future, and reduce their working capital needs. CFOs are expected to predict the future with a high degree of precision, yet they are only peripherally involved with managing the supply chain!

In the future, CFOs will likely find themselves in even more precarious positions, as Wall Street grows increasingly intolerant of errors and mistakes in forecasts. Even small inaccuracies in earnings projections can take an enormous toll on established companies' stock values.

CFOs typically do not have the tools or access to information necessary to scope their company's current financial situation, let alone predict the future. A critical gap is the inability to reconcile problematic invoices, purchase orders, and other documents. (Problematic documents often account for more than 20 percent of total documents in the FSC.) Such reconciliation is made difficult due to high error rates in fulfillment, changes in item numbers, poor documentation of back orders, mishandling of customer purchase order changes, and related problems.

CEOs are demanding that the CFOs issue "attainable" earnings projections when CFOs have little visibility into the financial aspects of the company's operations. These new demands create both new opportunities and new threats for every CFO.

To meet the new challenges and seize opportunities for success, CFOs need solutions to significantly advance the workings of their company's financial supply chain. The FSC parallels the physical (or material) supply chain and represents all transactions related to the flow of documentation and cash from the customer's initial order through reconciliation and payment back to the seller. FSC solutions enable CFOs to accurately manage their receivables, forecast their company's financial future, and reduce their working capital needs.

Traditional hedges against uncertainty are no longer viable and certainly too costly. Improved FSC processes can yield the timely, accurate information necessary for gaining a competitive advantage, through increased predictability, reduced reserves, and better use of working capital.

A $200 BILLION GOLDMINE
FOR FORTUNE 500 COMPANIES

Typical billion-dollar companies today spend $32 million annually for unnecessary working capital and inefficient processing functions, because they lack visibility into the FSC and receivables. By optimizing their FSCs, companies can

- Reduce their working capital needs by as much as 20 to 25 percent, using better invoicing control and cash flow management, saving nearly $15 million annually.

- Lower financing rates on required working capital by more than $4 million each year.

- Gain early warning into problems with any document in a commercial transaction that will likely cause invoice payment to be delayed 30 to 45 days past the due date, and then take corrective action to reconcile exceptions.

- Realize their prior investments in automating financial systems, with the savings from FSC processing equaling $13 million.

- Eliminate expensive, nonproductive float. Secure more favorable terms for the working capital based on the granularity and depth of financial visibility that will allow lenders to assess the real composition and quality of receivables.

When applied to the Fortune 500, efficient management of the FSC could save nearly $200 billion.

Just as manufacturing technology solutions have made it unnecessary for companies to use excess inventory as a hedge against uncertain demand, optimizing the FSC makes it unnecessary for companies to compensate for uncertain receivables with excess working capital.

As a result, CFOs can do their jobs more effectively: more confidently forecast earnings, provide more effective input into the enterprise's strategic direction, and potentially increase their job tenure.

In addition to significantly reducing the days of sales outstanding (DSOs), optimization of the FSC provides for faster payment processing through the accelerated flow of information to external logistics organizations and other third parties. Also, having access to FSC information constitutes a new customer relations channel that enables companies to resolve payment issues through fact-based negotiations.

MESS MANAGEMENT

The problem is 20 percent of all sales transactions have one or more data issues that cause reconciliation problems and delay of payment; change orders are a major cause of errors. It costs between $14 and $162 to process a receivable transaction. The 20 percent that are difficult to reconcile are at the high end of that range. More than half of accounts receivable balances in U.S. companies today are over 50 days outstanding. The 20 percent that are difficult to reconcile are, on average, in excess of 65 days outstanding.

The major headache is that no one knows for 45 days which invoices will be paid or rejected. This results in a complex set of commercial order and payment transactions. There is no single source of information across buyers, sellers, carriers, and financial institutions. The effort and cost to reconcile errors is substantial. In all cases, the seller bears the burden of financing the excess working capital. There is no ability to reconcile errors or gain visibility in real time. The reconciliation process is highly manual and itself error-prone. There is no linkage between the financial settlement process, including invoicing or bill presentation, and the delivery and receiving process. The ability to predict cash income and requirements is marginal.

The promise of enterprise resource planning (ERP) systems has not been achieved. ERP systems cannot provide the information for reconciliation or integration of the data in the diverse and unconnected internal application systems.

No ERP system integrates across business processes between buyer, seller, carrier, financial, and other support activities. Ironically, 90 percent of companies that have implemented a major ERP system increased their DSO by 10 percent—mostly due to the increased inability of their customers to reconcile invoices. Those companies took almost two years to return to the pre-ERP levels of DSO.

While great strides have been made to create procurement application systems, those systems are unable to connect the delivery and receipt processes with the financial and procurement processes. None of those systems can integrate delivery and receipt information; therefore, they are unable to reconcile invoices.

Industry has painfully learned that electronic data interchange (EDI) only speeds the pipeline and does not improve the process, while direct payment options [automated clearinghouse (ACH) and electronic funds transfer (EFT)] add value only to reconciled invoices but further complicate the ability to process those invoices that do not reconcile. Thus, the impact of the 20 percent nonreconciled invoices prevents the direct-payment option from replacing existing processes, and there is little value in companies maintaining multiple payment processes. Moving ordering to electronic commerce and utilizing electronic bill presentation does not identify or correct the basic underlying data documentation mismatches.

Increasingly the drive for electronic invoice presentation and payment (EIPP) is duplicating the unnecessary drive that occurred in the 1990s for online cataloging capability. Unless EIPP can present a reconciled invoice, it too is a partial fix that will not change the business processes nor add significant value. That is the main reason the utilization of procurement cards is less than 4 percent of all sales transactions. Procurement cards are a partial solution, like EIPP. Unless a procurement card can present a reconciled invoice, it too is a partial fix that will not change the business processes nor add significant value.

The benefits of EIPP require businesses to install and run a separate payment system for EIPP and regular invoicing. Businesses have a low appetite for installing and maintaining multiple payment systems and processes.

E-marketplaces will only exacerbate the mismatch of invoices, purchase orders, and receipt documentation. As has already been stated, in normal commerce between known buyers and sellers, 20 percent of invoices are nonreconcilable because of data errors. In an e-marketplace environment with unknown buyers and unknown sellers doing business through a third-party medium (the e-market) that percentage of nonreconcilable invoices will only increase, and the ability to reconcile will increase exponentially.

The financial supply chain is no longer just a technological or functional issue, but one with a scope that encompasses technology, business processes, and corporate strategy. Failure to recognize and leverage the potential of the financial supply chain will significantly handicap longer-term profitability and market positioning. The effective implementation of financial supply chain processes, across multiple industries, will define the very nature of competitiveness in this global economy.

The effective management of the financial supply chain offers companies a way to revolutionize their business, move to the next level of competitiveness, and achieve the type of breakthrough performance that creates new market leaders. Financial supply chains are not magic, but they can have magical effects.

THE BIG LIE: E-COMMERCE AND THE DIGITAL MARKETPLACE

Unfortunately, the expected potential of business-to-business (B2B) electronic commerce (EC) has not yet been realized. While business-to-consumer electronic commerce is becoming more omnipresent every day, the B2B environment has been lagging behind. The requirement for success in B2B EC is a ubiquitous, utility-like network connecting multiple buyers with multiple sellers. It must be akin to a new telephone network, achieving a critical mass with a common language and enabling a brave new world of complete digital commerce. The technology is there, the potential benefits are real, but the implementation has yet to be right.

Today, B2B EC coverage is less than 5 percent of both dollars spent and numbers of individual transactions. With the exceptions of the automotive, grocery, retail, and computer industries, it is still out of the mainstream of commerce. Why? Because the majority of B2B purchasing takes place for direct production materials, and most B2B e-commerce applications cover indirect materials, called MRO (maintenance, repair, and operating) supplies.

And so, most B2B EC application systems are still one-to-one, even proprietary, linkages, allowing one supplier to connect to one customer. They tend to be based on EDI, a 30-year-old technology that never gained widespread acceptance outside the Fortune 500.

It was expected that by now the Internet would have accelerated the acceptance and utilization of B2B EC. The Internet promises an open infrastructure that is software, hardware, and platform indifferent. But our analysis of almost 50 current Internet-based offerings to connect B2B EC buyers and sellers in a digital network would indicate the world of digital commerce is still far from a reality.

Here is what is wrong. The gap between potential and reality exists because the following two factors are missing from the current e-commerce and Web-based supply chain solutions currently offered in the marketplace. First, all the offerings require the buyer to enter the B2B EC process in a digital format. Yet the current order-entry transaction media is over 75 percent voice and fax. Not providing voice recognition, fax scan, or other customer translation capability excludes 75 percent of the buyers or forces them to adapt to the software's requirements. None offer asynchronous payment; that is, where the seller gets paid before the buyer pays. Second, no offering electronically integrates the delivery and receipt process that would allow real-time returns and claims resolutions and increased customer care. In most industries, despite the level of automation in the ordering process, the receipt process remains primarily a paperbound manual process. While estimates vary by industry (from a low of 15 percent to a high of 40 percent), a substantial number of deliveries cannot easily be processed for receipt or payment without a labor-intensive reconciliation process. In all but 4 percent of the time, the reconciliation process that delays delivery and payment is caused by the inability to match conflicting documents.

The companies that produced all these offerings fail to understand the basic nature of the existing commerce structure; they offer isolated areas of excellence, but not a complete "one-stop" solution. Some do not understand the critical differences between direct production material purchases and indirect maintenance, repair, and operating material purchases. For instance, production material is not ordered as individual shipments, but is released under major contractual relationships between the buyer and its major suppliers. Buyers do not search catalogs to buy production materials. Issues of quality, standards, reliability, delivery, and overall integration of the seller's materials into the buyer's production line make those buy and sell decisions a long and intense process.

The impact and benefits of the physical and information supply chains have not been realized by the financial supply chains. The great successes brought about by a renewed interest and effort to improve the physical and information supply chains reduced both the lead times and investment in purchasing, manufacturing, and shipping, plus dramatically reduced the cost of storage.

DATA CAPTURE AND DEPLETION PHENOMENA

The 1970s saw the development of enterprise-level software applications that purported to provide a wide scope of management information. Most applications initially focused on computerizing the paperbound financial tasks. Soon those software applications were borrowed from finance and applied to the physical supply of manufacturing and logistics. Reduced inventory forecast errors and resultant reductions of excess inventory levels became a real and attainable objective. Today, most companies have installed complex software applications that have automated the key elements of the financial supply chain administrative processes—order acceptance through invoice settlement. They have not, however, been applied to reduce the unknowns of working-capital requirements.

From order acceptance to manufacture, rich levels of information are captured and passed on to the next activity, providing a most accurate and complete envelope of commerce transactions and product and service characteristics. Yet in the information flows from manufacturing through invoice settlement that rich data bank is depleted and only summary information is passed through or accessible by downstream processes. See Figure 13–1 for a graphic display of the capture and subsequent depletion of data. Thus the shipping and invoicing documentation cannot be easily referenced to the complete envelope of commerce transactions and product and service specifics. In the over 20 percent of invoices that are not paid in a timely manner because of data inconsistencies; this inaccessibility to previously captured and now depleted information unnecessarily delays financial settlement.

FIGURE   13–1

Data Accumulation and Depletion Curve

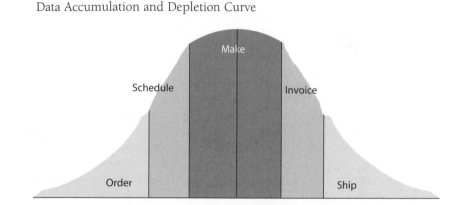

For the last 20 years, major corporations worldwide have invested billions of dollars in improving their information systems—attempting to achieve digital status. The perceived benefits of a comprehensive management information system (MIS) have been a powerful lure. Senior executives are mesmerized by the image of instant information, available at their fingertips. The growth of information giants, such as SAP, PeopleSoft, and Oracle, has relentlessly fed that dream. But today, instead of a digital marketplace, we have conflicting and competing software, hardware, protocols, and infrastructures. We are closer to a data Tower of Babel than to the brave new world promised.

The typical corporation has many systems. Corporations that proudly proclaim, "We are an SAP house," are really a patchwork quilt of application systems—SAP for financials and manufacturing, Marcam for purchasing and maintenance, i2 for forecasting, Oracle for database management, and Oracle (formerly PeopleSoft) for human resource management, Manugistics for supply chain management, plus a number of homegrown software applications. The corporation's internal information supply chain is neither seamless nor integrated. Ask a basic question on inventory levels, and the various systems applications will most likely provide four correct, but different, answers. It is information asynchrony. Each application system views the question in the context of separate time frames and reference points. As stated, the answers are correct, but they are also invalid.

The ability to synchronize information across the corporation is worse. Most corporations have customized their application software. That customization often dilutes the common digital standards and database integration that was an original goal of installation. In the extremely rare instance where both the seller and buyer have a complete SAP package, for instance, their ability to communicate is limited to translating one SAP version into a common communications application, and then retranslating at the other end for the second SAP version. With multiple software application systems and multiple versions of that software, corporations do not communicate electronically in a seamless and integrated process. When they do communicate, it is through various work-arounds, bypasses, and third-party translators.

The most important communication between corporations is, first, the order, and second, the payment.

In the United States, 80 percent of all purchase orders are still via voice, fax, or paper, or are nonexistent—resulting in orders that are in a nonstandard, nondigital format. Sellers must have an order-entry system that is capable of receiving orders in this multimedia and multiformat environment. The key value of the order-entry system is that it can convert those orders into a standard digital format that will be understood by the seller's downstream application systems. And most order-entry systems today are composed of human beings that enter the data manually. As the sales order travels through those various application systems, it frequently changes reference identifications (e.g., a sales order number becomes a different pick-n-pack number and a different invoicing and shipping number). In over 20 percent of the instances, the changes that occur in documentation are significant enough to produce invoices that are mismatched when compared to the buyer's retained hard copy of the purchase order and delivery receipt documentation. The result is the invoice is not paid within the expected time frame.

In the United States, over 90 percent of all invoicing or payment systems are not connected to the delivery system. Assuming the seller's invoice still reflects the buyer's original purchase order, it is sent to the buyer independently of the actual delivery of the product. The shipper (seller) initiates the delivery system by creating a bill of lading and delivering the goods and the bill of lading to a commercial carrier. The carrier creates its own set of documentation that has different reference identification numbers and application software. And so, the 12 blue conference room chairs that were ordered by the buyer are now labeled by the seller's invoice as one set (unit of issue is one dozen) of executive chair model ABC and are labeled by the delivering carrier documentation as three boxes of chairs not otherwise specified, knocked down four to a crate. The probability of that invoice speeding unchallenged through the buyer's accounts payable department is slim. This is further obscured by digital mismatches between competing shipping, delivery, and receiving application software, protocols, and nomenclature. In that environment, the chances for timely payment are slim.

CASH-TO-ORDER-TO-CASH CANYONS

The old maxim "Everything starts with the order" is financially incorrect. Whatever the industry or market segment, the vast majority of financial investments, capacities, alliances, and intellectual properties occur well before the order. The cash inputs are sunk into a steep and wide canyon. Excluding property and plant investments, we would estimate the average for manufacturing industries is for every $1 of sales orders received over $4 was invested 75 days prior to the order.

The inability to accurately forecast market demands and the requirements to rapidly respond to that demand when known necessitate this outpouring of cash.

The climb out of the canyon is also steep. The average days outstanding of unpaid invoices throughout all industries is over 50.

The emphasis on and successes within the physical supply chains over the last 30 years have had a significant impact on reducing the time and investment necessary before an order can be received. Purchasing management enhancements and effective systems integration have reduced forecast errors and unnecessary raw material and work-in-process inventory between suppliers, while decreasing lead times. Just-in-time (JIT), enterprise resource management (ERP), quality initiatives, and lean manufacturing techniques have shortened the manufacturing cycle with better output efficiencies and quality at reduced asset levels. Improved forecasting techniques have dramatically reduced the need for extensive storage of finished goods. Finally, the advent of EDI, the Internet, and e-commerce has allowed the ordering process to be reduced from days and weeks to seconds and minutes.

Unfortunately, the impact and benefits of the physical and information supply chains have not been realized by the financial supply chains. The great successes brought about by a renewed interest and effort to improve the physical and information supply chains clearly indicates those improvements and the necessity to, in parallel, reduce the lead times and investment in the financial side of the supply chain.

Industry has learned lessons from the physical and information supply chains that can be directly applied to the financial supply chain.

LESSONS LEARNED FROM THE PHYSICAL SUPPLY CHAIN

The drive to improve the physical supply chain taught industry three valuable lessons that are directly applicable and transferable to the financial supply chain:

1. Information is a viable substitute for inventory (and working capital).

2. Errors in quality in earlier stages do not improve by later stages.

3. Management hedging against the unknown is reduced by visibility.

Information Is a Viable Substitute for Inventory (and Working Capital)
Prior to the focus on the physical supply chain, lack of accurate and timely information could only be compensated for by excess working inventory. The inability to predict the range and depth of forecast errors required massive investments in inventory dispersed and isolated in numerous locations. The old maxim "If it isn't on the wagon, you cannot sell it" was accepted without challenge. Every wagon was loaded to capacity, and then new wagons were obtained and loaded. But since the early 1980s, when management information systems such as distribution requirements planning (DRP) and material requirements planning (MRP) (forerunners to ERP) were introduced, the levels of overall manufacturing inventory have fallen over 11 percent.

Substitute excess working capital for excess working inventory and the correlations are striking. Today, despite major advances in information technology, especially in enterprise management applications, the process of managing excess working capital is still obscure and inexact. The recent embarrassment of CFOs of major corporations discovering their earnings per share (EPS) estimates were seriously inaccurate only reinforces the concern that the information technology that spearheaded the improvements in the physical supply chain is missing from management of the financial supply chain.

Inventory used to be considered a necessary cost of doing business. Then information accuracy and visibility allowed industry to differentiate required inventory from excess inventory, resulting in substantial improvements. Today, excess working capital is considered a necessary cost of doing business. Soon, information visibility and the ability to precorrect invoices will change that view as well.

Errors in Quality in Earlier Stages Do Not Improve by Later Stages
In the days of long production runs, machine and labor efficiencies were the dominant theme of management. Nothing was allowed to stop the line. Even known quality defects were tolerated and not allowed to degrade production efficiencies. Quality was fixed at the end of the line. We even had a department called Final Assembly Quality Control tasked to perform that postproduction correction. Thus the $2 error in step two was corrected at a cost of $20 in the final step.

Today, with material costs the largest single cost of manufacturing, machine and labor efficiencies are secondary to quality throughout the line. The image of a drill press operator shutting down the line is no longer heresy, but preached as gospel. The same lesson is most applicable to the financial supply chain.

Today, 20 percent of invoices are rejected because data elements are irreconcilable. Most of those errors occurred prior to creation of the erroneous invoice. Compounding the difficulty to correct these quality defects is that most companies wait 45 days past invoicing to begin the reconciliation process. The cost and effort to correct an old invoice is considerably higher than preinvoicing corrections. Additionally, the excess working capital required to float the receivable during this long process adds no value to those companies.

Management Hedging against the Unknown Is Reduced by Visibility
The limits of information management required a Pareto analysis to effectively allocate scarce management resources. The concept of Pareto analysis has gained universal acceptance by management. Issues management was limited to the 80th percentile. Managers were trained to manage the A items, and they could afford the luxury of ignoring the B and C items.

In information-challenged environments, management by Pareto analysis is an appropriate conclusion. The problem remains that the devil is indeed in the 20 percent of the details that are excluded from Pareto analysis. No process or network can succeed when 20 percent of the universe is compromised. In a world of Six Sigma objectives, why do our management and information objectives accept one-sigma solutions?

The 1960s were an environment of cheap labor, abundant time, excess inventory, available assets, and easy money. The cost of poor hedging and exclusions by Pareto were acceptable. In the 1960s, we hedged errors with abundant resources and cheap costs of capital. Over the past 40 years we have fixed many of those problems. Yet today, surplus working capital is still the hedge in the financial supply chain, but it is no longer cheap.

OPTIMIZING THE FINANCIAL SUPPLY CHAIN

It is critical to reduce the process and information cycle times. Companies must remove the non-value-adding delays that result in decreased returns and increased costs throughout the network. This is not limited to within the organizational boundaries of the firm; it must smooth the efficiency of transactions between the firms in the network or chain as well as internal process transactions. That goal can only be obtained when all parties to the transaction are provided visibility to the physical and financial flows, status of investments, and costs. Current technology provides information richness for business intelligence capture and performance results.

The resultant known inefficiencies and added costs have been accepted as business as usual. Economic and competitive pressures are now forcing companies to rethink the financial supply chain in terms of reducing excess working capital. However, little has changed in the last 40 years in the reconciliation of outstanding receivables.

The amount of time required to process transactions in the 1960s was long and wasteful because the physical supply chain itself was fraught with inefficiencies. Companies prospered, in part, due to the lack of global competition, and in part, because all domestic companies were saddled with the same poor quality, demand forecasting limitations, and lack of financial supply chain visibility. They all used the same strategy to compensate for these problems and hedge against uncertain demand: excess inventory and excess working capital. The aim was to maximize productive capacities and labor utilization. Since the cost of capital was low (5 to 10 percent), cash reserve positions were routinely used. Companies relied on excess working capital and excess working inventory—and lots of it.

As the cost of inventory and capital began increasing during the late sixties and seventies, the "excess" strategy no longer worked. Not only was this excess strategy commonplace, it had been considered smart management practice: materials and resources were considered attractive assets that "pumped up" the balance sheet.

To remain competitive against the physical supply chain improvements initiated by offshore competitors, enterprises turned to MRP, DRP, JIT, statistical quality control, and other process technologies to cut costs, boost efficiency, enhance quality, and improve logistics. These information supply chain techniques and tools enabled enterprises to lower their costs while improving customer service.

These techniques and tools did not address, however, the underlying data mismatch problems within the FSC: the flow of information and money from the order-to-cash cycle. Excess working capital still plagues almost every global company today, regardless of industry. Moreover, until the options available from FSC are recognized, enterprises will continue to use an expensive hedge against the uncertainty of demand and out-of-control receivables, creating excess working capital.

The lack of synchronization within the demands for working capital and the visibility or reconciliation of funds creates the need for excess working capital, or nonproductive float to cover the unknown risk. This is a hedge against the lack of visibility into the FSC. It is a costly and ineffective hedge because it does not solve the visibility problems. A company with $1 billion in annual revenue can spend as much as $32 million a year on unnecessary float.

Improved FSC processes can provide, for the first time, an accurate snapshot of a company's cash flow, and credit and liquidity risk. Armed with this information, CFOs cannot only make accurate forecasts, but they also can propose alternative financial strategies likely to resonate well with lenders and corporate stakeholders. The liquidity risk that necessitates excess working capital can be reduced as a result of the lower float requirements made possible through cleaner order flows and early exception resolution.

Attention to FSC processes can pay handsome dividends to global organizations by reducing DSOs, accelerating the payment cycle, and reducing the necessary amount and cost of working capital. Once improved FSC processes are in place and fine-tuned, companies can extend the benefits throughout the physical and financial supply chains by facilitating communication and collaboration across buyers, sellers, carriers, and financial institutions. This represents a major opportunity for leveraging the core quantitative benefits from an optimized FSC.

A better way is to optimize the FSC and substitute information for float. The benefits are enormous: in addition to reducing the cost of float, the billion-dollar company could streamline its entire financial process and increase its margin by 22 percent.

THE NEW EMPHASIS ON THE FINANCIAL SUPPLY CHAIN

Ironically, the financial side of the business was the first function to actively embrace automation of its processes. Yet, that initial effort has been suboptimized because it never corrected the underlying issue—that 20 percent of invoices have data mismatches that delay payment.

Core financial functions have long been automated, first through stand-alone accounting programs for general ledger, accounts payable, accounts receivable, inventory, and other modules, and then through ERP. Many financial executives assume that with high-level accounting and ERP systems in place, they have a good handle on the FSC. Accounting, ERP, enterprise application integration (EAI), and other technologies can be excellent means of reporting on transactions and processes taking place within a company. However, they were never intended to function in an *intercorporate* FSC environment, where data needs to be extracted from all trading partners and full information must be provided to reduce the occurrence of exceptions from the current 20 percent to near zero. Thus the problems still exist.

Payments are delayed. The phrase "2 percent net 10 or net 30 days" applies in theory only; companies today typically receive payments in 45 to 60 days—the same length of time it took to get paid 40 years ago. DSOs are not reduced. Without visibility into the FSC, it is very difficult to correct the problems that generate delay-causing exceptions.

The ability to forecast with accurate, timely data is essential. Without visibility throughout the supply chain, forecasts are, at best, guesses and Wall Street often exacts severe punishment for guesses that miss the mark.

The FSC needs to optimize processes that perform the following core functions across the entire FSC:

- Extracting data noninvasively by normalizing information at the metadata level; in doing so, individual trading partners need not alter the structure or format of their data.

- Providing predictive value as to what problems will likely lead to delays in getting paid, such as inconsistent field formats within purchase orders, invoices, and other financial documents, or mismatched quantities.

- Tracking financial documents from order entry through reconciliation, including change orders, returns, and exceptions.

- Providing proactive intelligence and collaboration across business partners, including logistics and financial partners.

- Operating in real time or near real time to stay closely synchronized with the physical supply chain.

- Connecting delivery information with invoicing information.

By functioning in an intercorporate FSC environment, improved FSC processes enable trading partners to correct the small mistakes that kick out exceptions and bog down the entire supply chain in terms of the flow of cash. They also provide, for the first time, an accurate snapshot of a company's cash flow and credit and liquidity risk. Improved FSC processes can provide the means to anticipate, identify, and correct errors and omissions much earlier in the sales and fulfillment process, and ultimately to enable reconciliation in a timely way. By preempting data invoices, eliminating exceptions where possible, and forcing earlier resolution of exceptions, CFOs can more confidently use invoice information to predict cash flow.

With the traditional manual method of managing the FSC, exceptions occur behind the scenes, and selling companies typically do not know that they will not be getting paid on time until well into the payment cycle. With improved FSC processes, problems can be flagged in real time, even before an invoice has been sent. The FSC processes trigger an alert that a particular transaction has a high probability of becoming an exception. Corrective action can then take place so payment can proceed on a timely schedule.

If exceptions can be reduced to a minimum, CFOs can accurately plan for the working capital they will need. They will also be in a better position to prove the creditworthiness of their receivables; lenders can see the real composition of the monies owed rather than assessing an aggregate figure that can be skewed by a limited number of bad credit risks. FSC processes thus provide the granularity necessary to highlight winning customers and product lines and to prove that a substantial percentage of the company's receivables represent solid, timely cash.

Accurate and timely visibility into the true financial health of a company will do more than just improve credit risk ratings. It will allow access to the sophisticated capital markets of securitized receivables. These highly efficient sources of capital have long eluded most CFOs. These markets demand the accuracy and timely visibility that until now has not been available. In the past, the administrative burdens have limited securitized receivable programs to a small number of corporations with single or consolidated receivables that exceed tens of millions of dollars. Now the transaction capture of improved FSC processes will broaden the scope of securitized receivables by reducing the hurtle rate from tens of millions of dollars to tens of thousands of dollars. The ability to repackage subsets of receivables into various credit-level groupings will allow increased flexibility to the conduits or providers of securitized receivables programs.

Supporting research quantified that over 63 percent of all outstanding receivables took over 50 days to be settled. Upon investigation the true state of receivables is even higher. From our benchmarking research, we can segment outstanding receivables into two classes:

1. *Clean receipts.* Where the documentation matches, that is, where the key data elements on the purchase order match those on the invoice and the receiving ticket. Additionally, the delivery is not over, short, or damaged. These outstanding receivables are actually processed and paid within 30 days.

2. *Problem receipts.* Where the key elements of the documentation do not match or allow easy reconciliation. In most industries, the occurrence of problem receipts ranges from a low of 20 percent to a high of 40 percent. Additionally, over, short, and damaged deliveries account for approximately 4 percent of all deliveries. These outstanding receivables are rarely processed, reconciled, or paid before 75 to 90 days.

For most companies the vast majority of these problem receipts result in a substantially higher average number of days outstanding than that for all other receipts.

Additionally, these receivables result in a higher finance rate. The average for industry is between one to two interest points above prime, while the average for these receivables is closer to three interest points above prime.

These questions address a most pressing administration and data management issue—getting computer systems to be seamlessly integrated and to allow the connectivity of currently disparate information elements to be viewed as a continuous source of management information and operational controls.

Despite the growing implementation of ERP, all companies must solve the "digitization" problem before those ERP systems can provide their full potential. Some have made a substantial investment in customer care functions that process, verify, and translate those nondigital orders into a standard format as input into the first-level, customer-order management software. Unfortunately, most customer-order management systems do not integrate effectively with the downstream financial and movement control systems. Information must be reentered and reverified.

Additionally, this creates a burden for the customers, which adds to the time delays in financial settlement. The data stream that creates the invoice and the one that creates the bill of lading produce documents that, despite a common origin, are mismatched and difficult for the customer to reconcile.

Fundamentally, improvements to the financial settlement process would create cost savings and new opportunities for revenue generation. The following table summarizes how an innovative process would differ from existing financial settlement processes and what benefits are created for participating buyers and sellers.

Traditional Process	Innovative Process	Benefits
Financial settlement is simultaneous: the buyer's payment triggers the shipper's receivable. EFT is an example of the current process.	Financial settlement does not need to be simultaneous. The seller can be paid within a week, while the buyer can pay under normal terms of credit.	The seller and the carrier get their money in about one-fourth the time of the current process. Reduced administrative costs for sellers and carriers.
Factoring can help finance buyers' receivables, but the process is costly. In addition, financed receivables may carry a negative implication on a company's balance sheet.	Uses an existing credit card infrastructure (but no credit card) and normal terms of credit to facilitate and pay for short-term, off–balance sheet financing.	Improved accuracy and reduced cost of settlement through use of credit card network. Seller gains benefits associated with early payment in return for a small per-transaction fee.
While EFT is an electronic backbone, most of the related processes are manual, paper-intensive, and lack any consistent or standard process for communicating information.	Captures critical purchase order and sales order information electronically to replace or duplicate paper documents.	Process is faster and less expensive. All parties have access to greater information throughout the process.

The innovative process would provide significant business value to both buyers and sellers in the supply chain. Value would be created in these main areas:

Accelerating the payment process. On average, this payment process takes 40+ days, but frequently takes much longer. With these innovations, that time could be reduced to less than five days, creating a significant reduction in receivables for sellers [including original equipment manufacturers (OEMs), distributors, and carriers] without penalizing the buyer.

Reducing transaction costs for purchase of indirect materials. Transaction costs in this area are notoriously high: whereas the transaction cost for direct material typically averages 5 percent or less of the cost of the goods, for indirect materials these costs can comprise as much as 35 percent of the cost of goods. By reducing the administrative task to reconcile invoices, those transaction costs would be slashed.

Providing greater visibility and control of the process. This process is typically rife with redundant, manual tasks. Errors are also high, resulting in high levels of rework and exception processing. The ability to detect errors early in the process, often before an invoice is sent, would greatly reduce delays in settlement and provide forward visibility to the true financial nature of the firm.

These innovations would leverage the buyers', sellers', and carriers' existing core systems capabilities in supply chain management. The key benefits would be

- Electronic linkages between buyers, sellers, carriers, and banks
- Traceable delivery with electronic proof of delivery (POD)
- Financial settlement for goods and freight
- Accounts receivable factoring
- Data management, including buying trends and preferences
- Supply chain pipeline performance

VISION FOR THE FINANCIAL SUPPLY CHAIN

The current offerings in the financial supply chain utilizing electronic commerce all fail to understand the basic nature of the existing commerce structure; they offer isolated areas of excellence, but not a complete one-stop solution. The gap between potential and reality exists because two key factors are missing from the current e-commerce and Web-based financial supply chain solutions being offered in the marketplace—lack of asynchronous payment and inability to connect the delivery and payment processes.

No matter the industry, efficient payment systems are fundamental to business success. However, because of low perceived payback, many businesses have

neglected their payment processes in deference to other core function requirements. As a result, paper-based, manual-input systems are often found in today's
businesses, with outdated programming languages and computing hardware as
their foundation. This has put companies in the position of maintaining a staff to
preserve current operations as opposed to moving the company forward in their
core competencies. More importantly, as business processes change, the rigidity
of these legacy systems inhibits the company from responding quickly in a fast-
paced business environment.

What is needed are improvements in financial business processes that allow
real-time issue resolution and exception handling to enable companies to dramatically improve cash flow and significantly reduce the process costs associated
with accounts receivable. Process improvements should include

- Real-time reconciliation of commercial transactions
- Higher percentage of timely payments
- Significant reduction in costs associated with receivables transactions
- Increased cash flow with greater predictability
- Complete visibility into each commercial transaction
- Support for customer-specific business processes
- Access to more competitive financing terms
- Improvement in customer relationships

These improvements should be made by all partners in the supply chain, including buying organizations, selling organizations, logistics providers (carriers), and
financial institutions.

In summary, these process improvements would provide accurate and predictable information, which would help to lower days of sales outstanding (i.e., the
time it takes for a buying organization to settle payment with the selling organization) and allow for more efficient use of working capital. A more accurate and predictable cash flow might also raise the credit rating of the organization, providing
it with access to more competitive financing terms from financial institutions.

CHAPTER
14

INFORMATION SUPPLY CHAIN AND E-BUSINESS

ANTHONY TARANTINO, PH.D.
Senior Manager
BearingPoint

MARK SCHENECKER
Director, Standards Architecture
SAP

GIL PILZ
Director of Security and Directory Services
E2open, Inc.

INTRODUCTION

Joseph L. Cavinato, Ph.D., C.P.M., director of the A.T. Kearney Center for Strategic Supply Leadership (CSSL) at the Institute for Supply Management and ISM professor of supply management at Thunderbird, The Garvin School of International Management, defines the four sub-supply chains within an organization's overall supply chain. They exist in manufacturing and non-manufacturing enterprises, government agencies, and educational institutions.

Physical. The actual movements and flows within and between firms, transportation, service mobilization, delivery movement, storage, and inventories.

Financial. The flows of cash between organizations, incurrence of expenses, and use of investments for the entire chain or network, settlements, and accounts receivable, and accounts payable processes and systems.

Relational. The appropriate linkage between a supplier, the organization, and its customers for maximum benefit, including internal supply matter relationships throughout the organization.

Information. The processes and electronic systems, data movement triggers, access to key information, capture and use of data, enabling processes, and market intelligence.

Of the four, none has been more dynamic, complex, promoted, and over hyped than information supply chains (ISC), especially with the advent of e-business and e-commerce technology as a major enabler. Technology and market demands have sparked the need for major changes in business processes as enterprises race to compete in a global marketplace.

The term *e-business* refers to electronic methods, such as electronic data interchange (EDI), automated data collection systems, and Web-based tools to support a host of business-to-business (B2B) activities. At its most sophisticated, B2B means direct system communication between trading partners; for example, a customer's purchase order (PO) or change order is communicated directly to a supplier's order-entry or customer service system, all without human intervention. A less sophisticated, less costly, and more popular process involves buyers and sellers viewing and updating information via a Web-based business-to-human (B2human) user interface (UI).

This chapter addresses the information supply chain and e-business as they impact information flows within (intra enterprise), between (inter-enterprise), and among multiple levels (multi-tier) of enterprises. It also includes discussions of emerging e-business software tools, technologies, security, and corporate governance requirements around ISC.

A broad definition of *enterprises* is used to include a purposeful or industrious undertaking, especially one that requires effort or boldness, because much of this applies beyond the corporate world. A broad definition of *e-business* includes an overall strategy that is redefining business models, as differentiated from *e-commerce,* which is the execution of real-time business processes aided by Internet technologies. E-commerce is a facet of e-business.

HISTORICAL PERSPECTIVE
Vertical to Horizontal

The century-long transition from vertical to horizontal integration profoundly impacts information supply chains within and between enterprises. Henry Ford (1863–1947) championed vertical integration by manufacturing virtually everything required for his Model T cars. Ford's organization was the archetype of rigid vertical integration in manufacturing, distribution, and information with top-down authority and information flows. There was little need for robust information flows within and between Ford and its limited supply base.

Alfred Sloan developed a horizontal organization at General Motors with autonomous operating units that were encouraged to innovate. Information flows became more critical within and between operating units and the supply base. GM surpassed Ford in the early 1930s and became the world's largest industrial enterprise and standard setter for 40 years.

The automotive industry was one of the first to move from vertical integration to outsourcing all non-core manufacturing competencies. Taichi Ohno, the genius behind the Toyota Manufacturing System, added just-in-time (JIT) inventory management in the 1960s and 1970s. Successful information supply chains are mission critical in a horizontal, outsourced, JIT environment with daily inventory turns, ever-decreasing product cycles, and relentless demands to lower costs and improve quality and customer service levels internally and externally.

The vertical Ford and horizontal GM models were emulated by even the bitterest rivals to Western capitalism—the Soviets adopted the Ford model in the 1920s, and the Chinese Communists adopted the GM model in the 1950s. Vertical and horizontal organizations have a profound effect on information supply chains in all types of organizations.

Vertical and horizontal ISCs create what Harold Innis described in the 1950s as a bias of communication (believing one's own propaganda and ignoring external warning signs) that prevents rapid adaptation. Just as GM's horizontal ISC surpassed Ford's vertical one, domestic automakers were surpassed by Toyota with its JIT philosophy and execution.

E-business tools play a major role in vertical and horizontal intra-enterprise, inter-enterprise, and multi-tiered ISCs. While robust ISCs are required in all three areas, the collaborative nature of multi-tiered ISCs provides the best hope for minimizing the bias of communication.

Manual to Electronic

The telephone grew in importance in the 1960s and 1970s because it speeded procurement and supply chain processes. In the 1980s, the facsimile machine gained prominence. Private procurement regulations (Uniform Commercial Code—UCC) and federal aquistion regulations (Defense Aquistion Regulations—DAR and Federal Acquisition Regulations—FAR) have been amended to accept and encourage electronically transmitted documents.

In the 1970s, electronic data interchange (EDI) emerged. Data was translated between an enterprise's unique format and the standard format required and communicated via direct phone lines or through a third party or value-added network (VAN). This eliminated manual data input and reduced errors and processing times. By the early 1990s about a third of large corporations used EDI, primarily to transmit purchase orders and invoices. The high costs and complexity of EDI prevented wider adoption. With the advent of the Internet, some observers predicted the demise of EDI, but it continues to grow and to carry the large bulk of ISC data.

Just as EDI advanced *inter*-enterprise ISCs, in the 1980s more powerful desktops boosted *intra*-enterprise ISCs. Local area networks (LANs) enabled the exchange of information without sending data through a centralized mainframe or minicomputer. Wide area networks (WANs) linked mainframes and minicomputers, PCs, workstations, and LANs and made rules-based transactions, processes, roles, and responsibilities as well as electronic work flows, documents, forms, and secure remote access possible. Disparate systems could now be accessed: MRPII and ERP, quality, CAD/CAM, warehousing and inventory, traffic, financial, order management, and maintenance.

While EDI was expensive and complex, the Internet was and is relatively inexpensive and easy to use. The first generation of sites was passive—the seller could look at data but not update it. The next generation permitted suppliers to update data and buyers to approve or reject changes via electronic work flows—a true collaboration via a business-to-human process.

The benefits of and impediments to e-business have remained the same since the 1970s. It is a viable means to reduce overhead and operational costs while speeding the exchange of supply chain information; this is critical when cost increases cannot easily be passed to customers because of fierce global competition. The impediments to e-business remain primarily non-technical and solvable. These include the need for a greater strategic orientation and a change in skill sets of supply chain professionals, lack of standardization, and poor data accuracy.

INTRA-ENTERPRISE INFORMATION SUPPLY CHAIN

Ironically, information supply chains within an enterprise are often more complex, difficult, and less systematic than those between and among enterprises. For example, ordering and transferring materials between divisions and facilities, rescheduling deliveries and punishing inadequate performance, converting marketing forecasts into operational forecasts, tracking forecast accuracy, and holding forecasters accountable are typically more complex with poorer visibility within an enterprise than across enterprises.

The virtually universal deployment of intranets in the 1990s improved the intra-enterprise ISC process. An intranet typically includes a browser with one standard Windows interface with e-mail, calendaring, Web meetings, and instant messaging. Designed as a proprietary system, it improved communications and data transfer with enhanced controls and security.

In the 2000 edition of the *Purchasing Handbook*,[1] James T. Parker, C.P.M., described the benefits of an intranet. It is a relatively secure method to move business processes online by providing a common interface and communications environment. Data can be input without concern for where the information resides, thus enabling more complete and timely reporting because organizational data is provided. Information can be made available to employees and the public simultaneously. This is especially important when product designs require last-minute changes. Manual internal processes, such as sourcing, requisitioning, purchasing, releasing, receiving, and contract management, can be performed online to reduce manual and paper-intensive processes. Online training and documentation reduce costs while speeding and expanding the process. Internal coordination between departments can be facilitated, including timelier sharing of information and work documents. Intranets can be less expensive and quicker to install than

---

1 James T. Parker (2000). "Electronic Opportunities, and Electronic Commerce," *Purchasing Handbook*, 6th ed. New York: McGraw-Hill, pp. 418–419.

previous connectivity methods while allowing many more features, such as browsing and information posting. Advanced software and programming tools allow for the development of complex processes without the line-by-line code delays of legacy systems.

Instant messaging (IM), or chatting, is universally available at very low cost. Popular for personal use, IM is quickly gaining acceptance within enterprises. User-friendly virtual conferences can be activated within minutes. Errors and time frames are reduced because information is seen in real time. Physically remote associates of an enterprise can build a community or team and conduct real-time, internal, and confidential communications during meetings with customers and suppliers. After watching my teenage daughter and her friends simultaneously conducting multiple IM sessions while listening to music and doing homework, one can envision what is coming as this IM generation enters the business world. They have developed an electronic shorthand and keyboard speeds that are a marvel to behold.

E-mail is by far the dominate vehicle for intraenterprise ISC. It is easy to use, cost effective, works in real time, and is a proven means to collaborate and manage a variety of events. Proprietary and confidential documents can be quickly and easily transmitted. However, e-mail systems are vulnerable to security breaches and disruptions. There is no repository (electronic warehouse) in which to organize and store shared documents, no version control, and no viable means to create a hierarchy of users. There are typically no electronic work flows with alerts or time-outs to manage critical, time-sensitive, or repetitive events. *Collaboration management (CM)* software tools are widely available to address the shortcomings of e-mail.

Event management (EM) or risk management tools build on collaboration management by creating hierarchical work flows with alerts, reviews, and approvals for a host of ISC events ranging from the mundane and repetitive (disposition of rejected materials) to the strategically critical (timely reporting of material events under Sarbanes-Oxley). EM tools notify users about events via triggers or alerts, significantly accelerating the response to critical events, and focus users' attention on events (exceptions) that require immediate attention. Work flows can provide a decision matrix with reviewers, approvers, surrogate or alternate approvers, and time-outs with escalations. EM tools can link to messaging, collaboration, and knowledge management tools to provide a single, integrated platform for accessing all the information necessary to resolve events. EM tools provide a clear communication string and audit trail.

One other compelling reason to move critical and time-sensitive communication and collaboration from e-mail and IM to collaboration and event management is the effects of sensory overload from daily incoming e-mail, IM, and voice mail. The regulatory requirements for timely reporting under the Sarbanes-Oxley Act will not only compel enterprises to move very quickly in evaluating events, but in communicating their official response to the public. The ability to rapidly communicate and respond to critical events such as product recalls, epidemics, natural disasters, and major swings in supply and demand creates a competitive advantage.

INTER-ENTERPRISE INFORMATION SUPPLY CHAIN

Extranets are built on EDI technology and have a similar effect on inter-enterprise information supply chains. An extranet is a private internet-based network between an organization and its trading partners and customers. Typical features include a common user interface via a Web browser that enables users to view information in a standardized manner. The technology benefits are lower costs, a standardized software protocol, and a user-friendly and standardized interface. The business benefits are reduced cycle times for ordering, forecasting, and inventory management and reduced paperwork because purchase orders, acknowledgments, change orders, terms and conditions, advanced shipping notices, and invoices are transmitted electronically. Extranets provide near real-time review and approvals of critical ordering components such as price, lead time, quantity, and terms and conditions; true forecast collaboration in which customer forecasts are accepted or rejected by suppliers and exceptions (mismatches) are highlighted via alerts; and true inventory collaboration with customer requirements (minimums, maximums, buffer safety-stocks, kanban quantities) and inventory statuses (on-hand, in-transit, on-order) in which suppliers respond and exceptions are highlighted. Extranets offer early-stage inter-enterprise collaboration on product and life-cycle data and are a viable solution for customers and trading partners at all levels of technology sophistication.

Many of the benefits are soft, and some very large enterprises have yet to fully deploy extranets. In the Yankee Group's 2003 B2B Decision Maker Survey, 96 percent of respondents identified electronic communication with supply chains as a top corporate priority, and 66 percent said the need for improvement is urgent. However, the high costs and complexities of Extensible Markup Language (XML)-based solutions prevent adoption. Competing industry standards, such as RosettaNet and Open Applications Group (OAG), are troublesome for suppliers serving multiple industries. EDI, a proven technology, only requires additional resources in the existing solution.

Sales forecasts, open customer orders, and inventory stocking programs have historically driven enterprises. Today, market forces accelerate the trend to be purely customer-order-driven, a concept pioneered by the automotive industry which reduced waste to create a JIT or lean environment to respond to individual customer orders. This has evolved technologically to what AMR Research calls demand-driven supply networks (DDSN) in which point-of-sales data drives virtually all industries. A prerequisite is a robust extranet.

MULTI-TIER INFORMATION SUPPLY CHAIN

Julie S. Roberts described supply chains as multi-tiered, customer-driven, cross-functional, and an ongoing journey—not a destination.[2] "Supply chain management

---

2 Julie S. Roberts (2003). "The Buzz about Supply Chain," *Inside Supply Management*, July, vol. 14, no. 7, pp. 24–28

activities include good purchasing activities, but good purchasing activities are not necessarily true supply chain management activities (such as logistics or distribution)." Multi-tiers exist internally and externally for all types of organizations, and each additional tier of visibility adds strategic advantage. Understanding that the supply chain has multiple tiers beyond a supplier and a customer helps supply chain managers focus time and effort and make decisions that do not negatively affect other tiers.

In the 1980s, distribution requirements planning (DRP) emerged as the first software solution to address multiple tiers. It applied material requirements planning (MRP) logic to distribution—managing demand and inventory levels across multiple distribution centers, warehouses, hubs and spokes, and suppliers. With DRP logic, gross requirements are generated at a higher tier in the supply chain and combined with safety stocks and order modifiers to generate net requirements at lower levels. Like MRP, demand is time-phased, calculated against lead times and order modifiers, and dependent on demand at higher levels.

DRP solutions suffer from the compounding effect of needing to calculate order modifiers and service levels at each tier and location. It does not provide a network or global view and cannot optimize inventory and safety stock levels. Optimization engines emerged in the late 1990s to permit users to balance inventory carrying costs, customer service levels, cash flows, and other user-defined metrics. MRP proved impractical to balance customer service cost levels, and JIT and lean inventory management emerged. New multi-tier ISC solutions have surpassed those of DRP.

Multi-tier visibility solutions encompass ordering, inventory, engineering information, forecast and planning, and manufacturing and capacity. Lower tiers are alerted to customer demand changes. Sophisticated versions share product life cycle and end-of-life phase-out information and support Sarbanes-Oxley requirements and material traceability (Europe in 2006 and 200).

We will illustrate a fairly simple multi-tier process using a laptop computer seller:

Tier 1. A laptop computer seller outsources manufacturing to a Mexican contract manufacturer.

Tier 2. The contract manufacturer in Mexico buys a complete hard drive assembly from a hard drive supplier designated by the laptop manufacturer.

Tier 3. The hard drive manufacturer is located in China and obtains motors from its own motor division, an independent operating unit located in Mexico. The Mexican motor unit is running a different manufacturing and customer service system from that of the hard drive manufacturer.

Tier 4. The motor manufacturer buys application-specific integrated circuits (ASICS) from two suppliers, a U.S.-based supplier who can respond quickly and a lower-cost supplier in Singapore.

Relying on best-in-class inter-enterprise technology and business practices would result in the following:

Tier 1. The laptop computer seller uses B2B to communicate in near real time a purchase change order to the contract manufacturer's customer service system. The contract manufacturer runs an MRP calculation to determine the impact of the change. MRP is typically run or calculated daily, but the outputs must be evaluated and planned by humans, which is typically not done daily. Depending on the planning and procurement organization, multiple MRP runs may be needed as demand cascades down to items at lower levels in the bill of material. Even with fanatical dedication, this process can easily take one or two weeks.

Tiers 2–4. The process and cycle in tier 1 is repeated as the customer demand is converted from a gross to net requirement at each tier. Again, even with daily MRP calculations, pristine inventory, and bill-of-material accuracy, the process can consume one to two weeks per level.

All tiers. If all the systems are in perfect running order; B2B is used to communicate between each tier or level; and each planner, buyer, and customer service representative does his or her job as quickly as possible, it can easily require roughly four to eight weeks for the laptop computer's change in demand to reach the lowly ASIC supplier on the fourth tier or level.

With a multitier solution, all four levels receive the same demand change alert when the B2B information is transmitted. E-mail alerts can supplement system-to-system communications. Each level determines the effect of the change, sometimes requiring a call to the trading partner above them. Still, this can be done in a day or two, which translates to about a 95 percent reduction in cycle times with the assurance that the same information was received at the same time. Some call this one version of the truth, a profound accomplishment in most environments.

While the technical issues of multitier visibility are solvable, the business issues are more complex. For example, yields are critical in diverse manufacturing processes and, in some environments, yield information is as important to end users as order quantities. Therefore, manufacturers may be reluctant to share yields that tell where a product is in its life cycle or indicate that the manufacturer's processes suffer from wide yield variations when the customer is demanding six-sigma quality levels (literally 3.4 defects per million items).

Multitier execution has been the Holy Grail, where tiers are tied together in visibility and actionable outputs. Some call multitier visibility *light integration* and multitier execution *tight integration.* Attempts at tight integration where outputs of a higher tier become inputs for the next lower tier have been made in the automotive and high-tech industries. It requires bills of material, planning cycles, and synchronization of inventory balances. The odds of success are very low.

Early execution attempts failed because contracts required purchase change orders before suppliers could react to change signals from software solution and gross and net requirements were not aligned. Change at the top tier does not cascade proportionally. For example, a 50 percent increase in demand at the top may equate to no change or even a decrease in demand at lower tiers because of inventory balances, lot sizes, safety stocks, and open-order quantities.

A more realistic, and newly emerging, approach is to gather supply chain information from each tier and have a third-party solution create exception messages with alerts visible to all participants. Competitive advantage will go to whoever makes visibility and execution viable.

Most excess inventories, capacities, and higher expediting costs are due to delays and miscues in conveying changes. Successful application of multitier solutions will speed time-to-market, lower costs, minimize the pain of product end-of-life cycles, and reduce excess buffer inventories at each tier while improving responsiveness to changes in customer demand.

Thomas K. Linton, chief procurement officer for Agere Systems, sees value in multitier visibility for complex indirect goods and services such as hosted software providers and system integrators, many of which involve a complex array of subcontractors and outsourced processes. Today, visibility and collaboration processes are informal, imprecise, and labor intensive.

E-BUSINESS SOFTWARE TOOLS SUPPORTING INFORMATION SUPPLY CHAINS

Hosts of emerging software tools facilitate the movement toward e-business and change the nature of information supply chains.[3] To optimize their use, companies have to improve many existing business processes. These tools include

- Business intelligence (information management including spend analytics) with customizable dashboards and alerts

- Web-based sourcing with reverse auctions, multistage negotiations, and optimization engines

- Procurement with automated sourcing rules, approvals, and agreements across multiple organizations and locations

- Internet procurement with self-service requisitioning, parametric search engines, internal electronic catalogs, and punch-outs (round trips) to popular supplier catalogs

- Contract management with electronic warehouses and rules-based controls over terms and conditions

---

3 Parts of this section were copied with permission from the publisher, Institute for Supply Management™, from Anthony Tarantino (2003). "What's Holding Up the Purchasing Revolution," *Inside Supply Management*®, September, vol. 14, no. 9, pp. 34–39.

- Supplier collaboration portals, exchanges, and hubs
- Purchasing (individual) and supplier (enterprise wide) cards with summarized settlement
- Automated payables including evaluated receipts settlement (ERS)
- Advanced planning systems with optimization engines
- Collaboration and event management with document revision control and work flows
- On-demand and hosted supply chain collaboration tools with service-level agreements

Standing alone, each software tool offers the potential to improve the information supply chain process by lowering process costs, cycle times, and purchase costs, while improving supplier performance and customer service levels. In combination, they offer a revolution that will transform supply chains in ways unimaginable a decade ago.

Table 14–1 offers an overview of the current technology, what the technology attempts to improve, and the penalty for not deploying it.

The potential benefits of deploying the technology and related business processes are summarized in Table 14–2.

Many organizations struggle to effectively implement, deploy, and maximize software tools. Why is technology so far ahead of the user's ability to benefit from it? Much ISC software has been oversold and over-hyped. Newly developed ISC software tools have been so bug-ridden it often takes years to offer viable products and users experience painful software introductions. Software integration is also very new. Web-based supply chain management systems present opportunities to standardize and streamline processes that cannot be fully comprehended and implemented by decentralized organizations. The lack of a strong centralized planning group can result in underutilized facilities, excess inventories, and poor customer service. The complexity and sophistication of the new tools tax many organizations when it comes to supply chain staffing and organization, rationalizing the supply base for a given commodity, establishing long-term agreements, and ensuring and maintaining user-friendly catalog content. To successfully automate payments, purchasing and receiving data must be pristine, and Accounts Payable (AP) organizations may be downsized and centralized. Commodity-specific templates create a standardized and repeatable process, but do not exist in any form in most organizations, and there is no consensus about their content and use within larger, more sophisticated organizations.[4]

Supplier collaboration portals and exchanges permit suppliers to maintain order statuses, lead times, capacities, and order modifiers online. Most organizations

---

4 See Anthony Tarantino (2002). "What to Look for in a Good Sourcing Tool," *Inside Supply Management*®, November, vol. 13, no. 11, pp. 48–55.

TABLE 14-1

Current State Processes and Penalties for Not Deploying Technology

Technology	Typical Current Process	Typical Penalty
Business intelligence: spend analytics, information management	Spend, usage, supplier, and forecast data are disjointed and fragmented. Even the most fundamental data is often very difficult to obtain. There is little support for exception management, key performance indicators (KPIs), and summarized data.	The lack of viable data frustrates efforts to rationalize commodities and supply base and prioritize strategic sourcing and supplier relationship management efforts. Higher prices and inventory levels and poorer supplier performance and customer service levels result.
E-sourcing and auctioning tools	The sourcing process is manual, fragmented, and not standardized. Few enterprise wide negotiations are used to leverage volumes.	The lack of industry-accepted best practices in procurement typically requires 50 percent more resources for the same output (Hackett benchmark).
Purchasing	There is little use of blanket and contract purchase orders or sourcing rules to direct requisitions to supplier agreements. The review and approval process is manual—no electronic work flows.	The leaders enforce agreements with sourcing rules and electronic work flows. The lack of these tools and processes equates to added labor and price premiums for off-contract buys.
Internet procurement and supplier catalogs	Most indirect or expense procurement for goods and services is labor intensive and more difficult to automate and control as to contract compliance (greater maverick spending). Even highly repetitive items are not captured in electronic catalogs.	Without Internet procurement, supplier catalogs, and electronic processing and approval work flows, purchasing departments waste time on non-value-added activities. Maverick and off-contract buying can result in premiums of 5 to 25 percent.
Contract management	The process is typically manual and labor intensive with no electronic approvals or alerts, no viable means to apply standard templates and terms and conditions, and no clear audit trail.	With a manual process, contracts can expire without notifications. There is no viable means to capture the number and content of contract agreements, or there is a lack of consistency in the process.
Supplier collaboration portals and exchanges	There is a cumbersome process of acknowledging and maintaining purchase orders, capacities, forecasts, and lead times.	The process of managing viable data for orders, forecasts, and inventory is labor intensive, inconsistent, with poor checks and balances. Phone and e-mail communications are cumbersome and ineffective with inadequate audit trails.

(continued)

T A B L E   14-1

Current State Processes and Penalties for Not Deploying Technology (*Continued*)

Technology	Typical Current Process	Typical Penalty
Purchase and supplier cards	Low value buys go through purchasing or petty cash.	Purchasing resources are wasted on non-value-added activities. Petty cash has inadequate controls and high administrative costs.
Automated payables	A labor-intensive three-way matching (invoice-PO-receiver) process adds little value.	A manual payables process typically requires 25 to 50 percent more resources than an automated process, without improvements in controls.
Advanced planning systems	Planning is disjointed and tactical and assumes infinite capacity; no constraints are calculated; there are no means to optimize planning to balance costs, service levels, and other key factors.	Planning is labor intensive with unsatisfactory execution levels. Balancing customer service levels, margins, and cash flows is a manual and subjective process.
Collaboration and event management tools	Collaboration is disjointed and lacks security. E-mail transmission of documents makes version control impractical. It is difficult to manage critical events in a consistent, timely, and efficient manner.	Decision making and event management lack timely exchanges of communications and use unsecured documents, not under version controls. Results include delays in product introductions and changes, greater inventory levels and shortages, and lower customer service levels.
On-demand and hosted supply chain collaboration tools	Internal IT departments struggle to support wide ranges of disparate and disjointed supply chain solutions. Technology is too specialized to permit satisfactory internal staffing and support.	Service levels are many times inconsistent and unacceptable to internal users and trading partners even with high internal IT administrative and hardware costs.

have done a poor job measuring and rewarding suppliers, even though this is central to collaborative planning. Many purchasing groups have failed to make order and supplier maintenance a priority.[5]

Suppliers have been given few real incentives to support these tools and fear the commoditization of their products. The lack of accepted commodity and supplier code standards for electronic catalogs and content management translates into higher supplier costs with few demonstrable benefits. The promises of

---

5 See Anthony Tarantino (2002). "Why the Resistance to Supplier Portals?" *Line 56*, May, accessed at http://www.line56.com/articles/default.asp?ArticleID=3626.

TABLE 14-2

Leading Processes and Benefits in Deploying Technology

Technology	Leading Processes	Typical Benefits
Business intelligence: spend analytics, information management	Supplier and commodity rationalization, summarized and drill-down spend analytics, key performance indicator monitoring, desktop dashboards with alerts for out-of-tolerance situations.	Greatly enhances the ability to perform strategic sourcing, supplier rationalization, inventory- and service-level balancing, buyer and supplier performance measurements. Repetitive sourcing efforts are standardized and simplified with shorter cycle times. It is much easier to add additional bidders and source items more frequently. The results are lower costs and greater buyer and supplier performance.
E-sourcing and auctioning tools	Automated Requests for Quotations and Proposals (RFXs) with attribute-based scoring, weighting, and collaboration. Awards automatically converted into POs. Commodity-specific templates based on best practices and past successes simplifies the process.	
Purchasing	Multi organizational blanket and contract POs, planning system generated demand, automatic conversion of requisitions to POs based on approved supplier lists and sourcing rules.	The self-service, automated, and standardized features of procurement, Internet procurement, supplier collaboration portals, and contracts can yield a head-count reduction of 10 to 15 percent or a corresponding productivity improvement permitting buyers and planners to pursue more value-added activities.
Internet procurement	Self-service requisitions, catalogs with parametric and fuzzy logic search engines, punch-outs to popular MRO and expense supplier catalogs, work flow approvals and alerts	Buyer and supplier performance improves at lower cost levels. Inventory- and service-level imbalances are identified more quickly and consistently.
Contract management	Data warehouse with business rules, approval work flows, collaboration, and milestones. Apply standard templates and terms and conditions. Creates a complete and logical audit trail.	Collaborative planning with supplier portals and exchanges can reduce inventory levels while improving manufacturing throughput and the time-to-market.
Supplier collaboration portals and exchanges	Self-service view and update of POs, acknowledgments, advanced shipments, payment, inventory, capacity, lead time, and quality data.	
Automated payables and settlement	EDI, electronic funds transfer (EFT), evaluated receipts settlement (ERS), pay on receipt or auto pay, P-Card and ghost card with summary payments	Automating the payables process can yield head-count reductions of over 50 percent with improved controls.

(continued)

T A B L E   14-2

Leading Processes and Benefits in Deploying Technology (*Continued*)

Technology	Leading Processes	Typical Benefits
Purchase cards and supplier cards	Purchase cards issued to individuals and supply (or ghost) cards issued enterprise wide with summary payments processed through Internet procurement to provide approval controls.	Purchase and supply cards with monthly summarized billings and Internet procurement controls virtually eliminates purchasing involvement and substantially reduces accounts payables work-loads. When tied to Internet procurement, payment limits and correct General Ledger (GL) account codes can be enforced.
Advanced planning systems	Constraint-based planning with what-if capabilities and optimization engines that balance inventory, customer service, margins, capacity, etc.	Optimization gives the right balance among customer service, margins, and other key metrics.
Collaboration management (CM) and event management (EM) tools	Secure means of communication, collaboration, and event manage-ment within and between enter-prises. Document libraries with version controls; roles and responsibilities for group mem-bers; hierarchical work flows that include a decision matrix with reviewers, approvers, surrogate approvers, time-outs, and escalations.	CM provides visibility and controls about who may access and update documents and when. May include subscription alerts to advise members that a document has been updated so only the approved version is stored. EM creates hierarchical work flows with alerts, reviews, and approvals for a host of ISC-regulated events of interest to investors and government regulators. Together CM and EM provide an efficient, repeatable, and auditable process to handle recurring and critical events.
On-demand and hosted supply chain tools	On-demand and hosted supply chain software solutions with service-level agreements (SLA) requiring very high service levels or for the host to pay penalties.	Enterprises suffering from chronic disruptions and inconsistent service levels for software managed by internal information technology and residing behind their own firewalls are moving to a hosted, outsourced, or SLA model as a means to reduce events that will trigger Sarbanes-Oxley section 409 events. Offerings will include services ranging from sourcing and auctioning; trading partner collaboration; cataloging and internet procurement; and collaboration, event, and risk management.

greater market share and lower order-processing costs usually fail to materialize. Poor standardized naming conventions for suppliers, commodities, and items; poor adoption of standardized commodity coding systems such as the UN/SPSC; and poor international adoption of the DUNS (Data Universal Numbering System) system to classify suppliers results in poor spend data. Constraints can be overcome by a visionary procurement leader who is an advocate of the new technology and an agent for change.

Major strategic-level consulting organizations typically promote changes to current systems but often are not well versed on the latest software tools to make the changes beneficial. Major tactical-level consulting organizations are good at implementing supply chain software tools, but often lack the ability to attack the business changes to use such tools. In fairness, most clients limit engagements so the implementers do not have adequate budgets to address business processes and issues. Internal information technology (IT) departments are often measured by meeting arbitrary go-live dates, not by users' measures of success. Consultants and internal IT departments congratulate themselves for going live on time, but users fail to realize many of the benefits.

Emerging supply chain e-business tools provide the nucleus for a revolution in information supply chains. There are legitimate reasons for the delays and false starts, and clearly there are obstacles for even the most enthusiastic proponents and visionaries. However, those organizations at the forefront will enjoy lower costs and improved supply chain service levels.

INFORMATION SUPPLY CHAINS AND CORPORATE GOVERNANCE: SARBANES-OXLEY ACT (SOX)

There is a growing requirement for transparency within and among trading partners.[6] The excesses of the 1990s resulted in widespread support for enhanced government oversight regulations, federal and state prosecutions, and civil litigation by investor groups. The Sarbanes-Oxley Act of 2002 (SOX) may have a significant impact on ISCs in public, private, and foreign companies. The Securities and Exchange Commission (SEC) is not allowing a grace period or tolerance for ignorance in complying with the act, but its December 2005 recommendations will give some relief to small companies, those with a market cap under $700 million, by permitting them to perform their own audits.

E-business solutions can support compliance with sections 401, 404, and 409 of the SOX. Section 401 requires listing off–balance sheet transactions and obligations. For supply, this includes long-term purchase agreements and cancellation, minimum

---

6 Parts of this section were copied, with permission from the publisher, the Institute for Supply Management™, from Anthony Tarantino (2004). "The Impact of Sarbanes-Oxley Act on Supply Management," *Inside Supply Management*®, April, vol. 15, no. 4, pp. 16–17. Other parts of this section copied with permission from Anthony Tarantino (2004). "The Impact of Sarbanes-Oxley Act on Supply Management," E2open's White Paper, June.

usage, shelf life, and restocking charges. Restocking and cancellation charges (included in most long-term agreements) are listed as new triggering events requiring an 8-K filing. Most supplier managed inventory or SMI agreements obligate the buyer to consume minimum quantities and may require them to take possession of a minimum level of inventory within a designated period of time under "freshness" provisions. Capital and operating lease obligations, including fees for early termination, must be dealt with.

Even more complex is the ruling on *contingent off–balance sheet obligations*. This affects enterprises that sell through channel partners within indirect channel sales agreements or those that outsource manufacturing, distribution and logistics, and design. Off–balance sheet obligations may exist for consignment inventory, returns, and rebate programs with volume incentives, warranty, and special pricing agreements. Contract management tools can provide buyers with revision controls, work flows, and alterations when terms and conditions are accessed or updated. Event management tools can create secure communications and audit trails.

Section 404 calls for the creation and maintenance of viable internal controls over policies, procedures, training programs, and other processes beyond financial controls. Inadequate controls include insecure and unreliable communications such as chronic security breaches and virus-caused disruptions in e-mail services; poor visibility of open, valid purchase commitments that frustrate finance's efforts to forecast cash requirements; and inventory write-offs.

Collaboration management tools provide buyers and sellers with secure communications and document sharing, including revision controls, and notification to user groups when documents are accessed and/or revised. CM extranets can transmit, review, accept, or reject POs and change orders electronically with time-outs and exception flagging. Information management tools provide electronic dashboards to alert buyers to orders with past-due (historical) due dates, receiving imbalances, inactive POs, and other out-of-tolerance situations. Supply chain management tools provide a wide range of cycle counting and inventory control functionality to prioritize efforts and alert planners and buyers to potential excess and obsolete situations caused by product changes. Product life cycle management (PLM) tools are emerging to ease the inventory and cost pains for both product introduction and end-of-life. ISC extranets can facilitate the movement from user-planned and -owned inventory to vendor-owned and -managed inventory, including inventory balances, forecasts, and quantity requirements.

Section 409 requires reporting any material events that impact financial reporting such as late supplier deliveries that impact revenue projections, ERP system crashes that disrupt shipments, and poor inventory accuracy that leads to financial overstatement. Event or risk management tools provide key players with customized work-flow notifications and document sharing in a secure environment with clear audit trails. Multitier supply chain visibility solutions provide real-time visibility of supply disruptions that occur at one or more tiers and lead to more timely reporting. Emerging on-demand and hosted supply chain collaboration software solutions include service-level agreements (SLAs) requiring guarantees of high service levels.

Much of the SOXs impact on supply chain management is open to the SEC's interpretation and auditing guidance provided by the PCAOB (Public Company Accounting Oversight Board), which was created by the SEC to register, monitor and control auditors. Ultimately, it will be defined by civil and criminal courts. In site of company complaints about the excessive costs of compliance, robust compliance with sections 401, 404, and 409 is helping to restore investor confidence, improve efficiency, and increase responsiveness to changes.

EMERGING E-BUSINESS AND ISC TECHNOLOGIES

Business-to-Business (B2B) Integration

Despite demonstrated benefits, B2B integration has not been widely accepted or deployed, especially in small to midsized enterprises, due to technical and financial considerations. Even in large organizations, B2B adoptions have typically been limited to the largest trading partners.

One obstacle is the number of back-end e-business software packages in most enterprises, including customer relationship management (CRM), supply chain management (SCM), enterprise resource planning (ERP), product data management (PDM), product life cycle management (PLM), and industry-specific or process-specific applications. Standardizing on one solution is typically not a viable option because one solution cannot usually meet all of an enterprise's business requirements, and rapidly changing requirements are often best met by very specialized point solutions. By the time the large ERP providers catch up with the point solutions, the requirements have changed again. However, point solutions are often a risky choice due to their financial instability, limited customer base, and their potential as acquisition targets. Mergers, acquisitions, and outsourcing constantly lead to new solutions and requirements. It is impractical to hope for a homogeneous technological environment or for a single-source e-business solution to support robust ISCs, a problem that is compounded in B2B integration with trading partners. Point-to-point integration can work for small numbers of trading partners but has not proven to be scalable. Analyses over the years have shown B2B to account for less than 25 percent of trading partner transactions. There are too many disparate technologies and business processes for an enterprise and its trading partners to absorb.

The point-to-point nature of most B2B solutions and the existence of competing standards create a major problem. Traditionally, B2B solutions have relied on the implementation of a single technology model and integration standard to complete a point-to-point integration between trading partners. These standards, which started with EDI, now include RosettaNet use in the high-technology industry, Open Applications Group (OAG) used in the automotive industry, the Organization for the Advancement of Structured Information Standards (OASIS), and the Web Services Interoperability Organization (WS-1). No cross-industry standard has emerged, new standards continue to emerge, and adoption rates of standards groups are stagnating.

For example, within XML, there is SML, MathML, SVG, DrawML, ECE, ebXML (United Nations), cXML (RosettaNet), UBL (OASIS), xCBL (Commerce One), cXML (Ariba), and so forth.

Even if one standard were accepted as superior, enterprises with large financial and technological investments in their existing standards and protocols would resist change. The trend toward mergers, acquisitions, and outsourcing has also compounded the problem.

Point-to-Point B2B Integration and Client/Server Computing

The architecture of B2B solutions is analogous to the client/server computing model with heavy processing requirements at each endpoint. Each trading partner in an ecosystem must implement separate software synchronized with each other partner. B2B integration exhibits the same challenges in deployment, configuration, compatibility, maintenance, and overall cost.

First used in the 1980s, the term *client/server* refers to personal computers on a network. This was a dramatic shift from prevalent mainframe architectures and one that would improve usability and flexibility as well as optimize the hardware and software platforms. It became evident that client/server computing was particularly effective only with a small number of users. The installation and ongoing maintenance of a large client base proved quite expensive. For example, deploying a new version of client/server software required a synchronized ballet with hundreds of users and dozens of servers, all of which had to be updated simultaneously.

The Internet emerged a decade later and provided ubiquitous connectivity. Fundamentally, the architecture of the Internet moved processing back to a centralized model. The browser, a remarkably simple piece of programming code, provided a simple, elegant solution to the daunting maintenance and compatibility of client/server computing. IT professionals regained control of their computing infrastructure by implementing complex application software in a centrally managed environment that leveraged the simplicity of the browser on the desktop.

Organizations invested substantially to integrate their internal systems with their external trading partners using B2B integration technology. B2B servers exchange information across different platforms and assure message delivery. However, it is too costly and too complex for most organizations to create and maintain discrete point-to-point connections with a large number of trading partners, particularly those with fewer technical capabilities and resources.

An additional problem is that it requires tremendous technical competency for a trading partner to support many B2B protocols to satisfy its customers. Only the most dominant supplier can dictate the protocol to its customers, so all others deal with a multi-protocol environment, where many customers use many protocols and standards formats.

B2B Standards

Industry standards provide a set of services, application program interfaces (routines, protocols, and tools for building software applications), and transmission formats (protocols) that provide specifications to develop and enable multitiered, multicompany process management. The challenge is to allow a company the option of selecting the best protocol for its particular organization, while also allowing trading partners to embrace other standard protocols and data formats. If addressed, trading partners of any size can effectively participate in an ecosystem.

The secure, efficient exchange of information to support intercompany business processes is the real purpose of B2B integration. The selection of Web Services, EDI, RosettaNet, OAG, or any standard is irrelevant because the standard is not the value; it is merely an enabler.

Protocol Bridging

Protocol bridging is a concept borrowed from telephony. Telephone operators use a set of rigorous standards to bridge their network protocol with other operators. Bridging occurs in the background. The value to the user is the message transmission and quality of service. A protocol is a means to an end. In B2B integration, protocol bridging means each enterprise selects the standards that are optimal for its particular business needs and technical capabilities. One enterprise may prefer RosettaNet to OASIS, while another trading partner may prefer EDI to XML. Protocol bridging binds different protocols so that messages can be successfully transmitted.

The trading partner views all transactions in one format delivered over one protocol, just like a cell phone user sees all incoming or outgoing calls in one manner. This is a compelling proposition because it provides the opportunity for a trading partner to become technically competent in only one protocol and provides independence from new, emerging protocols.

The standards bodies can focus their efforts on the definition of the payload and business process rather than protocols. It is easier for a trading partner to address a new type of payload or a new business process than to acquire the technical expertise to integrate to a new protocol. The technical challenges can be formidable but should be transparent to supply chain members.

Intelligent Networks or Hubs Using an Integration Service Provider

Existing B2B integration consists of point-to-point connections. Each trading partner works one-on-one with another partner to define the process, connectivity, protocols, data formats, test scenarios, and operation and maintenance of the connection. Maintenance and synchronization problems abound. Changes made by a trading partner reverberate across the entire ecosystem. Every connection has to be reconfigured and retested before integration is reestablished.

Intelligent networks and hubs are designed to overcome these problems. According to Gartner, a *hub* provides reliable, secure message-based B2B data transport over Transmission Control Protocol/Internet Protocol (TCP/IP) networks (including the Internet). Hubs provide cost- and time-saving benefits and capabilities, including transactional messaging, gateways and adapters, a service delivery business model, high transaction performance, 24/7 availability, strong security services, low cost of ownership, many-to-many connectivity capability, and extensive management and administration capabilities.

According to SearchNetworking.com, a *dumb network*, such as the Internet, provides the physical interconnection between nodes with little processing to support signaling. Packets of data are transported. The intelligence is in end devices such as computers.

According to SearchNetworking.com, an *intelligent network* carries the intelligence for the operation within the network, for example, telephone networks. All the software, hardware, operations, support, and services methodology is included to support information supply chains. End devices, such as telephones and answering machines, are simple devices.

An *integration service provider* is a third party that manages the services delivered by an Intelligent Network, often in a hosted model with a service-level agreement guaranteeing access levels and help desk support. Integration requirements and primary integration costs of enforcement, persistence, testing, and transformation are shared by many small trading partners. The same level of technical discipline as a traditional B2B implementation is provided.

The hub provides all complex services and security such as enforcing rules to ensure that messages are sent only once and within specified time frames, inbound and outbound messaging infrastructure is secure and scalable, supporting virtually every document format and messaging protocol between internal enterprise application integration (EAI) infrastructures and trading partners. Many service providers in the middle deliver support for existing, defined B2B protocols and protocol bridging.

Another benefit is that software on the edge (known as a "thin" client as in "thin at the edge" as opposed to "thick at the edge") provides secure connectivity to the network. Most basic functionality required on the edge can be reduced to connectivity, and service required on the edge is ensured. Each connection uses a defined standard from the edge to the network—the standard is properly implemented as currently defined by the applicable standards body, since the connection appears as a point-to-point implementation to the B2B server on the edge. This protocol bridging may be to another integration service provider or directly to another trading partner. A trading partner can elect to connect to other trading partners via an intelligent network, but with its one chosen standard for protocol and data format. Existing B2B investments, such as EDI, are not lost. Intelligent networks extend the existing integration model. Enterprises can choose to integrate directly via point-to-point implementation or indirectly with an integration service provider or with a combination of methods.

THE FUTURE: THE RISE OF INTELLIGENT NETWORKS

The intelligent network model for B2B integration is not new.[7] Telephone operators bind the protocols of different networks. Bridging is part of the network that binds trades on the New York Stock Exchange. Each network insulates the user from the technical requirements of the protocol to focus on message content and business process synchronization.

Enterprises will continue to outsource design, manufacturing, and distribution activities. This trend, combined with a shift toward global sourcing and shorter product life cycles, forces enterprises to manage end-to-end processes that extend outside of their enterprise and across multiple supply chain tiers. Rising complexity makes it difficult for enterprises to get the right information at the right time to respond to changes and make informed decisions necessary to run their businesses. Complexity carries costs in the form of excess inventories, expediting fees, high materials management charges, lost sales, and wasted hours spent on manual processes.

There is significant confusion over B2B protocols, and B2B integration has proven repeatedly to be too expensive to deploy for small and medium-sized enterprises. Resolution comes from embracing all B2B protocols through protocol bridging to preserve the significant customer investments in existing B2B implementations and enable low-cost services on the edge. Bridging can be delivered in an intelligent network model similar to telephony.

Enterprise application integration coordinates various enterprise applications in an integrated enterprisewide system. Intelligent networks provide messaging infrastructure reliability and deliver a scalable solution that secures inbound and outbound information delivery from internal EAI infrastructures to trading partners across document formats or messaging protocols. The solution works with cross-industry or industry-centric standards such as OASIS, WBI, RosettaNet, and supplier-specific e-procurement data standards. The intelligent network delivers full B2B integration capabilities from provisioning to onboarding to the continual maintenance of the solution while lowering implementation costs, maintenance, and change management by leveraging the most costly aspects of B2B integration across many connections.

EMERGING SECURITY AND RELIABILITY REQUIREMENTS

Security grows in importance as enterprises move most of their information supply chain processes and transactions to intranets, extranets, and other Internet-based solutions. Failures can quickly shut down inter-enterprise, intra-enterprise, and tiered supply chains bringing investor lawsuits and criminal prosecution in the wake of Sarbanes-Oxley and other regulatory requirements.

---

7. Parts of this section copied with permission from E2open, Inc. (2004). "Moving from Point-to-Point B2B Integration to an Intelligent Network," E2open's White Paper.

Viable security systems contain the following:

Extensive monitoring, data collection, and fault management systems

Experienced staff in technology and operations, dedicated to system monitoring

Highly redundant and fault-tolerant systems including overlapping independent monitoring and alerting systems

Extensive infrastructure monitoring using specialized software tools

Deep application monitoring including
  - Transaction availability and performance monitoring from remote locations
  - Application-specific service quality monitoring
  - Specific log file monitoring
  - Optimal application recovery time monitoring, including rule-driven auto-recovery scripts based on event correlation driven by specialized software event engine
  - Simple Network Management Protocol (SNMP) monitoring

SNMP is an application layer protocol that facilitates the exchange of management information between network devices as part of the TCP/IP suite. It enables network administrators to manage network performance, find and solve network problems, and plan for network growth.

Systems Management Methodology

Viable security systems also contain the following characteristics. IT operations creates, follows, and maintains a set of standard operating procedures (SOPs) describing precise work flow, administration, deployment, and security steps. Multilayer security systems, including authorization policy direction and intrusion detection, prevent loss of intellectual property helping to maintain a competitive edge. IT operations works with software providers to assure scalable, stable, and maintainable solutions. A well-trained support staff, equipped with a state-of-the-art monitoring portal, is available on a 24/7 basis to resolve any technical issues. Access and modifications to production systems are limited to a select team of operators who follow clearly defined configuration management procedures to execute changes during prescribed maintenance windows. A configuration management system is in place to assure that systems can be deployed or restored quickly and cleanly. The combination of SOPs, customer support, weekly scheduled maintenance windows, standard platforms, extensive monitoring, and highly skilled system operators assures that service availability is high, well-defined, and predictable.

Viable security systems include the following hardware, software, and protocol components.

Firewall. A collection of components or a system placed between two networks through which all traffic must pass. Only authorized traffic, defined by the local security policy, is allowed to pass through, and the system is immune to penetration. The demilitarized zone (DMZ) is delineated by an external and an internal firewall. The external firewall protects and restricts access from the Internet into the DMZ. It provides controlled access to systems located in the DMZ.

Reverse proxy server or gateway. Acts on behalf of one or more other servers, usually for screening, firewall, caching (storing frequently used Web results locally for quick retrieval), or a combination of these. Typically, a proxy server is used within an enterprise to gather Internet requests, forward them to Internet servers, receive responses, and forward them to the original requester.

Intrusion detection systems. Inspect inbound and outbound network activity for suspicious patterns to identify network or system attacks attempting to break into or compromise a system. *Operating system security* occurs when systems in the DMZ have the latest level of operating system patches and the operating systems have been "hardened" to safeguard from attacks.

Authentication. The process of verifying the identity of a user, device, or other entity in a computer system prior to allowing access. Appropriate authentication techniques vary by type of user. *Single sign-on* (SSO) capability means a user's identity is passed across heterogeneous Web servers to eliminate separate sign-on. Once authenticated, the user's credentials are cached and used for the duration of the session on the reverse proxy in the DMZ. *Centralized privilege management (access control)* is the process of limiting access to authorized persons, programs, processes, or systems and is a common way to manage user privileges across mixed platforms, operating systems, Web servers, and applications.

Data confidentiality and integrity. Required when designated information is intended for a community of authorized users. Integrity is when computerized data matches the source documents, with no exposure to accidental or malicious alterations or destruction. *Audit trail and logging* is a sequence of records that shows who has accessed a computer system and the operations performed. Audit trails help maintain security and recover lost transactions. Accounting and database management systems include audit trails. *Session time-out* ensures that a session remains open for a predetermined time period and then closes the session and logs out the user.

Entitlement management. Controls user access and entitlements by implementing centralized authorization policy management for easier management of large numbers of user privileges and entitlements across all applications and platforms. It eliminates proprietary and redundant security mechanisms built into each application. *Internal and external audit* is an independent review to assess the adequacy of controls, compliance with established policies and operational procedures, and necessary changes.

Federated Identity Management

Federated identity management is when the accounts or identities of users ("corporate identity" within a company's intranet domain, account with a Web meeting provider, or account with an IM service) are linked to form a single global identity that spans multiple domains. Identity management is *federated* among individual domains. *Cross domain single sign-on* (CDSSO) occurs when users log into their home domain and access applications in other domains.

Disaster Recovery Preparedness

A viable disaster recovery program should include *redundancy* that is highly available and implemented in a fault-tolerant architecture so that if a component fails, a secondary unit automatically activates. Also critical are daily *backups* with on-site storage coupled with magnetic media storage for off-site archival storage and hot backups selectively restored onto test servers, on a recurring basis, for validation of both the backup and recovery procedures. *Facilities* should be in physically separated locations with *uninterruptible power supplies* (UPS) for protection from power anomalies and for an orderly shutdown if necessary. *Backup generators*, with ample supplies of diesel fuel on-site, should be provided at both physical sites to ensure continuous operation and to provide protection from power anomalies. *Security* should include control of physical access to hardware and equipment and online access to systems and data to prevent or mitigate loss from intentional damage caused from within or outside the organization. *Monitoring,* with status messages and alerts, should include all key infrastructure equipment (servers, routers, switches) and adjunct applications (gateways, application adaptors). The monitoring system receives events from hardware, applications, and network devices throughout the integration platform, consolidates them, and maintains rules to manage them with alerts. *Problem resolution* should include the capability to diagnose and resolve problems automatically or provide the tools to do so, route the right message to the correct resource, deliver the alert with the most effective means, confirm that the alert has been received and is being addressed, escalate the alert if it is not acted upon in a timely manner, and document the problem with root cause analysis and permanent corrective actions.

Reliability and security concerns will grow in importance over the coming years. Evidence is required that shared data is both physically and logically segregated, absolutely secure, and available 100 percent of the time. In the early days of MRP and ERP, users could live with hit-or-miss availability because they did not trust or use the system as part of the daily routines. Once users bought into the criticality of the systems, even a few minutes of downtime were intolerable. The system outputs went from piles of waste paper to closely guarded secrets.

CONCLUSION

What can supply chain professionals expect in the next four to five years? Expect a growing tendency toward geographically, culturally, linguistically, and technologically diverse enterprises, suppliers, and customers; a continuation of the global outsourcing trend; ever more demanding customers seeking greater visibility into the operations of suppliers' and tiers; ever decreasing product life cycles and end-of-life costs; fierce global competition with little ability to pass on cost increases; and competing e-business innovations claiming the greatest return on investment (ROI).

The situation may appear overwhelming. Competitors, customers, and suppliers are all going through the same conundrum. Contrary to the hype, no enterprise has addressed all these issues. Even the Toyotas and GEs of the world struggle to maintain dominant positions. Enterprises that tout their Six Sigma methodologies still suffer major product recalls. Many e-business and ISC solutions are cost effective, use proven technology, and have successful track records. ERP providers are adding e-business suites, and viable third-party solutions exist.

Readily available hosted ISC solutions remove much of the technical drudgery and administrative overhead and have been proven in demanding environments. For example, a large contract manufacturer with 19 sites located in Asia, Europe, and the Americas and six disparate back-end systems is using a hosted solution to connect to over 3,000 suppliers for purchasing, planning, and vendor-managed inventory transactions. The suppliers cover the entire range of technological sophistication—from B2B to dial-up connections. They average 500,000 transactions per week and have only one dedicated resource to support the product. Hosted ISC solutions also can work for small and technologically unsophisticated suppliers with a dial-up connection, e-mail, and a basic knowledge of Excel spreadsheets. Suppliers receive periodic e-mails with an Excel attachment that is opened and used to update order, inventory, or forecasting status. This Excel interface was referenced for over 2,000 suppliers.

How can a supply manager increase the chances of success in deploying e-business tools and achieving a robust information supply chain? It depends on people, internal IT, creativity, business change, and technology. Build a team of professionals unafraid of the future who understand that innovation and calculated risk taking are core elements of their jobs. Build a strong working alliance with internal IT to improve the chance of a successful initiative. Many IT people understand business issues, requirements, and business owners. Look beyond the immediate industry or business area for opportunities. American grocery stores were Taichi

Ohno's inspiration for the Toyota Manufacturing System. Technology is a means to assist in solving business problems; it is an enabler. Many e-business solutions fail to deliver their advertised benefits because they are not coupled with fundamental business change. Technology will always be ahead of our ability to absorb it into a business environment. The goal is to understand that this is not a project or series of projects, but an ongoing journey requiring continuous business improvement, training and education, and upgraded skill sets.

CHAPTER 15

RELATIONAL SUPPLY CHAIN: FROM ARM'S LENGTH TO ALLIANCES AND JOINT VENTURES

THE FUTURE OF SUPPLY CHAIN RELATIONSHIPS

Laura Birou, Ph.D.
Senior Consultant
ADR North America LLC

This chapter is devoted to a look into the future dynamics of effective relationships among supply chain members. An effective supply chain relationship is a dependable source of high-quality goods or services utilized to create value for the end customer thereby bringing a profit and competitive advantage to the provider. The purpose of the buyer-supplier relationship has not changed over time. However, the nature and characteristics of what makes these relationships effective has been dramatically altered by intense world-class competition and competitive pricing, a mass-customization strategy, just-in-time delivery, shortened product life cycles, and significant developments in information technology leading to 24/7 availability. These trends have created a need for heightened responsiveness and flexibility effectively altering traditional supply chain relationships. Leveraging these key relationships to their full potential is a cornerstone of value creation in the new millennium.

This knowledge has lead to the creation of a new supply management role: supplier relationship management.

With the growing importance of the Internet and other computer networks, companies have paid a great deal of attention to the customer side of their businesses. This has manifested itself in areas such as customer relationship management (CRM), and knowledge management (KM), and in the move from call centers to contact centers. Now many companies are applying the same emphasis on relationships to the supplier side. This has lead to a new solutions area: supplier relationship management (SRM). With SRM, enterprises employ a new way of thinking about the supply chain and supply chain transparency. Rather than specifically seeking the greatest short-term advantage in each transaction, customers and suppliers seek to work together for the long-term mutual advantage. This involves a level of trust and commitment that was often lacking in the shallow, transactional interactions that characterized the Internet boom, but it could provide a much greater payoff for companies willing to stick with this philosophy.[1]

To fully appreciate the magnitude of change in the nature of supply chain relationships and to understand the future, it is fruitful to take a brief look at the traditional view of supply chain relationships.

A LOOK AT THE PAST

Traditional supply chain relationships have been labeled "arm's length" in nature.[2]

> In the past, the buyer's role was primarily to maintain a large number of supply sources in order to pit suppliers against one another and negotiate the best deals. This unilateral approach created adversarial relationships in order to foster intense competition among suppliers. In the *short term*, this could be an effective approach to lower prices and enhance quality. This was often an effective approach to buying since it created value for the buying firm and its subsequent customers.[3]

The key distinguishing feature of this approach is the time frame: short term.

The focus of this strategy was short-term results with no commitment for future business for the supplier. Each interaction was transactional in scope, one transaction at a time, which fostered a win-lose mentality among the parties involved. Members of the supply chain were viewed as adversaries instead of partners, resulting in confrontational exchanges between buyers and suppliers. This is exemplified in the very early Chester L. Karras work titled *The Negotiating Game*, which dedicated chapter 2 to the topic of winners and losers. He exemplified the prevailing philosophy in stating:

> It is said that in a successful negotiation everybody wins. Let us be realistic. *In a successful negotiation both parties gain, but more often than not one party wins more than the other.* In this book we will find out why some people win and others lose; and losers make substantially larger concessions than necessary while winners do not.[4]

---

1 Romala Ravi and Katrina Menzigian (2003). "Supplier Relationship Management: Moving from 'Counterparties' to Collaboration," *IDC Executive Brief*, January, pp. 1–2.

2 Henrik Billgren (2003). "Battle of the Supply Chains: The Many Challenges in This Competitive Arena," *Global Logistics & Supply Chain Strategies*, July, accessed at www.glscs.com/archives/07.03.opinion.htm?adcode=30.

3 Ronald L. Meier, Michael A. Humphreys, and Michael R. Williams (1998). "The Role of Purchasing in the Agile Enterprise," *International Journal of Purchasing and Materials Management*, Fall, p. 40.

4 Chester L. Karras (1970). *The Negotiating Game: How to Get What You Want*, New York: Thomas Y. Cromwell, pp. 3–4.

While working at Hewlett-Packard, the author participated in a Karras Negotiations Training Program in 1983 where buyers were trained for a battle instead of a negotiation or resolution. The concept of a win-win negotiation did not become popular until the 1980s.[5] The shortcomings of the traditional arm's-length approach were widely publicized during the "Lopez tenure" at General Motors Corporation.

After years of trying to convince suppliers that they were "partners" in the General Motors supply chain, vice president of procurement Jose Ignacio Lopez de Arriortua

> had gotten rich and famous by squeezing nickels and dimes out of suppliers and pitting one company against another, sometimes employing their confidential plans against them. His practices did not alarm GM at the time. Indeed, General Motors touted Lopez' cost-slashing handiwork as a testament to its new thriftiness and offered him one promotion after another...[6]

Lopez was touted as a "purchasing czar" based on all the savings he was able to achieve for General Motors in the short term. The fallout of the Lopez method has been affectionately dubbed the "car wars" due to the destruction it caused in the relationships among General Motors' supply chain members.

A current use of the same relationship philosophy is the use of auctions as a competitive bidding technique to lower the cost of purchased goods or services. The Internet has provided companies with a tool that significantly increases the efficiency and visibility of the bidding process. An extension of the Lopez method is conveyed in the following example regarding the impact of auctions on supply chain relationships.

> The fact is that his [Lopez's] bullying of suppliers threatens to become standardized, institutionalized and automated with the advent of Covisint, the auto companies' Internet purchasing exchange, if the carmakers allow it. When the exchange was first announced, executives at GM, Ford Motor Co. and DaimlerChrysler could scarcely think about the trade exchange without drooling. Covisint's potential to cut purchasing and manufacturing costs, improve the balance sheet, and harvest cash with an eventual IPO was mightily arousing. All the car companies would have to do to improve their profitability was push a button, and watch the suppliers grind each others' profit margins to dust. Hoo boy! Reality began to set in when the auto companies realized that buyers aren't the parties who get to charge a fat commission, even if they own the marketplace. Suppliers began to revolt, too, when they realized that the auction aspects of the Internet exchange had the potential to treat them all like commodity providers, competing on nothing but cut-rate prices.[7]

---

5 Roger Fisher and William Ury (1981). *Getting to Yes: Negotiating Agreement Without Giving In*, New York: Penguin Books.

6 Jon Pepper (2000). "Lopez' Methods Are the Next Thing General Motors Should Exorcise," *The Detroit News*, May 24

7 Ibid.

According to Linda Michels, Chief Operating Officer of ADR North America LLC, a supply chain consulting firm, companies in the quest of cost savings are "auctioning-away their relationships" that they have spent years building.

Any supply chain organization should recognize the value of a traditional arm's-length relationship and utilize it when it is appropriate. Not all supply chain relationships are considered strategic and deserve the attention and level of invest-ment of more coupled buyer-supplier relationships. The place for the traditional arm's-length relationship in today's supply management environment should be reserved for short-term relationships, one-time buys, or real commodities, not the typical rebuy situation characteristic of the majority of supply chain relationships. Ideally, this form of supply chain relationship in the future will no longer be con-sidered the traditional form, but an exception to the mode of operation between members in the supply chain. "Critical to extracting competitive advantage from buyer-supplier relations, however, is a fundamental shift in perspective, away from an arm's-length, adversarial view of the buyer or supplier, toward a more trust-based, partnership orientation"[8] Part of this shift has been described as actually an "evo-lution" in range of possible relationship forms between buyers and sellers.

EVOLUTIONARY MODELS OF SUPPLY CHAIN RELATIONSHIP

Extending Charles Darwin's theory of evolution to the business world, the term *Industrial Darwinism* has been utilized to explain the external environmental pressures that create a "survival of the fittest" marketplace. Industrial Darwinism requires that organizations rapidly adapt to the demands of their market or face extinction. This need for rapid change and adaptability forces an evolution in the supply chain and the relationships among supply chain members. Those firms whose supply chains manage to evolve with the changing environmental demands stand the greatest chance of "surviving and thriving" in the highly competitive global market.

There are two evolutionary models that will be detailed in this section to serve as road maps for diagramming supply chain relationship evolution. The first model, *Five Levels of Evolution*, is a product of Poirier and Quinn and focuses on the nature of the interaction between the buyer and the supplier.[9] The second model is adapted from the *Seven Levels of Corporate Consciousness* model developed by Richard Barrett where the evolutionary framework is based on the philosophy of the interorganizational exchange.[10]

---

8 Akbar Zaheer, Bill McEvily, and Vincenzo Perrone (1998). "The Strategic Value of Buyer-Supplier Relationships," *International Journal of Purchasing and Materials Management*, August, p. 20.

9 Charles C. Poirier and Francis J. Quinn (2003). "A Survey of Supply Chain Progress," *Supply Chain Management Review*, September 1, pp 40–47.

10 Richard Barrett (1998). *Liberating the Corporate Soul: A Values-Based Approach to Building a Visionary Organization*, Woburn, MA: Butterworth-Heinemann.

FIGURE 15-1

The Five Levels of Supply Chain Evolution

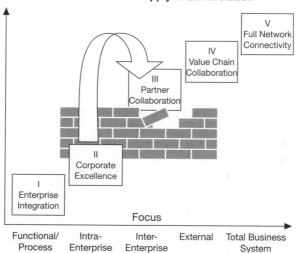

SOURCE: Poirier and Quinn (2003). "A Survey of Supply Chain Progress," *Supply Chain Management Review*, September/October, pp. 40–47.

The Five Levels of Evolution Model

This model was developed based on a survey conducted by Computer Sciences Corporation (CSC) and *Supply Chain Management Review* during the summer of 2003. The following information is taken all, or in part, directly from Poirier and Quinn's "A Survey of Supply Chain Progress."[11] The results of this survey indicated that a business enterprise moves through five levels of evolution in supply chain relationships on its way to the most advanced stage of supply chain management, as illustrated in Figure 15–1.

The following discussion describes in detail the level of integration between supply chain members at each stage. This discussion is provided so readers can reflect on the current state of operations within their own company and where their relationships fall in the evolutionary framework among members of their supply chain. Once the current stage has been determined, the Five Levels of Evolution model can then be utilized in a prescriptive capacity providing the reader with a road map of what needs to be done to proceed to the next level of evolution.

In *Level 1,* the company focuses on functional and process improvement. These efforts are internal to the organization and oriented around enterprise integration— that is, finding the best ways of executing the supply chain process steps by functional

---

11 Poirier and Quinn, "A Survey of Supply Chain Progress," pp. 40–47.

area. To guide their early efforts, many companies use the SCOR (Supply Chain Operations Reference) model of "plan, source, make, and deliver" developed by the Supply-Chain Council. In virtually every instance of Level 1 activity, the beginning emphasis is placed on two major areas—sourcing and logistics. The benefits of functional integration typically include a dramatic reduction in the number of suppliers and logistics services providers, rationalization of product offerings, and a leveraging of buying volume.

Unfortunately, most companies at Level 1 don't leverage scale across the entire enterprise. Content to find savings on a functional or business-unit basis, they adopt a stovepipe mentality that sees no advantage in centralizing any function or sharing any supply chain improvements. Collaboration between functions or business units is resisted. Communication systems to facilitate processing throughout the organization are nonexistent.

In *Level 2*, the supply chain evolution continues on an intraenterprise basis, as the company begins to recognize the savings being generated and strives for corporate wide excellence in its supply chain processing. Companywide assets are evaluated with an eye toward turning over portions of those assets to third-party providers more adept at handling the various supply chain activities. As the focus turns to integrating the organization to best provide end-to-end product and service delivery, the stovepipe mentality begins to disintegrate.

Those in purchasing and procurement transition to strategic sourcing roles and assume responsibility for the total buy at Level 2, achieving overall corporate leverage. These individuals begin to move to a higher level of buyer-seller relationship, as they segregate the supplier base and focus on the most strategic suppliers. Electronic purchasing is introduced here to handle the lower-value sourcing categories.

Logistics starts focusing on asset utilization and effectiveness of the delivery system. A key activity here is ensuring that the best provider is responsible for the process steps that assure accurate and timely delivery. Better flow of information through internal automation of transactional activities aids the loaders, shippers, and warehouse personnel in meeting customer demands. Improvements begin to show up in on-time deliveries and fill rates.

Demand management becomes an important factor at Level 2, as the company now realizes that forecast accuracy can be a major inhibitor to accurate planning and manufacturing. Near the completion of Level 2, some form of sales and operation planning (S&OP) typically goes into effect.

As illustrated in [Figure 15–1], a *cultural wall* inhibits progress past the second level in most organizations. This wall is built on a series of flawed premises: All good ideas must be generated internally; if we need help from the outside, our people aren't doing their job; and if we can get good information from the outside we'll take it, but we don't share our information with anyone.

Often it takes a visionary business leader to scale the wall and bring the others along. Once over the wall and into the external environment of Level 3, the company embarks on interenterprise activities and begins to form a business network with the help of a few, carefully selected business allies. The emphasis here is intentional as efforts to move forward with too many suppliers, distributors, and customers invariably bog down. The greatest successes start with a few, one-on-one relationships to build a framework for external partnering.

At *Level 3*, strategic sourcing reaches out to important suppliers, often inviting them to participate in the S&OP sessions, work on collaborative designs, and come up with solutions to match supply more closely with demand. The logistics, transportation, and warehousing functions establish global relations with qualified logistics services providers. As part of this effort, they introduce warehouse management systems and transportation management systems that enhance communication and visibility among all supply chain partners.

Marketing and sales enter the supply chain picture at this stage, empowering key customers to self-configure products and services often through an interactive online portal. Design and development take a decided leap forward in the third level. Leading-edge communication tools—based on Internet technology and a carefully designed communication extranet—are now used to shorten the time from concept to commercial acceptance.

In short, through a variety of tools and collaborative techniques, Level 3 finds business allies working together to discover savings through mutually beneficial initiatives that reduce cycle time, achieve faster time to market, and utilize assets more effectively. At *Level 4*, supplier and customer collaboration blossoms, as the organization moves forward with its positions in one or more networks. These collaborative initiatives create what is termed value chain constellations. In this advanced environment, the company begins working in earnest with a small base of upstream and downstream partners. Now the focus shifts to establishing a position of dominance in an industry for a particular network with the aid of the key end-to-end constituents.

At this level, new metrics appear in such areas as on-time delivery, fill rates, and returns to underscore the importance of satisfying customers. Network partners begin to use activity-based costing and balanced scorecards to turn the supply chain into a value chain of allies working toward the same strategic objectives. With information being shared electronically, network members can more readily identify opportunities to achieve higher performance levels. Joint teams are established to find solutions to specific customer problems.

On the supply side, supplier relationship management (SRM) is emphasized as the company works with key suppliers to enhance value for both parties. Collaboratively, they focus on the most important buy categories and look at the total cost of ownership to find any additional, hidden value that may have otherwise eluded them. A similar tactic is taken on the customer side. Customer relationship management (CRM) initiatives involving serious data sharing are launched with the goal of developing joint strategies and business goals that increase revenues for both parties.

Crucial to Level 4 progress, is the application of e-commerce, e-business, and cyber-communication techniques to enable end-to-end visibility across the value chain network. Two special features appear in this level—collaborative design and manufacturing (CDM) and collaborative planning, forecasting, and replenishment (CPFR).

Level 5, the most advanced stage of supply chain evolution, is more theoretical than actual. This level is characterized by communication connectivity across the total supply chain network. This is the world of full network collaboration and the use of technology to gain positions of market dominance. Only a few organizations in any given industry have reached this level. But those that do are moving to positions of industry dominance as they achieve unprecedented levels of order accuracy and cycle-time reductions across end-to-end networks that are completely electronically enabled.[12]

---

12 Ibid. Reproduced with permission of *Supply Chain Management Review*, Copyright 2003.

In this evolutionary model, the stages of evolution are characterized by the current strategic focus of the supply chain in developing the supply chain relationship. The distinguishing characteristic between each stage is the degree of integration and collaboration represented. Information technology facilitates achieving higher levels of integration and collaboration between members of the supply chain, advancing the evolutionary stage in tandem with the strategic focus. Level 1 in this model is representative of the traditional buyer-supplier relationships previously discussed where the focus is strictly on cost savings.

Of the 142 respondents to the survey of supply chain progress published in *Supply Chain Management Review* in September 2003, the majority placed their companies in the Level 2 and Level 3 stages of evolutionary development, a demonstrated movement away from the traditional supply chain relationship, but still a primarily internal organizational focus. Firms operating at these levels of evolution came from forest products and construction industries. Only 10 percent of the firms indicated that they had developed supply chain relationships higher in evolution than Level 3. Those firms came from high-technology, chemicals, manufacturing, and wholesale distribution including Boeing, Colgate-Palmolive, Wal-Mart, Intel, Kraft Foods, and Procter & Gamble. These findings highlight the significant opportunities still available for firms progressing through the stages of evolution.

The next evolutionary model, the *Seven Levels of Corporate Consciousness,* differs from the first in that the stages are determined by the demonstrated values of the corporation rather than the nature of the supply chain processes. These values serve to determine the caliber of the supply chain relationship developed between organizations.

The Seven Levels of Corporate Consciousness Model

The Seven Levels of Corporate Consciousness model was developed by Richard Barrett as a tool to identify and foster organizational relationships that are based on an alignment of corporate values. Ideally relationships that are based on the congruence of values would prove to be more responsive, dependable, and resilient and cause less friction or conflict over time. This model categorizes the existing values of an organization as survival, relationship, self-esteem, transformation, organization, community, and society. The model is evolutionary in nature as the developmental needs of an organization must initially satisfy the foundation of survival before the organization can progress to higher stages of evolution, similar to Maslow's hierarchy of needs. The stage of organizational evolution will determine the supply chain relationship capability of the organization. The following provides a description of each stage.[13] Figure 15–2 provides the visual model of this framework.

---

13 Adapted from Barrett, *Liberating the Corporate Soul.*

FIGURE 15–2

The Seven Levels of Consciousness

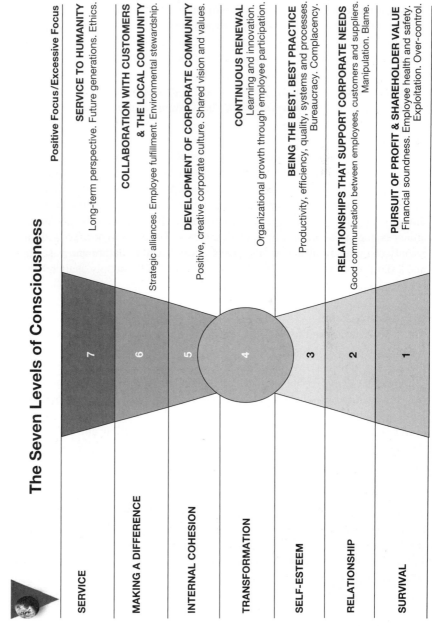

The Seven Levels of Consciousness

Positive Focus/Excessive Focus

SERVICE
7
SERVICE TO HUMANITY
Long-term perspective. Future generations. Ethics.

MAKING A DIFFERENCE
6
COLLABORATION WITH CUSTOMERS & THE LOCAL COMMUNITY
Strategic alliances. Employee fulfillment. Environmental stewardship.

INTERNAL COHESION
5
DEVELOPMENT OF CORPORATE COMMUNITY
Positive, creative corporate culture. Shared vision and values.

TRANSFORMATION
4
CONTINUOUS RENEWAL
Learning and innovation.
Organizational growth through employee participation.

SELF-ESTEEM
3
BEING THE BEST. BEST PRACTICE
Productivity, efficiency, quality, systems and processes.
Bureaucracy. Complacency.

RELATIONSHIP
2
RELATIONSHIPS THAT SUPPORT CORPORATE NEEDS
Good communication between employees, customers and suppliers.
Manipulation. Blame.

SURVIVAL
1
PURSUIT OF PROFIT & SHAREHOLDER VALUE
Financial soundness. Employee health and safety.
Exploitation. Over-control.

Reprinted with permission of Richard Barrett & Associates.

Detailed descriptions of the evolutionary stages are once again provided as a tool for the reader. To utilize this model, readers must be familiar with the dominant operating organizational philosophy, mission, and values of the company they work for and how these impact the company's business decisions. Often a company's stated or written philosophy, mission, and values differ from those that are operational in the culture. However, it is the operational ones that impact the day-to-day decisions that manifest themselves in the long run in the evolutionary level of the supply chain relationships. In addition, it is important to have the same level of knowledge regarding the members of your supply chain. Here, the old adage "Actions speak louder than words" can be of significant benefit.

Survival Level

The first and most basic need for an organization is financial survival. Every organization needs to make financial health a primary concern. When companies become too entrenched in survival, they develop a preoccupation with the bottom line and a deep-seated insecurity about the future. They attempt to allay their fears through excessive control and become territorial. They are not interested in strategic alliances; they view supply chain relationships as resources to be exploited for gain. Supply chain relationships at this level are traditional in nature and based on fear and a short-term orientation. The dominant concern of the supply chain relationship is cost and control.

Relationship Level

The second basic need for an organization is harmonious interpersonal and inter-organizational relationships with employees, customers, and suppliers. Companies that are too entrenched at this level see supply chain relationships as important not for what they can give, but for what they can take. They look at supply chain relationships purely from the perspective of getting their needs met. Companies at this level are strong on tradition and image and weak on risk taking, flexibility, and entrepreneurship. Rules are important because discipline and obedience are demanded in all supply chain relationships. There is a lack of trust of suppliers that severely limits the supply chain relationship.

Self-Esteem Level

The self-esteem level shows up in organizations as a desire for greatness. Organizations at this level want to be the biggest or best at what they do. Consequently, they are very competitive and are constantly seeking supply chain relationships as ways to improve cost effectiveness. Management is viewed as a science rather than an art. The focus is on improving supply chain fitness—productivity, efficiency, time management, and quality control.

Transformation Level

This is the pinnacle level where companies shift their perspectives from purely self-interest to interdependence with supply chain members. The focus is knowledge sharing and renewal of the entire supply chain. Accountability and responsibility for results becomes the operating norm across the supply chain as the culture transforms from control to trust, from punishment to incentives, from exploitation to ownership, and from fear to truth. The tyranny of the financial bottom line begins to disappear as supply chain success is measured against a broad set of metrics. Participation is invited and learning encouraged in the form of teams such as new product development, enterprise resource planning, process improvements, and quality enhancement. The importance of vision, mission, and values is recognized and becomes an integral component of the supplier selection process.

Internal Cohesion Level

The principal focus at this level is the development of supply chain potential or capability. The desire is for the highest levels of innovation, creativity, and productivity throughout the supply chain. This environment is achieved through building community spirit, synergy, and cohesion among supply chain members. Shared values, transparency, openness, equality, and trust are characteristic of this level. Risk taking is encouraged as failures are viewed as learning experiences and the risks and rewards are shared among supply chain members. The focus is on the integration of supply chain members into a cohesive whole operating in harmony with a purpose.

Making-a-Difference Level

The primary goals here are partnerships with customers and suppliers in a collaborative effort to be stewards of the earth's resources. Supply chain members voluntarily implement environmental practices and social policy that is for the betterment of the community. Their desire is to make a contribution to the local community. At this level, members of the supply chain embrace social responsibility and strive to be respected in their communities. Supply chain relationships take the form of strategic alliances and partnerships.

Service Level

At this level there is recognition of the interconnectedness of all organizations and the responsibility for the welfare of humanity. Supply chain strategy reflects the organizational values of ethics, justice, social activism, and philanthropy. Supply chain members are held to the highest ethical principles and the long-term implications of decisions, actions, and relationships.

The focus of this evolutionary model is on the caliber of the relationship based on shared values. An example of an organization utilizing community- and societal-level values in their supply chain is Starbucks Corporation. Howard Schultz, chairman of Starbucks, stated that,

> From the beginning, Starbucks has built a company that balances profitability with a social conscience. Starbucks business practices are even more relevant today as consumers take a cultural audit of the goods and services they use. Starbucks is known not only for serving the highest quality coffee, but for enriching the daily

lives of its people, customers, and coffee farmers. This is the key to Starbucks ongoing success and we are pleased to report our positive results to shareholders and partners (employees).[14]

In addition, Starbucks was recognized by *Fortune* magazine as number 8 on its list of America's Most Admired Companies and number 34 in its ranking of 100 Best Companies to Work For. Starbucks was once again listed among *Business Ethics* magazine's 100 Best Corporate Citizens.

This value system has a direct impact on Starbucks' supply chain relationships as illustrated in the following passage.

> Many of the world's 25 million coffee farmers are in crisis as low quality coffee has flooded the market in recent years. Starbucks is introducing Coffee and Farmer Equity Practices, or CAFE Practices. This program further refines the Company's global coffee buying guidelines meant to help ensure the future supply of high quality coffee and to promote equitable relationships with farmers, their communities, and the environment where coffee is grown. CAFE Practices is an evolution of the Company's Preferred Supplier pilot program that began in 2001. Further, the Company expects to help coffee farmers improve their crops and attract the same premium prices already paid by Starbucks. In January, Starbucks opened Starbucks Farmer Support Center in Costa Rica to provide agricultural support and training to coffee farmers, while stressing the importance of producing high quality coffee in a sustainable manner.
>
> "Starbucks buys only about two percent of the world's coffee beans, but as an industry leader and specialty coffee retailer with thousands of locations worldwide, we have an opportunity to lead change," Hay (senior Vice-President) said, "We are very excited about the positive impact Starbucks can have on coffee farmers, their communities and the environment."[15]

The first sections of this chapter have been devoted to understanding traditional arms-length supply chain relationships and to looking at the shift in supply chain relationships as evolutionary in nature. In the Five Levels of Evolution model (see Figure 15–1) the progression in the supply chain relationship is determined by the level of collaboration and integration between supply chain members. Evolution has also been presented (Figure 15–2) in the Seven Levels of Consciousness model, as progression in the values that govern the supply chain relationships. The next section will address those attributes that have been identified as characteristic of effective supply chain relationships. They represent the fundamentals or the foundations of supply chain relationships.

SUPPLY CHAIN RELATIONSHIPS 101

Sustainable, long-term, healthy supply chain relationships are characterized by compatibility, cooperation, communication, trust, and commitment. While these

---

14 Restaurant News Resources (2004). "http://www.restaurantnewsresource.com/article10172.html, May 23, accessed at http://www.restaurantnewsresources.com.

15 Ibid.

characteristics are essential for effective buyer-supplier relationships, the interesting thing is that none of them were taken from literature on supply chain management. The source of this information came from two books: *Relationships for Dummies*[16] and *The Complete Idiot's Guide to a Healthy Relationship.*[17]So while supply chain relationships are unique in that they are both interpersonal and interorganizational, they are still governed by the fundamentals that govern all relationships. Given the titles of these books, it would appear to trivialize the difficulty and complexity associated with developing and maintaining effective, healthy supply chain relationships. On the contrary, supply chain relationships behave just as do all human relationships. Some relationships are stronger, resilient, and harmonious and can stand the test of time, while other relationships are full of conflict, unreliable, and crumble under pressure. The challenge in the rapidly changing competitive environment characteristic of the new millennium is to select, develop, and maintain those supply chain relationships that can evolve over time to continually meet and exceed the needs of a dynamic relationship for the benefit and gain of all parties involved. Let's now examine each of the characteristics in more detail; the first is compatibility.

Compatibility

While it has been said "opposites attract," compatibility is significantly higher in relationships where the parties share the same values and similar goals.[18] Compatibility is the factor often attributed to for the success of long-term relationships as it transcends the characteristic period of new relationships and builds the bond of friendship that endures when the newness wears off. Supply chain relationships that rate high on compatibility outperform other supply chain relationships.

Compatibility is fostered interorganizationally by similarities in cultures, financial practices, power, values, and a shared history. Compatibility is usually assessed in supply chain relationships during the supplier evaluation and selection process. At this point in the relationship a site visit is often scheduled for the purposes of gathering information regarding the intangibles that impact a buyer-supplier relationship. It is the intangibility of these elements that makes it difficult to assess them and to quantify their impact.

Value congruence is one area of research that has progressed to help eliminate the intangibility of the assessment and impact of this dimension of compatibility. A full discussion of this assessment tool will be presented later in the chapter. Another method utilized by ADR North America LLC is to get the supply chain members to agree on the overriding principles that will govern the relationship, according to Linda Michels, Chief Operating Officer. Project Adventure, Inc., an experiential

16 Kate M. Wachs, Ph.D. (2002). *Relationships for Dummies*, New York: Wiley Publishing, Inc.

17 Judy Kuriansky, Ph.D. (2002). *The Complete Idiot's Guide to a Healthy Relationship*, Indianapolis, IN: Alpha: A Pearson Education Company.

18 Wachs, *Relationships for Dummies*.

learning organization, utilizes the Full Value Contract to engage all participants and to make sure that there are an agreed-upon set of values that the group will uphold.

> Developed by Project Adventure, the principles of the Full Value Contract are integral to many Adventure programs. A Full Value Contract fits the unique spirit and purpose of the group. It is a shared creation, developed in words that are understandable to all group members, that creates an emotionally and physically safe environment supported by all group members. All versions of the Full Value Contract ask the group: 1) to understand and/or create safe and respectful behavioral norms under which it will operate, 2) for a commitment to those norms by everyone in the group and 3) to accept a shared responsibility for the maintenance of those norms.[19]

The purpose of these exercises and assessments is to determine the degree of compatibility between individuals and organizations as it has a direct bearing on the caliber of the relationship formed. Cooperation is enhanced by compatibility, and it is also a key variable to supply chain relationships.

Cooperation

The change in supply chain relationships is accurately conveyed in the title from a publication by Ravi and Menzigian, "Supplier Relationship Management: Moving from 'Counterparties' to Collaboration."[20] The degree of collaboration is the measurement of the level of cooperation between supply chain members. The idea is for individual members of the supply chain to work together toward the accomplishment of common goals. Recognized interdependencies help to promote cooperation as the success of the entire supply chain is vital to the prosperity of all members.

> Rather than specifically seeking the greatest short-term advantage in each transaction, customers and suppliers seek to work together for long-term mutual advantage. This involves a level of trust and commitment that was often lacking in the shallow, transactional interactions that characterized the Internet boom, but it could provide a much greater payoff for companies willing to stick with this philosophy . . . collaboration doesn't mean customers and suppliers synching up their shipping schedules. Rather, they plan together for mutual, long-term benefit and they work in concert in the execution of the full life cycle, from sourcing to payment.[21]

Communication

To exercise a high level of cooperation and collaboration between organizations good communication channels must exist. Good communication is called "superglue #1" in the development and maintenance of effective relationships.[22] Good communication is essential to a supply chain relationship, and it involves direct communication and active listening. Currently many supply chains are held together by the "information highway" called the Internet. While this method of communication

---

19 http://www.pa.org, a Web Site of the nonprofit Project Adventure—see glossary.

20 Ravi and Menzigian, "Supplier Relationship Management."

21 Ibid.

22 Wachs, *Relationships for Dummies*.

is efficient, it falls far short on the dimension of effectiveness. Over 70 percent of communication is nonverbal including body language and voice inflection. That is why so many e-mail messages are misinterpreted by the receiver. Solving a simple problem using e-mail can require 20 or more e-mails between the parties involved, or one phone call! Computerized communication systems should be utilized for routine information exchange, not for problem solving and relationship building.

Findings indicate that open reliable communication between the buyer and the supplier lead to improved quality. When the communication from the supplier to the buyer is characterized in similar fashion, it leads to improved cost and delivery performance.[23] Open and reliable communication is dependent on the level of trust in the relationship. Full disclosure of confidential competitive company information requires a high degree of trust in the buyer-supplier relationship.

Trust

In the past five years there has been a noticeable growth in the body of research devoted to understanding the role of trust in supply chain relationships.[24] The element of trust has actually been elevated to the critical status when it comes to the development of long-term relationships among supply chain members. Trust is often portrayed as a static element; once it has been achieved, no further work needs to be done. The reality is that trust is fluid and dynamic. Trust is developed over time, one situation at a time. Covey refers to this as the "emotional bank account."[25] Each interaction results in a transaction; either a deposit or a withdrawal is made in the emotional bank account. If the interaction violates the trust between the two parties, a withdrawal is made. If the interaction reinforces the trust between the two parties, a deposit is made. When the account is in "the black," there is enough emotional capital to support a trusting relationship. If there have been too many withdrawals and the account is in "the red," the relationship is considered untrustworthy.

Trust is defined as "feeling you can rely on one another without question, and that you will not hurt each other; having confidence and faith in each other that you can depend on and count on each other without reservation."[26] Trust in

23 Leslie Richeson, Charles W. Lackey, and John W. Starner, Jr. (1995). "The Effect of Communication on the Linkage between Manufacturers and Suppliers in a Just-In-Time Environment," *International Journal of Purchasing and Materials Management*, Winter, pp. 21–28.

24 Ik-Whan Kwon and Taewon Suh (2004). "Factors Affecting the Level of Trust and Commitment in Supply Chain Relationships," *Journal of Supply Chain Management*, Spring, vol. 40, no. 2, pp. 4–14; Ashish Agarwal and Ravi Shankar (2003). "On-line Trust Building in E-Enabled Supply Chain," *Supply Chain Management: An International Journal*, vol. 8, no. 4, pp. 324–334; Mark Barratt (2004). "Understanding the Meaning of Collaboration in the Supply Chain," *Supply Chain Management: An International Journal*, vol. 9, no. 1, pp. 30–42; Patrick Jonsson and Mosad Zineldin (2003). "Achieving High Satisfaction in Supplier-Dealer Working Relationships," *Supply Chain Management: An International Journal*, vol. 8, no. 3, pp. 224–240; Adam Lindgreen (2003). "Trust as a Valuable Strategic Variable in the Food Industry," *British Food Journal*, vol. 105, no. 6, pp. 310–327.

25 Stephen R. Covey (1989). *The Seven Habits of Highly Effective People*, New York:Simon and Schuster.

26 Kuriansky, *Complete Idiot's Guide*, p. 9.

the supply chain is developed on the individual level, between buyers and sellers, and solidified by the actions at the organizational level. Often conflict arises when there is a disparity in the trustworthiness of the individuals and the organizations they represent. Individuals often inherit "corporate memories" according to Linda Michels of ADR North America LLC. Once a trust between supply chain members has been violated, it is never forgotten. The relationship can be repaired and overcome the violation of trust, but the relationship is never completely trusting again due to the "corporate memory."

Commitment

The element of trust is a predecessor in the relationship to the establishment of a long-term commitment.

> The existence of trust in a relationship reduces the perception of risk associated with opportunistic behavior. All the definitions of relationship commitment indicate that it involves continuity or a long-term orientation with both parties cooperating to maintain the relationship. Commitment is believing that an ongoing relationship is so important that it warrants maximum effort to maintain and ensure that it continues indefinitely.[27]

In relationship literature monogamy is cited as a contributing factor to the level of compatibility, trust, and commitment between two individuals.[28] In supply chain management, sourcing strategies designed to improve quality, communication, and loyalty and to reduce cost focus on supplier reduction to the point of single-sourcing strategies. It is an interesting parallel to draw between the importance of monogamy on interpersonal relationships and single sourcing on supply chain relationships. Another similarity is the practice of serial relationships in supply chain management, switching from one supplier to the next when the relationship is not operating as desired. "It is relatively easy to go from one failed relationship to the next, each time thinking that the previous relationship just wasn't meant to be—some people call this serial monogamy . . . Serial monogamy is the logical consequence of the 'more than one fish in the sea' philosophy."[29] Or in supply chain relationships this is the "there is more than one supplier out there" mentality. Often it is better to work toward improving an existing supply chain relationship than believe that a better relationship exists with a new supplier. The issue of loyalty and commitment can pay great rewards during difficult economic conditions.

The glaring change in the supply chain management paradigm in the area of relationships is the allowance for growth and development to take place over time, instead of the quick-fix mentality. This paradigm shift will alter the method of selecting supply chain members, the length and value of relationships, and the desired conflict-resolution methodology. What is next for firms such as Starbucks,

---

27 Kevin R. Moore (1998). "Trust and Relationship Commitment in Logistics Alliances: A Buyer Perspective," *International Journal of Purchasing and Material Management*, January, p. 25.

28 Wachs, *Relationships for Dummies*.

29 Blasé Harris, MD (1989), *How to Get Your Lover Back: Successful Strategies for Starting Over*, New York: Dell Publishing.

Boeing, Colgate-Palmolive, Wal-Mart, Intel, Kraft Foods, and Procter & Gamble, who have been identified as further along the evolutionary path? The final frontier is the establishment of visionary supply chains, capable of proactively engaging their environment in the pursuit of a competitive advantage.

VISIONARY SUPPLY CHAINS

These visionary supply chains will need to operate at "clockspeed," a term coined by Charles Fine in recognition of the rapid rate of environmental change confronting future supply chain relationships. Industry leaders will no longer be able to depend on the sustainability of a competitive advantage. Instead, they must learn to constantly remake themselves fast enough to capitalize on "temporary" competitive advantage.[30]

Visionary supply chains display six key characteristics: (1) a values-driven culture, (2) continual commitment to learning and self-renewal, (3) continual adaptation to internal and external environments, (4) strategic alliances, (5) a willingness to take risks, and (6) a values-based approach to performance measurement.[31] The most significant characteristic of visionary supply chains is their commitment and ability to continually renew and transform themselves to changing environmental conditions. They adapt as a chameleon does seeking to create harmony in their environment and reap the competitive benefits of this state.

The need for immediate reaction to market conditions has spawned the growth of "fused" relationships among the partners in a supply chain originally called "relationship marketing" by sales organizations.[32] These relationships have taken many forms and are usually described as partnerships or alliances.[33] A cornerstone in building a visionary supply chain involves the selection of partners that share similar cultural values. This value sharing or linkage of missions has been described as "co-missioning" in the literature.[34] The alignment of organizational cultural values between organizations linked in a visionary supply chain fosters the development of synergy and harmony in these fused relationships. There is an eight-stage process involved in building a visionary supply chain starting with the commitment of leadership to the creation of a values-driven culture among members of the supply chain. This is followed by a values assessment of each organization and an analysis of the values cohesion among the members of the supply chain. The remaining stages involve the steps necessary to improve the values cohesion between members of the supply chain. The ultimate goal of this approach is superior performance in the marketplace.

---

30 C. H. Fine (1998). *Clockspeed: Winning Industry Control in the Age of Temporary Advantage*, Perseus Books.

31 Barrett, *Liberating the Corporate Soul.*

32 Lindgreen, "Trust as a Valuable Strategic Variable."

33 Ellram, Lisa and Owen, R. V. (1996). " A Case Study of Successful Partnering Implementation." *International Journal of Purchasing and Materials Management*, vol. 32, no. 4, Fall 1996, pp. 20–28.

34 Covey, *The Seven Habits.*

Successful fused relationships are highly compatible and adaptable providing them the strength and resilience necessary to withstand a turbulent, competitive, and rapidly changing environment. For a fusion in the relationship to occur, there has to be a meeting of the minds and souls of the organizations. The fusion must be supported by an alignment and meshing of cultural values between the organizations referred to as value congruence. Value congruence is a process of assessing the level of similarity of values that exists between two organizations.

This approach to supplier selection and evaluation is unique in many ways. First of all, it is based on the displayed values of the organizations. Second, it is a two-way model versus the historical approach of one-way assessment where the buying organization evaluates the supplying organization. The values assessment in this methodology is conducted for both the buying and supplying organizations, and the analysis looks at the interaction of these two cultures. The more aligned are the cultural values between organizations, predictably, the higher the performance of the supply chain over the long run.

This chapter has provided a look at the past, a snapshot of the present, and a vision of the future of supply chain relationships. The chapter would be incomplete without providing the reader with some of the tools available to begin this evolutionary journey.

TOOLS

This section is not presented as a complete list of tools that foster effective supply chain relationships (team building, negotiations, effective listening, etc.); rather, it highlights some of the leading-edge strategic tools being utilized by visionary supply chain leaders.

Team-Building Exercises

A lack of cooperation between supply chain members can elicit a cry of, "Whose team are you on?"[35] Fortunately, there are tools available to help foster the development of teams. It is well recognized that teams follow a progression of forming, norming, storming, and performing. The breakdown or breakthrough usually happens at the storming stage when there is stress on the team. Because of the inter-organizational nature of supply chain teams, there is usually very little proactive team building done during the forming and norming stages of team development. It is usually only after the supply chain team is not performing as desired that the development of "team spirit" is considered.

Team building in supply chain relationships should be done proactively utilizing techniques that have been used for decades by groups whose lives depend on the functionality of the team such as firefighters and the military. These groups

---

35 Kuriansky, *Complete Idiot's Guide*, p. 115.

typically use simulation exercises like rope courses to build the trust, communication capabilities, an understanding of interdependence, and the effectiveness of the group. While rope courses may not be an option available to every organization, creative supply chain simulations can serve the same purpose. In addition, Hewlett-Packard has implemented supplier communications programs that are used as strategic information-sharing and goal-setting exercises. Deere & Company offers joint training programs to improve the team environment. There are many books that offer experiential exercises designed to facilitate team building. In addition, there are firms that specialize in this type of programming.

Supplier Relationship Management and Knowledge Management

As Nonaka stated, "In a world in which change is the only certainty, knowledge is the one and only lasting source of competitive advantage."[36] Knowledge management is a rapidly developing field of interest in many organizations. Internally, organizations are striving to find methods of capturing the "know what," or explicit knowledge, and the "know how," or tacit knowledge, of organizational members to improve the rate of organizational learning and to minimize the loss of organizational memory due to attrition. This methodology is also used interorganizationally primarily in the marketing arena to gain knowledge about the customer. With this knowledge, the marketing organization can customize product offerings, or provide higher service, to gain or retain valued customers.

The era has arrived to gain and utilize this same tool, knowledge management, between members of a supply chain. Spekman et al.[37] demonstrate that the principle of knowledge as a source of competitive advantage can extend from the individual firm to the whole supply chain creating an ability for the chain to learn and adapt, becoming a source of competitive advantage.[38]

Currently, buying organizations typically have explicit knowledge, "know what," regarding their suppliers, and this is being packaged by consulting firms and software providers as supplier relationship management. The value, however, resides in the tacit knowledge, the "know how," and that is the knowledge that most buying organizations lack regarding their suppliers. It is estimated that 10 to 20 percent of what organizations know is explicit knowledge. The real competitive advantage is derived from the 80 to 90 percent tacit knowledge that is much more difficult to share. Aristotle (350 BC) provides insight into how to gain the tacit knowledge in his teaching, "The end of theoretic knowledge is truth while that of practical

36 I. Nonaka (1991). "The Knowledge-Creating Company," *Harvard Business Review*, November–December, vol. 69, p. 96.

37 R. Spekman, J. Spear, and J. Kamauff (2002). "Supply Chain Competency: Learning as a Key Component," *Supply Chain Management: An International Journal*, vol. 7, no. 1, pp. 41–55.

38 Ray Collins, Tony Dunne, and Micahel O'Keeffe (2002). "The 'Locus of Value': A Hallmark of Chains That Learn," *Supply Chain Management: An International Journal*, vol. 7, no. 5, pp. 318–321.

knowledge is action."[39] It is the actions of the supply chain system that represent the critical "know how," or tacit knowledge.

> An important implication for managers is that an explicit knowledge of "best practices" does not provide value or competitive advantage any more than watching Tiger Woods swing a golf club will improve your golf game. Rather, it is tacit or applied knowledge, experiential in nature and obtainable only through practice, which adds value and enduring competitive advantage. It is important for managers to understand that it is tacit or applied knowledge that determines the effectiveness and competitiveness of an organization's actions, thus making applied knowledge a durable and robust construct.[40]

Knowledge of the entire supply chain system becomes crucial as it facilitates the ability of an organization to change, constantly adapting itself to its environment. "A firm's ability to adapt is based on two principles: first, having existing internal resources and capabilities that can be utilized in new ways, and second, being open to change or having a high 'absorptive capacity.'"[41] Knowledge sharing between supply chain members has only just begun, and the organizations that lead the way in implementing this tool will have a significant competitive advantage.

Values Audit
A tool that should be utilized in the supplier selection phase of relationship building is the values audit. The relationship between value congruence, organizational compatibility, and supply chain relationship performance has been previously discussed in this chapter in the Supply Chain Relationships 101 section. The values audit should be administered prior to final selection of a supplier to determine which supplier may be the most compatible. Relationships that are already established can also benefit from this exercise as it will serve to indicate which areas of the relationship are the primary causes of concern. The Corporate Values Assessment instrument developed and validated by Richard Barrett & Associates is an example of a validated tool that can be utilized to assess the cultural alignment between organizations in a supply chain.

Communication and Information Technology
It has been estimated that during the last five years, companies have spent approximately $10 billion dollars to improve their supply chain planning systems.[42] This

---

39 Aristotle, *Metaphysics*. Translated by W. D. Ross, Book II, Part I. December 1924.

40 William J. Christensen, Richard Germain, and Laura Birou, "Build-to-Order and Just-in-Time as Predictors of Applied Supply Chain Knowledge and Performance," *Journal of Operations Management*, vol. 23, issue 5, July 2005, pp. 470–81.

41 T. H. Davenport and L. Prusak (1998). *Working Knowledge: How Organizations Manage What They Know*, Harvard Business School Press, p. 65.

42 John Bermudez, Larry Lapide, David O'Brien, and Wendy Davis (2003). "Supply Chain Planning Implementations," *ASCET: Achieving Supply Chain Excellence through Technology*, July 27, accessed at www.ascet.com.

investment is expected to have a payback period of less than five years. System integration is one of the primary components of the the Five Levels of Evolution model and is a key driver of the evolution. The primary advantage sought through the technology is improved communication regarding information accuracy and timing. Improved communication is one of the foundations of an effective supply chain relationship. Future applications of this technology will encompass the area of knowledge management. There are many enterprise resource planning (ERP) tools available to select from. A detailed list will not be provided in this chapter.

The Supply Chain Relationship Journey
As we all know, relationships are a journey, not a destination. The goal of this chapter was to provide readers with *a* road map to help them on their journey and quest to improve the supply chain relationships that impact the performance of their organization. This chapter was not intended to be utilized as *the* road map as all relationships are unique and will follow their own course. The development of healthy and effective supply chain relationships will never be a linear process, just getting from point A to point B in a straight line. Instead the journey is dynamic, and the course may change many times during the journey. Enjoy the ride.

BIBLIOGRAPHY

Fawcett, Stanley E., and Alvin J. Williams, "Supply Chain Trust and Commitment: Practical Perspectives for Long Term Success." 2003 International Conference Proceedings (May 2003), accessed at www.ism.ws.

Germain, R., C. Dröge, and W. Christensen (2001). "The Mediating Role of Operations Knowledge in the Relationship of Context with Performance," *Journal of Operations Management,* vol. 19, no. 4, pp. 453–470.

Rognes, Jorn (1995). "Negotiating Cooperative Supplier Relationships: A Planning Framework," *International Journal of Purchasing and Materials Management,* October, pp. 12–18.

Manugistics, "Supplier Relationship Management: Transcending Traditional Relationships to Enable Collaboration and Profitability," Internal document, White Paper, accessed at www.manugistics.com.

PART 4

EMERGING ISSUES AND OPPORTUNITIES IN SUPPLY

A look to the future (Part 1), definition of strategic supply thrusts (Part 2), and building of chain subcomponents (Part 3) comprise the challenges for today's leading supply professionals. But, these new areas and expanded roles of the field give rise to new managerial and leadership issues and opportunities.

The chapters in this part present insights and key questions. How does one build, identify, grow, and apply the skills and talent needed for today's supply? What is the function and form of the viable supply management organization? What are the contributions to the organization that can be expected from today's expanded supply? How does one identify, meet, and overcome the risk challenges faced in the marketplace, economy, and global infrastructure? Finally, how does supply step up to the task of today's social responsibility?

CHAPTER 16

DEVELOPING SUPPLY MANAGEMENT SKILLS AND TALENT

WILLIAM S. McKINNEY III
President
McKinney and Associates, LLC
Director
Source One Management Services, LLC

INTRODUCTION

Developing today's competitive supply skills and talent is a challenge that is unmatched by any other period in the buying and purchasing field. The challenges and opportunities in the field are evolving and moving faster than at any other time in its history. This environment requires a focus on the supply capabilities that will be needed in the future and building for them starting today. The process begins with an assessment of the people and systems in a group or department to identify the gaps between today's performance and the requirements of tomorrow.

This chapter has two primary parts. The first identifies a broad scope of evolving and future supply management and leadership capabilities that leading companies have identified and are now applying for the future. The second details how one supply manager with experience in several companies is currently applying supply development.

PART I: EVOLVING AND FUTURE SUPPLY CAPABILITIES

In 2001 the Institute for Supply Management™'s (ISM) board of directors approved the definition of *supply* as the identification, acquisition, access, positioning, and management of resources the organization needs or potentially needs in the attainment of its strategic objectives.[1] By taking this leadership role in the field, ISM made this statement as a vision toward which purchasing groups could expand and play greater and higher supply performance roles in their organizations. This definition expands from traditional buying. It is an energetic definition that sees the role of

---

1 See www.ism.ws for the definition and a broader explanation.

acquiring resources in the broadest contexts, positioning the organization in the marketplace and actively fitting into the strategic initiatives of the firm or organization.

The new field definition gives rise to distinctions between buying, procurement, and supply as in the following spectrum of examples.

Buying

The traditional role of *buying* was as an administrative buying service for the organization, using the right product or service, right supplier, right quality, right price, right timing, right transaction method, and right delivery. This involved the following strong buying tasks:

- Processing orders
- Bidding and negotiating
- Expediting and tracing
- Making three-way matches
- Attaining price, delivery, and quality requirements

This longstanding role had purchasing in the position of following through to buy what the rest of the overall organization asked it to do. While it was largely a passive and reactive role, it was nonetheless one of value for over a century and still is in many stable settings to this day.

Procurement

Starting about two decades ago, some field leaders pushed out the boundaries of their activities and became involved earlier in the purchasing decision and execution processes. This broader practice was often referred to as *procurement* in order to make the distinction from pure buying. It included the buying tasks and many of the following additional roles:

- Making orders and the system more efficient
- Planning volumes
- Cost-managing the flow
- Negotiating systems
- Corralling buying power

Procurement professionals were taking on new roles and becoming involved in the buying process earlier with such activities as entering into larger and broader contracts, arranging the buy over longer periods, and directing attention to making the overall system efficient.

Supply

Today's *supply* scope is even broader yet. As the definition suggests, it includes the buying and procurement activities but expands further to include the following concepts:

- Anything on the supply side of the organization is fair game.

- New revenues are as important as cost savings.

- Supply can and should shape and influence the supply market and inbound chains of flows.

- The chain is physical, financial, information, relational (and more recently), also innovative.

- Supply results are measured in terms of the financial results of the overall company or organization.

- Supply accesses what the organization needs but does not have the capital, time, talent, or technologies to develop on its own.

Some key differences are noted between buying or procurement and supply. Supply is measured by its impacts upon the entire organization's performance. It entails integration with groups throughout the organization as well as beyond its legal boundaries. Finally, it is the opposite of being reactive or passive. Many of today's organizational senior managers expect supply managers to identify opportunities and take organization-wide or companywide initiatives to find value and bring it into the organization or company.

A spectrum of personal capabilities is present here. At the building-block level are the tasks needed for specific activities. For example, the creation and placement of an order involves tasks relating to requisitions, proper order creation, submission, monitoring, control, and eventual closeout. Skills are often referred to as the knowledge of and ability to combine one or more tasks into the accomplishment of an activity or creation of an output. In recent decades the term *competency* has arisen in strategic and organizational literature. Many definitions have been put forth, but most of them contain the following theme: *the ability to combine skills, systems, and knowledge together to produce a distinct competitive advantage.* Thus, competency is having the judgmental ability to combine many distinct resources and capabilities to produce an intended competitive effect.

In many of the organizations that are applying the broader concept of supply, some of the common competencies that are found are

- Integrating supply value into the business
- Identifying new areas of value capture from within the business
- Advancing change management, and acting as a catalyst or leader
- Managing and negotiating in multicultural environments
- Leading and managing across time zones and tiers of suppliers
- Managing projects
- Leading teams
- Possessing influence and reach

While these were primarily visionary ideas in this field in the 1990s, many examples are found throughout the world today.

One last feature of this field expansion is the nature of people's roles from the entry level to the top. At the entry level, the emphasis is upon learning and applying the right skills. As one progresses upward there is less emphasis upon skills (or even having to know them in detail) and more emphasis on the contribution that comes from having a broad range of competencies for flexing and time-demanding conditions. At this broader end of the field's spectrum the roles and contributions are less defined. Roles and responsibilities are situational as to how the organization competes for the roles it is designed to fulfill. Determining the appropriate action to pursue depends upon the timing, market shifts, and dynamic needs of the overall organization. The right talent is defined here first by those people who can scan and read situations, apply experience and wisdom as to future directions, and know how to lead and influence to attain the most successful outcomes.

PART II:
APPLYING TODAY'S NEEDS FOR A STRONG TOMORROW

The author is honored to share 30-plus years of experience with supply managers and those considering supply management as a career. This chapter will hopefully provide some guidance, excitement, and a desire to sharpen your skills to meet the demands of this ever-evolving field. The author's career includes more than 10 years on the global level, including living and working in the United States, Canada, and Europe—each country offering a unique environment. These experiences provided the author with the opportunity to be an active participant in many evolutions within supply management from the change in the desired end goal to a significant change in the way the process occurs within the organization.

The author began his career in a traditional buying role and moved through purchasing, procurement, and managing buyer—all transactional roles, as well as handling logistics, security, facility management, and package engineering. Figure 16–1 illustrates these changes by comparing traditional purchasing to the new world of supply management.

In the late 1990s, strategic sourcing became the mantra as the role of supply management expanded and changed dramatically. Strategic sourcing is a process used to evaluate a supplier's capabilities, financial wherewithal, and ability to be cost competitive and to deliver service or product quality. In addition, it utilizes a business plan approach that is significantly different than simply negotiating a price. Therefore the supply manager is suddenly no longer acting in a silo role under the auspices of purchasing or procurement, but now within a collaborative environment with other departments. Supply managers are required to not only know the suppliers and be able to negotiate favorable contracts and cost, but now they manage and actively participate in cross-functional teams. The creation of the cross-functional team approach demanded that supply managers also

FIGURE 16-1

Traditional Purchasing versus World Class Supply Management

Traditional Purchasing (The Old World)	World Class Procurement (The New World)
Price	Total Cost Focus
Domestic Regional Suppliers	Global Sourcing
Annual Agreements	Longer-Term Contracts
Opportunistic Co-Operation	Strategic Alliances
Focus on Local Materials And Service	Focus on Company-Wide Strategic Sourcing Leverage
Many Suppliers	World Class Suppliers
Functional Orientation	Cross Functional Teams
Efficiency Measures	Effectiveness Measures

develop the competency to manage change within the organization. The new scope of responsibility became global and expanded from handling direct spend (cost of goods items) to also include indirect spend (expense items), which are an emotional gold mine of savings opportunities, not for the faint of heart.

Do You Have the Right Skills?

The role of the supply manager has significantly changed over the past 30 years and will probably continue to evolve over the next 30 years. This part of the chapter provides an overview of the skills and competencies needed for today and beyond to enhance the understanding of this dynamic field and develop a solid understanding of the skills and competencies needed in today's competitive supply management career. It includes a discussion of the differences in the skills and competencies needed to manage direct and indirect spend.

Communication Skills

In many ways today's supply manager is a salesperson. An estimated 60 percent or more of a supply manager's time is spent on selling—selling an idea or a new process internally or negotiating or persuading suppliers externally. The most critical skill in sales is, without a doubt, exceptional communication. While most people focus on written and oral communication skills, listening is just as vital. An individual can be an excellent writer and wonderful orator, but unless he or she knows what the audience wants and/or needs, a sale will not result. Good listeners know their audience, understand their circumstances and restraints, and are acutely aware of their needs. This is easier said than done, especially in a corporate environment where many employees are protective of the existing process. These employees are called "snipers," and it is best to have them participate in the process because converted snipers can become your most loyal allies (while hidden ones become a detriment to progress).

Understanding the needs and needed results from internal constituencies and external suppliers will virtually ensure success in even the most difficult of environments. Because listening is the most important communication skill, the goal is to develop questions that are not prejudicial, but rather probing. For example, "What about the process does not work?" assumes the process does not work. "If you could change anything to make your job or your department's job more efficient, what would it be?" promotes more conversation and thought. Again, asking the right question is important, but listening to the response is critical.

Now that you are listening, let us move on to written communication. The ability to concisely and articulately describe a situation, present a new idea or approach, or even debate an established practice is a critical ingredient to success. Writing comes naturally to some, while others require more training (such as a business writing course) and practice.

Finally, oral communication is vastly important. Internal presentations or leadership of a project team require every bit as much persuasion and speaking ability as a presentation to a supplier. Some presentations are electric, such as when a new idea or benefit is met with total acceptance, while others are more pragmatic. In either case the supply manager is always "selling"; therefore developing good oral communication skills and a confident style is very important.

Project Management Skills

Leading or participating in a project management team is an excellent way to develop into a true leader. The cross-functional team approach is now viewed as the most successful method, and a supply manager is often actively participating in or even leading a team. The result of the effort is 100 percent correlated to the quality of the team and its leader. Each team member (many times members are from vastly different disciplines) comes with his or her own knowledge base and set of realities, so the project leader is challenged to create the team and its infrastructure.

The following are a few hints for successful project management. The first step is to identify the most appropriate stakeholders, because they will become the lifeline in terms of support. Some may even become a mentor and guide the supply manager through an unknown process or issue. Assemble a team of six to eight members from different disciplines that are respected within their area. These individuals are knowledgeable about their area of expertise, but not necessarily about the other areas. As stakeholders, each team member is affected by the project's outcome. Many people may be protective of the existing process or service and not accept the idea that change may improve the efficiency or significantly reduce cost. To understand the team, a leader must understand its members. (Remember the first skill—communication.) These individuals will also become the sales agents for the process in their area of influence. A good first step is to ask questions, probe each team member's needs and then ask more questions. Do not forget to really listen to their questions because frequently what is being verbalized is not really what is being asked. The old adage "read between the lines" is especially helpful in internal group dynamics.

Benchmarking is an integral part of the process to ensure success. Develop a good benchmarking process at the beginning, and use it as a tool to keep the project on track and monitor resources, costs, and success. Figure 16–2 lists seven important steps in a sourcing process. The figure also shows the differences between the actions taken by supply managers for the direct and indirect spend approaches for each step.

A good, solid implementation plan will always correct a flawed strategy, but the reverse does not hold true. This is particularly true in today's collaborative environment where so many people participate in a project. A strong implementation plan will guide the group toward a smoother implementation. In fact, while many can develop strategies, the most successful supply managers can implement and measure against the appropriate key performance indicators (KPIs) included in the implementation plan. Always keep in mind that compliance to the plan is key.

Are You a Skilled Risk Taker?

Risk taking is an art, and many live by the rule "ask forgiveness not permission." Risk taking is the willingness to accept new ideas and change even though there may not be a guaranteed improvement. Supply managers or project managers, however, should not throw caution to the wind. They should clearly evaluate the risks and the rewards, be open to other approaches, and not be afraid of controversy. Remember that the supply manager's initial or gut reaction may be the best way to proceed. However, if you are not willing to accept the risk and consequences (both good and bad), then you should not be leading a project team.

Creativity is another important skill because risk taking is closely related to creative problem solving. While it is important to analyze a situation and evaluate the risks and rewards, analysis should not paralyze you from thinking creatively and taking a risk. Creative thinking is important because in a cross-functional project team there will always be problems and different opinions or approaches, and the group may never be in total agreement. While problem solving is a skill requiring methodical analytical ability, creative thinking resolves obstacles in nonconventional ways and often on an immediate basis.

FIGURE 16–2

The Seven-Step Supply Management Methodology

Approaches required by supply management by sourcing step

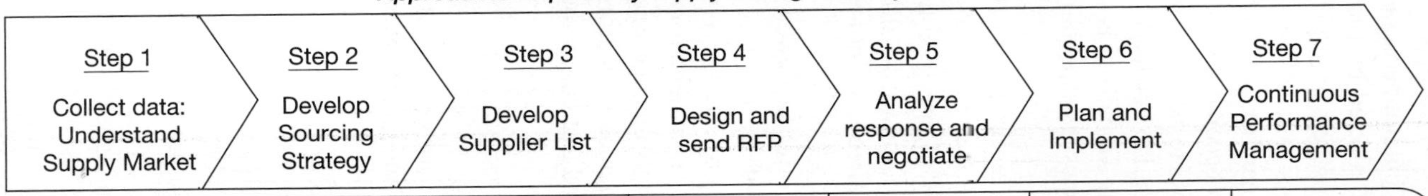

	Step 1 Collect data: Understand Supply Market	Step 2 Develop Sourcing Strategy	Step 3 Develop Supplier List	Step 4 Design and send RFP	Step 5 Analyze response and negotiate	Step 6 Plan and Implement	Step 7 Continuous Performance Management
Direct	• Gather data from existing systems and supply market • Forecasts are available	• Compile organizational /risk opportunity assessment • Benchmark	• Gather data/ measurements on historical and potential market providers	• Outline specific supply chain requirements and tolerances in RFP	• Finalize pricing and performance measures with suppliers and SC	• Develop integrated implementation team to ensure success	• Corp. Leadership meet regularly with supplier to review performance data
Indirect	• Overcome the fact that it is difficult to understand with high degree of certainty what you have bought • Operate less sophisticated systems • Stakeholder interviews	• Estimate leverage and organizational tolerance for supplier changes • May require new internal processes • Benchmark • Need incumbents info to gather spend	• Determine incumbents from payable data • Examine other sources for alternative suppliers	• Design RFP to have the flexibility to handle variations in demand and a high degree of customization in the services provided	• Negotiate pricing and performance measures while discussing options with stakeholders	• Introduce supplier (co-selling solutions) to stakeholders within different organizations • Change internal processes and manage change	• Review KPI periodically across multiple categories • Rely heavily on qualitative information

There are some who naturally "think out of the box" just as there are some who can sit at an easel and paint a landscape. If creativity does not come naturally to you, make sure someone who supports you is creative and fully involved.

Natural risk takers enjoy the challenge of a difficult situation or person and have no problem taking a risk. A safer way to temper risk taking is through a more deliberate and creative problem-solving approach. This often comes with age and/or experience.

Although there are many classes available to learn the fine art of risk taking, the best way to learn is through experience. If you are lucky enough to work in an environment that supports and fosters taking risks, you will learn quickly. If not, find a mentor either within the company or industry or outside, and start working on developing these skills. In this competitive world you will need to bring creativity and risk taking to the table in order to be truly successful.

The degree of risk taking will be different within each company. Some companies applaud "out of the box" thinking and have a high threshold for new ideas and processes, while others are risk-averse. So the first step is to determine how the company responds to creativity and risk taking and then develop your own style and approach. There will be times within your career that "what you can't do by diplomacy you must do by surgery" and that is your welcome to management.

Decision-Making Skills

The next critical skill in supply management is decision making. Although most decisions are made in a cross-functional team environment, that does not mean decisions are made on a consensus basis. Not everyone is going to be happy with the end result, much less the process. Many supply management experts have superior knowledge, excellent presentation skills, and commitment, but simply cannot make a controversial decision. Of course not all decisions are controversial, but all projects require decisions and some are difficult because of the many variables and diverse needs of the involved departments.

The following is how the decision-making process typically flows in the supply management process:

- All necessary research and information is completed.
- The team has agreed, and a starting point is established.
- The project leader has sold the idea to other internal stakeholders.
- The implementation plan is completed and accepted.
- The final decision is made.

Pretty logical, right? In many instances at least 50 percent of projects fail because the last step is not taken. As the leader, the supply manager must be able to evaluate each component, assess the risks and rewards, convince key stakeholders, and move to a decision.

Computer Literacy Can and Should Be Learned

In today's environment most do not have the luxury of full-time administrative assistance; thus computer literacy and familiarity with various software programs is another significant skill. Computer literacy is important and greatly reduces the time it takes to oversee and manage a project. The supply manager most frequently uses presentation software or spreadsheet software. Additionally, matrix and project management software are also crucial. Many efficient programs exist to enhance the project management process.

Supply managers must be able to recognize the value and evaluate the use of the continuous flood of e-commerce tools, from data gathering and electronic matching to auctions, inventory control, and cost comparisons. They are all computer-driven, and one cannot afford to avoid these areas due to a lack of computer skills.

Finally, from a bigger picture, the cross-functional project team should include an information technology (IT) representative whenever new products or services will require IT interface. IT can either be a lifesaver by saving you time in redesign, or a detriment, because of the lack of creative thinking in the overall project. Not all IT people are uncreative, but they tend to be less able to think out of the box, so be careful not to allow IT to run the project or define its scope based on its limitations. Rather, select IT representatives carefully and foster their creativity and innovative problem-solving approaches.

Additional Skills Needed to Become a World-Class Supply Manager

Three additional skills are fundamental and basic to the success of a supply manager: analytical problem solving, technical knowledge, and negotiation skills.

The supply manager must be comfortable analyzing and understanding the nuts and bolts of the project or process. Many supply managers come from a finance background and are comfortable with numbers. However, analytical problem solving is not only financial or cost-based; it almost always is much larger in focus. For example, in most cases, analytical skills are required when a supply manager is evaluating the potential outsourcing of a department or function. The analytical process involves more than a price review when following due diligence to determine whether outsourcing is appropriate from a cost, cultural, or service perspective.

Technical knowledge is an obvious need. A supply manager must have superior technical knowledge to manage the process and fully understand the end result. In many cases supply managers are generalists and maybe even catalysts to change. But they must always surround themselves with technical experts and then learn from them. The only exception, of course, is that within the cost of the goods-buying arena one must have vertical knowledge (feedstock to end product).

Finally, negotiation skills are another very important skill. In a cross-functional team, negotiating is simply part of the way to get things done. As persua-

sive sales people, supply managers learn early that they will always need to negotiate with external suppliers and even internal stakeholders.

Necessary Competencies for the Supply Manager

As a leader in supply management, a supply manager will need to demonstrate
competencies in many areas, including

- Team leadership participation and commitment
- Change management and accountability
- Development of others and empowerment

In the cross-functional team there are no "I"s and just one "we." Generally
speaking, an effective or productive cross-functional team requires six to
eight people. The team leader has the accountability, while the team as a whole
has the responsibility. Single accountability is important, regardless of how much
matrix management exists. When one person holds total accountability for the
project, that person will drive the success. A true leader will ensure that all team
members feel the same level of responsibility and commitment. For example, it is
critical that the leader assign tasks, lead segments, and level the workload from
the beginning; otherwise the team will never get to the end. Another significant
dynamic is team commitment, which leads to success on all levels.

Most people are averse to change for a variety of reasons, but mostly because
it is going to require something new of them personally or of their department. This
is true even when the end result will greatly improve their work, so be aware that
change is difficult and it is the supply manager's job to manage it so that the end
result can happen.

A supply manager's responsibility is to make change happen, and sometimes
that means not being the most popular person—at least in the initial stages of the
project or process. There are many aspects and skills to effecting and managing
change, and the best is to be a great facilitator (communication, again). A major
part of change management is getting stakeholders to buy in to the idea that change
will improve the process or product, that it will be worth the effort, and that better
overall cost management will be achieved.

Facilitating the change-management process is where you will find snipers—
you'll hear the remarks or see the hesitation or even destruction of an idea or process.
Now, before implementation, is the time to confront the snipers. Either eliminate
them from the project team entirely (not always possible) or disable them quickly
and make sure the team understands why. You will not only gain respect from other
team members, but also many times from the sniper.

Management Development Is Self-Development

Another important competency required to move to the next level of supply management is self-development and the development of others. The manager must
create the environment for people to understand and be committed to the project.

Many companies that tout their management development programs are just constantly moving people horizontally or vertically. To gain knowledge a person must be in a position long enough to be accountable. Many people actually excel at moving from position to position garnering no significant knowledge or understanding of what they are doing. These people are jokingly referred to as "Teflon people."

All these competencies are the building blocks of a world-class attitude. One way of knowing that the group or department has attained world-class status is when your staff, project team participants, or others outside your company begin to imitate your style or leadership skills.

Indirect versus Direct Supply Management

The future supply management group not only will be world class in managing direct spend, but also will be world class in managing indirect spend at the local, regional, and global level, and as a team leader or promoter of most company-sponsored projects.

Direct supply managers traditionally are technical experts who use deductive reasoning based on qualitative facts and have vertical knowledge working in a traditional buying organization, managing more well-defined goods and services. In fact, data drives the process. Generally there is little contact with internal constituencies, and so extensive experience in change management is not critical. The more traditional procurement techniques and expertise are critical to the overall success of direct supply management (see Figure 16–3).

The indirect supply manager must satisfy more internal constituents with a lower degree of specifications and sometimes a negligible amount of usable data. Further, the successful indirect spend supply manager will have finely tuned project management skills and must have the flexibility, category expertise, and developments skills to handle complex spend categories (see Figure 16–4).

It is important to differentiate between indirect and direct supply managers. Indirect spend is expenses other than salaries and the costs of goods sold. This includes telecommunications; office supplies; printed materials; advertising; merchant accounts; freight; warehousing; outsourcing of human resources; legal services or payroll; facility management; security; leases; computer equipment; maintenance contracts; benefits; waste removal; travel and travel agencies; rental cars and fleet vehicles; fuel; utilities; capital goods; uniforms; insurance; workers compensation costs; and maintenance, repair, and operating supplies (MRO).

Why are these expenses considered "emotional gold mines"? Indirect spend affects almost every department within the company, which means that virtually every area will be involved on some level in the cross-functional team. This explains the term *emotional* (remember that change of any type is not always embraced and sometimes leads to major resistance). Why a gold mine? Because these expenses represent a considerable spend with virtually no supply management involvement. Anyone with sales experience knows that sales are based on

F I G U R E   16–3

Required Competencies for Direct Supply Management

Required Competencies for Direct Supply Management

Characteristics	Required Competencies
• Quantitatively define specifications and monitor service levels • Quantitative data analysis drive the decision process with few intangibles impacting the analysis • Few internal constituents with minimal change management required • Experienced suppliers • Vertical intelligence • Cross-regional market expertise • Financial and trade regulatory issues	• Technical expertise in category • Quantitative analysis • Deductive reasoning based on quantitative facts • Traditional procurement techniques and expertise • Insights into the value-adding options and alternative by understanding inputs and the outputs of the manufacturing process • Cross-regional supply market understanding • Understanding of financial and trade regulations

F I G U R E   16–4

Required Competencies for Indirect Supply Management

Required Competencies for Indirect Supply Management

Characteristics	Required Competencies
• Difficult to precisely define specifications • Less predictable spend with limited data • Specifications are complex, dependent on intangibles and must be flexible enough to satisfy multiple end-users • Service many varied end-user groups • Compliance is often unmanaged and difficult to track • Inexperienced suppliers, especially in dealing with diverse business units • Multiple unrelated categories and/or projects	• Ability to handle limited data creatively • Organizational clout with user community • Extensive experience within the user community • Cultural understanding of the constituents' organization • Extensive internal network • Change management • Ongoing relationship management (coaching) with suppliers and internal constituents • Ability to manage several unrelated projects • Entrepreneurship-ability to"sell in" a program • Capable of driving consensus

relationships, and most of the suppliers of indirect items have long-term relationships with people in the buying organization, most of the time without the oversight of supply management.

It will be an emotional process to engage the team; however the gold mine is easily reached. Implementing a supply management process in these areas can result in excess of a 25 percent cost savings and even more over time. But, and this is a big but, this requires a change. No longer can someone use their favorite office supplier (unless it is the approved supplier). These are the most fertile grounds for cost reduction and the safest haven for snipers. The one area with few snipers but significant savings is telecommunications because it is such a siloed area with few involved in the actual operations of the organization. From a purely cost reduction perspective, these products and services are easily evaluated and a new process can be implemented.

Here is a true and classic example: XYZ company used eight or nine different limousine services. The company rationalized by selecting two services and reduced cost by more than 25 percent without impacting service. Sounds simple, but it was in fact a very difficult, even ugly process. Many people were accustomed to their drivers; they had long-established relationships and did not want to change in any way. The calls from the executives, not to mention their administrative assistants, questioned the quality and challenged the reduction in cost. However, over time, new relationships were established and acceptance came with the realization that the quality of service was equal to or better than the previous suppliers while achieving a significant cost savings (which means more time is spent on data gathering, estimation, and investigation). In addition, indirect supply managers must effect in some cases significant and emotional change within the organization and that requires excellent communication skills. Team leadership and decision-making ability are also critical to the successful indirect supply manager. See how these skills and competencies tie together?

In general, indirect supply managers must satisfy more internal constituents with a lower degree of specifications and sometimes a negligible amount of usable data. This all translates into a longer and more emotional process.

A very good friend, Bob Hutchens, a vice president with Booz Allen Hamilton in New York, with many years of experience, offered the following.

> I think that people need to remember that when you source directs you are not changing specifications. Although you may well change suppliers, generally you are buying a commodity that can be described scientifically (for example, by size or performance) and that can be bid on by packaging, chemical or other raw-material suppliers. The trick with indirects arises when you bring subjectivity into things like what constitutes a reasonable travel policy? What does a good advertising agency look like? Whenever I source directs, I have been able to obtain a 10 to 25 percent savings without changing specifications. Specifications, reductions or improvement typically result in an additional 5 to 15 percent savings, but because of the long lead-time, for stability testing or production testing, it is something that gets implemented outside of the sourcing process. When sourcing indirects you have to change

the behavior of many people who have a vested interest in maintaining the existing supplier relationship or arrangement. You can no longer use a specific supplier (airline) or agency (travel) or item (a specific brand of blue pens). These become very difficult to control and gain compliance. The bottom line, in my opinion, is that the supply manager handling indirects faces much more complexity and is challenged with balancing many more intangibles.

Successful careers also incorporate passion and fun. Passion is everything. The drive to do the best job possible in every circumstance and the willingness to go above and beyond expectations is what will separate you from others. World-class supply managers are passionate about their projects, about understanding the needs of others, persuading audiences, negotiating internally and externally, and most of all about implementing accurately and measuring correctly.

Passion must be managed and focused. To energize the cross-functional team with passion and a desire to supersede expectations is an art, but once that happens nothing will stand in the way of success—not the snipers, not anything.

Finally, there is fun that makes it all worthwhile. It may sound trite, but within appropriate business guidelines, fun is good and further energizes people and the team.

It is very disappointing that so many lack these skills in today's business environment. The competitiveness within the supply management industry is intense, but that does not mean that business life needs to be combative. Many projects require the leader to energize the project team—somehow unite them to act and respond as a team and not individual representatives for different departments. Silly slogans or outfits appropriate to the project may help boost motivation, create a bond, generate awareness, and energize the team.

Building Supply Talent

Above competencies is talent. Talent is the capability to quickly identify or capture the organization's needed imperatives and develop the needed competencies and supporting skills to bring about successful performance. Talent is less defined than competencies and skills, because it is largely situational and not known until a person is tested and performs. While talent means high performance in a current area, it is also the ability to develop for new, unexpected, and yet to be defined demands and opportunities. Organizational development researchers agree that persons with talent possess strong track records of accomplishments. They also develop new tools and approaches for new challenges and opportunities. And, they are able to transfer their skills and capabilities as they move from one area, discipline, or industry to others. Supply is a field that is ever-evolving, and the pace of change and transformation will no doubt accelerate in the future. Having talented people who can flex and develop tools and approaches needed for this undefined future is critical for competitive organizations.

CHAPTER 17

FUNCTION AND FORM IN SUPPLY MANAGEMENT ORGANIZATIONS

GREGORY M. MAGNAN, PH.D.
Associate Professor, Operations Management
Albers School of Business and Economics
Seattle University

STANLEY E. FAWCETT, PH.D.
Professor, Global Supply Chain Management
Marriott School of Management
Brigham Young University

INTRODUCTION

Four trends are dramatically shaping the business environment:

1. Global competition is increasing.

2. Technological life cycles are turning faster.

3. Customers are becoming more knowledgeable and demanding.

4. Financial markets are requiring firms to be more productive with capital and assets.

A likely result of this combination of factors is an increasing strategic role for the supply organization and a new mandate for supply management (SM): deliver better products and services and improved financial performance to the enterprise. The growing trend toward outsourcing (often just called "sourcing") of direct and indirect materials, services, and business processes widens the span of control and furthers the strategic importance of SM.[1]

The relationships between directives from a corporate level (driven by changes in the external environment), the strategies deployed in the supply management organization to support the directives, and the resultant impact on the

---

1 Robert M. Monczka, John D. Blascovich, and Joseph R. Carter (2004). "Strategic Outsourcing: Emerging Trends and Success Factors," presented at the 89th Annual International Supply Management Conference, April, Philadelphia, PA.

FIGURE   17-1

Supply Management Changes in Response to Corporate Directives

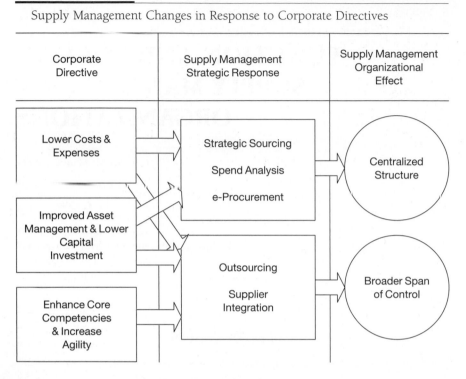

roles, responsibilities, and structure of the SM organization are portrayed in Figure 17–1. The expectation over the next five years is that global competition and pressure on financial results will drive firms to (1) further reduce the costs of purchased goods and services, (2) reduce business expenses by increasing business process outsourcing, and (3) drive firms to focus on core competencies and off-load under-performing assets, thereby increasing outsourcing.

There are two net results of the cost management and outsourcing effects for SM. First, an increasing amount of company spend will come under the control of SM. Subsequently, the increased need for control will drive a move toward centralization of part of the supply management organization. Second, the need for coordination with internal customers and external providers of goods and services will increase, broadening SM roles, responsibilities, and reach. For example, supplier selection and management processes will be applied to a wider variety of industries and commodity types. Facilitating relationships between internal customers and these external product and service providers will also be a growth business for SM. Ultimately, control and coordination factors will drive gains in overall strategic responsibility. In this scenario, a hybrid organizational structure is likely, with some elements of an SM organization decentralized to offer higher levels of service to internal customers and external partners, while maintaining a center-led function for leverage. The trend toward greater numbers of SM leaders reporting to the firm's executive team should also continue.[2]

This chapter addresses ways in which the supply organization is responding to these strategic effects, beginning with the changes to the roles and responsibilities of the supply organization, moving to the structural changes required to support the strategic changes, and ending with a look at other issues affecting the role and structure of SM, such as supplier integration, globalization, supply chain management, and trust.

CHANGES IN SUPPLY MANAGEMENT: ROLES AND RESPONSIBILITIES

The nature of business strategy focuses on the relationship between the firm (core competencies and capabilities, assets, organization structure, and performance) and the needs and demands of its external environment (competitors, technology, customers, investors, as well as suppliers) (see Figure 17–2). As its external environment changes, any company must react to the change through its business strategy. More rapidly changing environments require more agile companies. The feedback loop on financial performance in Figure 17–2 may cause further changes in strategy, as firms make adjustments to their strategy to meet financial objectives and targets.

Functional strategies should support the firm's business strategy, and as the business strategy changes, so must the functional strategies. At some point, changes in business strategy necessitate adjustments in the roles and responsibilities of the firm's functional organizations, either adding to or subtracting from the scope of duties.

Leenders and Johnson examined this issue in a study comparing changes to the roles and responsibilities of the SM function in 10 firms.[3] The majority of changes logged resulted in responsibilities and activities being *added* to the domain of SM, meaning that a wider array of goods and services were being purchased, more activities were managed by SM, and involvement in corporate activities was increasingly categorized as meaningful. At the studied companies, 65 commodities and services were added to SM responsibilities, while just 22 were deleted, indicating a shift to more items being run through the sample firms' SM organizations (see Table 17–1). Of the six acquisition categories the study used, services by far had the most additions (41 of 65), reflecting the trend to centralize overall company spend of all varieties, not just direct materials. Deletions were often items that were moving to full outsource (e.g., warehousing). The needs most commonly added to SM were dominated by services and included freight,

2 P. Fraser Johnson and Michiel Leenders (2004). "Supply Organizational Roles and Responsibilities." CAPS Focus Study, Tempe, AZ.

3 Michiel Leenders and P. Fraser Johnson (2002). "Major Changes in Supply Chain Responsibilities," CAPS Focus Study, Tempe, AZ.

FIGURE 17-2

Organizational Structure Drivers

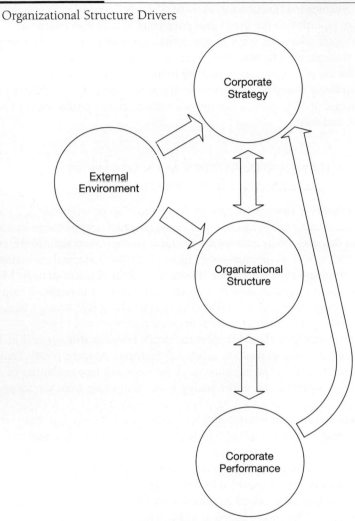

Adapted from P. Fraser Johnson (2003). "Supply Organizational Structures," CAPS Critical Issues Report, August, Tempe, AZ.

logistics, and transportation services; IT equipment; travel; consulting services; marketing and advertising; and subcontracted components.

Changes in activities within the total supply chain for which supply has responsibility were also tracked in the study. The top activities being added to SM's scope were

- Centralized coordination (10 of 10 firms)
- E-procurement (5 of 10 firms)

T A B L E   17–1

Supply Chain Responsibility Changes

Type of Category Change	Additions	Deletions	Total
What is Acquired	65	22	87
Supply Chain Activities	51	20	71
Role	11	1	12
Corporate Activities	31	1	32
Total	158	44	202

SOURCE: Michiel Leenders and P. Fraser Johnson (2002). "Major Changes in Supply Chain Responsibilities." CAPS Focus Study, Tempe, AZ.

- Logistics, transportation, and warehousing (5 of 10 firms)
- Processes and systems, and supply chain excellence (3 of 10 firms)
- Accounts payable (3 of 10 firms)

The increased variety of items purchased and the expansion of activities indicate an increasing role and span of control for the supply management function and hint at SM's potential impact on the financial performance of a firm. Companies in the Leenders and Johnson study also indicated that the SM organization's involvement in company matters was becoming much more meaningful and broad-based.

In a different study, Morgan also reports that many supply managers are taking on new responsibilities, experiencing increasing roles, or being more involved in company-level activities.[4] Services are well-represented among the areas being added. The new areas (with roles in parentheses) include

- New product design (strategy compliance)
- Logistics (restructuring)
- Reverse auctions (supervisor)
- Outsourcing (project manager)
- IT (outsourcing)
- Finance (cost reduction)
- Design (early supplier involvement)

---

4 Jim Morgan (2003). "How Buyers Are Changing," *Purchasing*, August 14, pp. 33–37.

- Contract labor (cost reduction)
- Inventory (cost reduction)

Just as the studies by Morgan and by Leenders and Johnson report that services are becoming a greater component of the supply management organization's responsibility, Porter notes that 95 percent of recently surveyed supply professionals indicate that supply management's influence over services spend is expected to grow in the next five years.[5] This may be an area requiring additional education for supply managers as a recent study indicates they consider the purchasing process to be different than that of materials, as well as being more complex than a material buy.[6]

CHANGES IN SUPPLY MANAGEMENT: FINANCIAL PERFORMANCE

As Figure 17–2 indicates, financial performance can be another driver of organizational change. If either the strategy or structure is out of alignment with each other or the external environment, financial performance is likely to suffer. The feedback loop may report that performance is lagging and therefore a change is required, in either the firm's strategy, its structure, or both elements.

At a more local level, the ability of the supply management organization to affect the financial performance of the firm is well-documented and forms the basis for the many calls for a more strategic role for SM.[7] Table 17–2 displays the relationship between SM actions and financial performance drivers and highlights the numerous linkages between the two. Actions in SM can affect the balance sheet (e.g., fixed and current assets), income statement (e.g., revenue enhancement through supplier involvement), and the statement of cash flows (e.g., cash-to-cash cycle time, payment terms, inventory levels).

Strategic Sourcing and Outsourcing

As the designated authority for purchasing in a company, one way that firms are responding to the need for improved financial performance is to require more of a firm's purchases be run through the SM organization. According to the recent

5 Anne Millen Porter (2003). "Controlling Total Spend," *Purchasing*, November 6, pp. 31–37.

6 Larry R. Smeltzer and Jeffrey A. Ogden (2002). "Purchasing Professionals' Perceived Differences between Purchasing Materials and Purchasing Services," *Journal of Supply Chain Management*, Winter, vol. 38, no. 1, pp. 54–70.

7 Lisa M. Ellram and Baohong Liu (2002). "The Financial IMPACT of Supply Management," *Supply Chain Management Review*, November, vol. 6, no. 6, p. 30; Stephen Timme and Christine Williams-Timme (2000). "The Financial-SCM Connection," *Supply Chain Management Review*, May–June, vol. 4, no. 3, pp. 32–43.

TABLE 17–2

Financial Measures and Supply Management Actions

Financial Driver	Financial Statement Element	Supply Management Action
Growth	Revenue Market share	Supplier design involvement Innovation Purchased goods
Profitability / EVA	Revenue Cost of goods sold Other cost clements	Operational excellence Purchase, freight, labor, transportation expense SMI programs, warehousing
Asset Management (ROA, ROIC)	Inventory Receivables Fixed assets Accounts payables	Inventory policy Payment terms Property, plant, equipment Systems and hardware Outsourcing/contract manufacturing
Cash Flow	Operating activities Investing activities Financial activities	Inventory management Order policy Payment terms Make/buy decisions

(Adapted from Ellram and Liu, 2002 and Timme and Timme, 2000)

survey by Monczka et al.,[8] outsourcing is being driven by six dominating factors, three of which come from financial performance goals and three from strategic factors (see Table 17–3). The top two responses—reducing operating cost and reducing capital investments—both directly affect the financial statements and support the profitability driver and asset management driver from Table 17–2. Focusing on core competencies certainly has support for strategic reasons,[9] but also allows firms to move underperforming assets off of their balance sheet, again touching the asset management driver in Table 17–2.

One response to the *reduce operating costs* driver in Table 17–3 is the use of strategic sourcing in supply management.[10] Porter notes that strategic sourcing

---

8 Monczka et al., "Strategic Outsourcing."

9 C. K. Prahalad and G. Hamel (1990). "The Core Competence of the Corporation," *Harvard Business Review*, May–June, pp. 79–91.

10 Peter E. O'Reilly (2002). "Achieving World Class Purchasing through Solving the Centralized vs. Decentralized Organizational Dilemma," presented at the 87th Annual International Supply Management Conference.

T A B L E   17-3

Outsourcing Drivers

Outsourcing Driver	Percent Indicating
Reduce Operating Costs	89%
Reduce Capital Investment	81%
Focus on Core Competencies	81%
Increase Flexibility & responsiveness	60%
Gain Access to Technology	60%
Turn Fixed Cost into Variable	58%

(Adapted from Monczka et al., 2001)

is "applying standard analytics-driven processes for sourcing any category of spend."[11] One of the analyses involves collecting data on the amount of money flowing out of the company to all suppliers (spend). Porter observed that corporate spend as a percentage of revenues has increased from 43 percent in 1996 to 48 percent in 2002, reflecting increased outsourcing. Additionally, the percentage of corporate spend controlled by SM organizations has increased dramatically, rising from 45 percent in 1996 to over 80 percent in 2002. More recently, Porter identified several firms with spend control percentages in the 90s (PPG, Delphi Automotive, Xerox, NCR, and Intel) and two firms with 100 percent of spend captured by a spend analysis system (IBM and Microsoft).[12]

Understanding corporate spend (how much business is being done with each supplier, what goods and services are they providing, who are the internal users, etc.) is the first step toward reducing prices paid and, eventually, costs. Areas in the company in which to look for spend data include purchasing and e-procurement systems, P-card databases, general ledger and accounts payable, enterprise resource planning systems, and inventory and materials management systems. The knowledge can also be used to aggregate spend across the company to drive costs down and margins up. Other benefits of spend analysis include better-managed supply base reduction programs, the formation of cross-functional commodity teams, and the creation of commodity strategies. Making it easy for internal users to categorize spend helps with compliance.

Technology certainly has had an impact on companies' ability to capture spend data. Violino reports that enterprise spend management (ESM) systems do require buy-in from users throughout the company to take the time to properly code monies spent (which of course assumes that spend categories have been pre-

---

11 Porter, "Controlling Total Spend."

12 Anne Millen Porter (2004). "Super Spend Analysis," *Purchasing*, March 18, pp. 28–42.

13 Bob Violino (2003). "Follow the Money," CFO, September, p. 15.

viously defined!).[13] Cleaning up data from purchase orders and other documents is also required, as is combining data from multiple legacy systems. Spend software, either purchased or built in-house, can offer real-time access to spend data, allow for deployment of policies like "no PO, no payables" (to require units to use the system), and facilitate aggregation of commodity spend across decentralized units.

New capabilities in information technology, combined with financial pressure to reduce costs and improve asset performance, have led to responsibility and role expansion in supply management. Similarly, increased outsourcing—both of services and business processes and of contract manufacturing—has altered the duties of the supply management function by adding to the breadth of goods and services procured, as well as to the role of SM in managing new commodities. Perhaps the long-awaited strategic role for supply management is not far off.

CHANGES IN SUPPLY MANAGEMENT: ORGANIZATION DESIGN

Historically, the firm's structure has changed along with its strategy in an effort to align the capabilities of the firm with the objectives of the strategy.[14] History also shows that there is no "one best way" to structure an organization; rather firms may adopt a variety of structures depending on internal and external conditions. Many firms will continue to adjust their structure in an effort to improve this alignment (and subsequent performance), even without a change in strategy (see Figure 17–2). A recent CAPS Research report concluded that structural change within the supply organization is now a constant theme.[15]

Supply management is one of the firm's boundary-spanning entities, meaning it interacts with the firm's external environment, extending beyond the boundaries of the firm. The trend toward outsourcing more business activities and processes is likely to continue, and data suggests the move toward purchasing globally will continue to grow.[16] The combination of purchasing a broader range of goods and services and an expansion of global sourcing increases the number and complexity of touch points between a firm and its suppliers of goods and services. What then is the appropriate structure of the supply organization?

Organization Design Elements

Before addressing design issues in the supply management organization, the broader structure and design at the corporate level should first be discussed. The

---

14 Alfred Chandler (1962). *Strategy and Structure*, Cambridge, MA: MIT Press.

15 P. Fraser Johnson (2003). "Supply Organizational Structures," CAPS Critical Issues Report, August, Tempe, AZ.

16 Robert J. Trent and Robert M. Monczka (2005). "Creating a World Class Global Sourcing Organization," *Sloan Management Review*, Fall, vol. 47, no. 1, pp. 24–32.

structure of an organization serves multiple objectives, from providing the frame-work for division of labor and specialization, to facilitating coordination across departments using integrative mechanisms, to defining the boundary of the organization.[17] Primary elements of organization design include

- Work specialization
- Coordination mechanisms
- Decision rights and authority
- Organization boundaries
- Formalization
- Span of control
- Centralization or decentralization
- Departmentalization (form)

Departmentalization addresses the way in which the assets and resources of the firm are ultimately configured. Classic options range from a functional to a divisional structure, with the divisional structure containing the option to split by product, process, customer, and geographic region. Functional structures maintain functional expertise and often use centralized control mechanisms. Companies that want to be more closely aligned to their products and customers may structure themselves along those lines, but often pay a price in duplicating functional resources across the divisions.

Matrix structures are a hybrid form that attempt to overcome the separation and cost challenges of functional and divisional organizations. Functional skills and groups are maintained, and resources are allocated to the corresponding divisional unit (product, region, or customer) in the gridlike structure. Anyone who has ever worked in a matrix organization knows the major challenge is figuring out how to work for two bosses! Functional organizations generally maintain performance management duties, with input from their divisional counterparts. Teamwork, efficient use of resources, and opportunities for growth are positives of the matrix structure, while power struggles and confusion reign as negative consequences.

At the corporate level, the decisions to adopt a functional or divisional structure, wide or narrow spans of control, and the appropriate coordination mechanisms are driven by a complex set of factors. Company strategy, size, and product complexity, along with environmental uncertainty, culture, technology and geographical spread are all factors that must be weighed before the correct structure is implemented. And even then, it's likely to change because of a change in strategy, leadership, or financial performance.

---

17 Nitin Nohria (1991). "Note on Organization Structure," Harvard Business School Publishing. Cambridge: MA.

When the corporation changes its structure, the ramifications of the change usually reverberate down to the functional groups in the company. In their study of shifts within SM, Johnson and Leenders found that major changes in supply management organization structure were actually caused by changes to the corporate structure of the firm, usually without consideration for effects in SM.[18] Of the 15 structural changes they identified in the 10 firms studied, *all* were initiated by changes at corporate. In each of the 15 cases, the primary driver for *corporate* structural change was cost reduction. In supply management, nine of the changes were moves toward increased centralization in SM, and six were headed toward decentralization.

Supply Management Design

Trent identifies organizational design as one of the four pillars of supply chain excellence (the others are human resources, information technology, and organizational measurement).[19] Not surprisingly, the basic design elements of structure present at the corporate level are repeated within the supply management organization. Rogers presents his variation of the design elements, one that is directed at the supply management function.[20] Figure 17–3 is a summary adaptation of his model. The six elements (tasks, people, information, decision making, rewards, and structure) are quite similar to those identified by Nohria,[21] but were selected by Rogers to be more accessible and appropriate to SM.

One major difference in approach is that Rogers' model reflects the organization and boundary-spanning role of SM, and the design philosophy therefore must account for internal customers, external suppliers, and the internal structure of the SM function. For example, information must be shared with the external supply community (e.g., forecasts, orders, designs), collected from and shared with the firm's internal customers (inventory levels, approved suppliers), and finally information must be shared within the supply management organization (supplier data, policies, performance to metrics). The boundary-spanning nature of SM dramatically increases the complexity of the task of determining the appropriate structure. Again, Rogers' model reflects the what, the who, and the how of work that gets done in SM and does so by addressing issues that are external to the firm, those that concern SM's relationship with internal customers, and finally, those things that matter to the people that work in the department.

---

18 P. Fraser Johnson and Michiel Leenders (2001). "The Supply Organizational Structure Dilemma," *Journal of Supply Chain Management*, Summer, vol. 37, no. 3, pp. 4–11.

19 Robert J. Trent (2004). "What Everyone Needs to Know About SCM," *Supply Chain Management Review*, March, vol. 8, no. 3, pp. 52–59.

20 Steve Rogers (2004). "Supply Management: Six Elements of Superior Design," *Supply Chain Management Review,* April, vol. 8, no. 4, pp. 48–55.

21 Nohria, "Note on Organization Structure."

FIGURE 17–3

Organizational Design Elements for Supply Management

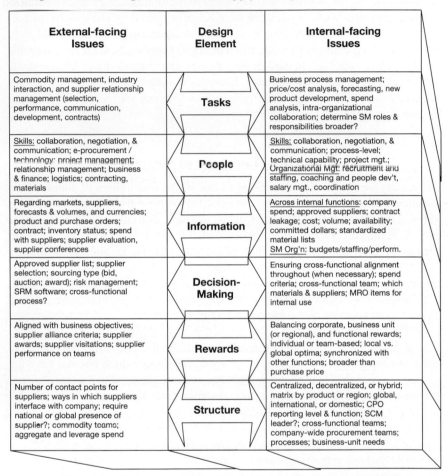

External-facing Issues	Design Element	Internal-facing Issues
Commodity management, industry interaction, and supplier relationship management (selection, performance, communication, development, contracts)	Tasks	Business process management; price/cost analysis, forecasting, new product development, spend analysis, intra-organizational collaboration; determine SM roles & responsibilities broader?
Skills: collaboration, negotiation, & communication; e-procurement / technology; project management; relationship management; business & finance; logistics; contracting, materials	People	Skills: collaboration, negotiation, & communication; process-level; technical capability; project mgt.; Organizational Mgt: recruitment and staffing, coaching and people dev't, salary mgt., coordination
Regarding markets, suppliers, forecasts & volumes, and currencies; product and purchase orders; contract; inventory status; spend with suppliers; supplier evaluation, supplier conferences	Information	Across internal functions: company spend; approved suppliers; contract leakage; cost; volume; availability; committed dollars; standardized material lists SM Org'n: budgets/staffing/perform.
Approved supplier list; supplier selection; sourcing type (bid, auction; award); risk management; SRM software; cross-functional process?	Decision-Making	Ensuring cross-functional alignment throughout (when necessary); spend criteria; cross-functional team; which materials & suppliers; MRO items for internal use
Aligned with business objectives; supplier alliance criteria; supplier awards; supplier visitations; supplier performance on teams	Rewards	Balancing corporate, business unit (or regional), and functional rewards; individual or team-based; local vs. global optima; synchronized with other functions; broader than purchase price
Number of contact points for suppliers; ways in which suppliers interface with company; require national or global presence of supplier?; commodity teams; aggregate and leverage spend	Structure	Centralized, decentralized, or hybrid; matrix by product or region; global, international, or domestic; CPO reporting level & function; SCM leader?; cross-functional teams; company-wide procurement teams; processes; business-unit needs

Source: Adapted from Steve Rogers (2004). "Supply Management: Six Elements of Superior Design," *Supply Chain Management Review*, April, pp. 48–55.

One of the design elements in Figure 17–3 is the *structure* of the function, for which the major internal questions revolve around centralization. We've touched on this concept a couple of times already in this chapter, so let's dig a bit more deeply into its meaning. *Centralization* refers to the degree to which purchasing is controlled at one central location for the entire firm.[22] *Decentralization* denotes that main purchasing is controlled at the business units or plants. A

---

22 Leenders and Johnson (2002). "Major Changes in Supply Chain Responsibilities."

hybrid structure lies in between, and in these firms, purchasing is shared between corporate offices and business units and operating plants. Tables 17–4 and 17–5 highlight the advantages and disadvantages of both centralized and decentralized supply management.

The primary benefits of a centralized SM organization are due to the aggregation of spend, supplier reduction, development of talent, strategic focus, and

TABLE   17–4

Advantages and Disadvantages of Centralization of Supply Management

Centralization	
ADVANTAGES	**DISADVANTAGES**
Greater buying specialization — proficiency	Narrow specialization and job boredom
Ability to pay for talent	Lack of job flexibility
Consolidation of requirements — leverage	Corporate staff appears excessive
Tendency to minimize legitimate differences in requirements	Tendency to minimize legitimate differences in requirements
Coordination / control of policies & procedures	Lack of recognition of unique needs
Effective planning and research	Focus on corporate requirements, not on business unit strategic requirements
Common or fewer suppliers	Most knowledge sharing one-way
Proximity to major organizational decision makers	Common suppliers behave differently in geographic and market segments
Critical mass	Distance from users
Firm brand recognition and stature	Tendency to create organizational silos
Reporting line — power — better prices	Customer segments require adaptability to unique situations
Strategic focus	Top management not able to spend time on suppliers
Cost of purchasing low — lower administrative costs	Lack of business unit focus
Better terms and conditions	Communication
Developing expertise / talent	Purchase Timing — speed
Supply chain coordination	Uncertainty
Compliance to policy easier	Customization costs
Accessible and complete management information	

T A B L E   17–5

Advantages and Disadvantages of Decentralization of Supply Management

Decentralization	
ADVANTAGES	**DISADVANTAGES**
Easier coordination/communication with operating department	More difficult to communicate among business units
Speed of response — purchase timing	Encourages users not to plan ahead
Effective use of local sources (supports lean)	Operational versus strategic focus
Business unit autonomy	Too much focus on local sources — ignores better supply opportunities
Reporting line simplicity	No critical mass in organization for visibility effectiveness — "whole person syndrome"
Undivided authority and responsibility	Lacks clout
Suits purchasing personnel preference	Suboptimization
Broad job definition	Business unit preference not congruent with corporate preference
Geographical, cultural, political, environmental, social, language, and currency appropriateness	Small differences get magnified
Greater appreciation for the operation	Reporting at low level in organization
Improved service from suppliers	Limits functional advancement opportunities
Reduced cycle/lead times from suppliers	Ignores larger organization considerations
	Limited expertise for requirements
	Lack of standardization
	Cost of supply relatively high
	Hides the true cost of supply
	Difficult to develop executive-level talent

compliance to policy. Each of these benefits aids in supporting the corporate directives of lower costs of goods and service and lower company expenses. But, there is a downside, most notably the real distance it places between SM and its internal customers and locations. The tendency to create a silo mentality and to lose touch with local suppliers are other notable costs.

Decentralized SM supports local suppliers, which may engender improved service and faster cycle times from those suppliers (a benefit for those engaged in lean manufacturing). Broader job responsibilities for employees in SM can improve job satisfaction. Finally, supporting business unit autonomy is a major benefit of the decentralized structure.

Hybrid approaches strive to obtain the cost savings and efficiencies of a centralized structure while continuing to offer service to local, autonomous units or factories. As discussed earlier, information technology is allowing for companywide spend analysis that can inform a central-led supply management team to aggregate that spend. Decentralized teams can remain in the field to support unique, localized needs.

One of the oldest of the age-old discussions is the one between centralization and decentralization.[23] The CAPS Research reports by Leenders and Johnson and by Johnson et al. highlight the true dynamism in changing structures.[24] All the studies, however, indicate that the pendulum is swinging toward centralization, or at least to the hybrid structure with a central-led supply management team. Of 13 changes identified in one study, 10 (77 percent) were moves toward centralization. Fully 75 percent of the firms in Leenders and Johnson's follow-up study employed some form of centralized or hybrid structure, with a centralized hybrid being the most common (41 percent).[25]

The shift received a boost 10 years ago, when *Fortune* ran an article extolling the virtues of centralization called "Purchasing's New Muscle."[26] Chrysler's head of procurement at the time, Thomas Stallkamp, was quoted on centralization's contribution to reducing costs, stating, "The advantages of decentralization don't show up in purchasing. We centralize buying to get the best prices from suppliers."[27] More recent studies have validated the trend. In a study by Ellram et al., 83 percent of their sample firms maintained a centralized (25 percent) or centralized-decentralized hybrid (58 percent) structure.[28] A CAPS Research benchmarking study of the aerospace industry indicates that 88 percent of indirect and direct goods are sourced through a centralized or centralized-decentralized structure.[29] Mayer presents a geographically spread health care organization that used information technology to centralize purchasing of $170 million in goods and services.[30]

---

23 Martin J. Carrara (1995). "To Centralize or Not—The Pendulum Keeps Swinging," *NAPM Insights*, June 1, p. 52.

24 Johnson and Leenders (2004) Supply's Organizational Roles and Responsibilities, CAPS Focus Study, Tempe, AZ.

25 Johnson and Leenders (2004) Supply's Organizational Roles and Responsibilities.

26 Shawn Tully (1995). "Purchasing's New Muscle," *Fortune*, February 20, vol. 131, no. 3, pp. 75–83.

27 Ibid., p. 78.

28 Lisa M. Ellram, George A. Zsidisin, Sue Perrott Siferd, and Michael J. Stanly (2002). "The Impact of Purchasing and Supply Management Activities on Corporate Success," *Journal of Supply Chain Management*, Winter, vol. 38, no. 1, pp. 4–18.

29 CAPS Research (2003). *Purchasing Performance Benchmarking Study for the Aerospace/Defense Industry*, Tempe, AZ.

30 Matt Mayer (2003). "How Centralizing Purchasing and AP Can Yield Significant Benefits," *Healthcare Purchasing News*, September, pp. 20–21.

Trent identifies "centrally coordinated supply teams" as a key component of the pillar "organizational design."[31]

Interestingly, Monczka et al. observe that the dilemmas facing SM today are similar to those that faced information technology organizations in the mid-1980s.[32] Back then, questions arose over the role IT would play in companies (either strategic or as an internal utility) and how it would be managed (internally or outsourced). Also, in 1990, Von Simson wrote that due to the strategic potential of companywide information (for functional integration and new opportunities), a centralized IT organization would be in a better position to see the overall needs of the company and champion integration, forming the strategic payoff of centralization.[33] Today, supply management is maintaining a centralized staff for much the same reason—to be in a position to see the overall spend in the company and leverage that spend across fewer suppliers.

CHANGES IN SUPPLY MANAGEMENT: GLOBALIZATION

As companies seek to be closer to customers or take advantage of lower input costs (e.g., materials, subassemblies, designs, and business processes), the prospect of sourcing outside the borders of a firm's home country becomes much greater. Complicating factors are many, however, and include distance and time delays, language and culture, currency issues, and importation and customs, which are becoming more complex due to increased security needs. To overcome these factors, firms must become more integrated and connected, managing processes, commodities, designs, suppliers, and information from a global perspective. It is a given that technology needs must also reflect the global nature of the requirements. Human resource needs differ greatly when moving toward a global buy, as supply management professionals are tasked with taming the many and varied challenges. Organization structures are clearly affected as the percentage of goods purchased from outside a firm's home country increases.

Trent and Monczka have developed a model that captures the maturity of a firm's sourcing efforts through five levels (see Figure 17–4).[34] The first level is simply to source all needs from domestic suppliers. Level II firms begin the maturation process by sourcing goods and services from international suppliers on an as-needed basis. New suppliers, lower input costs, supply disruption, changing exchange rates, and a declining domestic supply base are possible reasons to initiate the process. Level III firms purchase internationally as part of an overall sourcing strategy, yet are

31 Trent, "What Everyone Needs to Know."

32 Monczka et al., "Strategic Outsourcing."

33 Ernest M. Von Simson (1990). "The 'Centrally Decentralized' IS Organization," *Harvard Business Review*, July–August, pp. 2-6.

34 Trent and Monczka, "Pursuing Competitive Advantage" and "Creating a World Class Global Sourcing Organization."

FIGURE 17-4

Worldwide Sourcing Maturity Levels

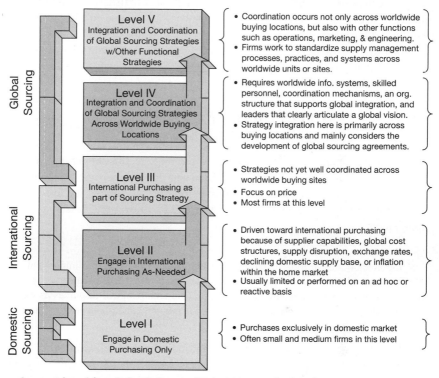

SOURCE: Adapted from Robert J. Trent and Robert M. Monczka (2002). "Pursuing Competitive Advantage through Integrated Global Sourcing," *Academy of Management Executive*, May, vol. 16, no. 2, pp. 66–80, and (2004). "Creating a World Class Global Sourcing Organization," Working Paper (currently under review).

mostly focused on price reductions. Buying sites scattered across the globe are not yet coordinated together to realize still greater efficiencies and speed.

Level IV firms begin to address the lack of coordination by implementing integrated information systems, hiring and developing skilled personnel, implementing coordination mechanisms such as periodic face-to-face meetings or teleconferences, and having leaders maintain and articulate a global vision. Finally, Trent and Monczka suggest that firms employ an organization structure that facilitates global integration. Although their studies do not advocate any particular structural form, they do encourage one that "features central coordination of global activities."[35] Level V firms take all that level IV firms do and ratchet up the level of integration, working to harmonize supply management processes across

---

35 Trent and Monczka, "Pursuing Competitive Advantage," p. 70.

worldwide sites, inevitably shifting the pendulum toward centralization. Supply management integration in a level V firm is extended to other functional areas within the firm, such as design engineering, manufacturing, and logistics. The use of cross-functional teams as an integrating mechanism is highlighted in their approach. Johnson and Leenders also report an increasing use of teams in supply management, indicating that the top two reasons for convening a cross-functional team were cost-reduction initiatives, followed by developing supply management strategies.[36]

SUPPLY CHAIN MANAGEMENT: ISSUES FOR SUPPLY MANAGEMENT

The supply management function is responsible for selecting and managing suppliers as well as managing the interface between the supplier and the company. These responsibilities are part of a larger umbrella of activities involved in the ultimate movement of materials, information, and money—that of supply chain management.

Fawcett and Magnan define supply chain management (SCM) as

> the collaborative efforts of multiple channel members to design, implement, and manage seamless value-added processes to meet the real needs of the end customer. The development and integration of people and technological resources as well as the coordinated management of materials, information, and financial flows underlie successful supply chain integration.[37]

Supply management's boundary-spanning role and relationship-building objectives are obviously necessary in this context. Benefits of well-executed SCM programs support the competitive and financial performance challenges highlighted at the beginning of this chapter. Working capital management, material and money velocity, and improved product performance are key performance areas.

Just as a maturity model was created for the development of global sourcing, one measuring a firm's development in the management of its supply chain was presented by Poirier and Quinn.[38] They also used five levels to model the evolution of their supply chain abilities, ranging from an internally focused SM organization that is establishing linkages between itself and just a couple of other functional areas (level I) to full network connectivity (level V). Just as most firms were in level III in the worldwide sourcing maturity model, most of the firms (90 percent) in the supply chain evolution model are in levels II and III.

---

36 Johnson and Leenders, "The Supply Organizational Structure Dilemma."

37 Stanley E. Fawcett and Gregory M. Magnan (2001). "Achieving Supply Chain Alignment: Barriers, Bridges and Benefits," CAPS Focus Study, Tempe, AZ.

38 Charles C. Poirier and Francis J. Quinn (2003). "A Survey of Supply Chain Progress," *Supply Chain Management Review*, September–October, pp. 40–47.

Other research indicates that few firms are realizing the potential of their SCM initiatives.[39] Somewhat counterintuitively, the barriers inhibiting achievement of objectives often are *inside* the four walls of the company, rather than on the integrative periphery (the issues faced in levels II and III in the supply chain evolution model). To better understand the barriers to supply chain integration, Fawcett and Magnan surveyed members of the former National Association of Purchasing Management (NAPM, now Institute for Supply Management), APICS: the Association of Operations Management, and the former Council of Logistics Management (CLM), now Council of Supply Chain Management Professionals.[40]

The data in Table 17–6 indicates that organizations are slightly more comfortable with internal integration efforts than with external, interorganizational forms of cooperation, findings corroborated by Poirier and Quinn.[41] About 60 percent of all respondents feel their organizations are somewhat to fully engaged in cross-functional integration within the firm (rating of 5 or higher). Tremendous variability in responses is revealed by the moderate mean of 4.67 (ratings ranged from 2 to 7). The relatively low scores for within-firm integration denote the difficulty of knocking down the walls that impede functional collaboration and may be viewed as a leading indicator for the challenges that await interorganizational collaboration.

The data indicates that most organizations are at early stages of intercompany collaboration. Respondents noted that forward integration efforts (mean = 4.33) are on pace with, or slightly ahead of, backward integration efforts (mean = 4.26). While individual companies find themselves at different points along the integration journey, it seems clear that organizations of all types and materials managers from all three functional areas are seriously talking about supply chain integration. Complete integration up and down the supply chain received the lowest rating, with a mean of 3.37 (just 26 percent rated it 5 or higher).

Ultimately, much resource-intensive work remains to be done to realize the full potential of supply chain integration. Within-firm integration is challenging; tackling issues such as aligning measures, meshing information systems, and sharing risks and rewards *across* organizations is even more difficult. Unless the fissures between companies, functions, and processes are reconciled, the breaches will continue to persist between an organization's suppliers and its customers.

Examining the functional responses reveals that logisticians perceive their organizations to be more fully engaged in integration efforts. Supply managers are the most hesitant in acknowledging their firms' efforts to engage in integrative endeavors. It is interesting to note that the largest gap in perceptions is found in the area of internal cross-functional integration. The purchasing mean was 4.30

---

39 Fawcett and Magnan, "Achieving Supply Chain Alignment"; Trent, "What Everyone Needs to Know."

40 Fawcett and Magnan, "Achieving Supply Chain Alignment."

41 Poirier and Quinn, "A Survey of Supply Chain Progress."

TABLE 17-6

Functional Perspectives on Firm/Supply Chain Integration

Integration Measure	Combined		Purchasing		Manufacturing		Logistics	
	Mean	% 5,6,7	Mean	% 5,6,7	Mean	% 5,6,7	Mean	% 5,6,7
Cross-functional process integration within the firm	4.67	60.55	4.30	48.10	4.72	65.70	4.95	66.60
Forward integration with valued 1st-tier customers	4.33	51.07	4.15	49.10	4.33	49.40	4.52	56.30
Backward integration with important 1st-tier suppliers	4.26	50.88	4.12	46.90	4.28	50.90	4.35	52.50
Complete forward and backward SC integration	3.37	25.80	3.28	25.70	3.27	23.90	3.53	27.80

compared to 4.72 for manufacturing and 4.95 for logistics, indicating that supply managers simply do not see the same emphasis on integration taking place within their organizations. Supply managers may be excluded from some cross-functional initiatives (or at least they feel that they are). By contrast, the customer-facing view of logistics—where companywide customer satisfaction initiatives are at the forefront—may foster an atmosphere more conducive to integration and collaboration. A final interesting point is that purchasers, the experts in establishing collaborative supplier relations, provided the lowest mean scores for backward integration. No other group should have a better feel for backward integration; yet, purchasers express greater reticence regarding upstream integration. This frustration represents a serious barrier to supply chain integration. Moreover, the fact that manufacturers and logisticians provide more optimistic evaluations of the progress being made in the area of upstream supplier integration suggests that many managers are at least somewhat caught up in the rhetoric of supply chain integration. Such differences in functional perspective promise to further impede the integration journey.

Functional Interaction

Coordination among functions is a critical requirement of effective supply chain integration and is an element in both maturity models discussed previously. Fawcett and Magnan asked respondents to indicate the degree to which cooperation and interaction takes place among functional personnel in their organizations.[42] Seven different dyadic relationships involved in the plan-design-source-build-deliver sequence were examined (see Table 17–7). The general level of function-to-function interaction is greater than existed in the broader arena of cross-functional process integration. Four functional, dyadic relationships obtained aggregate mean interaction scores greater than 4.90. Certainly, part of the increased interaction stems from the fact that the different dyads must work together on a day-to-day basis simply to perform their normal responsibilities. This finding suggests that the foundation is being established to move toward greater process integration.

Supply managers participate in the two most cooperative dyads, interacting at high levels with both manufacturing and logistics. Logisticians and production managers also participate in two of the top three interactive dyadic relationships. The relative strength of the most interactive dyads indicates that despite the challenges, strong intraorganizational relationships are forming. As firms outsource an increasing proportion of their direct requirements, the interaction between supply management and manufacturing will be increasingly critical to ensuring timely satisfaction of customer orders. The strength of the perceived levels of integration between logistics and the supply management and manufacturing functions is also encouraging. Together, these three functions have primary responsibility for the

---

42 Fawcett and Magnan, "Achieving Supply Chain Alignment."

TABLE 17-7

Cooperation & Interaction Between Internal Functions

Cooperation Between…	Combined		Purchasing		Manufacturing		Logistics	
	Mean	% 5,6,7	Mean	% 5,6,7	Mean	% 5,6,7	Mean	% 5,6,7
Purchasing & Manufacturing	5.21	69.97	5.57	77.30	5.51	77.70	4.65	57.10
Purchasing & Logistics	5.16	67.09	5.47	72.40	5.23	66.00	4.88	64.20
Manufacturing & Logistics	4.93	65.33	4.87	64.00	5.09	64.10	4.83	67.50
Engineering & Manufacturing	4.91	64.55	5.07	67.80	5.07	65.70	4.64	60.90
Purchasing & Engineering	4.39	47.68	4.78	60.30	4.53	54.90	3.96	31.20
Manufacturing & Marketing	4.13	40.86	4.18	40.10	4.07	41.70	4.14	40.50
Engineering & Marketing	4.07	38.21	4.25	44.80	4.24	43.20	3.79	28.60

entire order-fulfillment cycle. Increased cooperation among them will support the desires of companies to increase customer satisfaction while simultaneously increasing asset productivity and reducing operating costs.

Commitment to SCM

One important decision relating to the design of an organization's supply chain— one we have discussed already in the context of a single firm—is the governance infrastructure that will be used to coordinate the various players in the supply chain. Wagner notes that the appropriate tools for the product development phase differ from those for the industrialization phase.[43] Consequently, gaining an understanding of the infrastructures that can be used to successfully encourage commitment (in both phases) and help successfully integrate a supply chain should be a top priority for supply management professionals.

The Fawcett and Magnan CAPS Research study also included visits to over 50 companies to meet with managers throughout the supply chain.[44] A careful review of the interview summary statements suggests that most managers feel that four distinct types of commitment are vital to SCM implementation success.

1. *Top management commitment.* This is deemed to be a prerequisite to long-term SCM success. The very nature of SCM dictates that without the senior management commitment (including the CEO), the necessary vision will never emerge. Only top management can dedicate the resources needed to make SCM a top organization-wide priority.

2. *Broad-based functional support.* One of the greatest areas of frustration arises when a particular functional area commits itself to making the changes necessary to build a supply chain competency only to be thwarted by "backward-thinking" or "turf-protecting" managers in another area of the organization. Supply chain collaboration is inherently cross-functional—the value-added processes capable of delivering a real competitive advantage are almost always comprised of activities that reside across functional boundaries. Also, no single set of managers possesses all the information needed to make great "systemwide" decisions.

3. *Organizational and structural commitment.* To facilitate supply chain integration and provide the visibility and momentum to achieve true collaboration, the organizational structure must address internal barriers to integration. For many organizations, this change has taken place through the establishment of a senior-level supply chain position (e.g.,

---

43 Stephan M. Wagner (2003). "Intensity and Managerial Scope of Supplier Integration," *Journal of Supply Chain Management*, Fall, vol. 39, no. 4, pp. 4–15.

44 Fawcett and Magnan, "Achieving Supply Chain Alignment."

executive vice president of supply chain management). Other firms
have established supply chain groups or divisions, but these are often
housed within one particular function and fail to achieve real cross-
functional integration. Still other companies have put in place permanent (or at times, ad hoc) cross-functional supply chain teams (matrix
structure) composed of managers whose primary responsibilities still
reside in a specific functional area.

4. *Suppliers and customers.* Together with their trading partners, firms must
   collaborate in meaningful ways. Achieving success in this arena requires
   that senior-level managers aggressively and honestly sell specific supply
   chain initiatives. Good personal relationships, high-impact pilot programs, and trust are the foundation of interorganizational commitment.

Supply Chain Governance

Based on the survey and interview data, the following five supply chain infrastructure recommendations are proposed as a way of gaining organizational commitment and facilitating supply chain integration.[45] Supply chain leaders are using
a mix of the following infrastructures, providing balance to central-led supply
management (listed in order of their frequency of use):

1. *Ad hoc teams.* These teams are assembled and utilized on an as-needed
   basis to make supply chain–related decisions or to implement changes
   within the organization or the supply chain.

2. *Supply chain steering committee.* A supply chain steering committee
   should be established within organizations to help direct their supply
   chain–related activities.

3. *Supplier advisory council.* Key upstream members of the supply chain
   should be consulted on a regular basis through a supplier advisory council.

4. *Customer advisory board.* Organizations should establish a customer
   advisory board to help manage the interactions between their various
   functions and the downstream portion of their supply chain. This board
   should be comprised of key customers and should be facilitated by the
   executive-level vice president and the internal steering committee.

5. *Executive-level vice president of supply management.* Supply management–
   related functions such as marketing, purchasing, logistics, operations,
   supply chain management, and quality should report to an executive-
   level vice president within the organization.

---

45 Stanley E. Fawcett, Jeffrey A. Ogden, and Gregory M. Magnan (2004). "Supply Chain Commitment
and Governance: Establishing an Infrastructure to Support SC Integration," *Proceedings North
American Research/Teaching Symposium on Purchasing and Supply Chain Management,*
March, Tempe, AZ.

Trust in the Supply Chain

It is difficult to imagine a successful business relationship without trust as a foundational element. Unfortunately, trust is an intangible attribute that is widely recognized as a prerequisite to world-class supply chain performance, while at the same time being poorly understood by most managers. As a word, *trust* is frequently heard whenever supply chain alliances are discussed; yet, as an actionable and measurable concept, trust is difficult to explicitly define. In this respect, trust fits the old adage, "I'm not sure exactly how to define it, but I know it when I see it." As a result, the word trust is bandied about as if its frequent use can adequately fill the void in relationships, where distrust is perhaps a better descriptor of reality. This has led some managers to feel somewhat suspicious whenever they here the word trust; this is true especially at smaller firms where managers feel whipsawed about by their larger, more dominant supply chain "partners."

As part of their broader supply chain study, Fawcett, Magnan, and Williams included trust concepts in both the survey and the site visit and interview questions.[46] In response to the question, "What are the most important keys to alliance success?" no single word was mentioned more often or more prominently than trust. Managers consistently felt that an alliance's ability to create unique value-added capabilities depends on presence of trust. Without trust, neither alliance partner is willing to step out of traditional comfort zones to take on new roles and responsibilities. As managers discussed the other intangible attributes listed here that are needed to build great supply chain relationships, trust's importance was magnified.

- Collaborative and joint efforts
- Collaborative continuous improvement
- Creativity, innovation, and idea generation
- Mutual dependence
- Mutual commitment to the relationship
- Patience and perseverance
- Shared vision and objectives
- Understanding of each other's businesses
- Willingness to be flexible and tailor services

Trust permeates these fundamental intangibles. It is a core component of patience, idea generation, and valued personal relationships. Moreover, defining and measuring the collaborative, mutual, shared, or willing nature of key attributes remains an elusive challenge, placing great emphasis and stress on the notion of trust. Trust is needed for the preceding attributes to effectively bring the two sides of an alliance together to help each achieve greater success than they could alone.

---

46 Stanley E. Fawcett, Gregory M. Magnan, and Alvin J. Williams (2004). "Supply Chain Trust Is Within Your Grasp," *Supply Chain Management Review*, March, vol. 8, no. 3, pp. 20–27.

T A B L E 17–8

Appearance of Trust Mechanisms in the Supply Chain

MANIFESTATIONS OF TRUST	Combined		Purchasing		Mfg.		Logistics	
	Mean	% 5-7	Mean	% 5-7	Mean	% 5-7	Mean	% 5-7
Trust-based customer alliances	4.86	66.60	4.93	70.20	4.92	72.30	4.73	57.90
Trust-based supplier alliances	4.37	49.60	4.72	61.40	4.28	49.50	4.15	39.80
Shared value-added resources	3.95	36.00	4.11	39.80	3.68	29.40	4.08	39.60
Shared rewards/risks with suppliers	3.90	35.70	4.27	49.40	3.63	26.80	3.86	32.90
Resources Dedicated to Supplier Development	3.67	29.60	3.69	30.70	3.59	25.70	3.72	32.60
Shared rewards/risks with customers	3.57	28.30	3.79	35.40	3.39	24.10	3.55	26.40

Table 17–8 displays the survey results of the trust-related questions and some inherent inconsistencies. Respondents indicate that customer-facing alliances are further developed than those facing upstream (although the supply managers feel that they are in place). Areas that are opportunities to enhance trust are sharing-based: resources, rewards, and risks. While these concepts are often mentioned as foundational elements of higher-order relationships, the data indicates that companies have some work to do to really develop trust-based relationships in the supply chain.

SUMMARY

The increasingly competitive business environment, coupled with pressure for improved financial performance, is creating a strategic opportunity for the supply management function. Firms are responding to the environment by (1) concentrating on core competencies, which increases the amount of outsourcing activity in a company, and (2) directing more corporate spend through supply management. Combined, they broaden the roles and responsibilities, and consequently raise the strategic profile, of the supply management (SM) function.

Structurally, SM is moving toward central-led organizations to leverage the aggregated company spend. Some decentralized resources are still needed to support business units and maintain boundary-spanning duties (e.g., supplier involvement in new product development). Finally, SM will play a critical role in supporting companies as they expand and mature their supply chain management initiatives into the global environment. Internally, cross-functional relationships and process management are seen as necessary activities to prepare supply management and the firm for supply chain integration. Externally, new organizational forms are being applied in supply chain relationships to find the right balance between structure and cost, risk and reward, and trust and control. In many firms, it is the responsibility of supply management to manage the interface between supply chain partners and the rest of the firm, often leading the cross-functional— and sometimes cross-organizational—teams that seek to integrate the sometimes conflicting processes and objectives of multiple functions and firms.

CHAPTER 18

SUPPLY MANAGEMENT'S CONTRIBUTION TO PRODUCT AND SERVICE INNOVATION

R. DAVID NELSON, C.P.M., A.P.P.
Vice President, Global Supply Management
Delphi Corporation

JONATHAN R. STEGNER
General Director, Global Supply Management
Delphi Corporation

INTRODUCTION

We remember the "good old days" of purchasing as if it were yesterday . . . Tuesdays were good because one of our vendor reps, Harry, always brought cookies in for the whole department. Engineering knew Harry brought cookies, so they usually stopped by, too. That gave us the opportunity to meet with our engineers to share ideas about process improvement (should there be more or fewer chocolate chips?).

We always had Harry's purchase orders ready for him, along with all the return authorizations for the scrap and defective parts his company had sent during the past week. Manufacturing complained a lot about these parts, but Harry always took care of things.

Sometimes we would get behind in processing requisitions, especially if someone took a trip or a day off, because we would have to figure out how someone else tracked their orders and where they kept their PO log book. Those were exciting days.

And then there were the occasional battles with accounting. Accounting was slow to pay the vendors, but they usually tried to blame purchasing because the price on the PO was wrong, or the part number didn't match the invoice. Lots of people had to sign off before accounting could pay . . .

Were things really this bad in the "good old days?" You just might be surprised. Take a requisition. Make out a purchase order. Get three bids and accept the "best" one. That was purchasing's role. It is little wonder that purchasing got no respect from other parts of the company. The company expected little from us, and got little in return.

Contrast that with what world-class supply management operations are expected to do today. Today's competitive organizations put a premium on both strategic and technical proficiency. They seek out—and handsomely pay—those who can bring new thinking to corporate strategies and leadership. They are looking for professionals who understand sourcing strategies, cost structure, quality measurements, technology, communications, strategic planning, supplier development, and relationship building.

Ask yourself these questions: What if small companies could improve their competitiveness and chance of survival by adopting world-class supply management techniques? What if small to medium companies could improve their profitability 1, 5, or 10 times over? What if both large and small companies could accelerate their learning to leapfrog over the competition through cutting-edge technology and processes, thereby reaping "leapfrog" returns?

All these gains are possible using world-class supply chain practices and processes. Yet, traditional thinking about the supply chain prevents most organizations from fully moving from "the good old days" mentality to realize the incredible paybacks that are possible. For most smaller organizations, implementation of supply management best practices has only recently begun, and some still cling to traditional ways. While most larger organizations have evolved further, only a handful have managed to achieve world-class supply management capabilities.

This chapter examines supply management best practices and the three stages of supply management evolution: chaos/traditional, control/evolving, and future/step-function improvement.

While there are dozens of best practices, the ones we will focus on in this chapter relate to

- Price versus cost

- Quality

- Delivery

- Indirect and maintenance, repair, and operating (MRO) costs

- Training and career path planning

- Strategic sourcing and supplier performance

- Strategic planning and systems

PRICE VERSUS COST

How we think about price and cost is a direct reflection of where we are in our evolution.

Thirty years ago, when manufacturing costs occurred primarily within a company's own factories, manufacturers became very efficient at controlling internal costs. It made sense to put most cost management resources in-house because that is where most of the costs were. Purchasing took care of everything else by filling requisitions according to who would provide a part or service at the best price. Over the years, as companies became more concerned with asset management, they began outsourcing most of the parts they had made in-house. As purchased costs grew larger, companies that ignored supply chain efficiencies did so at their own peril.

Progressive companies now recognize that more and more of their manufacturing costs occur within the extended supply chain and that new tools and techniques are necessary to manage the supply chain as if it were part of the company. This, in turn, requires expertise beyond the purchasing skills of yesteryear. Unfortunately, many companies still focus most of their attention on internal costs instead of the 50 to 75 percent of their costs that occur within the supply chain. Some have not moved much beyond the traditional purchasing model of 30 years ago.

Stage 1: Chaos/Traditional

In the traditional stage, purchasing plays an administrative role and true cost management is nonexistent. Triggered almost entirely by requisitions, purchasing's first responsibility is to assign a purchase order number. At that point, purchasing is responsible for seeking three or more quotes and selecting the "best" bid. Often, this is based more on who knows whom, rather than on which supplier provides the best value to the customer.

In this approach, the measuring stick for determining the best quote is usually the "standard cost" for a part or commodity. This creature of standard accounting is computed once a year and is usually the last price paid. Once a month, a purchase price variance report shows how much was ordered and how prices compare to standard cost. Because suppliers are always raising prices, inflation might be 5 to 10 percent a year. Price variance is something purchasing is obligated to track but is powerless to control.

Stage 2: Control/Evolving

As companies begin to realize the shortcomings of standard cost accounting as a tool for managing costs, they look for a better way to track their own performance against outside benchmarks. External benchmarking is a hallmark of stage 2. One benchmark is the producer price index (PPI), which became popular during the 1970s as inflation heated up. The PPI is a family of indexes that tracks the average change over time in the prices domestic producers get for their goods and services. More than 10,000 PPIs for individual products and groups of products are released each month. Companies that track their costs according to the PPI consider themselves successful when their costs rise more slowly than the PPI.

The shortcomings of this approach are similar to the standard price approach. It does nothing to address true costs of producing a part, commodity, or service. It is price-driven, not cost-driven. For example, between January 1992 and January 1998, the PPI rose more than 12 percent. Companies using the PPI as their benchmark for cost performance looked at their own cost increases compared to the PPI

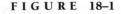

F I G U R E   18–1

Producer Price Index Compared to Two Companies' Performance

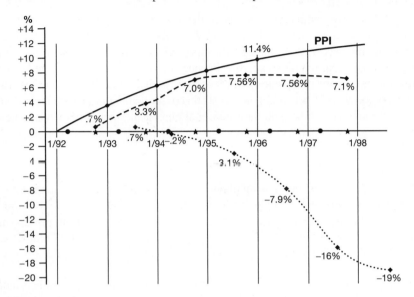

and made a judgment about their performance based on the difference. By that measure, the company represented by the green line on Figure 18–1 was doing well. In fact, the green company was doing about as well as most evolving companies will do just by picking low-hanging fruit. But it is not world-class.

Stage 3: Future/Step-Function Improvement

Now, look at the lower line on Figure 18–1. Not only did this company outperform the PPI, it actually reduced costs—by nearly 20 percent. Which company was it? Honda. What is the difference between a company that realizes moderate performance improvement and a company like Honda, which took 20 percent out of the cost of the 1998 Accord? The short answer is the first company focused mostly on price, Honda on cost. Focusing on price will get you a few percentage points below the PPI. A company that has done no supply management before can expect to get 5 to 20 percent gains at first. But this is not sustainable because the root causes of cost are never fully addressed. Instead, companies that focus on price tend to push costs down to their suppliers, instead of eliminating costs altogether.

Honda—and other world-class companies like IBM, Boeing, and Toyota— look deeply at costs up and down the supply chain and integrate their efforts to rid the value stream of inefficiency and waste. They do not stop at building effective cost structures inside their own organizations—they extend best-cost management practices to their suppliers. The first important step in true cost management is to develop cost standards. By building cost models, world-class organizations set target costs based on what a part or commodity should cost. They then track their costs against those standards.

The most important work occurs during a new product's initial design phase. World-class organizations take an integrated approach, involving suppliers, engineering, manufacturing, and supply management in early product development. This integrated approach can go well beyond the initial 10 to 20 percent that might result from a focus on price to reach continuous improvement and savings of up to 30 percent.

Supply management professionals today do not have all the cost management tools they need. Today's data and accounting systems cannot keep up with the speed of price changes, currency valuations, and other strategic issues. And yet, companies like Honda and Toyota have overcome these obstacles by designing and perfecting practices that get them closer to the answers than anyone else. Today, both Honda and Toyota view price as the outcome, not the goal. The goal is to eliminate all wastes, resulting in ever-lower costs and ever-higher value—inside their plants and among their suppliers. For most companies, to adopt that viewpoint—to attack price by focusing on cost—is an amazing transformation.

More companies in the future will be taking a "cost profit plan" approach to their finished products. This approach looks first at what customers are willing to pay. It then considers how much profit a company needs to make. The final step is determining how to manage costs for each part and commodity to enable the company to meet that profit target. This requires much more joint product development, in which customer and supplier work together to conceptualize and design new products. Honda and Toyota are doing this now. Model to model, they are integrating suppliers, engineering, manufacturing, and supply management.

Large customers with numerous suppliers are already starting to learn that working with suppliers to improve costs bears more fruit than continually beating them up over price. In the future they will recognize that involving suppliers in new model development allows suppliers' best ideas to be engineered into products, improving both costs and value.

In the future—10 to 15 years from now—we will see even more innovation and more universal adoption of techniques that world-class organizations are using to beat the competition. We predict that along with new systems and cost modeling tools, companies will be able to use best practices to reach step-function cost improvements of as much as 50 percent.

QUALITY

Perhaps the greatest turnaround in American manufacturing during the past 15 years has been in the area of quality. Quality leaders such as the electronics and automotive industries are now reaching levels that 10 years ago were thought impossible. To what do we owe this transformation?

Stage 1: Chaos/Traditional

In stage 1, quality is measured by returns; in other words, how many bad parts had to be sent back to the supplier, and it is not unthinkable for bad parts to reach as high as 10 percent of every shipment. Most companies in stage 1 accept this as part of doing business. For manufacturers, it means staffing a receiving and inspection department to find and report the bad parts. For their suppliers, it means sending more parts than ordered so that when defects are returned the customer has enough good parts to meet production schedules. One of the measures of a good purchasing department is how efficiently it is able to identify and return bad parts.

This mind-set was prevalent even into the 1980s. The authors remember a particular supplier that had been chosen as one of eight stamping suppliers for Honda's Ohio operations. This supplier almost immediately began sending bad parts. A number of Honda associates were sent to the supplier's factory to figure out what was wrong. The owner finally said, "My largest customer accepts 2 percent bad parts, and unless we send you more than 2 percent bad, don't give me any more calls." Before it was all over, Honda had 26 people in the supplier's plant, working on all aspects of the manufacturing process, ensuring that quality was built in and only good parts were shipped.

Stage 2: Control/Evolving

The previous story contrasts two philosophies of management. Working with Dr. W. Edwards Deming, Japanese companies had learned it was possible to improve quality by focusing attention on the root cause of problems and correcting those causes. These companies were intolerant of poor quality because they knew it was not necessary. Most American companies, on the other hand, looked at 1 to 2 percent bad parts as simply a cost of doing business. As customers began to see the level of quality that was possible, they refused to settle for shoddy workmanship. This put tremendous market pressure on American companies to level up their quality.

A traditional way of handling quality was to take a handful of parts flagged during inspection to company engineers and ask, "Will they work or not?" This was time consuming and costly. A breakthrough came when manufacturers designed statistical controls for quality. Tools like the Cpk, an index that defines the limits of acceptability for deviations from exact specifications, allow companies to design manufacturing processes so that fewer and smaller deviations result. Use of these techniques is one indicator of a company in stage 2.

As quality improves, it also becomes apparent that the old ways of measuring quality are insufficient. In the traditional way of looking at quality, 1 or 2 percent defective parts had the ring of success—until the meaning was considered. If a million bad parts were purchased, a 2 percent defect rate meant 20,000 bad parts were shipped back to the supplier. The Japanese were the first to realize that if you did away with percentages and simply looked at the number of parts, poor quality became much more visible. And more visibility meant more attention to the problem.

Rather than measuring quality by percentages, leading companies track defects in terms of parts per million (PPM). This is now industry's norm for measuring quality. To give an idea of how far some companies have progressed, consider that when Honda of America Manufacturing opened its first American plant in 1982, the quality of domestic parts was 10,000 PPM. Honda's goal was 300 PPM. Today, Honda's PPM rate is in the low single digits, as is the rate for an increasing number of companies all around the world.

Of course, these substantial quality improvements take more than redesigning manufacturing processes and tracking PPM. Processes cannot be adequately redesigned and quality can never increase unless you know what is causing bad parts in the first place. In today's evolving environment, leading companies employ root cause analysis to get to the initial reason for problems. It allows a company to treat the cause rather than the symptom. For example, you return home from a restaurant to find your entire kitchen covered with water. The sink is overflowing and the tap is running. In traditional quality control you would say the cause of the flooded kitchen is that you left the water running. You would fix it by turning the water off and mopping up the floor. Root cause analysis dives deeper by looking at the chain of events leading up to the flood.

One well-known example of root cause analysis is the Japanese process called the Five Whys. It analyzes problems by asking questions in the following way:

1. Why is my kitchen flooded? Because I left the water running.

2. Why did I leave the water running? Because I forgot it was on.

3. Why did I forget it was on? Because I was distracted by a phone call just as I was getting ready to turn it off.

4. Why did you get a phone call? Because I was late to meet my friend at the restaurant.

5. Why was I late? Because my watch had stopped.

In traditional thinking, you would be blamed for the flooded kitchen. Root cause analysis proves that the watch was at fault. By fixing the watch, you can prevent another flooded kitchen.

Stage 3: Future/Step-Function Improvement

Leading organizations no longer expect bad parts. While some bad parts are still a fact of life, the expectation is that every part will be good. Gone are receiving departments and parts' inspectors. Instead, companies push PPMs to ever-lower numbers. The leaders are doing this largely through lean supplier development and value stream mapping, a process that allows an engineer to see exactly where waste occurs during a manufacturing process so it can be removed.

The question of quality has not been completely answered. Bad parts on the production line are still a problem. But a few companies are now approaching zero PPM. The best of the best continue to keep that mind-set, even when they are leading the rest. Toyota, for example, consistently sets improvement goals of 20 to 30 percent per year. We may never reach absolute zero—every company shipping no bad parts. But the winners in the marketplace will consistently reach zero all or most of the time.

DELIVERY

The advent of the Internet has created a marketplace in which customers can realistically expect instant gratification. Online orders and overnight delivery services have revolutionized the way we buy and sell, forcing producers of goods and providers of services to think about fulfillment in a different way.

Stage 1: Chaos/Traditional

In stage 1, inflexible production and uncertain sales forecasts make inventory a necessity. The only way manufacturers can hope to meet orders quickly is to guess how much product is needed and to store it on-site for easy access when needed. It is not unusual for stage 1 manufacturers to house an entire month of inventory, or even several months of inventory early in the production process.

There are generally three kinds of inventory as shown in Figure 18–2:

- A inventory, representing 10 to 20 percent of the part numbers and 80 percent of the cost

- C inventory, representing 50% of the number of parts at little cost

- B inventory, representing everything in the middle

F I G U R E   18–2

The 80-20 Rule

Inventory Type	Percent of part numbers	Percent of total cost
A	20	80
B	30	15
C	50	5

There are few controls over how parts are managed. A-level parts are closely monitored and controlled, but less frequent attention is paid to B-level items (ranging from monthly to quarterly), and little attention is paid to C-level items after ordering large lots.

Stage 2: Control/Evolving

Even while holding large inventories, people know it is costing money. The transition to stage 2 occurs when people start asking questions about the purpose of large inventories. Inventory space takes up floor space that can be used for manufacturing. For all practical purposes, it is *wasted* space. And as the need for speed evolves and as companies begin to understand the concept of lean manufacturing, people begin to have a deeper discussion about whether the company needs inventory and, if so, how much is really needed.

In stage 2, financially driven metrics begin to drive smaller inventories. A month of inventory is suddenly too much. One of the great revolutionaries in the 1980s was Dell Computers, which proved it could win in the marketplace with virtually no inventory. Dell receives its parts, makes the computers, and ships them directly to customers—before paying for the parts financially. Inventory, or the lack of it, became a competitive weapon. The great advantage is that Dell does not need to pay for warehouse space and receive money from end customers to pay for parts. Companies within and outside the computer industry asked, "How can we do this?"

Stage 3: Future/Step-Function Improvement

Today, some companies outside the computer and electronics industries are beginning to approach zero inventories. When Honda of America built its second Ohio auto plant, it intentionally built a dock that could hold four hours of inventory. Suppliers were expected to respond accordingly. For example, a Honda wheel assembly supplier schedules deliveries to occur just before it is time to install them. As the vehicle nears completion, Honda scans the vehicle identification number and sends it electronically to the supplier. That is the supplier's cue to make the assembly and deliver it. By the time wheels need to go on, the assembly has been manufactured and delivered.

The impact of industry's new approach to delivery has extended beyond the warehouse to the financial houses on Wall Street. In 1980, investors accepted that a certain portion of a company's assets would be sitting in buckets or on skids. Today, they look at inventories and ask, "Why are you carrying so much?"

The tire assembly example is atypically fast compared to most manufacturing delivery systems. Yet, it is the wave of the future in which sequenced deliveries will be made in increasingly small periods of time—minutes instead of hours. As leaders think about getting into step-function improvement, they are going to be moving this idea of sequenced deliveries further and further up the supply chain.

INDIRECT AND MAINTENANCE, REPAIR, AND OPERATING COSTS

When it comes to tracking and controlling costs, manufacturers have traditionally focused most of their attention on direct materials and parts: the components that go directly into the final product. Yet, materials and services necessary to keep operations running—from computers, to uniforms, to travel—have gone largely ignored. This is like walking past a treasure chest without opening it. In some companies, indirect and maintenance, repair, and operating (MRO) costs can equal the spend for direct purchases, offering incredible savings to companies that apply strategic sourcing and cost management strategies to this overlooked area.

Stage 1: Chaos/Traditional

In the traditional stage, a company's approach to indirect purchasing is more or less identical to the purchase of direct materials: a requisition triggers a purchase order. Often, the requisition comes in with the supplier already identified and a number assigned. It is a totally tactical operation, and it is sometimes pure chaos. Purchasing receives the requisitions in big piles from people around the company who need to buy something "right now." Most suppliers will not ship anything without a purchase order (PO) number, because there is no possibility of getting paid—so purchasing frantically struggles to keep up. This sometimes results in tools or materials being purchased outside the system. For example, if Joe needs a hammer, he might just go to our regular supplier and buy a hammer directly. The chaotic nature of purchasing also results in a lot of POs going out "price advise"—which, in essence, means that the order placed asks the supplier to let the buyer know what the price will be. When approached this way, most suppliers sell on the high side because they have no incentive to offer a lower price.

Companies in the traditional stage are hampered by the inability to track costs accurately. Most processes are manual, so to see what was spent on a particular item someone has to open the accounting ledger and look for the cost. For a large company with thousands of purchased items this is a prohibitively labor-intensive exercise.

Stage 2: Control/Evolving

The advent of the personal computer changed everything. For the first time, annual purchasing activity could be analyzed and purchases could be tracked on spreadsheets. Using Pareto charts (80/20 rule), purchasing could identify the company's biggest suppliers and begin to slice and dice the information about the types of products purchased. Still, the challenges in stage 2 are formidable.

On the direct side, typically every part number is kept on a separate card and the buyer records every purchase order. However, that is not typical for indirect materials and services because of the overwhelming number of cards that would be required. If tens of thousands of cards are filed, someone must sit down and analyze the data. While PCs provided the ability to see more data than ever before, the data was not granular enough to reveal much. There is a need to see data on each facility—what is in each crib in each factory—especially for a large manufacturer.

Stage 3: Future/Step-Function Improvement

Just in the past five years, large companies have been able to use new data-mining tools to get at such numbers. And they are discovering what a gold mine regulation of MRO supplies can really be. For example, when Deere & Company began focusing on MRO supplies in 1997 and 1998, one of the commodities it looked at was gloves. Enterprisewide, the company spent almost $1.5 million a year on gloves, which represented 425 part numbers purchased from more than 20 different suppliers. Prices varied greatly, even among identical gloves sold by the same supplier to different facilities. By simply standardizing this one commodity and reducing the supply base to a single supplier, the calculated savings to Deere was nearly $500,000 a year. Multiply that by hundreds of other commodities, and it starts to look like real money.

In fact, for a company that has done no strategic sourcing at all, applying best practices to indirect costs can save 30 to 40 percent. This is significant. For example, in a typical company with $1 billion in sales and purchased costs of $400 million with indirect spend of $200 million, what effect would strategic sourcing have on the company's operating income? Typically, operating income is between 10 and 12 percent of sales, so in our example operating income would be about $110 million. Best practices applied to the $200 million of indirect spend will save 30 to 40 percent, or $60 million to $80 million. So, simply by applying best practices to MRO spend, a company could increase its $110 million operating income to $190 million. Here is another way to look at it. If labor costs are 8 percent of sales, or $80 million, by applying best practices just to MRO spend the savings could pay for the entire workforce with money left over.

These savings are not possible without a deep understanding of company spend, the suppliers with whom the company does business, along with a deep understanding of the company's business, coordination among divisions, and the support of senior management. For example, a large manufacturer with multiple plants will always need materials and services in common, such as lightbulbs. Everybody knows that it would be more economical to buy one lot of 3,000 lightbulbs than for three factories to buy 1,000 bulbs each. Yet, centralized purchasing is seldom the rule. So, suppliers are able to charge one factory one price and another factory another price. Factories are able to assign different part numbers to the same part, and nothing is ever easily tracked.

To realize the step-function improvement that is possible with proper attention to indirect spend, companies in the future will need to implement

- Capabilities for enterprisewide spend analysis
- Strategies for each commodity
- Purchasing policies to assure strategies are followed

- Executive support for strategies and policies
- Centralized authority for the most strategic and high-dollar purchases

Companies such as IBM recognized substantial opportunities to save big money in direct materials and MRO supplies, and set about controlling every single component of cost. CEO Lou Gerstner sought out and hired the right talent. He hired R. Gene Richter, a leader in the field, and placed him over the procurement function. He also created a policy (approved by IBM's board of directors) that put all purchases—every IBM dollar spent—under direct authority of Richter. And Richter made sure he had the right people in place by going outside the company if talent did not exist internally.

IBM did one other thing that most companies do not have the discipline for: when it reduced costs, it also reduced budgets. Working with one supplier, Richter's team created a tight linkage between savings and budget reduction. This is counterintuitive at a traditional company because the temptation is to buy more with the savings. But if you look at savings as an opportunity to buy what is needed at less cost, the difference can be returned to the bottom line.

IBM changed its approach because of a competitive crisis that forced it into sweeping changes and innovations. Most companies today have an opportunity to adopt best practices in the absence of a crisis. MRO is one area that, with a little attention, can provide an incredible payback.

TRAINING AND CAREER PATH PLANNING

Leaders in progressive organizations understand the need for training and career path planning. Each stage of supply evolution requires a different set of skills and knowledge. Identifying the critical skill and knowledge set and attracting, retaining, and developing people is a critical success factor in the evolution of a supply management organization.

Stage 1: Chaos/Traditional

In stage 1, training consists of learning how to read your paycheck, and career path planning means waiting for the department head to retire. That description is only a little unfair. There *is* training in stage 1, but it is usually how to do a particular set of tasks. For many years this approach was supported by limited availability of formal coursework for supply management or training focused on strategic issues. While this has certainly changed, leaders in stage 1 do not take advantage of what is now available. In stage 1 organizations, people come into purchasing only after being trained and employed in some other area. In other words, new purchasing employees learn on the job. Further, few organizations provide a clear path for advancement. Those who tend to excel at one set of tasks might be "moved up" to new positions without the preparation needed to assure their success.

The expectations of today's executives and the demands of today's supply chains have put increasing pressure on supply chain managers to become experts in both strategy and tactics. Basic purchasing training is no longer enough and has not been for years. This reality pressures leaders of stage 1 organizations to develop training and career path planning that fits changing business needs and expectations, and move into stage 2.

Stage 2: Control/Evolving

Joseph Cavinato, Ph.D., C.P.M., has written about the changing expectations for supply management, and those expectations tie directly in to the training needs of today. Dr. Cavinato has written that successful supply management professionals must know more about business, more about global issues, more about technology, and more about strategy, while at the same time knowing more about their own individual set of competencies. For example, departments must be

- Future-oriented
- Important to senior management
- Strategic in relation to the competitive imperatives of the organization
- Able to identify what will provide value and uniqueness to the organization's offerings in the marketplace

Dr. Cavinato also has described the characteristics of successful supply management *professionals*. He says that as *individuals,* we must

- Take a leadership role in seeking and driving new opportunities in the marketplace.
- Take a management role in systems and relationships.
- Become creators of new opportunities by developing strategies, systems, supply options, and revenue opportunities for our organizations.
- Become "needs enablers"; in other words, we must enable others in the organization to satisfy their own needs.

As people begin to do more networking and move between companies, and as top leaders begin expecting more out of their supply management people, a clearer definition emerges of what supply management skills are needed and the training necessary to get them.

Much of the hard work that has gone into describing the supply management professional of today has been led by professional organizations like the Institute for Supply Management™ (ISM). In fact, the evolution of ISM mirrors the evolution of supply management itself. In the 1960s, the organization was called the National Association of Purchasing Agents (NAPA), and that is what its members mostly were. During the 1980s, the organization's emphasis broadened as purchasing began to focus on quality measures, cost savings, and cost reductions.

NAPA became the National Association of Purchasing Management (NAPM) to describe more accurately what its members had become.

In 2001, NAPM changed its name to ISM. Because of its global reach and partnership with international purchasing organizations, it was no longer accurate to describe the group as the *National* Association of Purchasing Management. What once served purchasing agents in stage 1 organizations is now an institute concerned with the leveling-up of supply management in all its disciplines around the world.

Whereas NAPA probably began its training with how to do the buyer's job, ISM has worked more on helping managers and executives. ISM's certified purchasing manager program, specialized training programs, and sponsored research through CAPS: The Center for Strategic Supply Research and others have educated business leaders in the United States and around the world. Today, ISM offers something of value to people at every level.

More individual companies now take the initiative in offering their own specialized training. In developing managers, Honda exercises a philosophy of "go to the spot." When Honda began manufacturing in Ohio, the company sent a certain number of high-potential associates to Japan to gain more advanced knowledge from experts there. As the company has matured, Honda associates may be sent to experts anywhere in the world. Honda is not alone. Many other companies bring in their best and brightest from around the world to develop skills, sending them back to become experts in their own countries, businesses, or divisions.

Stage 3: Future/Step-Function Improvement

When accountants look for a job, they better be certified public accountants—a professional designation that shows they have met industry standards for expertise in accounting. When doctors graduate from medical school, they must serve a residency to prove they have both academic and practical knowledge necessary to make medical decisions on their own. The American accounting field has an organization called the Financial Accounting Standards Board (FASB) which creates principles of reporting financial performance for that field. There is no FASB of purchasing, no "generally accepted purchasing principles." But we may be getting closer, if progress in other areas is any indication. Great strides have been made, particularly at the university level.

Universities are a source of research, training, and people—important to the leveling-up process our field needs. We began seeing four-year purchasing degrees in the late 1970s and early 1980s. Through the 1990s, we began to see more MBAs and Ph.D.s coming into the discipline of supply chain management. There are now a number of recognized programs from which major companies can recruit.

This is where step-function improvement will occur in training—when companies are able to recruit formally educated supply management professionals with bachelor's or master's degrees in supply management and its various disciplines. It will occur when companies recognize ISM's certification designations (currently the Certified Purchasing Manager and as of 2008 the Certified Professional in Supply Management) as an important element in career path development. And it will occur when more and more companies draw students from formal programs into highly structured, discipline-focused internships.

For example, Deere & Company recruits interns from Arizona State University, Western Michigan University, University of Tennessee, Iowa State University, Michigan State University, University of San Diego, University of Wisconsin, Bowling Green State University, North Carolina State University, Western Illinois University, Northern Iowa University, North Carolina A&T, Western Ontario University, Monterrey Tech in Mexico, and the University of Stuttgart in Germany.

In contrast to traditional intern programs, which might put students to work organizing files or other administrative tasks, Deere focuses on providing meaningful work experience for students and applicable results for Deere. For example, one recent intern assigned to study a category of parts, consisting of nuts, bolts, and washers, gathered up samples and weighed and plotted their weight against the price. She then created a basic price curve for those commodities and segmented them according to the manufacturing processes. This enabled the intern to identify things that were not appropriately priced. Focusing on a simple commodity like fasteners is a good place to start because it allows students to get involved in the manufacturing process, analytical work, negotiations, and interaction with both supplier and customer.

Internship programs, if designed properly will allow a supply management organization to develop relationships with interns, professors, and schools. And the savings identified by students is well worth the investment—in our experience, 5 to 20 times the cost of the internship program itself. Not only that, but internships can serve as extended interviews for interns looking for postcollege jobs and supply management organizations seeking the best and brightest.

STRATEGIC SOURCING AND SUPPLIER PERFORMANCE

Strategic sourcing is a business model to select and develop suppliers in ways that drive down total acquisition costs while promoting more uniform strategies and processes. While it has taken many companies years to recognize the full value of strategic sourcing, it is one of the hallmarks of highly successful supply management organizations.

Most companies today continue to have numerous suppliers acquired over the years in a nonsystematic, nonstrategic fashion. For example, when Deere & Company began focusing on MRO supplies in 1997 and 1998, the company included gloves in its review. Remember the example of gloves at Deere? By simply standardizing this one commodity and reducing the supply base to a single supplier, chosen according to a strategic sourcing strategy, it was calculated that Deere would save nearly $500,000 a year.

While the focus of strategic sourcing is not supplier reduction per se, choosing the right suppliers usually means a leaner supply base. A coordinated sourcing strategy identifies the supply base of the future, providing a framework and process for choosing the right suppliers for the right products.

Stage 1: Chaos/Traditional

In organizations in stage 1, there is nothing very strategic about sourcing. Suppliers are chosen primarily on price. As mentioned elsewhere, the "right" price is determined using price variance standards, not true costs. While a supplier's delivery record is considered important, the focus in stage 1 is on whether a truckload of parts was delivered on time. There was no such thing as just-in-time delivery or the concept of small-lot, high-frequency deliveries, which today allows production schedules to be met without resulting in large inventories. Quality is measured according to how many bad parts have to be returned to the supplier, and almost no attention is given to a supplier's development or management capabilities or its willingness to work with customers collaboratively.

Instead, the basic process looks like this: Engineering creates a new product and creates a bill of materials. Manufacturing makes a decision about whether to make the part or buy it from outside. Prints and specifications are sent to purchasing, which sends quotes to companies that make the items. Purchasing then approves the best of three quotes. Job well done.

Stage 2: Control/Evolving

Leaders in stage 2 companies widely acknowledge that sourcing strategies can influence a company's competitiveness and that a big part of that competitiveness resides at the part and commodity level. While every company says it wants the most competitive supply chain, almost none has a way to measure competitiveness. Strategic sourcing provides those measurements. Strategic sourcing allows a manager to understand commodity-specific requirements for quality, cost, innovation, speed, and flexibility. It standardizes common core processes across departments or divisions to allow enterprisewide leveraging of pricing, volume, measurement, capabilities, and supplier relationships. Cross-functional teams and collaborative efforts allow companies to define expectations, evaluate suppliers, identify capabilities, and select the suppliers. In this way, strategic sourcing frames the customer-supplier relationship; it is not just a way to develop a single solution for a commodity or a supplier.

As companies become more in tune with the components of successful strategic sourcing, they adopt steps that move theory into practice. The following seven steps and their components describe what a best-practice strategic sourcing process is, in the author's experience.

Phase 1. Develop a business plan.
- State the business case for strategic sourcing.
- Understand the spend.
- Establish a multifunction strategic sourcing team.
- Create a charter.
- Understand key stakeholders.
- Decide how to communicate.

Phase 2. Develop a process plan.
- Establish a baseline (the current state).
- Define the desired mix of suppliers by segment.
- Include a work plan.
- Update the charter.
- Establish how communication will occur.

Phase 3. Gather data.
- Understand the current state.
- Create a hypothesis.
- Create a vision.
- Understand the industry.
- Understand the competition.
- Identify potential supplier.
- Identify benchmarks.

Phase 4. Evaluate the data.
- Narrow the supplier possibilities to a few.
- Begin to form a strategy.
- Determine the benefits.
- Create cost models.
- Determine what the barriers will be.

Phase 5. Select and develop suppliers.
- Define request-for-proposal process.
- Create a negotiation strategy.
- Select suppliers.
- Work through problems (corrective action and supplier development).
- Update the strategy.
- Prepare for implementation.

Phase 6. Implement.
- Identify the team.
- Determine what coordination will require.
- Integrate suppliers into the process.
- Establish performance measurement.
- Take corrective actions.

Phase 7. Performance measurement and continuous improvement.
- Manage the relationship and performance.
- Communicate.
- Continuous improvement.
- Follow up.

Figure 18–3 shows the relationship between commodity strategies (a strategy for every part, a strategy for every supplier), the strategic sourcing process, supplier management (including supplier development), and overall business strategies. A formal process is essential to align sourcing strategies with business strategies and

FIGURE 18–3

Strategic Supply Management

to help decision makers think about who to partner with and how to implement supplier relationships.

Sourcing leaders combine a strategic sourcing process with a number of organizational tools and best practices, including

- *A written strategy for every part and every supplier.* Which parts should be made and which ones should be bought? What standards must each supplier meet? To answer these questions, benchmark companies like Honda and Toyota give all their stakeholders input.

- *Multifunctional teams.* Sourcing teams that include purchasing, manufacturing, engineering, and suppliers make decisions about parts before one line is drawn on paper, before specifications are designed. These teams begin by looking at a part and how to create that part with the lowest possible cost designed in.

- *Centralized purchasing.* Implementing strategic sourcing fully requires control over spend, and this is more difficult with a decentralized purchasing organization. IBM realized this in the 1990s when it centralized purchasing and saved $1 billion through strategic sourcing.

- *Focus on high-cost, strategic parts.* It is impossible to devote 100 percent of organizational energy to 100 percent of the parts. It usually makes more sense to focus on the 20 percent of parts that have 80 percent of the cost.

- *Knowledge of the supplier's industry.* For every part, service, or commodity it is important to study and understand that industry. The more knowledge gathered about that industry, the easier it is to analyze a part and understand the product.

Focus on total costs. If there is a choice to buy from China or a supplier right next door and the part from China costs 40 percent less than the domestic supplier, consider total costs. This includes the cost of the part plus the costs of packaging and shipping from China, the risk of managing quality from 6,000 miles away, the cost of inventory, or the risk of obsolescence if the specifications change while the parts are in transit. Sometimes total cost includes the life of the end product—for example, the need to manufacture replacement parts adequate for the estimated life of the product.

Supplier involvement. Suppliers usually are the experts in the parts or services they are chosen to supply, yet customers historically have not treated them this way. Including suppliers at the earliest stages of product development is another critical element in successful sourcing strategies.

Supplier performance. A written strategy for every supplier includes written standards for performance. It is now possible, through new tracking and measurement tools, to assess supplier performance in a variety of ways. One of the responsibilities of a strategic sourcing team is to analyze performance data in the supplier selection process. An increasingly common tool is the stakeholder survey, which asks questions related to a supplier's past performance to gauge a supplier's potential to meet future performance standards. Best-practice companies such as IBM survey internal stakeholders to determine how purchasing's performance is viewed by both suppliers and other internal stakeholders.

If a company has been sourcing the traditional way and moves to our seven-step process, the difference might be compared to the difference between riding a horse to California and driving a car. Ironically, Honda and Toyota—the benchmarks when it comes to strategic sourcing—would never think to adopt a formal seven-step process. In fact, they might wonder why one was needed. That is because these practices are so ingrained in these companies' way of doing business that it is part of the corporate DNA. This is the difference between driving a car to California and flying an airplane.

Stage 3: Future/Step-Function Improvement

Step-function improvement in supplier performance results when a customer takes a hard look at its own practices and how they may affect a supplier's performance. In the traditional purchasing environment, suppliers were measured primarily according to price and on-time delivery. There was very little tracking of other performance indicators. In almost every instance, supplier performance was a one-way street. Suppliers performed to expectations (usually price) or they lost a customer. There was very little collaboration between customers and suppliers to identify costs, improve processes, and track results. True strategic sourcing changes that dynamic. Best-practice companies now insist that suppliers meet standards for both objective and subjective performance, including quality, cost, development capability, and management approach to the customer relationship. Best-practice companies today are slower to "fire" a supplier, instead looking at ways to improve results and establish a mutually beneficial arrangement.

STRATEGIC PLANNING AND SYSTEMS

Changing the perception of purchasing from primarily a tactical player to an essential strategic player in the organization is an important transition in the evolution from purchasing to supply management.

Stage 1: Chaos/Traditional

In organizations in stage 1, there is no such thing as strategic planning in purchasing. Purchasing practitioners are tacticians, measured by the efficiency with which orders are processed and defective parts counted. In years past, even if more had been expected of purchasing, it lacked the tools needed to be truly strategic. When Dave Nelson joined the workforce in the 1950s, purchasing was truly low-tech. The typical office copier was carbon paper and a manual typewriter. The typical calculator was paper, pencil, and a brain. Each part was assigned a purchase cost record (PCR) card. The PCR contained a complete description and history of the part—all handwritten. Each month the PCR cards were gathered, 100 to a tray, and purchasing met with production to synchronize. This process allowed purchasing to do the forecasting necessary to determine the next month's orders.

Stage 2: Control/Evolving

As supply management becomes recognized as an important influence on the company's bottom line, senior management increasingly includes supply management within its business plan. For the first time, supply management professionals will be expected to know their company's business plan and what the business objectives are and to create a business plan for purchasing aligned with the company's strategic objectives.

In stage 2, supply management moves toward multiyear plans detailing how purchasing will integrate into business processes across the company. This new approach leads to the adoption of leading procurement responsibilities, like attention to indirect, MRO, and every other aspect of the spend.

Stage 3: Future/Step-Function Improvement

Best-practices companies, and those looking for step-function improvement, invite supply management to the CEO's table, along with manufacturing, engineering, finance, and every other essential element of the company. While evolving companies span a variety of strategic planning models, an industry best practice, and one that will result in step-function improvement, gives purchasing responsibility for every part of the spend, not just the parts and commodities required for manufacturing. This, of course, requires some delegation. At some companies, the management team and board of directors write delegation policies placing responsibility for the company's entire spend with their supply management organization. While purchasing is given authority to delegate some of its responsibility (for example, delegating payroll to human resources), supply management is ultimately responsible. The stronger the policy, the more evidence there is of step-function improvement.

These new responsibilities and accountability require better tools and systems. A lot of tools have simply improved efficiencies. For example, procurement cards—credit cards that allow functional areas to make small, nonstrategic purchases—increase efficiency by automating small transactions while capturing all the data supply management needs to analyze the spend. Systems themselves have grown with computer technology. Enterprisewide systems, such as material requirements planning (MRP) and enterprise resource management (ERP), advanced as costs came down, allowing integration of purchasing systems and processes. As long as data collection is thorough and uniform across the enterprise (no small feat, especially in a decentralized organization), modern systems are fully capable of delivering detailed data analysis.

CONCLUSION

Where will supply management ultimately go? It is sometimes difficult to separate reality from hype. A reporter recently advanced the theory that the Internet eventually would make purchasing obsolete. That reporter believed there would be no more need for purchasing people because of reverse auctions, in which suppliers compete real-time by bidding lower as the auction proceeds. This reporter had fallen for the hype without thinking it through. To a certain extent, it is human nature to be wowed by the latest greatest tool, gadget, or toy. While supply managers will continue to search the next wonderful IT tool, reverse auctions and other tools are just that—tools. Like a chisel in the hand of a master sculptor, IT tools used properly can build a lasting legacy. In the hands of an amateur, they can produce a pile of rubble.

We remember the "good old days" of stage 1 development as if it were yesterday. And while this chapter has talked about how purchasing has evolved from those times and how supply management can realize huge benefits by taking some next steps, a few things should never be forgotten. For example, let's not forget good old Harry, the supplier rep who always brought cookies on Tuesdays. While Harry's job doesn't sound very strategic, he had at least one thing figured out—personal relationships were the grease that smoothed his company's relationships with its customers.

Today, that fact has been all but lost on some large supply management organizations. These companies are long on demands, short on trust; long on negotiations, short on information sharing; long on awarding the lowest bid, short on rewarding supplier innovation. This is a very traditional approach, and yet top-tier companies in every other respect often do not spend one minute thinking about the human element.

In contrast, we believe that the human element is the single most important indicator of whether a company or supply management organization will evolve and, eventually, realize step-function improvement. Togetherness—collaboration and cooperation among departments and up and down the supply chain—will be the hallmarks of tomorrow's most successful companies. And no amount of computer power, and no superfast Internet connection, can replace it.

CHAPTER 19

SUPPLY IN A RISK-SENSITIVE BUSINESS CLIMATE

GEORGE A. ZSIDISIN, PH.D., C.P.M.
Assistant Professor
The Eli Broad College of Business
Michigan State University

INTRODUCTION

Increasingly, firms and their management are coming to rely on lean supply chains to augment and enhance their own internal capabilities. These are also chains where waste and buffers in their various forms are actively identified, evaluated, and attacked. The goal is to replace the traditional "internal" factory (a system where the firm relied on its own capacities and capabilities to meet customer demand) with more effective and efficient supply chain systems. This new strategy can and does create significant competitive advantages for those firms willing to embrace it. Yet, there is a dark side to this new supply chain–based strategy. As firms become more reliant on the supply chain and as they seek to identify and eliminate waste, they are realizing that their supply chains have also become more susceptible to risk in supply.

Numerous examples of supply risk and its outcomes exist in business today. On August 14, 2003, electrical power in the American Midwest and Ontario was disrupted, with the resulting power outages lasting anywhere from minutes to days. The effects of this disruption were felt as far away as California, where Apple Computer was preparing to launch its much-anticipated G5 computer—the first mainstream personal computer featuring 64-bit processing. This launch was affected by the power disruption since Apple relied on an IBM facility in upstate New York to supply its chips. On September 21, 1999, a magnitude 7.6 tremor struck Taiwan, killing over 1,500 people. From a supply chain perspective, this earthquake hindered the supply of computer memory chips, affecting many firms' ability to meet anticipated consumer demand for the upcoming holiday season. Finally, on Tuesday, September 11, 2001, New York experienced the destruction of the World Trade Center towers due to terrorism. Companies such as American Express experienced significant losses in terms of their information databases.

The purpose of this chapter is to provide insights for understanding supply risk, its dimensions, and how firms can identify and mitigate that risk. The chapter will begin with defining risk and some of its sources in the upstream supply chain. Next, the critical dimensions of supply risk and two examples of tools for assessing that risk will be introduced. Several techniques for managing risk, based on its assessment, will conclude the chapter.

DEFINING SUPPLY CHAIN RISK

Risk and uncertainty have been studied in numerous business settings and have warranted significant investigation in corporate functions, such as in strategy, operations, accounting, and finance. A classic definition of *risk* is "the variance of the probability distribution of possible gains and losses associated with a particular alternative" (March and Shapira 1987, p. 1404). However, it has been found that few business managers define risk as so stated and instead focus on four aspects of risk: (1) the downside of risk, (2) the magnitude of possible losses as compared to its probabilities, (3) the distinction between risk taking and gambling, and (4) risk as a multifaceted construct (Yates and Stone 1992).

From these perspectives we see that risk can be further examined within the dimensions of probability and impact. The probability dimension involves the uncertainty associated with suppliers and the markets in which those suppliers participate. The impact of supply risk can result in the inability of supply management organizations to meet their customer requirements, supply discontinuity, and significant price increases that the organization cannot pass on to customers. These effects result in immediate and potentially long-term financial losses for the firm. Therefore, a formal definition of supply risk would be the potential occurrence of an incident with inbound supply in which its outcomes result in a financial loss for the firm.

Supply risk can manifest from many different sources. Two primary sources of supply risk are (1) individual supplier failures and (2) the markets in which these suppliers compete. Examples of individual supplier failures include capacity constraints, inability to reduce cost, quality problems, unpredictable cycle times, and volume and mix requirement changes. At times, risk can occur within an entire supply market or region. Examples of market risk sources include global sourcing, market capacity constraints, market price increases, and the number of qualified suppliers. A list of some risk sources prevalent in many supply chains can be found in Table 19–1.

CRITICAL DIMENSIONS FOR ASSESSING SUPPLY RISK

From understanding the sources of supply risk, we can assess all purchased goods and services by placing each into a two-by-two matrix classification according to its dimensions of probability and impact. In Figure 19–1, the supply risk profile for goods and services is classified into one of four quadrants: (1) low risk, (2) annoyance, (3) catastrophic, and (4) high risk. Low-risk items consist of circumstances where the probability that risk occurs is small and the impact on the organization is minimal. Items classified as annoyance consist of frequent failures with suppliers or the market but the impact on the organization is small. An example

TABLE 19–1

Examples of Supply Risk Sources

Source	Definition or Description	Supplier	Market
Capacity constraints	The inability of a system to produce an output quantity in a particular time period	X	X
Disasters	Any occurrence that causes great harm or calamity	X	X
Erratic cycle time performance	The time between purchase request to a supplier and receipt	X	
Financial health problems of suppliers	Profitability trends in cash flow and the existence of financial guarantees	X	
Global sourcing uncertainty	Political events and governmental policies that result in supply disruptions or significant cost incraeses		X
Inability to adapt to product design changes	The unpredictability of changes in product technology	X	
Inability to make process technological changes	The frequency of new ideas and emerging technology	X	X
Inability to make volume and mix requirements changes	Demand fluctuations in quantity and type for a component or service	X	
Inability to reduce cost	The act of lowering the cost of the same goods or services	X	
Inbound transportation problems	Methods to distribute, handle, and transport inputs	X	
Information system incompatibility	Information system capability of suppliers to transfer timely, accurate, and relevant information to buyers	X	
Legal liabilities	Legally enforceable restrictions or commitments relating to the use of the material, product, or service	X	
Limited supplier management vision	Supplier management attitude and ability to foresee market and industry changes	X	
Market price increases	Trends, events, or developments that may increase prices		X
Number of available and qualified suppliers	The existence of monopoly or oligopoly conditions in the supply market		X
Poor environmental performance	Activities such as selecting materials used, product design processes, and process improvements	X	
Poor inventory management practices	Supplier ability to manage raw materials, work-in-process, and finished goods and inventories	X	

T A B L E   19–1

Examples of Supply Risk Sources (*continued*)

Source	Definition or Description	Supplier	Market
Quality problems	The ability of suppliers to conform to specifications	X	
Shipment quantity inaccuracies	The gap between the actual demand requests and the quantity shipped	X	
Supply unavailability	Availability of strategic materials in terms of quality and quantity, and the relative strength of suppliers	X	X

F I G U R E   19–1

Matrix of Supply Risk Dimensions

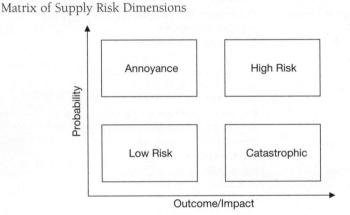

of this risk can be late shipments from suppliers that do not stop production. Although the impact may be small (i.e., increased inventory levels, production rescheduling), after a period of time, this form of risk can slowly drain a firm's profitability. Catastrophic risk occurs infrequently but can have devastating effects on a firm. For example, the defects associated with the interaction between certain Ford trucks and SUVs with the tires purchased from Firestone had a low probability of occurring but had devastating effects on Ford Motor Company as a customer, resulting in an estimated $2 billion loss (Truett 2001). High-risk circumstances involve both high likelihood and significant impact from supplier or market failures. Immediate managerial attention should focus on both the short-term and long-term implications of this risk classification.

This model can provide supply management professionals insight into appropriate tools that can cost-effectively mitigate supply risk. In order to classify purchased goods and services into this model, the risk must first be assessed. Two examples of tools that supply professionals can implement for managing risk are discussed next.

SUPPLY RISK ASSESSMENT TOOLS

An example of one supply risk assessment tool was created by a large European firm in the telecommunications industry. The supply risk assessment and measurement process was created to meet the legal requirements of KonTraG, which is a German law implemented in May 1998 to make investors aware of corporate risk. This amendment to German corporate law requires companies to treat risk-management information similar to financial information. The supply risk measurement process is one facet reported to top management as part of an overall balanced scorecard approach to measuring firm performance.

The supply risk evaluation process for this firm begins with a semi-annual meeting between the coordinator of the supply risk assessment process and each commodity manager. The risks associated with all commodities are evaluated for their impact on earnings before interest and taxes (EBIT) and reported on a quarterly basis to the coordinator of the risk assessment process.

There are 13 categories that are evaluated within the supply risk assessment and measurement process, as shown in Table 19–2. Each supply risk category is assessed using an 11-step process, summarized in Table 19–3. Purchasers and commodity managers assess their suppliers based on past experience and anticipated supply trends. The 11 steps focus on estimating the expected

TABLE 19–2

Risk Categories for Assessment

European Firm Example
Additional costs for cancellation due to lack of planning
Additional costs for transportation due to lack of planning
Additional costs for material obsolescence
Unexpected material price increase due to allocation
Unexpected material price increase due to yield problems
Unexpected material price increase due to change of specification
Missing parts due to late delivery
Missing parts due to supplier quality defects
Missing parts due to instability of supplier's country
Additional material costs due to single sourcing during ramp-up phase
Contractual risk
Investing in supplier improvement
Currency risk

SOURCE: Zsidisin (2001).

T A B L E   19–3

Supply Risk Assessment Process

European Firm Example

Step	Actions
1.	What is the impact on EBIT in million euros (mil. €) (before management implementation) for the current fiscal year?
2.	What is the probability of occurrence before risk-management implementation (in percent) during the current fiscal year?
3.	What is the impact on EBIT in mil. ? for the next fiscal year?
4.	What is the probability of occurrence before risk-management implementation (in percent) for the next fiscal year?
5.	Insert explanations for the key risk factors.
6.	List risk-handling measures to avoid the risk.
7.	Rate the implementation status of risk management: 1 = very low (0–19.9%) 2 = low (20–39.9%) 3 = medium (40–59.9%) 4 = high (60–79.9%) 5 = very high (80–100%)
8.	What is the impact on EBIT in mil. € (after risk-management implementation) for the current fiscal year?
9.	What is the probability of occurrence after risk-management implementation (in percent) during the current fiscal year?
10.	What is the impact on EBIT in mil. € for the next fiscal year?
11.	What is the probability of occurrence after risk-management implementation (in percent) for the next fiscal year?

SOURCE: Zsidisin (2001).

impact on EBIT, the probabilities of risk events occurring, and the measures or activities to be implemented for reducing risk. Estimates are made for both the current and upcoming fiscal year.

Within the process there is a trade-off between accuracy and speed. More accurate probabilities and the effects on earnings can be derived if additional information is obtained. However, deriving more exact data means that a significant degree of managerial effort would be required by supply management professionals that may not be offset by the benefits from engaging in supply risk assessment and measurement processes. In addition, the purpose of estimating supply risk is not to determine exact probabilities or effects on earnings. Instead, the process facilitates the *communication* of possible supply failures between the commodity and supply line managers, and the risk manager. In addition, the process prioritizes supply risk that warrants managerial attention and provides guidance for proactively reducing the chance that those risk events will transpire. The commodity and supply line managers are responsible for managing supply risk, and headquarters is responsible for reporting incidents and providing additional resources when required.

The second example of a supply risk assessment technique comes from a U.S.-based semiconductor manufacturer. The supply risk assessment tool was implemented in 1996 to ensure that potential supply issues are addressed early in the material's life cycle. This technique has also been introduced to key suppliers for their use to better assess and manage the supply risk encountered with second-tier suppliers and, eventually, their supply chains.

The risk assessment process involves a detailed 10-step procedure that is summarized in Table 19–4. The risk assessment process measures eight factors that are deemed critical to having a reliable, predictable, cost-effective supply of materials and services. These factors are (1) design, (2) quality, (3) cost, (4) availability, (5) manufacturability, (6) supplier, (7) legal, and (8) environmental, health, and safety impacts. Definitions for the eight attributes are shown in Table 19–5. A commodity manager evaluates each of these factors. In addition, there are subcategories within each factor that are assigned risk scores on a scale from 1 to 5, where 1, labeled "show stopper," is the highest risk and 5, labeled "qualified," is the lowest risk.

The two risk assessment tools can help guide supply professionals in their decisions on how to best manage their risk exposure. Information provided from these risk assessment tools can help classify the risk of inbound supply by its dimensions of probability and impact. As depicted in Figure 19–2, and discussed later, the risk management efforts can be classified as (1) risk monitoring, (2) risk transference, (3) risk mitigation, and (4) risk planning.

T A B L E   19–4

Supply Risk Assessment Process

U.S. Firm Example

Step	Activity
1.	Identify the material/service to be assessed.
2.	Identify the owner of the material/service who will be responsible for the risk assessment.
3.	Start the risk assessment scorecard.
4.	Review success criteria for each of the risk factors.
5.	Collect data.
6.	Determine risk level by comparing data to criteria on the risk assessment scorecard.
7.	Conduct impact analysis.
8.	Document risk level analysis and risk reduction plans.
9.	Track progress.
10.	Determine when to cease performing risk assessments.

Source: Zsidisin and Ellram (1999).

T A B L E   19–5

Risk Category Definitions

U.S. Firm Example

Risk	Definition
Design	Ability to complete the design, follow the design for manufacturing goals, validate the design, assess the materials interactions, and manufacture the item. This refers to both company and supplier design as well as to statements of work for service to outsourcing suppliers.
Quality	The direct and indirect materials, service, or product consistently meet requirements, and supporting processes are in place to enoure control
Cost	Determined by target costs from the customer, industry benchmarking, should-cost models, and make-or-buy decisions where appropriate.
Availability	Assessing the risk of the sourcing, unit volume requirements, and the material tooling (where applicable).
Manufacturability	Risk associated with manufacturing's ability to produce when material specifications are met. If the material has not yet been received, this may entail anticipating potential future problems, such as materials that meet specifications but do not meet design for manufacturing goals.
Supplier	Assessing and choosing suppliers of good financial health and manufacturing in politically stable or low-risk natural disaster areas. It also refers to instances when the firm becomes too large a percentage of a supplier's business, either through capacity or corporate revenue.
Legal	Risk associated with the substantive legal status of the material, product, or service, such as import-export restrictions and tax issues. Additional risk factors include legally enforceable restrictions or commitments relating to the use of the material, product, or service.
Environmental, health, and safety	Issues such as the handling and use of hazardous materials and compliance with EPA, OSHA, and other governmental agency policies by suppliers as well as this firm.

SOURCE: Zsidisin and Ellram (1999).

MANAGING SUPPLY RISK

The supply risk management techniques employed by supply management professionals should vary according to how that risk is classified, as discussed in the supply risk assessment section. An array of techniques is needed in order to manage risk from a cost-benefit perspective. For example, by using multiple supply sources, a firm may be able to help reduce its risk profile for the "catastrophic" classification (as shown in Figure 19–1), but the extensive use of this technique can lead to

F I G U R E   19–2

Risk-Management Classification Model

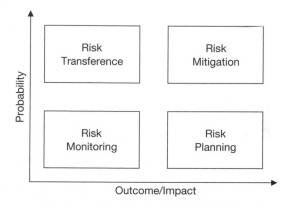

increased overall costs for the supply organization that can be better employed with other techniques. Each of the four supply risk management strategies is discussed, with some examples of suggested techniques that organizations can employ for efficiently and effectively managing its supply risk profile. Figure 19–3 provides a summary of techniques organizations can employ for better managing risk.

Purchases classified as *low risk* from the risk assessment, which entails low probability and low impact, do not require immediate action. Each of these items, however, should be periodically *monitored* for changes in its risk profile. For example, many organizations that relied on inbound shipments going through the port in Los Angeles had a low risk exposure for many of the items. However, when the International Longshore and Warehouse Union staged a work slowdown in the summer of 2002, the risk profile for some shippers changed from low risk to that of annoyance. After the work slowdown ended, for many of these purchases, the risk profile changed back to low risk.

Items and services classified as *annoyance,* which involves high probability and low impact, should be managed through *risk transference.* The goal for managing risk for this purchase classification is to transfer the firm's risk exposure, either to its supplier organizations or third parties, or by decoupling the firm's dependence on supply. As shown in Figure 19–3, several examples of transferring risk include writing penalty clauses for nonperformance into contracts with suppliers, indirectly developing suppliers (Krause 1997) through mechanisms such as promising suppliers current and future benefits, and using multiple suppliers to create competition that indirectly drives performance improvement and ,subsequently, reduces the firm's risk of supplier noncompliance for meeting requirements.

FIGURE 19–3

Summary of Risk-Management Techniques

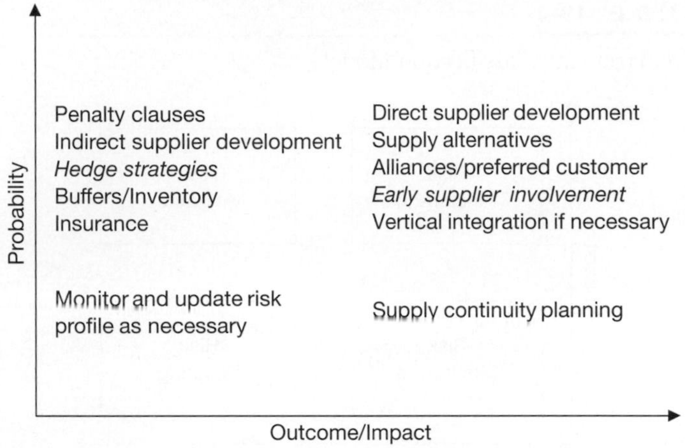

Two examples of risk transference are hedging and inventory management. Risk transference can occur through the use of intermediary financial instruments such as insurance and hedging. For example, Schlosser and Zsidisin (2004) describe how Hershey Foods is able to reduce its risk exposure of paying diesel fuel surcharges from carriers by purchasing future contracts on a related commodity—heating oil. In addition, business insurance can be purchased to help offset minor losses. One problem with hedging strategies and purchasing insurance is the cost involved to these financial intermediaries. Therefore, for certain types of risk that are not directly controllable, these instruments are appropriate for reducing the effects of risk when supply professionals know there is a reasonable likelihood of their occurrence (such as commodity price volatility and accidents). When there is some degree of control, particularly on the part of the supplier, it may be better to transfer that risk through contract clauses, when possible.

One other risk transference technique that has been employed by organizations for many years is managing inventory. If there is a relatively high chance that risk will lead to short-term stockouts, supply professionals should reevaluate their inventory management policies for adjusting inventory levels in response to the risk to which it is exposed.

The third risk classification is *catastrophic,* which consists of supply circumstances where the likelihood of risk occurrence is low but the effects on the organization are devastating. Under these circumstances, it is not logical for supply management organizations to invest a significant extent of sources in reducing the chance that risk occurs, since by definition these purchases have a very low probability of risk manifestation. However, in case the risk does transpire, supply management organizations should have a plan in place for quickly remediating any disruptions and minimizing its impact in terms of time and cost to the organization.

One example of this type of risk occurred with Ericsson in 2000 when one of their suppliers, a Philips Electronics semiconductor plant in Albuquerque, New Mexico, burned for 10 minutes from a lightning bolt strike. One problem reported by Ericsson was that it "did not have a plan B" for this event (Latour 2001). Because of the components shortage experienced with this natural disaster event, and additional problems that subsequently arose from this event, Ericsson reported an overall loss of $1.68 billion in 2000 for the company's mobile phone division. As a result, Ericsson has implemented a rigorous business continuity planning process in its firm to ensure that backup plans are in place in case a similar catastrophe occurs in the future.

The fourth and final risk classification is *high risk,* which consists of supply circumstances where both the likelihood and impact of risk occurrence is high and needs to be immediately addressed. In these circumstances, supply professionals need to create both short- and long-term plans for reducing the probability of occurrence and the impact these purchases can have on organizational performance. To immediately manage this risk, supply professionals need to find ways for opening their supply options. This can involve searching and qualifying new supply sources, taking ownership of tooling that can be moved to alternative locations, and developing contingency sources in the event that a specific supplier failure is imminent. All these activities focus on reducing the impact that supply failures would have on a purchasing firm's performance.

Purchases classified as high risk also need to be managed for the long term. One method for accomplishing this task is to improve organizational and inter-organizational processes. One technique appropriate for managing high-risk purchases, particularly in the new product development process, is early supplier involvement. For example, one firm in the aerospace industry that has been studied for its innovative early supplier involvement (ESI) process (Zsidisin and Smith, 2005) has also achieved a reduction in its risk exposure. Several sources of risk have been better managed at this firm from ESI, including the avoidance of being "priced" out of the market, having legal conflicts with suppliers, addressing quality problems, avoiding supplier capacity constraints, experiencing extended product development times, and managing changes in product design.

Other risk-management techniques suited for high-risk purchases involve creating closer working relationships with key suppliers, which can be accomplished by forming strategic alliances with critical suppliers and instituting direct supplier development programs with at-risk suppliers. Closer working relationships with suppliers can help create an atmosphere of cooperation between the two parties if potential supply problems are imminent. For these types of relationships, suppliers will be more willing to take the extra step in meeting their alliance partner's needs when supply problems occur or are likely. Solid relationships with suppliers can enable an organization to become a preferred customer to that supplier.

Direct supplier development, which consists of activities such as formally evaluating suppliers, training and education, and conducting site visits (Krause 1997) can also lead to reducing the likelihood of risk occurrence. Buying organizations get to understand their supplier organizations better and, in conjunction with assessment, can identify supply chain problems and work with those suppliers for rectifying issues that pose risk to the purchasing firm.

If the threat of supply risk is significant, some firms may also have the option to vertically integrate. This can be accomplished by acquiring suppliers to ensure control or by learning the current suppliers' processes and internally producing subassemblies in-house. This alternative should be a last resort but may be necessary if internal control becomes the only viable alternative for managing high-risk items.

CONCLUSION

With the advent of supply chain management, firms have experienced greater financial returns by replacing inventory with information. However, with these leaner supply chains, many firms have also become more susceptible to the risk inherent in outsourcing production inputs. As supply management professionals, we need to be cognizant of the risk that exists with our suppliers and supply chains. This chapter has provided a definition of supply risk, outlined various sources of supply risk, discussed the critical dimensions of supply risk to consider in its assessment, provided examples of supply risk assessment tools, and introduced a model for managing supply risk. Risk exists in virtually every supply chain, whether or not it is recognized. Only by taking proactive steps in identifying, assessing, and managing that risk can we realize the benefits of supply chain management without leaving our firms exposed to the unknown.

REFERENCES

Krause, D. R. (1997). "Supplier Development: Current Practices and Outcomes," *International Journal of Purchasing and Materials Management*, vol. 33, no. 2, pp. 12–19.

Latour, A. (2001). "Trial by Fire: A Blaze in Albuquerque Sets off Major Crisis for Cell-Phone Giants," *Wall Street Journal*, January 29.

March, J. G., and Z. Shapira (1987). "Managerial Perspectives on Risk and Risk Taking," *Management Science,* vol. 33, no. 11, pp. 1404–1418.

Schlosser, M., and G. A. Zsidisin (2004). Hedging Fuel Surcharge Price Fluctuations, www.capsresearch.org.

Truett, R. (2001). "Tire-Related Costs Mount for Ford," *Automotive News*, vol. 75, p. 45.

Yates, J. F., and Stone, E. R. (1992). "The Risk Construct." In J. Yates (ed.), *Risk Taking Behavior*, New York: John Wiley & Sons, pp. 1–25.

Zsidisin, G. A. (2001). "Measuring Supply Risk: An Example from Europe," *PRACTIX: Best Practices in Purchasing and Supply Management*, vol. 4, no. 3, pp. 1–6.

Zsidisin, G. A., and L. M. Ellram (1999). "Supply Risk Assessment Analysis," *PRACTIX: Best Practices in Purchasing and Supply Management*, vol. 2, no. 4, pp. 9–12.

Zsidisin, G.A., and M.E. Smith (2005). "Managing Supply Risk with Early Supplier Involvement: A Case Study and Research Propositions," *Journal of Supply Chain Management*, vol. 41, no. 4, pp. 44-57.

CHAPTER 20

PURCHASING SOCIAL RESPONSIBILITY—WHAT IS IT, AND WHERE SHOULD WE BE HEADED?

CRAIG R. CARTER, PH.D.
Assistant Professor of Supply Chain Management
College of Business Administration
University of Nevada

INTRODUCTION

"Safety Probe of GM Truck Tailgates Is Upgraded."[1]

"Quick Drug Review, Quick Recall."[2]

"Wilting Plants: Behind China's Export Boom, Heated Battle among Factories; As Wal-Mart, Others Demand Lowest Prices, Managers Scramble to Slash Costs; Rising Concerns about Safety."[3]

"Move by Honda Ups the Ante on Car Safety; It Will Equip Almost All Models with Side Curtain Airbags."[4]

"Socially Responsible—and Beating the S&P: High Quality Companies Tend to Have Good Records on the Environment and Treat Their Employees Well, which Results in Lower Turnover and Ultimately Lower Costs."[5]

---

1 Anonymous (2004). "Safety Probe of GM Truck Tailgates Is Upgraded," *Wall Street Journal*, February 24, p. D2.

2 Roman, M. (2000). "Quick Drug Review, Quick Recall," *BusinessWeek*, December 11, p. 56.

3 Wonacott, P. (2003). "Wilting Plants: Behind China's Export Boom, Heated Battle among Factories; As Wal-Mart, Others Demand Lowest Prices, Managers Scramble to Slash Costs; Rising Concerns about Safety," *Wall Street Journal*, November 13, p. A1.

4 White, J. B. (2003). "Move by Honda Ups the Ante on Car Safety; It Will Equip Almost All Models with Side Curtain Airbags," *Wall Street Journal*, October 30, p. D1.

5 Anonymous (2002). "Socially Responsible—and Beating the S&P: High Quality Companies Tend to Have Good Records on the Environment and Treat Their Employees Well, which Results in Lower Turnover and Ultimately Lower Costs," *BusinessWeek*, May 13, p. 118.

A manager in today's business environment needs only to consider these headlines from the *Wall Street Journal* and *BusinessWeek* to recognize that social responsibility, and the lack thereof, can significantly impact an organization's interface with consumers, shareholders, employees, regulatory agencies, and other stakeholders. These issues and others, including human rights, the environment, diversity, safety, ethics, and philanthropy and community involvement fall under the more encompassing umbrella of corporate social responsibility (CSR), which has been defined as "corporate activity and its impact on different social groups."[6]

Many of these issues might at first appear to fall under the broader jurisdiction of the corporation, rather than the more specific responsibility of the supply management function. What role then, does supply management have in CSR? Do activities such as environmental purchasing, minority business enterprise (MBE) procurement programs, and human rights issues at suppliers' plants, which have been researched and often managed as stand-alone activities, fall under a wider umbrella of purchasing social responsibility (PSR)? What is the current state of research in PSR, and where should our discipline extend to next, in terms of further research in this area?

In the next section of this chapter, the author will begin to answer these questions by first reviewing the existing stand-alone research that has examined individual dimensions of supply management's involvement in social responsibility, such as the environment and diversity. Afterward, the author will introduce and review the relatively recent literature that examines the more encompassing concept of PSR, a concept that the author defines as "purchasing activities that meet the discretionary responsibilities expected by society."[7] As will be discussed later in the chapter, this definition of PSR focuses on the discretionary activities of the supply management function, rather than ethical issues, which are considered to be at a more fundamental, building-block level of PSR.

In reviewing the PSR literature, the reader will be brought up-to-date regarding the current state of research in this area of supply management. Then, in the final section of the chapter, the author will suggest where the field of PSR needs to go next, in terms of both future research directions and managerial practices. This "future research" section of the chapter will highlight the need for improved performance metrics and the development of social responsibility audits, as well as the need for researchers to use complementary methodologies, including social network analysis, to address many of the broad gaps that still exist in this evolving stream of research.

---

6 Sethi, S. P. (1995). "Introduction to AMR's Special Topic Forum on Shifting Paradigms: Societal Expectations and Corporate Performance," *Academy of Management Review*, vol. 20, no. 1, pp. 18–21.

7 Carter, C. R., and M. Jennings (2004). "The Role of Purchasing in the Socially Responsible Management of the Supply Chain: A Structural Equation Analysis," *Journal of Business Logistics*, vol. 25, no. 1, pp. 145–186.

WHAT IS PSR AND WHERE ARE WE NOW?

The existing PSR literature can be largely divided into two areas: (1) the stand-alone literature that examines individual aspects or dimensions of PSR, such as environmental purchasing or the issue of the use of sweatshop labor by suppliers, and (2) the more recent and integrative literature that examines PSR as a broad, umbrella construct that encompasses these dimensions and others. While the PSR literature is more integrative, it is important to note that both streams of research were necessary and will continue to be necessary in the future. Specifically, it is essential to view PSR from a broad and holistic standpoint; at the same time, it is also important to take "deep dives" into specific dimensions of PSR in order to gain a better understanding of the particular nuances and practices of each set of activities. The next two subsections review the existing research from both of these areas, with a focus on the literature that had appeared in refereed, scholarly journals at the time that this chapter was written.

The Stand-Alone Literature

Diversity

The primary diversity issue that is discussed and examined in the supply management literature is that of purchasing from minority- and/or women-owned business enterprises (MWBEs). Krause et al.[8] employ a mail survey to examine MWBE sourcing from the perspectives of suppliers to a large manufacturing organization. The authors found that small minority suppliers (defined as organizations with less than $10 million in annual revenues) were on average (1) less optimistic about the manufacturing firm's minority supplier development program, (2) felt that there were more communication problems, and (3) believed that the customer was less committed to them, as compared to large minority suppliers (defined as firms with more than $10 million in annual revenues). Additionally, the authors discovered that minority suppliers that were not highly reliant on the customer (defined as suppliers selling "20 percent or less of their output to the customer firm") (1) were less likely to agree that the customer's supplier development program would help them to improve profitability and increase their ability to compete, (2) believed that communication was more of a barrier, and (3) felt they had more difficulty in advertising to and bidding with the customer, than did MWBE suppliers that were highly dependent (defined as suppliers with more than 20 percent of their revenues dedicated to the customer).

Somewhat similarly, Dollinger et al.[9] note that information asymmetry and complexity are potential barriers for MBE suppliers, due in part to a lower level

8 Krause, D. R., G. L. Ragatz, and S. Hughley (1999). "Supplier Development from the Minority Supplier's Perspective," *Journal of Supply Chain Management,* vol. 35, no. 4, pp. 33–41.

9 Dollinger, M. J., C. A. Enz, and C. M. Daily (1991). "Purchasing from Minority Small Businesses," *International Journal of Purchasing and Materials Management,* vol. 27, no. 2, pp. 9–14.

of support of these programs by corporate purchasers and managers who manage the programs, as compared to upper-level managers who might mandate the initiatives. Dollinger et al. suggest that some potential ways of overcoming these potential transaction costs include providing purchaser training, initiating supplier development activities such as quality control meetings for MBE suppliers, publishing and disseminating information to suppliers regarding purchasing procedures and current and long-run sourcing requirements, and providing buyers with lists of qualified MBE suppliers. Carter et al.[10] suggest that top management support, along with the inclusion of diversity sourcing criteria in the formal evaluations of supply management personnel, are significant antecedents to successful MBE programs. They find that the presence of a formal training program for purchasers is not significantly related to the extent of MBE purchases and suggest that informal training, including one-on-one interactions between an MBE coordinator and purchasers, may be more effective. Carter et al. find no relationship between government regulation and MBE sourcing and suggest that regulation likely acts as a minimum albeit important "hurdle" that does not help to explain variations in MBE spend above the level prescribed by law.

The Environment

The literature in this area of PSR has examined the involvement of supply management in a number of activities, including the purchasing of recycled and reusable inputs, the involvement of supply management in design for reuse and disassembly, the reduction of packaging material, asking suppliers to commit to waste reduction goals, and using a life-cycle analysis to evaluate the environmental friendliness of products and packaging.[11] Researchers have identified the following as being significant drivers and/or facilitators of these environmental activities:

- The degree of *coordination* between buyers and suppliers[11,12, 13]

- *Downstream members of the supply chain*, including not only the ultimate consumer, but also retailers and distributors[11, 14]

---

10 Carter, C. R., R. Auskalnis, and C. Ketchum (1999). "Purchasing from Minority Business Enterprises: A Cross-Industry Comparison of Best Practices," *Journal of Supply Chain Management*, vol. 35, no. 1, pp. 28–32.

11 Carter, C. R., and J. R. Carter (1998). "Interorganizational Determinants of Environmental Purchasing: Initial Evidence from the Consumer Products Industries," *Decision Sciences*, vol. 29, no. 3, pp. 659–685.

12 Narasimhan, R., and J. R. Carter (1998). *Environmental Supply Chain Management*, Tempe, AZ: Center for Advanced Purchasing Studies.

13 Walton, S.V., R. B. Handfield, and S. A. Melnyk (1998). "The Green Supply Chain: Integrating Suppliers into Environmental Management Processes," *Journal of Supply Chain Management*, vol. 34, no. 2, pp. 2–11.

14 Pohlen, T. L., and M. T. Farris II (1992). "Reverse Logistics in Plastics Recycling," *International Journal of Physical Distribution and Logistics Management*, vol. 22, no. 7, pp. 35–48.

- Individual employee initiatives[15, 16]
- The implementation of specific *goals*[11,12]
- A supportive organizational culture[15]
- Top management support [17, 15, 12]
- Employee *training*[11, 18]

Government regulation is an additional driver of environmental activities that has been cited in the broader management literature. However, there has been mixed evidence regarding the impact of regulation on environmental purchasing. Melnyk et al.[19] provide evidence of a positive relationship between environmental management systems and regulation, as does the case study research of Walton et al.[13] and the descriptive statistics shared by Min and Galle.[20] However, these latter two works discuss how regulation can also act as a barrier to environmental purchasing because of the frequent changes to existing regulation and the introduction of new regulation. The work of Carter and Carter[11] found no relationship between environmental purchasing and regulation. The authors suggested that the lack of such a relationship might be due to regulation acting as a barrier, along with inefficiencies in the U.S. environmental regulatory process, as compared to certain other countries such as Germany. It is important to note that the finding of no significant relationship between government regulation and environmental purchasing and supply chain management should not be interpreted to mean that regulation plays no role in the CSR and PSR arenas; as was discussed earlier in reference to supplier diversity programs, such regulation may well create a very necessary hurdle, or minimum level of compliance.

Relatively few studies have examined the consequences of environmental purchasing. Carter et al.[21] empirically examine the relationship between environmental purchasing and bottom-line firm performance, by combining survey and archival

15 Drumwright, M. E. (1994). "Socially Responsible Organizational Buying: Environmental Concern as a Noneconomic Buying Criterion," *Journal of Marketing,* vol. 58, no. 3, pp. 1–19.

16 Kopicki, R., M. J. Berg, L. Legg, V. Desappa, and C. Maggioni (1993). *Reuse and Recycling: Reverse Logistics Opportunities,* Oak Brook, IL: Council of Logistics Management.

17 Carter, C. R., L. M. Ellram, and K. J. Ready (1998). "Environmental Purchasing: Benchmarking Our German Counterparts," *International Journal of Purchasing and Materials Management,* vol. 34, no. 4, pp. 28–39.

18 Carter, C. R., and M. Dresner (2001). "Environmental Purchasing and Supply Management: Cross-Functional Development of Grounded Theory," *Journal of Supply Chain Management,* vol. 37, no. 3, pp. 12–27.

19 Melnyk, S. A., R. Calantone, R. Handfield, R. L. Tummala, G. Vastag, T. Hinds, R. Sroufe, F. Montabon, and S. Curkovic (1999). *ISO 14000: Assessing Its Impact on Corporate Effectiveness and Efficiency,* Tempe, AZ: Center for Advanced Purchasing Studies.

20 Min, H., and W. P. Galle (1997). "Green Purchasing Strategies: Trends and Implications," *International Journal of Purchasing and Materials Management,* vol. 33, no. 3, pp. 10–17.

21 Carter, C. R., R. Kale, and C. Grimm (2000). "Environmental Purchasing and Firm Performance: An Empirical Investigation," *Transportation Research E,* vol. 36, no. 3, pp. 219–228.

financial data. After controlling for organization size, leverage, and primary earnings per share, the authors found a significant relationship between environmental purchasing and net income and cost of goods sold.

Carter and Dresner[18] suggest that one reason for some of the conflicting findings in the broader environmental management literature regarding the relationship between environmental management and firm performance has been a failure to delineate between successfully and unsuccessfully implemented environmental projects. Successful environmental projects identified by case study participants in the research were those where quality, manufacturing performance, stakeholder relationships, and financial performance were improved, and where costs were decreased or remained unchanged *and* where environmental performance was improved.[18] These same authors suggest that barriers to the successful implementation of environmental projects include a lack of communication across functions and between firms, unreasonable requests by internal and external customers, technical difficulties, high costs, and organizational inertia. Potential work-arounds for these barriers include creating early buy-in by key constituents, providing training, using innovation, and identifying barriers during the early stages of a project's implementation.

Human Rights, Safety, and Philanthropy
Stand-alone scholarly supply management research in the areas of human rights, safety, and philanthropy has been scant. Recently, Emmelhainz and Adams[22] analyzed the codes of conduct in the apparel industry concerning sweatshop labor at supplier's plants. These human rights issues included paying a living wage to workers and avoiding inhumane working conditions in suppliers' factories. The authors suggest that these concerns have become more relevant to purchasing managers as a result of increased consumer awareness and greater regulatory assessment.

Other potential stand-alone streams of PSR research, including safety and philanthropy and community, have not appeared in scholarly journals. However, the next subsection of the chapter discusses these important components of PSR.

The PSR Literature

Most recently, this author has conceptualized the seemingly disparate areas that were highlighted in the earlier part of this chapter as dimensions of a broader, higher-order PSR construct. In Carter and Jennings,[7] my coauthor and I adapt and adopt Carroll's,[23, 24] framework, which is displayed in Figure 20–1, to test the

---

22 Emmelhainz, M. A., and R. J. Adams (1999). "The Apparel Industry Response to 'Sweatshop' Concerns: A Review and Analysis of Codes of Conduct," *Journal of Supply Chain Management*, vol. 35, no. 3, pp. 51–57.

23 Carroll, A. B. (1979). "A Three-Dimensional Conceptual Model of Corporate Social Performance," *Academy of Management Review*, vol. 4, no. 4, pp. 497–505.

24 Carroll, A. B. (1991). "The Pyramid of Corporate Social Responsibility: Toward the Moral Management of Organizational Stakeholders," *Business Horizons*, vol. 34, no. 4, pp. 39–48.

FIGURE   20–1

Hierarchy of Corporate Social Responsibility

Discretionary Responsibilities

Ethical Responsibilities

Legal Responsibilities

Economic Responsibilities

SOURCE: Adapted from Carroll[23,24]

hierarchical relationship between the ethical and discretionary social responsibilities of the supply management function. Our analysis of a second-order confirmatory factor analysis model showed that PSR is indeed a higher-order construct consisting of five distinct dimensions:

1. Diversity

2. The environment

3. Human rights

4. Philanthropy

5. Safety

The survey questions used to measure each of the five dimensions appear in Table 20–1. These five dimensions can be thought of as components of an umbrella PSR construct. While ethical issues were significantly correlated with several of these discretionary dimensions of PSR, they did not load on the higher-order PSR construct. These findings provide support for the model of Carroll that is displayed in Figure 20–1 and hold important implications for both researchers and managers.

T A B L E   20–1

PSR Survey Questions

PSR Dimension

The Environment (0.86)[†]

Currently, our purchasing function:[‡]

... Uses a life-cycle analysis to evaluate the environmental friendliness of products and packaging

... Participates in the design of products for disassembly

... Asks suppliers to commit to waste reduction goals

... Participates in the design of products for recycling or reuse

... Reduces packaging material

Diversity (0.82)[†]

Currently, our purchasing function:[‡]

... Purchases from minority- and/or women-owned business enterprise (MWBE) suppliers

... Has a formal MWBE supplier purchase program

Human Rights (0.86)[†]

Currently, our purchasing function:[‡]

... Visits suppliers' plants to ensure that they are not using sweatshop labor

... Ensures that suppliers comply with child labor laws

... Asks suppliers to pay a "living wage" greater than a country's or region's minimum wage

Philanthropy/Community (0.75)[†]

Currently, our purchasing function:[‡]

... Volunteers at local charities

... Donates to philanthropic organizations

Safety (0.73)[†]

Currently, our purchasing function:[‡]

... Ensures that suppliers' locations are operated in a safe manner

... Ensures the safe, incoming movement of product to our facilities

---

[†] Composite reliability.

[‡] These items were measured on a 7-point Likert scale where 1 = no extent whatsoever and 7 = very great extent.

Source: Carter and Jennings (2004)

The empirical results of the Carter and Jennings[7] study suggest that supply management researchers should acknowledge the interrelatedness of the dimensions of PSR within a broader framework of social responsibility. For academicians, this implies the need to research and consider particular dimensions of PSR within this broader scope of social responsibility. In summarizing these findings, the author is not suggesting that academics desert individual fields of study such as environmental purchasing or supplier diversity, but rather that researchers review and potentially integrate findings from these related streams of research when conducting literature reviews and developing hypotheses and theoretical models of stand-alone dimensions of PSR.

From the standpoint of supply management practice, the findings of Carter and Jennings[7] suggest that PSR programs should be managed in a similar fashion. Specifically, as organizations manage and promote their activities in one area of PSR, they should recognize how this might affect the management and promotion of others areas of PSR. Supply managers should leverage the knowledge and learning accrued in existing areas or dimensions of PSR when deciding how to implement and manage other PSR programs.

In the same paper, antecedents to PSR were examined.[7] The findings suggest that top management leadership has a direct and significant effect on PSR, as does an organizational culture that embodies values including fairness and the desire to be a good corporate citizen. Leadership by top management can also influence PSR by shaping an appropriate organizational culture, which then in turn impacts PSR; in essence, these findings suggest that executive-level supply managers can positively affect PSR by not only "talking the talk" but also by "walking the walk."

Additional antecedents to PSR found by Carter and Jennings[7] include employee initiatives and customer pressures. Further, while the individual values of supply management employees did not directly impact PSR, a significant mediating relationship was found to exist through employee initiatives. This finding suggests that PSR programs can be set in motion and managed regardless of employee values. However, employee values play a key mediating role when employees decide to initiate actions on their own. Additionally, managers should not ignore employee values when selecting personnel to develop or manage a PSR program.

Finally, in Carter and Jennings,[25] my coauthor and I examine some of the potential consequences of PSR. Here, it was found that PSR has a direct and positive effect on supplier performance. In addition, PSR can significantly improve supply chain relationships through increased purchaser commitment to and trust in PSR suppliers. Trust in turn engenders cooperation between purchasers and suppliers, which then leads to improved supplier performance.

The ISM Principles of Social Responsibility

In 2002, ISM's board of directors created a Commission on Social Responsibility (see Appendix A at the end of this chapter). The Commission was charged with creating the first group of social responsibility principles relating specifically to the supply management profession. Further, the Commission established the additional goals of increasing awareness of social responsibility among supply management

---

25 Carter, C. R. and M. Jennings (2002). "Social Responsibility and Supply Chain Relationships," *Transportation Research E*, vol. 38, no. 1, pp. 37–52.

professionals, and providing the tools, information, references, and other resources needed to aid supply managers in implementing socially responsible principles and initiatives. The principles of social responsibility established by the Commission can be found on the ISM Web site at www.ism.ws/SR/Principles.cfm; additional information and resources can also be found at this Web site.

After approving the work of the Commission, the ISM board of directors organized and created an ongoing Committee on Social Responsibility to continue the work of the Commission and to quantify the impact of the Commission's and Committee's work on the supply management profession. One of the first actions of the Committee was the implementation of a large-scale survey of the ISM membership. An e-mail survey was developed and sent to 11,119 members of ISM, of which 1,809 were returned as undeliverable, 152 were rejected as spam, and 157 generated out-of-office replies. In total, 1,163 usable surveys were returned, resulting in a 12.5 percent response rate. These respondents represented a broad range of industries, from manufacturing, service, and government and education.

In Carter,[26] the author replicated the findings from our earlier survey of the consumer products industries[7] by using the broad-based data from the ISM survey. The author found that the five dimensions of PSR that loaded on the higher-order PSR construct in the original study also loaded on a higher-order PSR construct in the case of the ISM data. Further, the factor structures of the second-order CFA were compared between service and manufacturing industries and found to be nearly identical, providing additional support for the assertion that PSR is an umbrella construct, consisting of, at a minimum, the five dimensions of diversity: the environment, diversity, human rights, philanthropy and community, and safety. These findings provide added support for employing PSR as a theoretical umbrella and lens that can be used to better understand the dimensions of PSR. From the standpoint of research in supply management, these findings further support the assertion that the broader CSR theory should be incorporated into research that examines the various dimensions of PSR. From a managerial standpoint, these findings indicated that supply managers must recognize the commonality among the dimensions of PSR and understand that similar drivers, barriers, and ways of overcoming those barriers likely exist: lessons learned in one sphere of PSR might be readily applied to programs and initiatives in other areas of PSR.

This summarizes the current state of research in PSR. In the last section of this chapter, the issue of future research, in terms of both management practice and additional research methods and topics, will be addressed.

WHERE SHOULD WE GO FROM HERE?

Perhaps the most significant gap that now exists in the area of PSR is the scarcity of use of consistent and well-thought-out performance metrics for most of the

---

26 Carter, C.R. (2004), "Purchasing Social Responsibility: A Replication and Extension," *Journal of Supply Chain Management*, vol. 40, no. 4, pp. 4-16.

dimensions of PSR. Many organizations are hesitant to initiate or expand PSR programs due to a perception that such programs will result in increased costs for the company. While the stand-alone extant research has begun to show that supplier performance and even organizational financial performance can improve when individual PSR programs are initiated, companies must still be able to develop and accurately measure the performance and cost outcomes of their PSR activities. Certainly standards such as ISO 14000 are excellent general guidelines that firms can use; however, supply managers must be able to measure the specific costs, benefits, and overall outcomes of their PSR activities. Here, tools such as life-cycle analysis (LCA), the balanced scorecard, and a total cost of ownership approach could be utilized.[27, 28, 29] Additionally, researchers and managers alike might more explicitly consider an organization's PSR and economic goals within the frameworks of sustainability and the triple bottom line.[30, 31]

A supply chain social responsibility audit would help organizations to not only avoid litigation, negative PR, and possible regulatory action, but also assist firms in more effectively managing suppliers and the purchaser organizations' own, internal processes. Existing social responsibility audits at the organization level consist of surveys, interviews, on-site inspections, and the development of an action plan to cope with deficiencies; however, the movement to conduct social responsibility audits of an organization is "farther along" in Europe as compared to the United States.[32] Further, the use of supply chain social responsibility auditing is at an even more emergent stage, and guidelines and standards are needed to ensure that supply chain social responsibility audits are conducted consistently across organizations.

One early innovator and developer of supply chain social responsibility auditing is the Body Shop. The firm was so successful in developing its supply chain social responsibility auditing that it was able to "sell" its processes to consulting firm KPMG in exchange for worldwide nonfinancial auditing provided by KPMG.[33]

27 Ellram, L. M., and S. P. Siferd (1998). "Total Cost of Ownership: A Key Concept in Strategic Cost Management Decisions," *Journal of Business Logistics*, vol. 19, no. 1, pp. 55–84.

28 Kaufmann, L. and S.M. Wagner (2003), "The Implementation of Purchasing Strategies Using a Balanced Scorecard Examining Barriers and Remedial Auctions," in: Proceedings of the 14th Annual North American Research Symposium on Purchasing and Supply Management, Tempe, AZ, pp. 589-609.

29 Nielsen, P., and H. Wenzel (2002). "Integration of Environmental Aspects in Product Development: A Stepwise Procedure Based on Quantitative Life Cycle Assessment," *Journal of Cleaner Production*, vol. 10, pp. 247–257.

30 Gladwin, T.M., J.J. Kennelly, and T. Krause (1995), "Shifting Paradigms for Sustainable Development: Complications for Management Theory and Research," *Academy of Management Journal*, vol. 20, no. 4, pp. 874-907.

31 Henriques, A. and J. Richardson (2004), The Triple Bottom Line, Does It All Add Up?; Assessing the Sustainability of Business and CSR, Earthscan Publications, London.

32 Logsdon, J. M., and P. G. Lewellyn (2000). "Expanding Accountability in Stakeholders: Trends and Predictions," *Business and Society Review*, vol. 105, no. 4, pp. 419–435.

33 Anonymous (1998). "KPMG and Body Shop Agree on Social Audit Swap," *Supply Management*, vol. 3, no. 25, p. 12.

Generically, the necessary criteria for the successful institutionalization of a social auditing and reporting process include the validity and trustworthiness of the process, the effective use of the results of the audit to create change in the organization, and the integration of the audit process with other auditing and data collection processes within the organization.[34] More specifically, it might be possible to model a supply chain social responsibility audit after the Malcolm Baldrige National Quality Award and the European Quality Award,[35] in order to ensure consistency in the auditing process across focal organizations and their supply chains. Melnyk et al.[19] found that the ISO 14000 certification process had a more positive impact on performance than did voluntary-based environmental programs. Thus the ISO 14000 certification process could be another excellent template after which to model a supply chain social responsibility audit.

Supply managers might also employ benchmarking to gauge their current PSR position vis-à-vis competitors in their industry. At the time the author wrote this chapter, a large-scale survey had just been completed by the Institute for Supply Management (ISM). This large-scale survey replicated the author's earlier PSR research from 2002 and 2004, by examining the level of involvement of supply managers in a very broad set of manufacturing, service, and government and educational industries. The results of this research, including a copy of the survey and summary statistics of the responses, should be available to the reader on the ISM Web site (www.ism.ws) by the time that this chapter appears in print. Supply managers can use the questionnaire to measure their organizations' current involvement in PSR activities and to benchmark their involvement against those of hundreds of other organizations in the manufacturing and service sectors. Supply managers should have multiple employees complete the ISM survey. Agreements across employees will provide some evidence of the reliability of responses. Conversely, a lack of agreement would be fertile grounds in terms of investigating why disagreements might exist across various areas or levels of the supply management function.

Managers must also understand not only the barriers that exist in implementing and managing PSR programs and activities, but also the most effective means of overcoming those barriers. Thus another valuable future research endeavor would be to expand upon the findings from the arenas of environmental purchasing and MBE sourcing to identify effective means of overcoming the barriers to these stand-alone PSR initiatives. For example, survey data could be used to examine the moderating effects of the tactics to overcome these barriers, through analysis of variance or regression analysis with mean-centered variables—empirical techniques that are not particularly sophisticated, yet not commonly employed in supply management research.

34 Dierkes, M., and A. B. Antal (1986). "Whither Corporate Social Reporting: Is It Time to Legislate?" *California Management Review*, vol. 28, no. 3, pp. 106–121.

35 Kok, P., T. van der Wiele, R. McKenna, and A. Brown (2001). "A Corporate Social Responsibility Audit within a Quality Management Framework," *Journal of Business Ethics,* vol. 31, no. 4, pp. 285–297.

On a final note, the stream of research in supply management in general, and even PSR in particular, has developed to the point that it is in need of additional research methods to complement the often used mail surveys and somewhat less often used case studies and interviews. Two additional methodologies that might be utilized are laboratory experiments and social network analysis. Laboratory experiments, which in contrast to surveys and field research have very strong internal validity, could be used to study the decision-making processes concerning PSR. This methodology could help to answer questions such as, "How do managers decide when and which specific PSR activities to initiate?" and "What are the trade-offs and specific criteria that managers consider when making these decisions?"

Social network analysis is a methodology that developed in the field of sociology[36] and can be used to study the social relationships among actors (in this case, employees) in an organization or even in a supply chain. The methodology allows researchers to examine the network of relationships and allows researchers to gain an understanding of how the role of informal power,[37] centrality in the network,[38] distance between employees and key decision makers,[39] and access to resources[40] can affect decision making. In the case of PSR, social network analysis could be used to gain clearer insights into the cross-functional and even interorganizational interplay that occurs as organizations initiate and continue to manage PSR activities.

CONCLUSION

Individual dimensions of PSR are not necessarily new areas of study. However, the recognition of the interrelatedness of these once seemingly stand-alone activities, under the broader umbrella of social responsibility, is a relatively new concept within supply management. PSR is, however, rapidly gaining traction and recognition as an important concept to both managers and academics. The establishment of ISM's Committee on Social Responsibility, the ongoing work of the Committee to provide information and resources to supply managers, and the growing number of organizations listed as supporters of the ISM Principles of

---

36 Tichy, N. M., and C. Fombrun (1979). "Network Analysis in Organizational Settings," *Human Relations*, vol. 32, no. 11, pp. 923–965.

37 Brass, D. J. (1984). "Being in the Right Place: A Structural Analysis of Individual Influence in an Organization," *Administrative Science Quarterly*, vol. 29, no. 4, pp. 518–539.

38 Brass, D. J., and M. E. Burkhardt (1992). "Centrality and Power in Organizations." In N. Nohria and R. Eccles (eds.), *Networks and Organizations: Structure, Form, and Action*, Boston: Harvard Business School Press, pp. 191–215.

39 Rice, R. E., and C. Aydin (1991). "Attitudes toward New Organizational Technology: Network Proximity as a Mechanism for Social Information Processing," *Administrative Science Quarterly*, vol. 36, no. 2, pp. 219–244.

40 Kilduff, M. (1992). "The Friendship Network as a Decision-Making Resource: Dispositional Moderators of Social Influences on Organizational Choice," *Journal of Personality and Social Psychology*, vol. 62, no. 1, pp. 168–180.

Social Responsibility, all indicate the mounting interest in PSR by industry. The growing number of subject tracks in areas such as the environment, diversity, and overall social responsibility, at academic conferences such as the Academy of Management, Decision Sciences Institute, and ISM, afford evidence that social responsibility is becoming an increasingly mainstream field of study for academicians. The suggested avenues for future research outlined in this chapter are but some of the possible starting points for additional PSR research. My hope is that this chapter will spur interest and activity to initiate and better manage PSR programs in the case of supply managers, and to undertake much needed further research in the instance of supply management scholars.

APPENDIX A

Institute for Supply Management's Principles of Social Responsibility

Social responsibility is defined as a framework of measurable corporate policies and procedures and resulting behavior designed to benefit the workplace and, by extension, the individual, the organization, and the community in the following areas (in alphabetical order) (http://www.ism.ws/SR/Principles.cfm):

I. Community
   1. Provide support and add value to your communities and those of your supply chain.
   2. Encourage members of your supply chain to add value in their communities.
II. Diversity
   1. Proactively promote purchasing from, and the development of, socially diverse suppliers.
   2. Encourage diversity within your own organization.
   3. Proactively promote diverse employment practices throughout the supply chain.
III. Environment
   1. Encourage your own organization and others to be proactive in examining opportunities to be environmentally responsible within their supply chains either "upstream" or "downstream."
   2. Encourage the environmental responsibility of your suppliers.
   3. Encourage the development and diffusion of environmentally friendly practices and products throughout your organization.
IV. Ethics
   1. Be aware of ISM's Principles and Standards of Ethical Supply Management Conduct.
   2. Abide by your organization's code of conduct.

  V. Financial responsibility
      1. Become knowledgeable of, and follow, applicable financial standards and requirements.
      2. Apply sound financial practices and ensure transparency in financial dealings.
      3. Actively promote and practice responsible financial behavior throughout the supply chain.
 VI. Human rights
      1. Treat people with dignity and respect.
      2. Support and respect the protection of international human rights within the organization's sphere of influence.
      3. Encourage your organization and its supply chains to avoid complicity in human or employment rights abuses.
VII. Safety
      1. Promote a safe environment for each employee in your organization and supply chain. (Each organization is responsible for defining "safe" within its organization.)
      2. Support the continuous development and diffusion of safety practices throughout your organization and the supply chain.

SOURCE: Institute for Supply Management™ Web site (www.iam.ws/sr/Principles.cfm)

COMPONENTS AND CAPABILITIES

This part includes descriptions, how-to information, and references for various tools and techniques that should be useful to supply management practitioners. These encompass a wide range of subjects, from electronic opportunities and electronic commerce to supplier performance evaluation. Supply management practitioners have available to them many tools and approaches to assist them in reaching the objectives of supply management that will support the broader objectives of their companies or other organizations for whom they are working. Some tools and techniques are somewhat sophisticated, for example, electronic approaches, while others, such as purchasing and supply negotiations, have been available and utilized for many years. To perform their jobs at the top of their profession, it is not enough for supply managers to simply know their supply chains; they must have some understanding of ways to improve the performance of the supply chain to the level required for the success of their organization.

The intention of this part is to introduce a number of these components and capabilities and provide some understanding of when and how they may be useful to improve supply management performance. For those who desire additional information or training in any of the subjects in this part, many of the chapters include references to additional sources of information, and the Institute for Supply Management™ and other organizations have available in-depth seminars, books, and other resources.

CHAPTER 21

TECHNOLOGY IN THE SUPPLY CHAIN

PHILLIP L. CARTER, DBA
Professor of Supply Chain Management
Harold E. Fearon Chair of Purchasing
W. P. Carey School of Business
Arizona State University
and
Executive Director
CAPS: Center for Strategic Supply Research

KENNETH J. PETERSEN, PH.D.
Associate Professor of Management
College of Business
Colorado State University

INTRODUCTION

New thinking about supply chain design, new paradigms of trading company relationships, the globalization of business, and the development of new information and decision support technologies have combined to give rise to remarkable changes in the way we view and manage supply chains. The technology-enabled supply chain has become a reality.

The purpose of this chapter is to examine the application of technology to key supply chain processes and to draw a linkage between these technologies and performance. Where appropriate, this chapter also identifies the benefits, costs, and challenges associated with the application of technology.

The following section describes supply chain processes in general and then reviews the application of technology to a number of key supply chain processes (purchasing, sourcing, and new product development). Following this discussion, a number of key technologies that have enabled one or more of these processes are reviewed. We conclude this chapter with a speculative discussion on the future of technology in supply chain management.

SUPPLY CHAIN PROCESSES

Supply chain processes, in increasing order of complexity, can be categorized as follows:

- *Data and information sharing*. Sending and receiving of information between trading partners. Typical types of information exchanged include
  - Production schedules
  - RFx [generic term for request for quotation (RFQ), request for information (RFI), or request for proposal (RFP)]
  - Shipping notices
  - Inventory visibility and tracking
  - Material discrepancy reports
- *Transactional*. Execution of commercial transactions between trading partners. Typical types of information exchanged include
  - Purchase order release
  - Purchase order confirmation
  - Payment of invoices
- *Collaborative*. Interaction of two or more trading partners to establish business relationships, plan and coordinate activities, solve business problems, and so forth. Typical types of information exchanged include
  - Product design
  - Demand forecasting and inventory planning

The challenges associated with e-enabling any process increase with the complexity of the process. We see evidence of this phenomenon from the 1970s when electronic data interchange (EDI) first e-enabled *data and information sharing* and *transactional* processes. Technology evolved steadily through the late 1980s and then boomed during the 1990s. While much of the "newness" of technology has now faded, we are left with the unmistakable conclusion that technology is critical to the enablement of *supply chain* processes. In fact, virtually all traditional supply chain processes, including purchasing, sourcing, supply-demand planning, logistics, supplier relationship management (SRM), product design and development, customer order fulfillment, sales and postsales management, and customer relationship management (CRM) have all been e-enabled. In the late 1990s and early years of the first decade of the twenty-first century, advancements in technology spawned the creation of entirely new supply chain processes, such as reverse auctions and electronic markets. These new processes often subsumed more traditional processes while simultaneously bringing new capabilities to bear.

The automation of traditional processes, individually or in any combination, has increased process efficiencies and effectiveness, resulting in lower total supply chain costs and greater responsiveness. In addition, new technologies have allowed the interconnection of enterprises and processes within the supply chain, creating the opportunity for new types of intra- and interenterprise cooperation and collaboration.

The drivers behind the automation of the supply chain processes are consistent with those that have always driven new developments in business, namely, the competitive priorities to reduce costs, increase service, increase quality, and speed new products to market. Figure 21–1 describes these forces and the need for the supply chain to deliver goods and services that are *perfect*, *exact*, *free*, and *now*.

Purchasing Process

The purchasing process was one of the first to receive the benefits of e-enabled automation. New applications were developed for the purchasing of indirect goods and services in the late 1990s, including both information exchange and transaction processes. The process for purchasing indirect goods and services is represented in Figure 21–2. The overall process starts with identification of need by a user and ends with payment. Within each of these processes are many subprocesses that

FIGURE 21–1

The goal of the supply chain is to deliver goods and services that are perfect, exact, free, and now.

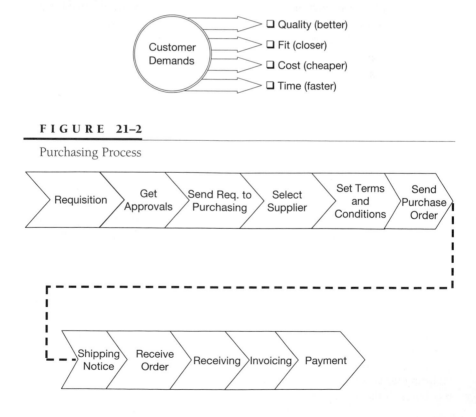

FIGURE 21–2

Purchasing Process

are not represented in this high-level diagram. Automation tools have been developed for each of the processes and subprocesses within the overall purchasing cycle.

The purchasing process starts with a user requisition. Technology has put an electronic requisition on the user's desktop, along with automatic access to account numbers, authorization routing, employee identification, and tracking numbers.

Once a user has completed the requisition, it is automatically routed to managers, budget officers, and others who must approve it. These individuals typically receive notification of the pending requisition by e-mail. Follow-up e-mails for past-due approvals are also often included in the system. The approval path can be tailored for each kind of requisition (e.g., office supplies versus computer equipment), for different users (e.g., administrative assistants versus corporate officers), and for different spending authority levels.

Once the appropriate approvals have been received, the requisition is automatically routed to a supply manager for action. A traditional buying process may take place at this point or a preselected supplier may be used. An electronic purchase order (automatically populated with the appropriate information from the requisition and terms and conditions) can be completed and sent to the supplier using mail, electronic fax, e-mail, or, in more sophisticated systems, directly to the order-entry system of the supplier.

In more sophisticated implementations, electronic catalogs are available on the desktop of the user. Users can browse through e-catalogs from preapproved suppliers for preapproved goods or services at contracted prices. Once the required item is found in the e-catalog, the system automatically populates the requisition with all the information required to specify the item. After the necessary approvals are obtained, the order can flow directly to the supplier, without stopping for the supply manager's approval.

More advanced purchasing systems also often include a capability to manage contracts over time. When a supply manager initiates a contract, it is then stored in a central database and is accessible by the supply manager at a later time as well as by other supply managers throughout the firm.

Automated purchasing systems work best for tightly specified items. This is often not the case for services, such as legal and advertising, where many variables come into play. In such cases supply managers have traditionally relied on broad contracts with firms to provide services, without closely specifying the services. The required services are not requisitioned by users as described above, but rather general outlines are specified and the service firm is expected to provide the details. This condition is changing as third parties (e.g., e-markets) have tackled the task of providing detailed descriptions for services, making them easier to specify (and to buy through the e-markets). This work has made it possible to create catalogs for services that can be made available to users for requisitioning purposes.

Automated purchasing systems have found great application in both manufacturing firms (for indirect goods and services) and in service firms, where most purchases fit the traditional definition of indirect items.

For direct goods in manufacturing firms, the purchasing process is different in many respects and is often handled by subapplications of material requirements planning (MRP) and enterprise resource planning (ERP) systems. Most of the requisitions are orders generated by MRP systems. After review, companies will often send these orders through EDI (or other e-enabled technology) to their first-tier suppliers. These processes have not changed much in the past 20 years. Upon receipt of the goods or services, either central receiving or the users will review the order and annotate the purchase record with the required receiving information. This information can then be automatically routed to accounts payable, which has the electronic purchase order, electronic invoice, and electronic receiver to make the three-way match. This match may occur automatically, and if no problems arise, a traditional payment or electronic payment can be issued automatically.

Benefits
The benefits of automating the purchasing process include increased efficiency and increased effectiveness. The efficiencies include the ability to reduce purchasing staff, to reduce the overall purchasing cycle time, and to reduce the rate of errors generated during the process. Effectiveness comes about from using the system to enforce purchasing policies, reduce maverick buying, standardize and manage demand, and aggregate demand from across the organization. Of course none of this can happen with just the implementation of the technology itself. Appropriate company and purchasing policies must first be developed. Technology allows these policies to be enforced throughout the organization as very little can be bought without using the system and the system is the embodiment of the policies and procedures.

Challenges
There are two main areas of challenge to implementing automated purchasing systems. The first is the calculation of the return on investment (ROI) of a purchasing system. These systems are expensive, with a total cost in the several millions of dollars for a large company. In addition to the initial cost of software, a company must also plan for training costs, ongoing maintenance costs, and possibly network and computing upgrade costs.

The calculation of ROI for a purchasing system is challenging because the efficiency gains are difficulty to quantify. More importantly, the efficiency gains are not realized unless the company is prepared to make improvements in its processes coincident with the introduction of the purchasing system. For example, many companies that have introduced such systems have discovered that their requisition and purchase order approval systems are cumbersome and slow. Resources are required to change the approval system in order for the company to gain the maximum possible efficiency from the new technology. Further, many of the quantifiable efficiency savings can result only if personnel are *actually* removed from the payroll. Many companies prefer to reassign people to higher-level tasks, which may well be the right decision but confounds the calculation of savings.

The second area of challenge is change management. Installing new systems is never easy and can be particularly challenging for a purchasing system that touches many parts of the organization. While change management is a critical topic with applications to much of what is discussed in this chapter, it is a more general topic that is outside of the scope of this chapter.

Sourcing Process

Unlike the purchasing process, the sourcing process for *both* indirect and direct goods and services has undergone tremendous change due to the implementation of new technology-enabled tools. Because the sourcing process involves higher-order collaborative processes, it has been more challenging to automate than the purchasing process. Further, collaboration with suppliers may occur within any of the major processes from product design through customer order fulfillment.

Because the product design process plays such an important role in determining the overall performance and design of the supply process, it is discussed separately below.

Once a product design has been set, the total need for parts and services must be determined. This process depends on data about forecasted demand and current inventories from other functions. ERP and customer relationship management databases may be employed here, along with bills of materials to generate forecasted need by time period.

Much has been done to automate the request for information, request for proposals, request for quotations (RFx) from the supply base. Many third-party suppliers have developed e-enabled tools that systematize the collection of information for the requests, the sending of the information to suppliers, the return of the requested information from the supply base, and the analysis of the information. Cumbersome and often ad hoc, spreadsheets have been replaced with online templates that are prepopulated directly from company databases.

Following the analysis of the RFx, the buying company must decide how to award the business. Electronic reverse auctions (e-RAs) have been increasingly used for this purpose. E-RAs are discussed in more detail in a later section. If e-RAs are not used, a company may rely on the traditional sealed bidding process or an open negotiation with one or more suppliers. Other than having better sources of data about total spend with a supplier and total projected need, e-enabled automation has not changed the traditional negotiation process substantially.

FIGURE 21–3

The Sourcing Process

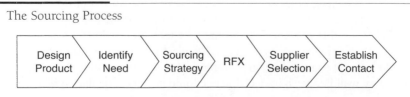

Benefits

There are many benefits associated with e-enabled sourcing. However, the main benefit that accrues from e-enabled sourcing is that sourcing managers are able to set better sourcing strategies. These improved sourcing strategies are possible because of access to better information. This information often comes in the form of better access to spend for a given or related set of purchased goods and materials as well as better and more timely access to public and private information related to the purchased goods and services. For instance, sourcing managers are often provided with a "heads-up display" that contains news and market information related to their commodity. Other benefits from e-enabled sourcing stem from the fact that e-enabled sourcing *requires* the creation of better specifications. Further, e-sourcing both removes time from the process as well as enables the more firm establishment of specific time-oriented process steps. This enables a relatively shorter process to move more smoothly.

Challenges

There are numerous challenges to developing and implementing an e-sourcing tool set. One of the biggest challenges faced by most e-sourcing teams is a lack of data integrity coupled with the dilemma of how to standardize (often referred to as "clean") the data quickly while simultaneously proceeding in the absence of this clean data.

System integration also represents a significant challenge to the implementation of e-sourcing tools. E-sourcing systems require information from various parts of the firm, and integration efforts to connect the e-sourcing application with these other areas of the firm are often difficult and frequently run over cost and time budgets. Excellent work processes should drive the e-sourcing integration effort, while the ease of use of the e-sourcing tools should drive their adoption. The rapid adoption and full utilization of the e-sourcing tools should drive the return on investment of e-enabled sourcing. Therefore, the suite of available e-sourcing tools must be fully understood and integrated.

User training and access also present a significant and often overlooked challenge to the successful implementation of e-sourcing tools. Often, the bulk of the available resources for the e-sourcing implementation project are allocated to software development, while relatively few are allocated to user training and access. This often results in the completion of a system which users do not understand and often do not have sufficient access to.

Product Design and Development Process

In order to be competitive, it is necessary for a firm to develop its new products and services in collaboration with many different functions within the firm as well as key external partners. The most common external partners are customers and suppliers, but other external partners (technical experts, consultants, etc.) will often be involved as well.

Product design and development solutions are among the most complex to develop and perhaps the furthest from maturity. This is largely due to the highly complex integration needed for product design as well as the disparate data standards for describing parts and products. Despite the complexity and immaturity of the tools, the value gained from even partial automation is highly significant for many companies. The opportunity to significantly affect cost and profitability exists because of the large impact design decisions have on long-term supply chain costs.

E-enabled product development applications may be thought of as either asynchronous or synchronous in nature. *Asynchronous* product development applications are of a more traditional nature, requiring users to interact with the product development process on a serial basis. For instance, an engineer might make a modification to a design and then pass the modified design to a key supplier for evaluation for possible impact on components that that supplier is designing. *Synchronous* product development applications allow users to interact with other users and the development process on a parallel basis (simultaneously and collaboratively). For instance, engineers from a manufacturer and any number of geographically disparate suppliers and other experts might meet to simultaneously work on a product design, interacting with the design and each other on a real-time and virtual basis. Synchronous collaborative product development tools are on the leading edge of supply chain product development and are the most likely place from which many of the breakthroughs in the new product development process will hail. Both asynchronous and synchronous new product development collaboration can be applied to either manufacturing or nonmanufacturing situations. Nonmanufacturing examples might include new menu items for restaurant chains, new methods of delivery for entertainment products such as music or video, and new products or delivery methods for financial service industries.

Asynchronous Product Development Collaboration

Most of the e-enabled applications that new product development teams use today are asynchronous. Common applications include document management, global data and design vaults, stand-alone CAD/CAM systems, project management, groupware, teleconferencing, e-mail, Internet-based meeting solutions, and threaded messaging systems. These applications have provided product development teams the ability to collaborate in a basic way from different physical locations.

Synchronous Product Development Collaboration

The latest developments in e-enabled new product development are currently in the areas of *integrated new product development applications* and *collaborative product commerce* systems.

Integrated Product Development Applications. Integrated product development applications (e.g., www.onespace.net) allow product development team members and key stakeholders to interact with each other using the basic capabilities provided in asynchronous product development applications, but in real time with each other. For instance, using these tools, a designer, a supply manager, and a supplier can connect to a collaborative environment to view a three-dimensional (3D) model of a design and discuss how part and material substitutions might improve the total cost of the design.

Collaborative Product Commerce. Collaborative product commerce (CPC) is an extension of the integrated product development applications that also integrates the rest of the company and the supply chain. The focus of CPC is to extend new product development into product life-cycle management and supply chain management. For instance, a third-tier supplier could have access to the product development environment directly as opposed to indirectly through several supply chain tiers.

Challenges

There are many challenges to the use of e-enabled applications in support of new product development. For instance, if the technology is not readily accessible to all members of the development team and other key stakeholders, appropriate reviews may be delayed, potentially causing the development process to move down the wrong path, causing additional expense and a longer concept-to-customer development time.

As product development applications move to a more full-featured and integrated state, more network and computing infrastructure is required. For the members of a new product development team to view the same 3D representation of a product design in real time requires very capable servers and clients as well as a very fast Internet connection.

Given that the new product development process is one of the key processes that give a firm its unique competitive advantage, security around product designs is critical to the success of any e-enabled product development application. Each member of the team (internal or external) as well as other key stakeholders must be allowed access to the appropriate parts of the design, but in most cases, not the design in its entirety. However, in a collaborative environment, the design itself exists on a server that is exposed to the Internet. Therefore, good application design, business rules, and network infrastructure (security, firewalls, etc.) are important to success.

As is true with all the new technology-based tools, the organization must be capable of making changes to accommodate them. In more collaborative new product development environments, it is often the case that the new product development team requires more organizational flexibility than organizational structures usually allow. An important consideration when establishing a collaborative new product development environment is that the organizational structure will support and not hinder the process.

FIGURE 21–4

The New Product Development Process

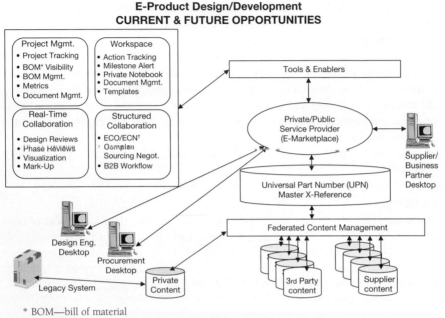

E-Product Design/Development
CURRENT & FUTURE OPPORTUNITIES

* BOM—bill of material
† ECO/ECN—engineering change order/engineering change notice

Benefits

The benefits of a strong e-enabled new product development process are substantial (see Figure 21–4). A large part (in excess of 80 percent) of the total cost of a product is established during the new product development process. E-enabled sourcing allows for improved product designs which in turn reduces the total cost of the product and significantly shortens the time-to-market. Further, e-enabled sourcing can improve the efficiency of the product development team by reducing the number of meetings and providing better access to the resources necessary to do the best job. Finally, the significant travel cost typically associated with new product development projects may also be reduced.

E MARKETS—PUBLIC, INDUSTRY-SPONSORED, AND PRIVATE

E-markets are one of the new supply chain processes made possible by Internet technologies. At their most basic level, e-marketplaces match the supply and demand of trading partners and automate the transactions between them. Public e-markets emerged first, soon followed by quasi-public, industry-sponsored e-markets, and then by private, company-sponsored e-markets or portals.

FIGURE 21–5

Public E-markets: Many to Many

Public E-markets

At their most basic level, public markets (commonly called e-markets) provide the opportunity for companies to buy and sell through a third party (see Figure 21–5). As originally developed, public markets had a vertical (industry, e.g., grocery) orientation or a horizontal [cross-industry, e.g., maintenance, repair, and operating (MRO)] orientation. However, the importance of this distinction has faded as public markets have settled into niches within industries and with product lines. Public markets in the form of commodity and stock exchanges have been around for many years. These exchanges were for highly similar goods (e.g., hog bellies) that had multiple transactions per day. Internet technology made possible the creation of public marketplaces for virtually all goods and services, not just commodities with high levels of transactions.

At the height of the dot-com boom, up to 10,000 electronic public marketplaces were estimated to have been established and doing business on the Web. However, a careful search in 2000 by CAPS Research could only identify about 1,000 e-markets with a Web presence, and only about 500 of these could be induced to communicate in any way. Whatever the maximum number of e-markets at any time, only a relatively few survived the dot-com bust. Among the survivors, many are providing robust and useful services to their customers, both buyers and sellers.

Close examination of the functioning e-markets reveals that many offer more than just a convenient mechanism to conduct transactions. In fact, for many, transactions are the least important of a broad array of sourcing and purchasing services. Figure 21–6 illustrates the parallelism between the services offered by e-markets and the sourcing-purchasing subprocesses.

E-markets represent an opportunity to outsource many of the sourcing-purchasing processes to a third party (Figure 21–6). Viewed from this perspective, it is not surprising that they had great difficulty in attracting business from purchasing professionals whose job tasks they wanted to capture. Of course, not all e-markets offer all these services. Some concentrate on the sourcing process, while others concentrate on making markets (often through reverse auctions) or focus on handling transactions.

F I G U R E   21–6

E-market Services and the Sourcing-Purchasing Process

Purchasing Process

Design and plan	Develop sourcing strategy	Identify relevant supply base	Purchase		Transact and execute	Improve contin-uously
			Product/ service	Value-added services		

E-market Services

Design and plan	Develop sourcing strategy	Identify relevant supply base	Make the Market		Transact and execute	Improve contin-uously
			Product/ service	Value-added services		

Benefits

Public e-markets can provide transactional efficiencies as well as market effectiveness. The efficiencies from automating purchasing processes have already been addressed. The potential big gain is in the ability of markets to present new products and new suppliers in niche markets to buying companies. E-markets can substantially reduce the search time and greatly increase the probability of search success for supply managers. Additional services, such as shipping, insurance, and training, may also be readily available.

Challenges

Although the surviving e-markets are creating a history of stability, their staying power is always in question. Also their ability to adequately vet suppliers remains uncertain in some cases. Supply managers continue to use untested e-markets with caution, limiting both the potential benefits and potential risks.

Industry-Sponsored E-markets (Consortia)

At the height of the dot-com boom, many industry executives, financial and purchasing, upon viewing the apparent success of public e-markets, thought that they had a better idea. The idea was to create quasi-public markets tailored to the specific needs of their industry. In doing so they would accomplish several objectives. First, they would create an e-market that would be responsive to the needs of the industry. Second the market could be staffed with people experienced in the industry and could rapidly develop tools and applications best suited to meeting the needs of the industry. Third, the market could provide better security and protection for sensitive company and industry data. Lastly, investment in the marketplace could provide (apparently) a handsome return for the investing companies, when the market grew large enough to justify an IPO. Given the volume of transactions within the major industry groups, it was reasonable to expect that industry marketplaces could grow quickly and substantially.

Most of the industry-sponsored e-markets were founded and initially funded by the buy-side of the industry. Suppliers were quickly invited, or coerced, to participate, sometimes as equal partners and owners and sometimes not. Different industry-sponsored e-markets developed different applications, depending on the "pain points" in the industry. Many worked on developing industry applications (e.g., CPFR, Collaborative Planning Forecasting and Replinishment) that did not affect a company's competitive position, but could increase the overall efficiency of the industry. Others focused on developing industrywide standards for describing products and transactions.

The success of the industry-sponsored e-markets has been uneven. Some (e.g., Covisint in the auto industry) have gone out of business, while others (e.g., Exostart in the aerospace industry and Quadrum in the mining industry) have continued to grow and provide an array of valuable services. Success and failure depended on the willingness of the industry to support the e-market with investment resources (i.e., people and capital) and with business (e.g., transactions, reverse auctions).

As industry-sponsored e-markets have evolved, it has been apparent that some of the greatest industry pain points, and therefore needs to be met, revolve around standards for data exchange and product description. These are complex issues to resolve, even within one company, and become exponentially more difficult as more companies and suppliers try to rationalize standards among themselves. More and more of the consortia are turning to third-party standard writing bodies, e.g., RosettaNet and UCC, for help with these knotty problems. One of the major contributions that consortia can, and probably will make, is building the infrastructure to seamlessly connect the trading partners within the industry.

Industry consortia provide a number of services in addition to standards development that are not easily provided by public e-markets. Consortia can aggregate demand across buying companies and use this larger demand to strike more favorable relationships with suppliers. This may be done with reverse auctions or using more traditional bidding and negotiation techniques.

The aggregation potential extends to transportation and logistics also. Here the potential is not just to negotiate better prices, but to truly impact the efficiency of the industry by aggregating and rationalizing transportation loading across the country. By aggregating loads, partial truckloads and empty back hauls can be minimized, saving money for all concerned. However, this coordination is not easily accomplished and requires considerable decision analysis skill and computing power.

Lastly, consortia can host secure private e-markets for their participants, the topic of our next discussion.

Benefits

Industry-sponsored marketplaces address key industry pain points that can be best solved through industry collaboration. Pain points are those processes that have a significant impact on costs, quality, or the value of the product from the customer's viewpoint. For example, collaborative planning, forecasting, and replenishment are key challenges for the consumer packaged goods (CPG) industry. They address the issue of how to ensure that the right goods are in the right place at the right time while minimizing the inventory, transportation, and logistics costs.

Industry consortia have the advantage of sharing the development costs across several or, in some cases, many companies. The quasi-independent governance structure gives the consortia a flexibility not found in their parent companies. Also the consortia have industry experts to call upon for advice and help. Lastly, they have a readily identifiable market with companies that have some disposition to use their services and a financial stake in their success.

Challenges

Unfortunately, disposition does not always turn into action. The founding companies have generally not dictated that supply managers use the services of the industry consortia. Additionally, by addressing mostly industrywide issues, the consortia cannot address some of the specific issues of their customers. Finally, industrywide issues are often the most difficult and take the most time and resources to impact. Some ran out of resources before they could develop profitable services.

Private E-markets

Private exchange functionality is more diverse than that found in consortia and public e-markets. Companies use private portals on both the buy and sell sides to create competitive advantage within their supply chain and to accelerate the implementation of tools and applications that are not readily available to competitors. On the buy side, companies create private portals (private e-market places) to provide a common interface and access point for their supply base. The portals typically include company-specific applications to support their purchasing, supply, and supply chain processes. Within the portal, the supplier may have its own private space through which it may access such information as demand forecasts, inventory reports, performance evaluations, and new product design information.

The procurement tools developed and/or managed by private exchanges (e-RFx, e-catalogs, auctions, data mining) are similar to those of consortia, though they leverage individual organization opportunities rather than cross-enterprise opportunities. In addition to developing and/or managing purchasing tools, private exchanges have built a diverse array of tools to address other value chain processes. These tools vary from one company to another, but include product development, supply chain network integration, and sales and marketing. The value created by these tools varies substantially depending on the value chain processes addressed.

Those that address product design, for example, potentially have to substantially reduce supply chain costs. Other tools, such as discrepant material disposition, are important, but more limited in their impact.

A list of applications found in one company portal include

- Electronic exchange of business, technical, and cost data for component parts

- Online tool to facilitate the creation, tracking, and sharing of procurement contracts

- Electronic access for suppliers to technical design data

- Electronic data interchange (EDI)—electronic exchange of business information between the company and suppliers

- Electronic data management and communication system for supply chain collaboration

- Strategic Web-based solution for purchase and invoice exchange

- Electronic bidding and sourcing exchange between company and suppliers

- Electronic medium for supply assessment and the manufacturing materials replenishment

- Collaborative system to manage product quality

Other companies have implemented different, company-specific applications in their portals that address issues and opportunities of strategic importance.

Benefits

Portals provide companies with the opportunity to increase both efficiency and effectiveness in supplier relationships. The internal efficiencies of automating data and information and transaction processes within the company have already been discussed. Additional efficiencies accrue from standardizing the supplier side of the transaction. Effectiveness gains come from automating collaborative processes with suppliers, as discussed in the section on product design.

Challenges

The challenges with portals are twofold. First, because they are company-specific, the company has the total burden of developing and deploying the process. Unlike consortia, there is no one to share the burden. This has resulted in inordinately long and uneven portal development. Secondly, private portals are all somewhat unique. This forces suppliers to integrate with the portals of all their major customers, adding to supply chain costs at the supplier level. Unlike industry consortia, there is no common interface for the industry. Because many companies, on the buy side, participate in industry consortia as well as have their own portals, suppliers must integrate with both!

The staying power of consortia versus portals has yet to be played out. It seems likely that the industry integration tools under development by consortia will eventually replace the commodity-type tools, for example, automated purchasing systems, found in company portals.

REVERSE AUCTIONS

In the mid-1990s, a new electronic sourcing tool emerged that has had, and is continuing to have, a profound impact on the way in which firms source goods and services from current and potential external suppliers. This tool, while known by other names (e.g., online negotiation) is the electronic reverse auction (e-RA).

In its *basic* form, an e-RA is an online, real-time dynamic auction between a buying organization and a group of prequalified suppliers who compete against each other to win the business to supply goods or services that have clearly defined specifications for design, quantity, quality, delivery, and related terms and conditions. These suppliers compete by bidding against each other online over the Internet using specialized software by submitting successively lower price bids during a scheduled time period. This time period usually is only about an hour, but multiple extensions of a few minutes are usually allowed if bidders are still active at the end of the initial time period.

The dramatic growth of the use of e-RAs has been facilitated both directly and indirectly by a number of converging internal and external developments and forces, including

- An intense need by firms to reduce costs of externally sourced goods and services (often 60 percent or more of total costs) to become or remain competitive in the challenging economic environment of the late 1990s and early years of the first decade of the twenty-first century.

- Aggressive initiatives by firms to rationalize (usually reduce) their supply base and give more business to fewer suppliers or, alternatively, add new sources as a hedge against risk

- Increased ability through integrated ERP systems to aggregate company-wide demand for sourced goods and services and thus facilitate standardization and stockkeeping unit reduction

- Widespread ability for supply managers and suppliers to economically communicate in real time, worldwide, via the Internet

- Development of robust, user-friendly Internet-based software systems to support worldwide e-RA events that either are hosted by a third party or designed to be run by the buying company with little or no outside assistance.

- Many buying organizations, for the past few years, have enjoyed a buyers' market where excess supplier capacity exists, and suppliers are willing to reduce prices, in some cases, just to cover variable costs.

- Intense initiatives by suppliers to reduce their total costs often have resulted in increased margins that may not have been passed on to their customers in price reductions, especially if they enjoy differentiated oligopoly or niche market power

- Recent order-of-magnitude improvements in quality and cycle time reductions resulting in buying companies viewing superior quality and service as givens and thus shifting their emphasis toward *low price* as a major sourcing decision variable

- Emergence of sophisticated and disciplined *strategic sourcing* processes that enable supply managers to systematically use various e-tools (including e-RAs) to increase their competitiveness

- Increased emphasis on global sourcing due to a combination of drastically improved quality of goods and low labor costs from developing countries

The birth and acceptance of the e-RA tool has not been without controversy. For some, its process is anathema to the long-term benefits associated with collaborative and cooperative buyer-supplier alliances. This perceived conflict primarily is caused by the tool's emphasis on awarding business based on aggressive price competition (the classical arm's-length coercive, competitive model) instead of long-term total cost of ownership (TCO) considerations. However, for a growing number of firms, e-RAs have found an appropriate niche in the strategic sourcing tool kit where they are used to source goods and services that are highly standardized or can be replicated by competitors and where switching costs are insignificant. In contrast, those suppliers of strategic items where alliance-level supplier relationships are critical usually are not subjected to e-RA sourcing. Generally, suppliers asked to participate in e-RAs, especially incumbent suppliers, do so reluctantly for fear of losing business.

To this day, there continues to be an ongoing controversy between some sourcing professionals and their top corporate managements regarding the acceptance of awarding business on the basis of lowest TCO versus lowest price. Sourcing professionals argue that higher prices can often result in lower total costs due to nonprice variables such as suppliers' superior quality, service, technical ability, and long-term commitments between the two entities. Part of this controversy is caused by the difficulty of measuring the components of total cost versus the transparency of measuring reductions in price. As a result of this transparency, in these times of economic challenge, most top managements not only embrace the use of e-RA tools, but in some cases, seeing the impressive results of early e-RAs, they set aggressive goals for e-RA use in sourcing their firm's annual requirements. This is especially the case when top management learns that the documented return on investment from e-RA use can run as high as 10 to 1. This is not to imply that TCO criteria for awarding business through an e-RA event is not used or accepted. To the contrary, there is a growing acceptance of its use as more sophisticated e-RAs (and other e-sourcing tools) are developed.

Benefits of E-RAs

Direct Cost Reductions

Without a doubt, the major benefit from the use of e-RAs is the potential for measurable direct cost reduction of purchased goods and services through either price reductions or believable TCO reductions. In general, reported reductions in price (or TCO) are double-digit percentages in the range from 10 to 20 percent over historical prices.

Biddable Attributes

Is everything a company buys a candidate for e-RA application? The answer clearly is no. Especially exempt from e-RA use are (1) items or services that do not have clearly defined attributes that competing suppliers can translate into unambiguous specifications (e.g., software development and skilled contract labor), (2) highly differentiated strategic items supplied by firms that are tightly coupled through strategic alliances with the buying firm (e.g., jet engines for an aircraft manufacturer), (3) when switching suppliers would result in unacceptably large change costs (e.g., unique, proprietary process with no acceptable substitutes, and recertification of flight hardware by the FAA, DOD, NASA), (4) when the volume or value of the item is so low that the potential savings do not cover the cost of holding the event.

In general, the major biddable attributes of a good or service are

- Items can be clearly specified (design, terms, and conditions) and translated into prices a supplier will commit to charge the buyer for the item(s) being auctioned.

- There is a strong likelihood that the current price is sufficiently higher than the market price so as to make the e-RA event cost effective.

- Switching costs are acceptable.

- A sufficient number of qualified, competitive suppliers exist in the marketplace.

- These qualified suppliers are willing to participate in an e-RA.

If good specifications can be written and if a competitive supply market exists, then e-RAs are a viable approach to purchasing the good or service. In fact, a benefit is the need to prepare these unambiguous specifications. The converse is also true. E-RAs for commodities that are controlled by just two or three major suppliers will generally not succeed. Likewise, e-RAs for which suppliers were provided with incomplete or confusing specifications result in suppliers bidding on essentially different items. The results are often that the low bid is not acceptable because it was not responsive to the intended buy.

E-RAs Can Create Markets

Clearly, the development and use of e-RAs has created competitive, relatively efficient markets for many goods and services where none previously existed. While this "market making" only approaches the efficiency of the organized stock, commodity, and currency exchanges, it is substantially more effective in determining market prices than are the traditional static sealed bid or tender processes still in wide use throughout the world. Suppliers traditionally have used a marketing strategy that relies upon supply managers' lack of knowledge about market prices and acceptable substitutes for their products and services. In addition, suppliers spend considerable effort to differentiate their products to divert attention from price to nonprice features. E-RAs, on the other hand, provide a practical mechanism to bring several suppliers together with one buyer to "make a market" for a broad range of nonpure commodities such as highly engineered parts, specialty chemicals, PCs, MRO supplies, and services such as temporary labor, maintenance, and transportation.

Cycle Time Savings for Supply Managers and Suppliers

The use of traditional processes for sourcing goods and services can consume several weeks, months, or more. The cycle time from issuing a RFx to contract award can be painfully long and consume a substantial amount of time and effort from professional supply managers. Much of this time is spent in managing several rounds of information sharing and negotiation with competing suppliers. On the other hand, preparation for planning and holding an e-RA event often requires a substantial up-front effort to assure that an auction will produce good results. A successful e-RA requires much greater time and preparation up-front, in order to correctly and adequately specify the requirements, select suppliers to participate in the event, and communicate and coordinate with suppliers. In addition, post-e-RA event negotiations also can consume substantial time and effort. However, the trade-off between these extra up-front and back-end efforts versus the hour or so taken to "negotiate" an acceptable price can result in a substantial net reduction in the cycle time for the RFx-to-contract award cycle. This cycle time reduction is in the range of "no significant reduction" up to 40 percent over traditional sourcing processes. The result of this greater up-front preparation is a significant shortening and compression of the negotiation period into a 30- to 90-minute event.

Many suppliers believe that e-RAs not only decrease the negotiation phase of the sales process, but also improve cash flow because buying firms make faster decisions. Like their buyer counterparts, suppliers also emphasize the decrease in negotiation cycle times, where multiple face-to-face price negotiations that might have occurred over several weeks are condensed into a period of a few hours. Finally, suppliers have found that the scheduling process of an e-RA can minimize the possibility of supply managers postponing bid deadlines.

Increased Supply Managers' Reach

Since most e-RAs are hosted through standard (secure) Internet connections, the reach to include qualified suppliers worldwide is increased substantially. Some integrated e-procurement systems (usually provided by third parties) include semi-automated release, receipt, and analysis of RFxs in multiple language formats. These RFxs are sent electronically to suppliers that are identified by the buying firm and to other potential suppliers that may have been prequalified by the service provider. This expanded reach results in an effective and speedy supplier search mechanism.

Total Cost Analysis
While TCO analysis of bids is available in most e-RA systems, it is used *explicitly* only by the most advanced user of the tool. Some systems allow for the integration of a dozen or more variables to be factored into a price bid during the event. This is usually done by adjusting each supplier's bid price up or down based on a pre-e-RA analysis of each competing supplier's performance in relation to the nonprice variables. Often, these variables are weighted to reflect their relative importance. On the other hand, supply managers that announce that the business may not be awarded to the low price bidder are *implicitly* considering nonprice factors in determining who will win the business, and thus are de facto users of the TCO criteria.

Price Visibility
E-RAs offer the unique opportunity for supply managers to gain insight into price levels, market prices, price elasticity (as related to various volumes), and price rigidity (from powerful oligopolies) from suppliers that participate in the event. The use of e-RAs, however, will not guarantee that the low-price bid is the true market price. This is because the low bidder may be willing to go even lower, but the competitors in the event are not. Nonetheless, price visibility, in general, is more transparent through e-RAs than in traditional sourcing processes. This knowledge of markets and prices can result, in some cases, in a power shift from strong suppliers to weaker buyers not previously attainable prior to the information revealed though preevent RFx submissions, the event, and postevent analyses.

Transparency of the Purchasing and Supplying Processes
If fairly administered, both the buying firm and the supplying firms have a clearer level of transparency into the purchasing and supplying processes. Buying firms spend more up-front time defining specifications for the items to be auctioned, determining what suppliers are qualified to be awarded the business, and gaining insight into the supply market's nature by analyzing preevent, event, and postevent behaviors. Likewise, suppliers have a clearer picture of what they are expected to deliver, have an opportunity to retain current business or gain new business, and are less impacted by nonrational decisions made by supply managers or internal customers that want to maintain the status quo.

Overall Process Efficiency and Productivity
Users of e-RAs report that they are able to spend less time on managing the tactical and operational logistics of sourcing, thus enabling them to spend more time on such strategic sourcing functions as spend analysis, opportunity assessment, market evaluation (e.g., performing Porter's five-forces analysis), developing

commodity sourcing strategies, identifying potential suppliers, current supplier development, supplier evaluation, and contract administration. Since the e-RA event drastically shortens the cycle time of price (or TCO) negotiation, more time also can be spent on preevent planning and postevent negotiation issues.

Other and Indirect Savings
The effective use of e-RAs can result in a ripple effect of cost reduction in such areas as shorting the cycle time of new product introduction, higher inventory turnover, quicker introduction of lower-cost materials, more effective use of sourcing professionals, and, in some cases, head-count reduction due to automation of some components of the sourcing process.

Benefit/Cost Justification
E-RA users seem to have little trouble justifying the cost to set up and run e-RAs versus their documented hard and soft benefits. Reported payback can be achieved after the first few uses of the tool. (One user reported that the investment in an e-RA system paid for itself during the first five minutes of the first event!) Nonetheless, there has been some resistance to the fees charged by full-service providers of e-RA events. These providers have listened to their customers and have responded by developing less expensive do-it-yourself systems that are rapidly gaining acceptance.

Dysfunctional Aspects of E-RAs

Like any tool, e-RAs can be misused or, even if used appropriately, can result in a dysfunctional outcome. Some of the causes of poor results are

- Inadequate up-front event planning and unclear item specifications and auction rules
- Insufficient training in the use of the e-RA system (supply managers and suppliers)
- Allowing unqualified bidders to participate
- Misreading the market and setting a reserve (maximum) price that is too far below the market price, resulting in no bidder responses
- Awarding business to a supplier at a price so low it cannot deliver as specified or severely threatens its survival
- Targeting the wrong commodity where the market will not be responsive or may even refuse to participate
- Holding repeated e-RA events for the sole purpose of pressuring incumbent suppliers to reduce their prices
- Use of an e-RA that results in destroying the trust and mutual interdependence between the buying company and a key strategic alliance supplier

Benefits to Suppliers

As discussed earlier, most incumbent suppliers indicate they are reluctant participants in e-RA events, but rarely refuse the chance to retain their current business or increase their business if supplier consolidation is an objective of the e-RA. In contrast, contender suppliers appreciate the chance to develop new business through their e-RA participation. In addition, suppliers also gain valuable insight into their competitive environment through their own postevent analysis of the outcome. If they win the business while maintaining a decent margin, that indicates they probably are competitive. Likewise, if they lose the business to a competitor, that indicates their cost structure and/or their margin requirements may need to be leaner.

Other potential benefits to suppliers might include lower marketing/sales costs, quicker award-nonaward cycle times (sometimes awards are announced at the end of the event or a day or two later versus weeks or months under traditional sourcing processes), and constructive feedback from some supply managers as to why they won (or lost) the business if they were (or were not) the low-price (or highest-ranked) bidder.

STANDARDS, TECHNOLOGY, AND INTEGRATION

Electronic Data Interchange

The need to share key business information within and between firms has been recognized as critical to the success of supply chain management for many years. Electronic data interchange (EDI) represented the first set of technology standards and associated electronic methods of sending and receiving business documents between supply chain partners. During the early days of EDI a variety of different standards for information sharing were developed and placed into use. Most of these standards were proprietary in nature and were not themselves interoperable. In the late 1970s the Accredited Standards Committee (ASC) began the process of creating a more uniformly adopted standard. EDI gained traction with large firms in the 1980s, but failed to become the technology standard that would integrate the business community. Major obstacles to the adoption of EDI included (1) the slow and complicated standards-setting process and (2) the high cost associated with the implementation of an EDI-based system.

The World Wide Web

With the advent of the World Wide Web (WWW), it became possible for nearly any user to create and share information electronically. However, this method of sharing information [(called Hyper Text Transfer Protocol (HTTP)] was much better suited to the consumer-to-consumer (C2C) and business-to-consumer (B2C) environments than to the business to business (B2B) e-commerce environment. In essence, HTTP provided a simple way to display well-formatted, aesthetically pleasing documents for consumption by human beings.

The problem in using HTTP to support B2B e-commerce is found in its inability to describe the elements of a Web page (called a metalanguage) in a computer-interpretable method. For instance, assume that you were browsing the catalog of one of your approved suppliers and you found a page that included a part name, description, picture, specification, price, availability, terms, and so forth. You would likely have enough context from the page and the process that you used to navigate the page to immediately understand that the "price" on the catalog was indeed the *purchase price*. If the price included a discount for early payment, you would immediately understand that there were two different prices on the page and the meaning of each. However, without a metalanguage to provide the higher level meaning of price, the computer would lack the necessary context to be able to interpret price, discount price, or any other element on the page.

Extensible Markup Language

Extensible Markup Language (XML) was developed to provide the descriptions necessary to enable a computer to interpret the specific information elements contained within a document (or data stream). To extend the previous example, the computer would understand that the page contained a "no-discount" price as well as a discounted price (if, for instance, payment was received by the supplier within 30 days of delivery).

However, while XML provided this metalanguage capability, it did not provide the specific definitions of the elements to be described. In other words, XML provided the ability to describe price but did not provide the business definition of price. Thus XML became a tool around which new standards for information sharing could be written.

Just as the EDI standards proliferated in the 1970s causing a slowing of the adoption of this technology, XML standards likewise proliferated in the late 1990s and early years of the first decade of the twenty-first century. XML standards were created by groups representing industries and business functions, e-commerce companies, standards-setting bodies, and others. In the end, the promise that XML would provide the unifying technology for the sharing of a standardized and agreed-to set of business information became less certain.

XML Business Standards

The Standards
There are many organizations that have created XML-based standards to allow business partners to share information. Many of these standards are based around business functions. Some of these include XBRL (Extensible Business Reporting Language) in accounting and finance, HR-XML (Human Resources—Extensible Markup Language) in human resources, and RosettaNet in supply chain management. Other standards are industry-focused. Some of these include cdmXML

(Construction, Manufacturing and Distribution Extensible Markup Language) in the construction industry and IXRetail (International XML Retail) in the retail sector. Some standards like ebXML (Electronic Business XML) are cross-industry and cross-function. Nearly every constituency has become involved in some way or another in the XML standards-setting process.

An Example: RosettaNet

The following discussion will use RosettaNet as an example of an XML-based e-business standard. RosettaNet was originally founded as a supply chain management XML standard primarily focused in the electronics industry. Since its inception, it has set its sights on becoming an international XML standard that crosses industries and functions.

All business-oriented XML standards must start by clearly defining the business process that the XML standard is written to support. In the case of RosettaNet, these business processes are defined as partner interface processes (PIPs). RosettaNet has established PIPs in a variety of business process areas including: (0) administration, (1) partner, product, and service review, (2) product introduction, (3) order management, (4) inventory management, (5) marketing information management, (6) service and support, and (7) manufacturing. Within each of the higher-level business processes exists some number of subprocesses. For instance, within (3) order management, RosettaNet has identified (3A) quote and order entry, (3B) transportation and administration, (3C) returns and finance, and (3D) product configuration. If we exam the (3A) quote and order-entry subprocess, we will find 14 individual PIPs. One of these PIPs (3A1) describes the process for requesting a quotation (see Figure 21–7).

In support of the process described in Figure 21–8, RosettaNet provides all the documentation (XML-dialogs, message choreography, etc.) necessary for a firm to understand and implement this PIP to share information with business partners.

Web Services

One of the challenges of sharing information between supply chain partners surrounds the process of connecting the supply chain partners' systems (e.g., SAP, Siebel) together such that XML-based data can easily flow back and forth. We often think of connections of this nature as *point-to-point* solutions. Recognizing that we have many suppliers and many customers, creating these point-to-point solutions is both difficult and costly (recall the discussion of consortia versus e-markets).

Web services is a new technology that allows the integration of business partners' systems without the traditional cost and complexity of establishing the point-to-point connection just described. Interestingly, Web services also allows for these connections to be made from computer to computer without intervention or prompting by human beings.

FIGURE 21–7

PIP 3A1 Business Process

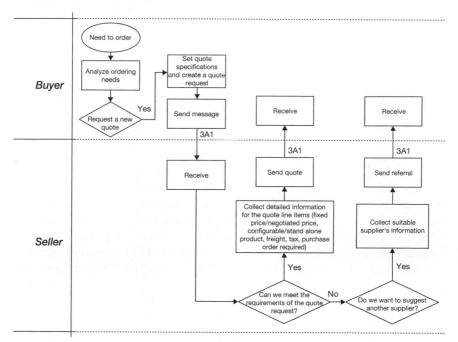

SOURCE: http://www.rosettanet.org/rosettanet/Rooms/DisplayPages/LayoutInitial?Container=com.
webridge.entity.Entity%5BOID%5B0CB57A9DA92DD411842300C04F689339%5D%5D
Reprinted by permission from RosettaNet, www.rosettanet.org

FIGURE 21–8

Radio Frequency Identification (RFID)

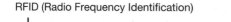

RFID (Radio Frequency Identification)

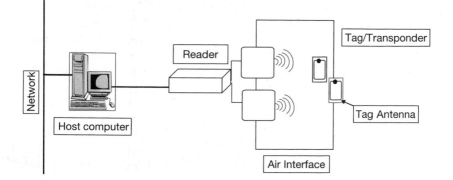

Web services are really made up of four main components: (1) XML, (2) SOAP, (3) WSDL, and (4) UDDI. We have already discussed XML; the following list details the remaining three standards that comprise Web services.

- *SOAP* (Simple Object Access Protocol) provides the capability for Web services to communicate with one another over the Internet.

- *WSDL* (Web Services Description Language) describes each Web service and provides instructions on how to connect to the Web service.

- *UDDI* (Universal Discover, Description, and Integration) provides a directory of Web services that are available.

Hence, Web services promises to be one of the more exciting technologies in the arena of supply chain integration.

The majority of Web services success stories are in the B2C environment. For instance, Kinko's has employed Web services to provide users of Microsoft Office with the ability to print directly to one of Kinko's print centers using the Print button within each of the Microsoft Office applications. Dollar Rent-a-Car created a Web service that allows customers of Southwest Airlines to book Dollar rental cars without leaving Southwest's Web site. Early adopters of Web services in the B2B environment include Boeing Company (IONA) and British Telecommunications (Clear Cape).

RFID

Radio frequency identification (RFID) is one of the newest technologies to be deployed in the supply chain. RFID is already widely used by consumers at the gas pump and fast-food restaurants. For example, in 1997, Mobil introduced its Speedpass system that lets customers wave the tag in front of the pump to record their transaction and debit their account. The E-ZPass highway toll collection system also uses RFID. More recently Wal-Mart and the U.S. Department of Defense have mandated that certain of their suppliers attach RFID tags to supplied goods. METRO Group, the world's fifth-largest retailing company, will soon begin using RFID technology throughout its entire process chain. Beginning in November 2004, approximately 100 suppliers initially will affix RFID chips to their pallets and transport packages for delivery to 10 central warehouses and around 250 stores within the METRO Group's sales divisions Metro Cash & Carry, Real hypermarkets, Extra supermarkets and Galeria Kaufhof department stores.

RFID is a data collection technology that uses electronic tags to store identification data and a wireless transmitter gun to capture it. The tag is also known as an electronic label, transponder, or code plate. RFID tags consist of microchips that store encoded product data and an antenna that wirelessly transmit those data. The transmission is over radio frequency waves that are activated when placed in the transmission field of a reader or transmitter gun. RFID does not require line-of-sight reading and can contain unique item-level information. RFID tag sizes vary from large active tags to the new 0.2-mm passive microdot.

Challenges

There are several issues with RFID technology. Perhaps the most important is the lack of standards for the technology and the radio frequencies used. Today there are at least 11 competing standards that will have to be rationalized before RFID will be widely used. Secondly, the ROI for RFID is very uncertain. Part of this uncertainty stems from the competing technologies, but much of it concerns benefits. Although RFID could make available information about the exact location of every piece of inventory, this benefit is yet to be demonstrated for most goods. More information does not mean that all the information will be used. Consider that many years passed before companies began to effectively use all the information collected by bar code readers at retail checkout lanes. RFID promises to multiply the amount of information available to supply chain managers by several magnitudes.

Benefits

Potential applications of RFID in the supply chain include

- Advanced planning and optimization
- Real-time and bidirectional communications to help reduce the bullwhip effect
- Increase forecast accuracy
- Improve order fulfillments and inventory replenishment
- Event messages triggered by the RFID reader
- Task and resource management
- Warehouse management
- Product life-cycle management
- Mobile supply chain management

Potential benefits to retailers and other buying organizations include

- Increased in-stocks
- Reduced labor cost
- Improved customer service
- Reduced shrinkage
- Lower costs
- Increased revenue
- Decreased working capital
- Reduced fixed capital

Commodity Codes and Identification Codes

With the advent of the new technology, there has been a growing use of the value of assigning commodity codes to all purchased goods and services. The technology makes the assignment of commodity codes feasible and practical. Once implemented, commodity codes can become the basis for analysis of the total spend in a company.

Commodity codes are often confused with identification codes, but they are different and have different uses. Identification codes unambiguously identify an item. Some examples are

- Social security number—identifies people

- Uniform Code Council (UCC) code—identifies products

- Part number—identifies parts

The digits in an identification code may or may not have significance. For example some part numbers, in addition to uniquely identifying the part, may give some information about where and when it was manufactured. Other part numbers are essentially random, contain no other information, and serve only to uniquely identify a part and tie it to a master record in a computer system. Identification codes are used for inventory tracking, warranty records, accounting and costing, and so forth.

Commodity codes, also called classification codes, group similar items into common categories and indicate the relation of the items to other items. Commodity codes are typically hierarchical in structure. At the bottom of the hierarchy are a large number of narrowly defined categories of goods and services. These categories aggregate into broader categories, until the top of the hierarchy is reached. The top includes a relatively small number of broadly defined categories.

The digits in a commodity code indicate the categories and subcategories in which an item is a member. The digits correspond to the hierarchical definition of the overall coding scheme.

Characteristics of Good Commodity Code Schemes

Good commodity code schemes allow for "drill-down" and "roll-up" analyses. The results of an analysis conducted on items at one low-level category can be aggregated with the results from items of another category at the same low level. These results from all of the categories at this low level can be aggregated (rolled up) to intermediate categories. The results from the intermediate categories can then be aggregated (rolled up) to the highest categories of goods and services. The specificity of the analysis can be tailored to the need of the business, within the overall constraints of the coding scheme. In general, companies conduct spend analyses at the level of a "contractible group," that is, the group or category of goods and services that might be purchased from one supplier.

Another good attribute is that the scheme assigns unique codes to each classification. This allows commonality across business units, companies, and countries. In addition, the scheme needs to be consistent; that is, the scheme should include each item in only one category. Finally, the scheme must be complete. It must include, or must be able to accommodate, all purchased products and services (within the limits of the schema.)

The United Nations Standard Products and Services Code (UNSPSC)

The United Nations Development Program and Dun & Bradstreet created UNSPSC by merging their separate commodity classification codes into a single open system. The Electronic Commerce Code Management Association (ECCMA), a not-for-profit membership organization, oversees the management and development of the UNSPSC.

The UNSPSC has gained increasing use with the advent of automated purchasing systems for indirect goods and services. It has all the desirable attributes previously discussed and is gaining acceptance by an increasing number of firms. (The complete code can be found at www. unspsc.org.) In a 2003 CAPS Research survey of large companies 45 percent of the responding companies indicated that they use UNSPSC commodity coding. Another 17 percent indicated they plan to use UNSPSC codes in the future. Only 9 percent of the respondents indicated that they do not plan to use UNSPSC commodity coding in the future.

The UNSPSC has four levels of classification. The highest-level classifications are called *segments* and are represented by two-digit codes ranging from 10 to 94. Example two-digit codes are

[30] Structures, Building and Construction Components and Supplies

[31] Manufacturing Components and Supplies

[32] Electronic Components and Supplies

The next level of classification is four-digit codes, within each of the two-digit codes. This level of the scheme is called *families*. Families within Segment 32 include

[32 10] Printed circuits and integrated circuits and microassemblies

[32 11] Discrete semiconductor devices

[32 14] Electron tube devices and accessories

Within the families are six-digit codes called *classes*. Classes within Family 32 10 include

[32 10 15] Circuit assemblies and radio frequency (RF) components

[32 10 16] Integrated circuits

Finally, within the classes are eight-digit commodity codes. Commodity codes within the 32 10 15 class include

[32 10 15 02] Printed circuit assemblies (PCAs)

[32 10 15 17] Couplers

[32 10 15 28] Modulators

Note that the code 32101528 does not identify a specific modulator. An identification code (i.e., a part number) would be needed for that purpose.

The UNSPSC actually allows for a fifth level of classification called *business function*. This level is rarely used however.

UNSPSC Classification Rules

While classifying goods and services may see straightforward, some difficult choices can arise. For example, consider batteries, which could be classified in any of the following segments:

25000000 Commercial and Military and Private Vehicles and Their
    Accessories and Components

26000000 Power Generation and Distribution Machinery and Accessories

32000000 Electronic Components and Supplies

39000000 Electrical Systems and Lighting and Components and
    Accessories and Supplies

In fact, batteries are assigned to Segment 26. To resolve classification ambiguities, UNSPSC uses a hierarchy of rules. The rules are

1. Classify with other products that serve a common purpose or task

2. Classify with other products that are made by a similar process

3. Classify with other products that are made from the same material

Even these rules may not resolve all issues, so the panel of experts overseeing the scheme must exercise some judgment.

Several e-commerce companies have adopted the UNSPSC as the standard for constructing e-catalogs. This has increased the rate of adoption of the UNSPSC as a standard. However, it has not been universally adopted, even for indirect goods and services. Moreover, other commodity codes are firmly entrenched for the direct materials in some industries. For example, the Standard Transportation Commodity Code (STCC) is a publication containing specific product information used on waybills and other shipping documents. The STCC uses a seven-digit numeric code to represent 38 commodity groupings. Similarly, NIGP maintains a commodity code used by local and state governments. Finally, eCl@ss is a commodity-coding scheme developed in Germany and is similar to, but different from, UNSPSC.

Benefits

Commodity codes can be the basis for a spend analysis, which can lead to great cost savings. Combined with a supplier coding scheme, the spend analysis can help a company understand its total spend across various business units. This, in turn, can lead to standardization of products and services, aggregation of the resulting demand, and leverage within the marketplace. By aggregating at the "contactable level," companies can group goods and services in a request for bid or in negations. Without the benefit of commodity codes, spend analysis becomes a tedious, labor-intensive, and time-consuming task.

Challenges

Unfortunately, in some companies the most widely used commodity code is 00 or 99, or some other code that indicates "other" or "unknown." Of course such coding has no value. The first challenge is to get all the purchased goods and services coded correctly as the scheme is being introduced, which can be a resource-intensive task. The second challenge is to get commodity codes correctly assigned on an ongoing basis. Fortunately, new software helps with both tasks. Artificial intelligence software can read the parts description in item masters and based on this correctly classify the goods in over 90 percent of the cases. (This assumes that the item masters are in good shape.) Additionally, software is available that classifies goods and services on the fly. That is, as requisitions are completed the software automatically assigns the correct commodity code, relieving the user from the burden of having to look up a commodity code and preventing the dreaded 00 code from being assigned.

FUTURE AND PROMISING TECHNOLOGIES AND APPLICATIONS

This section of the chapter will discuss several emerging technologies that may have an impact on supply chain management as they mature. These technologies are (1) intelligent agents, (2) data mining, and (3) network infrastructure (including wireless).

Intelligent Agents

Intelligent agents have received substantial attention in recent years. An intelligent agent may be thought of as a system situated within and a part of an environment that senses that environment and acts on it, over time, in pursuit of its own agenda and so as to affect what it senses in the future. In essence, intelligent agents are software programs that work autonomously toward the completion of a given mission. General classes of intelligent agents include (1) information filtering agents, (2) information retrieval agents, (3) advisory agents, and (4) performance agents.

Possible supply chain management applications for intelligent agents abound. For instance, say you have a requisition for which no current source of supply exists. An intelligent agent could be used to scour the Internet for not only potential suppliers, but also the best pricing and delivery terms. This same agent might then place its findings directly into a spreadsheet for your review.

In preparation for a reverse auction, a buying company might employ an intelligent agent to help establish a market basket of goods and services that optimizes a group of supplier core competencies and capabilities. While this intelligent agent would use product availability and capacity information from the suppliers to create an optimal market basket, it would not share the supplier's strategic capacity information with the buying firm. The buying firm would only receive advice from the intelligent agent on the best combination of required goods and services, thus likely leading to a better outcome for both the buying and supplying companies.

Data Mining

While businesses have done a remarkable job of capturing and storing terabytes upon terabytes of structured and unstructured data on many parts of their supply chain processes, they have not been able to integrate and use this data to the degree that might be possible (refer to the discussion of RFID). For instance, many companies collect information on contracts, sales forecasts, quality problems, hard and soft cost savings, and so forth. Unfortunately, this data is difficult to work with in its entirety. Data mining software offers the possibility of being able to use this relatively unstructured data to ferret out relationships that may exist in our supply chain processes but are not obvious or approachable using traditional data analysis tools. As an example, consider some of the types of data described earlier. If we used data mining software to examine this data, we might find that there is a relationship between how much forecasting information we share with our suppliers and their pricing of the forecasted goods or services. We might also find that this relationship is not the same for all suppliers. This is to say that some suppliers may be able to use the additional forecasting information to improve their cost competitiveness while others may not. The rapid advances in computer hardware have allowed data mining technologies to advance rapidly. This technology is continuing to advance at a rapid rate and may turn out to deliver significant value to supply chain managers.

Network Infrastructure

The Internet is constantly evolving. As an example, in 1998 the government announced the creation of the Abilene network backbone that would span the United States and allow data to pass at a rate of 2.5 gigabits per second. This network was completed at the end of 1999 and is currently being upgraded to 10 gigabits per second. As another example, an MCI-based research team has recently been able to pass data between two points at a rate of 40 gigabits per second using technology compatible with its 10 gigabits-per-second backbone. Typical users of the Internet currently see only a very small fraction of this rate (50 kilobytes per second to 5 megabytes per second). At the same time that we are seeing significant improvements of Internet speed, we are also finding that the Internet itself is on its way to becoming pervasive. The Internet may be accessed wirelessly by handheld computers, personal digital assistants, cellular phones, laptops, wrist watches, home appliances, and automobiles. Several airlines have announced the availability of wireless Internet service on flights. The increasing speed and pervasive nature of the Internet is changing the way we live and work. It is changing the expectations of our employees as well as many of our business processes. It is important that we keep a careful eye on the advancements in Internet technology as these changes will likely allow us to both improve our existing processes as well as develop entirely new processes. As tangible examples of how this might occur, you might look at the advent of Internet-based meetings (Microsoft Live Meeting, Webex, etc.) and their effect on the reduced cost structure for employee travel in many firms.

CONCLUSION

The future holds both developments in technology and the improved application of new and maturing technologies to real-world business problems. Many of today's mainstream technologies (e-purchasing, electronic reverse auctions, portals, etc.) will reach maturity in the near future. We are likely to see significant advancements in the areas of e-enabled supply chain integration and the subsequent abilities of firms to develop new processes that leverage their access to better and more timely information.

BIBLIOGRAPHY

Auto-ID Center (2003). Business Research Track. February 26.

Beall, S., et al. (2003). *The Role of Reverse Auctions in Strategic Sourcing*. Tempe, AZ: CAPS Research.

Desktop Engineering. February 2000.

E-Commerce Exchanges: Making Informed Decisions, Applying Best Practices. Tempe, AZ: CAPS Research and McKinsey and Company, 2002.

Engineering Automation Report. May 2000.

Flynn, Anna (2004). *Developing and Implementing eSourcing Strategy*. Tempe, AZ: CAPS Research.

www.accenture.com

www.amrresearch.com/content/view.asp?pmillid=17427&bhcp=1

www.epcglobalinc.org

www.future-store.org/servlet/PB/-s/1qd2emc1e8xinlcv9udm1bdf30j15r7zra/menu/1000154_l2/1089657398122.html

www.rosettanet.org

www.sap.com

"Is It an Agent, or Just a Program? A Taxonomy for Autonomous Agents." *Proceedings of the Third International Workshop on Agent Theories, Architectures, and Languages*, Springer-Verlag, 1996.

RFID Journal, www.rfidjournal.com.

RFID: UPC of the 21st Century, Manhattan Associates.

SAP Lab (China): SAP & Auto-ID in China.

SAP White Paper: SAP Auto-ID Infrastructure.

Scientific American, January 2004.

Using the Lens of Economic Value to Clarify the Impact of B2B e-Marketplaces. Tempe, AZ: CAPS Research and McKinsey and Company, 2000.

CHAPTER 22

SUPPLIER PRICE AND COST ANALYSIS

Michael E. Smith, Ph.D., CQA
Associate Professor of Management
& International Business
MBA Program Director
Western Carolina University

Lee Buddress, Ph.D., C.P.M.
Associate Professor and Director,
Supply and Logistics Management Program
Portland State University

INTRODUCTION

Supplier price and cost analysis has received considerable attention as organizations seek cost savings, a subject central to the esteem of supply management activities in many organizations. This concern has been so pivotal to the reputation of supply managers that most introductory supply management texts contain an early example showing how cost savings from effective supply management add considerably more to the organizational bottom line than do considerably larger increases in revenue driven by increased sales. The simple fact is that the reader can easily make the argument that a dollar saved through his or her efforts at cost containment translates into a dollar on the bottom line, a result that may require many dollars in increased sales revenues. It is that simple! The intent of this chapter is to provide you with a strategic context for considering price and cost analysis, an understanding of what is involved, and a view of the practical applications of such analyses.

Let us begin with a look at some of the recent changes in the supply management profession and how those changes have impacted the role of supplier price and cost analysis. Undoubtedly, most readers are aware of past practice in the profession, when purchasing personnel sought to pit supplier against supplier in a competitive contest that was aimed at obtaining the lowest possible purchase price for necessary supplies and services. Some organizations may still operate where at least part of the purchases are still administered in this way; indeed, one could argue that certain widely available commodities, which do not represent strategically critical categories for the organization doing the purchasing, should be purchased in a manner similar to that described.[1] However, readers should also be aware of the importance of concerns beyond just the immediate purchase price.

For example, as the supply management profession has advanced, a central message to supply management professionals has been that they should attend to the total cost of ownership: the cost of obtaining something, getting it to the point of use, conversion and customer support, etc., that is, purchase price plus all other costs of a given product throughout its lifetime.[2] In many cases, the lowest total cost has been found to be for materials or services where the actual purchase price is somewhat higher than that of products priced lower because of better quality and other factors of product performance. This example illustrates the importance of strategic guidance for the use of supplier price and cost analysis, a fact compounded by the increasingly strategic nature of supply management in general.

WHAT IS PRICE?

From our perspective, price is the amount that we might expect to pay for materials or services that we seek to purchase. At first glance, we can see that this price must consist of two primary elements if the supplier is to survive. First, the supplier must cover all relevant costs associated with the product we are purchasing, for failure to do so is to plan for business collapse. Secondly, businesses need to derive adequate profit from sales if they are to continue to be our suppliers.

This is a simple idea, but it covers the basics of one of the most fundamental models for pricing. Cost-plus pricing remains exceedingly common, but belies a lack of strategic understanding on the part of many marketing managers because it ignores the concept of customer value.[3] The standard approach has been to start production, determine costs (after the fact), determine the markup, and set the price. At this point, the organization is gambling on a value proposition that may not satisfy customers.

A modern alternative is to determine what the customer needs (up front, not as an afterthought) and then determine what price, given satisfaction of customer needs, would be competitive in the market. Thus, there is an increasing focus on designing products to provide the value in both product function and product price that the customer is seeking.[4] This modern approach relies on the firm's strategy to guide exploration for customer needs that align firm purpose and competencies.

1 L. Buddress and A. Raedels (1998). "Using Criticality Grids to Determine Negotiation Strategies," *Proceedings of the 83rd Annual International Purchasing Conference*, Tempe, AZ: National Association of Purchasing Management (now the Institute for Supply Management™), pp. 384–388. This document is available online at www.ism.ws.

2 There is extensive literature about total cost of ownership, including a chapter in this book. Another reference readily available through the Institute for Supply Management™ is L. M. Ellram (1994). *Total Cost Modeling in Purchasing*, Tempe, AZ: Center for Advanced Purchasing Studies.

3 T. T. Nagle and R. K. Holden (2002). *The Strategy and Tactics of Pricing: A Guide to Profitable Decision Making*, Upper Saddle River, NJ: Prentice Hall.

4 Ibid.

Strategy also guides decision making about the amount of the price that represents margin. From this point, target costs at the component level can be determined, and product design can be developed within the constraints of customer requirements and the target costs.

Note that in the case of the tactical, cost-based pricing, costing was not strategic and might be compared to attempts at successfully steering your car to an important destination while looking back at the territory you have already passed. Such an after-the-fact approach can only be successful for those who are exceedingly lucky, and strategic decision making is about minimizing the role of luck in determining organizational success. In the second approach, pricing is derived before the decisions that determine the profitability of sales at a given price. Thus, strategic pricing is more like driving in a responsible manner, with forward vision aimed at the course we wish to steer. Pricing aimed at profitably producing customer value increases the odds that the customer will be well served while also increasing the probability for a positive organizational outcome.

This conceptual background underlies at least part of the logic for implementation of many innovative practices in systemic supply chain management (SCM). For example, early supplier involvement (ESI) in product design can be implemented to gain supplier assistance in meeting both function and price requirements for new products. Suppliers can help an organization ensure that new products meet price targets when they are informed of target component prices and they have input into component materials and designs. In a recent case, a supplier of aeronautical engines found that ESI coupled in this way to target pricing was successful in reducing costs and enhancing product performance.[5]

As the ESI example shows, we see progress among supply management professionals in using price analysis with a strategic focus on customer and organizational needs. This presentation now turns to a more substantial look at the elements of price analysis.

PRICE ANALYSIS

Since price represents what we pay, or what we expect to pay, in the proactive stance, price analysis can be seen as concerned with this amount. To the extent that price is determined by cost elements, discussion will largely be reserved for the cost analysis section later in this chapter. Price analysis represents a macro concern, whereas cost analysis delves into the cost elements that affect the total cost. In their sum, the elements of cost drive the price. Thus, this section deals with the big picture, and in cost analysis the discussion will turn to justification for the individual cost elements.

Price analysis is a comparative process that seeks to establish reasonable purchase price thresholds relative to market conditions. Such an analysis does not

---

5 M. E. Smith and G. A. Zsidisin (2002). "Early Supplier Involvement at MRD," *Practix: Best Practices in Purchasing and Supply Chain Management*, vol. 5, no. 4, Tempe, AZ: CAPS Research, pp. 1–5.

necessarily require knowledge of the cost structure of the supplier, but, instead, evaluates the extent to which the sum of the cost elements is justified given prevailing prices for the item or similar items. This essentially represents analysis for benchmarking of prices.

Supplier Pricing Strategies

Sellers utilize a number of pricing rubrics, and each represents a way of arriving at and supporting a price quotation. As such, supply management professionals should be aware of the basic classifications and how they are applied. Traditional pricing strategies can be seen as cost-based, market-based, or a hybrid of cost- and market-based strategies.[6]

Cost-plus pricing and pricing based upon rules of thumb both represent cost-based pricing strategies. In both cases, the seller utilizes cost estimates to establish price. In the case of cost-plus pricing, as already described, the price is established so as to cover variable costs plus contributions toward fixed costs and profit. The challenge in executing a cost-plus strategy is that those doing the pricing must have a good understanding of the firm's overall cost structure and the costs associated with production of the particular product in question.

Pricing that is based upon rules of thumb appeals to marketing managers with a sales force that is not adequately aware of the firm's cost structure to execute cost-plus pricing effectively. In this case if, for example, direct costs for a product are known, those costs would have some estimate of the necessary markup to cover indirect costs and profit added to the direct costs. Such rules of thumb are frequently based upon overall contribution margins for the firm's entire product line and are particularly likely to be used when organizations don't know their true costs. This situation is quite common, since many firms have inadequate costing information. It should be clear that when rules of thumb are applied to pricing, there is considerable risk for the firm in not applying a large enough markup. An obvious way to guard against such risk is to exaggerate the necessary markup, a potential source of excessive price quotes and something that price analysis should seek to uncover.

Purely cost-based strategies only really work if the selling firm can reasonably assume a monopoly such that the purchasing firm must buy the product from the supplier. Where competition exists, successful pricing must take market conditions into account. When buyers have a choice, sellers must price competitively, whatever their costs. This force clearly has tremendous impact on pricing and is one that has long been exploited by purchasing personnel, even to the extent of developing competition where none exists. For the selling firm, such price pressure often requires aggressive cost reduction in order to maintain profitability.

With market-based strategies, demand and competition enter the pricing decision. Such pricing strategies require effective market research to determine the extent of current and future demand for a product. Higher demand generally sup-

---

6 K. B. Monroe (1990). *Pricing: Making Profitable Decisions*, 2nd ed., New York: McGraw-Hill.

ports higher prices and is often the result of limited competition. Where there is effective competition and demand is readily met, prices generally have to be lower to accomplish sales of the product. Obviously, innovative products enjoy a period when the market supports higher prices. Generally, the appearance of such opportunity tends to promote the development of competition. It is the likely entry of competition that drives many organizations to engage in a skimming strategy, where they price the product high early in the product's life cycle in order to capture as much profit as possible before competition forces price reductions.[7]

Effectively, cost-plus pricing can be rendered a hybrid strategy when the supplier takes market conditions into account when establishing the magnitude of the margin.[8] Thus, the seller might reduce the size of the margin to gain market share and, perhaps, to drive out competition.

In introducing pricing strategies, we referred to these conventions as traditional approaches. The approaches that have so far been described in this section are traditional in that they are more tactical than strategic. It is likely that when these strategies are in effect, price analysis will uncover marked deviations from the market, and forceful cost analysis may be necessary in order to find actionable improvement opportunities if you plan to continue with the same supplier (i.e., supplier development is implemented with the aim of maintaining the relationship with the supplier).

As previously noted, marketing managers who are aware of the strategic impact of pricing increasingly seek to adopt value-based pricing in a proactive manner, such that pricing affects product design and production decisions instead of trying to find a way of rendering past design and production decisions profitable, a much more reactive stance.[9] When strategic pricing truly is in effect (i.e., the profit margin intended by the selling firm is reasonable, and the value proposition has been based upon solid market research), price analysis should find that the established price compares well with the market. Any other finding would suggest that strategic, value-based pricing was not systematically applied. When this is the case, the findings from price analysis should drive aggressive cost analysis efforts to uncover the source of deviations from the market.

Market Influence on Pricing

Since price analysis is aimed at determining if pricing is reasonable from a market perspective, the type of market within which your supplier is operating represents a critical input into the process. Prices are likely to be lower in markets where there is competition than in markets without competition.

In order for perfect competition to exist, there must be many firms, each small relative to the total size of the market. This requirement prevents any given firm from

---

7 R. Monczka, R. Trent, and R. Handfield (2002). *Purchasing and Supply Chain Management*, 2nd ed., Cincinnati, OH: South-Western.

8 Ibid.

9 Nagle and Holden, *The Strategy and Tactics of Pricing*.

influencing price (although, collusion or the formation of a cartel could bring about such influence, reason enough for such activity to generally be prohibited in the United States). Another requirement for perfect competition is that the product must be standardized. This prevents competitive advantage through differentiation. Perfect competition, at least in theoretical purity, is rare, but many standard materials purchases may come close.[10] In such cases, prices are subject to easy comparison and are likely to be quite consistent from supplier to supplier, since price premiums favorable to the supplier are likely to be detected, reducing patronage. Price reductions are readily matched by competitors, thus resulting in reduced profits for any firm attempting to capture market share in this manner. Price should be determined by the market in such cases.

Monopolistic competition, like perfect competition, results when there are many producers. However, unlike in the case of perfect competition, while the products are similar, they are subject to some differentiation. Under monopolistic competition firms tend to maximize profits.[11] In such markets, differentiation and lack of dominating control present opportunities for negotiating favorable deals, and volume purchasing may obtain preferable pricing. In price analyses, market comparisons are readily available, but adjustments need to be made for any differentiation of the specific product in question.

Where relatively few suppliers dominate the market, they are operating in an oligopolistic market. Traditionally, suppliers frequently wield price advantage in an oligopoly. However, with expanding markets, including globalization, traditional oligopolies (e.g., the steel, automobile, and appliance industries) have seen reduction of seller power with respect to purchasers.[12] Thus, in price analyses, we should generally expect to see competitive pricing and attractive options from our suppliers since oligopolies are increasingly difficult to maintain in a global marketplace.

In a monopoly, in which one firm is the entire market, the supplier is free to determine production and pricing, except where government has regulated them. While government deregulation of many industries and the rapid pace of technological change have reduced the prevalence of monopolies in recent times, in many cases, the supply management organization may not have many alternatives or the alternatives may be imperfect at best. For example, while an industry may not be monopolistic, patents and proprietary products create situations where a particular product is effectively insulated from competition. Accurate pricing information for comparison purposes is unlikely to be available, so price analysis may not be meaningful. Further, where formal or effective monopolies exist, purchasing influence should be considered to be minimal. Without influence, there may be little that can

---

10 J. K. Shim and J. G. Siegel (1998). *Managerial Economics*, Hauppauge, NY: Barron's Educational Services.

11 Ibid.

12 Monczka, Trent, and Handfield, *Purchasing and Supply Chain Management*.

be done to effect supplier pricing changes, which may minimize the value of either price or cost analysis, since there may be little return on the expenditure of resources.

To the extent that market conditions allow meaningful price analyses, prices can be found to be acceptable, too high (the case that most people assume), or too low (thus, not providing for sustainable operation of the supplier's firm). If the price is too high, the cause might be a lack of strategic alignment; that is, the pricing strategy of the firm is in conflict with your needs. On the other hand, if excessive costs are at the root of high prices relative to the market, discussion of the strategic use of cost analyses later in this chapter will suggest alternatives that you can pursue.

If you suspect that the price from a critical supplier is too low, you may also want to engage in cost analysis in order to determine if the firm is profitable, if its costs can be cut without jeopardizing what you are purchasing, or if in the final analysis you may need to pay more so that you can protect your firm's interests by supporting sustained operation of a valued partner.[13]

With knowledge of pricing strategy and market structure in hand, you are positioned to seek meaningful pricing comparisons.

Sources of Information for Price Analysis

The Internet represents a garden of plenty for anyone seeking information for price analyses. First, prices can be obtained for just about anything by simple searches. In the extreme, comparisons can be found by use of online reverse auctions. However, it may be the case that many have been persuaded to utilize reverse auctions to substitute for doing the hard work to consistently know market pricing and contain prices on an ongoing basis. Organizations that have not been making consistent use of price analysis and good purchasing practices may be able to obtain large price reductions by using reverse auctions, at least in the short term as the prices that they are paying come into alignment with the prevailing market. Where good purchasing practices have been consistently applied, price reductions following a reverse auction should be relatively small, since the utilization of comparative price information should ensure that competitive prices have been paid for necessary materials.

While the general market represents a source for direct comparison, market changes can readily be observed for many commodities through the Institute for Supply Management™'s (ISM) *Report On Business*® (available monthly either in *Inside Supply Management*®, the membership magazine for ISM, or online at www.ism.ws). This report lists commodities that are reported by supply management

---

13 Early suggestion of this concern was provided when R. David Nelson, C.P.M., described auditing suppliers to make sure that the suppliers were charging enough to sustain business operations. This issue is addressed at several points in R. D. Nelson, P. E. Moody, and J. Stegner (2001). *The Purchasing Machine: How the Top Ten Companies Use Best Practices to Manage Their Supply Chains*, New York: The Free Press.

professionals as in short supply or up or down in price (or, in volatile cases, some-times commodities are reported both up and down). Broader economic influences on prices can be found through the U.S. government's Bureau of Labor Statistics Web site at www.bls.gov. Of particular interest is its producer price index (PPI). The first information that you are likely to encounter is the commentary on the current PPI, an aggregate measure that addresses changes in selling prices received by domestic organizations. Along with the PPI, the site also includes pric-ing information on numerous commodities and industries. For commodity and industry indexes the information provides price differences relative to a reference base from 1982 to 1984. The numbers in the tables reflect percentage differences relative to that base.

For example, at the commodity level, preliminary results (adjustments are frequently made up to four months after a period is first reported) for May 2004, made available in June 2004, show that diesel fuel was selling for 121.1 percent (inflation adjusted) of the reference 1982–1984 prices, up from 87.9 percent of the reference price in May 2003. In real terms, producers were getting lower prices in 2003 than they were in the reference period. Real prices increased rapidly toward May 2004 (a result that will not surprise any supply management professional), and producers were receiving more for diesel at this point than they were during the reference period. At the industry level, the petroleum refining industry was receiving a price (preliminarily) that was 154.1 percent of the reference period in May 2004, up from 109.1 percent in May 2003.

Additional resources include *Purchasing* magazine, which has monthly cov-erage of commodity pricing, and industry magazines related to your particular industry. The U.S. Department of Commerce (www.commerce.gov) supplies a large number of economic indicators, including industrial commodity indexes. Readers may also want to make use of commercial commodity indexes (for example, those offered by Dow Jones). While these indexes are aimed at investors, since they reflect daily fluctuations and provide analyses, such indexes can prove a valuable source of information including political and social events that might be important indi-cators of changes in volatile commodities.

While these sources can prove useful in determining the extent to which the prices you are paying are reasonable, they should also help you to be aware when price increases are coming.

Is a Price Increase Justified?

Your supplier has informed you that prices are going to go up. Is a price increase justified in this particular case? If you are regularly monitoring business trends and trends in commodities that are critical to your business, you may already have recognized that news of a price increase was coming. In such a case, the news just confirms what you expected, and the major question may be the extent of the increase.

You should also be aware when raw materials or products that your supplier requires in order to produce for you are increasing in price. In the first case, the market is speaking, and comparable prices are increasing. In the second case, costs are increasing, and market prices will soon rise.

Finally, our business practices and demands often impact supplier costs— costs that must be passed on to us if the supplier is to continue in business. For example, new quality demands or frequent changes in our forecast demand have implications that reasonably will result in increased prices. Thus, while we frequently seek to understand the supplier's cost structure in determining the appropriateness of price increases, we should also look to our own practices as a potential cause of increasing costs (and a potential source of cost containment or reductions).

Pricing Consistency

Frequently, suppliers present a range of prices for an item where the price depends on the quantity purchased. Such price schedules are either for particular quantities or for a range of quantities. Economies of scale, such as being able to spread fixed costs or lot costs such as setup costs over larger quantities, are the justification for the lower prices for larger quantities. Consistency of pricing across such price schedules means that as larger quantities are purchased, the average price in each price range, or for each larger quantity, should be less than for smaller quantities. This is not always the case. Opportunities for price negotiation are provided by such price-list inconsistencies. To determine if inconsistencies exist in a price schedule, a technique known as quantity discount analysis can be used. The example in Box 22–1 illustrates the general process for such an analysis for price range schedules.

When you have industry-standard products sold in a competitive marketplace, competitive pricing information along with awareness of external causes of price pressure may represent a cost-effective way to accomplish ensuring that the prices you are paying are appropriate. While price analysis is not as detailed and precise as cost analysis, it has the advantage of being relatively easy, not requiring cooperation and information from your suppliers, requiring relatively few resources (i.e., low in cost), and being relatively quick. Cost analysis is appropriate when price comparisons are not readily available and when detailed examination of supplier costs is desired in order to improve cost containment efforts, particularly when the supplier and the supply management organization can engage in collaborative efforts to reduce costs.

WHAT IS COST?

Cost is the value of resources required to produce a given good or service. In the context of this chapter, the term *cost* will be used to refer to the sum, or total, of all the categories of cost, including direct and indirect costs. Thus, the total cost associated with a given product can be broken down into components through cost analysis.

B O X   22–1

Quantity Discount Analysis

Price Range Price Breaks

(prices change according to quantity ranges).
To determine whether this is a consistent price schedule, it must be determined if there is an incremental decrease in the cost of each unit after each price break. This can be most easily done by setting up a table as follows where lines a and b are the quoted price schedule.

Line	Item				Price Breaks			
a	Quantity range (units)	0	1–10	11–20	21–30	31–200	201+	
b	Price per unit ($)	0	20.00	15.00	13.00	10.00	8.00	
c	Total cost at each minimum quantity (a min. × b) ($)	0	20.00	165.00	273.00	310.00	1,608.00	
d	Maximum quantity at each price range (c for next highest range. Divided by b for this range)	0	8	18	24	160		
e	Total cost at each maximum quantity (b × d) ($)	0	160.00	270.00	312.00	1,600		
f	Difference in total cost at maximum quantity (difference in e amounts) ($)		160.00	110.00	7.00	1,288.00		
g	Difference in quantities between maximum quantities (difference in d amounts)		8	10	6	136		
h	Price per unit per price range (f/g) ($)		20.00	11.00	7.00	9.47		

Notice that the per-unit price increases in the fourth range compared to the third range. This inconsistency provides a potential basis for price discussion and/or negotiation.

The information necessary for supplier cost analysis can be obtained in one of three ways.[14] In the first two approaches, information is obtained directly from the supplier, and in the third approach, costing is estimated through modeling. Information obtained from the supplier has the obvious benefit of being potentially both more comprehensive and more accurate. Where there is attention to obtaining cost information from our suppliers, the realization that such information is being used by the customer can also serve to promote attention to both the process

---

14 D. K. Burt, W. E. Norquist, and J. Anklesaria (1990). *Zero Base Pricing: Achieving World Class Competitiveness through Reduced All-in Costs*, Chicago: Probus Publishing.

of costing and the reasonableness of the associated costs on the part of the supplier. Thus, requesting cost information may substantially accomplish the cost containment that you desire.

Cost information can be obtained from the supplier either because of the relationship that your organization has with the supplier, or because of requirements as part of a request for proposal for a new purchase. Generally, in order to gain voluntary provision of costing information, a long-term relationship will be required. Among the benefits of trusting relationships is access to information and commitment to working together for mutual gain.

When suppliers are required to provide cost information at the time of new or expanded purchasing, there may be problems with completeness and accuracy of information. Further, compliance does not bring with it the same level of intention and effort that we can obtain when we are working with committed partners.

Finally, where cost information is not available from the supplier, cost modeling provides a tool for determining and understanding the behavior of key cost drivers. The next section describes ways to decompose cost information when such information is available and concludes with a discussion of cost modeling.

COST ANALYSIS

In a strict sense, analysis is the act of decomposing something into its component parts. Thus, cost analysis implies an attempt to determine the actual cost of producing something by seeking to determine the costs associated with various aspects of its production. In supply management, our concern is to establish the extent to which the prices we pay are reasonable and amenable to reduction. This suggests that supply professionals need to understand how the overall costs that figure in the purchase price arise (recall that this is only part of the total cost of ownership, which includes the selling organization's profit plus the purchasing organization's costs associated with ownership and use of the product). This requires looking at those costs that directly relate to production of each unit of the product (the direct costs) and those costs that are incurred in managing and providing for the production of the product as part of the overall production mix of the organization (the indirect costs).

Direct costs include labor actually attributable to production of the product and the materials utilized in the product. The relationship of these elements to the value of the product is obvious. The analyst may question the extent to which the correct methods or materials are used to be cost effective, in which case, this may become the focus of target and should costing as well as value analysis and engineering activities. Such activities are aimed at containing costs by bringing new thinking and product design to bear on meeting customer needs in a cost-effective manner. Innovation in supply management techniques, currently including ESI, may be required in order to impact these cost elements. However, the values of direct costs in product pricing are generally relatively easy to establish. Such is not the case for indirect costs.

Indirect costs include many categories of overhead. While some overhead is essential to the operation of any business, how overhead applies to a given product in aggregate form or at the unit level is frequently difficult to establish. As previously noted, these decisions and the extent to which such costs are considered reasonable are always the province of judgment.

If a supplier produces only one product, the firm's overhead must all be covered by the price charged for that product. Thus, allocation of overhead becomes a relatively easy matter, and each unit can be assumed to require overhead activity that is simply the total of overhead costs divided by the units produced. There are not many firms for which such simple logic applies.

When there are multiple products and multiple product lines, allocation of overhead and capital expenses becomes convoluted at a rate that accelerates rapidly as the complexity of the firm increases. In firms with multiple product lines and multiple divisions, we have never seen a situation where there was internal agreement about how overhead was allocated, because any approach that is taken will impact how various divisions and products are viewed from the perspective of profitability. If such disagreement is common within the firm, there should be little surprise that supply managers often question overhead allocation. The problem of overhead allocation is made worse by the fact that in many cases, overhead costs may exceed the cost of materials in a given product.[15] Such a reality provokes obvious interest among supply professionals in ensuring that suppliers are containing overhead costs.

Overhead costs need to both be allocated reasonably and be reasonable. Overhead and indirect costs should not be allocated to a given product except when they are reasonably necessary. For example, we would object if we were buying a mature product and found that the supplier was allocating engineering overhead across all its products, since none of that engineering effort was presently being directed toward design of our product. As another example, if we have a long-term contract for a given product, the allocation of sales overhead to our product would not be appropriate, since the sale has already been made and there is presumably no sales activity directed toward the account at this time.

One of the first challenges in evaluating the extent to which overhead costs are reasonable is to determine the method used to allocate such costs. A traditional method has been to allocate overhead based upon the revenues associated with a given product. Implicit in this approach is that it must cost more to manage a product that yields more revenue. Thus, a given product is assigned overhead costs that are equivalent in ratio to the total of overhead costs in the same ratio as are the product's revenues relative to the firm's (or division's, etc.) total revenues for a given period. Another approach is to allocate overhead in the same manner, but instead of using revenue as the basis for allocation, direct labor represents the comparison ratio.

---

15 Ibid.

BOX 22-2

Do You Prefer Overhead Allocation Based upon Revenues or Direct Labor Costs?

A company has two divisions. One division is involved in manufacturing office furniture systems and the other division provides businesses with office services, including printing, geographic information systems (GIS), mailing, and other services. As is the general case, material costs are more significant than are labor costs for the manufacturing division, and labor costs are the major cost for the office services division. The company follows typical practice for many firms by pooling overhead costs and allocating them based upon a single driver. The difference between allocation based upon revenues and allocation based upon direct labor is illustrated in the following table.

Overhead Allocation	Manufacturing	Office Services	Total
Revenues	$1,287,564	$978,465	$2,266,029
Direct labor costs	321,891	684,926	1,006,817
Total overhead			**613,545**
Revenue based	348,618	264,927	613,545
Direct labor based	196,158	417,387	613,545

Note that if overhead is allocated based upon revenues, the manufacturing division is allocated considerably more overhead costs than is the services division. The situation is reversed if overhead is allocated based upon direct labor costs. Your preference as a supply manager would depend on the division with which you are doing business.

Both revenue-based and direct-labor-based schemes for allocation of overhead suffer from obvious flaws. In the case of revenues, the product with the greatest revenues is frequently well-established, and thus, overhead is allocated to a product that probably requires relatively little effort outside of those associated with direct costs. Likewise, new products, etc., often require considerable activity beyond direct costs. Similarly, direct labor is not a reliable estimator of overhead activity.

This is the premise at the heart of a shift toward activity-based costing. Under such an approach, overhead costs are assigned to a product in proportion to the amount of overhead activity generated by that product. Assuming that overhead costs within a firm or division are appropriate, activity-based costing certainly represents a refinement in assigning those costs to production and is an approach likely to find favor with purchasers seeking to understand the roots of costs associated with products that they buy.

Activity-based costing provides numbers that are more accurately reflective of the costs associated with a product, but no approach for assigning overhead costs can assure that the associated costs are reasonable. Generally, reasonable costs are those that are minimally required to accomplish production now and into the future.

This applies to both direct and indirect costs. The analyst can only assess reasonableness from the perspective of what is required. This means that the analyst must understand the work being done and how management of this work must be accomplished. Generally, this can only be accomplished by experience. That is, the analyst must answer the question of what a given activity should cost. Such "should costing" may require the use of specialists from outside the supply management profession. By using such specialists (engineers, machinists, etc.), supply professionals can leverage their experience in determining reasonable costs. It bears noting that with increasing outsourcing, the previous internal experts may be particularly adept at producing should-cost figures.

For example, in should costing a compressor fan, there is need to determine foundry costs and machining costs. By finding experts who know about foundry work, the supply professional can determine the work and associated costs for producing the rough fan. The supply professional then needs to work with experts on machining to determine the costs of removing metal and finishing the final form. Increasingly, organizations are also finding that it is useful to capture their cost experience for tasks, such as those just described, utilizing modern knowledge management techniques (i.e., the use of databases) for future reference.

In services, supply professionals need to be aware that the intangible nature of the work to be accomplished may render the utilization of trained professionals within the disciplines for which services (e.g., lawyers, engineers, and training) are being sought critical to efforts at cost containment. Guidance from such experts promotes an understanding of activities that need to be completed by contractors, such that an accurate statement of work can be completed. Careful development of the statement of work may be critical, because these statements go a long way toward ensuring the accuracy of should costing. Every activity within a statement of work represents a cost element both for cost estimates and for the actual tasks to be accomplished. Greater detail relating to statements of work, particularly with respect to purchasing consulting services, can be found in Chapter 35 of this book.

In addition to classification as direct and indirect, costs can also be classified according to the extent to which they vary with levels of production. Costs that vary directly with changes in the number of units being produced are termed variable costs. Such costs include direct materials and labor. These costs should remain relatively constant from a per-unit perspective.

Fixed costs vary from a per-unit perspective. Such costs include the cost of the plant, production equipment, and associated costs such as insurance and taxes. In an idealized sense, truly fixed costs remain, even if there is no production. Obviously, some costs fall between fully variable and truly fixed costs. These costs vary in a stepwise fashion with changes in production, such as is the case when certain types of labor and equipment have to be added at certain points in order to meet production demand, or they may vary in another pattern that roughly parallels changes in production. We can term such patterns as stepwise and semivariable cost patterns. In order to understand costs that do not remain constant across the entirety of the relevant range of production (i.e., the range of production levels that are required or will be required for our purposes), we must understand capacity limitations facing the supplier.

The importance of fixed costs and those that are not proportionally variable with production is that they are the source of economies of scale. To the extent that fixed costs are constant, at least in the near term over the relevant range of production, larger production volume yields a smaller per-unit fixed cost. Thus, the total cost for a given unit is often smaller if the unit is part of a large volume, because the sum of variable costs plus a smaller portion of the fixed costs is lower than is the sum of (constant) variable costs plus a larger portion of the fixed costs with smaller production quantities. Semivariable costs, depending upon the behavior of these costs within the relevant range, may also yield unit cost advantage, but the extent to which this is the case depends on precise production levels and must be verified.

Such economies of scale are very attractive but also often overstated. For example, Toyota has shown that by better managing smaller production volumes so that inventories are reduced and production wastes are minimized, they can reduce unit costs below those of automotive manufacturers emphasizing large production volumes.[16] In the case of Toyota, work process innovations have resulted in reduced overhead requirements in order to control and manage production. In seeking cost reductions, the effective supply manager must look beyond the numbers and simple models in order to understand the processes that yield the cost numbers. Understanding that how work is organized affects cost numbers has been an important part of the Toyota success story.

By analyzing cost information and categorizing costs according to direct, indirect, variable, and fixed categories, a supply manager can prioritize concerns. In fact, the greatest power might be found in combining the categories. For example, direct costs are readily traced to production of the supplies that we are purchasing. Further, to the extent that direct costs are variable, the cost elements to which such costs apply are directly consumed or used in production. Accomplishing changes in these costs may require product and/or process redesign and a great deal of shared design effort. Alternatively, supply managers often accomplish cost reductions by helping suppliers improve their purchasing practices. At the very least, direct variable costs are likely to provide a situation in which analysts agree with supplier costing.

Indirect costs are not subject to direct tracing to the cost object. As previously noted, the approach to assigning such costs to a given product is through allocation. Allocation of fixed indirect costs represents a situation where well-intentioned people with different points of view can readily disagree. For example, the extent to which a supply professional feels that costs associated with

16 H. T. Johnson and A. Bröms (2000). *Profit beyond Measure: Extraordinary Results through Attention to Work and People*, New York: The Free Press. See also J. P. Womack and D. T. Jones (1996). Lean Thinking: Banish Waste and Create Wealth in Your Corporation, New York: Simon & Schuster.

corporate headquarters or a plant in which many of the supplier's product lines (many of which are sold to other customers) should be allocated to a given product for which a cost analysis is being conducted is likely to differ from how the supplier sees such allocation.

Thus, supply management professionals are much more likely to question cost allocations associated with fixed indirect costs than to contest direct variable costs. In the first case, divergence arises out of questions of appropriateness and judgment at a relatively high level. In the latter case, informed divergence requires a much deeper understanding of readily traced costs. The supply manager contesting direct variable costs must either possess or obtain consultative (perhaps based upon resources internal to the organization, but perhaps not) competence to understand materials and processes essential to production of what is purchased.

Between these two extremes are fixed direct costs, such as supervisory personnel directly associated with production of the purchased product, and variable indirect costs, such as utility costs associated with production of multiple product lines. Of the two, once again we see that indirect costs provide considerable grist for contention. However, the astute supply professional can also often find room for substantial savings in fixed direct costs, particularly since such costs may be excessive given patterns in our consumption of production capacity.

The concepts discussed here can as well be applied to services as manufacturing. For example, the concept of unit costs can be applied to the delivery of telephone services or data processing. In such cases, the unit of interest may readily be determined by observing how revenues are generated, for example, by minute for telephone service and by hour for data processing. Fixed, variable, and semifixed costs could be determined just as would be the case for a manufacturing setting (equipment versus labor, etc.), as could also direct and indirect costs (direct labor versus headquarters, supervision for services to multiple customers, etc.).

While many other approaches can be taken in categorizing costs, these basic categories have proven useful in supply management. Additional information regarding presentation of costing information can be found in managerial accounting texts, as well as among the works cited here.

We now turn our attention to other concepts useful to supply professionals seeking cost savings. One of the major tools available to the cost analyst in determining the extent to which costs can be reduced is based upon the concept of the experience, or learning, curve.

The Learning Curve

One of the most important relationships in the analysis of cost, and of particular concern in predicting decreasing costs, is the learning curve. In simple terms, the learning curve represents quantification of the benefits that derive from experience doing work, but this benefit is only available where learning can take place. That is, generally we expect the greatest benefit from learning where the greatest labor is involved or where there are highly complex processes associated with creation of a good or service. The greatest impact from learning usually occurs in the early stages of production of a new or significantly revised product, or following implementation of a new or modified production process. In highly automated work, we would not expect to see much benefit from learning, except to the extent to which the operators learn to make better use of the technology.

The learning rate is equal to the amount or cost of labor that unit N of production requires compared to unit $N/2$. In other words, as cumulative production doubles, to what extent is labor reduced? For example, if for a particular product it is observed that as cumulative production doubles, labor requirements per unit decrease by 20 percent, then the 20 percent is called the *learning rate* and the process would be said to have an 80 percent *learning curve* (100 percent – 20 percent = 80 percent).

The learning rate can vary considerably, but experience suggests that for labor-intensive products, learning curves of approximately 60 percent are possible, while for highly automated processes, the curve may be 95 percent or higher.

Cost savings from learning apply to both manufacturing and the production of services, so as long as labor is involved. Services that contain a routine element of labor are good candidates for a learning effect, for example, professional services if information must routinely be collected and standard forms or statements produced (these are often also subject to some degree of automation as the process becomes clear).

To determine the learning rate, you can review recent production or, if data are available, compare the current process with similar processes for which the rate is known. In other cases, you may have to observe the process. Once the learning rate is known for a given process, you can apply the concept in estimating cost reductions.

Tables and instructions for calculating the learning rate directly from observations over a period of production are available in many operations management texts.

Our discussion of cost analysis up to this point has assumed access to cost data. When such data are not available, the supply professional can still estimate cost elements utilizing cost modeling.

Modeling Costs

Building models that utilize cost elements to estimate or essentially forecast supplier prices is a common practice in supply management. Such models serve both to establish and determine the levels of variable costs (post hoc cost analysis to see what costs are and should costing to determine what costs should be if accompanied by product and process knowledge) and as a tool for use by supply management and sales personnel in costing new production (should costing to see what costs should be, and target costing to establish costs to be met in new products).

A simple, underappreciated approach to investigating the relationship between a variable and product cost is through the use of graphical analysis. In order to do such an analysis, the supply professional constructs a scatter diagram, portraying the cost driver on the horizontal (x) axis and that driven, the product cost, or some element thereof for more detailed analyses on the vertical (y) axis. A point is then plotted for each datum consisting of the value for the cost driver and the relevant cost. If, when this is done, the points approximate a line that ascends, we have a positive relationship between the driver and the cost. A positive relationship indicates that as the value of the cost driver increases (e.g., as the size of a product increases, suggesting that more material is required in its production), the cost increases (e.g., the purchase price that we pay). Figure 22–1 provides such a scatter diagram.

If the line descends as we move to the right, we have a negative relationship. A negative relationship indicates that as the magnitude of a suspected driver increases (to use the same example, as size increases), the cost decreases (we pay less, as might be the case when it is difficult to make something in a small size, resulting in lower product yield).

Other patterns might also be observed and can be interpreted in a similar manner. For example, it may be the case that a product is costly to make in either small or large sizes, but relatively less expensive midrange. In such a case, we would expect that a curvilinear pattern would exist between size and purchase price, with relatively high prices on both extremes, and a lower price for medium-sized

F I G U R E   22–1

Scatter Diagram for Price as a Function of Size for Hypothetical Seals

Note the positive correlation, such that as size increases, the organization has been paying more for the seals. In this case, $r = .97$ and $r^2 = .94$, suggesting that most of the purchase price can be explained by the size of the seals. In most cases, the relationship will not be this clear.

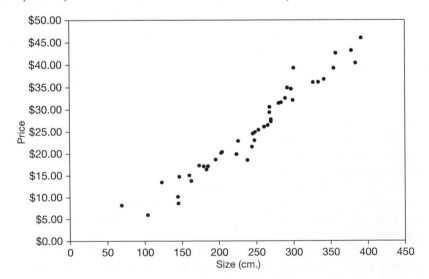

product (and, if this is not the case, it might induce the supply professional to seek explanations for high midrange prices or to express concern about inadequate pricing in order to recover costs at one of the extremes).

While scatter diagrams provide considerable power in a simple and readily interpreted tool for investigating costing, they should be accompanied by causal logic, since the observed pattern represents the correlation. That is, unless you have reason to believe that something is important in costing, you may want to be cautious about interpreting a relationship as indicating that something does cause differences in cost.

One additional note: The correlation coefficient provides an indication of how strong of a relationship exists. Excel can provide you with the correlation coefficient (look under Tools and then in the scroll-down list that appears when you click on the Data Analysis add-in—additional instructions are available through Excel help). You should be aware that the standard correlation coefficient only applies to a linear relationship and, hence, will underestimate the extent of curvilinear relationships (although transformations can be applied to overcome this, a topic that is covered in advanced statistics texts). If you square the correlation coefficient (r^2), this provides you with the proportion of the variation in cost that is accounted for by your proposed cost driver (obviously, the higher r^2, the more important the proposed cost driver).

More sophisticated models can be constructed using linear regression, once again available under the analysis add-in under the Tools menu item in Excel. Although many resources are available to aid you in such efforts, including basic coverage (often under the topic of forecasting) in most business statistics textbooks, NASA's Johnson Space Center provides an online *Parametric Cost Estimating Handbook* that is a rich resource for adventurous practitioners (available at www.jsc.nasa.gov/bu2/handbooks/index.htm).[17]

Conceptually, this is a relatively easy task, often only requiring that we analyze information that we should have available in commodity databases for critical purchases. In one common incarnation, the person seeking to do such modeling obtains the prices for recent acquisitions, along with a listing of salient product features for each purchase (this should make the value of a commodity record obvious). These elements are then assembled into a database, and a regression analysis is conducted to relate product features to purchase price.

For example, imagine that your firm manufactures a product for which O-rings are an important feature (the product must be assembled so that oil is sealed in and environmental contaminants sealed out). You might then obtain the purchase price along with product and order features. These rings vary in both diameter and the specific formulation of the ring material.

---

17 This URL provides access to a handy online version that is easily searched and browsed. A second edition, sponsored by the Department of Defense, and now titled *Parametric Estimating Handbook*, can be downloaded from the International Society of Parametric Analysts (ISPA) Web site at http://www.ispa-cost.org.

The regression analysis dialogue in Excel makes easy work of conducting a regression analysis. Once you have the price (the dependent variable) and various potential price predictors (the independent variables, such as ring material) placed in columns, you select the Tools menu item at the top of the screen, then select the data analysis add-in (you may have to install the add-ins, if you have not already done so), and then select Regression Analysis from the listed options in the new list that will appear. At this point, a new dialogue box appears. You can then enter the addresses or select the cells for the independent variable and the dependent variables, just as you would in the dialogue boxes for other tasks in Excel. If you have labeled the columns to reflect the variables, you should also select the Labels box, so that Excel will use your labels to label the results. In general, it is desirable to have the results of the analysis displayed on a new worksheet, so that there is no danger of overwriting data.

If you are going to use regression analysis on a regular basis, you may find that the constraints associated with Excel, including a requirement that the variables that you are analyzing be placed contiguously (side by side) in columns, becomes a real problem if you decide that one or more variables should be omitted from the analysis. Instead, a dedicated statistical analysis package may be worthwhile since they will provide you with much more power and, in spite of the apparent complexity of these packages, ultimately make your task much easier.

SPSS is a very powerful package that is readily available, but its apparent complexity may intimidate relatively new users (www.spss.com). An alternative statistics package that may have a slightly flatter learning curve and is used in many business statistics courses is Minitab (www.minitab.com).

An example of regression cost modeling was recently conducted by a student who is a purchasing manager at an organization that makes gaskets (the details have been fictionalized to protect the identity of the business). We started by looking at size and composition of the gasket and attempted to predict purchase price on a per-gasket basis. For composition of the gaskets, we coded the materials as an ordinal variable (i.e., we ranked the presumed costs of the materials, but did not specify precise costs since these supplier costs were not known). The output from such an analysis is depicted in Figure 22–2. Note that the model is significant (see the ANOVA portion of the output), and the r^2 suggests that the model accounts for about 93.5 percent of the variance in pricing (but in multiple regression the r^2 is considered an optimistic estimate; the adjusted r^2 at 0.929 or 92.9 percent represents a better estimate of the population). Thus, the model is very efficient as a predictor.

The summary for the coefficients tells us that the estimated cost is $8.90 plus 0.57 times the value for the type of material, plus 0.03 times the size of the gasket in centimeters. This use of unstandardized coefficients allows us to estimate price, but it fails to tell us which factors were most important in determining price, since the units associated with each unstandardized coefficient is that used in measuring the particular variable. The standardized coefficient is stated in terms of standard deviations, and thus, the dimensions are the same for each of the slope coefficients, allowing comparison. Note that while size had a smaller unstandardized coefficient than material, it has the larger beta coefficient, indicating that it is more important in determining the price of the gasket than is the type of material. Note also that both coefficients are significant (if we set significance at $p = 0.05$, as is generally used).

The summary report in Figure 22–2 is from SPSS. The report in Excel would look similar, except that it does not provide Beta coefficients. Although this example illustrates a successful modeling attempt, such is not always the case. The minimum level at which a model should be considered successful is a matter of

---

F I G U R E   22–2

Regression Output (from SPSS)

Regression

Variables Entered/Removed[b]

Model	Variables Entered	Variables Removed	Method
1	Material, Size[a]		Enter

a. All requested variables entered.

b. Dependent Variable: Price

Model Summary

Model	R	R Square	Adjusted R Square	Std. Error of the Estimate
1	.967[a]	.935	.929	.9315

a. Predictors: (Constant), Material, Size

ANOVA[b]

Model		Sum of Squares	df	Mean Square	F	Sig.
1	Regression	261.779	2	130.890	150.853	.000[a]
	Residual	18.221	21	.868		
	Total	280.000	23			

a. Predictors: (Constant), Material, Size

b. Dependent Variable: Price

Coefficients[a]

Model		Unstandardized Coefficients		Standardized Coefficients	t	Sig.
		B	Std. Error	Beta		
1	(Constant)	8.900	.818		10.880	.000
	Size	3.737E-02	.005	.758	7.039	.000
	Material	.575	.264	.235	2.180	.041

a. Dependent Variable: Price

judgment, but in general, if your model accounts for less than about 70 percent of the variance in pricing, it will not be very helpful in understanding how pricing is being accomplished. Under such circumstances, there is often temptation to resort to mathematical sophistication instead of addressing a more fundamental message.

When Models Fail

Given any set of data, it is possible to fit those data if you are willing to resort to a polynomial of high enough order. The hunt for such a solution may attract the attention of some, but the practical importance of such endeavors is nonexistent. While wasting a great deal of effort, beyond some reasonable level, the search for a way to fit your data will lead only to a one-time solution, because it will fit your current data but fail to fit data in the future. Such solutions are not useful in our context because cost modeling is fundamentally about gaining an understanding of what is happening in order to predict and manage the future.

Once again, your best judgment is required in this situation, but when sensible efforts, given reasonable data, fail to produce a useful model, it is time to take a look at the processes that yielded the data. Are you using consistent processes in making your purchases? Do your suppliers have a consistent process for pricing? It is safe to assume that when there are consistent processes, we should be able to model those processes. Conversely, when a reasonable model is not found, it may serve as a valuable indication that management intervention is required in order to ensure that a process for doing the work is designed and implemented.

There are many approaches to modeling costs, and study in this area can be richly rewarding. However, do not lose sight of the extent to which our numbers are just ways of summarizing the complexities of products and work. Perhaps the most important information from efforts at cost analysis is the extent to which we actually understand the processes that are summarized in the numbers that we scrutinize. Ultimately, good processes can be modeled, and when we have the right processes, we will get good data, and cost prediction and containment become real possibilities.

USING COST ANALYSIS IN
LEADING-EDGE SUPPLY MANAGEMENT

As previously noted, supply management professionals will claim that a major reason for avoiding cost analysis is that they fear damaging relationships with critical suppliers. We believe that this unfortunate perception is the result of a long history in which purchasing was conducted primarily to coerce the lowest possible purchase price out of suppliers using any means possible to browbeat suppliers into a competitive struggle that resulted in wins for the purchasers at the expense of the suppliers. The upside of the fear is that supply professionals have clearly gotten the message that the old ways are not appropriate to today's business environment. The downside is that many supply professionals may not be as cost effective as they could be, which we have seen to result in surprising claims of price savings when relationships are once again exposed to competition.

Another problem that supply professionals confront in conducting cost analyses is in obtaining the information that they need. Since cost information is usually obtained from the supplier, we are counting on the accuracy of that information when inaccuracy may favor the supplier. Thus, supply management professionals need to be able to assess the accuracy of cost data by comparison to independent figures. This can be done by either obtaining comparisons from several suppliers or by developing our own cost estimates. Thus, in working with suppliers on cost analyses, the supply manager is challenged both by potential inadequacies of previous efforts and by potential inadequacies in information and knowledge. These possibilities reasonably provoke a certain amount of fear as supply professionals approach suppliers with new requirements.

The truly effective supply manager does not ignore cost analysis in order to save relationships. Instead, she or he uses price and cost analysis to drive successful relationships with suppliers. At the leading edge, the tools of price and cost analysis are being used to promote win-win solutions that ensure that our partnerships with suppliers create sustainable levels of profit while delivering cost-effective products into the marketplace. One realm where we see this occurring is when value engineering and target costing are used collaboratively between purchasing organizations and suppliers early in the product design process to ensure successful, cost-effective new products. Such target costing brings a new level of performance to early supplier involvement.

A recent report in *Practix* described how a manufacturer in the aeronautical industry utilized value engineering and target costing to drive effective ESI implementation.[18] For new products, value engineering focuses on determining and successfully meeting customer requirements while minimizing costs. In order to accomplish product design that meets these requirements, target costing establishing the presumed market price (i.e., what the market will bear) for the final product allows internal experts in both product and production process technology to establish realistic target costs at the component level. The challenge is to establish aggressive but realistic targets. Many supply management organizations find management of such activities challenging because of lack of experience and lack of accurate, clean data.

Such activities can also be used with services. For example, in providing business services, customer requirements for a particular service (e.g., design, layout, and printing of business documents) can be determined, a market-competitive price can be established, and then the materials incorporated into the service along with the process for delivering the service can be designed to accomplish such a price. Note that a higher degree of standardization in the delivery of the service than is often observed may be necessary to obtain the advantages of value engineering in the service setting.

---

18 Smith and Zsidisin, "Early Supplier Involvement at MRD."

Likewise, the selection of suppliers that are capable of collaborating on projects at the initial design stage can be challenging. Supplier selection for ESI projects needs to incorporate engineers, commodity experts, and sourcing personnel in a process that draws upon internal knowledge of the industry and of supplier performance. Only organizationally mature suppliers, with adequate competencies, who are strategically aligned with your organization and have a history of excellence in supplier performance, are good candidates for engagement in ESI.

Sharing target costs and the bases of their derivation with the potential suppliers is critical to driving cost reductions. Only with such understanding can potential suppliers begin to contribute to the design of the product and make progress in production process design. Final selection of suppliers should incorporate knowledge of their core competencies, capabilities and progress in product development, and evidence of successful performance. Supplier selection should also incorporate consideration of technical and rough pricing information provided by the supplier.

Target costing based upon a value focus can help to ensure that designs address customer needs in a cost-effective manner, instead of having design efforts fall prey to a tendency toward excessively elegant, and costly, designs. Early involvement of supply professionals and suppliers in product design helps to ensure that cost containment is designed into the product proactively, instead of relegating cost containment to a reactive afterthought.

We now turn our attention to how the supply function can work to ensure that supply management activities are also designed and managed in a cost-effective manner.

SUPPLY MANAGEMENT'S ROLE IN SUPPLIER COST CONTAINMENT

There are many approaches, tools, and techniques that can be applied to managing supply relationships that are presented in this book. They all potentially have cost implications. It is critical to remember that our intent is to create value for the customer, so anything that we do in managing these relationships should add performance that exceeds the costs of the activity, or the activity should reduce costs.

Problem identification and containment may also have tremendous cost implications. Supply management techniques that address risk are intended to positively affect value by reducing potential costs. However, care should be exercised to ensure that these activities are cost effective.

When we look to value creation in supply relationships, it should be clear that today's supply professional has a role in assisting suppliers in cost containment. It is not enough to demand that suppliers reduce costs. We must also make sure that our supply management practices do not drive costs up for our suppliers. What do we do that increases prices?

How we order, forecasting failures, the time performance that is demanded, inflexibility in specifications, and how we pay suppliers all have cost implications. For example, the process for ordering and the timing of orders can increase administrative and paperwork costs, as well as requiring unnecessary setup costs of our suppliers. To a substantial extent, careful implementation of e-commerce solutions has substantial potential to reduce these costs, but so does old-fashioned communication.

While how we communicate can increase supplier costs, so can what we communicate. When we fail to provide accurate forecasts, costs incurred by the supplier can include unnecessary setups and changeovers, rushed orders, and excessive inventories. One solution is to develop better internal forecasting capabilities. Perhaps more elegant is to work with the supplier to reduce lead time in both organizations and between them such that forecasts do not need to extend so far into the future. At the limit, forecasting accuracy is greatest when lead times are short enough that actual demand drives production.

Creating situations where delivery timing does not create problems for suppliers is another area where the best solutions are the result of joint effort between the organizations. Only through understanding of the constraints on each party can equitable, cost-effective solutions be reached.

The previous section on ESI in this chapter makes it clear that joint efforts in product design can have tremendous cost-reducing potential when the purchasing organization leverages core competencies of world-class suppliers. Concurrent design with suppliers can go a long way toward addressing costly specifications, as well as addressing inventory costs, raw material issues, and such concerns as design for manufacturability (which, if ignored can result in incredibly costly production problems and/or extensive redesign).

In some cases, development of the competencies and the ability to collaborate in design will require time and supplier development since the number of world-class suppliers is limited. In any case, specification flexibility, where such is possible, has long been associated with cost savings.

Finally, when cost is at issue, it is common to hear discussion of delaying supplier payment and other payment techniques aimed at easing cash flow for the purchasing organization. There may be situations in which there are no alternatives, but in general, such behavior merely increases costs for the supplier. Ultimately, such costs must be passed on to the customer. A fundamental reality is that there are no free lunches, so we pay in the end!

Supply professionals who work diligently to streamline supply management practices with the purpose of value creation not only ultimately reduce costs, they also enhance supplier relationships. Such endeavors require knowledge of current organizational practices and a constant search for new solutions.

Negotiations represent an important part of resolving supplier cost concerns. In particular, in a rapidly evolving business climate, ongoing negotiations may be one of the most important aspects of cost containment.

TABLE 22–1

When to Negotiate*

Issue	Aim of Negotiations
Price of materials incorporated in the purchased product is likely to increase.	Develop contractual provisions for price escalations.
Setting standards for price, quality, timeliness, and service.	Develop contractual provisions regarding trade-offs among requirements.
Quality concerns.	Promote supplier understanding of requirements and implications.
Uncertainty about design efforts, materials content, and labor required for new products.	Reduce uncertainty.
Rapidly changing requirements.	Develop a process for dealing with changes.
An internal customer has established specifications that favor a particular supplier and/or a stated supplier preference.	Internal negotiations need to determine the legitimacy of the preference; where not legitimate, the importance of flexibility needs to be emphasized. Negotiations with the supplier need to be conducted in such a manner as to ensure that the supplier does not take advantage of the situation.

*Burt et al. present an extended discussion of this topic.[19]

COST AND PRICE IN NEGOTIATIONS

All too frequently, those with technical aptitude toward price and cost analyses lack the social orientation necessary in effective negotiators. However, attaining necessary cost and pricing information, as well as resolving the issues that result from useful price and cost analyses, requires effective negotiation techniques. Those most effective in promoting cost-driven value must accomplish analytical competence while also recognizing and leveraging opportunities for negotiation.

While specific advice for the process of negotiation is covered elsewhere in this book, we will present some guidance regarding situations requiring negotiation and the aim of negotiation efforts in resolving issues that can impact cost. In general, negotiation is warranted whenever there is a lack of clarity or potential for a lack of clarity regarding requirements and how costs are to be addressed. Negotiations should address provisions for likely events and clarification of areas of potential misunderstanding. Table 22–1 presents a summary of cost-related negotiation issues.

While the situations presented in Table 22–1 are generally related to formal negotiations, opportunities for informal negotiations exist any time that there are

19 D. K. Burt, W. E. Norquist, and J. Anklesaria (1990). *Zero Base Pricing: Achieving World Class Competitiveness through Reduced All-in Costs*. Chicago: Probus Publishing

two or more perspectives on a course of action. Even informal discussions of future activities can have profound cost implications, and the wise supply professional should be vigilant in seeking to influence resolution toward cost-effective supply performance that results in mutual benefits for the supplier and the purchasing organization.

SUMMARY

Supplier price and cost analysis is a valuable part of the work for supply management professionals today. When such analyses are conducted within a strategic framework, they can support appropriate supplier relationships and form the foundation of an enhanced reputation for the supply management profession.

There are a large number of avenues for the conduct of price and cost analyses. Figure 22–3 provides a flow diagram for decisions related to use of the tools discussed in this chapter. Fundamentally, when market dynamics provide a reasonable framework for determining the appropriateness of prices, traditional price analysis may prove adequate to your purposes, since the major concern is competitiveness of the pricing you are receiving from your supplier.

FIGURE 22–3

Flow Chart for Supplier Price and Cost Analysis

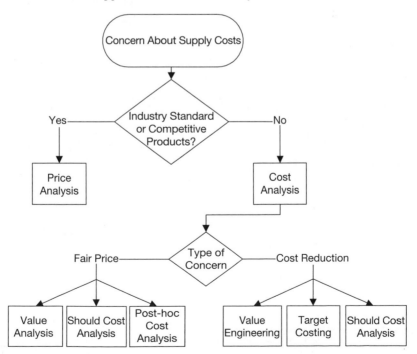

When competition is either absent or substantially compromised by critical differentiating product features, it is generally not reasonable to assume that traditional price comparison techniques will meet your needs. In such cases, cost analysis may be useful. However, the monopolistic nature of the market dynamics may not justify such efforts, since the supply manager may effectively have little choice but to pay the supplier's price. In general, a collaborative relationship with the supplier will be required in order to obtain cost information and for cost analysis to be useful in reducing product prices. For example, joint product design represents a context where cost information may be supplied by the supplier and where cost analysis may be effective.

If price increases are your primary concern, and pricing concerns are limited to overall market dynamics (e.g., general inflationary pressures) or commodity fluctuations for critical components of the purchased product, an informal price analysis may prove useful. Your scanning of the environment may allow you to address the appropriate course with price analysis, often without the need for a formal process (see the section titled "Is a Price Increase Justified?" earlier in this chapter).

This chapter has provided a brief overview of tools and techniques available to aid supply professionals in accomplishing their role in cost containment. These approaches should be applied with caution, judgment, and a clear view of how the relationships with the suppliers affected by price and cost analyses fit within the strategy of the organization employing the person conducting such analyses. As noted earlier, it may well be the case that price and cost analyses are often avoided because of fears that their use can be damaging to supplier relationships. There is

---

B O X 22–3

Recap of Cost Analysis Terms

Value engineering. Proactive design activities focused on meeting the customer's product performance requirements at the lowest possible cost.

Value analysis. Analysis of product and process design after design activities have been completed. During production, value analysis focuses on improving the product or producing the product less expensively.

Target costing. Establishing the price of a product before product and process design activities. This generally respresents the maximum price at which it is presumed that a product will be competitive in the marketplace. Target costing can be done at both the final product level and the component level. At the component level, target costing is based upon decomposing the target cost for the final product so as to establish the component costs necessary in order to meet the target cost for the final product. Target costing provides goals at the stage in design activities when product and process changes can readily be made to meet the targets.

Should-cost analysis. Establishing the best-case costs for production of a product once the product has been designed.

Post hoc cost analysis. Attempting to reconstruct cost elements from available information. Cost modeling represents a post hoc approach to cost analysis.

little reason to fear such damage in situations where professionals make appropriate use of the tools as described here. For greater detail on the technical aspects of price and cost analysis, there are numerous articles and texts available, as well as information available on the Internet. The books listed in the Bibliography are likely to be of particular interest to readers engaged in supplier price and cost analysis. However, clarity about your strategic intent and a clear sense of your purpose in conducting such analyses will always be your best guide in how to proceed.

BIBLIOGRAPHY

The books listed here are particularly useful as references in supplier price and cost analysis.

The following two books provide good coverage of the tools and techniques associated with supplier price and cost analysis:

Burt, D. K., W. E. Norquist, and J. Anklesaria (1990). *Zero Base Pricing: Achieving World Class Competitiveness through Reduced All-in Costs.* Chicago: Probus Publishing.

Newman, R.G. (1992). *Supplier Price Analysis: A Guide for Purchasing, Accounting and Financial Analysts.* New York: Quorum Books.

The following two books provide a solid foundational presentation of strategic and supplier management aspects of supplier price and cost analysis:

Nelson, D., P. E. Moody, and J. Stegner (2001). *The Purchasing Machine: How the Top Ten Companies Use Best Practices to Manage Their Supply Chains.* New York: The Free Press.

Östring, P. (2004). *Profit-Focused Supplier Management: How to Identify Risks and Recognize Opportunities.* New York: AMACOM.

CHAPTER 23

TOTAL COST OF OWNERSHIP

LISA M. ELLRAM, PH.D., C.P.M., CMA
Richard and Lorie Allen Professor of Business
Professor of Supply Chain Management
College of Business
Colorado State University

INTRODUCTION

On a hot summer day, a swim in a nice, refreshing pool may sound wonderful. If you live in a place like Florida or Arizona, it also may sound great that many people have built-in swimming pools, because when purchasing a preexisting home, there is a high probability that it will come with a pool. Some people really want a pool. Others, who have never had a pool, might view it as a nice, but not necessary amenity. They won't pay extra for it, but if it is there, they may use it on occasion. But many of these "accidental" pool owners become disgruntled later when they realize the true cost of owning their "free" pool. The water is constantly evaporating and needs to be refilled. That can increase the water bill by $120 a year. And then there is the pool pump, which runs 4 to 6 hours a day in the cooler months and 8 to 10 hours a day in the warmer months. That adds up to about $300 a year in incremental electricity bills. The pool needs to be drained and acid-washed each year, for another $150. Then there are maintenance issues, such as problems with the pump, the skimmer, or the vacuum. These can add an average of another $500 per year. If you hire a service to clean the pool and monitor the chemicals, that is about another $1,200 per year. For people having a pool put in, the cost of the pool is considerably more than the initial investment. Even if you move into a house that already has a pool, there is still an additional cost of around $2,270 a year to own a pool, assuming you do not heat the pool.

As shown in Table 23–1, if you use the pool 20 times per year, the true cost of using it (not including the initial investment) is $113.50 per usage! Some people might think this is a small price to pay for their own private pool. Others would be appalled. What we have just done is looked at the total cost of ownership of a pool. While it gave us the answer to the question regarding what it costs to own a pool that was included with an existing house, it did not give us the answer to whether or not we should have a pool. That is where human judgment and preference comes in.

TABLE 23–1

Total Cost of Ownership for the Operating Costs of a Swimming Pool[*]

Item	Annual Cost ($)
Extra water	$120.00
Additional electricity to run pump	300.00
General maintenance and repairs	500.00
Annual acid wash and fill	150.00
Weekly cleaning and chemicals	1,200.00
Total annual operating costs	2,270.00
Cost per use assuming 20 uses per year	113.50

[*]Assumes that the swimming pool exists in a home that we purchase, so there is no initial investment.

This chapter explores the concept of total cost of ownership, which is defined here as a philosophy for developing an understanding of all relevant supply chain-related costs of a particular purchase transaction or process. From a business standpoint, the process can be an internal process such as accounts payable, a supply chain process such as customer fulfillment, or the outsourcing of a process. In supply chain management, total cost of ownership often focuses on the cost of doing business with a particular supplier for a particular good or service.[1] Total cost of ownership (TCO) considers total cost of acquisition, use and administration, maintenance, and disposal of a given item or service. As will be presented later, TCO modeling does not actually require precise calculation of all costs, but looks at major cost issues and costs that may be relevant to the decision at hand. Total cost of ownership analysis focuses on quantifiable costs. The soft issues that cannot be quantified, such as user preference, must still be considered in a nonquantifiable way in the final analysis.

FRAMING TCO

In understanding the proper use of TCO analysis, it is important to frame it versus other cost management approaches. *Price analysis* involves analyzing a supplier's price, including terms and conditions, without reference to the underlying costs. *Cost analysis* focuses on how much it costs for the supplier to produce and deliver an item or service to its customer. It includes elements such as labor, packaging, raw materials, overhead, and transportation. Understanding such costs may be helpful when performing a sophisticated TCO analysis. It is also relevant if the supplier is willing to work with the organization on reducing TCO. Such cooperation is growing in practice.

Cost from a buyer's perspective is analogous to the TCO concept. Rather than simply buying based on price, the buyer should have a method for determining what

---

1 Mary Lu Harding (1996). "Defining and Calculating TCO," *NAPM InfoEdge*, August, vol. 1, no. 14, pp. 1–8.

a particular purchase really costs the organization, including more obvious issues such as transportation, duties, and on-time delivery, and more difficult to identify issues such as the cost of a supplier field failure and the education, training, and administrative support required to work with a supplier.

Total cost of ownership is not a new technique by any means.[2,3] It is a philosophy receiving increased visibility and concern among organizations for a variety of reasons, including the growing emphasis on strategic cost management.

STRATEGIC COST MANAGEMENT

Strategic cost management focuses on getting the best value. The premise of strategic cost management is that costs should never be managed or reduced in isolation. Rather they should be managed while simultaneously considering the value proposition of the organization, and the supply chain in which the organization operates. Managing costs without relation to the bigger picture can lead to value erosion.[4]

Likewise, total cost of ownership analysis should always be conducted in the context of how decisions affect other members of the supply chain and the value provided to the customer. With that in mind, any change that an organization undertakes that is not completely transparent to the customer must be analyzed in the context of how it affects revenue, as well as costs associated with serving the customer. As an example, a well-known manufacturer of printers suffered from early product failure when one of its suppliers switched to a cheaper grade of plastic to save money. Looking only at price, this was a good decision. However, ultimately, the company had to put a fix in place to resolve the customers' problems, or suffer long-term loss of reputation, good will, and sales. The fix cost considerably more than the amount saved on the inexpensive plastic.[5] Thus, it was a poor decision from a TCO perspective.

Globalization and Outsourcing

Two significant and accelerating trends that require TCO modeling for valid data analysis and decision making are globalization and outsourcing. As firms buy increasingly from places like China and Central America due to low prices, they may incur a number of other costs. These include costs such as increased inventory levels, higher transportation costs, differential quality levels, differential reliability levels,

---

2 Joseph L. Cavinato (1992). "A Total Cost/Value Model for Supply Chain Competitiveness," *Journal of Business Logistics,* vol. 13, no. 2, pp. 285–301.

3 Lawrence P. Carr and Christopher D. Ittner (1992). "Measuring the Cost of Ownership," *Journal of Cost Management,* Fall, pp. 42–51.

4 John Shank and Vijay Govindarajan (1993). "Strategic Cost Management," chapter 2 in *Strategic Cost Management: The New Tool for Competitive Advantage*. New York: Free Press, pp. 13–28.

5 Lisa M. Ellram, Wendy Tate, and Corey Billington (2004). "Understanding and Managing the Services Supply Chain," *The Journal of Supply Chain Management,* vol. 40, no. 4, pp. 17–32.

and other costs that go beyond price. In order to make a valid decision, the organization needs to take a big-picture perspective such as that provided by TCO analysis. For example, when HP decided to outsource and offshore some of its assembly operations to Brazil, a TCO analysis that incorporated the impact on revenue helped clarify and improve its decision.[6] However, global conditions are constantly changing, so the analysis must be updated for future decisions.

Likewise, TCO analysis can help an organization understand the costs of an outsourcing decision that extend beyond price. These include costs such as management, training, security checks, reliability, and IT investments. The hidden costs of outsourcing IT and software development overseas are so great that experts from the Gartner Group advise that it should not be considered unless the anticipated savings exceed 25 percent.[7] These additional costs, such as employee turnover, learning, and productivity differentials are the types of issues that TCO attempts to capture and quantify, either directly or through a sensitivity analysis. An example of a TCO analysis of an outsourcing situation will be presented throughout this chapter as part of the five-step approach to TCO analysis.

Other Issues Driving TCO

The development of activity-based cost management (ABCM) has been an important tool to facilitate the use of TCO analysis and automation of TCO. Organizations such as Compumotor[8] and Nortel[9] have used concepts from ABCM to create overhead allocations to assign activity-based costs to suppliers, providing an automated method for performing TCO analysis on routine purchases.

Related to this, there is growing recognition that there are many hidden activities or *cost drivers* within organizations and in dealing with suppliers that render the use of simple accounting data or price alone highly inaccurate for decision purposes. TCO analysis keys in on those cost drivers and hidden costs to support improved analysis and decision making.

Finally, the concept of supply chain management is really beginning to take hold in organizations throughout the world. Supply chain management recognizes that all the costs of an organization's network, from earliest supplier through final customer, and even disposal, are interdependent. TCO analysis supports supply chain management efforts by recognizing and analyzing how an organization's costs and performance impact, and are impacted by, the cost and performance of the

---

6 Lisa M. Ellram and Ed Feitzinger (1997). "Using Total Profit Analysis to Model Supply Chain Decisions," *Journal of Cost Management,* July–August, vol. 11, no. 4, pp. 12–22.

7 Ed Parry (2003). "Gartner: Offshore Outsourcing Horse Has 'Left the Barn.'" *SearchCIO.com*, July 8, Accessed at http://searchcio.techtarget.com/qna/0,289202,sid19_gci913695,00.html (accessed March 22, 2004).

8 Paulette Bennett (1996). "ABM and the Procurement Cost Model," *Management Accounting*, March, pp. 28–32.

9 Lisa M. Ellram (1994). *Total Cost Modeling in Purchasing*. Tempe, AZ: Center for Advanced Purchasing Studies.

TABLE   23–2

Price versus Cost: Kodak Example
Purchase of Programmable Logic Controller: The "Iceberg" Model

Cost Element	% of Purchase Price
Purchase Price	100%
Engineering	75
Installation	100
Commissioning	12
Parts and service	15
Maintenance	50
Training	5
Equipment Retirement	10
Total	367

Source: From Ellram and Edis (1996).

organizations with which it does business. TCO analysis can be performed at a dyadic level or by incorporating any or all parts of the supply chain.

An Example

Table 23–2 illustrates that total cost of ownership may be multiples higher than price, thereby invalidating price as a selection criteria. This example is based on Kodak's TCO analysis of programmable logic controllers (PLCs).[10] PLCs were being purchased by Kodak at the plant level throughout the world, based on price. A group within Kodak whose mission was to find cost savings and leverage opportunities was convinced that this low-price emphasis, which was causing proliferation of models and manufacturers of PLCs, was actually creating higher total costs for the company.

In order to build a business case for creating a global PLC contract, Kodak performed a TCO analysis, as in Table 23–1. Kodak determined that it could cut 25 to 50 percent of the 367 percent total cost of ownership of PLCs by using a common PLC worldwide. This analysis was used successfully to demonstrate the benefits of a global contract and to gain cooperation of plants throughout the world.

A FIVE-STEP APPROACH TO
DEVELOPING A TCO ANALYSIS

Figure 23–1 shows the five-step approach to TCO analysis that is presented in this section. The approach presented here is an iterative process that captures the key issues in successfully implementing TCO.

---

10 Lisa M. Ellram and Owen R.V. Edis (1996). "A Case Study of Successful Partnering Implementation," *International Journal of Purchasing and Materials Management,* Fall, vol. 32, no. 4, pp. 20–28.

F I G U R E   23–1

A Five-Step Approach to Implementing TCO Analysis[11]

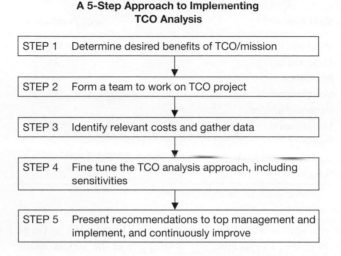

A 5-Step Approach to Implementing TCO Analysis

STEP 1	Determine desired benefits of TCO/mission
STEP 2	Form a team to work on TCO project
STEP 3	Identify relevant costs and gather data
STEP 4	Fine tune the TCO analysis approach, including sensitivities
STEP 5	Present recommendations to top management and implement, and continuously improve

Step 1: Choosing a Project for TCO Analysis

Not every purchase, outsourcing situation, or process analysis is an ideal candidate for TCO analysis. TCO analysis can be complex and time consuming, so there should be some initial assurance that the potential benefits of the analysis will outweigh the costs. Table 23–3 shows some of the characteristics that make a purchase well suited for TCO analysis, in order to demonstrate the dramatic difference between TCO and price.

Early success is important in implementing total cost of ownership concepts. An early success, with many dollars involved, and a high level of organizational visibility will create ongoing support for TCO as an approach to doing business and may also help overcome some of the organizational politics and barriers that are part of every organizational change process. It is important that early TCO projects not be controversial; for example, they should not include huge layoffs or encourage offshore outsourcing. If early projects create much controversy, the benefits of TCO can become lost in internal politics. TCO analysis will develop a bad connotation in the minds of many, impeding the probability of its success for current and future projects.

An example of a successful TCO project that met many of the criteria for a pilot TCO project is outsourcing of maintenance, repair, and operating (MRO) supplies by a major manufacturer of high-tech medical testing equipment (Hi-Tech). It chose to outsource management of its MRO operations because there were big

---

11 Stan Fawcett, Lisa M. Ellram, and Jeffrey Ogden (2007). *Integrated Supply Chain Management.* Prentice-Hall, forthcoming.

TABLE 23–3

Characteristics of Item for Pilot TCO Project

The firm spends a relatively large amount of money on that item.
The firm purchases the item with some degree of regularity in order to provide some historical data, but more importantly, to allow opportunities to gather current cost data.
Supply Management believes the item has significant transaction costs associated with it that are not currently recognized.
Supply Management believes that one or more of the currently unrecognized transaction costs is individually significant.
Supply Management has the opportunity to have an impact on transaction costs, via negotiation, changing suppliers, or improving internal operations.
Those purchasing and/or using the item will cooperate in data gathering to learn more about the item's cost structure.

Source: From Ellram (1993).

dollars involved, many unrecognized costs, multiple qualified suppliers available, and major performance problems it felt could be addressed by TCO. It was also relatively noncontroversial. Hi-Tech was counting on significant savings for this high-visibility project. They currently had hundreds of suppliers providing them with thousands of low-value items.

Step 2: Forming a Team

Once a promising project has been identified for TCO analysis, it is essential to identify who to involve in the analysis process. Participants will vary depending on the project under consideration. At a minimum, the TCO analysis team should include supply management, finance and accounting (for credibility as well as expertise), users, key stakeholders, and any functional and technical experts. TCO analysis is most effectively performed in a team setting. Because TCO analysis is time consuming and complex, it is important to gain the commitment and cooperation of others in advance. Before proceeding, it is important to consider the following: What is in it for others? Why should they cooperate? How will it improve their job environment or company performance? Gaining participation of others in TCO analysis may be a sales job. It is important to consider who will be affected by the outcome of the TCO analysis. Key stakeholders should be invited to provide input, so they can be co-opted into the process. Team membership and accountability for the MRO outsourcing team are shown in Table 23–4.

Step 3: Data Gathering and Analysis

It is important to keep the scope of the TCO analysis reasonable—make sure benefit exceeds cost. A good way to get this information is through brainstorming with

T A B L E   23-4

Team Participation in MRO Outsourcing

Name	Expertise	Contribution to Team	Contribution to Job
Nicole	Accounts payable	Understand current/proposed payment processes	Incorporate improved payment process into operations.
Justin	Finance	Help gather project cost data, including inventory investment	Early finance involvement will improve decision making.
Lynette	Line supervisor	Understands importance of MRO, actual performance of current suppliers, and key performance issues	Day-to-day job is affected by these suppliers.
Carson	Purchasing—MRO	Understands scope of project and current suppliers	Will have an impact on managing future MRO providers.
Sophie	Union-labor liaison	Understands current labor contract can point out potential problems in advance	Head off labor problems in advance.

the team. This entails using a round-robin method, asking each team member to name a TCO cost for that project while someone takes notes. This continues until all ideas are exhausted. Once you believe you have listed all key cost drivers, combine like items. These should then be classified according to pretransaction, transaction, and posttransaction costs. Pretransaction costs are those that occur prior to the receiving of goods or performance of the service. Transaction costs are incurred at time of purchase, whereas posttransaction costs are incurred after the service is performed or after the item has been received and inspected. The major cost elements that fit into each of these categories are shown in Figure 23–2. This tool is designed to help you remember the key cost drivers. It is not as important to put costs in the correct category or transaction versus pretransaction as it is to simply remember to consider all the costs.

Table 23–5 provides partial results from a brainstorming session on Hi-Tech's potential MRO outsourcing. The team must then determine which of the costs identified are really relevant to the decision. Relevant costs are those that are significant and will vary among decision alternatives. For example, inspection costs may be a large cost for an organization. However, if the inspection costs will remain unchanged regardless of the supplier chosen or alternative pursued, these costs are not relevant to the decision because they will not affect the decision outcome.

Process mapping should also be part of every TCO analysis. This is a way to verify that all key cost drivers have been identified and to expose inefficiencies that could be eliminated, further reducing the TCO. Thus, Hi-Tech also mapped the current MRO process and found it riddled with inefficiencies, as shown in Figure 23–3. As a result of this mapping, they decided to work on significantly reducing the supply base, having suppliers manage the inventory, and create a highly automated

FIGURE 23–2

Major Categories for the Components of Total Cost of Ownership Analysis

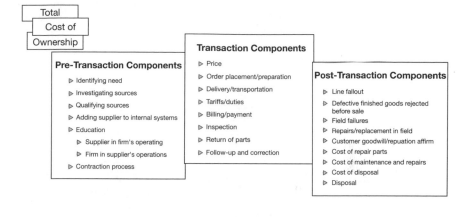

TABLE 23–5

Key Cost Drivers of Current Operations

Cost	Potential Outsourcing Impact
Pretransaction	
Order placement	Decreased internal cost—supplier monitors inventory and initiates replenishment rather than internal.
Transaction	
Receiving	No change due to union labor commitments
Transportation-related costs	Some increase due to smaller, more frequent shipments
Price	Unclear—larger guaranteed volume offset by smaller individual orders and additional required services
Breaking down orders	Eliminated, as required parts will be delivered to point of use by supplier
Inspection/counting	Same quantities verified.
Posttransaction	
Other administrative activities	Significant decrease because of paperless process, fewer orders, etc.
Obsolescence	Significant decrease due to smaller, more frequent (daily) deliveries

SOURCE: From Ellram and Maltz (1995).

process. This would result in significant potential savings in head count, as well as reductions in inventory and obsolescence. Hi-Tech had to work closely with the union to accomplish these objectives.

In the case of the MRO decision, after the process was changed, not all the costs initially identified in Table 23–5 were relevant to the decision. Table 23–6

FIGURE 23-3

Process Flow Diagram—Current MRO System

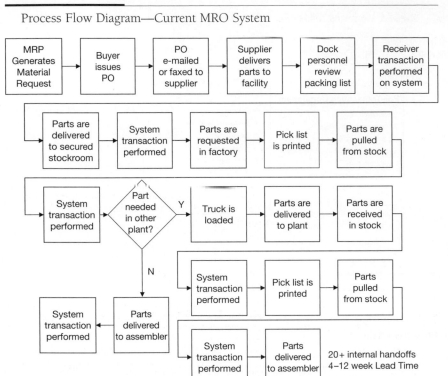

shows the costs that actually turned out to make a difference and explains how those costs were affected.

Once you have determined which costs are relevant, it is time for the team to gather data on the costs. In general, TCO analysis is conducted on a spreadsheet. Spreadsheets provide the flexibility to readily change cost categories and amounts as new information is gathered.

For those relevant costs where it is easy to gather data, the data should be gathered. Examples of such costs typically include price, transportation, and duties and tariffs. There are numerous others depending on the type of analysis. For those costs for which data are not readily available, such as the cost of shutting a line down due to a parts shortage, the team should go to the next step, sensitivity analysis, before spending a great deal of time gathering data.

Step 4: Fine-Tuning TCO and Sensitivity Analysis

Determining which costs are truly relevant to the decision is supported by performing a sensitivity analysis. A sensitivity analysis involves changing certain parameters in the TCO analysis to determine how the changes affect the outcome of the

T A B L E   23–6

Cost Elements Affected in This Outsourcing Analysis—MRO

Cost Element	How Affected
Transaction	
Price	Renegotiated
Transportation	Freight included in price and more frequent shipments under proposed system
Interest	Reduced cost due to carrying lower inventory levels
Posttransaction	
Obsolescence	Reduced due to smaller orders under new system
Pre- and posttransaction	
Support	Supplier will provide many more services, such as
	• Counting inventory
	• Placing orders
	• Breaking down orders once reviewed
	• Providing one monthly invoice
	• Investigate new products and sources of supply
	Reduction of data processing and database management as number of suppliers will be significantly reduced

Source: From Ellram and Maltz (1995).

analysis. This often involves reconsidering the critical assumptions and estimates included in the model. For example, if there is a cost or assumption that is very difficult or time consuming to determine with great accuracy, the team may be comfortable developing a "range" of values it believes to be reasonable. In the MRO example, the team might be able to determine the cost per minute of a certain line being down, but cannot accurately determine how many minutes per year a certain supplier might cause the line to go down. They are comparing this to a supplier that guarantees it will cause no downtime at all. In such a situation, the team should perform a sensitivity analysis, reanalyzing the total model with different assumptions about how long the line goes down for a certain supplier. They might determine that it is somewhere between 0 and 100 minutes per year. They will plug each assumption into the model, run the model, and compare the results.

Changing model assumptions is very fast and easy in a spreadsheet. If the model gives the same recommendation, the team knows that it is not worth spending the time to get very accurate downtime data for this decision; their best or worst estimates will give them the same recommendation. Thus, sensitivity analysis can actually improve decision making and lower the workload of the team. However, if they get a different recommendation with 0 or 100 minutes, they know that they should invest in getting more accurate data, because this downtime issue is truly a major cost driver that can make or break the decision. Sensitivity analysis also allows us to examine how an outcome would vary if we decide to change one of the assumptions or processes.

T A B L E   23-7

Sensitivity Analysis on Pool Ownership

---

1. Assume we do our own cleaning, so the only cost is chemicals at $150/year.
   $2,270 (old TCO) – (1,200 old cleaning + 150 new cleaning cost) = 1,120/year
   The cost per use is based on 20 uses per year and $55.10 per usage.

2. Assume we have children that use the pool several times a day in the summer and in the evenings after school in the warm months. Then our pool usage is 350 times per year.
   Cost per usage under original assumptions = $2,270/350 = $6.49/usage
   Cost per usage if we clean = $1,120/350 = $3.05/usage

Looking back at the opening example with the preexisting pool, cleaning costs are a big driver. What if we decide to clean the pool ourselves? As shown in Table 23–7, it would cost about $150 for chemicals (plus our time) instead of $1,200 per year. Our new TCO is $1,120 per year, or $55.10 per usage. This might make a potential pool owner decide that she will maintain the pool herself. Imagine that the pool owner had children who love to swim. Let's look at how our cost per use would change if we change our assumptions about how frequently we use the pool. We had an annual operating cost of around $2,270 per year. Assume we have children that use the pool several times a day in the summer and in the evenings after school in the warm months, so our pool usage is 350 time per year. With a total annual cost of ownership of $2,270, our cost per usage drops to $6.49. If we decide to clean the poor ourselves, with a TCO of $1,120, the cost per usage drops to $3.05! This is starting to look like a very good deal for anyone who has to keep children entertained when they are off school.

The point is that the answer that you get from TCO analysis depends heavily on the assumptions you employ in the model. Thus, varying cost and performance estimates to see how sensitive the model is to changes in those estimates should be done for all key assumptions. Elements should be varied simultaneously to capture the interaction effects among variables. Just as in the situation for difficult-to-calculate costs, if the decision recommendation changes as the estimates change, the team should investigate those cost elements more carefully. The goal is to improve its level of confidence. If the decision recommendation is unaffected as the estimate changes, the analysis is robust. Thus, it is probably not worth the time to gain greater certainty of the value for that variable. Sensitivity analysis helps assess the risk associated with a decision by easily answering what-if questions (Ellram, 2006).[12] When the team is comfortable with the analysis, it is ready to use the data in decision making and/or present the results to top management.

In addition to the quantitative data, the team must consider qualitative factors and factors that are difficult to quantify. In the MRO example, the firm was laying off staff. This could create morale issues. Was the savings worth enough to "pay"

---

12 Lisa M. Ellram (2006). "TOC: Adding Value to the Supply Chain" Proceedings of the Worldwide Research Symposium on Purchasing and Supply Chain Management, April 6–8, San Diego, CA. CD-Rom.

for this factor? The organization was also becoming very dependent on a handful of multiline distributors. Could this increase its risk of being out of stock? How difficult would it be to find alternate sources? These are just a few of the noncost factors that the team should consider. The team should research and present relevant facts and potential issues related to the noncost factors, both positive and negative.

Step 5: Present Results and Implement

The team should present the key findings of its analysis to management. This should include the TCO assessment, sensitivity analysis, and the qualitative issues for which it could not develop a cost. In the case of the MRO outsourcing, this included goodwill as employees were laid off, possible repercussions with the union, and the possibility of losing some expertise in certain areas of MRO as technology changed. Top management accepted the team's recommendations to outsource MRO, and it was successfully outsourced. The benefits of the analysis were presented as in Figure 23–4. What this figure shows is that based on the original price (using 100 as the base), plus additional costs of interest, support, obsolescence, and transport, the TCO was 108.9 percent. The new price, including interest, support, obsolescence, and transport, was 104 percent. The relevant comparison was the old TCO of 108.9 percent to the new TCO of 104 percent, not the old price of 100 percent. Better yet, the second year after this was implemented, the TCO dropped to about 98 percent, versus 108.9 percent. This was a tremendous unanticipated benefit as a result of standardization and simplification suggested by the suppliers.

In addition, the team presented the original process flow diagram as in Figure 23–3, and the new process flow diagram as in Figure 23–5. Being able to visually demonstrate the change in the process was very compelling.

F I G U R E   23–4

Analysis of Cost Breakdown MRO—Total Input Cost Index

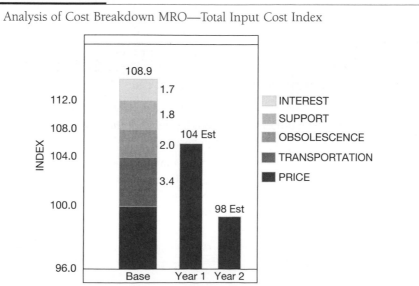

FIGURE 23-5

MRO Material Flow—As Outsourced

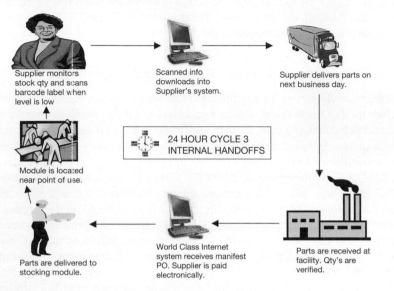

Supplier monitors stock qty and scans barcode label when level is low

Scanned info downloads into Supplier's system.

Supplier delivers parts on next business day.

Module is located near point of use.

24 HOUR CYCLE 3 INTERNAL HANDOFFS

Parts are delivered to stocking module.

World Class Internet system receives manifest PO. Supplier is paid electronically.

Parts are received at facility. Qty's are verified.

IMPLEMENTATION ISSUES

Implementing TCO is not without difficulty, even after a successful analysis. The first critical issue, as mentioned earlier, is that the firm must move away from a price orientation to a TCO philosophy. Supply management may have to demonstrate that a TCO philosophy is a superior way to manage and understand costs. Case studies indicate that the most effective proof of TCO effectiveness may have to come through a successful TCO pilot project. "Knowing comes from doing and teaching others how."[13]

Second, few firms have accurate cost information for the pretransaction, transaction, and posttransaction cost components in Figure 23–2. For most firms, data gathering will begin as a significant manual effort. Thus, much energy may have to be devoted to

1. Developing a process flow chart, to highlight the firm's pretransaction, transaction, and posttransaction cost elements

2. Determining which cost components are significant enough to warrant tracking. This can be done by using Pareto's law and sensitivity analysis. There are probably a few key cost components that make up the majority of TCO expenses for a given item.

---

13 Jeffrey Pfeffer and Robert I. Sutton (2000). *The Knowing-Doing Gap.* Boston: Harvard Business School Press.

3. Determining how those significant cost components will be calculated and monitored

4. Gathering and summarizing the relevant cost component data

5. Analyzing the results

Third, the firm needs to alter its metrics to value TCO results rather than price only. This can help motivate people to support desired initiatives.[14]

Fourth, a firm must determine how and where TCO will be used in the organization. Will it be a tool reserved for critical items or more broadly used? Will TCO be used to select suppliers, manage costs with current suppliers, or allocate purchases among suppliers? Will one TCO model be used to provide the data to support all those efforts? The proposed scope will have an impact on the way in which a TCO approach is implemented and on whether a one-time analysis or an ongoing system would be most effective.

Continuously Improving TCO

TCO analysis should not be treated as a static, one-time analysis. Projects that are justified using TCO should be reanalyzed or audited, after the project has been implemented for a reasonable time period, perhaps six months to a year. The analysis should consider the following:

- Are results as expected? Why or why not?

- Were any key cost elements or benefits overlooked that should be considered in future analyses?

- Were any key assumptions or sensitivities significantly in error? Could this have been prevented?

- Is there anything else that can be learned for future TCO analysis?

It is also important to monitor and report the actual TCO project results so that TCO gains visibility in the organization and that those involved in TCO analysis get proper recognition. TCO can be applied at many levels, as shown in Figure 23–6. Operationally, TCO information can be used to select and manage suppliers on a day-to-day basis. Tactically, the information can be used to improve routine processes. At a strategic level, TCO can be used to support the determination of what the organization should make versus buy, and where to focus for maximum results.

SUMMARY

This chapter provides a brief overview of TCO concepts and methods. While the concept of TCO is relatively simple, its execution may be complex. There may be internal political issues and rewards systems that hinder TCO progress. Lack of time

---

14 Pfeffer and Sutton, ibid.

Various Levels of Analysis Supported by a TCO[15]

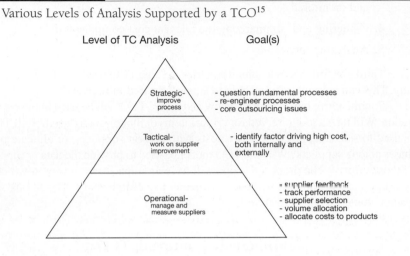

and data availability can be important issues. Those interested in TCO analysis are urged to investigate TCO processes and have a good understanding of their own organizational reward structures and political issues before proceeding further with TCO development and implementation. The five-step approach presented here is equally applicable to the analysis of goods, services, processes, and outsourcing. Added expenses and complications of global sourcing and outsourcing make TCO analysis even more critical today.

15 Lisa M. Ellram and Sue P. Siferd (1998). "Total Cost of Ownership: A Key Concept in Strategic Cost Management Decisions," *Journal of Business Logistics,* vol. 19, no. 1, pp. 55–84.

CHAPTER 24

NEGOTIATIONS

Brian G. Long, Ph.D., C.P.M.
President,
Marketing and Management Institute, Inc.

INTRODUCTION

Perhaps the most important tool of the supply management professional is the ability to successfully negotiate agreements of all types. Indeed, for some supply managers the ability to negotiate becomes the key factor in their performance as supply managers. A supply manager who cannot negotiate effectively is, therefore, of little value to the supply management department or the firm. However, negotiation is a tool. Nothing more, nothing less. Its purpose is to secure the best possible long-term agreement for the supply manager's firm or organization, consistent with the concept of lowest *total* cost.

NEGOTIATIONS
A Brief History

No one is exactly sure where commercial negotiations began, except to say that some form of negotiation was probably associated with our very early attempts at commercial enterprises. When ships first sailed to what is now China to buy silk and spices, they certainly found it necessary to perform some kind of bargaining ritual with the sellers. Indeed, early negotiation was most probably influenced by the Chinese culture more than anything.

Negotiations in commercial enterprises during the 1,000-year period of the Dark Ages were limited by the small scope of the "cottage manufacturing" operations. In the era of shop tradespeople, manufacturing skills, such as shoemaking, bookbinding, blacksmithing, and coopering, were passed on from generation to generation. These small entrepreneurs had to be skilled in everything from accounting to production to customer service. If raw materials were required, it was essential that they become skilled in purchasing. Because profit margins usually left only enough money for a meager living, negotiation skills were essential when purchasing raw materials. If poor-quality materials were purchased resulting in an unacceptable final product, the customers went elsewhere and the entrepreneur starved. If too much was paid for the materials, there was no profit margin left and again the entrepreneur starved. Hence, negotiation skills, along with the so-called tricks of the trade, were passed on from generation to generation.

With the dawning of the Industrial Revolution came the factory, and soon thereafter came the first purchasing agents in the late nineteenth century. Unlike today's firms, early industrial sellers customarily set prices at or near cost plus 10 percent. Negotiations for purchasing agents were therefore more apt to focus on quality, delivery, service, and other aspects of the purchase. It was not really until the 1930s when the lid came off pricing and salespeople were frequently given the authority to set the price at any level to which the focus of negotiation shifted.

Today's Negotiation Environment

In the new age of just-in-time (JIT) manufacturing, strategic alliances, single sourcing, and supply chain management, many old methods of negotiations are no longer viable. Our purpose is therefore to focus on the new kinds of negotiation skills necessary to implement the modern supply management practices that are now mandated by recent evolutions in the supply management profession. More changes may have taken place in the profession in the last 15 years than occurred in the previous 50. Management's enlightened understanding of supply management's role in the organization has put supply managers under more pressure to show bottom-line results, but at the same time to lower inventories, elevate quality, and improve services by negotiating what would have seemed like impossible agreements just a few years ago.

Traditional Purchasing
Thirty years ago, the job of purchasing was very different. The typical purchasing manager was thought to be a gatekeeper, guardian of the treasury, and funnel through which every expenditure for the purchase of goods and services should pass. Because of the large dollars purchasing was often spending, it had the power to demand compliance from suppliers. A sign hung on the wall in one purchasing office read, Have You Kicked a Vendor Yet Today?

In the world of crowded file cabinets, mountains of catalogs, and vaults filled with archived purchase records, the purchasing manager was the person who "knew where to go to buy things," which often resulted in the requisitioner being more than willing to simply file requisitions and wait for fulfillment. Little attention was paid to the fact that the cost of transactions for both buyers and sellers was rising rapidly. It took until the 1990s for many firms to realize that these rising costs now meant that purchasing was no longer adding value to well over half the transactions passing through the average purchasing office.

Traditional Negotiation Training
For more than 50 years, purchasers let the sellers set the negotiation agenda. To these traditional sellers, negotiation was a game. The seller would begin by offering to sell for a very high price, and the buyer would counteroffer with a very low

price. Then the games began. Both buyers and sellers would try to trick each other into an agreement. At least half the discussion was something less than honest. Tricks and lies were thought to just be part of the "game." Furthermore, to these negotiators, "a lie was not a lie when the truth was not expected." Therefore, traditional negotiation training taught both buyers and sellers to (1) use tactics and tricks, (2) creatively lie, and (3) artfully badger the other party. Purchasing negotiation was viewed by buyers and sellers as well as others in the organization as simply beating down the seller's price—sometimes at the expense of delivery, quality, and goodwill.

Supply Management's New Role
The current supply management literature is filled with strategies and buzzwords that didn't exist 30 years ago. Such concepts as partnering, strategic alliances, JIT, supplier certification, supplier consolidation, global sourcing, and at least a half dozen other terms demand a new approach to negotiation. The absurd thought of "playing games" with a JIT supplier speaks to the fact that traditional negotiation systems have little or no place when implementing modern purchasing practices.

The Supply Management Environment
Most strategists believe that purchasing has evolved into supply management, which implies a much broader horizon of responsibility as well as multiple levels of negotiations. Instead of in-baskets filled with seemingly endless stacks of requisitions, the majority of a supply manager's work will be that of administering a series of large contracts for complete commodity groups. In terms of negotiation, the focus will shift from relatively small, day-to-day purchases to large, multiyear contracts. Negotiation skills, therefore, must focus in three directions: first, the task of negotiating multiproduct, long-term supply management agreements; second, bridging the gap between end users and the suppliers; and third, ironing out difficulties, revising systems, monitoring controls, and otherwise maintaining proper performance.

KEY STRATEGIC APPROACHES

Even though some approaches to negotiation are clearly outdated, at least four primary strategies are prevalent in today's negotiation environment. Although it is also possible to think of these strategies as a continuum ranging from hard to soft, there are some key benchmarks of each of these systems.

Power Negotiation

The supply manager always has the age-old power of the almighty dollar. Until the seller has an order, the seller really has nothing. Therefore, the more money a buyer has to spend, the greater the power.

If the buyer (or seller) does not have power, then the power negotiator usually attempts to develop some form of artificial power. Catching the seller in an excess inventory situation or discovering that a salesperson is coming up short for a monthly quota would temporarily shift power to the buyer side. For the sellers, age-old practices like backdoor selling or stalling the negotiations until no time exists to talk with another seller are just a couple of options for creating an imbalance of power in the seller's favor. In the past, most large firms did not really negotiate with their sellers. They simply brought their power to bear and demanded better pricing, service, quality, and delivery. Sellers who did not comply were punished with smaller orders or no orders at all.

Positional Bargaining

When buyers and sellers decided to make a game out of negotiations, they established a simple rule: Sellers would always start high, and buyers would always counteroffer with some kind of a low and unacceptable number. Both parties would then proceed to defend their respective positions and maneuver the other party with a series of tactics and tricks.

Everyone likes a game, primarily because games are a form of entertainment. However, everyone recognizes that games are not reality. Major difficulties arise when gamesmanship is projected as a way of doing business. The best solutions to business problems seldom emerge from game strategies. For these reasons, some people regard negotiation as a game. When a game strategy fails and they fall short of their goals, they don't understand why.

Traditional negotiators have a win-lose attitude. They believe that in order to gain, someone must lose. Both parties are therefore supposed to sit at the table and bat these offers back and forth until one party, presumably the weaker of the two, gives in and accepts a less-than-optimum agreement.

Win-Win Negotiation

Negotiation is not a game. Negotiation is business, and it should be conducted as business. To be transacted effectively, business must be conducted in a win-win manner. The win-win theory of negotiation endorses the growing belief that good suppliers can greatly improve the success of the supply manager's firm or organization. It does away with the zero-sum or fixed-pie notion of traditional negotiations and assumes that, if properly negotiated, agreement can benefit both parties.

Win-win negotiators look at agreements through the eyes of the parties who are going to perform them. Agreements written on mere pieces of paper do not get up and walk out into the plants and perform. Agreements don't perform, but people do, and these people must be motivated to perform if we are to expect to receive the greatest value from the contract. If people lack incentives, they will think of numerous reasons why not to perform or, sometimes even worse, perform poorly.

Win-win negotiators often focus on common ground, because it is the basis for all movement in negotiation. The more common ground you have, the closer you are to an agreement. American industry has been severely criticized lately for its short-term "quarter to quarter" mentality. Win-win negotiation, in answer to these criticisms, is therefore more concerned with the long run than short run. A win-win negotiator looks down the road saying, "Where are we going to be in three years? Let's not sacrifice the present for the future." The other party is then considered to be a partner in success, not an opponent or adversary.

Benevolent Negotiation

In the age of strategic alliances and long-term cooperation between buyers and sellers, it is clearly possible to lean too far in the seller's direction. The benevolent negotiator makes the assumption that a seller, if just given the reins, will automatically look out for the buyer's best interest. Proponents will point to isolated examples of success where sellers did, in fact, take over a complete project and provide excellent quality, top-notch service, and reasonable prices.

Benevolent negotiation, therefore, is a classic example of too much of a good thing. Even though the seller may make public announcements and even perform acts that appear to be in the buyer's interest, the fact remains that the selling firm is under pressure for profitability just like any other firm. It is still the buyer's responsibility to look out for his or her firm's best interest and to secure better performance from the seller at each and every negotiation. The core of the supply manager's job is still supplier management and cost reduction.

Forming Strategic Alliances

A logical extension of win-win negotiation is to form a permanent, long-term relationship whereby both parties agree to work with one another for their combined best interest. For the supply manager, this kind of arrangement implies setting aside traditional bid-buy purchasing in favor of selecting a supplier who is willing to *continuously* update and improve price, quality, and service to meet the buyer's changing needs. Since this kind of arrangement requires the commitment of the entire selling firm from one end to the other, the supply manager's role becomes that of a contract manager. For the supply manager, negotiations now take place between the buyer and various departments within the selling company in order to secure compliance.

Since negotiating a strategic alliance requires a team effort, it almost goes without saying that it takes a unified commitment of the entire firm or organization to make it work. The establishment of this kind of arrangement obviously requires considerable more time than a normal contractual arrangement. More importantly, it requires considerable time to maintain the relationship and keep it on track once the agreement is formed. Procedures must be established for holding regular update meetings and resolving both small and large problems as they occur. Failure to regularly and openly communicate is one of the major causes for alliances falling apart.

Despite hundreds of books and articles advocating the strategic alliance, the concept remains one of the most elusive. Almost every seller *claims* to be interested in a long-term relationship. It is a frequently used opening line. However, it takes the commitment of the entire selling firm to make a strategic alliance work. The salespeople themselves are often unable to secure the performance of their own firms.

Alliances, as well as most other types of relationships, require mutual trust. Building and maintaining trust, therefore, becomes one of the greatest tasks for both buyers and sellers. However, changes in ownership of either firm, changes in the business environment, or changing from a goal of mutual cooperation to one of financial self-interest are just a few of the ways that alliances can be destroyed.

Finally, since negotiation is a people process, it turns out that it is usually people problems that cause strategic alliances to fall apart. In today's age when people are frequently moved to different positions around firms and organizations, keeping all parties on both the buying and selling side working together is a major problem.

THE PRAM NEGOTIATION MODEL

Negotiation is a process, not just an event. As illustrated by Figure 24–1, PRAM stands for plans, relationships, agreements, and maintenance. These constitute the

F I G U R E   24–1

The PRAM Model: The Win-Win Negotiation Process

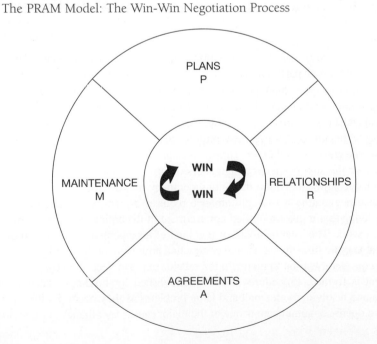

primary steps in any long-term negotiations situation and form the blueprint by which many contemporary supply managers manage their suppliers.

Although planning is easily recognized as an important step, the modern supply manager concentrates on building a positive relationship with the supplier. Japanese negotiators seldom think of doing business before they feel at ease with the other party both personally and professionally. They depend on relationships to pave the way for an agreement, as well as to ensure that it will be properly carried out. On some occasions they will spend years developing a relationship before they conduct business.

With an adequate plan and a good relationship, forming an agreement should be much easier. The goal at this stage is to be in a problem-solving mode so that both parties can reconcile differences and hopefully come up with an agreement.

The last step is maintenance. As the name implies, the goal of maintenance is to maintain the other three steps in the negotiation process as well as pave the way for future negotiations. The PRAM model is therefore round to imply that the process is ongoing. Because of the nature of the industrial market, most supply management negotiators find themselves facing the same sellers and the same markets over and over again. It would therefore be a major mistake in any negotiation to sacrifice the present for the future.

The concept of continuous improvement implies that the negotiation process should get better every time the buyer and seller go around the PRAM model. After many successful negotiations augmented by continuous improvement, the buyer and seller should ultimately attain a nearly perfect business relationship. However, maintaining the momentum of continuous improvement is one of the most difficult tasks for a buyer, or seller, to accomplish.

Negotiation Planning

Although almost everyone concedes the importance of negotiation planning, they simultaneously note that their planning is often inadequate. Some have even characterized their planning as "ready, fire, aim," which really means that whatever planning is done is sometimes done right at the negotiation table itself or in brief recesses or caucuses.

Many inexperienced negotiators approach a negotiation with the idea that "I don't know what I want, but I will know it when I see it." Such an approach makes it fairly easy for a skilled seller to redefine the situation to simply match the seller's objectives—at the buyer's expense.

State of Mind

Perhaps the most important factor determining the outcome of a negotiation is the state of mind of both parties as they embark upon the negotiation. For instance, a seller who has already been told by someone with authority that the decision has already been made in their favor will come to the table ready to smugly walk away with an agreement while making no concessions at all. Other factors influencing state of mind include everything from reputations to rumors to how fairly each party felt they were treated last time.

Timing is also important. Take the case of a salesperson that has just closed three large contracts for 10 to 20 percent above the going market price. Would such a salesperson be in the mood to talk discounts? Hardly. In fact, until you bring the salesperson back down to earth, it will be difficult to conclude any type of a reasonable agreement.

Another set of factors relates to the tone of the markets that both parties face. A seller's market puts pressure on the salespeople to hold the line on prices and grant practically no concessions that cost money. Conversely, a buyer's market puts pressure on the supply manager to demand better pricing and more concessions. However, a wise negotiator looks toward the future in an attempt to ensure the long-run profitability and survival of both firms. This does not, imply, however, that outside factors such as foreign competition should not be considered when negotiating a long-term agreement with a domestic seller.

In this same context, it is wise to remember that all the planning in the world cannot overcome all forces of supply and demand. When the price of copper rises 10 percent and the entire market accepts the price increase, a buyer will be hard-pressed to negotiate a price below the current market without providing some kind of additional incentives to the seller. Typical concessions may include long-term purchase guarantees, early payment, or other incentives of equal value.

The Supply Manager's Key Issues

Negotiation planning must include a system for listing the issues of the negotiation itself, as well as the optimistic and pessimistic outcomes for each of these issues, generally known as the settlement ranges. Each of these issues should also be prioritized so that those issues that are most important are considered at all times.

Some issues recur in almost every negotiation, such as price, quality, service, warranty, and terms of sale. Other issues, such as return policies, restocking charges, engineering changes, rights to technical data, on-site inspections, and various seller certifications will be unique to each negotiation.

The Seller's Key Issues

Analyzing the issues for your firm or organization is important, but equally important is putting yourself in the other party's shoes. Most of the issues that are important to the supply manager are also important to the seller. The task then becomes determining targets, settlement ranges, and priorities that constitute the best estimate of what the other party will expect from this negotiation. As illustrated by Box 24–1, the concept of a complete settlement range for both buyer and seller appears like a table of possible outcomes. In the case of delivery time in Example A, the two parties should be able to reach an agreement somewhere between 3 and 10 weeks. In the case of price in Example B, the settlement range is between $1,500 and $2,200.

B O X   24-1

The Settlement Range

Example A: Delivery Time

Buyer's Perspective		Seller's Perspective
Ideal Settlement Position − − − −	2 Weeks	
	3 Weeks − − − − Least Acceptable Position	
Target Settlement Position − − − −	4 Weeks	
	5 Weeks	
	6 Weeks	
	7 Weeks − − − − Target Settlement Position	
	8 Weeks	
	9 Weeks	
Least Acceptable Position − − − −	10 Weeks	
	11 Weeks	
	12 Weeks	
	13 Weeks	
	14 Weeks	
	15 Weeks − − − − Ideal Settlement Position	

Example B: Price

Buyer's Perspective		Seller's Perspective
Ideal Settlement Position − − − −	$1,400	
	1,500 − − − − Least Acceptable Position	
	1,600	
Target Settlement Position − − − −	1,700	
	1,800	
	1,900 − − − − Target Settlement Position	
	2,000	
	2,100	
Least Acceptable Position − − − −	2,200	
	2,300	
	2,400	
	2,500	
	2,600 − − − − Ideal Settlement Position	

With the goals of both parties side by side, planners must now devise a plan or strategy to reconcile the two sets of goals. This step requires creative thinking. It is often much more difficult to come up with a win-win solution than simply demand the acceptance of your position, offer to split the difference, employ standard negotiation techniques, or put up a good fight in the hope that the other party will give in before you do. A good negotiation planner thinks of opportunities to expand the pie beyond the boundaries of the existing agreement and considers as many things as possible that benefit both parties. Many of these concessions, such as using the buying firm's name in an advertisement, cost no money at all!

Power

Even in the enlightened era of win-win, power is still reality. The outcome of any negotiation still favors the power party. However, it is also the power parties that are able to set the overall tone of the negotiation. As previously noted, the power that a supply manager always has is the power of money. Sellers must sell to survive, and the seller who walks away without an order still has nothing. It has been said that money talks. Therefore, more money equates to more power. When the dollars are large enough, the sellers will listen, even though they might not like what they hear. Modern supply managers, therefore, consolidate their purchases into a big enough package that it attracts the attention of the seller. However, the supply manager who goes into the market with only one small order will probably find the seller to be underwhelmed—unless more business is in the offing.

The power that the seller often has is the power to do the job and do it right. A seller with a proven record of on-time delivery, top-notch quality, excellent service, and ease of order placement is clearly in a position of power. A competing seller offering to do the "same job for 10 percent less" is looked upon by the buyer with a skeptical eye. Discharging an incumbent seller that is causing practically no trouble for the supply manager is not easy, even though economic circumstances may dictate the necessity.

Unscrupulous sellers may try to develop artificial power or take power away from the supply manager. The so-called backdoor seller tries to get a product or service "spec-ed in" or committed before the supply manager even finds out what is going on. In other instances, the seller may wait until the supply manager is in a time bind, is short on inventory, or does not have time to qualify a new suppler.

Cost Analysis

Although a separate topic by itself, cost analysis is sure to grow in importance for supply management negotiators. One of the major goals of supply managers is and will continue to be long-term cost reduction. Therefore, supply managers must come to the table ready to discuss and analyze realistic prices.

One of the key factors that must be researched prior to the negotiation is the seller's major cost drivers. For some firms, it is obvious. In the case of service organizations, it is labor. When plenty of qualified labor is available, costs should remain relatively stable. In the case of a goods-producing firm, the cost drivers are often labor and materials. If the materials prices are stable, pricing should be stable. If, however, the cost of a key raw material were to rise or fall, so should the end price of the final product.

Developing Long-Term Relationships

Historically, buyer-seller relationships were frowned upon. It was generally thought that relationships detracted from the objective decision-making process and sometimes put supply managers as well as other members of the firms in compromising positions. Some larger firms even developed elaborate rotation patterns to keep the supply managers from getting too familiar with the sellers.

Many of these considerations related to the fact that relationship development seemed to be almost synonymous with seller-sponsored entertainment. Typical activities included lunch, dinner, golf, baseball games, and other activities often designed to put the buyer in a positive frame of mind.

Although the concept of purchasing ethics can be a separate subject by itself, it is sufficient to say that any form of excessive seller-sponsored entertainment is probably designed to develop a win-lose relationship and, therefore, obligate the supply manager. In response, some firms as well as most governmental units and government contractors simply wrote policies to disallow such activities altogether.

However, the modern supply management negotiator now faces a need to develop long-term relationships with a limited number of suppliers. A modern relationship is different because

1. At least part of the time, a positive, well-developed relationship will be the key to resolving problems. Not only are the communication channels more open, the willingness of people inside the selling organization to go the extra mile is greatly enhanced.

2. Sellers will still say things to supply managers outside of the office that they will not feel comfortable saying in the office. Restricting communication to taking place only in the office may inhibit negotiation outcomes.

3. Every conversation is a relationship development opportunity. Relationships do not have to be built while spending money. For instance, a plant tour costs nothing but introduces the supply manager to the firm or organization.

4. In order to negotiate long-term cost reduction, it is necessary to have a relationship with all of the departments and individuals in the selling firms that influence cost. This requires broadening the buyer-seller relationship to include a much wider circle of people.

5. Many supply management departments have developed a policy of reciprocity for activities like lunch and dinner. Under this system, the supply manager picks up the check about half the time.

6. Excessive entertainment is not necessary or productive. Going to lunch can be a useful relationship development activity that does not have to cost excessive amounts of money.

Relationship Components

Building "Like"

In days gone by, buyers were trained to put salespeople down. They would not return phone calls. They would leave the seller waiting in the lobby just to make themselves look more important. They would even be downright rude on some occasions.

In today's environment, the opposite is true. Supply managers are accommodating and polite to sellers, but still businesslike. They consider the seller's time to be important and make every effort to keep scheduled appointments. They also return phone calls to legitimate sellers. All of these and other activities are aimed at getting the seller to like the supply manager personally.

Other aspects of "like" are psychological. For instance, remembering the seller's name and company is important. Taking an interest in the seller personally also helps to build a bond.

Building Respect

If the seller likes the supply manager, the relationship is one-third complete. But like without respect is of little or no value as far as a business relationship. For the supply manager, respect has many dimensions. Being the real decision-making authority is certainly of maximum importance. However, being knowledgeable about the subject matter may be just as important. The supply manager is not expected to be a technical expert—just knowledgeable enough about the product, service, or commodity to carry on an intelligent conversation. This allows the seller to communicate effectively. Otherwise, many sellers will say that they have been talking to the wrong person.

Building Trust

Perhaps the most illusive of the three, building trust requires patience and time. Part of trust is conferred by the organization by placing authority in the hands of the buyer. Another part of trust comes from professional stature such as a C.P.M. (Certified Purchasing Manager) certificate hanging on the wall. But the most important part of trust comes from working together over a long period of time.

As illustrated by Figure 24–2, all three factors overlap. At the same time, different circumstances may require different proportions of each factor, depending on the marketplace, the dollars involved, the complexity of the issues, and the goals and objectives of both firms.

Finally, it is wise to remember that the purpose of a good relationship is to (1) improve communication, (2) increase creativity, (3) enhance problem solving, (4) provide a buffer for human error, and (5) make both parties feel good about the agreement. A relationship that only opens the door for the seller to sell more products or services has little place in modern supply management and should be avoided.

Negotiating the Agreement

Good negotiation planning and a positive relationship are essential to laying the groundwork for actually forming a final agreement. However, even this firm

Relationship Components

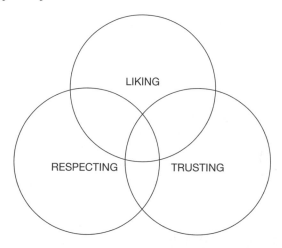

foundation still requires skill, patience, and perseverance in order to reach an agreement.

It is essential to get off to a good start. This involves a continuation of the good relationship that, hopefully, has already been developed. A good place to begin the discussion is with the common ground that brought you together in the first place. Before proceeding further, this is usually a good time to ask any questions that you may have regarding clarifications of the subject matter of the negotiation.

What you do next will set the tone for the entire negotiation. For instance, it would be tempting to jump in and start negotiating random issues without first looking at the overall picture. If you expect the seller's help in solving problems, you must first draw them into the process. Many modern negotiators advocate *jointly* making a list of those factors where there is agreement and those where there is disagreement prior to trying to solve any of the problems. The areas of agreement—the common ground—form the foundation of the entire business relationship. The areas of disagreement—the problems—are what stand in the way of forming not only the present agreement but often future agreements as well.

The Myopia of Tactics and Tricks

Traditional tactics often create the poorest possible business agreements. Entering a negotiation session by telling lies or playing tricks encourages the other party to tell lies and play tricks. As the negotiations progress, both parties simply lie to each other, until one of the parties convinces the other to accept a lie as truth. The parties commit the agreement to writing, which becomes of course a culmination of lies. Both parties sign the agreement with their fingers crossed behind their backs and shake hands as though they had both reached an agreement. Of course, the chances are good that one or the other party won't perform. When asked why, an honest defector will probably say, "What do you mean, perform? That agreement was a lie. We thought you knew that. That's how business is done in our industry."

Some negotiation books are primarily a discussion of tactics and tricks, and many seminars are conducted every day that advocate these practices. Box 24–2 describes some of the typical win-lose tactics that are still practiced by some sellers and still advocated by some buyers as well. The fact remains that some people like to read books and attend seminars that make them come back feeling bigger and stronger than they actually are, even though many of the ideas they have learned are really fantasies. Business does not exist in a fantasy world.

Modern supply managers also avoid falling into the traps of traditional negotiations. For instance, they avoid defend-attack spirals where one party is badgered into responding with a counterattack. This often results in the other party escalating the attack. Ultimately, the talks may break off with both parties screaming at each other.

B O X   24-2

Typical Win-Lose Tactics

- Appeal to Profitability
  "At that price, we're not making any money …"
- Stone Wall (hard nose) Tactics
  "That's the best I can do. Take it or leave it."
- Stalling
  "Sorry to put off our meeting, but we need more time to prepare …"
- Flattery
  "You are my favorite customer …"
- Established Policy as a Barrier
  "I'm sorry, my hands are tied …"
- Artificial Legal Leverage
  "The law says that we must sell to everyone for the same price."
- Moral Appeals
  "If I don't close this sale, we will have to lay people off …"
- Loyalty
  "But we have been your loyal supplier for all these years …"
- Emotional Appeals
  Crying
- Rhetorical Answers
  "Before I answer your question, you must first tell me …"
- Authority Variation
  "I am only authorized to offer …"

Conversely, modern negotiators try to make the other party feel at ease throughout the entire negotiation. If the talks are not successful, both parties still recognize that there may still be an opportunity to do business in the future.

Recesses and Caucuses

When time is passing but no progress is being made, it is often wise to call a recess or a caucus. The distinction between a recess and a caucus is that of degree. In a recess, both parties leave the room with an agreement to resume the discussion at a later time, such as an hour later or even a week later. In a caucus, just one group leaves the room. In both instances, the purpose is for both buyers and sellers to rethink, redefine, and develop fresh approaches to the problem.

Failure to call a recess or caucus when progress is not being made can be a major mistake. When no progress is being made, the parties may begin to wear on each other's nerves and destroy the positive atmosphere of the negotiations. In team negotiations, a recess will allow both teams to brainstorm as well and redefine and recollect their thoughts.

Frequent Errors at the Table

1. *Coming unprepared.* If you do not know what you want or need, then the seller is apt to exert a right of prominence and help you—to the seller's advantage. Furthermore, the sellers may feel that they have wasted their time trying to deal with a person or team that has little or no appreciation for what they have to say.

2. *Committing too soon.* There is nothing that the seller would rather hear than that you or your company have already decided to give the seller the business. In the case of an electronics firm that was negotiating with a component company for its latest model, the electronics firm printed the catalog containing the component before the negotiations were completed. Having seen the catalog being prepared for printing, the seller felt little need to comply with any of the buyer's requests.

3. *Inappropriate body language.* All good negotiators read body language. What is not said is often more important than what is actually said. In the case of a head negotiator disagreeing with a point being made by the seller, she did not see that another member of her team was nodding in agreement. In short, three little nods resulted in a less-than-favorable agreement.

4. *Disclosure of competitive terms.* There is nothing the seller would rather know than the exact terms they have to beat. The seller's state of mind then shifts to believing that any offer that is marginally superior should be acceptable.

5. *Team disagreement.* In the right time and place, there is certainly nothing wrong with devil's advocates. However, the negotiation team *must*

B O X   24-3

At the Negotiation Table: Some Do's and Don'ts

DO Focus on problems, not personalities

DO Identify as much common ground as possible

DO Make the other party feel PHYSICALLY comfortable

DO Make the other party feel MENTALLY comfortable

DO Share information when the seller shares with you

DO Explore additional business opportunities

DON'T Slip into traditional negotiation by making immediate counteroffers

DON'T Talk too much or oversell your ideas

DON'T Make derogatory comments about competitors

DON'T Reject seller's ideas prior to discussion

DON'T Irritate the other party

DON'T Dangle business opportunities that are not yours to offer

---

present a united front at the negotiation table. When someone is asked to join the team, it is assumed that the person is a *team* player.

6. *Dos and don'ts.* Finally, as illustrated by Box 24–3, there are some dos and don'ts that should be followed in almost every negotiation.

Maintaining Momentum

Professional negotiators often refer to a point in a negotiation session where the tide turns and the entire agreement begins to fall into place. This point often occurs when you and the other party have reached a mutual solution to a difficult problem. This is, of course, positive momentum.

In terms of negative momentum, it is sometimes just a few wrong words that tell the seller that you are ready to accept the agreement on the seller's terms. For instance, assume that your management has determined that you must obtain better quality, pricing, delivery, or services from a supplier. Opening the negotiations with a phrase like, "I'm sorry I have to ask for this …," implies you are not really committed to your own firm's goals. The seller will now feel little or no need to work with you to deliver the better terms that your firm requires.

A similar problem relates to apologizing for doing your job. Assume that the salesperson for a long-term supplier encounters a competing salesperson in the lobby. You simply explain that it is your job to keep abreast of the market and explore other alternatives. In this same context, if asked during a negotiation if you are looking at other alternatives, one of the worst things you could imply would be that you have already dismissed the possibility of ever dealing with alternative suppliers.

When to Walk Away

It is again important to emphasize that positive agreements cannot always be accomplished. Before walking away, it is wise to ask yourself a few important questions:

1. What is (or are) the key issue (or issues) that are standing in the way of the agreement? Are they essential to the success of the agreement? Is there any way that they can be resolved at a later time without jeopardizing the essence of the present agreement?

2. Are your goals unreasonable? Have you asked for more than the seller appears to be able to realistically provide? Are you asking for performance or concessions that exceed the authority of the seller with whom you are negotiating?

3. Would a recess help? If you gave the seller or sellers a chance to rethink, regroup, brainstorm, call the home office, or otherwise redefine the situation, could the situation change?

4. What is your next best alternative? If there are other sellers to investigate and the prospect of accomplishing your goal still seems feasible, then you may owe it to yourself and to the alternate seller to take a look. However, getting up and walking away when there is no other viable alternative will put you in a bad negotiation position when you have to come back to beg forgiveness and accept the seller's terms.

If the decision is still to walk away, then one last step is still essential. The explicit nature of the problem or problems that stood in the way of the agreement *must* be made very clear. The seller must believe and understand that you, as the negotiator, are not to be personally blamed for the unfavorable outcome. Furthermore, if the sellers leave the negotiation still focused on the impasse problem, then they will probably continue to think of a potential solution.

Finalizing the Agreement

When is a negotiation concluded? To a modern negotiator, the answer is easy. The agreement is concluded when all the problems are solved and both parties are happy. No more, no less. However, old-school salespeople often bombard the supply manager with so-called closing tactics similar to those illustrated in Box 24–4. The purpose of using closing tactics is to hurry up the decision process and force the supply manager to make a decision—in short, to get the supply manager to quit shopping.

When relationships are positive, is it still necessary to put the agreement in writing? Because of the large number of people who must interface with the agreement on both the buying and selling side, the answer is yes—not that they don't trust each other, but simply in recognition of the fact that both parties will probably forget details of the agreement as time passes.

B O X   24-4

Typical Closing Tactics

- Artificial Time Constraint
  "This offer is only good until 5:00 p.m. today."

- Rhetorical
  "Would delivery next Thursday be good, or would you prefer Tuesday?"

- Physical Action
  "But it is already on the truck and headed this way ..."

- Piecemeal
  "Let's just agree on the basics now and work the details out later ..."

- Advance Commitment
  "Your production supervisor has already agreed ..."

- Ben Franklin
  "Let's list why you should buy today rather than another day ..."

- Puppy Dog Close
  "I left it for the department to try out 30 days ago, and they want to buy it ..."

- Time Constraint
  "In order to meet your delivery, I have to call the order in right now ..."

- Inducement
  "If I can have the order now, I can throw in ..."

- Closing Bomb
  "I think this is an agreement you can live with ..."

- All-Inclusive Concession
  "If all it takes to close this deal is to ..."

- Fait Accompli (Fact Accomplished)
  "But it's already installed and running ..."

Debriefing

With a signed document firmly in hand, the debriefing is one last thing that many negotiators overlook. In negotiations, this debriefing should not take more than a few minutes. However, in the long term, 10 minutes worth of immediate debriefing is worth more than four hours of planning time six months or a year from now. It is essential to keep in mind that supply managers must deal with the same people and same companies over and over again. Box 24–5 illustrates a debriefing checklist.

Negotiation Maintenance

When negotiating for a vase in an antique store, the performance of the agreement is immediate. Regardless of the wisdom of the purchase, rendering payment gives you the right to immediately leave the shop with your prized merchandise. Future performance is only a marginal consideration because you may never have cause to visit the same store or deal with the same person again.

B O X   24-5

The Debriefing

Take just a few minutes after the sellers have departed and ask yourselves the following questions:

1. Are WE reasonably happy with the negotiated outcome? If not, can we do better next time, or should we begin looking for another supplier?

2. Do THEY appear to be reasonably happy with the outcome? If not, the sellers may drag their feet on performance. The seller may also begin looking for another customer.

3. Did out win-win solution work? If we introduced a plan, did the sellers buy into it? If not, how could it have been improved?

4. What did we do right? What were the key elements of the negotiation that persuaded the seller to accept our terms?

5. What did we do wrong? What were our major mistakes? How could they have been avoided? Is there any permanent damage that we must fix?

6. What information should we have ready for next time? If we need more cost information or a better analysis of the market situation, the time to begin data collection is NOW, not two days before the contract is due.

7. What goals can we realistically accomplish next time we meet? The concept of continuous improvement says that our next agreement should improve.

Purchasing negotiation is quite different. Even the novice negotiator realizes that closing the agreement is really only the beginning. Indeed, the agreement can only be judged to be successful if proper performance is forthcoming. For some agreements, the total performance may actually take place over many months or even years. The concept of negotiation maintenance, therefore, is the process of keeping the agreement on track from inception to completion.

Role of the Internet

For buyers and sellers, the Internet is one of the most powerful communication tools ever invented.

1. *Discovery of new sources.* Even with trade publications, trade shows, line card files, catalogs, and direct-mail fliers, the Internet will almost always yield a host of new potential suppliers. This is especially true of foreign suppliers who have not yet advertised in the standard directories or exhibited at local or regional trade shows.

2. *Tracking current suppliers.* Because of the online availability of newswire services, it is especially easy to keep track of major news releases from most major companies. This can provide the supply manager with early warning notices about pending problems with suppliers, as well as financial information about publicly traded firms. Tapping the online business section of local newspapers in the seller's hometown can provide similar information.

3. *Commodity information.* Especially for commodities that are represented by trade associations, a wealth of information is often available detailing price trends, capacity issues, legislation, and other news about the respective commodity. For commodities traded on the open market such as most of the major nonferrous metals, grains, lumber, and food products, the Web can provide daily or even real-time updates on spot market and futures market trading.

Showing Commitment

In order for the other party to perform, you must create a feeling of total acceptance. One of the worst things that you can do is to create the impression that you are still shopping even after you have reached an agreement. The seller may feel that you are about to renege or that the agreement has no future—even though there has not yet been any performance to be judged.

Courtesy is also an element of commitment. For instance, a new contractor who is introduced to the various departments around the organization feels much more welcome. These introductions not only begin the process of building relationships among the people who must work together but also create the feeling of commitment.

Keep on Planning

Good negotiation planning is a never-ending process. A good negotiator is always thinking ahead to the next negotiation. In addition to filing all the planning notes at the conclusion of the negotiation, it is wise to continue to collect and file useful information all year long. In the age of e-mail, it is wise to keep an electronic file of any messages that may be important in the future. The same is true of electronic articles for trade publications and other data sources that may relate to the commodity or the supplier.

Relationship Maintenance

It only takes a few minutes to regularly touch base with the other party so that both parties are at ease with one another. Holiday greeting cards also help, but they are not effective unless they are personally signed by the buyer.

Agreement Maintenance

It isn't always the supplier who drops the ball. It is often someone on the buyer's staff who fails to provide certain paperwork or someone in engineering who fails to provide engineering drawings in a timely manner.

ENHANCING NEGOTIATION SKILLS

Finally, the questions must be raised as to what supply managers can do better to prepare for the future and what areas the supply manager should emphasize when hiring and training new personnel. There are 10 key areas that should be the focus of these efforts.

1. People Skills

In the old school, purchasers were taught that being overly friendly could be regarded as a sign of weakness. Being a little mean and nasty on occasion would therefore let the sellers know who was boss and command their respect. As the old school gives way, people skills now appears to be one of those areas where the supply managers may be highly undertrained—or even mistrained.

In today's environment, there is often more money to be saved negotiating inside the organization than outside. Building relationships inside the firm is just as important to the supply management profession of the future as building external relationships. Altogether too many supply managers and their jobs are protected by company procedures demanding that all requisitions of a certain size must go through the supply management department. In the age of empowered department managers, this may not occur in the future.

Finally, the nature of the buyer-seller relationship is being redefined. All the buyer needed in the past was to have a good relationship with the salesperson. In today's environment, as well as the supply management environment of the future, the supply manager's relationship will be with the supplier's entire organization.

2. Team Skills

Too many people in all phases and at all levels in many firms went through team-building seminars in the late 1980s and early 1990s with their fingers crossed behind their backs. In private, they said, "Teams are a great idea, but they won't work at our company." Needless to say, many firms will find it necessary to revisit the concept of team building in order to create the intraorganizational effort necessary to make supply management agreements work as they should.

In other instances, team building is necessary to get supply management back on the team. Some firms that were successful in team building created teams that did not include the supply management function. At least some supply managers have lamented in retrospect that they did not adequately assert themselves regarding the importance of including supply management on the team.

3. Cost Analysis

Old-school purchasers were often taught to badger for a lower price with little or no knowledge of what the actual price ought to be. Old-school sellers dreamed of opportunities to close particular sales at outlandishly high prices and earn large commissions.

In the supply management environment, most pricing will be based on some form of cost-plus pricing. Pricing according to market demand, regardless of whether the current market favors the buyer or seller, will be obsolete for most commodities. Sellers of the future will be asked to submit cost data for securitization and will guarantee certain margins and be rewarded for cost reductions.

Purchasers will work with sellers to take unnecessary costs out of the system resulting in price reductions.

However, altogether too many supply managers of today are not cost accounting literate. When asked to define the basic differences between job order and process cost accounting, they come up short. This level of illiteracy must be bridged for the supply manager of the future.

Finally, there is the elusive concept of calculating total cost. It sounds easy, but actually negotiating on the basis of total cost requires a whole new perspective and set of skills.

4. Target Pricing

One purchaser proudly declared, "Target pricing? I've been using it for years. I pick a price and tell the seller to meet it or forget it." Sadly, many people today think that target pricing is really just some form of "take it or leave it" negotiations. In actuality, target pricing involves a detailed analysis of all factors that contribute to price, including materials, services, expertise, inventory, and almost every other imaginable business expense. For obvious reasons, it has worked well for firms who attempt to outsource products they are already manufacturing. In the future, this tool will be used for other procurements as well, especially in the service arena.

5. Computer Literacy

No serious observer disputes the notion that the computer is the most important tool used in business today. With the cost of computer hardware and software continuing to fall, even the very smallest supply management operations are now managed with the help of the computer.

For negotiation planners, management's emphasis on the bottom line often demands that costs be spreadsheet-analyzed and discussed as part of a normal negotiation session. Therefore, a modern negotiator must be flexible enough with spreadsheet programs to manipulate the numbers on a computer right at the negotiation table.

6. Internet Literacy

Since all negotiations are built on information, it seems obvious that one of the best sources of current, up-to-the-minute information in today's environment is the Internet. While negotiators in the past were encouraged to go to the library to keep abreast of market trends and supplier financial information, modern negotiators should locate and bookmark Internet sites to track as many relevant information sources as possible. Prior to any major negotiation, it would be wise to scan the Net for any new information or new sources that may have been posted since the last contract negotiation.

7. International Cultural Literacy

As previously noted, negotiation is a people process. An old Shakespearean phrase advises, "When in Rome, do as the Romans do." As supply managers are increasingly asked to board airliners and cross borders to negotiate agreements, it becomes essential that successful negotiators know and understand the customs and thinking processes of the people with whom they must deal. Whereas many firms doing business around the world, as well as many colleges and universities, regularly provide various forms of cross-cultural training, it becomes the responsibility of all professional negotiators to thoroughly study and understand the true nature of the people with whom they must deal.

If time does not permit formal training, it is still possible to find at least some information about other cultures on the Internet. In addition, most large bookstores also carry books designed to provide updates to last-minute travelers who must quickly bring themselves up to speed on a country and culture for which they have little or no experience. However, the biggest mistake supply managers often make is to automatically assume that "the customer is always right" and that learning about the other party's culture is therefore unnecessary.

8. Master of Commodity Information

In the past, purchasers gleaned clout from being *the* person who knew where to go to find things. With supply management agreements in place for many commodities, this task is shifting to the seller. In the supply management environment, supply managers of the future will have to become the people with the latest and best information about their respective commodities.

An old-school solution to the problem of adequate market information was to rely on sellers to provide updates on the market. Is this the fox watching the chicken coop? Not necessarily. But the fact remains that the seller is not always the best source for this kind of information.

Where will supply managers look for commodity information? In several places. First, most news organizations, periodicals, newspapers, 10-Ks, press releases, opinions, rumors, and every other form of human communication will probably be available on the Internet within the next 10 years. To the nonsupply management professional, this information overload will be overwhelming.

However, a new breed of skilled supply managers will sort out, classify, and clarify this information into a powerful managerial tool. Like other phases of the purchasing process, this process sounds easy, but it is not.

A second source of purchasing information comes from trade periodicals that are often on the supply manager's desk but unread. In the age when everyone is being asked to do more with less, altogether too many supply managers go from month to month without adequately digesting the latest information at their fingertips.

Not all this newfound information will come from either the printed or electronic media. For instance, the supply manager of the future should attend about three trade shows per year for the purpose of updating the firm's information on leading-edge technologies and potential new sources. Again, the Internet is a good source; e-newsletters for a variety of sources are available.

9. Commodity Training

The salesperson for an automotive door latch manufacturer lamented a recent sales call. A new supply manager had just been reassigned to purchasing door latches without a moment's training about the technical aspects, Department of Transportation (DOT) regulations, or quality issues associated with automotive door latches. Five minutes into the conversation, the salesperson concluded that the buyer didn't really know "a door latch from a throttle plate." He further noted that it was probably going to take him several months to teach the purchaser everything that he needed to know about door latches. In the mean time, the purchaser had already concluded their first meeting by badgering for a lower price.

In the supply management environment of the future, commodity training will be essential. Sellers will simply not put up with supply managers with whom they cannot carry on an intelligent conversation about the commodity. Conversely, technically trained requisitioners may become just as frustrated. Months of training are often required before sellers are even allowed to make their first sales call. In the future, similar requirements will be demanded of the supply management professional. In the absence of this training, both requisitioners and sellers may conclude that the supply manager is not adding value to the transaction and may elect to exclude them from the entire process, except perhaps for processing some of the necessary paperwork.

10. Contract Writing

In today's environment, hundreds of transactions are processed daily utilizing the standard purchase order form supported by the standard terms and conditions preprinted on the back. Many of today's supply managers are not even aware of the meaning of all of these T's and C's, let alone their impact.

In the supply management environment of the future, the purchase order will be utilized for mid- to high-value spot purchases only. The majority of the supply management agreements will utilize individually negotiated terms and conditions to fit the nature of the commodity and the individual needs of both the buyer and seller. An effective negotiator will therefore need to be trained in the skills necessary to write the contract terms for each major contract. Altogether too many of today's supply management agreements contain terms that were actually prepared by the sellers themselves.

11. Macrosupplier Cost Management

A lot of the top retail firms of today owe their success to a few fairly simple purchasing philosophies. First, they don't listen to sob stories about how costs have gone up and price increases are necessary. They simply ignore these price requests, and if necessary, buy elsewhere. Second, they believe the world is the marketplace, and they insist on world-competitive pricing, recognizing that "Made in U.S.A." or "Made in Canada" doesn't count for much in the marketplace, whether any of us like it or not. Third, they expect the seller to unconditionally stand behind the product in terms of service and 100 percent refunds. Finally, they expect the sellers to work with them on cost reduction, marketing, inventory reduction, and a whole host of other things. Although this sounds relatively harsh for an environment of cooperation and strategic alliances, it is a reality that the purpose of supply management is not just to shift costs around but also to reduce them based on a total-cost environment. This will be a key challenge to negotiations of the future.

12. Management of Suppliers

Old-school purchasers registered disgust with a seller by simply placing the business elsewhere. Future supply managers will become management consultants to the supplier base and help them with any phase of their business operation. When negotiating large contracts and demanding better pricing, quality, and services based on large volume, supply managers will also earn the right to criticize and manage certain aspects of the seller's business. During the life of the agreement, the focus of the negotiations will then shift to individual negotiations with the seller's personnel in order to bring them up to speed. This by itself will require a whole new set of skills on the part of the supply manager.

CHAPTER 25

COST-SAVING TECHNIQUES IN SUPPLY MANAGEMENT AND THE SUPPLY CHAIN

Ralph G. Kauffman, Ph.D., C.P.M.
Associate Professor and Coordinator
Supply Chain Management Program
University of Houston–Downtown

INTRODUCTION

If one were to survey business managers and ask them what type of activity or result comes to mind first when the term *purchasing* or *supply management* is mentioned, it would not be surprising to discover that "cost reduction" would be the first thought many of them would have. Indeed, several years ago when Bob Nardelli became CEO of Home Depot, one of his first big efforts was to centralize buying. A primary objective of this was to reduce costs by making it easier to get volume discounts from suppliers.[1] Lists of objectives for supply management always include something that indicates cost reduction or cost control. According to Monczka et al.,[2] buying at the "right price" is the number one item in a list of purchasing requirements necessary to supporting operational requirements. While these examples refer to price reductions, there are also many other ways to reduce costs such as reducing inventory or simplifying supply chain processes.

What techniques can reliably be used to reduce costs in the supply chain? This chapter is intended to provide some answers to this question. The chapter is organized around a five-step best-practice approach that starts with organization activities and proceeds to discuss what is necessary to know about supply chains to reduce their costs.[3] How to determine cost reduction potential, selection of cost reduction targets, implementation of changes, and follow-up and evaluation to assure continuous improvement make up the remaining steps of the approach. The final section of the chapter is a discussion of various supply chain cost reduction techniques.

---

1 Dan Morse (2004). "Home Depot Posts 39% Jump in Net Amid Strong Sales," *The Wall Street Journal*, February 25, p. B7.

2 Robert Monczka, Robert Trent, and Robert Handfield (2005). *Purchasing and Supply Chain Management*, 3rd ed., p. 31. Mason, OH, USA, Southwestern, a division of Thomson Learning.

3 Thomas A. Crimi and Ralph G. Kauffman (2003). "Looking for Cost Savings in the Supply Chain," *Inside Supply Management®*, March, vol. 14, no. 3, p. 6.

The chapter includes many references to articles on cost-saving techniques and approaches from the Institute for Supply Management publication *Inside Supply Management*® and its predecessor ISM publication *Purchasing Today*® over the past several years. Most of these articles are available at www.ism.ws and provide more in-depth and varied discussion of specific cost reduction techniques than can be included in this chapter. The monthly ISM publication *Inside Supply Management*® should be on the reading list of anyone who wants to reduce supply management costs. It regularly contains pertinent articles on the entire range of supply chain cost reduction techniques.

SUPPLY CHAIN COST REDUCTION BASICS

Cost reduction in the supply chain can be obtained from two main sources:[4]

1. Change what is purchased, processed, or sold; who the supplier or customer is; how and when the item is purchased, processed, or sold, and delivered to the point of use; and who is responsible for each step in the supply chain process and for the overall success of the process.

2. Increase the velocity of material in the supply chain to reduce total cycle time in the supply chain. Reduce subcycle times. Execute faster and reduce inventories throughout the supply chain.

The cost reduction techniques discussed in this chapter all relate to one or both of these two main sources of lower costs in the supply chain. These sources of cost reduction are shown in relation to a simplified supply chain flowchart in Figure 25–1.

In reality, supply chains are much more complex than the depiction in Figure 25–1, often giving the appearance of a network rather than a chain (refer to Figure 25–2). However, for purposes of analysis and to identify likely cost reduction targets, they must be broken down and separated into individual chains.

To identify cost reduction targets and implement changes to achieve cost reduction, detailed information must be known about a company's supply chains. This includes knowing how much is being spent for purchase of materials and services throughout a supply chain. In addition to spend data for each major supply chain, it must be known who are the members of the chain including suppliers, customers, and providers of transportation and other services; all inventories in the chain; and all costs and cycle times across the chain. Process mapping techniques are an excellent way to organize this information and to facilitate communication and analysis. Because there will be multiple organizations and companies involved in most supply chains, a cross-functional team approach that includes representation of all affected parties should be used to collect information, analyze it,

---

4 Ralph G. Kauffman (2003). "Cost Savings in the Supply Chain," in *Business Briefing: Global Purchasing & Supply Chain Strategies*, CD-ROM Reference Section, Elizabeth Boulton, Editor, London: Business Briefings, Ltd., November.

FIGURE 25-1

Two Sources of Cost Savings in the Supply Chain

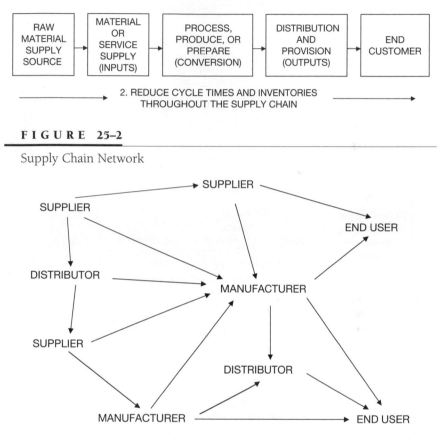

FIGURE 25-2

Supply Chain Network

determine cost reduction opportunities, plan changes to reduce costs, implement changes, and follow-up to maintain savings achieved.

A FIVE-STEP BEST-PRACTICES FRAMEWORK FOR SUPPLY CHAIN COST REDUCTION

The following five steps can be used to identify, implement, and achieve the benefits of cost savings[5]:

1. Organization and support.

2. Know your supply chain.

---

5 Crimi and Kauffman, "Looking for Cost Savings in the Supply Chain."

FIGURE 25-3

Five-Step Best-Practices Framework to Implement Cost Reduction in the Supply Chain

STEP	ACTIONS
1 Organization and Support	• Organize • Know overall organizational goals and strategies • Roughly estimate supply chain cost reduction potential • Gain support of management • Form cross-functional teams • Involve all stakeholders

2
Know Your Supply Chain
	• Gain knowledge of your supply chain:
	  ○ Members
	  ○ Money
	  ○ Material/Services
	  ○ Information
	  ○ Cycle times

3
Select Targets and Build the Business Case
	• Select cost reduction targets
	  ○ Significant
	  ○ Achievable
	  ○ Prioritize
	• Determine implementation requirements
	• Develop metrics to measure results
	• Build business case for each target
	• Obtain management and stakeholder approval to implement

4
Implement Improvements
	• Implement improvements
	  ○ Communicate changes to be made
	  ○ Train personnel
	  ○ Practice, pilot implementation, parallel operation
	  ○ Implement

5 Evaluate and Improve	• Monitor, evaluate, improve • Measure results using metrics developed • Identify changes to be made • Practice continuous improvement

3. Select targets, and build the business case.

4. Implement improvements.

5. Evaluate and improve.

Refer to Figure 25-3 for a summary of actions required at each step of the process.

Step 1. Organization and Support

Obtaining Management Approval

The first activity in approaching supply chain cost reduction is to organize for it and obtain management approval to proceed. In many organizations, a mandate from top management may be necessary to achieve the necessary cooperation of all affected segments of the company for a successful supply chain cost reduction initiative. To gain management support to begin a cost reduction effort, the cost reduction initiative must be shown to support the company's goals and strategies. Therefore, a thorough understanding of these is essential. Also, after cost reduction targets have been identified and management approval for implementation is sought, the business case presented must have a good fit as an integral piece of the process of achieving the organization's goals. For example, if a company has a strategy of producing the highest-quality product in its particular market, attempting cost reduction by procuring the cheapest production materials regardless of quality would not fit.

Estimates of cost reduction potential and what may be required to achieve that potential are necessary to obtain management approval to proceed with a cost reduction initiative. In large organizations it may not be practical to target the entire corporation for cost reduction. Therefore, considerations such as relative cost competitiveness, quality problems, and service problems can be used as indicators of where in the organization an initial effort should be directed. Another method of identification of potential cost reduction targets is to identify the materials and services for which the most money is being spent.

An additional alternative for obtaining estimates of cost reduction potential is to conduct benchmarking analyses of key processes, costs, and prices to determine how one organization compares to others or to cost or price references. At this stage of the cost reduction process, it is not important to be extremely precise since the objective is only to obtain estimates that will convince management to approve proceeding with more detailed cost reduction activities. Armed with estimates of significant cost reduction potential, management approval to proceed should be easily obtained.

The Cost Reduction Team

Once management approval of a cost reduction initiative has been secured, cost reduction must be organized as a team effort. The cost reduction team must include representation from each part of the organization and from outside organizations such as suppliers and customers who are necessary to the success of the cost reduction effort and/or are likely to be affected in some significant way by cost reduction activities. This is very important because the participation of these groups will be necessary to obtain agreement on what cost reductions are possible and how to achieve them. Having all the key stakeholders on the team will also ensure inclusion of their input and concerns, and of their ideas and cooperation, in making the cost reductions happen. To determine which groups to include, consider that some requirements for cost reduction achievement could include: changed or new information systems, revised specifications for purchased items or services, changed responsibility for inventory management, and changes in suppliers of materials or services. Assure that the team has knowledge and (preferably) experience in applying current concepts, techniques, methods, processes, and systems to reduce supply chain costs.

Plan and Schedule
A final organization activity is to lay out a plan and time schedule for conducting the remaining steps of the cost reduction process.

Step 2. Learning Activities

Study your supply chain to determine how it operates, what and where costs are being incurred, what are the principal cost drivers (such as number and frequency of orders, number of inventory items, number and frequency of payments or shipments), and what has to be done to reduce current costs. Create a process map (refer to Figure 25–1 for a summary example) of the supply chain. Determine what constitutes customer value and how value can be added to information, product, and money flows. At this stage, the cost reduction team must get more detailed information on the key supply chains in order to more specifically identify potential cost reduction targets.

Identify and Detail Key Supply Chains
Which supply chains are key to company operation and success should be evident from data collected to obtain management approval to proceed with a cost reduction initiative. For each key supply chain it is necessary to know the following:

- Who are the members of the supply chain? (Include all members, e.g., suppliers, third-party service providers, internal customers, departments, clients, outside customers, distributors, and transportation companies). How do the members relate, communicate, and do business with each other?

- Where is the money in the supply chain (purchases, inventories, services, and process and transaction costs)?

- What and where are the material and services in the supply chain (locations and sources of supply, use, and disposition)?

- Where is the information in the supply chain (e.g., information system records, files, transaction records)? How can it be determined what is happening in a supply chain over time?

- How long are the cycle times in the supply chain (e.g., order-delivery cycles, cash-to-cash cycles)?

- What are the main cost drivers in the supply chain, and what determines cost levels?

- Where is cost incurred in the supply chain? What is the amount and frequency of cost at each location of occurrence?

- Who is responsible for each supply chain cost?

- Where are the cost-determining decisions made? Who makes these decisions, and why are the decisions currently made the way they are?

Process mapping, either using software or simply a large piece of paper on a wall with sticky notes attached, is an excellent way to record this data so that all members of the cost reduction team will have the same view of the supply chain under study.

Identifying Cost Reduction Targets

Where are the money, material, and activity in a supply chain? The locations of the greatest concentrations of these three things in a supply chain will also usually be the locations of the greatest cost reduction potentials. To be able to identify potential cost reduction targets and to measure the results of cost reduction efforts, the current costs must be known. In a supply chain the largest source of cost is usually purchased materials and services for operation of the company or other organization. In addition to purchases directly for use in company operations, there are support purchases such as office supplies; maintenance, repair, and operating (MRO) materials and services; travel services; employee benefits; capital equipment; and real estate, just to name some of the most common items. While the supply chain is sometimes thought of as including only direct operating materials and services, costs of all these other items are usually very significant and, more important for a cost reduction initiative, often not well managed in terms of getting the best value for the money spent. All these items together make up what is called the *spend* of the company. If spend details are known, identification of the details of supply chains is simplified.

Spend Identification and Analysis

Before any supply chain cost can be reduced, it must be known that money is being spent as a result of purchasing an item or that cost is otherwise being incurred. It is also necessary to know the relative amounts being spent on various products and services. This information makes it possible to place priorities on cost reduction efforts. The determination of how much is being spent, on what products and services, from which suppliers, and by which parts of the organization is called *spend analysis*.

Spend identification can be accomplished by searching company records such as contained in an enterprise resource planning (ERP) system, a purchasing system, other accounting systems, or from accounts payable files of what has been paid and to whom. If company records are not complete or not well organized for identifying spend, major suppliers can be asked to provide information on what and how much they have sold to the company over a recent period of time. One of the best ways to completely identify spend, however, is to use spend analysis software and techniques that have been developed by organizations such as Analytics, Inc.[6] These are specifically designed to identify all spend and produce data that can be analyzed for the purposes of identifying cost reduction potential.

---

6 Analytics, Inc., 15 Meigs Avenue, Madison, CT 06443 (203/318-0400), www.analytics-usa.com.

Regardless of the source of data, it is necessary to know the following:

1. What products and services are being purchased or used.

2. How much is being spent on each item per year.

3. The unit cost of items purchased and of activities performed in supply chain processes. For purchased items, both price and total cost should be known.

4. Quantity per year of items or services purchased and of activities performed.

5. From which suppliers or in-house source are items obtained and how much is obtained from each source. Where are the sources of supply located.

6. Special circumstances such as seasonal supply or demand for items.

7. What part of the organization makes the decision to purchase or use items and when to purchase or use them.

8. Purpose or use of product or service.

9. Who sets specifications for items.

10. Where, organizationally and geographically, is the item used.

With this data, opportunities can be identified to reduce costs. In particular, spend analysis can enable, among other benefits,[7]

- More centralized sourcing to reduce costs and control spending

- Support for supplier negotiations to reduce costs or improve service

- Consolidation of the supply base

- Standardization of purchased products and services

- Improved management of demand levels

Identify Other Supply Chain Costs

If spend analysis is used, then the next activity is to identify other supply chain costs that are not part of spend. In-house activities and services such as inventory management (incoming, outgoing, MRO), warehouse operations, transportation services, inspection and other quality management activities, receiving and shipping activities, and investment recovery and recycling activities are examples of supply chain costs that may or may not be included in spend. Other costs include supply chain process costs, transaction costs such as costs of releasing orders, and information systems costs. Also for supply chain processes, cycle time data should be collected to identify the time length of key cycles such as customer order delivery for finished products, production materials order delivery, and cash-to-cash in various segments of the supply chain. The same types of information

---

7 Scott Elliff (2004). "The Importance of Visibility and Data on Enterprise Spending," *Inside Supply Management*®, May, vol. 15, no. 5, p. 42.

should be collected for these activities as described previously for spend and cost items. The reader may want to review Chapter 23, Total Cost of Ownership.

Step 3. Select Targets and Build the Business Case

In this step of the process the first activity is to look at the identified spend and costs and make some approximate division of the spend items in order to identify cost reduction priorities. A simple way to do this is to apply the technique called ABC analysis that is frequently applied to inventories. It is generally true that for any organization, if all its costs for purchases and other supply chain activities are analyzed, a relatively small number of items account for a relatively large amount of the total costs. A typical breakdown might be as shown in Figure 25–4.

This analysis identifies which cost items account for the largest chunks of total costs. Supply chain cost reduction initiatives directed at these items should have the potential for the largest cost reductions. Also, by focusing on the relatively few class A items, a large proportion of the total cost or spend is included in the analysis. This is a somewhat crude approach, but if spend information is limited, it may be the only practical one. A more refined approach is to divide the spend and other costs into four groups according to the amount of cost and the impact or importance of each item to the company. This approach will allow improved tailoring of cost reduction techniques to particular groups of spend or cost. A term that is frequently used for this approach is *portfolio analysis*. An example of this breakdown is shown in Figure 25–5.

F I G U R E   25–4

ABC Classification: Typical Approximate Breakdown of Supply Chain Costs

ABC CLASS	PERCENT OF TOTAL ITEMS	PERCENT OF TOTAL COST
A	About 20	About 80
B	About 30	About 15
C	About 50	About 5

F I G U R E   25–5

Spend and Cost Analysis Portfolio: Types of Purchases and Cost Items

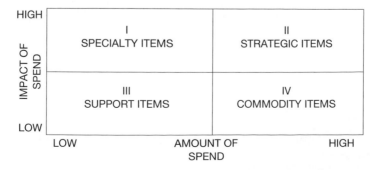

Examples of spend or costs represented by each quadrant of Figure 25–5 include

Quadrant I: specialty items. Relatively small spend or low-cost items, certain spare parts or other MRO items, occasionally used production materials, special transportation services, or inspection processes used only occasionally.

Quadrant II: strategic items. Production materials used in large quantities may be custom-made or specially made items, items critical to the success of the company, or strategic services such as those involving high levels of technology and expertise.

Quadrant III: support items. Office supplies, common MRO items, lubricants, cleaners, maintenance tools and equipment, nonspecialized maintenance services, and generally commodity items that are relatively low cost and/or not used in large quantities.

Quadrant IV: commodity items. Low-cost materials and services used in relatively large quantities. Basic commodity materials such as steel and other metals and some chemicals, for which a ready supply is generally available.

Some cost reduction techniques that may be applied to the costs in the quadrants of Figure 25–5 are indicated in Figure 25–6.

F I G U R E   25–6

Purchases and Cost Types and Cost Reduction Techniques

	LOW ← AMOUNT OF SPEND → HIGH
HIGH IMPACT OF SPEND **LOW**	**I – SPECIALTY** • Standardize • Substitute • Simplify • Supplier Partnerships • Strategic Alliances • Supplier Stocking • Supplier-managed Inventory **III – SUPPORT** • Process Improvements • Reduce Transaction Costs • Reduce Number of Transactions • Systems Contracting • Supplier Stocking	**II – STRATEGIC** • Shared Cost Reduction Initiatives • Partnerships • Strategic Alliances • Supplier Design Involvement • Global Sourcing • Strategic Sourcing **IV – COMMODITY** • Consolidate Volume • Total Cost Analysis • Global Sourcing • Standardize • Simplify • Supplier Stocking • Supplier-managed Inventory

What the portfolio approach does is allow focus on cost items that are both high-impact and high-cost, where the ABC approach focuses mainly on cost. To relate the two approaches, quadrants II and IV would generally contain the A items. Quadrants I and III would contain C items and most of the B items. There may be some B items also in quadrants II and IV since the actual distribution of items would be a continuum and not an exact separation into the quadrants.

Identification and Prioritization of Cost Reduction Targets

To identify and prioritize cost reduction targets, the focus must be on items and activities that represent large amounts of cost. For these areas in the supply chain, ask how changes might be made that would reduce the cost of the item or activity. Consider, for example, the following:

- Change specifications or substitute different material.
- Improve forecasting to reduce inventories.
- Apply e-business approaches to reduce transaction and process costs.
- Reduce the number of suppliers.
- Combine purchase volumes to gain negotiation leverage or additional services from suppliers.

These and other techniques will be discussed later in this chapter in the section Supply Chain Cost Reduction Techniques. Application of these techniques to the identified purchases and costs will result in a list of cost reduction targets. This list must then be prioritized by potential cost reduction and ease and time required for implementation. This will provide a target list with four segments:

1. High-cost reduction potential; easy, quick implementation
2. High-cost reduction potential; difficult, lengthy implementation
3. Low-cost reduction potential; easy, quick implementation
4. Low-cost reduction potential; difficult, lengthy implementation

The items in category 1 should be given top implementation priority unless certain items in other categories have additional considerations such as a better fit with achieving company goals or an urgent need for cost reduction in a particular area. Category 4 items should be given lowest priority, with category 2 and 3 items assigned intermediate priorities.

Another prioritization approach is to survey possible cost reductions that have been identified from the foregoing and rate them in terms of sustainability and achievability.[8] This approach consists of attacking costs in the following order:

1. Price reductions
2. Landed supply chain costs: inbound costs other than price

---

8 Joseph L. Cavinato (2004). "Sustainability—A Layered Approach," *Inside Supply Management®*, February, vol. 15, no. 2, p. 26.

3. Transaction costs: reduce process time and cost

4. Inventory costs: carrying and acquisition

5. Process costs: unseen costs such as those resulting from cycle times

6. Investment in assets: capital equipment, real estate

Business Case Development

Regardless of the method of prioritization and selection, for each target selected for implementation, a detailed business case must be developed. Each business case should include

- Identification of expected results
  - Targeted cost reduction amount or range
  - When the expected cost reduction will be achieved (timing)
  - How implementation of the business case contributes to achievement of organization or company goals
  - How implementation of the case is aligned with and supports organization or company strategies

- Identification of what must be done to achieve the cost reduction target
  - Who must be involved or affected
  - What each party must do
  - Implementation plans including time schedules
  - Detailed costs of implementation including any capital investment required

- Discuss performance metrics and post-implementation monitoring. Show how success will be measured

- Present plans for continuous improvement to assure continuation of cost reductions

Management approval of the business case is the next step. If the cost reduction team carefully prepares the case, and stakeholder buy-in is obtained by the team, management approval should not be a problem.

Step 4. Implement Improvements

Communicate changes to be made to all affected parties. Determine what training may be needed and for whom. Arrange for and conduct training. Pilot test process and procedure changes. Effect the implementation.

Step 5. Evaluate and Improve

Using metrics developed by the cost reduction team (such as total cost of ownership, total cost per unit, order response time, order-delivery cycle time, average inventory value, average inventory value per line item), measure results and compare them to the goals and expectations. Adjust implementation as necessary. Practice continuous improvement to maintain cost reductions achieved.

SUPPLY CHAIN COST REDUCTION TECHNIQUES

This list is not in any particular order but is divided into general categories where most frequent application of the techniques might be expected to occur. Also, the list is not exhaustive but merely representative of the more common techniques that are used in supply chain cost reduction initiatives. References provide sources of additional information.

Supply Management and Sourcing

- *Apply competitive bidding to significant purchases.* Use as a very effective tool to determine if the organization has been paying premium prices for materials or services. Invite only qualified bidders and maintain the integrity of the process by not revealing individual bid information to competing bidders.

- *Strategic sourcing initiatives.* Determine key material and service items necessary for company success and develop best sources and methods of supply for those items.[9]

- *Global sourcing.* Search worldwide markets for materials and services. The objective is to identify qualified suppliers and obtain the best value regardless of the location of supply. Use total-cost analysis to compare costs, particularly where significant transportation is involved.

- *Volume leveraging.* Capture as much spend as possible in particular material or service categories to enable reduced costs through economies of scale and to support more competitive negotiation with suppliers, for example, use of national supply agreements to supply multiple sites by one supplier.[10]

- *Reverse auctions.* Obtain best price or other objective through real-time online supplier bidding for purchases.[11]

---

9 Julie S. Roberts (2002). "Sourcing Strategically: It's Your Move," *Inside Supply Management*®, March, vol. 13, no. 3, p.33; Dian K. Castle (2003), "Strategic Sourcing," *Inside Supply Management*®, November, vol. 14, no. 11, p. 8; Pierre Mitchell (2002). "E-Sourcing Tools Can Improve Strategic Sourcing Processes, but Proceed with Caution," *Inside Supply Management*®, March, vol. 13, no. 3, p. 46; and Philip L. Haury (2004). "Making the Most of Strategic Sourcing Software," *Inside Supply Management*®, February, vol. 15, no. 2, p. 14.

10 Robert Goss, Jr. (2004). "Developing and Benefiting from National Agreements," *Inside Supply Management*®, February, vol. 15, no. 2, p. 6.

11 Ernest G. Gabbard (2003). "Electronic Reverse Auctions: The Benefits and the Risks," *Inside Supply Management*®, October, vol. 14, no. 10, p. 32; and Robert L. Neumann (2001). "The Basics about Reverse Auctioning," *Purchasing Today*®, November, vol. 12, no. 11, p. 18.

- *Effective negotiating.* Achieve the best deal from or among supply chain members by having complete information and by applying effective preparation and techniques.[12]

- *Supplier integration.* Reduce the number of suppliers of materials or services by finding ones with multiple capabilities or the ability to manage other suppliers. This can be implemented to remove tiers from the supply chain as a result of vertical integration, or to remove supply chain members horizontally and thereby reduce the number of suppliers. Vertical integration has the potential to increase the speed of material through the chain, while horizontal integration can facilitate process costs and improve volume leveraging potential.[13]

- *Change supplier relationships; partnerships, and strategic alliances.* Implement longer-term contracts, strategic partnerships, or alliances to reduce acquisition, process, or other costs of ownership, or to improve quality. Relationship changes can also be from long term to short term if, for example, a change in a particular market makes it more advantageous to use a spot market purchase strategy instead of a long-term commitment strategy.[14]

Inventory and Materials Management

- *Eliminate obsolete inventory.* Review records and/or perform physical inspection of inventories to determine what is no longer required for operations and maintenance. Dispose of surplus by returning to suppliers, selling to recyclers or to other users, or selling to scrap market.

- *Investment recovery initiatives.* Manage material and equipment surplus systematically to recover as much of the original cost and investment as possible. Requires good data on all materials and equipment owned, including capital equipment, to identify what is needed and what is not needed for the ongoing operations of the business.

- *Reduction of number of inventory locations.* Use supplier-owned or supplier-managed inventories, drop shipments, or warehouse consolidation to obtain the service required but with fewer inventory locations.

---

12 Joseph L. Cavinato (2000). "Don't Leave Money on the Table," *Purchasing Today®*, April, vol. 11, no. 4, p. 16; Allie Keaton (2001). "Negotiations: Do You Have the Right Stuff?" *Purchasing Today®*, December, vol. 12, no. 12, p. 6; and Dianna Wike (2002). "Revisiting Negotiation Fundamentals," *Inside Supply Management®*, May, vol. 12, no. 5, p. 16.

13 Roberta J. Duffy (2001). "Value through Integration," *Purchasing Today®*, March, vol. 12, no. 3, p. 36.

14 Scott Beth and Marshall Wood (2001). "Partnerships in a Down Market," *Inside Supply Management®*, December, vol. 12, no. 12, p. 4; Patrick Campbell and William M. Pollard (2002). "Ending a Supplier Relationship," *Inside Supply Management®*, September, vol. 13, no. 9, p. 33; and John Yuva (2004). "Achieving Sustainable Cost Savings," *Inside Supply Management®*, February, vol. 15, no. 2, p. 22.

- *Reduce average size of inventories.* Evaluate safety stock levels, and implement just-in-time techniques with frequent deliveries. Apply Pareto or ABC analysis, and study inventory order quantities and order points to assure that appropriate management techniques are applied to achieve the required service level with the smallest possible stocks.[15]

- *Supplier-maintained or -managed inventories and systems contracting.* Place inventories and/or responsibility for their management in the supply chain where they can be most efficiently sized and managed to meet user requirements at the lowest cost. In some cases that location may be at a supplier facility or may mean supplier management of inventories at user locations.

- *Change mode of transportation.* If the physical characteristics of the materials will allow it (i.e., relatively light weight and small size) transportation inventories can be reduced and warehouse consolidation made possible by replacing location-enabled material access with transportation-enabled access.[16]

- *Improve forecasting to enable operation with fewer and/or smaller inventories.* Better forecasting will enable upstream supply chain members to operate more efficiently with fewer or smaller "just in case" inventories.

Cost Analysis and Improvement
Also see Chapter 23 for more detailed information.

- *Total cost of ownership analysis.* Analyze all cost components involved in a supply chain or a segment of a supply chain to determine the lowest total-cost combination. This allows the cost effects of alternatives and trade-offs to be considered and evaluated.[17]

Process Improvement Techniques

- *Process improvements.* Increase value or decrease cost by modifying any phase of a supply chain process. For example, reduce order-entry

---

15 Marilyn Gettinger (2003). "Examining and Reducing Inventories," *Inside Supply Management®*, April, vol. 14, no. 4, p. 12; and Tony Noe (2002). "Inventory Control—An Oxymoron?" *Inside Supply Management®*, August, vol. 13, no. 8, p. 10.

16 Joseph L. Cavinato (2001). "Buying Transportation Today," *Purchasing Today®*, October, vol. 12, no. 10, p. 16.

17 Sanjit Menezez (2001). "Calculating the Total Cost of Ownership," *Purchasing Today®*, May, vol. 12, no. 5, p. 16; Mary Lu Harding (2001a). "Total Cost of Ownership—Inventory Materials," *Purchasing Today®*, June, vol. 12, no. 6, p. 18; Mary Lu Harding (2001b). "Total Cost of Performance—Services," *Purchasing Today®*, July, vol. 12, no. 7, p. 18; Mary Lu Harding (2001c). "Total Cost of Ownership—MRO," *Purchasing Today®*, August, vol. 12, no. 8, p. 15; and Mary Lu Harding (2001d). "Total Cost of Ownership—Capital Equipment," *Purchasing Today®*, September, vol. 12, no. 9, p. 16.

cost by changing from central to decentralized ordering against established contracts.[18]

- *Transaction cost reduction.* Decrease the cost to process a supply chain transaction. For example, change material or service order entry from paper documents to e-processes. Can be applied at any stage of a transaction cycle: ordering, transportation, storage, billing, or payment.

- *Cross-organizational synergies.* Identify opportunities to share best practices or coordinate sourcing programs across a company to reduce costs. This is often accomplished through cross-functional teams. For example, packaging expertise that reduced cost in one part of an organization may enable cost reductions in other parts of the same organization if the expertise can be shared.

- *E-procurement or other e-business initiatives.* Apply information systems and Internet techniques to improve the productivity of supply chain personnel and to reduce process and transaction costs in the supply chain.[19]

- *Benchmarking.* Compare how something is done in one organization with how it is done in other organizations. Determine how best to do it and change processes accordingly.[20]

- *Supply performance metrics.* Determine what and how to measure to determine supply chain performance and/or results of supply chain cost reduction or improvement initiatives.[21]

- *Apply JIT and other lean manufacturing or processing techniques.* Reduce waste at every step of the supply chain. If efficient in terms of total cost, operate with smaller shipments, lot sizes, and inventories to reduce inventory holding costs.

- *Cycle time reductions.* Reduce the total time it takes to complete one, several, or all the elements of a supply chain cycle from initiation to completion and payment or other accounting. For example, using e-business processes in place of paper documents or using air transportation in place of land service.[22]

---

18 Mitch Millstein (2002). "Examining Business Process Improvement Theories," *Inside Supply Management*®, August, vol. 13, no. 8, p. 12.

19 Stephen Bradley, Paul Chae, and George Hughes (2002). "Evaluating E-procurement Systems for the Supply Network," *Inside Supply Management*®, January, vol. 13, no. 1, p. 16; and Christopher Berger (2002). "Procuring E-procurement," *Inside Supply Management*®, April, vol. 13, no. 4, 24.

20 D. Steven Wade (2002). "Benchmarking in an E-procurement Environment," *Inside Supply Management*®, July, vol. 13, no. 7, p. 44.

21 Sam Farney (2003). "Metrics Drive Supply Chain Collaboration," *Inside Supply Management*®, July, vol. 14, no. 7, p. 21; and William D. Agee, Jr. (2003). "System Design for Supplier Performance Measurements," *Inside Supply Management*®, August, vol. 14, no. 8, p. 11.

22 Richard Porterfield (2000). "Time is Money, but How Much?" *Purchasing Today*®, January, vol. 11, no. 1, p. 16.

Design- and Specification-Related Techniques

- *Material or service substitutions.* Achieve cost savings by identifying and qualifying acceptable material or service alternatives that meet specification requirements but have less total cost than existing materials or services (e.g., plastic for metal, or a standard part for a custom part).

- *Quality changes.* Change products or processes to reduce material quality costs or improve the performance of materials, equipment, or services (e.g., changing to an alternate material that has increased durability but the same cost as the previously used material).

- *Standardization and simplification.* Reduce the number of specifications, products, or material or service variations to reduce process costs, inventories, and enable cost-reducing economies of scale (e.g., use of the same parts in multiple products or versions of the same product).

- *Product design improvements.* Enhance the functionality or performance of material, equipment, or service by changing the design of existing products or through supply management involvement in the new product design process (e.g., designs that enable use of the same parts in multiple products or that minimize production costs for parts and other materials).

- *Value analysis and engineering.* (Also see Chapter 28 for more detailed information.) Compare cost versus function of materials or services purchased. Determine the best materials and parts to purchase from a manufacturability viewpoint. Supply management involvement in product and process design can contribute to the effectiveness of these initiatives. In procurement of services, for example, reduction of service costs can be reduced by analyzing statements of work in service contracts to ensure exact and correct work descriptions are used.

Price and Cost Analysis

Also see Chapter 22 for more detailed information.

- *Outsourcing of noncore activities.* Evaluate company activities to determine whether improvements in efficiency or effectiveness can be gained from contracting with outside organizations for their executions. This is usually restricted to "noncore" or noncritical activities (e.g., information systems operation and equipment maintenance).

- *Help suppliers to buy better.* Cooperatively contract with suppliers for items that are used in common between the supplier and buyer organizations, review supplier sourcing practices, and suggest improvements.

- *Systematic spend analysis.* Continuously and/or cyclically monitor all significant spending. Apply structured periodic analysis of spending to identify areas of potential cost reduction.

- *Price and cost analysis and shared cost reduction initiatives.* Analyze prices and costs of materials and services to determine cost reduction potential. This requires a knowledge of markets and processes for the product and service categories analyzed. An example result would be identification of purchased materials and services that are high profit for their suppliers and may provide negotiation opportunities to reduce costs, materials, and services that suppliers can make at a lower cost by changing processes or materials. When used in the context of a supplier partnership or strategic alliance, this technique can contribute to establishment of an arrangement where the partners or alliance members share costs and benefits of improvements to the supply chain.[23]

- *Target pricing.* Determine a price that your organization is willing to pay for a given material or service, based on knowledge of costs and markets. Seek suppliers that will provide the requirements for a price at or below the target. For example, if your company is about to develop a new product for a previously unserved market segment, and market research indicates a maximum price that can be charged to gain significant share in that market, backing off the required profit and the expected manufacturing or processing, administrative, and overhead costs from that price leaves a total target cost for acquisition of parts, materials, and services.

CONCLUSION AND SUMMARY

The keys to successful cost reduction in supply management and the supply chain are

- Take an organized approach such as the five-step best-practices framework in this chapter.
- Employ teams that represent all stakeholders in the cost reduction effort.
- Know your supply chains—members, volumes, activity, etc.
- Know cost-saving techniques.
- Know the overall goals and objectives of your company or organization.
- Get management on board, and develop convincing business cases.
- Employ metrics to determine performance, set goals, and measure results.
- Follow-up and apply a continuous-improvement program.

---

23 Henry Garcia (2002). "Price Economics," *Inside Supply Management*®, June, vol. 13, no. 6, p. 16; and Robi Bendorf (2002). "Supplier Pricing Models," *Inside Supply Management*®, May, vol. 13, no. 5, p. 18.

CHAPTER 26

CONTRACT AND SUBCONTRACT WRITING AND MANAGEMENT

ERNEST G. GABBARD, JD, C.P.M., CPCM
Director of Strategic Sourcing
Allegheny Technologies

INTRODUCTION

The supply management profession is no longer a profession where the supply manager merely places purchase orders, but has evolved to establishing and managing comprehensive contracts with strategic suppliers. Therefore, a key characteristic that distinguishes a progressive supply management professional is the ability to handle complex transactions that require contractual coverage beyond the basic or standard purchase order (PO). Contract writing skills must be combined with effective contract administration and management to ensure that the contracting parties obtain the rights established in their contract. The supply manager's new role is therefore often that of contract writer and contract administrator or manager. The focus of this chapter will be to provide practical advice on these subjects for the supply management professional. Refer to Chapter 31, "Legal Aspects of Purchasing and Supply," Chapter 36, "Intellectual Property and Technology Acquisition," and Chapter 42, "Supply Management in the Public Sector" for information applicable to particular aspects and situations of contract preparation.

DEFINITIONS

The best place to start in our coverage of this important subject is to establish definitions for several key terms. The following definitions are used for the respective terms in this chapter.

> *Contract. Black's Law Dictionary* defines a contract as "a promise, or set of promises, for breach of which the law gives a remedy, or the performance of which the law recognizes as a duty." The Uniform Commercial Code (UCC) 1-201 defines a contract as "the total

legal obligation which results from the agreement of the parties ..."
Therefore, in this chapter the term *contract* will be used to describe
the documents that govern the relationship between a purchaser and
a supplier. While these definitions provide a general foundation, it
is important to note that a contract may be formed orally or in writing
and can be found to exist without a formal document entitled "contract." It is also important to note that a simple, standard purchase
order is a contract that establishes the parties' agreement on key
elements of their relationship.

Subcontract. A subcontract is a type of contract within the definitions outlined for *contract*; however, this chapter will distinguish the subcontract,
due to its significance in the acquisition of goods and services.There are
two definitions of a subcontract that apply in a procurement context,
depending upon whether the procurement takes place in a commercial
environment or in a federal acquisition environment. The following
definitions will apply for the respective environments:

Commercial subcontract. Black's Law Dictionary gives this definition: "A
contract for a portion of a principal contractor's obligation to its customer." In other words, a subcontract is used to purchase materials and
services to support higher-tier contracts for sales to the supply manager's
commercial customers.

FAR subcontract. Federal Acquisition Regulation (FAR) 3.502-1 gives
this definition: "A contractual commitment to procure from a lower-
tier supplier," in support of a federal government contract. This subcontract is used to purchase materials and services to support
higher-tier contracts with ultimate sale to a federal or state government entity.

RFx. This term will be utilized to describe the mechanism for obtaining
proposals from suppliers. There are many formats for such purposes,
such as request for information (RFI), request for proposal (RFP), request
for quote (RFQ), and invitation for bid (IFB). However, there is not
universal agreement on the meaning of each of these terms, so it will
be appropriate to use RFx to describe this phase of the procurement
process.

Supply management. The evolution of procurement has resulted in many,
varied titles for procurement professionals. The contemporary scope of
our professional responsibilities generally encompasses more than just
the traditional placement of PO for procurement of material and services.
Therefore, the term supply management is utilized to indicate the more
comprehensive function of our profession in the contemporary business
environment. Supply management as defined by the Institute for Supply
Management™ is the identification, acquisition, access, positioning, and

management of resources the organization needs or potentially needs in the attainment of its strategic objectives.

CONTRACT WRITING

The experience of this author indicates that many of the problems encountered in the administration and management of a contract had their genesis in the contract formation stage; that is, careful contract drafting could have avoided a later administrative problem. Therefore, a comprehensive discussion of contract administration should start with a review of some basic principles of contract writing. It is impractical to completely cover such a broad subject in this limited space. However, the following are some key elements of contract writing, which will apply to virtually any contract.

Start at the RFx Stage

The procurement process starts with the solicitation of proposals, and the contract drafting process should commence concurrently. It is important to ensure that any terms and conditions (T&C) that the purchaser intends to be included in the ultimate contract are incorporated into the RFx. If an attempt is made to subsequently insert substantive contracting terms after proposals are received, suppliers may have to revise pricing or other proposal elements to address such new terms; therefore, the key is to consider the end result desired in the contract when drafting the RFx. In recognition of this reality, the supply manager should not simply focus on purchase price or contractual T&C. Critical elements of a comprehensive RFx are

1. General description of item or service.
2. Quality requirements.
3. Logistics and delivery requirements (when and where).
4. Payment provisions (how much and when).
5. Commercial terms and conditions—warranty, liability, etc.
6. Rules for submittal of proposals by suppliers.
7. Mechanism for asking questions or obtaining clarification of RFx requirements.
8. Request for financial condition of supplier or format to provide such information.
9. The detailed specification and/or statement of work. This is critical to obtaining responsive proposals and to creating a meaningful contract. These documents are the source of a large portion of contractual disputes, because there is often inadequate attention paid to them during the RFx and contracting phases of the procurement process.

Consider the Circumstances and Requirements for Each Transaction

There is really no boilerplate that will provide appropriate language for all substantive transactions. Practicality necessitates the use of some standardized clauses; however, experience indicates that such clauses can be a trap if utilized indiscriminately. Any critical language desired in the contract should be included in the RFx. The professional supply manager should therefore custom tailor clauses for all significant issues that must be addressed in the contract. The supply manager will need to look to alternate sources such as their law department or formbooks for appropriate clauses to adequately cover some of the more complex issues. However, a good general rule is to never incorporate specific language provided for one contract into another contract without reviewing it for applicability. If in doubt, consult with the law department or outside legal counsel.

Use Templates, but Be *Cautious*

The modern electronic work environment enables the supply manager to utilize contracting templates so that he or she does not have to create each contract from scratch. Such templates can save significant time; however, they can be dangerous if not carefully utilized. The author has frequently seen contracts for procurement of services that contained provisions intended for purchase of a commodity. This is usually because the drafter utilized a template but overlooked the need to remove provisions that were inappropriate for this specific transaction. Unfortunately, the drafter may have also failed to include important provisions for that transaction by inappropriate use of the wrong template.

Use a Checklist

There is a common misconception that checklists are for the novice, rather than the seasoned contracts or sourcing professional. A true professional should never draft a contract for a significant transaction without a checklist to ensure that all substantive issues are addressed. An important aspect of this recommendation is to find the right checklist for contract drafting. There are many such checklists available in the commercial market. Truly comprehensive checklists should also provide a discussion of each contractual issue for consideration, rather than just a title for each recommended clause. It should also provide sample language for each contractual clause. With any checklist, the supply manager should be careful to *not* automatically utilize any recommendations without some consideration of the necessity and/or language for the specific transaction.

Place Emphasis on the Specification or Statement of Work

As noted earlier, a substantial portion of the problems experienced during the administrative phase of a contract result from inadequate attention to this portion of the RFx and the resulting contract. While most supply managers consider the specification or statement of work (SOW) to be the primary responsibility of technical or other departments, it is incumbent upon the supply manager to ensure that this document is clear and comprehensive. Even if the supply manager does not completely understand the technical aspects of the procurement, he or she must learn enough about the specification or SOW to ensure that the supplier is receiving unambiguous direction on how to satisfy the specific requirements of this procurement. It should be recognized that a specification or SOW that is too restrictive can result in higher prices, and one that is too loose may result in poor supplier quality. Therefore, a *balance* is needed to provide a solid foundation for the contract.

Selection of Suppliers for the Source List

This is a critical aspect of the sourcing process. If the supply manager does not exercise caution and discretion at this stage, the resulting contract may be of limited value. It is imperative that suppliers be adequately qualified *before* we provide them with an RFP or allow them to submit a proposal; that is, this is the time to eliminate questionable sources—not after they have submitted a proposal. The source list should be developed considering current and previous suppliers, as well as other resources that provide qualitative information about prospective suppliers. A great source for such information is the experience of other supply managers, who purchase similar products or services. This is where a network of supply management colleagues can be an invaluable resource.

Minimum Terms and Conditions

What are the minimum contractual provisions that almost every contract should contain? This question is difficult to answer, because differing circumstances can require widely differing contractual coverage. The content of each contract should be appropriate for the nature of the transaction and should consider such elements as the type of commodity or service, the dollar value of the procurement, whether it is a domestic or an international procurement, and whether work is to be performed on the organization's premises. Figure 26–1 provides a summary of items that should be included in the simplest PO as well as the more significant contract for complex items. Obviously, this is not an all-inclusive list but rather a baseline or starting point. The T&C recommendations provided in Figure 26–1 are for a contract to purchase goods. However, when purchasing services, the supply manager should be aware of the need to provide additional or supplemental terms, since the UCC and state commercial codes do not apply. Figure 26–2 is a checklist

F I G U R E 26–1

Checklist for Recommended Minimum T&C

- Scope and description
  - Product or service required?
  - Specifications referenced or cited?
- Duration of contract
  - Start date?
  - End date(s)?
- Price
  - What is included?
  - What is not included?
  - Tax? Delivery?
  - Pricing validity period?
- Delivery
  - When?
  - To where?
  - Who pays?
  - FOB point?
- Inspection
  - Where?
  - When?
  - Acceptance?
- Warranty
  - When commenced?
  - How long?
  - For what?
  - Materials?
  - Workmanship?
- Payment
  - When due?
  - Prompt payment terms?
- Damages and liabilities
  - Indemnification?
  - Insurance?
- Disputes
  - How to resolve?
  - Mediation?
  - Arbitration?
- Termination
  - For convenience of purchaser?
  - For default of seller?

FIGURE 26–2

Checklist for Recommended T&C—Services Contracts

- Scope of work
  - Carefully describe the service to be provided, in as much detail as possible.
  - How will the quality be assured? What standard will be required?
- *Changes clause.* Changes in scope are much more likely with service contracts.
- Warranty
  - There are no UCC warranties, so describe what warranty of work is needed.
  - How and when will warranty work be performed?
- *Work disruption.* Should provide the process to follow if work is disrupted.
- Payment
  - May need to provide progress payments to fund services.
  - Ensure that progress payments never exceed percentage of work completed.
  - Ensure that lower-tier subcontractors are paid by supplier to avoid liens.
- *Subcontracts.* Require approval of any subcontractors before utilization.
- Contractor employees
  - Ensure that they are classified as independent contractors.
  - Require adherence to supply management organization's policies and procedures when on organization's premises.
  - Reserve right to remove contractor employees for behavioral issues.
- *Third-party liability.* Obtain indemnification and/or insurance.
- *Environmental compliance.* Require indemnification and obtain insurance where possible.
- *Termination.* Reserve right to terminate for failure to comply with any contract obligations.
- *Completion.* Incorporate liquidated (agreed upon) damages clause to ensure performance or receive compensation where the service is critical.

of recommended items that should be carefully considered when purchasing services. This is especially true when the service is to be performed on the premises of the supply manager's organization. When service providers enter the organization's premises, significant legal issues arise that should be covered in the contract. It should be recognized that the actual language utilized to cover these items would also depend on the circumstances. The contract T&C are the vehicle with which the parties allocate the risks and responsibilities; therefore, the contract drafter must ensure that all risks are identified and covered in the contract document.

This is a serious task with significant consequences. A formbook such as mentioned earlier can provide language to be considered and tailored for each particular circumstance.

While there are other aspects to contract drafting, this author's experience indicates that the vast majority of issues that create contracting and/or legal problems can be traced to the foregoing items.

SPECIAL SUBJECTS FOR CONTRACT COVERAGE

There are a few subjects that are worth special attention with respect to the discussion of contract writing. These are protection of intellectual property and resolution of disputes with suppliers.

Intellectual Property

There can be significant intellectual property (IP) issues when procuring materials and/or services in the modern commercial environment. These can be in the form of IP belonging to the supply manager's organization, the supplier organization, or third parties. While volumes have been written about each type of IP and related laws, there are a few essential elements that are relevant to the procurement and contracting professional. The best place to start is to be able to identify the basic forms of IP. These are

1. *Patents.* Provide the patent holder with the right to exclude others from using, making, or selling the covered invention for a specified period (usually 20 years). The supply manager must ensure that patented products or the drawings and specifications for such products are not inadvertently compromised by failure to assert the organization's patent rights in the contract or correspondence with a supplier.

2. *Copyrights.* Provide protection against copying, reproduction, or use in any manner not authorized by the copyright owner. There are many forms of copyrightable material; however, in a commercial environment the most common is computer software. Computer software piracy has become a major problem for many organizations and can result in significant liability. Supply managers must ensure that their organization adequately protects the copyrighted material of both their employer and that of their suppliers. All such materials should be clearly marked with copyright assertion so that there is no doubt about ownership rights and the need for protection.

3. *Trade secrets.* May include any information, including formula, pattern, compilation, program, device, or process that derives economic value from not being generally known or readily ascertainable by other persons. This type of IP is perhaps the least obvious, yet it is sometimes the most

valuable to an organization. There is no federal law on trade secrets, and state laws vary. The critical action for the supply manager with respect to such IP is to (1) clearly identify all such information as "proprietary," (2) limit access within the supply manager's and supplier's organizations, and (c) require a clear nondisclosure agreement with the supplier and any third party who is granted access.

Protection

All forms of IP should be protected as noted earlier. Such protection should initially be in the form of a nondisclosure agreement (NDA). This is essentially a stand-alone contract under which both parties agree to protect each other's IP.

Such NDA should be accompanied by a clear company policy requiring all employees to safeguard the IP of their organization and/or their suppliers. The supply manager can be the catalyst for such a policy and should set the example for protecting intellectual property rights.

Dispute Resolution

Disputes with suppliers will inevitably occur; therefore, it is important to provide for a method of resolution in the contract—preferably without resort to litigation. There are several ways to resolve such disputes, and the following are the most common:

1. *Negotiation.* The parties can agree to require negotiation at increasing levels within the supply manager's and supplier's organizations. The purpose of such escalation to higher levels is to remove the dispute from the originating parties who may lack objectivity, due to their involvement in the genesis of the dispute. This can provide the easiest and the most cost-effective method of resolving disputes.

2. *Mediation.* Some contracts provide for resolution of disputes by mediation. This format requires the utilization of a neutral third party (mediator) who guides the contracting parties through a discussion of the issues and potential solutions. The mediator provides an objective perspective but cannot rule on the dispute. If the parties fail to agree on a solution, other methods must be pursued. Mediation is a voluntary process; therefore, it should be established as the format of choice in the contract, if desired.

3. *Arbitration.* As with mediation, a third party guides the contracting parties through a discussion of the issues and potential solutions. However, in arbitration, the arbitrator *does* have the authority to provide a decision on the dispute. Arbitration is also a voluntary process, so it should be established as a choice in the contract, where desired.

4. *Litigation.* Although no form of dispute resolution is without some negative aspects, litigation is generally the least favorable option. Litigation tends to be more costly and more time consuming than other options, and it creates an adversarial relationship that may make future transactions with this supplier virtually impossible. It should therefore be considered as a last resort for resolution of supplier disputes.

FORM OF CONTRACT

Written Contracts

The supply manager should know when a contract must be in writing and what constitutes a sufficient "writing" to establish a contract. This is covered in depth in Chapter 31, "Legal Aspects of Purchasing and Supply"; however, a few points should be mentioned in the context of our coverage of contract writing:

1. The UCC and most state laws require a contract in writing for a sale of goods over a certain value, such as $500, and/or when the contract cannot be performed within one year of the contract date. The National Conference of Commissioners for Uniform State Laws (NCCUSL) has recommended that this threshold be raised from $500 to $5,000. States will be implementing this recommendation over several years; therefore, the effective date of this change will be based upon each state's time frame.

2. The common law of contracts generally has no requirements for writing of service contracts, except as mentioned in Chapter 31. However, it is generally in both parties' best interest to also have a written record of their agreement for performance of services.

3. The requirement for a writing can be satisfied by an exchange of correspondence between the supply manager and seller and does not require a document entitled "contract." It is therefore important to ensure that all correspondence with suppliers is controlled to guard against inadvertent contractual commitment.

4. The writing requirement is not always satisfied by electronic exchanges of correspondence or documents. This is changing with the implementation of the Uniform Electronic Transactions Act (UETA) and the Electronic Signatures in Global and National Commerce Act (E-SIGN) as mentioned in Chapter 31. However, it may be prudent for the parties to agree to be bound by electronic exchanges until such laws are somewhat uniform and universally implemented. The essential elements of such an agreement are incorporated as Figure 26–3.

5. The requirements for a writing are not necessarily the same in an international procurement and contracting environment. Caution should therefore be exercised when forming contracts in this environment. Legal counsel advice will likely be more necessary for international contracts than for domestic (U.S.) ones.

FIGURE 26–3

Electronic Commerce Agreement (Example)

This Electronic Commerce Agreement is made by and between the following parties in order to facilitate their transacting business via electronic communications.

Purchaser: _____

_____

_____

Seller: _____

_____

_____

1. Parties Intend to be Bound by Electronic Exchanges

   Both parties to this agreement hereby evidence their intention to be bound by the electronic exchanges as described herein and specifically agree as follows:

   (*a*) The parties agree that no separate "writing" shall be required order to make their electronic transactions legally binding, notwithstanding any contrary requirement in any law.

   (*b*) To the maximum extent permitted by law, the parties hereby agree that the electronic exchanges will be adequate to satisfy the requirement of any writing which may be imposed by any law.

   (*c*) The parties agree that no "signature" shall be required in order to have legally enforceable electronic transactions between them.

2. Offer and Acceptance

   Electronic transmission of an order by Purchaser to Seller shall be effective as an offer when it is received on the Seller's terminal. Said offer shall be accepted by Seller in any one of the following ways:

   (*a*) Via electronic transmission of an acknowledgment, acceptance, or receipt of the offer; or

   (*b*) The shipment of the goods called for in the offer.

3. Terms of the Transaction(s)

   The terms of any electronic transaction shall be those terms and conditions which may be contained in the electronic data transmissions, plus the terms and conditions attached hereto as *Exhibit* ___.

4. Miscellaneous

   A. Nothing in this agreement shall be deemed to create any responsibility of either party to buy or sell any specific goods. This agreement is solely intended to facilitate the handling of electronic transactions between the parties. Neither party shall be entitled to or required to do any

---

(Continued)

F I G U R E   26–3

Electronic Commerce Agreement (Example) (*Continued*)

---

certain amount of business with the other, nor shall either party be required to do business with the other for any certain period of time.

B. This agreement may be terminated by either party by giving _____ days written notice to the other. Such termination of this agreement shall not affect any transactions entered into before the effective date of the termination, even if the performance of such transactions is to take place after the effective date of termination.

C. While it is the intent of both parties to use electronic transmission to the extent practical, this agreement does not preclude the exchange of documents by other methods when required by special circumstance.

D. Each party shall adopt and maintain reasonable security procedures to ensure (1) that documents transmitted electronically are authorized, (2) that its business records and data are protected from improper use, and (3) that the security of access codes and electronic identification codes is maintained.

E. This agreement shall be governed by the laws of the State of

_____.

Author's note: The adoption of the Uniform Electronic Transactions Act (UETA) by the National Conference of Commissioners on Uniform State Laws (NCCUSL) created a foundation for uniform recognition of electronic media to form a contract. However, it may be several years before all state legislatures enact the proposal as law in their respective states. In addition, the Electronic Signatures in Global and National Commerce Act (E-SIGN) provides federal law on this subject, but it only applies to interstate or international transactions and is preempted by a state's adoption of UETA. The UCC is also being revised; however, as of early 2006, no states have yet implemented the NCCUSL recommended revisions. Therefore, it is prudent to utilize a form of this Electronic Commerce Agreement to cover electronic transactions until the law on this subject is settled.

Letter Contracts

As noted earlier, contracts can be formed with an exchange of communications, so it is not unusual for parties to establish *letter contracts,* pending finalization of a formal contract document. This enables the supplier to commence work without delay, which can work to the benefit of both the supply manager and the supplier. However, this can also be risky, unless some parameters are established with such letter contracts. The following should be included as a minimum in the correspondence establishing a letter contract:

1. Contractual requirements, including incorporation of the specification or statement of work, delivery and performance schedules, etc.

2. Citation of any T&C accepted by both parties, even though not all T&C may be agreed upon at this stage.

3. Schedule for final negotiation and agreement to be established. This recognizes that the letter contract is incomplete and forces the parties to not let the final agreement languish until after the work is complete.

4. Financial limitations should be established to provide funding of only a portion of the anticipated cost or price. This also provides an incentive for the parties to finalize agreement on all aspects of the transaction. Such a limitation is generally established as a "not-to-exceed" amount in the letter contract.

Purchase Orders

The most common form of a purchase or sales contract in the commercial environment is the PO issued by the supply manager. Because of its simple form and the inherent focus on the description of what is purchased on the front of the form, the PO is often not treated as a contract. All parties must recognize the PO as a contract, which creates legal rights and obligations. The T&C that are generally contained on the reverse side of the PO form are very significant and should be reviewed with the supplier whenever possible. The supply manager should be particularly sensitive to the acknowledgment copy of the PO, which the suppliers often execute and on which suppliers often take exception to the supply manager's T&C. As noted in the "battle of the forms" discussion in Chapter 31, the acknowledgment copy of the PO should not be filed away without review and response to suppliers if necessary to preserve the supply manager's contract T&C. As noted before, the standard PO T&C for purchase of goods may not be appropriate or adequate for the purchase of services. Therefore, the supply manager must carefully scrutinize standard PO language when it is used for noncommodity purchases.

Blanket Purchase Agreements

Supply managers and suppliers often create blanket purchase agreements (BPAs) to provide a mechanism for the supply manager's organization to periodically order materials and/or services from suppliers without the need to create a new contract for each requirement. The BPA establishes the T&C to apply to such transactions and may or may not create an obligation to purchase. The BPA should clearly indicate the intention to commit to purchase or merely to establish the mechanism to order, when desired. The supply manager's organization generally issues release orders against the BPA, with reference to its terms. Caution should be exercised if the BPA covers a long period, since price adjustment may become necessary. It is also possible that a product may become unnecessary, and a long-term BPA could oblige the supply manager to purchase unwanted supplies. The BPA should therefore be used with some caution.

Is the Contract for Goods or Services or Both?

Determining the appropriate contract form will often depend on whether the transaction is for goods or services or both. If the transaction is for both, a hybrid contract will be necessary, which covers the relevant issues for the specific procurement. In such a case, the predominant purpose for the transaction or contract will determine whether it will be interpreted as a contract for goods or a contract for services. It is therefore important for the supply manager to make the contract clear as to the intended predominant purpose for this transaction.

SELECTION OF APPROPRIATE CONTRACT TYPE

As procurement gets more complex, the supply manager will need to consider using more sophisticated contracts. The standard firm, fixed-price purchase order or contract may not be appropriate for all transactions; therefore, the following summarizes the options available.

There are many types of contracts that could be utilized; however, the three general types are

Fixed price. The seller receives compensation for the product or service, based upon a predetermined price, which generally includes the seller's profit. There are variations of this contract type that are covered later in this chapter.

Cost based. The seller receives compensation for the product or service based upon the seller's cost to perform the contract and deliver the product or service. The seller also generally receives an additional fee for its effort, which is tantamount to its profit. There are also many variations of this general contract type.

Time and material. This is similar to the cost-based type of contract, and some people categorize this as a type of cost-based contract; however, there is generally a fixed profit built into the labor rate paid to the seller, and no profit or markup for the materials. There may be exceptions, which could make this tantamount to a cost-type contract.

The selection of contract type is a primary determinant of who will bear the financial risk of the transaction(s).

In a firm, fixed-price contract, the seller bears the financial risk, since it receives the agreed-upon price, even if its cost to perform is significantly greater than forecasted. The seller also reaps an additional reward (profit) if its costs are less than forecasted.

In a cost-based contract, the supply manager bears the financial risk, since he or she will pay the seller for the costs incurred to perform, generally with some limitations. There are variations of the cost-based contract that enable the supply manager and seller to share the costs and even adjust the fee (profit). This becomes a sharing of the risks associated with the contract or transaction.

In a time-and-material (T&M) contract, the supply manager bears most of the financial risk of the transaction, because he or she is compensating the seller at a fixed hourly rate, including profit for the amount of labor needed to perform the work. In order to minimize this risk, the supply manager generally establishes a maximum number of hours or dollar limit with the seller. Prior approval would then be required before the seller could exceed such a limit.

VARIATIONS
Fixed-Price Contracts

Firm, fixed-price contracts are sometimes adjusted to cover changes in circumstances. For example, the contract may cover a commodity that could fluctuate in price over the life of the contract. A mechanism is then incorporated into the contract to enable adjustment of the price based upon such a fluctuation. This creates a fixed-price, economic price adjustment (FP-EPA) contract. It is important to establish parameters to limit the amount of exposure to which the supply manager will be subjected; that is, the price will be adjusted up to a maximum (*specified*) percentage per year.

Another variation would be where the supply manager is willing to allow the seller to obtain extra compensation, in return for exceeding some predetermined objective or goal. For example, if the supply manager needs the product or service provided on an accelerated basis, the supply manager and seller could agree to an incentive to compensate the seller for beating its contractual delivery or performance requirement(s). This is known as a fixed-price incentive (FPI) contract.

Cost-Type Contracts

There is almost no limit to how many different variations of the cost-type contract can be created by the supply manager and seller. However, the primary variations are cost-plus fixed fee; cost-plus incentive fee; and cost-plus award fee. In all variations, the seller receives the cost incurred to perform, plus a fee, which depends upon the circumstance. The critical element in all cost-type contracts is to establish a clear definition of *allowable* costs that can be charged to the contract. Since the supply manager is paying the seller's costs, the supply manager should ensure that the allowable costs are defined appropriately for the circumstances. Once the allowable costs are established, the supply manager and seller must establish the appropriate fee for the transaction. The primary variations in the fee structure are

Cost-plus fixed fee (CPFF). The supply manager agrees to pay the seller a fixed fee in addition to the seller's allowable costs. The dollar amount of the fee is agreed upon in advance and is not dependent upon the final costs. The seller will generally estimate its costs in determining the amount of the fee, but the fee will not change, even if actual costs deviate from the estimates. For example, a seller's estimated costs for a particular project are $100,000 and the parties agree that the seller will be paid for its allowable costs, plus a fixed-fee of $10,000. If the seller's actual costs are on target, it will be paid a total of $110,000 ($100,000 costs plus $10,000 fee). If the seller's costs are only $90,000, then the supplier will be paid a total of $100,000 ($90,000 costs plus the $10,000 fee). However, if the seller's actual costs are higher, say $120,000, then the supply manager will pay $130,000 ($120,000 costs plus the $10,000 fee). As may be noted, the seller's fee is the same in all cases, but the costs recovered depend upon the circumstances.

Cost-plus incentive-fee (CPIF). The supply manager agrees to pay the seller a target cost, plus an incentive fee. The fee is variable dependent upon how accurately the seller estimated its costs. In this case the supply manager and seller are sharing the risk of cost overrun and also sharing the potential reward of cost underrun. If the seller's actual costs *exceed* the target cost, the agreed-upon fee (profit) is reduced by some proportion, until there is no fee left. If the seller's actual costs are *less* than the target cost, the fee (profit) is increased, based upon a formula established in the contract. This obviously provides a financial incentive for the seller to control costs more than with a CPFF contract.

Cost-plus award fee (CPAF). The supply manager agrees to pay the seller a target cost, plus a target fee, with preestablished minimum and maximum levels. The actual fee paid is usually based upon the supply manager's subjective assessment of how well the seller is performing the contract; that is, the financial risk is related to contract performance, rather than just financial performance, as is the case of the CPIF contract. It is not a popular contract type due to the extensive administrative effort required by both the supply manager and the seller. If this contract variation is used, it is imperative that the supply manager and seller establish *very clear* criteria for judging the quality of the seller's performance.

For all cost-type contracts, the Federal Acquisition Regulation (FAR) prescribes limitations on fee percentages that may be allowed and extensive descriptions of allowable costs. These change periodically, so the FAR should be consulted when utilizing such contracts or subcontracts.

For any adjustable contract, it may be appropriate to establish levels that the price cannot go above or below during the contract period. These levels are known, respectively, as *ceilings* and *floors* and can provide an effective method to control prices during the life of the contract. Such parameters should be tied to third-party, independent indices where possible, to ensure that the supplier does not have direct control of the elements which may result in price adjustments. These indices should be carefully selected during contract negotiation and incorporated into the contract; for example, during a period of volatility in petroleum products, the purchase of petroleum products could be tied to the General Industrial Oils Index, published by the U.S. Bureau of Labor Statistics (www.bls.gov).

DELEGATION OF RESPONSIBILITY OR AUTHORITY

When the supply manager intends to have the supplier interface directly with other organizations, there should be a clear understanding of who has the responsibility to monitor supplier performance, and the extent of the authority of that individual or department. The supply manager should be certain that any requests for contractual changes resulting from this monitoring activity are required to be processed in writing and that they flow through the supply manager's organization.

Contractual language should also be included that clearly outlines the authority of the supply manager's representative(s) for monitoring and recording contract performance and documenting compliance (or noncompliance). A sample of such a designating clause is provided here.

Administrative Authority

The supply manager will designate representative(s) who shall have authority and responsibility to perform the following tasks on behalf of the supply manager:

1. Provide interpretation of the scope and specification for work to be performed under this contract;
2. Monitor performance of the work to ensure compliance with the work schedule(s);
3. Inspect performance against the scope/specification, and report compliance and/or deficiencies;
4. Obtain and review Work Progress Reports; and
5. Initiate "stop work" orders, to suspend work in accordance with other provisions of this contract.

Such representative(s) will not have authority to effect changes or modifications to the contract or any contractual provisions. Contracting authority is expressly reserved for the contracting/procurement office that executed the original contract.

SUBCONTRACTING
Commercial Subcontracting

As noted in the definition section, anytime an organization purchases material and/or services to support a sale to its customers, that organization is technically *subcontracting* a portion of its obligations to lower-tier suppliers. Although the term is often used to identify only significant purchases by a purchaser, every purchase order could be considered a subcontract, if the item purchased is used to support a sale to the end customer of the purchaser.

The most important element of any subcontract is that the document incorporate any and all major obligations that the purchaser intends to have performed by the subcontractor. This is often referred to as the *flowdown* of those obligations. If the supply manager fails to include such requirements in lower-tier subcontracts, the supply manager's organization will be responsible to perform such obligations. This is because there is no *privity of contract* between the supply manager's customer and the supply manager's suppliers. Therefore, it is often prudent to have the supply manager review the organization's sales contracts to ensure that all material terms flow down to the suppliers through the subcontract document(s).

Federal Subcontracting Environment

A unique feature of the federal subcontracting environment is that the subcontract is subject to a set of complex federal acquisition regulations—only some of which apply. It is also concurrently subject to the Uniform Commercial Code, as generally implemented by a state commercial code.

The distinctive aspect of a subcontract in the federal acquisition environment is that the material or service is being obtained to ultimately support a purchase by the U.S. Government (USG) under a prime contract between the USG and the prime contractor.

Although not often apparent, it is important to note that the subcontract is essentially a commercial contract; therefore, the primary governing body of law in the *subcontracting* environment is commercial contract law [not the Federal Acquisition Regulation (FAR) or federal law]. This generally takes the form of state versions of the Uniform Commercial Code.

The FAR is applicable *only to the extent incorporated* by the parties in the subcontract. It should be noted that the FAR is not a body of law, nor does it have the force or effect of law in the subcontract environment. While many federal laws may apply to such procurements, they apply because they are federal laws—not because they are part of the FAR. In such instances, the FAR is only the implementing vehicle for such laws. Examples of these are the Procurement Integrity Act, small-business legislation, and affirmative action legislation. A graphic depiction of the foregoing principles applied to the FAR environment is provided in Figure 26–4.

Since FAR clauses are not automatically applicable to or incorporated into the subcontract, the supply manager must understand the significance of ensuring the incorporation of the appropriate FAR clauses into each transaction. This is the flowdown of a FAR obligation to a lower-tier subcontractor. This is particularly important when a specific clause gives the government a right that requires collateral action on the supply manager's part with the supplier, for example, the changes clause or the termination for convenience clause. Since there are no comparable rights in commercial law, the supply manager's company could be "caught in

FIGURE 26–4

Contracting Relationships

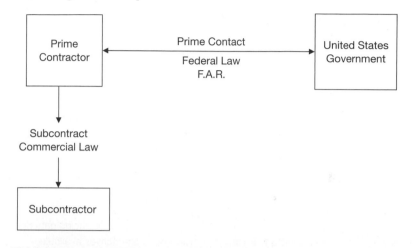

- The Subcontract is a "Commercial" Relationship/Contract

- Commercial code (state law) governs, <u>unless</u> we agree otherwise in the subcontract, or federal statute specifically requires compliance by subcontractor

- F.A.R. will apply only to the extent incorporated into the subcontract

between" if the government were to exercise such a right in the company's prime (sales) contract and the supply manager could not concurrently do likewise with his or her major suppliers; for example, if the USG terminated the prime contract under the FAR termination for convenience clause, the prime contractor would need to terminate all underlying subcontracts that existed to support the prime contract. If the termination for convenience clause were not incorporated into the subcontract(s), there would be no legal right to terminate the subcontract(s).

It is not only important to ensure flowdown of appropriate FAR clauses to the supply manager's suppliers, but to ensure that some of them are incorporated into the subcontract in their entirety and not just by reference. For example, the federal government's right of access to records and/or audit clause(s) would require significant modification to be acceptable in a subcontract. This is because it is doubtful that a subcontractor would grant the supply manager's company the same rights, which the prime contractor is obliged to grant to the government. Therefore, caution must be exercised when determining the method of incorporating the requirements of a specific FAR clause into the subcontract.

Comparison

To provide insight into the significant differences between the FAR and the UCC for federal subcontracting, a summary comparison of selected provisions of the FAR

F I G U R E   26–5

FAR and UCC—Distinctions

FAR/Government	UCC/Commercial
Actual contracting authority required	Apparent authority sufficient
Formal T&C and mandated clauses	Informality and many implied terms
"Offer" and "Acceptance" unequivocal	Equivocal and/or contrary terms can create a contract
Specific ethics and standards of conduct	Generally good faith and company policy
Warranties only as expressed	Implied and express warranties
Specific inspection and acceptance criteria	Implied and statutory terms for inspection, acceptance, and rejection
Damages for contractor default limited	UCC provides for excess costs, plus incidental and consequential damages
Unilateral convenience termination right	No collateral rights!
Changes clause (unilateral)	No collateral rights!
Cost data required over dollar threshold	Generally no cost or pricing data rights
Disputes resolution procedures and limits	Numerous alternatives available
Formal competition required	No such requirement to compete
Authority to audit seller's books	Not generally!

and UCC is provided as Figure 26–5. As may be concluded, the FAR establishes a very structured, formalized method of contracting, while the UCC promotes unstructured, informal contracting, based on the intent of the parties, rather than on the content of the documents. It may also be noted that there is significantly more flexibility in the commercial contracting environment. Of particular concern to the subcontracting professional are the areas where there are significant differences between the FAR and the UCC.

Recognizing the uniqueness of the subcontracting environment and understanding the relationship of the FAR and UCC in this environment is imperative for the professional supply manager. Such recognition and understanding will enable the parties to correctly assess their respective rights and obligations during contract formation and administration. It will also ensure that these rights and obligations are not *inadvertently* different than anticipated or desired by the contracting parties.

Proposal Evaluation

If a supplier provides a responsive proposal and unequivocally accepts all elements of the RFx, evaluation of proposals is relatively easy. However, suppliers often take exception to key elements of the RFx, and the supply manager must be able to identify any differences, determine the impact of such exception(s), and reconcile or resolve those differences that may be essential to the particular transaction. Each of the elements or sections of the RFx outlined earlier should be compared to the suppliers' proposal to ensure the supplier's responsiveness. A spreadsheet will be valuable to compare each of the proposals with all other proposals for each material or significant element. Merely comparing the prices proposed by the suppliers could lead to an erroneous conclusion; that is, the lowest price may be conditioned upon a material deviation from the requirements outlined in the RFx.

This is another critical phase of the procurement process, and the supply manager must devote adequate time to analyze the quality of the supplier's proposal, since this will have a direct impact on the quality of the resulting contract.

The supply manager should also consider the financial viability of the supplier. Despite the commercial attractiveness of a proposal, the supply manager must ensure that the supplier is capable of providing the required materials and/or services and that the supplier will be around to perform the contract. While there are many sources of such information, the most commonly used are (1) annual reports and operating statements, (2) Dun & Bradstreet reports, and (3) banking references. If the supplier's financial statements are complex, the supply manager may need to obtain assistance from his or her organization's financial personnel to interpret the data.

CONTRACT ADMINISTRATION AND MANAGEMENT

The well-drafted contract will often be of limited value, unless that contract is properly administered to ensure that the supply manager's organization receives all the benefits anticipated when it was drafted. Therefore, good contract writing must be accompanied by effective contract administration, which includes any actions necessary to ensure that all contract rights are received and that all contract obligations are performed. The level of contract administration or management required will depend upon the complexity of the product or service and on many variable circumstances. However, following are some key elements of contract administration and management that should be applied in all circumstances to ensure optimal supplier performance of the contract requirements. As may be noted, effective contract administration and management is a very *active* process and involves many diverse functions.

1. An overriding consideration for the supply manager is that the purchasing organization can inadvertently waive their contractual rights if they do not enforce or reserve those rights. This can take many forms, but consider two examples:

    a. A supplier delivers nonconforming parts, which are not rejected in a timely manner. The failure to reject such parts could result in a waiver of contractual rights and affect the supply manager's subsequent remedies under the contract.

    b. A supplier repeatedly delivers product late, and the supply manager fails to notify the supplier that this is a breach of contract and is not acceptable. Failure to do so could ultimately result in a waiver of the supply manager's contractual right to timely delivery. The supply manager must immediately notify supplier of any late delivery and reaffirm the right to on-time delivery in the future.

2. Performance management and tracking reports must be incorporated and maintained to ensure contract compliance. Such requirements should be established in the contract document and reaffirmed in the contract abstract, as elaborated in the "Contract Abstract or Work Summary" section later in this chapter. The criteria for measurement of contract performance should be clearly established in the contract and may include

   a. Delivery measures. Actual delivery compared to promised delivery

   b. Service measures. Supplier responsiveness to the needs of the supply manager's organization

   c. Cost measures. Actual cost compared to historic, target, or benchmark costs

   d. Quality measures. Actual quality compared to specifications or historic quality

3. Effective written communication between the supply manager's organization and its sellers is the *key* to effective contract management. All outgoing correspondence should be logged and suspended to ensure a timely response is received from the seller. All incoming correspondence should likewise be logged and suspended to ensure a timely response is sent to the seller. In the latter case, timely support from other company departments, such as Engineering, Quality Assurance, and the Program Office may be essential to providing responses.

4. Early identification of performance problems is paramount to avoidance of schedule delays, which would ultimately impact the ability of the supply manager's company to meet its obligations. The first indicators of such supplier problems are generally

   a. A delayed response to correspondence—particularly correspondence requesting or confirming seller performance schedules.

   b. Supplier requests for delays in scheduled performance reports or performance reviews.

   c. No visible or apparent progress on seller reports and progress charts during performance reviews.

   d. When percentage of progress payments exceeds percentage of performance completion. If this occurs, the supply manager loses a significant lever with which to obtain timely contract performance.

5. What if the supplier has not actually breached the contract, but the supply manager has reason to believe that breach is imminent? Must supply managers wait for the actual breach to occur? If the supply manager has reason to believe that the supplier will not perform future obligations, he or she may take action to request that the supplier provide written

assurance of its capability and intent to perform. This is pursuant to UCC 2-209, under the following circumstances:

a. The supplier has failed to perform previous installments, for example, repeated late deliveries or previous delivery of nonconforming parts.

b. The supplier repudiates its obligation; for example, the contract becomes less attractive commercially, and the supplier advises it does not intend to perform.

c. Circumstances indicate that breach is likely; for example, the supplier has become financially unstable and may go out of business.

6. Immediate written response to any indications of performance or schedule delays is imperative. A seller must be clearly held accountable for any identifiable delays, up to and including legal and contractual "show cause" and "termination" procedures. Failure to do so could result in a waiver of the supply manager's contract rights.

7. Enforcement of the contractual milestone schedule. If a detailed milestone schedule is incorporated in the initial purchase contract, it will be easier to withhold payments when milestones are missed, thereby maintaining adequate leverage to ultimately ensure timely performance.

8. Create and maintain a master contract file, where original contract documents are secured and controlled. It is imperative that all parties recognize these documents could someday be critical to prove the supply manager's legal rights. They should therefore be treated as significant legal documents. Access to master contract files should be controlled, and such files should be secured when not being used by the supply manager. This file should include at least:

a. A copy of the RFx

b. A copy of the supplier proposals

c. The original contract, including any specifications or other attachments and exhibits

d. A copy of all amendments, changes, or other contract addenda

e. All incoming and outgoing correspondence

f. Minutes of any project meetings or supplier review meetings

g. Progress or performance reports

h. Payment authorizations and records of payments

i. Quality assurance reviews or audits

j. Summaries of supplier performance issues

k. Summaries of supplier remedial actions

CONTRACT ABSTRACT OR WORK SUMMARY

This is one of the most significant tools available to the supply manager for effective contract administration and management. This is the document in which complex contractual requirements are summarized for all internal stakeholders. Without this document, every internal stakeholder or recipient of the purchased product or service must read the entire contract and interpret the requirements contained therein. This would be time consuming and inefficient and could create multiple, differing opinions of the organization's contractual rights and obligations. Absence of such an abstract or summary could also result in unintended breach of a contractual obligation or inadvertent waiver of a contract right.

The contract abstract or summary can take many different forms, dependent upon the scope and complexity of the contract. It can be a one-page summary of key rights and obligations, or it could require a complex matrix of each contract clause with assignment of responsibility for compliance with each clause. Creation of such a document should be the first step in contract administration and management.

In order to prepare the abstract or summary, the administrator will need to read every element of the contract. He or she will then need to determine the appropriate level of detail required in the abstract or summary. It is suggested that the following will be needed, as a minimum, irrespective of complexity:

1. Description of product or service being procured

2. Description of quality requirements for each product or service

3. Packaging or marking requirements

4. Summary of price(s) for each product or service

5. Delivery or performance dates for each product or service

6. Delivery terms, with clear designation of freight on bill (FOB)

7. Description of event(s) that constitute acceptance of the product or service

8. Summary of warranty provisions, with a clear description of when the warranty starts and the method to obtain warranty repair of replacement

9. Listing of supplier reports, with due date(s) for each report

10. Method for handling and protecting any supply management–provided intellectual property (IP)

11. Method for handling and protecting any supplier-provided IP

12. If performance is on the supply manager's premises, ensure the following:
    a. Receipt of insurance certificate
    b. Acknowledgment of security requirements
    c. Receipt and understanding of supply management's safety standards
    d. Assurance of supplier compliance with the supply manager's workplace rules
    e. Assurance of supplier compliance with environmental rules and regulations

13. Payment terms, with prompt payment discount, if any

14. Key contact person(s) for both purchaser and seller

15. Contract term, with requirements for extension, if any

Other requirements can be added as necessary for more complex contracts. If multiple organizations are responsible for receiving, inspecting, and accepting the product or service, the abstract or matrix should indicate the organization and/or person with the responsibility and authority to perform those tasks. For complex contracts, it is advisable to hold a kickoff meeting of all internal stakeholders, to ensure a complete understanding of all contractual rights and obligations. This should include a review of product or service specifications, contract deliverables, key performance dates, billing and payment processes, and respective roles and responsibilities of each of the stakeholders in the supply manager's organization. This can result in much more effective contract administration and management. However, it should be noted that the ultimate responsibility for supplier performance resides with the supply management organization. The supply manager's role in creating the contract abstract is therefore critical to contract compliance.

Supplier Kickoff Meeting

A meeting of the supply manager and supplier organizations is also appropriate wherever the requirements for contract performance are complex and include multiple departments within each organization. Such meetings should include a review of the contract responsibility matrix and should ensure agreement and understanding of the contractual requirements for both organizations. The more complex the contractual obligations, the more important this step will become.

Contract Amendments

Exceptional contract drafting and administration necessarily requires that any changes of circumstances be documented to ensure continuity of the continuing legal rights and obligations of the contracting parties. Such documentation is generally accomplished with a contract modification or amendment. The key to effective contract amendments is that the drafter devotes as much effort and expertise to the amendment as was utilized on the original contract. Some critical elements of effective contract amendments are

1. Sequential numbering and stated effective date for each change
2. Reference to the specific provisions that have changed
3. Verification that all other provisions remain unchanged
4. Control of the process to ensure amendments are properly approved and executed

Comprehensive procedures should be established and followed by all parties to ensure that the process of amending contracts is effective.

If the supply manager is unprepared, contract amendments can be costly. Since the supplier is already under a contract, it might be impractical or impossible to switch suppliers when circumstances change; therefore, the supplier is often in a position to price any contract changes with a much higher profit margin than was obtainable during the initial contract negotiations. Such vulnerability can be minimized by the following:

1. Provide for the possibility of changes in the contract. The supply manager should always reserve the right to make modifications, with an appropriate adjustment in price and/or schedule. Where possible, the contract should also provide a mechanism for pricing any changes required during contract performance. One method is to limit the price for any changes to the supplier's actual cost for performing the changed work.

2. When changes are needed, the supply manager must focus on the specifics of the change and be aware of the prospect that the supplier may attempt to renegotiate items in the contract that have not changed. This is why any change must be carefully documented and evaluated to ensure that unaffected portions of the contract are not inadvertently changed.

3. Whenever possible, the contract amendment should be negotiated before work proceeds on the changed portion of the contract. This will enable the supply manager to ensure that there is agreement on the cost and schedule impact of the change before it is performed. Obviously, the supply manager is vulnerable to supplier gouging if the work has already been performed before the contract amendment is negotiated.

4. Document and communicate the changes with the same diligence as was utilized in the original contract. All such changes should be formalized in a written document and executed by responsible parties. Clearly state which specific contract terms are being revised, and indicate that "all other terms remain unchanged." This will avoid any ambiguity on the intentions of the parties.

5. Ensure that the amendment is distributed to all recipients of the original contract. Also revise the contract abstract or work summary to reflect any changes created by the amendment and ensure that all internal stakeholders receive the revision.

6. The supply manager should be sensitive to the prospect that too many contract amendments may make the contract of questionable value; that is, after 20 contract amendments, what does the contract really say? There may be circumstances when a new contract is appropriate to replace one that requires multiple, significant amendments.

Contract Breach

During the administration of the contract, the supply manager may determine that the supplier has failed to perform an obligation provided for in the contract. This could be delivery of a nonconforming product or a delinquent performance. Such a failure is considered to be a breach of contract. The supply manager should take the following actions *in a timely manner*:

1. Notify the supplier of the contract breach, and make a specific demand for the supplier to comply with the contractual requirements. This notice should reaffirm the rights of the supply manager's organization, outline specific action required of the supplier to remedy the breach, and provide a due date for the supplier's remedial action. It is not appropriate to terminate the contract at this stage unless the breach is so onerous as to require such action. In fact, the law generally requires that the purchaser provide the supplier with an opportunity to "cure" the breach.

2. If the supplier cures the breach, the supply manager should document any financial or other damages incurred as a result of the breach and file a claim with the supplier. The supply manager should also advise the supplier that future performance is expected in accordance with the contract, to reaffirm that any previous acceptance of late delivery or non-conforming parts does not constitute a waiver of future contract rights.

3. If the supplier fails to cure the breach, the supply manager should notify the supplier of intention to terminate the contract. This notice should indicate that the supply management organization reserves its legal rights to reprocure elsewhere, at the seller's expense, and/or take any other action provided by law. It is important for the supply management organization to carefully document all actions taken to recover from the supplier's breach in order to support subsequent claims against the supplier. All such actions must be taken in a timely manner.

4. Whether the supplier has cured the breach or not, it is important to document the supplier's performance failures for evaluation on future procurements. Such documentation can provide evidence and justification to not award to this supplier or to adjust this supplier's prices to reflect the risk of procuring from this supplier.

It should be noted that supply management organizations could also breach a contract. The most common breach by supply management is failure to make payments in accordance with the contract requirements. Other obligations that must be met to avoid breach of contract by the supply management organization include

1. Providing customer-furnished material or tooling relied upon by the supplier

2. Providing the supply management organization's drawings or specifications in a timely manner

3. Providing timely approval of supplier documents, such as designs or design changes

4. Providing timely access to the supply manager's facilities where required to perform the supplier's obligations

Supply management should set up an internal system to monitor and report such obligations and ensure that both the supply management organization and the supplier organization perform their respective contractual obligations in a timely manner.

Contract Termination

Contractual relationships may be ended before the completion of performance by the parties by termination of the contract. This may be accomplished by mutual agreement, such as where the parties decide they no longer desire to complete their respective obligations.

Termination can also be made unilaterally, where one of the parties has failed to perform and the law allows the nonbreaching party to terminate the relationship "for default." Refer to Chapter 31 for more information; however, it is appropriate to point out in this chapter that it is valuable to reserve the right to terminate a contract for specific reasons when the contract is drafted. This is known as a *default* termination clause. Commercial codes may provide such a legal right; however, the course of action will be much clearer if it is established in the contract.

It may also be appropriate to reserve the right to terminate the contract for no reason at all, other than that it is no longer considered a desirable or valuable relationship. This is known as a *convenience* termination clause. This is particularly important when the supply manager's organization has such provisions in the sales contract to its customers. Without such provisions in the supply management organization's contracts with suppliers, the supply management organization could be vulnerable; that is, if the supply manager's customer terminates the sales contract under a termination for convenience clause, but the same right does not exist in the procurement contract(s), the supply management organization could be obliged to purchase the supplier's product or service, even though there is no longer a need for it. There is generally no legal right under commercial law to unilaterally terminate a contract; therefore, such a right must be established in the contract, if desired.

CONTRACT CLOSEOUT

When delivery of a product or service is complete, it is tempting to merely place the contract file into a cabinet for disposition at some future date. However, the experienced supply manager knows that it is important to first perform a review of the contract file to ensure that all contractual rights have been obtained and that all contractual obligations have been performed.

A comprehensive checklist should be used to review the contract file before it is shuffled off to storage. At a minimum, such closeout questions as the following should be answered:

1. Have all products been received, inspected, and accepted?

2. Have all related services been performed according to the contract SOW?

3. Have any claims and/or disputes been completely resolved?

4. Have all warranty periods expired and warranty claims been satisfied?

5. Has all customer-furnished material (CFM) been returned to the supply manager?

6. Has any supplier-provided (loaned) material been returned to the supplier?

7. Has any consigned material been purchased or returned?

8. Have all invoices been received and paid?

9. Have all notices required by the contract, for example, notice of contract nonrenewal, been issued?

10. Are all original contractual documents placed in the master contract file for storage?

When the supply manager is assured that all elements of contract performance are complete, he or she must consider:

Storage. Where will the contract file be stored, and for how long? It may be necessary to store the contract file in a readily accessible location for a period of time until all closeout questions and issues have been completely satisfied.

Retrieval. When the file is moved to long-term storage, how will the administrator retrieve the file in the event of litigation or other activity necessitating access?

Retention. When a file is stored, it should be determined how long it must be retained before destruction. The supply management organization's record-retention policy should provide basic guidance on how to retain what documents and for what period. However, many federal, state, and local laws will often require retention for specific time frames, so caution must be exercised in establishing the retention period. All files should be carefully marked with such retention information, and an index should be created to provide a summary of applicable file destruction date(s).

Electronic format. Storage, retrieval, and retention requirements could be satisfied by utilization of electronic files, rather than paper files. However, many laws requiring record retention may not recognize the validity of electronic files. Therefore, such legal requirements must be determined before the storage format is decided. Special caution must be exercised in protecting electronic files in any event, since they must be protected against corruption or alteration. This probability is not as likely or as problematic with paper documents.

CONCLUSION

The contract writing and management process should clearly allocate and administer the rights and obligations of both the supply management and supplier organizations. This process must clearly

1. Start with the preparation of the RFx
2. Include comprehensive terms and conditions, which consider the circumstances
3. Involve more than just the supply management professionals
4. Include internal dissemination of appropriate contractual requirements
5. Ensure all rights and obligation are performed in a timely manner
6. Carefully document contract performance and contract changes
7. Ensure closeout activities are performed at contract completion

Professional performance of these important tasks is critical to the supply management organization and will distinguish the supply manager as a valuable professional on the organization's management team.

CHAPTER 27

QUALITY MANAGEMENT

RICHARD A. GOULD
Chief Solution Provider
R G Management Solutions

DENNIS R. ARTER, PE
Certified Quality Auditor
Columbia Audit Resources

PATSY BALL–BROWN
Brown & Associates Quality Consulting, Inc.

DAN CREININ
Product Manager
Böwe Bell + Howell

LINDA HOWE GARRIZ
Manager, Quality Assurance
Alcon Manufacturing, Ltd.

THOMAS I. SCHOENFELDT
President
Schoenfeldt Services, Inc.

TRACI VAN ARSDALE
TVA Associates

INTRODUCTION

Objective

This chapter will focus on quality management and its impact on the overall procurement of products and services. The significance of quality in the customer-supplier relationship will be addressed, and practical quality tools for both the customer and supplier will be presented.

Quality management has a direct impact on the supply management function. As the use of quality management tools spreads throughout what have traditionally been "nonquality" departments or organizations, it is imperative that all personnel understand the basics of quality management and the tools employed in the quality discipline.

There is a science to quality that can make a significant positive contribution to a company's bottom line. Studies on the leveraging effect of quality point to the financial impact of good versus bad quality, and an even stronger positive impact with an effective supplier quality management program.[1]

In the past it has been thought that purchasing did not like to talk about quality in general, and supplier quality in particular, because of the relationships that purchasing personnel have with their suppliers. However, since a strong supplier quality management program can have a significant impact on the success of the company, quality personnel must have an influential seat at the corporate table, rather than being a reactive player when something goes wrong. It is expected that the reader will come away with an appreciation for the important role quality management plays as a teammate of the supply management professional.

BACKGROUND

By studying the history of the quality movement, it can be concluded that there have been three eras of quality. The quality control era was started by the early pioneers, principally at Western Electric Corporation, and consisted mostly of inspection activities. While still practiced today, it is but part of the total approach to quality. The quality assurance era began after World War II, primarily with military and nuclear applications. It added the element of defined manuals, procedures, and drawings to the quality movement. It peaked in 1994, with the ISO 9001 approach of "Say what you do and do what you say." Remnants of this philosophy can be seen today when it is suggested that the answer to every problem is to revise or generate another procedure. The current quality management era began in the mid-1990s with earnest consideration of the organizational systems used to achieve results. Total quality management, the Malcolm Baldrige National Quality Award, Six Sigma, Lean, and ISO 9001:2000 are all manifestations of this systems approach.

It is to be noted that as one era progressed to the next the older tools and ideas were not discarded. Quality management is an additive process.

What Is Quality?

Quality can mean different things to different people. Some well-known quality advocates (or gurus) have developed their definitions of quality, such as

---

1 The Aberdeen Group (2002). "Measuring Supply Chain Success," *The Supplier Performance Benchmarking Report*, December, www.aberdeen.com.

- According to the late Dr. W. Edwards Deming, a Bell Laboratories statistician who developed many of the statistical process control methods used today, quality is "nonfaulty systems."[2]

- According to Dr. Joseph Juran, who developed the "quality trilogy" consisting of quality planning, quality control, and quality improvement, quality is "fitness for use."[3]

- According to the late Philip Crosby, who developed the idea of "zero defects" (doing things right the first time), quality is "conformance to requirements."[4]

- According to Dr. Armand Feigenbaum, who developed the concept of total quality control, quality is "a customer determination that is based on the customer's actual experience with the product or service, measured against his or her requirements—stated or unstated, conscious or merely sensed, technically operational or entirely subjective—and always representing a moving target in a competitive market."[5]

- According to the American Society for Quality, quality is "a subjective term for which each person has his or her own definition. In technical usage, quality can have two meanings: (1) the characteristics of a product or service that bear on its ability to satisfy stated or implied needs and (2) a product or service free from deficiencies."[6]

These definitions show that quality does not have a simple definition. Each customer of a product or service defines it. Suppliers must continuously listen to their customers to find out what their requirements or definitions of quality are and develop ways to meet them.

Finally, a more contemporary definition of *quality* is as follows.

A systematic approach to the search for excellence. Synonyms: productivity, cost reduction, schedule performance, sales, customer satisfaction, teamwork, the bottom line.[7]

This concise definition can be easily understood. Quality is a journey, not a destination; therefore, it is right to look at quality as a search. Quality is also a technical discipline, so it must be systematic, and excellence is the quality goal sought by all. The synonyms define excellence in today's business world. Things that are not to be wasted are talents (productivity), resources (cost reduction), and time (schedule performance). Corporate expectations (sales) as well as market

2 Donna C. S. Summers (2003). *Quality*, 3rd ed., New York: Prentice Hall.

3 J. M. Juran (1988). *Juran's Quality Control Handbook*, 4th ed., New York: McGraw-Hill.

4 Philip B. Crosby (1979). *Quality is Free*, New York: Penguin Group.

5 Armand Feigenbaum (1983). *Total Quality Control*, 3rd ed., Ontario, Canada: McGraw-Hill Ryerson.

6 Summers, Quality.

7 American Society for Quality, Milwaukee, WI. Taken from a wall poster, ASQ staff author unknown.

expectations (customer satisfaction) must be met. Today's environment favors collaboration (teamwork) that benefits everyone (the bottom line).

Quality is defined in the context of relationships. The better the relationship, the more the customer will share with the supplier and vice versa, creating a strong relationship.

Customer Responsibilities to Suppliers

Effective customer-supplier relationships are built upon complete and open communication. There are responsibilities that a customer has to a supplier in the relationship. These responsibilities are generally related to new product (services are also considered a product) development and quality, and materials practices (planning, procurement).

First, it is important that the customer involve the supplier early in the development of new products. The supplier is the expert in his or her product. With the supplier's early involvement, clear specifications can be developed, with clearly defined parameters and quality requirements that are mutually agreed upon as being vital to success. These parameters will be used to monitor quality and performance on an ongoing basis.

Second, the use of just-in-time (JIT) procurement is a significant factor contributing to success. Several planning disciplines must be implemented as prerequisites to an effective JIT process. Demand stability must be pursued so that customers can accurately forecast their requirements to suppliers. Forecasts must be frequent and give the supplier as much forward visibility of requirements as possible. Accurate forecasting, blanket purchase order coverage, and a "pull" system that releases material from the supplier based on actual consumption will be used. The customer must tightly control inventories, which not only reduces waste but also protects the supplier from sudden changes in demand.

Finally, the customer must treat the supplier as a long-term partner and not sacrifice this relationship based on short-term opportunistic minor price variations.

Customer Expectations from Suppliers

Once the customer has fulfilled its responsibilities, then certain things may be expected from the supplier.

First, it is expected that the supplier be a leader in its particular business. As such, it will maintain open communication with the customer and establish product development partnerships that result in rapid time-to-market for the customer's products.

Second, suppliers are encouraged to adopt JIT practices in their internal operations and with their suppliers and subcontractors in order to improve productivity and reduce waste.

Third, suppliers must commit to long-term cost reductions. As the volume of business increases, the supplier will realize improvements that result in cost reductions to be passed on to the customer. Experience-curve pricing models may be used early in the relationship to project future price reductions in a predictable manner.

With the security of a long-term relationship, the supplier can commit to aggressive downside flexibility where temporary production line interruptions stop releases for material. Conversely, suppliers must also have an aggressive upside capability, being able to respond quickly to increased business opportunities.

Regarding quality, suppliers must continually strive for the highest quality levels throughout their operations. They must demonstrate quality philosophies and systems that represent a true customer satisfaction focus and a continuous-improvement mind-set at all levels. To attain these levels of quality, thc supplier will be expected to implement advanced quality disciplines.

QUALITY MANAGEMENT TOOLS AND TECHNIQUES FOR SUPPLIERS
Measuring and Monitoring

Measuring and monitoring are part of the continuous-improvement processes used by customers and suppliers in the manufacturing and service industries. There is a difference between measuring and monitoring. *Measuring* is a discrete act of taking and recording qualitative or quantitative data. *Monitoring* involves gathering data over time, to look for trends or patterns. Suppliers perform both measuring and monitoring using tools such as the following.

Inspection

Inspection is classic *quality control*, where data is taken on items or activities by trained people and compared to requirements in order to make an acceptance decision. Often, employees or operators are the best ones to perform the inspection, as they are able to immediately make appropriate corrections.

Process Measurement

One of the biggest contributions to improved quality has been scientific monitoring of the various processes. Tools, such as statistical process control, allow the supplier to detect and then correct variability in the process.

Peer and Management Review

Suppliers are expected to perform peer reviews of documents before they are actually used for production. (This is also known as *document review*.) If products are produced from the supplier's own design, the supplier is expected to perform design reviews.

In addition to checking the quality characteristics of the product or service, managers and supervisors should monitor the performance of employees and equipment. This is often referred to as "management by walking around."

Internal Audit

An internal audit is performed by the supplier to verify that things are going as planned. It is the process of "comparing reality with requirements."[8] An audit is an important tool in detecting and correcting problems. Suppliers should implement internal audits of their quality, safety, and environmental control systems as a way of improving their performance and providing customers with assurances. The audit has two inputs—documented requirements and actual performance. The output of the audit is a report, with overall conclusions and positive and negative findings.

There are four fundamental rules for an internal audit.

1. *Audits provide information for decisions*. Audits provide stakeholders with processed information on the health of the operations.

2. *Auditors are qualified*. Competent auditors are objective, knowledgeable of the technical processes, and able to assess and communicate the results to others.

3. *Auditors measure against agreed-upon requirements*. Documented requirements are defined by external sources such as standards, regulations, and purchase orders, or by internal sources such as manuals, procedures, plans, and drawings.

4. *Audit conclusions are based on fact*. Auditors gather data from the operations, examine the data, and present *findings*, which are subjective statements of a problem supported by one or more facts as evidence. Finally, auditors report their overall conclusions, positive and negative, about the management controls being applied within the scope of the audit.

Statistical Process Control

Statistical process control (SPC) is a methodology where data (statistics) is used to control the output of a process. Data is gathered from the process to determine whether the process is operating within the expected limits or whether it should be adjusted.

SPC is implemented on one or more characteristics of the process that are determined to be important to the overall performance of the product or process. In a manufacturing process, dimensional information can be gathered directly off the manufacturing line. In a service industry, data may be gathered using stopwatches and general observations.

Data may be any of the following:

- Dimensional (e.g., size, weight, height, circumference)

- Physical (e.g., tensile strength, pH, elasticity)

---

8 Dennis R. Arter (2003). *Quality Audits for Improved Performance*, 3rd ed., Milwaukee: Quality Press, p. 18.

- Process (e.g., heating time, cooling time, flow)

- Activity (e.g., days late, mislabeling, data entry)

After the data is gathered, SPC software is usually used to analyze it according to well-defined statistical formulas and criteria.

SPC is used to meet three goals:

1. Achieve a stable process

2. Maintain a stable process

3. Improve overall process capability

Achieving a Stable Process

To achieve a stable process, variation in the output of the process must be measured. No two variables—people, parts, finished product, equipment, measuring instruments—are exactly alike. Although the differences may be slight, they still exist.

Variation in the output of a process can be of two types—common cause variation and special cause variation. Common cause variation is random variation inherent in the process. It exists even under ideal situations. Special cause variation is anything that occurs as a result of factors that are not always present in the process. Some examples of special cause variation include

- Batch-to-batch changes in raw material used in a process

- Small, incremental changes over time, due to tool wear or other mainte-nance issues

- Sudden, permanent change due to equipment failure or malfunction

Special cause variation can result in deteriorated process output results and should be identified and eliminated to achieve a stable process and to determine the true capability of that process.

Maintaining a Stable Process

In order to maintain a stable process, the ongoing capability of the process must be determined. Process capability must not be confused with the ability of the process to stay within the specification limits. A stable process, one that is statis-tically in control, may not be capable of meeting specification requirements. If this is the case, improving overall process capability should be an immediate goal. If a process is out of control, it must be stabilized—brought into a state of statistical control, with the sources of special cause variation identified and elim-inated—before the process capability can be improved.

Improving Overall Process Capability

To improve overall process capability, three measures relating to the output of the process should be considered: process *mean*, or average; process spread, or *vari-ability*; and process shape, or *distribution*.

As process capability is improved, the process mean will be very close to the nominal specification requirement, the process spread will be smaller, and the shape of the distribution will resemble the normal (or bell-shaped) distribution.

Control Charts

Control charts are graphical representations of data that help predict the output of a process and help determine the process capability. They have a solid centerline, representing the process average, and dashed lines, representing the upper and lower control limits. Data points are considered to be out of control if any of the following conditions occur:

- A point falls outside either control limit, indicating a possible increase in variability of the process.

- Seven points in a row are on one side of the centerline, indicating a possible process shift.

- Seven points in a row are steadily increasing or decreasing, indicating a possible trend.

Variables Control Charts
Variables data is measured to a prescribed accuracy. This data is plotted on variables control charts, such as X-bar and R charts, to track the performance of variables data over time.

Capability Index
The capability index C_{pK} is a common measure of process performance. It compares the process average to the nominal specification and the process spread to the specification limits. It is used only in situations with symmetrical specification limits around a nominal or target specification requirement. Larger values of C_{pK} indicate a better capability, because the processes are closer to the nominal specification and the process spread is less.

Attributes Control Charts
Attributes data can be classified as either conforming or nonconforming (e.g., good or bad). This data is plotted on attributes control charts, known as p-charts, np-charts, c-charts, and u-charts. These charts track attributes data over time: p-charts track the proportion nonconforming, while np-charts track the actual number of nonconforming units in the sample; c-charts track the number of non-conformances found in the sample, and u-charts track the number of nonconformances found in each unit.

SPC helps the supply manager as a tool that is used to determine a root cause of an issue. If the root cause can be pushed back to a supplier material issue, this affects the criteria under which the materials are purchased. From a supplier relationship management perspective there are benefits to tracking such issues:

- *Process improvements.* Significant improvements in yield, productivity, or quality may be realized.

- *Reduced costs.* Particular material may not require as tight control over a certain characteristic. This may allow purchasing contracts with more suppliers, improving competition for business and lowering overall costs.

Total Quality Management

The Department of Defense popularized the term *total quality management (TCM)*, which was defined as a series of "continuous improvement activities involving everyone in the organization—managers and workers—in a totally integrated effort toward improving performance at every level."[9]

Although there are many versions of TQM programs, some of the common principles include

- *Leadership from senior management.* Senior management demonstrates a commitment to quality and a customer focus that is visible to all levels of the organization by establishing clear, visible quality values and goals and providing the resources, performance measures, and reward and recognition programs for the achievement of these goals.

- *Customer-focused quality.* The customer is seen as the company's highest priority. The customer defines the quality of the product, and the top priority is to continuously improve quality.

- *Employee involvement and teamwork.* A successful organization has a well-trained, empowered workforce that participates fully in the quality improvement activities of the company. Teamwork is an essential element to solve problems and improve business processes.

- *Continuous improvement.* Continuous-improvement activities in every operation, function, and work process in the company focus on reducing defects and errors, reducing cycle times, eliminating non-value-added activities, streamlining processes, eliminating waste, and improving customer responsiveness.

- *Data-driven approach to solving problems and improving processes.* A quantitative approach to problem solving and the statistical analysis of process data recognizes most problems are process-related and are not caused by individual employees. Data is collected and analyzed, and actions are taken by those in the best position to act—the workers in the process.

TQM has seen much success but has also seen many failures in companies. Some of the most common reasons attributed to failures of TQM in organizations include lack of senior management involvement and commitment, lack of middle

---

9 David L. Goetsch and Stanley B. Davis (2002). *Quality Management: Introduction to Total Quality Management for Production, Processing, and Services*, 4th ed., New York: Prentice Hall.

management support for team activities, implementation by part-time resources whose normal job responsibilities often interfered with team progress, lack of a process for selecting and reviewing projects, and efforts not directed at achieving tangible, measurable results.

Six Sigma

Sigma is a measure of variation, and Six Sigma translates into producing no more than 3.4 defects per million products.

Motorola, the 1988 recipient of the Malcolm Baldrige National Quality Award, introduced the concept of Six Sigma in 1986. The concept spread to other U.S. corporations, including General Electric. The 1997 General Electric Annual Report reported: "Six Sigma, even at this relatively early stage, delivered more than $300 million to our 1997 operating income." In 1998, GE's Annual Report declared savings due to Six Sigma of $750 million, and by 2002, annual savings of $2 billion was reported.[10] This level of return on investment caused companies to take serious notice of Six Sigma.

The Six Sigma Forum of the American Society for Quality provides the following definition of Six Sigma: "A methodology that provides businesses with the tools to improve the capability of their business processes. This increase in performance and decrease in process variation lead to defect reduction and improvement in profits, employee morale and quality of product."

The major elements of Six Sigma are as follows.

Strategic Focus by Senior Management
Senior management comprise the Leadership Council and are responsible for setting the vision, objectives, and leadership for the program; communication of the Six Sigma initiative to the organization; ensuring adequate resources are provided; ensuring a solid infrastructure for Black Belt selection and training; participating in project selection, support, and review; and ensuring a reward-and-recognition program is in place.

Strong Infrastructure to Support Six Sigma Initiative
The Six Sigma initiative includes many individuals who are trained in the tools needed to carry out the following roles:

- *Implementation Champion.* A senior manager who is responsible for the day-to-day management of the Six Sigma initiative, designs the infrastructure, and acts as a liaison between the Leadership Council and the Project Champions.

- *Project Champion.* A senior manager who oversees a Six Sigma project and works with the team to ensure adequate resources are provided and any bureaucratic barriers are eliminated.

---

10 General Electric Annual Reports (1997, 1998, 2002). Letters to Stakeholders.

- *Master Black Belt.* The expert on the Six Sigma tools and concepts who is responsible for the training and mentoring of the Black Belts and Green Belts.

- *Black Belt.* An individual who is responsible for leading, executing, and completing projects and is highly trained on the Six Sigma tools.

- *Green Belt.* An individual who is trained on a subset of the Six Sigma methodology and tools. This individual is typically a member of a Black Belt team who may work on small-scope projects in his or her department.

- *Other support.* Members of the finance, information technology, and human resources departments also support Six Sigma projects.

Dedicated, Highly Trained Black Belts to Lead Projects

Black Belts are the key to the success of Six Sigma. A Black Belt typically receives four weeks of training conducted over a three-month period. Black Belts work full time on their projects. Successful Six Sigma implementations report savings of $150,000 to $230,000 per project, with an average of four projects per year completed.[11]

Structured Process for Six Sigma Projects

The process used in Six Sigma projects is called DMAIC (define, measure, analyze, improve, and control). Each step has specific requirements as well as statistical and quality tools for its completion:

- *Define.* What needs to be improved is clearly defined.

- *Measure.* The baseline performance of the process is measured, the process flow is defined, the process capability is measured, and the measurement system is evaluated.

- *Analyze.* The data is analyzed and an improvement plan developed.

- *Improve.* Improvements are made to the current process and measured for success.

- *Control.* A control plan is put in place so that improvements are sustained.

Six Sigma has been implemented successfully in both large and small firms in manufacturing as well as service and administrative environments. Despite these differences, the successful companies have all had several elements in common: a committed management team, dedicated Black Belts representing the company's top talent, and a focus on tangible, measurable results.

---

11. Mikel Harry, Ph.D., and Richard Schroeder (2000). *Six Sigma: The Breakthrough Management Strategy Revolutionizing the World's Top Corporations*, New York: Doubleday.

ISO 9000:2000

In December of 2000 the nearly 100 member countries that participate in the International Organization for Standardization (ISO) approved the three-part ISO 9000:2000 standard, comprised of

- Q9000-2000—Quality Management Systems—Fundamentals and Vocabulary
- Q9001-2000—Quality Management Systems—Requirements
- Q9004-2000—Quality Management Systems—Guidelines for Performance Improvements

The stated scope of the ISO 9001:2000 standard is as follows:

The International Standard specifies requirements for a quality management system where an organization

1. Needs to demonstrate its ability to consistently provide product that meets customer and applicable regulatory requirements, and
2. Aims to enhance customer satisfaction through the effective application of the system, including processes for continual improvement of the system and the assurance of conformity to customer and applicable regulatory requirements.[12]

ISO 9001:2000 is the standard that has the specific requirements that must be met in order for an organization's quality management system (QMS) to be certified by an approved third-party registration body (registrar). Once an organization is certified, the registrar will usually perform regularly scheduled surveillance audits of the QMS.

The standard is built upon the foundation of eight quality management principles as described in Q9004-2000.[13] They are

Customer focus. The identification and measurement of customer satisfaction are important.

Leadership. Top management involvement in the QMS is critical.

Involvement of people. The QMS is to be deployed throughout the entire organization.

Process approach. Process analysis is done and all hand-off points are identified.

Systems approach to management. Interrelated processes are managed as a system.

Continual improvement. Improvement of overall performance must be a permanent objective.

---

12 ANSI/ISO/ASQ Q9001-2000, p. 1.

13 These eight principles are similar to the core values in the Malcolm Baldrige Criteria as discussed in the following section of this chapter.

Factual approach to decision making. Decisions are based on the analysis of facts and data.

Mutually beneficial supplier relationships. Systems to ensure beneficial customer-supplier relationships are necessary.

The ISO 9001:2000 standard contains five main clauses that address the following aspects of the QMS:

Quality management system. Defines such things as requirements for a quality policy, quality objectives, the quality manual, and procedure requirements.

Management responsibility. Defines such things as top management commitment and involvement as well as requirements for planning, document control, quality records, organizational structure, and a management review system.

Resource management. Defines such things as material, utilities, required purchasing controls, plant and equipment, access to data, human resources, and education and training.

Product realization. Defines things such as contract review, design controls, process controls, handling, storage, control of nonconforming product, delivery, and service controls.

Measurement, analysis, and improvement. Defines such things as internal audit requirements, process and product measurement, data analysis, and corrective and preventive action.

Requiring a certificate from a supplier showing that it is registered to an international standard such as ISO 9001:2000 will not guarantee a better product. From a customer's perspective, an ISO 9001:2000 certification should indicate that the supplier is capable of delivering a consistent product.

Baldrige Award Criteria Framework

The National Institute of Standards and Technology (NIST), an agency within the U.S. Department of Commerce administers the Malcolm Baldrige National Quality Award Program.[14] This program was established in 1988 to promote economic growth and strengthen U.S. competitiveness among for-profit business enterprises. Since the inception of the program, the "Criteria for Performance Excellence" have been used by thousands of organizations, including small-to-large service and manufacturing firms, for conducting self-assessments as well as to apply for the award. The program now also includes criteria for education and health care organizations.

---

14 2004 Baldrige National Quality Program, Criteria for Performance Excellence. NIST, U.S. Department of Commerce, Gaithersburg, MD.

On an annual basis, NIST administers the award application process. A written feedback report is provided to all award applicants, based on demonstration of the effectiveness of approaches in addressing the criteria, their deployment, the fostering of organizational learning, integration and results. The criteria includes a set of 19 results-oriented requirements designed to focus on creation of value for customers and the business. These requirements are divided among seven categories. Scoring guidelines make up the second part of the assessment architecture, and are used to determine a point value based on an organization's responses to the criteria requirements in each category.

Criteria Categories

The seven Baldrige Criteria for Performance Excellence Framework categories are

1. *Leadership.* Used to assess how senior leaders set and deploy company values, directions, and performance expectations, as well as the organization's governance system of fiscal accountability and independence in internal and external audits; how senior leaders review organizational performance and capabilities; and how the company addresses its public and community responsibilities and ensures ethical behavior.

2. *Strategic planning.* Used to assess how an organization develops and deploys strategic objectives and action plans.

3. *Customer and market focus.* Used to assess how an organization determines customer and market requirements, expectations, and preferences, and how the organization builds relationships with customers.

4. *Measurement, analysis, and knowledge management.* Used to assess how an organization selects, gathers, analyzes, manages, and improves its data, information, and knowledge assets.

5. *Human resources.* Used to assess how an organization's work systems and employee learning and motivation approaches enable employees to develop and utilize their full potential in alignment with the company's overall objectives and action plans.

6. *Process management.* Used to assess the organization's processes for creating customer and organizational value, including how input from customers, suppliers, and partners is obtained and used to improve performance.

7. *Business results.* Used to assess an organization's performance, relative to competitors, in key business areas including customer satisfaction, product and service performance, financial and marketplace performance, human resource results, operational performance, and governance and social responsibility.

The criteria framework also consists of an Organizational Profile that is used to serve as a guide for organizational performance management. It includes the business and regulatory environment, key relationships, and strategic challenges. In defining its key relationships, the company is asked to assess the role suppliers play in the value creation process and what associated supply chain requirements and communication mechanisms exist.

Category Scoring Guidelines

Categories 1 to 6 focus on an organization's processes used to address the criteria items. Four factors are considered in assigning a percentage value:

1. *Approach.* The appropriateness and effectiveness of the methods employed

2. *Deployment.* The extent to which the process is applied consistently and used by appropriate work units

3. *Learning.* The refining of processes through cycles of evaluation and improvement

4. *Integration.* The extent to which the applicant's approaches are aligned with organizational needs

Category 7 focuses on an organization's outputs and outcomes in achieving the criteria items. The four factors used to evaluate results and assign a percentage value in this category are

1. Current levels of performance

2. Rate and breadth of performance improvements

3. Performance relative to competitors

4. Linkage of results to key factors identified in the Organizational Profile

Customer-Supplier Partnerships

Successful customer-supplier partnership relationships are based on the elemental building blocks of trust, openness, factual representations, mutual concern for one another's best interests, and common or shared goals.[15] These relationships are characterized by common language; open and consistent communication; trust, sharing, and an open attitude; predictable behavior; and truth, holding one another accountable, and continuous improvement.

Common Language

A partnership must have a common language in which to communicate. From the company's standpoint, it means receiving all its information in a common format

---

15 Adapted from Bruce Moeller (2003). *Tying Supplier Inputs to Outputs*, Oak Brook, IL: EMNS, Inc. Used with permission.

from its supplier partner and being able to use the information to make data-based decisions.

Open and Consistent Communication

A steady communication of quality information in an open and nondefensive posture will unearth problems, misunderstandings, and opportunities early. Quality information encompasses a wide variety of measurements that can be used to improve operational productivity and improve overall supplier relationships. A centralized measurement system has the potential to help achieve real cost reductions and improvements in yield. It is imperative to identify and quickly put into action processes to contain or limit the risk associated with problems or to take advantage of opportunities.

The benefits of open and consistent communication of quality information can be staggering. According to the AMR Research Report, "Adding Quality Management to Supplier Collaboration," September 25, 2002,

> An automotive manufacturer reduced its defects over all suppliers from 2,000 to 700 parts per million over one year by updating supplier ratings continuously and managing supplier corrective actions on its supplier portal. An electronics manufacturer reduced the average time to implement corrective actions at a supplier from 10 days to 3 days by using e-mail notification and online status tracking. Another firm reduced the average time from 30 days to 10. An Aerospace and Defense (A&D) manufacturer reduced its incoming receiving backlog by 83 percent over a one-year period by catching certification documentation problems at the time of shipment. An A&D manufacturer improved its data integrity for quality tracking from 50 to 92 percent overnight by installing a system that forced data collection at the time a quality problem was detected.

Trust, Sharing, and an Open Attitude

Supplier partners must be treated with the appropriate sharing, trust, and openness. Free-flowing and real-time communication and sharing of data leads to focused performance and continuous improvement.

Predictable Behavior

Companies have distinct personalities or cultures that are predictable and provide insight into how they behave in different business circumstances. With comprehensive and integrated knowledge of the supply chain, the behavior of each participant in the chain can be shown. Cause-and-effect analyses show trends having adverse effects on the customer-supplier relationship.

Truth, Holding One Another Accountable, and Continuous Improvement

A data-driven customer-supplier relationship does not deal with anecdotal evidences and perceptions. Partners are held accountable for the quality of documentation and expectations, responsiveness, creativity, analytical abilities, yields, costs, and other measurable characteristics. Supplier partners will strive toward continuous improvement and higher degrees of performance that determine success for both partners.

QUALITY MANAGEMENT TOOLS AND TECHNIQUES FOR SUPPLY MANAGERS

Measuring Provided Goods and Services

Measuring is a discrete act of gathering qualitative or quantitative data. Often, the customer will perform inspections of or tests on supplier-provided materials. This is usually done to determine if materials are acceptable or occasionally to adjust customer processes to account for variances in supplier materials.

Inspection is the act of measuring something and comparing the data to acceptance criteria. When customer employees perform the inspection at their own site, it is called *receiving inspection*. When customer employees (or their agents) perform the inspection at the supplier site, it is called *source inspection*. A source inspection can be quite expensive, but it is often more economical when purchasing large or expensive items, such as jet engines or underground storage tanks.

Testing is the act of measuring something to determine its properties. Occasionally, the customer may wish to test received items as an added assurance of quality or to verify accompanying certificates. When an accredited independent laboratory performs this testing, it is called *conformity assessment*. Conformity assessment is often used in international trade of commodity items, such as grain or switches.

Monitoring Supplier Performance

The customer must monitor supplier performance. The customer may wish to require and then examine *certificates of conformance* that accompany the shipment. (Note: A *certificate of compliance* adds process and system elements to product conformity and is nearly impossible to truthfully affirm.) Customers should only request certificates of conformance for critical items, when nonconformance would have a dramatic effect on cost, production, or risk. As a better measure, customers can monitor supplier performance over time, using metrics such as on-time delivery and quality variations.

Supplier Audit

There are three types of audits: first party (evaluation of your own activities), second party (evaluation of your supplier activities), and third party (examination by the government or an accredited independent registrar). Please refer to part II of this chapter for a discussion of the general model and the four fundamental principles of the audit.

Audit Planning

In auditing, as in all other aspects of supplier management, there is no equality. As defined by the customer, some suppliers are more important than others depending on the cost, production, and risk contributions of the individual suppliers. Critical suppliers should receive the most attention. They are generally audited 6 to 18 months apart. Important suppliers are generally audited 18 to 36 months apart. Commercial suppliers are audited by exception. The customer's audit program manager (also known as the *audit boss*) should prepare an annual audit schedule, including supplier audits, to meet the needs of all stakeholders. It is a good idea to work with the supply manager on the supplier audit schedule. All suppliers listed on the audit schedule should receive notification from the assigned buyer at the beginning of the yearly audit cycle.

Nine Steps of Audit Preparation
The following steps are required to prepare for the supplier audit:

1. Define the purpose of this audit.

2. Define the scope of activities and functions to audit.

3. Verify the authority to perform the audit.

4. Assemble a team of one to three auditors for the supplier audit, and designate a team leader.

5. Informally contact the supplier to determine the documents (requirements) for the audit.

6. Study the supplier's documents and its production processes.

7. Formally notify the supplier of the audit by sending the audit plan via the assigned buyer.

8. Conduct a document review of the supplier's requirements.

9. Prepare audit work papers to guide the audit team members while on-site.

The audit team leader typically performs step 5 (informal notification) about six weeks prior to the site visit. Formal notification should occur a month before the site visit. Prior to any on-site activities, the audit team members should produce their own flowcharts of the supplier's processes. All this communication before the audit will result in more thorough and beneficial results.

Audit Performance
Once on-site, the audit team should conduct a brief (15 minute) opening meeting with its supplier counterparts. Then, the team will gather and analyze data from five principle sources:

1. Physical characteristics of processes and products

2. Sensory inputs, such as seeing and smelling

3. Paperwork (documents and records)

4. Interviews with supplier personnel at all levels

5. Patterns that the data from sources 1 to 4 make

As the data is gathered, the audit team members, both individually and together, will start to see strengths and weaknesses and begin to draw audit conclusions. These preliminary conclusions should be shared with the supplier as they arise, rather than waiting until the end of the audit. This promotes a spirit of trust and allows the supplier to provide additional information.

Audit Reporting

A supplier audit typically lasts two days. Prior to departing the site, the auditors meet with the supplier's managers to share the audit results. This is called the *closing meeting*. In the spirit of *no surprises*, any misunderstandings should be resolved before this meeting occurs. The audit team leader presents the team's overall conclusions, along with any specific positive or negative findings. Leaving draft finding sheets with the supplier will allow the supplier to address any problems right away.

Once they return home, the auditors prepare their formal report. After they agree on its contents, the audit team leader gives the report to the audit program manager, who then gives it to the affected supply manager. The supply manager should formally transmit the report to the supplier, along with any request to correct identified problems.

Audit Follow-up

The customer should make sure the supplier corrects any serious problems detected by the audit. Often, the team leader (or audit program manager) will transfer the problem statement from the *Finding* sheet(s) to a *Supplier Corrective Action Request (SCAR)* form. These are included in the audit report package and sent to the supplier. The supplier should respond to the request within 30 days with the plans for correcting the problems. The original auditors may or may not be involved with any subsequent follow-up on these supplier promises. Nevertheless, since problems could affect future business, they need to be corrected by the supplier and verified as such by the customer.

Quality Planning and Supply Management

Quality planning is an important part of the overall supply management process. Supply managers and quality engineers must collaborate to ensure suppliers are cognizant of all quality requirements that are to be met by the supplier operationally and by the supplier's products specifically. As noted earlier in the section "Customer Responsibilities to Suppliers" in part I of this chapter, one of the key elements in the customer-supplier relationship is complete and open communication. Quality planning is dependent upon such communication.

Communication is critical to ensure all requirements and expectations are defined prior to finalizing any agreement with the supplier. When developing the requirements, it is advisable to seek the supplier's advice within the supplier's area of expertise. All functions involved in defining the requirements, such as engineering, supply management, quality, purchasing, manufacturing, and service must provide their input to the requirements and specifications. Supply management and quality ensure that documentation reviews, product design reviews, and specification reviews are performed to make sure all expectations have been clearly and completely defined in the purchase order or agreement.

In addition to all the technical requirements for the purchased product, the planning must also include consideration of how the supplied product is to be determined acceptable (source inspection, receiving inspection, testing, sampling plans, etc.), how communication to the supplier of the product status is to be accomplished, and how the customer will disposition purchased product that is found to be defective.

As part of the quality planning, the customer must be apprised of how the supplier will control the quality of the product. The supplier will prepare a documented quality plan that details the process for manufacturing its product. This plan will define all the process steps and identify those that are critical to the product meeting the customer's requirements. The method to be used to control the product quality at each of the critical steps in the process will be defined, such as the type of SPC chart or method to be used (see the section, "Statistical Process Control" for more detail), the test or inspection to be performed, and the equipment to be used.

Finally, effective planning by the quality and supply management personnel, in collaboration with the supplier, will lead to a long-term relationship that is based on well-planned, clearly understood, and openly communicated expectations.

The Supply Management Professional and Quality

The supply management and quality functions act together for overall corporate improvement and success. This interaction may best be illustrated by considering the following scenarios:

In the first scenario, a supply manager has found a new source of supply for a particular good that costs significantly less than the current source of supply. After performing some investigation, it is found that the company is reputable and supplies similar materials to competitors. With the volume that the company is purchasing, the initial price offer can be improved by another 5 percent, reducing total spending by over $500,000. However, an additional process step will have to be performed for the goods to be of the appropriate quality for the manufacturing process.

In the second scenario, a quality engineer returns from a supplier audit and finds that a component will improve efficiency by 2 percent annually by using a material that costs approximately three times the price currently being paid. Finished goods quality will rise and in-process defects will decrease, but it will have a significant impact on the supply management professional's ability to reduce total spending.

How do these scenarios affect the interaction between the quality and supply management professionals? Would it be possible to use the supplier's material and possibly change some design parameters to accommodate the less expensive materials without affecting product quality? Should the quality and design teams involve the supply management professional earlier on in the process to see if there is a potential for reduced cost? If quality and the supply management personnel are measured against goals of improved overall quality, then it may be acceptable to add another step in the manufacturing process, as long as the overall product quality improves and the cost of the finished product goes down.

The key to ongoing improvement is to have a team of quality and supply management professionals involved in the early stages of any new supplier program. This allows for the potential of vast improvements in quality and overall cost.

CONCLUSION

This chapter has focused on how quality management, quality tools, and interaction of quality and the supply management functions are necessary for any enterprise to be successful. The importance of mutually beneficial customer-supplier relationships has been stressed, and the emergence of supply chain management only reinforces the necessity of close collaboration between quality and supply management.

According to the article "Supply Chain Management: A New Opportunity," by Greg Hutchins in the April 2002 issue of *Quality Progress*, the American Society for Quality's flagship periodical, "... one of the hottest topics of interest to quality professionals today is Supply Chain Management." The links in the supply chain are the many and varied customer-supplier relationships that form the chain. One of the major challenges in managing an effective supply chain is making sure that all time spent in any operation adds value. Activities that do not add value need to be minimized or eliminated. A structured process of quality management working with supply management in dealing with suppliers will improve cycle time by minimizing or eliminating non-value-adding activities while improving and assuring consistent quality from suppliers in the chain. Customers and suppliers must use quality tools such as statistical process control, Six Sigma, Lean, benchmarking, and auditing to achieve the levels of quality required by today's marketplace.

Companies must develop an objective process of selecting suppliers that is best for their particular business or industry, and stick to it. The selection process must be data-driven, not based on emotion. Data describing the supplier's capabilities relative to criteria such as cost, quality, delivery, technical support, and attitude, from both the supplier and internal company stakeholders should be collected and evaluated.

The process must also include an audit of the supplier's quality management system and manufacturing processes including process controls to be used, and ongoing monitoring of supplier performance, with frequent and continual open communication between the customer and supplier.

The digital age has provided companies with many opportunities to improve their relationships with suppliers through open communication and sharing of information and data. With increased levels of electronic capabilities and e-commerce, there are greater opportunities to take advantage of the communication tools available so as to accelerate progress in supplier relationships. By digitizing processes, sharing information, and moving from anecdotal to data-based decisions, the whole supply chain benefits from improved products, streamlined processes, and overall healthier supplier-customer relationships. As quality management principles are adopted and quality tools are used by all involved in the supply management functions, more comprehensive relationships will be established between customers and suppliers.

ACKNOWLEDGMENTS

Members of the Customer-Supplier Division (CSD) of the American Society for Quality (ASQ) have written this chapter. The ASQ is a leading authority on quality, with more than 104,000 individual members and 800 organizational members. The society's goals are to advance learning and quality improvement and facilitate the exchange of knowledge to improve business results and create better workplaces. The CSD's mission is to continually research, develop, and communicate the quality concepts, body of knowledge, and technologies to improve supplier performance and increase customer satisfaction.

To contact the ASQ call 1-800-248-1946. The ASQ's Web site is www.asq.org. The CSD's Web site is www.asq.org/cs/.

CHAPTER 28

VALUE ANALYSIS

LAWRENCE J. CLARK, C.P.M.
Sodus Central Schools

OVERVIEW

In today's business climate, supply managers are significant team members. They are adept at helping their companies succeed in a rapidly changing marketplace. Working with marketing, engineering, and production is crucial in getting quality products released quickly. Speed to market, cost reduction, and improved design depend on teamwork. Value analysis is a technique that brings the various departments together to work for a common goal. In recent years this process has been pushed forward in the product life cycle. Often it is combined with the concept of *design for manufacturability* (or, for nonmanufacturing situations, *design for execution efficiency*). Thus value analysis has changed from an afterthought in the design process to a strategy in product development. It attempts to eliminate *unnecessary cost* at the outset, rather than trying to reduce it later. Although value analysis originated and is often associated with manufacturing, it is applicable to nonmanufactured products and services.

HISTORY

Value analysis originated at the end World War II in order to deal with material shortages. Substitutions had to be made, and in many cases the replacements were more suitable. Larry Miles of General Electric wanted to continue its use as a cost reduction–product improvement strategy. With Roy Fountain, an electrical engineer, Miles, a supply manager, developed the first value analysis plan. In 1952 they organized workshops to train GE employees in various plants. Those extensive workshops typically involved 40 to 60 hours of training. Initially, value analysis was considered strictly a purchasing tool. Now it has moved forward in the product life cycle to combine with *value engineering*. Gradually it has expanded to include other functions, such as engineering and marketing. As value analysis has evolved it is being used earlier in the product life cycle. Many companies, especially smaller ones, have adopted a less formalized approach, using shorter sessions and pulling in team members as they are needed. It has also been adapted for use in businesses outside of manufacturing.

BENEFITS

The benefits of value analysis are extensive and far exceed any cost associated with the program. There is a potential for

- Reduced labor costs
- Lower cost of goods
- Improved quality
- Better performance
- Increased customer satisfaction
- Preservation of scarce resources
- Increased profitability

THE BASIS OF VALUE
Definitions

Note: The various concepts and use of the term *product* throughout this chapter should be interpreted as also applying to nonmanufactured output, such as services, in addition to physical products. The purchaser of services is concerned with efficiency of service execution. They can apply value analysis principles to improve quality while lowering costs.

- *Value analysis.* Value analysis is the organized and systematic study of every element of cost in a part, material, or service to make certain it fulfills its *function* at the lowest possible cost. Value analysis also employs techniques that identify the functions the user wants from a product or service; it establishes by comparison the appropriate cost for each function; and then it causes the required knowledge, creativity, and initiative to be used to provide each function for that cost.

- *Value engineering.* The terms *value analysis* and *value engineering* are used synonymously in this chapter, and value analysis will be used to represent both concepts. Generally speaking, however, value engineering can be thought to be applied early in the design process, after several production runs have been completed, as opposed to later in the product life cycle. Since value analysis or value engineering is strictly a team effort, freedom of suggestions from both engineering and supply management are necessary. Supply management must question engineering specifications, and engineering must question supply management practices such as sourcing and award decisions based on price.

- *Concurrent design.* Concurrent design centers on the consideration and inclusion of product design attributes such as manufacturability, procurability, reliability, maintainability, schedulability, and marketability in the early stages of product design. To achieve this, design engineers work with supply management, manufacturing, and marketing, as a *cross-departmental team*, in the areas of developing specifications, interchangeable parts, and part substitutions. It bears a close resemblance to value analysis and value engineering in that it involves a multidepartmental group working together to reduce cost. In many organizations it appears that value analysis programs have evolved to become part of concurrent design programs.

For a manufactured product example see Figure 28–1, and for a nonmanufactured product (service) see Figure 28–2. Both figures are located near the end of the chapter.

Functions: Primary and Secondary

The key to value analysis and value engineering is to understand how a part fulfills its function. For instance, the *primary function* of the watchband is to hold the watch to the wrist. It can perform this work whether it is plastic or gold. A *secondary function* is to allow the watch to be worn during participation in sports. If this is the case, then the soft plastic band would be more appropriate than the gold-plated band. The plastic band holds the watch on the wrist comfortably. It also has a lower cost and is safer to wear. There are other examples. A jewel case for a compact disc has a primary function to *protect* the *CD*. The secondary function may be to *hold* the *jacket* that helps sell the CD.

Function is that which the product or service must do to make it perform and sell. For example, a knife *cuts material* and a thermometer *measures temperature*. Define the function by using just two words, a verb and a noun. This prevents an attempt to apply more than one simple job at a time to the item being analyzed. It is important to note that while function definitions describe the desired result, they do not define the means to achieve the end. There are always several choices one can make on how to proceed. A complex product or process may have several functions and even subfunctions. Function analysis is performed so that the purpose of the product or service can be fully understood. The product or service is described as a number of word pairs, verb and noun, rather than by name or process.

Value

Value can be defined as the lowest end cost at which the function can be accomplished at a given time and place and with the quantity required. Value has no direct relationship to cost. Some items that cost less than a similar product accomplish the function in a superior manner. For example, a premium paid for overnight shipping increases the cost of a product but probably does not add to its value from the supplier's viewpoint. However, it is important to consider value in the customer's eyes. Value analysis is a technique that lowers cost but maintains worth, from the end users perspective. It does not cheapen the product.

Value Analysis in Action

Probably the best way to understand value analysis is to look at a case of it being used. A good example is the humidifier that went from a metal to a plastic drip pan. The function of the drip pan is to *hold water* as it drips from the condenser coil. A plastic drip pan can *hold water* as well as a metal one, but there is value in making the change. Plastic is cheaper, quieter, weighs less, and does not rust. It won't dent or scratch as easily. The substitution of plastic in this case resulted in a lower cost without lowering quality from the customer's point of view.

Checklist: Test for Added Value in a Product or Service

Here are 15 questions to ask regarding the product or service being considered:

1. Does an item component part or phase of service contribute value to the product?

2. Is the cost proportionate to the product's usefulness?

3. Does the product have secondary functions or phases that can be broken out?

4. Has the product's function changed over time?

5. Does the product require all its features, parts, components, or phases?

6. Do original specifications or standards still apply?

7. Can specifications or standards be changed?

8. Is there a better replacement or method available for the intended use?

9. Can the product or item be eliminated?

10. Can a useful part be made, or a more expedient service employed, at a lower cost?

11. For a product, can a standard part be found that will accomplish the function at a lower cost?

12. Is the product produced using proper tooling, considering the quantities used?

13. Can another dependable supplier provide the product for less? Alternatively, can you make the item or provide the service more efficiently yourself?

14. Can you work with your suppliers to reduce cost?

15. Can long lead times be reduced allowing the product to get to market faster?

Selecting a Product or Service to Be Value-Analyzed

To make the most of value analysis techniques, it is important to give consideration in selecting the products, parts, processes, or services to be analyzed. You want to look at items that can give you dollar returns on your efforts. It is best to start with components that have a high dollar value. Here is a list of things you can look for:

1. High annual dollar value or expense
2. Intricacy or complication in design
3. Low yields or high scrap expense
4. Labor-intensive or time-consuming processes
5. Complex processes with many operations
6. An assembly that can be reduced to a single part
7. Parts that can be standardized or used in several applications
8. Obsolete or hard-to-obtain components
9. Older raw materials that now have better substitute materials available
10. Items with inconsistent quality or performance

The Purpose of Value Analysis

The cooperation and participation of other departments, such as marketing, engineering, and production are important to the success of any value analysis effort. In order to optimize teamwork among the various departments, management should be involved. To win management's cooperation, it is important to convince them that value analysis will maintain or improve quality while reducing costs. It is important to link value analysis to a product's success in the marketplace. Value analysis helps to improve a product's performance, quality, marketability, maintainability, and reliability. It may also assist in making products available sooner.

Quality

A decision as to suitable quality must involve *technical quality* and *economic quality*. Regardless of the degree of technical suitability, the item must be procurable at a satisfactory cost on a continuous basis. Consequently, economic quality includes technical quality as well as cost and availability factors. Reappraisals of the material, product, and process selected are necessary from time to time because applications, competition, and customer expectations change. Quality must be maintained or enhanced. Otherwise, any savings will be inconsequential as sales and reputation decline.

Performance

No matter how attractive in appearance or how solidly built, if the product does not function efficiently, it will not sell. In value analysis, the goal is equal or improved accomplishment of the function at a lower cost. In some cases, cost may be increased to achieve better performance or to reduce maintenance costs. Value is still added because of improved product marketability.

Marketability

The primary aim of business is to produce products or services that find a ready market and provide a reasonable profit. All items must have the necessary degree of sales appeal, whether it is in

- Effectiveness of operation
- Efficiency of operation
- Low repair or maintenance costs
- Esteem value

Value analysis recognizes that marketability must be maintained or improved.

Maintainability

Maintainability is an important feature affecting the total end cost of a product to a customer. Regardless of the initial quality of components and initial marketability of the product, if a value analysis study results in increased maintenance costs for the customer, then any savings realized would sooner or later be wiped out by decreased sales and loss of goodwill.

Reliability

It is equally important that the required *reliability* of a product be preserved or improved by the value analysis recommendation. Suppose an electrical relay performed perfectly for half its expected life and then malfunctioned, shutting down a production line. Suppose a commercial water heater would only work 98 percent of the time! What would happen to customer goodwill, and to profits?

Teamwork and Speed-to-Market

Because of the cross-departmental nature of value analysis, it seems reasonable that it would be combined with concurrent design principles and moved forward in the product life cycle. Design, working together with manufacturing and supply management, can make many of the value substitutions before the release of a new product. This not only gets the product to market faster but saves money by avoiding costly redesigns and downstream waste in procurement and assembly. The cooperation among departments improves the manufacturability of the product. When product development works simultaneously with supply management and assembly early in the design cycle, many of the procurement and manufacturing issues are resolved by the time a product is released. A key factor here is that in modern economies the first products in the marketplace are often the most successful.

The Process of Value Analysis

If the project involves reviewing a service, the team membership may include service and support personnel. Value Analysis and concurrent design can be used to review any service that can be divided into sections with quantifiable costs. Value analysis should follow an organized application of specific techniques. The goal is to follow a plan similar to the way a scientist follows procedural steps in an experiment. In the completion of complex operations, having a method to follow is important. To finish with a quality product, a contractor follows a blueprint, a writer follows an outline, and an assembler uses a bill of material. The key is to follow a systematic plan in order to get the best results from value analysis in the shortest amount of time.

Value analysis is easiest to implement in companies where the cost of goods or services is an issue. Intense competition in the marketplace tends to drive the task of adding value and avoiding excess cost. Competition also pushes the need to move value analysis forward in the design process. Speed-to-market with new products is important in the face of intense competition and shortened product life cycles.

Work within a Team

Value analysis is a team effort. The different departments working alone cannot do as well collecting information and making proposals that affect others. Better results are achieved in a team environment. In small companies where the lines between departments may be loosely drawn, an informal work group might be effective, as long as issues are looked at from all points of view. It is important to include representation from marketing (with customers), engineering, design, service, production, supply management (along with suppliers), and quality. Supply management often takes a lead, performing the initial cost analysis on the target product or service and then selecting items with economic feasibility for investigation. Teams should report successes—particularly to senior management. Regular reporting of cost savings and product improvements not only lend credibility to the effort but can encourage others to join or form a value analysis team.

Value Analysis Job Plan

The job plan is the organized application of specific techniques in order to achieve the best results. A rational sequence of events is followed in identifying value and reducing cost without diminishing quality. Traditionally, it was considered important to follow formal procedures to the letter. Now, especially in smaller organizations, procedures are being followed on a more casual basis. On small or simple projects informal techniques can be effectively used, especially where team members have previous experience with value analysis. Although it varies with size and type of enterprise, a typical job plan includes the following steps:

- Preparation
- Information

- Analysis
- Creation
- Synthesis
- Development
- Presentation
- Implementation
- Follow-up

Preparation Phase

Before starting the study, the team lists all areas that will be improved by the assessment's results. They should list any roadblocks they expect to encounter and any action plans to consider in overcoming obstacles. These lists must be updated as the investigation continues. This procedure helps to limit unfortunate surprises later in the execution or implementation phase. The team can then select the product or service that will most benefit from cost reduction and improvement. An item challenged by new competition in the marketplace is a good candidate, as is an item that has a high dollar impact on a company's revenues. The team should review all the components of a product or service, and sort them by cost. Typically, it pays to review the high-dollar items first. Each item is assessed carefully for its function. Then ideas are presented, perhaps by brainstorming, for ways to substitute better materials, components, or processes. Finally, an estimate is made of annual savings that should be achieved through the improvements made. This is a tangible way to measure the project's success.

Information Phase

The objective of the information phase is to gather relevant information and to make known opportunities for improvement. This phase includes

- Establishing performance perimeters
- Determining customer acceptance
- Gathering meaningful costs
- Obtaining details of manufacturing methods or processes, or breaking the service into assessable parts
- Determining quality aspects
- Defining objectives
- Analyzing costs
- Performing a Pareto analysis to separate the significant few items from the trivial many
- Defining functions and developing a *function logic diagram*

- Allocating costs to functions

- Focusing on *opportunity areas* or *problem statements* upon which to apply creative efforts

The manufacturing value analysis team should accumulate bills of material, cost information, assembly procedures, and other relevant facts. A service team might accumulate a list of tasks, cost information such as pay rates, and what procedures are required to perform the service. Typical questions at this phase are

- What tasks are involved in performing the service and how long do they take?

- What other major costs or expenses are involved in performing the service including travel and transportation, tools, supplies, contract labor, advertising and communication outlay.

- Should we compare machining to casting costs?

- Will plastic substitute for metal on that component?

- Is there an easier or quicker way to put that assembly together?

- Can we add customer services without increasing the labor involved?

- Can a paraprofessional perform some of the duties of a professional in a given service?

- Is there a better or more efficient way to deliver a service?

Prepare a list of questions that will need to be answered in the attempt to reduce unnecessary cost. Involve others from outside the team in searching for knowledge, for example, a machine operator, a supplier, or even a customer.

Analysis Phase

The objective of the analysis phase is to evaluate ideas and select ones worthy of development. Steps in this phase include

- Listing advantages and disadvantages for each idea

- Estimating the impact on cost, performance, and quality

- Selecting approaches with the best yield for resources required

- Comparing against objectives

In this phase the question is, "What will the changes cost?" Estimate the dollar value of each proposal. Select those ideas that reduce cost but do not negatively affect value in the customer's eyes. The parts and costs for a product or service should be broken down into functional areas, and the cost associated with each area should be identified. Total cost should be compiled, which may require some estimates of hidden costs. To achieve a more accurate estimate, use actual costs rather than standard costs. Items to consider in this phase include suppliers' input, prices, order lot sizes, drawings, or design specifications, and information about manufacturing methods. Service items to be considered might include time sheets, travel expenses, rent, or construction costs.

Creative Phase

The objective of the creative phase is to generate a large quantity and variety of unjudged ideas. The creative phase should include the following steps:

- Writing down all ideas for each stated opportunity area or problem statement
- Using generic terminology to enhance generation of different means to accomplish goals
- Calling upon outside experts, consultants, or suppliers

At this time various techniques are applied using the information gathered earlier. Here the question "What else will do the job?" is asked. Creativity is important in evaluating the function, or job, a part performs. Avoid dismissing ideas offered by team members. Usually all suggestions are recorded, and then the team reviews the proposals and picks those most likely to succeed. During this phase, as ideas and concepts arise, the team leader may ask someone in the group to "champion" specific ideas or concepts. If no one volunteers, the idea or concept may be dropped. Those who do volunteer are charged with investigating the feasibility and economics of the idea or concept. This champion concept can result in a series of solutions, which are likely to be implemented.

Synthesis Phase

The objective of the synthesis phase is to select the most value worthy ideas from those generated in the creative phase. Each idea is looked at carefully as a return on the investment of performing the value analysis. Potential cost savings are calculated for each idea. The ideas which promise the greatest returns for a product or service are selected. Typically in manufacturing parts that offer the greatest dollar savings are chosen. For a service it may be a task that offers a lower dollar savings, but correspondingly costs much less to implement. Total potential return on investment, not just dollar savings should be considered in selecting which ideas to exploit.

Development Phase

The objective of the development phase is to expand selected ideas into workable value improvement proposals. It includes

- Developing ideas into decisions
- Engineering or redesigning, with enhancement of good points and strengthening or eliminating weak points.
- Determining how to design, produce, alter, and assure quality

- Consulting suppliers and specialists
- Determining total system impacts
- Preparing the implementation plan

Presentation Phase
The objective of the presentation phase is to obtain the approval, support, and resources necessary for implementation. It includes

- Combining proposals into reports for distribution
- Presenting value improvement recommendations with their anticipated financial and nonfinancial impacts
- Obtaining necessary commitments and resources

Implementation Phase
The objective of the implementation phase is to obtain results from the improvement proposals. The steps include

- Following the established implementation plan
- Conducting regular management reviews
- Applying value techniques to resolve problems
- Documenting results

Follow-up Phase
The objective of this phase is to track the progress of the effort and make plans to correct any problems that have developed. Here you will apply precise evaluation techniques and measure savings. Figure out how much you are saving per part and multiply it by annual use. Total up all the savings on all the product's parts and report the entire reduction in cost. This is how the value analysis team shows it is successful and worthwhile to the organization. For a service, determine the value of a segment of the method or procedure used. Then compare it to the original cost.

Approaches to Value Analysis

The most common approach for a company beginning value analysis is to create a value analysis committee composed of representatives from marketing, customer service, design, supply management, and production. It is also beneficial to have representatives of internal customers sit on the committee to insure their point of view is represented acceptably. This committee operates most effectively when it employs the workshop method to review possible opportunities. The workshop approach encourages free discussion and exchange of ideas on how the function of the various items studied can be performed at a lower cost. Value analysis workshops have led to a number of refinements of the basic principles and procedures.

In recent years many companies have moved the value analysis forward in the product life cycle. Historically, value analysis was applied at the mature stage of a product's life. This was the point where competing products had established themselves in the marketplace. It was felt that the mature stage was the appropriate time to lower costs to stay ahead of rivals in the marketplace. In today's economy that theory does not work so well, especially with products like the personal computer. Many product life cycles have been shortened dramatically. By the time the competition catches up, it's time to begin design of a new product, rather than to fix the old one. Concepts like total quality management (TQM) and concurrent design compel manufacturers to consider releasing high-quality products quickly. Typically, the first product in a particular market gets the largest share. Usually it keeps its leadership role, especially if it is a correctly designed, quality product. Prompting marketing, manufacturing, and design to work together on the front end helps to avoid expense and speeds the release of new designs.

Creative brainstorming is the process of stimulating an uninhibited flow of ideas, however outlandish they may seem at first, from the team. In such sessions negative thinking, that is, expressing skepticism or derision toward another team member's expression, is not permitted. The theory underlying this approach is that the fear of being laughed at will suppress a person's willingness to share thoughts. Another rule is to record all ideas no matter how frivolous they may seem at first. Judgment is deferred until later phases of the analysis after all propositions have been considered carefully.

Leapfrogging is a technique of value-analyzing comparable products in a company's line to identify their best features and characteristics. These are combined into a hybrid or fused product that, in turn, is value-analyzed to bring additional creative ideas from the team. This process has, in some cases, enabled a company to enter a new market with a superior product that is priced competitively.

Value Analysis and Concurrent Design
Many organizations have combined value analysis and value engineering into one operation. The next logical step has been to apply it to development projects with concurrent design principles. Concurrent design, as defined earlier, centers on the consideration and inclusion of product design attributes, such as manufacturability, procurability, reliability, maintainability, schedulability, and marketability, in the early stages of product design. To achieve this, design engineers work with supply management, manufacturing, and marketing as a cross-departmental team. The team works on specifications, interchangeable parts, and part substitutions. Concurrent design bears similarities to value analysis in that a cross-departmental team undertakes to reduce cost and improve the product. However, concurrent design principles lack the systematic and somewhat scientific approach in avoiding cost. In many cases it appears that value analysis programs have evolved into concurrent design programs.

There are several benefits to the concurrent design approach including reduced cost of goods, nimble release of new product to market, and merchandise more in touch with customer requirements. Often as much as 70 percent of the cost of manufacturing is determined in the design stage. For example, once a mold for a part is built and paid for, it is difficult to achieve cost reduction on that part. This is due to the fact that the cost for tooling has already been paid. The bulk of production savings come from improvements in design rather than savings in material, labor, or overhead. Therefore, it pays to examine a product for cost reductions as it is being developed.

The best way to avoid costs in a product is to bring in the downstream departments such as production, supply management (including suppliers), and marketing, for their input. This should be done before the design is finalized. Organizations can accomplish this by having regular design review meetings, which include members of all departments, right from the inception of a new project.

There are many ways supply management professionals can contribute to a design before it is fixed. In developing specifications, they may help a designer revise tolerances and features. This is accomplished by reviewing plans with potential suppliers. For example, a machine shop might recommend new material that holds tolerances better than the material originally specified. This will result in lower fabrication costs. Supply managers can often recommend parts that meet functional requirements at a lower cost. In one instance a supplier, at a design-review meeting, recommended a low-cost diode laser. It replaced a helium-neon laser in a portable-sighting device. This substitution reduced the cost by several hundred dollars and the product weight by several ounces.

Supply management is often in a position to recommend *interchangeable* or common parts. It already knows what it is buying for other products. Making some of these parts common parts to several assemblies reduces inventory and brings the benefits of lot-size buying. A classic example here is Eli Whitney's use of interchangeable parts. He produced exact replicas of any part on his rifle. This enabled mass production and the accompanying reduction in costs. Whitney's demonstration to the war department, of disassembling and mixing parts and then reassembling rifles, resulted in increased sales. Part *standardization* is important. Efforts should be made to utilize off-the-shelf rather than custom parts to perform a function. Standardized parts typically have shorter lead times, lower prices, and better warranties. In addition, salvage values are usually higher for standardized parts, in case the project changes. Supply management is in a good position to take the lead in implementing value analysis techniques in the forward design meetings.

SUMMARY—STEPS TO TAKE IN SETTING UP A VALUE ANALYSIS PROGRAM

Value analysis achieves the greatest benefits when it is implemented as a *continuous-improvement* process. A supply management professional can follow these steps to start a project in his or her company.

> *Step 1. Obtain senior management approval.* A value analysis program will not work unless there is a climate for cultivating an ongoing group. A management sponsor such as a president, vice president, or

general manager must be identified to oversee the program. The sponsor should have corporatewide responsibility, and authority. He or she must be committed to the program. The sponsor provides motivation and funding, evaluates the proposals, and makes decisions on implementation.

Step 2. Identify a value manager. The value manager receives direction and objectives from the management sponsor, organizes workshops, and administers the program. The value manager should identify projects for value analysis, as well as track and report on the value team's progress.

Step 3. Appoint a workshop facilitator. The workshop facilitator instructs team members in value analysis principles and techniques and leads the team in applying them to a specific project. The facilitator must have an in-depth knowledge of value analysis principles and methods and how to apply them. He or she must have a sense of where and how to uncover improvement opportunities, plus have the ability to manage a multi-disciplined team. The facilitator should be able to guide the members in stimulating creative output, without being viewed as a source of solutions.

Step 4. Integrate the value program with other improvement projects. Many organizations already have some programs such as concurrent design, total quality management, and just-in-time. These programs should be integrated with value analysis under the banner of improving competitiveness through better value. Objectives should be aligned with organizational goals.

Step 5. Plan for implementation. It is crucial to plan for implementation from the start. The plan should be documented, describing how value improvement recommendations are to be evaluated. Resources must be made available to accomplish the approved recommendations.

Step 6. Obtain cross-functional support. A value analysis program requires cross-organizational support; it needs to be a program in which all organizational elements have a role and a commitment.

Step 7. Select a project. A prudent plan of action is to begin simple and then move to more sophisticated projects. Choose the ones that tie into strategic objectives. Value analysis study projects are usually identified by management insight or through the use of organization diagnostics. For each project it is imperative that the specific objectives and scope be clearly stated and understood. Although value analysis can be applied to almost any area, typical projects include products, production processes, and/or other information processes that have problems such as
- High cost
- Unsatisfied needs
- Redundancy or unnecessary functions
- Repetitive problems (multiple bottlenecks)

- Waste (time, effort, money, material)
- Complexity of time or consumption

Step 8. Select a team. Once the project is defined, select a team representing the elements of expertise necessary to address the project. Team members should be capable, respected, and able to obtain the support of their departments; they should also have an unbiased viewpoint. Choose a team leader from the group.

Step 9. Collect data. Information for analysis should be collected, with the value manager, the facilitator, and the team leader working together to identify what is required. The nature and extent of the data depends on the project and the objectives but typically includes facts on cost, resources consumed, cycle times, suppliers, and known problems. Customer or field data may also be required. The team leader has the overall responsibility to see that the data is collected but may delegate the actual collection to various team members.

Step 10. Conduct the workshop. The value manager and facilitator work together on workshop preparation, making arrangements for items such as meeting facilities, equipment, and letters of invitation. The workshop should be a full-time commitment during which the participants need to focus their attention on the project without having their thoughts interrupted by other commitments.

Step 11. Implement approved projects. Approved recommendations enter into the implementation stage. Sponsors should hold monthly or bimonthly implementation progress review meetings. Those responsible for implementation report their progress and problems.

Step 12. Recognize and reward success. It is important for management sponsors to realize that implementing value improvements can be frustrating work. An important role of the sponsor is to support and encourage those working on implementing value improvements.

Step 13. Track and record the benefits. Shifting priorities or changing management can have an impact on an ongoing value analysis program. Should the program come under scrutiny, success and continuation can be achieved by keeping well-documented records of audited savings and other benefits.

Step 14. Repeat the procedure. Project selection is an ongoing process. As soon as the first project moves into implementation, the next project and workshop should be taking form.

Figure 28–1 and Figure 28–2 are examples of a value analysis project that came about in an effort to reduce lead time and improve speed to market for a new product. The product was a scanning tunneling microscope. The function of the head, shown in the figure, was to enclose the probe and sample. Additional benefits were realized in cost, customer maintainability, and faster release to market.

FIGURE 28–1

The Welded Can

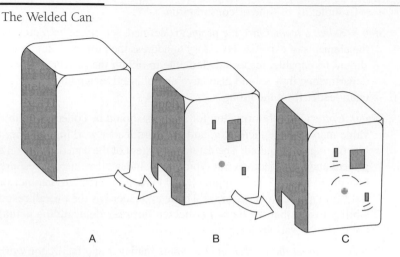

A   B   C

Before Value Analysis

    A. The custom-size unfinished steel-drawn can was purchased from a manufacturer. Lead time is 8 to 12 weeks, due to the manufacturer's production schedule.

    B. At the sheet-metal fabricator the cutouts and holes were machined or milled into the formed can. It is difficult to fixture and hold the part because of material flexing and the rounded corners. Machining adds three to four weeks to the lead time.

    C. The can is painted and silk-screened. Rounded corners make it difficult to align silk-screened registration marks. One to two weeks is added to the lead time.

    D. The cover is inspected and shipped. Total lead time at this point is 13 to 19 weeks. There are frequent rejections due to dimensional accuracy problems.

After Value Analysis

    A. The raw material is changed to aluminum sheet, eliminating the steel-drawn can, saving lead time and expense.

    B. The aluminum sheet is sheared, and holes and slots are punched instead of machined. A slot is added to facilitate customer removal of the cover without removing the knob, providing easier maintenance. Punching is inexpensive and faster than machining. Also, holes and slots are easier to locate on flat sheet as opposed to the rounded, flexible can.

    C. The material is bent to shape.

    D. The seams are welded and ground to a smooth finish.

FIGURE 28–2

The Welded Can

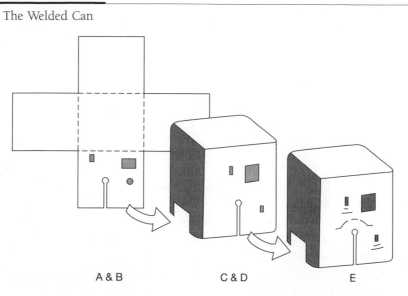

A & B   C & D   E

E. The can is painted and silk-screened. The new lead time is four to six
weeks total. The total cost of the part is reduced by about $8.00.
Product maintenance is simplified.

The following is an example of a value analysis project that came about in
an effort to reduce the cost of office cleaning.

Before Value Analysis

Company X had a contract to clean offices that had been in place for a number of
years. The specifications for what was to be done, how it was to be done, and how
often it was to be done were very general and vague. Other than requiring cleaning
five nights per week, the rest was pretty much up to the contractor. Discussions
with the cleaning contractor revealed that each office was vacuumed, all work
surfaces dusted, and trash containers emptied nightly. Additional work was done
nightly in restrooms and hallways. Basically all cleaning chores were repeated
each night. Company X's supply manager contacted several supply managers in
other companies who had office cleaning contracts and found that the current
cleaning cost was above what most others were paying and that most other supply managers had more detailed cleaning specifications in their contracts than did
Company X.

After Value Analysis

It was determined through experimentation that vacuuming of offices was not
required nightly and that dusting of work surfaces also was not needed every day.
Vacuuming was changed to every third night and dusting to once per week. Other

tasks were also similarly spread out. By alternating which parts of the office received the various treatments, the contractor was able to carry out the revised schedule with fewer personnel. The supply manager for Company X prepared and competitively quoted a new contract that explicitly stated what the various cleaning tasks were and when and how they were to be done. Company X realized an acceptable level of cleaning at a significantly reduced cost.

FOR FURTHER READING

Carbone, J. (1996). "Value Analysis: For Some More Important Than Ever," *Purchasing*, June 20, pp. 33–34.

Farrell, P. (1982). *Aljian's Purchasing Handbook*, 4th ed , New York: McGraw-Hill.

Mazel, J. L. (1996). "New Value Analysis Emphasizes Greater Supplier Involvement," *Supplier Selection & Management Report, April,* vol. 96, no. 4 (New York: Management & Administration, Inc.).

Miles, L. D. (1972). *Techniques of Value Analysis and Engineering.* New York: McGraw-Hill.

Miller, J. (1993). "The Evolution of Value Analysis," *NAPM Insights*, February, pp. 13–14.

Morgan, J. (1995). "Where Has VA Gone?" *Purchasing*, June 1, pp. 34–37.

Mudge, A. E. (1971). *Value Engineering: A Systematic Approach*, New York: McGraw-Hill.

Napolean, L. J. (1993). "Reaping the Benefits," *NAPM Insights*, December, pp. 26–27.

Raia, E. (1992). "Taking Out the Cost," *Purchasing*, June 4, pp. 41–57.

Raia, E. (1993). "VA Contest Winners," *Purchasing*, June 3, pp. 55–64.

Stundza, T. (1997). "Purchasing Evolves into Supply Management," *Purchasing*, July 17.

"Value Analysis Contest" (1994). *Purchasing*, June 2, pp. 33–39.

"Value Analysis Report" (1991). *Purchasing*, June 6, pp. 61–71.

Brown, J. (1992). *Value Engineering: A Blueprint*, Industrial Press Inc. New York, NY ,

Clark, L. J. (1997). "Understanding and Applying Value Analysis and Value Engineering," *NAPM InfoEdge*, December.

Cooper, R., and R. Slagmulder (1997). *Target Costing and Value Engineering*, Productivity Press Inc., New York, NY

Dell'Isola, A. (1997). Value Engineering: Practical Applications for Design, Construction, Maintenance and Operations, R.S. Means Company. Kingston, MA

Fowler, T. C. (1990). *Value Analysis in Design*, Van Nostrand Reinhold. New York, NY

Harris, K., C.P.M. (2004). "Improving Products and Processes with Mini Value Analysis," *Inside Supply Management*®, September, pp. 6–7.

Hartley, J. L. (2000). "Collaborative Value Analysis: Experiences from the Automotive Industry," *Journal of Supply Chain Management*, Fall, pp. 27–32.

Park, R. (1998). Value Engineering: A Plan for Invention. Saint Lucie Press.

SAVE International Society for Value Methodology (Value Analysis, Value Engineering, Value Methodology), www.value-eng.com. Shilito, M. L., and D. J. DeMarle (1992). *Value, Its Measurement, Design and Management*, John Wiley & Sons.

Younker, D. (2003). Engineering: Analysis and Methodology, Marcel Dekker.

CHAPTER 29

FORECASTING FOR SUPPLY MANAGEMENT

ALAN RAEDELS, PH.D., C.P.M.
Professor Emeritus of Supply and Logistics Management
Portland State University

INTRODUCTION

Forecasting is one of the most important activities any manager, especially a supply manager, can ever undertake, yet this is an activity that few organizations do well. For example, a company which will remain nameless invited a colleague and me to develop a forecast for raw materials, parts, and components. Our approach was straightforward. We suggested all they needed to do was use their material requirements planning (MRP) system to explode the bills of material from the master schedule. The company's response was very revealing. They didn't use the MRP system because sales and marketing could not (or would not) forecast more than five minutes ahead. The supply manager felt a more accurate forecast (and one less costly) could be developed using historical usage data and assuming the demands for the various items were independent rather than developing the forecast based upon the production plan.

STATUS OF THE FORECASTING PROCESS

Forecasts are necessary for a variety of tasks such as scheduling, planning the acquisition of goods and services, and determining resource requirements such as personnel, funds, and capital equipment. An article by Wisner and Stanley reports that studies of forecasting processes have shown that

- In a survey of electronic firms, half the respondents had total responsibility for price forecasting.

- Maintenance, repair, and operating (MRO) supply purchasers relied on price indexes to forecast price increases.

- Individuals responsible for forecasting often held titles such as director of sales, vice president of manufacturing, and national sales manager.

- When respondents were asked to indicate which techniques they used most often, the highest response was for judgmental methods.

- As the complexity of the forecasting model increased, the frequency of use decreased.

- When respondents were asked to identify the most common cause of forecast error, responses included seasonality, promotions, lack of communication, and over optimism.

- Another area in which respondents indicated they experienced difficulty was in short-term forecasting for individual items.

- The most common strategies for dealing with forecasting error included overtime, excess inventory, flexible worker schedules, and flexible worker skills.

- Less than half the supply management managers interviewed formally review the historical accuracy of their forecasts.[1]

These results do not paint a rosy picture of the status of forecasting in organizations today. The objective of this chapter is to provide supply managers with some simple tools and knowledge to improve their organization's forecasting process. This chapter first discusses what the supply manager needs to forecast. Then it reviews the various types of qualitative (judgment) and quantitative (time series and causal) models available to forecast quantity. Next, it looks at the tools for forecasting the availability of materials, including the ISM *Report On Business*. Lastly, it looks at the tools available for forecasting price.

What Do Supply Managers Forecast?

The supply manager must forecast in at least three different dimensions: quantity, availability, and price. Quantity forecasting involves estimating demand and usage requirements in both the near term and the long term. Availability forecasting is looking at market conditions, economic conditions, and technology changes. Price forecasting is concerned with determining how to ensure that the organization pays the appropriate price for the goods and services it purchases.

Why do supply managers need to forecast? To anticipate *change*! Change can come from many sources. It can be in our supply base or in our customers' markets. There are many factors that may cause change in our supply chain or in our requirements from the supply chain.

- *Technology.* Changes in technology can come from our supply base in the form of new or modified components and materials. It can also come in the form of new requirements from the customer.

- *Annual or long-term budgets and plans for operations and company expansion or contraction.* These impact ongoing requirements and requirements for capital items. These frequently require forecasts of quantity, availability, and price.

---

1 Joel D. Wisner and Linda L. Stanley (1994). "Forecasting Practices in Purchasing," *International Journal of Purchasing and Materials Management,* Winter, pp. 22–29.

- *Demographics.* Changing population demographics will affect supply availability and product demand.

- *Law.* As laws are enacted, they may affect the availability of supply.

- *Taste and needs.* A change in customer desires or needs may affect demand.

- *War and the threat of war.* The threat of war may cause stockpiling which can cause shortages, even if the war doesn't take place and can cause a slowdown if the war doesn't happen.

- *Mergers and acquisitions.* A merger or acquisition may result in a change in management which may change your relationship with the supplier, or the supplier may drop the product you purchase from them.

- *Strikes and the threat of strikes.* These have the same effect as war and the threat of war.

- *Global economic conditions.* Markets are now world markets. The supply base is becoming more global, especially at the second- and third-tier supply levels. Your first-tier supply may be domestic, but its supplier or its supplier's supplier has a good chance of being non-domestic. Therefore, what is happening in other economies will have a direct influence on our supply chain.

- *Nature: depletion, discovery, and disaster.* Natural resources are generally controlled by oligopolies, and as a result, the price and availability are controlled. Also, a natural disaster, such as an earthquake, hurricane, or tornado, can destroy a supplier's facility creating shortages in an industry. Examples include the Japanese earthquake in Kobe in 1995 which affected Toyota's brake supplier and the floods in the central United States in 1993 which caused major disruptions in rail and truck transportation. Fire can create problems as well as when a major chemical producer's Louisiana plant caught fire, cutting the industry capacity, for at least a year, by 50 percent.

- *Environmental concerns.* The supply manager will need to monitor and anticipate the ever-changing environmental legislation and standards such as ISO 14000.

- *Supply chain security and terrorism.* A new factor that needs to be considered is disruptions to the supply chain caused by terrorist attacks and the need in many industries to have secure supply chains year-round.

The Forecasting Process

The process to develop a forecast requires

1. Determining what is to be forecasted, the accuracy required, the frequency of the forecast, and the purpose of the forecast. Is the item to be forecasted

Forecasting—When to Use Each Method

Qualitative	Quantitative	Causal
Data scarce	Past data available	Past data available
No past data	Relationships/trends stable	Relationships clear & stable
New products	Short run accuracy needed	Need to identify turning
Advanced tools too costly	Need forecasts frequently	points
No ideas on causality		Some explanatory variables
Data too costly to collect		controllable
Participation desired		High cost of inaccuracy
Short run accuracy not		
needed		

a commodity? Is it freely traded or cartel controlled? Is the forecast for production planning or for general sales? If it is for planning, is it for production planning or for budgeting? If it is for budgeting, the forecast will need to be in currency rather than units. Is the forecast for quantity, availability, or price? Is the forecast for daily, weekly, monthly, or annually? Until these questions are answered, the chances of a relevant forecast being developed are quite small.

2. Selecting the model or models to be used and collecting the appropriate data. Be sure the data will be available when you need to make a forecast. See Figure 29–1 for a list of conditions for when each type of model is most often used. After collecting the data, review it for missing values and outliers. Missing values need to be estimated if a time series model is being used. The forecaster can use the average of the observations on each side of the missing value.

3. Developing the forecasting model and testing it. The usual rule of thumb is to use two-thirds of the data to develop the model and one-third to evaluate the model's performance.

4. Make your forecast considering all the available inputs, not just the model's number. Always give a range of outcomes. Remember, the only sure thing about a forecast is it is wrong.

5. Review the model at least quarterly to ensure it is still appropriate.

FORECASTING QUANTITY
Qualitative Methods

Qualitative methods are forecasting models based on the collective judgment of individuals. Four of the most common are the Delphi method, market research, executive opinion, and sales force composite.

Delphi Method

The Delphi method is used when there is little information about what the future holds. This technique involves a panel of respondents who answer questions about a future scenario. Then the answers are compiled and fed back to the panel with no indications of who said what. The process continues until the group reaches a consensus. This technique is often used for technological forecasting as well as new product introduction.

Market Research

Market research involves surveying potential customers to determine their future buying plans. Although the sample selection may seem highly mathematical, the results simply represent buyer opinion or plans.

Executive Opinion

When all else fails, ask management! Experienced executives may have experienced similar situations previously and can bring that experience to bear on the current problem. This method is quick and may perform reasonably well on aggregate forecasts of sales.

Sales Force Composite

The sales force composite starts with each salesperson estimating his or her sales for the coming forecast period by product and by customer. These estimates are given to the sales manager who aggregates them and makes adjustments. The sales manager then gives the results to the next level up who repeats the process. This process is repeated until it reaches the top of the organization. The top executives review the forecast and make changes. These changes are then passed down the organization for setting sales goals. The advantage of this process is that it is participatory. The downside is that it can take two or three months to develop.

Time Series Methods

A time series is a plot of a series of values where the only independent variable is time. This implies that the past predicts the future. Every time series has four components: trend, seasonality, cyclical, and randomness. These are illustrated in Figure 29–2. There are a number of time series models that can be used. We will look at four of the more common ones: moving average, exponential smoothing, simple linear regression, and the decomposition model. Time series models are most often used for short-term forecasting.

Moving Average

This model works best when there is no trend in the data and the data varies above and below a stable average or mean. The simple moving average model involves taking the average of some number of periods as the forecast of the next period's demand. For example, a three-period moving average would be the sum of the

FIGURE 29–2

Time Series Components

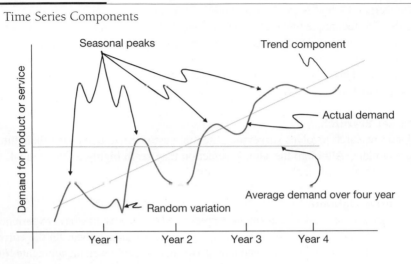

demand values for periods 1, 2, and 3 which is then divided by 3. This creates the forecast value for period 4. This model will always lag changes in direction of a series. Figure 29–3a and b shows the calculations for a data set and the graphs of the actual and forecast values. The earliest you can forecast for, using a three-period moving average, is period 4. The forecast for period 4 is the average of the actual values for periods 1 through 3. This would be

$$F_4 = \frac{A_1 + A_2 + A_3}{3} = \frac{1,690 + 940 + 2,625}{3} = 1,752$$

The weighted moving average is the same except that the various demand values are given weights between 0 and 1, which must sum to 1. For example, if we give the most recent data a weight of 0.5; the next period back, a weight of 0.3; and the third piece of data, a weight of 0.2, then our forecast for period 4 is

$$F_4 = 0.2A_1 + 0.3A_2 + 0.05A_3 = (0.2)(1,690) + (0.3)(940) + (0.5)(2,625) = 1,933$$

When we try a four-period moving average, notice how the line is more stable than the three-period model. When using a moving average equal to the number of periods in the seasonal cycle, the effect is to eliminate the seasonality from the data leaving the underlying trend line. We will use this fact in developing decomposition models later.

Exponential Smoothing
Exponential smoothing is a special form of weighted moving average. This model can be used when more weight is desired on more recent data (as compared to the moving average model which puts the same weight on the data from each past time period that is included). More weight on more recent data may be desired due to

FIGURE 29-3A

Moving Average Example

Quarter	Sales	3 per	Error	|error|	error^2	4-per	error	|error|	error^2
1	1690								
2	940								
3	2625								
4	2500	1752	748.33	748.33	560003				
5	1800	2022	-221.67	221.67	49136	1939	-138.75	138.75	19252
6	900	2308	-1408.33	1408.33	1983403	1966	-1066.25	1066.25	1136889
7	2900	1733	1166.67	1166.67	1361111	1956	943.75	943.75	890664
8	2360	1867	493.33	493.33	243378	2025	335.00	335.00	112225
9	1850	2053	-203.33	203.33	41344	1990	-140.00	140.00	19600
10	1100	2370	-1270.00	1270.00	1612900	2003	-902.50	902.50	814506
11	2930	1770	1160.00	1160.00	1345600	2053	877.50	877.50	770006
12	2615	1960	655.00	655.00	429025	2060	555.00	555.00	308025
13		2215				2124			
			124.44	814.07	847322		57.97	619.84	508896
			Bias	MAD	MSE		Bias	DMA	MSE

F I G U R E   29–3B

Moving Average Example Graph

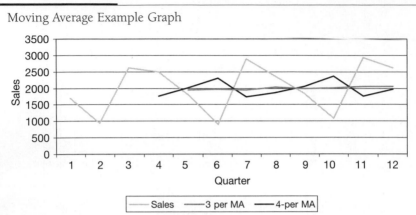

greater accuracy of recent data or because there is a trend in the data that would cause a moving average forecast to significantly lag the trend in making a forecast. Another advantage of exponential smoothing is the small amount of data required. This makes it useful for organizations that have a large number of finished products or other items to forecast.

The forecast for the next period is the forecast for this period plus some percentage of the forecast error which is the actual value for the current period minus the forecast for the current period. The weight is between 0 and 1. Using our data from the previous example, a weight of 0.2, and the forecast for period 1 of 1,690, the forecast for period 2 is

$$F_2 = F_1 + \alpha(A_1 - F_1) = 1{,}690 + 0.2(1{,}690 - 1{,}690) = 1{,}690 + 0 = 1{,}690$$

The forecast for period 3 would be

$$F_3 = F_2 + \alpha(A_2 - F_2) = 1{,}690 + 0.2(940 - 1{,}690) = 1{,}690 - (0.2)(750) = 1{,}540$$

Figure 29-4a shows the results of the exponential smoothing model using weights of 0.2 and 0.3. Notice in the graphs in Figures 29–3b and 29–4b that the exponential smoothing, as well the moving average models, always lags any change in direction.

Trend Projections

Trend projections are used when it is desired to determine if a set of data is changing in some relatively consistent manner over time, for example, the growth of demand for gasoline over a particular number of years.

A common method to do trend projections is to use simple linear regression to fit a straight line to a set of data points. Linear regression allows the supply manager to estimate a straight line of the form $y = a + bx$ to the data by minimizing the sum of the squared error values (the difference between the actual and forecast

FIGURE 29–4A

Exponential Smoothing Example

Quarter	Sales	Exp-.2	error	|error|	error^2	Exp-.3	error	|error|	error^2
1	1690	1690				1690			
2	940	1690	-750.00	750.00	562500	1690	-750.00	750.00	562500
3	2625	1540	1085.00	1085.00	1177225	1465	1160.00	1160.00	1345600
4	2500	1757	743.00	743.00	552049	1813	687.00	687.00	471969
5	1800	1906	-105.60	105.60	11151	2019	-219.10	219.10	48005
6	900	1884	-984.48	984.48	969201	1953	-1053.37	1053.37	1109588
7	2900	1688	1212.42	1212.42	1469953	1637	1262.64	1262.64	1594262
8	2360	1930	429.93	429.93	184842	2016	343.85	343.85	118232
9	1850	2016	-166.05	166.05	27574	2119	-269.31	269.31	72526
10	1100	1983	-882.84	882.84	779412	2039	-938.51	938.51	880809
11	2930	1806	1123.73	1123.73	1262759	1757	1173.04	1173.04	1376023
12	2615	2031	583.98	583.98	341033	2109	506.13	506.13	256166
13		2148				2261			
			208.10	733.37	667064		165.82	760.27	712335
			Bias	MAD	MSE		Bias	MAD	MSE

FIGURE   29–4B

Exponential Smoothing Example Graph

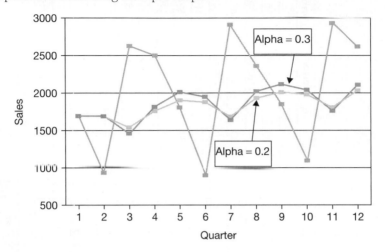

values). The calculations are programmed on many calculators and all computer spreadsheets. If we run a regression on the four-period moving average values shown in Figure 29-3a, the results are

$$\text{Forecast for period } x = 1,925 + 16.5(\text{Period number})$$

The period number is the quarter number. To forecast for quarter 1, year 4, the quarter number would be 13. The forecast would be 2,139.5 or 2,140.

Decomposition Models

Decomposition models seek to identify the trend and seasonal components of a time series. These models are useful for forecasting sales or demand for products that exhibit both trend and seasonality. They do this by first taking out the seasonality using a centered moving average and then using linear regression to identify the trend component. The seasonal factors are obtained by dividing the actual by the centered moving average value for that period where the number of periods in the moving average is equal to the length of the seasonal cycle.

Causal Methods

Causal methods try to identify the variables that have a cause-and-effect relationship with the variable being forecasted. These models are more complex and take longer to develop than qualitative and time series models. They are used when it is important to predict turning points and when some of the variables can be controlled.

Multivariate Regression

Multivariate regression uses multiple variables that are assumed to have an effect on the variable being forecasted. For example, to forecast monthly sales of bathtubs, the forecaster might look at the number of new housing permits issued, the number of multifamily housing permits issued, and the number of remodeling permits issued. The one thing the forecaster must be cognizant of is the availability of the data at the time the forecast is to be made. For example, July data may not be available until late August or September. Therefore, using July's data to forecast July's sales is not appropriate since the data is not available.

Econometric Models

Econometric models consist of multiple multivariate regression equations used to model sectors of the economy. These models are not generally used for forecasting a single company's sales. Rather they are used to model an industry or sector on the economy. If a supply manager has access to econometric models, they could be used to predict the effect on the manager's company from changes in the economy and how such changes might affect the demand for purchased materials and services.

MODEL EVALUATION

There are three commonly used measurements that are used to compare forecasting models. The first is the average forecast error. The forecast error is the difference between the actual demand for a period and the forecasted demand for that period. The average error therefore is the sum of the forecast errors divided by the number of observations. The problem with using the average error as a criterion is that it ignores the magnitude of the errors as long as they sum to 0. For example, model A has forecast errors of −5 and +5 and model B has forecast errors of −10 and +10. The average error is 0 for both, but model A is clearly preferred.

The second measure of forecast error is the average of the absolute values of the forecast errors. Known as the mean absolute deviation (MAD), it is calculated by summing the absolute values of the forecast errors and then dividing by the number of observations. Using the preceding example, model A would have a MAD of 5 and model B would have a MAD of 10. The MAD lets the forecaster see the average magnitude of the errors ignoring the sign. It also gives equal weights to the error terms no matter the magnitude.

The third measure is the mean squared error (MSE). The MSE is calculated by summing the squares of each of the forecast error values and then dividing by the number of observations. Using the same example, model A would have an MSE of 25 and model B would have an MSE of 100. The MSE gives more weight to the larger errors resulting in models that try to avoid large errors.

It is important to only forecast to the accuracy of input data. If your smallest unit of measure is the nearest tens, then develop your forecast to the nearest ten.

To evaluate the effectiveness of the forecasting process Gilliland suggests using what he calls the forecast value added (FVA) which is the change in forecast accuracy due to an activity in the forecasting process.[2] In other words, is the forecast error less than doing nothing? Four basic approaches for the do-nothing forecast are using the average of the demand, the demand for the previous period, the moving average of the demand, and the demand value for the same period in the previous year. If the forecast model is not better than the do-nothing approach, then your forecasting process needs improvement.

FORECASTING AVAILABILITY AND LEAD TIMES

The second area supply managers must forecast is availability of supplies. This involves understanding the supply markets and how they relate to general economic conditions. There are several tools that the supply manager can use to look at the economy. These include the ISM *Report On Business*®, the Federal Reserve's Industrial Production Index and capacity utilization rate, the Conference Board's Index of Leading Indicators, and industry publications.

There are many factors that can affect material availability. These include

Factory utilization rates. If utilization rates are high, an increase in demand can cause prices to rise as well as indicate shortage potential.

Lead times. As demand increases and capacity doesn't grow as fast, lead times will increase.

Inventory levels. If inventory levels are high, then lead times should be relatively short.

Supply chain issues. Supply chain issues include problems with second- and third-tier suppliers.

ISM'S *REPORT ON BUSINESS*®

The ISM *Report On Business*® is an excellent source of information about the economy. It consists of two surveys taken monthly of supply chain professionals. The manufacturing survey, released the first working day of the month, covers NAICS codes 311–339 which cover the manufacturing sector of the economy. The non-manufacturing survey, released on the third working day of the month, covers the rest of the economy. Both surveys have over 300 respondents. Respondents are selected based upon the importance of the NAICS to the gross domestic product (GDP) and by region. Each survey consists of a number of questions where the respondent only has to indicate whether the item is higher, the same, or lower than the previous month.

---

2 Michael Gilliland (2002). "Is Forecasting a Waste of Time?" *Supply Chain Management Review*, July, www.manufacturing.net/scm/article/CA232251.

FIGURE 29–5

ISM *Report On Business®* Indexes

Manufacturing	Non-Manufacturing
PMI	
Production	Production/Business Activity
Inventory	Inventory
New Orders	New Orders
Employment	Employment
Supplier Deliveries	Supplier Deliveries
Backlog of Orders	Backlog of Orders
New Export Orders	New Export Orders
Commodity Prices	Prices
Imports	Imports
Customers' Inventories[1]	Inventory Sentiment[1]
Additionally, Buying Policy is reported for Capital Expenditures, Production and MRO in average days.	

Both reports also include lists of commodities that are reported to be up in price, down in price, or in short supply.
[1]Note: Customers' Inventories and Inventory Sentiment are not measuring the same thing.

What Information Is Available?

Figure 29–5 lists the indexes that are reported each month. Additionally there are lists of items that are are in short supply, up in price, and down in price. This information is available each month at the ISM Web site www.ism.ws/ISMReport/index.cfm. The (PMI) is a composite index that is the weighted average of the manufacturing production, new orders, employment, supplier deliveries, and inventory index values. There is no composite index for the non-manufacturing sector; however the non-manufacturing production index is called the Business Activity Index. Many of the ISM indexes lead comparable activity indexes published by the government and other organizations. The following table presents the relationships between the ISM indexes and relevant federal government indexes.[3]

ISM Index	Federal Government Index	Peak	Trough
New orders	Manufacturing new orders	+5	−1
Inventories	Manufacturing and trade inventories	+5	0
Prices	Consumer price index	+8	+7

3 Alan Raedels, Lee Buddress, and Michael Smith (2002). "You Can Predict the Next Recession," in *Proceedings of the 13th Annual North American Research/Teaching Symposium on Purchasing and Supply Chain Management,* Tempe, AZ, pp. 367–378.

The data is presented as diffusion indexes. Diffusion indexes are a form of change index and are calculated by summing the percentage of respondents that indicate the measure is higher plus one-half of the percentage of respondents that indicate that the measure is the same. For example, if 40 percent of the respondents say prices are higher than last month and 30 percent indicate prices are the same as last month, the diffusion index would be

$$DI = 40 + 0.5(30) = 55$$

If the value of the diffusion index is above 50, it indicates the economy is expanding, while a value below 50 indicates the economy is contracting. If there is significant seasonality in the index, a seasonal adjustment factor is applied to obtain the published index value. The advantage of change indexes is that they lead the actual value of the measure. If the index goes from 55 to 57, it indicates the measure is increasing at a faster rate, while if it goes from 55 to 53, it indicates the measure is increasing at a decreasing rate. Likewise, an index value that changes from 45 to 43 indicates the measure is contracting at an increasing rate, and a move from 45 to 47 indicates a slower rate of contraction. The supplier deliveries index is the opposite of the other indexes. When the economy is growing, demand starts to exceed supply and supplier deliveries start to get later than scheduled. So, worsening deliveries indicates an expanding economy.

Raedels, Buddress, and Smith have proposed an economic index that is the average of the production, new orders, employment, and supplier deliveries indexes for both the manufacturing and non-manufacturing surveys.[4] These two index values are then weighted by the contribution of each sector to the gross domestic product. The resulting value is called the Economic Index. Figure 29–6 shows the performance of the index since 1997. Note how the index led the 2001 recession by two months. The index is available at http://artwo.home.comcast.net/wsb/ISM/ISMGraphs-3.html.

How to Use the Information

The first step is to plot company and industry information and compare it with the relevant ISM indexes. When comparing company data such as production, new orders, and employment to the ISM data, remember the ISM indexes are change indexes while the company data is absolute; therefore the ISM indexes should indicate change prior to the change being observed in the company data.

Next, look at the macroeconomic trends and evaluate the general direction of the economy. Relevant items to look at would include producer price indexes, the Index of Leading Indicators, the Industrial Production Index, the capacity utilization rate, the consumer price index, unemployment levels, and the federal funds rate. Figure 29–7 shows the performance of several of these key indicators over the last 25 years. The shaded areas indicate the periods during which the National Bureau of Economic Research (NBER) has declared the U.S. economy

---

4 Ibid.

FIGURE   29–6

Economic Index

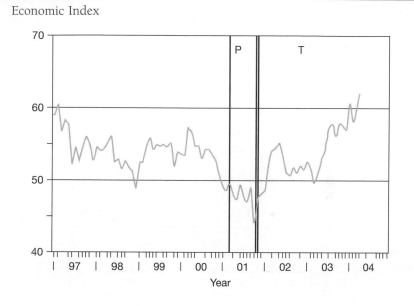

was in a downturn or recession. Notice how the factory utilizations declined in 1990–91 and 2000. Also see how the federal funds rate was lowered starting in 1989 to offset the coming recession of 1990–91 and also in 2000–2001 to offset the slowdown of 2000–2001. Two other valuable indicators are the Index of Leading Indicators (ILI), published by the Conference Board, and the Industrial Production Index (IPI) published by the Federal Reserve.

The ILI leads upturns in the economy by 1 to 7 periods (median of 1) and downturns by 7 to 16 periods (median of 11).[5] The IPI lags upturns by one to three months and leads downturns a median of five months. First, as the economy improves, you can expect the capacity utilization to begin to move upward causing lead times to rise and inflation (shown by the change in the CPI) to increase. By being able to observe when these events are happening, the supply manager can determine the appropriate strategies for dealing with suppliers. For example, when the capacity utilization is low, it might be an opportunity to work on process and product improvements with a supplier because the supplier now will have the time to work on its processes.

Look at what is going on in other areas of the country. There are a number of regional business surveys published each month and are accessible from the ISM Web page at www.ism.ws/ISMReport/index.cfm#regional. The regional surveys allow you to look at areas of the country where your suppliers and/or your customers are located to determine if there are any differences that might be useful.

---

5 Ibid.

FIGURE   29–7

Economic Indicators

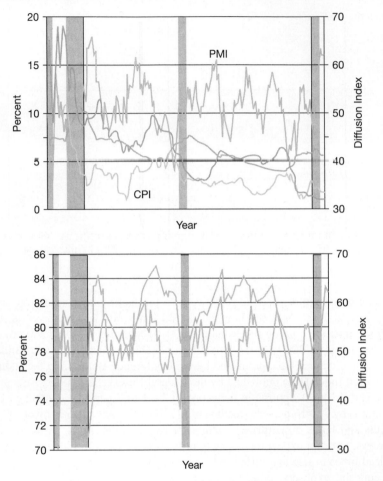

Read the "Market Trends" page in *Inside Supply Management®*. This page regularly presents information on commodities, present and future, each month.

FORECASTING PRICE

Prices are probably the most difficult factor for the supply manager to forecast. Prices are the result of a complex set of factors including demand, availability, industry capacity, political situations, requirements, lead time, and requirements. It is important that an organization define its objectives before developing a price forecasting system. For example, if an organization desires to maximize its bottom line, then the objective is to determine the level and timing of the highs and the lows. If the objective is to "follow the crowd," then a buying strategy can be developed that is based on expected deviations from averages.

Baker suggests that there are two types of price forecasting approaches: fundamental and technical.[6] Fundamental models use supply-and-demand inputs, while technical approaches involve a gestalt analysis of the relevant forces that affect prices. Baker proposes several decision-making systems for price forecasting. They include

Intuition. Based on years of experience and reliable sources of information with complete awareness of the decision's effect on the business.

Statistical or econometric models. Forecasting of deviations from the model to provide a better fit with the market situation.

Comparable-year and seasonal analysis. A combination of supply-and-demand analysis and price-movement analysis.

Bullish-bearish analysis. Uses a ranking of all opposing forces in the market, ranking them based on their estimated strength and probability of occurrence to produce a price forecast giving direction, level, and time.

Producer Price Indexes

Producer price indexes (PPIs) are available for a large number of commodities. The downside is the data is not available until 11 to 15 days after the month in question. PPIs give you an idea where the prices have been relative to the past. The important thing to do is to compare them against your material price data for the same time period. For example, using aluminum as an example, Figure 29–8 shows the metals and metal products PPI versus aluminum prices. We see that the PPI indicated the turning point at least by one quarter four out of five times between 1994 and 2000. This type of information could be very valuable to a supply manager in determining whether to lock in long-term contracts.

For example, Figure 29–9 shows the quarterly prices for aluminum plotted against the ISM Price Index. Note that in three of the six price turns, the ISM Price Index led the turn by two quarters; in two of the cases the price index led by one quarter; and the last case was coincident with the price change.

Hedging

Hedging is a technique for minimizing the effects of prices that vary over time or must be fixed for a time in the future. Hedging is taking equal and opposite actions on the spot and futures markets to reduce the risk of large changes in cost. "The key

---

6 John D. Baker (1995). "Purchasing Price-Volatile Commodities: Risk Control and Forecasting," in *Proceedings of the 80th International Purchasing Conference,* Tempe, AZ: National Association of Purchasing Management.

FIGURE 29–8

Example Price Forecast Using the PPI

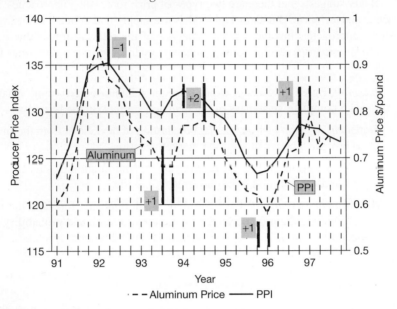

FIGURE 29–9

Example Price Forecast Using the ISM Price Index

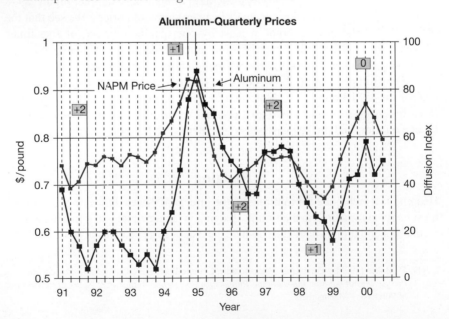

benefit to hedging is the reduction of price volatility because it helps companies manage their cash flow better and more predictably."[7]

SUMMARY

Forecasting is as much art as it is science. No one technique or model will work in all situations. The supply manager must understand the markets and the factors that cause change in the markets in order to develop realistic forecasts. The Appendix to this chapter lists sources of information for forecasting based on an article by Motlok and Pie.[8]

ADDITIONAL REFERENCES

Helsmoortel, Martin L. (1995). "Using Key Economic Indicators," *NAPM Insights*, January, pp. 30–32.

Kauffman, Ralph G. (1994). "Making the NAPM *Report On Business*® Work for You," *NAPM Insights*, October, pp. 62–64.

Raedels, Alan R. (1995). "Tracking Inflation's Effect on Prices," *NAPM Insights*, January, pp. 6–7.

Using the NAPM *Report On Business*® to Forecast Purchase Trends, CD-ROM, NAPM, 1996.

APPENDIX

The following list offers resources for gathering data on economics and forecasting. This list is not all-inclusive, but should serve as a starting point.

Commodity Trade and Price Trends, published by the International Bank for Reconstruction and Development/The World Bank, lists prices for food, nonfood, fuel, metal, and mineral commodities in international markets. Published annually; Contact Johns Hopkins University Press, Journals Division, 701 W. 40th Street, Suite 275, Baltimore, MD, 21211; 410/516-6900.

Doane's Agricultural Report (www.doane.com) provides prices for primary livestock and grains. Released weekly; Contact Doane Information Services, 11701 Borman Drive, St. Louis, MO, 63146; 314/569-2700.

The Economist (www.economist.com) provides commodity price indexes and foreign exchange rates. Published weekly; Contact Economist Newspaper, 10 Rockefeller Plaza, 10th Floor, New York, NY, 10020; 212/541-5730.

---

7 Cheryl C. Lewis (1998). "Hedging Your Bets," *Supply Chain Management Review*, July 16, www.manufacturing.net/scm/article/CA116498.

8 Tracey Motlok and Carolyn Pye (1996). "Forecasting Tools," *Purchasing Today*®, June, pp. 32–33.

Plastics Technology (www.plasticstechnology.com) provides plastics prices. Published monthly. Contact Bill Communications, Inc., 633 Third Avenue, New York, NY, 10017; 212/592-6570.

Statistical Service Current Statistics contains a variety of commodity prices. Released monthly. Contact Standard and Poor's Corporation, 25 Broadway, New York, NY, 10004; 212/208-8000.

The Timber Bulletin (www.unece.org/trade/timber), released by the United Nations, provides prices for forest products in several international markets. Published monthly. Contact United Nations Publications, Palais des Nations, CH 1211 Geneva 10, Switzerland; 22.34.28.06.

The International Monetary Fund's *International Financial Statistics* includes prices for several primary commodities. Released monthly. Pricing also includes the *International Financial Statistics Yearbook*. Contact the International Monetary Fund, 700 19th Street NW, Washington, DC, 20431; 202/473-7430.

American Bureau of Metal Statistics (www.abms.com), P.O. Box 1405, Secaucus, NJ, 07094; 908/905-6699; fax 908/905-7755. Compiles industry statistics for nonferrous metals.

American Iron and Steel Institute (www.steel.org), 1101 17th Street NW, Washington, DC, 20036; 202/452-7100; fax 202/463-6573. Compiles iron and steel industry statistics.

American Paper Institute, 260 Madison Avenue, New York, NY, 10016; 212/340-0600. Maintains library.

American Petroleum Institute (www.api.org), 1220 L Street NW, Washington, DC 20005; 202/682-8000; fax 202/682-8030. Maintains library.

American Textile Manufacturers Institute (www.atmi.org), 1801 K Street NW, Suite 900, Washington, DC, 20006; 202/862-0500; fax 202/862-0570. Maintains library.

Cadmium Council, Inc., Greenwich Office Park, Building 2, Greenwich, CT, 06830; 203/625-0911; fax 203/625-0918. Maintains library.

Copper and Brass Servicenter Association (www.copper-brass.org), Adams Building, Suite 109, 251 W. DeKalb Pike, King of Prussia, PA, 19406; 215/265-6658; fax 215/265-3419. Compiles statistics.

Copper Development Association (www.copper.org), 260 Madison Avenue, New York, NY, 10016; 212/251-7200; fax 212/251-7234. Compiles market statistics and research.

Electric Power Research Institute (www.epri.org), 3412 Hillview Avenue, Palo Alto, CA, 94304; 415/855-2000; fax 415/855-2954. Maintains library.

International Magnesium Association (www.intlmag.org), 1303 Vincent Place, Suite 1, McLean, VA, 22101; 703/442-8888; fax 703/821-1824. Compiles industry statistics.

Metal Treating Institute (www.metaltreat.com), 302 Third Street, Suite 1, Neptune Beach, FL, 32266; 904/249-0448; fax 904/249-0459. Compiles statistics.

Textile Research Institute (www.triprinceton.org), P.O. Box 625, Princeton, NJ, 08542; 609/924-3150; fax 609/683-7838. Maintains library on textile-related topics.

Western Wood Products Association (www.wwpa.org), Yeon Building, 522 SW Fifth Avenue, Portland, OR, 97204-2122; 503/224-3930; fax 503/224-3934. Compiles statistics.

The Conference Board (www.tcb-indicators.org) provides numerous fore-casting-related publications, including *Business and Economic Outlook: How Will the Century Close?*, a 38-page report; the *International Economic Scoreboard,* a quarterly publication; and the semiannual *World Outlook.* Publications are $25 for association members and $100 for nonmembers. For information on related publications, contact the Conference Board, 845 Third Avenue, New York, NY, 10022-6679; 212/759-0900; fax 212/980-7014; e-mail info@conference-board.org.

The Economic Forecasting Center's (robinson.gsu.edu/efc/) publications include: *Forecast of the Nation,* issued quarterly, *Monthly Projections*; *Consumer Price Index,* issued monthly; *Producer Price Index,* issued monthly; and *Weekly Commentary.* For more information, contact the Economic Forecasting Center, Georgia State University, University Plaza, Atlanta, GA, 30303; 404/651-3282; fax 404/651-3299.

Government Resources

The U.S. Government Printing Office offers numerous economic and forecasting tools, including the following:

Agricultural prices, Agricultural Statistics Board reports (www.usda.gov/nass/aggraphs/agprices.htm). Provides comparative information on prices received by farmers for commodities and services, interest, taxes, and farm wage rates. Issued monthly.

CPI detailed report (www.bls.gov/cpi/home.htm). Reports on consumer price movements of urban consumers and urban wage earners through statistical tables and technical notes. Released monthly.

Current industrial reports (www.census.gov). Presents tables and statistics based on a survey of manufacturers on the total production, value, ship-ment, and consumption of various products manufactured by industries in the United States. Released monthly.

Economic indicators (www.gpoaccess.gov/indicators/index.html). Includes economic information on prices, wages, production, business activity, purchasing power, credit, money, and federal finance. Issued monthly.

Federal Reserve data (www.federalreserve.gov/rnd.htm). Various economic data published by the Federal Reserve.

Natural Gas Monthly (www.eia.doe.gov). Provides state and national data on production, storage, imports, exports, and consumption of natural gas. Issued monthly.

Producer price indexes (www.bls.gov/ppi/home.htm). Comprehensive report on price movement at the primary market level, arranged by stage of processing and by commodity. Issued monthly.

Situation and outlook reports. Contain information on supply, demand, and price research published by the Economic Research Service of the Department of Agriculture. Issued quarterly.

Internet Resources

The following Internet sites offer economic and/or forecasting information:

www.sec.gov/edgarhp.htm. The Securities and Exchange Commission's EDGAR (Electronic Data Gathering, Analysis, and Retrieval) database. Offers information, including annual and financial reports, on U.S. publicly held companies.

www.access.gpo.gov. The Government Printing Office's home page. Offers information on economic indicators.

www.lib.lsu.edu/bus/economic.html. Internet Economic and Statistics Resources. Offers a weekly economic briefing and a summary of economic indicators in the United States and worldwide.

http://wpcarey.asu.edu/seid/. Arizona State University's L. William Seidman Research Institute. Offers lists of forecasting publications available for purchase, including an economic forecast of Mexico.

www.eia.doe.gov/oiaf/aeo/. The Annual Energy Outlook. Includes historical and projected information on the energy market.

www.cob.ohio-state.edu/edu/dept/fin/osudata.htm. Ohio State University's economics- and forecasting-related home page. Offers links to numerous forecasting- and economics-related sites, including Bloomberg's financial information; Hoover's Online, with information on public and privately held U.S. companies; Media Logic, with economic indicators; and Standard and Poor's online site.

Freelunch (www.economy.com/freelunch/). Free access to over 100,000 economic, financial, and demographic data series.

Institute for Supply Management™ (www.ism.ws). Source for *Report On Business*® and access to regional surveys.

CHAPTER 30

LOGISTICS OF SUPPLY MANAGEMENT

M. Theodore Farris II, Ph.D., CTL
Associate Professor of Logistics
Executive Director, TLEF Center for Logistics Education and Research
University of North Texas

WHAT IS LOGISTICS?

The Council of Supply Chain Management Professionals (CSCMP) (formerly the Council of Logistics Management) was originally founded as the National Council of Physical Distribution Management (NCPDM) in St. Louis, in January 1963. The NCPDM was formed by a visionary group of educators, consultants, and managers who envisioned the integration of transportation, warehousing, and inventory as the future of the discipline. At that time, physical distribution was just beginning to edge its way into the corporate lexicon and make its considerable presence felt in the business community. The professional organization evolved to focus on logistics, with a mission to "lead the evolving logistics profession by developing, advancing, and disseminating logistics knowledge."[1] More recently with the name change CSCMP will have a broader emphasis on the entire supply chain. The organization defines logistics management as

> that part of supply chain management that plans, implements, and controls the efficient, effective forward and reverse flow and storage of goods, services and related information between the point of origin and the point of consumption in order to meet customers' requirements.

Logistics management activities typically include inbound and outbound transportation management, fleet management, warehousing, materials handling, order fulfillment, logistics network design, inventory management, supply-and-demand planning, and management of third-party logistics services providers. To varying degrees, the logistics function also includes sourcing and procurement, production planning and scheduling, packaging and assembly, and customer service. It is involved in all levels of planning and execution—strategic, operational, and tactical. Logistics management is an integrating function, which coordinates and optimizes all logistics activities, as well as integrates logistics activities with other

---

1 http://cscmp.org/Website/AboutCSCMP/Definitions/Definitions.asp.

functions including marketing, sales manufacturing, finance, and information technology."[2] It is in this context that this chapter addresses the logistics of supply management.

In their article "Some Thoughts on Logistics Policy and Strategies,"[3] LaLonde and Mason offer eight key principles of logistics management that serve as an excellent guide toward the strategic and tactical management of logistics. They are as timely today as they were when they were first published, and this chapter utilizes these principles as the "blocking and tackling" basics for logistics management.

Principle One—Selective Risk

The principle of *selective risk* suggests utilizing a multiechelon approach to both inventory and customer management. Do not treat all parts or all customers the same. Shift from a policy of 100 percent service to a policy of selective risk where critical items or customers receive higher service levels, and less critical items or customers receive lower service levels.

The logistics manager should design logistics systems so that the system performance objectives are directly related to the importance of the product or customer in the firm. To accomplish this, consider using the management tool of Pareto analysis. As an Italian economist, Pareto Vilfredo published *Cours d'économie politique* in 1897, which investigated the distribution of wealth in Florence, Italy. What became known as *Pareto's law* suggested that 80 percent of the wealth was held by 20 percent of the population. Over the years, Pareto's law has proved remarkably resilient in empirical studies throughout a number of situations, including the distribution of the value of parts and the makeup of the typical customer base for a firm.

When applying Pareto's law in parts management, a typical means of classifying parts includes a combination of the value of the part and the annual usage. For example, the Tucson manufacturing site of International Business Machines (IBM) designated parts into the following categories:

Classification	Magnitude (Part Cost × Annual Usage)	% Total Part Numbers	% Total Value of Inventory Held
1 (High)	$40,000	2.6%	68.0%
2	$3,000–$39,999	8.8	23.6
3	$800–$2,999	10.1	5.2
4	$200–$799	14.6	2.1
5	$20–$199	28.1	0.9
6 (Low)	$0–$19.99	27.6	0.1
Other	No cost/no usage	8.0	0.2

2 http://cscmp.org/Website/AboutCSCMP/Definitions/Definitions.asp.

3 Bernard J. LaLonde and Raymond E. Mason (1985). "Some Thoughts on Logistics: Management Challenges for the 1980s," *International Journal of Physical Distribution & Materials Management*, vol. 15, no. 5. pp. 5–9.

Close management of the top two classifications of inventory captured 91.6 percent of the total value of inventory but focused on only 11.4 percent of the parts. Using Pareto analysis one can determine where to leverage management focus to gain the greatest return.

In their classic article "Staple Yourself to an Order" Shapiro, Rangan, and Sviokla cite four "lessons learned" in the management of customer orders.[4] One of these lessons is order selection and prioritization of orders based on the importance of the customer. A typical means of classifying customers emphasizes profitability in order to consider where best to earn the next additional dollar of revenue. By emphasizing service commitment to the top customers as identified by Pareto analysis, the logistics manager can focus effort and policies where the rewards are highest.

This concept may be applied throughout logistics operations to strategically focus on the areas of greatest return. Inbound and outbound transportation management should consider emphasis of closer working relationships with critical carriers to help drive cost out of the process. Warehousing and materials handling should focus on key parts by placing them closer to the shipping dock to reduce handling distance, cycle time, and cost. Order-fulfillment policies should recognize differences in customers and treat them accordingly. Inventory management policies should emphasize management of high-magnitude parts in supply-and-demand planning.

The principle of selective risk will enable the logistics manager to dedicate the proper amount of time and effort to each part or customer relative to the part's or customer's importance to the business process.

Principle Two—Information Selectivity

The principle of *information selectivity* suggests that information is as much of a resource to the decision maker as capital, human resources, and facilities. Information should be treated with the same operational, tactical, and strategic importance of any other resource of the firm. Historically the cost of computers and information has dramatically decreased over time. As a result, the manager is flooded with a multitude of data. It becomes imperative to design and implement logistics information systems that produce a focus on actionable and significant events.

In logistics and supply chain management a managerial tool that has recently been receiving notice is the concept of *real options*.[5] Real options correct the traditional financial concept of net present value which assumes the value of information is linear. The use of real options recognizes that more and better information is typically known nearer the decision and that each option holds value.

---

4 Benson P. Shapiro, V. Kasturi Rangan, and John J. Sviokla (1992). "Staple Yourself to an Order," *Harvard Business Review*, vol. 70, no. 4, July/August, pp. 113–125.

5 For further information regarding real options, consider Tom Copeland and Peter Tufano (2004). "A Real-World Way to Manage Options," *Harvard Business Review*, vol. 82, no. 3, pp. 90–99.

Real options analysis can more accurately value the opportunities under conditions of uncertainty where management can exercise discretion.

The implication to the manager is that logistics, and supply chain management, is a series of choices, or options. Each option holds value. Decisions regarding deferral of a decision, expansion or reduction of project scale, or the choice to abandon or switch all can be valued using real options. As a result the manager can value the flexibility of his or her decisions, increase visibility of risk, and subsequently mitigate exposure to risk.

The principle of information selectivity will enable the logistics manager to focus on actionable and significant events. Coupled with the concept of real options, the manager can reduce the risk associated with uncertainty.

Principle Three—Information Substitution

The principle of *information substitution* suggests that the primary target for the logistics manager should be the transformation of information for inventory. There are two different types of inventory. *Optimum inventory* is that inventory immediately required to support the needs of the business. Typically only cycle or working stock is classified as optimum. *Overage inventory* is inventory that is not immediately required to support the needs of the business. This includes anticipation or seasonal stock, transit stock, decoupling stock, and safety stock. Improved information may result in reductions of each type of overage inventory.

- *Anticipation or seasonal inventory* is inventory held in anticipation of customer demand or uncertain events. Improved demand information from customers which project future needs on a timely basis will result in lower anticipation stock. Anticipation inventory may be a strategic choice if the cost of a stock-out is too great. Another form of anticipation stock may occur if there is an upcoming price increase and the supply management professional determines the point at which it is less expensive to hold additional inventory than to pay higher prices.

- *Transit stock* represents inventory in transit moving from one location to another. Improvements in shipment tracking information have provided better visibility for customers and suppliers and have, at least in theory, reduced the amount of inventory in the supply chain.

- *Decoupling stock* represents the inventories that result from unequal lot sizes experienced throughout the process. The nature of many manufacturing processes results in unequal lot sizes throughout the process and in the accumulation of inventory. For example, the masking process of wafer fabrication in computer chip production results in hundreds of raw chips, while mounting each chip takes place one at a time. Instead of investing in hundreds of units of mounting equipment, the chip manufacturer will accept an accumulation of decoupling inventory just before the mounting operation as a part of the process. In this example it is less expensive to hold decoupling inventory than to invest in the capital equipment necessary to level out the production process. Design of just-in-time (JIT) production attempts to reduce the variation in the lot sizes which results in a reduction in the decoupling inventory in the process. In addition, it has been estimated that "most material in a manufacturing process spends 95 percent of its time waiting."[6] Much of this time is waiting for information to proceed to add value or authorize the next movement. Improvements in the flow and timing of information will result in decoupling inventory reduction. The decision to hold decoupling inventory or invest in additional capital equipment is one of the many economic trade-offs that must be considered by the logistics manager.

- *Safety stock* represents inventory that is held to protect against uncertainty in supply and demand. One part of the traditional formula used to calculate the level of safety stock for a given service level is based on the uncertainty of the supplier to provide the inventory when promised. The other part of the formula is based on the uncertainty of demand by the customer. For both parts, improved information may be used to reduce uncertainty and subsequently reduce the amount of safety stock inventory required to provide the same level of service. Some experts consider safety stock to be a strategic choice. Other experts view safety stock as an excess protecting against problems that should be resolved.

The principle of information substitution will enable the logistics manager to use improved information to reduce inventories and their associated costs.

Principle Four—Transaction Simplification

The principle of *transaction simplification* suggests the logistics manager should improve the efficiency and effectiveness of the transactional processes of the firm by upgrading systems to remove human intervention; linking collection transmission and storage of data of information sets within the system or between the system and the outside suppliers, customers, or third-party providers; and gaining efficiencies from cooperation among parties involved in the transaction.

Another lesson cited by Shapiro et al. is the need for the simplification of orders both vertically and horizontally.[7] They imply that the complexity of the order process results in uncertainty between levels of management (vertically) and between areas of activity (horizontally). Part of the simplification process involves improvement in communication between involved parties.

---

6 George, Michael L. (2003). *Lean Six Sigma: Combining Six Sigma Quality with Lean Production Speed*, New York: McGraw-Hill.

7 Shapiro et al. "Staple Yourself to an Order."

The rise of the Internet and advancing computer technology has improved the ability for companies to facilitate better communication. Inbound and outbound transportation management companies such as Qualcomm and @Track have enabled the ability to closely track shipments in transit and automatically communicate the status of the shipment to all parties involved. Federal Express and United Parcel Service (UPS) both offer electronic shipment tracking at a minimum of seven stages (or handshakes) within the shipping process. Warehousing and materials handling operations are developing radio frequency identification (RFID) at the part number level which further systematizes the order process (see chapter 21, "Technology in the Supply Chain" for more information). While development is in the early stages, leading users, including Wal-Mart and the Department of Defense, may serve to press the implementation forward.

Ryder Supply Chain Services and Cisco Systems have developed a supply system to support the fulfillment of spare and replacement parts to Cisco Systems' customer engineers who are charged with minimizing downtime of Cisco Systems' server customers. As a third-party logistics services provider, Ryder manages strategic pockets of Cisco Systems' inventory throughout the country ensuring support 24/7. Cisco Systems maintains continuous online visibility of the levels of inventory held at the Ryder locations. When a part is withdrawn from inventory and sent to fulfill a field request, there are 12 checkpoints where tracking is updated and the current location of the part is electronically updated for Cisco Systems, Ryder, and the customer engineer.

The principle of transaction simplification will enable the logistics manager to simplify and streamline transactions between trading partners through the use of technology.

Principle Five—Variance Reduction

The principle of *variance reduction* suggests that in any logistics system there are a series of linkages between demand and supply points. Failure to accurately anticipate demand leads to erosion of the system productivity as can be measured by excessive inventory, increased overtime, and increased stock-outs. A logistics manager can significantly influence the productivity of the system by reducing unplanned variance in the system.

Variation results in uncertainty. There are two principle types of uncertainty: that stemming from demand uncertainty and that stemming from supply uncertainty. To reduce uncertainty of demand, order fulfillment activities may use customer relationship management (CRM) software which may be configured to allow for customer tracking and to enhance customer service and help desk support, as well as inventory management. Companies such as Wal-Mart have taken the customer-supplier relationship a step further by using communication to facilitate supply. Wal-Mart provides point-of-sale information to Procter & Gamble each time a unit of Procter & Gamble product is sold at a specific store. Such information provides Procter & Gamble with immediate awareness of consumer demand and pushes the management of inventory down to the supplier's level. Procter & Gamble can plan manufacturing accordingly and benefits from precise demand information provided at the earliest possible moment.

To reduce uncertainty of supply, companies have turned to shipment tracking, electronic data interchange (EDI), and enterprise resources planning (ERP) utilizing technology to share production schedules with suppliers and improve communication quality and speed. Anyone familiar with the MIT Beer Game[8] knows that the lack of communication throughout the supply chain coupled with uncertainty of customers' needs results in a bullwhip effect. This effect was first pointed out by Lee et al. in 1997.[9] Conceptually, it suggests that great variations in inventory occur farther away from the end consumer, much like someone cracking a whip. Variation in the shape of a bullwhip is minimal close to the hands but increases farther down the end of the whip. This uncertainty in the supply chain may result in excessive and costly variations in inventory. Reduction of this uncertainty can result in significant cost savings.

Relative to inbound and outbound transportation management, studies have shown that shippers prefer reliability of delivery over speed of a shipment.[10] Uncertainty in a shipment delivery time means a firm must hold protective inventories just in case the shipment is late. The greater the variation in the reliability of the delivery time, the greater the amount of protective inventory. Average transit time is typically known ahead of time, and a firm can generally plan ahead. The management of carriers, both inbound and outbound, should include measurements of both reliability and average transit time.

Reducing the amount of unplanned variance will enable the logistics manager to reduce uncertainty throughout the logistics system and subsequently lower overall cost.

Principle Six—Inventory Velocity

The principle of *inventory velocity* suggests the entire process must be managed to facilitate the flow of inventory from raw material to the end user. A logistics manager must focus efforts on both the level of inventory and the velocity of inventory (turnover). Inventory turnover is a key performance indicator that reflects the efficiency and effectiveness of a process. Turnover is measured as the number of times inventory must be replaced during a period of time (usually a year).

$$\text{Inventory turnover} = \frac{\text{Cost of goods sold}}{\text{Average inventory}}$$

---

8 http://beergame.mit.edu/default.htm.

9 Hau L Lee, V. Padmanabhan, and Seungjin Whang (1997). "The Bullwhip Effect in Supply Chains," *Sloan Management Review*, vol. 38, no. 3, Spring, pp. 93–103.

10 Michael A. McGinnis (1979). "Shipper Attitudes toward Freight Transportation Choice: A Factor Analytic Study," *International Journal of Physical Distribution & Materials Management*, vol. 10, no. 1, pp. 25–33.

The logistics manager can manage the metric by manipulating inventory so that the firm uses proportionally less inventory for each unit of sales. While this is easier said than done, this may typically be accomplished by using a multiechelon approach to parts and customers. Three variables affect the value of the inventory held:

1. *Cost per unit.* If the cost per unit of inventory changes, the value of the inventory will directly change as well. It is possible to change the method of costing inventory,[11] but the frequency of changing the method of costing is limited due to tax laws. The alternative is to reduce the total cost paid per unit, which is a typical performance measurement placed on the purchasing professional.

2. *Schedule of production supporting demand.* A change in the production schedule will directly influence inventory levels. An increase in the production schedule will bring additional inventory assets into the firm. Unfortunately most firms discover that a reduction in the production schedule does not result in a corresponding decrease in inventory because the change in the schedule typically occurs after the inventory is resident in the firm. Process initiatives such as JIT emphasize producing exactly what is required using cycle stock and only holding strategic overage inventory when it is profitable to do so. A level, or consistent, schedule is much preferred over one that has frequent changes and will result in a higher inventory turnover.

3. *Time to produce.* Much of a firm's inventory is tied up in the production process. Speeding up the time to produce a unit will reduce the amount of time the raw materials, components, and possibly finished goods are resident as inventory. Cycle time reduction (CTR), JIT, and quick response (QR) philosophies incorporated through the process emphasize keeping the product in motion and reducing wait times throughout the process. Increasing the velocity of the inventory will reduce the amount of inventory and will result in a higher inventory turnover.

Inventory turnover is not a particularly new concept to many managers, but measuring it both throughout the entire firm and on a part number basis is. Aggregate inventory turnover can mask dramatic differences in turnover levels for various parts. Increasing inventory turnover will result in lower carrying costs, reduced waste, and greater utilization of assets.

Another metric that is receiving increased notice is the concept of cash-to-cash. Cash-to-cash is very easy to calculate and is defined as "the time from when you pay your supplier to the time that your customer pays you."[12] There are three variables associated with cash-to-cash:

---

11 These methods are first-in first-out (FIFO), last-in first-out (LIFO), and first-in last-out (FILO).

12 M. Theodore Farris II and Paul Hutchison (2002). "Cash-to-Cash: The New Supply Chain Management Metric," *International Journal of Physical Distribution and Logistics Management*, vol. 32, no. 4, pp. 288–298.

1. Days of accounts payable

2. Days of supply (inventory)

3. Days of accounts receivable

Cash-to-cash is calculated as follows:

$$\text{Cash-to-cash} = \text{Days of accounts receivable} +$$
$$\text{Days of supply (inventory)} - \text{Days of accounts payable}$$

Some companies, such as Dell Computer, utilize the metric in their annual report as a means of measuring improvement. Through the ever-evolving Dell model, Dell Computer has improved its cash-to-cash from minus 4 days to better than minus 30 days. This means that Dell Computer receives payment from its customer more than 30 days before it pays its suppliers.[13] Velocity may be measured using cash-to-cash and may be readily compared against competitors.[14] In addition, cash-to-cash performance has been directly tied to improved profitability.[15] The logistics manager utilizing cash-to-cash as a metric must take care to understand the impact of changing firm variables on trading partners on both ends of the supply chain. Proper analysis may determine that the firm wishes to hold additional inventory if it can hold it at a lower total cost than a customer. As a result, the inventory holding savings achieved by the customer may be shared between companies and drive additional cost out of the supply chain.

Mapping of a process is not new, but as companies further develop their involvement in supply chain management, mapping of the entire process including all the logistics activities helps offer insight into previously hidden opportunities. The benefit of supply chain management results from the fact that when two processes connect there is typically an opportunity for improvement where both organizations protect their process from the uncertainty stemming from the other. As the entire process is managed, the logistics manager should consider mapping the entire process to identify these opportunities. Most times these opportunities for improvement are found in stockpiles of inventory. Mapping may initially start using a macro map as shown in Figure 30–1 for the Food Service and Drinking Places and then expanded in detail as required. Through understanding of the process by mapping, the logistics manager may find cost and time saving opportunities by shifting the ownership of processes or reducing "protection" built into the process by the owner.

Managing inventory velocity will enable the logistics manager to manage and improve the flow of inventory from raw material to end user. As a result, pockets of inventory may be eliminated and asset turnover will improve.

---

13 Paul Hutchison and M. Theodore Farris II (2004). "Managing Cash-to-Cash to Increase Firm Value," *Today's CPA*, March/April, pp. 18–29.

14 M. Theodore Farris II and Paul Hutchison (2003). "Measuring Cash-to-Cash Performance," *International Journal of Logistics Management*, vol. 14, no. 2, pp. 83–92.

15 Sonen Luc (1993). "Cash Conversion Cycle, and Corporate Profitability," *Journal of Cash Management*, vol. 13, no. 4, July/August. pp. 53–58.

FIGURE 30–1

722 Food Service and Drinking Places Industry Supply Chain Macro Map

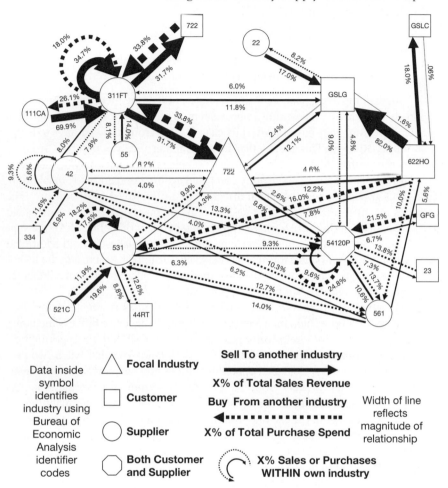

Original map created by Michael Gallia for LSCM4860 Advanced Logistics Problems course project at the University of North Texas.

Principle Seven—Postponement

The principle of *postponement* suggests it is possible to reduce the amount of inventory necessary to meet target customer service levels through optimizing the primary cost trade-off between a reduction in inventory investment against the cost of transportation, information systems, or additional production or processing systems. There are two basic forms of postponement:

- *Geographic postponement* occurs when the product is not committed to a specific geographic location but is stored in a central location.

Consider the cost of additional transportation compared to the reduction in inventory that may occur by holding inventory in a centralized location. One entrepreneur in West Texas recognized this opportunity in supplying pipeline valves to the oil fields. One particular valve cost $10,000 but was rarely needed. The cost of not having the valve available when it was needed was cost prohibitive, so all field locations held the valve in inventory. This was the case with many valves used in the oil fields. The entrepreneur purchased these valves for pennies on the dollar and set up a centralized warehouse location in the oil fields to supply the valves quickly, as needed, using premium transportation. By consolidating demand of many locations into a central warehouse and coupling it with the ability to deliver as needed, the entrepreneur was able to draw cost out of the process for the oil field companies and still earn a profit.

- *Value-add postponement* occurs when there is a delay in the personalization of the product in the manufacturing process. The longer the personalization can be delayed, the less time inventory will need to be held. Personalizing early requires the firm to commit inventory and resources to a dedicated unit. Any change in the order will directly affect the dedicated unit. The ability to manufacture a generic unit until last-minute personalization allows the firm to operate with more flexibility and less inventory. For example, consider the local paint store. Customers are offered a multitude of colors but sitting on the shelf is a generic, unpersonalized base paint. Personalization comes from the on-the-spot mixing of pigments with the base paint. Imagine how much inventory the paint store would have to hold if it had to hold millions of color choices. Delaying personalization allows the paint stores to provide better customer service at a lower cost.

The principles of geographic postponement and value-add postponement will enable the logistics manager to dedicate the proper amount of time and effort to each part or customer relative to each part's or customer's importance to the business process.

Principle Eight—Shared and/or Shifted Risk

The principle of *shared and/or shifted risk* suggests shifting the logistics cost structure from a fixed cost base to a variable cost base. By shifting costs to a supplier upstream in the channel or downstream to a customer, the logistics manager can shift fixed investment cost and risk outside the firm. Shifting risk may involve modifying the distribution channel, utilizing outsourcing, or shifting responsibility for activities or management of assets.

Each company has a core competency. That is, that thing that they do best. Shifting or sharing risk suggests utilizing the core competencies of other companies so your company can focus on what it does best. This synergistic effort will yield the greatest gains.

It is possible to shift responsibility to hold inventory to a supplier upstream in the channel. This is a common technique used in JIT. The Dell Computer manufacturing process is designed where Dell Computer does not own its cycle stock until it needs it. Dell Computer will receive an order and send a manufacturing bill of materials to the assembly area. Adjoining the assembly area are open truck trailers containing parts owned by Dell suppliers. When the assembly technician removes the required parts out of a trailer, the supplier is electronically notified that a part has been removed and Dell "officially" purchases the part. When the inventory in the trailer drops to a predetermined level, the supplier sends another trailer of parts. Instead of anticipating customer requirements, placing anticipatory orders on the suppliers, and holding inventories, Dell Computer has pushed the risk back to the suppliers.

Other firms have pushed the ordering process and associated costs down the channel to the customer. Service Merchandise offered showrooms of products where customers placed their order at a computer terminal inside the store. With the rise of e-tailing, many firms have placed their product catalogs online allowing customers to electronically place their orders, and order fulfillment takes place outside of the traditional bricks-and-mortar store.

Opportunities to outsource logistics functions ranges from third-party warehouse management and transportation services to providing customer service functional support in India. In most cases the variables in the business decision to outsource continue to follow the traditional make versus buy decision.

For example, a firm may consider whether it is best to open a private warehouse or utilize a public warehouse company. A private warehouse offers more control but requires a higher up-front cost. The purchase of a warehouse becomes an asset on the company balance sheet but represents another activity that the company must manage. Selecting to use a public warehouse will offer the company more flexibility in the amount of committed warehouse space and time spent in a location. Typically the use of public warehouses makes the most sense when a company is entering into a new marketplace, launching a new product, lacks available capital, sells a seasonal product, or is uncertain regarding warehousing needs. A private warehouse makes more sense when the storage needs are constant and capital is available to invest into facilities.

The Container Store had experienced aggressive growth over recent years. It had outgrown its present warehousing space but was faced with a variety of growth scenarios. The Container Store needed to have a warehouse plan that matched its growing needs. Instead of using a public warehousing strategy, the Container Store applied the concept of *real options* to commit to a new private warehouse and purchased two options to utilize adjoining space in future years. Doing so allowed the Container Store to have warehousing space as it was required without a high up-front investment.

When sharing or shifting risk, the logistics manager must consider the effect throughout the supply chain and keep in mind the concept of minimizing the total cost of the process. Sharing and shifting risk may be applied throughout the logistics process. Most will occur as a hybrid between private and public services. For example, inbound and outbound transportation management may consider use of a full-service carrier in place of a private fleet, warehousing and materials handling may utilize a third-party provider, or a company may choose to offer both electronic order fulfillment and traditional bricks-and-mortar outlets. In addition to the third-party provider concept, the logistics manager may also consider utilizing a fourth-party provider. A fourth-party provider is similar to the outsourcing concept of a third-party provider except that it offers services for managing information.

The principle of shared and/or shifted risk will enable the logistics manager to shift the logistics cost structure from a fixed cost base to a variable cost base so the company can focus on core competencies.

SUPPLY CHAIN SECURITY

With the tragic events of September 11, 2001, came another variable adding to the complexity of supply chain management. Security of the supply chain impacts both international and domestic supply. While international trade dropped after these tragic events in 2001, there were still over 2,461 million tons imported using ocean freight and over 14 million tons imported using air freight.[16] The Transportation Security Administration (TSA) reports that in 2003 less than 5 percent of international air cargo was physically screened; between 10 to 12 percent of ocean containers entering the Port of Houston were screened by the U.S. Coast Guard in 2003.[17] In 2000 there was an average of 31,709 NAFTA border truck crossings per day with inbound clearances taking significantly longer than outbound clearances, and longer average delays on the southern border than on the northern border.[18] The California Transportation Institute estimates the average queue to enter the United States with motor freight through the border town of Laredo to average in excess of five days.[19]

Faced with the possibility of an increasing focus on security, the supply management professional should understand the ramifications:

- International shipments will require longer transit time.

- There likely will be increased scrutiny on shipping document accuracy.

- Transaction costs will increase to compensate for the additional security expenses.

---

16 Measured in tonnage, comparing 2001 against 2000, international ocean imports dropped 6.9 percent and international air imports dropped 8.3 percent. *U.S. Department of Transportation, Bureau of Transportation Statistics (2002)*, National Transportation Statistics 2002, BTS02-08 Washington, DC: U.S. Government Printing Office, December.

17 *Dallas Morning News*, September 9, 2004.

18 *Commercial Vehicle Travel Time and Delay at U.S. Border Crossings*, Federal Highway Administration, June 2002.

19 www.cati.csufresno.edu/cab/rese/96/960301/mex2.html.

- Ongoing relationships between customers and suppliers will help facilitate the smooth flow of goods. Therefore the cost of switching to a different supplier will increase and companies will emphasize maintenance of current international relationships over switching.

CONCLUSION

Each year it seems another set of buzzwords has been developed and is being promoted as the latest solution. The eight principles of logistics should serve as a foundation to the logistics manager to be implemented in a synergistic fashion throughout the logistics process and the entire supply chain.

CHAPTER 31

LEGAL ASPECTS OF PURCHASING AND SUPPLY

Updated for Seventh Edition by
HELEN M. POHLIG, JD

Sixth Edition Authors
CONSTANCE CUSHMAN, JD

MARTIN J. CARRARA, JD, C.P.M.

LAW AND THE SUPPLY MANAGEMENT PROFESSIONAL

Legal principles, rules, and requirements permeate the daily activities of supply management professionals. They establish the supply manager's power to act and to contract on behalf of the organization. They form the framework for every transaction with every supplier, determining whether an agreement is enforceable in court and what remedies are available if it is breached. In many ways they govern even routine administrative actions of supply managers, their suppliers, and their internal customers. Every supply management professional needs a command of basic legal concepts and a knowledge of relevant statutes.

Sources of Law: Common Law and Statutory Law

The basic legal concepts for commercial transactions in this country come from *agency law* and *contract law*. Both agency law and contract law originated in the old English *common law*, which is a body of legal principles based on historical customs, reason, and justice that developed over time as courts made decisions on a case-by-case basis. The common law in this country continues to evolve through the ongoing development of case law. In deciding cases, judges look to prior judicial decisions for established precedents and make adaptations only to account for changing conditions and societal needs. The common law is followed throughout the United States, except in Louisiana.

Over the years, many jurisdictions have codified certain legal principles in statutes. Statutory law consists of written rules of law enacted by legislatures at the federal, state, or local level, which may either formalize or override the rules of common law or address issues never dealt with under the common law. Going beyond common law, lawmakers have developed many regulatory systems to achieve a variety of purposes, from protecting competition to safeguarding workers and preserving the environment. While judges cannot change statutory laws, they do interpret these laws when their application to the facts of a particular case is unclear.

The U.S. Constitution prescribes the areas of law that are within the jurisdiction of the federal government, leaving the balance of law within the purview of the individual states. Much of commercial law, including contract law, is left to the states; however, because the Constitution gives the federal government authority over interstate commerce and to ensure equal protection of the laws for all Americans, a myriad of federal statutes (including antitrust, health and safety, labor, and environmental laws) impose on business requirements and constraints with which the supply management professional must be familiar.

In addition, the realities of global commerce bring to bear not just our own country's laws, but those of other countries and of international bodies. Treaties between sovereign states bind their participants to apply agreed-upon rules to commercial transactions across national boundaries.

All of these—common law, case law, statutes at all levels of government, court interpretations of statutes, and international treaties—weave together to create a legal system that makes contracts enforceable or not, sets out the mechanisms for enforcement, and dictates what supply managers can and must do as they contract with suppliers.

AGENCY LAW

In business, typically individuals act on behalf of the organizations for which they work, and their actions are governed by the principles of agency law. Agency law establishes the power and authority whereby supply management professionals act on behalf of their employers. It also establishes some of the duties and ethical responsibilities of the supply manager, so in many ways, agency law is the bedrock of supply management professionalism.

Agency Law and the Authority of the Agent

The *law of agency* simply says that when one person acts as an *authorized* agent of another, the acts of the agent become those of the person (or entity) for whom the agent is acting—usually called the *principal*. All corporations, being invisible, intangible, and existing only in contemplation of the law, must act through agents. Therefore most supply managers and salespeople are agents of their organizations. If agents act in the manner in which they have been authorized to act, the organization is bound by their commitments. If agents act beyond the scope of their authority, the organization may not be bound, and the agent may be personally liable for any commitments made.

Problems usually arise with the definition of *authorized*. There are three types of authority, each having its own legal effect.

The first is known as *actual authority*. What the organization says the employee may do, either in express oral statements or in writing is known as *express actual authority*. Some call this "job description" authority because it is often part of the job description, the statement of what the individual has been hired to do for the organization. Purchasers have express purchasing authority, salespeople have sales and marketing authority, and engineers have design and engineering authority. When employees take action or make statements that lie outside their express authority, they may or may not bind the organization.

Then there is *implied actual authority*, which is authority implied by the law to make it possible for agents to carry out their express actual authority. For example, if an organization expressly authorizes an individual to enter into contracts with suppliers on its behalf, necessarily the individual may seek quotes, enter into discussions, and reach agreement on terms and conditions. Otherwise it would not be possible to enter into contracts. All agents in the organization have both express and implied actual authority although the exact nature of that authority varies from agent to agent.

Finally the law also recognizes the concept of *apparent authority*, which is the authority that arises in law because of the way the principal acts toward third parties. Even if an employee does something outside of his or her authority, the employer or principal may honor the transaction, thus making it appear that the employee has authority. A pattern of honoring unauthorized actions creates apparent authority because it gives outsiders a valid expectation that such conduct is allowed. If written organization policy gives only the supply management department express authority to enter into contracts with suppliers, but the accounts payable department routinely pays invoices for supplies or services ordered by personnel outside of supply management, it has effectively given these nonsupply management personnel apparent authority to make these purchases. This is the practice commonly known as *back-door procurement.*

In an organization where the procurement function is highly centralized, lines of actual agency authority are usually well defined in written policies and are fairly well adhered to. In a decentralized setting, written policies are often less complete or current, and employees and suppliers often rely to a greater extent on apparent authority. Reengineering the procurement function, or introducing new technologies such as procurement cards or electronic contracting, often causes organizations to reexamine and redefine their contracting lines of authority, including rewriting of policies and procedures. When they do so, they are invoking the principles of agency law.

In summary, supply professionals must be concerned with two aspects of agency authority:

1. How can an organization's procurement activities be run to ensure that contracts are made only by individuals with express contracting authority, and so avoid or at least reduce backdoor procurement? Up-to-date written policies spelling out which job titles carry contracting authority are best, because they establish actual authority. In addition

to formal policies, there must be a program of internal education and communication so that all organization employees know, and are periodically reminded about, what they can and cannot commit to. As a second line of defense, programs aimed at informing suppliers exactly who within an organization has procurement authority (with whom the suppliers can deal) are also useful.

2. When negotiating with suppliers, how can an organization make sure the resulting agreements will be enforceable? The best way to ensure enforceability is to be alert to situations where salespeople may be exceeding their authority. Be aware that salespeople in general have less authority than purchasers. If there is any question, clarification should be sought from someone high up in the supply organization. It may be advisable to have the contract signed by the supplier's vice president of sales.

Agency Law, the Duties of the Agent, and Purchasing Ethics

With the powers or authority a principal confers on an agent go duties and responsibilities. Because principals place their trust in agents to act in their place, all agents have a fiduciary duty to act solely in the best interest of their principals. The agent must "stand in the shoes of" the principal, acting on behalf of the principal, with only the principal's interests in mind. Personal or private interests of the agent must not influence the decision at all. And it is not just the principal's financial interests that the agent must serve. The agent must at all times act within the law and in good faith toward third parties when acting on behalf of the principal. The agent must do nothing that would cause the principal to be exposed to accusations of unfairness, sharp practice, or wrongdoing—certainly not criminal wrongdoing. These fiduciary obligations exist whether the agency relationship is one of express or apparent authority. They are the essence of purchasing ethics standards—and the standard of behavior is a very high one.

Because ethical requirements are often closely related to agency law, agency law provides solutions for some ethical dilemmas. When a possible problem of conflict of interest arises, such as a circumstance that might make a purchaser seem to be less than completely independent of a supplier (for example, a purchaser is related to one of the organization's suppliers), the ethical problems can often be cured by disclosure of the details to the organization, accompanied by the organization's consent to the arrangement. By consenting to the arrangement, the principal expressly authorizes the agent to continue to represent the principal in the matter. The principal has declared a belief that its best interests are served by continuing the arrangement and has expressly authorized the conduct.

Over the years, and generally in response to situations where people seriously violated their fiduciary and ethical responsibilities, legislatures have passed laws creating criminal and civil sanctions for certain unethical behavior. Similarly, because individuals often need more explicit guidance concerning their fiduciary and legal obligations, over the years organizations and professional associations have tried to spell out these requirements—and they often incorporate the legal standards into their formal ethics policies. As a result, corporate ethics policies, the *ISM Principles and Standards of Ethical Supply Management Conduct*, and state and local laws overlap with each other in many respects. Sometimes the differences can be confusing.

For example, the laws on bribery essentially provide that if a purchaser takes *anything* of value that might sway the buying decision, however trivial it might be, it is a bribe. In order for the government to prosecute it as a crime, however, there must be some criminal intent. By contrast, most organizations' ethics policies assume that a payment of anything substantial to the purchaser will affect the buying decision and would be unethical, whether or not there is any bad intent, but they allow minor or trivial gifts or favors. The mid-1980s saw increased concern with bribery and ethics in the government contractor area. Therefore the rules are more stringent and the enforcement more rigorous if a purchaser is buying items for use in connection with a government contract.

Similarly, the antitrust laws regulate the actions of both individuals and organizations to preserve fair competition. Buying on the basis of reciprocity is often against organization policy, and it could also be illegal under the antitrust laws if such a practice results in the lessening of competition or in the restraint of trade. Favoring one supplier over another for reasons other than price, quality, and service may be unethical and can create serious legal concerns if there is a government contract in the picture. Agreeing with other purchasers not to do business with a certain supplier can be unethical and may be a boycott and considered a restraint of trade under the antitrust laws.

What all this comes down to is still the same basic standard: agents must act solely in the interest of their principals and of no other person, including themselves; and agents must do nothing that would cause the principal to violate the law or act unfairly toward its trading partners. Good common sense, alertness to situations that can look bad, and full disclosure and discussion with management and legal counsel about questionable situations are very good ways to remain inside both legal and ethical boundaries.

CONTRACT LAW

Most of the day-to-day activities of supply management professionals involve the law of contracts. Every purchase, whether for goods or services, is a contract between the purchasing organization and the supplier, governed by the principles of contract law. Like agency law, contract law originated in the common law of England and is part of the law that is left to the states, not the federal government, to address. Generally speaking, the law of the state where the contract is formed and performed will apply to that contract, but the growth of interstate and global commerce has meant that the law of contracts has been shaped to a very large degree by a process of developing uniform statutes that are designed to codify certain legal principles in a consistent manner from state to state within the United States and even across national boundaries. The most notable example is the Uniform Commercial Code (UCC). It is the product of extensive work, over several decades, by the National Conference of Commissioners on Uniform State Laws (NCCUSL) working together with the American Law Institute (ALI). By the late 1950s a version had been developed that eventually saw widespread adoption by the states.

Article 2 of the UCC applies to the sale of goods, which until fairly recent times was the dominant context of interstate trade. In making decisions in cases involving the sale of goods, courts look first to the written rules of the UCC as adopted in the state whose law applies to that contract, and then to case law when the UCC rules require interpretation or do not answer the specific question at hand. The UCC does not apply to contracts for services, which until recently tended to be much more local in nature. To resolve disputes in the service area, courts look to case law, although they may apply UCC rules by analogy to contracts for services. Where a contract is for a sale of both goods and services, courts may make a determination as to which—the goods or the services—predominates. If the contract is predominantly for the sale of goods, then the UCC will be applied. The common law will be applied where services comprise the predominant part of the contract. Application of one body of law or another may appear confusing, and it can be, but the essential concepts of law are fairly consistent for goods and services.

Although the UCC is a set of rules governing commercial transactions, it is merely a model recommended by the NCCUSL and must be adopted by individual state legislatures before it has the effect of law. Each state chooses whether to make changes to the model text before enacting the statute that governs transactions in its jurisdiction. As a result there may be variations in the statutory provisions as well as the judicial interpretations of the UCC from state to state. (In a dispute between contracting parties from different states, in the absence of an express provision providing which state's laws shall govern, the court hearing the dispute will make that determination based upon its own conflicts of laws rules.)

The UCC is under constant review in an effort to keep it current with changing commercial realities. Much of what organizations contract for these days does not fall neatly into the old categories of "goods" and "services." Software license agreements are a good example—the owner sells not the product but only the right to use the software in restricted ways. Also, systems development contracts mingle hardware, software, services, and expertise. In the past decade, the explosion of information technology and electronic commerce generated a great many commercial transactions for which the old rules were out of date—they just didn't fit. The NCCUSL and the ALI collaborated for years to revise UCC Article 2 and draft new laws to govern information technology and electronic commerce transactions. The result of their efforts—proposed amendments to UCC Article 2 as well as two new uniform laws—may help to alleviate some of the problems of outdated legal rules.

Proposed Revisions to UCC Article 2

From the late 1980s until 2002 committees within the NCCUSL worked on drafting revisions to UCC Article 2 in an attempt to make it more responsive to current business practices. The original idea to completely overhaul the law was dropped in the mid-1990s in favor of discrete amendments to the existing law. The NCCUSL and the ALI finally approved those amendments in 2002 and 2003. While the revisions are now available for adoption by state legislatures, no rush to adopt the changes has been evidenced. Some of the amendments address issues related to electronic commerce. For example, the term *writing* is replaced throughout the law with the term *record*, which is defined as "information that is inscribed on a tangible medium or that is stored in an electronic or other medium and is retrievable in perceivable form." There are also new definitions for the terms *electronic*, *electronic agent*, and *electronic record*. Other proposed changes will be discussed throughout the remainder of this chapter.

Uniform Computer Information Transactions Act

As part of the revisions to Article 2, the drafters originally intended to create a new section of the UCC—Proposed UCC Article 2B—to address issues related to software licensing. Because of controversy concerning some of its provisions, the proposed law was instead promulgated by the NCCUSL in 1999 as a stand-alone act known as the Uniform Computer Information Transactions Act (UCITA). It is not part of the UCC and to date has only been adopted by two state legislatures—those of Virginia and Maryland. State lawmakers in at least four other states—Iowa, North Carolina, Vermont, and West Virginia—have demonstrated their dissatisfaction with the law by passing legislation that specifically prohibits application of UCITA to software contracts in those states. Additional information about this law and its current status in the states is available online at Web sites listed in the Appendix at the end of this chapter.

Uniform Electronic Transactions Act and E-Sign Legislation

To address the issues of electronic commerce more directly the NCCUSL, also in 1999, adopted another stand-alone law known as the Uniform Electronic Transactions Act (UETA). Unlike UCITA, the UETA was quite popular among state legislatures and was quickly enacted as law in the vast majority of states. It addresses a variety of issues related to electronic commerce. The UETA does not modify substantive contract law. Rather it functions as a bridge between the existing legal concepts of the common law and/or the UCC and the way business is actually being done in the electronic environment. In effect the UETA makes electronic records the equivalent of written documents and makes electronic signatures the equivalent of handwritten signatures for legal purposes. An electronic signature is defined in the law as "an electronic sound, symbol or process that is attached to or logically associated with a record and that is executed or adopted by an individual with the intent to sign the record." More information about UETA, including a listing of states that have enacted it is available online at Web sites listed in the Appendix at the end of this chapter.

In 2000 the U.S. Congress also got into the act with its enactment of the Electronic Signatures in Global and National Commerce Act, better known simply as E-Sign legislation. This law, effective October 1, 2000, is far less comprehensive than the UETA and simply legitimizes electronic signatures for contracts. The federal law applies to interstate or foreign commerce but may be preempted by a state's adoption of the UETA.

International Contract Law

In the context of international contracts, the laws of the different countries whose businesses are trading with each other come into play. Each country has its own contract laws, but to foster predictable and reliable business dealings a great many countries have joined together by treaty to create a common body of contract principles, the United Nations Convention on Contracts for the International Sale of Goods (CISG), to govern international transactions. Just as states do with the Uniform Commercial Code in the United States, countries must voluntarily decide to be bound by the CISG, and like the UCC the CISG governs only goods transactions. It applies to international sales contracts between parties in countries that are signatories (the United States is a signatory), unless the contracting parties specifically opt out. This means that if an organization based in the United States enters into a contract with an organization located in another country that is also a signatory to the CISG, the CISG applies to their contract unless the written agreement expressly states that the CISG does not apply. A provision saying, for example, that the laws of New York govern a particular international contract between two parties whose countries have signed the CISG will have the effect of making the CISG apply, since the treaty provisions signed by the United States are the controlling law in every state. While the CISG was modeled on and largely resembles the UCC, significant provisions vary. For this reason, it is important to be sure what law applies, and what it says, when contracting with businesses in other countries. Many organizations that regularly engage in international goods transactions routinely opt out of the CISG.

There are other laws and treaties that have a bearing on international contracts. These include the various international trade agreements; the import and export laws (including quotas and customs duties) of the different countries; the banking, currency exchange, and credit laws; tax laws; and commercial bribery laws. A discussion of these provisions is beyond the scope of this chapter. Many excellent references exist, some of which are listed in the Appendix at the end of this chapter.

CONTRACTING WITH SUPPLIERS

The sections that follow discuss general principles of contract law, many of which are the same whether the UCC applies or not. Specific references to the UCC are made where the UCC provides clarification of or actual changes in common law principles of contracting. Remember that the specific details of the law may vary depending on if and how the UCC has been modified when enacted by the legislature in a particular state.

Definition of Contract

People use a variety of terms when referring to the relationship that exists between a purchasing organization and a supplier—an agreement, a contract, a purchase order, an understanding, a letter of intent, etc. The relationship may or may not be documented in writing. In many organizations there is a distinction drawn within supply management between *purchasing*, which typically involves the acquisition of goods, and *contracting*, which involves the acquisition of services. From a legal perspective, however, it is all contracting. What one calls the relationship or the document in which it is memorialized does not determine whether it constitutes a contract in the legal sense of that term. What matters is whether the actions of the parties create a contract. In effect a contract is a promise or a set of promises that creates legal obligations. The UCC defines the term *contract* as "the total legal obligation which results from the parties' agreement as affected by this Act and any other applicable rules of law." A contract may be defined as an agreement that courts will enforce. So what makes an agreement legally enforceable; that is, what makes an agreement a contract?

Essentials of a Valid Contract

Four essentials must be present to create a valid and enforceable contract:

1. *Agreement.* In order to enter into an agreement, the parties must "mutually assent" to the same terms. This concept is often referred to as reaching a "meeting of the minds." Mutual assent is typically manifested through the process of *offer* and *acceptance*, in which one of the parties makes an offer to enter into a contract and the other party accepts that offer, thereby creating a contract (if the other essential elements of a valid contract are present). Offer and acceptance are discussed in greater detail later.

2. *Competent parties.* In order for a contract to be enforceable it must have been made between parties with both the legal capacity and the authority to form a valid contract. Incompetency (i.e., lack of such legal capacity) arises where, at the time of entering into the contract, one of the parties

(1) is a minor, (2) suffers from some mental infirmity, or (3) is under the influence of drugs or alcohol. In most states majority (i.e., when one is no longer a minor) is reached at age 18; the exceptions are Alabama (19 years), Mississippi (21 years), and Nebraska (19 years). Most contracts involving incompetents are *voidable* at the incompetent's option, which means that the incompetent party has the choice of either enforcing the contract or acting as if no contract had ever been made. Both parties to a contract must also have the necessary authority to contract (refer to the previous discussion of agency law). All competent individuals have the authority to contract for themselves. A corporation, however, must be represented by an agent who contracts for it. Supply management professionals are agents of their organizations and customarily possess the authority to contract for the organization, although such authority may be—and typically is—restricted by the principal.

3. *Legal subject matter.* The subject matter of a contract must be lawful for the contract to be enforceable in a court of law. The subject matter cannot be immoral, against public policy, or outright illegal. Contracts that are illegal are void, which means that the contract is considered never to have existed at all. For example, commodities that require a license to procure, hold, or use or services that require the service provider to be licensed to perform such services cannot be the subject of an enforceable contract unless the parties have the requisite licenses.

4. *Mutual consideration.* To be enforceable, a contract must be supported by mutual consideration passing between the parties. The existence of consideration is generally what distinguishes promises that will be enforced from those that will not. *Consideration* is defined as something of value for which the parties bargain. It is a performance or a return promise, and it may be in the form of a gain or a detriment. It may be a promise to do something that one is not obligated to do (such as a promise to purchase goods or services from a certain supplier), or it may be a promise not to do something that one has a legal right to do (such as an agreement not to compete). A promise to buy goods or services and a promise to sell goods or provide services are sufficient consideration to support each other. The common law was very strict in insisting that consideration be passed between the parties if there was to be an enforceable contract. Modern contract law and the UCC have relaxed these rules to some extent. Although courts will not enforce a contract that does not provide for mutual consideration, courts do not measure the equality or relative value of each party's consideration. That is left for the contracting parties to evaluate in their negotiations when forming the contract. Past consideration, which is a promise made by one party *after* the other party has already performed, may not be used to enforce a contract because it is not bargained for and does not induce the other party's act or promise. For example, a contractor's promise not

to disclose confidential information that is made after the information has been provided to the contractor will probably not be enforceable because the owner of the information has already performed by providing it to the contractor.

If a valid contract exists, the court will next examine what the terms and conditions are in that contract, and the facts concerning what each party has done, to determine whether and how to enforce the contract.

Creating the Agreement: Contract Formation Process

There is a required choreography, a certain set of steps and exchanges, that must take place in order to bring a contract into existence in the eyes of the law. Sometimes they take place in one conversation or exchange of documents. In other cases they take place over a long period of extended negotiations and then are reflected in a master document that both parties sign to indicate that they are "in agreement." Either way, every contract will reflect the presence of these steps. Understanding them equips the supply management professional to perform them smoothly and to exercise his or her rights in an effective and timely manner.

Offer

The first step to be taken in the formation of a contract is for one of the parties to make an offer. An *offer* is a promise by the maker, communicated to the other party, promising to enter into a contract under certain conditions if the other party accepts the offer. The party making the offer is called the *offeror*, and the person to whom the offer is directed is known as the *offeree*. Since an offer invites acceptance by the offeree, it gives the offeree the power to form a contract.

To be valid, an offer must be made with the intention of the offeror being ready and willing to enter into a contract with the other party. This intention of the offeror is determined under an objective standard, which means that a determination is made whether a "reasonable person" in the position of the offeree would have believed that the offeror intended to enter into a contract when the offer was made. Thus, an offeror cannot avoid the contract by claiming that the offer was made in jest. Offers generally must be made to a specific party and must identify the contracting parties and the subject matter of the contract. If a purported offer is anything less than a complete indication of a willingness to enter into a contract with the offeree, it is only an "invitation to do business." Invitations to do business do not have the legal effect of an offer and cannot ripen into a contract—they do not invite acceptance. Thus, advertisements, catalogs, and price sheets issued by a supplier are generally not considered offers to sell, but merely invitations to prospective purchasers to make an offer to buy. Similarly, a request for quotation or request for proposal issued by a supply management organization is not an offer to buy, but merely an invitation to prospective suppliers to make an offer to provide some goods or service.

A purchasing entity may be either an offeror or an offeree. An offer to buy might be expressed by saying or writing "I will buy 12 gross of your #2 pencils at $14 per gross" to a pencil manufacturer. That would make the pencil manufacturer the offeree. Or the pencil manufacturer could first say, "I will sell you 12 gross of my #2 pencils at $14 per gross." In this example, the pencil manufacturer is the offeror and the purchaser is the offeree. In negotiations between a buyer and a seller, it is not uncommon for both to make several offers before an agreement is reached. In such instances both the buyer and the seller act at times as offeror and as offeree.

Four possible fates may befall an offer. An offer may (1) *lapse* due to the passage of time, (2) be *rejected* or subject to a *counteroffer* by the offeree, (3) be *revoked* by the offeror, or (4) be *accepted* by the offeree. The first three of these possibilities, lapse, rejection or counteroffer, and revocation, result in the termination of the offer. Only acceptance, the fourth possibility, results in the formation of a contract.

Termination of Offer

Lapse. An offeror may specify a time limit within which the offer must be accepted, and if it is not accepted by the offeree within that time period, it will have expired. Thus, an offer that states "this offer is good for 10 days" may not be accepted on the eleventh day or beyond. Offers are effective when they are received by the offeree. However, if the offer states it is good for a certain time period from a date specified in the offer, then the time period for acceptance begins to run from that date. If no time limit is specified, the offer will expire after a reasonable time period. UCC Section 1-204 provides that a "reasonable time" depends upon "the nature, purpose and circumstances of such action." An offer that is communicated orally, such as in a telephone conversation between a supplier and a purchaser, is generally considered to have terminated at the conclusion of the conversation, unless the offeror states otherwise.

Rejection or Counteroffer. An offer may be rejected at any time before acceptance by the offeree. Once an offer is rejected by an offeree, it is terminated and it cannot be renewed by the offeree. It can only be renewed by the offeror. An oral rejection is effective. However, any rejection must be communicated to the offeror before it is effective. Thus, a rejection that is mailed to the offeror is not effective until the offeror receives it. A counteroffer by the offeree is treated as a rejection of the offer and the making of a new offer by the original offeree to the original offeror. Thus, an offeree who makes a counteroffer can no longer accept the original offer.

Revocation. Revocation of an offer is the act of the offeror. The common law allowed an offer to be revoked at any time prior to acceptance, no matter how it read. Revocation was allowed because the offeror received no consideration from the offeree to keep the offer open. Therefore the offeror was free to revoke at will.

For the sale of goods, the UCC provides an exception to this general rule that an offer is revocable any time before its acceptance. Under Section 2-205 an offer made in a signed writing by a merchant that expressly states that it will be held open cannot be revoked. (A *merchant* is defined in Section 2-104 as one who deals in goods of the kind—thus, suppliers and purchasers can be merchants.) Such offers—referred to as *firm offers*—remain open, and therefore subject to acceptance by the offeree, for the time period specified in the offer, or if no time is specified for a reasonable time, but not to exceed three months in either event. A revocation must be received by the offeree before it is effective.

Acceptance of Offer

It is at the point of acceptance of an offer that a contract is formed between the parties. Acceptance must be made by the offeree to whom the offer was made, and it must be made in the manner prescribed in the offer. The offeror is deemed the "master" of the offer and may specify the required means for acceptance of the offer. Section 2-206 of the UCC states that an offer may be accepted in any reasonable manner unless otherwise stipulated in the offer; but an attempt by an offeree to accept by any means other than that specified by the offeror will be invalid.

An offer may invite acceptance by (1) the making of a return promise by the offeree, or (2) performance by the offeree.

An offer that looks for a promise in return results in what is known as a bilateral contract. In a bilateral contract, there is an exchange of promises between the parties, and each party is obligated to fulfill its promise to the other. For example, suppose party A (the offeror) says to party B (the offeree), "I agree to pay you $500 if you agree to paint my house this weekend." If B accepts this offer and promises to paint A's house this weekend, then that promise is B's acceptance of A's offer and a bilateral contract is formed in which both A and B are obligated to keep their respective promises. If B does not paint A's house over the weekend, B will be in default of the contract and A will be entitled to recover from B any damages suffered as a result of B's breach.

Alternatively, an offer may invite acceptance in the form of a performance by the offeree, forming a unilateral contract in which only the offeror has made a promise. Returning to our example, suppose that A said to B, "I will pay you $500 if you paint my house this weekend." Note that A did not ask B to promise to paint the house. At no time is B obligated to paint A's house, but if B does paint A's house this weekend, that performance is B's acceptance of A's offer. A unilateral contract will be formed in which A is obligated to keep the promise to pay B the $500.

UCC Section 2-206(1)(b) provides that an order for prompt or current shipment is viewed as an offer that invites acceptance either by a prompt promise to ship or by prompt shipment. For illustration, let's return to the example where a supply management organization makes an offer to a pencil manufacturer in the form of a purchase order to buy 12 gross of its #2 pencils at $14 per gross. If the pencil manufacturer accepts the offer by promising to sell that quantity of pencils at that price, such as by returning an order acknowledgment, then a bilateral contract is formed and both parties are obligated to make good on their promises. If, however, the supplier responds to that offer by shipping the pencils, then it is this act of shipment that constitutes acceptance and creates the unilateral contract obligating the purchasing organization to keep its promise. Note again that with the unilateral contract in the latter example, the offeree, or supplier, was never obligated to ship, but once it did ship, that performance formed a unilateral contract that created an obligation on the part of the offeror, or purchaser.

Under common law, an acceptance is valid only when it is a "mirror image" of the offer, which means that it unconditionally accepts all the terms of the offer. A nonconforming acceptance is a counteroffer. A counteroffer is a *rejection* of the original offer and is itself a new offer, giving the other party (the original offeror) the power to accept the counteroffer. Modern business forms made mirror images difficult to achieve. A purchaser's purchase order and a supplier's proposal to sell or its acceptance of an offer to buy will usually contain preprinted terms and conditions that are written in that party's favor. The chances of such forms being mirror images of each other are, of course, minimal. This led to the problem known as the "battle of the forms" where the buyer and seller exchange preprinted forms in the hope of forming a contract on their own terms without attempting to reconcile the differences of their respective terms through negotiation.

UCC Section 2-207, entitled "Additional Terms in Acceptance or Confirmation," attempted to eliminate the battle of the forms. The first part of the section says that an acceptance, if "definite and seasonable," can act as an acceptance even though it states terms additional to or different from those offered. The primary requirement here is that it must be very close to an acceptance (i.e., all the basic terms are in agreement and only minor differences exist between the forms).

The second subsection UCC Section 2-207 deals with the additional terms in the acceptance. Between merchants, such additional terms become part of the final contract unless (1) the offeror has already made clear that acceptance can include only the terms of the offer, (2) the additional terms materially alter the contract, or (3) the offeror has previously objected to any additional terms or objects to them within a reasonable time after receiving the acceptance. No mention is made here of different terms because they are deemed to have been objected to because they are different.

The third subsection handles offers and acceptances that do not make a contract under the first subsection, but the contract is performed by the buyer and the seller. This situation is sometimes referred to as a *contract by conduct* because the parties are acting as if they have a contract even though their exchanged communications do not create a contract. If a disagreement arises between the parties after the goods have been delivered, the paperwork exchanged by the parties (the purchase order and the supplier's proposal or sales acceptance) are laid side by side and compared. Those terms found in both parties' documents are included in the final contract. Additional terms proposed in the acceptance will be included if they qualify as immaterial under the second subsection, discussed previously. Those terms on which the parties disagree are discarded, and the appropriate UCC sections that deal with that subject matter will be substituted. Although Section 2-207's purposes are laudable, it sometimes creates more problems than it solves. Section 2-207 is helpful in solving the battle of the forms but does not provide clear-cut guidelines as to when an acceptance is "definite and seasonable" and when it is not. If the supply management organization wants to be sure of the terms that will govern a transaction, it is advisable to negotiate the terms up front. Many supply professionals accomplish this by negotiating a "master agreement" with suppliers with whom they will have ongoing purchases. The master agreement sets forth the terms and conditions that will govern subsequent orders, which incorporate the terms of the master by reference.

Timing of acceptance may be significant. In the majority of jurisdictions an acceptance is effective when it is sent by the offeree, not when it is received by the offeror, since it is at this point in time that a meeting of the minds occurs and, thus, a contract has been formed. This affects revocation of an offer because an offeror *cannot* revoke an offer where the offeree has already sent an acceptance (because the offer was already accepted at the time the acceptance was sent) even though the offeror has not yet received the acceptance. This is sometimes referred to as the *mailbox rule* because the acceptance is considered effective when it is dropped into the mailbox. Applied to other delivery methods, acceptance is effective when the offeree has released control of the acceptance document (for example, has clicked "send" on an e-mailed acceptance).

Oral Contracts and Writing Requirements

As stated earlier, every contract will reflect the process of creating an agreement through the exchange of offer and acceptance, much of which often takes place in conversations. The next question is, How much of this agreement must be in writing? Some types of oral contracts are enforceable, but certain types of contracts require written evidence of the existence of the contract in order for the contract to be enforced in a court of law. This requirement for a *writing* has its roots in an English law known as the Statute of Frauds, which was intended to prevent fraudulent contract claims. Under this law, contracts that cannot be completed within one year from the time the parties enter into the contract must be evidenced by a writing in order to be enforced. Note that the rule speaks of contracts where completion within one year is *impossible*. Even if it is unlikely that a contract will be completed within one year, if it is possible that it may be then it does not fall within this rule. In addition to the one-year rule, UCC Section 2-201(1) provides that any contract for the sale of goods of $500 or more is not enforceable "unless there is some writing sufficient to indicate that a contract for sale has been made." (Note that under the proposed revisions to UCC Article 2, the threshold amount is increased to $5,000.) Also most real estate transactions (except short-term leases) require written documentation in order to be enforced.

It is not necessary for the parties to have entered into a formal written contract to satisfy these writing requirements. The writing does not have to be in any particular form provided that it identifies the parties and the subject matter of the contract, indicates that a contract has been made, states with reasonable certainty the essential terms of the contract, and is signed by the party against whom enforcement is sought. The writing requirement may be satisfied by a memorandum, and it may be satisfied by taking multiple documents together to evidence that a contract had been formed. Section 2-201 also provides that no writing is necessary to make the contract enforceable if (1) the goods are to be specially manufactured for the buyer and the seller has begun production of them or made commitments for their procurement, (2) payment for the goods has been made by the buyer and accepted by the seller, or (3) goods have been received and accepted by the buyer.

Modification

Once a contract has been created, any change to the substance of the agreement, the terms and conditions of the contract, is, in effect, a new contract. Common law rules require consideration to pass between the parties in order to modify an existing contract. For the sale of goods, UCC Section 2-209 states that the parties may modify an existing contract with no consideration. However, any modification of a contract involving the sale of goods where the contract as modified is valued at $500 or more must be in writing to satisfy the Statute of Frauds. A modification may also require a writing if the original contract has a provision that requires changes to be in writing in order to be effective.

Contract Terms and Conditions

So far, we have discussed the choreography, or what we might call the mechanics of how a valid contract is put together so as to be enforceable in a court of law. All of that is merely the preliminaries, because the content of the agreement will establish just what the parties expect to give and receive by way of the contract. The content is reflected in the contract terms and conditions. Some of these are standard terms that the supply management organization will want to include in every contract. Lawyers refer to these as *boilerplate* because they can be recycled from contract to contract almost as though the contract is being manufactured on an assembly line. Even boilerplate content should be reviewed to be sure it is appropriate in a particular contract. Other terms and conditions might be described as *special* because they are drafted with the particular contract needs in mind. Still other terms, like warranties, may be included in the agreement by operation of law, although the parties can modify them to a certain extent.

Warranties
A *warranty* is an assurance of the existence of some fact or a promise that some fact will exist in the future. When one party makes a warranty, the other party may

rely upon that warranty and may recover damages (i.e., hold the warrantor liable) should the fact prove to be untrue. There are two general types of warranties: (1) express warranties and (2) implied warranties.

Express Warranties. Under common law, statements of fact (as opposed to statements of opinion) made by the supplier create express warranties. UCC Section 2-313(1) provides that express warranties are created by the seller of goods by (1) a promise or affirmation of fact, (2) a description of the goods, or (3) a sample or model, which is part of the basis of the bargain with the buyer. The warranty in the latter two cases is that all the goods will conform to the description, sample, or model. Section 2-313(2) states that the seller does not need to use the words *warrant* or *guarantee* to make an express warranty, but the statements made must pertain to facts and cannot be merely opinions.

Implied Warranties. Implied warranties are created by operation of law, rather than by any statements made by a party. For services, the common law in a few states provides an implied warranty that the work will be performed in a "workmanlike" manner. (When contracting for services, however, purchasing organizations will usually be much better served by inclusion of express warranties than by reliance on such generic implied warranties in the common law.) For the sale of goods, the UCC provides the following implied warranties:

- *Implied warranty of merchantability* (Section 2-314). This is an assurance that the goods will be of average quality and will be fit for ordinary purposes for which they are generally used.

- *Implied warranty of fitness for particular purpose* (Section 2-315). This warranty is an assurance that the goods are suitable for the particular use intended by the buyer. It arises only where a seller knows of a buyer's intended use for the goods, and the buyer relies upon the seller's recommendation in selecting the goods.

The UCC also provides three additional warranties. Although it does not term them "implied warranties," these warranties, nevertheless, are created by operation of law and are often referred to as "constructive warranties." They are

- *Warranty of title* [UCC 2-312(1)(a)]. This is an assurance that the seller has legal title to the goods and has the authority to transfer such title to the buyer.

- *Warranty of freedom from encumbrances* [UCC 2-312(1)(b)]. This is an assurance by the seller that there will be no liens on or security interests in the goods at the time title is transferred to the buyer.

- *Warranty against infringement* [UCC 2-312(3)]. This is an assurance that the goods do not infringe upon the patent or other intellectual property rights of any third party.

Disclaimer of Warranties

Although the UCC allows warranties to be disclaimed (i.e., negated), there are rules for how this is done. For example, UCC Section 2-316(1) denies effect to any disclaimer of an express warranty that is inconsistent with express warranty language. This means that if there are both words or conduct of warranty and words or conduct of disclaimer that are inconsistent with each other, the language of warranty will override the disclaimer. In order to disclaim the implied warranty of merchantability, UCC Section 2-316(2) requires specific use of the word *merchantability* in the disclaimer language. There is no requirement that the disclaimer of merchantability be in writing, but if it is, it must be "conspicuous," meaning it has to stand out from the rest of the contract language so as to be noticeable. No special language is required to disclaim fitness for particular purpose, but this disclaimer must be in writing and must be conspicuous. Use of the words *as is, with all faults,* or similar language will also exclude both the warranties of merchantability and fitness for particular purpose [UCC 2-316(3)(a)]. In addition Section 2-316(3)(b) provides that there is no implied warranty with respect to an obvious defect if the buyer has had the opportunity to examine the goods prior to contracting and fails to notice the defect. This rule does not, however, apply to hidden ("latent") defects. Finally, Section 2-316(3)(c) provides that implied warranties may be excluded or modified by course of performance, course of dealing, or usage of trade. (Course of performance refers to the conduct of the parties under a particular contract, course of dealing refers to prior conduct by the parties in a series of past contracts, and usage of trade refers to any practice widely accepted in a particular trade or industry.)

UCC Gap Fillers

The common law of contracts is built on the principle of "freedom of contract," allowing the parties to a contract to freely choose the contents of their contract. The UCC generally adopts this principle of freedom of contract, providing in Section 1-102 that the "effect of provisions of this Act may be varied by agreement . . ." However, the UCC will supply certain provisions in the event that they are not specifically addressed by the parties. In the absence of express terms in the contract, these default rules of the UCC, sometimes referred to as *gap fillers,* will automatically apply to the agreement. The following paragraphs discuss the UCC treatment given to quantity, delivery, price, and payment terms.

Quantity. Every contract for the sale of goods must contain a provision for a fixed or determinable quantity of the item. The UCC will *not* insert a quantity term if the parties have not themselves agreed to the quantity. In effect, if the parties have not agreed to a quantity term, they really have not had a meeting of the minds and thus do not have a valid contract. It is noteworthy to remember from the earlier discussion on offers that, to be valid, offers generally must be specific as to quantity. The common law insisted that the quantity in a contract be fixed, but subsequent interpretations and UCC Section 2-306 recognize the validity of both *output* and *requirements* contracts. Contracts based on the output of a seller or on the requirements of a buyer for a specific period are acceptable without having to specify a precise quantity. With these types of contracts, however, sellers cannot tender and buyers cannot demand quantities unreasonably disproportionate to any stated estimate. If no estimate is included in the contract, the actual quantity tendered or demanded cannot be unreasonably disproportionate to any normal or otherwise comparable prior output or requirements.

Delivery. Delivery terms in a contract specify (1) the time and place when the seller has completed its performance under the contract, (2) when title and risk of loss pass from the seller to the buyer, and (3) which party bears the expense of the transportation. If the parties do not specify the place of delivery in their agreement, UCC Section 2-308 provides that "the place for delivery of goods is the seller's place of business" unless the parties know that the goods are located in some other place, in which case that other place is the place for delivery. Therefore, the default rule is that the buyer is obligated to pick up the goods at the seller's location or at some other location where they may be.

It is most common, however, for the parties to intend that the supplier will ship the goods to the purchaser's location. The UCC provides for the use of the free-on-board (F.O.B.) trade terms as a simple method for specifying the place of delivery. Section 2-319 defines two F.O.B. terms: (1) F.O.B. place of shipment and (2) F.O.B. place of destination. When specifying F.O.B. place of shipment, the seller's performance is completed when it delivers the goods into the hands of a common carrier for shipment to the buyer's location, and the buyer is responsible for the transportation costs and any risk of loss [Section 2-509(1)(a)]. F.O.B. place of destination means that the seller's performance is not completed until the goods are delivered to the buyer's location. It requires the seller to bear the cost for transportation, and, under Section 2-509(1)(b), risk of loss remains on the seller until the goods arrive at the location specified by the buyer. In addition to these F.O.B. terms, supply management professionals involved in sourcing from foreign suppliers should be familiar with the *Incoterms* (international shipping terms) promulgated by the International Chamber of Commerce. Additional information about Incoterms is available online at the Web sites listed in the Appendix at the end of this chapter. They provide trade terms generally used for international shipments. (Note that under the proposed revisions to UCC Article 2, all the delivery terms currently found in the UCC would be eliminated, which means that widely used abbreviations like *F.O.B.* would no longer be defined in the law. Contracting parties would have to write their own terms, use the Incoterms, or rely on usage of trade, course of dealing, or course of performance to determine delivery obligations.)

Price. It may surprise some supply professionals to know that they can form a valid contract even without specifying the price. Price is, of course, an important component of any purchase contract, but some purchases are made without a price showing on the contract or purchase order, and price need not be included to make the contract valid. UCC Section 2-305(1) provides that, absent a specified price, the price shall be "a reasonable price at the time for delivery."

Price adjustment clauses are often used in longer-term contracts to provide for future variations in price due to changes in the supplier's costs for raw material. In this manner, suppliers do not have to cover in the original price quotation all future potential cost changes that may or may not occur in their raw material costs during the contract term. An adjustment clause permits both the buyer and the seller to keep the price of the contract at a current *level*. An adjustment clause, drawn properly and fairly for both parties, can provide for price increases (escalations) or decreases (de-escalations) as the market may dictate. The clause should also specify the base index that will best reflect price changes in the commodities involved in the supplier's product.

Payment. Section 2-310(1) provides that unless otherwise agreed, "payment is due at the time and place at which the buyer is to receive the goods ..." Note that the buyer's payment obligation is tied to its *receipt* of the goods, even if the agreement provides for delivery F.O.B. place of shipment. This means that although the seller will have completed its performance obligation when it delivered the goods into the hands of the common carrier, the buyer is not obligated to perform (i.e., pay for the goods) until a later time. Section 2-511 further provides that tender of payment by the buyer is a condition to the seller's duty to tender and complete delivery. Section 2-507 makes tender of delivery of the goods a condition to the buyer's duty to pay for them. These two sections operate to render the duty to deliver and the duty to pay concurrent conditions. The end result is that the default payment rule under the UCC is cash on delivery. The supply management organization will typically negotiate for credit terms at the time of contracting with the supplier. Such terms may include a credit period after receipt of the goods and possibly a cash discount for prompt payment of the invoice within a specified number of days after the material has been received. The credit period and the cash discount period come only to those who ask for and get them from the supplier. Contracting parties are cautioned to be specific in their payment terms; simple phrases like *net 30* may not have the same meaning for all concerned, and the law does not define that term.

PERFORMANCE OF THE CONTRACT

Performance of the contract refers to the fulfillment of the obligations agreed to by the parties when they entered into the contract. The failure to perform any contractual obligation, without legal excuse, may constitute a *breach* of contract and give rise to remedies for the other (nonbreaching) party.

In a contract for services under common law, the obligation of the supplier is to perform in the manner and within the time frame agreed and that of the purchasing organization is to accept performance and to pay in accordance with the contract. A breach arises where there is a partial or total failure to perform or where there is some defect with the performance. If the breaching party has "substantially" performed, then the breach is deemed immaterial. An immaterial breach is merely a "partial" breach, which may entitle the nonbreaching party to money damages but does not release that party from its obligations. The determination of whether a party has substantially performed is dependent upon the facts of the particular situation, and in making this determination courts will generally consider the following factors:

- The hardship on the breaching party if a total breach is declared
- The extent to which the breach deprives the nonbreaching party of the expected benefit of the contract
- The amount of benefit that has been bestowed on the nonbreaching party
- Whether the breach was inadvertent or intentional
- The likelihood that the party will be able and willing to cure the breach

For the sale of goods, UCC Section 2-301 describes the general performance obligations of the parties as follows: "The obligation of the seller is to transfer and deliver and that of the buyer is to accept and pay in accordance with the contract." The supplier is obligated to make timely delivery of conforming goods, and upon receipt of those goods the purchasing organization may inspect them for compliance with the contract description and is then obligated to accept and pay for them. These obligations will be discussed more fully in the following.

Delivery of the Goods

Under UCC Section 2-503(1), the seller is required to "put and hold conforming goods at the buyer's disposition.…" *Conforming* means that the goods are "in accordance with the obligations under the contract" [UCC Section 2-106(2)]. If the contract is a *place of shipment* type contract, then the seller tenders delivery by placing the goods in the hands of a common carrier (UCC Section 2-504). In a *place of delivery* type contract, the seller tenders delivery when it makes the goods available to the buyer at the particular destination point [UCC Section 2-503(3)]. Section 2-503(1) requires the buyer to "furnish facilities reasonably suited to the receipt of the goods."

Under UCC Section 2-513, the buyer has the right (not an obligation) to inspect the goods before accepting or paying for them. The purchasing organization must check the exterior of the containers or cartons after the delivery of the goods to make certain that no apparent damage was done to the goods during the delivery process. The carrier will want a receipt signed by the receiver indicating that no apparent damage has occurred. (Note that issuance of such a receipt does *not* constitute acceptance of the goods by the buyer.) If there has been apparent damage, that fact must be noted on the carrier's receipt, and the carrier's representative must be given the opportunity to inspect the goods and the packaging material. The contracting party who had the risk of loss for safe transit must file the appropriate claim with the carrier.

Acceptance of the Goods

Acceptance must be distinguished from receipt of the goods. *Acceptance* is a legal act indicating that the buyer acknowledges that the delivered goods conform to the contract. To make certain of this fact, the buyer should inspect the goods for quality. This inspection is in addition to the normal receiving inspection for damage during shipment. The buyer has the right to inspect the goods for compliance with the contract description before accepting the goods. However, the buyer under a COD shipment or a financing shipment may have to pay for the goods before inspection can be accomplished. Thus, payment may occur before acceptance because the buyer is not required to "accept" the goods until they have been inspected and meet the buyer's approval. The buyer accepts the goods if (1) the buyer notifies the seller that the goods are accepted, (2) the buyer fails to give the seller notice of rejection within a reasonable time after receipt of the goods, or (3) the buyer uses the goods or otherwise acts in a way that is inconsistent with the seller's ownership (UCC Section 2-606).

Payment

If the goods or services have been furnished in accordance with the contract requirements, the buyer is obliged to pay, in the manner and within the time frame specified by the contract.

Rejection of the Goods

If inspection discloses any variance from the contract description, under UCC Section 2-601 the buyer may accept the whole, reject the whole, or accept any commercial unit(s) and reject the rest. The UCC has adopted the "perfect tender" rule, which means that the buyer may reject the goods for any reason, however slight. The seller must be notified of the rejection and given the reason(s) that the delivery is being rejected. A buyer who fails to particularize any defect loses the right to claim damages for that defect. After notice of rejection is received, if the time for performance by the seller has not yet expired the seller is given an opportunity to "cure" such defects by making another conforming delivery or curing the defects in the original goods within the contract time (UCC Section 2-508). Upon rejection of goods, the buyer is under a duty to reasonably care for the goods subject to the seller's disposition of them.

Revocation of Acceptance

What happens if the purchasing organization discovers a defect after acceptance of the goods? If the defect "substantially impairs the value of the goods" to the buyer, UCC Section 2-608 allows the buyer to revoke the acceptance of the goods under either of the following conditions:

1. The buyer was aware of the defect when the goods were accepted, but the buyer accepted on the reasonable assumption that the defect would be cured.

2. The buyer was not aware of the defect at the time of acceptance due to the difficulty of discovery of the defect or due to the seller's assurances.

This section provides that the buyer must notify the seller within a reasonable time from when the defect was discovered or should have been discovered by the buyer. Failure to give this notice will cause the buyer to be barred from any remedy.

DISPUTE RESOLUTION

Once goods have been rejected, or a prior acceptance has been revoked for a valid reason, the buyer is no longer under any obligation to make payment. Sometimes this is the end of the matter, because the other party realizes its error and does not claim payment. But if payment has been made and not returned, or if other adverse consequences resulted from the breach, or if the supplier disagrees that the goods or services were defective or claims that it was not given the proper notices or opportunity to cure the defect, the resulting dispute may end up in court.

In the same fashion, for services contracts, when all goes well, the contract document is simply the road map to performance, clarifying the expectations and guiding the behavior of the contracting parties. But circumstances change, and documents are imperfect, either because something is left out or the language can be read in more than one way. Often, the parties to a contract find themselves in disagreement about what performance is required, and they resolve their disagreements either by clarifying the contract terms by mutual agreement or by turning for interpretation to the courts or to some form of alternative dispute resolution. In other cases, there may be no real difference of understanding, but circumstances make performance more costly or more difficult for one of the parties, and that party chooses to walk away from part or all of the agreement. Left in the lurch, the aggrieved party can either accept, renegotiate, or sue—taking its adversary to court.

If a dispute ends up in litigation, the court will review the merits of the case and consider what remedies to order. But any resort to court must be taken in a timely manner.

Statute of Limitations

A statute of limitations is a legislative act that establishes the time period in which a party must seek to enforce its rights. After this time has passed, the aggrieved party is barred from bringing any legal claim against the other party. For the sale of goods, UCC Section 2-725 sets the statute of limitations at four years, which means that a legal action for breach of a contract for the sale of goods must be brought within four years from the time that the breach occurs. (Note that five states have modified this section of the UCC to reflect different time periods: Colorado—three years, Oklahoma—five years; Mississippi, South Carolina, and Wisconsin—six years.) The statute of limitations for breach of a services contract varies from state to state and may depend on whether the contract is oral or written; periods range from 1 to 25 years.

Remedies

The basic remedy for breach of a contract is *compensatory damages*, which are damages paid to the injured (nonbreaching) party in order to put that party in the position it would have been in if the contract had not been breached. This is sometimes referred to as giving that party the "benefit of the bargain." Damages are awarded to compensate for actual injuries resulting from the breach. Compensatory damages include *general damages,* which are money damages for the diminution in value caused by the breach (i.e., the difference in value between what was received and what should have been received had the contract not been breached). They also include *special damages,* which are damages for injuries caused indirectly by the breach such as lost business, personal injury, or property damage. Special damages are only recoverable if they were reasonably foreseeable at the time the parties entered into the contract.

Another remedy that may be available for breach of contract, although used much less often than awards of money damages, is an order for specific performance. When ordering specific performance, a court directs the breaching party to do what it promised to do. Before applying this remedy, the court must determine that

- Money damages would not provide an adequate remedy to the injured party.
- Some irreparable injury will occur if specific performance is not ordered.
- Consideration under the contract is sufficient.
- The contract is not unconscionable.
- The contract terms are sufficiently clear and unambiguous to be enforced.
- The injured party has not breached the contract in any way and is prepared to perform its obligations.

The UCC does not provide specific performance as a remedy for sellers; only buyers of goods may take advantage of this particular remedy.

Breach by the Purchasing Organization

When the supplier has performed and the purchasing organization fails to make payment when it is due, the supplier has the right to sue for the contract price under the common law and under UCC Section 2-709. For the sale of goods, the supplier may also recover *incidental damages,* which are the seller's costs associated with transportation, care, and custody of the goods, and so forth (UCC Section 2-710).

Breach by the Supplier of a Contract for Services

Where the failure to perform by the supplier is trivial and innocent and the cost of correcting the work is unjustified, the purchasing entity may recover compensatory damages equivalent to the diminution in value between the performance as delivered and the performance for which it actually contracted. For example, if a contractor installed a different manufacturer's pipe than was called for in the contract but it was of the same grade as the pipe specified, the contractor will have substantially performed because the deviation, while intentional, was trivial. The measure of damages will be the diminution in value, if any. It simply would not make any sense to require the contractor to tear apart the structure, rip out the installed pipe, and install the specified brand of pipe.

Where the breach by the supplier is intentional and where the defect is so great that the supplier has not substantially performed, the remedy for the breach may be the cost for completing the performance or the cost for correcting the performance.

Breach by the Supplier in a Contract for the Sale of Goods: Delivery of Nonconforming Goods

When the buyer has accepted nonconforming goods shipped by the seller, the UCC provides the following remedies:

- *General (direct) damages* [UCC 2-714]. The difference between the value of the goods as delivered and their value had they been delivered as provided in the contract.

- *Incidental (direct) damages* [UCC 2-715(1)]. The costs associated with receipt, inspection, storage, and transportation of the goods.

- *Consequential (special) damages* [UCC 2-715(2)]. These include any losses realized as a result of the breach that the seller had reason to know about at the time of contracting, including economic losses such as lost profits, and any damage to property or personal injury resulting from the breach.

Breach by the Supplier in a Contract for the Sale of Goods: Failure to Deliver

UCC Sections 2-711 and 2-712 provide that when a seller fails to make delivery, the buyer may *cover,* which means the buyer may buy the goods from another seller and recover the difference between the price paid to that supplier and the contract price with the original supplier. Alternatively, the purchasing organization may recover damages measured by the difference between market price and contract price (without having actually to purchase replacement goods). In either case, the purchasing organization may also recover incidental and consequential damages.

Alternate Dispute Resolution

Court proceedings are expensive, time consuming, and adversarial. They erode or destroy the communication and cooperation needed for successful relationships between purchasing organizations and suppliers. When disputes arise, by far the best practical course for those wishing to continue doing business together is for the parties to deal with each other directly and to clarify or update their contract. When this is possible, it keeps costs down and helps ensure successful completion of contract performance. Contract provisions can help support informal resolution of disputes by setting up effective mechanisms for contract administration.

Sometimes it is not possible for parties to resolve their disputes themselves. Each is wedded to its own position and has a hard time seeing the merits of the other side. To help keep costs down and to speed up decision making, parties now often seek ways to make their contracts enforceable without resorting to litigation in the courts. They may do this by including in their contract documents specific provisions spelling out alternative dispute resolution (ADR) mechanisms which they agree will bind the parties should a dispute arise. Such ADR mechanisms commonly include mediation, conciliation, arbitration, and minitrial.

Mediation is a mechanism to bring in a neutral, trusted third party who helps clarify the issues and assists the parties to find a mutually agreeable resolution of the dispute. Mediators do not make binding decisions, and if mediation is not successful, the parties may go on to court or arbitration, whichever the contract provides. Conciliation involves even less intervention by the third party. The conciliator simply facilitates the parties getting together to find their own resolution.

Arbitration is more formal and typically results in a binding decision. The contract document may spell out procedures for selecting an individual or panel of arbitrators and for presenting the controversy to the arbitrator for a ruling. If binding arbitration is specified, the arbitrator's ruling ordinarily cannot be appealed to court unless the agreed-upon procedures were not followed. For this reason it is very important to spell out in the contract what rules will govern the arbitrator and what, if any, law the arbitrator must follow in making a decision. When the arbitration is nonbinding, either party, if dissatisfied with the arbitrator's decision, may pursue litigation.

Either a mediator or an arbitrator may suggest a minitrial, or a formal presentation of evidence and arguments by both sides in the dispute. If the setting is mediation, this formal presentation sometimes helps each party see the merits of the other side and fosters a settlement of the dispute. In an arbitration, it provides a structure for the panel or decision maker to learn all the facts and hear the positions of the parties before making a decision.

The contract language adopted by the parties at the outset can help them deal with disputes in other ways as well. When courts or alternative adjudicators consider contract disputes, they must determine a number of threshold issues before they can turn to the particular facts involving performance or breach of the contract. These issues include: Is this the correct forum for resolving the dispute? What law applies to the contract and performance questions under dispute? Are the correct parties before the court? Have the parties complied with all the formalities required to invoke the court's jurisdiction? Has the dispute been brought to court in a timely manner? In their contract documents, parties can and should address each of these threshold matters. Thus, for example, the parties can agree that disputes will be presented to the courts in the home state of one of the parties and that that state's law will be used to decide the dispute. Or, in an international contract, they could agree that the CISG will govern and that an arbitrator will hear the dispute following the procedures established by an organization such as the American Arbitration Association (AAA). If the parties do not clearly address these issues in their contract documents, whatever court is presented with the case must invoke legal principles to decide these procedural matters before hearing the merits of the case. This process will increase the time and cost of litigation, and in addition, the decision may not be what any of the parties would have wished.

Once it has resolved the threshold questions, the adjudicator can consider the merits of the case, by reviewing the contract text, the facts concerning contract formation and performance, and the applicable law. The parties will present factual evidence by way of witness testimony, documents, and perhaps other physical evidence such as samples of the items purchased. The records kept by the purchasing organization will play a critical role in establishing the facts at trial, including intent of the parties where the contract language is ambiguous, and the circumstances of performance or breach. The fact finder will draw inferences not just from what the records contain but from what they have left out. Incomplete or damaged records may lead to adverse findings against the party that should have kept the records.

Following the principles described earlier in this chapter, the adjudicator will decide whether there was a valid contract, and if so, what were its terms and what exactly do they mean; whether on the facts presented there has been a breach; and, if so, what the remedy should be—to order performance or to provide for payment of damages and in what amount. By having a clear understanding of their rights and obligations under common law, the UCC, and other statutes, supply management organizations and their suppliers can develop contract documents and contract administration protocols that make disputes, if not easy, at least easier to resolve.

After considering the evidence on all these questions, the court or arbitrator will make a decision and will issue a formal judgment stating the substance of the remedy. Parties can appeal court decisions and some arbitration rulings to higher courts, and still more time may elapse before the case has resulted in a final judgment. The winning party may then invoke yet another judicial mechanism to enforce and collect on the judgment.

REGULATIONS AFFECTING SUPPLY MANAGEMENT

The old expression "there oughta be a law" captures the idea that for every wrong, there must be a remedy, and that remedy might well be a statute. Over the years, American lawmakers have responded to a great variety of problems with detailed laws spelling out what people and organizations must do to correct the problem, with paperwork requirements to ensure compliance, and with penalties for not complying. The "granddaddy of them all" for procurement is the body of antitrust laws, which were created in response to the great monopolies of the early industrial revolution and which establish the principles of free and fair competition that are at the heart of American domestic commerce. In addition, laws that address issues of corporate governance and reporting; fair labor practices; occupational safety and health; nondiscrimination on the basis of race, age, or gender; affirmative action contracting policies; equal opportunity for individuals with disabilities; and a myriad of environmental concerns all establish regulatory schemes that impose requirements on those entering into contracts. Supply management professionals must familiarize themselves with these regulatory requirements in order to help their organizations comply.

Antitrust Laws

The antitrust laws (the Sherman Act, the Clayton Act, and the Federal Trade Commission Act) prohibit agreements that create unreasonable restraints of trade. Since all contracts restrain trade to some degree, the question before the court in most antitrust litigation is whether a contract does so unreasonably. A full trial on all relevant issues is often necessary, and the results are often difficult to predict. However, there are some fairly clear rules.

Agreements on pricing are illegal. Supply professionals should not agree with fellow purchasers (whether or not competitors) on any aspect of pricing.

Reciprocal agreements may be anticompetitive if they foreclose a substantial amount of trade. Therefore, as a general rule, supply management professionals should not agree to buy any products on the basis of a reciprocal agreement on the part of the supplier to buy the purchasing firm's product.

Exclusive dealing arrangements may also be anticompetitive. An agreement to purchase all requirements from a single source could be anticompetitive if the purchasing organization accounts for a substantial amount of the total market for that product. Similarly, an agreement to purchase all the output of a certain organization could be anticompetitive if that organization accounted for a large share of the amount of that product available. Exclusive dealing arrangements of a substantial nature should always be reviewed by the organization's legal counsel.

The Robinson-Patman Act prohibits an organization from charging different prices for the same product to two different buyers if that difference would have an adverse effect on competition and is not justifiable. In general, purchases of items used in a business (such as office supplies) could not affect competition. If one organization gets a lower price on office supplies than another, typically it would not be a big enough factor in the total cost structure to have any effect on the sales prices of its own products. However, getting a lower price than a competitor on items the firm resells (such as a purchaser acquiring a commodity for resale) could have such an effect. Likewise, if purchasers have reason to believe suppliers are charging their competitors more than they themselves are being charged, consultation with the organization's legal counsel may be appropriate. The Robinson-Patman Act also prohibits a buyer from "knowingly inducing" a supplier to sell its product at a lower price than the supplier charges the buyer's competitors. *Knowingly inducing* are the key words in this section of the law.

Other Key Regulatory Laws

Supply management professionals should be aware that there are a number of other laws that affect their dealings with suppliers and their role within their own organizations. Detailed treatment of these laws is beyond the scope of this chapter. Supply managers, nonetheless, must be generally aware of their existence and should seek appropriate legal counsel for guidance in these areas. Following is just a small sampling of some additional regulatory laws affecting the supply management function.

Labor and Employment Laws
Labor and employment laws govern how organizations may obtain and interact with contracted labor. Often the parties' actions will override the express language of the contract. For example, it is not enough that a contract for temporary labor states that the relationship is that of an "independent contractor." In some cases the actions of the purchasing organization may be deemed to create an employment relationship, obligating the organization to provide employee benefits for the contract workers. Some laws, such as regulations issued by the Occupational Safety and Health Administration (OSHA), dictate safety precautions that must be taken—both by the contractor as well as by the organization that is obtaining the contracted services.

Environmental Laws
Federal and state laws as well as regulations issued by the Environmental Protection Agency (EPA) and other administrative agencies affect how organizations may obtain, handle, and dispose of certain materials categorized as hazardous. These laws may impose *criminal* penalties as well as civil penalties, and penalties may be imposed upon individuals as well as their employers. Hazardous materials laws also require certain labeling and communications to employees who will be coming into contact with the materials.

Sarbanes-Oxley Act
The Sarbanes-Oxley Act was adopted by Congress in 2002 in an attempt to restore public confidence in corporate governance after a number of corporate scandals surfaced. The law, which took effect in July 2003, applies to publicly traded companies

but is often used as a guide for privately held companies and nonprofit organizations as well. While much of the law focuses on regulation of the auditing profession, it includes some provisions of particular concern for supply management. In general the law requires

- Maintenance of records that accurately reflect transactions and asset dispositions

- Proper recording of transactions, and assurance that receipts and expenditures are properly authorized

- Prevention or timely detection of unauthorized material transactions

More specifically the law requires the disclosure of off–balance sheet obligations, which could include long-term purchase agreements. It also calls for disclosure of material events that impact financial reporting. Such material events may include late supplier deliveries and inventory inaccuracies. Supply management professionals should familiarize themselves with specific practices and procedures established within their own organizations in response to this law.

ELECTRONIC COMMERCE

Any aspect of commercial transactions that once were performed face-to-face or through the exchange of documents written on paper and signed in ink can now be conducted exclusively by electronic means and at a distance between parties that never see or speak to each other. In the most extreme examples, organizations can buy and sell in large quantities instantaneously through Internet transactions conducted by electronic agents acting without direct human intervention, with no paper document or inked signature at any point, from order to delivery to payment. The enormous time and money savings generated by these technologies yield great competitive advantage, and it is no wonder that organizations pressed forward without waiting for laws to be spelled out. Organization representatives make commitments by telephone, fax, or e-mail, and their business counterparts perform and receive payment, assuming that things will work out and that the laws will catch up when they have to.

Just as interstate and global shipping and trade created new circumstances that required the law to change and adapt, so too information and communication technology advances have outpaced developments in the laws governing commercial transactions. As in the past, generally accepted business practices sometimes become codified in statutes; some laws develop in the context of court cases when judges try to make a fair decision after things go wrong. What seems to be happening today is similar to what has happened over the centuries: business people make business decisions based on practicality and common sense, sometimes taking risks in order to make money; and courts, legislatures, and uniform laws commissions look to the fundamental principles of the old laws and try to make them work in the new settings.

A few examples will illustrate some of the major issues.

Under common law and the UCC, to be enforceable in court certain contracts must be evidenced by a writing that is signed by the party (or its authorized agent) against whom enforcement is being sought. This requirement protects against fraud and mistake. In today's digital world, the requirement for a writing is being replaced by a requirement for a "record" (which could be entirely electronic) and the signature requirement is being met by elaborate "authentication" mechanisms to ensure that the parties to the electronic transaction actually are who they appear to be and that the record of the transaction has not been tampered with during transmittal. Other authentication mechanisms increasingly supplement or substitute for signatures in the credit card and electronic banking environment at the retail and consumer level: knowledge of your mother's maiden name, or the first or last digits of your social security number. Encryption technology provides electronic means to keep records as though they were physically locked in a sealed container, protected from any alteration—just like old-fashioned original paper documents with initials on every page.

Or take the basic concept that a contract is formed when there is an *offer* and an *acceptance* in substantially identical terms, between competent parties and for a legal purpose. If both parties have established the required electronic systems, an electronic purchasing agent following programmed instructions can browse an online catalog, identify the required product, place the order, and even send payment; on the other side, the electronic seller's agent can process the purchase and order delivery. The required "meeting of the minds" is entirely figurative, but the contract transaction appears to have taken place.

Now consider what happens when problems in performance arise. In today's world we can expect that even with a traditional paper contract agreement many communications between the parties take place electronically during the course of performance and that some of them may actually modify terms of the original contract as the parties try to work matters out. If the dispute is presented to a court to adjudicate, the electronic communications will likely become evidence in court, possibly on an equal footing with the original paper contract document.

What about the Internet purchase that goes wrong? Is the contract governed (for purposes of court decisions) by the law of the state where the buyer is located, where the seller is located, or where the Internet service provider is located? Will the contract be viewed as one for goods, or services, or a mixture? Or (as with Internet sales of software) will it be interpreted as a license, not a sale at all? Will a court find that the bugs in the software were a breach of warranty? What about a disclaimer of warranty that the purchaser never had a chance to read?

Courts have been wrestling with these and a myriad of other issues presented by electronic commerce. New laws such as the Uniform Electronic Transactions Act, the proposed revisions to UCC Article 2, and to a lesser degree the Uniform Computer Information Transactions Act, all discussed earlier in this chapter, will go a long way to clarifying many of the issues. As with any new law, however, it may still take a number of years before all the answers are clear because the legislative enactments are still subject to judicial interpretation and application.

Well-advised supply management professionals will not rely entirely on model statutes and court decisions. A better approach is to develop standard forms of agreement for the organization's electronic trading partners, to serve as a master contract or umbrella agreement for all electronic transactions. In much the same way as any blanket agreement that is executed using purchase orders or releases, such a master contract can spell out agency authority and limits; set up authentication protocols; identify electronic order, delivery, acceptance and payment methods; state any warranties or disclaimers; and select dispute resolution procedures including applicable laws. Such trading partner agreements must be drafted with the same level of care that goes into any partnering-type agreement.

CONCLUSION

As this chapter has shown, supply management activity involves many areas of law. The various rules are often complex, and detailed treatment is beyond the scope of this chapter. The purpose of this chapter is simply to raise supply management professionals' awareness of the various laws affecting the performance of their duties. They should be better able to recognize potential problems before the problems materialize so that they will know when to seek legal counsel or other appropriate advice. This awareness can help supply management professionals and their employers avoid many legal disputes and obtain optimum outcomes when such disputes are unavoidable.

APPENDIX

Internet Resources

American Bar Association (www.abanet.org). Includes a comprehensive listing of ABA publications on business and commercial law, international trade, environmental regulations, technology, and ethics, as well as on links to other law-related sites.

American Law Sources On-Line (www.lawsource.com/also/). Includes information and additional links for American, Canadian, and Mexican law.

Business Laws, Inc. (www.businesslaws.com). Information on books, forms, and subscriptions available for order.

Cornell University Law School (www.law.cornell.edu/states/index.html). Provides access to legal resources from each of the 50 states and the District of Columbia. Also includes a Uniform Law Locator to help identify where in a particular state's laws specific provisions of the UCC may be found.

FindLaw (www.findlaw.com). Provides a comprehensive set of legal resources on the Internet suitable for legal professionals, businesses, students, and individuals. Resources include Web search utilities, cases and codes, legal news, and community-oriented tools, such as a secure document management utility.

International Chamber of Commerce (ICC) (www.iccbooksusa.com and www.iccwbo.org/index_incoterms.asp). Sites offer information about the Incoterms both in a read-only format and for sale.

Pace University School of Law (www.cisg.law.pace.edu). Includes the text of the CISG treaty, an updated list of the signatories to the treaty, general information on the application of the CISG, as well as annotations of the text itself (providing case references). It is a good starting point for other aspects of international law as well.

University of Pennsylvania School of Law (www.law.upenn.edu/library/ulc/ulc.htm). Contains the working drafts for UCC sections in the process of revision. From time to time press releases relative to the UCC will be posted here as well.

CONTRACT WRITING INTERNET RESOURCES

Association of Technology Procurement Professionals (www.caucusnet.com). Sponsored by International Computer Negotiation, Inc. Association membership provides access to a document library that includes various contract-related forms for information technology (IT) contracting.

The Leadership Companies, Inc. (www.leadershipworldwide.com). Provides Document Management Technology (DMT) software applications, business processes, management guides, textbooks, and educational programs for achieving excellence in purchasing and supply management. DMT applications are sold either as a low-cost ASP Internet solution through www.contractsonline.net or as an enterprise intranet solution to medium and large companies.

The Outsourcing Institute (www.outsourcing.com). Provides outsourcing information, outsourcing research, outsourcing networking opportunities, and customized outsourcing services and solutions to the outsourcing industry.

University of North Carolina–Charlotte (www.uncc.edu/unccatty/contract.html). Includes a contract review checklist for use by procurement professionals at the University of North Carolina–Charlotte. Useful for any contract writer.

CHAPTER 32

PRINCIPLES OF MANAGING INVESTMENT RECOVERY INVENTORY: THE APPLICATION OF REVERSE LOGISTICS

GARY L. STADING, PH.D.
University of Houston–Downtown

INTRODUCTION

Managing investment recovery inventory requires a distinct and different management philosophy from typical "salable" inventory. The philosophies for managing these types of inventories are somewhat complicated and involve applying the challenging theories of reverse logistics (Stock 1998). Most business models are built to assist business professionals in managing inventory that can be sold, liquidated, or "turned over" in the open market. The goal of most types of inventory is to sell it quickly and convert it to cash. The goal of recovered inventories also includes selling the inventory, but other goals are relevant as well.

Stock (1998) acknowledges that while recovering inventory reduces costs and increases revenues, growing legal requirements are mandating that companies focus on recovering inventory. In addition, companies are shouldering social responsibilities for recovering inventory. Organizational mandates like the ISO 14000 standards continue to grow in importance, establishing requirements that companies may elect to follow in the future.

Investment recovery inventory has additional benefits. Often, this inventory is held as maintenance inventory in case a critical machine or process is shut down. Recovered inventories, like maintenance and supply (M&S) inventories, are held as replacement parts for machine repairs. Therefore, investment recovery groups of most companies play a critical role in not only the reverse logistics (recycling) process of equipment and materials, but also in the M&S arena as well.

The investment recovery departments of most companies are responsible for recovering some value associated with assets that have been decommissioned from service. Often, those assets are old and have been used for many years. In addition, the technology is often outdated and sometimes may not be available on the open market. Original suppliers can conceivably have gone out of business or no longer be in existence. These circumstances, however, may not mitigate the value of the asset in either real or book value on the open market. The value of an asset can be held in many ways including as a whole unit replacement or as a disassembled individual replacement part. Oftentimes, there are buyers available as appreciators of the equipment. In each of these scenarios, investment recovery groups of companies play an important role for those companies in gathering, warehousing, organizing, cataloging, and eventually disposing of these surplus assets.

The assets or inventory held by many investment recovery groups of most companies are not limited to recovered items. The sources of surplus inventory in many companies appear from such places as surplus from projects, extra items ordered as spares, and project changes. Surplus arising from those types of sources can easily involve new items and new technologies. Therefore, the inventory held by investment recovery groups is not limited to old and recovered equipment, but often includes new equipment and new technologies.

Recovered stock, whether it is new equipment or old, can be a golden find for some engineers working on project designs and implementations. The one piece of equipment that was ruled out because it was cost prohibitive against a project budget could easily have been saved because the investment recovery team happened to have one in its warehouse, or that old technology that is no longer made might be found in its warehouse also. These types of scenarios typify an investment recovery team's story of success. The benefits brought to a company by such a group can result in millions of dollars of savings for most major companies. Beyond the savings, there is the opportunity to safely utilize dormant inventory that could otherwise be costly or environmentally unfriendly if disposed of by alternative means.

Managing investment recovery inventory is a complex undertaking. This chapter will attempt to provide a brief overview of some of these complexities. The topics covered will include the reasons why investment recovery continues to grow in strategic importance for companies. A description of how investment recovery inventory is characterized and segmented will be provided. This is followed by a discussion of the requirements for distributing the inventory, and the inherent obstacles facing an investment recovery group are also presented. The importance of valuing the inventory is described, and finally the importance of systems for tracking inventory is discussed.

REASONS WHY COMPANIES MAINTAIN INVESTMENT RECOVERY GROUPS

The reasons why companies maintain investment recovery groups, while complex, are fundamental and compelling. First and foremost, a significant amount of money is saved and generated by these relatively small groups of employees. In accounting terms, this money is "hard savings," meaning the money generated is directly added to the coiffures of the company and not just added through an accounting entry. When a piece of equipment is sold at some price higher than would have been realized through scrapping it out; real cash is added to the bottom line. The recovered inventory saves money while reflecting a positive image in terms of goodwill for customers (Minahan 1998).

Second, the inventory that is maintained in these groups is used in conjunction with maintenance and supply inventory to maintain a store of inventory that is used as an emergency backup for critical processes. When something breaks down in the process, these stores are used to bring the line back up. Many times the inventory is obsolete and held for years, but when that piece breaks down, it is immediately available instead of forcing a company to wait for that part to be ordered.

The investment recovery program is an inventory source that provides immediately available materials. This inventory is sourced mainly from a combination of a buildup of surplus inventory and recovered items. These sources of inventory, while not inexpensive, occur as an inherent part of operating a business. Therefore, it is prudent for the company to utilize this type of inventory.

Finally, it is environmentally the correct thing to do, and even in some cases, the legal responsibility of the company. The investment recovery group prevents some materials or many pieces of equipment from becoming scrapped out and landfilled. These groups provide a big part of the overall recycling and reuse programs of many companies. They function as a significant portion of the moral and legal obligation of a company to recycle components and parts in the business.

The International Organization for Standardization (ISO) is an organization born out of the European Union (EU). Its function has been to establish standards and requirements for doing business with member countries of the European Union. The ISO has established a set of environmental measurement standards referred to as the ISO 14000 standards. These standards establish a protocol for setting policies, forming strategies, planning the process, implementing objectives, and measuring and reviewing the progress for the environmental management process in companies (see Stock 1998 for a broader discussion). This type of regulatory expectation in recovering inventory can only be expected to grow in the future.

Regulatory expectations are complex, so it is important to consult a qualified expert when considering safety and environmental issues. Government legislation has impacted a number of the processes involved with inventory recovery efforts. For instance, the Resource Conservation and Recovery Act (RCRA) affects the product cycle from the conception through the recovery process for a number of products that may be hazardous to human health. The Comprehensive Environmental Responsibility, Compensation, and Liability Act (CERCLA) regulates the cleanup of certain hazardous substances, and the Hazardous Materials Transportation Act (HTMA) regulates the transport of hazardous materials. A full discussion of these and other safety and environmental issues is beyond the scope of this text. For more information on environmental and safety considerations see the Web sites at the end of this chapter for both the EPA and OSHA.

CHARACTERIZING INVESTMENT RECOVERY INVENTORY

There are several characteristics common to recovered inventory. One of the primary characteristics is that the sourcing of this inventory is usually unpredictable. This may seem counterintuitive because it would seem the decommissioning of a process or a project would be carefully scheduled and planned. While this is true, many times there are circumstances in which the decommissioning occurs and is not planned. In addition, many equipment surpluses occur beyond the planning and scheduling process. Equipment surplus occurs during project implementations, refurbishments, upgrades, and even decommissioning. Equipment, parts, or materials that may have been missed, unaccounted for, or even hidden away tend to show up at different times during the life cycle of a functioning process from the implementation all the way through a decommissioning. The list of examples of how, why, and when the inventory appears is expansive, but the primary characteristic of this inventory is that the sourcing of this inventory is unpredictable.

A second primary characteristic of this type of inventory is that it is a demand creation venture; the demand for this inventory needs to be created. Demands come from internal and external customers. Internal customers include project managers, engineers, and maintenance personnel. External customers include competitors, complementary companies, suppliers, companies from other industries, and brokers. While the list of potential customers is vast, identifying those customers and disposing of this inventory is a complicated effort. Customers and potential users of this inventory need to be told about this inventory so that they can buy it. Investment recovery professionals should be prepared to market to not only these groups of potential users but others as well. Finally, the managers, professionals, and employees of the inventory recovery department often find that while they are faced with a tremendous and complex marketing effort, they are usually operating on a very slim marketing budget.

The third primary product characteristic of recovered inventory is inventory condition. Many engineering professionals and project managers make a big assumption that this type of inventory will be in a well-used condition with little or no product life left available. In reality, often the equipment is in good shape and could be new. Sometimes the technical standards reports, generically referred to as MTRs (mill test reports), are available with the equipment. Regardless of the apparent condition of the equipment, it is often worth the time of the project engineer evaluating its use to physically go and look at the equipment being considered.

Because of these primary characteristics of unpredictable sourcing, unpredictable demands, and the unknown condition of the equipment, investment recovery inventory is not necessarily a good application of traditional inventory modeling. Economic order quantities, reorder points, and other traditional inventory management techniques may not be necessary or helpful for managing investment recovery inventory. Therefore, other management techniques discussed later may be helpful in managing these inventory levels.

PLACING THE INVENTORY

Investment recovery groups in companies face a multitude of daily challenges inherent with recovering this type of inventory. The first major challenge is where to place the inventory. The demands of this type of inventory, however, go beyond placing the pieces into the process when the line goes down. Investment recovery inventory levels will quickly grow to uncontrollable levels if additional end uses for this inventory are not identified. This is one of the major functions of management in an investment recovery group. Inventory is coming in, and inventory levels are building; the inventory has to go somewhere besides storage.

If a group's only charge is to sell the inventory on the open market, this alone would be a major challenge for investment recovery groups. Since recovered inventory requires placement into other channels as well, the placement challenge is even greater. Professionals in the investment recovery group are often not prepared for the marketing challenges because they draw personnel from groups like inventory managers, warehouse managers, materials managers, and supply management. The personnel of these departments often come from operational positions or materials management positions and often do not have vast amounts of marketing experience. The success of an investment recovery group depends to a large degree on marketing. Demand for this inventory has to be created both within the company and external to the company. Engineering groups need to be told that this inventory exists to encourage usage of this inventory in their projects. Maintenance people need to know this inventory is available so they can use this inventory in their repairs and preventative maintenance programs. Regardless of the complexities, placing the inventory still begins with the four marketing P's of product, placement, promotion, and pricing.

Product Knowledge

The first of the four P's is product or in this case product knowledge. Gaining knowledge or an expertise of the product is often difficult because recovered inventory originates from so many sources. The professionals attempting to market this product need a certain degree of knowledge. It is useful to become knowledgeable with the major classes of inventory and specifically the major pieces in inventory. The more knowledgeable professionals working in this area become on the product, the more capable they will become at finding outlets as well. It sometimes helps to segment recovered inventory.

A popular segmentation of recovered inventory is into the following general categories.

- Maintenance and supply (M&S) inventory
- Surplus inventory (excess and raw materials inventory)
- Capital equipment (including machinery)
- Real estate (involving buildings and land)

- Materials, chemicals, and products
  - Off-specification
  - Downgraded
  - Wastes
  - Byproducts

This list can be thought of as segmenting the investment recovery inventory between inputs (sourced goods), products (completed goods), real estate, and project materials. Any of these segmentations may be slightly different between types of companies or businesses because segmentation is extremely susceptible to the type of industry a business is in. Companies will sometimes segment by product type. Some popular categories include the following: pipes, valves, and fittings; plates and structural pieces; electrical components like wiring, transformers, conduit, breakers, and motors; instrumentation like controllers, transmitters, and indicators; catalyst and support materials; columns, vessels, and drums; vehicles, trailers, and emergency escape vessels; warehouse furnishings and material handling equipment; mechanical equipment like compressors, pumps, and gearboxes.

Product knowledge is enhanced by a careful collection of associated data with recovered inventory. Inventory recovery professionals can then have the benefit of accessing records instead of relying on their own knowledge of these wide and varied products. Recording as much information as possible from recovered inventory often proves prudent. The type of information collected includes the following:

- Product name
- Product description
  - Condition description
  - Source
  - Known engineering-related information (e.g., gpm, psig, Hz)
  - Asset or product number
  - Model and/or serial number
  - Original manufacturer
  - Original purchase information (e.g., purchase order number, price)
- Current location
- Recommended disposition information
  - Category (e.g., scrap, resale, hold for maintenance)
  - Recommended price
  - Potential customers

An example of a form designed to collect this information is shown in Figure 32–1. It is generally a good idea to identify inventory with this information through some sort of automated system such as a bar code system or a radio frequency identification tag system. The importance of accurate information regarding recovered inventory cannot be understated.

F I G U R E   32–1

Surplus Equipment Report and Asset Disposition Request

SURPLUS EQUIPMENT REPORT and
ASSET DISPOSITION REQUEST

			DATE

GP 8639 (8-90)

DIVISION #	DIVISION NAME	TYPE OF OPERATION	LOCATION (CITY, STATE)

1. EQUIPMENT DESCRIPTION

DESCRIPTION OF EQUIPMENT

MANUFACTURER	MODEL NUMBER	SERIAL NUMBER	QUANTITY
YEAR MANUFACTURED	CONDITION OF EQUIPMENT	SPARE PARTS ☐ YES ☐ NO	DRAWINGS/MANUALS ☐ YES ☐ NO

2. PROPOSED DISPOSITION

☐ SALE $_____   ☐ OTHER_____

☐ TRANSFER $_____   Corporate Investment Recovery Consulted? ___Yes ___No

3. TO BE COMPLETED BY THE FACILITY CONTROLLER

ASSET AMOUNT $	RESERVE AMOUNT $ AS OF (DATE)	NET BOOK $
GUIDELINE CLASS YEAR SUFFIX	EQUIPMENT NUMBER, IF APPLICABLE	

4. APPROVALS

Obtain approvals in the following sequence. Refer to the Financial Handbook if you have any questions.

1. ORIGINATOR	DATE	5. REGIONAL/GROUP MANAGER (AS REQUIRED)	DATE
2. ENGINEERING MANAGER	DATE	6. CORPORATE INVESTMENT RECOVERY MANAGER	DATE
3. FACILITY CONTROLLER	DATE	7. VICE PRESIDENT (AS REQUIRED)	DATE
4. FACILITY MANAGER	DATE		

5. INVESTMENT RECOVERY

ITEM NUMBER	CATEGORY CODE NUMBER	ESTIMATED MARKET VALUE

6. DISPOSITION OF EQUIPMENT

☐ SOLD $_____   ☐ SCRAPPED

☐ TRANSFER $_____   ☐ ABANDONED

☐ TRADE-IN $_____   ☐ DONATION

WHITE - INVESTMENT RECOVERY   YELLOW - FACILITY CONTROLLER   PINK - ORIGINATOR

Placement

Being knowledgeable of various distribution outlets and customers helps achieve placement, the second P. Networking is essential and includes both internal and external customers. Investment recovery groups must maintain relationships with internal engineering and supply management groups throughout their own company. Distribution channels, however, do not stop there, and the networking should expand beyond the internal borders of a company.

A list of potential customers should include, but not be limited to, distributors, contractors, and scrap dealers. Distribution outlets should also have a network list of other investment recovery groups from similar companies and even companies that are traditional competitors in the salable product arena. While it may seem counterintuitive for direct competitors to trade between themselves, one company's investment recovery group may have a component that a particular competitor does not. Selling or bartering that product for another turns out to be good business for both companies because savings and benefits occur both ways. Therefore, even direct competitors can become mutual customers in the inventory recovery arena.

Disposal of recoverable assets does not have to be limited to a sale or a reuse of that asset. A number of avenues exist for disposing of recoverable assets, including but not limited to the following list:

- Sell the inventory.
  - To other companies
  - To after-markets
  - Through informal networks and industry associations
  - To dealers and reclaimers
  - Through auctions (many types and methods of auctions are available)
  - By bartering or trading (trading usable assets between companies)
  - By brokering the inventory (contracting an agent to sell it for you)
  - Through consignment (allowing someone else to sell it for you)
- Use or reuse the inventory.
  - Hold for M&S.
  - Redeploy.
  - Return the inventory to the original manufacturer or producer.
- Donations (giving the asset to a charitable entity and taking the write-off)
- Scrap or dispose of as a waste (be careful to follow all environmental regulations)

The placement and marketing of inventory for an investment recovery group cannot be limited to internal customers and needs to encompass a wide range of potential options. Figure 32–2 provides a flow diagram depicting the decision process associated with the deployment of recovered inventory. In addition, various organizations exist to help or assist with any of the options listed. The Investment Recovery Association is a good place to collect additional information on the available options (see the Web sites listed in the References section at the end of this chapter).

FIGURE 32–2

Decision Sequence to Maximize Recovery

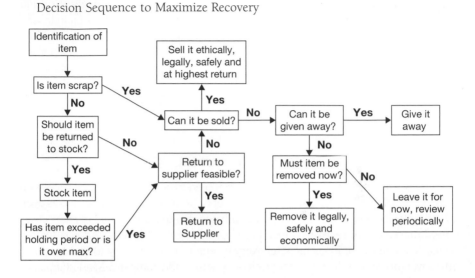

Promotion

Promotion, the third P, is important in investment recovery. Investment recovery groups have to promote their inventory to both internal and external customers. All groups of potential customers need to know what is available. The promotion of these products has to be just as hard to internal customers as to external customers. If engineers, for example, are designing or building a process, they do not necessarily think about pulling inventory from their internal investment recovery warehouse to complete a project. This process is helped in some companies because the investment recovery group is allowed to review a project design prior to implementation. This practice allows investment recovery groups an opportunity to suggest potential money saving alternatives for buying new inventory. Promotion outside the company is equally important. Engineers, designers, contractors, and so forth, have to be aware of what's available before they'll consider using this inventory as an option.

Pricing

Pricing, like the other three P's, is important for the investment recovery group. Pricing is extremely complex for an investment recovery group because both internal and external pricing strategies have to be considered. The investment recovery group has to not only deal with the same issues with pricing that exist in a company's marketing department, but it also has to deal with internal issues. The major external issues include determining the going rate for the equipment, what the competition is doing, the appropriate costs that need to be covered, and what the markup should be.

Determining the internal pricing strategies includes those same issues that other internal departments face. Transfers are typically a source of negotiation and argument between internal departmental managers. The negotiation includes the following arguments: should the transfer price be the going market price, should it just cover variable costs, should it cover all costs, or should it cover at least a portion of the fixed costs in addition to covering the variable costs. These arguments are consistent with transfers of many types of inventory within companies and are also true for investment recovery groups. Unfortunately, this is an age-old debate and one that is not easily resolved.

MARKETING SUMMARY

Often investment recovery professionals are forced to perform marketing tasks with either an extremely limited marketing budget or no budget at all. This makes even the simplest of marketing tasks exponentially tougher to achieve, and in many cases good marketing of recovered inventory does not get achieved. This results in a continual buildup of investment recovery inventory or at the very least disposal of the inventory at less than optimal profit or benefit to the company. Most companies would derive a benefit by specifically allocating a budget for the marketing efforts within their investment recovery group.

On many occasions, professionals in investment recovery groups start with limited marketing experience; these personnel often leave an investment recovery group having gained a vast exposure to marketing through experiential trial by fire. Marketing, in general, is a complex science, and investment recovery operations are not exempt from the necessity of this function. Good marketing training and efforts in the investment recovery arena tend to pay dividends for companies. An entrepreneurial spirit is helpful for employees of a corporate investment recovery group.

LOGISTICAL OBSTACLES FACING INVESTMENT RECOVERY GROUPS

Beyond the task of placing the recovered inventory somewhere, the investment recovery group faces other daily challenges. One of the major challenges is non-uniformity. Not only is the inventory nonuniform in type, but it is also nonuniform in size and shape, which makes the inventory complicated to handle and store.

Investment recovery groups face another obstacle in that stores of recovered inventory exist all over the world. This type of inventory is not conducive for pooling into one location for storage. The first reason for this is that transporting this inventory to one central location would be prohibitively expensive, oftentimes costing many times greater than the value of the inventory itself to transport. The second reason this inventory isn't centralized is that oftentimes countries will not release it for political reasons. This can be an issue even when a use or a customer is identified for the inventory, but the political battle is not worth the red tape if the inventory is just being moved for storage reasons.

Other reasons for not pooling this inventory into central locations include not having enough storage space at one location and encountering heavy duties and taxes on the transfers to and from foreign countries. Regardless of reasons, having this inventory spread out all over the world is a common obstacle. Therefore, because of these logistical considerations, investment recovery groups require an effective communication tool to manage the inventory.

The investment recovery inventory management system should be user-friendly and should include the same master planning, material requirements planning, multi-item management, and distribution requirements planning systems that primary inventory management systems utilize [see Vollmann et al. (1992) for a broader discussion of inventory management systems]. This is necessary so that investment recovery professionals can manage their inventory and communicate inventory availability to both their internal and external customers.

Other obstacles for investment recovery groups occur when the inventory lacks or is missing official paperwork conferring the quality level. One example includes the previously discussed MTRs (mill test reports), but other types of inventory may require some other form of certification and may even involve safety information. For instance, chemicals or materials being recovered may be missing material safety data sheets (MSDS). These are typically provided by original manufacturers, but for recovered materials, these documents may be harder to secure. It is this paperwork, or the equivalent confirmation of quality status, that engineers and designers often need to place equipment or materials into service. Engineers, designers, project managers, and so forth, need these quality inspection reports to avoid liability issues that might occur. At the very least, an equipment inspection may need to be done to confirm the number of years, hours, and so forth, of useful life left in the inventory being considered for use. Recovered materials may need to go through quality control testing to confirm quality status.

Sometimes, the designers or users can inspect the inventory being considered and make a reasonable guess themselves. Inspection, however, can be difficult due to logistical or technical issues. It is often prohibitive to have this inventory inspected or tested, whether it is designers conducting the inspection themselves or the investment recovery group having the inspection done.

Whether considering inventory being located half a world away, or considering inventory of unknown quality levels, or encountering some of the other obstacles previously mentioned, the inherent challenges add up to the same issues. Investment recovery groups need to place the inventory, reduce building inventory levels, and secure value from that inventory. These are the logistical challenges facing investment recovery groups.

BASIS OF MANAGEMENT: VALUING THE INVENTORY

Valuing the recovered inventory is important, and investment recovery groups need to keep track of the value of their inventory. There are several reasons why inventory needs to be valued, but the three most prevalent reasons are (1) investment recovery groups need to be able to price their inventory appropriately, (2) they need to be able to show amounts of savings that are brought to the bottom line, and (3) they need to know which inventory should be tracked, monitored, and managed closely. Valuing this type of inventory, however, is not necessarily done by conventional methods and differs slightly for investment recovery groups.

There are many ways of valuing recovered inventory, but most methods should include an assessment of two factors. The first factor involves an assessment of the criticality. The second factor involves assessment of the financial worth of the part from an accounting value. A short explanation of each factor is offered next. These assessments are relative and should be developed based on individual relevance for each unique company.

The first method of inventory valuation is replacement value. This applies to inventories held to provide quick spare parts to keep a process operating. If this situation applies to particular inventory being held, that inventory needs to be considered for the appropriate level of criticality to the process.

The second method of inventory valuation is measured through the monetary valuation of the inventory. As a point of procedure in managing and controlling the inventory, each piece should have an assessed value. In assessing the value of a recovered inventory item, three components should be considered. They are (1) the original cost of the part (or at least the current replacement cost if purchased on the open market), (2) the price that can be commanded by the inventory item on the open market, or (3) how many useful years of service life does the item have left.

An investment recovery professional can easily become confused by the many accounting conventions that are commonly used by companies for valuing inventory assets. For example, a short list of common methods of valuing inventory follows:

Acquisition cost	Opportunity cost
Actual cost	Out-of-pocket cost
Appraisal method	Replacement cost
Average cost	Retirement method
Avoidable cost	Salvage value, or some value based on any possible depreciable life left on the asset (which includes the annuity method)
Composite depreciation	
Current cost	
Declining and double declining balance	Sinking fund
	Standard cost
Double interest depreciation	Straight-line depreciation
Fully absorbed cost	Sum of the years
Future cost	Sunk cost
Historical cost	Traceable cost
Imputed cost	Variable cost
Incremental cost	

It is easy to see why an investment recovery professional can get confused in attempting to value recovered inventory because sometimes even accountants get confused with so many methods of valuation. Unless otherwise specified by company policy, it is usually better to keep the valuation of recovered inventory simple and to consider the three criteria listed above: understanding the original cost, understanding the amount of useful life remaining on the asset, and the market price available for the inventory.

Finally within investment recovery groups, understanding relevant operational costs is just as important for recovered inventory as it is for salable inventory. Often with recovered inventory, the item purchase cost is not necessarily high, but the holding cost is important. Understanding this cost is important for capturing savings and for motivating the placement of inventory into proper disbursement channels. The costs associated with managing recovered inventory are high because the out-of-pocket expense (direct costs) are high, the costs of managing large amounts of inventory (indirect costs) are high, and the value of the space to store that inventory is costly.

The major components included in the holding cost of recovered inventory includes the cost of capital, costs of taxes and insurance, the cost of the storage space, obsolescence, spare parts, shrinkage, and administrative costs. Storage and physical costs include depreciation or rent, cost of equipment, and environmental and liability costs. Obsolescence includes shelf life, loss of documentation, and the cost of outdated technology. Administrative costs include, in addition to the direct and indirect costs, charges like computer time and cost of disposition. Understanding these costs is important for effectively managing this inventory and to account for costs, savings, and ultimately profitability.

In summary, valuing the recovered inventory is important, and investment recovery groups need to track the value of recovered inventory. Some of the most prevalent reasons why investment recovery groups need to understand the value are that they should be able to price their inventory appropriately whether selling the inventory or bartering it, they need to be able to show amounts of savings, and the value should be understood if even for donation benefit.

SYSTEMS FOR TRACKING INVENTORY ITEMS

Systems for tracking recovered inventory refer to entire management systems. The key components of the system include the following: an organizational structure that facilitates reverse logistics strategies, a policy committing to environmental performance, a planning process supporting the effort, measurable objectives and goals, implementation programs and support tools, training programs, and a measurement and review process. The importance of the management system implementation cannot be overstated; a good system in place is important for complying with the growing environmental pressures and considerations of today's economy [see Daugherty et al. (2002) for a more in-depth discussion].

A good management process begins early in the reverse logistics process through a process called life-cycle analysis (LCA). Life-cycle analysis conceptually means that through the planning process, the most cost-effective approach for product management is chosen which achieves the least cost of ownership over the life of a product (Stock 1998). In other words, if a new product is developed and marketed in a cost-effective and profitable fashion, but the product ultimately costs the company more money to retrieve and recover down the road in its life cycle (cutting into its earnings), then the product launch is not healthy for the company. Life-cycle analysis is the planning process that includes estimating and planning for the recovery early in the planning process [see Stock (1998) for a broader discussion].

Many companies have inventory information systems available, but often complications mitigate the usefulness and effectiveness of such systems. For instance, oftentimes, separate inventory systems exist in the same company at separate company locations. This creates a communications barrier within the same company [see Blumberg (1999) for more discussion].

Sometimes inventory management professionals do not fully utilize capabilities of inventory management systems. For instance, many times the ABC analysis capability of a system is "turned off." Regardless of the inventory system being used to track and manage inventory, almost all the systems have an ABC analysis capability. An ABC inventory management system is an industry standard system used for typical salable inventory allowing inventory managers to assign A, B, or C classifications indicating how closely the inventory type needs to be managed or watched. The classification is typically an annual cost volume usage measure calculated by multiplying the unit cost by the annual usage. The A items then will account for about 20 percent of the items, B items will account for about 30 percent of the items, and C items will account for about 50 percent of the items.

If an inventory management feature is turned "on" in companies, many times a variation of the feature can be used. Individualizing the system can be effective for investment recovery groups. In particular to the ABC system, for example, classifying recovered inventory on a cost volume usage measure may not be effective, but classifying the inventory on an item criticality or an item value system could be very effective and should be considered.

In summary, investment recovery systems should be thought of as an active management system. The management system includes clearly establishing policies, strategies, goals, objectives, measurements, and reviews (audits). In achieving effective management for recovering investments, the planning must encompass the recovery up front and early in the process. Life-cycle analysis is proving to be one effective method of accomplishing this mission. Disjointed management systems should be linked, but even with disjointed information systems, certain capabilities can still be utilized though some reconfiguration may be required.

CONCLUSION

The management of investment recovery inventory is complex. It begins with carefully identifying established management systems and commitment. It includes understanding the inherent obstacles seen in this industry. Management of this inventory must also include understanding and capturing not just the costs of this type of inventory but also the value of this inventory. Identifying the criticality of this inventory is important. In all cases, marketing this inventory and getting it placed is instrumental to driving costs down and achieving profitability within the investment recovery group in an organization. The reasons for recovering inventory through reverse logistics programs are compelling including the continued growth of legal and social demands for maintaining such programs. Investment recovery groups need to utilize information systems capabilities to achieve profitability. Even when faced with mounting environmental considerations, in the end, it will be the investment recovery programs that show profitability support to the company line that will be the surviving model over those programs that are seen only as an expense to the bottom line.

REFERENCES

Blumberg, D. R. (1999). "Strategic Examination of Reverse Logistics and Repair Service Requirements, Needs, Market Size, and Opportunities," *Journal of Business Logistics,* vol. 20, no. 2, pp. 141–159.

Daugherty, P. J., M. B. Myers, and R. G. Richey (2002). "Information Support for Reverse Logistics: The Influence of Relationship Commitment," *Journal of Business Logistics,* vol. 23, no. 1, pp. 85–106.

Minahan, T. (1998). "Manufacturers Take Aim at End of the Supply Chain," *Purchasing,* vol. 124, no. 6, pp. 111–112.

Stock, J. R. (1998). *Development and Implementation of Reverse Logistics Programs.* Oak Brook, IL: Council of Logistics Management.

Vollmann, T .E., W. L. Berry, and D. C. Whybark (1992). *Manufacturing Planning and Control Systems.* Homewood, IL: Irwin, Inc.

USEFUL WEB SITES

Council of Supply Chain Management Professionals (formerly the Council of Logistics Management): www.cscmp.org

Environmental Protection Agency (EPA): www.epa.gov

Investment Recovery Association: www.invrecovery.org

Occupational Health and Safety Administration (OSHA): www.osha.gov

Recycler's World: www.recycle.net

CHAPTER 33

SUPPLIER PERFORMANCE EVALUATION

MARY LU HARDING, C.P.M., CPIM, CIRM
Harding & Associates

MICHAEL HARDING, C.P.M., CPIM
Harding & Associates

INTRODUCTION

Measurements drive behavior. Supplier measurements define the criteria for acceptable performance, monitor performance over time, and lead both parties to take action based on the data. The *only* purpose for collecting data is to act on what it says; the evaluation process should include actions to be taken when performance is unacceptable, acceptable, or superior. Data assists supply managers in assessing supplier performance objectively.

The real work of supply management is determining what the organization values and defining the parameters of the measurement system. When properly defined, the measurement system assists in creating a supply base that best serves the business needs of the organization. First, supply management must define what it wants for specific results. For example, if price is the most important measure, low price is what the organization will get. Delivery, quality, low inventories, and profitability will be secondary.

Supplier performance is inextricably linked to supply management's performance. As supply management is evaluated, so will it measure suppliers. Both aspects of these measurements will be discussed in this chapter.

TRADITIONAL MEASUREMENTS

Commonly, organizations (both practitioners and software providers) rely on the time-honored measures of price, delivery, and quality. Although traditional methods of calculating these measurements have some inherent problems, they will be reviewed first, and then alternative measurements will be discussed.

Price

How do you know when you have achieved the best price? Several thorny issues can arise when determining an appropriate measure of price. One involves the use of standard cost accounting. In organizations that use a standard cost system (primarily manufacturing), an internal standard cost is established for each item before the beginning of a fiscal year and stays in place for that year. Differences between internally established standard costs and actual prices paid are tracked as variances. A standard cost system establishes a consistent valuation for inventory and helps determine the cost content of end products. However, standard cost systems become counterproductive when purchase price variance is used as a measure of a supply manager's or a supplier's effectiveness.

Typically, supply management establishes standard costs since they are in the best position to predict future prices. When variance to those standards is also the measure of supply management performance, political games often result. How is success defined? If a favorable variance is defined as success, there is an incentive for supply management to set high standards. Then actual prices less than standard cost can be achieved easily, and supply management will be "successful." If any variance is bad, and achieving the standard defines success, then hitting that number at any cost will be the resulting behavior—even if it means walking away from a cost savings opportunity or exerting destructive pressure on suppliers.

Using standard cost as a measure of a supply manager's or a supplier's performance doesn't work very well even in the most enlightened environments. Commodities can experience market moves in price which may not be predictable a year in advance. If actual prices go up, supply management and the supply base look like they are performing badly when that may not be the case. If prices go down, they look like heroes although they've done nothing to earn it. In neither case was the price change due to any creative efforts on the part of supply management or the supplier.

Other cost accounting systems measure actual price variances from the last price paid, a budget amount, or an engineering estimate. The belief is that if supply management and suppliers provide prices as expected, the buying organization will have acceptable and predictable costs. A standard or budget cost becomes a stake in the ground from which movement can be measured.

Comparison to a target is a comforting measure of price for those who are not involved in the negotiations. For example, general management and finance are often so distant from price-establishment negotiations that it is difficult for them to tell how well the job was done. Was the result the best that could be obtained? The more removed one is from an actual negotiation, the harder it is to know. Comparing the result to a target is one way that these noninvolved people can measure results. The problem arises in establishing the validity of target costs and in the behavior that hitting an artificial number creates. Those doing the actual work know what can be achieved. Focusing on an artificially established number can blind them to what is really desirable (or possible) creating destructive behavior and sub-optimum results.

Other methods of price measurement foster appropriate behavior in both supply management and the supply base better than variance to a standard or a target cost. These include measurement of price trends, cost savings and cost avoidance, contribution to profit, and affordable cost.

Price Trends

A trend measurement is better than a point measurement or performance to a pre-set target because it shows context and history. Rate of change (slope) and degree of variation are readily apparent. Trend measurement also does not foster political games as much as hitting an artificial number.

To measure price trends, plot time on the *x*-axis and price on the *y*-axis. The slope of the curve shows the rate of change of prices. Trends can be plotted for individual items or aggregated prices for a commodity or supplier. To determine goodness, a trend can be compared to industry averages or affordability. An example is shown in Figure 33–1.

Cost Savings

Measurement drives behavior. If you want suppliers and supply managers to get creative to control prices, then measure and reward that activity. One way is to measure cost savings and cost avoidance. If guidelines for documentation and calculation are established appropriately at the beginning, these measurements are less prone to game-playing than variance to standard cost.

F I G U R E   33–1

Price per 1,000, PN 84732-1. From Able Corporation.

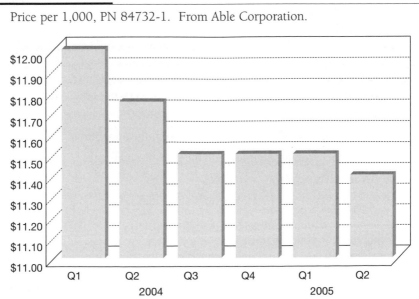

Since standard or target cost is an artificial number, measure cost savings against prior *actual* cost. Request that the following data be captured and reported with each cost savings claimed:

1. Prior price: contract or PO number, date, quantity, unit price

2. New price: contract or PO number, date, quantity, and unit price

3. Total cost savings (unit price difference × quantity over which it applies)

4. Short description of what was done to achieve the savings

This information allows a savings to be audited, which is very important for internal credibility. It also demonstrates that the savings has substance. A comparison of quantities shows that it was not simply due to reaching the next volume price break. A description of what was done to generate the savings provides information to credit creative effort and good ideas. These good ideas may be transferable to other supply managers and commodities, and they provide a basis for rewarding talented supply managers and suppliers. (*Caution:* Be careful not to give a supplier's good ideas to their competitors or ethics problems as well as supplier disenchantment will result.)

Credit supply management and suppliers for the extended dollar amount saved. If the savings is for one purchase order, extended savings is the unit price difference multiplied by the quantity on that purchase order. If a price change is permanent, credit the difference in price times the average annual quantity used. After a year's credit, the new price becomes the norm, or the savings can be extended for additional years if conditions warrant. Accumulate total savings by supplier, supply manager, and as a grand total so that it can be publicized internally to generate recognition for supply management and for good suppliers.

Cost Avoidance

Cost avoidance is remission of legitimate charges that supply management negotiates away and a supplier agrees to waive. Examples include penalty charges, setup charges, and supplier absorption of cost increases. Since there is no record of a prior charge paid, documentation of the prior condition is very important. Request that the following data be captured and reported for each cost avoidance claimed:

1. Documentation of the initial charges from the supplier

2. Documentation of the final settlement of those charges

3. Total dollar savings

4. Description of what was done to achieve the savings

Appropriate documentation allows for an audit to ensure that facetious data is not being used. If your organization is wary of cost avoidance or has had a history of abuse, keep cost savings and cost avoidance data separate until credibility is reestablished. Measuring and crediting cost savings and cost avoidance sends a message to supply managers and suppliers that cost issues matter and individual efforts are recognized and rewarded. Documentation of what was done to achieve the savings provides the basis for training supply management staff in what is possible. Joint efforts to control costs between supply management and suppliers can result in a deeper level of relationship.

Contribution to Profit

An objective of business in the private sector is to produce a profit. Regardless of its other objectives, if it does not produce a profit, it will not continue to exist for long. Top management is typically measured and rewarded based on the company's profit performance while others are measured and rewarded based on cost control. Top management has the better deal. They have latitude to make decisions that improve profitability. A very important measure of supply management's cost-effectiveness is contribution to profit. When supply management measures and reports contribution to profit, top management is better able to understand the value they contribute to the company.

To determine contribution to profit:

1. Obtain a costed bill of material (or bill of labor for services) for your end product or service. This shows its purchased cost content.

2. As supply management reduces the cost of any component in this bill of material or services, its total cost content will be lowered.

3. As prices increase for other components, its total cost content will increase.

4. The *net change* in total cost content becomes supply management's contribution to the profitability of that product or service.

Using total cost content as a measure of effective price control gives supply management needed flexibility to look for genuine opportunity and not get sidetracked working areas with little or no opportunity. Suppliers can be measured on genuine level of performance rather than against an artificial target. For example, a good supplier may negotiate a price increase based on legitimate increases in costs beyond what they can absorb. If they work together with you to keep the increase to a minimum and cut costs where possible, they can get some degree of credit for cost containment and level of effort even if the price increases somewhat. Another commodity may have more opportunity for cost reduction. Supply management is measured on the sum total of all material costs, which is a more balanced measure.

Delivery

On-time delivery is a major concern for everyone in the buying organization, and supply management can spend an ever-increasing amount of time expediting. Measuring true delivery performance may not be a simple process. In many organizations using computer-generated data, delivery performance compares the due date on a purchase order to the receipt date recorded at receiving.

Data integrity can be an issue. Keeping due dates current is a primary responsibility of supply management. For example, an expedited shipment delivered (as requested) before its original due date will be recorded as early (and possibly refused or returned) if the original due date was not changed in the supply manager's system. The supplier will be penalized in their delivery performance for acting as requested.

If due dates are not well maintained, delivery performance measurements rapidly lose credibility with suppliers, and if inaccurate data is used against them, it can cause relationship damage. (Also monitor receiving for data integrity. A backlog on the docks can create inaccurately recorded delivery dates.)

What is the appropriate reference date against which a delivery should be measured? Some use a supplier's promised delivery date, while others use the requestor's need date. Using a supplier's promise date increases the likelihood that the shipment will be on time (increasing delivery predictability), but the buying organization's needs may not be served. Need dates may change and/or be a stretch, but using them is a more accurate reflection of a supplier's flexibility in meeting actual customer demands.

What window of time is appropriate for your organization to define as *on-time*? Organizations that have many deliveries and tightly scheduled unloading docks may define on-time as a 30-minute window during which a supplier's truck is scheduled to unload. Other examples include the due date only, the due date plus or minus one day, up to five days early but no days late, or within the week.

Once delivery expectations are defined and an on-time window identified, delivery performance is calculated as an attribute measurement. Each delivery is compared to its on-time window. Either it was delivered within that window, or it was not. All deliveries are measured, and delivery performance is calculated as

$$\text{Delivery performance} = \left[\frac{\text{Deliveries on time}}{\text{Total number of deliveries}} \right] \times 100 = \% \text{ On-time}$$

Another consideration in maintaining valid delivery performance measurements is point of title transfer. For shipments sent FOB Origin, the supplier legally "delivered" the goods when they loaded them onto a carrier at their facility. If there were delays in transit, the buying organization owns both the goods and the problem. Since suppliers are measured by dock receipt date, they have a right to challenge legitimacy of your data. Manual correction can be time consuming. Deliveries shipped FOB Destination do not have this problem since delivery measurement and transfer of ownership are at the same point.

Quality

Most organizations track the quality of incoming material, recording the following: supplier, purchase order number, item, and lot number of the incoming item and whether it passed or failed inspection. They total the number of lots rejected from each supplier and compare it to the total number of lots received, yielding a percentage often called a *reject rate*. They may also notify the supply manager when there is a quality problem. A history is developed which accumulates problem information by supplier, by part number, and by specification revision.

Incoming inspection results do not provide a complete picture of a supplier's quality performance. Latent defects, line fallout, or random failures may not be apparent until the product is well into the usage process or even in the hands of the final customer.

Capture data as far into the life of the item as possible, and make certain that suppliers understand the scope of the data collection involved in reporting their quality performance. If the only information available is from incoming inspection or an initial user, understand that only a portion of the errors will be detected and reported.

Some software systems, such as more advanced versions of Manufacturing Resource Planning (MRP II) or Enterprise Resource Planning (ERP), can accumulate and report errors throughout the process and provide the results to supply management and quality. If it is used in the supplier evaluation process, data from these sources must distinguish supplier-assignable errors from internal errors. Rules for determining responsibility for the error must be clear in order to maintain the integrity of the process and the perception that responsibility is fairly assigned.

Correlation of data between a supplier's quality system and that of the supply manager is a major issue in establishing a valid quality measurement process. Are both organizations measuring the same thing? Are they using the same measurement methods? Ensuring that the two quality systems are compatible and capable of yielding the same results is fundamental to the credibility of a quality rating system and its results. Additional information on quality management is contained in Chapter 27.

Combining the Data

A single numeric score by which each supplier can be compared against others is useful. A cutoff score can be determined as a threshold of performance at which a supply manager starts to ask if a supplier requires assistance or should be deleted from the qualified supplier list.

Supply management must define acceptable performance by category. For example,

1. Ninety percent of invoices must not exceed standard or target cost.

2. Ninety-five percent of lots received must pass incoming inspection without objection.

3. Eighty-five percent of lots received must be on time.

4. An accumulated score of 90 percent (90 + 95 + 85 = 270/3) is acceptable performance.

Supply management may also add subjective input to the process including:

- Causes of poor performance (adding sanity to the numbers), that is, unclear specifications, commodity price changes, and so forth.

- Maintaining balance. It may not benefit the buying organization to have a supplier who is 100 percent in price and delivery and only 70 percent in quality.

- Allowing time to meet with poor-performing suppliers to determine causes and correction strategies.

- Making certain that a critically important but poor-performing supplier is not automatically dropped.

This combination of data and cut score provides a basis for discussion with current and potential suppliers about expected versus actual performance. Performance can be monitored, definitions can be negotiated, and issues can arise that promote healthy discussions between buyers and suppliers. The cut score should be reviewed periodically to ensure that it reflects the buying organization's needs as driven by its market, desired margin, customer, and quality requirements.

THE QUESTIONING

Are price, delivery, and quality alone the right measures of supplier performance? They are desired results, but will the traditional measures produce those results? That is,

- Is price performance against a preset standard, budget, or estimate a sign of goodness? Is a standard cost established nine months ago relevant today?

- If a critical item is needed in one week, but a supplier promises and delivers in four weeks, did the supplier deliver on time?

- If random and latent errors are only found by the process or customer, is incoming inspection the proper place to measure supplier quality performance?

- Even if price, delivery, and quality goals are met, will the buying organization meet its profitability goals?

Predictable supplier performance may no longer be sufficient. Better measures include

1. Affordable prices in a changing market
2. Delivery of goods and services when needed
3. Quality tracked through the process and evaluated by the end customer

Affordable Prices

Suppliers' (and supply management's) ability to meet the cost needs of the organization should be the measure of their success. Redesign, cost reduction, process improvements, material substitutions, and the acceptability of quoted prices can all be measured against what is affordable. Affordability is determined as follows:

1. Sales determines the market selling price of the final product that will yield the desired market position and sales volume. For example, a company must price its product at $75 to achieve its goals.

2. This information is given to finance to break down into its component costs, for example, material cost $30, labor $10, overhead absorption $15, and profit $20.

3. A costed bill of material and labor is reviewed by engineering to ensure its accuracy.

4. The accurate bill of material with a total affordable price of $30 is given to supply management. If it can buy all components on the bill for $30, the desired margin and price position can be achieved. If it can buy the materials for $28, it has contributed an added $2 per finished unit to profit. Individual prices for components are irrelevant; only the total matters. To contribute to profit, supply management needs to know what is an affordable cost. Refer to Figure 33–2 for an example.

FIGURE 33–2

Affordable Prices. Once an affordable price has been established, supply management and the supplier begin to reduce cost/price on a business need. Their progress can be reported in this chart. Once a price goes below the 100 mark, supply management and the supplier begin to contribute to the profit of the buying company.

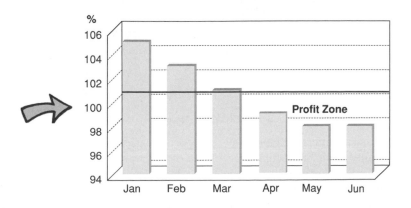

Delivery When Needed

Delivery should not be driven by a supplier's comfortable lead times. Suppliers' response time to customers must conform to a customer's requirements, not the other way around. Delivery to quoted lead times is not acceptable performance if those dates do not meet a customer's needs. Traditionally, buying organizations have compensated for long supply lead times by increasing inventories. The cost associated with this practice may no longer be affordable. If an organization must respond to its customer in 10 days, suppliers have less than 10 days to deliver the required materials. Only "need" dates have any meaning. Refer to Figure 33–3 for an example.

FIGURE   33–3

Supplier Delivery Performance. The only two dates that matter are the *need* and *delivered* dates. Where the two match, there is acceptable delivery. Data may be displayed by major part number or by averaging all part number deliveries on a periodic basis or by dollars of goods purchased. Be aware that averaging can hide performance problems. Need may also be expressed in terms of hours.

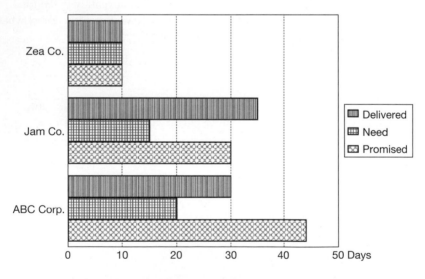

Tracking Quality

Supplier quality must be judged by total performance throughout product life. Good quality results in customer acceptance of the product with minimum investment by the producer to ensure that quality. It does a buying organization little good if the purchased materials pass incoming inspection and latent defects appear in the product in the customers' hands. Create a process that tracks supplier-assignable defects throughout the usage process and reports that information to supply management so corrective action can be taken with suppliers.

Data from these measures may be analyzed by item number (especially for large-dollar items), by supplier (listing all part numbers provided by a supplier), or by supply manager and supplier. An example is shown in Figure 33–4.

FIGURE 33–4

Supplier Assignable Errors

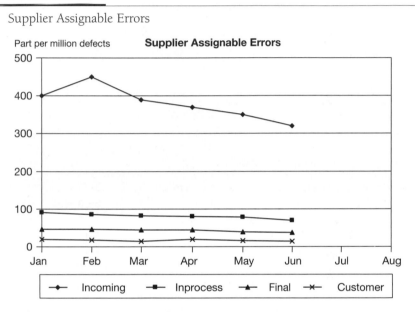

This information gives supply management the required tools to migrate suppliers to a point where they not only meet their customers' needs but contribute to their customers' profitability. Once these needs are met, customers can begin to reduce their investment in hedge inventories and quality overhead.

A BETTER PLACE

There is a point beyond the common measurements that embraces the intent behind the measures. If suppliers perform to our real needs, our operating costs improve, which also contributes to profit.

Cost of Inventory

Consistent delivery when needed creates a financial benefit just as failure to meet delivery requirements creates a cost. A large portion of that cost is in inventory. The longer a supplier's lead time and the greater the uncertainty of delivery, the more inventory a customer will carry as insurance. Generally accepted accounting practice (GAAP) values inventory as an asset. However, it can also be a liability to cash flow if it exceeds an affordable level. Most organizations use a cost to carry inventory that is relatively low (about 20 percent per year) based on the cost of money (interest rates) plus taxes, insurance, space, and obsolescence. However, if one included *all* overhead costs, the true cost to carry inventory would be much higher.

The Cost of Carrying Inventory

Recognized Costs	Approximate % per Year
Interest rate of money	5–10%
Taxes (vary from state to state)	2–5
Insurance	2–3
Space (occupancy, and utilities)	5
Obsolescence reserve	7–20
Total	20–30%
Unrecognized Costs	
Personnel (warehousers, inventory controllers, etc.)	10–15%
Capital equipment (fork lifts, racks, etc.)	5–10
Computation costs (hardware + transactions)	3
Secondary quality costs (reinspection)	5–10
Rework, handling damage, additional loss	5–10
Total	50–75%

Source: Michael Harding and Mary Lu Harding, *Purchasing*, 2nd ed., Barron's Educational Series, Hauppauge, New York, 2001, p. 198.

A more comprehensive view of the cost to carry inventory has led organizations to question their dependence on it. It is possible to factor the cost of inventory into purchase decisions. For example, Acme Drill Company carries one week of inventory per week of supplier lead time for steel. It has three steel suppliers and calculates inventory carrying costs at 75 percent. Usage is 5,000 pounds per year, and Acme's standard cost is $12.50. Supply management requested quotes for a new high-speed steel rod size and received the following:

Supplier	Price	Lead Time (weeks)
Able Corp.	$12.25	10
Baker Co.	$12.65	7
Charlie Inc.	$13.10	2

If purchase price variance is a heavily weighted measure, supply management may be inclined to buy from Able Corp. to stay below standard cost and create a favorable variance (knowing full well that increased inventory will be a result), but if price is adjusted for the cost of inventory, the results change:

$$\text{Carrying cost per week} = \frac{75\% \text{ per year cost to carry}}{50 \text{ weeks per year}} = 1.5\% \text{ per week}$$

Therefore,

Time factor = Quoted price $\times$ 1.5% per week cost to carry $\times$ Weeks of lead time

Supplier	Price × Time Factor	Adjusted Price
Able Corp.	$12.25 + $12.25(0.015 × 10)	$14.09
Baker Co.	$12.65 + $12.65(0.015 × 7)	$13.98
Charlie Inc.	$13.10 + $13.10(0.015 × 2)	$13.46

When total cost (including inventory) is used to make the decision, suppliers quickly understand that they must compete on lead time as well as price.

Cost of Quality

Since the 1980s, an ever-increasing number of companies calculate the cost of quality [also called the price of nonconformance (PONC)]. More advanced companies seek the root causes of quality problems at all stages of their business and know their associated costs. [Activity-based costing (ABC) has been helpful in this effort.] When the cost of supplier-assignable errors is understood, these costs can be added back to the quoted price to determine cost of quality (purchase price plus average cost of quality from a given supplier). *Note:* While this discussion is based on manufacturing situations, service industries also have costs of quality, such as inspection and (if the service is not performed correctly) rework. Cost of quality includes the internal costs listed in the following table.

Incoming	In-Process	At Customers
Inspection	Scrap	Repairs
Sorting	Rework	Premature failures
Added inventory	Poor yields	Warranty work
Added handling	Nonfunctional tests	Lost reputation
Added space	Longer lead times	Lost sales
Administrative costs		Delayed revenue

The greater the value added to the product, the higher the cost of quality.

The average cost of quality in American industry ranges from 7 to 11 percent of the cost of sales. Suppliers who increase these costs must be made aware of the quality (and cost) problem associated with their products. Conversely, a supplier whose products are uniform and predictable and who lowers the buyer's cost of quality is contributing to lower costs and higher profits. For example, a purchased part is found defective at final inspection. The associated costs to that point are

Cost if the Part Is Scrapped

Purchase price	$2.00
Incoming inspection	0.04
Value-added labor	3.25
Final inspection	0.06
Discard cost (if part is scrapped)	$5.35

Cost if the Part Is Repaired

Purchased price	$2.00
Incoming inspection	0.04
Value-added labor	3.25
Final inspection	0.06
Rework cost	1.00
Cost to make a bad item good	$6.35

The cost for that component ranges from $5.35 to $6.35 instead of its $2.00 purchase price.

Measuring Total Cost Impact

Combine price, delivery, and quality into a single measure of contribution to profit (expressed in dollars). For example, a supply manager buys 1,000 widgets at $5.00 each. The affordable price is $4.75, but $5.00 was the best the supply manager could obtain. Delivery is promised in eight weeks, but the widgets are needed in three weeks. (*Note:* See the discussion on lead time later in this chapter for information on how to cost delivery time.) Twenty-seven widgets are found defective at final inspection, and three defects find their way to the end customer. The total cost impact is as follows:

Profit or (loss) on the buy	=	($0.25)	×	1,000	=	($250.00)
Late delivery [5 wk × 1.5%]	=	$0.375/unit	×	1,000	=	(375.00)
Cost of finding 27 defects	=	$8.00/unit	×	27	=	(216.00)
Cost of customer's repairs	=	$26.00/unit	×	3	=	(78.00)
Gain or (loss) of profit	=					($919.00)

A total loss of $919.00 on the purchase of 1,000 widgets equals a loss of $0.919 each. So the total cost was $5.92 each. Conversely, when suppliers meet an organization's need for affordable pricing, delivery, and quality or beat current performance goals, they are measurably contributing to the organization's profit.

Measurements drive behavior. Measuring both supply management and suppliers on all cost factors and contribution to profit frees supply managers to make *business* decisions rather than price decisions, and the buying organization will reduce its costs.

PUTTING IT ALL TOGETHER

In addition to price, delivery, and quality, there are many other attributes of supplier performance that organizations measure. *Anything* that adds to the total cost of the item or service can be a part of the performance measurements, including policy issues that the buying organization values in its suppliers. Since the array of issues spans a diverse spectrum, it is useful to have a common denominator so that a bottom-line result can be calculated and used to compare a supplier's performance both to its own past performance and to other suppliers. Money is a good common denominator. When all issues are translated into their dollar impact, the sum of all measurements represents the supplier's total cost to the organization.

Issues generally fall into three categories: cost, performance, and policy. Cost issues include price plus any other ancillary costs that the supply manager will ultimately pay such as transportation costs and setup charges. Performance issues include delivery, quality, lead time, inventory, and any other measure of performance the buying organization chooses to include, such as responsiveness or flexibility. Policy issues include those attributes that a buying organization values in suppliers and wishes to foster or reward such as disadvantaged business status, recycled content in the product, or socially responsible practices of any kind.

Calculating Total Cost

Total cost is the sum of all cost, performance, and policy factors the buying organization wishes to measure. Since purchase decisions are often made on the basis of unit price, a good measure of total cost is to calculate it per unit also. *Unit total cost* is the purchase price amended by the addition of all other factors (translated into their per-unit monetary impact).

Cost issues are the easiest to include since they are already stated in monetary terms. Simply convert any ancillary charge into its per-unit impact. To do that, divide each charge by the number of units over which it applies. A *unit* is the unit of measure in which the price is quoted (each, roll, dozen, etc.). For example, if transportation charges are $14.95, and there are 100 units in the shipment, then the per-unit transportation cost is $0.15 each ($14.95/100).

The financial impact of performance issues can be determined exactly or approximated. Organizations that use activity-based cost systems may have calculated the cost of dealing with non-quality, supplier lead time, or non-delivery. If exact figures are available, use them. If they are not available, approximations will suffice.

Performance evaluations are primarily used for comparison purposes: comparing a supplier's performance to its previous history to measure improvement or comparing suppliers to each other to make sourcing decisions. When the purpose is comparative, approximations derived from the same formula can provide valid results.

Estimates are acceptable as long as they are *relatively* valid. A formula for approximating performance can be considered valid as long as

- It makes sense; that is, it is relevant to the issue the organization wants to measure and can be calculated without undue difficulty.

- It can be applied across suppliers and used to validly differentiate performance.

Cost of Non-Delivery

If a supplier delivers early, you will pay for the items sooner and carry the inventory longer. If a supplier delivers late, peoples' time is consumed to replan the work schedule and/or expedite delivery. If lateness is chronic, you may carry safety stock and/or alter the production schedule. All of these cost money. Calculating actual dollars expended can be time consuming and may vary with each situation.

A simple method for incorporating the cost of non-delivery into total cost calculations is to use the *non*-delivery performance percentage as a price adder. For example, if Able Corp. delivers on time 85 percent of the time, then it is not on time 15 percent of the time. Multiply Able's quoted price by 15 percent and add that amount to the base price as the cost factor for its non-delivery performance. The better its delivery performance, the lower the cost adder it bears. Since each supplier bears the cost of its own non-performance, it is a fair way to differentiate between suppliers.

On-Time Delivery Calculations Example

Factor	Able Corp.	Baker Co.	Charlie Inc.
Quoted price	$10.00	$11.50	$12.00
On-time delivery	+$1.50	+$1.27	+$0
1 – % on time	(85% on time)	(89% on time)	(100% on time)

Cost of Non-Quality

The actual costs of non-quality include the overhead costs of incoming inspection, a reject materials stockroom, the administrative expense of a materials review board, and the cost of the materials return process. They also include rework expenses and quality fallout from your production processes due to defective or marginal incoming materials. For services, non-quality costs will include the costs of supervision, negotiating with a supplier for correction, and the cost of correction or doing a job over. An organization that uses activity-based costing may have allocated the costs of quality into a separate cost pool. If so, that provides a good base for allocating quality costs to suppliers in proportion to the consumption of those resources that they use.

If actual costs are not available, a measure of percent defective components, percent reject shipments, or percent service performance failures or corrections can be used as a price adder in the same manner as a non-delivery percentage. For example, if 8 percent of Baker Company's shipments are rejected, then Baker's price is multiplied by 8 percent, and that amount is added to the base price to compensate for your costs of handling non-quality shipments. The higher the supplier's quality, the lower the cost factor it bears. Since each supplier bears the costs of its own non-performance, this is a fair relative measure of quality.

Quality Calculations Example

Factor	Able Corp.	Baker Co.	Charlie Inc.
Quoted price	$10.00	$11.50	$12.00
Quality	+$1.30	+$0.92	+$0
% Rejected	(13% rejects)	(8% rejects)	(No rejects)

Cost of Lead Time

Lead time is a performance factor. Items or services with a lead time of 4 weeks will be managed differently than those with 12 weeks. Items with a long lead time limit the flexibility you have to change your schedule to accommodate changes in business. They may also be a major driver of safety stock inventory. Since measurements drive behavior, measuring lead time as a cost factor also sends a message to the supply base that lead time matters and less is better.

To create a formula for the cost of lead time, start with the cost of carrying inventory stated as percent per year. Divide it by 52 to obtain the percent per week.

Determine if that formula is strong enough to send the appropriate message to suppliers about how much you value lead-time reduction. If it does not carry the weight you deem appropriate, increase the percent per week until its appropriate. Formulas of 1 to 2 percent per week are typical. Once an appropriate percentage has been determined, multiply it by the supplier's quoted lead time (in weeks). This becomes the multiplier for unit price:

$$\text{Cost factor for lead time} = \text{Inventory carry cost as \% per week} \times \text{Lead time in weeks} \times \text{Unit price}$$

Lead-Time Calculations Example

Factor	Able Corp.	Baker Co.	Charlie Inc.
Quoted price	$10.00	$11.50	$12.00
Lead time	+1.00	+1.04	+0.84
1%/wk	(10 weeks)	(9 weeks)	(7 weeks)

Subjective Performance Measures

Subjective performance characteristics (such as responsiveness or flexibility) matter and can be measured if you are willing to find a way to quantify them. To do that, first define what you mean by the term. For example, define *responsiveness*. There may be two aspects: (1) a responsive attitude, in which the supplier is open and willing to listen to your requests, and (2) responsive actions in which the supplier either did or did not do what you requested.

Secondly, devise a method to track performance. How many requests for flexibility were made? To how many of those did the supplier respond appropriately?

Any performance measure must eventually be defined and tracked in order to be useful. If there is no agreement on definition or no desire to track performance, the characteristic cannot be measured, and using it in a supplier evaluation while definitions are mushy is opening the door for disagreement and potential chaos.

Any performance measurement can be calculated as a percentage: how many total occurrences were there, and in how many of those did the supplier respond well?

Percentages can be applied as price adders by calculating that percentage of the quoted price and adding it into the total. Remember to use the non-performance percentage as the price adder.

Including Policy Factors

Policy factors are those issues that an organization wants to foster or reward in its supply base, such as disadvantaged business status, recycled material content, consensual reciprocity, or compliance to social policy standards. Compliance to a policy is usually an attribute measurement: either suppliers comply with the policy standard or they don't. To incorporate any policy factor into supplier measurements, the following steps are necessary:

1. Define the policy factor.
2. Define what constitutes compliance.
3. Define how much the organization values the issue.

To define organization values, ask the policy's sponsors (usually general management), "If all other factors are equal, up to how much more are you willing to pay to incorporate this issue?" The answer establishes a measure of value. It does not mean that the organization will necessarily pay any more; it simply defines a boundary between enough and too much. Once a boundary is defined, it can be used for measurement.

In unit total cost calculations, if a supplier complies with the policy issue, credit its total cost by the amount of the defined limit. This creates a positive incentive for the supplier to comply. For example, an organization values green buying and wishes to foster the use of recycled materials, so it establishes a 5 percent credit for recycled content of a certain level. Suppliers that meet the requirement receive a 5 percent credit in total cost. Suppliers that do not meet the requirement are not penalized, but they receive no credit.

Social Policy Calculations Example

Factor	Able Corp.	Baker Co.	Charlie Inc.
Quoted price	$10.00	$11.50	$12.00
Recycled content?	No	Yes	Yes
Credit (–5%)	–0	–0.58	–0.60

Unit Total Cost

When all measurement factors have been defined and their dollar impact calculated, add the cost factors together with the price to obtain unit total cost. An example is shown in the following table.

Unit Total Cost Calculations Example

	Factor	Able Corp.	Baker Co.	Charlie Inc.
Cost factors	Quoted price	$10.00	$11.50	$12.00
	Shipping ($/Quantity)	+0.09 ($8.98/100)	+0.07 ($700/100)	+0 (Supplier-delivered)
	Discounts (Prompt pay)	–0.20 (2% 10 Net 30)	–0.06 (0.5% 10 Net 30)	–0.12 (1% 10 Net 30)
Performance factors	On-time delivery (1 – % on time)	+1.50 (85% on time)	+1.27 (89% on time)	+0 (100% on time)
	Quality (% Rejects)	+1.30 (13% rejects)	+0.92 (8% rejects)	+0 (No rejects)
	Lead time (1%/wk)	+ 1.00 (10 weeks)	+1.04 (9 weeks)	+0.84 (7 weeks)
Policy factors	Recycled content? (-5%)	+0 (No)	–0.58 (Yes)	–0.60 (Yes)
Unit total cost		$13.69	$14.16	$12.12

In this example, cost factors, performance factors, and policy factors are all evaluated in dollars and can be compared to each other as well as across suppliers. Unit total cost can be used to select suppliers and to measure their changing performance over time.

If a supplier is new and there is no history of performance, request that they provide at least three references (specific name and telephone number) to other organizations who purchase this specific product. Contact them. Ask them what they measure and how (to get an understanding of the validity of their measurements). Then ask them how this supplier has performed over the last year. Although a supplier can provide extraordinary service to customers once in a while, it is very difficult to do that for multiple customers consistently. If the information provided by these references is consistent, it is a reflection of the operating system by which the supplier does business, and you can be reasonably sure that the service you experience will be in the same range.

Using Unit Total Cost

A total measurement plan such as unit total cost accomplishes several business objectives:

1. It allows disparate issues to be combined into a coherent measurement plan.

2. It provides a method by which all groups within an organization can have access to the supplier selection and measurement process, ensuring that their issues are included.

3. It makes clear the basis on which suppliers are selected and retained, educating everyone about how these decisions are made.

4. It gives a supplier clear information about what issues matter and how they are weighted so that suppliers understand what comprises good performance.

Often for the first time, suppliers have specific information about how their performance affects their competitive position, what they can do to compete, and how much it is worth to them to improve performance.

Measuring Service Suppliers

When services are rendered, there can be a host of subjective assessments as to their quality, timeliness, and cost-effectiveness. Quantifying performance can be a challenge. In order to have something against which to measure service performance, it is imperative to document expectations up front. The various forms of services can make measurement more difficult. Some of those difficulties include

- Users may be uncertain of the final product at the time the order is placed.
- User expectations may be unrealistic or unclear.
- Both users and providers make assumptions.
- Personal services may vary based on personalities (i.e., physician, consultant).
- Job definition may change in the middle of the work.
- People within either organization may change during the work.
- The unforeseen may occur.
- Funding may change.

Supply management's job is to assist all parties to define their performance expectations, costing formulas, and acceptance criteria. These should be clearly spelled out and incorporated into either the Statement of Work in the contract or in a separate section of the contract for services. For example, an order for product development services might incorporate the following:

1. What work is to be done? Define the project and its scope.
   Design a new shoe sole that will last three years in average use.

2. Who will do the work? Specify the people and skills.
   Mr. W. B. Anderson and three A-level polymer engineers

3. What is the time frame?
   Work will begin on September 1, 2005, and conclude with a finished
      product on or before May 1, 2007.

4. Progress reporting
   Written progress reports will be submitted by the 28th of each month
      to Vice President K. L. Beep and meetings will be held on the 5th
      of each month to review status. What are acceptance criteria? When
      will both parties know work is finished?
   Blueprints and specifications will document a product that meets the
      three-year criteria. Three samples will be submitted to K. L. Beep.

5. What legal issues need to be covered?
   We will own all patentable features of the new sole, and you will assist
      us to obtain the patents.

6. How are changes approved and documented? Plan for changes in time,
   scope, and costs! Create a process to accommodate and document
   inevitable changes.
   All changes to scope or funding will be submitted to Vice President
      K. L. Beep for approval.

7. How are costs determined?
   Project effort = $200,000
   Hourly rate (hours to be documented) = $40.00/hour
   Machine hours (to be documented) = $90.00/hour
   Materials as invoiced = actual cost
   Overtime is not allowed
   Estimated project cost = $350,000

8. How will payments be made?
   Costs will be itemized and invoiced monthly. The last $50,000 will be
      paid upon successful testing of the sole—no later than June 25, 2007.

Once the criteria are defined, measurements may be recorded as either attribute (yes or no) or variable (numeric) data. It is important to track all major issues:

How Did the Supplier Perform Against These Criteria?

	Yes	No
Was the new sole produced?	X	
Were the specific talents utilized?	X	
Were date commitments met?	X	
Were costs and estimates met?	X	
Were the agreed-to reporting and documentation procedures followed?		X

Regardless of the type of service, up-front agreement on deliverables will provide the criteria against which to measure performance. Issues such as these can be treated as policy issues with established values and credits. Quantitative issues can be treated as performance issues using the nonperformance percentage as the price adder.

CONCLUSION

Measurements drive behavior. A good measurement system will engender the desired behavior in both supply management and suppliers and will lead to the desired business results. To develop a good measurement system:

1. Define desired business results.

2. Define what behavior will generate those results.

3. Construct measurements that will measure that behavior. (Be careful to think through what people will do as a result of a measurement. Misdirected measurements can produce counterproductive behaviors.)

4. Make a measurement as simple as possible, numeric, and preferably translatable into dollar impact.

5. Allow *all* the people in the organization who have a vested interest in suppliers to participate in the measurement establishment process. (Quality, new product development, materials management, production, and purchasing all have issues to measure and want a vote in how suppliers are performing for them. Users want a say in the selection and measurement of service suppliers.)

6. Make measurements clear to suppliers so that they know what is expected of them and how their performance will be measured.

7. Act on the results of the measurements. Use them to drive business decisions.

ITEM AND
INDUSTRY PRACTICE

Many supply management concepts, processes, practices, and techniques are more or less equally applicable across the entire spectrum of products, services, industries, environments, and situations. We have tried to provide a broad variety of such topics in the other sections of this seventh edition of *The Supply Management Handbook*. Some items and industries, because of the nature of their requirements for materials and/or services; the characteristics or requirements associated with the acquisition, use, or distribution of these items; the supply management environment or situation in particular industries; or some combination of these and other factors, contain unique aspects that merit special consideration. As an example of a special supply management situation, supply managers in process industries, such as chemicals, petroleum, and some food products, have found that much of the literature, reference material, and training resources for supply management is directed at manufacturing industries that assemble products from parts or other materials. While this situation has changed somewhat in recent years, there is still relatively little supply management informational material and attention directed at process industries where most purchasing and other supply management activities are directed at capital equipment or services.

To ensure adequate coverage of these types of subjects, this section of *The Supply Management Handbook* includes chapters on supply management practices for particular types of items and industries. In this section, specific chapters are devoted to raw materials and commodities, MRO and other indirect materials and services, software and intellectual property, capital assets, services in general, and construction services. In addition, specific chapters are devoted to the special supply management environments and requirements found in service industries, process and extractive industries, and public administration organizations.

CHAPTER 34

RAW MATERIAL AND COMMODITY SUPPLY MANAGEMENT

H. Ervin Lewis, C.P.M.
President
Lewis and Associates

INTRODUCTION

Raw materials are generally regarded as initial inputs to a manufacturing process. Examples might include steel, synthetic resins, and rubber compounds. Manufacturers that assemble products for sale consider manufactured parts and components as raw materials. Commodities are generally viewed as the natural materials from which manufactured items are produced. Examples include oil, minerals, ores, and agricultural products that are used in the manufacturing process.

The terms *raw materials* and *commodities* are not mutually exclusive. In some cases, original commodities are used in production of goods that then become raw materials for other manufacturers. So, what would be considered a commodity by one firm could be the basic raw material for another. For example, ore is used in the production of steel. Steel is then used by automobile manufacturers as a key raw material. In this case, ore is raw material for the steel producer and steel is raw material for the automobile manufacturer.

Because raw materials are incorporated into the final product, they are referred to as direct materials. Generally, direct materials are purchased differently than indirect materials such as repair and operating supplies used to support a manufacturing process. Note the following key differences in supply management environments between direct and indirect materials or services.

Characteristic	Direct Materials	Indirect Materials and Services
Supplier base	Small, controlled	Larger, somewhat less controlled
Purchase decision	Dependent, automated	Independent, sometimes ad hoc
Ordering process	Relatively simple, autogenerated, no order-by-order approval	More complex requisition, purchase order (PO), order-by-order approval required
Product/price information	Bill of material (BOM), contract pricing	Sourcing, request for quotation (RFQ), individual PO
Involved in process	Supply and primary users	Supply and many users

THE LINK BETWEEN RAW MATERIALS
AND ORGANIZATIONAL SUCCESS

There are three broad areas of activity in which a manufacturing organization's profitability may be influenced. They are the acquisition of goods and services, conversion of those goods and services into a salable product, and marketing of that product. Given that 55 to 60 percent of corporate America's revenues are used to acquire needed goods and services, the greatest leverage for cost takeout lies in optimizing value through the acquisition of goods and services. Further, each dollar of cost takeout by supply management goes directly to net income before taxes. Because raw materials represent a high percentage of an organization's total goods and services expenditure, they also offer the greatest opportunity to reduce that expenditure. Accordingly, sound management of raw materials acquisition generally offers the most significant impact on unit cost of manufactured goods. Manufacturing cost per unit, in turn, impacts market price for finished products, profitability, market share, and ultimate success of the organization.

MULTITIER SUPPLIER MANAGEMENT

Primary suppliers are often called first-tier suppliers. Sources used by first-tier suppliers are called second-tier suppliers, and so on. Consider a first-tier contract for parts made from strategic metals that originate from second-tier sources in South Africa. Given that first-tier supplier performance is dependent on reliable performance of second-tier sources, multitier supplier management may be necessary.

Multitier supplier management may involve more than two tiers. Consider a first-tier contract for preassembled dashboards for automobiles. The preassembler may produce the dash cover and source instruments to be installed from second-tier sources. The instrument manufacturers may, in turn, source parts for those instruments from third-tier sources, and so on.

There are generally two situations when multitier supplier management is used. The first seeks to manage risk and ensure continued supply through multiple tiers, as just described. The second occurs when a number of suppliers to a supply management organization use the same raw material and the aggregated volume is large. In this case, the supply manager may have more leverage than either of the first-tier suppliers and may contract with the second-tier source on behalf of first-tier suppliers. The targets in this case are usually lower pricing, better service, and assurance of supply to the first tier.

A supply management organization should carefully assess risks associated with multitier sourcing. Risk assessment, combined with criticality of the raw material, may demand multitier management.

KEY MACRO-INFLUENCES ON RAW MATERIAL
SUPPLY MANAGEMENT STRATEGY

Both internal and external influences must be factored into raw material purchasing strategies. Key macro-influences include internal operating and marketing strategies. A sales forecast leads to a manufacturing plan, including capital and operating budgets. Supply strategies are then developed to meet the planned needs of manufacturing and other supporting functions. Value-adding support of operating strategies requires close supply management coordination with operations.

Supply management's plans also incorporate market and economic conditions, and other financial influences that lead to specific financial strategies. While they may take many forms, the following purchasing strategies are commonly implemented with financial results in mind.

1. *Deliberate timing of purchases.* A purchase timing strategy is generally based on anticipated changes in the market or economy. As examples, this strategy may seek to take advantage of price trends, or it may seek to avoid paying more than average price by spreading purchases uniformly over a price cycle.

2. *Hedging.* There is risk involved in purchasing commodity raw materials at today's prices to produce products for future delivery. The technique of hedging is premised on a belief that customers will expect future pricing of those products to reflect then-current commodity raw material prices. For example, consider a current purchase of raw wool fleece to produce fabric that will be sold and delivered months from now. If, in the interim, the price of raw wool falls, future product prices will tend to decrease. If raw wool price rises, future product prices will tend to rise. Note the following example of hedging such risk.

Current Actions

A. Buy in the spot market 100,000 pounds of raw wool fleece at $0.36/lb and use the wool to produce fabric for sale.

B. Sell a futures contract for 100,000 pounds of raw wool fleece at $0.36/lb for delivery in 120 days.

120 Days from Now

A. *Scenario 1.* The price of raw wool fleece is up to $0.42/lb. Buy 100,000 pounds of raw wool fleece at $0.42/lb to cover promised delivery under the futures contract. This will result in a $6,000 loss. However, fabric made from the wool will also sell at a higher price, theoretically gaining back the $6,000 and breaking even.

B. *Scenario 2.* The price of raw wool fleece is down to $0.32/lb. Buy 100,000 pounds at $0.32/lb to cover promised delivery under the futures contract. This will result in a $4,000 gain. However, fabric made from the wool will also sell at a lower price, theoretically $4,000 lower, thereby breaking even.

This example depicts a perfect hedge. However, because of the costs of hedging transactions and delays in the impact of raw material price changes on the price of finished goods, a perfect hedge is rare. Still, these costs are usually small compared to potential losses, and hedging is a way to ensure against such risk. It is important to understand that the objective of hedging is not to make money, but to avoid losing money.

3. *Hand-to-mouth purchasing.* A hand-to-mouth strategy seeks to purchase in small quantities to meet immediate need. This is usually in response to anticipated price decreases.

4. *Forward purchasing.* Forward purchasing strategies seek to purchase in excess of immediate need, but not in excess of planned future needs. This strategy is typically implemented in anticipation of price increases. This creates a need to advantageously balance savings on the price of goods with increased cost of inventory.

5. *Speculative purchasing.* Speculative strategies are also implemented in anticipation of price increases. However, purchase quantities are typically in excess of anticipated need with a view toward selling the excess at a profit after prices rise sufficiently. The risk is that any unused or unsold inventory may have to be salvaged at a loss.

The level of criticality of raw materials will also influence supply management strategies. Since price, quality, and availability of raw materials are critical to organizational success, supply management strategies give equally critical consideration to supplier capability and the kind of supplier relationship most likely to optimize final value.

Each of these macrofactors will be broken into many micro-influences for thorough evaluation during market analysis and the supplier analysis phase of a raw material supply plan.

MARKET ANALYSIS

Market analysis seeks to identify factors or conditions that influence availability, quality, and pricing of required materials. Generally, if supply exceeds demand, materials are readily available and prices tend to fall. If demand exceeds supply, the risk of interrupted supply rises and prices tend to rise. Accordingly, market research should seek to understand current world supply and demand and their trends in the short and long term. Further, supply of natural commodities may be limited by natural scarcity, curtailed ability to bring them to market, or actions taken by supplier cartels. Decreased commodity supply will have a similar impact on availability and pricing of raw materials produced from those commodities. So, market analysis should include factors such as

1. *Economic conditions.* As economic activity and demand increase, prices and production levels tend to rise.

2. *Industrial capacity.* This refers to a particular industry's worldwide production capacity, including where the capacity is located and what is required to bring it to market.

3. *Factory utilization.* The rate at which industrial capacity is utilized is measured as factory utilization. Rising factory utilization indicates ris-

ing demand. Increased demand generally leads to higher pricing and potentially to longer lead times.

4. *Market structure.* Market structure includes the number of suppliers, the nature of those sources, where they are located, and the level of competition. To better understand this issue, consider a continuum with perfect competition at one extreme and pure monopoly at the other. All points between the extremes represent varying levels of imperfect competition. Note the following graphic.

Perfect Competition   Imperfect Competition   Pure Monopoly

Perfect competition exists when prices and availability are influenced only by the laws of supply and demand. Pure monopoly exists when a single supplier controls the entire supply of a given commodity or raw material. Since the federal government owns some productive resources and influences many industries through antitrust legislation, the markets in which supply managers operate represent neither perfect competition nor pure monopoly. A practical exception is a supplier's monopoly power when marketing patented or otherwise proprietary products. Generally, supply managers operate in the area represented as imperfect competition, which represents varying combinations of purchaser and supplier position strength. This is commonly referred to as relative position strength. As market structure moves more toward perfect competition, purchaser position strength rises. As market structure moves more toward pure monopoly, supplier position strength rises.

5 *Important relationships between primary products and by-products.* For example, caustic soda is a by-product generated during the production of chlorine. Caustic soda price and availability rises and falls with chlorine output. Accordingly, a supply manager who is researching the caustic market will be interested in chlorine markets and production levels.

Market Analysis Factors Related to Global Sourcing

Until the 1960s, purchasing professionals in the United States were generally less concerned with world events. That was before the oil crises and market share gains by foreign products. Supply managers today recognize the reality of a global market and that market analysis should be performed from a global perspective. Specific analysis factors include the following.

1. *Monetary exchange rates.* Since payment for foreign goods is typically in the supplier country's currency, the final U.S. dollar price of materials depends on the exchange rate at the time of payment. Accordingly, analysis of international markets should include exchange rates, trends, and whether or not the foreign currency purchase should be hedged.

2. *Payment process.* Payment to a foreign supplier will likely include a letter of credit or a bill of exchange. A supply manager's commitment to pay a foreign supplier using these instruments increases the need for precontract assurance of supplier reliability.

3. *Import duties.* An import duty is essentially a tax levied by the government on goods imported into the country. Market analysis should reference the *Harmonized Tariff Schedule of the United States Annotated;* published by the U.S. Office of Tariff Affairs and Trade Agreements to provide applicable tariff rates and statistical categories for goods imported into the United States. This schedule will help determine if duties apply to needed materials and, if so, the type and value of duty. Payment of duty essentially raises the price of imported goods.

4. *International transportation.* Since international transportation is generally more costly and complex than domestic transportation, it deserves more scrutiny. Further, supply managers should understand any requirement for special vehicles or containers and the important characteristics of various ports of exit and entry, such as capacity of on-site materials handling equipment and storage facilities. In some cases, the cost of transportation may approach the cost of materials. That makes logistics an important factor in purchase decisions.

5. *Documentation requirements.* Documentation requirements for imported materials generally include export license, import declaration, certificate of origin, invoice, insurance certificates, and a bill of lading. Some importing firms are able to deal with these complexities in-house. Others use broker services.

6. *Convention for the International Sale of Goods (CISG).* The CISG is a body of law enacted to bring uniformity to rules governing international sales contracts. It was adopted by the United States in 1986. This body of law represents a compromise of the diverse laws and legal philosophies of the United States, Europe, and Latin America and covers the sale of goods between signatory countries. CISG law is different in many ways from the Uniform Commercial Code. Further, it is important to know that the CISG will govern contracts with foreign suppliers in signatory countries, even if a U.S. firm's purchase order is made to a U.S. representative of the foreign supplier and sent to a U.S. address. However, a supply manager can opt out of CISG law and apply the UCC if both parties agree and the choice of law is stated in contract documentation.

7. *Different freight terms.* While free-on-board (FOB) terms still apply to domestic transportation, international shipments are under a different set of transportation rules, the International Commercial Terms (Incoterms). Incoterms were developed by the International Chamber of Commerce and differ in a number of ways from FOB terms to accommodate the

different shipping modes, laws, and traditions that apply to international shipments.

8. *Cultural differences.* Each country has its own culture, developed over long periods by influences such as law, religion, social norms, and level of development. Violation of a cultural norm may be seen as deeply offensive by a foreign supplier, even if unintentional, and it could affect a business relationship. Country-specific information on law, social expectations, currency, and other cultural norms are available from the U.S. Department of Commerce, foreign consulates, and most of the major international accounting firms. However, even with focused preparation, it is unwise to assume a clear understanding of the many subtleties inherent in a foreign culture.

9. *Other issues and risks related to foreign sourcing.* This might include environmental regulations, trade restrictions, and geopolitical issues related to a foreign government. Market analysis should also recognize that international trade agreements come and go, giving rise to other risks associated with international supply. They include increased uncertainty in the market, differing rates of industrial growth or technology break-throughs, and the possibility of political instability. Changes in any of these influences could change a good sourcing decision into a bad one. Accordingly, market analysis should identify, evaluate, and incorporate risk factors as appropriate.

In addition to their influence on contract terms and conditions, the state of markets, supply chain issues, and potential risks identified through market analysis help define purchaser expectations and supplier relationship strategies.

QUALITY

Experienced supply managers recognize that end product quality is directly linked to the quality of input raw materials. Given that the quality of raw material inputs influences production efficiency, conversion costs, and market acceptance of final products, the purchase price may be a small part of the overall cost to acquire and use a raw material. Accordingly, supply managers should focus on the total cost of acquiring and using materials, and that demands close attention to quality. Given the critical importance of raw material quality management, it should begin at the earliest practical stage. Refer to Chapter 27 for additional information on quality management. Key influences on quality of purchased materials include:

Well-developed, concise specifications

Clear communication of quality expectations

Capable suppliers

Metrics that accurately display adherence to quality specifications

Commodities

Physical properties are critically important when purchasing commodities. Among others, physical properties include density, coefficient of thermal expansion, thermal conductivity, and electrical conductivity. Purity and types of impurities have a significant influence on quality, processing efficiency, and yield. Supply management professionals use historical performance data to determine the impact on processing of various types of impurities. They then manage the level and type of impurity through appropriate specifications.

Raw Materials

Mechanical properties are critically important when purchasing materials that have been converted from commodities. Mechanical properties relate to a material's fitness for a particular application and how it reacts under specific conditions. The level and type of impurities are also important when purchasing converted raw materials, but for different reasons. As examples, impurities in raw materials used to make value-added products influence characteristics such as strength, hardness, grain structure, conductivity properties, and yield. Additionally, the level and type of impurity will impact the relative ease of working a material (machining, shaping, cutting, finishing). Because raw material quality has such a critical impact on organizational success, leading-edge firms manage it through formal quality management processes, such as total quality management (TQM), quality function deployment (QFD), and a Cpk metric, which is a statistical measure of a supplier's process capability.

DEVELOPING A RAW MATERIALS SUPPLY PLAN

Develop Supply Management Needs and Expectations

It is best to clearly understand the supply management firm's needs and expectations relative to raw materials before seeking information on the capability of potential suppliers.

There are generally three dimensions for consideration.

1. *Expectations relative to the acquisition process.* This involves a plan to streamline the raw material acquisition process. General objectives are to eliminate non-value-adding activity, automate the process to the fullest practical extent, and seek to include value-adding concepts. For example, one process industry firm uses a critical chemical in large quantities. The firm keeps two days of inventory in two large storage tanks and receives more through a daily inflow of tank cars. The net result is that the majority of inventory of this chemical is always in tank cars, in transit to the supply manager's firm.

2. *Expectations relative to purchased materials.* Expectations relative to purchased materials are generally managed through quality and perform-ance specifications, such as a parts-per-million metric for defects, a Cpk specification, or specific yield requirements.

3. *Expectations relative to supplier performance.* These expectations typi-cally involve the supplier's attitude toward customer service and assis-tance. Considerations might include rapid response to purchaser needs, assistance with inventory, joint continuous process improvement, will-ingness to offer its expertise in a highly collaborative environment, and dedication to mutually beneficial results.

A supply manager's documented needs and expectations will greatly influence supplier selection criteria and supplier relationship strategy.

Develop a Supplier Relationship Strategy

After defining expectations, supply managers should direct attention to how those expectations will be met. One part of that process is to identify the kind of supplier relationship most likely to facilitate achieving key objectives. So, the supplier rela-tionship is an integral part of procurement strategy. It should be planned and implemented with specific goals in mind. Since raw materials have a direct and sig-nificant impact on organizational success, raw material supplier relationships are generally high level. Examples might include a certified supplier relationship or a supplier alliance. For more critical applications or where there is potential for other mutual benefit, a strategic supplier alliance might be in order.

Establish a Supplier Performance Road Map

A supplier performance road map begins with a carefully developed set of supply management expectations in all areas of supply management interest, including a supplier relationship strategy. The supplier is then advised of the supply manager's expectations early in the process, as opposed to allowing the supply manager's expec-tations to be shaped by supplier capabilities. The resulting supply strategy should clearly establish the supplier's performance plan; the roadmap. While supplier capa-bility must ultimately be factored in, addressing supply management expectations first facilitates increased supply management influence over supplier contribution.

Identify and Evaluate Potential Suppliers

Domestic raw material or commodity supply sources may be identified by use of the Internet, various industrial directories such as the Thomas Register, trade shows, past experience, or through input from other knowledgeable individuals.

Evaluation data may be obtained indirectly from published information and from other knowledgeable individuals. Additionally, information might be gathered directly from a supplier through the use of expression of interest (EOI) or request for information (RFI) processes.

An EOI request describes materials on which bids will be requested, including essential information about specifications, scope, timing, and other performance expectations. This process familiarizes potential suppliers with supply management's expectations. Suppliers then respond to indicate their interest in competing for the business.

An RFI is used to gather information on a supplier, the supplier's products, and any other area of interest to the supply manager. Similar to the EOI process, a request for information alerts the supplier that it is being considered and, depending on how the request for information is designed, can serve as a supplier pre-screening process. Requests for information should seek whatever information is of interest to the supply manager and may include the following:

1. Names, addresses, contact names, telephone and telefax numbers, and Web site for the supplier's primary, subsidiary, and other business interests.

2. North American Industry Classification System (NAICS) codes and type of business operated by the supplier, its subsidiaries, and other business interests.

3. Ownership structure for all business interests (partnership, corporation, etc.)

4. Business status (small, minority, historically underutilized, foreign, etc.)

5. Names, titles, length of service, education, and backgrounds of managers and other key employees

6. A copy of organizational charts

7. Financial information (banking relationships, annual reports, 10-K report, etc.)

8. Systems infrastructure and electronic commerce capability

9. Customer and other references

10. Facilities (age, size, insurance coverage, any hazards, etc.)

11. Key equipment lists

12. Evidence of quality control philosophy and methods

13. Process capabilities

14. Engineering and design capabilities

15. The nature and organization of supply management and logistics

16. Inventory levels and how they are managed

17. Instrumentation and calibration management

18. Process reliability

19. Warranty policy

20. Records retention and storage

21. Research and development capability and commitment

22. Product price

23. Cost and expense distribution

24. Ability to segregate overhead costs by process

25. Delivery capability

Identifying potential foreign suppliers is less complex in today's global economy. The U.S. Department of Commerce assists U.S. firms in dealing with foreign suppliers by publishing world trade reports and overseas business reports that provide information on imported materials by country of origin. International trade expositions such as the Leipzig and Hanover Fairs in Germany and the International Exhibition of Chemical Engineering in Paris provide access to foreign suppliers and technology.

International trade directories such as *International Business and Trade Directories* (Grey House Publishing, Millerton, N. Y.), *International Dun's Market Identifiers* (Dun & Bradstreet, New York), and the *World Trade Directory*, one of many directories that may be accessed through the World Wide Web, offer information on foreign sources.

Foreign embassies and consulates provide information on specific companies in their home country through direct assistance and catalogs.

Select Potential Suppliers

After gathering sufficient information, potential suppliers may then be compared and evaluated against supply management's requirements. A weighted-point supplier evaluation process is most common. The following steps are typical of a weighted-point evaluation process.

1. Develop evaluation criteria. Note again that evaluation criteria should not be built around perceived supplier capabilities. Instead, they should directly reflect the requirements of the supply manager's organization.

2. Assign a weight to each criterion. The weight assignments will reflect the relative importance of each criterion compared to the others.

3. Assign each supplier a rating (say, 1 to 10 with 10 being the best) on each criterion.

4. For each supplier, multiply the weight times the rating for each criterion.

5. The supplier whose weight × rating values sum to the highest number is considered the highest-rated supplier.

While a typical supplier evaluation will consider many additional variables, here is a simple demonstration of the rating process using only quality, price, and delivery.

		Supplier A		Supplier B	
Evaluation Criteria	Weight	Rating	Weight × Rating	Rating	Weight × Rating
Quality	0.5	7	3.5	9	4.5
Price	0.3	10	3.3	9	2.7
Delivery	0.2	8	1.6	9	1.8
Sum of weight × rating			8.4		9.0

In this case, supplier B rates higher than supplier A and, in the absence of other extenuating circumstances, would be the first choice. Though subjective in nature, the perception of supplier service may be evaluated on the same 1–10 scale. The service category would then be assigned a relative weight, entered into the weighted-point rating process, and allowed to influence the outcome.

A significant level of cross-functional buy-in to the final supplier selection can be achieved by involving a cross-functional team in developing supplier selection criteria and weights. The team should represent supply management, key operations employees, and other functions with vested interest in the outcome.

A supplier evaluation may also include elements that aid in assessing risk. The following questions help identify useful risk-related evaluation factors.

1. Is the supplier relationship of strategic importance to the purchasing firm?

2. Is the supplier a single or sole source?

3. Can another supplier be sourced within an acceptable lead time?

4. What are the ramifications of poor supplier performance?

5. What are the ramifications of supplier insolvency?

After potential suppliers are evaluated, commercial negotiations may begin with those ranked highest.

Negotiate the Raw Materials Supply Contract

There are generally three dimensions in preparing for negotiations. They involve strategic, administrative, and tactical planning. Consistent with a mutually beneficial agreement, strategic planning seeks to identify goals that, when achieved, measurably optimize contributions to the purchaser firm's strategic objectives. This will require the negotiator to understand his or her firm's competitive imperatives and key objectives. Elements of strategic planning typically manifest themselves in the form of key metrics. Administrative planning involves the logistics of getting people and information in place for negotiations. Tactical planning involves matters such as setting interim objectives, studying issues and potential problems, and planning concessions.

To the fullest practical extent, a negotiator should seek to gather and understand the following relevant information.

1. Negotiation objectives. This should include both the supply manager and supplier objectives. This should be accomplished as a first order of business in the negotiation process.

2. Price data. This refers to the supply manager's target and maximum prices.

3. Cost data. This refers to any information available on the supplier's cost structure, and any in-house costs estimates. This information facilitates a more useful estimate of the supplier's target and minimum pricing.

4. Records of previous negotiations and results achieved.

5. Any potential learning curve applications or other economies related to volume.

Additionally, an assessment of relative purchaser to supplier position strength is usually helpful and might include developing estimates on the following.

1. *How badly the supplier wants the contract and the supplier's relative certainty of getting it.* This involves issues such as adequacy of supply, level of competition, supplier financial condition, availability of substitutes, and product strength.

2. *Amount of time for negotiations.* This refers to the relative urgency to arrive at an agreement. Generally, the party under the greatest pressure to conclude an agreement is likely to concede more.

3. *Supply manager's availability of other options.* Other sources for the same material or the availability of substitutes tend to strengthen the supply manager's position.

Sound negotiating practice will address all pertinent issues, including matters such as acceptance criteria, point of acceptance, warranties, and confidentiality.

Cost Management

Since raw materials constitute a large percentage of finished product cost, the total cost of acquiring and using a raw material is a prime consideration in supply agreements. It is generally agreed that quality should not be sacrificed for cost reduction. Instead, supply managers should seek to reduce cost through elimination of non-value-adding activity, advantageous use of technology, increasing the efficiency of materials, and building useful economies of scale. Examining each element in the process of acquiring and using a raw material typically uncovers opportunities to lower overall cost.

Elements of Cost

The following are typical elements of cost related to acquisition and use of raw materials.

1. *The cost of materials.* Subjects for analysis include both the cost of original commodity materials and any added cost of conversion if goods produced from commodities are being acquired.

2. *Transportation.* This includes all costs to have materials delivered for use. If sourcing from a foreign country, costs will include duty, documentation, and brokerage charges.

3. *Inventory.* Excessive inventory ties up capital that could otherwise be generating a return. Accordingly, supply managers should seek to minimize the value of inventory. Given an acceptable service level, inventory turnover rate is a key measure of effectiveness. It is calculated as follows.

$$\text{Annual Turnover Rate} = \frac{\$ \text{ Value of Monthly Usage } \times 12}{\text{Average Inventory Value}}$$

Leading-edge practice seeks supplier agreements in which the supplier owns raw material inventory until used by the purchasing organization.

The need to minimize inventories increasingly results in smaller quantities delivered in smaller time windows. This pressures suppliers to shorten manufacturing cycle times and produce more products in relatively smaller lot sizes. A supplier's ability to satisfy such expectations leads to two purchaser benefits. First, it lowers costs related to holding inventory. Second, it eliminates potential inventory obsolescence resulting from changing designs or product mix.

4. *Costs added during conversion.* This refers to costs associated with assembly or other manufacturing processes using purchased raw materials. This will be influenced by a material's efficiency of use, such as the ease with which they are handled, stored, machined, and shaped. Quality-related costs are a significant impact, as defects lead to off-spec goods, rejects, and a higher per-unit cost of conversion. As described earlier, the yield of input materials will impact final cost of conversion. Note the following example of the effect of yield on conversion cost.

Raw Material

Supplier	Price per Unit	Yield	Final Product Cost per Input Unit (Price/Yield)
A	$1.00	0.98	$1.02
B	$1.00	0.95	$1.05

There are two different but related aspects to the effect of yield on raw material cost per unit of finished product. The first involves dimensional characteristics of purchased raw material. For example, if rectangular parts are being stamped from sheet metal, the supply manager should carefully study the stamped part size in relation to the overall sheet dimensions. If final dimensions of the stamped part are 10 inches $\times$ 8 inches and $\frac{1}{16}$ inch all around is required for cutting and burnishing the part, then the yield is maximized if the length and width of the sheet metal is in multiples of 10 $\frac{1}{16}$ inches in one direction and 8 $\frac{1}{16}$ inches in the other direction. Obviously, any part of the sheet not consumed adds to waste, decreases yield, and increases the raw material cost per unit.

The second aspect deals with the effect of impurities and how a material reacts during further processing. If, for example, 100 pounds of material enters a manufacturing process, but, due to in-process removal of impurities, only 96 pounds of it goes into the finished product, the yield factor would be 96 percent. Similarly, if 100 parts are entered into an assembly operation and 4 cannot be used due to defects, the yield is 96 percent.

There are always material losses during a manufacturing process. Since any yield less than 100 percent adds to the raw material cost per unit, supply managers should diligently pursue a high yield as part of quality specifications.

Draft and Issue a Supply Contract

Given that supplier relationship failures are usually due to differences in expectations, supply managers can facilitate value-adding relationships by ensuring that the contract language and terms reflect a mutually beneficial agreement. This includes understanding what drives each party's costs. In this framework, a successful agreement revolves around the interests of both parties and in finding ways to satisfy both sets of interests.

Hazardous Materials

If contracting for hazardous materials, or any materials that would require a costly cleanup if spilled in transit, supply managers should carefully insulate their firms from liability. First, be sure the materials are properly packaged for transport. Second, be sure the carrier is adequately insured against costs of an environmental cleanup of the materials should they be spilled during transport. Finally, write FOB destination contracts so that the supplier retains the risk of loss during transit.

USING THE INTERNET

Electronic commerce over the Internet facilitates rapid, global communication. It is useful in identifying potential sources and provides an electronic avenue through which to communicate supply management needs and expectations to a large number of potential suppliers around the world. Supplier response to an electronic RFQ essentially results in a reverse auction where bidders see a real-time ranking of bids, but without bidder identification.

Since interfacing will occur electronically, supply managers must provide online bidder access to drawings, specifications, quality expectations, delivery requirements, and any other information required to respond with an informed bid. Supplier prescreening is critical and can often be accomplished over the Internet. However, a prescreening process is intended to facilitate a go/no-go supplier decision and should not substitute for a more thorough supplier analysis.

Reverse auction software providers operate their systems differently, so supply managers are advised to thoroughly investigate software requirements and relative ease of use before engaging in competitive electronic bidding.

ADMINISTER THE RAW MATERIALS CONTRACT

Contract administration refers to any contract-related activity that occurs between contract award and final closure. General objectives of contract administration are to protect supply management's interests by ensuring fulfillment of respective contract obligations, ensuring fair resolution of problems, and equitably adjusting contract terms and costs as appropriate. More specific objectives include monitoring performance to ensure that

1. Delivery schedules are maintained.

2. Costs remain within the agreement.

3. Materials are being consumed at predicted levels.

4. Both raw material and end product quality conform to specifications.

5. Any changes to specifications or contract terms are warranted.

6. Expectations of both parties are being met.

VALUE LEVERAGING TECHNIQUES
Economies of Scale

When more than one operating unit within a firm uses a given commodity, material, or family of components, there may be opportunities for economies of scale. That is achieved when multiple units using the same or similar raw materials agree to aggregate their demand, thereby facilitating larger-volume supply agreements. Increased contract volume leads to at least the following potentially significant cost takeout opportunities.

1. Increased negotiating strength. Larger volume makes a contract more important to a supplier. Suppliers are usually willing to lower profit margins and improve service in return for significant volume increases.

2. The ability to leverage increased value per dollar spent on administration and training.

3. More effective supplier relationship management.

4. Improved transportation costs. These can usually be negotiated if larger volumes of materials are transported.

Additionally, significant economies of scale facilitate negotiation for cost-based pricing.

Cost-Based Pricing

Supplier costs and operating expenses typically do not increase in direct proportion to increases in business volume within the same contract. This provides a cost removal opportunity if supplier profit is negotiated based on the actual cost of goods plus actual expense. That is, any fixed costs or expenses that do not increase with volume should not be reflected in pricing for additional volume. Further, a supplier may not pay the same level of sales commissions on a large volume of committed business. Any commissions or other variable expenses that are economized through volume agreements should also drop out of the pricing structure. Cost-based pricing simply means that, for any given contract, no supplier cost or expense should enter the pricing structure unless it is actually expended by the supplier. If they do, they simply become additional profit. This is a major benefit of economies of scale and can lead to significant cost takeout. It is a matter for negotiation.

Price Analysis

Price analysis is essentially a comparison of competitive pricing or a comparison of available pricing to purchaser objectives. Sound analysis is premised on the notion that supplier prices should be fair and should provide the supplier a reasonable profit, while providing the purchaser with reasonable value. Information on spot, futures, and option commodity prices may be obtained from the *Wall Street Journal*, the *Journal of Commerce*, and the *New York Times*. Information on agricultural products may be obtained from the U.S. Department of Agriculture. Industry publications such as *Metals Week* (McGraw-Hill) and the *Paper Trade* (Lockwood Trade Journal Company) provide pricing information specific to their industry.

Sources of pricing information on value-added products include published price lists with various discount structures, competitive quotes, or prices negotiated based on identifiable added value such as may be found in economies of scale. Consider the following continuum.

Standard,	Proprietary,
Readily Available Goods	Made to Order, Nonstandard Goods

$\longleftarrow$ ———————————————————————— $\longrightarrow$

High Purchaser Position Strength	High Supplier Position Strength

Price analysis is a useful tool when materials are available from a number of sources and competitive pricing is available. In this environment, purchaser position strength is relatively high compared to the supplier. Price analysis is less useful when sourcing unique, complex, nonstandard goods as the market is less competitive and sufficient comparative pricing may not be available. In this case, supplier position strength is high relative to that of the purchaser. When sourcing complex, nonstandard goods, cost analysis is the more useful tool.

Cost Analysis

Cost analysis seeks to develop an informed, reasonable estimate of cost to produce a product. The technique is useful when purchasing manufactured components. A good starting point is simply to request a cost breakdown from the supplier. The supplier's cost structure can then be tested through analysis. Analysis might include the assistance of engineering or other technical personnel, estimating costs based on other items of similar complexity, or estimating costs though intelligent, informed analysis of each element of cost. Such analysis would typically consider the following.

1. *Direct materials.* Commodity prices are generally available through commodity price guides or market-based quotes. The cost of direct material per unit of finished product may be estimated by determining the amount of material, number of components, and so forth, in one unit of the product and multiplying it by the unit cost of the material. For example, if a polypropylene chute contains 12 pounds of polypropylene and the market price of polypropylene is $0.36 per pound, then direct material cost for one chute is 12 x $0.36, or $4.32.

2. *Direct labor.* Original equipment manufacturers can advise on the capacity of their equipment and the number of operators required. Labor rates may be obtained from the Bureau of Labor Statistics Average Hourly Earnings data. With equipment output rate, operator time per unit, and average wage rates for the industry, a supply manager can reasonably estimate the labor cost per unit. Again, in-house technical personnel may offer assistance.

3. *Manufacturing overhead.* In the absence of better information, the following guide is useful. For manual supplier operations, supplier manufacturing overhead cost per unit is typically estimated at 1 time the direct labor cost; for semiautomated operations, 2 times the direct labor cost; and for fully automated operations, 3 times the direct labor cost.

4. *General selling and administration (GS&A) expenses.* In the absence of better information, GS&A expenses are usually estimated between 32 and 45 percent of total production costs.

So, a supplier's total cost would be the sum of direct material per unit, direct labor per unit, overhead, and GS&A expenses. Add a reasonable profit, and the supply manager has a starting point for negotiations.

Learning Curve Application

If purchasing unique items such as new or redesigned parts for a new-model-year automobile, it is reasonable to expect a manufacturer to become more efficient as it produces additional units. This is referred to as a *learning curve effect*. A learning curve depicts the percentage of efficiency improvement gained through learning. This improved efficiency results in reduced time required to produce one unit. These improvements will continue at a diminishing rate until all gains through learning are exhausted. As per-unit time to produce reduces, so will the unit cost of labor, leading to a reduction in total unit cost. The supply manager's challenge is to negotiate the reduction in cost into the purchase price.

The actual slope and shape of a learning curve depends on the percentage of improvement as multiple units are produced. The general rule is that production time per unit reduces by the percentage of learning each time the number of units produced doubles. For example, a 90 percent learning curve implies that the time to produce a unit will reduce by 10 percent each time the output doubles. If 100 minutes were required to produce one unit, then doubling output to 2 units would require 90 minutes per unit (0.90 × 100). Doubling output to 4 units would require 81 minutes per unit (0.90 × 90). Doubling again to 8 units of output would require 72.9 minutes per unit (0.90 × 81), and so on.

Early Supplier Involvement

In a quest for lowest total cost, a supply manager must consider the operating requirements of the various technologies employed to produce a product. Suppliers to those processing technologies typically possess great expertise in how their materials might be used to greater advantage. Given that up to 80 percent of a product's cost may be locked in at the design stage, simplifying or improving a design can reduce product cost or make the product more desirable. Either contributes to organizational goals. If involved sufficiently early in the design process, suppliers can offer valuable assistance in achieving these goals.

Early supplier involvement also implies early communication to suppliers on supply management's objectives and raw material needs, thereby enhancing supplier opportunity to assist in achieving the supply manager's goals. The following key areas may be favorably impacted through early supplier involvement.

1. *Design assistance.* Where long-term trust is established, supplier technical personnel may work with purchaser design teams to optimize a new product design. Such collaboration may also lead to supplier assistance with product prototypes, models, or samples.

2. *Assistance in the manufacturing process.* Suppliers know more about their products and may suggest ways to better utilize them in manufacturing. Highly collaborative supplier relationships often involve sharing manufacturing systems information. Such an exchange often identifies other mutually beneficial opportunities, such as outsourcing some pre-assembly to the supplier. The purchaser would then buy partially manufactured goods and finish them on purchaser manufacturing lines. The objective is to identify all mutually beneficial, value-adding opportunities.

3. *Suggestions for improved cost management.* Suppliers may offer insight into managing product development costs and potential manufacturing costs using their materials.

4. *Quality requirements.* With sufficient advance notice, suppliers can help develop quality requirements and prepare to meet purchaser expectations through timely process development, capability studies, and acquisition of any special equipment that may be needed.

5. *Assurance of material availability.* Supply managers should clearly understand which suppliers are capable of meeting their raw material demands. This information may be difficult to obtain without early collaboration with potential suppliers. Early collaboration will further facilitate supplier mobilization to meet purchaser demand.

6. *Reduced time to market.* A primary objective of early involvement of raw material suppliers is to reduce product development time and, consequently, time-to-market. In addition to assistance in the design phase, suppliers may help eliminate redundancies in development, manufacturing, and distribution.

Given that benefits from early supplier involvement are enhanced through highly collaborative, mutually beneficial supplier relationships, these relationships should be planned with specific goals in mind. As already noted, this makes the nature of a supplier relationship an integral part of a material-specific purchasing strategy.

Early Supply Management Involvement

In a competitive business environment, the acquisition process may involve a degree of trade-off between functionality and cost. Providing assistance to ensure that such trade-off decisions are made with a focus on long-term optimal cost is a key supply management role. It follows, then, that benefits from early involvement of raw material suppliers will be enhanced when supply management professionals are also involved early.

With sufficient advance notice, supply management professionals can expedite identification and qualification of suppliers well in advance of actual purchases, thereby avoiding less effective fast tracking late in the process. Since they are generally better trained in dealing with suppliers, supply management professionals often act as the conduit between suppliers and internal design and manufacturing. This will further enhance supplier planning to meet supply management's organizational needs.

The supply management professional should ensure proper attention to confidentiality and take steps to ensure that all in the collaboration circle understand confidentiality requirements.

Cross-Functional Teams

Innovative supplier relationships, creative contracts, early supplier and supply management involvement, or any other strategy that impacts across an organization will require organization-wide support. These strategies must be presented to involved functions in ways that gain their support. Best practice involves those whose support is needed in developing and implementing supply management strategy. An effective cross-functional team tends to create needed support as team members discuss and promote team activity in their respective functions. Additionally, a cross-functional team fosters creativity and innovation. Leading-edge firms consider cross-functional teams as key to effective strategy implementation.

ORGANIZATIONAL MANAGEMENT'S MIND-SET IN A GLOBAL ECONOMY

Today, more than ever, supply management functions in a global economy. Business and industry face increased and smarter competition, and shrinking margins. To maintain viable margins, firms aggressively seek to remove costs at all levels in the organization. This demands evaluation of expenditures in terms of value received, often while operating with fewer human resources. Each function in a company is expected to develop a strategy that looks beyond the tactical aspects of the function to focus on overall organizational success. The ultimate business of supply management professionals is not to release orders, receive materials, and pay invoices. While these and other tactical activities are important, they are a means to an end. That end is ultimate success of the firm, and that is where procurement strategies and metrics must be focused.

METRICS

Raw materials must satisfy a range of demands as they pass through various manufacturing technologies. Since the processes employing the various technologies may have their own operating peculiarities and material specification requirements, each is typically measured in terms of efficiency and cost. While these interim technology or departmental metrics are important, objectives of a raw material supply plan should target lowest total cost from a whole company perspective. That may require some trade-offs in terms of specifications that favor one interim process over another. So, while leading-edge companies pay attention to interim single-process metrics, the ultimate focus is on optimizing the total cost to produce and, through that, on measurable contribution to achievement of organizational strategic objectives.

To senior management, the ultimate measure of organizational success is an acceptable rate of return on the value of assets (ROA) deployed to operate the business. Influences on ROA include things like selling price, better customer relations, improved competitive strength, and greater market share. Raw material procurement is in a position to exert significant positive leverage on each of these influences by taking out costs related to acquisition and use of raw materials. As costs reduce, margins improve and selling price may be reduced. Lower market price for finished goods leads to more customers, greater strength in the market relative to competitors, and increased market share. Keep in mind that cost take-out is much broader than cost reduction. Cost reduction implies reduction in the price per unit of materials, and that can only go so far. Cost takeout implies that any cost, wherever it lives in the organization, is fair game. That logically includes influences like process improvements, better material yields, lower total manufacturing cost per unit, and reduced time-to-market. As already noted, suppliers can often assist in meeting these goals where expectations are established and supported through collaborative, mutually beneficial relationships.

Given that a key raw material procurement objective is to measurably reduce the cost of raw materials and improve return on assets deployed, the following metrics are logical.

1. *Reduction in cost of raw material per unit of finished product.* This could be measured as an absolute number or as a percentage of total cost per unit. The absolute number would provide an ongoing macroview of trends in raw material costs. The percentage of total cost per unit will provide a view of raw material cost relative to other costs of goods.

2. *Contribution to return on assets deployed.* Return on assets deployed is the product of percent profit on sales multiplied by the asset turnover rate. Consider the following firm.

Annual sales = $1,000,000,000

Profit on sales = $100,000,000

Percent profit on sales = 10% (Profit on sales/Annual sales)

Assets deployed (cash, receivables, inventories, other fixed assets) = $400,000,000

Asset turnover rate = 2.5 (Sales/$ Value of assets deployed)

Return on assets deployed = 25% (Percent profit on sales × Asset turnover rate)

Recall that every dollar saved by supply management goes directly to net income before taxes. Suppose supply management documented

$6,000,000 in cost takeout. The pretax effect on ROA is shown by reducing profit by $6,000,000, thereby reducing the percent profit on sales to 9.4 percent. Under this scenario, ROA would be 9.4 × 2.5 (% Profit on sales × Asset turnover rate) = 23.5%, a difference of 1.5 percent. Therefore, supply management's contribution to ROA is 1.5 percent.

3. *Earnings per share (EPS).* For public companies, supply's contribution to earnings per share would be meaningful. This may be calculated by backing the dollar value of supply's contribution out of net income before taxes, deducting income taxes at the same rate, and dividing net income after taxes by the number of shares outstanding. The difference between earnings per share with and without supply's contribution is the purchasing impact on EPS.

Lower-level, tactical metrics are important to supply management because they indicate trends and measure ongoing impact on the influences that lead to meaningful strategic metrics. However, the ultimate measure of success lies in strategic metrics that visibly and measurably link supply management's contribution to organizational competitive imperatives. These are the new expectations of supply management professionals, particularly those who purchase raw materials.

CHAPTER 35

INDIRECT MATERIALS MANAGEMENT

Lee Buddress, Ph.D., C.P.M.
Associate Professor of Supply and Logistics
Director, Supply and Logistics Management Program
Portland State University

Michael E. Smith, Ph.D., CQA
Associate Professor of Management and International Business
MBA Program Director
Western Carolina University

INTRODUCTION

The acronym *MRO* (maintenance, repair, and operating) is familiar to most involved in supply management. MRO materials comprise the goods necessary to operate an organization, aside from materials that go directly into an organization's products. Today, indirect purchasing has been expanded to include a wide variety of other activities and represents the acquisition of all goods and services necessary for the continued operation of the organization except those materials directly consumed by the production process. In some organizations, these purchases represent two-thirds of all company expenditures. For that reason, and in recognition of the expanded role of this purchasing activity, this section will refer to indirect purchases, rather than MRO purchases. The MRO term will continue to be used specifically to apply to maintenance, repair, and operating materials purchases.

Every organization has some form of indirect purchasing. Even pure service businesses need office supplies, janitorial services, and occasionally, consultants. This chapter will discuss the characteristics that make indirect purchasing somewhat different from purchases of direct materials. Goals, objectives, and strategies for indirect purchasing will be developed. Tools for indirect purchasing and inventory management will be described, followed by performance measures and other related topics. In some organizations, indirect purchasing is perceived as somewhat less important than the purchase of direct materials. While it is obviously vital that an organization maintain a smooth flow of materials for production, it should be equally obvious that without the necessary energy, lubrication, and maintenance, production will just as quickly halt. It is the purpose of this chapter to explain that while some of the characteristics of indirect purchasing are different from those of direct purchases, indirect purchasing is of equal importance.

INDIRECT SUPPLY CHARACTERISTICS

In one organization, at the same time it purchased 8,900 production parts, it bought, on a continuous basis, more than 40,000 different indirect materials. In one survey, the average value of an indirect purchase order was $125. In another survey, the average value was $167. Two characteristics are immediately apparent: (1) many indirect purchases are of low value, perhaps less than the administrative cost of generating the order, and (2) there is amazing variety in indirect purchases—from pencils to capital equipment and capital projects, and a wide variety of services. Increasingly, indirect supply managers are responsible for energy purchases and negotiating rates with a wide variety of service providers. The scope of activity is one of the differentiating characteristics of the indirect purchasing function.

Indirect Supply Problems

Indirect purchases are typically required for every location of an organization. In many organizations, such requirements extend to mobile service personnel, who are likely to have on-location requirements that must be met. Consider, for example, an electrical utility operating in numerous states, and the requirements associated with emergency repairs. This raises several problematic issues for indirect supply managers. How might an organization make sure goods are available when and where they are needed, with necessary controls, while still enabling the organization to maximize its aggregate purchasing leverage? If multilocation contracts have been negotiated to achieve broad availability while attaining advantageous pricing, how will the organization effect compliance and avoid "maverick spending" (purchases made outside of the contract)? The succeeding sections will address these and other key components of an integrated indirect purchasing program.

Objectives of Indirect Supply Management

The first objective of indirect supply management is the development of strategy and focus for the entire scope of indirect materials and services supply. That carries forward to commodity or category strategies and finally to strategies for each significant supplier. Underlying these strategies are the fundamental goals of assuring continuity of supply, minimizing administrative costs, and reducing cycle times. These strategies provide focus and direction to all who work in the indirect supply area.

Development of Indirect Supply Strategy

Any functional strategy must be consistent with the overall organizational strategy. The strategic planning process begins with the definition of an organization's mission. This is a concise statement defining the underlying purposes for the existence of the organization. The second step is to establish a vision statement. What does management intend for the organization to become in X years. Thereafter follow the strategies that detail the means by which the organization will progress from its present position to where the vision statement directs. Finally, performance measures are established to encourage employees to do the things that are necessary to proceed from the present position to that defined by the vision statement.

Strategies typically have three fundamental characteristics. First, they are long-term action plans, detailing what must be done now so that the vision can be achieved. Second, a strategy involves the commitment of organizational resources to a specific course of action. Finally, the underlying objective of any strategy is the creation of competitive advantage.

Strategies for indirect materials management will conform to the preceding model. Categories of commodities, products, or service groups are defined. Examples include electrical supplies, safety supplies, janitorial service, and bearings. For each one, a strategic plan is developed. For example, an organization may analyze its office products purchasing and inventory processes. If it were determined that the organization has six office products suppliers and three office product storerooms, the strategy for the commodity might be to develop and use a formal supplier performance measurement system to reduce the number of suppliers to two. Additionally, the organization may choose as a commodity strategy the use of a systems contract. A key feature of this type of contract is rapid turnaround of orders. If orders are filled and delivered within 24 hours, very little, if any, inventory is necessary. Having evaluated the characteristics of the remaining suppliers, individual strategies can be developed to improve the costs and performance of each.

The type of product being acquired will significantly influence development of strategy. Commodities or industry standard products will require substantially different strategies than custom products or those that are patented or incorporate proprietary technologies. Commodities or industry standards are likely to be substantially market-driven transactions. Other strategies may focus on the acquisition of technology or on the development of long-term supplier relationships.

Criticality Grid Applications to Indirect Purchasing

A criticality grid is a tool to evaluate the importance of a product to the ongoing operations of an organization and to assess the difficulty of the marketplace from which it must be acquired.[1] Criticality grids are useful to categorize strategies based on product type and marketplace conditions. Highly critical markets are those involving such things as proprietary technologies or patented products. In these sole-source situations, a supplier may have transactional power because of limited alternatives. Markets may also be termed critical when conditions of high market concentration, high price volatility, or high supply-industry capacity utilization exist.

---

1 Lee Buddress and Alan Raedels (1998). "Using Criticality Grids to Determine Negotiation Strategies," *Proceedings of the 83rd International Purchasing Conference*, Tempe, AZ: NAPM, pp. 384–388.

On the other end of the scale are commodities, industry standard products, or products that have many substitutes. These typically have highly competitive marketplaces that offer buyers choices among several suppliers, so materials are comparatively easy to obtain. In between are differentiated industry standards—those where customer preferences for one brand or another may have a large influence. Hammers may be a standard, common-use item, but every trade has its favorite brand and hammer characteristics. Somewhat less competitive conditions may result for these items.

In terms of product criticality, at the low end of the scale are items of little importance to the organization, of little use, or incorporating unimportant technologies. High criticality occurs where volumes are high, dollar expenditures are high, or the item is highly price sensitive. Similarly, if the material is pervasive, for example, throughout a product line, or incorporates key operating characteristics, it may be critical in nature. This tool provides a conceptual framework for indirect purchasing analysis and decision-making. Figure 35–1 illustrates the grid and its elements.

Each of the quadrants of the grid has differing usage and marketplace characteristics that call for different strategies. In the lower left quadrant, industry standard products are acquired in relatively low volumes. Pricing and administrative costs will be primary concerns. Supplier selection decisions will be driven by material costs and by the supplier's ability to minimize the administrative costs of doing business. Does the supplier have the capability to automate these transactions? Does the supplier accept purchase cards? Either of these options is substantially less expensive, administratively, than generating a formal purchase order. Any mechanism that enables indirect purchasing managers to minimize the costs of acquiring these low-dollar, low-volume materials will be attractive.

F I G U R E   35–1

Market and Internal Criticality

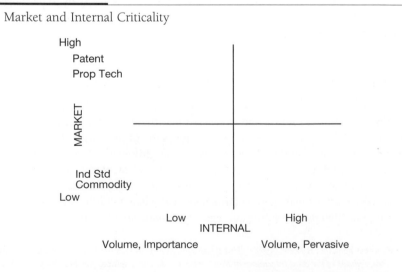

In the lower right quadrant are the same materials—industry standards—but now the requirement is for higher volumes. As such, while price will still be a significant determinant, continuity of supply and quality will be deciding factors. Long-term relationships with suppliers often develop for these requirements. Termed *operational alliances*, these agreements may span several years. They are characterized by comparatively low levels of interaction, typically involving users and supply personnel from the buying organization and sales and marketing personnel from the supplier.

The most frequent buyer-supplier relationship found in the upper right quadrant is a strategic alliance. This form differs from an operational alliance primarily in the degree of interaction between the two firms. Ordinarily, there are engineers, quality management personnel, maintenance personnel, operations managers, and supply and logistics managers representing the buying firm, while similar functions are involved from the supplying organization. This results in a close, collaborative, long-term relationship between the firms.

The final quadrant, the upper left, is perhaps the most difficult for indirect supply managers. Here, the organization is acquiring proprietary technology under conditions where there is not sufficient purchasing volume to generate meaningful negotiating leverage. Not infrequently, these transactions assume "take it or leave it" characteristics. In negotiation, there is a saying as follows, "The longer the shadow of future interaction, the more likely the two sides are to reach a satisfactory conclusion." For this reason, indirect supply managers often evaluate future requirements perhaps several years ahead to assess the future interactions between the firms. If it appears that the use of the proprietary technology is to increase over time, this may generate the leverage to enable the indirect supply manager to negotiate or work toward a strategic alliance. If, on the other hand, it appears that future requirements will be stable or declining, this may provide a powerful argument to engineering or maintenance to look for ways to minimize or eliminate requirements from what is otherwise a difficult market situation. Figure 35–2 illustrates the application of these strategies to the various categories of requirements.

TOOLS FOR INDIRECT PURCHASING MANAGEMENT
Forecasting

While many will argue that it is impossible to predict machine breakdowns, and therefore to forecast maintenance purchases, the authors will argue that this is but one small part of the forecasting task of indirect supply managers. With appropriate tools, at least general forecasts can even be made for maintenance purchases.

The motto of traditional maintenance was, "If it ain't broke, don't fix it." Of course, the problems with this philosophy are that the machine only breaks when it is most needed, and when it breaks under load, not only must the failed parts be replaced, the failure often causes damage to nonwear parts that otherwise

F I G U R E   35–2

Managerial Objectives

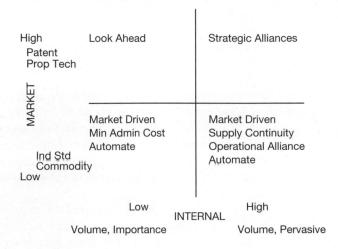

would never need replacement. In addition, the failure usually leads to rush deliveries and overtime repair.

The concepts of preventive maintenance suggest that with data about reliability of wear components of a machine, it is possible to determine life expectancy and schedule repair work to be done *before* something breaks. By definition, such systems are forecastable and indeed *require* forecasting. This also highlights how important it is for indirect supply managers to work closely with maintenance personnel to determine the preventive maintenance schedules and to ensure that parts, especially those with long lead times, are available according to the schedule.

The primary purposes of forecasting are to minimize uncertainty and to anticipate change. If an activity continues with relatively little change, automation is a likely tool for its management. For activities that change frequently, such as MRO and other indirect purchasing activities, forecasting becomes a critical tool in their management. To sustain operations without forecasting usually demands substantial excess inventories. This is especially true when applied to MRO inventories.

A number of other chapters in this text provide discussions of forecasting processes and techniques; it is the purpose of this section to extend those concepts to the indirect purchasing environment. Since it is impossible to plot a trend in a seasonal environment with less than three years of data, and since many organizations exhibit seasonal demand patterns to some degree, it is essential that sufficient data be maintained. In addition to historical maintenance records, such as for overhaul frequency, machine breakdowns and other repairs, essential information is often available from equipment manufacturers.

Most capital equipment manufacturers maintain "recommended spares" lists that indicate what parts may need to be replaced on a regular basis. Most equipment suppliers also have a general notion of the frequency of such repairs. From internal and other sources such as machinery and maintenance handbooks it is possible to determine the average life cycles of common components. In conjunction with maintenance personnel and using this information, it is then possible to construct a maintenance schedule (forecast) incorporating all expected repairs.

If it is known that a particular type of engine has a mean time to failure of 10,000 hours, an organization will likely set an overhaul target at something less to forestall catastrophic failures. If the target is 9,000 hours, and the rate of use is known, it is a simple matter to calculate the date on which the target will be reached. Assume the engine has 5,000 hours on it today. The machine will run two shifts (say 14 hours total) per day, five days per week. With 4,000 hours to go until overhaul, and with a usage rate of 70 hours per week, it will be just over 57 weeks until an overhaul is required. Not only is this information useful in scheduling the availability of necessary parts (especially those with long lead times), it is essential for budgeting purposes, as well. There is a significant impact on inventories from failure to forecast. Just-in-case inventories will grow, not just from the need to protect against the lack of planning, but from safety stock calculations, as well.

Safety stock requirements are a function of variability in demand occurring during the lead time for acquisition. If an automated system is used to calculate safety stocks, consider what the computer sees. First, there is a relatively stable demand for a part for normal usage. Then, a spike in demand occurs at overhaul time. The automated system perceives the difference between normal usage and overhaul usage as large demand variability against which it must protect with large safety stocks. Excluding the special projects such as overhauls from the automated safety stock calculations will result in a significantly lower level of safety stock required to protect against stockouts *under normal circumstances.*

Even in situations where overhaul kits are delivered directly from the supplier to the machine under repair, many organizations, as a means of tracking parts usage, enter the overhaul materials into the inventory database as if they had been put on the shelf and then issued to the overhaul job. For obvious reasons, it is recommended that this practice be avoided.

The forecasting tasks for indirect purchases are every bit as important as those for direct materials. Forecasts of requirements for copy paper, electrical supplies, pipe, valves and fittings, bearings, safety supplies, and any other indirect material necessary to support ongoing operations are necessary to ensure availability and as the foundation for contract negotiations with suppliers. While most organizations spend large sums to develop forecasts of customer demand, they often overlook the second half of the forecasting equation: forecasts of supply availability and price. Forecasts of requirements must be played against supplier capabilities and supplier capacities to ensure availability. If machines are out of service because indirect purchasers failed to forecast that the supplier would be on strike when parts were needed, such deficiencies are likely to be career limiting.

Lead-Time Management

If an organization has two suppliers, one that quotes six weeks lead time (say an offshore supplier) and *always* delivers on time, and a second supplier (perhaps a domestic one) who quotes two weeks lead time, but often takes three, which is the best supplier? Conventional performance measures would clearly favor the first. On-time delivery is, according to many surveys, the most highly prized of supplier attributes. But is the first supplier really best in today's highly volatile business environment?

Lead-time management may be one of the most important tasks of indirect supply managers. Lead times affect indirect materials in a number of ways. They influence inventory levels, replenishment rates, responsiveness to changes in demand, stockout rates, and even the determination of orders as "rush" or "routine." There are two definitions of rush orders. An *internal rush* is an order that must be processed outside of its chronological order of receipt. If a buyer stops work on one order to process another, clearly it is a rush. From the supplier's view, any order that requires delivery in less than the supplier's normal lead time is a *rush*. By working with suppliers to help them better understand future requirements and to identify elements of lead time that can be reduced, rush orders are automatically reduced. Considering the fact that in some organizations rush orders represent as many as half of all indirect purchase transactions, this is a critical issue. Reduced cycle times, increased flexibility, and increased on-time deliveries all argue for considerable focus to be directed, by both buyers and suppliers, toward reducing lead times. Many organizations track standard deviations of lead times as a supplier performance measure. If the standard deviation of lead time exceeds the actual lead time, it is an obvious indicator to both parties that delivery time is inconsistent and significant attention is needed.

Standardization

There are two concepts that sound much alike but differ substantially in terms of their source and implications. Industry standards are products that are manufactured to the same specifications by all firms in the industry, or are functionally interchangeable. For example, copy paper of similar grade from one manufacturer is interchangeable with that of any other supplier, and the functioning of a standard light switch remains the same, independent of its manufacturer.

Company standardization, on the other hand, is a management decision-making process that evaluates need and product availability. What is the specific requirement, and what are the products available to fill that need? From those available, one is chosen to become the organization's standard. Henceforth, at each recurring requirement for that product, the organization's standard will be used. Whenever an industry standard can be used as the organization's standard, it will be beneficial. Typically, industry standards cost somewhere between 25 and 50 percent less than similar, custom-made products.

Periodically, an organization's requirement cannot be met with industry standard products. In such situations, clearly, a custom product will be required. To realize the benefits of standardization, whenever such a need recurs, the same custom product will be employed.

Benefits from standardization are several. The purchasing benefits include aggregating purchase volume to generate quantity discounts. Supplier support increases proportionally as a firm's volume increases. As a standardization program is implemented, inventory diversity declines. This typically results in a decrease in inventory investment, while coincidentally increasing inventory fill rates. Maintenance productivity increases markedly as variety declines. Part prices decline as volumes increase, as well. Finally, quality is improved as consumption is concentrated on the suppliers who provide superior products and minimum variability.

Life-Cycle Cost Analysis

Capital equipment purchases involve extensive analyses of the total costs of ownership over the useful life of the equipment. It should be noted that useful life spans will differ between organizations. Upon buying a new machine, the firm may plan to replace it in 10 years. At that point, the machine may have reached the end of its intended use for the first purchaser, but others may find the machine suitable for further use. The machine, therefore, has salvage value (the machine's value on the used equipment market). With this in mind, a life-cycle cost analysis may be developed.

The purchase price is the obvious starting point in analyzing a machine's total cost of ownership. Installation is the next cost element. It is not unusual for firms to spend several times the cost of the machine in installation costs. In addition, such costs may vary significantly between machines.

Operating costs are now estimated. For example, because of its design, one machine may be able to perform the same tasks as another, but with a smaller motor. Over the projected 10-year useful life span, the electricity cost difference may be substantial. Expected costs of maintaining the machine over its useful life must be considered, as well. The machine with the smaller motor may cost less to operate, but the motor may need more frequent maintenance or replacement. Routine maintenance costs and intervals, as well as major overhaul costs and their frequency will be included.

At the end of its useful life, equipment must be removed and disposed of. If, as mentioned, the equipment can be sold, the proceeds will be deducted from the total cost of ownership. Alternately, there may be significant disposal costs involved if, for example, a transformer that is being replaced contains PCBs or other environmentally damaging material.

Life-cycle cost analysis, then, is the sum of the costs to acquire, install, maintain, and operate the equipment over its useful life, plus disposal costs, or less salvage value. Comparisons of life-cycle costs (total cost of ownership) of competing machines usually produces a different purchase decision than one based solely on purchase price. See also Chapter 23, "Total Cost of Ownership."

A related issue has to do with negotiation for spare parts pricing and availability. All too often, spare parts are an afterthought to the acquisition of the machine. Only when parts are needed do the issues of price and availability arise. At this point, negotiating discounted pricing is nearly impossible. Considering that spare parts often carry significant markups, paying full list price is, at the least, distasteful.

Parts availability is another problem that benefits from early indirect supply involvement. Does the supplier routinely have, on the shelf, the parts that may be needed, or must they come from a distant warehouse? Worse yet, must they be made after the order is placed? Some capital equipment manufacturers, by policy, only keep parts on the shelf for a specific number of years. If an organization plans to use a machine for 10 years and the supplier only actively supports the machine with off-the-shelf parts for 7 years, the time to discover this is before the purchase order is signed, so additional support can be negotiated and written into the agreement.

It is important, then, that indirect supply managers be involved in the capital equipment acquisition process very early. Spare parts pricing, availability, service costs, and support are key elements in the purchase decision process and can be advantageously negotiated only before the ink is dry on the purchase order.

Warranty Management

Warranties of one form or another come with most products we purchase. Indeed, the Uniform Commercial Code grants buyers four critical warranties: express warranty, implied warranty of merchantability, warranty of title and against infringement, and implied warranty of fitness for a particular purpose. Section 2-316 of the Uniform Commercial Code allows suppliers to exclude or modify warranties, but the exclusion must be in writing and conspicuous.[2] Refer to Chapter 31, "Legal Aspects of Purchasing and Supply," for more details related to warranties.

Warranties are often subject to negotiation during indirect purchases. This is particularly critical, as indirect purchases are often of maintenance parts or spares. Manufacturers typically offer warranties of quality for specific periods. An electric motor manufacturer may, for example, offer a 90-day warranty against defects in materials or workmanship. If the motor is to be immediately installed, this may be a period sufficient to uncover any manufacturing defects. What if the motor is to be put into inventory as an emergency spare, only to be used upon failure of the one presently in service? In such a circumstance, the warranty period may expire while the motor is still on the shelf. For this reason it is especially important that indirect supply managers negotiate warranties that only begin as of the date of installation. This is a critical issue for MRO materials and spares.

An underlying assumption of the preceding paragraph is that an organization has a process or procedure by which it tracks dates of installation for all its

2 American Law Institute, National Conference of Commissioners on Uniform State Laws (2003). *Uniform Commercial Code 2003 ed., Official Text and Comments.* Eagan, MN: West Publishing.

MRO parts and equipment for which warranties are significant. Such a system may be incorporated in MRO maintenance software, or it may be as simple as a wire-on tag attached to the part, upon which the mechanic notes the date of installation. That, along with a dated work order, is often sufficient for suppliers to use to replace parts or equipment that failed during the warranty period.

Indirect Inventory Management

One of the commonly held notions of indirect inventories is that there is always too much of it, but the right goods are never there. This is all too often true. Several conditions contribute to these perceptions. First, the array of indirect materials is typically several times as varied as the items held for production. Second, item-by-item predictability may be difficult, and finally, the values of indirect items may literally be from pennies to millions. Spare parts may not be used for years, and then several may be needed in quick succession resulting in a stockout. Frequent-use items may be needed several times each month. The sum of these characteristics equates to the need to manage these inventories somewhat differently from direct materials.

Risk Sharing

If an organization had several manufacturing locations throughout the country, all producing the same product with the same machinery, traditionally a full set of parts was held at each location. Since the turnover for many MRO parts often is close to only one time per year, significant dollars were parked on inventory shelves only to be used intermittently. Today, many organizations have elected to trade inventory for premium transportation by holding slow-moving items in only one or two locations and using airfreight to move them to the required location. While airfreight is obviously more expensive than truck transportation, lower inventories and lower inventory carrying costs result in a significant net savings, overall.

Inventory Calculations

There are several important inventory numbers managers must have to make informed decisions. The first is inventory carrying cost. It is often surprising to see how much it really costs to carry inventory. For typical manufacturing firms, this cost may range between 35 and 50 percent of the inventory value per year.[3] This means that if an item were purchased for $10, stored on the shelf, and issued and replenished as necessary throughout the year, it would cost between $3.50 and $5.00 per year to store, care for, and issue the item. This cost is in addition to the $10 price of the product and is an annual cost for as long as the item stays in inventory.

---

3 J. Heizer and B. Render(2004). *Operations Management, 7th ed.* Upper Saddle River, NJ: Prentice-Hall.

A fair average cost for industrial firms is approximately 40 percent. While this may seem costly, an examination of the elements of cost may illustrate its accuracy.

Inventory carrying costs are all costs associated with inventory that would disappear if the inventory were eliminated. There are many different ways authors have sorted the costs associated with maintaining inventories, but regardless of how they are classified, the following costs must be included.

> *Capital investments.* To hold inventories, an organization must have a warehouse, pallet racks, forklifts, fax machines, and other equipment in which it must invest (typically about 10 percent of the average inventory value).

> *Cost of capital.* This cost represents the annual cost of the money invested in inventory (typically approximately 8 to 15 percent of the average inventory value).

> *Labor costs.* Costs for those working in the warehouse include both wages and fringe benefits (typically about 15 percent of the average inventory value).

> *Variable costs.* This category of carrying costs includes such things as utilities (heat, light, phone, etc.), allowances for shrinkage and obsolescence, taxes and insurance (typically about 5 to 10 percent of the average inventory value).

> *Tracking costs.* This last category of carrying costs incorporates such activities as data entry costs, the value of computer time devoted to tracking inventories and inventory report generation (typically about 2 to 5 percent of the average inventory value).

Calculating Carrying Cost

After the values for each of the preceding cost categories are determined, they are now summed. The total of those costs is then divided by the average inventory value and then multiplied by 100 to arrive at the carrying cost as a percent of the inventory value. For example, if a firm invests $100,000 in order to hold inventories, and the cost of capital is $80,000, labor costs (wages and fringe) are $150,000, variable costs are $50,000 and tracking costs are $30,000, then the total of these costs is $410,000. If company records indicate that the average inventory value is $1,000,000, we can compute average carrying costs as 41 percent of the inventory value (($410,000/$1,000,000) × 100 = 41%). This represents the cost of storing, maintaining and caring for the $1,000,000 inventory for one year. Note that this is a recurring, annual cost, in addition to the money already invested in the inventory. It should also be noted that the costs of carrying inventory typically are not exemplified by a smooth curve but by a step function. Adding another warehouse worker increases costs in a step, as does adding another forklift. As inventories decrease, costs decline in a similar step-by-step fashion.

It is important that indirect supply managers have an accurate assessment of carrying costs to realistically evaluate special buying opportunities. If a one-time discount is offered, or if a price increase is imminent, supply managers may elect to purchase more than immediate requirements. How much to buy will be determined by balancing purchase savings with carrying cost increases associated with longer holding periods until use. Without precise inventory carrying costs, economic order quantity (EOQ) calculations will likewise be inaccurate.

During the process of evaluating inventory carrying costs, inventory labor costs were determined. Under the traditional application of inventory carrying costs, the value of the inventory or of an individual item is multiplied by the carrying cost to determine the holding cost per year. For example, if an item costs $10 to purchase and the inventory carrying cost is 40 percent per year, then by multiplying the two together, an annual holding cost of $4 is defined for that item. The flaw in this process is that there is no consideration for the usage of that item, that is, its turnover ratio. One $10 item may have an average usage of twice per year, while another $10 item may turn eight times per year—yet (assuming the same average inventory) they are both given the same carrying cost. Ideally, the costs for warehouse labor would be assigned to each item based on the number of transactions, rather than as a percentage of inventory value. To do so requires only that the dollar value of warehouse labor be divided by the total number of inventory transactions to determine a cost per transaction. However, organizations don't commonly track inventory transactions. In lieu of that information, the following method may be used to roughly estimate inventory transactions.

To determine an estimate for the number of inventory transactions, two additional statistics must be known. First the number of SKUs (stockkeeping units—distinct items in inventory) must be determined. This is ordinarily readily available as a part of the inventory statistical database. Additionally, the turnover ratio for the inventory must be found. This calculation is easily made by dividing the annual total value of issues from inventory, at cost, by the average inventory value. For example, if the total value of maintenance goods issued to the shop during the past year was $10 million, and the average maintenance inventory value was $2 million, then the turnover ratio for the maintenance inventory would be 5. This number tells managers that *on average* (important words) all items in inventory have been issued and replenished 5 times per year. From another perspective, if inventory is viewed, not as parts on the shelf, but as stacks of dollar bills, the turnover ratio tells managers how much use they are getting from the money invested in the inventory.

If there are 5,000 SKUs in inventory and the inventory has a turnover ratio of 5, then as a rough approximation, there would be 25,000 inventory transactions per year. If, as in our example, the warehouse labor cost was $150,000 and the number of inventory transactions was 25,000 per year, then the rough approximation of the warehouse labor cost per transaction would be $6 ($150,000/$25,000). This leads to the question of whether or not it makes good managerial sense to keep low-value items within the formal inventory system where it may cost more to issue and replenish the items than they are worth. Spending $6 in warehouse labor to issue a $1 item may not be cost effective. This is a special concern for indirect supply managers, as many of the MRO inventory items fall into this category.

The labor cost per transaction and the characteristics of spare parts inventory performance combine to argue for the necessity to create three categories of indirect or MRO inventories: expensed, spares, and active. These categories are necessary because the differing characteristics of the classes cause different managerial tools to be applied. To solve the low-value problem, an expensed inventory category is created.[4] All such low-value goods are expensed as they arrive and are no longer a part of the formal inventory. In essence, the material is presumed to be consumed immediately upon receipt (treated as a current expense) and is typically kept in point-of-use bins. By removing these low value items from the formal inventory system, users no longer need to requisition them from stores, and they are no longer tracked or counted as part of the formal inventory. Frequently, a supplier-managed inventory contract is put in place to minimize the administrative costs associated with managing these low-value items. Two bin inventory systems are commonly seen with these items. Examples include fasteners, O-rings, and minor shop supplies.

Spare parts are typically kept because they have long lead times and are not available locally. Indeed, many firms have emergency spares that have never been used. Extended lead times for these parts and the risk of not having them in the event of a breakdown dictate they be held in inventory. Since the expected turnover ratio for spare parts is (hopefully) around one, by including this inventory with the active items, the managerial tool (the turnover ratio) is distorted downward. Creating a category called Spares and moving all the items that are expected to turn slowly into it solves this problem.

The remaining inventory is where the majority of the indirect dollars and the majority of the inventory activity remain. It is here that the majority of managerial attention is likewise concentrated. Such classifications as pipe, valves, and fittings; bearings; electrical supplies; and safety supplies are examples.

Consignment Inventories

Consignment inventories represent a fourth category for some organizations. Under this process, a supplier consigns its inventory to the buyer's warehouse. The inventory is still owned by the seller, but it is carried in the buyer's inventory, to be paid for upon use. While the prospect of acquiring inventory without paying for it is attractive, it should be noted that consignment inventories are a method of sharing inventory carrying costs. The buyer may not need to pay upon receipt, thus eliminating one element of inventory carrying cost; however, all other costs are still to be borne by the buyer.

---

4 Other names for this inventory category include 'bin stock', 'free issue' or other similar titles.

Typically, these agreements contain several key clauses, the first of which deals with minimum turnover ratios. It is unrealistic to expect a supplier to furnish goods at no charge, only to be stored indefinitely without a sale. A negotiated turnover ratio usually must be met, or the item is returned to the supplier. A second clause addresses the situation where the supplier wants to reclaim some of its inventory for an immediate sale. In such cases, the parties commonly agree that the buyer may exercise a right of first refusal. If the buyer has no immediate need, the supplier is typically allowed to take the goods, and they are to be replenished as soon as possible. If there is an immediate requirement, the buyer may exercise the right of refusal, at which time, the buyer is charged for the goods.

A third critical clause in consignment agreements defines the method by which the buyer and seller will dissolve their relationship. If the buyer deems it necessary to change suppliers, what will happen to the consigned inventory, especially if some of it is custom-made? Obviously, the deposed supplier will be reluctant to take the material back, while the new supplier may be equally reluctant to purchase the material from the old supplier. The buying organization, having grown used to the availability of consigned inventory, will likely be uninspired by the prospect of purchasing the material from the departing supplier. Indirect supply managers are cautioned to make sure this issue is negotiated *before* the consignment agreement is signed, while everyone is on friendly terms and the negotiation is easy. If left until later, when both sides are angry, the separation process may well end up in court.

INVENTORY PERFORMANCE MEASURES
Turnover Ratio

This commonly used indicator of the frequency of inventory usage is typically kept for the inventory as a whole but may be tracked for classes of inventory or for individual items. From another perspective, if inventory is viewed, not as parts on the shelf, but as stacks of dollar bills, the turnover ratio tells managers how much use they are getting from the money invested in inventory. The calculation method was discussed previously. As noted, spare parts may have a turnover ratio of about one, while active inventory items may turn from 4 to 20 times per year, or more.

Inventory Response (Fill) Rate

There may be some debate as to the applicable definition for *response rate*. Is it the percentage of line items filled by the due date, the percentage of line items in one shipment, or the percentage of orders shipped complete, without back orders or substitutions? Regardless of the internal definition agreed upon within an organization, some measure of response is typically kept. From the customer's perspective, only the latter definition is meaningful.

Organizations often set managerial goals for response rates. In doing so, indirect inventory managers are reminded that the seemingly obvious goal of 100 percent requires massive investments in inventory, as ever-larger safety stocks must be maintained to increase toward 100 percent the probability that the inventory quantity on hand will meet any possible demand variability. As a consequence, managers typically set goals for less than 100 percent. If the goal is 98 percent for a particular item, management recognizes that for 2 percent of the orders, there will be stockouts, and accepts this in exchange for the additional inventory investment that must be made to exceed that goal.

MANAGING THE INDIRECT PURCHASING PROCESS
Materials

Contract Types

There are several contract forms that are especially applicable to indirect supply management. Before proceeding with this section, readers are encouraged to delete from memory all previously held definitions of contract types. Instead, please note the product characteristics and managerial objectives leading to the creation of a particular contract type. Think how many different definitions there may be among your colleagues for the term *blanket order*.

Blanket Orders

For purposes of this discussion, the term blanket order will be used to describe an agreement that serves the following situation. Often it is necessary to acquire from local suppliers a few, relatively low-value items on an irregular basis. If the mechanic occasionally needs to pick up a few parts from the hardware store, and if it costs $100 in administrative expenses to generate a purchase order, we hope to avoid spending $100 to buy $40 worth of parts. This is the classic small-order problem. If an organization uses purchase cards, this is an ideal application for them. Not all firms use them, however.

In this situation, a mechanism is needed to minimize administrative costs while still allowing the mechanic (and others, as necessary) access to needed materials. An agreement may be struck with the hardware store whereby a single purchase order number will be issued to cover all materials needed during a single month. The supplier keeps track of what was purchased, by whom, each item's value, and the account to which each item is to be charged. At the end of the month, the list is totaled, and an invoice is submitted. Administratively, several transactions are treated as one, with only one attendant administrative cost. In effect, one purchase order "blankets" numerous purchases. When using such agreements, most organizations fix restrictions on the total value of monthly purchases and limit the individuals authorized to use them. This form of agreement, then, is designed to minimize administrative costs to acquire relatively low-value items with sporadic and unpredictable usage.

Supplier (Vendor) Managed Inventory Contracts

Another situation confronting indirect supply managers is the replenishment of common inventory items. Again, the issue is the minimization of administrative costs, while ensuring material availability. For active or expensed inventory items, it is often possible to negotiate a supply agreement where the supplier manages the buyer's inventory of the goods the supplier sells. On a predetermined schedule (usually weekly) the supplier checks the inventory of the goods being supplied, determines the usage since the last check, and sends goods to bring inventories back to their maximum levels.

Systems Contracts

For situations where an organization requires significant volumes of industry standard products, primary managerial concerns are continuity of supply, competitive pricing, minimum inventories, and a minimum of administrative cost. One tool that addresses all these objectives is a systems contract. Two differentiating characteristics of this type of agreement are fast turnaround time and that users deal directly with the chosen supplier.

The development of such a contract begins with the development of company standards from within the product offerings of suppliers. For example, office products catalogs contain multiple options for every product type. Firms typically select specific products to become company standards.

Orders are placed electronically or by fax on a daily basis. Deliveries occur within 24 hours in cities or usually within 48 hours in outlying areas. This rapid response enables buying organizations to operate with a minimum of inventories of contracted items.

This contract form has multiple advantages in that it allows the aggregation of an organization's needs across long (often multiyear) time frames to maximize leverage. It also addresses the small-order problem (where the administrative costs to generate a purchase order may be more than the goods are worth) by enabling users to deal directly with suppliers without involving the purchasing department. Supply management has done its job by selecting the best supplier and negotiating the terms under which the firms will do business. Having done that, supply management adds no value to small individual transactions for, say, one individual's needs for office products. This contract form has proven successful for a wide variety of indirect materials requirements, such as office products, electrical supplies, plumbing supplies, safety supplies, bearings, and other similar categories. These contracts are typical of the operational alliances formed between buyers and suppliers of industry standard products and are often multiyear.

A common question arising from the implementation of this type of contract is whether, by not involving supply management, users may overbuy. It should be noted emphatically that policing is *not* a supply management function. If an individual overbuys, that is an issue between the individual and the supervisor who has managerial control over the accounts to which the purchases are charged. This is an individual disciplinary issue and should be treated as such. Usually it only takes one well-publicized incident to put a stop to any such transgressions. This is similar to the issues raised when issuing purchase cards to individuals.

Advantages of this form of contract include dramatically reduced inventories, rapid response, high fill rates from information sharing, and most importantly, the minimization of involvement of the supply management organization in a multitude of small orders for common items. Repeatedly, organizations have seen thousands of transactions annually with which the supply management organization no longer needs to be involved.

All too often, indirect purchasing activity is concentrated on this sort of transaction to the exclusion of a focus on strategic activities, further reinforcing the view of some top managers that this is a clerical function. This form of contract addresses these concerns.

National and Regional Corporate Contracts

Frequently, it is advantageous for organizations to aggregate demand for like products across multiple locations. This is especially true for indirect materials, as standardization often leads to this sort of opportunity. In such cases it is common for a central supply management entity to negotiate a contract for such goods with a supplier capable of supplying at least an entire region, if not nationwide. Office products can be used as a suitable example. Almost without exception, an organization's locations from sales offices to manufacturing plants will all require office products. Several office product suppliers offer nationwide capabilities. Pricing should be significantly better in aggregate than if purchased location by location. The advantage to the organization, as a whole, may be significant. However, acceptance of such agreements at the local level may require disrupting long-standing relationships with local suppliers. Individual locations may be very reluctant to comply.

Failure to achieve local acceptance of such corporate agreements clearly negates the benefits, but there may be valid reasons for local reluctance. On occasion, service from a more distant national supplier may be slower than from a local supplier. Loss of a large local account may even jeopardize the continued existence of the local supplier. Compliance with national agreements must be tempered with some degree of flexibility.

Reasonable forecasts of requirements may enable a more distant national contract holder to ensure product availability. Larger, national contract holders may have the resources to offer consignment inventories as another way to ensure availability without increasing inventory investment. In situations where a small local supplier is dependent on a large local buyer, as a matter of social responsibility, it may be desirable to purchase at least part of the local requirement from the local supplier.

Acceptance of corporate national or regional contracts may have its foundation in the formation of the agreement. First, an organization must have firm assurances that the bidders for national contracts truly have the capability to supply all locations promptly and with consistency. Many organizations, after full evaluation, conclude that a few regional contracts may offer nearly the same economies of scale as a national contract, but with better service. Commonly, organizations considering national or regional contracts will include all major consumers of that product category in the supplier evaluation and selection committee.

By example, one major worldwide electronics manufacturer, when developing global purchase agreements, invites representatives of all major using locations to report to headquarters with all their commodity knowledge and information. This commodity team then evaluates all known suppliers, using information brought by team members and developed by the central organization. The team then makes the supplier selection and develops the agreement. Acceptance is assured, since all major users were involved in the selection process and understand the selection criteria and the advantages offered by the selected supplier. Without such buy-in by all major users of the commodity, the contract is sure to fail.

Evergreen Contracts

There are many situations where indirect buying and supplying organizations find it mutually advantageous to form long-term relationships that may not be directly tied to specific purchases or volumes. In such cases, the agreement may have no specified goods nor an expiration date. Commonly, there is a clause to the effect that the agreement can be terminated by either side upon written notice to the other X days or months prior to termination. The notion is that the agreement will continue in force for as long as both sides find it beneficial. An example of this type of agreement is the situation where a firm employs significant numbers of a particular manufacturer's engines. In exchange for first access to new engine models and technologies, the using firm agrees to act as a test facility for those new engines and technologies. These agreements are commonly found in strategic alliances.

In any long-term agreement such as systems contracts, supplier managed contracts, or corporate contracts, there are several critical clauses that must be included. The first is the price change mechanism. If a several-year contract is put in place, how will prices be equitably adjusted, both up and down, over the life of the agreement? In situations where purchases are made from distributors, it is common to find cost-plus agreements, where the distributor's price from the manufacturer plus a negotiated margin will determine the buyer's invoice price. Typically these agreements include the right for the buyer to audit the supplier's books as it chooses, and this mechanism is *easily* auditable, an important characteristic. The authors wish to add a caution, here. Often organizations become fixated on discovering the supplier's "true" cost after any volume discounts, advertising allowances, rebates, and such. This focus often leads to auditing nightmares. To be effective, the pricing mechanism needs to be easily and cleanly auditable. If the manufacturer's invoice plus a negotiated margin equals a fair price, then that should be sufficient. In Chapter 22, "Supplier Price and Cost Analysis," other pricing mechanisms and the use of commodity indexes are discussed.

A second important long-term agreement clause is one that relates to technology. The situation of concern is for a competing supplier to develop a breakthrough technology while the buyer is committed to a now noncompetitive supplier. This clause typically states that if a competing supplier develops new technology, the contracted supplier has a specific period of time to develop a competing technology or the buying company is released from the contract.

Related Tools and Concepts

Purchase Cards

As noted previously, one of the continuing difficulties of indirect purchasing is the small-order problem. It often costs organizations more than $100 in administrative expenses to generate a purchase order. When the typical indirect purchase value may be less than the administrative cost of the transaction, organizations look for less expensive ways to make these acquisitions. One of the tools designed to address this problem is the purchase card. Similar to credit cards, purchase cards may significantly reduce the administrative cost of these low-value transactions. They eliminate the need to set up credit accounts with suppliers from whom there are only infrequent, low-value requirements. Transaction costs in these circumstances may be significantly reduced.

The issue of control is immediately raised as nonpurchasing personnel are granted cards and the authority to purchase. To address this concern, the use of purchase cards may be limited by dollar value per day, per transaction, per week, or per month. They also may be limited to just the specific types of businesses intended by the using organization.

Like any tool, if used for the intended purpose—minimizing the administrative cost of *low-value, nonrepetitive* transactions—they are very effective. Like any tool, if abused, they quickly become problematic. As noted earlier in the discussion of systems contracts, there is always a risk when granting authority to purchase. Traditionally, the purchasing, receiving, and accounts payable functions have been segregated to minimize the possibility of "creative" transactions. Firms have been willing to accept the risk of placing all those activities in the hands of a single individual in exchange for the opportunity to minimize transaction costs for *low-value, nonrepetitive* transactions. As noted in the discussion of systems contracts, transgressions in the use of purchase cards are individual disciplinary issues between the cardholder and the supervisor.

Integrated Supply

As a concept, one-stop shopping has a certain appeal. As applied to indirect purchases, it typically involves the selection of a single supplier for all necessary MRO materials. Several nationwide distributors advocate this process. If they don't have it, they will get it. In addition, the integrated supplier often offers to staff and manage a firm's toolroom, as well. Receiving all MRO materials from one supplier is attractive in terms of minimizing administrative costs, but integrated supply equates functionally to outsourcing the MRO purchasing function. There is a significant difference in perspective from an organization whose primary function is to sell product and one whose charge is to make goods available when and where needed at the least *total* cost. If considering such an arrangement, organizations should proceed cautiously, being careful to identify all the true costs related to such a program.

One of the chief objections to integrated supply is that organizations may lose technical support from local suppliers. Many firms come to depend on suppliers for technical information, training, and advice. Problems involving electrical systems, welding, hydraulics, and others frequently benefit from supplier assistance. Those contacts may be lost upon the adoption of an integrated supply system from a single supplier. For this reason, and several others, a number of organizations that have experimented with integrated supply have abandoned it.

There is a version of integrated supply that has proven widely successful. Single sourcing—electing to buy all of a particular product type from a single supplier—is popular. This amounts to integrating across a single commodity or product classification. For example, if an organization buys much of its requirement for electrical supplies from one supplier, but buys specific brands from other suppliers, it may be effective to arrange that the primary supplier procure from other dealers the specific parts on behalf of the buying organization.

In effect, this converts several first-tier suppliers from whom only small quantities are purchased to second-tier suppliers. This accomplishes the dual objectives of reducing the supplier base and minimizing the administrative costs of acquiring electrical supplies while maintaining the all-important access to technical expertise.

Collaborative Planning, Forecasting, and Replenishment

The concept of *collaborative planning, forecasting, and replenishment* (CPFR) is no less applicable or important to indirect purchases than to those for production. Any time an organization has continuing high-volume requirements, it is to the benefit of both the buying organization and the supplier to collaborate to meet those requirements. It is incumbent on the buying organization to develop realistic forecasts and to share them with important suppliers. Since a fundamental strategy of supply management is to minimize supply chain costs, sharing of forecasts allows suppliers to prepare and deliver necessary materials without having to rely on large inventories.

The industrial distribution industry has been undergoing consolidation for several years. This is a special caution for indirect supply managers, as supplier performance frequently changes following a change of ownership. At times, new owners reduce inventories or otherwise change their operating characteristics. Discounts and terms may change, and on-time delivery performance and lead times may be altered, as well. In other instances, marginal suppliers are helped by an infusion of cash and managerial talent from new owners and become superior suppliers. At the least, a change in ownership is cause for close observation of the supplier's performance for a considerable time after the change.

F I G U R E 35–3

Application of Tools to Categories

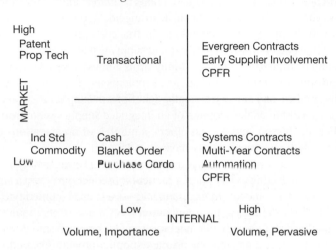

Returning to the criticality grid discussed earlier, and recalling the objectives of each of the quadrants, it is now possible to determine which types of agreements and tools best apply to each of the categories of indirect purchase transactions, as illustrated in Figure 35–3.

Services

Statements of Work

Indirect supply management has increasingly become involved with service contracts as organizations outsource functions previously accomplished by employees. Such activities as janitorial services, grounds maintenance, building maintenance, and copier and other office machine service agreements are common. Communications contracts, energy contracts (electricity and gas supply contracts, for example), and contracts for construction and remodeling all require detailed and exact descriptions of supplier activities. Additionally, contracts for such activities as electric motor rewinding and machine maintenance and overhaul pose further difficulty since the exact work to be performed may not be known until the machine is disassembled. In such cases, it is common to negotiate agreements with suppliers defining the hourly rates for various activities. Further, many firms form contracts defining ranges of activity with a negotiated amount tied to each level. Minor repairs, intermediate repairs, and major overhauls may each have specific rates. The caution here is to clearly define the characteristics of each category and the points of division between them.

Statements of work are to services what specifications are to products or materials, except that they often are much more difficult. Services don't come with part numbers. Development of thorough, complete statements of work are critical to successful service contracts. For example, organizations frequently outsource janitorial services. Ordinarily, such services include emptying waste baskets and cleaning restrooms. But what does "'empty waste baskets'" mean? Not only should the basket be emptied, but perhaps the buyer also wants a plastic bag in the basket. What kind of plastic bag? What size? What mil thickness? Will the contractor be allowed to reuse the bag if it is not soiled?

When the contractor is asked to clean a restroom and mop the floor, what does "mop the floor" mean? With just water? With a disinfectant? What kind? Rinse afterward? There are several points here. First, it is incumbent upon the buyer to fully and completely describe the service the contractor is to provide. This is a complex and time-consuming task, but it must be done for several reasons. If it is done well, the rest of the transaction typically proceeds smoothly. If it is done haphazardly, there will be conflicts and dissatisfaction on both sides. Each of the elements of the statement of work represents a cost element to the contractor and also represents a component of performance evaluation. If the statement of work is developed thoroughly, both sides know exactly what is expected, what is to be provided, and how performance will be measured. This is obviously a more protracted process than ordering by part number and can be equated to the development of specifications for a custom product. In almost every sense, a service agreement is a custom application and requires the same sort of analysis, planning, and design as a custom-engineered component.

There is a definitional distinction between *make or buy* and *outsourcing*. The former is a fluid decision, revisited periodically. Under some conditions, an organization may itself perform the activity. Other conditions will lead to buying the service (or material); even so, the organization retains its internal capability. Outsourcing typically results in the decision to eliminate the internal capability and to depend on suppliers thereafter. Outsourcing, however, does not relieve the buying organization of the responsibility to continue to manage the function. All too often organizations outsource a maintenance service and then forget to actively manage the activity, perhaps even more intensely than when the activity was performed internally. The importance of this intense management of outsourced activities cannot be overstressed.

One of the more difficult service agreements to administer is one for a consultant. Nevertheless, a statement of work should be carefully constructed to include the specific tasks expected of the consultant, a thoughtful and thorough definition of the problem(s) to be examined, and, most importantly, the particular deliverables and timetable for completion of the project. The same cautions previously noted with regard to materials purchases also apply to service agreements. At times consultants, like manufacturers, have capacity constraints. Consultants should be prohibited from outsourcing or subcontracting the work without written permission from the buyer. The consulting contract should also include agreements about the specific level of personnel (or even names of specific persons) to be assigned to the project, and the hourly rates for their services. Finally, the consultant should provide an estimate of the number of hours required to complete the project. Many organizations have seen consulting projects, especially for information technology

(IT) services or software development, balloon beyond any expectation because the buying organization did not spend the necessary time to clearly define the needs of the project and because the consultant was not asked to provide a realistic cost estimate. Situations like this may suggest the use of contracts with "not to exceed" values.

INFORMATION SYSTEMS AND TECHNOLOGY APPLICATIONS IN INDIRECT MATERIALS MANAGEMENT

Indirect purchasing offers many opportunities to automate routine transactions. As illustrated in Figure 35–3, those transactions involving repetitive requirements for industry standard products are particularly appropriate. Inventory replenishment is often accomplished in this way, with minimums, maximums, and supplier infor mation entered for each item to be controlled in this manner. As the computer system tracks current balances of each item, when the balance on hand reaches or goes below a predetermined minimum, the computer notifies the supplier's computer to replenish the item. In one large international organization, more than 60 percent of all indirect materials orders are automated, going directly to predetermined suppliers without the necessity of purchasing intervention.

It is not the intention of this chapter to develop a lengthy discussion of the capabilities of various software systems. Suffice it to say that it is critically important to involve all the organization's operations—purchasing, logistics, inventory management, and production management—in the software selection decision. All too often, the authors have seen selection decisions driven by finance, accounting, and information technology departments, only to find that they are operational disasters. One organization could find all information necessary to create an order from only two screens in its legacy system. In the new system, it takes seven. In frustration, purchasing has reverted to hard copies as being easier than searching through seven screens. The point is to be extremely careful in the selection process to ensure that all necessary functionality is contained in the new system and that the new system is not unnecessarily complex.

On the other end of the spectrum are really proficient systems that provide ready information about all elements of material flow. Order transmittals and acknowledgments, advance ship notices, in-transit tracking, bar code reading, radio frequency technologies, real-time inventory tracking, order tracking through the production process, finished goods storage, and outbound shipment tracking are just some of the functionalities available from more advanced systems. Today, it is imperative for indirect supply managers to be technologically proficient, as most of these functions are, at least to some degree, systems driven.

Impacts of Global Supply Chains

Nuts and bolts come from China, grinding wheels from Great Britain, bearings from South Korea or Brazil, gloves from Indonesia. In short, indirect materials come from all over the world. While this often leads to lower prices, transaction complexity increases sharply. Lead times stretch out, leading to increased pipeline inventories, while security processes further increase lead times. Quality concerns often lead to the use of independent inspection agencies to assure quality before the material is loaded into a container. Indeed, many letters of credit require a satisfactory inspection certificate prior to payment. Many MRO materials are suitable candidates for global sourcing, especially industry standard products, since their specifications are known and there are many available suppliers.

In comparing domestic and offshore suppliers it is essential to develop a total landed cost for each. What does it cost, in total, for the products to be delivered to the receiving area? Domestically, transportation costs and payment terms would be included, in addition to price. Alternatively, inland transportation, wharfage and handling, port charges, stevedoring charges, ocean freight, customs costs, paperwork costs, and inland transportation are considered, in addition to price. While foreign suppliers may offer attractive prices, only by examining total landed costs can the indirect supply manager determine if the deal is beneficial.

Counterfeit Goods

As indirect supply managers increasingly acquire materials from global sources, the possibility of finding counterfeit goods in the supply chain increases. One automaker estimates that of all parts sold with its brand name worldwide, 40 percent are counterfeit. Other instances of counterfeit indirect materials include electrical connectors in military helicopters, circuit breakers in nuclear power plants, aircraft parts, and even such common products as nuts and bolts. It is therefore imperative for indirect supply managers to thoroughly understand their supply chains and the reliability of the firms in them.

Another related concern is the advisability of using aftermarket parts. Commonly, several companies offer parts to fit a particular machine. An original equipment manufacturer (OEM) may charge more for parts than does an aftermarket supplier, so there is an obvious temptation to save money by buying the aftermarket part. However there is a responsibility to ensure that the aftermarket part is truly the equivalent of the OEM part. While the aftermarket part may be less expensive, it may require more frequent replacement, it may fail under use, or otherwise may not deliver the service of the OEM part. This is not to suggest that the aftermarket part *may not* be as good as, or even better than, the OEM part. It is the responsibility of indirect supply management to make that determination.

Security and Sustainability

Increased safety and security concerns are evident in many aspects of indirect supply management from border crossing delays and attendant increased costs, to computer virus attacks. Increased global sourcing and dependence on technology tools highlight reasons for apprehension. In response to these, and other risks, many firms are developing formal risk analysis and risk mitigation plans. Suppliers may be asked to develop problem prevention plans to assure buyers that operations can continue even if the supplier suffers a disaster. Everything from political risk to labor disruptions to natural disasters are considered. Supply chains are evaluated for all critical parts. The goal begins with problem avoidance. If an organization buys from an offshore supplier (e.g., an electric utility buys a replacement transformer from a South Korean supplier), it is important to know that the West Coast Longshore contract will expire just when the product is to arrive at a West Coast port. Rerouting to a Gulf port may avoid a potential lengthy delay.

The secondary goal is the mitigation of the adverse event, once it has occurred. For example, a key producer of antifreeze suffers a plant explosion just as winter approaches. If an organization operates equipment through the winter, this may represent increased costs or even a shutdown. The formal risk evaluation and mitigation process leads to planning in a calm environment, rather than crisis decision making.

Indirect supply managers are frequently responsible for the development and operation of environmental responsibility programs. From recycling to the selection and use of less environmentally damaging or hazardous materials, these activities are of increasing importance and visibility, often being the result of top management directives. Handling, storage, and disposal of hazardous material is a never-ending responsibility. Minimizing facility emissions in terms of air or water quality are equally important as they represent not only politically sensitive issues but increasingly costly ones, as well.

Systems Integration for Indirect Supply Management

Indirect supply management incorporates a multitude of disciplines from maintenance and engineering to purchasing and supply management, inventory management, logistics, forecasting, and scheduling. In addition, this function may be responsible for the acquisition of energy, capital equipment, and a multitude of services across many disciplinary lines. As a governing notion, all these disciplines and activities must be managed collectively, not independently. These functions are interdependent and interrelated to the degree that separate management leads inevitably to decisions that may maximize performance of one to the detriment of others. Understanding realistic lead times is critical to maintenance project scheduling. All too often, maintenance schedules are completed, and then purchasing is informed of material or service needs. Airfreight, overtime, and rescheduling often result. Purchasing large quantities may lead to lower prices but may also decrease the performance of indirect inventories. Coordinating the activities and information flow among all these parties is facilitated by today's hardware and software technologies. Enterprise resource planning software has a great influence on indirect supply management because it enables all interested parties and functions, even outside the organization, to access the same information to develop and coordinate schedules, plan for future requirements, and ensure material availability and control.

CONCLUSION

This chapter has identified characteristics that differentiate indirect supply management from other supply activities. Great variety, typically small individual orders, requirements from virtually every firm location, inventories that serve many different functions with different performance characteristics, and the implementation of integrating technologies make this a challenging activity. The criticality grid and numerous contract types were introduced as tools to assist in achieving goals of ensuring availability with a minimum of administrative cost. Indirect materials inventories pose another indirect supply management challenge. Several methods were discussed that facilitate control of the several classes of indirect inventories. Underlying all the activities of indirect supply management are the functional, commodity, and supplier strategies developed to improve overall performance. These are the tools that enable indirect supply managers to provide necessary materials and services at a minimum total cost across the entire spectrum of organizational locations and needs.

CHAPTER 36

INTELLECTUAL PROPERTY AND TECHNOLOGY ACQUISITION

LESLIE S. MARELL
Attorney at Law
Law Offices of Leslie S. Marell

The successful acquisition of software and other technology requires knowledge of various types of legal principles. These principles are drawn from a number of areas of the law, including the law of contracts, employment, and intellectual property.

Part 1 of this chapter will introduce the concept of intellectual property and provide an overview of the four principal types of intellectual property. The final section of Part 1 will address the common myths and misconceptions surrounding intellectual property. Part 2 will apply these intellectual property principles to the acquisition of software and other technology as well as identify and discuss the key issues involved in the technology acquisition agreement.

PART 1: WHAT IS INTELLECTUAL PROPERTY?

Intellectual property consists of creations of the mind that are given the legal rights often associated with real or personal property. The rights that are given are a function of statutory law (i.e., law created by the legislature). These statutes may be federal or state laws, or in some instances, both federal and state laws govern various aspects of a single type of intellectual property. The term *intellectual property* is commonly used to refer to the bundle of rights conferred by each of the following four fields of law:

1. Trade secret (also known as *confidential* or *proprietary* information) law

2. Copyright law

3. Trademark law

4. Patent law

Some people confuse these areas of intellectual property law, and although there may be some similarities among these kinds of intellectual property protection, they are different and serve different purposes.

Trade Secret Law

Virtually all states have adopted a portion or modified version of the Uniform Trade Secrets Act, which was drafted by the National Conference of Commissioners on Uniform State Laws in 1970 and amended in 1985. Under the Uniform Trade Secrets Act, a trade secret is defined as information or know-how that (1) is not generally known in the business community, (2) provides its owner with a competitive advantage in the marketplace, and (3) is treated in a way that can reasonably be expected to prevent others from learning about it. Trade secrecy is based on a simple idea: by keeping valuable information secret, one can prevent competitors from learning about it and using it. While the legal community refers to this type of information as *trade secrets,* businesspeople typically refer to this information as *confidential* or *proprietary.*

The information can be an idea, written words, a formula, a process or procedure, a technical design, a customer list, a marketing plan, or any other secret that gives the owner an economic advantage.

Trade secret law protects the owner of the confidential information against unauthorized use, copying, or disclosure. However, in order to protect the confidential information, the holder of a trade secret must do more than put a confidentiality notice on his or her materials. He or she must actually maintain the secrecy of them. This requires, among other things, that the recipient of the information agree in writing to maintain the secrecy of the confidential information.

The reward for developing and maintaining a trade secret is that it may last forever; however, others are merely prohibited from misappropriating it. Anyone is free to independently develop the same information.

Unlike copyrights and patents, which are governed by federal law, trade secrecy is *not* codified in any federal statute. Instead, it is made up of individual state laws and is based on such state laws, common law, and contractual provisions. However, the protection afforded to trade secrets in every state is much the same. Trade secret protection attaches automatically when information of value to the owner is kept secret by the owner. There are no formal registration requirements.

In order to ensure that a company's trade secrets remain confidential, all recipients of the trade secrets should sign a confidentiality agreement, also known as a nondisclosure agreement (NDA). Simply marking a document "Proprietary" or "Confidential" may not be enough to legally require that the recipient keep the information confidential.

A nondisclosure agreement (or confidentiality agreement) is a contract in which a party who is given access to trade secret information promises that information conveyed will be maintained in secrecy and not disclosed to others. The creation of a confidentiality agreement is really the creation of a confidential relationship. Generally speaking, such confidential relationships can usually be created both in writing and orally. It should be noted, however, that while some court cases in some jurisdictions do allow the oral creation of such a relationship, and some court cases in some jurisdictions do allow actions to be used as evidence of the creation of such a relationship, *you should never rely on or anticipate that a court will enforce an oral agreement or an agreement based only upon action.* This is true because it is exceedingly difficult, if not impossible, to prove the existence of an oral agreement and/or actions that suggest the creation of such an agreement. Obtaining signed nondisclosure agreements consistently is the single most important element of any trade secret protection program.

Copyright Law

A copyright is a form of protection provided by the federal laws of the United States (and most other countries) to those who create what the law refers to as "original works of authorship." Copyright protects only the *expression* of the idea, concept, or discovery in a computer program, book, or movie; it does not protect any ideas, concepts, or discoveries embodied in the work. In fact, the U.S. Copyright Act states that, "In no case does copyright protection for an original work of authorship extend to any idea, procedure, process, system, method of operation, concept, principle or discovery ..."

Copyright protects all kinds of works of authorship. These include literary works (software programs, computer databases, designs, documentation, training manuals); musical works (songs, advertising jingles); dramatic works (plays, operas); choreographic works (ballets, mime); motion picture and other audiovisual works; sound recordings; pictorial, graphic or sculptural works (photographs, posters, maps, cartoons); and architectural works (building designs).

Copyrights provide their owners with the exclusive right to reproduce, display, perform, distribute, and prepare derivative works from the copyrighted work. The owner has a monopoly on his or her fixed *expression* of an idea, but does *not* have a monopoly on the idea itself. Others are free to independently create even an identical work and to make whatever use they wish of the ideas embodied in the copyrighted work.

Ideas are not protected by copyright law because protecting an idea would take the idea out of the public domain and prevent others from using the idea to create their own independent and original works of authorship. Such an occurrence would frustrate the very purpose of copyright law, which is to stimulate creativity and provide the appropriate incentives to foster the creation of more artistic works.

For example, a description of a new machine can be copyrighted, but this would only prevent others from copying the description. It would not prevent others from writing a description of their own or from making and using the machine.

The *first sale doctrine* is an exception to the exclusivity rights given to owners of copyrights. The first sale doctrine allows owners of lawfully made copies of a work (e.g., a book) to sell, rent, or otherwise dispose of their copies of the book without the authorization of the copyright owner. In 1990, software rental was exempted from the first sale doctrine. However, a revision to the U.S. Copyright Act in 1999 permits the owner of a computer program to make copies essential for use of the program as well as an archival copy, and permits the transfer of the copy so long as he or she transfers all copies.

Before March 1, 1989, all published works had to contain a copyright notice (the © symbol followed by the publication date and the copyright owner's name). This is no longer necessary in the United States. Under current law, a work is automatically protected by copyright upon its creation, that is, as soon as it is "fixed in any tangible medium of expression." Even so, it is always a good idea to include a copyright notice on all works distributed to the public. Registration of the copyright with the U.S. Copyright Office is optional; however, the copyright must be registered before an infringement lawsuit is filed.

The copyright owner has the exclusive rights to *reproduce* (copy, duplicate), *modify* (also known as the derivative works right because it is the right to modify the work to create a new work, e.g., a movie made from a novel), *distribute* (to sell, rent, or lease to the public), and *publicly display and perform* (show the work at a public place).

When you acquire a copyrighted work, you have the right to use that copyrighted work only to the extent that your use does not *infringe* (violate) the exclusive rights of the copyright holder. For example, when you acquire a music CD, you have the right to play that CD on any CD player, including a CD player not belonging to you. However, your ownership of the CD does not give you the right to make copies of that CD or incorporate all or any part of the music into another medium.

One who violates any of the exclusive rights of a copyright owner is an infringer. A copyright owner can recover actual damages or, in some cases, statutory damages from an infringer. The federal courts have the power to issue injunctions (orders) to prevent copyright infringements and to require that the infringer stop the infringing activity. Most copyright infringement cases are civil cases. However, copyright infringement can also be a criminal offense.

Under current law, the copyright term for works created by individuals is the life of the author plus 70 years. The copyright term for "works made for hire" (see next section) is 95 years from the date of first publication (distribution of copies to the public) or 120 years from the date of creation, whichever expires first.

Ownership of Copyrights

As a general rule, the creator of a work owns the copyright. This means that when a company retains an independent contractor to develop, design, or create a work, the independent contractor, *not the company,* will own the copyright to the work. *Works made for hire* are an important exception to the general rule.

If a work is created by an *employee* as part of his or her job, the law considers the product a work made for hire, and the employer will own the copyright. Therefore, as an employee, whatever works you create are owned by your employer.

In addition, if the creator is an *independent contractor*, the works will be considered works for hire *only* if (1) the parties have signed a written agreement stating that the work will be a work for hire, *and* (2) the work is commissioned as a contribution to a collective work, a supplementary work, an instructional text, answer material for a test, an atlas, motion picture, or an audiovisual work. *Thus, unless there is a contractual agreement to the contrary, and the work fits within one of the preceding categories, the independent contractor owns the copyright.*

Note that the preceding list for independent contractors is very limited. The items likely to be purchased such as computer programs, designs, photographs, and catalogs are not listed. Merely including the "work made for hire" language is not enough to ensure that your company obtains ownership to the copyright in most cases.

In order to effect a transference of the copyright ownership to your company, you should have a contract that includes language in which the independent contractor transfers ("assigns") the copyright in the creation to your company. The following is example language of an independent contractor assigning his or her copyright rights in the work to the company.

> Independent Contractor assigns and transfers to Company all right, title and interest worldwide in and to the Work and all proprietary rights therein, including, without limitation, all copyrights, trademarks, design patents, trade secret rights, and all contract and licensing rights.

When You Don't Need a License or Permission to Use Copyrighted Work

You don't need a license to use copyrighted work if your use is "fair use" or the material is in the public domain. The fair use of a copyrighted work is not an infringement of copyright. The fair use exception to the copyright owner's rights permits limited use of copyrighted material for purposes such as criticism; news reporting, teaching (nonprofit), research, and comment. Examples of fair use are quoting passages from a book in a book review and summarizing an article with brief quotations for a news report.

It is not always easy to tell whether a use of a work is fair use or unfair and an infringement. Determinations are made on a case-by-case basis by considering four factors: (1) the purpose of use, (2) the nature of the copyrighted work, (3) the portion used, and (4) the effect on the potential market for the copyrighted work.

Public domain works are not protected by copyright and can be used by anyone. For example, the plays of Shakespeare are in the public domain. In addition, works created by federal government employees as part of their official duties are not covered by copyright. Works enter the public domain in several ways: the term of the copyright expires, or for works created before March 1, 1989, the copyright owner failed to properly use a copyright notice.

COPYRIGHT LAW AND THE INTERNET

Much of the material that is on the Internet is protected by copyright. If you want to use material you found on the Internet in your own project—on a Web site, in a Web product, or in some other medium such as a newsletter—don't assume that you are free to use the material. If the material is in the public domain, you do not need permission. However, if it is copyrighted, unless fair use or some other exception to the copyright owner's rights apply, you need permission.

Digital Millennium Copyright Act

In 1998, Congress enacted the Digital Millennium Copyright Act which, among other things, dealt with the issues of software piracy and copyright violations on the Internet. In general terms, the Act

- Makes it a crime to circumvent antipiracy measures built into most commercial software
- Outlaws the manufacture, sale, or distribution of code-cracking devices used to illegally copy software
- In general, limits Internet service providers from copyright infringement liability for simply transmitting information over the Internet
  - Expects Internet service providers, however, to remove material from users' Web sites that appears to constitute copyright infringement

Trademark Law

A trademark is any visual mark that accompanies a particular product, or line of goods, and serves to identify and distinguish it from products sold by others and to indicate its source. A trademark may consist of letters, words, names, phrases or slogans, numbers, colors, jingles, symbols, designs or shapes, or combinations of any of these. Common trademarks include "Coke," "Intel," the picture of an apple with a bite taken out of it, and "The Ultimate Driving Machine." As a general rule, to be protected from unauthorized use by others, a trademark must be distinctive in some way.

A service mark is the same as a trademark except that it identifies and distinguishes the source of a service rather than a product. The terms *trademark* and *mark* are commonly used to refer to both trademarks and service marks.

The word *trademark* is also a generic term used to describe the entire broad body of state and federal laws that cover how businesses distinguish their products and services from the competition. Each state has it own set of laws establishing when and how trademarks can be protected. There is also a federal trademark law called the Lanham Act which applies in all 50 states. Generally, state trademark laws are relied upon for marks used only within one particular state, while the Lanham Act is used to protect marks for products that are sold in more than one state or across state or national borders.

A trademark is registered by filing an application with the U.S. Patent and Trademark Office (USPTO) in Washington, DC. Registration is not mandatory; under both federal and state laws, a company may obtain trademark rights in the states in which the mark is actually used. However, registration provides important benefits. These include the mark's owner is presumed to have the exclusive right to use the mark nationwide, and anyone who begins using a confusingly similar mark after the mark has been registered will be considered a willful infringer. This means that the trademark owner can collect larger damages. The owner of a registered trademark is entitled to use the symbol ® after the mark. The ™ symbol is used to denote marks that have been registered on a state basis only or marks that have not yet been officially registered by the USPTO.

Patent Law

Patent law protects inventions and processes ("utility" patents) and ornamental designs ("design" patents). Inventions and processes protected by utility patents can be electrical, mechanical, or chemical in nature. Internet-related works protectible by utility patents include communications protocols, data compression techniques, interfaces, encryption techniques, online payment systems, and information processing technologies. Examples of works protected by design patents are a design for the sole of running shoes, a design for sterling silver tableware, and a design for a water fountain.

A patent for an invention is the grant of a property right to the inventor, issued by the USPTO. The term of a new patent is 20 years from the date on which the application for the patent was filed in the USPTO or, in special cases, from the date an earlier related application was filed, subject to the payment of maintenance fees. U.S. patent grants are effective only within the United States, U.S. territories, and U.S. possessions.

The right conferred by the patent grant is, in the language of the statute and of the grant itself, "the right to exclude others from making, using, offering for sale, or selling" the invention in the United States or "importing" the invention into the United States. What is granted is not the right to make, use, offer for sale, sell, or import, but the right to exclude others from making, using, offering for sale, selling, or importing the invention.

There are strict requirements for the grant of utility patents and design patents. In order to be patentable, the invention must meet several basic legal tests and be sufficiently "innovative." Generally, in order to obtain a patent, the invention must meet each of the following criteria:

- *Novel.* Unique compared to previous technology in one or more of its elements

- *Nonobvious.* Surprising to a person with ordinary skills in that technology

- *Useful.* Possessing a sufficient degree of utility

In the United States, a patent is obtained by submitting an application and fee to the USPTO. Once it has received the application, the USPTO assigns an examiner who is knowledgeable in the technology underlying the invention to decide whether the invention qualifies for a patent and what the scope of the patent should be.

Until fairly recently, computer software was thought not to be patentable on the grounds that it consists of mathematical algorithms. Mathematical algorithms had long been considered to be unpatentable as abstract methods for solving problems and not tied to a particular use. Also, they were considered to be akin to laws of nature and unpatentable on that ground as well.

However, a series of decisions by the Court of Appeals for the Federal Circuit during the mid to late 1990s significantly modified this view by permitting patents to be issued with respect to software if the process the software implements or the machine it creates when combined with hardware is the subject matter of what is being patented, not the computer code itself.

Each of these four types of intellectual property may be used to protect different aspects of software, although there is a great deal of overlap. The supply manager should be aware of their application to software in order to construct a meaningful software acquisition agreement.

Intellectual Property Common Myths and Misconceptions

The following are some of the more common intellectual property misconceptions and explanations of their inaccuracies:

1. The work I want to use doesn't have a copyright notice on it, so it's not copyrighted.

   Why it's wrong: Although most published works contain a copyright notice, it's optional for works published after March 1, 1989. Copyrights automatically vest upon completion of the document. Just because a work doesn't have a copyright notice doesn't mean the work is unprotected by copyright. In fact, it probably is.

2. In order to have a copyright in something, you must register the copyright with the U.S. Patent and Trademark Office.

   Why it's wrong: Registration of a copyright is helpful as a procedural matter if you want to sue someone for infringement. However, registration is not required in order to have a copyright.

3. I don't need a license from the owner because I'm using only a small amount of the copyrighted work.

Why it's wrong: It's true that de minimis copying, that is, very small amounts of copying, does not infringe a copyright. But the courts have found it very difficult to tell where de minimis copying ends and copyright infringement begins. Copying a small amount of copyrighted work is an infringement if what is copied is qualitatively substantial. Copying any part of a copyrighted work is risky. It's better to get permission or a license to use.

4. If I hire a computer programmer to write a program or a photographer to take pictures of my company's product for its brochure, my company owns the copyrights in the resulting work because the program or pictures were specially made for and were paid for by my company.

   Why it's wrong: This is a common misunderstanding. The copyright law vests ownership of the copyright in the author. In the above cases, the authors are the computer programmer and the photographer. The person commissioning or paying for the work is *not* entitled to copyright ownership.

5. If I put a clause in my contract with the independent contractor stating that the items he or she creates are "a work-made-for-hire," I will then own the copyrights.

   Why it's wrong: The copyright laws define a work-made-for-hire that is not prepared by an employee to include nine rather restrictive items. The items likely to be purchased such as computer drawings, photographs, catalogs, and designs are not listed. Merely including the "work-made-for-hire" language is not enough to ensure that your company obtains ownership to the copyright. Your contract should include language in which the independent contractor assigns the copyright to your company.

6. If I give my supplier a copy of our company's drawings which are stamped "Proprietary," the supplier is then obligated to keep the drawings confidential.

   Why it's wrong: Simply informing the supplier of the trade secret status is not enough. In addition, your supplier must promise to treat the information in confidence. You should ensure that your supplier signs a nondisclosure agreement before you give him or her the drawing.

7. If our company licenses one copy of an accounting program, we are entitled to install that program on our local area network. All members of our accounting department then will be entitled to access the program from their personal computers.

   Why it's wrong: You are entitled to install the program in your centralized computer. However, multiple access from the remote terminals would be just as much an infringement as if you made separate copies of the program. The exception would be if you had obtained a site license.

8. We receive a subscription of a technical magazine. Based on the "fair use" doctrine exception in the copyright law and for educational purposes, we can make copies of it to distribute to all the engineers of our department.

Why it's wrong: "Fair use" is a legal defense against a claim of copyright infringement. Simply put, the fair use privilege permits a person to make limited use of a copyright owner's work without asking the owner's permission. The following are generally considered to be fair uses: (a) criticism and comment, (b) research, (c) nonprofit educational uses, and (d) news reporting.

Note that except for news reporting, the uses are primarily for nonprofit educational purposes. In a well-known case, Texaco was found guilty of copyright infringement when the one subscription it purchased was copied for distribution for a number of the members of its technical department. In finding Texaco liable for copyright infringement, the court found that the distribution of the copies benefited Texaco commercially and was not nonprofit in nature.

9. Our engineers are free at any time to reverse-engineer a device or disassemble a software program.

Why it's wrong: Reverse engineering is perfectly legal so long as it doesn't violate another's patent or copyright rights. If the hardware is not subject to patent protection but rather trade secret protection, reverse engineering of the device is permissible. So long as there is no patent on the hardware and provided there is no contract prohibiting reverse engineering, the hardware may be reverse-engineered.

Software, however, which is usually subject to copyright protection, is another matter. The courts generally hold that reverse-engineering or decompilation of a software program is permissible as a fair use exception to the copyright only when (a) reverse engineering or decompilation is the only available means to study the unprotected elements of a program (the ideas, function principles, etc.) and (b) the copier has a legitimate reason for seeking such access (such as development of a compatible or complementary program that does not cause the copyright owner economic harm).

10. If our company no longer requires the maintenance services for our computer system because we are outsourcing our entire information systems function, including the computer equipment, we automatically have the right to terminate the maintenance contract.

Why it's wrong: A party to the contract does not have an automatic right to terminate a contract due to business reasons. The right to terminate for breach by a party is a remedy at law (in other words, it does not have to be written anywhere in the contract). However, the right to terminate for the convenience of a party (even if necessitated by business decisions) is not automatic and must be written into the contract (making it a remedy in contract).

11. Our company has a substantial computer system for which we have licensed many software programs. We want to outsource the operation of the system to a third party. When we negotiated the software licenses, we did not consider the possibility of outsourcing. Some of our software licensors are demanding additional royalties. Since we already paid the license fee and are paying yearly maintenance, we do not have an obligation to make payment.

Why it's wrong: Typically, a software license expressly prohibits sublicensing or assignment (transferring) by the licensee without first obtaining the licensor's consent. The license will probably limit your company's operation of the software to employees of the company, and not third parties. If the original license did not contemplate the possibility of outsourcing, there will have to be a new negotiation and the licensor may try to demand additional money.

PART 2: TECHNOLOGY ACQUISITION
Technology Development and License Agreements

The License Agreement

Software or technology that exists is generally acquired vis-à-vis a license agreement between the owner of the technology *(licensor)* and the customer *(licensee)*. A *license* is the permission given by the licensor to the licensee to use the technology in a specific, limited manner but does not grant any ownership interest in the technology. Most software contracts today grant the party acquiring the software a *license* to use the software, rather than transferring ownership through the purchase process.

The Development Agreement

Development agreements are not licenses, per se, since they usually relate to the creation of software or other technology. The type of agreement contemplated is an agreement in which the customer approaches the developer to produce a new product, software program, technology, or major modification of an existing product or technology to meet a particular customer need. Once the technology is developed, the customer will acquire the technology either as its owner or as a licensee. Two major purposes of the development agreement, therefore, are the development of the technology and the determination of ownership of the newly developed technology. If the customer acquires the technology vis-à-vis a license, the ultimate agreement becomes both a development and license agreement.

In discussing the issues applicable to these agreements, the acquisition of software will be the technology contemplated. However, the principles identified apply to the acquisition of any technology. The following are some of the major issues that should be addressed in the license agreement and/or development agreement.

Development of Design Specifications and Technology

One of the major distinctions between the license agreement and the development agreement relates to the development of the detailed technical and performance specifications ("specifications"). The license agreement assumes an existing software product whose specifications have been developed. This is not the case in the development agreement whose primary purpose is to create a new software product. Specifications for the software do not, in fact, exist but are to be developed during the course of the agreement.

In the development agreement, it is the customer's responsibility to ensure that the software to be developed is defined as specifically as possible. Frequently, this is the most difficult step in the entire process and is generally the first function to be performed by the developer. Prior to the development of the specifications, the customer should write a generalized statement of the desired capabilities and functions required of the software. After the developer's preparation of the specifications, the customer should thoroughly review the specifications for its final approval and prior to the commencement of the actual development of the software. Preparation of the specifications is a step for which the customer almost always accepts an obligation to pay, whether the desired software is ever developed or not. Once the specifications are approved, they should become the basis for all further performance by the developer under the agreement.

The software to be developed should be made available for evaluation by the customer in several phases so that the work product can be evaluated as work progresses. In such instances, it is possible to test and accept each portion of the software as it is completed with payments for the completed portions being made upon the customer's acceptance of each portion. Additionally, a portion of the total payment due should be withheld until the entire software program is completed, tested, and found to perform in accordance with the specifications. The sums withheld should be large enough to ensure that the developer cannot abandon the project short of completion and still make a profit.

The customer should be able to terminate the development agreement at any time on relatively short notice if the customer becomes dissatisfied with the progress of the work. Alternatively, the developer's right to terminate the agreement should be limited. The equities mandate this approach. If the customer is solely dependent upon the developer to complete the work, the customer could suffer great detriment if the work is 90 percent complete and the developer decides not to continue. Conversely, the detriment to the developer if the customer elects to terminate the effort at this point is relatively minor, if the customer pays for work performed to the date of termination.

Ownership of the Intellectual Property

An area of frequent controversy in the development agreement is the issue of ownership in the resulting software. Since the customer will have paid for development of the resulting software and confidential customer information is likely included in the software, the customer will want to own the resulting work product including any developed specifications and all copyrights therein. On the other hand, if the developer has substantial experience and/or intends to incorporate previously developed technology into the software, the developer may well consider that the developer should own the resulting software with the customer having only a license.

As a practical matter, most customers do not gain any benefit from ownership, as contrasted to a license to use, since the software is intended for their internal business. Additionally, if the customer owns all rights to the software, the developer will have one customer for the software and will have limited financial incentive to enhance, improve, and maintain the software. In many cases, it may be better for the developer to win the ownership argument and keep all rights, while granting the customer a very broad right to use the software under a nonexclusive license. Then, for each license for the software the developer subsequently sells, the developer pays the customer a small royalty. The royalty terminates when the user recovers the cost of the software development. While this is a common solution, there are no industry guidelines for the amount of such royalties. Note, however, that this approach would be inappropriate if the underlying technology of the software were proprietary to the customer. This important issue of ownership should be finalized before the development work begins or monies are paid since the customer loses leverage once performance commences.

Type of License

Exclusive or Nonexclusive. Off-the-shelf software is generally licensed on a nonexclusive basis. With custom software, however, competing interests come into play. On the one hand, the customer will want either to acquire all rights to the customized software or an exclusive license to restrict its competitors from acquiring and using the software. This is particularly true if the customer funded the development of the customized software. On the other hand, the developer will want to market the software to others to make greater profits and recoup its development costs, if it funded the development in whole or in part.

Scope of Use. The scope of the license defines the approved user(s), the equipment upon which the software can be used, the business location(s) where the software can be implemented and maintained, and any limitations on business uses and applications. This key element goes to the very core of the agreement between licensor and licensee. Depending on the type of license, the licensor will want to limit the use of the software to specific equipment, specific users, or number of users, number of seats (terminals), or specific location(s). If the customer contemplates any possibility of expanding the use at any time to other locations, affiliated companies, personnel, or the like, these discussions and corresponding license fees are best discussed up front in the negotiations of the license agreement, when the customer has the most leverage. Otherwise, when the need arises, the customer may unexpectedly discover that additional licenses are significantly more expensive than the initial license fees. If a customer has subsidiary or affiliate operations, it is advisable for the initial license to provide that the software may be used by those operations as well.

The following are examples of the different types of licenses and their scope of use:

- *Corporate or enterprise*. Licensee may utilize the software on any CPU (seat or machine) anywhere within the corporation.

- *Site*. Licensee may utilize the software on all CPUs at a physical location.

- *Concurrent use*. Licensee may utilize the software for the maximum number of people who will be running the software simultaneously.

- *File server*. Licensee may utilize the software on a per-server basis for as many seats or users as are attached to that file server.

- *Machine*. Licensee must purchase a license for every machine on the network using the software.

- *Individual*. Licensee must purchase a license for every person who will use the software.

Development Fee, License Fee, and Terms of Payment

Development Fee. There are two basic ways to pay for the development of custom software: (1) on a time and materials basis or (2) with a fixed price agreement. Time and materials agreements have several drawbacks for the customer. First, they give the developer a strong incentive to provide less experienced, less expensive programmers. Second, because the developer makes more money the longer the project takes, there is no financial incentive to guarantee that the project will be completed on time. To give the developer some incentive to finish the project in a timely manner, the customer should place a cap on the developer's total compensation and possibly pay a bonus for early or timely completion.

Another way to encourage the developer to finish the work as quickly as possible is to pay a bonus based on the number of hours billed. The fewer the hours, the higher the bonus. This may result in getting the project completed faster as well as saving the customer money in the long term. Any bonuses should be phased. The following is an example of a bonus clause incentivizing timely performance:

> As an incentive to timely performance, Developer shall be paid a bonus as follows:
>
> *(a)* The total number of hours billed by Developer under this Agreement shall be multiplied by $___ if the total number of hours billed is ___ or less.
> *(b)* The total number of hours billed by Developer shall be multiplied by $___ if the total number of hours billed is ___ or less.
>
> There shall be no bonus if the total number of hours billed by Developer under this Agreement exceeds ___ hours.

The other payment option is for the customer to pay the developer a fixed price for the entire project. In theory, this payment scheme favors the customer by giving the customer certainty as to what the project will cost. However, as a practical matter, fixed price agreements often do not end up favoring the customer as much as one would think. If the fixed price originally agreed upon does not provide the developer with fair compensation, the customer will probably end up paying the developer more money. Otherwise, the developer may quit or deliver a hastily completed product.

Perhaps the optimum approach involves combining the two payment approaches. The developer's services would be paid on a time and materials basis up until the point at which the detailed specifications are finalized. After completion of the detailed specifications, it becomes possible to enter into negotiations for a fixed price for the development of the software. The contract should address the possibility that the parties are unable to reach agreement on the fixed price. In that event, the contract should specify that the developer be paid for services performed, and the customer be entitled to ownership of the specifications and work performed.

License Fee. In the case where the software is licensed, it is important to identify what is and is not included in the license fee and what is encompassed in any additional fees. Types of fees include license fees (one-time, annual, or monthly), installation fees, training fees, and maintenance fees.

If there are annual license and/or maintenance fees, customers should insert a price protection clause into the contract. This is accomplished by putting a maximum limit on the annual rate of increase. The following is an example clause relating to increases in annual maintenance fees:

> The annual maintenance fee is subject to change by Licensor following the end of the one year period upon ninety (90) days' prior written notice to Licensee; provided, however, that such maintenance charge shall not be increased more than one in any one year period and in no event shall any increase exceed ___% of the maintenance charge applicable to the preceding year.

Terms of Payment. Whether contracting for development or a license, the customer should avoid paying too much money up front. Software suppliers will press for as much of the fees up front as possible. Paying most of the fees early on reduces the customer's leverage in ensuring that the project is done right.

Instead, payments should be spread out according to the anticipated deliverables or milestones in developing and/or implementing the software. The customer should pay the supplier as the customer receives, tests, and accepts each deliverable. If the deliverable is not acceptable (i.e., does not meet contractually defined criteria), then the customer is not obliged to pay until it does. Knowing that payment is contingent on delivering functioning software will motivate the supplier to do the job correctly and on time. In the event the supplier does not deliver, the customer has much less invested in the project if it chooses to terminate the agreement.

The following are examples of milestones used in the licensing of a complex software system:

- Execution of license
- Detailed specifications approved
- Completion of preliminary testing by supplier at its site
- Completion of preliminary testing by supplier at user's site
- Training of users
- Delivery of software documentation
- Online system implementation
- Completion of final integrated acceptance test
- Final Acceptance (This is an event that will be defined in the Contract and should be capitalized)
- 30 days after Final Acceptance

Acceptance

Acceptance is a key event in any software acquisition agreement. The purpose of an acceptance provision is to ensure that the software delivered and installed does in fact operate in accordance with all specifications and contract requirements. If the software does not operate as required, the customer should have the right to reject the software, send it back, and receive a refund of either all payments made if there is a license agreement, or all payments made subsequent to the customer's approval of the specifications. Significant to proper acceptance are (1) clear, detailed, and unambiguous functional and design specifications and (2) detailed, objective, and meaningful acceptance criteria and a test plan tailored to the needs of the customer.

In the license agreement, the optimum approach is to obtain the right to evaluate the software during a test period before paying or committing to pay for the software. Desirably, the licensee should have the right to test the software and return it after the evaluation, at the licensee's option (for any or no reason), and before any payment is made to the licensor. Upon completion of the licensee's evaluation, its decision to retain the software would constitute its acceptance. A word of caution—a licensee who has had an evaluation period during which the licensee did not test the software, but accepted it anyway, or who tested it but did not return the software, will have a little ability to complain of significant defects or failure of the software at a later date.

One key to successful software testing is to conduct testing of each module of a software system and then conduct system or integrated testing. The development of a comprehensive test plan is critical to determine whether or not the software has met the acceptance criteria. It should be possible to fail the test, quantify the failure, and determine what changes are required to pass the retest.

Acceptance of the fully implemented software should be the triggering event for the following:

- Final payment to the licensor
- Commencement of warranty period
- Commencement of support and maintenance obligations
- Warranties

Express Warranties. An express warranty is a promise or statement made by a seller regarding the quality, quantity, performance, or characteristics of the product or service sold. The developer or licensor, in making an actual promise about how the software will work, whether orally or in writing, is making an *express warranty*. While an express warranty can be created by using words such as *warrant* or *guarantee*, there are no magic words necessary to create a warranty. Representations made by salespeople, sales literature, statements at product demonstrations, proposals, manuals, and specifications can all constitute express warranties. Express warranties can last for any period of time, from a few months to the lifetime of the software.

Customers often seek an express warranty from the developer or licensor guaranteeing that the software is free from defects and will meet the functional and design specifications established. This is an increasingly difficult area for negotiation as fewer software suppliers will warrant the performance of their software because of the risks inherent in these promises. Software can and often does fail, so the supplier won't commit that it will run error free or get fixed if it "breaks."

Whatever the final outcome, it is important that all promises and agreements about the software be written into the contract. If these promises (including reference to the developer or licensor's proposal) are not included in the contract, they will likely *not* be binding on the supplier.

The following are express warranties the customer should consider including in the agreement:

- Warranty of software performance
- Warranty against disablement
- Warranty of compatibility (with hardware or other software)
- Warranty against infringement of a third-party intellectual property right

An equally important aspect of the warranty clause is the issue of the customer's remedies (rights) should the software not comply with the supplier's promises (warranties). Although suppliers are not likely to give a money-back guarantee, they should be willing to refund fees paid if they breach the performance warranty because the software never worked. This is a complex area of drafting in the agreement but may be the most important. Because software projects can and do fail, the remedies for the customer must be "make whole" remedies: a refund of all fees paid. Anything less than that will allow the developer or licensor to potentially profit from a deal in which it overcommitted or failed to perform.

A middle ground would be to draft a partial refund based on the portion of the software that does work, or a discount if the software lacks promised functionality. Software licenses will often restrict the remedy for a failed software product to remedying the failed product. That begs the question: What if the licensor never does get it to work?

Negotiate for some kind of ending to the cycle of failure and repair. One method provides for "three strikes" and then the licensor is out. Another would provide a period of time to cure the failing software, after which the customer is entitled to a refund of fees related to the failed software.

The following is an example of a customer warranty clause relating to software performance:

> Licensor warrants that the Software is free from material defects and will operate substantially in accordance with the documentation listed in Exhibit __ for twelve (12) months following acceptance by Licensee.
>
> If, at any time within the twelve (12) month period, the Software is considered by Licensee not to be in conformance with this warranty, Licensee shall promptly notify Licensor of such nonconformance. Licensor shall respond as required in the Error Correction section of the Paragraph entitled "Maintenance."
>
> If a nonconformance is not corrected within thirty (30) days of the original notification to Licensor, or if an acceptable plan for correcting the nonconformance is not established during such period, Licensee may, by giving Licensor written notice thereof, terminate this Agreement and return all copies of Software to Licensor or verify in writing that the Software has been destroyed and Licensor shall refund to Licensee all fees paid by Licensee pursuant to this Agreement.

Implied Warranties. In every commercial transaction involving the sale of goods, certain representations by the seller are assumed to be made, even if no words are written or spoken. These representations are implied by state laws based on the Uniform Commercial Code (UCC). In the past, a number of courts have disagreed on whether software qualifies as a "good" governed by these state UCC laws, but today the trend appears to be that the UCC applies to off-the-shelf and custom software sales and license transactions.

There are four implied warranties:

1. Implied warranty of title
2. Implied warranty against infringement
3. Implied warranty of merchantability
4. Implied warranty of fitness for a particular purpose

Disclaimer of Warranties. There is no requirement that the developer or licensor provide any warranties at all. The implied warranties (and any express warranties) may be expressly disclaimed (negated) by the developer or licensor.

Term, Renewal, and Termination

Term. The effective date of the license will be specified in the agreement or will be the last date that a party executes the agreement. The termination date could either be unspecified (a perpetual license) or specified (a limited term or subscription license). The licensee must be assured of receiving a license for a sufficient time period. Generally, if the license is for a short, fixed time period (e.g., one year), the licensee will be required to pay an additional fee to renew the license.

If the license is perpetual, the licensee will generally pay a one-time license fee and then be permitted to use the license in perpetuity thereafter. Even with a perpetual license, however, the licensor will want to have the ability to terminate the license in the event the licensee breaches the license agreement. The right to terminate should always be preceded by notice to the licensee and a period of time during which to cure the default.

Renewal. If the license is a limited-term license, the agreement may include a renewal provision. Typically, however, licensors use automatic renewal or "evergreen" provisions. The following is an example of an evergreen provision:

> This Agreement shall automatically renew for successive one (1) year periods unless terminated in writing by either party at least thirty (30) days prior to the expiration of any one year period.
>
> A contract tip for licensees: Users who want to reevaluate the software license every year should insist that renewal occur only upon payment of the renewal license fee. In addition, the user should reserve the right to terminate at any time.

Termination. A developer or licensor should not have the right to terminate a development or license agreement unless the customer breaches its terms. In a development agreement, the developer should not have the right to cancel a project unless the customer fails to pay an undisputed amount after notice and a period to cure. This protects the customer from the developer having unwarranted leverage in a dispute. If the developer can walk away from an implementation because of a problem with customer relations, the customer will be at the developer's mercy.

In a license agreement, the events constituting default should be very clearly specified. Additionally, in the event of an alleged breach by a licensee, the licensor should be required to provide a reasonable notice period and an opportunity to cure or dispute the alleged breach. This will avoid a situation where the licensor terminates the license with little or no warning or for a reason that the licensee disputes, leaving the licensee with no software and little time to replace it.

Conversely, the customer should have the absolute right to terminate a development or license agreement at will. In the case of a software license, the licensee should be prepared to sacrifice previously paid license fees, however. If the licensee's plans for using the software change, licensors won't usually give a refund.

In the case of a development agreement, the customer should always be able to terminate the developer for dissatisfaction or budget cuts. The developer may negotiate for a termination charge. Consider whether the developer has legitimate costs to recover from the sudden termination. If the termination charges are not warranted, the customer should pay only for work performed.

Termination Protection. Unexpected termination of a software license can severely impair the licensee's ability to process its business, particularly in the case of software that performs a crucial function of the licensee's business operation. Therefore, the termination provision should be drafted in a manner to protect the user from unexpected terminations and provide necessary assistance from the licensor in order to implement an orderly transition to another software system.

Often, the transition to another software program will result in a need to transfer the existing data to another format. In such a case, the licensee may require specialized knowledge of the former system possessed only by the licensor. In any type of termination setting, whether in a default or nondefault scenario, such assistance should be provided for in the license agreement.

Training

A comprehensive, well-thought-out training plan may be important, particularly with large, complex integrated systems. Key issues to address are

- How much will the training cost? (What is included in the development or license fee?)
- How many employees can be trained?
- What is the course curriculum? (How important is it to review the training course?)
- How many instructors will be needed?
- Where will training occur?
- When will training occur?
- Who will pay for travel and provide training facilities?

Maintenance and Support

Response and repair times should be specifically stated as well as all the developer or licensor's support and maintenance obligations such as providing bug corrections, modifications, and enhancements.

Confidentiality

If the customer will be providing the developer or licensor with any of its trade secrets, such as business procedures, customer lists, computer programs, and the like, the agreement should include nondisclosure provisions.

Assignment

The supplier's license agreement will undoubtedly have a restriction on the licensee's right to assign (transfer) the license to a third party. Two possibilities exist with regards to assignment: the licensee's company is acquired by another company; or the licensee decides to outsource the operation of its data processing function to a third party. For these potential reasons, the licensee should carve out exceptions to the restriction against assignment. The following is an example clause:

> Upon advance written notice to Licensor, Licensee may assign this Agreement, at no charge, to a parent, subsidiary, a company acquiring the interests of Licensee, or a successor in interest carrying on the business of Licensee. In addition, Licensee shall have the right, at no charge, to assign this Agreement to a third party who assumes the responsibility of Licensee's data processing function.

The Source Code Escrow Agreement

If the customer negotiates the right to ownership of the software in a development agreement, the customer attains all rights to the specifications, including software source code. However, in the license agreement, the licensee typically does not obtain a copy of the source code.

If the software supplier goes out of business or simply stops maintaining the software, this will cause great harm to the licensee. In the case of a computer system, the customer's system may be rendered virtually useless. The customer may be forced to obtain a replacement source, the cost of which could be substantial.

The source code is the code used by the developer to create the software. It is typically in a different computer language than the object code (the language the licensee uses to read, install, and use the software) and is considered to be valuable proprietary information belonging to the licensor. Without the source code, the licensee cannot perform regular maintenance on the system.

On the one hand, the source code (relating to software) will be a trade secret of the licensor and the licensor will be reluctant to provide it to third parties. However, the licensee will want to make sure that the software will be maintained no matter what happens to the licensor.

One approach to resolving the interests of both licensee and licensor is to establish an escrow account into which the source code is deposited. As the name implies, this involves having the software owner deposit a copy of the source code (and appropriate documentation) into "escrow." This device is used, for example, in purchases of real estate, where the buyer does not want to pay until he or she gets the title, and the seller does not want to transfer title until he or she gets paid.

Problems with Escrow Agreements

Bankruptcy. Under the federal bankruptcy laws (which take precedence over state laws and private contracts) the bankruptcy trustee has no obligation to turn over the escrow data to the licensee unless such a clause is specifically included in the escrow agreement. Therefore, a clause similar to the one that follows should be included in the escrow agreement:

The parties acknowledge that this Source Code Escrow Agreement is an "agreement supplementary to" this Development and License Agreement as provided in Section 365(n) of Title 11, United States Bankruptcy Code (the "Code"). In any bankruptcy action by Licensor, failure by Licensee to assert its rights to retain its benefits to the intellectual property encompassed by the Software pursuant to Section 365(n) of the Code, under an executory contract rejected by the trustee in bankruptcy, shall not be construed by the courts as a termination of the contract by Licensee under Section 365(n) of the Code.

Defining Events of Default. Events that trigger the licensee's access to the source code are usually termed "events of default." In order to avoid disputes that will delay distribution, these events must be listed very specifically. They may include

- Filing of bankruptcy by licensor
- Licensor going out of business
- Failure of the licensor to maintain the software
- Discontinuance by licensor of production of software
- Failure of licensor to maintain the software in a timely manner
- Consistent quality problems

Source Code Must Be Current. If the source code is not current, it will likely be useless. Therefore, it is critical that the source code in escrow be periodically reviewed to ensure currency. The simplest approach in the contract is to put a provision in the escrow agreement requiring that the licensor maintain the information in escrow as current. However, this could be the least effective method if the licensor does not comply. It will be important, therefore, that the agreement provide that the licensee be able to monitor compliance. Another approach is to require that the escrow agent (or independent third party) monitor the source code to ensure that it reflects the current state of the software.

Expediting Dispute Resolution. If the licensee claims an event of default and the licensor says there is not, the escrow agent is going to be subjected to various demands. To address this potential, escrow agreements are typically drafted to allow for arbitration to resolve disputes. While arbitration is generally less costly and speedier than a court case, the process may still be time-consuming.

One approach to speed up the process is to require an expedited arbitration where both parties agree that the arbitration will take place in a certain way and within certain time frames. In addition, the parties can agree that the escrow agent also act as the arbitrator.

CONCLUSION

Contracting for technology involves knowledge of principles from several areas of law: contracts, intellectual property, and employment. A major purpose of this chapter is to identify and demystify a number of key concepts within each of these areas as they apply to technology contracts. Once the supply manager understands the issues, he or she will be better equipped to engage in more productive contract discussions with his or her legal department and supplier. The ultimate end goal of this process is to create a contract document that clearly defines the deal between the parties, addresses the obvious and more subtle issues involved, and creates guidelines to resolve possible "what could go wrong" scenarios.

CHAPTER 37

CAPITAL AND ITS IMPACT ON THE ORGANIZATION

Bruce J. Wright
President
B. Wright & Associates and Total Systems, Inc.

WHAT IS CAPITAL?

There are many definitions of capital and the use of capital in an organization. The idea of capital is discussed and debated by many people and organizations. Capital is normally considered as something of value to the holder of the capital; thus a sunset to an artist has a great deal of value, but a driver facing a sunset could have a negative value perspective. There is a basic premise that capital only goes where it is invited and remains only if made to feel welcome. This is very true when considering the purchase of capital assets.

Capital is another word for positive value normally represented by money, and *expenditure* denotes the trade of money or value for something else of value. This in a direct sense is the definition of a capital expenditure. This is probably why there is such a broad application of the term in organizations. Accounting has attempted to apply its own definition by making capital expenditure synonymous with depreciable asset. In today's world of management accounting, this is not a true definition of the term. Capital expenditure is more aligned with the term *fixed asset* in today's world. A fixed asset is any asset that lasts more than a year, with an impact on shareholder value, and is considered by management worth controlling. This is much broader than the current accounting definition. The current accounting definition is determined by each organization relative to time and value related to materiality. Relative to time, the government has issued asset depreciation ranges (ADRs) for all types of equipment that might be used in an organization. These ADRs, however, start at three years. This means that if an asset, which might be very costly, has a life of less than three years, then the organization has the option of expensing the asset rather than depreciating it. On the value side, companies are allowed to set what they feel is material in accounting for depreciation related to an asset. In some companies this is as low as $500, while in others it may be as high as $5,000 and in some rare instances even more than that if agreement of auditors and taxing authorities is obtained. Most companies are currently at a level around $1,000. This assessment of materiality affects the accounting process, but it doesn't necessarily reflect the desires of management. Normally management will want to keep track of any asset that is significant to the outcome of the organization mission and is not included in an inventory process. This relates to the current concern for shareholder value and the return on invested capital represented by value that lasts more than a year and is used to manufacture cash.

Some other business definitions of capital assets are (1) renovation of worn or obsolete production, distribution, or service facilities or the replacement of these facilities, (2) new production, distribution, or service facilities or expansions of a product or product line, (3) research and development, improved working conditions, or investments that might be required by the government through regulations to improve the health and welfare of workers or the community, and (4) any material expenditure of money that extends the economic life of current assets.

The definition of a capital expenditure really depends on the organization and the way the organization looks at the use of funds. There are several very general accounting definitions, but within reasonable bounds, the decision is left to the individual organization. It is important in supply management that we understand and influence the policies of management related to capital spending and then model the organization of the supply management group after this.

When buyers purchase a capital asset, they should be ready to make sure that the money they are spending will return value to the organization they are involved with and also to the shareholders of the organization. The placing of value in the organization is a partnership between the buyer and the user of the asset. The user must provide a means of use for the asset that will return to the organization through revenue generation, cost saving, or cost avoidance that will exceed the cost of the capital that supply management must use in obtaining the asset. The only exception to this is when assets must be purchased because of laws or regulations or when the assets are part of a strategic mission.

Impact of Capital Assets on the Organization

Capital assets are the tools by which an organization works and creates value. The improper decisions in a capital process can be very detrimental to the organization. In today's world, there is a movement to use the value of the capital assets purchased as a measure of management performance. In the use of value-added evaluation, there is a capital charge that is taken before the benefit to the shareholder is calculated and management is limited in bonuses until the cost of capital taken on the capital base is achieved.

In all organizations, the application of capital assets is important to the success of the organization. As more and more organizations become fully automated and e-commerce becomes more and more a focus of the organization, the application of the relationship of capital assets to the success of the company in all types of organizations becomes more important. Although many organizations have made the transition to fully utilizing automation and e-commerce, there are still many that have not or are still in the process of doing so. Organizations must exercise care in selecting their capital asset base to avoid damaging the ability to compete and support the organizations mission and the flexibility required in servicing customers and markets.

Capital Expenditure Environment

Successful capital expenditures depend upon four conditions:

1. *Timing.* Usually the saying "Strike while the iron is hot" applies. Timing of capital expenditures can mean the difference between success and failure.

2. *Direction.* Proper direction of a capital expenditure is imperative if budgets and deadlines are to be met. Capital buys must reflect the strategic planning of the organization.

3. *Support.* This means both top management and supervisory support. Without proper support, failure is assured.

4. *Coordination.* Coordination of capital expenditures is required to make sure full use is given to resources available and employed by the organization.

Supply management needs to be involved from the strategic planning process of a capital buy. When supply management is involved, there is normally a much better result achieved in the buy process. There is a balance that must be struck in a capital buy; this is the balance between the technical side of the buy and the business side of the buy. If the technical side of the buy is completed before the business side is undertaken, we are often left with a position where the asset fits the situation technically but we miss the opportunities of negotiation of price, delivery, warranty, service, and many of the other values of the business side of the buy. On the other hand, if the business side is undertaken before the technical side is ready, we can get a piece of equipment that fits the values of supply management but does not fit the form and function required for success in a strategic position of the organization. There must be a balance in the business and technical side of the buy with the business side leading. This leadership is normally seen in the negotiation of terms and conditions (T&C) and the initial sourcing of the supplier at the point of planning for the buy. The T&C of the buy should not be on the back of the purchase order where they are often found in organizations. They should be separated and placed up front in the buy. Standard Ts&Cs define the playing field for both the supplier and the buyer and should be handled when the sourcing process is first initiated. This is when the buyer is in the best negotiating position, when the supplier is not yet in a position of being a supplier for the organization. It is best to initiate contact with suppliers by negotiating the Ts&Cs and getting them out of the way so that an alliance is formed and the rest of the buy can take place without problems on how the two parties will conduct their business. Many businesses are placing their Ts&Cs on the Internet. This allows all segments of the organization the opportunity of referring suppliers to the Web site. It also allows a prospective supplier the opportunity of reviewing the Ts&Cs and after accepting them, being given an approved supplier position so that engineers and others can then start developing the technical side of the capital buy.

Capital Control

The control of capital depends on the development and use of reliable methods of assessing the impact of projects on the profits of the company. There must be adequate coordination of the direction of the company to ensure continuity of the company's capital spending program.

Misdirected capital spending increases operating costs and ties up needed funds that many times reduces profits and creates unneeded excess capacity. Failure to make good capital decisions at the right time can increase product cost and jeopardize a company's competitive position.

Capital invested in the right place at the right time will increase a company's strength and competitive position and provide the basis for effective strategic planning.

THE ENTERPRISE RESOURCE PLANNING MODEL

The planning part of an organization normally includes five planning thrusts: strategic plan, capital forecast, revenue forecast, cash forecast, and operating forecast (see Figure 37–1). These plans and forecasts must be coordinated and related to the operating process that will translate into actions that move the organization forward. These plans should be dynamic rather than static. In the past, companies have set their plans once a year and then they have set about to execute those plans. In this type of environment, many times the plans are set and then they are put away until the results are in when they are brought out and it is just coincidence if they are achieved or exceeded. It seems in many organizations that every year starts with an exercise called "Surprise." Everyone is surprised if the revenue forecast coordinates with the capital forecast and if the operating forecast supports the strategic plan. To be really effective, the planning cycle must be a dynamic process that continues through time and is not limited to the artificial constraints of an accounting year or period.

The Enterprise Resource Planning Model is a model of information flow and coordination in an organization. This process is divided into three areas, planning, actual, and historical. This process allows us to make sure that everything we do within the organization is connected and has a purpose and that the various elements of the process do not just hang out as islands or territories in the organization.

FIGURE 37-1

Enterprise Resource Planning Model

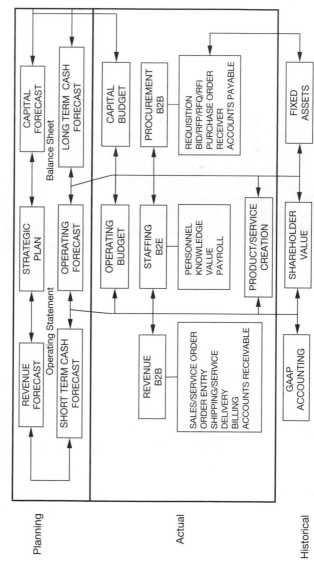

CAPITAL PROCUREMENT, EVALUATION, AND CONTROL TOOLS

The capital procurement process deals with the right-hand side of the Enterprise Resource Planning Model (see Figure 37–2). The ability to achieve success and fulfill the conditions of capital procurement, evaluation, and control depends on the use of the proper tools related to the process. These tools are the strategic plan, capital forecasting, operating forecast, appropriation request, and capital budget.

Strategic Plan

There are generally two methods used when top management performs its strategic planning responsibilities: intuitive-anticipatory planning and formal systematic planning. Both are important and must not be underestimated. In many corporations there are conflicts between these two approaches because there are different thought processes that are involved in completing them. However, formal planning cannot be done without management intuition. If the accounting and information systems are correctly tailored to support the managerial characteristics of looking ahead and anticipating the future, it will help managers improve their intuition.

The strategic plan is an analysis of the opportunities, challenges, and expectations presented by the internal and external environment of the business. It is the process of setting goals and then analyzing the various processes that will allow

FIGURE 37–2

Capital Expenditure Process

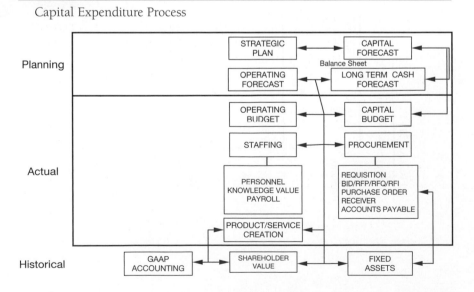

the organization to accomplish those goals. The interaction and information that supports the strategies of the organization come from the capital forecast and the revenue forecast. These two forecasts give management the insight into where revenue will be generated and where capital must be invested to make the organization capable of taking advantage of the opportunities of the industry. The strategic plan provides the framework for the formulation of a good capital, revenue, and operating forecast. The strategic plan takes into consideration as many long-range external and internal factors as possible, and it is the reflection of the thinking and desire of top management, the board of directors, and the shareholders as to the position of the company in the future. The planning horizon for the strategic plan should be such that decisions are made with as much flexibility as possible. This horizon is usually based on the capital intensity of the firm, the firm's ability to maneuver, and the points listed previously. The greater a firm's ability to maneuver or the more volatile the industry, the shorter the strategic planning process.

Capital Forecasting

The capital forecast is the second step in the capital procurement cycle and one of the most important tools in control of capital and optimizing the expenditure of capital funds. The reason for this is that the wise use of capital is the basis for accomplishing the strategic plan. It is also the basis for determining how large an operating force will be needed to support the effort required to achieve the goals and objectives of the strategic plan as a result of capital projects and the ongoing requirements of the organization. It gives an indication of the firm's potential production and therefore sales. There are several other areas served by a formal capital forecast. Some of these are

> *Forecasting cash requirements.* Capital forecasts assist in the forecasting of the timing and amount of cash required and thus enable corporate management to plan for additional financing if required. Plans can also be made to defer or abandon certain projects if insufficient funds are available or if the costs would exceed the amount that management is willing to invest in capital expansion. Such revisions can be made before operating units go to the trouble and expense of compiling the details of their operating forecast.

> *Determining operating targets.* The capital forecast is most useful in apprising management of their operating personnel's plans for cost reduction, product and service improvement, additional capacity, or new products or services. The necessity of preparing a forecast of capital requirements forces managers to make more realistic appraisals of their overall goals and objectives. Supply management should be involved here in determining the industry position on general availability, suppliers, lead times, and sourcing possibilities.

Elimination of duplication. A formal capital forecast helps to avoid such duplication as similar capital projects being undertaken by two operations. It also lessens the possibility that an operation may be permitted to purchase a capital asset that is available elsewhere within the company.

Project priorities. A capital forecast is essential in selecting and assigning priorities to projects, the sum total of which usually far exceeds the funds available.

Most companies require that proposed projects be rated as to their degree of urgency or desirability. They will generally fall into three broad categories:

1. *Must projects.* Projects that affect the continued operation of the company and management and for which there is usually no choice about whether they will be done or not. Often they are needed to satisfy a regulatory requirement or an emergency replacement of existing capacity. In addition, there are special projects sometimes termed *pet projects;* these are strategic projects that in no way reflect a return on investment but are the perks of management. These might include a corporate airplane, corporate yacht, or other projects that are included in the image of the organization rather than directly related to direct operations.

2. *Want projects.* Projects that provide some type of real improvement and are desirable from their risk-reward position. These are projects that show low risk and high return and will be of direct benefit to the bottom line of the company. Hopefully the bulk of the projects in an organization will fall into the want category.

3. *Wish projects.* Projects that carry either a high risk or relatively low reward for the company. These are projects that may be out of the company's operational expertise but may show a high reward potential. Normally, these projects are undertaken only after the first two categories are exhausted.

Compatibility with Company Objectives The capital forecast as part of the Enterprise Resource Planning Model makes it easier to detect projects that are not compatible with the strategic plans of the company. Many times, parts of the strategic plan will remain confidential to the point that operating management will not be fully aware of their impact. A formal forecast enables management to eliminate or defer any projects that are at cross-purposes with the strategic plan.

Operating Forecasts

Operating forecasts are the coordination point of the effect of capital forecasts and revenue forecasts, and generally this process contains the most recognized steps in the planning cycle. An operating forecast is the basis of the operational planning and control system. The operating forecast provides the plan by which management will attain the company's goals. It is a forecast that will carry the operational figures on a dynamic basis. It will also provide a tool for recording the assumptions related to the forecast and the operating effect of management and capital decisions.

The operating forecast is normally made up of two sets of information, deterministic information and probabilistic information.

Deterministic Information

1. *Strategic plan.* This is the set of information that provides management with the opportunity to set "par" for the organization in establishing goals and objectives that will be carried out by the organization.

2. *History.* History provides the trends and relationships that will allow us to project a good forecast on a moving basis. The historical information is usually represented by trends and causal relationships. The causal relationships are often called ratios by the accounting group.

3. *Industry.* Industry information is used to predict what will happen as a result of the influences outside of the organization. Industry information is usually related to the trends of industry and the success of other organizations within the industry. The measure against the success of other organizations is called benchmarking.

4. *Geopolitical.* This is a review of the political and regulation environment that the organization finds itself in and the ability to work within the boundaries of this environment both internally and externally.

Probabilistic Information

Management perception comes in two thrusts:

1. Magnitude

2. Confidence

Operating management should be able to review the direction of events and input its perception to this direction in these two areas. In fact operating management should have the ability and responsibility to communicate the assumptions by which the figures in the forecast could change, and it should provide the relative range of the change where the information is critical to the outcome of the organization segment. Confidence can only be expressed in terms of probability and ranges. There are two types of ranges in a capital buy, the revenue range and the cost range. Because a capital expenditure is always evaluated on a cash in, cash out basis, these ranges naturally deal with cash in (revenue) and cash out (cost) with supply management coordinating the cash out in the purchase process and the operating management coordinating the revenue generation or the cost savings.

Operating forecasts provide the final step in forecasting of the timing and amount of cash required. The operating forecast along with the revenue budget, staffing budget, supply management budget, and capital budget coordinated with the operating flows of information provide the tools necessary to keep a close control on cash requirements and capital expenditures. At this point the request for capital should be completed and evaluated. In order to complete this process, the outflows of cash must be brought together with the inflows of cash and the resulting effect on the organization evaluated.

Appropriation Request

The appropriation request is used by the project sponsor and supply management to submit the capital request in detail and transfer the project from forecast to budget. Funds are committed to the project only after complete review of the appropriation request. The appropriation request is reviewed at the levels of management required and determined by the dollar limit of approval given to each management level. Large projects would require the approval of the president and board of directors, while small dollar outlays could be handled by a line manager. Supply management should be involved with the initial information gathering to determine possible prices, specifications, deliveries, and other factors that will affect the ultimate buy. Supply management should be careful to protect the integrity of the buy related to competitors and others in the industry.

Capital Budget

The capital budget provides management a tool that assists in appraising the relative merits of projects proposed and controlling the funds that are approved for the purchase of the capital equipment and services involved. Once a project is approved and made part of the capital budget, it should be in a position where supply management can go ahead with final sourcing and negotiation of items related to formation of a purchase order with potential suppliers.

CAPITAL ACQUISITION REQUIREMENTS

The process involved in establishing a successful capital acquisition process depends on the success of the following processes:

1. *Creative search for investment opportunities.* This is the first step in the capital expenditure program. A company must give ample opportunity to its managers to identify the best capital investment opportunities.

2. *Long-range plans and projections for the company's development.* This is the step called strategic planning. This is the process of upper management that develops a plan for the growth and position of the company given the company's resources, the market, and the company's financial condition.

3. *Forecast and study of demands for funds.* A good program for the determination of the sources and uses of funds for the company is essential for success in a capital investment program.

4. *Correct yardstick of economic worth.* There are many methods of determining the return on the investment in a capital project, and each of these methods has positive and negative points. [Return on investment (ROI) alternatives will be discussed in the section, "Cost of Capital."] Each company must decide what constitutes the correct yardstick and then use it consistently.

5. *Realistic estimation of economic worth of projects.* This includes the subjective (ranking according to management outlook) and objective (ranking according to ROI tools) determination of a project worth.

6. *Standards for screening investment proposals.* This includes the establishment of some type of "hurdle rate" and levels of approval that are consistent with company size and direction. The hurdle rate and approval levels should be set taking into consideration company goals, economic circumstances, and risk.

7. *Expenditure controls by comparison of authorizations and specifications.* This is the control imposed during the outlays of funds to make certain that the expenditures do not get out of control.

8. *Candid and economically realistic postcompletion audits.* The audit is probably the most important of the steps in ensuring that the capital program will remain viable over a long period of time.

9. *Investment analysis of candidates for disposal.* This step is to make sure that past investments are still performing according to the needs of the organization.

10. *Forms and procedures.* This step is company dependent and should be determined after the needs and requirements of the company and management are determined.

Capital Asset Evaluation

In the evaluation of an asset, the project sponsor and supply management must coordinate in establishing the cash flows that will affect the outcome of the purchase. The first premise that must be understood is the corporate purpose or objective. The corporate purpose or objective is to maximize, as far as is possible in the presence of uncertainty and imperfect information, the value to the stockholders or other owners that is generated or represented by the enterprise. This criterion underlies all decisions about optimal asset, financial, and operating structures.

The maximization of shareholder wealth is not the only purpose in business, but it should be one of the dominant ones and should be in relationship to the strategic plan, long-range health, and survival of the corporation.

The maximization of business return to shareholders depends on a balance of resources, both capital and operational, with the potential of gaining profit or position in a given marketplace. This is accomplished by maintaining a balance in the strategic planning process between long-range use of capital and current requirements of operating processes. Along with this, a close monitoring and analysis of actual results and the projection of these results to test forecast thinking is essential in this process.

General Capital Analysis

When a good capital forecast and budget process are part of the coordinated planning cycle, it makes it easier to detect projects that are not compatible with the strategic plans of the company. Many times, parts of the strategic plan will remain confidential to the point that operating management will not be fully aware of their impact. A formal forecasting process with an appropriation process enables management to eliminate or defer any projects that are at cross-purposes with the strategic plan.

The general categories of projects, found in the section, "Capital Forecasting," are those the organization *must* do, those they *want* to do, and those the organization has a desire to do but for reasons of risk or fit, they are projects that will be undertaken only if there is ample capital and management for the musts and wants.

Hurdle Rate

A hurdle rate is the rate of return on investment in capital that will ensure continuing operations and provide a desired level of return for the shareholder. The starting place in determining the hurdle rate is to understand the present cost of the capital. The cost of capital is the return required by those that provide the capital utilized in order to keep them happy. For example, if a bank requires a certain interest rate before it will lend money, the interest rate required by the bank is the cost of that type of capital.

The second factor in the determination of shareholder return is return on invested capital (sometimes called ROIC). This is determined by looking at the performance of the company related to the capital invested by the shareholders.

Cost of Capital

The cost of capital is the average rate of earnings that investors require to induce them to provide all forms of long-term capital to the company. Operationally this cost is the weighted average cost of the various classes of the long-term capital, that is, long-term debt, preferred shareholders' equity, and the common shareholders' equity.

Components of the Cost of Capital
The following is a breakdown of the components and an example that will illustrate how the cost of capital is calculated:

Long-Term Debt		$ 500,000
Preferred stockholders' equity		200,000
Common stockholders' equity		
Common stock	$300,000	
Paid in surplus	100,000	
Retained earnings	300,000	
Total common equity		$ 700,000
Total capital		$1,400,000

Weighted Average Cost Method
This method examines the various components of the capital structure and applies the weighting factor of after-tax cost to determine the weighted cost of capital. The following examples will show the formation of the weighted average cost of capital.

Long-Term Debt. There are two considerations when looking at long-term debt:

1. The present cost of debt
2. The availability of the financing method

Long-term debt includes bonds, mortgages, and long-term secured financing.

Bond Cost. Let's say we can issue bonds with face values of $100 per bond and it is estimated that the bond will generate $96.00 net proceeds to the company after discounting and financing costs. The normal interest is $14.00 or approximately $9.00 after taxes (assuming a 35 percent tax rate). To obtain the cost, we divide the after-tax interest by the proceeds:

$$\frac{\$9.00}{\$96.00} = 9.475\%$$

which is the after-tax cost of bond financing.

Mortgage and Long-Term Financing Costs. Our banker has informed us that our long-term rate is two points over prime and prime is currently 10 percent, which puts our lending rate at 12 percent. With a 35 percent tax rate it comes to a 7.8 percent cost. Our banker has informed us that our mortgage rates are presently 11 percent, which would give us an after-tax cost on mortgage money of 7.15 percent.

Weighting the Cost of Long-Term Debt. To weight the cost of long-term debt, we take the average of the costs of long-term debt which would give us

$$7.48\% \frac{7.8\% + 7.15\%}{2}$$

and multiply the long-term debt ($500,000) by that factor, which will give us a weighted average cost of $37,400.

Preferred Stock Costs. We must take the present market value or an estimate of that value less discounts or finance costs and divide dividends or cash flow per share by this value. For example, assume preferred stock is $100 per share less $2 finance costs (or $98.00 proceeds) and cash flow or dividends on preferred stock are $11.00 per share.

$$\frac{\$11.00}{\$98.00} = 11.2\% \text{ after-tax cost of preferred stock}$$

To weight preferred stock, we multiply the after-tax cost of 11.2 percent by the preferred stock value ($200,000) which gives us a weighted average of $22,400.

Common Equity Costs. Common equity has three components—common stock, paid in surplus, and retained earnings. From the stockholder's viewpoint, all three are costs. If retained earnings are used in the business, the stockholders cannot use them elsewhere to earn money, and therefore they carry an opportunity cost.

Common Equity Valuation. Stockholders invest because they expect to receive benefits that will be equivalent to what they would receive on the next best investment when risk is considered. Stockholders look for two benefits from common stock:

1. Current operating performance
2. Capital appreciation from growth

The valuation of common equity must take into consideration both the present and future earnings of the stock.

Weighting the Cost of Common Equity. We consider the present market price of the stock less issuing costs. For example, assume $100 per share less issuing costs of $15 (or proceeds of $85 per share). This is divided into the future earnings per share estimated by investors or reliable analysts. If we use $12 per share, then the weighted cost will look like this:

$$\frac{\$12}{\$85} = 14.1\% \text{ after-tax cost of common stock}$$

Using the 14.1 percent and the total common equity value of $700,000 we have a weighted average of $98,700.

Total Weighted Average Cost of Capital. A summary of the three components gives us the weighted average cost of capital. The formula for figuring this is as follows:

$$
\begin{aligned}
\text{Long-term debt} &= \$500,000 \ \times \ 7.48\% = \$37,400 \\
\text{Preferred stock} &= 200,000 \ \times \ 11.2\% = 22,400 \\
\text{Common equity} &= \underline{700,000} \ \times \ 14.1\% = \underline{98,700} \\
\text{Total capital} &= \$1,400,000 \phantom{\ \times \ 14.1\% = {}} \$158,500
\end{aligned}
$$

Thus the weighted average cost of capital is

$$
\frac{\$158,500}{\$1,400,000} = 11.3\%
$$

Use of the Cost of Capital. The 11.3 percent weighted cost of capital serves as one input into the formulation of the hurdle rate or the basis of evaluation of the capital expenditure. We know that we should not accept any capital investment that earns less than 11.3 percent after tax. This figure actually forms a *minimum* goal for management in order to satisify the external expectations of the debt, lease, and shareholders. This completes one of the factors in establishing our hurdle rate.

The other factor that we would not be willing to violate for a long-term period of time would be return on invested capital (ROIC). Every organization has investors that have put money into the organization either through loans or through an equity position, and each of these individuals or organizations wishes a return on their invested capital. This is a ratio that is fairly easy to obtain and gives the investor or any other interested party a good gauge, over time, of the health of the organization.

The formula for ROIC is a ratio represented as follows:

$$
\text{ROIC} = \frac{\text{Operating income before interest and taxes}}{\text{Total liabilities} + \text{Equity} - \text{Current liabilities} - \text{Accruals} - \text{Reserves}}
$$

This ratio should normally be higher in a service organization than it will be for a manufacturing firm; the reason for this is the difference in the level of the asset base required in manufacturing versus service and the higher risk level in the service industry brought on by easier entry from the outside.

If an organization lets this ratio trend lower, it is jeopardizing its ability to return value to investors through the use of the capital invested.

In addition to the bases provided by the cost of capital and/or the return on invested capital there are other factors that must be taken into account before we finally come to a hurdle rate for the evaluation of capital equipment. The following is a list of these factors.

1. *Zero return projects.* There are some projects that must be undertaken for other reasons than the maximization of shareholder value. These reasons fall in the areas of complying with government regulations, civic responsibilities, work responsibilities, and work quality improvement. Another area that might be considered a must would be the management priorities. Examples of the first type of project would be smokestack scrubbers, pollution control devices, or other non-revenue-producing projects. The second type of project might be a corporate aircraft or yacht. Our

hurdle rate must be high enough to compensate for this type of project. An evaluation of the percentage of our total capital outlay that will go to this type of project will help determine the effect of zero return projects on the overall requirement for capital and the effect on the return on invested capital.

2. *Replacement projects.* Many times we will be faced with the replacement of worn-out equipment in order to just maintain our market position. These projects will usually show a fair return on investment, but often this return is below our current cost of capital or return on invested capital. Because of this, other projects must make enough return to make the overall rate of return either equal to or above the cost of capital and the return on invested capital.

3. *Overhead.* Because the evaluation of a capital expenditure is based on incremental cash flow based on the project itself, there is normally no consideration in the project itself for overhead. This is added to the hurdle rate to make sure the return covers the portion of overhead that should be supported by this project.

4. *Relative risk.* Another factor in our hurdle rate is the risk factors of the projects we expect to undertake. As the risk increases, it is natural that we would expect to receive a greater return for that risk. Most companies will set a minimum hurdle rate for prime projects and then increase that rate according to the risk of that project relative to prime projects.

Hurdle Rate. After evaluation of the preceding factors, we can then settle on a hurdle rate or series of hurdle rates depending on our approach. Generally most companies find the addition to cost of capital or ROIC to get to the hurdle rate to be about four to six points for must projects and another four to six points for estimating errors and management reach. Another approach is to take 1.5 times the cost of capital and add it to the cost of capital to make sure the project makes the grade. This is by no means a scientific standard, and each company should come to its own determination of what its hurdle rate should be to achieve the desired stability and long-term health.

FINANCIAL RETURN ANALYSIS

Methods for evaluating capital expenditures vary from rough rule-of-thumb or visual inspection techniques to sophisticated discounted cash flow methods. It is very important that we recognize the advantages and limitations of each of the various techniques in common use today.

It should be remembered that mathematical analysis of capital expenditures is only a guide to investment decisions and not the decisions themselves. Also, the precise nature of the results of quantitative analysis can obscure errors made in the formulation of the original problem. Care must be taken to apply the procedures consistently to all projects. Further, it is extremely important that all cash flows, relevant to a project, be identified and entered into the computations even if this involves making several estimates. Normally in a return analysis, the supply management group and the operating group should work together in establishing the cash flows. Supply management should determine the cost of the business side of the capital expenditure, and the project sponsor should determine the operating costs and savings and the resultant excess cash flows.

Management should be aware of the assumptions implicit in the calculation method being employed, including limitations as well as advantages of those methods. It is understood that with must projects supply management will try and make the best business decisions related to obtaining the asset and accomplishing the requirement of the asset usage. There is no use in evaluating the must projects by the hurdle rate because it is known that they will not accomplish a return on the investment required. The goal is to keep the cash requirements to a minimum and still accomplish the requirements of the project.

All other projects are normally evaluated using a combination of the following five methods, which gives management input to the decision process related to the asset.

The examples used in this section are all based on a simple project with a life of three years plus the investment year with the following flows; this is the capital evaluation calculation example at the end of the section.

Year	Outflows	Inflows
Investment year	(1,000)	0
Year 1	(800)	1,200
Year 2	0	400
Year 3	0	900

Nondiscounting Investment Evaluation Techniques

There are two basic nondiscounting methods used in evaluating capital expenditures—accountant's rate of return and payback. These techniques use cash flow data without any direct attempts at adjusting for the time value of money.

Advantages

1. Simple to calculate.

2. Based on easily understood ideas and produce "apparently" useful answers.

3. Can be used as coarse screening devices to pick out high-profit projects that are so clearly desirable that they require no refined return estimates and to reject quickly those projects that show such poor promise that they do not merit thorough analysis.

Disadvantages

1. No consideration for the timing of cash inflows and outflows.

2. No consideration for the timing of tax savings based on the decision to expense part of an investment outlay or from writing off capitalized costs over the life of the project.

3. No consideration for the cost of capital.

The Accountant's Rate of Return

The accountant's rate of return may be defined as the percentage yield that the income anticipated from a project will earn on the investment. There are a variety of possible ways to calculate this measure, some of these are

1. Total profit/Average investment

2. Average annual profit/Total investment

3. Average annual profit/Average investment

The definitions of these factors are as follows:

Total profit = Total net inflows – Total net outflows

$$\text{Average annual profit} = \frac{\text{Total profit}}{\text{Number of years in project life}}$$

Average investment = Nondepreciable portion + (1 – Tax rate)(Depreciable portion)

An example of the accountant's rate of return using the preceding example would be

Total profit (Inflows – Outflows) = $2,500 – $1,800 = $700

$$\text{Average annual profit} = \frac{\$700}{3} = \$233$$

Average investment = 0 + (1 – 0.34) ($1,800) = $1,188

The accountant's rate of return in each case would be

Method 1. $700/$1,188 = 58.92%

Method 2. $233/$1,800 = 12.94%

Method 3. $233/$1,188 = 19.61%

Use of the Accountant's Rate of Return. If there are no budget constraints, select all projects above an arbitrary rate of return cutoff; if there is a budget constraint, then select projects with the highest rates of return.

Advantages. This method gives a cash-on-cash return without taking the time value of money into consideration. It may be a more accurate measure for long-term projects that have high returns in later life.

Disadvantages

1. Depends heavily on arbitrary accounting rules and does not distinguish between cash flows and accounting allocations.

2. The use of averages in the calculation of cash flows compounds the problems of timing individual cash flows.

3. The three techniques listed to calculate the return can produce different rates of return for any one proposal, leading to uncertainty as to which method is best.

4. Ignores the time value of money and uneven flows of money.

Payback

Payback is the year (or fraction of a year) at which the sum of the outflows of cash equals the sum of the inflows of cash; or the year (or fraction) at which the sum of flows equals zero.

Example of Payback

	Inv. Year	Year 1	Year 2	Year 3
Net flow for year	($1,000)	$400	$400	$900
Cumulative flow	($1,000)	($600)	($200)	$700

$$\text{Payback period} = 2 \text{ years} + \frac{(\$200)}{\$900} \text{ years} = 2.22 \text{ years}$$

Use of Payback. If there are no budget constraints, accept all projects with a payback period that is less than some arbitrary cutoff period; if a budget constraint exists, select projects with the shortest payback period. Care should be taken in using this decision tool that long-term survival is not compromised by short-term gains.

Advantages of Payback

1. It concentrates on cash flows early in the life of the project. Payback is useful for appraising risky investments because cash flows can be estimated with some certainty in the early life of a project.

2. It is an adequate guide for companies with poor liquidity positions, that is, with high outside cost of capital and severely limited internal cash generating ability in comparison to a high volume of profitable investment opportunities.

Disadvantages of Payback

1. It does not consider earnings after the year of payback. This may lead to rejection of highly profitable projects that would produce revenue streams later on.

2. Payback measures the liquidity of a capital investment program and not profitability over the project's economic life.

3. It does not provide results that can be measured against the current rate of return on investment for the company or the cost of capital.

4. When major outflows occur in more than one period, there is a possibility of confusing results.

Discounting Investment Evaluation Techniques

The three major techniques most widely used, taking into consideration the time value of money, are internal rate of return (IRR), excess present value index, and net present value.

Advantages of Discounting Methods

1. The timings of investment and cash flows are weighed so as to reflect the differences in the value of near and distant cash flows.

2. Discounting concentrates on cash flows and does not include arbitrary accounting allocations.

3. The total economic life of the project is considered.

4. The timing of tax savings is reflected.

Disadvantages of Discounting Methods

1. Management is not, in general, as familiar with discounting as it is with the more commonly used nondiscounting methods.

2. The precise nature of discounting calculations often obscures the difficulty of making annual cash flow estimates and the many assumptions implicit in the calculation method to arrive at such estimates.

Internal Rate of Return

This method has many different names, among them are return on capital employed, discounted cash flow, return on capital, and return on net capital. The definition of IRR is that rate of return which would discount all cash flows of the project to zero. We compare this rate to our hurdle rate for the class of project to determine the worth of the project to the company, and also we compare this rate to the cost of capital to make sure that the project will return to the shareholders and others that hold capital interests.

Example of IRR (Trial and Error Method)

	Cash	Factor	@ 20%	Factor	@ 30%	Factor	@ 27%
Inv. Year	(1,000)	0	(1,000)	0	(1,000)	0	(1,000)
Year 1	400	0.8333*	334	0.7700*	308	0.7850*	314
Year 2	400	0.6944*	278	0.5925*	237	0.6175*	247
Year 3	900	0.5787*	521	0.4556*	410	0.4878*	439
Total	700		132		(45)		0

*Present value factor of $1.

The exact return would be 27.14 percent, but again keep in mind that the cash flows that are the basis of the return calculation are really only estimates. In fact this would be a good time to look at the ranges of expenditure and the ranges of returns and evaluate the return based on those ranges.

Use of IRR. If there are no budget constraints, choose projects with rates of return above the hurdle rate. If there are budget constraints, choose projects with the highest rate of return.

Advantages of IRR. It is strictly comparable to the hurdle rate and the cost of capital ratios, so the relationship between indicated rate of return and the value of money to the company is apparent.

Disadvantages of IRR

1. It is assumed that all future cash flows can be invested at a rate identical to the original rate for the project.

2. When periodic net inflow and net outflow are staggered over time, there may be more than one yield rate that satisfies the condition of discounting all flows to zero.

3. There is no direct way of evaluating projects for which only the costs can be stated, for example, mandatory projects such as smokestack scrubbers.

Excess Present Value Index (EPVI)

This is an index derived from comparing the present value of outflows to that of inflows. It is used to rank and compare proposed investment projects. The higher the project index, the more profitable or desirable the project.

Example of EPVI. The formula for the excess present value index is

$$\text{EPVI} = \frac{\text{Net inflows discounted at hurdle rate}}{\text{Net outflows discounted at hurdle rate}}$$

	Actual	@ 20%	Actual	@ 20%
Inventory year			(1,000)	(1,000)
Year 1: 0.8333	1,200	1,000	(800)	(668)
Year 2: 0.6944	400	278		
Year 3: 0.5787	900	521		
Total	2,500	1,799		(1,668)

$$\text{EPVI} = \frac{\$1,799}{\$1,668} = 1.08$$

Use of EPVI. If there are no budget constraints, choose projects with an EPVI greater than 1. If there are budget constraints, choose projects with the largest EPVI.

Advantage of EPVI. The EPVI may be used as an index of investment profitability and, therefore, to place all alternative opportunities on a comparable easy-to-understand basis.

Disadvantages of EPVI

1. There may be problems in defining the expenses associated with the investment.

2. The two types of flow must be discounted separately.

Net Present Value (NPV)

The net present value is the sum of net cash flows, discounted by the hurdle rate.

Example of NPV

	Cash	Factor	@ 20%
Investment year	(1,000)	0.0000*	(1,000)
Year 1	400	0.8333*	333
Year 2	400	0.6944*	278
Year 3	900	0.5787*	521
NPV			132

*Present value factor of $1.

Use of NPV. If there are no budget constraints, choose all projects with a positive NPV; if there is a budget constraint, then choose projects with the largest NPV.

Advantages of NPV

1. Cash flows are discounted at the hurdle rate or at the minimum acceptable rate of return on capital investment.

2. It involves only one discounting sequence.

3. The method makes a minimum of implicit assumptions.

4. The NPV calculates directly the amount of discounted contribution to a firm's profit, which is the logical quantity to be maximized.

5. Risk can be factored in with relative ease by raising or lowering the hurdle rate according to the risk of the project.

6. Investment projects of different types (replacements, new investments, required investments) can be evaluated using NPV and can be strictly compared.

Disadvantages of NPV. None, other than those listed under general disadvantages for discounting methods.

STEPS IN A PROJECT EVALUATION PROGRAM

1. Establish a hurdle rate.

2. Determine the evaluation techniques to be used (you may use more than one).

3. Rank the projects available.

4. Make the decisions that will make the project evaluation meaningful.

5. Complete a capital request for transfer from forecast to capital budget making process.

6. Set the criteria and timing for postcompletion audits and determine audit criteria.

Example of Capital Evaluation Calculation

Revenues and (Investment Outlays)

Example Information

		Time Period		
Project	0	1	2	3
A	(1,000)	25	50	1,600
B	(1,000)	1,100	100	100
C	(1,000)	1,000	325	50
D	(1,000)	400	400	850
E	(1,000)	$400*	400	900

*$1,200 Inflow – ($800) Outflow = $400.

	Accountant's Rate of Return (on Average Investment)		Period Payback (PP)		Yield Method (DCF) × (IRR)		Excess Present Value Index (EPVI)*		Net Present Value (NPV)*	
Project	Rate (%)	Rank	PP	Rank	Yield (%)	Rank	EPVI	Rank	NPV	Rank
A	45.0	1	2.58	5	19.2	5	0.98	5	(21)	5
B	20.0	5	0.91	1	24.5	4	1.04	4	44	4
C	30.0	3	1.00	2	28.3	1	1.09	2	88	3
D	43.0	2	2.24	4	25.7	3	1.10	1	103	2
E	26.0	4	2.22	3	27.1	2	1.08	3	133	1

*@ 20% cost of capital.

The preceding table illustrates the problem with using just one of the evaluation methods. You will notice that all five projects have the same investment or cost of acquisition. The variation is in the cash flows after the acquisition of the asset. It can be seen that depending on the adjustment of the cash flows, each of the projects can come up number one. For this and other reasons, we suggest that the organization use at least payback period, IRR, and NPV.

In order to apply the preceding evaluations, it is imperative that a good job of revenue and cost evaluation be completed. This is often termed life-cycle value analysis.

Life-Cycle Value Analysis

Simply stated, life-cycle value analysis estimates the total revenues and costs related to an individual project, including acquiring, installing, using, maintaining, and, in some instances, removing and disposal. These factors are then compared to the revenues or cost savings that will be generated as a result of the process. In reality, it makes sense to pay a somewhat higher price for an item if it has greater productivity gains and a lower maintenance cost than an alternative item from another source. Life-cycle value analysis provides a sensible alternative to the emphasis on low acquisition cost only. Its use has recognition and support from many organizations including The Coca-Cola Company and Intel Corporation.

There are 11 essential steps involved in the determination of the life-cycle value analysis for a project:

1. Determination of purchase and installation price

2. Establishment of operating profiles

3. Establishment of utilization factors

4. Identification of revenue elements

5. Identification of critical revenue elements

6. Identification of cost elements

7. Determination of critical cost elements

8. Calculation of costs at current incremental values

9. Escalation of current labor and material costs over the life of the project

10. Discounting of all costs and revenues to a base period

11. A summation of all discounted and undiscounted costs and revenues

The project should be shared by supply and operating management with the assistance of accounting. It is often best to utilize a range process with life-cycle valuation with a modeling technique to determine the probability of success (exceeding the hurdle rate), the business exposure involved (a business's worst position related to the business's best position), and where operations and supply should spend their time to improve the value through revenue enhancement or cost reduction. Companies are using Monte Carlo modeling to accomplish this evaluation. The Monte Carlo method is a simulation technique for assessing risk and aiding in decision making by providing information on the likelihood of possible results from different decisions that could be made.

SUPPLY MANAGEMENT'S ROLE IN THE ACQUISITION OF CAPITAL EQUIPMENT

The role of supply management in the capital process is to provide the business side of the purchase. This process relates to the 10 "rights of purchasing. The buyer must optimize the following "right" areas:

1. Capital asset

2. Place

3. Time

4. Price

5. Quality

6. Quantity

7. Warranty or guarantee

8. Service

9. Terms (both shipping and payment)

10. Contract

It would be ideal if supply management could be involved from the strategic planning process right on through to the disposition of the asset after the productive life is over; however, in most cases this is not possible. Factors such as culture, past practices, and tradition may inhibit the buyer's participation in some areas of the acquisition process. It is vitally important that the buyer coordinate the 10 rights of purchasing.

Right Capital Asset

This is the process of review of specifications, drawings, and statements of work for clarity and competitiveness. It is important to start coordination with users on the requirements of the technical side of the buy as soon as possible.

Right Place

This process relates to supplier sourcing and coordination of the place of purchase with the rest of the procurement processes. Finding and developing sources of supply is an ongoing and important function in the area of capital equipment purchasing. Normally the time span between capital evaluation and requisition is fairly short, and the more we can do in preparing for the actual purchase, the better off we will be.

One of the important parts of supplier sourcing and time processes in many capital acquisitions is a supplier visit. It is important that the buyer understand and qualify the supplier before the bid and contract process takes place. This is the time that the buyer should introduce the company's terms and conditions to the supplier and make sure that the supplier is willing to comply with the stated terms and conditions or that differences are negotiated at this point in time. There are several other reasons why a buyer would visit a supplier before the actual purchase of the equipment.

The buyer should determine the following:

1. Can the supplier deliver?

2. Does the supplier have the equipment to complete the order?

3. Does the supplier have the workforce and equipment to meet the desired delivery date?

4. Is the supplier involved in programs such as value analysis, TQM, ISO 9000, or other quality or value programs, and how will this affect the supplier's ability to handle our order?

In addition the buyer should make contacts that will assist in troubleshooting and preventing or resolving problems when they occur.

Supplier visits provide the buyer with education. Valuable insights into an industry or into a procedure may be gained through a supplier visit. Because of such knowledge gained, visits to every new source may not be necessary.

Courtesy would dictate that notice is given to a supplier before bursting upon the scene. A proper warning of your intent to visit allows the people involved to coordinate their schedules to allow all interested parties to be available, for instance, technical people and sales managers. Furthermore, a previous announcement of your intent to visit allows the company to put its best foot forward.

Right Time

Time relates to the coordination of the purchase with the requirements of the organization. This is where the statement "strike while the iron is hot" fits.

At the beginning of the process it is good to provide each one of the prospective suppliers with a booklet of the terms and conditions. These terms and conditions are usually found on the back of the purchase order or as part of a contract which is probably the worst place in the world to have them. Terms and conditions should be agreed to before the contracting process is ever started. This way the groundwork will already be laid and the process of developing a good working relationship can begin right up front.

An overview of the project should be given and should include a discussion of how it fits into the overall plan and purpose of the company. This step follows and is a natural extension of the terms and conditions. It can also follow and use the format used for presentation of the project to company management and other parts of the internal organization.

Another timing factor is the coordination of timing of installation, production, and other time constraints of either the supplier or the user of the equipment. This also relates to the management of project records and status including

1. Bid, RFP, RFQ, and RFI processes
2. Purchase contract issue
3. Authorizations
4. Changes and adjustments
5. Expediting log including final receipt and acceptance

Right Price

This is often thought of as obvious in the purchase process; however, the balance of monetary value against the rest of the rights is very important in a capital acquisition to optimize both use and shareholder value.

Right Quality
Quality is a perception of the parties involved. It is very important that the buyer understand the quality requirements so that there is again a balance of the quality against the price and the other elements involved.

Right Quantity
Although there is not a question of quantity related directly to the purchase, this relates to the quantity of spare parts and where they will be maintained and any other quantity such as quantity of time for training and time for support.

Right Warranty
Warranty is often a negotiable item related to price and quality. Again it is a balancing process.

Right Service
Service with capital equipment is very important. Many times a negative service contract will be included. This means that payment for service will depend on the uptime of the equipment. The supplier will receive the most from the contract if the equipment is always in top operating condition.

Right Terms
This right deals with both shipping terms and payment terms. Payment terms could include progress payments, while shipping terms should determine when the title of the equipment transfers.

Right Contract
The right contract will address the following areas at a minimum:

1. The clarity of specifications, drawings, and statement of work and inclusion of this in the contract.

2. The expected level of performance of the equipment and personnel involved and the remedies if performance, including quality, does not occur.

3. The expected schedule of performance to meet delivery requirements of the organization and the relationship of maintenance and spare parts to the operation.

4. Warranty, guarantee, and service agreements including the action to be taken if defaults occur.

5. The price and payment schedule relating to all parts of the equipment and services to be delivered as a result of the contract.

It is obvious that the issues in the contract and in the 10 rights of the procurement process must be coordinated with the capital team prior to preparation of a bid, RFP, RFQ, and RFI; again during the analysis process; and finally during the preparation and execution of a negotiation plan.

CONTRACT NEGOTIATIONS

Note: For a more complete discussion of negotiating, refer to Chapter 24.

Negotiation should be the least troublesome method of settling disputes and/or establishing agreement. Negotiation may be exploratory and serve to formulate viewpoints and delineate areas of agreement or contention. It may aim at working out practical arrangements. The success of negotiation depends upon whether (1) the issue is negotiable (that is, you can sell your car but not your child); (2) the negotiators are interested not only in taking, but also in giving; are able to exchange value for value; and are willing to compromise; and (3) there is a trust level between negotiating parties. If there isn't an element of trust, then there will be a plethora of safety provisions and protections that will render the agreement unworkable.

An excellent definition of *negotiation* comes from the U.S. Air Force:

> A mutual discussion and arrangement of the terms of a transaction or agreement. Negotiation is the use of argumentation and persuasion, not to win an argument, but to resolve issues—not an individual issue—but the whole problem. Negotiation is not the process of giving in or mutual sacrifice in order to secure agreement. It is an attempt to find a formula which will optimize the interests of both parties.

It is a specialized process of communication called *bargaining,* by which means a buyer or a seller reach agreement on the issues involved that will reflect a balancing of the interest of the two parties. Negotiation is the application of facts and logic supported by the strengths of a bargaining position to achieve valid and necessary business objectives. Procurement by negotiation is the art of arriving at a common understanding through bargaining on the essentials of a contract such as delivery, specifications, prices, and terms. Because of the interrelation of these factors with many others, it is a difficult art and requires the exercise of judgment, tact, and common sense. The effective negotiator must be a real shopper but not a haggler, alive to the possibilities of bargaining with the seller. Only through an awareness of relative bargaining strength can a negotiator know where to be firm or where he or she may make concessions in position. In a simple statement, negotiations must result in an agreement that is acceptable to both parties.

LEASE VERSUS BUY ALTERNATIVES

What is a lease? What is the difference between an operating lease and a capital lease? The answers to these basic questions can be given from an economic, legal, Securities and Exchange Commission (SEC), accounting, financial, IRS, or industry point of view. Which is right? The answer depends upon the needs of the person asking the question. For the sake of this definition we will rely heavily upon the accounting definitions given by the Financial Accounting Standards Board (FASB), since the Board governs the accounting practices of virtually all public corporations. Then too, reliance will be placed upon IRS terminology and classification since taxes are such a crucial element in any decision concerning leases.

In general a lease is viewed as a contract between a lessor (owner of an asset), and a lessee (user of an asset), where the lessor grants the temporary possession and use of an asset to the lessee. This is usually for a specified period less than the asset's economic life at a fixed periodic charge (rental charge or lease payment). However, even though a contract labeled as a "lease" might contain these characteristics, it will not necessarily be considered a lease from an accounting or IRS point of view.

FASB Accounting Definition of a Lease

The FASB in its Statement No. 13, "Accounting for Leases," divides all leases into two basic classifications. A lease is either a capital lease or an operating lease. A capital lease is not really considered a true lease at all, but rather is a *sale* of equipment from the lessor's viewpoint and a *purchase* from the lessee's viewpoint; whereas, an operating lease is a true lease from both the lessor's and lessee's viewpoints.

Capital leases can be further subdivided into three types of lease. They are a sales-type lease, a direct finance lease, and a leveraged lease where the lessee wants to use as little of the organization's money as possible.

According to FASB Statement No. 13, "If at its inception a lease meets one or more of the following four criteria, the lease shall be classified as a capital lease by the Lessee. Otherwise, it shall be classified as an operating lease."

1. The lease transfers ownership of the property to the lessee by the end of the lease term.

2. The lease contains a bargain purchase or bargain lease renewal option.

3. The lease term is equal to 75 percent or more of the estimated economic life of the leased property.

4. The present value at the beginning of the lease term of the minimum lease payments equals or exceeds 90 percent of the fair market value (FMV) of the leased property at the inception of the lease. (The FMV of the property is to be reduced by any investment tax credit or energy credit retained by the lessor prior to determining the 90 percent base).

The lessor's discount rate shall be the implicit rate in the lease.

The lessee's discount rate shall be his or her incremental borrowing rate unless the implicit rate in the lease can be determined and that rate is lower.

Criteria 3 and 4 are ignored when the beginning of the lease term is within the remaining 25 percent of an asset's economic life. This situation occurs when used assets are leased during the last 25 percent of their economic lives.

If none of the aforementioned criteria are met, then the lease is considered a true lease and is referred to as an *operating lease*.

Lease and Purchase Cost Evaluation

To facilitate the identification of pertinent lease costs, Table 37–1 subdivides leasing costs into direct and indirect costs. Direct costs are generally the initial, subsequent, and terminal financial costs that form an integral part of the lease. Indirect costs are represented by executory and other miscellaneous costs that are not integrally related to the lease but are incidentally related such as taxes and insurance.

Costs of purchasing an asset with the proceeds of either an installment loan or with internally generated cash will be categorized in the same manner as leasing costs. The purchase decision format appears in Table 37–2.

TABLE 37–1

Lease Cost Format

	Amount	Tax × Factor	Present Value × Factor	= Total
Add Direct Leasing Costs				
Initial costs				
Advance rental payments	_____	× _____	× _____	= _____
Security deposit	_____	× _____	× _____	= _____
Lease origination fee	_____	× _____	× _____	= _____
Subsequent costs				
Lease payments	_____	× _____	× _____	= _____
Excess use charges	_____	× _____	× _____	= _____
Lease termination costs	_____	× _____	× _____	= _____
Exercise of purchase option	_____	× _____	× _____	= _____
Add Indirect Leasing Costs				
Sales tax in advance	_____	× _____	× _____	= _____
Sales tax with payments	_____	× _____	× _____	= _____
Insurance expense	_____	× _____	× _____	= _____
Maintenance	_____	× _____	× _____	= _____
Fuel costs	_____	× _____	× _____	= _____
Accounting costs, etc.	_____	× _____	× _____	= _____
Total present value of costs to lease				$_____
Deduct Leasing Benefits				
Depreciation tax shield	_____	× _____	× _____	= _____
Return of security deposit	_____	× _____	× _____	= _____
Total present value of leasing benefits				$_____
Net present value of leasing				$_____

TABLE 37–2

Purchase Cost Format

	Amount	Tax × Factor	Present Value × Factor	= Total
Add Direct Purchasing Costs				
Initial costs				
Down payment	_____	× _____	× _____	= _____
Service charge	_____	× _____	× _____	= _____
Sales tax	_____	× _____	× _____	= _____
Compensating bank balance		×	×	=
Subsequent costs				
Periodic payments	_____	× _____	× _____	= _____
Purchase termination costs (none normally)	_____	× _____	× _____	= _____
Add Indirect Purchasing Costs				
Insurance expense	_____	× _____	× _____	= _____
Maintenance	_____	× _____	× _____	= _____
Fuel costs	_____	× _____	× _____	= _____
Replacement costs	_____	× _____	× _____	= _____
Additional facility costs	_____	× _____	× _____	= _____
Accounting costs, etc.	_____	× _____	× _____	= _____
Total present value of costs to purchase				$_____
Deduct Purchasing Benefits				
Return of compensating bank balance	_____	× _____	× _____	= _____
Interest tax shield (per assumptions)				_____
Depreciation tax shield (per assumptions)				_____
Total present value of purchasing benefits				$_____
Net present value of purchasing				$_____

Explanation for Lease versus Buy Analysis

1. Some leases require delivery and installation charges to be paid by the lessee.

2. Security deposits are sometimes required to be paid in advance to give the lessor additional collateral security and to compensate the lessor for any excessive wear and tear on the leased asset at the time of its return to the lessor.

3. Percentage rentals are based upon a fixed percentage of the lessee's gross revenue in excess of a base amount. The percentage rentals are generally paid by the lessee in addition to the normal periodic rentals.

4. The amounts of some lease payments are tied to increases in the prime rate or to increases in the consumer price index.

5. Should the lessee expect usage of the equipment beyond that allowed in the lease, then excess use fees will be charged by the lessor.

6. At the end of the lease term, one of several alternative actions will be taken depending on the terms of the lease and the needs of the lessee. The equipment may be purchased by the lessee.

7. At the termination of the lease the contract might require the lessee to pay a penalty for excess use (e.g., mileage on trucks beyond a specified maximum) or for repairs and maintenance required to bring the equipment up to a specified working order and condition. Should the lessee anticipate such additional costs, they should be included as costs under the lease alternative.

8. In net leases, executory costs such as sales tax, property tax, insurance, and maintenance are required to be paid by the lessee.

9. Replacement costs are incurred when equipment is obtained from the lessor to replace equipment temporarily out of service due to extraordinary breakdowns.

10. Under certain full-service leases, fuel costs can be minimized. For example, many Ryder Truck leasing agreements provide for the purchase of fuel from company outlets at prices below retail. With rising energy costs, these savings could became a decisive factor in the lease versus buy decision.

11. When compared to purchasing equipment, the leasing of the same equipment generally requires substantially less accounting and bookkeeping.

12. Miscellaneous costs are those expenses that are unique to the leasing of particular types of equipment. For example, some equipment requires special licenses and permits, for example, trucks used in interstate commerce.

13. Sublease income expected from the lessee's anticipated leasing of the equipment to others should be deducted from the lease costs.

14. In the event the lessee does not expect to receive a refund of the security due to anticipated excess wear and tear of the equipment, such loss becomes a future noncash tax deduction.

15. In many cases it is more advantageous to the purchaser of equipment to capitalize costs of delivery, installation, closing and service fees, and licenses and permits. Such capitalization allows the purchaser to

take energy credit on the capitalized costs. Moreover, these costs can be subsequently depreciated resulting in additional tax benefit.

16. At times banks and other financial institutions also require security deposits in addition to a down payment when loaning on an installment purchase. Such a deposit is not tax deductible to the purchaser.

17. Compensating bank balances are cash deposits required to be held in the purchaser's checking account with the banker-lender. Since the cash outlay is held by the bank without any payment of interest, it represents a nontaxable outflow in the initial year, and a nontaxable inflow at the time the loan is paid off.

18. Recent installment loan agreements have provided for payments that increase as the prime rate increases. Therefore, forecasting of future prime rates is required.

19. In order to keep installment loan payments to a minimum, some banks allow the purchaser to pay a large balloon payment at the end of a loan term. This type of loan structuring makes the installment loan very comparable to leases that require large guaranteed residuals to be paid at the end of the lease.

20. Ownership of equipment oftentimes entails costs that would not ordinarily be incurred under a full-service lease. For example, spare parts and supplies inventories must be maintained to support equipment maintenance. Significant added costs of ownership are represented by these incremental support costs. Should any of these support costs represent capital expenditures, these should be added to the initial cost of purchasing. Later on, these capitalized costs would result in depreciation tax shields available to the purchaser as benefits of ownership. Remember to add only those costs that are incremental, that is, those variable costs that will be incurred only as a result of purchasing the equipment.

21. Equipment that is owned qualifies for depreciation under IRS rules. Depreciation results in tax savings that are equal to the income tax rate multiplied by the annual depreciation charge.

22. Interest is included in the installment loan payments listed earlier as a purchasing cost. Since interest is tax deductible, it results in a tax savings equal to the interest paid times the tax rate.

23. If the equipment is assumed salvaged prior to the end of its economic life in order to make the purchase alternative equivalent to the shorter-term lease alternative, then the salvage proceeds represent a savings. However, such proceeds must be adjusted for tax consequences. If the equipment is salvaged for more than its book value (tax basis or undepreciated value), then taxes must be paid equal to the tax rate times the gain (ignoring any capital gain opportunities). Should the salvage value be less than the book value, a tax benefit would be earned in an amount equal to the loss times the tax rate. In either case, the additional tax expense or benefit must be deducted or added to the salvage value.

CONCLUSION

Executive management, line management, and supply management make up a team that is charged to deliver shareholder value for the owners of the organization. This is accomplished by executive management providing a clear vision of the expectations within the organization. Line management provides the evaluation of its capability in accomplishing these expectations, and supply management assists in managing the external relationships to the value requirements.

These external relationships can be evaluated through the following relationship:

$$\frac{\text{Cash return}}{\text{Invested capital related to the weighted average cost of capital}}$$

Capital asset acquisition affects the cash return by making the operation more efficient and effective. The cost of invested capital is managed through the effort of supply management in determining value and negotiating position. The capital management part of the organization affects two of the three parts of the value relationship and becomes one of the important focuses of the organization.

CHAPTER 38

PURCHASING SERVICES

Lori Yelvington, CPCU
Assistant Vice President, Procurement Governance
Allstate Insurance Company

OVERVIEW

According to a Bureau of Economic Analysis (BEA) report released in August 2004, the service sector accounts for approximately two-thirds of the nation's gross domestic product (GDP). Of the nearly $11 trillion that is spent in the United States each year, $7 trillion is spent on services, while the remaining $4 trillion is spent on durable and nondurable goods and investments.

In contrast, supply management organizations have focused primarily on the procurement of direct and indirect goods. In recent years, supply management departments have expanded their efforts to include the purchase of services. The result has been the realization that purchasing services has many elements that are quite different from purchasing goods and often requires additional knowledge and skills.

Research organizations have also recognized this increased focus on services purchasing. In 2003, the CAPS Research (CAPS) released a research paper entitled "Managing Your Services Spend in Today's Services Economy." The study found that among responding companies, services spend is 11 percent of total revenue and 30 percent of total purchase spend. This is compared to indirect goods which are 9 percent of sales and 23 percent of total purchasing spend and direct goods which are 18 percent of sales and 44 percent of total purchasing spend. CAPS also noted that services spend is expected to increase approximately 13 percent over the next 5 years.

The CAPS study reported that the average number of service suppliers for an organization is 2,321 but ranges from 100 to 14,000 suppliers among the study participants. The median number of service suppliers is 900.

Finally, CAPS survey respondents reported that organizations source, procure, and manage goods more efficiently and effectively than services, or bundled goods and services. In fact, 70 percent of participants said that purchasing services is more difficult when compared to buying goods and that it is more difficult to manage the delivery of services relative to managing the delivery of goods.[1]

---

1 CAPS Research (2003). "Managing Your 'Services Spend' in Today's Services Economy," Tempe, AZ: CAPS Research.

TYPES OF SERVICES

Organizations purchase a multitude of services that can be categorized as follows:

- *Professional services.* Consulting, accounting, financial services, legal, temporary office staff

- *Marketing services.* Advertising, media, inbound and outbound telemarketing, data management

- *Facilities services.* Cafeteria, construction, equipment maintenance, facility maintenance, janitorial, landscape maintenance, real estate, security, utilities, courier, mail, printing, and copying

- *Information technology services.* Computer equipment, installation and maintenance, disposal, telecommunications

- *Human resource services.* Benefits administration, medical, payroll, travel, lodging, meals, recruiting, relocation, outplacement, employee education and training

DIFFERENCES IN PURCHASING SERVICES

The purchasing of services is similar to purchasing goods in that a traditional sourcing process is followed. Commodity managers leverage the supply and demand of the markets and request proposals from qualified suppliers. A specific contract is needed both for goods and services to identify the terms and conditions under which the agreed-upon goods and services will be delivered.

However, many significant differences exist when purchasing services. Services are not tangible goods—you can't touch, feel, or inspect the item being purchased. This makes it extremely important that the supply manager defines the requirements and the services being sought in the formal proposal. The services must also be thoroughly described in the contract or statement of work to ensure that both the supply manager and the supplier understand what is expected and how it will be evaluated. Figure 38–1 provides a list of suggested elements for a thorough statement of work (SOW).

Many services are highly technical. Sourcing personnel should involve their client subject matter experts (SMEs) in all aspects of the sourcing process. The input of these individuals is necessary to ensure that the ultimate service purchased meets all the requirements of the user area. Outside experts should also be consulted when warranted. Currently engaged consultants can often provide a perspective on the industry and price points. User groups, particularly in the technology, telecommunications, and advertising industries, are very informative and insightful. Additionally, other companies are often willing to share information and learnings that they have experienced in similar projects. These outside entities provide good support and balance for the internal SMEs.

Unlike hard good purchases, it is often difficult to identify qualified suppliers when a specialized service is requested. Requests for information (RFIs) are common

FIGURE 38–1

SOW Template Guidelines

Headings	Suggested Content
Project overview and purpose	Description of project background and overall work in simple terms.
Key assumptions	Detail of all understandings that will drive costs or requirements.
Scope	Functional, technical, and services. Geographic and business area. Start and end date of project.
Approach	Define whether project is results- or resources-based. If results-based, define the desired end result and allow the supplier flexibility to deliver based on its experience. If resources-based, provide specific definitions (how many, for how long, and at what rate). Include service-level agreements (metrics, standards, remedies and penalties).
Deliverables and performance	Specify the required delivery and completion dates for each item of deliverable products and services. May include interim milestone dates.
Approval and change control process	Specify any reviews or approvals required from the purchaser, and state the performance measurement criteria. Outline the process for how changes in scope will be handled from a pricing and contract addendum perspective.
Inspection, test, and acceptance	Define any required in-process tests or inspections, who will perform them, criteria for acceptance, and the time period for remedy.
Staffing and costs	Specify whether payment will be based on hourly rates or a fixed fee. Make every attempt to unbundle costs to enable pricing transparency. List key personnel on engagement. Clarify if travel expenses are included in fixed fee; require that the supplier follows the buyer travel policy. Cap expenses at 10%–15% of fees.
Project management	Describe requirements and the management data needed.
Supplier responsibilities	Checkpoint meetings should include agendas, status of each deliverable, problems, notes, etc., in writing.
Buyer responsibility	Include items such as who will supply equipment and the specifics as to which personnel will be accessible to the supplier.

(Continued)

FIGURE 38–1

(Continued)

Headings	Suggested Content
Agreement not to compete	Use only if project work is truly a competitive advantage or unique deliverable. Provide a list of competitors for whom the supplier cannot do work for a certain time period.
Warranties	Default to professional services agreement (PSA) unless it is a high-risk project. Outline how the supplier will warrant the outcome and results, including how it will be measured.
Information security	May have additional requirements outside of the PSA, especially if customer data is involved.

in the services arena when searching for capable suppliers. An RFI can be used prior to a formal bid process [request for proposal (RFP)] to determine which suppliers have both the capacity and the ability to perform a needed service for an organization.

Services purchasing is much more political than the purchase of goods. The internal alignment regarding the selection of a service supplier is often more difficult to achieve than the actual negotiation with the supplier. Many executives have relationships or a history with specific service providers. Managers may prefer a given supplier based on anecdotal information, with little basis in fact. In addition, client departments often perceive that the supply management organization makes selection decisions based on price alone.

The selection of services is more subjective than the selection of goods. It is important to reach agreement on the selection criteria and the weight of each criteria element prior to evaluating the various bids. For example, the following categories might be chosen as scoring criteria for a consulting project:

Project team. Assessment of core team based on past experience of similar engagements or ability to demonstrate its understanding of the purchaser's needs

Resources. Assessment of the supplier's depth and breadth of resources and its ability to ramp up the project and manage the resource pool

Approach and project plan. Assessment of the supplier's ability to demonstrate a logical and effective approach to the project and how skills will be transferred to the customer

External insight and experience. Understanding and insight into the customer's industry and how the supplier's insight and experience can be leveraged

Fee and pricing structure. Level of fees, as well as willingness to place fees at risk based on tangible deliverables

Intangibles. Assessment of any "differentiators" that set the supplier apart from the others

Once these criteria are identified and agreed upon, weights should be assigned prior to sending out the RFP. A possible weighting structure might be

Project team (20%)

Resources (30%)

Approach and project plan (20%)

External insight and experience (15%)

Fee and pricing structure (10%)

Intangibles (5%)

By setting the criteria and weights before the bids are received, the supply manager can avoid emotional issues and relationship considerations that might arise during scoring and selection. Refer to Chapter 33, "Supplier Performance Evaluation," for examples of supplier scoring and evaluation. Unlike goods, services are not returnable. The contract and statements of work must be very specific as to the details of what the supplier will be doing. Every possible scenario must be anticipated with details on how each situation will be handled. This should include changes in volume, changes in business strategy, definitions of acceptable performance, consequences for unacceptable performance, and specifics as to who determines acceptable or unacceptable performance.

Background checks and security concerns are very important components in the sourcing of services. When a supplier's employees are going to be on the premises, or interfacing with customers, it is important to make sure that a background check is performed. The contract or statement of work should specify the thoroughness of the background check, how far back the search should look, how this will be audited, who will pay for the background checks, and what will ensue if certain items are discovered in the background check. Also, security and privacy of customer and employee data, as well as other confidentiality provisions, are elements of services purchasing that must be considered.

Finally, services are much more difficult to track and analyze, depending on a company's accounting system. A manufacturing company usually tracks items by part number, making it relatively easy to determine how much is being spent on a specific part or parts. However, services are usually lumped into a ledger or cost element as "professional services" or "facility services" or "marketing services," making it extremely difficult to analyze buying patterns.

These and other considerations make the purchase of services much different than the purchase of goods.

THE SERVICES SOURCING PROCESS

The goal of any sourcing project is to optimize the value of externally purchased goods and services. Or in more simple terms, the goal is to get the best-quality goods or services at the most cost-effective price.

There are many variations on the process of purchasing services. To ensure that an organization optimizes the value of the purchased services, the process that it follows in procuring the service should include the following eight steps.

Step 1. Establish a Working Team

This step may be formal or informal, depending on the size of the project. As mentioned earlier, many services are highly technical. It is very helpful to form a cross-functional team that includes client subject matter experts. These individuals will add valuable insight and expertise on the service being purchased. Since they are the ones who will ultimately have a working day-to-day relationship with the supplier, it is essential that they buy in to the selection decision. Financial experts are another important piece of the cross-functional team. They will be called upon to analyze suppliers' pricing proposals and to verify the financial health of potential suppliers. Technology experts are also often needed on the team to verify that the technology that a supplier proposes to use or build will successfully integrate with the company's future and/or current technology. Finally, supply management expertise on the team ensures that a consistent and nonbiased process is followed. It will ultimately be supply management's responsibility to achieve a fair and thorough contract and to ensure that both parties abide within the terms and conditions. The client may feel awkward enforcing contract terms, since he or she usually interacts with the service provider daily. Supply managers provide value to the client by acting as an unbiased third party when contract and service issues arise.

Step 2. Define the Requirements

This step is crucial to any services sourcing initiative. An internal client may wish to purchase a particular service and engage his or her supply management department to assist and guide them. Often, the internal client cannot effectively articulate what it is that it would like to purchase. It is important, at this point to rigorously describe the requirements. This includes defining what need is to be fulfilled by the purchase, what part or parts of a process will be performed by the supplier, what deliverables are expected at the end of the project, how much the client is budgeting for the purchase, and what is the time frame for both supplier selection and project completion.

In some cases, the service is already being performed by a supplier. In these instances, it is also important to define the parameters of the current contract, including termination provisions and contract expiration dates, the satisfaction levels with the current supplier, the reasons the current supplier was selected, and what has changed since that selection occurred. Also important are key leverage points and improvement opportunities with the current supplier.

Sometimes, client departments engage in conversations with suppliers prior to involving the supply manager. When this occurs, the supplier may volunteer to define the project requirements for the client. This often results in a much broader scope of service (and cost) than was originally intended by the client and makes it difficult to scale back the project to the original scope. For this reason, it is highly recommended that clients work with their supply managers when defining desired services engagements. Suppliers can be utilized as a resource to fill in the gaps, but overall project specifications and deliverables are best when defined by the client.

Step 3. As-Is Assessment

The as-is assessment contains two pieces. The first is an internal spend analysis to determine what is currently being spent on the particular service, who is buying it, and from whom. The second part is an analysis of the industry and the suppliers within that industry.

The internal spend analysis is often more difficult to perform than the external industry analysis. The first difficulty arises when a major sourcing effort is begun. Often the goal of such a project is to consolidate the supplier base to leverage the company's entire spend in that category and achieve better pricing. Thus, it is essential to understand how much is currently being spent on the particular service. Each department in an organization may define a service differently, making it very difficult to aggregate the expense for analysis.

Additionally, one supplier may provide multiple services to a company. It is important to understand each commodity and avoid lumping the entire spend into one category. For example, an information technology department may hire a supplier to do some architectural design and project management, and code this work as "contract programming." The marketing department may hire this same supplier to help it organize and map its prospecting databases and code this work to "professional services." The corporate strategy department may hire the same firm again to assist it in defining the corporate data strategy and code the work to "management consulting." The supply management department must identify and define the exact service that it is sourcing.

Another difficulty is that, depending on a company's accounting structure, similar work could be coded to a multitude of accounts. This makes it extremely challenging to gather information on firms that are doing similar work throughout the company. Many companies use the account "professional services" to include a conglomeration of all types of service provider expenses, adding to the difficulty to analyze spend.

The ultimate goal of the internal spend analysis is to determine how much is being spent on a particular service, how many suppliers are currently providing the service, and at what cost. One of the most eye-opening results of this analysis is often the fact that one supplier may be contracting with multiple areas of a company for the same service at differing price and service levels. Once this information is obtained, the sourcing analyst can work with the cross-functional team to determine the sourcing strategy and any opportunity for consolidation and savings. If the service has never been purchased before, the sourcing analyst can proceed to industry and supplier analysis.

Industry and supplier analysis enables the sourcing team to understand what the marketplace has to offer. The more information gathered about different suppliers and their relation to the industry as a whole, the more value and savings that can be achieved from the process. SMEs on the cross-functional team are often a good source with experience and knowledge of the industry and the players in the industry. Benchmarking studies can provide information about the quality and prices that are typical for the industry. Consultants and prior employees are also another good source of information. A multitude of research tools are available to help with this inquiry:

- Internet
- Chamber of Commerce
- Yellow Pages
- Dun and Bradstreet
- Libraries
- Industry publication trade magazines and journals
- Benchmarking studies
- Lexis-Nexis
- Thomas Registry
- ISM Supplier Directory

It's important to use multiple research tools to verify information and not to place too much emphasis on one tool. Many companies find that the data gathered in this step contradict what has traditionally been thought to be fact. Organizations may believe that the "deal" they are receiving from a service supplier is superior. A fact-based analysis may reveal that one part of the organization is subsidizing another part or that the supplier is earning a profit on its account well in excess of the supplier's total corporate profit. The most effective sourcing projects result from those teams that have thoroughly researched a service and its industry and are well informed about all aspects of the pricing, delivery, customer satisfaction, reputation, and supplier practices. Knowledge, in this case, is truly power.

Step 4. Request for Information and Request for Proposal

The next step is to prepare a request for information. RFIs are most often used when a large number of suppliers have been identified and the organization needs to obtain additional supplier information to narrow the base of potential suppliers. When only a few suppliers are identified as candidates, an RFI is not usually necessary. RFIs typically contain higher-level questions on organizational capabilities and pricing. Once the RFI is received, the number of potential suppliers can be reduced to a manageable level and a formal request for proposal (RFP) can be prepared.

An RFP requesting services should include background information about your company and the objectives of the project, detailed requirements of the project, and guidelines on how and when to respond.

The RFP should also define the criteria by which each respondent will be evaluated and scored. Typical criteria include

- *Organizational capabilities.* Is the organization large enough and does it have the geographic footprint to adequately provide services to your company? Is it financially healthy?

- *Competitive pricing.*

- *Service.* This includes account management, flexibility, and responsiveness.

- *Technology.* This includes the organization's ability to report on its performance, compliance, and tracking capabilities.

- *Other value-added offerings.* Is there anything that the supplier is including in its proposal that will bring additional value to your company?

The cross-functional team should prepare a scoring model with weights assigned to each of the criteria. Each organization and each sourcing project values different criteria. In many instances of services purchasing, price is the lowest-valued criteria. Service and other value-added components typically carry greater weight. The integrity of the scoring process depends on setting these weights and criteria before responses are received. This avoids emotional or other influences on the scoring process.

RFPs for services vary considerably in length and detail. On one hand, for a management consulting engagement, the RFP may consist of a very brief description of the engagement and deliverables desired. The responding consultants are encouraged to creatively design how they will approach the engagement, and therefore, very little guidance is given in the RFP. One or two weeks is allowed for a response, at which time, each consultant is invited to present to the scoring team their formal proposal. Each consultant is given the same amount of time to present, and a winner can be selected in a very short period of time.

On the opposite spectrum, an RFP to select a call center supplier may be several hundred pages long. This may include detailed requirements as to how calls are to be handled, staffing qualifications and levels, account management specifics, performance measures, issue escalation and resolution processes, disaster recovery specifics, and technology provisions and requirements. Significant guidance is given in the RFP to ensure that both buyer and seller understand what is expected and how service delivery will be measured. In RFPs such as these, the supply manager's contract terms and conditions may be included to enable a speedier contracting process, once a supplier is selected. If a potential supplier is unwilling to comply with certain contract terms, it is better to reveal that early in the process and possibly eliminate that supplier. One or two months may be allowed for the response, at the end of which time, formal presentations may or may not be invited.

Step 5. Score the RFP Responses

Scoring the RFP responses can be done in a variety of ways. Because the selection of a service provider can be very subjective, it is essential that all parties on the selection team participate in the scoring. The previously developed scoring model should be used to provide an objective and fact-based measurement of the supplier responses relative to the supply manager's requirements. Scoring can be done either by assigning a numerical value to each of the supplier's responses (i.e., a poor response receives a 1 and a good response receives a 5) or by ranking the supplier responses to each question (i.e., if there are seven suppliers, the best answer receives a 1 and the worst answer receives a 7). The team members responses should then be aggregated and each section weighted based on the previously agreed upon weights.

Step 6. Evaluate

The evaluation part of the process is extremely important because this is where the team should be examining and testing the suppliers responses to the questions.

One very critical area that should be scrutinized is volume commitments. Suppliers are often willing to respond that they are able to handle large volumes of additional business. The sourcing team should look for evidence that the desired level of volume has been handled in the past or that substantial adjustments and resources have been added to the supplier's business processes. One way to ensure this is for the supply manager to arrange a pilot or testing phase. For example, a supplier who is being hired to provide on-site maintenance and troubleshooting for PC equipment on a countrywide basis, could be tested during a pilot period. The supply manager might devise fictional problems in various areas of the country to test availability and response time of the service supplier. Another example is a supplier who is being hired to provide office supplies to hundreds of locations countrywide. The supplier might well be able to handle the volume of supplies being purchased; however, the supply manager should also ensure that the supplier is able to handle an enormous amount of small orders and is prepared to handle the distribution and shipping in a timely manner. Finally, software provides a unique challenge when it is purchased for a large-scale implementation. The buyer should test the software to its full capacity and bring it to where response times are at the limit.

Another area that should be investigated thoroughly is the proposed account management. Call centers or service centers, in particular, present a unique challenge. Suppliers often staff these centers with a given number of employees who are dedicated to a particular company's call handling. They often have swing employees who are available to help during busy times. The sourcing team should ensure that the amount of dedicated call handlers and management personnel is sufficient to handle the "normal" volume. The client should not be depending on swing employees to service their normal level of activity. Additionally, when a company contracts with a staff augmentation firm or consulting firm, the supplier often places on-site management staff at the buyer's location. The sourcing team should ensure that the amount of on-site management staff is sufficient. Too many managers can add cost and loss of productivity to the account, whereas too few managers can cause confusion and lack of direction among the supplier's employees.

Suppliers often offer electronic billing for their services. The supply manager should make sure to understand the possible cost implications to his or her own company, which may result when he or she tries to understand and verify the billing. This is particularly true in the telecommunications field.

Step 7. Negotiate an Agreement

Once the RFP responses are scored, the team should select one or two suppliers to be in the "zone of consideration." It is often advantageous to negotiate with two finalists, because this maintains competition throughout the process. If an impasse is reached with one supplier, the second supplier is already at the negotiating table.

As with any sourcing initiative, the key to strong negotiations is preparation and information. The internal client and the supply management employees should present themselves to the suppliers as one united front, with one spokesperson. Similar to hard goods negotiations, the team should agree upon what they are willing to pay for the service and keep it among themselves!

One particularly challenging aspect to negotiations for services occurs when the client department engages its supply management partners at this point in the process. The client may have already engaged the supplier for a project and at this point, turns over the contracting and negotiations to supply management. In some cases, the supplier is scheduled to begin work on premises the next day. This makes it extremely difficult to achieve a favorable price or contract with the supplier, because any leverage that the company may have had has been given away. Clients should be counseled that even if they would like to single-source a project and not receive bids, they should not let the supplier know that this is the case. The illusion of competition should be maintained, if possible, so that supply management is able to negotiate a favorable deal.

This also applies when the decision is made to stay with the incumbent supplier. Incumbents often feel that they are untouchable and that, once ingrained in a company's processes, they are there to stay. Once again, constant competition, or the threat of such is a good thing! A company should always bring competition to its supplier base. Better pricing as well as increased service levels will inevitably be the result of a competitive threat.

Step 8. Contracts and Statements of Work

A good way to accommodate clients with a speedy contracting process for services is to have a master service agreement (MSA) or a professional services agreement (PSA) in place with major suppliers. The PSA should contain all the legal provisions, such as liability, warranties, confidentiality, and termination clauses. Once this is completed with a supplier, it does not have to be renegotiated each time the supplier is engaged. Statements of work (SOWs) can be attached to the master agreement for each body of work or project that the supplier is hired to perform. (See Figure 38–1 for suggested elements.) The SOW contains business issues such as project scope and objectives, time line, project deliverables, buyer versus supplier responsibilities, fees, invoicing, specific personnel assigned to the project, and the change process to be followed.

Good statements of work are arguably the most critical component to services purchasing. Unlike the purchase of goods, service contracts are not governed by the Uniform Commercial Code (UCC). Service contracts are governed by common law. There are a multitude of unanticipated situations that can occur in any project, and a thorough SOW will provide for such circumstances. The SOW should thoroughly describe the scope of work and how it is to be accomplished. Specific deliverables, along with a time line for these deliverables, should be clearly stipulated. Performance standards and their definitions should also be included, as well as the frequency of these measures. If all these elements are thoroughly articulated, there will be little or no possibility of misinterpretation by either party.

Performance metrics should be measurable. Occasionally, contracts are executed with performance measurements for which no measurement system exists. When developing the SOW, a company should ensure that the data needed for the measurements is available and that the provider has the capability to gather the data. The performance measures should also be set at a level that is adequate. If a supplier consistently exceeds a standard, the standard may be too low. Industry and competitor benchmarks are helpful in these instances to set attainable, yet challenging standards. Subjective performance standards should also be avoided, unless a well-articulated methodology is laid out in the SOW.

Often when a consultant or professional is hired, a company executes a confidentiality agreement with the supplier. This is particularly important when the supplier is exposed to strategic or proprietary information. The contract itself should also contain a noncompete clause, prohibiting the supplier's employees from working on a similar project with a competitor firm.

In many instances, contracts should contain language regarding advertising constraints and brand name usage. One of the marketing tools that professional service firms use frequently is client lists or case studies. Companies with powerful brand names should ensure that they protect the brand with contract provisions that prohibit unauthorized use of their name in any type of advertising or marketing materials. This is also a useful negotiating tool for many companies, who are willing to allow their name to be used in exchange for pricing or service concessions.

Another important element in a services contract is audit rights. When a supplier is engaged to provide a service for a client, it is advantageous for the client to have the right to audit those services and to audit the financials of privately held suppliers. These provisions should be included in the contract, as well as details on who will perform the audit (often a third party), who will select the auditor, how often the audit will be performed, and who will pay for the audit.

Rate cards are often negotiated in service agreements and should be attached to the statement of work or the final contract. The procurement associate should ensure that a supplier does not have multiple rate cards within one company. If a supplier is working on a number of projects at one company, the company should be benefiting from the aggregated volume of work, in the form of lower rates or volume rebates. It is very important to identify all possible work that a supplier may do for a client to avoid excessive, out-of-scope fees, once the contract is executed. A la carte billing should be avoided, if possible, and should be stipulated as such in the SOW. Finally, the use of subcontractors should be thoroughly addressed.

The most optimal rates are achieved when the sourcing team can link prices or price increases to an external index or a set of competitor price points.

Contract Maintenance

After the contract is executed and work has begun, contract maintenance responsibility usually resides with the supply management department. Contract maintenance begins with active management of key milestone dates, service and performance levels, pricing, and report cards, both for the supply manager and the supplier. An electronic contract database is very helpful to organize a company's contracts by commodity manager, supplier, contract end date, and notice period date. Periodic performance reviews with the supplier are very helpful in structuring performance management and allow a forum for issues to be surfaced by both parties.

SUPPLIER PERFORMANCE MANAGEMENT

The ongoing management of service suppliers and their performance is becoming an increasing focus for supply management departments. Once a company has completed supplier consolidation and has sourced each commodity several times, additional value can be extracted from supplier relationships through a rigorous and disciplined approach to supplier performance management (SPM). SPM is a collection of processes that allows a company to classify its suppliers and manage different classifications appropriately. It also allows a company to allocate the most experienced employees to its most strategic suppliers and to work with these suppliers to identify ways to mutually add value to the relationship. SPM also improves communications and business interaction with a firm's suppliers and increases the ability to measure performance. This is accomplished because each segment is managed differently, according to the actions determined to be "best practices" for that segment.

The first step in optimal SPM is to segment an organization's suppliers. Supplier segmentation can be accomplished using a couple of models (see Figure 38–2 and Figure 38-3). Linear segmentation categorizes suppliers according to strategic importance.

FIGURE 38–2

Single-Dimension Supplier Segmentation

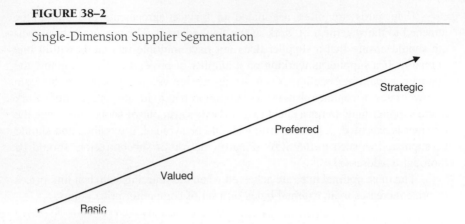

FIGURE 38–3

Multidimensional Supplier Segmentation

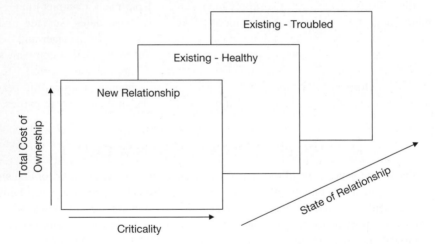

However, this methodology has several weaknesses:

- The extreme classifications (strategic and basic) are easily defined, but it is much more difficult to distinguish the middle players, which is how most suppliers are classified.

- This method works best for new suppliers and does not address the current health of the relationship.

- This method does not provide guidance regarding how to proceed with the relationship.

- This method does not allow for efficient and effective supply management resource allocation.

A more functional model is a three-dimensional one that classifies suppliers according to relationship health, total cost of ownership, and criticality of the service A supplier should first be categorized by the health of the relationship. A relationship is either new, healthy, or troubled.

A new supplier relationship is one that is still in a probationary period and has not yet graduated to healthy status. New suppliers have usually not done prior business with the company and are unfamiliar with the firm's internal processes. In some instances, a new supplier could be a current supplier providing a new offering or program. The objective of this relationship is to manage the supplier to a healthy relationship.

A healthy supplier relationship is one in which all parties (client, supply management, and supplier) are satisfied. The supplier is meeting all the service-level agreements (SLAs), and the internal client is satisfied with the service being provided. The objective of this relationship is to ensure that the supplier sustains the required level of performance and, thus, remains healthy. The majority of a firm's suppliers should be in this category.

A troubled supplier relationship is one in which the buyer stands to suffer a significant loss of value or is exposed to increased risks that were not contemplated in the original agreement. Typical characteristics of a troubled supplier include failure to achieve results and meet SLA commitments; supplier financial, labor, or supply problems; internal client not satisfied with the service; and poor communication with the supplier. The objective of SPM in this case is to either bring the supplier back to a healthy state or exit the relationship.

Once the health of the relationship is identified, suppliers should be plotted on the next two dimensions, total cost of ownership and criticality. Total cost of ownership primarily represents the purchase price of the service. However, other factors, such as testing, installation, service and maintenance, R&D, and disposal, should also be considered. Supplier criticality is determined by factors such as touching the customer or employee, depth of integration, absence of alternatives, and alignment with the buyer's goals and values.

Plotting major suppliers according to this model allows a firm to achieve an overall view of their supplier base. It is also helpful to represent the direction that the firm desires to move with each major supplier as shown in Figure 38–4.

To properly implement SPM, a firm should establish best practices and tools (or templates) for each segment. This ensures that the proper amount of management and resources are focused on suppliers in each quadrant (see Figure 38–5).

Illustrative best practices for the segments are as follows.

New Supplier Best Practices

- Define SLAs.
- Hold an orientation meeting with the supplier to acquaint it with the company's internal processes (code of ethics, travel policy, etc.).
- Coordinate checkpoint meetings.

FIGURE 38–4

Current and Desired Relationships Should Be Plotted

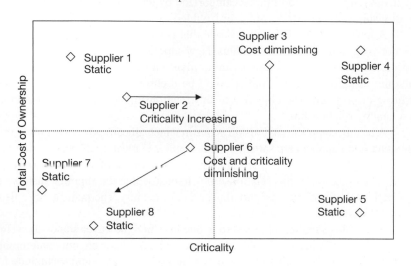

FIGURE 38–5

Supplier Segmentation—Best Practices Should Be Developed for Each Segment

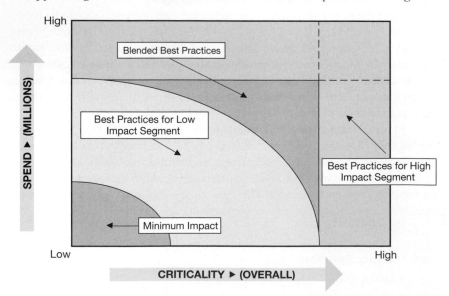

Core Best Practices for All Suppliers

- Determine key performance metrics if SLAs are not defined in the contract. Track performance against these.
- Review company and supplier compliance to contract quarterly.
- Benchmark competitiveness of the contract semiannually.
- Review and refine contingency plan annually.

Healthy High-Impact Best Practices

- Analyze supplier performance and customer satisfaction monthly.
- Meet with supplier to discuss performance monthly.
- Update key stakeholders in company of supplier status.
- Meet with internal client and supplier to forecast and establish goals annually.

Healthy Low-Impact Best Practices

- Analyze supplier performance and customer satisfaction monthly.
- Meet with supplier to discuss performance monthly.
- Update key stakeholders in company of supplier status.
- Meet with internal client and supplier to forecast and establish goals annually.

Troubled High-Impact and Low-Impact Best Practices

- Prepare analysis and communication of the situation and offer recommendations for solutions.
- Meet with supplier to determine resolution and how it will be measured.
- Document resolution action plans and update the contract and scorecard as needed.
- Track performance.

Best practices should be tailored to each company's internal practices and culture. Segmentation and best-practice refinement should be revisited at least annually.

Once SPM is established with a firm's major suppliers, commodity managers should develop an SPM plan each year for their suppliers. The SPM plan details the actions that the commodity manager plans to undertake with each supplier or group of suppliers over the next 12 months. This exercise is helpful because it forces supply associates to review the management of their suppliers each year. It also provides a work plan for management to assess a commodity manager's performance and progress.

CONCLUSION

Services purchasing and the ensuing management of suppliers presents a clear challenge for supply management professionals. Requirements must be thoroughly defined in the bid process. This requires a cross-functional team approach to ensure that all elements are considered. Rigorous analysis of the proposals ensures that the client will receive the level of service that it anticipated. A thorough contract and statement of work is also essential in a services sourcing engagement. All contingencies must be anticipated and accounted for. Since the performance criteria are often subjective, it is essential that the SOW provide as much definition to performance measurement as is possible. The sourcing team must also be very familiar with the industry to evaluate pricing proposals and service levels. Finally, supplier management is a critical element to ensure that the appropriate value is derived from every supplier. The supply manager must create a plan for each supplier that will guide him or her on an appropriate course of action throughout the term of the supplier relationship. By accomplishing all this, supply management can truly add value to a company's bottom line, as well as ensure a high level of performance from all of its suppliers.

CHAPTER 39

CONSTRUCTION SERVICES SUPPLY MANAGEMENT

BRUCE J. WRIGHT
President
B. Wright & Associates and Total Systems, Inc.

ELEMENTS IN CONSTRUCTION BUYING

Construction buying is unique in many ways, not the least of which is the uncertainty of the purchase. In construction, innumerable types of contractors supply many kinds of construction services. Each contractor has its own unique character and technical talents, but they all have one thing in common—high uncertainty. Where there is high uncertainty, there is the presence of two options, risk and opportunity. Contractors manage high risks and opportunities related to intellectual property, labor and craft problems, human motivation, jurisdictional disputes, weather conditions, material coordination, and job complexities.

Construction buying is infrequent for most supply managers. At best the supply managers have a working knowledge and a good background in purchasing services; however, most contract for new facilities or construction only infrequently. The customary procurement methods and policies often are very different from those prevailing in the world of construction.

In purchasing for manufacturing or service operations, the description of the good or service to be purchased is usually definable and reasonably precise with other elements of the buy measurable and controllable. Supply managers are normally accustomed to dealing with prices that can be questioned and analyzed and then agreed upon. One of the big focuses in today's supply management is the establishment of policies and procedures that tend to provide for consistent and long-term relations with suppliers where continuing analysis of price and cost is frequently conducted, computing rather precisely the amounts of raw material, labor and production resources, support costs, and technology costs that are required to produce the quality product the end customer desires.

Construction contractors perform their services for an organization according to a set of criteria generally known to them, but supply managers may be using these criteria for the first, and possibly only, time. This adds to the uncertainty of the purchase and requires tools that will measure that uncertainty as well as solidify the desired outcome of the relationship. Most organizations have gone to contracting for deliverables rather than time and materials with a set profit margin and only cost changes after the contract is agreed upon. There are some elements that are controlled by neither the buyer or seller, for example, weather and government regulations.

CONSTRUCTION PROJECT PROCESS

The construction project process generally follows the following flow:

Strategic plan

Capital evaluation

Request for proposal

Bid or request for quote

Negotiation for deliverables

Purchase order (contract)

Strategic Plan

Normally the construction project process starts with a strategic decision to expand, update, or otherwise change or increase operating capability. Management should determine the focus and outcome of this project relating to the customers, share-holders, and employees. With this start, it is also important to evaluate the expectations of other groups of people that will be affected by the project. For example suppliers, the government, the local community, and other groups will have expectations in the outcome of the project. It is very important in a construction project to manage expectations and optimize the outcome of these expectations so that when the project is completed, it will not only be accepted but also supported by all concerned.

Capital Evaluation

The next part of the process is the general evaluation of resources available to support the project. This includes monetary capital, people capital, and market capital. Monetary capital deals with the range of expenditure anticipated by management. People capital relates to the personnel from both supply management and user areas that will be dedicated to the project, and market capital determines the expected shareholder position as a result of the project. It should be understood that this is an initial look, so the ranges of commitment could be wide and varied.

Request for Proposal

With most construction projects the purchasing organization does not have the information or the expertise to establish a bid or quote process directly, so most organizations will go through a request for proposal. This process is now deemed to be a request for intellectual property with recent legal changes, and it should be treated as such. Oftentimes an architectural firm will be used first to establish the elements of the construction and the desired quality and structural integrity. It is often called a two-step purchase. The first step is to get the architecture firm to create the requirements, and then the supply manager takes those requirements and goes to general contractors to have them bid or quote on the requirements.

In this step it is important to understand the relationship of the request to the outcome of the process. When sending out a request for proposal to multiple parties, care should be taken to agree to a confidentiality or secrecy agreement at the time of the proposal to protect both parties. From the supply manager's point of view, there should be care taken not to use either the information of the proposal or the company information for other purposes than the construction without the express approval of the buyer organization. Likewise, the proposer does not want the information in the proposal used by either the purchasing organization or other parties for gain outside of the proposal. Care should be exercised to make sure that ideas from one proposal are not arbitrarily provided to other proposers without first acquiring the rights to those ideas. When acquiring the rights to ideas, care should be taken to make sure that an agreement for the use of the proposal is signed by both parties.

There are three levels of agreement normally used in a proposal process:

1. *License to use.* If no other stipulation is agreed to by both parties, the buyer upon the purchase of the proposal has the license to use the information internally only in the buyer organization. This is normally sufficient in a construction project except where ideas or software will be included in subsequent operations. When this is desirable, then the second level of agreement should be undertaken.

2. *Right of resale.* When intellectual property is going to be used in a product or service produced by the construction, an agreement should be made related to the right of resale. Normally the one making the proposal will want a royalty arrangement, while the buyer would be better off if it can negotiate a bulk agreement. Whichever is established, the agreement needs to be part of the payment of services for the proposal.

3. *Right of title.* The final state of agreement sometimes used is the right of title. This means that the one making the proposal turns over the right of title to the buyer. This right includes the right to prohibit the proposal creator from using the ideas after the completion of the purchase order. The buyer is given the right to patent, service mark, trademark, or copyright the idea involved. This is not often done but should be considered where the identification of the construction will become an integral part of the image of the organization.

In most cases the first level will be enough, but the buyer should consider the ultimate position of the intellectual property before establishment of payment for the proposal.

If the company that makes the proposal also becomes the general contractor for the project and carries the construction to completion, then we would go directly to negotiation of the contract and not make this a two-step process. However, this is not always the case, and so the proposal step is often very important.

Bid or Request for Quote

The bid or request for quote is the next step after management, users, and the supply managers are satisfied with the direction, quality, look, and functionality of the project. Normally the bid or quote will go out to general contractors that will hire and coordinate the activities of subcontractors in completing the project.

It should be understood that with the bid process, all parties should be given the same chance to submit their best position the first time and that, although often violated, the ethics of a bid is that it is not negotiable. All bidders should have the same possibility of success.

It is understood that the quote will be the initial starting place for the contractor and that there will be negotiation in all areas of the contract. If the supply manager does not have expertise or time, then the bid process is often best. If there is some expertise and there is a desire to optimize value, then the quote process is normally the best to follow.

Organizational Strategy

There should be consideration of a variety of construction contracting strategies when planning for a construction project. The construction supply manager, along with the other members of the management team, should carefully analyze the options at this point in the planning process to ensure selection of the organizational strategy that best suits the project. There are normally three strategies employed.

1. *Turnkey organizational strategy.* The design approach, sometimes referred to as the *turnkey* method, involves the selection of a single firm to accomplish the complete design and construction of the project. Using this strategy, the supply manager delegates full authority and responsibility to the design builder. The supply manager typically provides the deliverables the completed project is expected to meet— such things as operating and performance characteristics, cost, site location, aesthetic appeal, and schedule requirements. In addition, the turnkey builder is sometimes obligated to meet other special requirements such as matching an existing facility, use of local materials, architectural style, and the mechanical and electrical systems or equipment preferred. Within these general specifications and requirements, the turnkey contractor must complete the project.

2. *General contractor organizational strategy.* The general contractor strategy, sometimes referred to as the traditional contracting strategy, encompasses the use of a bid package, with a request for proposal, that

has been developed by the buying organization's design staff or by an independent architectural-engineering firm under a separate contract as indicated earlier. The bid is typically completed by several general contractors, and the contract is awarded to the successful bidder for the *construction* of the project. This strategy is most often utilized for small to mid-sized construction projects. On some projects, where a variety of trade skills are required, the general contractor will, in turn, subcontract portions of the construction work to other more specialized contractors, sometimes referred to as *subs.* The primary difference between the general contract and the design-build strategies is that in the general contract approach the design function is accomplished by the buying firm or by a separate design organization.

3. *Construction management organizational strategy.* In today's sophisticated environment the construction management or team approach is used. The term *construction management* has been used to describe any variations and hybrid approaches to the more conventional turnkey and general contract approaches, borrowing concepts from both. Because of these variations in definition, construction buyers must ensure that they understand exactly what is meant when analyzing a specific proposal for construction management and look to writing the agreement in relation to deliverables rather than general objectives. Members of the construction management group may or may not perform some of the construction work, or supervise laborers, artisans, or other subcontractors. Clearly, though, they do oversee each of the contractor entities that the buyer has employed. The construction manager's staff is made up of personnel experienced in project management, scheduling, estimating labor relations and jurisdiction, engineering, purchasing and expediting, personnel management, accounting, and performance measurement.

Negotiation for Deliverables

With a turnkey process, normally the negotiation for deliverables is left to a general outcome bond. With the other two, there is generally a construction manager appointed in the supply management group that will coordinate the efforts of the organization and the contractor with the time frame or the project and ensure the final balance of the expectations of the various groups involved. A key element of the construction manager's responsibility is to work with the architect during design to ensure that all deliverable issues are adequately considered. Sometimes referred to as *preconstruction design*, this involvement during the design work distinguishes a construction manager from a general contractor. Without question, this is an important advantage of the construction management organizational strategy. Proponents of construction management also point out that it puts the management team in a position to oversee the specialty contractors, and at times even the general contractor. They believe that a general contractor often "wears blinders" when it comes to recognizing the need for improving performance. Of course, construction management involves an additional level of management, which costs an additional 1 to 5 percent of the total project cost. But it may be a real bargain if optimization of the outcome expectation relates to the outcome of the project and increases the performance of all the operating units.

For years general contractors, themselves, have offered construction management services along with their general contractor duties. This generally is still the case. It can be difficult, however, for a general contracting firm also to serve as its own construction manager, because the firm's personnel often are too involved in the actual construction process to discern mismanagement.

The construction management or general contractor organizational strategy may or may not be the best strategy for a supply manager to utilize. There are other means of gaining the advantages that impartial, objective construction management can accomplish. First, the buying firm may have the expertise internally to do it; second, the general contractor may be willing and quite able to designate a construction management team that reports to a different part of the contractor's organization; and, third, the architect-engineer may also be able to carry out this role.

Regardless of the strategy used, there should always be strong, effective construction management present that will have the responsibility for performing the management function of making sure that the deliverables and expectations are met. The construction management or general contractor concept will have an impact on the bidding and quoting contractors, and they should be aware prior to the process what the expectations will be.

In reviewing the three major contracting strategies just described, several conclusions can be drawn. An analysis is presented in Figure 39–1. The following general comments are offered concerning specific characteristics:

1. *Significant buyer firm involvement required.* The major effect of an organizational strategy or general contract is to dictate commensurate management involvement in project-specific activities. Depending on the subsequent assignment of responsibilities within the boundaries of any given strategy, the supply manager's management involvement varies greatly.

2. *Contract pricing alternatives.* Although described in more detail later, pricing alternatives depend to a great extent on the establishment of deliverables and negotiation of prices on the deliverables. In the absence of any other influencing factors, such as the competitive nature of the contracting marketplace, completeness and firmness of design information, and general economic uncertainty, the ability to secure firm fixed price contracts increases as each contractual performance period and the scope of work decreases.

3. *Single contractor risk.* With the turnkey process, everything is placed in the hands of a single contractor. As the number of outside contractors

FIGURE 39–1

Contracting Strategies Relationship

Characteristic	Turnkey	General	Management
Issued contracts	Few	Moderate	Many
Size of contractor	Large	Midsize or small	Large
Service scope	Extensive	Moderate or limited	Extensive
Scope definition at contract start	Preliminary	Extensive	Extensive
Contractor's project responsibility	Extensive	Moderate	Moderate or limited
Schedule flexibility	Extensive	Limited	Extensive
Scope change frequency	Low	High	Moderate
Price contingency	Large	Small	Moderate to large

in a project increases, the risk vested in any one contractor decreases. Potential negative impacts resulting from failure, termination, or inadequate performance from any one contractor are reduced when the total project scope is distributed among a number of outside organizations. The benefits of this spreading effect on risk must be weighed against the demands for increased management and control.

4. *Contractor control capabilities.* As the relative scope of work and company size increases, internal management and control capabilities typically improve. Larger design-build contractors usually maintain more extensive management and project control capabilities than do smaller, specialized contractors that typically work on a restricted scope, within the environment of controls provided by others.

5. *Contract formation and administration requirements.* Two major factors influence the scope of contract management duties and the difficulties with which they are performed. These are the *organizational approach* selected by the supply manager and the *pricing alternative* used for each contract. Disregarding pricing considerations, contract formation and administrative efforts increase in direct proportion to the number of contracts issued for a given project.

Only by understanding the impact, features, and benefits of each strategy can a construction buyer make a rational selection of a single strategy or develop an effective hybrid strategy and then successfully implement the strategy chosen.

Purchase Order (Contract)

The buyer-seller relationship and related agreements in construction buying deals with situations not typically found in the average industrial purchasing situation. The prospective construction service buyer must be fully aware of all the issues and their related effect on the outcome before attempting to analyze the wide variety of contract pricing alternatives available. A brief description of the key contractual alternatives follows.

Fixed Price Types

Lump sum fixed. This is a single price commitment related to bid or quote specifications and drawings. Changes by the supply manager to the concept or scope of the job add to this total. All market cost increases are borne by the seller, and the original price for the defined job is fixed. This pricing type is used primarily for small to medium-size, well-defined projects and some large construction projects that are well defined and properly negotiated. Deliverables and design must be well established to avoid large contingencies in the price.

Lump sum with escalation. In addition to the contract price, escalation of labor and material costs are paid by the buyer. This pricing type is also used on projects where design is well established but may involve an extended or loose schedule that inhibits the possibility of obtaining a fixed price or involves work in an industry that is highly volatile.

Fixed deliverable price. A dollar amount for each work deliverable described in detail; all segments of work added together constitute the entire project cost. The segment of work can be for worker-hours of labor or for all material and worker-hours or for any other combination. This pricing type is used for a wide range of construction and contracting services: temporary office help, security services, construction materials and so on, or for other trades work where quantities may not be completely established for the work in question.

Cost-Plus Types

The following five types of contract pricing alternatives are all cost-plus. In each one, the buying firm reimburses the contractor for all costs plus an overhead percentage (usually based on costs) plus a contractor's profit.

1. *Cost-plus, fixed profit.* The contractor is reimbursed for all direct costs and for overhead and administration at a predetermined percentage of the labor costs. The contractor's profit is a fixed amount. The profit amount is altered only if the specifications and scope of the job are changed from the original contract agreement. This pricing type can be used for all types of construction in which there are insufficient design specifications to bid a pure fixed price, but the specifications are complete enough to avoid a percentage fee arrangement.

2. *Cost-plus, percentage profit.* The contractor is reimbursed for all direct costs plus a percentage of labor costs for overhead and administrative expenses. In addition, a contractor's profit is calculated as a straight percentage of direct cost and overhead. This pricing type is used for construction contracts where work cannot be adequately defined to permit incentives or where the schedule is so tight that a prediction of work conditions is impossible to make. Obviously, this is a risky pricing arrangement for the supply manager.

3. *Cost-plus, incentive profit.* The contractor is reimbursed for all costs of labor, material, equipment, and tools, plus a markup on all labor costs to cover administrative expenses, plus an *incentive* profit. The incentive profit is built around a target estimate as part of the contract, either in the form of a target worker-hour figure for the total job or a total dollar target of the cost of labor, materials, tools, and equipment. This type of contract often includes a floor of 60 to 70 percent and a ceiling of 110 to 135 percent of the target. If the contractor succeeds in billing under the target, it receives a percentage of this difference (usually a specified dollar amount for each hour of labor less than the target, until this figure, when added to the fee, reaches the ceiling). If the contractor exceeds the target, it loses a given amount per hour for all worker-hours or costs above the target, until the fee has been reduced to the floor. This pricing arrangement can be used for all types of construction where the percentage of drawings and specifications completed prior to contract establishment are insufficient to determine a fixed price and yet are sufficient for the contractors to create an accurate target.

4. *Cost-plus, upside maximum.* The contractor is reimbursed for all costs including labor, material, equipment, tools, overhead, and administration, plus a percentage markup on all labor costs and a markup for profit according to the contract schedule of prices. Each contractor on the final contract has three lump-sum figures. The most likely figure is called the *target* lump sum, the second figure the *maximum,* and the third figure the lump-sum *floor.* Contractors are paid for all their costs plus a percentage markup for overhead and a markup for profit up to the floor (if costs plus overhead and profit are below the floor, there can be a buyer-contractor sharing of savings). Any additional costs are paid, plus a percentage markup for overhead only from the floor to the target; costs only are paid from the target to the maximum; the buyer pays nothing above the maximum. This pricing arrangement is used for any type of construction where the scope or specification definition is too vague for a guaranteed maximum price but sufficient to avoid a lesser type of incentive contract.

5. *Cost-plus, guaranteed maximum price (GMP) or fixed price incentive.* The contractor is reimbursed for all costs, including labor, material,

equipment, tools, overhead, and administration. In addition, it receives a percentage markup on all labor costs and a markup for profit based on the contract schedule of prices, up to a guaranteed maximum dollar amount. If the scope and specifications change during the course of the job, the supply manager and the contractor agree on a new guaranteed maximum; otherwise, the original maximum remains fixed. This pricing type is used for all construction in which a reasonable amount of engineering is performed and the scope is well defined.

Cost-Plus Reimbursable Fee Types

The following two types of contract pricing differ from cost-plus types in the sense that the buyer pays all direct costs and a fee to the contractor. The fee reimburses the contractor for all indirect costs, administrative overheads, and profit.

> *Cost-plus reimbursable, fixed fee.* The profit and overhead stay fixed unless there is a major change of scope, and the contract allows for such profit and overhead alteration. The buyer pays all direct costs as incurred.

> *Cost-plus reimbursable, incentive fee.* This contract permits the contractor to alter the fee if the work is performed with fewer worker-hours or at a lower labor cost than originally calculated. A target for total hours or total labor cost is established for the contract. If the contractor's actual labor cost is less than the target, the fee is increased; if the target is exceeded, the fee is decreased in accordance with a formula agreed on in the contract terms.

Time and Materials

This specialty type of cost contract is structured so that an all-inclusive labor rate is charged for every worker-hour of work performed. The rate includes the labor cost, supervision, insurance, taxes, tools, field and home office expenses, and profit. The material factor is the actual cost of materials billed at the price paid by the contractor, less the trade, quantity, and cash discounts. This pricing arrangement is used frequently for pricing extra work that cannot be defined well in advance or for field work where unknown requirements or conditions may surface during performance of the work.

SELECTING THE PROPER PRICING ALTERNATIVE

The numerous types of construction contract pricing alternatives simply reflect the fact that a wide variety of construction projects are carried out under greatly different operating conditions. Generally, there is no single pricing alternative that is best. The best choice varies depending on the various elements of the project. A key consideration in selecting the pricing alternative is the assignment of risk and the required management controls necessary to minimize risks. Many supply managers are using modeling techniques such as discussed later to assess the risks and opportunities of these types of processes.

The Use of Modeling in Construction Purchasing

What will that construction project cost? What will it cost to finish that construction job? How much will productivity increase if we install that new equipment in our plant? How many worker-hours will it take to design that new system? And so on. In other words, "What is your best estimate?"

Estimating is an integral part of planning. And supply managers do a lot of it. Many seem to be on an "estimating merry-go-round." Much of our time is devoted to estimating costs, productivity, profits, and a multitude of other performance measures. And around and around it goes. It very much looks like "the business is estimating."

Doing a good job of estimating brings plaudits and profits. Doing a poor one can bring bankruptcy. It's not surprising then that we spend a lot of time and money on estimating. We harness rivers of data. We filter the data. We polish the data. We reflect upon the data. Then, finally, we make our selection of "the right number," holding it up for the world to see. From all appearances, this number represents our best thinking. But does it? Almost never! Our best thinking can seldom be captured in one number. The sad fact is that no matter how good of a job we do, there's one safe bet—the actual cost of the construction project will be different than our estimate. The question is, How much different is it likely to be? Often enough, it's very different, and we end up getting buried under a big cost overrun or have problems with a contractor cutting corners because of problems with the relationship of costs and profits.

Generally when a cost overrun occurs, particularly a large one, a serious search is begun to pinpoint the reasons. Anyone who had anything to do with the estimate is likely to fall under suspicion. The problem however is one of method, not of humans. Simply put, our traditional method of estimating construction projects often fails to cope with the realities of the modern world.

The Real World Is Not a Spreadsheet

Although it may take the form of an electronic spreadsheet, traditional estimating is nothing more than the application of simple arithmetic. Each item in the estimate is described with one—and only one—number. To arrive at our bottom-line estimate, we add, subtract, multiply, and divide these numbers as if they were absolutes (sometimes, they take on an almost biblical importance). But, what you see is not what you get. The real world is not as neat and tidy as our spreadsheets. The real world is populated with probabilities and ranges of possibilities, not single-point numbers frozen in time and space just waiting for us to count on them with certitude. In fact, about the only thing we can count on is uncertainty. In other words, the real world is probabilistic. What we need is an analytical technique that comes to grips with this unavoidable fact.

This doesn't mean that our traditional estimating technique should be abandoned. It simply means that, once we have completed the estimate, we need to apply an analytical tool that will give us the answers to such vital questions as: What is the probability of success (living up to expectations) in this construction project? If it gets bad, how bad can it get, and if it gets good, how good can it get? (beware the use of best-case, worst-case scenarios), and Where should we direct management to spend time to take advantage of minimizing risk or increasing opportunity?

What's Critical and What's Not

Estimating is either conceptual or detailed in nature. If it is preliminary, for order of magnitude, it is classified as conceptual. If it considers low-level details, it is classified as detailed. Whether conceptual or detailed, estimating can be defined as the method we use to forecast the bottom-line cost of a project, based upon our forecast of the value of each element that plays a role in determining that bottom line. The traditional estimate contains a "target" estimate for each such element. When all these targets are combined in the proper arithmetic fashion, they produce a target estimate of the bottom-line cost of the project.

The typical estimate has numerous elements. But Pareto's law (the law of "the significant few" and "the insignificant many") tells us that only a few are critical. It is this phenomenon that both sets up the problem and allows us to solve it. Since there are but a few critical elements, it's quite possible that a majority of them will go in the wrong direction and thus lead to a cost overrun. On the other hand, their small number allows us to concentrate our analytical energies on them to see how the project is likely to unfold. But which elements are critical?

In order to decide which elements in the estimate are critical, we first must decide what's critical as far as the project's bottom-line cost is concerned. Specifically, what maximum variation in bottom-line cost, caused by variation in a single element, are we willing to tolerate? That threshold value is called the critical variance of the bottom line. A substantial amount of empirical evidence indicates that this threshold occurs in the neighborhood of 0.5 percent in conceptual estimates and 0.2 percent in detailed estimates. (If the bottom line measures profit rather than cost, the threshold values are approximately 5 percent and 2 percent, respectively.) Using this rule of thumb, if the bottom-line cost of a project in a detailed estimate is $1,000,000, then the critical variance of the bottom line is $2,000.

The critical elements in the estimate can now be identified. Specifically, a critical element is one whose actual value can vary from its target, either favorably or unfavorably, by such a magnitude that the bottom-line cost of the project would change by an amount greater than the critical variance. Thus, in the previous example of the $1,000,000 detailed estimate, any element in the estimate that can change the bottom-line cost, either favorably or unfavorably, by more than $2,000 is classified as a critical element.

This rule of thumb has been successfully applied in hundreds of projects of all types. They ranged in size from $100,000 to $12 billion, and well over 90 percent of those projects had fewer than 30 critical elements each.

It is important to note that the deciding factor in determining criticality is an element's potential for variation, not its magnitude. For example, an element may account for a very large portion of the bottom-line cost of the project but have very little or no potential for variation. In other words, the actual value of the element cannot be sufficiently different than its target, either favorably or unfavorably, to produce a bottom-line change that is greater than the critical variance. Such an element is noncritical. On the other hand, another element may account for a very small portion of the bottom-line cost but can vary from the target, either favorably or unfavorably, by such a degree that the bottom-line change would be greater than the critical variance. An element such as this is critical.

Uncertainty: Measure It to Manage It

In the real world, the actual value of a critical element can be any of hundreds or thousands of values. For example, if a critical element's target is 16,000 worker-hours and its actual value can be anywhere between 14,000 and 20,500 worker-hours, then counting only the whole numbers, the actual can be any one of 6,501 possibilities, only one of which is the target of 16,000 worker-hours. Although there are relatively few critical elements, there is a tremendous number of ways in which their possible values can combine in the real world to produce the actual bottom-line cost of the project. For example, if there are just 10 critical elements, each with only 10 possible values, they can combine in 10 billion possible ways to produce the actual bottom-line cost. Is it any wonder why our estimates are never right?

In a word, the problem is uncertainty. Uncertainties in the critical elements combine and cascade through the estimate to produce the uncertainty at the bottom line. If this uncertainty is to be dealt with effectively, it must be measured. We're accustomed to measuring all sorts of things. Why, then, don't we measure uncertainty, the biggest potential killer in most projects? The answer is simple: There hasn't been an easy way to measure it, at least not until the advent of current computer technology.

Range Estimating in Uncertainty

Range estimating picks up where the traditional methods leave off—it tells us the possibility of having a cost overrun, it tells us how large the overrun can be, it tells us what to do now to eliminate or reduce that risk, and it tells us how much contingency to add to our estimate to reduce any residual risk to an acceptable level.

Range estimating does all this by breaking the problem down into its component parts. The uncertainty of each critical element is assessed by the organization experts, and then, with the use of a computer, these individual uncertainties are put together in such a way that the uncertainty at the bottom line can be measured. Surprisingly, the entire process requires only a modest amount of effort.

It must be emphasized that range estimating is not an estimating system. It is a decision technology that is employed as an adjunct to traditional estimating.

The Range

As its name implies, range estimating utilizes a simple but effective measure of uncertainty: the range. The range is specified by three parameters: the probability that the element's actual value will be equal to or less than its target as provided by the best experts we have in the organization, a lowest estimate that is so low there is less than a 0.5 percent chance an actual happening could be lower, and a highest estimate that is so high there is less than a 0.5 percent chance an actual happening could be higher. This process is often called Six Sigma. This is explained in the following example.

An element having a target of $10.05 has the following range: a probability of 75 percent, a lowest estimate of $7.80, and a highest estimate of $14.35. This means there are 75 chances in 100 that the actual value will be equal to or less than $10.05. (And, indirectly, it also means there are 25 chances in 100 that the actual value will be greater than $10.05.) If the actual value is equal to or less than $10.05, it can be any value from $10.05 down to $7.80. If the actual value is greater than $10.05, it can be any value from $10.06 up to $14.35.

As is apparent in this example, the probability parameter measures the likelihood of an underrun (and, indirectly, the likelihood of an overrun), whereas the lowest and highest estimates measure the degrees of potential underrun and overrun. The lowest and highest estimates form the boundaries of the range. The greater the uncertainty, the farther apart the boundaries of the estimate and the broader the range estimate. This is often referred to as establishing a Six Sigma range so that there is less than a 1 percent chance a happening will be out of the range.

Specifying the lowest and highest estimates follows a quantitative guideline. Specifically, the lowest estimate is set low enough such that there is less than one chance in 100 that the actual value can be any lower. Similarly, the highest estimate is set high enough such that there is less than one chance in 100 that the actual value can be any higher. In other words, the lowest and highest estimates lie beyond the 1st and 99th percentiles, respectively. However, as far as range estimating is concerned, the lowest and highest estimates serve as the outermost boundaries of the range. Looking at it another way, the range is nothing more than a contingency, one that considers potential underruns as well as potential overruns and makes it so the outcome has no surprises.

Some people have difficulty quantifying probabilities. In such cases, it is often helpful to elicit a qualitative assessment and then translate it into quantitative form. The first step is to ask if it is likely, unlikely, or equally likely as unlikely that the element's actual value will be equal to or less than its target. In other words, what is the likelihood that the actual value will not overrun the target?

An answer of *equally likely as unlikely* means that the probability is 50 percent. *Likely* means that the probability is greater than 50 percent and its specific value must yet be determined. *Unlikely* means that the probability is less than 50 percent and its specific value must yet be determined.

If the answer is *likely*, the next step is to ask if it is somewhat, very, highly, or extremely unlikely that the element's actual value will be equal to or less than its target. *Somewhat* suggests a probability of 40 percent, *very* 30 percent, *highly* 20 percent, and *extremely* 10 percent. Again, if there is difficulty in making a selection between two qualitative assignments, the corresponding midpoint probability should be used. Thus, if there is difficulty making a choice between *highly* and *extremely*, then a probability of 15 percent is appropriate.

By assessing each critical element in the form of a range, we can better articulate our perception of the future—certainly much better than by mentally wrestling with all the critical elements simultaneously. When specifying the range, we take into account all foreseeable circumstances. This ability to look at critical elements in terms of extremes dampens undue optimism or pessimism and thus encourages realistic assessments of their uncertainties.

Furthermore, range estimating puts the critical element's target into proper perspective. The target is but a single number in a spectrum of possible numbers. The range, no matter how subjective it may be, is far more valuable for decision making than any single number from within it—including the target. This makes six tons of sense. How could the target, a single number, be as valuable as the range from which it comes? Most of us understand this dangerous deficiency in single-point estimates and, if we are given a choice, make use of ranges to describe the future. Crudely put, by using ranges rather than single targets, we prefer to be approximately right rather than exactly wrong.

There are several computer-based programs that will allow the buyer to create a model with the contractor. Most of the good construction management firms now use models in project management and evaluation of project processes. These programs are available on the Internet and from software providers.

CONTRACT CONTENT FOR PROTECTION OF THE BUYING ORGANIZATION

It is generally best to have two segments to the agreement between the buying organization and the contractor. The first is the terms and conditions agreement that is executed up front during the capital evaluation phase. This provides an umbrella agreement that can cover relationships with the suppliers under any conditions. It should contain the boilerplate and only needs to be executed once. The other segment is the construction contract or contracts between the buyer and the contractor. The makeup of typical terms and conditions and the construction contract can very well follow a general pattern including the principal segments described next.

Terms and Conditions Agreement

The Recital

It is good protection for the buyer to describe carefully the parties to the contract, including the company's official location and name. The recital should include a fairly comprehensive description of the project, whether the contract is for specialty work or is a general contract for the entire job. The recital sets the position of the parties in the terms and conditions agreement and sets a standard for all contracts under its umbrella. It puts the burden on the contractor to perform the work in keeping with the buyer's overall project expectations, whether specifically spelled out in later paragraphs or not.

Method and Manner of Performance

The status of the supervisors and the employees of the contractor must be specified, indicating that they are not employees of the buying organization and that the level of competence of the personnel will be subject to approval of the buyer. This should also be done for any subcontractors or other personnel acquired by the general contractor.

   The contractor has an obligation to comply with all laws. It must also adhere to reasonable work practices so that adjoining property owners are not annoyed by noise, pollutants, or material handling operations, and so forth, and it should establish adequate protection against fire, theft, and storm damage. The contractor needs to establish and enforce job practices relating to the safety and welfare of employees. This includes adequate training to ensure compliance with all federal, state, and local laws on safety and health.

   The contractor must agree to perform its labor relations function in keeping with its labor contract agreement, consistent with actions in the buyer's best interest. Any overtime practices or retroactive agreements with unions that would be to the buyer's detriment should be limited to only those approved by the buyer

Taxes

A statement regarding the method of handling all taxes in the best interest of the buying organization is required. Taxation of construction equipment and some materials varies between states and between the owner and the contractor.

Accounting System

The buyer should specify the accounting system to be used by the contractor so that the final records are compatible with the firm's own system. The contractor should agree to safeguard the buying organization's rights with respect to the waiver of liens against the purchased property for any unpaid bills including those to subcontractors and suppliers.

Changes

The contract should include a mutually agreed upon system for establishing official changes to the contract. This includes changes in scope and changes in compensation for the contractor.

Assignment of the Contractor and Subcontractors
The contract should definitely define the acceptability or unacceptability of the contractor or subcontractor assigning any of the rights of the contract to another third party.

Advertising
The buyer should reserve the right to approve, prior to release by the contractor, any information about the project. This avoids misleading advertising and protects the buyer from erroneous statements.

Force Majeure
Since contractors invariably insist on protection from job completion defaults occasioned by acts beyond their control (riots, strikes, acts of God, etc.), it is well to have the exact words of this provision agreed to by both parties before the job starts.

Arbitration
The buying organization should have the privilege of specifying its desires about settlement of disagreements between the buyer and the contractor through the use of courts of law or perhaps by means of the arbitration process.

Governing Law
It is common practice to include a provision in the contract that says the contract, and the rights, obligations, and liabilities of the parties, should be construed in accordance with the laws of the state in which the buying firm is located, or perhaps where the facility is being built.

Equal Employment Opportunity
Without question, the contract should include provisions that require the contractor and all subcontractors to comply with U.S. Executive Order No. 11246, as amended September 24, 1965, and the rules, regulations, and relevant orders from the Secretary of Labor.

Binding Effect of Contract
Once the basic contract provisions are agreed upon, the contract should contain a clause stating that it is binding on both parties and their respective successors, assigns, subcontractors, heirs, executors, administrators, receivers, and other representatives.

Entire Agreement
A statement should be included to the effect that the terms and conditions and the contract, including all its appendixes and amendments, constitutes the agreements between the parties relative to the project or projects undertaken by the parties and that these agreements supersede any previous agreements or understandings.

Contract Elements

The Scope
A description of the individual contract scope needs to be established. The work to be performed by the contractor should include all specifications, drawings, and other official documents. This includes applicable codes around which the proposal was made and the contract is being formed. It usually includes the technical specification and the general conditions of the contract.

Work to Be Performed by the Supply Manager
To have a complete meeting of the minds for both parties, it should be clear what support the buying organization customarily and specifically provides for the contract in question.

Acceptance by Buyer Organization
This section defines the agreed-upon method by which the buying organization both partially and finally accepts the work. For some types of construction jobs, the buyer needs to assume control of certain parts of the job before the entire job is completed; this is frequently the case when certain types of training are required. Both parties should also agree on the definition of what constitutes final acceptance before payment of any retained compensation.

Title to Work Ownership
A mutually satisfactory statement concerning the timing of the title transfer for the job is important; ownership of materials and equipment is particularly significant. In this section it is important to fully define the relationship of both parties to intellectual property.

Compensation
The methods used to compensate the contractor must be described completely. This description should be prepared carefully to establish the most practical means of administering the contract, both in the field and the office. Construction contracts contain some provisions, such as retention of payment and partial payment for uninstalled but received goods, that are not normally present in purchase orders for materials and equipment. They are typical in construction contracts, however, and can be made very workable.

Schedule of Payments
The exact timing to which both parties have agreed for submitting invoices or for approving deliverables if no invoicing is used and making payments should be stated in the contract. At times it is desirable to pay for some costs such as materials and equipment rentals on a monthly basis and for others such as salaries on a more frequent basis. Reimbursements by the buyer for payments to subcontractors must also be scheduled.

Contracts that include a fee or separate profit usually define the payment schedule for the fee or profit. Incentive fee or profit contracts should hold back enough of the fee or profit to make necessary adjustments for contractor performance. A retention of 5 to 10 percent, depending on the size of the project, is usually considered reasonable. This "hold back" is to help supply an incentive for the contractor to finish the job as early as possible and to avoid errors or omissions.

Termination
When writing a termination or deferment provision to the contract, give careful attention to the numerous details of the physical movement of people and material and the ultimate costs of these activities. It is much better to do this prior to the start of work on the job.

Suspension of Work
It is customary for the buyer to retain the right to extend the schedule of work to be performed or even to suspend the work and direct the contractor to resume work when appropriate, with equitable adjustment of the contract for added costs caused by the suspension.

Liability
Suitable indemnification of the buying organization and the "hold harmless" provision to be furnished by the contractor should be detailed in the contract. If possible, buyers also frequently attempt to include a provision to the effect that the cost for any rework required, due to lack of performance of the contractor, will be borne by the contractor. Contractors usually accept this provision only up to stated dollar limit.

Patent Infringement
The contractor should agree to protect the buyer from any patent infringements by the equipment suppliers from whom the contractor buys and protect the buyer against any suits because of a contractor-created infringement.

Schedule for Performance of Work
It is the contractor's responsibility to schedule the various components of the job so that requirements can be met without planned overtime. Without a precise, yet realistic, schedule for performance of the work, important completion dates may not be met and cost overruns may be experienced.

Progress Reports
Monthly (or more frequent) progress reports usually are required from the contractor. The specifics of this provision should be included in the contract.

Standard Construction Industry Contract Forms
Construction buyers developing contract terms and general conditions for a construction project for the first time would do well to borrow a set previously used

successfully for a similar type of project. The American Institute of Architects (AIA) has prepared many standardized contract and general condition forms. One in particular, AIA Document A201 "General Conditions of the Contract for Construction," includes many of the protective features just discussed. It is also a familiar and accepted document by most construction contractors. When utilized with a project-specific supplemental document developed by the construction buyer and legal counsel, this can be a very useful document for construction contracting purposes. AIA documents can be obtained by writing to the AIA at 1735 New York Avenue, NW, Washington, DC, 20006.

CONCLUSION

The entire cycle of construction buying is clearly an extremely demanding pur chasing assignment. Yet, because of the infrequent timing and the magnitude of most construction jobs, the buying task is filled with opportunities to provide unique and effective service to the organization. It should be looked at as an opportunity, not a burden.

CHAPTER 40

SUPPLY MANAGEMENT IN THE SERVICE INDUSTRIES

Aaron D. Dent
Former Vice President, Supply Chain Management
Delta Air Lines

Johnathon Baker
Director, Supply Chain Management
Corporate Operations & Supply Chain Strategy
Delta Air Lines

Craig Reed
Director, Supply Chain Management
Fuel & Airport Services
Delta Air Lines

INTRODUCTION

Supply chain management is now being leveraged by leading companies in the services industries as a primary strategy for improving cost, increasing speed to market, and accessing innovation. Service companies are starting to explore all areas within their control to increase competitiveness and improve overall customer service. Only recently have service companies realized the value proposition in managing the supply chain to improve their internal efficiency as well as to act as an extension of services to their customers.

Supply chain management has long been understood in the manufacturing sector. However, companies in the services sector have often taken a back seat to manufacturing companies in the application of supply chain management practices. Only recently are service companies starting to recognize the opportunities to reduce cost, mitigate risk, and add value to the end customer through supply management techniques. Supply chain value is directly reflected in the company's top (revenue) and bottom (profit) lines. In many cases, supply management is a company's primary competitive advantage. The major reason for this change of view in the service industries is the transition of the global (and, in particular, U.S. and European) corporate structures from industrial-based economies where the focus is on the production of goods to service-based economies where tasks and expertise may be outsourced or procured from other sources to satisfy a need and/or customer demand. Wal-Mart Corporation is a primary example of this phenomenon. This is the largest company in the world with revenues greater than $285 billion. A significant part of its success is due to the development of processes and systems that allow more efficient and effective management of its supply of goods. Wal-Mart's supply chain management operation is a primary competitive advantage.

SERVICES COMPANY

What is a services company? *Fortune* magazine defines a service corporation as a company that derives 55 percent of its revenues from nonmanufacturing activities. Service companies traditionally provide sales, marketing, financial, and utility or transportation services to their end customers. Over the last 50 years many companies that began as manufacturing companies are now considered services companies. IBM is one example of such a company. In 1956 IBM manufactured machines and technical systems that increased companies' control over processes. This was done predominately through design, development, and manufacturing of equipment and software products for sale to end customers. Today IBM still manufactures systems, but it now derives almost half of its revenues from service activities such as consulting and outsource services management for customer companies. General Electric is another large company that now derives significant revenues from financial services, while 50 years ago it was mainly a manufacturing company. The truth of the matter is that while many companies provide services, all companies manage and purchase services. The critical difference between companies is whether or not they have a structured process in place to acquire and manage services and service support products. Only with a structured process can a company identify value opportunities and apply the appropriate frameworks and tools to reduce cost and risk and maximize revenue.

Services versus Manufacturing

The evolution of the supply chain management professional and profession has, until relatively recently, occurred mostly in the manufacturing sector. This has been more a result of necessity than by chance. The early manufacturers of goods traditionally worked in vertically integrated factories. Raw materials such as steel, rubber, and iron ore would go in at one end of a production facility, and out the other end would come a completed component or system, or, in some cases, a finished good like an automobile. As competition increased for manufacturers, and end customers started demanding better cost and quality of finished goods, the manufacturing companies had to find more competitive ways to get the parts and components they needed. This led to the need for greater specialized skills for buying professionals as they now were required to procure more complex parts. This drove them to find, and in some cases develop, sources to meet the demands of their organization. In these types of organizations the cost of direct goods purchased can

FIGURE 40–1

Manufacturing Company Spend Profile

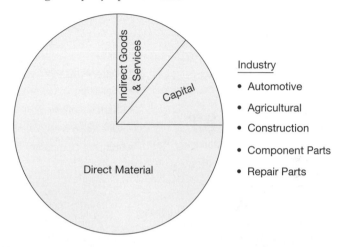

Industry

• Automotive

• Agricultural

• Construction

• Component Parts

• Repair Parts

be more than 75 percent of the total cost of the product being manufactured. Because of this, there evolved a heavy focus on the management of direct goods since they had such a direct effect on overall profitability (see Figure 40–1). In this environment the part or process would be the same for each plant or facility location, allowing for standardization that could be managed and measured, with success based on the tangible outcome of the product being purchased.

Service corporations, on the other hand, have a different cost structure. These companies traditionally have been revenue focused and customer driven. Since service companies are primarily a group of activities and products coming together to satisfy a specific consumer need, the percentage cost of direct goods purchased relative to total spend is much less than in manufacturing companies, in some cases as low as 20 percent of the cost of the service product sold. The remaining 80 percent of spend is in capital equipment and indirect goods and services such as marketing and advertising (see Figure 40–2). Traditionally, because of the nature of the service delivered, most service companies have enjoyed rather robust returns, so the need to focus on cost was not the primary driver for this sector. As a result of trying to anticipate or satisfy customer demand, overall business strategies and tactics tended to drive all supply management decisions. In this environment the supply management professional was tasked with doing the paperwork after the deal was crafted with a service or product provider by someone else. Because of this process the supply management function was missing the opportunity to maximize the value of the product or service to the corporation. But now, because of increased global competition and the advancement of technology, most service corporations have to focus more on cost while still meeting customer expectations. In addition it is much harder to measure the benefit or effectiveness of a service because of its intangible nature. For example, what constitutes good customer service is a perception of the

FIGURE 40–2

(a) Services Company Spend Profile, and (b) Specialized Services Company
Spend Profile

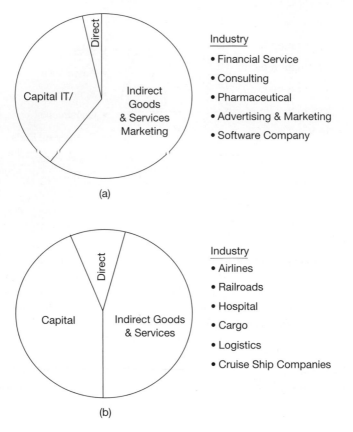

(a)

Industry
- Financial Service
- Consulting
- Pharmaceutical
- Advertising & Marketing
- Software Company

(b)

Industry
- Airlines
- Railroads
- Hospital
- Cargo
- Logistics
- Cruise Ship Companies

customer receiving the service. Technology is a primary driving force behind this
transition due to the commoditization of services and products offered by providers
like airlines and automotive dealerships. Today a consumer can obtain enough information via the World Wide Web to be as smart as the salesperson when engaging in
the acquisition of a product or service. Detailed specifications, cost information,
quality expectations, and competitive analysis data are all available to assist the
consumer in making a more informed choice. This wealth of information has
increased the buyer's power and has forced many companies to compete on price,
thus driving down profits. In order for companies to prove their worth to their customers and their ultimate value to their shareholders, they must focus on the level of
overall service to the customer that yields maximum value at the least cost possible.
As a result of this change service industry supply management professionals have
seen an increased role in responsibility, accountability and expected results, as it
relates to value creation and delivery for the corporation.

Some typical types of items purchased by service companies include

- Equipment for providing services
- Equipment to be provided to customers
- Maintenance parts for equipment
- Information technology equipment
- Information technology services
- Building maintenance
- Temporary employees
- Building construction
- Furniture (office and other)
- Food
- Vehicles
- Training
- Uniforms
- Products for resale
- Paper
- Printing
- Transportation services
- Logistics services
- A large variety of business services such as advertising, consulting, insurance, financial, banking, and legal

Contribution and Capabilities

At the highest level, a supply management department exists to deliver value to its company's shareholders. In order to deliver value, it is essential to clearly articulate supply management's role or contribution to an organization. The following elements are critical to realizing the potential value of a supply management department: utilizing technical and cross-functional knowledge and perspective to influence all aspects of the supply chain, defining and executing commodity strategies, creating and maintaining capabilities, and positioning and structuring supply chain functions for success.

Utilizing Technical and Cross-Functional Knowledge and Perspective to Influence *All* Aspects of the Supply Chain

Supply management is in a unique position to partner with the various areas of its company to drive business strategy. In working with internal customers, supply management understands the strengths, weaknesses, opportunities, and threats to its business segment partner. In working with suppliers, supply management understands industry best practices, as well as what its company's competitors are doing in a specific business segment. Therefore, supply management has an obligation to partner with the business to support and drive business strategy. In this role, the supply management professional must act as an advisor, a collaborator, and an owner while following a disciplined approach. The depth and manner of this involvement varies by commodity criticality, complexity, and business segment maturity.

There are six general steps in the life cycle of a commodity (refer to Figure 40–3). They include (1) identifying the business need, (2) developing a commodity strategy, (3) negotiating with the supplier(s), (4) managing the supplier(s), (5) utilizing the asset, and (6) disposing of the asset. In the first step, identifying the business need, the business must take on the ownership role. Given the cross-functional knowledge and perspective that supply management professionals have, they must play an active role as a collaborator and advisor to the business during this step. In developing the commodity strategy, negotiating with the supplier(s) and managing the supplier(s), supply management must take the ownership role with the business acting as an advisor when needed. The last two general steps in the life cycle, utilizing the asset and asset disposition, are often owned by the business. Typically, supply management will act in an advisory capacity for these steps. At the conclusion of the asset disposition step, the commodity life cycle starts over again with identifying the business need.

Defining and Executing Commodity Strategies

The first component to defining and executing commodity strategies is to align plans and objectives across all stakeholders. In order to be successful a cross-functional

FIGURE 40–3

Commodity Lifecycle

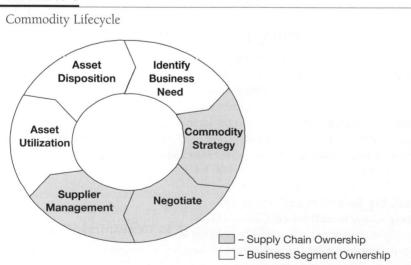

team, consisting of at least the key stakeholders, needs to be established. This team will seek to understand, and in some cases define, the future state of the commodity or service as it relates to the future state of the corresponding business segment(s). Supply managers should attend staff, leadership, and strategy meetings within the business segment(s). They should also make themselves visible and take a proactive approach.

The next component of defining and executing commodity strategies is to promote value awareness and discipline. In understanding value, it is critical for supply management, suppliers, and the business segment to have the same definition. One of the best ways to accomplish this task is to conduct workshops with all key stakeholders to broaden and establish alignment on the definition of value for the particular commodity. Workshops can also be an effective method to clarify roles and responsibilities with the business segments. It is extremely important to continuously communicate progress, success, and learnings through the utilization of a disciplined approach, such as a strategic sourcing process. (*Note:* We will discuss strategic sourcing in more detail in the next section.)

The third component of defining and executing commodity strategies is providing alternatives. Supply management professionals must be credible and flexible enough to provide alternative buy options regarding products and services, timing, supplier, and so forth. Another key value driver is creative options relating to processes and technological enablers.

Creating and Maintaining Capabilities

There are five main capabilities that are critical to supply management excellence. They include people, process, enablers, knowledge, and culture. We will examine each of these capabilities in detail.

Having the right people with the right skills and competencies should be the number one priority for any supply management department. The capability of supply management professionals can be measured on three elements: technical skills, management skills, and leadership competencies. Technical skills include areas such as strategic sourcing, financial analysis, total cost of ownership (TOC) and design-to-cost, logistics, process design and improvement, e-commerce and information technology (IT), and contract management. Management skills include areas such as resource planning and management, meeting leadership, consensus building, change management, team building, financial assessment, and value-based decision analysis. Leadership competencies include areas such as enhancing your own effectiveness, bringing about positive action, connecting to the customer, operating with intensity, acting and understanding why, and activating the organization. Expectations for mastery of these three areas should depend on job responsibilities and relative career stage. Entry-level supply management professionals should excel at the technical skills with less focus on the management skills and leadership competencies. Midlevel managers should excel at both the technical skills and management skills and be proficient in the leadership competencies. Senior-level supply management executives should excel in all areas.

FIGURE 40-4

Strategic Sourcing Process

Define strategic opportunity	Baseline current state	Conduct industry analysis	Develop sourcing strategy	Select supplier and negotiation	Implement	Monitor results and continuous improve- ment

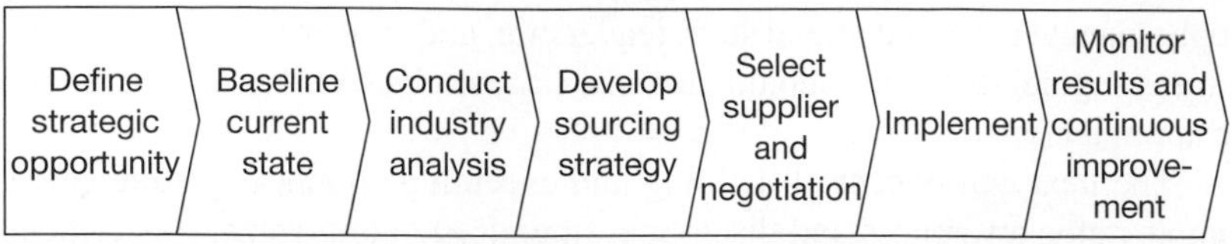

Simply defined, processes are rigorous methods of converting thought into action. Effective and efficient processes are critical to supply management success. The strategic sourcing process is the backbone to any strategic supply management organization. An example of a strategic sourcing process can be found in Figure 40-4.

The first steps in any strategic sourcing process are about gaining knowledge. In order to ultimately be successful in delivering value, the supply manager and his or her cross-functional team must understand the strategic opportunity. During this phase of the process, it is critical for the team to be creative, think broadly, and dream of what is possible. The team must think well beyond cost savings, the typical value driver for supply management. The team should consider value drivers such as revenue generation, joint marketing, and equity ownership just to name a few. This is such a critical step because it sets the stage for the entire process. After the strategic opportunity is defined, the team must understand its current state as well as the latest trends in the industry. Once the team has gathered and assessed all this information, it is ready to develop the sourcing strategy. The sourcing strategy will dictate the approach taken during the supplier selection and negotiation phase. There are many methods and tools available for today's supply managers with regard to supplier selection and negotiation. Among the most popular are electronic RFxs [request for information (RFI), request for proposal (RFP), and request for quotation (RFQ)], reverse auctions, private offers, decision analysis, and face-to-face negotiations. Any combination of these can be utilized with the situation dictating the optimal approach. Once the supplier is selected and the contract is in place, the focus shifts to implementing the supplier, along with any new or redefined processes identified previously in the strategic sourcing process. Upon completion of the implementation, results must be monitored, and an effort to continually improve becomes the focus of the supply management professional.

As mentioned earlier in the process section, there are many tools or enablers available in today's environment. There are technology solutions for most of supply management's processes in varying degrees of maturity. Some of these solutions include spend analysis, program management, negotiation solutions, contract development and management, and supplier performance management. It is extremely important for the supply management organization to define its strategy before identifying the processes and enablers needed to execute the strategy.

In order to achieve excellence, an organization must leverage knowledge to continuously improve. Knowledge is created every day in supply management through the utilization of a strategic sourcing process, continuous-improvement efforts with suppliers, and benchmarking activities. The key is to capture the relevant data, facts, insights, and opinions. Capturing knowledge and utilizing knowledge can create significant value for any supply management organization.

Creating a visible values-based environment that nurtures continuous improvement in all other capabilities is the aim of most culture-focused initiatives. In order to create this type of culture, an organization needs to clearly identify its values and embrace them. Ultimately, an organization's culture is judged by the attitudes and behaviors of those in it.

Positioning and Structuring the Supply Management Function for Success

Most companies today recognize the importance of supply management to their overall success. In fact, many companies have created a C-level position [chief procurement officer (CPO), chief purchasing officer, or vice president of supply management] for the leader of their supply management organization. In order to realize the value promise, it is critical for the supply management function to be on equal footing with the business segments it supports. There are two structures where this is evidenced: matrix and centralized (refer to Figure 40–5). This positioning needs to be evidenced in the executive leadership of a company. Once

---

FIGURE 40–5

Supply Chain Management Structural Options

Structures	Pros	Cons	Examples	World Class
Decentralized				
Each area of a company acquires goods & services on its own	• Ease of acquisition	• Tactical sourcing • No consolidation of spend • Little ability to leverage • Unmanaged supply base • Little demand management • Cross-divisional issues not considered	• Home Depot*	NO
Matrix				
Center-led sourcing using common processes and tools, with matrix reporting	• Greater spend consolidation leveraging power and cross-commodity coordination • Healthy friction between SCM and the Business	• Risk of supply base confusion • Slower decision-making	• John Deere • American Express • Delta Air Lines • American Airlines	YES
Centralized				
All sourcing and supply management activities consolidated at the CPO level.	• Maximized leverage • Clear ownership of supply base • Speed in decision-making • Strong demand management	• Business disempowered	• General Motors • Ford • IBM	YES

> Increasingly, Fortune 500 Companies are recognizing the benefits of "organized" SCM efforts and are actively installing CPO's to lead them.

*Home Depot transitioning to Matrix structure.

the supply management function is positioned appropriately from a leadership perspective, it is essential to create the right structural relationship between supply management and the partner business segments. A good start to this structure would be an executive council that would consist of the CPO, the business segment executives, and potentially the CEO of the company. The role of this council would be to identify business opportunities, resolve conflicts, and monitor progress. Another important aspect of the organizational structure is the relationship between the business segment executive and its respective supply management leader.

Ideally, the supply management leader would have a dotted-line reporting relationship to his or her business segment executive. The supply management leader's role would be to actively participate in discussions regarding the strategic direction of the business segment as well as dealing with the day-to-day issues.

Prerequisites to Success in
Service Industry Supply Management

There are several prerequisites to success in service industry supply management. These include

- Securing senior management commitment and sponsorship
- Establishing "healthy friction" between supply management and the business units through cross-functional collaboration
- Creating an internal incentive structure to drive behavior
- Establishing objective, reliable performance metrics for internal performance and supplier performance
- Implementing a supplier relationship management strategy
- Achieving enough early successes to initiate momentum that leads to institutionalization of successful practices

Leaders in service industry supply like IBM, Delta Air Lines, and UPS have succeeded in fulfilling these prerequisites and are now able to count on supply management value contribution every year.

How to Determine the Need for Supply
Management Excellence in a Service Company

There are two filters that give an indication of the need for supply management excellence in a service company. The first is the noninternal labor spend of the company as a percentage of sales. If a service company has greater than 25 percent spend as a percentage of sales, sourcing and supplier management is relatively important. This typically means that the company's outsourced needs go well beyond office supplies, furniture, and so forth, and into goods and services that are core to the company operations. Two examples are Delta Air Lines and IBM. Delta's noninternal labor spend as a percent of sales is 62 percent, indicating a high degree of reliance on the supply base to run its operations. IBM has a 44 percent noninternal labor spend as a percentage of sales with the same implications. If a company has less than 25 percent, supply management will not be a primary value driver and will focus on optimizing procurement of nonstrategic goods and services.

For service companies that pass the first filter, the second filter is historical average profit as a percentage of sales. It is necessary to use a historical average since a single year's profit can vary based on extraordinary events as well as non-operating gains and losses. A company with an extraordinarily high profit as a per-centage of sales is less likely to view supply management as a primary value driver, making the need for supply management capability beneficial but not critical. Examples include Microsoft with a 25 percent profit as a percentage of sales and The Coca-Cola Company with 20 percent. In these companies, the focus will likely remain on growth and exploration of new business opportunities versus optimiza-tion of cost. However, it should be noted that these companies are increasingly using supply management to scan the market for innovation as well as to create more efficient and effective ways to get product to market globally. For companies with a relatively low profit as a percentage of sales, supply management is a key lever to creating and enabling value. In these companies, excellent supply manage-ment capability is mandatory or essential for survival and represents a sustainable competitive advantage. The median profit as a percentage of sales for the Fortune 500 was 4.6 percent in 2002.

Profit Percentage of Sales Analysis to Determine Need for Supply Management Capability

> 11% profit/sales	supply management excellence is beneficial
< 11% but >4.6%	supply management excellence is important
< 4.6% but >0%	supply management excellence is mandatory for success
< 0%	supply management excellence is essential for survival

Companies with noninternal labor spend of greater than 30 percent and a profit as a percentage of sales below 4.6 percent should be very aggressively building supply management capability and represent some of the most untapped opportunities for supply management professionals. Moving forward, these are the companies that will seek talent with supply management experience from manufacturing to deliver similar value in the service industry.

CONCLUSION

It is obvious that the service industries have come of age with regard to supply chain management. As services have become more commoditized and accessible as a result of the application of technology, service industries have realized that their supply chains need to be managed in ways somewhat similar to the approaches that historically have been more common in manufacturing companies. A structured, organized approach to supply management, using the suggestions in this chapter, will help to move any service company toward utilizing the potential benefits of supply management to achieve the strategic objectives of its organization.

CHAPTER 41

SUPPLY MANAGEMENT IN THE PROCESS AND EXTRACTIVE INDUSTRIES: INTEGRATION INTO SUPPLY CHAIN MANAGEMENT

Thomas A. Crimi, C.P.M.
Chevron International Exploration and Production Inc.
CIEP Learning and Development Coordinator

S. R. (Randy) Dean
Supply Manager
BHP Billiton/New Mexico Coal

INTRODUCTION

Processing and extractive industries such as chemical, mining, petroleum, and petrochemical companies share many functions with other manufacturing and service-oriented industries. However, in some important respects these industries are different from manufacturing and also from each other. This chapter focuses on the effects of those differences on supply management responsibilities and activities in these industries. It also reflects on the transition of purchasing into supply chain management.

The expectations of top managers of major corporations have changed significantly in recent years. They now realize that good management of supply chains, including purchasing, materials management, transportation and logistics management, quality management, and time management can make major contributions to the bottom line and help their organizations gain and maintain competitive advantage. Globalization is now accepted as a way of life, the normal way of doing business. More and more companies have adopted a global view of their operations in order to survive and thrive. Many corporations have been transitioning from the traditional purchasing or "tactical paradigm" and are now aware of or taking advantage of, improvements and benefits that could come from a global supply chain.

THE NATURE OF SUPPLY MANAGEMENT IN THE PROCESS AND EXTRACTIVE INDUSTRIES

Supply management activities in process and extractive industries contrast sharply in some respects with a typical manufacturing company or a service company. First, compared to manufacturing, there may be no end-product components to purchase at all, or if there are components and materials, they may be much smaller in number and variety than those in a manufacturing organization, although purchase volumes may be enormous. In the mining environment, for example, almost all noncapital purchases are made to support the maintenance of mining equipment necessary for the extraction of ore. A small mining operation may require a warehouse containing over 20,000 catalogued items just to support the maintenance of operating mining equipment. Second, the importance of capital purchases frequently is much greater than in either the manufacturing or service industries. Most of the process and extractive industries are very capital equipment intensive. Mining, petroleum production, and chemical and other processing industries all use large quantities of capital to acquire and construct production and processing facilities and to provide the equipment necessary to support the operation of the facilities. A third area of differentiation is the relative importance of purchased services. While this difference may be growing smaller with the increased utilization of outsourcing by most industries generally, in some of the process and extractive industries purchased services can amount to over half of all annual purchase dollars.

The remainder of this chapter will discuss these and other key aspects of supply chain management in the process and extractive industries including effects of location of activities and multiplicity of business sites; impact of technology; use of strategic sourcing and alliances with suppliers; effects of economic cycles; importance of maintenance, repair, and operating (MRO) items, capital purchases, and purchased services; the nature of inventory and materials management in these industries; use of global sourcing; and some miscellaneous trends.

LEASE AND ROYALTY OBLIGATIONS

In the petroleum exploration and production industry in particular, many operations are conducted on properties that are jointly owned by various entities including private companies, government entities, and individuals. Some of these owners are compensated for their ownership in cash, based on the amount of production. Others elect to share in both the revenues and expenses on a percentage basis. Procurement activities can be affected by the lease or operating agreements that govern such situations. For example, such arrangements may include audit provisions or requirements for partner approval for certain purchases and for asset sales.

LOCATION OF ACTIVITIES AND
MULTIPLICITY OF BUSINESS SITES

The extractive industries, such as mining and petroleum exploration and production, must necessarily operate where deposits exist of the materials they produce. Often these locations are far from markets and commercial centers. Sometimes (often, in the petroleum and mining industries) operating locations are literally on the floors of oceans or lakes or in tundra, desert, or jungle areas. Many extractive industries operate in remote and sometimes hostile environments that may contain both environmental and political hazards and risks. The chemical and petrochemical industries, on the other hand, are more likely to be located in or near commercial or population centers. Because of the geographical dispersion of both raw material deposits and processing and consuming centers, operating locations can be quite numerous. In the petroleum industry, for example, individual operating locations for any one company may number in the thousands and be geographically dispersed worldwide. Process industries that purchase their raw materials usually have fewer operating locations. However, their raw material suppliers are often agricultural or extractive industries that frequently do have numerous and dispersed locations.

Remote and sometimes numerous operating locations generate additional and special activities and challenges for supply management that are not often present in industries that have few locations and are near commercial and population centers. For example, in remote locations for extractive industries the supply function must frequently procure and arrange for communications equipment and/or services, logistical services, and furnishing and operation of employee living quarters. Construction of maintenance, administrative, and living facilities at operating locations is common in the mining industry. Another challenge is the transportation of capital equipment, operating materials and supplies, and personnel from commercial centers to the remote location, and transportation of the produced ore, petroleum, or other materials from the production site to processing and consuming centers. Providing for transportation service may itself generate additional supply requirements such as materials and construction services to build pipelines, roads, or railway and dock facilities. For international locations, packing, security, and transportation factors may be of equal or greater importance when compared to the quality and price of the material itself. Use of freight forwarders, security services, chartered aircraft or vessels, or other special transportation often are routine aspects of supply management in the international operations of these industries.

Limited, and seasonal, access to some locations can create logistical problems that require months of planning to acquire and secure a full year of supplies for the operations. Mines and production facilities north of the Arctic Circle, for example, require movement of bulk materials, equipment, construction materials, and fuel over engineered ice roads that are only available for two to three months of a year.

A supply manager, when faced with the problem of how to provide supply management services to dispersed and/or remote locations, particularly new operating locations, must first assess the locations in terms of infrastructure (transportation, commercial, political, and possibly residential), supply facilities and capabilities, available services, and nearness to supply centers. These factors must be evaluated in relation to the material and service requirements of the operation, as well as local content and local business development expectations. The supply base must be evaluated in relation to service, leverage, and synergy capture. From this assessment, any deficiencies can be identified and a supply plan developed that addresses deficiencies and provides for all supply and transportation requirements including construction, start-up, and operation of the facility.

In some geographically dispersed operations, such as petroleum exploration and production, purchase volumes are relatively small, and operating locations usually have some level of purchasing authority and responsibility, for example, small spot or emergency requirements, with strategic procurement activities conducted from a headquarters or other central location. Mining and process industry operating locations tend to be much larger and usually contain a supply structure at each location, perhaps with global agreements as guidelines for procurement activities. Strategic sourcing is a necessary core competency of supply chain management in these industries to attain competitive advantage in the global economy.

It is common that many remote locations are subject to aboriginal agreements that require procurement of operational materials and services from local, tribal, and governmental businesses. In such situations, supply professionals often must help develop existing local businesses to be able to supply the materials and services that they require. Aboriginal agreements often require a commitment to increasing the amount of business over time. Such commitments may require practices outside of commonly accepted supply principles in order to meet the agreement requirements.

IMPACT OF TECHNOLOGY

Different technologies used in the various parts of process and extractive industries cause their purchasing focus to address specific aspects of each industry such as exploration for ores, minerals, and petroleum; development and operation of mines and oil and gas production; transportation of the produced material; processing or refining; and marketing activities. One result of this focus has been the formation of strategic supplier alliances with primary product and process technology suppliers. As the technology used by these industries has developed and become more complex, it has required a tremendous amount of specialty item procurement and procurement of engineered equipment unique to a particular industry. At the same time, equipment quality has improved and reduced the need for replacement or backup material.

The technology of communications has improved to facilitate immediate contact and the accurate transmittal of drawings, specifications, and equipment data. Remote locations, no matter where located on the globe, have virtually instant communication capability with any other global location via satellites and microwave technology.

Technology has also improved the purchasing process. Electronic commerce has enabled requisitioning, ordering and contracting, invoicing, and payment processes to become more efficient and to reduce ordering and delivery cycle times and inventories required. Global enabled supply-and-demand chain management is now a common best practice integrating order-demand capture, sourcing, procurement, order fulfillment, logistics, payment, and customer relationship management.[1] Companies have invested in enterprise resource planning (ERP) technologies such as SAP, Oracle, and J.D. Edwards in order to optimize global operations and to expand and link systems and applications across business units worldwide so supply chains can be managed on a global basis. As a result of these capabilities, transaction costs have been and are continuing to be drastically reduced. Information technologies have also improved both tactical and strategic planning. This has enabled the concept of strategic sourcing to become more viable in these industries, which tend to have long planning horizons and long-term project buying with a large impact on many commodity families.

STRATEGIC SOURCING

Most industries in the process and extractive group are mature industries. As a result, they are not experiencing rapid overall growth, have relatively stable overall supply needs, and have embraced strategic sourcing as a primary procurement enabler. These industries have become highly systematic in directing their supply activities using plans to develop and manage supply bases that are consistent with their organizations' strategic objectives. The trend in many of these industries is, in effect, to create an extended enterprise by obtaining the full potential of integrating suppliers into their long-term business processes. Strategic sourcing is also a central process within a larger industry trend toward supply chain management. It involves a cross-functional team utilizing commodity, spend, and market analysis with a request for information (RFI), a request for proposal (RFP), negotiation strategies, and category management.

STRATEGIC ALLIANCES

Many process and extractive industries rely heavily on supplier alliances to provide domestic and global requirements for materials and services. The ability to share risks between suppliers and buyers in areas such as developing new technologies and serving remote and/or hazardous locations is one reason for the attractiveness of strategic alliances to these industries. Alliances also fit well with a strategic sourcing strategy of concentrating on best-in-class suppliers to reduce total cost of ownership while maintaining competitive purchase prices. An example is leveraging

---

1 Julie Murphee (2002). "Globally Enabled Supply Chain Series." *iSource*, August–September, p.40.

MRO purchases through strategic alliances to reduce overall prices paid. Use of alliances is also consistent with significant personnel reductions that have taken place through reengineering in many of these industries. In addition, alliances are part of many organizations' plans to use suppliers as an "extended enterprise" to help further reduce overall supply chain costs.

In remote areas where the supply base is limited, it is becoming more common for competing companies to form alliances, cooperatives, and consortiums in order to use existing suppliers and to leverage overall purchasing capabilities for all companies. In the mining industry, for example, mining companies are creating supply alliances with primary customers (e.g., coal mines with power generators) in an effort to keep the overall cost of the customers' end product down and enable the mining companies to compete effectively in the customers' markets. Organizations tend to group their supply agreements into strategic, preferred, and logistical or basic categories in order to utilize different supply chain management approaches.

There is a growing trend globally for companies to contract directly with manufacturers, rather than with distributors. Many companies are realizing that manufacturers are the leverage point for product pricing, while the distributor is key to product support and service. Many global agreements are being developed where the manufacturer defines product pricing and the individual operating sites select particular distributors for the products, based on local service levels. This allows the site to have access to the best on-site service, at the best price, and can also facilitate the meeting of aboriginal contract requirements.

ECONOMIC CYCLES

The extractive industries, perhaps more than any other industry group, are supply chain victims of their own success. As commodity prices for the raw materials produced by the industries increase, the prices of finished products consumed by the industries also increase. Steel, petroleum products, and petroleum product derivatives are heavily used by the industries. As the prices for these products increase, the challenge for the supply professional grows. This significant correlation of cause and effect is a ripe area for the industries to consider as a cost containment initiative in the future.

Because many of the process and extractive industries produce basic commodity-type materials that are sold in global markets, economic cycles have a significant impact on their business, particularly on product demand and on the prices they receive for their products. Although technology has enabled a reduction in the historically long lead times required to find and develop mines and oil fields or to design and construct new processing plants, lead times are still long relative to many other industries. In addition to the time required for design, procurement, and construction, environmental, governmental, and local issues can extend new projects by weeks, months, or years, depending on the project. These industries must therefore try to conduct a delicate balancing act with the objective of providing adequate supply but not so much supply that, in economic downturns, they experience severe negative effects on prices of their produced products. Such a balancing act has been very difficult to implement in practice. One result has been the creation of cartels in several of these industries over the years in attempts to restrict supply and increase product price. Tin, diamonds, and petroleum are three noteworthy examples. Generally, these efforts eventually fail, and the additional supply attracted by artificially high prices causes market glut and depressed prices, sometimes for extended periods.

Another impact on the petroleum and mining industries is deregulation of the electrical power industry in the United States. The potential of increased competition has caused companies who were in only one area of the industry to diversify into various other areas including exploration, production, transmission, and distribution.

The significance of these developments for supply management are that specialized supply communities that cater to the process and extractive industries also tend to wax and wane with the buying industry. In good times a seller's market often prevails, and in bad times a buyer's market develops. The swings in the petroleum industry from 1980 through 1999, for example, have seen two high-activity periods with accompanying seller's markets followed by two periods of very low activity and resulting buyer's markets.

The recent economic explosion in China is creating an enormous challenge for supply professionals. While the Chinese industrial market has helped to drive up the price of raw products such as copper, manganese, bauxite, iron ore, coking coal, thermal coal, natural gas, and crude oil, the Chinese are also consuming finished products at a high rate. The market is compensating for the demand increase by applying surcharges to products and freight in an effort to prevent having to change base pricing principles. This is a good example of the delicate balance that often exists between supply and demand, and the supply management challenges created when it gets out of balance.

MRO PROCUREMENT

The changes in the approach from traditional purchasing of MRO materials to the broader concept of *supply chain management* for MRO materials and services best illustrates the transition to supply chain management. The purchasing of MRO materials is a significant part of purchasing in the process and extractive industries. MRO purchasing may account for only 20 to 25 percent of the purchasing spend in these industries, but it may account for 75 to 80 percent of a supply management department's resources. There are opportunities to achieve significant savings in this area by utilizing total cost of ownership analysis in conjunction with using major suppliers as alliance partners, that is, the extended enterprise. Many companies have implemented consignment, supplier stocking, and outside operated warehouse management programs in an effort to reduce personnel and inventories. "Distribution" companies have evolved that offer, through a consortium of suppliers, multiple product lines, warehouse management, and purchasing systems as a means to reduce total cost of ownership.

This extended enterprise approach applied to MRO purchases is a strong industry trend that enables firms to focus on consolidation of the supply base; better leveraging of purchase dollars; reductions in inventory, workforce, and transaction costs; and continuous improvement. All these efforts can provide significant cost reductions and improvements in supplier service and the delivery of products. The strategic focus in the MRO area in these industries is characterized by firms identifying, developing, certifying, and forming alliances with global best-in-class suppliers for major groups of MRO commodities. A relative comparison of some characteristics of process and extractive MRO and typical manufacturing purchasing would likely yield the differences shown in the following table.

Relative Situations Concerning MRO Purchases*

Characteristic	Process and Extractive Industries	Manufacturing Industries
Cost controls	Low	High
Dollar value per order	Low[†]	High
Usage history	Low[†]	High
Buyer expertise	Low	High
Administrative order cost	Same	Same
Number of purchase orders	High	Low
Number of suppliers	High	Low
Emergencies (frequency)	High	Low

*Electronic commerce [electronic data interchange (EDI)], autofax, and evaluated receipts have changed many of the transaction issues for MRO purchasing. In addition, the use of automatic max-min MRP-type systems has drastically reduced personnel requirements in MRO warehousing. The trend toward alliances has also reduced the supply base in both groups of industries. MRO purchasing activities have now evolved into supplier management and integration, with strategic category management a critical part of the landscape.

[†]High for the mining industry.

Many companies are exploring the idea of sharing their MRO contracts with their service partners. The idea of MRO distributors providing products to business partners under contracted pricing and terms is a relatively new concept. Because leveraging capabilities might reduce partners' pricing for MRO materials, it can be possible to reduce the cost of services and at the same time increase leveraging capabilities. Many partners are small and not capable of leveraging MRO materials on their own. It is a basic principle of partnering to help partners reduce their costs in order to reduce total cost.

CAPITAL PURCHASING

In the extractive industries in particular, and also in some of the process industries, capital purchases sometimes dominate the overall purchases of materials because purchased components for the firm's produced or manufactured end products may be small, of little importance, or nonexistent. For example, in the oil- and gas-producing industries, most purchases are capital materials to construct facilities and/or to keep the physical plant, or oil field operating, capital equipment, or services. In the mining industry the majority of purchases are for the maintenance of large capital equipment and the purchase of that equipment. The product that is mined or otherwise produced from the earth includes few if any purchased ingredients.

The procurement of capital equipment differs from other materials in a number of respects, including that often each purchase involves substantial amounts of dollars and takes place after a long purchasing cycle that may include design services and several levels of negotiations (see Chapter 37, "Capital and Its Impact on the Organization," for more information). When purchasing MRO materials, for example, a major alliance supplier may be selected based on price, quality, logistics, and service overall for a broad range of products, and the business relationship is maintained with this supplier until there is reason to change (see Chapter 35, "Indirect Materials Management"). In contrast to this, for each major equipment purchase there will very likely be separate and long-term negotiations with diverse suppliers. Because of the specialized nature of much of the capital equipment, most capital maintenance items such as parts must be purchased from the original equipment manufacturer (OEM). Unlike MRO purchasing, there is generally not an automatic continuing relationship with the same supplier, with some exceptions if the item is purchased on a regular basis.

Lead times for capital purchases are generally much greater than for other materials. Specifications also may be more flexible than those for other types of purchases. One factor affecting specifications is that the equipment options for the same functionality from alternative sources may vary in characteristics to some degree. One other differentiating factor in capital purchasing is that very often related equipment, spare parts, materials, and services may be required to be purchased along with the capital equipment. In situations where spare parts are held in inventory, it may be necessary to consider the cost of carrying spares if a decision is made to change the OEM. Purchase decisions for capital should include the item price, costs of obsolescence and availability, and costs of carrying and/or changing inventories of spares. Standardization of capital equipment can contribute to reduced total cost of ownership through reduction of spare part inventories. Repurchase surveys, installation services, and training services are additional major dimensions of capital purchasing.

PURCHASED SERVICES

Services procurement is substantially different from procurement of materials. For example, services cannot be stored; therefore availability and delivery timing of services have heavy weights in supply management planning and evaluation.

The major categories of purchased services in the process and extractive industries include technical, operational, mechanical, construction, professional, and transportation and related services. Historically, services in some of the extractive industries have been largely purchased at decentralized operating locations and by various parts of the organization. As the industries seek to improve leverage with suppliers through reducing numbers of suppliers, the tendency is to move to more central coordination and/or cross-functional team approaches to procuring services and on a companywide basis where applicable. There appears to be a strong trend toward using strategic alliances in services procurement as numbers of suppliers are reduced. Alliances with service providers can also be used to share development and operational risks in hostile operating environments. In some cases materials and services are combined in one alliance arrangement.

Most services that are used by these industries are evaluated in a *make-or-buy* fashion to determine if a better value can be obtained by providing the service internally or by purchasing it through an outsourcing arrangement. Many services such as maintenance, engineering and design, and administrative services that historically were provided internally have been outsourced by many process and extractive companies.

The supply function has traditionally neglected the areas of health, safety, environment, and community (HSEC) in its contracting efforts. It is common that these issues are covered in standard terms and conditions of contracts. As global companies become more accountable for their performance in these areas, supply will need to take on an increasing role in the selection of service contractors based not only on price and service but also on the contractor's performance in these HSEC areas. One large mining company recently reported that 78 percent of all serious accidents and deaths that occurred in their operations happened to employees of contractors.

Services provided to the extractive industries are often perilous activities. Operations are often located in environmentally sensitive areas where surface disturbances can last for decades. Chemicals are used that can harm people, flora, and fauna. People are expected to work in severe climatic conditions. Supply should play a key role in reducing these risks through the supplier selection process.

INVENTORY AND MATERIALS MANAGEMENT

Inventory and materials management issues are significant in these industries where inventory carrying costs can range from 20 to 30 percent annually. Inventory levels are often driven by the cost of equipment downtime if repair parts are not available when needed. Inventories may include MRO and other operational support items that have not been put on a supplier-stocked, just-in-time delivery program. Other items that may be inventoried include raw materials, containers, packaging materials for some process industries, and certain capital equipment and equipment parts including so-called long-lead-time insurance parts for critical pieces of capital equipment. Most organizations do have very substantial just-in-time, supplier stocking, or integrated supply programs. Safety stock issues are usually minimal but may be dependent on the remoteness of the operation and the availability of parts and services. Cycle times are closely tracked to minimize inventory investment. Systems that track responsiveness to customer demand are used, particularly in the MRO materials supply area. The key focus there is to get MRO materials from the supplier directly to the location where needed, at the exact time needed, and in the quantity required. Electronic commerce technology has facilitated inventory reduction programs by improving communications content and speed and making possible delivery of materials within hours of the request for material. Investment recovery has become a major initiative as the industry seeks to coordinate organizational efforts to reuse idle surplus equipment and materials or dispose of them through external sales.

Almost all the process and extractive industries are 24/7 operations. Inventories must be based on supporting that operating requirement. Wherever maintenance inventories are located or whoever owns them, availability when needed is critical. Integrated supply business models have become an effective process to reduce inventory carrying costs. Inventory carrying cost applications have grown in the industry since the 1990s. The industry has made more strategic efforts at identifying and supporting inventory management and investment recovery best practices.

GLOBAL SOURCING

A global scope to supply management activities is not new to many process and extractive industries. Because of the location of raw materials or of mineral or petroleum deposits, these industries have had to operate on a global basis for many years. However, as the world has become more developed and communications capabilities have improved, true global supply management has become both possible and necessary. Historically, most material, equipment, and service requirements may have been purchased in the United States, Europe, or Japan and shipped to wherever needed. Procurement cycles were long, and much inefficiency had to be accepted. Today, there are likely supply alternatives in a number of locations across the globe, and transportation and communications technologies have reduced the time required for the procurement cycle. Supply management activities in a global context have also taken on additional meaning as the process and extractive industries have matured. An increasing number of domestic industrial manufacturers (e.g., sources of materials and equipment needed by process and extractive industries) have moved part or all of their operations overseas or established multiple locations in different countries. This move by manufacturers and suppliers has created an opportunity for global companies to better utilize alliances worldwide. In addition, the majority of large industry members have exploration, production, mining, process, refining, or marketing operations in a number of different countries.

One of the major challenges of procurement in a global setting has to do with the significant variability in quality, service, dependability, and pricing from various sources of supply in different countries. A key challenge to the supply management professional is to balance the advantages of global supply with the requirements of individual operating site requirements. The leveraging advantages of global alliances are sometimes outweighed by service and availability needs of operating locations. The impact of exchange rates also makes buying commodities in various markets a variable task that has to anticipate rapid changes in pricing due to currency fluctuations.

Countertrade activities can also be a significant factor in global sourcing due to capital requirements, logistical considerations, or host country requirements. Countertrade or barter activities are usually complex procurement arrangements since the valuation process changes over time and objective and consistent pricing benchmarks are not easily established or tracked.

Given the current and developing capabilities of many industrialized or industrializing countries, global sourcing is a necessary part of developing a competitive supply base. Two key aspects of global business relationships are cultural and communication differences between buyers and sellers. Philosophy, political considerations, customs, and business practices can create barriers to effective procurement activities.

Cost pressures are also placing the spotlight on global supply management opportunities. There are new competitors in traditional markets. There is new access to emerging markets. There are procurement opportunities to redefine the supply chain; redesign supply base relationships; and realign processes, people, and technology to enable the organization to sustain and maintain competitive advantage through effective global sourcing. Strategic sourcing has become, in many organizations, a core competency in which leading industry members have invested significant resources. These successful companies have utilized global sourcing to keep their organizations on the cutting edge of cost and technology by being able to realize breakthrough opportunities in locations all over the world. Procurement in this sense is perhaps best thought of as a "global sourcing process" with the objectives of maximizing leveraging advantages, improving services, and reducing costs.

MISCELLANEOUS TRENDS

A number of management trends are shaping current supply management processes in the process and extractive industries. A continuing increase in the utilization of cross-functional teams for sourcing and purchasing is one example. Early and immediate involvement of supply management on planning and operations teams is necessary to achieve the best possible supply management contribution to development and operating activities. Along with this is the trend toward embracing best practices within the industry. Continuous-improvement efforts permeate supply management activities at all levels and are a permanent feature of many organization's business process. Benchmarking of supply management activities to compare one's own performance with that of peer organizations are becoming more commonplace, with CAPS: The Center for Strategic Supply Research having a major role in assisting various industry efforts. Some of the process and extractive industries for which CAPS has compiled benchmarks include chemical, mining, and petroleum.

CONCLUSION

In summary, the process and extractive industries in the early twenty-first century are characterized by moving toward world-class supply chain management, evolving supply base relationships, and a realignment of parallel processes, people, and technology. In today's world, competitive advantage through global enabled supply chains is a critical goal with e-procurement as a key enabler. By advancing total cost of ownership concepts the process and extractive industries are focused on reducing production, transportation, processing, and marketing costs and promoting standardization while providing world-class service to internal and external customers. Consequently, the role of change management has increased significantly in these industries as they find themselves in the early years of the new millennium and its opportunities for new vision. Globalization, with salient advances in technology, has produced a momentum of its own, creating the need for global supply chains to be developed, implemented, and optimized.

CHAPTER 42

SUPPLY MANAGEMENT IN THE PUBLIC SECTOR

HENRY F. GARCIA, C.P.M.
Consultant and Trainer
Asentrene

INTRODUCTION

The public sector is extremely diverse, encompassing federal as well as state and local governments, special jurisdictions (e.g., publicly owned utilities, school districts, hospital districts, and energy districts), and nonprofit as well as not-for-profit private corporations and organizations.

Public entities consist primarily of federal, state, county, and local governments. They also include some schools, universities, and hospitals that are operated as public-sector governmental entities, such as, public schools on federal land, state-controlled universities, and federal hospitals.

Quasi-public jurisdictions include public utilities; authorities that operate bridges, tunnels, transit systems, or ports; public school districts; and colleges and universities that are state-related but have separate organizational structures and governing boards. For example, while utilities are subject to operating and rate-setting provisions set by public utility commissions, they are formed as public corporations with independent boards of directors. Similarly, many state-related universities are organized as corporations under constitutional provisions that place their management in the hands of independent boards of governors or regents.

Private nonprofit and not-for-profit organizations include charitable groups, societies, and institutions (e.g., churches, charities, and hospitals); private education-related organizations (e.g., schools, colleges, and universities); and other education- and research-related corporations (e.g., independent research and development institutions, philanthropic foundations, and professional societies). These organizations are characterized by their relative independence from control by public entities. They have tax exemptions as charitable, educational, or trade-related organizations, and they are governed by independent boards of directors and/or trustees.

In this chapter, the term *public sector* incorporates all three types of public-sector organizations. Any differentiation among these types will be explained in the following sections. It should be noted, however, that the most prevalent interpretation of the term public sector relates to tax-supported entities, jurisdictions, and organizations. Many of the examples offered in this chapter relate to the federal government, because it alone represents a buying organization that accounts for the expenditure of a disproportionate share of aggregate taxpayer dollars compared to all the rest.

Although the terms *procurement* and *purchasing* remain more prevalent than the term *supply management* in the public-sector literature, many public-sector organizations have adopted supply management as a complement or substitute for procurement or purchasing.

Difficult economic times have led to budget overruns as the demand for goods and services increases while revenues decline. Governments, including federal, state, county, and local entities, have experienced budget shortfalls in the past few years, and budget shortfalls are expected to continue. Many nonprofit and not-for-profit organizations, too, have seen a decline in revenue from investment income, charitable contributions, and research and grant receipts. Nevertheless, their expenditures on goods and services, especially among state, country, and local governments, have maintained a steady upward trend. For example, the federal government spent $586.5 billion and state, county, and local governments expended $1,034.5 billion on goods and services in 2002, according to the 2003 edition of the *Statistical Abstracts of the United States*. Together, these expenditures among only government entities within the public sector accounted for about 15 percent of the 2002 gross domestic product (GDP). If all other public-sector organizations were included, it is believed that the ratio of these expenditures to GDP for 2002 would approximate 20 percent. Government expenditures on goods and services may be considered contracyclical, because they do not rise or fall consistently with the prevailing business cycle.

The exercise of the purchasing and supply management function in the public sector is confronted with an increasingly complex environment characterized, in part, by rapidly emerging technologies and technological substitutions, progressively growing concentration ratios in certain domestic industries, substantially expanding product diversity and choice through global competition, incrementally rising environmental concerns, and a systemically changing emphasis on product and service quality and best-value purchase decisions—all within an intrinsically constraining operational context (i.e., a "fish bowl"). In addition, the exercise of the purchasing and supply management function is expected to balance the dynamic tension between satisfying socioeconomic objectives and realizing cost-based initiatives, provide the rationale for establishing strategic supplier alliances or partnerships with select suppliers of goods and services, and retain the public trust by maintaining economy and efficiency in the allocation of scarce fiscal resources. Along with these usual competing and often conflicting demands, the purchasing and supply management function is confronted with greater budgetary restraints, higher demands for flexibility and responsiveness, and limited strategic support from within.

Moreover, the purchasing and supply management function, particularly within the federal government, is undergoing a reinvention founded on acquisition reform. The roles and spectrum of responsibilities of purchasing and supply management professionals continue to change. In addition, the gradual emergence of an empowerment culture, allowing public-sector managers the flexibility to prioritize the use of fiscal and operational resources in exchange for greater responsibility and accountability for improvements in service production and delivery has contributed to a shift to decentralization from centralization of the purchasing and supply management function's procedures, processes, and practices.

Through the careful and judicious application of supply management and supply chain management principles and practices, purchasing and supply management professionals in the public sector will evidence that they have the requisite knowledge and skills set to improve their organizations' efficiency and effectiveness, while mitigating the various factors that impede the expansion of purchasing and supply management's role in this sector.

SUPPLY MANAGEMENT AND SUPPLY CHAIN MANAGEMENT DEFINITIONS

The Institute for Supply Management™ (ISM) defines *supply management* as "the identification, acquisition, access, positioning, and management of resources the organization needs or potentially needs in the attainment of its strategic objectives."

The ISM's definition of *supply chain management* (SCM) is "the design and management of seamless value-added processes across organizational boundaries to meet the real needs of the end customer. The development and integration of people and technological resources are critical to successful supply chain integration." When applied to a specific industry, SCM can be considered to cover a "wide set of interdependent, cross-industry business strategies that can reduce costs, expand revenue and increase market share through improved efficiency and effectiveness," according to a definition offered by Gartner, Inc., a recognized leader in providing research and analysis on the global information technology industry. From a logistics management perspective, the Council of Supply Chain Management Professionals (CSCMP) (formerly the Council of Logistics Management) defines SCM as follows: "Supply chain management encompasses the planning and management of all activities involved in sourcing and procurement, conversion, and all logistics management activities." This definition implies the coordination and collaboration with channel partners [e.g., suppliers, supply intermediaries, third- and fourth-party service providers, and end users (customers)] through the integration of supply and demand management within and across organizations. These definitions relate to the public sector, but the implementation of SCM in this sector has been operationally problematic. The federal government, for example, strives to emulate private-sector organizations in the steady adoption of SCM, because when properly implemented SCM can mitigate costs, improve product or service delivery, and enhance product or service quality.

Whether in the public or private sector, SCM is based on ensuring that an organization's customers and consumers benefit from the reduction or avoidance of material costs (e.g., total cost of ownership); implementation of a quality culture (total quality management, continuous improvement, quality management system, ISO 9000 and 14000 series, and others like Kaizen, Six Sigma, and zero defects); and execution of service support activities (e.g., customer relationship management, supplier relationship management, and customer chain of service).

ORGANIZATIONAL DIFFERENCES BETWEEN THE PUBLIC AND PRIVATE SECTORS

Within public entities, the purchasing and supply management function is accomplished by organizations that employ acquisition, contracting, and logistics systems whose policies, procedures, practices, and processes are specified or influenced by federal, state, county, and local laws, regulations and ordinances. In addition to the acquisition of necessary products and services, many public entities, specifically the federal government, often use their purchasing activities to further certain socioeconomic goals. Some quasi-public jurisdictions as well as private nonprofit and not-for-profit organizations, whose legal charter specifies fiscal support, directly or indirectly, from public entities as well as grants and donations from businesses and individuals, can apply select private-sector policies, procedures, practices, and processes in the conduct of their purchasing and supply management operations.

The purchasing and supply management function within public entities tends to be highly codified, with formal competitive bidding as the customary method for determining source and price. Public entities not only give essentially every interested supplier equal opportunity to bid on a particular requirement, but also generally permit accessibility to information regarding purchasing transactions to anyone who is interested or has a need to know. In addition, purchasing and supply management operations are subject to close scrutiny by legislative bodies, media companies, and interested taxpayers.

The purchasing and supply management function in quasi-public jurisdictions is often subject to legal, regulatory, and statutory controls, and, like public entities, their operations are open to public inquiry. Typically, however, purchasing and supply management policies, procedures, processes, and practices in these jurisdictions provide more operating flexibility than do those associated with public entities.

The purchasing and supply management function in private nonprofit and not-for-profit organizations can apply policies, procedures, processes, and practices that conform more to generally accepted business practice than to governmental laws, regulations, or ordinances. Their purchasing and supply management affairs are subject to less public scrutiny than those of public entities or quasi-public jurisdictions.

OPERATIONAL DIFFERENCES BETWEEN THE PUBLIC AND PRIVATE SECTORS

Setting aside the private sector's profit motive, some of the salient differences between the purchasing and supply management function in the public versus the private sector include sources of funds (e.g., taxes, donations and contributions, and, to a limited extent, profits from the sale of goods and services); spheres of influence and oversight, including political interference; and legislative and executive mandates such as those related to the implementation of various socioeconomic programs.

Tax Dollars

Specific to public entities and generally applicable to quasi-public jurisdictions, expenditures on goods and services (i.e., cost of purchases) are a direct cost to the taxpayer. Because the total cost of ownership related to these expenditures is passed directly to the taxpayer, public entities that spend taxpayer dollars on goods and services are under intense public scrutiny to exercise their fiduciary responsibility in the protection of taxpayers' interests. Media organizations, seeking to uncover waste, fraud, and abuse within public entities, frequently use "freedom of information" provisions of federal legislation as well as state and local statutes and ordinances to secure access to all communications and information, based upon the concept that these items are public property. Moreover, many constituencies, composed of taxpayer and watchdog groups, are highly organized and intensely vocal—much more so, for example, than the typical loosely knit consumers of goods and services produced and provided by private-sector organizations. In fact, some of these constituencies, including taxpayers and members and consumers of quasi-public jurisdictions as well as nonprofit and not-for-profit organizations, even play a formal part in the governance of the entities, jurisdictions, and organizations with which they are affiliated. The effect is to make it virtually impossible for all public-sector organizations to ignore any of their constituency groups when making decisions, especially expenditures on goods and services. Public-sector organizations can mitigate the arguably intrusive nature of public scrutiny by guarding against conflicts of interest in supplier selection based on familial, fraternal, and financial relationships and securing the best value by making acquisition decisions based on overall value rather than just acceptance of the lowest price, creation of minibid or backdrop contracts, and use of cooperative purchasing agreements.

Public Scrutiny

Using best-value criteria such as improved delivery, cost reduction, better maintenance standards, and reliance on supplier experience, a public entity's purchasing and supply management professionals can enhance the benefit to the taxpayers because best-value procurement shifts the burden of creatively solving acquisition-related problems from the buying entity to its supplies. Although the application of best-value procurement practices among public- and private-sector organizations may be conceptually the same, the use of this time-honored principle is easier to implement in the private sector because purchasing and supply management professionals usually do not have to provide written rationale or documentation to justify the use of best-value criteria for award determination among competing sources. Unlike private-sector organizations, public entities like departments and agencies of the federal government must justify in writing the rationale for supplier selection, especially when awards of significant dollar value are made. Best-value criteria generally are related to some form of numeric scoring methodology because the expenditure of taxpayer dollars requires that legally defensible documentation be in place to sustain possible protests from unsuccessful suppliers and inquiries from oversight groups.

Legislative Oversight

In addition to public scrutiny over entities' expenditure of taxpayer dollars, congressional oversight of federal programs, dependent on the U.S. Congress as the source of appropriated funds, is often intense—bordering at times on micromanagement. Public entities and quasi-public jurisdictions as well as some nonprofit and not-for-profit organizations tend to purchase a variety of products and services, some of which are technically complex, frequently costly, and commonly without commercial application. Colleges and universities have alumni and other benefactors who, rightfully or not, sometimes feel compelled to exert influence on how their dollars are spent on these products and services. Moreover, these alumni and benefactors as well as student factions and faculty groups seek to advance special agendas. For example, diverse interests among the faculty may create conflicting priorities and often promote backdoor selling, frustrating the effectiveness of the purchasing and supply management function.

Compliance with Laws

Public entities and some quasi-public jurisdictions, in the conduct of their procurement-related activities, must comply with federal, state, county, and local laws, regulations, and ordinances that impose the attainment of such socioeconomic objectives as environmental sensitivity and small, disadvantaged, and minority business preferences. Concerning this sensitivity, the Environmental Protection Agency issued final guidance on purchasing products based, in part, on environmental attributes such as recycled-content percentages, energy- and water-efficiency ratings, lower toxicity, and the use of renewable resources pursuant to Executive Order 13101—Greening the Government through Waste Prevention,

Recycling, and Federal Acquisition—in 1998. With respect to these preferences, the Department of Defense (DoD) issued a final ruling implementing Section 816 of the National Defense Authorization Act of 1990 for Fiscal Year (FY) 2003 that extends the objective of awarding 5 percent of all contract dollars to small disadvantaged businesses as well as other minority organizations to FY 2006.

Among the many laws that affect the acquisition of goods and services by public entities and some quasi-public jurisdictions are the laws of agency. These laws, whether applicable to "special agents" or "general agents," govern the relationship between an agent (employee or third-party provider) and his or her principal (employer or issuer of the third-party contract) with respect to the authority and responsibility of these individuals to purchase goods and services on behalf of entities and jurisdictions. These laws differ among states and the federal government. The creation of agency authority to purchase goods and services remains restrictive, and the extent of the agent's authority given by the principal (i.e., entity or jurisdiction) will be contingent on the laws that pertain to the principal issuing the authority. For example, contracting officers have the authority to commit funds on behalf of the federal government, and this is the actual or express authority intrinsic to the contracting officer's warrant. The chief procurement officer of a jurisdiction, via the actual or express authority also known as "job description" authority, is granted the authority and responsibility to purchase goods and services on behalf of the jurisdiction. Third-party providers can receive "implied authority" by ratification, but the process is more complex and can be perilous to the third-party acting outside of a written contract. By contrast, the private sector can use all forms of agency authority (i.e., actual or express and implied) in the conduct of its procurement activities. All public-sector organizations engage, to the extent possible and permissible, in supplier selection processes that are open, inclusive, equitable, and competitive.

Similarities with the Private Sector

In certain respects, however, the purchasing and supply management function in the public sector, in general, is similar to that in the private sector. Public-sector purchasing and supply management professionals face many challenges, analogous if not identical to their private-sector counterparts. The fundamental objective for these professionals in both sectors is to identify sources of needed goods and services and to acquire these goods and services when needed as economically as possible, within specified quality standards, requisite delivery periods, and expressed budgetary and price constraints. Consistent with this objective, the purchasing and supply management function must react quickly, effectively, and efficiently to the desired requirements, while maintaining policies and practices that conform to sound business practice. To this end, many public-sector purchasing and supply management professionals, contingent on any limitations imposed by their entities, jurisdictions, and organizations, can base their procurement decisions on best value and negotiation instead of adhering solely on the lowest responsible bid. These professionals, albeit cautiously and deliberately, are adopting modern professional techniques and methods, including those associated with supply management, to ensure that the purchasing and supply management function fully supports their organizations' needs.

Quasi-Public Organizations

Public utilities as quasi-public jurisdictions, for example, can apply purchasing and supply management practices akin to those in the private sector. These jurisdictions, whose revenues are obtained from the sale of their products and services, may not be dependent on taxpayer support. In fact, they may provide a portion of their revenues and/or may even contribute services in lieu of taxes to the public entities that own or oversee them. Depending on their charter, some utilities have the latitude to conduct their purchasing and supply management functions along the lines of private-sector- or investor-owned utilities, rather than as tax-supported jurisdictions. Unlike some specific purchasing and supply management practices related to source selection at the public entities under whose control they operate, utilities are able to restrict their bid list to a reasonable number of qualified firms using methods ordinarily employed in the private sector. Public utilities often have no requirements to advertise for competitive bids or to open bids to the public.

Stewardship

Notwithstanding any similarity with the private sector, the practice of purchasing and supply management in the public sector is primarily a stewardship function, because it involves the expenditure of someone else's money to support services and activities that a public-sector official has decided, in advance, should be provided. The technology-based and computer-related processes, inherent in the application of purchasing and supply management, support the efficient and effective exercise of this function. In an article entitled "Defending Taxpayer Dollars" appearing in the February 2003 issue of *Government Procurement,* Commander Steven Dollase, director of acquisition policy at the U.S. Navy's Naval Inventory Control Point, was quoted as saying, "As government agencies continue to adopt technologies to better utilize our fiscal resources, we are hopeful that the public's confidence in our stewardship of these resources will be further enhanced." Having an agency responsibility to obtain what is needed when it is needed, while demonstrating proper stewardship, demands openness and de jure compliance from public-sector purchasing and supply management professionals. In the case of public entities as well as certain quasi-public jurisdictions and private nonprofit and not-for-profit organizations, the service demands (and the resources to satisfy those demands) emanate directly or indirectly from taxpayers. As a result, the public purchasing and supply management function has evolved into a controlled, yet open, process that is prescribed by a myriad of laws, regulations, and ordinances; rules and regulations; judicial and administrative decisions; and policies and procedures. These legal, regulatory, administrative, and procedural constraints (which cover everything from who is authorized to purchase a particular good or service to who can and cannot supply this good or service) complicate and frequently delay the seemingly simple process of securing needed goods and services generally attributed to the private sector.

Moreover, these same constraints discourage the approbation of a paradigm shift from traditional purchasing to supply management, the latter of which relies on successful, long-term strategic alliances or partnerships to reach its full potential. The allocation of contracts, in the federal government as well as state, county, and local governments, may be made on the basis of socioeconomic engineering. In federal contracting, for example, agencies or entities are constrained by the provisions of the Competition in Contracting Act of 1984, and they are faced with the precarious reconciliation of maintaining a fair and open competitive posture in contract award selection and adopting private-sector practices that may restrict competition. The federal government enacted the Government Performance and Results Act of 1993, Federal Acquisition Streamlining Act of 1994, Federal Acquisition Reform Act (aka Clinger-Cohen Act) of 1996, and the Services Acquisition Reform Act of 2003, in part, to promote cooperation and collaboration with supply chain partners. These acts as well as other legislation (e.g., Section 800 of the National Defense Authorization Act of 1990) and executive orders (e.g., EO 12931, October 13, 1994) are in response to federal acquisition reform generally considered to have begun with the 1986 Packard Commission.

An example of an organization adopting federal acquisition reform initiatives is the General Services Administration (GSA). The GSA's transformation, influenced by federal legislation and reflective of a service-dominated and customer-driven marketplace, has allowed it to deliver better-quality goods and improved services to its federal customers through implementation of programs such as the Federal Supply Service (FSS) and the Federal Technology Service (FTS). The FSS offers federal customers outstanding service and reduced prices for commercial off-the-shelf (COTS) items, and the FTS provides these customers with exemplary service and expanded selection of technology-based and value-added solutions to information technology and network-related problems and issues. This federal agency has realized that acquisition reform does not obviate adherence to federal laws and regulations, but it acknowledges that such reform has modified these laws and regulations to facilitate the procurement of goods and services for and foster the delivery of expanded service to its customers.

ABA Model Procurement Code

Although each of the 50 states in the United States has its own body of legislation and regulation, the American Bar Association's Model Procurement Code for State and Local Government, originally published in 1979, offers a degree of standardization in acquisition-related terminology and practice among the state, county, and local governments. This code can aid state, county, and local governments in the creation of statutes and ordinances that provide these public entities with policy guidance and statutory language for managing their procurement-related operations, direction for the administrative and/or judicial resolution of disputes relating to contract award, and a set of ethical standards for governing public and private participants in the acquisition and contracting processes. Subsequent revisions may permit greater flexibility among purchasing and supply management professionals by allowing them to be more responsive to operating needs, especially the more complex ones. These professionals, operating within the fishbowl of public entities and quasi-public jurisdictions, are challenged not only with legal, regulatory, administrative, and procedural oversight and control, but also with a resultant risk-adverse culture that inhibits innovation and change as well as discourages strategic planning and new program implementation. Moreover, this culture promotes a confusing authorizing environment that hinders collaborative communication and encourages a divisive workplace that exacerbates turf battles and political interference.

In addition, other cultural barriers (e.g., civil service regulations, administrative micromanagement, and functional silo organizational structures) that so effectively hamper change in any structural or regulated environment are demonstrative of many public-sector organizations. The absence of a competitive market operating in the public sector differentiates it from the private sector, even though the functions associated with purchasing and supply management often are identical.

The private sector has accelerated the adoption of modern, information-based supply management systems, in order to remain competitive in the global marketplace, while the public sector generally has encountered significant resistance—delaying the implementation of such systems among the various organizations. Among the reasons for this resistance, particularly among public entities, is that the shift from a centralized to a decentralized structure (even an eclectic matrix system demonstrative of effective cross-functional teaming, supplier partnering, and customer synthesizing) to optimize organizational fluidity and operational flexibility worries some public-sector purchasing and supply management professionals. These entities traditionally have not participated in such teaming and partnering, regarded their roles and spectrum of responsibilities as climbing to a strategic position within their organizations, nor experienced intense pressure from internal or external sources to embrace supply and supply chain management principles and practices. The most significant reason for this resistance, and perhaps the most consequential, is the perceived threat or risk of job attrition or loss from those responsible for implementing supply management (i.e., those management and staff members in such functional departments or divisions as purchasing, finance, inventory management, logistics and transportation, and operations). They remain comfortable with the old way of doing business and exhibit a resistance to change that is a natural part of every complex change effort.

ROLES AND RESPONSIBILITIES IN THE PUBLIC SECTOR

The purchasing and supply management function in a public-sector organization plays several roles that distinguish it from its counterpart in the private sector. These roles may include, but are not limited to, being

- A planner for requirements definition, goods and services acquisition, and channel selection through identification and specification of goods and services, evaluation and selection of suppliers, and assessment and adoption of distribution channels

- An implementer of policies, procedures, processes, and practices that, in addition to promoting and securing the maximum permissible and practicable competition through detailed, prescribed procedures, must also champion laws, regulations, and ordinances that govern the purchasing and supply management function and may include small, disadvantaged, and minority business participation as well as environmental protection issues

- A defender of the decision-making processes associated with securing goods and services through documentation of various analyses such as market competition, cost/price, cost-benefit, present value and product elasticity, budget variance, and source selection and evaluation

- A provider or procurer of often thousands of different types of goods and services for a wide variety of internal customers that, in turn, utilize these goods and services to operate their entities, jurisdictions, and organizations or add needed infrastructure and facilities

- A marketer of business opportunities that must seek out as many potential supply sources as possible or practicable, accurately and attractively communicate needs to those potential sources, and maintain effective relationships and communication with both the successful and the unsuccessful suppliers

The responsibilities of the purchasing and supply management function in a public-sector organization can be viewed in terms of both the specific products and services it secures for its internal customers or end users and the various functions it discharges in the course of supplying these products and services.

Products and Services Purchased

Public-sector purchasing and supply management professionals typically purchase a large number and variety of products and services. In general, the items purchased are COTS items that can be secured without the need for custom design and manufacturing or major modifications. Obvious exceptions include items such as weapons systems for the DoD; specialty vehicles such as fire trucks; construction for state, county, and local entities; state-of-the-art research equipment for universities and research institutions; and professional services as well as specialty or customized hardware and software for all public-sector organizations. A typical public entity, for example, will purchase literally thousands of different items within the course of a single year. Among the items that account for a large part of these expenditures are office supplies and equipment, computer hardware and software, telecommunications equipment, food, furniture, and vehicles. Public-sector organizations also are turning increasingly to private-sector companies for the delivery of various services.

Functions Performed

The purchasing and supply management function in the public sector supports its fundamental mission of supplying goods and services to those who require them in an efficient and timely manner. In general, these functions include

- Cultivating a proactive approach to requirements definition, goods and services acquisition, and channel selection within the context of allowable competitive sourcing
- Centralizing management for strategic oversight and decentralizing execution for tactical implementation of supply management
- Taking advantage of modern management tools such as the balanced scorecard, process reengineering and redesign, Web-based financial and budgetary system, and supplier-customer resource management
- Developing, organizing, and maintaining formal (qualifying) lists of potential suppliers
- Assisting internal customers or end users in designing, researching, and preparing written, competitive solicitations or specifications and evaluating the offers received in response to the specifications
- Ensuring continuity of supply through coordinated planning and scheduling, supplier alliance and partnership contracts, and appropriate levels of inventory
- Assuring the quality of purchased goods and services through standardization and simplification, quality inspection, and contract administration
- Participating, via cross-functional teams, in decisions on whether to make goods in-house or buy from outsourced suppliers
- Documenting procurement actions and making pricing or other nonproprietary data reasonably available to those requiring or requesting it
- Advising top or senior management, using functional staff and others, on such matters as market conditions, new products, product improvements, and opportunities to build goodwill among the constituent and business communities

These roles and responsibilities are executed under the glare of the public spotlight and without allowing suppliers to benefit from political influence or advantage. Mitigating political influence or advantage can be accomplished by educating oversight groups on the fair and equitable treatment of suppliers, giving suppliers due process, and ensuring all procurement decisions are documented and defensible. Moreover, these roles and responsibilities are carried out consistent with an organization's mission and vision as well as broad public policy goals. Although the fabric of public entities, quasi-public jurisdictions, and private nonprofit and not-for-profit organizations, encompassing the public sector, may be dominated by entrenched bureaucracies, change, albeit problematic, is not impossible to implement through a dedicated and decisive approach to procurement reform via adoption of supply and supply chain management procedures and practices.

EVOLUTION OF SUPPLY MANAGEMENT AND SUPPLY CHAIN MANAGEMENT

Purchasing, formerly consisting of a series of clerical and transactional processes involving the acquisition of goods and services usually from the lowest responsible bidder or select suppliers, has evolved into supply management. Supply management incorporates twenty-first century technology-driven, relationship-based, and competition-sensitive (private sector only) business practices into the integrative management of supply-related functions within an organization. To achieve and maintain the effective and efficient exercise of this function, supply management professionals must have a pragmatic understanding of supply management's role in the organization. Moreover, they must acquire and sustain the requisite skill set to successfully execute the policies, procedures, practices, and processes related to supply management within the context of the new business paradigms, some of which have been mentioned previously. Many of these paradigms apply as well to public-sector organizations.

A seminal study conducted by the CAPS Research, in cooperation with the Institute for Supply Management™ (ISM), Arizona State University, and Michigan State University, produced in 1995 a report entitled "Purchasing and Supply Management: Future Directions and Trends." This was followed by a collaborative research project conducted by CAPS, ISM, and A.T. Kearney, Inc., that resulted in the 1998 report entitled "The Future of Purchasing and Supply: A Five- and Ten-Year Forecast." These reports identified key issues or "change drivers" that affect the acquisition of goods and services by the public and private sectors through the use of supply management principles and practices. While the emphasis of these reports is in the private sector, public entities, especially the federal government, are also affected to some degree by these same drivers. Therefore they continue to adopt private-sector methods and techniques in the procurement of goods and services to achieve greater efficiency in process execution and better management of limited fiscal resources. Among these issues or drivers are the following:

Supply Management Responsibilities and Activities

Many public-sector organizations anticipate a continued decrease in purchasing's responsibility for tactically oriented tasks. This shift in responsibilities reveals a large-scale movement away from tactical commitments and toward strategic or value-adding tasks. Notwithstanding this shift, key tactical activities will continue to include supplier evaluation, selection, and development, including cross-functional and cross-enterprise teams. The number of purchasing-related groups, organized by commodity, will continue to decrease gradually, while the number of those groups, organized by end item or identified as hybrid structures usually associated with project management, are anticipated to increase. Along with the reduction of tactical activities, most organizations, especially those in the private sector, are increasing the supply management function's responsibility for reduction of the supplier base and development of strategic alliances with preferred suppliers for critical goods and services. Public-sector organizations, however, often are precluded by laws, regulations, and ordinances from restricting access to procurement opportunities, especially for small businesses or small disadvantaged businesses as well as for minority, women-owned, or historically underutilized businesses. Documented circumstances and selective relaxation of certain procurement-related laws, regulations, and ordinances, nonetheless, have empowered public-sector organizations, including public entities, to prudently reduce their supplier bases. Those so empowered are expected to pursue a continued increase in strategically focused and externally focused purchasing-related responsibilities.

Although competitive bidding will continue to be used, especially among public entities, to ascertain market prices for nonstrategic items, many of these items will be outsourced by quasi-public jurisdictions as well as nonprofit and not-for-profit organizations to third-party buyers or consortia to conduct the bidding. Moreover, several public-sector organizations will continue to purchase most nonstrategic products and services under master contracts, some of which will be negotiated by consortia that have leveraged and buying expertise. These organizations will follow an emerging trend for the continued use of third-party purchasing by primarily private-sector firms pursuing all forms of competitive advantage possibilities.

Moving toward establishing win-win relationships in the context of strategic alliances, many public-sector organizations are looking at total cost as a criterion, thus allowing win-win relationship building to lower total costs. Quite a few public-sector organizations, emulating private-sector firms, are expected to use integrative (win-win) versus distributive (win-lose) negotiations, as they move away from adversarial and toward collaborative relationships with suppliers.

Supplier Outsourcing

Within public entities, the federal government for example, continues to change its perception of supplier importance and of the purchasing and sourcing process toward achieving its strategic missions and objectives. As stated previously, public-

and private-sector organizations alike will increase their reliance on external suppliers as a source of product and service enhancement. Strategic sourcing, the creation of supplier alliances and partnerships with select suppliers, will drive SCM initiatives and strategies, even in the public sector, to achieve cost and technology advantages. This type of sourcing implies outsourcing noncore functions, reengineering procurement-related functions, and using the Office of Management and Budget (OMB) A-76 process.

This process is defined in the OMB Circular A-76 that established the federal government's policy for the competition of commercial (private sector) activities related to outsourcing, and it requires that federal government departments and agencies conduct competitive sourcing studies—comparing costs and benefits related to specific functions currently performed in-house with the same costs and benefits as if these functions were to be accomplished by private-sector organizations. The intended outcome of this process is to allow commercial functions to be performed in a cost-effective, process-efficient manner. This circular distinguishes between federal government activities that must be performed by federal government employees from those that could be performed by employees of private-sector organizations. Circular A-76 also establishes competition standards that determine whether federal government employees should perform functions that can be considered private-sector activities. Moreover, this circular states that the potential outsourced organization must comply with procurement integrity, ethics, and standards of conduct, including restrictions found in 18 U.S.C. § 208 prohibiting a federal government officer or employee from participating "… as a government official in any 'particular matter' in which he or she has a financial interest."

Many public-sector organizations anticipate sustained growth in their outsourcing activities to attain short- and long-term cost reduction and performance improvement. These organizations continue to evaluate their outsourcing decisions through systematic decision processes requiring determination of core competencies in all aspects of organizational and operational performance, logistics management, and service delivery. A 2003 congressional report entitled "Noncompetitive Federal Contracts Increase under the Bush Administration," indicated that the federal government spent $107 Billion or 60 percent more on noncompetitive contracts in FY 2003 than the $67 billion spent in FY 2000.[1] Commenting on this report, Representative Henry Waxman (D-Calif.), ranking member of the House of Representatives Government Reform Committee, said, "Increasingly, the administration is turning over essential government functions [via the A-76 process] to the private sector, and it has jettisoned basic safeguards like competition and supervision that are needed to protect the public interest." Outsourcing, however, is expected to remain an integral part of many public-sector organizations' long-term strategies.

Supply chains will form upstream and downstream from dominant firms that will prevail because of their size, technology leadership, or distribution systems

---

1 Taken from an article in *Federal Computer Week* at www.fcw.com dated June 3, 2004. This article, titled "Feds Increase Noncompetitive Contract Spending," was written by Michael Hardy.

among other reasons. Notwithstanding the Small Business Reauthorization Act of 1997, federal government departments and agencies can consolidate goods and service requirements, previously provided by several suppliers (primarily small businesses), into a single bundled contract with a large supplier if the department or agency can document consolidation is necessary, prudent, and unchallengeable, and the department or agency can demonstrate that it would derive "certain measurably substantial benefits from the consolidation, as compared to the benefits it would derive if the requirements were not bundled."[2] Federal government procurement-related activities, especially those associated with the development of supply management programs, continue to focus, to the extent possible and permissible, on the reduction of the existing supplier base. The rationale for this focus is due, in part, to the realization that maintaining a large supplier base naturally results in increased variability (e.g., in lead times, material consistency, service excellence, specifications and requirements interpretation, transportation and delivery costs, and relationship integration). Public entities, especially state, county, and local governments limited by statutes and ordinances from restricting access to procurement opportunities, find the reduction of the supplier base more problematic. Consistent with changes already taking place within the public, quasi-public, and private non-profit and not-for-profit segments of the public sector, the trend toward strategic alliances or partnerships with select suppliers focuses on developing collaborative relationships with these suppliers. As the public sector looks to the private sector for adoption of its commercial standards and best practices, early supplier involvement, implicit in these alliances or partnerships, depends on relaxation of procurement-related regulations and greater flexibility in the execution of the procurement process. Creation of virtual supply chains, via the public sector's use of e-commerce and e-procurement, is expected to continue over the next decade, and public-sector organizations may choose to enter into term contracts without the usual entanglements associated with procurement-related laws, regulations, and ordinances.

Supply Base Management and Systems Development

Organizations, including those in the public sector, increasingly are willing to take direct action to develop supplier performance capabilities. A formal supplier measurement system provides an efficient way to express performance requirements throughout the supply chain. Some type of common performance metrics can be established in particular for supply chains that have a common set of core performance measures tied directly to an organization's strategic as well as tactical performance. Several trends have emerged in supply management performance measurement. The continuous improvement in cost, quality, and delivery performance from suppliers will be required for maintenance of an organization's service delivery position in an increasingly complex and fiscally constrained public-sector environment. Continued innovation in the evolution of supply management strategies

---

2 Quote taken from the text of the Small Business Reauthorization Act of '97.

and activities will be integral to reinforcing the contributions of the purchasing and supply management function to the success of public-sector organizations. Chapter 4 of the May 2004 report by the Aberdeen Group and Government Computer News states, "The Supply Management in the Public Sector reaffirms that government agencies will never fully embrace full-scale supply management until legislators impose measures and incentives to drive continuous improvements in supply performance and cost reductions." This report asserts that state and local governments continue to lag the federal public sector and, of course, the private sector in adopting supply management principles and practices, particularly those associated with streamlining procurement-related operations as well as using technology solutions in supply management-related processes.

E-commerce technology supports electronic efficiency efforts. Suppliers are becoming more integrated and involved throughout the supply chain. The Internet will be the front end for proprietary information systems that are becoming pull-based and conducive to applying demand-pull purchasing philosophies as a seamless interface between supplier and purchaser. Integrated information systems will facilitate supply chain integration despite rapid changes in technology and marketplaces. Public-sector organizations can expect continued growth of and emphasis on the use of Web-based systems for interactions among their suppliers and end users (i.e., internal customers and various external constituencies).

ADOPTION OF SUPPLY MANAGEMENT IN THE PUBLIC SECTOR

Confronted with budgetary constraints, inflexible and obsolete systems, reduced workforces, and increasing pressure for performance improvements in efficiency and effectiveness, public-sector organizations, in particular public entities, are availing themselves of already successful supply management practices in the private sector to ameliorate the effects of legacy purchasing and materials management procedures and practices. Public entities are striving to demonstrate new levels of competence and sophistication through the transition from purchasing to supply management. Concurrently, citizens, businesses, and politicians are demanding new levels of service delivery. Faced with these dual challenges, today's public entities must look for new business models, including those related to, for example, acquisition planning and resource allocation, fixed asset investment, inventory control, facility and equipment maintenance, logistics management, and relationship management. The intent is to realize the "best bang for the buck" of taxpayer dollars and to exploit opportunities for improvements in labor (workforce) and capital (facilities and equipment) productivity.

Many public entities have begun the process of improving productivity by making significant investments in enterprise resource planning (ERP), supplier relationship management (SRM), and customer relationship management (CRM), also known among public entities as "constituent relationship management," as part of decision support software systems. Information technology firms, leveraging the booming SCM market, are attracting public entities' interest in improving their service-to-the-citizen mandate through adoption of technology-based tools that complement their zeal to offer service delivery that is better, cheaper, and faster. The original technology focus of their implementations (rather than a focus on organization transformation), however, has meant that few public entities have yet to realize the full benefits of their investments. Notwithstanding the absence of a profit motive, public entities are concerned with the wise expenditure of taxpayer dollars. Mr. Jim White, senior vice president of public sector, aerospace and defense, and airlines at Dallas-based i2 Technologies Inc., has been quoted as saying, "With pressures on the budget, and citizens wanting more for their tax dollars, there is an embracing of the idea, 'We've got to do things better. The old school of good is good enough is no longer good enough.'"[3] Quasi-public jurisdictions and private nonprofit and not-for-profit organizations, in general, have experienced greater success in the gradual adoption of these software systems as part of evolving emphasis on supply management.

Despite the shackle of legal and regulatory impediments and the bondage of cultural and bureaucratic inertia, the demand for the change to supply management has been growing within the public sector, notwithstanding the absence of a competitive marketplace. Karen D. Schwartz identifies seven factors that affect the transformation from traditional purchasing to supply management.[4] These are

1. Secure top management commitment and high-level leadership approval to capitalize on modern, information-based methodologies that support supply chain efficiency and effectiveness to mitigate barriers to change.

2. Focus on core competencies by examining which elements of public-sector organizations are inherently sector-specific and/or truly core competencies of each organization and by competing the rest—recognizing that competition is the critical incentive needed to achieve higher performance at lower cost. This is a reference to the "A-76" process whereby federal government organizations (entities) must demonstrate to their leadership and federal government inspector generals and/or auditors that the function they perform must be accomplished by federal government employees and this function cannot be accomplished by non-federal government personnel.

3. Outsource whenever appropriate to ensure that public-sector organizations take advantage of their core competencies, which may lie in many of the elements of the supply chain, while always maintaining a competitive orientation, especially in the application of best-value acquisition strategies.

---

3 Trish Williams (2000). "New Climate Sparks Government Demand for Supply Chain Management," *Washington Technology*, November 25, vol. 15, no. 13, http://www.washingtontechnology.com/news/15_13/tech_features/1827-1.html.

4 Karen D. Schwartz (2001). "Streamlining Links in the Supply Chain," *Government Executive*, March 1, www.govexec.com/features/0301/0301managetech.htm.

4. Develop a customer focus by emphasizing and providing maximum end-user value—resulting in improved customer satisfaction and reduced costs, because allocation of fiscal resources are prioritized on the basis of better source selection and excellent product and service quality.

5. Minimize distrust and stress security and confidentiality, critical cultural barriers to successful supply management implementation, through continuous collaboration via cross-functional teaming (possibly including suppliers and customers), demonstrated dependability by way of professionalism (including competence and dedication), and patronized public-spiritedness via retention of the public trust (including ethical behavior conflict of interest avoidance).

6. Use the right supplier performance metrics and link contractual incentives to them through the use of end-to-end performance and cost measures as well as incentives that are directly linked to those measures.

7. Adopt proven supply chain technology by investing in technological products (i.e., COTS hardware and software) that offer documented scalability, life-cycle savings, and improved productivity, instead of merely customizing manual systems that simply digitized their current processes, to realize benefits of world-class approaches already adopted by the private sector.

Arguably, the most critical of these seven factors is the first. Without top management's resolute commitment and leadership, the resulting progress, if any, will be protracted and problematic. With the exercise of energetic leadership, public-sector organizations truly can become world-class, and taxpayers, users, and supporters will benefit from this transformation.

Application of Supply Chain Management in the U.S. Postal Service

The successor to the Post Office Department, the United States Postal Service (USPS) was established by the Postal Reorganization Act of July 1, 1971, as an independent, self-supporting federal agency within the executive branch.

PWC Consulting, formerly the consulting arm of PricewaterhouseCoopers, the audit and tax firm, produced a report, dated December 21, 2001, entitled "USPS Purchasing and Materials Organizational Effectiveness in Supply Chain Management Phase IV Report: Organizational Guidelines Implementation Plan Business Case" wherein it presents the business case for the USPS, a quasi-public government-owned corporation, reengineering and redesigning its purchasing and materials organization to take full advantage of SCM as a vehicle to mitigate the effects of rising costs and increased competition. The Background section of this report offers the salient rationale for the transformation of traditional purchasing to supply chain management. It states, in part, "At the heart of SCM are advances in technology that have allowed companies to streamline processes and collaborate with suppliers like never before." Like many companies, USPS has embraced SCM as a potential source of competitive advantage and has made significant progress over the last few years implementing SCM.

In 1999, the USPS began transitioning to an SCM strategy and process. As an independent government agency, the USPS, by law, is self-sustaining and does not depend on "appropriated funds" from the U.S. Congress. Therefore, no tax dollars are used to support any USPS operations. Realizing that it could no longer operate under its traditional business plan or philosophy, the USPS decided to adopt private-sector business procedures and processes, including SCM.

Because SCM is dedicated to the mitigation and reduction of cost, also known as bottom-line contributions, measuring SCM accurately for these contributions involves the establishment of value added measurements or metrics. Measurable value can be broken down into three categories: (1) cost reduction, (2) cost savings, and (3) cost avoidance. An example of cost reduction is a measurable decrement in the cost of purchasing parts or services. The Postmaster General mandated that the USPS reduce its total cost by $5 billion over the next five years, beginning in 2000. The supply chain management division of the Postal Service set a goal of $1 billion over the five-year horizon. According to Keith Strange, former vice president of supply management for the U.S. Postal Service, embracing SCM policies and practices has permitted the USPS to document savings of $820 million as of the third quarter of 2003. The USPS projects that its supply chain management division will more than exceed its target savings of $1 billion before the end of 2004.

Mr. Strange acknowledges that the Postal Service uses the verification and validation method, as directed by the Comptroller General of the United States. In order for cost abatements to be credited to the implementation of SCM, one of the Comptroller's divisions, part of the U.S. General Accounting Office, must validate any cost reductions through events or actions taken directly by the USPS. Cost avoidance is commonly grouped with the cost reduction. Because it is difficult to measure objectively, cost avoidance often is not reported. By streamlining its purchasing and materials processes, the USPS found that it could realize cost avoidance by not being penalized for late payment, late deliveries, and missed orders. Moreover, the USPS discovered that cost savings could be established by aggressively using online purchasing procedures, commonly referred to within the USPS as e-buy. (Note: *E-buy* is a term of art used by the USPS, and it can refer to e-purchasing or e-procurement.) As an intangible benefit from transitioning to SCM, the supply chain management division's staff is excited and more enthusiastic. By changing from its traditional transaction-based activities to an SCM process, staff members believe that they have impacted significantly the efficiency and effectiveness of USPS operations. Mr. Strange states, "By in large as the people within supply chain management or even our internal clients who are working with us on supply chain initiatives … people are excited by it, people enjoy it." By developing strategic alliances or partnerships with suppliers, the need to maintain an extensive list of suppliers to potentially engage in a bidding war is minimized. Forming strategic alliances or partnerships with limited (select) suppliers is a win-win proposition. The USPS has reduced its supplier base over the last three years. The magnitude of USPS operations made paring its supply base a major undertaking. Nevertheless, Mr. Strange indicated that implementing SCM principles, processes, and practices allowed the USPS to cut the total number of suppliers from 31,000 in 2001 to 25,000 in 2002. In addition, the USPS has established a strategic alliance with Federal Express (FedEx). Under this alliance, the USPS contracts for space on FedEx airplanes to transport Express Mail, Priority Mail, and First-Class Mail, and FedEx locates overnight service collection boxes at post offices nationwide.

   Moreover, the USPS has assertively pursued outsourcing as another vehicle to mitigate or reduce costs. The Institute for Supply Management™ describes outsourcing as a process that "involves sourcing using a supplier that provides a complete item or service rather than buying the components and manufacturing them in-house." Through the implementation of outsourcing, the USPS has created cost savings by reducing capital equipment expenses, supply-related expenditures, and labor costs.

   While full support exists at the executive level, pockets of resistance still persist in the mid- to upper-management levels within the USPS. According to Mr. Ray Jacobson, manager of material management for the USPS, key managers and contract specialists throughout the system have resisted the move to SCM. The introduction of any new system provokes change and the perceived loss of authority and power. A key factor in the successful implementation of SCM is the total support of top management. Without this support, any SCM initiative will be plagued by resistance and failure. Apathy and overly optimistic expectations will ruin any chance of success. Educating USPS employees to the potential benefits of SCM remains a paramount concern.

   In order to maintain its self-sufficiency status, the USPS must use all its resources (i.e., labor and capital) competently to sustain its profitability. The implementation of SCM at the USPS has contributed to cost reduction, cost savings, and cost avoidance. Through the judicious use of supplier selection, strategic alliances, and outsourcing, the USPS has leveraged the benefits of SCM to enhance its service capability and delivery.

Application of Supply Management at the City of Los Angeles Department of General Services

In an effort to mitigate the traditional, albeit archaic and ineffective, method of acquiring goods, the Los Angeles Department of General Services contracted with PeopleSoft, Inc., to initiate the supply management system (SMS) project. A reengineering project, SMS uses PeopleSoft's supply chain management technology (software) to significantly reduce inventory levels, decrease procurement contract volume, and shorten accounts payable cycle time. In addition, the successful implantation of this reengineering project resulted in the elimination of warehouse space and associated labor-related costs. This SMS project also realized the consolidation of inventory purchases—cutting the number of warehouses and slashing the supplier base.

Moreover, other benefits from the implementation of PeopleSoft's SMS included

- Better use of cross-functional teams in supplier and inventory item (storekeeper units) selection
- Increased deployment of cost savings and avoidance initiatives
- Improved automation of the purchasing and supply management function
- Revised integration of procurement, inventory management, and accounts payable processes
- Enhanced compatibility of information technology hardware and software support
- Improved communication and collaboration among city agencies affected by warehouse consolidation
- Better management of fiscally related considerations (e.g., budgets, operational costs, accounting processes)

The realignment of human capital and reengineering of business processes elevated the visibility of an integrated procurement, inventory, and accounts payable function as a major contributor to a more efficient and effective use of taxpayer dollars. In addition, city user departments were satisfied with the implementation of the SMS project. Department managers saw the benefits of this integrated approach as evidence that supply chain management works to the best interests of all city departments.[5]

CONCLUSION

Some of the major trends that have impacted significantly the acquisition, management, and utilization of goods and services during the last decade include

- Cooperative purchasing
- Automation and information technology
- Green procurement
- Outsourcing
- Best-value purchasing
- E-commerce and e-procurement
- Strategic alliances and partnerships

---

5. "Universal Supply: Supply chain management saves millions for city of Los Angeles," http://www.govtech.net/govcenter/solcenter/?id=78489.

The principles and practices of supply management are consistent with these trends, and these principles and practices are used in or facilitated by the implementation of these trends among public-sector organizations. Purchasing and supply management groups within public entities, quasi-public jurisdictions, and private nonprofit and not-for-profit organizations have made only incremental strides in fully embracing and implementing supply management. Legal, regulatory, and administrative restraints coupled with restrictive policies, procedures, processes, and practices have sustained a risk-adverse operational culture among many public-sector organizations, in particular public entities, that has delayed adoption of supply management initiatives.

The combined effects of budgetary constraints, inflexible and obsolete systems, reduced workforces, procurement reform actions, and increasing pressure from multiple oversight groups for performance improvements in the efficient and effective exercise of the purchasing and supply management function are expected to intensify the slow but steady pace of incorporating supply and supply chain management into purchasing and supply management operations within public-sector organizations. The documented experiences with the application of supply management in the private sector serve as examples of the benefits to be derived from this application. Public stewardship can be maintained; public trust can be retained; and public confidence can be reclaimed. These accomplishments, especially by public entities that use supply management practices in support of their purchasing and supply management operations, will become continuously visible and vulnerable in the rotating fishbowl of public scrutiny.

SUPPLY MANAGEMENT INFORMATION RESOURCES: INSTITUTE FOR SUPPLY MANAGEMENT™

The Institute for Supply Management™ (ISM) is the oldest and largest supply management institute in the world. Founded in 1915, the ISM has more than 40,000 members in 80-plus countries, continually extending the global impact of supply management. The ISM works with more than 170 affiliated associations within the United States and is actively expanding its affiliate presence into other countries, including Canada, France, Hong Kong, Mexico, and South Korea.

The ISM's ongoing mission is to lead supply management, a task which is done primarily through education, research, standards of excellence, influence building, and information dissemination—including the renowned monthly ISM *Report On Business®*.

The Institute relies heavily on its strong and active membership base. While all supply management professionals benefit from the ISM, members of this prestigious institute have access to a bevy of information and resources that are unmatched. Each day ISM members turn to their professional institute for benefits such as the award-winning magazine *Inside Supply Management®*, an expansive Online Career Center, the ISM Resource Center (including the innovative Research on Demand), discounts on a variety of products and programs, networking opportunities, and the ability to be identified as one who is dedicated to the supply management profession.

The ISM has long been at the forefront in the education of supply management professionals, through public seminars, conferences, Web-based products, self-study workbooks, books, and other media. The ISM also provides a platform for professionals, academics, and consultants to showcase their research, experiences, and best practices. Simply put, the goal of ISM's ongoing educational efforts is to ensure its members and other supply management professionals develop the knowledge and skills needed to do well and to help their organizations succeed.

PROFESSIONAL CREDENTIALING

Supply professionals interested in self-fulfillment, improving their skills, and creating opportunities for promotion, recognition, and more earning potential can benefit from earning ISM's professional designation—the Certified Purchasing Manager (C.P.M.). Established in 1974, the C.P.M. was the first internationally accepted standard of competence and knowledge for the profession. Since the program's inception, more than 40,000 professionals have earned the C.P.M. credentials.

ISM continues to lead supply management by developing a new professional qualification that will be relevant internationally and reflect the expanded education, skills and experience needed to be a successful supply management professional. The development of the Certified Professional in Supply Management™ (CPSM) further enhances ISM's mission to lead supply management. Today's professionals are facing both increasingly complex supply relationships and a greater reliance on technology. ISM assumes the responsibility to raise its professional and educational standards to meet the current and future demands of the profession. The new qualification will be available in 2008.

LEADING BY EXAMPLE

The ISM keeps its members and other supply management professionals informed of the latest trends and best practices being used today. It also provides leadership training on the local and national levels and numerous opportunities for industry leaders to meet and share ideas. One such initiative is the A.T. Kearney Center for Strategic Supply Leadership at ISM. This center is an exclusive thought-development forum of chief purchasing and supply officers and other senior executives who collaborate to detect and interpret the challenges and opportunities of the next three to five years. The Center synthesizes this future vision through executive forums and programs that build competitive business and supply capabilities today, while providing unique executive development and networking opportunities. Each of the Center's programs is designed with executives in mind.

The ISM has also created the *Principles of Social Responsibility*, designed to increase awareness and to provide tools for the development of a proactive supply management social responsibility program within the organization. Focusing on seven key areas within an organization, these principles have already gained support in several leading corporations, institutions, and organizations.

Learn more about this ever-evolving and constantly improving institute—and how it can help you—by visiting its Web site today: www.ism.ws.

You can also reach the ISM by phone (800/888-6276 or 480/752-6276, extension 401), e-mail (custsvc@ism.ws), or by mail (PO Box 22160, Tempe AZ, 85285-2160).

The ISM is a member of the International Federation of Purchasing and Supply Management (IFPSM).

I N D E X